DISCRIMINATION LAW

This is the second edition of a work which offers comprehensive coverage of the relevant UK and European Community law with a critical analysis of that law. Structured so as to be accessible to the student approaching discrimination law for the first time, the book is sufficiently detailed and analytical to appeal to the well-informed reader (practitioner and otherwise), and to provide those engaged in research with a solid base for further independent study. For the undergraduate student studying discrimination law as a free-standing subject or as part of a wider course, the book provides a 'one stop shop'; for the postgraduate student, too, it provides a challenging core text for any discrimination law course.

While the pace of change in this area is breathtaking, the author has endeavoured to state the law as it was on 8 April 2005, thus taking into account the Disability Discrimination Act 2005.

DISCRIMINATION LAW: TEXT, CASES AND MATERIALS

Second Edition

Aileen McColgan
Professor of Human Rights Law
King's College, London
Barrister, Matrix Chambers, London

·HART·
PUBLISHING
OXFORD AND PORTLAND, OREGON
2005

Hart Publishing
Oxford and Portland, Oregon

Published in North America (US and Canada) by
Hart Publishing c/o
International Specialized Book Services
5804 NE Hassalo Street
Portland, Oregon
97213-3644
USA

Hart Publishing is a specialist legal publisher based in Oxford, England.
To order further copies of this book or to request a list of other
publications please write to:

Hart Publishing, Salter's Boatyard, Folly Bridge,
Abingdon Road, Oxford OX1 4LB
Telephone: +44 (0)1865 245533 or Fax: +44 (0)1865 794882
e-mail: mail@hartpub.co.uk
WEBSITE: http//www.hartpub.co.uk

British Library Cataloguing in Publication Data
Data Available
ISBN 1–84113–484–8 (paperback)

Typeset by Hope Services (Abingdon) Ltd.
Printed and bound in Great Britain by
Page Bros Ltd, Norfolk

This book is dedicated
to my beloved parents Eithne and Sam

Contents

Table of Cases

Table of Statutory Instruments and Codes of Practice

Table of Legislation

United States of America

EUROPEAN

Publisher's Note

The author and publisher gratefully acknowledge the authors and publishers of extracted material which appears in this book, and in particular the following for permission to reprint from the sources indicated.

Oxford University Press Journals: *Oxford Journal of Legal Studies*: (S Poulter, 'Muslim Headscarves in School: Contrasting Approaches in England and France' (1997) 64, 66–7, S Hannett, 'Equality At The Intersections: The Legislative And Judicial Failure To Tackle Multiple Discrimination', (2003) 66–108) *The Industrial Law Journal*: Lucy Vickers 'The Employment Equality (Religion or Belief) Regulations 2003' (2003) 191; C McCrudden, 'The Northern Ireland Fair Employment White Paper: a Critical Assessment' (1988) 162–3; J Davies, 'A Cuckoo in the Nest? A 'Range of Reasonable Responses, Justification and the Disability Discrimination Act 1995' (2003) 170–1, 178–81; K Wells, 'The Impact of the Framework Employment Directive on UK Disability Discrimination Law', (2003) 261–2, 272; K Ewing, 'The Human Rights Act and Labour Law' (1998) 275, 288–9; S Fredman, 'Marginalising Equal Pay Laws' (2004) 282–3; L Flynn, 'Gender Equality Law and Employer's Dress Codes' (1995) 256–60; H Oliver, 'Sexual Orientation Discrimination: Perceptions, Definitions and Genuine Occupational Requirements' (2004) 15–18, 18–19; B Ryan, 'Employer Enforcement of Immigration Law after s.8 of the Asylum and Immigration Act 1996' (1997) 140–1, 141–3, P Skidmore, 'EC Framework Directive On Equal Treatment In Employment: Towards A Comprehensive Community Anti-Discrimination Policy?' (2001) 128; K O'Donovan and E Szyszczak, 'Redundancy Selection and Sex Discrimination' (1985) 253–4; J Lewis, 'Refusing to Allow Job Sharing' (1989) 246–7; M Connolly, 'Discrimination Law: Justification, Alternative Measures and Defences Based on Sex' (2001) 313-18; C McCrudden, 'Rethinking Positive Action' (1986) 230–2, 233–4; Mark Bell, 'Equality and the EU Constitution', (2004) 250; Marzia Barbera, 'Not the Same? The Judicial Role in the New Community Anti-Discrimination Law Context' (2002) 90–91; L Barmes and S Ashtiany, 'Diversity Approach To Achieving Equality: Potential And Pitfalls (2003) 282, 290–1; P Skidmore, 'Sex, Gender and Comparators in Employment Discrimination Law' (1997) 51, 54–6.

Oxford University Press: D Pannick *Sex Discrimination Law* (1985); 'Women's Rights in Employment' by E Collins and E Meehan in G Chambers and C McCrudden (eds) *Individual Rights and the Law in Britain* (1994).

Dr Wilson McLeod of the University of Edinburgh for 'Autochthonous language communities and the Race Relations Act', *Web Journal of Current Legal Issues*, (1998).

AB Academic Publishers (for extracts from *International Journal of Discrimination Law*: 'Religion or Belief and the Workplace', 104–06; 'The Operation of The Fair Employment (Northern Ireland) Act 1989—Ten Years On' (2002), 29–31, 112–13; L Dickens, 'Gender, race and employment equality in Britain: inadequate strategies and the role of industrial relations actors'; R Townshend-Smith, 'Justifying Indirect Discrimination in English and American Law: How Stringent Should the Test Be?'

Sweet and Maxwell (*Public Law*): L Lustgarten, 'The New Meaning of Discrimination' (1978) 190–3; M Bryan, 'Discrimination in the Public Provision of Housing: the Commission for Racial Equality Report on Housing in Hackney' (1984); S Robilliard, 'Should Parliament Enact a Religious Discrimination Act?' (1978); K McEvoy and C White, 'Security Vetting in Northern Ireland: Loyalty, Redress and Citizenship'; D Pannick, 'Homosexuals, Transsexuals and the Law', (1984); G Appleby and E Ellis, 'Formal Investigations: the CRE and the EOC as Law Enforcement Agencies', (1984) 247, 341, 343–5. (*European Law Review*) E Ellis, 'The Definition of Discrimination in European Sex Equality Law' (1994) 567–8; H Benyon and N Lowe, 'Mandla and the Meaning of "Racial Group"' (1994) (*Law Quarterly Review*) E Ellis and G Appleby, 'Blackening the Prestige Pot? Formal Investigations and the CRE' (1984); J M Thomson, 'Note on the Porcelli case' (1983).

MIND: 'Lesbians, gay men, bisexuals and mental health' (1996).

Continuum Publishing: from B Hepple and E Szyszczak (eds), *Discrimination: The Limits of Law* (London, Mansell, 1992): B Hepple 'Have 25 Years of the Race Relations Act in Britain Been a Failure?'; M Coussey, 'The Effectiveness of Strategic Enforcement of the Race Relations Act 1976'; T Modood, Cultural Diversity and Racial Discrimination in Employment Selection'; S Fredman and E Szyszczak, 'The Interaction of Race and Gender'; B Parekh, 'The Case for Positive Discrimination'; E Szyszczak, 'Race Discrimination: The Limits of Market Equality'; M Coussey, 'The Effectiveness of Strategic Enforcement of the Race Relations Act 1976'; V Sacks, 'Tackling Discrimination Positively in Britain'.

1

Introduction

Introduction

Discrimination, which thirty years ago was barely recognised in domestic law, is now the subject of a wealth of legal attention. Prohibitions on discrimination figure strongly in international law. The first recital to the Universal Declaration of Human Rights, for example, recognises 'the equal and inalienable rights of all' and the first two articles of the declaration provide that 'All human beings are born free and equal in dignity and rights' and that 'Everyone is entitled to all the rights and freedoms set forth in this Declaration, without distinction of any kind, such as race, colour, sex, language, religion, political or other opinion, national or social origin, property, birth or other status.' The International Covenant on Civil and Political Rights (ICCPR) and the International Covenant on Economic, Social and Cultural Rights (ICESCR), through which the Universal Declaration is given effect, both regulate discrimination. Article 26 of the ICCPR, for example, provides that:

> All persons are equal before the law and are entitled without any discrimination to the equal protection of the law. In this respect, the law shall prohibit any discrimination and guarantee to all persons equal and effective protection against discrimination on any ground such as race, colour, sex, language, religion, political or other opinion, national or social origin, property, birth or other status.

The ICESCR requires contracting parties (Article 2.2) to 'guarantee that the rights enunciated in the present Covenant will be exercised without discrimination of any kind as to race, colour, sex, language, religion, political or other opinion, national or social origin, property, birth or other status,' an approach adopted also by the European Convention on Human Rights (Article 14). Many of the other regional instruments (the American Covenant on Human Rights, the African Charter on Human and People's Rights; the European Social Charter of 1961 and revised Social Charter of 1996 and the recently adopted Treaty Establishing a Constitution for Europe, for example) proscribe discrimination either generally or in relation to the rights provided therein while the Charters, together with the ICESCR, ILO Conventions, the International Conventions on the Elimination of all Forms of Racial Discrimination (CERD) and on the Elimination of all Forms of Discrimination against Women (CEDAW) and the Convention on the Rights of the Child, all contain detailed provisions by which discrimination is to be eliminated and equality furthered.[1]

---

[1] For general discussion of these and other international provisions see A McColgan, 'Principles of Equality and Protection from Discrimination in International Human Rights Law' [2003] *European Human Rights Law Review*, 157–75.

These international provisions are mentioned here to give a flavour of the context in which domestic discrimination law operates. Between them they include a rich variety of approaches varying from blunt prohibitions on differential treatment on listed (and, in some cases, unlisted) grounds to richly detailed substantive requirements (such as, for example, Article 10 ICESCR which requires a reasonable period of 'paid leave or leave with adequate social security benefits' for maternity and Article 7 of the Convention on the Rights of the Child which provides that children shall be registered immediately after birth and 'shall have the right from birth to a name, the right to acquire a nationality and, as far as possible, the right to know and be cared for by [their] parents').[2] Most of the international provisions, whether ratified by the UK or not, are not directly applicable in domestic law (though in cases of genuine ambiguity the courts will adopt an interpretation of legislation which is consistent, rather than inconsistent, with international obligations undertaken by the state if the words of the statute are 'reasonably capable of bearing such a meaning').[3] But, as we shall see below, the implementation in the UK of the Human Rights Act 1998 has had the effect that Article 14 of the European Convention on Human Rights, together with a number of other provisions of the Convention which are particularly relevant to discrimination, have been given a form of effect in domestic law. The contours of these provisions are considered at various points throughout the book and there is a brief explanation at 14–19 below of how the HRA operates. But the discussion of the HRA is only by way of context and background for the most part in a book whose focus is on the detailed statutory regulation of discrimination.

Discrimination and the Common Law

The other context in which that statutory regulation operates is the common law. As Sandra Fredman has made clear in her book *Women and the Law*,[4] the historical approach of the common law to sex discrimination left much to be desired, the judiciary itself being responsible for doctrines such as coverture by which 'the very being or legal existence of the wife is suspended during the marriage or at least incorporated and consolidated into that of the husband under whose wing, protection and cover she performs everything.' It was not until 1991 that domestic law accepted that the rape of a woman by her husband was a legal possibility.[5] And gains for women in terms of enfranchisement and child custody on divorce were won very slowly by legislative reform in the teeth of determined judicial resistance. Public employers' attempts to pay men and women equally were struck down in *Roberts v Hopwood* [1925] AC 578 as the pursuit of 'some eccentric principles of socialistic philanthropy.' Nor were the common law's inadequacies in the context of discrimination restricted to the field of sex: in *In re Lysaght* the High Court upheld the validity of a legacy to fund training of British-born non-Jews and non-Roman Catholics.[6] According to that

---

[2] The US and Somalia are the only states which have not yet ratified this, the most widely accepted of, the United Nation's Conventions.

[3] *Garland v British Rail Engineering Ltd* [1983] 2 AC 751 (HL), *per* Lord Diplock. In addition, as in *Wilson v United Kingdom* (2002) 35 EHRR 523, international obligations can enter into domestic law via the interpretation of Convention provisions by the ECtHR.

[4] (Oxford, OUP, 1997).

[5] *R v R* [1992] 1 AC 599.

[6] [1966] 1 Ch 191. See also *Scala Ballroom v Ratcliffe* [1958] 3 All ER 220.

Court the stipulation, though 'undesirable . . . [was] not . . . contrary to the public policy.' Nor, according to the House of Lords in *Blathwayt v Baron Cawley*, was a testamentary condition excluding those who were or became Roman Catholic.[7] Conor Gearty cites *In re Lysaght*, together with *Schlegel v Corcoran* (1942) IR 19 and *Scala Ballroom (Wolverhampton) Ltd v Ratcliffe* [1958] 1 WLR 1057, as illustrative of 'a system of laws which prioritized . . . interests in property and contract to the exclusion of other public interests.'[8] In *Schlegel*, an Irish court upheld the reasonableness of a refusal to transfer rooms to a Jewish dentist on the grounds that the practice 'may, under Mr Gross, develop a Jewish complexion . . . such an anticipation is not groundless in a locality with a number of Jewish residents.' And in *Scala* the English Court of Appeal upheld the legality of a bar on non-white entrants to the ballroom as 'a course which [the company was] entitled to adopt in [its] own business interests.'

In *Nagle v Feilden* [1966] 2 QB 633 the Court of Appeal reinstated a claim struck out by the lower courts that the discriminatory refusal by the Jockey Club to grant a woman a training licence was 'unlawful and in restraint of trade and contrary to public policy.' Lord Denning remarked that the refusal of training licences to women 'may well be said to be arbitrary and capricious,' women being perfectly capable of training horses, although he did suggest that a different approach might be appropriate in relation to 'an unsuitable occupation for a woman, like that of a jockey or speedway-rider.' The case did not mark a turning point in the judicial approach to questions of discrimination. In *Amin v Entry Clearance Officer, Bombay* [1983] 2 AC 818 the House of Lords ruled, by a majority, that sex discrimination in the context of immigration fell outwith the SDA (this aspect of the decision is considered in Chapter 4). Their Lordships further ruled that, this being the case, the discrimination was not open to challenge. According to Lord Fraser, with whom all of their Lordships agreed on this point: 'not all sex discrimination is unlawful . . . Discrimination is only unlawful if it occurs in one of the fields in which it is prohibited by [the SDA].' More recently too, in *Bernstein v Immigration Appeal Tribunal & Department of Employment* [1988] Imm AR 449, Lord Justice Mann made the same point in which he ruled that 'sex discrimination of itself is not unlawful. It is unlawful only in circumstances prescribed by the [SDA].'

In *R v Admiralty Board ex parte Lustig-Prean, R v Ministry of Defence ex parte Smith* [1996] QB 517 the Court of Appeal upheld a ban on gays in the military against *Wednesbury* challenge. Simon Brown J (as he then was), in the Divisional Court, had remarked on the lack of evidence put before him to justify the ' "blanket, non-discretionary, specific," "status based" ban' but had ' "albeit with hesitation and regret," ' decided that the ban was not so irrational as to fail the *Wednesbury* test which requires the court to be satisfied that the administrative action at issue 'is beyond the range of responses open to a reasonable decision-maker.'[9] The Court of Appeal upheld his decision. The Court accepted the submission of David Pannick QC, for the claimants, that:

---

[7] [1976] AC 419. See also *Horne v Poland* [1922] 2 KB 364, in which the High Court accepted that race discrimination in the provision of insurance was potentially reasonable, and *Cumings v Birkenhead Corporation* [1972] Ch 12 in which the Court of Appeal upheld the *vires* of an education authority rule that children who had attended Roman Catholic primary school would be considered only for Roman Catholic secondary schools. In *Cumings* Lord Denning insisted that a rule allocating places in according to hair 'or, for that matter,' skin colour 'would be so unreasonable, so capricious, so irrelevant to any proper system of education that it would be *ultra vires* altogether, and this court would strike it down at once.'

[8] 'The Internal and External 'Other' in the Union Legal Order: Racism, Religious Intolerance and Xenophobia in Europe in P Alston, M Bustelo and J Heenan (eds), *The EU and Human Rights* (Oxford, OUP, 1999) 327, 341.

[9] Divisional Court citation from M Bowley QC, 'The Strasborg Flight is Boarding Now' (1996) 1 *International Journal of Discrimination and the Law* 376, 376–7.

The court may not interfere with the exercise of an administrative discretion on substantive grounds save where the court is satisfied that the decision is unreasonable in the sense that it is beyond the range of responses open to a reasonable decision-maker. But in judging whether the decision-maker has exceeded this margin of appreciation the human rights context is important. The more substantial the interference with human rights, the more the court will require by way of justification before it is satisfied that the decision is reasonable in the sense outlined above.

But it went on to decide that the policy, which was justified by the Ministry of Defence on the grounds of 'morale and unit effectiveness, the . . . role of the services as guardian of recruits under the age of 18, and . . . the requirement of communal living in many service situations,' was not irrational. Pannick argued that the first reason was rooted in irrational prejudice, the second also in the assumption 'that homosexuals were less able to control their sexual impulses than heterosexuals,' and that, while '[t]he lack of privacy in service life was . . . a reason for imposing strict rules and discipline [it was] not a reason for banning the membership of any homosexual . . . each of the appellants had worked in the armed forces for a number of years without any concern being expressed or complaints made about inappropriate behaviour.'

Above all, Mr Pannick criticised the blanket nature of the existing rule. He placed great emphasis on the practice of other nations whose rules were framed so as to counter the particular mischiefs to which homosexual orientation or activity might give rise. He pointed out that other personal problems such as addiction to alcohol, or compulsive gambling, or marital infidelity were dealt with by the service authorities on a case by case basis and not on the basis of a rule which permitted no account to be taken of the peculiar features of the case under consideration.

The Master of the Rolls, with whose judgment the others concurred, ruled that 'The threshold of irrationality is a high one. It was not crossed in this case.'

In *Smith & Grady v UK*[10] the ECtHR ruled that the ban breached Article 8 of the ECHR.

Smith & Grady v UK (1999) 29 EHRR 548

Judgment:

. . . each State is competent to organise its own system of military discipline and enjoys a certain margin of appreciation in this respect . . . it is open to the State to impose restrictions on an individual's right to respect for his private life where there is a real threat to the armed forces' operational effectiveness, as the proper functioning of an army is hardly imaginable without legal rules designed to prevent service personnel from undermining it. However, the national authorities cannot rely on such rules to frustrate the exercise by individual members of the armed forces of their right to respect for their private lives, which right applies to service personnel as it does to others within the jurisdiction of the State. Moreover, assertions as to a risk to operational effectiveness must be 'substantiated by specific examples.' . . .

The core argument of the Government in support of the policy is that the presence of open or suspected homosexuals in the armed forces would have a substantial and negative effect on morale and, consequently, on the fighting power and operational effectiveness of the armed forces . . .

---

[10] *Lustig-Prean & Beckett v UK* (1999) 29 EHRR 548 was in similar terms.

The Court notes the lack of concrete evidence to substantiate the alleged damage to morale and fighting power that any change in the policy would entail. . . Given the number of homosexuals dismissed between 1991 and 1996 . . . the number of homosexuals who were in the armed forces at the relevant time cannot be said to be insignificant. Even if the absence of such evidence can be explained by the consistent application of the policy, as submitted by the Government, this is insufficient to demonstrate to the Court's satisfaction that operational effectiveness problems of the nature and level alleged can be anticipated in the absence of the policy . . .

. . . The Government . . . underlined that it is 'the knowledge or suspicion of homosexuality' which would cause the morale problems and not conduct, so that a conduct code would not solve the anticipated difficulties. However, in so far as negative attitudes to homosexuality are insufficient, of themselves, to justify the policy . . . they are equally insufficient to justify the rejection of a proposed alternative . . .

The Government maintained that homosexuality raised problems of a type and intensity that race and gender did not. However, even if it can be assumed that the integration of homosexuals would give rise to problems not encountered with the integration of women or racial minorities, the Court is not satisfied that the codes and rules which have been found to be effective in the latter case would not equally prove effective in the former. The 'robust indifference' . . . of the large number of British armed forces' personnel serving abroad with allied forces to homosexuals serving in those foreign forces, serves to confirm that the perceived problems of integration are not insuperable . . .

The Court . . . notes the evidence before the domestic courts to the effect that the European countries operating a blanket legal ban on homosexuals in their armed forces are now in a small minority. It considers that, even if relatively recent, the Court cannot overlook the widespread and consistently developing views and associated legal changes to the domestic laws of Contracting States on this issue.

In *Smith & Grady* the ECtHR specifically addressed the contention of the UK Government that the claimants' access to judicial review (the exercise of which had eventually resulted in their application to that Court) was sufficient to constitute an effective remedy in respect of ECHR violations as required by Article 13 of the Convention which provides that: 'Everyone whose rights and freedoms as set forth in this Convention are violated shall have an effective remedy before a national authority notwithstanding that the violation has been committed by persons acting in an official capacity.' The British Government argued that irrationality review was sufficient to meet its obligations under Article 13.[11] The Court disagreed, ruling that 'even assuming that the essential complaints of the applicants before this Court were before and considered by the domestic courts, the threshold at which the High Court and the Court of Appeal could find the Ministry of Defence policy irrational was placed so high that it effectively excluded any consideration by the domestic courts of the question of whether the interference with the applicants' rights answered a pressing social need or was proportionate to the national security and public order aims pursued, principles which lie at the heart of the Court's analysis of complaints under Article 8 of the Convention.'

In the previous edition of this book I was sceptical about the argument put by Jeffrey Jowell, that equality is a 'constitutional principle' in English common law,[12] pointing out

[11] Relying on *Vilvarajah v UK* (1991) 14 EHRR 248 in which the ECtHR accepted that proceedings by way of judicial review could amount to an effective remedy for the purposes of Art 13 in a case in which (as there) the test applied in judicial review proceedings coincided with the ECtHR's approach under the relevant provision of the ECHR (Art 3, in a case concerning extradition and expulsion decisions made by the Secretary of State).

[12] 'Is Equality a Constitutional Principle?' (1994) *Current Legal Problems* 1.

that many of the cases relied upon by Jowell resulted in decisions striking down attempts to take ameliorative action in favour of disadvantaged groups.[13] But I suggested that the decision of the Privy Council in *Matadeen v Pointu & Ors* [1999] 1 AC 98 might mark a significant change in the common law's approach to discrimination.

The case concerned a challenge to a change of education rules which had the effect of disadvantaging students who were not studying an oriental language. The claimants argued that, Mauritius being a signatory to the ICCPR, its constitutional prohibitions on discrimination must be read so as to give effect to Article 26 of the Covenant, which provides (as we saw above) that 'the law shall prohibit any discrimination and guarantee to all persons equal and effective protection against discrimination on any ground such as race, colour, sex, language, religion, political or other opinion, national or social origin, property, birth or other status.'

Lord Hoffmann stated, for their Lordships, that 'treating like cases alike and unlike cases differently is a general axiom of rational behaviour. It is, for example, frequently invoked by the courts in proceedings for judicial review as a ground for holding some administrative act to have been irrational.' He went on to declare that the protection of the rights guaranteed by Article 26 did not require the incorporation of that provision as such into domestic law, this on the basis that 'the power to quash the Minister's decision as unreasonable, under the principles in *Associated Provincial Picture Houses v Wednesbury* [[1948] 1KB 223], would have been entirely adequate to secure compliance with the equal treatment provisions of Article 26.'

In the last edition of this book I suggested that 'On the assumption that this declaration is to the effect that discrimination contrary to international obligations should, *per se*, be regarded as contravening *Wednesbury*, it marks a significant recent change in administrative law,' citing the decision of the Court of Appeal in *ex p. Smith*. The impact of the decision is further considered below. But it should be noted that *Matadeen* raised as many questions as it answered. Immediately after making the statement extracted above Lord Hoffmann went on to declare that:

> the very banality of the principle [of equality] must suggest a doubt as to whether merely to state it can provide an answer to the kind of problem which arises in this case. Of course persons should be uniformly treated, unless there is some valid reason to treat them differently. But what counts as a valid reason for treating them differently? And, perhaps more important, who is to decide whether the reason is valid or not? Must it always be the courts? The reasons for not treating people uniformly often involve . . . questions of social policy on which views may differ. These are questions which the elected representatives of the people have some claim to decide for themselves. The fact that equality of treatment is a general principle of rational behaviour does not entail that it should necessarily be a justiciable principle—that it should always be the judges who have the last word on whether the principle has been observed. In this, as in other areas of constitutional law, sonorous judicial statements of uncontroversial principle often conceal the real problem, which is to mark out the boundary between the powers of the judiciary, the legislature and the executive in deciding how that principle is to be applied.
>
> A self-confident democracy may feel that it can give the last word, even in respect of the most fundamental rights, to the popularly elected organs of its constitution. The United Kingdom has traditionally done so; perhaps not always to universal satisfaction, but certainly without forfeiting its title to be a democracy. A generous power of judicial review

---

[13] These included *Prescott v Birmingham Corporation* [1955] Ch 210 and *Hopwood* itself.

of legislative action is not therefore of the essence of a democracy. Different societies may reach different solutions.

Matadeen was relied upon by the defendants in *Gurung v Ministry of Defence* [2002] EWHC 2463 Admin to argue that the courts ought not to intervene in a case in which race discrimination was alleged. McCombe J drew a distinction between the ground upon which discrimination was alleged in *Matadeen* and that at issue in *Gurung*:

> [in a] lecture given by Lord Steyn on 18 September 2002 in honour of Lord Cooke of Thorndon [he] says:
> 'The anti-discrimination provision contained in Article 14 of the European Convention is parasitic in as much as it serves only to protect other Convention rights. There is no general or free-standing prohibition of discrimination. This is a relatively weak provision. On the other hand, the constitutional principle of equality developed domestically by English courts is wider. The law and the government must accord every individual equal concern and respect for their welfare and dignity. Everyone is entitled to equal protection of the law, which must be applied without fear or favour. Except where compellingly justified distinctions must never be made on the grounds of race, colour, belief, gender or other irrational ground. Individuals are therefore comprehensively protected from discrimination by the principle of equality. This constitutional right has a continuing role to play. The organic development of constitutional rights is therefore a complementary and parallel process to the application of human rights legislation.'[14]
> I cite that passage in demonstration of the continued force of the common law principle of equality and generality of its application. I emphasise the passage where Lord Steyn says that, 'Except where compellingly justified distinctions must never be made on the grounds of race [or] colour' . . .
> Th[e *Matadeen*] decision obviously leaves intact the common law principle of equality of which Lord Steyn spoke in his lecture. Moreover, given the terms of the Constitution of Mauritius which proscribed discrimination on racial grounds, it can hardly have been thought that concepts of racial discrimination might not be properly justiciable . . .

McCombe J went on to rule that race discrimination was 'irrational and inconsistent with the principle of equality that is the cornerstone of our law.' In *R (Association of British Civilian Internees: Far East Region) v Secretary of State for Defence* [2003] QB 1397 the Court of Appeal rejected an argument, based on *Matadeen*, that a (non-racist) distinction drawn between categories of British citizens on the basis of their place of birth contravened the 'common law principle of equality.' According to Dyson LJ, for the Court:

> We do not find it necessary to determine whether there is a free-standing principle of equality in English domestic law, since we did not hear argument on the point. We do not, however, think that the Privy Council in *Matadeen's* case was propounding such a principle. It seems to us that what Lord Hoffmann was discussing was how the Wednesbury test should be accommodated in cases of alleged unjustified discrimination . . .
> whether the question is considered in *Wednesbury* terms, or on an application of a free-standing principle that like cases should be treated alike unless there is a valid reason for treating them differently, the complaint in the present case must be rejected. We have already given our reasons for concluding that the decision to exclude those who did not satisfy the birth criteria was not unreasonable in the *Wednesbury* sense. If a free-standing

---

[14] Now at (2002) 18 *European Human Rights Law Review* 723.

principle of equality were to be applied, it would have to be on the basis that the court would give the minister a margin of appreciation to determine what was a valid reason for treating internees differently. In our view, the minister's decision to exclude those British subjects who did not satisfy the birth criteria fell comfortably within the margin of appreciation that should be accorded to him by the court. Our reasons are essentially the same as those which led us to conclude that the challenge to the birth criteria fails on an application of the *Wednesbury* test.

The future development of the common law principle of equality (assuming such a principle exists) is beyond the scope of this book. One point which should be made is that the law tends to lead rather than follow in these matters: if the grounds upon which one person receives less favourable treatment than another have to be seen as invidious before the discrimination is seen as irrational, there will be a time lag between social change and legal prohibition. In *Short v Poole* [1926] Ch 66 Warrington LJ made the oft-repeated statement that the courts could strike down as *ultra vires* 'an act of the public body, though performed in good faith and without the taint of corruption, was so clearly founded on alien and irrelevant grounds as to be outside the authority conferred upon the body.' He gave an example there of a teacher dismissed 'because she had red hair, or for some equally frivolous and foolish reason,' while upholding the decision to dismiss the claimant, a teacher, because she was a married woman.

Domestic Statutory Prohibitions on Discrimination

Existing Provisions

The main domestic legislation concerned with discrimination consists (in chronological order):

- the Equal Pay Act 1970 (EqPA)
- the Sex Discrimination Act 1975 (SDA)
- the Race Relations Act 1976 (RRA)
- the Disability Discrimination Act 1995 (DDA)
- the Fair Employment and Treatment (Northern Ireland) Order 1998
- the Employment Equality (Religion or Belief) Regulations 2003 (RB Regs), and
- the Employment Equality (Sexual Orientation) Regulations 2003 (SO Regs)

These provisions cannot be considered in isolation from the wider context; in particular, EU law and the Human Rights Act 1998. These are considered further below. All but the most recent of the domestic provisions have been extensively amended over time. The SDA and the EqPA operate together, the latter dealing exclusively with discrimination in contractual terms of employment. The scope of the SDA, RRA, FETO and DDA is broadly similar, all but the SDA regulating discrimination in contractual terms of employment. But only the RRA applies in full to discrimination by public authorities and imposes positive duties thereon. The Northern Ireland Act 1998 imposes duties on Northern Irish public authorities across a range of grounds. The DDA 2005 imposes positive duties on public authorities and prohibits discrimination by them on grounds related to disability. The Act is considered throughout the book, those provisions dealing with public authorities primarily in Chapters 3 and 5. The Equality Bill 2005, which made similar provisions in relation to sex discrimination, did not survive the dissolution of Parliament in advance of the May 2005 general election but the Government indicated that similar legislation would be an early priority in the event of a Labour victory. The SDA, RRA, DDA and FETO all apply well beyond employment to housing, education, access to goods and services etc (though with important differences between the DDA and the other Acts). The SO and RB Regs, by contrast, only regulate discrimination in relation to employment and third level education, though the Equality Bill 2005 proposed the extension of the prohibition on religion and belief discrimination to cover access to goods, facilities and services and education more generally. The scope of the various legislative provisions is considered in Chapter 4, and their enforcement in Chapter 5 while Chapters 6–10 consider specific issues arising in connection, respectively, with sex, race, disability, religion or belief (and, in Northern Ireland, political opinion), sexual orientation and gender reassignment.

There are differences between the legislative regimes in their approach to discrimination as well as in the circumstances in which it is regulated. The most noteworthy of these differences is perhaps between the DDA and the other provisions, in that the DDA explicitly imposes duties of reasonable adjustment on employers and service providers etc. But there are also variations in definitions of indirect discrimination and approaches to harassment which result from EC initiatives, and significant differences between FETO and the other regimes. These are discussed in Chapter 2 while the DDA's unique approach to discrimination is considered further in Chapter 8 and FETO's in Chapter 9. The approach of the legislative provisions to positive discrimination is the subject matter of Chapter 3.

It will become apparent to any reader of this book that the domestic provisions on discrimination are complex and, at times, lacking in coherence or consistency. Piecemeal reform over the years has resulted in a tangle of acts and regulations whose variety owes little to principle and much to happenstance. A degree of such development is probably unavoidable—Marzia Barbera pointed out recently in the *Industrial Law Journal* that 'What le[ads] certain differences to be considered unlawful before or in place of others [is] not some "natural and permanent" quality, but the meaning that this difference assume[s] in a given historical context, within a given community.'[15] Thus legislation from the EU has focused initially on sex (and nationality), only more recently on the other grounds, necessitating not only the implementation of new legislation (such as the SO and RB Regs) but the amendment of earlier provisions. Some inconsistency has perhaps been inevitable in the short term. But what has emerged is a hierarchy of grounds which does not have any principled defence. It may be that some grounds of discrimination do require greater levels of protection than others. But the current hierarchy is not grounded in any defensible rationale.

The SDA and RRA were originally very similar (though the application of the EqPA rather than the SDA to contractual discrimination renders challenges to sex-related pay differentials more, rather than less, problematic). The DDA in its original form was considerably weaker, but the ongoing implementation of its provisions together with its amendment in line with EU and domestic pressures has significantly strengthened the Act, a trend which has continued with the passage of the DDA 2005 (see further Chapters 3, 4 and 8). The RRA overtook the SDA in 2000 with the implementation of the Race Relations (Amendment) Act 2000, which was passed in response to the racist murder of teenager Stephen Lawrence in 1993, and the widespread 'institutionalised racism' disclosed by the

---

[15] 'Not the Same? The Judicial Role in the New Community Anti-Discrimination Law Context', (2002) 31 *Industrial Law Journal* 82.

subsequent *Macpherson* report.[16] The 2000 Act extended the application of the RRA to public authorities and imposed positive obligations on them. The Act is also more protective than both the SDA and the DDA as it applies other than to employment, having been amended to give effect to the definitions of indirect discrimination and harassment and the shifting of the burden of proof provided for by the Racial Equality Directive. On the other hand these new definitions do not apply to discrimination on grounds of nationality or colour (save to the extent that the latter also amounts to discrimination on grounds of 'race or ethnic or national origins'), so protection in relation to these forms of discrimination in the employment context is weaker than under the SDA (which was amended in 2001 to give effect to the Burden of Proof Directive whose provisions, however, apply only in relation to employment, broadly defined). Beneath the RRA, SDA and DDA come the SO and (prior to the expected reintroduction of the Equality Bill) the RB Regs, which apply only to employment and third level education, and under these the SDA as it applies to discrimination on grounds of married status (only in the employment context) and to discrimination on grounds of gender reassignment (only to direct discrimination and only in the employment context). Having said this, the implementation of the Gender Recognition Act 2004 (see further Chapter 10) significantly improved the position of trans people (though it has not rendered discrimination against them unlawful as such).

It is not altogether surprising, in light of the above, that the past decade or so has seen increasing pressure for a total overhaul of domestic discrimination/equality legislation so as to replace the current jumble with a comprehensive and comprehensible, coherent and principled structure. The need for such reform has increased with the expansion of protected grounds over recent years but until August 2004 the British Government had set its face firmly against root-and-branch reform (by contrast, plans are well under way in Northern Ireland to create a single equality Act there). In May 2004, however, the DTI published proposals for the creation of a Commission for Equality and Human Rights whose remit (see further Chapter 5) would extend to all the regulated grounds (including age, which will be regulated from the end of 2006) and to human rights. And in August 2004 the Government declared that a review of equality and discrimination legislation to create a single equality act would be one of the first tasks of the CEHR. The proposals for the CEHR found their way into the Equality Bill 2005 but no further details of single equality legislation have been made available at this stage.

Age Discrimination

The Employment Equality Directive prohibits direct and indirect discrimination, harassment and victimisation, on grounds of sexual orientation, religion or belief, disability and age. In these respects the age-related provisions of the Directive do not differ from those concerning discrimination on grounds of sexual orientation and religion or belief[17] and it is likely that eventual legislation will reflect the pattern of the SO Regs and the RB Regs (considered throughout the book and, in particular, in Chapters 10 and 9 respectively).[18]

---

[16] FETO, which applies only in Northern Ireland and regulates discrimination on grounds of religious and political belief, imposes monitoring and review obligations on employers (see Chs 4 and 9) and applies the new definitions of indirect discrimination and burden of proof etc. to employment-related discrimination.

[17] The disability provisions are somewhat different, providing as they do for a duty to make reasonable adjustments.

[18] Though the ECNI suggests that direct discrimination in this context should be replaced by a prohibition on 'disadvantage on the grounds of' (ECNI, Response to the DTI Age Consultation 2003 *Equality and Diversity: Age Matters* 10.

The SO and RB Regs were passed under the European Communities Act 1972, which permits only those provisions reasonably necessary to achieve compliance with EU law. The age-related provisions of the Directive are to be implemented by regulation in the UK by 2 December 2006 despite the new commitment to a single equality Act, given the time scale involved and the fact that it will take some years even to have the CEHR up and running, more for it to complete a review of discrimination law. The Government has begun the consultation process on the content of the age-related legislation. The DTI published *Equality and Diversity: Age Matters* in July 2003 with a view (para 1.20) to 'develop[ing] draft regulations in the light of responses to this consultation . . . consult[ing] on them in the first half of 2004 [and] . . . lay[ing] the legislation before Parliament by the end of 2004.' That timetable has slipped, the latest government announcement being that draft regulations will be consulted on in summer 2005 and the legislation brought into force in October 2006, assuming a Labour victory in the May 2005 elections.

Where the age regulations are likely to differ significantly from those dealing with sexual orientation and religion or belief is in relation to defences. The Employment Equality Directive provides (Article 4) that:

. . . Member States may provide that a difference of treatment which is based on a characteristic related to [age] shall not constitute discrimination where, by reason of the nature of the particular occupational activities concerned or of the context in which they are carried out, such a characteristic constitutes a genuine and determining occupational requirement, provided that the objective is legitimate and the requirement is proportionate.

This, the genuine occupational requirement (GOR) defence, is common to all the grounds covered by the Directive and is relatively non-controversial in its application in this context. According to *Towards Equality and Diversity* (para 5.15) 'One example might be a requirement for child actors to play the parts of children in, say, a performance of *Oliver.*' Of much broader potential application, however, are Recital 14 of the preamble and Article 6 of the Directive which provide as follows:

Recital 14

This Directive shall be without prejudice to national provisions laying down retirement ages.

Article 6

1. . . . Member States may provide that differences of treatment on grounds of age shall not constitute discrimination, if, within the context of national law, they are objectively and reasonably justified by a legitimate aim, including legitimate employment policy, labour market and vocational training objectives, and if the means of achieving that aim are appropriate and necessary. Such differences of treatment may include, among others:
   (a) the setting of special conditions on access to employment and vocational training, employment and occupation, including dismissal and remuneration conditions, for young people, older workers and persons with caring responsibilities in order to promote their vocational integration or ensure their protection;
   (b) the fixing of minimum conditions of age, professional experience or seniority in service for access to employment or to certain advantages linked to employment;
   (c) the fixing of a maximum age for recruitment which is based on the training requirements of the post in question or the need for a reasonable period of employment before retirement.

2. . . . Member States may provide that the fixing for occupational social security schemes of ages for admission or entitlement to retirement or invalidity benefits, including the fixing under those schemes of different ages for employees or groups or categories of employees, and the use, in the context of such schemes, of age criteria in actuarial calculations, does not constitute discrimination on the grounds of age, provided this does not result in discrimination on the grounds of sex.

Article 6 does not set out a closed list of circumstances in which discrimination on grounds of age may be justified. *Age Matters* suggests that the types of objectives which could be justified in line with Article 6 include (para 3.15): 'health, welfare, and safety—for example, the protection of younger workers; facilitation of employment planning—for example, where a business has a number of people approaching retirement age at the same time; the particular training requirements of the post in question—for example, air traffic controllers, who have to undergo 18 months theoretical and practical training at the College of Air Traffic Control, followed by further on the job training; encouraging and rewarding loyalty; the need for a reasonable period of employment before retirement.'

Age Matters reported (para 2.1) that 50 per cent of respondents to the Government's initial consultation document on the new directives (*Towards Equality and Diversity*, 2001) believed that they had either experienced or witnessed age discrimination at work. The most commonly perceived form of age discrimination (22 per cent of those reporting age discrimination) consisted in being forced to retire at a particular age. But although *Age Matters* recognised (at para 4.5) that a 'powerful way' of transmitting the desired message that 'age discrimination is not acceptable . . . would be to abolish employers' mandatory retirement ages'; and that 57 per cent of respondents to *Towards Equality and Diversity* opposed compulsory retirement ages. But Trade and Industry Secretary Patricia Hewitt announced in December 2004 that the age regulations would impose a default retirement age of 65 at which employers would not have to justify mandatory retirement. The effect of such a default age was considered in the consultation document:

DTI, *Age Matters*, paras 4.25–4.26

. . . With such a default age employers would, of course, still be free to continue employing people beyond the age . . . or indeed to set a retirement age higher than the default age.

Either approach might help us move towards the culture change already begun by employers themselves and reinforced by the Age Positive campaign to focus on ability and not age. The outright abolition of non-justified mandatory retirement ages would send a stronger signal. On the other hand, some businesses have said that allowing the default option of a retirement age . . . might allow them to manage their workforces effectively and operate productively—providing them with more certainty when it comes to workforce planning.

The decision to embrace a default retirement age was very controversial: it had been suggested that deadlock between the DTI (which favoured such a provision) and the Department for Work and Pensions (which did not) was to blame for delays in the production of the draft regulations. The December 2004 announcement was all the more unwelcome to many as *Age Matters* had floated a possible default retirement age of 70. The legality of the Government's proposal remains to be assessed.

Age Matters identified a number of areas in which the implementation of the age-related provisions of the Employment Equality Directive will require legal change. These include the age-related upper limit for unfair dismissal claims (though as the document points out, a dismissal in connection with a justifiable or default retirement age is likely to be fair). Basic unfair dismissal awards and statutory redundancy pay are currently calculated in part by reference to age, a practice which will have to end, although the Government favours retention of the long-service element of the award for redundancy despite the indirectly discriminatory impact of this on younger workers.

DTI, *Age Matters*, paras 6.12–6.13

. . . the primary purpose of the [redundancy payment] scheme is to ensure that employers compensate qualifying redundant employees for the loss of expected continued employment in the job. It does not compensate for 'loss of rights in the job.' However, the weighting of payments in favour of more senior employees appears to be a widely supported aspect of the scheme.

We have, therefore, taken this opportunity to review the rationale for the scheme itself. We have concluded that it should henceforth have the supplementary purpose of ensuring that employers recognise, in the amount of any payment to which a redundant employee is entitled, the extent of that employee's past commitment to the business. We believe that, by reference to this supplementary purpose, the use of length of service as a factor in the payment calculation remains justified and appropriate. We propose, therefore, to retain this provision.

The Consultation Paper suggests that discrimination in relation to recruitment, selection and promotion could be justified in line with Article 6 of the Employment Equality Directive in 'exceptional cases' in which 'the length of time a potential recruit would have with a company would [have the result that their recruitment would] not make business sense.' It also suggests that 'legislation should allow employers to provide pay and non-pay benefits based on length of service or experience, which might otherwise amount to unlawful direct or indirect discrimination, if they can justify doing so' in line with Article 6.

DTI, *Age Matters*, paras 8.4–8.6

The 269 responses to *Towards Equality and Diversity* identified a number of practices that might be based on seniority, length of service or experience. These included additional annual leave, long service awards, trainee pay, incremental pay, and redundancy pay. Such arrangements:

- are accepted ways of recognising loyalty. Employers feel that that has nothing to do with age and should not be outlawed—all employees are potentially eligible if they remain in service;
- provide incentives for staff;
- particularly incremental pay, reward experience.

We propose that legislation should allow employers to provide pay and non-pay benefits based on length of service or experience, which might otherwise amount to unlawful direct or indirect discrimination, if they can justify doing so.

The benefits of many seniority provisions are widely accepted. The Directive clearly envisages that where such arrangements amount to direct discrimination they can be justifiable. Therefore, we propose to make specific provision for employers to be able to justify seniority conditions by reference to the aims set out in paragraph 3.15 [above]-specifically, encouraging and rewarding loyalty.

Seniority practices which are indirectly discriminatory will also be able to be justified . . .

Retirement ages have repercussions, as we saw above, not only for unfair dismissal and redundancy, but for recruitment and training, etc. The question whether employers will be able to justify their own mandatory retirement ages will turn on individual cases, though the legislation could be more or less permissive on this issue. But the suggested state imposition of a default retirement age is problematic for a number of reasons. One potential difficulty is the non-regression principle: at present there is no state retirement age (as distinct from state *persionable* age) and so the imposition of a default retirement age might be regarded as reducing protection from age discrimination.[19] Michael Rubenstein, writing in the *Equal Opportunities Review* prior to Hewitt's announcement, suggested that 'What to do about mandatory retirement is the single most important equal opportunities issue facing the government today.'[20] He argued that a mandatory retirement age 'is entirely inconsistent with eliminating arbitrary age discrimination' and countered the arguments put forward in favour of mandatory retirement ages by suggesting that 'the loss of dignity from being dismissed for cause has to be weighed against the loss of dignity of being thrown out of a job before you are ready and willing.' Pointing out that the assumption of declining capability in older age, coupled with an unwillingness to retire, is an 'offensive stereotype,' he stated that 'Experience in countries that have abolished mandatory retirement teaches us that there will continue to be a "normal" retirement age without mandatory retirement. Most employees will retire voluntarily when they can afford to. That means that they will retire at the minimum age at which they are entitled to a full pension.' Rubenstein decried the December 2004 announcement as a 'shameful surrender' (137 *Equal Opportunities Review*), and pointing out that Recital 14 of the preamble to the directive appears to refer only to *pre-existing* state retirement ages. The *Equal Opportunities Review* suggested that a legal challenge is 'inevitable'. Others have expressed concern at the prospect that the implementation of the Directive will be used to increase state pensionable age. The Equality Commission for Northern Ireland (ECNI) has warned against confusing removing mandatory retirement ages and increasing state pensionable age, and the TUC launched a national campaign against raising pensionable age in 2004.

Discrimination/Equality and the HRA

The Human Rights Act gives effect in domestic law to the provisions of the ECHR which are appended to the Act. As is the case with international equality provisions and the common law, the HRA is outside the scope of this book. It is mentioned here only because (a) it has implications for the interpretation of the statutory provisions here considered and (b) it forms a significant part of the context in which those provisions operate. So, for example, although the new legislation on sexual orientation discrimination applies only to employment, the House of Lords recently ruled in *Ghaidan v Godin-Mendoza* [2004] 2 AC 557 (see Chapter 10) that discrimination against same-sex partners in the provisions of the Rent Act 1977 breached Articles 8 and 14 of the Convention, and relied on the HRA to interpret the 1977 Act so as to provide the same benefits to same-sex as to heterosexual couples. Equally, although the new provisions regulating discrimination on grounds of

---

[19] Though the cut-off for unfair dismissal claims at the normal retirement age may amount to the same thing for these purposes.
[20] 'Mandatory retirement and the dignity canard' 131 *Equal Opportunities Review*.

religion or belief apply only in relation to employment, the Court of Appeal recently accepted in *R (on the application of Begum) v Headteacher and Governors of Denbigh High School* [2005] EWCA Civ 199, which is discussed in Chapter 9, that Article 9 of the Convention (which protects freedom of 'thought, conscience and religion') applied in a case involving a dispute about the application of school uniform rules to a Muslim pupil.

All of the incorporated provisions of the European Convention are of potential significance in the context of discrimination, this because they can provide a 'hook' for the application of the parasitic Article 14 which provides that:

> The enjoyment of the rights and freedoms set forth in this Convention shall be secured without discrimination on any ground such as sex, race, colour, language, religion, political or other opinion, national or social origin, association with a national minority, property, birth or other status.

Article 14 could be pleased in conjunction with Article 2 (which protects the right to life), in a case in which discrimination in access to life-saving treatment was alleged, with Article 5 and/or 6 (which protect rights to liberty and fair trials) where discrimination in the criminal justice system was at issue, or in conjunction with Article 12 where discrimination concerned entitlement to marry. These provisions will not be further considered. There are, however, a number of Convention provisions which are of particular relevance to discrimination because they may themselves be brought into play by discriminatory treatment. Perhaps the most important of these are Articles 3, 8 and 9 and Article 1 of the First Protocol to the Convention which provide, respectively, as follows:

Article 3
No one shall be subjected to torture or to inhuman or degrading treatment or punishment.

Article 8
1. Everyone has the right to respect for his private and family life, his home and his correspondence.
2. There shall be no interference by a public authority with the exercise of this right except such as is in accordance with the law and is necessary in a democratic society in the interests of national security, public safety or the economic well-being of the country, for the prevention of disorder or crime, for the protection of health or morals, or for the protection of the rights and freedoms of others.

Article 9
1. Everyone has the right to freedom of thought, conscience and religion; this right includes freedom to change his religion or belief and freedom, either alone or in community with others and in public or private, to manifest his religion or belief, in worship, teaching, practice and observance.
2. Freedom to manifest one's religion or beliefs shall be subject only to such limitations as are prescribed by law and are necessary in a democratic society in the interests of public safety, for the protection of public order, health or morals, or for the protection of the rights and freedoms of others.

Article 1 of the First Protocol to the Convention
Every natural or legal person is entitled to the peaceful enjoyment of his possessions. No one shall be deprived of his possessions except in the public interest and subject to the conditions provided for by law and by the general principles of international law.

The preceding provisions shall not, however, in any way impair the right of a State to enforce such laws as it deems necessary to control the use of property in accordance with the general interest or to secure the payment of taxes or other contributions or penalties.

Article 3 may be brought into play by discrimination on grounds of race, the European Commission having accepted in the *East African Asians* case that race discrimination may amount of itself to 'inhuman and degrading treatment' contrary to that provision.[21] The ECtHR has ruled that Article 8 has been breached by discrimination on grounds of sexual orientation, both by itself (as in *Smith & Grady v United Kingdom*, above) and in conjunction with Article 15 (*Mouta v Portugal* (2001) 31 EHRR 47). Not all sexual orientation discrimination will breach Articles 8 and/or 14 (see, for example, the decision in *Fretté v France* [2003] 2 FCR 39).[22] But Article 8 is likely to be implicated by such discrimination notwithstanding *X v Y* [2004] IRLR 625 (further discussed in Chapter 10) in which the Court of Appeal ruled that the dismissal of a gay man on the grounds that he had been cautioned for engaging in consensual sex in a toilet did not bring Article 8 into play, this on the basis that the sexual activity concerned was not 'private.' It is also likely to be engaged by sex discrimination such as, for example, some forms of sexual harassment. The relevance of Article 9 to religious discrimination is obvious, while Article 1 of the First Protocol permits challenge to the discrimination in, for example, pensions (at least if of a contributory nature).[23]

The Convention rights are binding only upon the state, but they include positive obligations to secure and protect the rights from interference by private actors as well as merely negative prohibitions on active interference by the state. Thus, for example, in *Young, James & Webster v UK* Appl. 7601/76 (1977) Yearbook XX 520, the Commission ruled that the UK had breached Article 11 of the Convention (which protects the right to freedom of association) by permitting a state of affairs to exist in which workers could lawfully be sacked for refusing to join a trade union. And in *Stedman v UK* (1997) 23 EHRR CD the Commission accepted (in the case of a private sector employee) that 'if a violation of one of [the Convention] rights is the result of non-observance of [the State's obligation under Article 1 of the Convention to "secure to everyone within [its] jurisdiction the rights and freedoms defined in . . . [the] Convention"] in the domestic legislation, the responsibility of the State is engaged.' But the degree of positive obligation to protect Convention rights from interference by others is not as strong as the obligation on states not themselves to interfere. And a significant 'margin of appreciation' is provided to Contracting States as to the manner of protection.

The Commission accepted, in *Rommelfanger v Germany* (1989) DR 151 that the positive obligations imposed on Contracting States by Article 10 (freedom of expression) required some measure of protection to be afforded to private sector employers. But these obligations required only that 'a reasonable relationship' existed 'between the measures affecting freedom of expression and the nature of the employment as well as the importance of the issue for the employer.' Discrimination by a private employer in connection with a worker's

---

[21] (1973) 3 EHRR 76, EComHR, para 207; followed by the Court in *Cyprus v Turkey* (2002) 35 EHRR 30, paras 30–6.

[22] *Cf* the decision of the Constitutional Court of South Africa in *Du Toit and de Vos v Minister for Welfare and Population Development* 2002 (10) BCLR 1006 (CC) that laws restricting adoption to married couples discriminated unconstitutionally on grounds of sexual orientation.

[23] *Purja v Ministry of Defence* [2004] 1 WLR 289, *R (Carson) v Secretary of State for Work and Pensions* [2003] 3 All ER 577. The Convention position is set out by the ECtHR in *Gaygusuz v Austria* (1996) 23 EHRR 364 and, more recently, *Poirrez v France* 30 September 2003, App No. 40892/98.

political beliefs or activities will not necessarily establish an 'interference' by the state with the worker's Convention rights.

The HRA became fully operational throughout the UK in October 2000. The most significant provisions for our purposes are ss.3 and 6 which provide as follows:

S.3(1) So far as it is possible to do so, primary legislation and subordinate legislation must be read and given effect in a way which is compatible with the Convention rights.
(2) This section—
    (a) applies to primary legislation and subordinate legislation whenever enacted;
    (b) does not affect the validity, continuing operation or enforcement of any incompatible primary legislation; and
    (c) does not affect the validity, continuing operation or enforcement of any incompatible subordinate legislation if (disregarding any possibility of revocation) primary legislation prevents removal of the incompatibility.

S.6(1) It is unlawful for a public authority to act in a way which is incompatible with a Convention right.
(2) Subsection (1) does not apply to an act if—
    (a) as the result of one or more provisions of primary legislation, the authority could not have acted differently; or
    (b) in the case of one or more provisions of, or made under, primary legislation which cannot be read or given effect in a way which is compatible with the Convention rights, the authority was acting so as to give effect to or enforce those provisions.
(3) In this section 'public authority' includes—
    (a) a court or tribunal, and
    (b) any person certain of whose functions are functions of a public nature
    but does not include either House of Parliament or a person exercising functions in connection with proceedings in Parliament . . .
(5) In relation to a particular act, a person is not a public authority by virtue only of subsection (3)(b) if the nature of the act is private.

Section 4 provides that the courts (High Court and above) may issue 'declarations of incompatibility' where a provision whose validity is protected under s.3 (that is, essentially, a provision of primary legislation) cannot be interpreted consistent with the Convention. Section 2 provides that the courts must take into account the jurisprudence of the Convention organs when interpreting Convention provisions (though they are not bound by it) and s.7 provides that:

(1) A person who claims that a public authority has acted (or proposes to act) in a way which is made unlawful by section 6(1) may—
    (a) bring proceedings against the authority under this Act in the appropriate court or tribunal, or
    (b) rely on the Convention right or rights concerned in any legal proceedings,
    but only if he is (or would be) a victim of the unlawful act.

Only public authorities (and, in relation to their public functions, 'hybrid' public/private bodies) can be sued directly under the HRA. But s.3 HRA applies whether the parties are public or private (*Ghaidan*) and in this way the Act is given a measure of 'indirect,' 'horizontal' effect. Indirect horizontal effect also results from the inclusion of courts and tribunals as public authorities, with the effect that they are obliged to give effect to the

Convention rights where possible (but not—see the decision of the House of Lords in *Wainwright v Home Office* [2004] 2 AC 406—to create new causes of action in order to do so). Someone dismissed by a private or hybrid employer on grounds of sexual orientation is not able to sue directly under the HRA (employment being regarded as a private function). But she will be able to argue that the unfair dismissal provisions should be interpreted so as to comply with her Article 8 and 14 rights to be protected from sexual orientation discrimination. The Court of Appeal accepted in *X v Y* that dismissals which would breach the Convention would generally be unfair regardless of whether the employer was private or public (see Chapter 10). And it may be, notwithstanding the decision of the House of Lords in *MacDonald v Ministry of Defence, Pearce v Governing Body of Mayfield School* [2003] ICR 937, that the SDA ought to be interpreted to cover a refusal to hire someone because of her sexual orientation (see further Chapter 10). This is of limited importance now in the employment context because of the implementation of the SO Regs, which regulate discrimination in employment and third level education. But the question whether the SDA can be interpreted, post HRA, so as to apply to sexual orientation discrimination remains of practical importance in those other areas (access to goods and services, housing and education other than third level) which fall within the scope of that Act but not of the SO Regs. The same is true at present in relation to religion, the RB Regs applying more narrowly than the RRA which, pre HRA, was interpreted to apply to Jews and Sikhs as 'racial groups' but not to Muslims on this basis (see Chapter 9).

There may be scope under the HRA for extending the boundaries within which discrimination is currently regulated. In particular, the implementation of the HRA is likely to impact on the scope of judicial review and to result in further expansion of the irrationality limb of review. But in addition to the limitations discussed in the preceding paragraphs, the scope for discrimination-based claims under the HRA is restricted for the reasons discussed by Keith Ewing in the following extract, and in the text which follows it. Dealing with the area of employment, Ewing warns that:

K Ewing, 'The Human Rights Act and Labour Law' (1998) 27 *Industrial Law Journal* 275, 288–9, footnotes omitted

. . . it would be a mistake to be over optimistic about the potential of incorporation for there are several reasons for thinking that the progress here too will be measured in inches rather than miles.

The first of these is the very narrow approach to the construction of the Convention adopted by the Strasbourg authorities, at least in relation to its application to employees. In *Ahmad* [(1981) 4 EHRR 126] the Commission held that there had been no violation of the applicant's article 9 right to freedom of religion, partly because the content of the right could 'as regards the modality of a particular manifestation, be influenced by the situation of the person claiming that freedom,' including any employment contract to which he or she was a party. And in *Stedman*, where the applicant was dismissed by her employer 'for refusing on religious grounds to accept a contract which meant that she would have to work on Sundays,' the Commission concluded that the applicant had been dismissed 'for failing to agree to work certain hours rather than for her religious belief as such and was free to resign and did in effect resign from her employment.' Although directed to take these decisions into account, controversially the British courts are not bound by the Strasbourg jurisprudence, which they are free to disregard. It would indeed be disappointing if the courts were to take the view that Convention rights could be qualified by contract, and they would be rightly excoriated were they to adopt the formalism of the Commission's reasoning in *Stedman*.

The second reason for caution, however, is that the rights in the Convention are by no means unqualified. Indeed as the Commission reminded us in *Ahmad* 'the freedom of religion, as guaranteed by Article 9, is not absolute, but subject to the limitations set out in Article 9(2).' This has important implications for any court or tribunal faced with a complaint that a dismissal breaches a Convention right. The applicant will first have to establish that the right claimed is in fact a Convention right, a not inconsiderable obstacle in view of the fact that much of the jurisprudence is so embryonic, and in view of the fact that the content of the right can be determined by the contract itself. Consideration will then have to be given to the second paragraph in cases relating to articles 8–11 which permit restrictions where 'prescribed by law' and 'necessary' in 'a democratic society,' on a number of grounds including in each case 'the rights and freedoms of others.' Assuming that restrictions imposed by the contract of employment are restrictions 'imposed by law' (though *quaere* the position of implied terms where there is a self evident lack of transparency), the rights and freedoms in whose interests restrictions may be imposed presumably will include those of employers: it is a fair bet that commercial and business considerations will not always take second place.

The utility of the HRA as a weapon against discrimination is limited by the concept of discrimination adopted by the Convention organs. Violations of Article 14 are not generally found unless the discrimination at issue is direct and overt. The ECtHR referred, in the *Belgian Linguistics* case, to the 'aims *and effects*' (my emphasis) of legislation.[24] But, according to Harris *et al*, 'the burden upon the applicant to establish that it exists is severe.'[25] And the Court tends to evaluate indirectly discriminatory treatment according to its aims, failing to take into account its disparate impact. In *Abdulaziz v UK* (1968) 1 EHRR 252, for example, in which the ECtHR rejected a complaint that an immigration rule indirectly discriminated against men from the Indian sub-continent, the Court ignored the disparate impact of the rule and simply examined the purpose behind it. And in *Dudgeon v UK* (1981) 4 EHRR 149, the Court accepted the imposition of differential ages of consent for homosexual and heterosexual sex by focusing on the protective intent of the (higher) homosexual age limit without considering whether such arguments justified the differential treatment of homosexuals, as distinct from the restriction of intercourse with young persons generally. The decision of the ECtHR in *Thlimmenos v Greece* (2001) 31 EHRR 14, discussed in Chapter 9, does indicate a willingness to consider what might be characterised as indirect discrimination in domestic law, and this willingness was reiterated more recently in *Hoogendijk v Netherlands* 6 January 2005 App No 58641/00 as it had been in *Pretty v UK* (2002) 35 EHRR 1. But *Thlimmenos* remains the only case in which indirect discrimination has been accepted as having breached the Convention.

EC Law and Discrimination/Equality

Existing Provisions

Many reservations have been expressed about the potential of the HRA as an anti-discrimination tool given the shortcomings of the Convention rights, in particular in their

---

[24] (1968) 1 EHRR 252.
[25] D Harris, M O'Boyle and C Warbrick, *Law of the European Convention on Human Rights* (London, Butterworths, 1995), 477.

application to employment. Of more significance, at least in relation to employment, are the many equality-related provisions of EC law. These include Articles 12, 13, 39 and 141 TEC which provide, respectively, as follows:

Article 12

Within the scope of application of this Treaty, and without prejudice to any special provisions contained therein, any discrimination on grounds of nationality shall be prohibited.

The Council, acting in accordance with the procedure referred to in Article 251, may adopt rules designed to prohibit such discrimination.

Article 13

1. Without prejudice to the other provisions of this Treaty and within the limits of the powers conferred by it upon the Community, the Council, acting unanimously on a proposal from the Commission and after consulting the European Parliament, may take appropriate action to combat discrimination based on sex, racial or ethnic origin, religion or belief, disability, age or sexual orientation.
2. By way of derogation from paragraph 1, when the Council adopts Community incentive measures, excluding any harmonisation of the laws and regulations of the Member States, to support action taken by the Member States in order to contribute to the achievement of the objectives referred to in paragraph 1, it shall act in accordance with the procedure referred to in Article 251.

Article 39

1. Freedom of movement for workers shall be secured within the Community.
2. Such freedom of movement shall entail the abolition of any discrimination based on nationality between workers of the Member States as regards employment, remuneration and other conditions of work and employment.
3. It shall entail the right, subject to limitations justified on grounds of public policy, public security or public health:
   (a) to accept offers of employment actually made;
   (b) to move freely within the territory of Member States for this purpose;
   (c) to stay in a Member State for the purpose of employment in accordance with the provisions governing the employment of nationals of that State laid down by law, regulation or administrative action;
   (d) to remain in the territory of a Member State after having been employed in that State, subject to conditions which shall be embodied in implementing regulations to be drawn up by the Commission.
4. The provisions of this article shall not apply to employment in the public service.

Article 141

1. Each Member State shall ensure that the principle of equal pay for male and female workers for equal work or work of equal value is applied.
2. For the purpose of this article, 'pay' means the ordinary basic or minimum wage or salary and any other consideration, whether in cash or in kind, which the worker receives directly or indirectly, in respect of his employment, from his employer.
   Equal pay without discrimination based on sex means:
   (a) that pay for the same work at piece rates shall be calculated on the basis of the same unit of measurement;

(b) that pay for work at time rates shall be the same for the same job.

3. The Council, acting in accordance with the procedure referred to in Article 251, and after consulting the Economic and Social Committee, shall adopt measures to ensure the application of the principle of equal opportunities and equal treatment of men and women in matters of employment and occupation, including the principle of equal pay for equal work or work of equal value.

4. With a view to ensuring full equality in practice between men and women in working life, the principle of equal treatment shall not prevent any Member State from maintaining or adopting measures providing for specific advantages in order to make it easier for the underrepresented sex to pursue a vocational activity or to prevent or compensate for disadvantages in professional careers.

Article 13 may not be directly relied upon as a source of rights, but operates instead to provide a Treaty basis for the adoption of Directives (to date the Racial Discrimination Directive and the Employment Equality Directive, which came into force in July and December 2003 respectively): 'the Treaty does not [in this context] speak the language of rights, but the language of power.'[26] Articles 12 and 39, by contrast, can be relied upon as a source of individual rights and the ECJ confirmed in *Roman Angonese v Cassa di Risparmio di Bolzano SpA*, Case C–281/98 [2000] ECR I–04139 that Article 39 had direct horizontal as well as vertical effect (that is, it can be relied upon as against private as well as public sector employers).[27] Article 141 similarly operates both as a basis for EU directives and a source of individual rights which may be enforced against private and public sector employers. The enforcement of EU law in the domestic courts is considered in Chapter 5.

In addition to Articles 13, 39 and 141, a number of EU directives regulate discrimination. These include, most significantly:

- Council Directive 75/117—the Equal Pay Directive
- Council Directive 76/207—the Equal Treatment Directive, as amended by Council Directive 2002/73/EC
- Council Directive 79/7 and 86/378—the Social Security Directives
- Council Directive 92/85—the Pregnant Workers' Directive
- Council Directive 97/80—the Burden of Proof Directive
- Council Directive 2000/43—the Racial Equality Directive
- Council Directive 2000/78—the Employment Equality Directive

All but the final two of these directives are relevant only to sex discrimination/ equality, the Racial Equality Directive regulating discrimination on grounds of ethnic or national origin (but not nationality), and the Employment Equality Directive regulating discrimination on grounds of religion or belief, sexual orientation, disability and (as of December 2006 in the UK) age. The material scope of the directives is limited, in the case of all but the Racial Equality Directive, to employment and (in the case of sex alone) social security. The Racial Equality Directive applies also to discrimination in education, goods and services, housing, social security and social advantage, etc (see further Chapter 4), while in December 2004 a new directive was adopted on equal treatment of men and women in access to goods and services (Council Directive 2004/113/EC, see Chapters 4 and 6). In October 2005 amendments to the Equal Treatment Directive will be implemented to bring that Directive

---

[26] M Barbera, above n 15, 86.
[27] See further Ch 7 for a discussion of the limitations of Article 39.

broadly into line with the Employment Equality directive and incorporate into its text the ECJ jurisprudence. The substance of these directives is considered throughout the book.

The New Constitutional Treaty

The Treaty Establishing the European Community is to be replaced by the Treaty Establishing a Constitution for Europe which, although it has been agreed by the European Council in June 2004, has yet to be ratified by the Member States (this being the precondition for its entry into force). Final entry into force is likely to take in excess of two years. Parts I and III of the Treaty, so far as relevant here, broadly reflect the current Treaty Establishing the European Community. They contain a significant number of provisions dealing with discrimination/ equality. Non-discrimination and 'equality between women and men' are included among the 'values' of the European Union (Article I–2), with the effect that they are explicit criteria for union membership and breach can result in suspension of membership rights. The 'objectives' of the Union also include combating discrimination and promoting 'equality between women and men, solidarity between generations and protection of the rights of the child' (Article I–3). Non-discrimination on grounds of nationality is accorded special mention (Article I–4) and Article I–44 imposes a duty on the EU to 'observe the principle of the equality of citizens.'

Part II of the Treaty, which incorporates the Charter of Fundamental Rights adopted in December 2000, is considered further below. Part III sets out detailed legal provisions including those which are now Articles 13, 39 and 141 TEC. These provisions are found as Articles III–8, III–18 and III–108 respectively of the Constitutional Treaty. (Article III–8 retains a requirement for unanimity in relation to legislation against discrimination on grounds of sex, sexual orientation, religion or belief, race and disability. This, as Mark Bell observes,[28] contrasts with the qualified majority voting approach otherwise generally standard in the new Treaty.)

Article III–2 reproduces Article 3(2) TEC: 'In all the activities referred to in this Part, the Union shall aim to eliminate inequalities, and to promote equality, between men and women' while new Article III–3 provides that 'In defining and implementing the policies and activities referred to in this Part, the Union shall aim to combat discrimination based on sex, racial or ethnic origin, religion or belief, disability, age or sexual orientation.'

The Charter of Fundamental Rights set out in a single text the range of civil, political, economic and social rights of European citizens and others resident in the EU. Its legal status was uncertain prior to its incorporation into the Constitutional Treaty and a degree of uncertainty remains as a result of Article II–52(5) which states:

> The provisions of this Charter which contain principles may be implemented by legislative and executive acts taken by Institutions and bodies of the Union, and by acts of Member States when they are implementing Union law, in the exercise of their respective powers. *They shall be judicially cognizable only in the interpretation of such acts and in the ruling on their legality* (my emphasis).

Article II–20 provides that 'everyone is equal before the law' and II–21 that 'Any discrimination based on any ground such as sex, race, colour, ethnic or social origin, genetic features, language, religion or belief, political or any other opinion, membership of a national

---

[28] 'Equality and the EU Constitution' (2004) 33 *Industrial Law Journal* 242.

minority, property, birth, disability, age or sexual orientation shall be prohibited.' National origin does not feature in Article II–21(1), though Article II–21(2) provides that 'Within the scope of application of the Constitution and without prejudice to any of its specific provisions, any discrimination on grounds of nationality shall be prohibited.' The Explanatory Memorandum prepared at the instigation of the Praesidium of the Convention which drafted the Charter provides that this should be interpreted in line with Article I–4(2) (currently Article 12 TEC), which was interpreted by the ECJ to afford protection only in relation to nationals of EU states. Article II–22 provides that 'The Union shall respect cultural, religious and linguistic diversity' and Article II–23 that 'Equality between men and women must be ensured in all areas, including employment, work and pay. The principle of equality shall not prevent the maintenance or adoption of measures providing for specific advantages in favour of the under-represented sex.' Articles II–24 and II–25 recognise the rights of children and of the elderly and Article II–26 provides that 'The Union recognises and respects the right of persons with disabilities to benefit from measures designed to ensure their independence, social and occupational integration and participation in the life of the community.'

The Constitution is far from perfect in its treatment of equality. Mark Bell remarks that the amended Explanatory Memorandum draws a distinction between 'rights' (which are enforceable) and 'principles' (which do not, according to the Memorandum, 'give rise to direct claims for positive action by the Union's Institutions or Member States' authorities'). Among the provisions declared by the Memorandum as giving rise to 'principles' rather than 'rights' are Articles II 25 and II–26 (notwithstanding their titles, which refer to the *rights* of the elderly and disabled respectively). The European Commission's network of legal experts on the application of Community law on equal treatment between women and men, in its 'Observations on the [then] Draft Treaty establishing a Constitution for Europe' (September 2003), expressed its concern over 'the distinction between legal rights . . . and "programmatic" provisions or *principles*, which, as such, do not create enforceable rights or positive claims for individuals, but which must first be implemented.' The Experts suggest that:

> women (and men) have, until now, benefited from the recognition of the *right* to equal treatment. This gives individuals a better legal position than weaker provisions on programmes, objectives etc. of public authorities' action. Moreover, Article 141 EC Treaty, for instance, provides that the Member States 'shall ensure that the *principle* of equal pay for male and female workers for equal work . . . is applied'. Although this provision uses the term *principle*, giving rise to an argument in *Defrenne II against* direct effect of (then) Article 119, the ECJ has recognised an enforceable right to equal pay. It is a matter for the judiciary, in particular for the ECJ, to determine whether a provision involves an enforceable right or not.

As Bell points out, the weight to be attached by the ECJ to the original and amended Memoranda (both of which are referred to as interpretive guides in the preamble to the Constitution) remains to be seen. But the Committee of Experts go on to point out that Article II–23 is significantly weaker than old Article 3.2 TEC which provided that: 'In all the activities referred to in this Article [all the activities of the Union], the Community shall aim to eliminate inequalities, and to promote equality, between men and women.' According to the Committee:

> the Charter falls short of the *acquis communautaire*, because [*inter alia*] in addition to a clear and precise prohibition of discrimination which may be enforced in the courts (Article II–21) and to the principle of gender equality in all areas (Article II–23(1)), it does not state

explicitly that there exists a *positive obligation* to eliminate gender inequalities 'in all areas,' as Article 3(2) EC Treaty currently does [and] the so-called 'positive measures' mentioned in the Charter are presented as a matter of exception to non-discrimination, rather than as a means to achieve real equality, thus disregarding the current Community concept of substantive gender equality as reflected in the EC Treaty and recognised by ECJ case law.

Positive action is permitted under Articles II–23 and II–26 but these provisions, by contrast with Article III–108 (currently Article 141 TEC) do not explicitly recognize positive action as being aimed at 'ensuring full equality in practice', rather than being a derogation therefrom.

M Bell, 'Equality and the EU Constitution' (2004) 33 *Industrial Law Journal* **242, 250, footnotes omitted**

Overall the formal equality concept tends to dominate the equality provisions of the Constitution, both in terms of equality as a general principle of law and in the right to non-discrimination . . . Positive action is only unequivocally anticipated in respect of sex; it is neither specifically authorised, nor prohibited, in respect of other grounds. The absence of any legal protection for positive action for ethnic minority groups stands out as a significant omission. Indeed, this contrasts with [CERD] which obliges states to adopt appropriate positive action measures. Furthermore, in the light of the positive action clauses in both the Racial Equality and Framework Employment Directives, the Constitution should have provided a firmer and more consistent commitment to substantive equality by recognising the legitimacy of positive action in respect of any of the 'Article 13' grounds of discrimination.

Bell comments on willingness of the constitution 'to engage the union with positive duties' (for example Article I–3(3)) but warns that: 'Whilst the legislative procedures foreseen in Article III–8 may not facilitate action, Article I–3(3) creates an expectation that discrimination and equality will remain central items in the EU policy profile.' He goes on to remark that 'the risk associated with provisions [such as Articles I–3(3), II–22 & II–23] is that they remain attractive sentiments, but fail to be translated into concrete actions. The generality of the commitment hinders the identification of specific consequences for Union policy-making. Therefore, it may be more important that positive duties are also introduced into Part III [which sets out detailed equality provisions].'

Discrimination and Disadvantage

A variety of statutory prohibitions cover discrimination based on sex (including gender reassignment), race, disability, sexual orientation and religion or belief (as well as, in Northern Ireland, political opinion). These 'protected grounds' have not been plucked out of the air, legislation having followed the recognition of disadvantage suffered by women, ethnic and religious minorities, disabled people, gay men, lesbians, bisexual and transgendered people.

The disadvantages suffered by these various groups, and the extent to which these disadvantages persist, are discussed in Chapters 6–10. What is of interest here to note is that, with the exception only of the DDA, legislation passed in recognition of the disadvantage suffered by particular groups (women, ethnic and religious minorities, gay men, lesbians, bisexual and transgendered people) has taken a formal approach to equality, rather than seeking to prohibit discrimination on the grounds of membership of the disadvantaged group. In other words, the SDA prohibits discrimination on grounds of sex[29] rather than discrimination against women; the RRA prohibits discrimination on racial grounds rather than discrimination against black people, Asians, African Caribbeans, etc, and the FETO prohibits discrimination (in Northern Ireland) on the grounds of religious belief or political opinion, rather than discrimination against Catholics/ Nationalists. The DDA, by contrast, prohibits discrimination only against the disabled.[30]

The significance of the DDA's asymmetric approach is that it permits all forms of positive steps to be taken to ameliorate the disadvantage suffered by the disabled, whereas the other legislation allows only such positive steps as are expressly permitted (see Chapter 3) or which do not contravene the general prohibitions on 'discrimination' discussed in Chapter 2. While there have not been a great number of claims brought under the RRA or SDA by white people and men respectively challenging attempts to reduce the disadvantage experienced in particular spheres by women and persons of particular ethnic minority background, the symmetrical approach to discrimination adopted under those Acts has stifled efforts which might otherwise have been made to achieve increased substantive equality.[31]

The other problem with the symmetrical approach to discrimination/equality lies in the conceptual difficulties generated by the comparator approach with which it is associated. These difficulties have resulted in the symmetrical approach having come under increasing question in recent years. As Marzia Barbera remarks, the Racial Equality and Employment Equality Directives begin to move away from the 'traditional concept of discrimination [which] refers to a situation where the person who claims to be discriminated against is, in all relevant aspects, the same as her or his comparator, and nevertheless suffers a disadvantage,' to an understanding of discrimination which is about 'difference' rather than 'sameness.' Thus 'discrimination also occurs when a person is, in some relevant aspects, different, depending on her or his group characteristic (such as race, gender, religion beliefs, disability), and is adversely affected because of this.'[32] It incorporates a 'a concept of discrimination as violation of the dignity of a person, that is as an absolute right not to be disadvantaged or humiliated by virtue of one's subjective characteristics (and not merely not to be "more" disadvantaged'), as well as providing some positive rights.

Indirect discrimination is one element of the 'difference' approach though, as Lizzie Barmes and Sue Ashtiany have recently pointed out: 'even if a complainant can establish that a practice has such systematic negative impact on a protected group that it is *prima facie* indirectly discriminatory, there is the possibility of objective justification. The implication is that treating people the same with discriminatory consequences is less problematic than when differential treatment is discriminatory. Secondly and more fundamentally, a finding of indirect discrimination does not render differential treatment acceptable. Rather a new, non-discriminatory way must be found to treat both groups the same.'[33] The new

---

[29] Or being married or undergoing or having undergone gender-reassignment, see further Chs 6 and 10.

[30] Save only where the discrimination takes the form of victimisation, discussed in Ch 2.

[31] Women-only railway carriages would, for example, breach the SDA, but fear of attack prevents many women from travelling after dark.

[32] Above n 15, 89.

[33] 'Diversity Approach To Achieving Equality: Potential And Pitfalls' (2003) 32 *Industrial Law Journal* 274, 279.

Directives replace 'the 'disproportionate effect' test with the 'particular disadvantage' test in the context of indirect discrimination. This goes some way towards a more substantive approach (although it leaves intact the weaknesses identified by Barmes and Ashtiany). More particularly, they explicitly prohibit harassment as a form of 'discrimination.'

Marzia Barbera, 'Not the Same? The Judicial Role in the New Community Anti-Discrimination Law Context' (2002) 31 *Industrial Law Journal* 82, 90–1, footnotes omitted

Harassment in fact does not require a comparison, but rather focuses on the violation of the dignity of a person and on the creation of an intimidating, hostile, humiliating or offensive environment, and yet it is considered to be discrimination. Finally, a separate form of discrimination refers to the failure of the employer to provide reasonable accommodation for a person with disabilities, in order to enable such person to have full access to, or advancement in, employment.

By recognising that difference matters in itself and requires changes in the way it is dealt with, in order to eliminate the disadvantage historically resulting from difference, Community law is clearly paying a debt to the feminist legal theory that has disentangled the principle of equality from comparative evaluation, which is generally considered intrinsic to it. The new notion of discrimination tends to go beyond the traditional structure of the anti-discrimination principle, which presupposes the presence of a subject (who represents the 'norm') with whom anyone who claims to have been a victim of inequality must compare his/her own condition in order to be entitled to equal treatment, and this notion appears to rely in some cases on the substantive test already used by the ECJ in *P v S* [Case C–13/94 [1996] ECR I–2143, and in *Dekker* (Case C–177/88 [1990] ECR I–3941).

Sandy Fredman (extracted below) suggests that a further weakness with the 'equal treatment' paradigm is its aim, which was to 'free individuals from their group characteristics' in pursuit of 'a colour blind and gender-neutral world, where individuals could thrive as individuals free from stereotypical assumptions.' While this approach is 'at the heart of the business case for equality, on the grounds that selection on merit rather than according to stereotypes or prejudice yields a better workforce,' it 'requires all individuals to conform to the same norm [and] ignores the fact that cumulative disadvantage makes it difficult for members of out-groups to attain the prerequisite merit criteria [and] the positive aspects of group identity, aiming at assimilation rather than pluralism.'

Fredman's recognition of the positive aspects of group identity chimes with the current rhetoric which tends to emphasise 'diversity' as much as, or more than 'equality.' Fredman warns, however, that 'diversity has often been narrowly focused on the business prospects of the employer,' and Barmes and Ashtiany, who make a similar point, also highlight the lack of fit between 'diversity' and the current legislative framework:

Barmes and Ashtiany ('Diversity Approach To Achieving Equality: Potential And Pitfalls' (2003) 32 *Industrial Law Journal* 274, 282, 290–1, footnotes omitted

The diversity perspective deviates from the traditional legislative model in two main ways. First, despite taking the individual as the starting point, the diversity perspective operates far less individualistically than the law. In practice, as the case studies demonstrated, it takes a systemic approach. So organisational measures to achieve change are central. Individual complaints are not needed to initiate action and there is no necessity to engage with apportioning blame for past wrongs.

Secondly, the diversity perspective's emphasis on concrete steps to enhance inclusiveness, with the particular concern to accommodate difference, contrasts with the traditional legal model's resistance to any differentiation on a prohibited ground. In effect, the diversity perspective countenances differential treatment on grounds of race and sex, or in relation to other barriers to participation, so long as the objective is to promote diversity. In other words, the diversity perspective envisages positive action, in the sense of measures targeted to redressing difficulties faced by particular groups or individuals and always provided the steps taken do not give anyone an unfair advantage . . .

[But] the centrality of individualism remains a problem. At an abstract level . . . judging diversity from the standpoint of the individual collapses into meaninglessness because everyone is unique. To illustrate, it would be perfectly rational from the individual point of view to regard highly homogenous groups, for example the judiciary, as wholly diverse because each member has their own distinctive talents, experiences, outlooks and tastes, not to say quirks or idiosyncrasies. The error of this thinking is that it treats vastly different phenomena as equivalent . . . just a few facts are determinative of a great deal about a person's life chances. This is the hallmark of a profoundly unequal society. In a more equal world no doubt much, much less could be predicted from broad and imprecise measurements . . . to pretend that we live in that world, as the diversity focus on accommodating individuality of all kinds does, is a serious error. Most importantly, in theory at least, it dramatically under-estimates the difficulties and obstacles typically encountered by members of disadvantaged groups compared to others.

Barmes and Ashtiany go on to highlight some of the difficulties of a move from formal to substantive equality, citing *Lommers v Minister van Landbouw, Natuurbeheer en Visserij* Case C–476/99 [2002] ECR I–02891 (see further Chapter 3) as illustrative of the delicate balance which needs to be struck between recognising realities and perpetuating stereotypes (there in relation to women's responsibility for childcare). They also draw attention to the difficulties of conflicting 'diversities':

For example, what if the question were whether to accommodate intolerance or sexism rooted in religious belief? It seems clear that an employer should refuse to make room for such difference in order that certain basic entitlements of all individuals be respected. Moreover it appears that this is what the diversity perspective would require. Yet this conclusion begs the question: what is it about a given dilemma that will enable an employer to tell that it is individuals' essential sameness that should be insisted upon?

Barmes and Ashtiany state an 'urgent need for some carefully tailored ground rules to be set by the law, especially regarding the resolution of conflicts between equality norms.' Some guidance is suggested by Fredman.

S Fredman, *The Future of Equality in Britain* (EOC, 2002) 11–16, footnotes omitted

Breaking the Cycle of Disadvantage
The first step is to move beyond the assumption of a 'neutral' approach, which regards as invidious all distinctions on grounds of gender, race, disability, age, religion and sexual orientation. Instead, the problem should be conceptualised in terms of actual disadvantage. On this understanding, equality laws target disadvantaged groups, not advantaged groups. Thus, according to Canadian jurisprudence, the purpose of the equality guarantee is: not only to prevent discrimination by the attribution of stereotypical characteristics to individuals, but also to ameliorate the position of groups . . . who have suffered disadvantage by exclusion from mainstream society as has been the case with disabled persons. It aims particularly at persons or groups who have been subject to historical disadvantage, prejudice and stereotyping.

Central to this approach is the recognition that equal treatment of all can in fact be deeply inegalitarian. Instead, as Sen argues 'equal consideration for all may demand very unequal treatment in favour of the disadvantaged. The demands of substantive equality can be particularly exacting and complex when there is a good deal of antecedent inequality to counter.' [34]

Redressing disadvantage involves several different dimensions. One is to concentrate on distribution of resources and benefits, particularly, in the form of under-representation of a particular group in jobs and training places. This is often seen as an 'equality of results' approach . . . A second dimension, complementing the first, is to concentrate not so much on outcomes, but on the facilitation of choice . . . If effective freedom of choice is genuinely to be achieved, measures need to be taken to ensure that persons from all sections of society have a genuinely equal chance of satisfying the criteria for access to a particular social good. This requires positive measures such as education and training, family friendly measures and adaptation of the built environment. It may go even further, and challenge the criteria for access themselves, since existing criteria of merit may themselves reflect and reinforce existing patterns of disadvantage. In other words, it is crucial not just to open the gates but also to equip people to proceed through them.

Such an approach goes further than helping individuals change themselves. There are limits to the extent to which people can change. It is not sufficient to show that a person is unable to do the job as pre-defined. Instead, the employer or service provider is under a duty to institute changes to the job or the environment so far as practicable in order to facilitate participation . . . An important result of targeting disadvantage, rather than aiming at neutrality, is that a claim by a relatively advantaged member of society, on this approach, is dealt with very differently from a claim by a disadvantaged member. Provisions aimed at women or ethnic minorities will not be discriminatory as against men or members of the majority provided they aim to redress discriminatory disadvantage. Similarly, provisions specifically aimed at ameliorating labour market difficulties experienced by older workers will not be discriminatory as against younger workers . . .

Promoting Respect for the Equal Dignity and Worth of All
The second main principle of equality is that of a fundamental right to respect for our common humanity, dignity and worth. Dignity is a cornerstone of human rights: the Universal Declaration of Human Rights and many other bills of rights declare that the inalienable rights of all persons derive from the inherent dignity of the human person. Dignity has also has been extensively used to give substantive force to equality . . . the core of the modern notion of dignity is that all individuals deserve respect on the grounds of their innate humanity. Rationality, efficiency or desirability cannot be used as preconditions for equal respect. Human beings should not be used as objects, nor as means to ends, but always as ends in themselves. The dignity principle attacks the stigma, stereotyping and denigration inherent in much racism, homophobia, sexism and other forms of discrimination. As a Canadian judge recently stated, the purpose of equality is to 'prevent the violation of essential human dignity and freedom through the imposition of disadvantage, stereotyping, or political or social prejudice, and to promote a society in which all persons enjoy equal recognition at law as human beings or as members of . . . society, equally capable and equally deserving of concern, respect and consideration.' It is important to define dignity consistently with the other three central principles, namely redressing disadvantage, facilitating identity, and promoting participation within community . . . Care should also be taken to ensure that a conception of dignity is sensitive to actual distributions of power and wealth . . . Dignity is clearly central to the concerns of many groups subject to discrimination. It has particular resonance for disabled people, who find themselves subjected to a

[34] Citing *Inequality Re-examined* (Oxford, Oxford University Press, 1992).

host of humiliating experiences when proper accommodation has not been made for their needs. It rings true too for the many groups subjected to sexist, racist, homophobic, anti-Semitic or anti-Islamic abuse . . .

Affirming Community Identities
It has been argued above that it is necessary to move beyond a 'colour-blind' view of equality and to focus on disadvantage. But it is also important for equality to aim towards a positive affirmation of the individual as a member of the group. This is based on the recognition that there is no abstract, universal individual, but that individuals are partly constituted by their group membership. Moreover, this is an enriching characteristic, part of the positive identity of individuals, strengthening community ties and enhancing democracy. The aim is not to abstract the individual from her characteristics, but to change the public space to reflect and respect them . . . At the same time, communities can themselves be parochial and exclusive. Such communities, while displaying intense internal bonds, can also create strong oppositional forces between Self and Other, so characteristic of racism and other forms of discrimination. As Putnam puts it, it is crucial to 'ask how the positive consequences of social capital—mutual support, cooperation, trust, institutional effectiveness, can be maximized and the negative manifestations—sectarianism, ethnocentrism, corruption—minimized.'

Facilitating Full Participation in Society
The full participation and inclusion of everyone in major social institutions is fundamental to social equality. As has been recognised in other jurisdictions, equality law should specifically compensate for the absence of political power of minority groups, groups 'to whose needs and wishes elected officials have no apparent interest in attending.'
Participation extends across many levels, whether in the workforce, the political arena, the health service, or education . . . Participation rights are also key to ensuring genuine equality for religious, ethnic and cultural minorities. Ethnicity is not static, but is part of an ongoing dynamic interaction both between those who regard themselves as within the group and between the group and the dominant culture. Active participation of the groups in question is therefore crucial if intervention is to avoid being patronising, erroneous and unlikely to succeed.

Fredman's approach is supportive of a movement away from a formal commitment to equal treatment which remains strongly characteristic of the approach to discrimination in domestic law. The legality of positive discrimination is considered further in Chapter 3, but the discrimination/difference debate is sampled here to indicate its centrality to current thinking about equality and discrimination. Hugh Collins goes further again and suggests that discrimination law is best understood as being concerned with the social inclusion of 'out-groups,' rather than a commitment to formal or even substantive equality.

H Collins, 'Discrimination, Equality and Social Inclusion' (2003) 66 *Modern Law Review* 16, 17, 27–8, footnotes omitted

Equal treatment demands impartiality in the sense of forbidding criteria such as sex or race from providing grounds for differentiation. Yet the aim of anti-discrimination laws cannot be reduced to equal treatment. A closer inspection of the legislation reveals three kinds of deviations from a simple equal treatment principle. In some cases, different rather than the same treatment is required. In the case of discrimination against pregnant women, for instance, the law mandates different treatment of women rather than the same treatment as men. Similarly, different treatment of disabled persons is required in many respects, in order to enable them to gain access to work and other opportunities. In a second type of deviation, equal treatment is itself not permitted, if it causes unjustifiable 'indirect discrimination' or 'disparate impact.' Here formal equal treatment becomes unlawful where a rule or practice disproportionately operates to the disadvantage of one of the protected groups, and the rule or practice cannot be objectively justified. A third kind of deviation permits preferential treatment for protected groups in certain circumstances, in order to redress a prior history of disadvantage. The exact scope of permitted positive discrimination is deeply controversial, no doubt because it is perceived as conflicting sharply with the equal treatment principle. These three deviations reveal that we cannot understand the aim of anti-discrimination laws by reference to a straightforward equal treatment principle. The question becomes how can we account for the law in a way that both recognises the force of the equal treatment principle and acknowledges its deficiencies as a complete explanation of the aims of the law?

Conventional accounts of the aim of anti-discrimination laws try to answer that question by using another conception of equality, one that furthers a substantive or distributive goal. Deviations from equal treatment are justified by reference to the pursuit of goals such as equality of results, equality of resources, or equality of opportunity. For example, it is argued that permitting claims for 'indirect discrimination' or 'disparate impact' serves the purpose of reducing institutional barriers to the achievement of a distributive goal such as more equality in results or fairer equality of opportunity . . . Although the precise conception of substantive equality remains ambiguous in such formulations, it certainly seems possible to justify deviations from the equal treatment principle by reference to some distributive conception of equality. The problem for justifying the aims of anti-discrimination laws becomes rather to restrain or confine the force of a substantive conception of equality. This problem arises because there is always a tension between the equal treatment principle and substantive conceptions of equality . . .

Equality justifications for anti-discrimination laws lack a determinate view of how to constitute the groups for comparison. The principle that different groups should be treated equally (in otherwise similar circumstances) does not describe how these groups should be composed. Any group can claim that it is not being treated equally and demand that it should receive protection from the law. The groups might be comprised by reference to genetic endowments, socially constructed categories, legal classifications such as nationality, or some other criterion of classification. What is crucial is that the group is able to claim plausibly that membership of the group puts individuals at a disadvantage. One effect of the indeterminacy of protected groups under the equal treatment principle is that the province of anti-discrimination laws always remains contested. In contrast, social inclusion provides a more determinate criterion for the composition of protected groups. The question is whether the group is one that in practice has been disproportionately socially excluded compared to the population as a whole . . . social inclusion is not interested in whether the group is classified by unalterable genetics, socially constructed qualities, or legally imposed characteristics, factors which are sometimes used to determine the scope of discrimination laws under equality justifications. Nor is it interested in whether the group is regarded with disrespect. The composition of groups is determined by reference to the objective of social inclusion, which can draw upon any system of classification. Examples of this variety might include single parents (regardless of sex) or residents in particular postcodes that include high levels of minority ethnic exclusion.

There are very significant differences between the approaches espoused by Fredman on the one hand and Collins on the other. But they share a recognition of the limitations of the symmetrical, equality-as-equal-treatment approach to discrimination. It is likely that developments over the next few years both at EU level and as a result of the incorporation into domestic law of Article 14 and increasing awareness of the systemic nature of much discrimination[35] will prompt serious reconsideration, in the drafting of any single equality Act, of the standard 'symmetrical' approach to statutory discrimination provisions. While it may be unrealistic to expect a wholesale replacement of the comparator approach with a definition of discrimination which is linked to disadvantage, it is not unlikely that the symmetrical, comparator-based approach will be supplemented other than (as at present) only in relation to 'harassment' regulated by the Race and Employment Equality Directives (see further Chapter 2).

Both Fredman and Collins help us to see that there is nothing inherently wrong with asymmetrical approaches to equality/ discrimination law. Fredman, in particular, also provides insights as to how apparently competing equality rights can be balanced without the creation of a rigid hierarchy of rights against discrimination. Such hierarchies are not restricted to UK domestic law: EU law creates a hierarchy with (EU/EEA) nationality at the top followed by race and gender, followed by sexual orientation, disability and religion/belief. And in the US the Supreme Court has created a hierarchy where discrimination on grounds of race and illegitimacy can only be justified on 'strict scrutiny' review, sex discrimination on 'intermediate' review and all other discrimination on 'rational basis' review.[36] But rigid hierarchies of protected grounds are not inevitable. Fredman cites the Government's statement, in *Equality and Diversity: Making it Happen* that 'the interests of all groups served must carry equal weight. It would be quite wrong for any group either to predominate or be marginalised' and suggests that 'This underscores the need to "level up," legislating for all the strands on the model already adopted for race.' She continues:

S Fredman, *The Future of Equality in Britain* (EOC, 2002) 29–31

. . . even if a levelling up solution is adopted, there may still be conflicting claims by different groups. Particularly complex is the conflict between gender and ethnicity or religion. A recent UN expert report found that women from particular ethnic groups who wish to challenge aspects of their cultural or religious traditions which are harmful to them, such as arranged marriages or abuse within the family, may be denied the right to do so by their own communities: 'Often community leaders seek to de-legitimize women's demands as "western" and therefore alien to the norms of the community.'[37]

However, a commitment to multiculturalism by the State might mean that these women find little protection from the law: 'Fundamental human rights of minority women remain unmet as the State seeks to be "culturally sensitive and tolerant" . . . The danger inherent in this approach is that it accommodates the application of differential standards of human rights to those who are in greater need of State protection by virtue of their vulnerability and powerlessness within minority communities.'

Similar potential conflicts arise in other areas. A commitment to retaining older workers can function as a bar to recruitment of minority workers or women. Religious equality can be used to justify a bar on gay, lesbian or bisexual people. Or there may be conflicts between different disadvantaged groups for the same scarce resource, such as jobs, or university places. Should we distinguish between degrees of disadvantage, and focus action on the most disadvantaged at the expense of the lesser disadvantaged?

There are no easy answers to these questions. But helpful guidance is provided by the principles of breaking the cycle of disadvantage, promoting respect for the dignity and

---

[35] See, eg, the 'discovery' of 'institutionalised discrimination' in the wake of the murder of Stephen Lawrence, discussed in Ch 7.

[36] See further A McColgan, *Women under the Law: the False Promise of Human Rights* (Longman, 2000).

[37] Citing UN Division of Women Expert Group Report, 13–14.

equal worth of all, affirming community identities and facilitating full participation in society. Multiculturalism cannot be fashioned in such a way as to infringe on the dignity of any person. Thus equality for one group cannot be based on stigmatising or demeaning the dignity of others, excluding them from society, or requiring them to hide their true identity or to assimilate to other norms.

Of course, it could be argued that dignity itself is a culturally biased concept, and there is no reason why the dominant group's notions should be imposed on others. This in turn is addressed through a reassertion of the principle of participation. Women's voices within their communities may well be silenced or marginalized. As Patel points out: 'Many relations between the state and minority communities are mediated through unelected self appointed community leaders, who are men, usually from socially conservative backgrounds with little or no interest in women's rights or social justice. Most are from religious backgrounds and their interests lie in preserving the family and religious and cultural values.'[38]. . . .

The suggested principles are also helpful in mediating the conflict between religion and sexual orientation. Should a religious group be entitled to claim that they believe that homosexuality is sinful? Here dignity and disadvantage can be used to delineate the rights to minimise the conflict. While an individual is entitled to believe what her religion dictates, it is not an affront to her dignity to prevent her from acting on beliefs which infringe the equality rights of others. The right to respect and dignity is at the core of the right to sexual orientation equality, and therefore cannot be infringed by conduct in the name of religious belief . . .

Multiple Discrimination

Fredman touches on the potential difficulties faced by (for example) minority women who can find themselves entangled both by racism and sexism. The problems suffered by those who are vulnerable to disadvantage and discrimination on the basis of more then one characteristic have been increasingly recognised in recent years by commentators and discrimination activities, if not by the legislators. Thus the Home Office appointed Working Group on Forced Marriage recently pointed out the reluctance of some service providers to tackle forced marriage for fear of being seen to 'meddl[e] in religious traditions or cultural norms' and went on to warn that this 'mismatch of understanding about cultural differences and how these fit in to a diverse, multi-cultural, multi-faith society' resulted in 'some victims of forced marriage who had sought help [feeling] that they had been denied access to services that would have been available to women fleeing other forms of violence and abuse.'[39] And in its response to the Government's White Paper on a single human rights and equality commission the EOC remarked that 'It is simply not defensible in today's society that a black lesbian couple would have a remedy if they were refused accommodation in a hotel because they are black but not if they are turned away because they are lesbians.'[40] The point being made by the EOC was that discrimination on grounds of race

---

[38] Citing P Patel, 'An Urgent Need to Integrate an Intersectional Perspective' (CRE Notes on Gender and Racial Discrimination) 8.

[39] 'A Choice by Right: The Report of the Working Group on Forced Marriage'.

[40] EOC, *Towards Equality And Diversity—Making It Happen*: A Response From The Equal Opportunities Commission, para 40.

in access to goods and services is regulated, whereas discrimination on grounds of sexual orientation is not. But the example is illustrative of another difficulty highlighted also by Skidmore in his critique of the Racial Equality and Employment Equality Directives.

P Skidmore, 'EC Framework Directive On Equal Treatment In Employment: Towards A Comprehensive Community Anti-Discrimination Policy?' (2001) 30 *Industrial Law Journal* **126, 128, footnotes omitted**

Harassment suffered for example by Turkish or Moroccan workers within the Community may not be adequately addressed. . . Whilst in theory they will be protected against discrimination on grounds of their religion and ethnic origin once the Directives come into force, Community law offers them no assistance where the discrimination is based on their nationality. This is problematic because multiple and overlapping discrimination is therefore unlikely to be recognised adequately. Where a person is disadvantaged because she is 'foreign' or 'other,' the acts of the discriminator are not necessarily motivated within narrow legal paradigms of discrimination based on a single criterion such as 'religion' or 'ethnic origin', but are located within societal structures which seek to marginalise those who do not comply with prevailing norms. If the Directive is to be successful in assisting some of the most disadvantaged workers in the Community, the challenge for the Court of Justice will be to develop an interpretation of the Community equality norms which is sensitive to these problems of multiple discrimination and which overcomes the apparent rigidities of the legislation . . .

The practical difficulties caused by multiple discrimination are considered in Chapter 5 in which the recent decisions of EAT and the Court of Appeal in *The Law Society v Bahl* [2003] IRLR 640/ *Bahl v The Law Society* [2004] IRLR 799 are considered. In essence, a black woman who complains of race and sex discrimination must establish, in relation to each incident complained of, that she has been treated less favourably on grounds of *either* race *or* sex, or race *and* sex (separately). A tribunal must, however 'separate out the two strands of race and sex from the mix.' This places insuperable difficulties in the path of a tribunal who may not know (any more than a person who discriminates against her) whether the treatment is on grounds of race or sex or, in the EOC example used above, race or sexual orientation.

The difficulties posed by multiple discrimination (or, more accurately, discrimination alleged by anyone who differs on more than one ground from a heterosexual white man with no disabilities and no demanding religious beliefs) are considered in more detail in the following extract in which Sarah Hannett, like Fredman above, advocates a movement towards a substantive, rather than symmetrical, approach to discrimination.

S Hannett, 'Equality At The Intersections: The Legislative And Judicial Failure To Tackle Multiple Discrimination' (2003) 23 *Oxford Journal of Legal Studies* **65, 66–108, footnotes omitted**

. . . Anti-discrimination law conceives of claimants as possessing a singular set of social characteristics: for example, inclusion in the category 'black' or inclusion in the category 'woman.' Further, the sealed nature of the grounds protected ensures that such social attributes are 'defined as if they have fixed, unchanging essences.' As a result, any differences between the individuals of a particular sex or racial group are rendered invisible . . .

'multiple discrimination' can occur in at least two ways: where the grounds of discrimination are additive in nature, and/or where the discrimination is based on an indivisible combination of two or more social characteristics. The former, 'additive discrimination,' describes a situation where an individual 'belongs to two different groups, both of which are affected by [discriminatory] practices.' The latter, commonly referred to as 'intersectional discrimination,' 'arises out of the combination of various oppressions which, together, produce something unique and distinct from any one form of discrimination standing alone' . . .

The facts of *Nwoke v Government Legal Service & Civil Service Commissioners*[41] illustrate additive discrimination. The claimant, a Nigerian-born woman, applied for a post in the Government Legal Service. During the interview the Board ranked all the claimants from 'A' (the highest) to 'E' (the lowest). The claimant received a ranking of 'E'. The evidence established that the white claimants were graded higher even if they possessed a lower degree class. Further, although white women were graded higher, they were less likely to be appointed than men, and, if appointed, were paid less. In addition, the only person on a temporary contract with the GLS not to be permanently appointed was a black woman. Nwoke successfully alleged race and sex discrimination. The adverse treatment Nwoke suffered was additive or double discrimination: she was discriminated against because she was both a woman, and black. Nwoke thus faced a double burden in her job application.

In contrast, adjusting the facts of Nwoke demonstrates how intersectional discrimination operates. Suppose that roughly equal numbers of women and men were appointed, that approximately equal numbers of blacks and whites were appointed, but that no black women were appointed. Applying the SDA and/or the RRA as they currently stand, Nwoke may be unable to show sex or race discrimination. For the purposes of the SDA, Nwoke has not been discriminated against: she has not been treated 'on the ground of her sex . . . less favourably than . . . a man' as the generic group 'woman' has not suffered adverse treatment. Neither has Nwoke been discriminated against on the basis of her race under the RRA: she has not been treated 'on racial grounds . . . less favourably than . . . other persons' as blacks as a whole have not suffered disproportionate treatment. However, as a black woman she may have suffered discrimination.

The concept of multiplicity is not unique to marginalised groups in society. Every individual has a sex, race, religion, sexual orientation which to varying degrees influences his or her life. Indeed, the ubiquitous comparator in antidiscrimination law, the white male, implicitly reflects a multiple construction of race and sex. However, the pervasive nature of sexism, racism, homophobia and disability discrimination ensure that the consequences of failure to recognise, and provide, effective remedies for multiple grounds of discrimination may be most profound for those in marginalised groups. Such failures produce what has been described as a 'single-axis framework' with a triple effect. First, such a framework presumes that a core experience of adverse treatment is common to all individuals sharing that particular social characteristic, regardless of any others possessed. Therefore, it assumes communality of a woman's experience of discrimination, flattening any social characteristics that women might not share such as race, sexuality, class, or disability. Such essentialism suggests that racism, for example, is merely a further form of oppression suffered by black and Asian women, to be added to a shared experience of sexism, instead of recognising that adverse treatment suffered by women of ethnic minorities may be a qualitatively different experience. Accordingly: 'The result of essentialism is to reduce the lives of people who experience multiple forms of oppression to additional problems: 'racism + sexism = straight black women's experience,' or 'racism + sexism + homophobia = black lesbian experience.' Thus, in an essentialist world, black women's experience will always be forcibly fragmented before being subjected to analysis.'[42]

---

[41] 28 *Equal Opportunities Review* 6.
[42] Citing A Harris, 'Race and Essentialism in Feminist Theory' (1990) 42 *Stanford L Rev* 581, 588.

The practical consequences of essentialism are reflected in the presumption of anti-discrimination legislation that one remedy fits all. But legal changes trumpeted as improvements for women as a generic group may not in fact represent gains for all. Analysing these problems in relation to black and Asian women in the United Kingdom, Diamond Ashiagbor highlights the manner in which differing economic and cultural circumstances impact upon the utility of anti-discrimination statutes.[43] One example she cites is the recognition by European and domestic courts that unequal treatment of part-time workers could constitute indirect sex discrimination due to its disproportionate impact on women. But studies show, for example, that black women are more likely than white women to work full time. Thus undoubted improvements for white women may not impact as extensively upon the lives of their black and Asian counterparts.

A second, and related, consequence of a 'single-axis framework' is that each ground is isolated from any other: 'it is assumed that it is possible and appropriate in the context of redressing relations of inequality to consider the social characteristic of each [ground] in isolation.'[44] Accordingly a successful claim of discrimination requires a claimant to describe his or her adverse treatment as occurring along a single axis, regardless of how it was perceived. Thus claimants who regard adverse treatment suffered as having occurred due to an indivisible combination of race and sex discrimination, for example, find that anti-discrimination statutes cannot adequately address the problem.

The final consequence of a 'single-axis framework' relates to structural disadvantage. Structural disadvantage, which has been heavily theorised in relation to gender, refers to 'the powerful institutional forces which drive so many women into low paying, low status jobs and which obstruct the career paths of many others.' Yet as Ashiagbor explains, an assumption of homogeneity in the analysis of gendered structural disadvantage ensures that the differing types and causes of structural disadvantage facing black and Asian women will be overlooked . . .

Under the existing statutory regime, a claimant has fewer procedural and institutional difficulties in claiming additive discrimination than intersectional discrimination. Whilst a single anti-discrimination statute would provide greater conceptual access and flexibility than current statutory arrangements, even the discrete nature of the SDA, RRA and DDA do not prevent a claimant pleading more than one ground. Procedurally, claims of additive discrimination can be, and sometimes are, made in a single application to an employment tribunal. . . . Intersectional discrimination is more troublesome. The structure of the SDA, RRA and the DDA . . . cannot conceive of a claim that is not merely additive, but in fact alleges intersectional discrimination as a result of an indivisible combination of more than one social characteristic. Procedurally, such a claim is impossible under existing statutory arrangements. Thus the claimants in *Burton and Rhule* or in *Coker and Osamor* [see Chapters 2 and 4] could not claim discrimination against them as black women . . .

In some of these cases the claimant gained a remedy, despite pleading only one ground. Does the conceptual divergence between the kind of discrimination actually suffered and that redressed by a court matter? It does, for two reasons: first, ignoring one aspect of the discrimination suffered implies a hierarchy of grounds, and neglects the differences within groups. It implies that if you are black or Asian, you are male, and that if you are a woman, you are white. Second, the misfit causes difficulties in selecting a comparator in both direct and indirect discrimination claims and may prevent the applicant making a successful claim.

---

[43] Citing D Ashiagbor, 'The Intersection between Gender and "Race" in the Labour Market' in S Sheldon (ed), *Feminist Perspectives on Employment Law* (London, Cavendish, 1998) 139.
[44] Citing N Iyer, 'Categorical Denials: Equality Rights and the Shaping of Social Identity' (1993) 19 *Queen's Law Journal* 179, 192.

However, the approach of the American courts suggests that whilst a holistic anti-discrimination statute and enforcement commission may alleviate some of the procedural and institutional difficulties outlined above, these improvements may be limited to claimants pleading additive discrimination, and not to those seeking a remedy for intersectional discrimination. Rather, a revised conception of what constitutes intersectional discrimination is needed. Such a conceptual shift demands consideration of who should or could be the beneficiary of intersectional discrimination.

An expansive concept of multiple discrimination clearly creates the potential for permutations and combinations of claims across races, sexes, religions, disabilities and sexualities. It allows consideration of the ways in which 'groups come to be constructed by discriminatory practices.'[45] Under our existing ideology of formal equality, every individual represents a potential claimant of multiple discrimination, regardless of race, sex, etc. This resonates with a subjective conception of the adverse treatment one perceives that one has suffered.

However, in identifying a distinction between additive and intersectional discrimination, one acknowledges that sometimes the discrimination suffered may be qualitatively worse (ie double the burden), or qualitatively different (ie a unique experience of adverse treatment by say, black women) respectively. The former can be largely accommodated by the creation of a holistic anti-discrimination statute. Conceptually and practically, additive discrimination retains the simplistic, discrete analysis of grounds preferred by judges, and allows a correspondingly clear comparator to be selected.

It is more difficult, and more controversial, to identify who the beneficiaries of intersectional discrimination might be, and/or should be. Considering intersectional discrimination to be qualitatively different treatment raises the question of what the differences might turn on. Is it only certain groups who can claim to experience intersectional discrimination? For example, throughout this article black and Asian women have been described as encountering intersectional discrimination. But what is it about black and Asian women that makes the adverse treatment that they suffer qualitatively different from the adverse treatment meted out to black and Asian men, or to white women? Similarly, what is it about lesbians that make the adverse treatment suffered qualitatively different from the adverse treatment experienced by gay men, or by heterosexual women? And why do we not perceive white men to suffer from intersectional discrimination as defined above?

The answer stems from disadvantage: that historically black and Asian women, lesbians and others have carried a disproportionate discriminatory burden. Continuing to frame legislation in terms of difference rather than disadvantage, particularly in cases of alleged intersectional discrimination, 'obscure[s] the historical and continuing realities of inequality facing the subordinated group within each ground.' Furthermore, in addition to fundamentally misconceiving the social mischief the legislation should be targeting, this approach rules out any structural protective or remedial measure that addresses disadvantage. In contrast, recognising that there is something qualitatively different about certain types of intersectional discrimination implicitly moves away from traditional notions of formal equality that demand symmetry. Hence a real commitment to addressing intersectional discrimination requires a shift towards a substantive equality paradigm. . . .

Enacting a single anti-discrimination statute with a corresponding single commission would overcome some of the existing conceptual and practical barriers to pleading multiple heads of discrimination, whether additive or intersectional . . . But wider questions of the efficacy of anti-discrimination statutes to address the social inequalities caused by discrimination which impact particularly upon those who find themselves in more than one

---

[45] Citing K Abrams, 'Title VII and the Complex Legal Subject' (1994) 92 *Michigan Law Review* 2479, 2497.

historically disadvantaged social group. As noted above, problems of structural disadvantage for women resonate particularly severely with black and Asian women. The underpinning ideology of the anti-discrimination statutes, formal equality, or equality of treatment, may be insufficient to tackle such disadvantage. The statutes are individualistic: they demand an individual claimant, and award an individual remedy. Inherent in the scatter-gun approach of current anti-discrimination law is the idea that 'what is complained about is abnormal.' This cannot provide acknowledgement or redress for institutionalised or structural discrimination. Similarly, the symmetrical nature of the statutes reflects the ideology of equal treatment: discrimination against men is as impugned as discrimination against women; discrimination against whites is as deserving of censure as discrimination against ethnic minorities. Accordingly, the 'legislation is framed in terms of difference rather than disadvantage: it constructs the problem to be tackled as race and sex discrimination, rather than as discrimination against and disadvantage of women and certain ethnic groups.'[46] This model prevents a remedial response targeted at disadvantage. Thus although a united anti-discrimination statute may be one mechanism by which the problems of a claim of multiple discrimination can be alleviated, the difficulties of those who attempt to claim multiple discrimination are merely a further illustration of the lack of transformative potential of an anti-discrimination regime premised on equality of opportunity.

---

[46] Citing N Lacey, 'From Individual to Group? A Feminist Analysis of the Limits of Anti-Discrimination Legislation' in *Unspeakable Subjects: Feminist Essays in Legal and Social Theory* (Oxford, Hart Publishing, 1998) 25.

2

'Discrimination'

'Discrimination' is the subject matter of this book, and it is the concept which ties together all the legislation here considered. The concept of 'discrimination' is not unique to the legislation generally regarded as central to the study of that subject. The Trade Union and Labour Relations (Consolidation) Act 1992 prohibits employment-related discrimination on grounds of trade union membership and non-membership (ss.137–8, 146, 152–3) and the Employment Rights Act 1996 prohibits discrimination on grounds that someone has exercised any of the rights provided by the Acts (ss.44–7 and 99–104). The Employment Relations Act 1999 also prohibits discrimination on a number of grounds. But what is of particular significance in the case of the legislation here studied is the central importance to them of the discrimination prohibition.

Most of the legislation here under discussion utilises similar concepts of 'discrimination', direct and indirect, and all of it prohibits 'victimisation' (see below) which is categorised as a form of discrimination. Also prohibited is the issue of instructions to discriminate. This too is considered below.[1] The Disability Discrimination Act 1995 differs from the other statutory provisions in that it imposes duties to make reasonable accommodation to the needs of disabled persons rather than prohibiting indirect discrimination, and has only recently been amended to prohibit 'direct' discrimination as such. Prior to October 2004 it itstead prohibited 'disability-related discrimination' (to use the Disability Rights Commission's terminology). This is defined more broadly than direct discrimination but is subject to a justification defence. This type of discrimination survives the Act's amendment but the narrower 'direct' discrimination is not subject to any general justification defence (see further Chapter 8).

Direct Discrimination

The concept of direct discrimination applies across the regimes under discussion though, as was mentioned above, in the case of the DDA only since 1 October 2004. Section 1(1) of the Race Relations Act 1976 provides that:

> A person discriminates against another in any circumstances relevant for the purposes of any provision of this Act if—
> (a) on racial grounds he treats that other less favourably than he treats or would treat other persons. . .

[1] Pressure to discriminate and the provision of assistance to discriminators are considered in Ch 4.

The same concept of direct discrimination is used by FETO, the Employment Equality (Religion or Belief) Regulations 2003 (RB Regs)[2] and the Employment Equality (Sexual Orientation) Regulations 2003 (SO Regs),[3] the prohibited grounds of discrimination consisting, respectively of 'religious belief or political opinion', 'religion or belief' and 'sexual orientation.'[4] The scope of these protected grounds is considered in Chapters 9 and 10. The approach taken by the Sex Discrimination Act 1975 (SDA) is similar rather than identical, s.1(1) providing that:

> A person discriminates against a woman in any circumstances relevant for the purposes of any provision of this Act if—on the grounds of her sex he treats her less favourably than he treats or would treat a man . . .

The significance of this is that, whereas the RRA protects from discrimination against A on grounds of B's race (where, for example, B is A's sexual partner, or child, or is a customer against whom A is instructed to discriminate on grounds of race),[5] the SDA protects only against discrimination on grounds of a claimant's *own* sex. Those concerned with discrimination strongly favoured the application of the broader, RRA, approach to the RB and SO Regs and in this they were successful (the broader 'on grounds of' religion or belief, etc was in any event necessary to conform with the wording of the Employment Equality Directive (Council Directive 2000/78)). The SDA is less protective in this respect than are the other legislative provisions with the practical effect that it cannot be used in order to challenge discrimination based on the sex of a person's sexual partner (ie, discrimination connected with sexual orientation). So, too, is the DDA which, in apparent contravention of the Employment Equality Directive (see Chapter 8), continues to protect only disabled persons themselves (save in the case of victimisation).

Prior to its amendment in October 2004, s.5(1) DDA provided that a person discriminated against another where 'for a reason which relates to the disabled person's disability, he treats him less favourably than he treats or would treat others to whom that reason does not or would not apply' (this in addition to the duty of reasonable accommodation imposed by the DDA and discussed in Chapter 8). This is wider than 'direct discrimination' (see pp 40ff below) and is discussed in Chapter 8. The Act now includes, in addition, a definition of direct discrimination (new section 3A(5)):

> A person directly discriminates against a disabled person if, on the ground of the disabled person's disability, he treats the disabled person less favourably than he treats or would treat a person not having that particular disability whose relevant circumstances, including his abilities, are the same as, or not materially different from, those of the disabled person.

This coexists with the broader definition of discrimination above (now s.3A(1)). Its significance is that, whereas disability-related 'discrimination' under the DDA is capable of justification (s.3A(3)) ('if, but only if, the reason for it is both material to the circumstances of the particular case and substantial'), s.3A(4) provides that 'treatment of a disabled person cannot be justified under subsection (3) if it amounts to direct discrimination falling

---

[2] SI 2003 No. 1660.

[3] SI 2003 No. 1661.

[4] The Equal Pay Act (EqPA) does not define 'direct' (or 'indirect') discrimination—indeed, the term 'discrimination' is not even employed by the Act. But, as we shall see in Ch 6, the concepts of direct and indirect discrimination have a significant role to play for the purposes of that Act.

[5] See discussion of *Showboat v Owens* [1984] ICR 65 below and in Ch 7.

within subsection (5).' This serves to bring the DDA into line with the other legislation by removing the general justification defence to 'direct' disability discrimination. However, the test for justification of other types of discrimination under the DDA remains significantly easier to satisfy than that which applies in relation to the other protected grounds. This is further discussed in Chapter 8.

Intention, Motivation and Stereotypes

The definition of direct discrimination appears relatively straightforward. But, particularly in the early application of the SDA, the courts at times appeared reluctant to apply it in its full force. The first case to reach the Court of Appeal under that Act was *Peake v Automotive Products*.

Peake v Automotive Products Ltd [1978] QB 233

The claimant challenged his employer's practice of allowing women to leave the factory five minutes before men. Men and women finished work at the same time, but women were permitted to leave first, according to Lord Denning, 'in the interests of safety so that the women should not be jostled or hurt in the rush through the gates when the men leave work.'

Lord Denning MR:

Although the [SDA] applies equally to men as to women, I must say it would be very wrong to my mind if this Act were thought to obliterate the differences between men and women or to do away with the chivalry and courtesy which we expect mankind to give womankind. The natural differences of sex must be regarded even in the interpretation of an Act of Parliament. Applied to this case it seems to me that, when a working rule is made differentiating between men and women in the interests of safety, there is no discrimination contrary to s.1(1)(a). Instances were put before us in the course of argument, such as a cruise liner which employs both men and women. Would it be wrong to have a regulation: 'Woman and children first?' Or in the case of a factory in case of fire? As soon as such instances are considered, the answer is clear. It is not discrimination for mankind to treat womankind with the courtesy and chivalry which we have been taught to believe is right conduct in our society.

Goff and Shaw LJJ agreed with the Master of the Rolls, the latter on the basis that 'The [SDA] was not, in my judgment, designed to provide a basis for capricious and empty complaints of differentiation between the sexes' and that 'discrimination' against men or women 'involves an element of something which is inherently adverse or hostile to the interests of the persons of the sex which is said to be discriminated against.' The decision in *Peake* was described by Peter Wallington as one 'redolent of all the values that the [SDA] had sought to lay to rest . . . a contribution from the Court of Appeal which must rank as intellectually one of its weakest in recent years.'

P Wallington 'Ladies First—How Mr Peake was piqued' [1978] *Cambridge Law Journal* 37, 39, footnotes omitted

A person who refused to employ women as bricklayers because he envisaged that they would be embarrassed by the language used by the male employees, or the landlord who kept women out of his dockland pub because they might be molested by drunken male customers, would not be discriminating. That in itself is bad enough—women are capable of making such judgements for themselves without the need for a judicially-sired wet-nurse—but what must cause greater concern is the formidable burden of proof if some element of subjective hostility on the part of the respondent needs to be proved in every case of discrimination. Proof of discrimination even on an objective standard of conduct is difficult enough: it would be well-nigh impossible if the respondent could put on his best honest expression, disclaim any malevolent intent towards the applicant, and wait for the Tribunal to shelter behind the burden of proof and dismiss the claim.

The difficulty with the approach of the Court of Appeal in *Peake* is that it is just the attitudes of 'chivalry' and those regarding the 'natural differences of sex' which are in large part responsible for the disadvantages suffered by women which the SDA attempted to eradicate. Recognition, albeit belated, of this prompted the Court of Appeal in *Ministry of Defence v Jeremiah* to modify the approach it had adopted in *Peake*.

Ministry of Defence v Jeremiah [1980] QB 87

Mr Jeremiah complained that that, whereas men who volunteered for overtime were required to work in the 'colour-bursting shop' (an unpleasant environment in respect of which work attracted an additional premium), women who worked overtime were not so required.

Lord Denning MR:

A woman's hair is her crowning glory, so it is said. She does not like it disturbed: especially when she has just had a 'hair-do'. The women at an ordnance factory in Wales are no exception. They do not want to work in a part of the factory . . . which ruins their 'hair-do' . . .

   Mr Jeremiah has little regard for chivalry or for the women's hair-dos. He is a modern man. He says that there should be equality between the sexes. Either the women should be required to do their stint (in the colour-bursting shop), just like the men. Or the men should not be required to do it any more than the women . . . it is plain that Ministry of Defence here discriminated against Mr Jeremiah. They required him to work in the dirty shop. They treated him less favourably than they treated a woman; and they did it on the ground of his sex, because he was a man . . . the Ministry relies on *Peake v Automotive Products Ltd* . . . There were two grounds for the decision. Now on reconsideration, I think the only sound ground was that the discrimination was *de minimis*. Counsel for Mr Jeremiah told us that on a petition to the House of Lords, they refused leave to appeal for that very reason. They thought that the decision was correct on the *de minimis* ground.

   In these circumstances, the other ground (about chivalry and administrative practice) should no longer be relied on . . .

The categorisation of the discrimination in *Peake* as de minimis is questionable, Peter Wallington pointing out that the difference in time worked by men and women amounting to two days per annum. The existence of a de minimis defence to a discrimination claim has been accepted by Buxton LJ in the recent Court of Appeal decision in *Jiad v Byford* [2003] IRLR 232, which concerned the question when a claim could be struck out as 'scandalous, misconceived or vexatious.'[6] This case and the broader issue of detriment are considered in Chapter 4.

---

[6] See further Ch 5.

Direct discrimination may consist in treating people differently *simply* because of a difference in sex, racial group, etc.[7] But it will more commonly consist in treating them differently on the basis of attributes stereotypically associated with persons of either sex or a particular racial group.

T Modood 'Cultural Diversity and Racial Discrimination in Employment Selection' in B. Hepple and E Szyszczak (eds), *Discrimination: the Limits of Law* **(London, Mansell, 1992), footnotes omitted**

Stereotyping is an intellectually crude, patronizing and unfair method of providing a context in which to judge individuals who are deemed to be of a collective type; in the extreme case individuals are seen completely in terms of a collective type. The greater the ignorance about a group of people by an outsider or observer, the greater the reliance on a stereotype (which may not be completely unfavourable to the group). It follows that to decrease the use of unfavourable stereotypes one has to increase the level of knowledge about the groups and to make sure that the knowledge used is not only of the outsider's generalizing type but includes some understanding of how the group understands itself, of what it believes to be some of its distinctive qualities or virtues. We need to allow favourable as well as unfavourable generalizations to come into play. The more one knows about a group the more one is able to penetrate beyond the group to the individual; it is when the context is easily understood and taken for granted that the individual stands out and so can be noticed in his or her own right. The less familiar one is with the group, the less one is able to perceive the individual for 'they all look alike' (not just in terms of physical appearance but also in terms of behaviour). See for instance how easily all assertive Muslims have been branded as 'fundamentalists' by the media, and indeed how there was no media interest in Muslim concerns until they were seen as a threat. The choice, then, is not between identifying someone as an individual and identifying him or her as a group member; without understanding the group, one lacks the context for identifying the variables out of which individuality is composed. Until one can penetrate into the forest one cannot see one tree as being different from another.

   These generalities are relevant to the employment selection process. Consider the cultural variables of an interview for example. What I have in mind are the following types of features: desired length of interview, desired ratio of talk between interviewer and interviewee, length of introductions, eye-contact, posture, body language, deference, willingness to talk about oneself and various areas of one's life, tendency to answer directly or in circumlocutions and elaborate context-setting ways, standards of politeness and informality, willingness to 'sell oneself' and inhibitions about boasting, sexual modesty, anxieties built up from previous rejections and fear of discrimination, etc. How we treat and evaluate other people in an interview is dependent on how we relate to them, how comfortable we are with them. The very same qualities that in one individual may be perceived as pushy and aggressive may in another be commended as the raw materials to be developed into leadership skills. The difference in perception may be nothing more than racial—or for that matter, sexual— prejudice. Such prejudice may be unconscious and unexamined because it is shared and reinforced by our own peer group and, when combined with a lack of familiarity with the nuances of a different cultural manner, is bound to produce mutually unsatisfactory interviews and fail in bringing out or identifying the capabilities of ethnic minority candidates. Where we as selectors do not make an effort to guard against unconscious discrimination, we invariably select those individuals who are most like ourselves—for after all not only are they the people it is easiest to get close enough to for their strengths to be spotted, but they

---

[7] In such a case an employer, if replying honestly, would affirm that the reason for the differential treatment was the difference in sex, race, etc.

are the ones whom we are likely to feel we had a good interview with because they are the individuals that we are likely to enjoy the experience of being with. Conversely, with those that we don't easily hit it off with, we do not make the same effort to seek their positive qualities and therefore undervalue them.

Stereotyping was recognised as a form of direct discrimination in *Skyrail Oceanic Ltd v Coleman*.

Coleman v Skyrail Oceanic Ltd (trading as Goodmos Tours) [1981] ICR 864

The claimant, a travel agent, was dismissed when she married an agent from a competing firm. Both employers had agreed that Ms Coleman should be dismissed on the assumption that her husband would be the primary breadwinner. The Court of Appeal re-instated the tribunal's decision that she had been dismissed on grounds of sex, EAT having overturned that decision in the meantime ([1980] ICR 596.

Lawton LJ (with whom Sir David Cairns agreed):

The foundation of Mr Lester's submission [for the plaintiff] that there had been unlawful discrimination against Mrs Coleman because of her sex was . . . [the employer's] evidence when he said: 'We [decided to dismiss her] on the assumption that the husband was the breadwinner.' The respondents made no inquiries about the financial position of the husband. Had they done so they would have discovered that he was earning a modest wage of £46 per week net, which in 1978 would have provided a poor standard of living for himself and his wife if she did not make any contribution to the family income . . . I am satisfied that the dismissal of a woman based upon an assumption that men are more likely than women to be the primary supporters of their spouses and children can amount to discrimination under the [SDA].

The problem which Mr Lester had to overcome in this case was that the respondents had a reason for dismissing Mrs Coleman which had nothing to do with her sex. What mattered to them was the fact that she was on intimate terms with an employee of a rival firm. Mr Lester submitted, however, that what triggered off their decision to dismiss Mrs Coleman was their assumption that her husband would be the breadwinner after their marriage. It was this which led them to treat her less favourably than they would have treated a man in their employment who happened to have a wife working for a rival firm . . .

There was evidence that the respondents and Mr Levinson of the rival firm had discussed the problem arising from the fact that they were employing a married couple. Following this discussion Mrs Coleman had been dismissed because of the assumption which was made. The evidence is not clear who made the assumption. It seems to me likely that the assumption was made by both the respondents and Mr Levinson in the course of their discussion; and even if it was not, it was made by the respondents . . .

[Counsel for the employers] also submitted that the evidence did not establish that the respondents discriminated against Mrs Coleman on the ground of her sex. The assumption which they made had no sexual connotation because a breadwinner can be of either sex. This is so; but, in the circumstances of this case, the assumption was that husbands are breadwinners and wives are not. Such an assumption is, in my judgment, based on sex.

Shaw LJ (dissenting):

The circumstances which give rise to this appeal have been recounted in the judgment which has just been delivered. I need not, therefore, dwell in detail upon the history. I must acknowledge at the outset that it appears to me to be trivial and banal even when topped up with much legalistic froth. However, this court is required to examine the claims erected upon it. The appellant asserts that the respondents discriminated against her on the ground of her sex and that she was unfairly dismissed by them. In the light of the history those claims are, in my view, artificial and pretentious; but the ... Tribunal thought otherwise and their only concern appears to have been as to how great a sum they could award to this excessively outraged victim of sex discrimination. As the other members of this court are of the mind that on the evidence there is a narrow factual ground for awarding her some-thing, though it be a small sum, I must take a little time to explain why I consider Mrs Coleman's claim to be unmeritorious and an abuse of the idealistic principle sought to be embodied in the [SDA] ...

Before the appellant was married, the respondents had a legitimate ground for terminat-ing her contract of employment with them. Their only obligation then was to give her due notice and to avoid any implication that she had been guilty of impropriety as an employee. Her relationship with a fiancé in the service of a competing organisation made her contin-ued employment with the respondents a source of risk which they were not called upon to accept. If she had been told this and given due notice that would have been the end not only of her employment with the respondents, but of any possible claim against them. Whatever tears she may have shed because of her dismissal at a time when she was contemplating marriage, no solatium could have been extracted or extorted from her employers. She would have had to be content with such consolation as her fiancé and her family could give her. When she had dried her tears she would have had to look for new employment and to have counted herself lucky to find it, as she has indeed done ...

After the appellant had made her original claim for unfair dismissal, the respondents were incautious enough to assign a purported reason for her dismissal. Those who advised her pounced upon this as a manifestation of sex discrimination and the Industrial Tribunal embraced the proposition and awarded her a thousand pounds for the injury thus done her. This appears to me to make nonsense of s.1 of the [SDA]. Mrs Coleman gave evidence before the Tribunal. She does not appear to have been asked whether she would have been more content (or would have suffered less) if (i) her husband had been dismissed and she had not, or if (ii) both her husband and she had been dismissed. If either of those events had occurred no cry of 'unfair discrimination because I am a woman' would have availed her before the Industrial Tribunal. Had she appeared there in those circumstances not even the most unrestrained sympathy could have evoked support for a claim resting on so unreal a foundation. This reductio ad absurdum demonstrates, in my view, that the appellant's claim is founded on a fallacy ...

Each employer might have adopted the harsh expedient of respectively dismissing the husband and the wife. They might have tossed a coin to decide which of them should dis-pense with the services of the embarrassing employee. The tears might still have followed, but no execrating noises about sex discrimination ...

This was so unmeritorious a case on the facts that I deplore the encouragement given to the appellant to pursue what was at best a phantom claim. The promotion of such claims can only have the consequence of bringing the laudable aims of the legislation against sex discrimination into disrepute. The principles which the [SDA] are designed to promote and protect are disserved when it is sought, with all the attendant anxieties and expense to oth-ers, to apply those principles to cases as empty as the present ...

Shaw LJ's blustering dissent notwithstanding, *Coleman* was followed by EAT in *Horsey v Dyfed CC* [1982] ICR 755 to rule in favour of a woman disadvantaged by the assumption that she would subordinate her career to that of her husband. And more recently, in *R (European Roma Rights Centre) v Immigration Officer at Prague Airport* [2005] 2 WLR 1, the House of Lords overturned a decision by the Court of Appeal ([2004] QB 811) which permitted the application of stereotypical assumptions that Roma travelling to the UK were more likely than others to be prospective asylum seekers.

The cases thus far considered suggest (*Jeremiah*'s disapproval of *Peake* being taken into account) that a respondent's motive for treating the claimant less favourably will not preclude a finding of discrimination as long as that discrimination was '*on the grounds of* sex or race, etc. The prohibited ground does not have to be the sole ground for the less favourable treatment (*Owen & Brigg v James* [1982] ICR 618, Court of Appeal) but it must be 'the principal or at least an important or significant cause of the less favourable treatment.'[8]

The lack of any requirement that the discriminator be motivated by the prohibited ground was confirmed by the House of Lords in *R v Birmingham City Council ex parte EOC*.[9] The same decision established that 'less favourable treatment' occurred when a plaintiff was deprived of a choice which was valued by her and by others on reasonable grounds.

R v Birmingham City Council ex parte EOC [1989] AC 1155

The case was brought by the EOC because, the Council having fewer grammar school places available for girls than for boys, it set the pass mark higher for the former in the '11 plus' examination by which children in the area were selected for secondary education. The House of Lords ruled that, in order to establish that the girls had been discriminated against, it did not have to be shown that grammar school education was better than the alternative. Lord Goff went on to consider, for their Lordships, the meaning of 'on the grounds of sex.'

Lord Goff:

There is discrimination under the statute if there is less favourable treatment on the ground of sex, in other words if the relevant girl or girls would have received the same treatment as the boys but for their sex. The intention or motive of the defendant to discriminate, though it may be relevant so far as remedies are concerned . . . is not a necessary condition to liability . . . if [it were] it would be a good defence for an employer to show that he discriminated against women not because he intended to do so but (for example) because of customer preference, or to save money, or even to avoid controversy.[10]

This statement of the law seems clear. But it did not settle the meaning of 'on the grounds of' within s.1(1)(a) of the SDA and RRA. Only one year later, the House of Lords considered the matter once again in *James v Eastleigh Borough Council*.

---

[8] Reaffirmed in *Nagarajan v London Regional Transport* discussed below. By contrast, in the US the Civil Rights Act 1991 reversed the decision of the Supreme Court in *Price Waterhouse v Hopkins* (1989) 490 US 228 to the effect that the prohibited reason in a mixed motive case must at least 'tip the balance.' *James v Eastleigh Borough Council* and *Nagarajan* used the 'but for' test adopted *restrictively* by a US Court of Appeals in *Lewis v University of Pittsburg* 33 US Cases 1091 (1983) (ie, to require that the discriminatory reason had to tip the balance), see D Pannick, *Sex Discrimination Law* (Oxford, OUP, 1985), 87. But the House of Lords, in adopting the 'but for' test in these cases, did not do so restrictively but, as we saw above, expansively to deny the need for motivation. It may be that the discriminatory reason may *either* satisfy the 'but for' test or, in a case where a discriminatory motive is established (this not being necessary in a 'but for' case), be an 'important and significant cause.' In *Chamberlin Solicitors v Emokpae* [2005] EWCA 142 the Court of Appeal supported the guidance set out in *Barton v Investec Securities* (EAT) [2003] ICR 1205 which was to the effect that, in order to discharge the burden of proof imposed by one SDA (see Ch 5) an employer had to establish that treatment was 'in no sense whatsoever on the ground of sex'.

[9] Prior to this see *R v Commission for Racial Equality, ex p Westminister Council* [1985] ICR 827.

[10] Citing *Jenkins v Kingsgate (Clothing Productions) Ltd* [1981] ICR 715 *per* Browne-Wilkinson J and *R v Secretary of State for Education and Science, ex p Keating* (1985) 84 LGR 469 at 475 *per* Taylor J. See also Lord Denning MR in *Ministry of Defence v Jeremiah* discussed at p 41 above.

***James v Eastleigh Borough Council* [1990] 2 AC 751**

The applicant had been charged entrance to the local swimming pool on the grounds that, both he and his wife being aged between 60 and 65, she but not he had reached state pensionable age upon which free entrance depended. A county court and the Court of Appeal had rejected the applicant's complaint of direct discrimination, the latter on the ground (per Browne-Wilkinson VC) that s.1(1)(a) SDA imposed a subjective test which was satisfied only if either the covert or the overt reason for the treatment complained of was sex.

Lord Bridge:

. . . the statutory pensionable age, being fixed at 60 for women and 65 for men, is itself a criterion which directly discriminates between men and women in that it treats women more favourably than men 'on the ground of their sex' . . . It follows inevitably that any other differential treatment of men and women which adopts the same criterion must equally involve discrimination 'on the ground of sex'. . . .

The Court of Appeal's attempt to escape from these conclusions lies in construing the phrase 'on the ground of her sex' in s.1(1)(a) as referring subjectively to the alleged discriminator's 'reason' for doing the act complained of. As already noted, the judgment had earlier identified the council's reason as 'to give benefits to those whose resources would be likely to have been reduced by retirement' and 'to aid the needy, whether male or female.' But to construe the phrase, 'on the ground of her sex' as referring to the alleged discriminator's reason in this sense is directly contrary to a long line of authority confirmed by your Lordships' House in [*ex parte EOC* above].

Lord Goff's test, it will be observed, is not subjective, but objective. Adopting it here the question becomes: would the plaintiff, a man of 61, have received the same treatment as his wife *but* for his sex? (My emphasis) An affirmative answer is inescapable.

Lord Goff:

. . . As a matter of impression, it seems to me that, without doing any violence to the words used in [s.1(1)(a)], it can properly be said that, by applying to the plaintiff a gender-based criterion, unfavourable to men, which [the Council has] adopted as the basis for a concession of free entry to its swimming pool, they [sic] did on the ground of sex treat him less favourably than it treated women of the same age, and in particular his wife. In other words, I do not read the words 'on the ground of sex' as necessarily referring only to the reason why the defendant acted as he did, but as embracing cases in which a gender-based criterion is the basis on which the complainant has been selected for the relevant treatment. Of course, there may be cases where the defendant's reason for his action may bring the case within the subsection, as when the defendant is motivated by an animus against persons of the complainant's sex, or otherwise selects the complainant for the relevant treatment because of his or her sex. But it does not follow that the words 'on the ground of sex' refer only to cases where the defendant's reason for his action is the sex of the complainant and, in my opinion, the application by the defendant to the complainant of a gender-based criterion which favours the opposite sex is just as much a case of unfavourable treatment on the ground of sex . . .

. . . as I see it, cases of direct discrimination under s.1(1)(a) can be considered by asking the simple question: would the complainant have received the same treatment from the defendant but for his or her sex? This simple test possesses the double virtue that, on the one hand, it embraces both the case where the treatment derives from the application of a gender-based criterion, and the case where it derives from the selection of the complainant because of his or her sex and on the other hand it avoids, in most cases at least, complicated questions relating to concepts such as intention, motive, reason or purpose, and the danger of confusion arising from the misuse of those elusive terms.

Lord Ackner concurred with Lords Bridge and Goff. Lords Griffiths and Lowry gave dissenting speeches, Lord Griffiths on the ground that the Council had not discriminated against Mr James 'because' he was a man, Lord Lowry on the ground that Lord Goff's 'causative construction not only gets rid of unessential and often irrelevant mental ingredients, such as malice, prejudice, desire and motive, but also dispenses with an essential ingredient, namely the ground on which the discriminator acts . . . the causative test is too wide and is grammatically unsound, because it necessarily disregards the fact that the less favourable treatment is meted out to the victim on the ground of the victim's sex.'

Lord Griffiths characterised as 'an attractive feature of our national life that those who provided entertainment and travel facilities gave generous treatment to old age pensioners by providing them free or at concessionary rates,' and found it hard to believe that the SDA was intended to put an end to this practice. He accepted that:

> adopting pensionable age as the criterion to judge whether a person is living on a pension is to adopt a broad brush approach. But given that it is the intention to give the concession to those who are living on a pension and thus of reduced means, it appears to me to be the only practical criterion to adopt. It would be quite impossible to interrogate every person as to whether they were or were not living on a pension or to apply some other form of means test before admitting them to the swimming pool . . .
>
> Obviously imposing a retirement age of 60 on women and 65 on men is discriminatory on the grounds of sex. It will result in women being less well off than men at 60. But what I do not accept is that an attempt to redress the result of that unfair act of discrimination by offering free facilities to those disadvantaged by the earlier act of discrimination is, itself, necessarily discriminatory, 'on the grounds of sex.' The question in this case is did the Council refuse to give free swimming to the plaintiff because he was a man, to which I would answer, no, they refused because he was not an old age pensioner and therefore could presumably afford to pay 75p to swim.

The benefit of the 'but-for' test is that it avoids analysis of the motivation for discrimination. On the other hand, it is clear from Lord Griffiths' dissent that the approach does not permit a distinction to be drawn between negative and positive discrimination—that is, between discrimination which perpetuates existing disadvantage and that which is designed to ameliorate it. This is further considered in Chapter 3.

The 'but for' test was reiterated by the House of Lords (Lord Browne-Wilkinson dissenting) in *Nagarajan v London Regional Transport*, a victimisation case also considered below. All their Lordships agreed that the term 'by reason that' in the victimisation provisions had to be interpreted consistent with 'on the grounds of' in the context of direct discrimination.[11] Lord Browne-Wilkinson argued that the decisions in *ex parte EOC* and in *James v Eastleigh* did not establish the 'but for' test as the sole, objective, test for direct discrimination. While his Lordship accepted that Lord Bridge had, in *James*, expressly preferred what the former termed an 'objective approach' to s.1(1)(a) (ie, one which asked 'was a substantial cause of less favourable treatment the race or sex of the applicant?'),[12] he suggested that Lord Goff himself did not fully accept the 'but for' test.

---

[11] This has subsequently changed—see discussion of *Khan v Chief Constable of the West Yorkshire Police* below).

[12] Or, in a victimisation claim, the fact that the claimant had done a protected act.

Nagarajan v London Regional Transport [2000] AC 501

Lord Browne-Wilkinson, dissenting:

. . . It is to be noted that Lord Goff picks his words carefully. He finds the 'but for' test a useful practical approach to determining the discriminator's reason 'in the majority of cases.' Moreover, it is to be noted that his formulation is purely subjective: the question is whether the applicant would have received the same treatment 'from the defendant.' The 'but for' test is not a rule of law but a rule of convenience depending on the circumstances of the case. I find it difficult in these circumstances to know exactly what was decided by the James case. Although it is binding on your Lordships I do not regard the question under section 1 as finally determined: it may require to be revisited in the future . . . The only yardstick (in the field of direct discrimination) must be the mental state of the alleged discriminator. To dismiss somebody who comes from an ethnic minority is not, per se, unlawful. Only if what lies within the mind of the employer is the race of the employee and it is that factor which provides the reason why the employee is dismissed does one come into the field of race discrimination at all.

There can be no doubt that the mental state of the alleged discriminator is important to whether direct discrimination has occurred. But the categorisation as 'objective' of the 'but for' test is flawed. The race, sex, etc, of the employee does lie within the mind of the direct discriminator in a *James v Eastleigh* situation in that s/he *knowingly* and *intentionally* applies a criterion which itself *directly* discriminates as between men and women/ different racial groups, etc.[13] Thus, contrary to the view taken by Lord Browne-Wilkinson in *Nagarajan*, it is not the case that the 'but for' test requires a finding of discrimination simply on the basis of less favourable treatment accorded to a ethnic minority worker than to another.[14] This was recognised by Lord Nicholls who, with Lord Steyn, delivered the majority speeches:

Nagarajan v London Regional Transport [2000] ICR 877

Lord Nicholls:

. . . in every case it is necessary to inquire why the complainant received less favourable treatment. This is the crucial question. Was it on grounds of race? Or was it for some other reason, for instance, because the complainant was not so well qualified for the job? Save in obvious cases, answering the crucial question will call for some consideration of the mental processes of the alleged discriminator. Treatment, favourable or unfavourable, is a consequence which follows from a decision . . . The crucial question just mentioned is to be distinguished sharply from a second and different question: if the discriminator treated the complainant less favourably on racial grounds, why did he do so? The latter question is strictly beside the point when deciding whether an act of racial discrimination occurred. For the purposes of direct discrimination under section 1(1)(a), as distinct from indirect discrimination under section 1(1)(b), the reason why the alleged discriminator acted on racial grounds is irrelevant. Racial discrimination is not negatived by the discriminator's motive or intention or reason or purpose (the words are interchangeable in this context) in treating another person less favourably on racial grounds . . . If racial grounds were the reason for the less favourable treatment, direct discrimination under section 1(1)(a) is established . . .

[13] The knowing and intentional application of indirectly discriminatory criteria is (intentional) indirect discrimination, see *London Underground v Edwards* [1995] IRLR 355, *JH Walker Ltd v Hussain* [1996] ICR 291.
[14] Or, for that matter to a woman than to a man or vice versa, or to a white worker than to another.

The same point was made in *James* . . . The reduction in swimming pool admission charges was geared to a criterion which was itself gender-based. Men and women attained pensionable age at different ages. Lord Bridge . . . described Lord Goff's test in the *Birmingham* case as objective and not subjective. In stating this he was excluding as irrelevant the (subjective) reason why the council discriminated directly between men and women. He is not to be taken as saying that the discriminator's state of mind is irrelevant when answering the crucial, anterior question: why did the complainant receive less favourable treatment?

The prohibition of discrimination on grounds of sex, race, etc, in the absence of any general justification defence, has created a battle ground. This was evident in cases such as *Peake* and *Jeremiah* and in Shaw LJ's dissent in *Coleman* and, though the 'plain meaning' arguments gained the ascendancy in the *EOC* and *James* cases, as well as in *Jeremiah* and *Coleman*, the dissatisfaction of elements of the judiciary rumbles on. Lord Browne-Wilkinson was particularly strongly wedded to a narrow approach to 'direct' discrimination which minimized the sphere within which discrimination which appeared appropriate, justifiable or in some sense inadvertent would nevertheless breach the relevant legislation. He maintained this approach throughout his career despite being in many ways ahead of his time in embracing the anti-discrimination legislation of the 1970s with a degree of enthusiasm (see, for example, the decision in *Showboat v Owens* below). Lord Browne-Wilkinson's fellow Law Lords refused to follow his vision in *Najarajan* but it is evident from the decision of the Court of Appeal in the *Roma* case that the wheel has to be re-invented continually for judges without a great deal of experience in the statutory regulation of discrimination.

Legitimising Direct Discrimination: 'Appropriate' Comparators

The decision of the Court of Appeal in the *Roma* case illustrates—as did *Peake* in its time—that the courts sometimes accept as legitimate discrimination for which statute does not provide a justification defence. The other way in which this has occurred has been through the manipulation of the comparator requirement.

Most of the legislative provisions considered in this book permit a claim on the basis of a hypothetical comparator alone.[15] Whether an actual or a hypothetical comparator is used, s.5(3) SDA provides that:

A comparison of the cases of persons of different sex . . . under section 1(1) . . . must be such that the relevant circumstances in the one case are the same, or not materially different, in the other.

The RRA, FETO, SO Regs and RB Regs are all in similar terms and s.3A(5) DDA, as we saw above, incorporates into that Act's definition of direct discrimination a requirement for comparison between the disabled person's treatment and that of a real or hypothetical person without the same disability 'whose relevant circumstances, including his abilities, are the same as, or not materially different from, those of the disabled person.' It has been noted above that no general justification defence is provided under any of the legislation in respect of 'direct' discrimination. But we shall see, below, that ss.5(3)/ 3(4) and Article 3(3) may operate covertly to permit the justification of direct discrimination under the SDA, RRA and FETO respectively.

---

[15] *Cf* the EqPA and the Part-time Workers and Fixed-term Work Regulations discussed in Ch 6.

In *Showboat Entertainment Centre Ltd v Owens*, EAT upheld a finding of race discrimination against an employer who dismissed the claimant for his refusal to obey an instruction to exclude young black people from his place of work (an amusement centre). Much of the decision dealt with the applicability of s.1(1)(a) RRA to discrimination against someone other than the claimant, a matter further discussed in Chapter 4. But the final point dealt with by EAT was the employer's argument that, in order to satisfy s.3(4) RRA, the treatment received by the claimant had to be compared with that which would have been meted out to another manager who refused to obey a racist instruction.

Showboat Entertainment Centre Ltd v Owens [1984] ICR 65

Browne-Wilkinson J (for the Court):

. . . Although one has to compare like with like, in judging whether there has been discrimination you have to compare the treatment actually meted out with the treatment which would have been afforded to a man having all the same characteristics as the complainant except his race or his attitude to race. *Only by excluding matters of race can you discover whether the differential treatment was on racial grounds.* Thus, the correct comparison in this case would be between Mr Owens and another manager who did not refuse to obey the unlawful racialist instructions [my emphasis].

The approach taken in *Showboat* certainly seemed consistent with that subsequently adopted by the House of Lords in *James v Eastleigh*, in which Lord Bridge declared that:

Because pensionable age is itself discriminatory it cannot be treated as a relevant circumstance . . . It is only by wrongly treating pensionable age as a relevant circumstance under s 5(3) that it is possible to arrive at the conclusion that the provision of facilities on favourable terms to persons of pensionable age does not involve direct discrimination under s 1(1)(a) . . . On a proper application of s 5(3) the relevant circumstance which was the same here for the purpose of comparing the treatment of the plaintiff and his wife was that they were both aged 61.[16]

In *Dhatt v McDonalds Hamburgers* [1991] ICR 238, however, the Court of Appeal permitted a race-related circumstance to be considered for the purposes of s.3(4) RRA. The claim was brought by a man of Indian nationality who was dismissed by McDonalds because of his failure to satisfy his employers that he was entitled to work in the UK. His passport was stamped in such a way as to indicate his entitlement to work, but McDonalds did not recognise this stamp as sufficient to comply with their requirement, imposed only in respect of non-EEC workers, of evidence of entitlement to work. On the face of it, Mr Dhatt had clearly been discriminated against contrary to s.1(1)(a) ('racial grounds' being defined by s.3(1) RRA as 'any of the following grounds, namely colour, race, *nationality* or ethnic or national origins' (my emphasis)). 'But for' the fact that he was not an EC national, he would not have been dismissed because of his failure to provide evidence of his entitlement to work. Despite this, the claim was rejected by a tribunal, EAT and the Court of Appeal.

All three Lords Justice of Appeal accepted the relevance of the decisions in *Showboat* and in *James* but distinguished the latter on the basis that, while the council had freely chosen to condition free entrance on directly discriminatory criteria, here McDonalds had, *per* Neill LJ, a 'general responsibility to ensure that those who work in his business comply with the law.' Stocker LJ agreed that employers had a 'public duty to assist in the enforcement

---

[16] Although Browne-Wilkinson LJ in the Court of Appeal [1990] QB 61 took a different view.

of the immigration laws. They had, in my view, no alternative but to enquire whether or not an applicant was lawfully entitled to accept employment. Such an enquiry for this purpose did not arise in the case of British citizens or those from EEC countries.' The Court of Appeal took the view that this was sufficient to render a job seeker's nationality a 'relevant circumstance' under s.3(4). Lord Justice Neill did not attempt to distinguish the dicta in *Showboat*, but Stocker and Staughton LJJ agreed that *Showboat* did not lay down any principle of 'universal application.'

The Court of Appeal in *Dhatt* purported to rely on the employers' legal obligation to read into s.3(4)'s 'relevant circumstances', in a claim of nationality discrimination, the factor of nationality. If it were the case that the failure so to do would prevent employers from meeting their legal obligations, this would perhaps have been inevitable. But s.41 RRA provides that a discriminatory act is not unlawful under the RRA if it is done:

(a) in pursuance of any enactment or Order in Council or
(b) in pursuance of any instrument made under any enactment by a Minister of the Crown or
(c) in order to comply with any condition or requirement imposed by a Minister of the Crown (whether before or after the passing of this Act) by virtue of any enactment.

In *Hampson v Department of Education and Science* [1991] 1 AC 171 which is considered in Chapters 4 and 7, the House of Lords took a restrictive approach to s.41(b). Their Lordships did not consider s.3(4) RRA. But, if the approach taken by the Court of Appeal in *Dhatt* were correct, s.41 would be otiose and Ms Hampson's claim would certainly have failed. Not being in possession of a UK qualification (or, perhaps, a three-year equivalent as proscribed by the Secretary of State for Education), the claimant's appropriate comparators would have been others similarly failing to comply with the regulations as applied. All such persons would, it must be presumed, have been given equally short shrift by the Secretary of State.

Section 5(3) SDA has also given rise to difficulties in connection with pregnancy. Taken to its logical conclusion, the 'but for' approach might have permitted the British courts to find that pregnancy discrimination necessarily amounted to direct discrimination on grounds of sex. A woman dismissed on grounds of pregnancy could claim that, 'but for' the fact of her sex, she would not have been so treated.

In *Geduldig v Aiello* (1974) 417 US 484 the US Supreme Court refused to accept that pregnancy discrimination amounted to sex discrimination, upholding the exclusion of pregnancy from a state unemployment insurance plan on the grounds that:

[t]here is no risk from which men are protected and women are not. Likewise, there is no risk from which women are protected and men are not . . . The program divides potential recipients into two groups—pregnant women and nonpregnant persons. While the first group is exclusively female, the second includes members of both sexes.

By contrast, the Supreme Court of Canada in *Brooks v Canada Safeway* [1989] 1 SCR 1219 ruled that 'pregnancy cannot be separated from gender.' There the Court found that the exclusion of pregnancy from an insurance policy contravened the equality provisions of Canada's Charter of Rights: '[t]he fact . . . that the plan did not discriminate against all women, but only against pregnant women, did not make the impugned distinction any less discriminating.'

The UK courts focused on the 'relevant circumstances' of the appropriate comparator under ss.5(3) of the SDA, and defined those circumstances so as to defeat direct discrimination claims based on pregnancy (and, as we shall see in Chapter 10, sexual orientation).[17] European developments eventually forced the British courts to accept pregnancy discrimination (though not, as yet, sexual orientation discrimination) as direct sex discrimination, a development further discussed below and in Chapter 10. Meanwhile, the decision of the Court of Appeal in *Dhatt*, discussed above, illustrates the potential of s.5(3) SDA and its equivalents to undermine the prohibition of direct discrimination and, in particular, of the 'but for' test.[18]

The House of Lords has recently recognised the difficulties to which the hunt for an appropriate comparator can give rise. *Shamoon v Chief Constable of the Royal Ulster Constabulary (Northern Ireland)* [2003] ICR 337 involved a complaint under the Sex Discrimination (Northern Ireland) Order 1976, which is materially identical to the SDA. The claimant was a chief inspector whose appraisal duties were removed from her after a number of complaints had been made against her in connection with her conduct of appraisals. Her sex discrimination claim was upheld by a tribunal but dismissed by Northern Ireland's Court of Appeal (to which claims from tribunals go directly) on the basis that her chosen comparators—two male chief inspectors—were not similarly situated (this because no complaints had been made against them in connection with their performance of appraisals).[19]

The House of Lords agreed that the actual comparators relied upon by the claimant were inappropriate and that the tribunal had given no reasons to justify the finding of sex discrimination. Their Lordships did, however, make some interesting observations about the question of comparators. Lord Hope pointed out that:

> the choice of comparator requires that a judgment must be made as to which of the differences between any two individuals are relevant and which are irrelevant. The choice of characteristics may itself be determinative of the outcome . . . This suggests that care must be taken not to approach this issue in a way that will defeat the purpose of the legislation, which is to eliminate discrimination against women on the ground of their sex in all the areas with which it deals.[20]

Lord Nicholls, with whom Lord Rodger agreed on this point, noted that the general practice of tribunals was to ask, first, 'whether the claimant received less favourable treatment than the appropriate comparator (the "less favourable treatment" issue)' and to treat this question effectively as a 'threshold which the claimant must cross before the tribunal is called upon to decide' the second question—'whether the less favourable treatment was on the relevant proscribed ground (the "reason why" issue).' He accepted that this practice could be 'convenient and helpful' but stressed that there was 'essentially a single question: did the claimant, on the proscribed ground, receive less favourable treatment than others [received or would have received]?' The 'sequential analysis' could 'give rise to needless problems' 'especially where the identity of the relevant comparator is a matter of dispute.

---

[17] See also the decision of the ECJ in *Grant v South West Trains* Case C–249/96 [1998] ECR I–3739 discussed in Ch 10.

[18] See also the decision of the ECJ in *Hlozek v Roche Austria Gesellschaft mbH* Case C-19/02 [2004] All ER(D) 132 for a case in which that Court ruled that the claimant and his comparators were not analogously situated.

[19] Actually the materially identical Art 7 of the NI Order.

[20] Having noted Sandra Fredman's critique of the comparator approach (see *Discrimination Law*, Oxford University Press, 2001, 96–9).

Sometimes the less favourable treatment issue cannot be resolved without, at the same time, deciding the reason why issue. The two issues are intertwined.'

In the instant case Lord Nicholls pointed out that it was not possible to answer whether the claimant's chosen comparators were appropriate without addressing the question why she had been relieved of her appraisal duties: if the reason was connected with the complaints against her the comparators were not appropriate. But the action taken against her may have had nothing to do with the complaints, in which case the comparison she advocated would have entailed 'comparing like with like, because in that event the difference between her and her two male colleagues would be an immaterial difference'. Equally, the question whether the claimant was less favourably treated than a hypothetical comparator:

is incapable of being answered without . . . identifying the ground on which she was treated as she was. Was it grounds of sex? If yes, then she was treated less favourably than a male chief inspector in her position would have been treated. If not, not. Thus, on this footing also, the less favourable treatment issue is incapable of being decided without deciding the reason why issue. And the decision on the reason why issue will also provide the answer to the less favourable treatment issue.

On the basis of this analysis Lord Nicholls concluded that tribunals:

may sometimes be able to avoid arid and confusing disputes about the identification of the appropriate comparator by concentrating primarily on why the claimant was treated as she was. Was it on the proscribed ground which is the foundation of the application? That will call for an examination of all the facts of the case. Or was it for some other reason? If the latter, the application fails. If the former, there will be usually be no difficulty in deciding whether the treatment, afforded to the claimant on the proscribed ground, was less favourable than was or would have been afforded to others.

Lord Nicholls' approach fits well with the domestic model of direct discrimination which permits claimants to establish discrimination in relation to a *hypothetical* comparator. Once it has been established that the treatment complained of was *by reason of* a protected ground, the comparator question is largely a formality save in cases in which the discriminator alleges that *differential* treatment was not *less favourable* (as, perhaps, if single-sex toilet facilities were to be challenged).[21] But Nicholls' approach does not solve all the problems to which the analysis of discrimination gives rise. Indeed it is perhaps precisely because of the difficulties associated with determining the reasons for differential treatment that a comparator-driven approach can appear attractive. The House of Lords' embracing of the 'but-for' test in *James v Eastleigh* was intended to avoid unnecessary confusion as to intention, motive, etc. It operates in practice by emphasising what Lord Nicholls referred to in *Shamoon* as the 'less favourable treatment' question over the 'reason why' question. In order to determine whether a claimant would have been treated more favourably 'but for' her sex, the question required by s.5(3) SDA is whether a similarly situated man was or would have been treated more favourably than she was. But as their Lordships generally recognised in *Shamoon*, the answer to this may depend on the characteristics assigned to the 'similarly situated' man or other relevant comparator.

Particular examples of this arise in the context of pregnancy dismissals and discrimination against gay men and lesbians. In the case of pregnancy the question is whether the

---

[21] Note that s.1(2) RRA provides that: 'for the purposes of this Act, segregating a person from other persons on racial grounds is treating him less favourably than they are treated.'

similarly situated man requires a similar period of absence from work. Or—because pregnancy can only happen to women—must that which is inevitably connected with it be excluded from the 'relevant circumstances' under s.5(3) SDA? In the case of discrimination against gay men and lesbians the question is whether the similarly situated woman or man respectively is one who (a) would or does have sexual relationships with men (where the claimant is a gay man) or women (where the claimant is a lesbian); or (b) one who has or would have sexual relationships with members of their own sex In either of these cases, the difficulties are not alleviated whether (as in *James*) an objective 'but for' test is adopted or whether (as suggested by Lord Nicholls in *Shamoon*) the 'reason why' test is brought to the fore. If the former then all hangs on the choice of comparator. If the latter the question is whether discrimination connected with pregnancy, on the one hand, and discrimination against gay men and lesbians, on the other, is discrimination which ought in principle to be recognised as *sex* discrimination.

The approach adopted by the House of Lords in *James* was liberal and purposive in defining direct discrimination widely without requiring malign motivation on the part of the discriminator (though its impact on the potential of positive action to redress disadvantage are discussed in Chapter 3). But the *James* approach does not do away with the need to ask questions about reasons for discrimination and whether they are properly categorised as coming within the protected grounds or not. It is clear from the decision in *James* that differential treatment which is based on criteria which themselves directly discriminate between men and woman will directly discriminate on grounds of sex. Equally, differential treatment which is based on criteria which themselves directly discriminate on racial grounds will directly discriminate on racial grounds. It follows from this that, if a woman were dismissed *solely because* she was pregnant she should be regarded as having been discriminated against on grounds of sex. There is in principle no need in such a case to identify a comparator but, to the extent that one is required by s.5(3) SDA,[22] he must simply be a man if the dicta in *James* is to be given effect. A man in the same relevant circumstances—whatever those circumstances were—could not possibly be pregnant and would not therefore have been sacked.

But once the reason put forward for the dismissal of a pregnant woman is something other than the fact of pregnancy *itself* (as, for example, where the employer points to the period of required leave or the flouting of moral standards by an unrepentant single pregnant woman) the picture is muddied. The question which arises under the 'reason why' approach is whether these reasons are reasons of sex. That which arises under the 'less favourable treatment' approach is whether the comparator should in the first example need a comparable period of leave and whether, in the second, he should be someone similarly morally tarnished in the eyes of the discriminator or whether, on the other hand, the same approach is required as would be applied if the reason for the dismissal was the fact of pregnancy *itself*. This is certainly desirable and—in the absence of other adequate legal protection from pregnancy-related discrimination—crucial if women are to be permitted even the most minimal claim to an even playing field at work. It is also required by EU law, the ECJ having ruled in a succession of cases that pregnancy discrimination is sex discrimination regardless of the precise reason for the differential treatment (see further Chapter 6). But the fact that this answer has been supplied in the pregnancy context for reasons which are extraneous to the model of discrimination adopted by the SDA does not supply a principled answer which necessarily ought to be applied in other circumstances.

---

[22] *Webb v EMO Air Cargo (UK) Ltd (No 2)* [1994] QB 718, discussed in Ch 6.

We will return to direct discrimination in considering positive discrimination in Chapter 3, in which the issue of proof is considered, and in Chapters 6–10 which deal individually with each of the protected grounds. Here it is sufficient to conclude from our initial consideration of direct discrimination the importance of the 'but for' test; the fact that reliance on stereotypical views of women (men, persons of different racial or national groups, etc.) is directly discriminatory; and the potentially problematic role of the requirement that the 'comparison of the cases of persons of different sex [race, etc] . . . must be such that the relevant circumstances in the one case are the same, or not materially different, in the other.'

Harassment and Discrimination

Catharine MacKinnon has defined sexual harassment as 'the unwanted imposition of sexual requirements in the context of a relationship of unequal power',[23] Canada's Labour Code as:

> any conduct, comment, gesture or contact of a sexual nature
> (a) that is likely to cause offence or humiliation to any employee; or
> (b) that might, on reasonable grounds, be perceived by that employee as placing a condition of a sexual nature on employment or on any opportunity for training or promotion.[24]

The European Commission's Recommendation on the Protection of the Dignity of Men and Women at Work defines sexual harassment in the following terms:

> conduct of a sexual nature, or other conduct based on sex affecting the dignity of women and men at work [which] . . . is unwanted, unreasonable and offensive to the recipient; is used . . . as a basis for an [employment] decision; and/or . . . creates an intimidating, hostile or humiliating work environment for the recipient.

The US Equal Employment Opportunity Commission (EEOC) in 1980 produced guidelines on sexual harassment which defined harassment as a violation of Title VII's prohibition on sex discrimination.[25] And in Canada, the Supreme Court recognised sexual harassment as sex discrimination in *Janzen v Platy Enterprises Ltd* Manitoba's Court of Appeal had ruled that sexual harassment did not amount to discrimination this on the basis that (*per* Twaddle JA): 'harassment and assault are acts, whilst discrimination and random selection are methods of choice' and that 'Only if [a] woman was chosen on a categorical basis, without regard to individual characteristics, can . . . harassment be a manifestation of discrimination.' The Supreme Court allowed the plaintiff's appeal:

---

[23] *Sexual Harassment of Working Women: A Case of Sex Discrimination* (New Haven, Yale University Press, 1979) 1.

[24] RSC, 1985, c. L–2, 247.1.

[25] EEOC, Guidelines on Discrimination Because of Sex, 29 CFR 1604.11(a) (1985).

Janzen v Platy **(1989) 1 SCR 1284 (SC)**

Dickson CJ (for the Court):

When sexual harassment occurs in the workplace, it is an abuse of both economic and sexual power.

Sexual harassment is a demeaning practice, one that constitutes a profound affront to the dignity of the employees forced to endure it. By requiring an employee to contend with unwelcome sexual actions or explicit sexual demands, sexual harassment in the workplace attacks the dignity and self-respect of the victim both as an employee and as a human being.

Perpetrators of sexual harassment and victims of the conduct may be either male or female. However, in the present sex stratified labour market, those with the power to harass sexually will predominantly be male and those facing the greatest risk of harassment will tend to be female . . .

Sexual harassment as a phenomenon of the workplace is not new. Nor is it confined to harassment of women by men, though this is by far the most prevalent and significant context. It may be committed by women against men, by homosexuals against members of the same sex. According to a Canadian survey published in 1983, women reported far more exposure to all forms of unwanted sexual attention than did men. Forty-nine per cent of women (as compared to 33 per cent of men) stated that they had experienced at least one form of this kind of harassment. The frequency of sexual harassment directed against women was also significantly higher. In the case of sexual harassment experienced by women, most (93 per cent) of the harassers were men, while men complained of harassment by women (62 per cent) and men (24 per cent) . . .

There appear to be two principal reasons, closely related, for the decision of the Court of Appeal of Manitoba that the sexual harassment to which the appellants were subjected was not sex discrimination. First, the Court of Appeal drew a link between sexual harassment and sexual attraction. Sexual harassment, in the view of the Court, stemmed from personal characteristics of the victim, rather than from the victim's gender. Second, the appellate court was of the view that the prohibition of sex discrimination in s. 6(1) of the Human Rights Act was designed to eradicate only generic or categorical discrimination. On this reasoning, a claim of sex discrimination could not be made out unless all women were subjected to a form of treatment to which all men were not. If only some female employees were sexually harassed in the workplace, the harasser could not be said to be discriminating on the basis of sex. At most the harasser could only be said to be distinguishing on the basis of some other characteristic.

The two arguments raised by the Manitoba Court of Appeal may in fact be seen as alternate formulations of the following argument. Discrimination implies treating one group differently from other groups, thus all members of the affected group must be subjected to the discriminatory treatment. Sexual harassment, however, involves treating some persons differently from others, usually on the basis of the sexual attractiveness of the victim. The harasser will typically choose one, or several, persons to harass but will not harass all members of one gender. As harassers select their targets on the basis of a personal characteristic, physical attractiveness, rather than on the basis of a group characteristic, gender, sexual harassment does not constitute discrimination on the basis of sex.

This line of reasoning has been considered in both Canada and the United States, and in my view, quite properly rejected . . .

The fallacy in the position advanced by the Court of Appeal is the belief that sex discrimination only exists where gender is the sole ingredient in the discriminatory action and where, therefore, all members of the affected gender are mistreated identically. While the concept of discrimination is rooted in the notion of treating an individual as part of a group rather than on the basis of the individual's personal characteristics, discrimination does not require uniform treatment of all members of a particular group. It is sufficient that ascribing to an individual a group characteristic is one factor in the treatment of that individual. If a finding of discrimination required that every individual in the affected group be treated identically, legislative protection against discrimination would be of little or no value. It is rare that a discriminatory action is so bluntly expressed as to treat all members of the relevant group identically. In nearly every instance of discrimination the discriminatory action is composed of various ingredients with the result that some members of the pertinent group are not adversely affected, at least in a direct sense, by the discriminatory action. To deny a finding of discrimination in the circumstances of this appeal is to deny the existence of discrimination in any situation where discriminatory practices are less than perfectly inclusive. It is to argue, for example, that an employer who will only hire a woman if she has twice the qualifications required of a man is not guilty of sex discrimination if, despite this policy, the employer nevertheless manages to hire some women.[26]

It is clear from the decision of Manitoba's Court of Appeal in *Janzen* that the characterisation of 'harassment' as 'discrimination' is not uncontroversial. At the EU level the argument has been settled by the express categorisation of harassment as a form of discrimination by the Race and Employment Equality Directives which provide that 'discrimination' includes 'harassment' which is in turn defined as 'unwanted conduct [which] relates to a protected ground and which takes place with the purpose or effect of violating the dignity of a person and of creating an intimidating, hostile, degrading, humiliating or offensive environment,' though they go on to provide that 'In this context, the concept of harassment may be defined in accordance with the national laws and practice of the Member States.' Council Directive 2002/73/EC, which comes into force in October 2005, amends the Equal Treatment Directive to define sexual harassment as a form of sex discrimination. Meanwhile, however, the status of sex discrimination and of discrimination on grounds of colour or nationality (as distinct from 'race or ethnic or national origins') is governed by the domestic case law, considered below.

The domestic law on harassment is extremely complex. The implementation of the Race and Employment Equality Directives means that harassment related to sexual orientation, to religion or belief or to race, ethnic or national origins or, in the employment context, is defined as discrimination under the SO Regs, the RB Regs the RRA and the DDA respectively. Further, the definition of 'harassment' is in some respects broader than that provided by the new Directives.

Section 3A RRA, to which s.3B of the DDA as amended and Regs 5 of the SO Regs and the RB Regs are materially identical, provides that:

(1) A person subjects another to harassment . . . where, on grounds of race or ethnic or national origins, he engages in unwanted conduct which has the purpose or effect of—
    (a) violating that other person's dignity, or
    (b) creating an intimidating, hostile, degrading, humiliating or offensive environment for him.

The consultation exercise which preceded the amendment of the RRA uncovered a clear perception that 'detriment' would occur for the purposes of the domestic discrimination provisions where unwanted conduct which discriminated on the relevant grounds (see further Chapter 4) had the purpose or effect either of violating the recipient's dignity, or of creating an intimidating, hostile, degrading, humiliating or offensive environment for the

---

[26] Citing *Brooks v Canada Safeway* [1989] 1 SCR 1219.

recipient. In view of the prohibition on levelling-down in Article 6(2) of the Racial Equality Directive, a disjunctive rather than conjunctive approach to (a) and (b) was adopted. Section 3A(2), however, in common with the equivalent provisions in the DDA, SO Regs and the RB Regs, provides that:

> Conduct shall be regarded as having the effect specified in paragraph (a) or (b) of sub-section (1) only if, having regard to all the circumstances, including in particular the perception of that other person, it should reasonably be considered as having that effect.

The inclusion of this expressly objective test was controversial, a number of consultees having taken the position that this amounted to a levelling down of the existing protection from harassment. That argument is considered in Chapter 4. It should be noted that, save where the express definition of 'harassment' applies, harassment amounts to actionable discrimination only where (in addition to constituting 'less favourable treatment' on a protected ground, discussed below, it amounts to a 'detriment' within the relevant legislation (see further Chapter 4).

The other apparent shortcoming of the UK's approach is its substitution of 'on grounds of' for the Directives' 'relates to'. The former rubric is tainted by the comparator-driven approach considered below and, if it has the effect of importing this approach into the application of the amended provisions, will be inadequate to implement the Directives. The draft regulations by which the government proposes to transpose Council Directive 2002/73/EC maintain this approach (defining 'harassment' as unwanted conduct etc which is 'on the ground of [the victim's] sex'/ gender reassignment), although they also prohibit 'sexual harassment': unwanted etc 'verbal, non-verbal or physical conduct of a sexual nature' and less favourable treatment on the ground that a person has rejected or submitted to unwanted conduct of either variety. This still leaves possible gaps in coverage (where, for example, a woman is exposed to an environment in which women are routinely disparaged and spoken of in derogatory, though not explicitly sexual, terms). We know from *Pearce v Governing Body of Mayfield Secondary School* [2003] ICR 937 that gender-specific conduct is not, as such, conduct 'on grounds of' sex. So unless such conduct is either *motivated* by sex, in which case it will amount to direct sex discrimination, or *explicitly* sexual, it will fall outside the scope of the proposed legislative prohibition.

That sexual harassment could amount to sex discrimination contrary to the SDA was recognised by Scotland's Court of Session in *Strathclyde v Porcelli*.

Strathclyde Regional Council v Porcelli [1986] ICR 564

The case was brought by a woman laboratory technician driven from her job by the sustained verbal and physical harassment, of a sexual nature, to which male colleagues had subjected her. A tribunal rejected her sex discrimination claim on the grounds that the reason for the harassment lay in her aggressors' dislike of her, and that a man who was so disliked by them would have been treated equally badly. On this ground the tribunal found that she had not been treated less favourably than an (equally disliked) man would have been and had not, therefore, been discriminated against contrary to the SDA. EAT allowed an appeal, a decision upheld by the Court of Session.

Lord Emslie (P):

Section 1(1)(a) is concerned with 'treatment' and not with the motive or objective of the person responsible for it. Although in some cases it will be obvious that there is a sex related purpose in the mind of a person who indulges in unwanted and objectionable sexual overtures to a woman or exposes her to offensive sexual jokes or observations that is not this case. But it does not follow that because the campaign pursued against Mrs Porcelli as a whole had no sex related motive or objective, the treatment of Mrs Porcelli by Coles, which was of the nature of 'sexual harassment' is not to be regarded as having been 'on the ground of her sex' within the meaning of s.1(1)(a). In my opinion this particular part of the campaign was plainly adopted against Mrs Porcelli because she was a woman. *It was a particular kind of weapon, based upon the sex of the victim, which . . . would not have been used against an equally disliked man* [my emphasis].

The Industrial Tribunal reached their decision by finding that Coles' and Reid's treatment of an equally disliked male colleague would have been just as unpleasant. Where they went wrong, however, was in failing to notice that a material part of the campaign against Mrs Porcelli consisted of 'sexual harassment,' a particularly degrading and unacceptable form of treatment which it must be taken to have been the intention of Parliament to restrain. From their reasons it is to be understood that they were satisfied that this form of treatment—sexual harassment in any form—would not have figured in a campaign by Coles and Reid directed against a man. In this situation the treatment of Mrs Porcelli fell to be seen as very different in a material respect from that which would have been inflicted on a male colleague, regardless of equality of overall unpleasantness . . .

Lord Grieve:

In order to decide whether there ha[s] been a breach of s.1(1)(a) consideration . . . ha[s] to be given . . . to the weapons used against the complainer. If any could be identified as what I called 'a sexual sword,' and it was clear that the wound it inflicted was more than a mere scratch, the conclusion must be that the sword had been unsheathed and used because the victim was a woman. In such a circumstance there would have been a breach of s.1(1)(a).

Treatment, whether it is apparently sexualised or otherwise, will also amount to sex discrimination (less favourable treatment on grounds of sex) in any case where sex is the motive (eg, where a manager or colleagues do not wish to work with women and so take steps to drive out women workers). The problem arises where the treatment is not *motivated* by sex, but nevertheless takes a sexualised *form*.[27] The strength of *Porcelli* is its recognition that such treatment can be *on the ground of* sex. The same is true, by analogy, of racist conduct and conduct directed, for example, at a worker's disability or other protected characteristic.

It is clear from the decision of the Court of Session in *Porcelli* that harassment connected with sex would not automatically involve discrimination under the SDA (similarly with race, disability, etc, under the relevant legislation). While a claim of discrimination will be made out as long as the particular type of 'weapon' used would not have been used on a person of the opposite sex/ a different racial group, etc, such a claim would generally be defeated by a credible claim that the same weapon (whether sexual assault or, arguably, race, religion or disability-specific abuse) had or would have been used against a man, or a person not having the particular characteristic targeted. This point is illustrated by the decision in *Stewart v Cleveland Guest (Engineering) Ltd* [1996] ICR 535 in which the conduct complained of consisted in the display of pictures of semi-naked women in a workplace in which '[t]he conditions . . . tended to be suggestive of the treatment of women as sex objects, not as people' and '[m]anagement had encouraged a general ethos that was male

---

[27] Unless it amounts to a criminal assault, harassment under the Protection from Harrassment Act 1997 or that the failure to protect from harassment amounted to a breach by the employer of implied contractual terms relating to, for example, trust and confidence or health and safety.

orientated.'[28] EAT upheld a tribunal decision that a woman constructively dismissed in connection with the display had not been subject to sex discrimination on the basis that 'the display . . . was neutral. A man might well find [it] . . . as offensive as the claimant did'[29] and that, accordingly, no sex discrimination had occurred.

Ms Stewart's sex discrimination claim failed because neither the tribunal nor EAT accepted that she had been sexually harassed. In *British Telecommunications plc v Williams* [1997] IRLR 668, Morison J expressed the view that, where sexual harassment (or, by implication, other forms of harassment) was proven, it would *always* amount to direct discrimination. Morison J cited *Porcelli* in support of the proposition that: 'Because the conduct which constitutes sexual harassment is itself gender-specific, there is no necessity to look for a male comparator. Indeed, it would be no defence to a complaint of sexual harassment that a person of the other sex would have been similarly so treated.' But in *Smith v Gardner Merchant Ltd* [1999] 1 ICR 134 a majority of the Court of Appeal disagreed, Ward LJ remarking that it was precisely on this issue that the Court of Session in *Porcelli* had differed from Scottish EAT and stating that: 'it is not the case that because the abusive conduct is gender-specific that there is no necessity to look for a male comparator; but it is rather the case that *if it is gender-specific*, if it is sex-based, then, in the nature of the harassment, it is almost certainly bound as a matter of fact to be less favourable treatment as between the sexes' (my emphasis). Ward LJ's approach, was condemned by Michael Rubenstein in his commentary to the IRLR report. Pointing out that it would provide a defence, on a sex discrimination claim, to an employer guilty of sexual harassment who would harass (or had harassed) an employee of the opposite sex as well, Rubenstein declared (IRLR 'Highlights', September 1998) that the approach:

> would be risible, if it did not threaten to do such damage to sexual harassment law. It is, indeed, difficult to credit that a sexual assault on a woman will amount to sex discrimination only if the perpetrator would not sexually assault a man. This is the conclusion demanded by the Court of Appeal in *Smith v Gardner* which, although it claimed to follow *Porcelli*, seems to narrow it in asserting that treatment which is 'sex-based' or 'gender-specific' (such as, for example, grabbing a woman's breast) is not *per se*, but only 'almost certain . . . as a matter of fact' to amount to sex discrimination (because it is unlikely that, for example, a man who committed an indecent assault upon a woman would also indecently assault a man (or do so in the same manner).

In *Sidhu v Aerospace Composite Technology Ltd* [2001] ICR 167, the Court of Appeal accepted that, while in each case a finding of direct race discrimination required that the claimant 'show that he has been treated less favourably by the discriminator than the discriminator treats or would treat other persons in the same circumstances,' nevertheless (*per* Peter Gibson LJ):

> in certain cases the comparison need not be demonstrated by evidence as to how a comparator was or would be treated, because the very action complained of is in itself less favourable treatment on sexual or racial grounds. Thus in a sex discrimination case if it can

---

[28] According to the tribunal's decision.

[29] Ms Stewart also successfully claimed constructive dismissal on the ground that, given the way in which management had handled her complaint, she had had to leave. *Cf* the recent decision of EAT in *Moonsar v Fiveways Express Transport Ltd* [2005] IRLR 9 in which judge Ansell recognised that, 'viewed objectively the exposure of a woman to internet pornography downloaded onto her colleagues' computers clearly had the potential effect of causing an affront to [her] . . . and as such could be regarded as degrading or offensive to [her] *as a woman* [my emphasis].'

be shown that the less favourable treatment meted out to a woman was only because she was a woman, it follows that the woman was treated less favourably than a man [citing *Porcelli*]. In the jargon of employment lawyers, that conduct is gender-specific. So also if a person is harassed or abused because of his race, that conduct is race-specific and it is not necessary to show that a person of another race would be treated more favourably . . .

More recently, however, the House of Lords decision in *Pearce v Governing Body of Mayfield School* has cast doubt on the *Porcelli* decision on which the recognition by domestic case law of harassment as discrimination rests.

Pearce v Governing Body of Mayfield Secondary School [2003] ICR 937

So far as is relevant here the case concerned complaints of sex discrimination based on the subjection of a lesbian teacher to sustained harassment which included the use of taunts such as 'lesbian', 'dyke', 'lesbian shit', 'lemon', 'lezzie' or 'lez'. The argument that discrimination on grounds of sexual orientation could and should be regarded as discrimination on grounds of sex was comprehensively rejected by the lower courts and, in turn, by the House of Lords (this aspect of the decision is considered, together with the joined case of *Macdonald v Ministry of Defence*, in Chapter 10). But a subsidiary argument made by Ms Pearce was that the use by her harassers of gender-specific taunts itself amounted to less favourable treatment on grounds of sex. This argument was dismissed by the lower courts, which considered themselves bound by *Smith v Gardner Merchant*, and by the House of Lords.

Lord Nicholls:

Sexual harassment is only prohibited by the Sex Discrimination Act if the claimant can show she was harassed because she was a woman. Section 1(1)(a) requires the employment tribunal to compare the way the alleged discriminator treats the woman with the way he treats or would treat a man. In any case where discrimination is established, this exercise must involve comparing two forms of treatment which are different, whether in kind or in degree. It also involves the tribunal in evaluating the differences and deciding which form of treatment is less favourable.

   The suggestion in some cases that if the form of the harassment is sexual or gender-specific, such as verbal abuse in explicitly sexual terms, that of itself constitutes less favourable treatment on the ground of sex, could not be reconciled with the language or the scheme of the statute. The fact that harassment is gender-specific in form cannot be regarded as of itself establishing conclusively that the reason for the harassment is gender-based, 'on the ground of her sex.' It will be evidence, whose weight will depend on the circumstances, that the reason for the harassment was the sex of the victim, although in some circumstances, the inference may readily be drawn that the reason for the harassment was gender-based, as where a male employee subjects a female colleague to persistent, unwanted sexual overtures. In such a case, the male employee's treatment of the woman is compared with his treatment of men, even though the comparison may be self-evident. However, the observation of Lord Brand in *Strathclyde Regional Council v Porcelli* that if a form of unfavourable treatment is meted out to a woman to which a man would not have been vulnerable, she has been discriminated against, and the observation of Lord Grieve in the same case that treatment meted out to a woman on the ground of her sex would fall to be regarded as less favourable treatment simply because it was sexually oriented, could not be approved insofar as they were suggesting that it was not relevant whether the claimant was treated less favourably than a man where the harassment is sexually oriented. Similarly, Morison J read too much into *Porcelli* when he said in *British Telecommunications plc v*

Williams that it would be no defence to a complaint of sexual harassment that a person of the other sex would have been similarly so treated.

In the case of Ms Pearce, the natural inference to be drawn from the homophobic terms of abuse was that the reason for this treatment was her sexual orientation, even though the form which the abuse took was specific to her gender. The issue under s.1(1)(a) cannot turn on a minute examination of the precise terms of the abuse. Ms Pearce had not put forward any evidence that a male homosexual teacher would have been treated differently. Therefore, she did not establish that the harassment was on the ground of her sex.

Lord Hope (having cited the second paragraph of Lord Emslie's extracted above):

The key to a proper understanding of this passage is to be found in the fact that the Lord President has identified sexual harassment as a particular form of treatment which was to be distinguished from other forms of unpleasantness. Having done so the application of the comparator test became a formality, because the tribunal's findings indicated that this form of treatment would not have featured in a campaign against a man. But I do not think that he is to be taken as laying down any principle. What he was doing . . . was examining the question whether the tribunal had correctly applied the provisions of s.1(1)(a) to the facts which it found proved . . .

In my opinion Morison J read too much into Porcelli when he said in *British Telecommunications plc v Williams* that it would be no defence to a complaint of sexual harassment that a person of the other sex would have been similarly so treated. It was precisely because the tribunal's reasons showed that they were satisfied that sexual harassment in any form would not have been used in a campaign which Coles and Reid directed against a man that Lord President Emslie felt able to say that if they had asked themselves whether Mrs Porcelli had been treated less favourably than a man they would have been bound to answer the question in the affirmative. In so far as Lord Grieve and Lord Brand may be taken to have been suggesting that this was not a relevant question where the harassment is sexually orientated, I would disapprove of their observations. I respectfully agree with the way Ward LJ dealt with *Porcelli* in *Smith v Gardner Merchant Ltd.* As he said, the conclusions in that case were conclusions of fact and Morison J was wrong to elevate them into a principle of law.

There is no escape, then, from the need to resort to a comparison. The words 'less favourable treatment' in s.1(1)(a) render this inevitable. It may be that the conduct complained of is so specific to the claimant's gender that there is no need to do more than to ask the question, to which the answer may well be, as Ward LJ put it in *Smith v Gardner Merchant Ltd, res ipsa loquitur* . . . But that conclusion may be more easily drawn in cases of sexual harassment which do not involve any homophobic element than in cases such as those of Mr Macdonald and Ms Pearce where the context for the abuse is the abuser's belief that the victim is a homosexual. This is because those who abuse homosexuals tend to pick on them not because of their gender but because they are homosexual. The form which the abuse takes may well be specific to the gender of the person who is being abused, but this is because the terminology which is used to describe homosexuals and the acts which they can perform with each other tend to vary according to the gender of those who are involved in this relationship. That is not to exclude the possibility that an abuser may treat a woman who is a homosexual less favourably than he would treat a male homosexual. That may indeed happen, and an employment tribunal must always be alert to this possibility. But whether this is so will be a question of fact in each case.

Lord Rodger went further, disapproving of the approach taken by Lord Emslie in the *Porcelli* case (as distinct from its subsequent application in the *BT* case. According to his Lordship, *Porcelli* had involved a 'widening' of the concept of sexual harassment from the 'classic cases' in which conduct has a sexual motivation to cases 'where the motivation of the harasser was not sexual,' and the decision though 'influential . . . is not satisfactory':

> What [Lord Emslie did was] to hold that the tribunal should have segregated the incidents with a sexual content from the rest and should have considered, separately, the way that the men treated Mrs Porcelli in those incidents. I regret that I am unable to agree with that approach, which depends on reading s.1(1)(a) as if it spoke of the person treating the woman less favourably *in a material respect*. There is, of course, no warrant for adding any such words and, as Lord Grieve points out, counsel for the education authority had argued against it. But it is only if the provision contained some such words that a tribunal would be justified in dealing separately with the various items making up the alleged discrimina- tor's treatment of the woman. In fact the section simply envisages a comparison between the way the alleged discriminator treats the woman and the way he treats or would treat a man. In the absence of any qualifying words, this must mean that a comparison is to be made between the whole of the alleged discriminator's treatment of the woman and the whole of his treatment of the man . . .
>
> No words should be read into s.1(1)(a). The provision requires the employment tribunal to compare the way the alleged discriminator treats the woman with the way he treats or would treat a man. In any case where discrimination is established, this exercise must by definition involve comparing two forms of treatment which are different, whether in kind or in degree. It also involves the tribunal in evaluating the differences and deciding which form of treatment is less favourable. That is an exercise for the judgment of the tribunal, with its lay members using their experience and acting rather like a jury. Although the exer- cise may be more complicated, the same applies where the alleged discrimination takes the form of a course of conduct against the woman. The tribunal must compare that course of conduct as a whole with any action, or with the whole of any course of conduct, that the alleged discriminator pursues or would pursue against a man in similar circumstances. On the basis of that comparison the tribunal decides whether the alleged discriminator treats the woman less favourably on the ground of her sex than a man in similar circumstances.

Lord Rodger's views did not command majority support, Lord Hobhouse agreeing with Lord Nicholls and Lord Scott with all three judgments extracted here. But the approach of the House of Lords is no ringing endorsement of the principle for which *Porcelli* has come to stand, and highlights the inadequacy of the 'make do and mend' approach which UK lawyers, lacking any tailored harassment prohibition upon which to rely, have been forced to adopt. This development is perhaps of limited significance given the legislative definition of harassment as discrimination in the context of sexual orientation, religion or belief, race (race, ethnic or national origins) and, from October 2005, sex. But the old provisions continue to govern harassment on grounds of nationality or colour (save to the effect that such harassment also amounts to harassment on grounds of 'race, ethnic or national ori- gin'), non employment-related harassment connected with disability, sex and (in Northern Ireland) religion and belief.[30] It is a matter of serious concern, then, that the jurisprudence of the domestic courts does not fully recognise harassment as a form of discrimination.

---

[30] At least, in the case of sex, until the implementation (December 2007) of Council Directive 2004/113/EC, further discussed in Chs 4 and 6. Note also the point made above that the use of the 'on grounds of' terminology may serve to perpetuate the approval taken by the House of Lords in *Pearce*.

Victimisation

All the discrimination legislation here under consideration (the SDA, RRA, DDA, FETO, SO Regs and RB Regs) prohibits 'victimisation' which is defined in each case as a form of discrimination. Section 4 SDA provides that:

(1) A person ('the discriminator') discriminates against another person ('the person victimised') in any circumstances relevant for the purposes of any provision of this Act if he treats the person victimised less favourably than in those circumstances he treats or would treat other persons, and does so by reason that the person victimised has—

   (a) brought proceedings against the discriminator or any other person under [the relevant legislation];[31] or

   (b) given evidence or information in connection with proceedings brought by any person against the discriminator or any other person under [the relevant legislation]; or

   (c) otherwise done anything under or by reference to [the relevant legislation] in relation to the discriminator or any other person; or

   (d) alleged that the discriminator or any other person has committed an act which (whether or not the allegation so states) would amount to a contravention of [the relevant legislation],

   or by reason that the discriminator knows that the person victimised intends to do any of those things, or suspects that the person victimised has done, or intends to do, any of them.

(2) Subsection (1) does not apply to treatment of a person by reason of any allegation made by him if the allegation was false and not made in good faith.

Sections 2, and 55 and Art 3 respectively of the RRA, the DDA and the FETO are in materially identical terms as are regs 4 of each the SO Regs and the RB Regs. A straightforward application of the victimisation provisions occurred in *Northern Health and Social Services Board v Fair Employment Agency*,[32] in which the claimant sued successfully in respect of a remark made by one member of an appointments panel to another to the effect that he had previously made a complaint under the FEA (as it then was). The Fair Employment Agency ruled that the making of the remark amounted to discrimination by way of victimisation 'in the arrangements the employer makes for the purpose of determining who should be offered employment.' Northern Ireland's Court of Appeal agreed.[33]

Cases such as *NHSSB v Fair Employment Agency* aside, the victimisation provisions have not served adequately to protect discrimination complainants from dismissal and other ill-treatment. Research has shown extraordinary rates of attrition in relation to sex

---

[31] The SDA also prohibits victimisation in relation to proceedings brought under the EqPA and the sex discrimination provisions of the Pensions Act 1995.

[32] Unreported 20 September 1994, available on LEXIS. See also *Bameih v Crown Prosecution Service* 41 *Equal Opportunities Review Discrimination Case Law Digest* 3–4, a case in which 'extra care' was written on the interview notes of the claimant, who had previously complained of discrimination, marks were awarded subjectively, no proper records kept and hers was the only performance not properly marked.

[33] More recently, in *St Helens MBC v Derbyshire* [2004] IRLR 851, EAT ruled that employers had victimised a group of equal pay claimants by informing staff that the cost of the women's claims could 'make provision of the service economically unviable' and that redundancies would ensue, and by writing to the claimants urging them to reconsider their claims in light of these threats. EAT, *per* Cox J, ruled that victimisation did not require threat of disciplinary or other sanctions.

discrimination and equal pay claimants, both successful and unsuccessful. Alice Leonard, for example, found that only 17 of 70 successful claimants remained with the same employer a couple of years later.[34] One difficulty which arises in relation to any provision concerned with the intentions of an actor (here the alleged discriminator) is that of proof. This issue is discussed more generally in Chapter 5. The difficulties inherent in proving discrimination are not unique to the victimisation provisions. But additional hurdles have been imposed in this matter by the interpretive approach taken by the courts to victimisation.

In *Kirby v Manpower Services Commission* [1980] ICR 420, EAT ruled that the victimisation provisions required that the claimant be less favourably treated than a person who had acted similarly, but other than in connection with the relevant Act. Mr Kirby had been demoted because he breached his duty of confidentiality towards client employers by reporting to the Council for Community Relations racially discriminatory actions taken by them. EAT accepted the employer's argument that, as any employee who had 'give[n] away information of this kind or information which [was] received in confidence would [have been] treated on broadly the same basis,' the victimisation claim failed.

The first victimisation claim to reach the Court of Appeal was *Aziz v Trinity Street Taxis Ltd* [1989] 1 QB 463, in which that Court characterised as 'absurd' the approach taken by EAT in *Kirby*. The Court ruled that a finding of victimisation did not require the complainant to demonstrate that s/he had been less favourably treated than someone who had not done an act under (a)–(d) above ('a protected act'). Slade LJ, for the Court, declared that:

> [a] complaint made in reliance on s 2 necessarily presupposes that the complainant has done a protected act . . . If the doing of such an act itself constituted part of the relevant circumstances, a complainant would necessarily fail to establish discrimination if the alleged discriminator could show that he treated or would treat all other persons who did the like protected act with equal intolerance. This would be an absurd result.

Slade LJ identified as the 'clear legislative purpose of s.2(1) . . . to ensure, so far as possible, that victims of racial discrimination shall not be deterred from' seeking redress. This being the case, it might be assumed that the Court of Appeal would replace the *Kirby* test with one more likely to afford protection. But in *Aziz* the Court of Appeal replaced the approach taken in *Kirby* with one whose effect was precisely the same.

Mr Aziz, a taxi driver, formed the view that he was being unfairly treated by TST, a company of which he was a member and which promoted the interests of taxi drivers in Coventry. He was concerned that some of his fellow members who were sympathetic in private would not be so publicly, and he tape-recorded some conversations with them. He subsequently filed a race discrimination complaint as a result of which the existence of the tape recordings became public and, after Mr Aziz's race discrimination complaint was dismissed by a tribunal, he was expelled from TST. His victimisation complaint was rejected by tribunal, EAT and the Court of Appeal.

The Court of Appeal accepted that Mr Aziz had been treated 'less favourably than . . . [TST] treat[ed] other persons' in that he had been expelled from membership. But the industrial tribunal found that the expulsion had been by reason of Mr Aziz's breach of trust, rather than because of any link between his actions and the RRA. This being the case,

---

[34] A Leonard, *Pyrrhic Victories: Winning Sex Discrimination and Equal Pay Cases in the Industrial Tribunals, 1980–1984* (London, HMSO, 1987). See also J Gregory, *Trial by Ordeal: A Study of People Who Lost Sex Discrimination Cases in the Industrial Tribunals in 1985 & 1986* (London, HMSO, 1989).

Slade LJ declared that the less favourable treatment suffered by Mr Aziz could not be regarded as having been:

> by reason that the appellant had (within the meaning of s 2(1)(c)) 'otherwise done anything under or by reference to' the RRA . . . on the true construction of s.2(1), if the necessary causal link is to be established, it must be shown that the very fact that the protected act was done by the complainant 'under or by reference to' that legislation, influenced the alleged discriminator in his unfavourable treatment of the complainant.[35]

Despite the criticism directed at *Kirby* by the Court of Appeal in *Aziz*, the practical effect of the decisions is the same. Under *Aziz*, Mr Kirby would have had to establish, not that he was less favourably treated than someone who had made the complaint to the CRE, but than someone who had not made a complaint. So far, so good. But Mr Kirby would then have had to establish that his less favourable treatment was *by reason that* his act was connected with (in that case) the RRA (in another case it could equally have been the SDA, DDA or FETO). This, in turn, would have required him to establish that he had been less favourably treated than a person who had acted similarly, but other than in connection with the RRA. Yet this is precisely the test which was applied to him by EAT, but which was dismissed by the Court of Appeal in *Aziz* as 'absurd.'[36]

The result of the decision in *Aziz*, as it had been of *Kirby*, was that the victimisation provisions did not provide protection in respect of less favourable treatment which an employer can suggest was motivated, however unreasonably, by the complainant's actions themselves, rather than the relationship between those actions and the relevant discrimination provisions. This approach has, however, been altered by the decisions of the House of Lords in *Nagarajan v London Regional Transport* and in *Chief Constable of West Yorkshire Police* v *Khan* [2001] ICR 1065. In *Nagarajan* their Lordships overruled the Court of Appeal's decision ([1998] IRLR 73) to the effect that a victimisation complainant must prove that the less favourable treatment was consciously influenced by the claimant's commission of a protected act. A tribunal had found an interview panel's assessment of the claimant, who had taken action under the RRA against the organisation on previous occasions, inexplicable and so, given the knowledge of the interviewing panel members of the background, had felt bound to draw an inference of victimisation. Both EAT and the Court of Appeal disagreed, Peter Gibson LJ for the latter requiring 'conscious motivation' on the part of the alleged discriminator. The House of Lords reinstated the tribunal's decision.

Nagarajan v London Regional Transport [1999] ICR 877

Lord Nicholls:

All human beings have preconceptions, beliefs, attitudes and prejudices on many subjects. It is part of our make-up. Moreover, we do not always recognise our own prejudices. Many people are unable, or unwilling, to admit even to themselves that actions of theirs may be racially motivated. An employer may genuinely believe that the reason why he rejected an applicant had nothing to do with the applicant's race. After careful and thorough investigation of a claim members of an employment tribunal may decide that the proper inference to be drawn from the evidence is that, whether the employer realised it at the time or not,

---

[35] See also the decision of the Court of Appeal in *Cornelius v University College of Swansea* [1987] IRLR 141.

[36] Albeit in relation to the question whether the claimant had been 'less favourably treated,' rather than whether that treatment was 'by reason of' his having done a protected act.

race was the reason why he acted as he did . . . If . . . the discriminator treated the person victimised less favourably by reason of his having done one of the acts listed in section 2(1) . . . the case falls within the section. It does so, even if the discriminator did not consciously realise that, for example, he was prejudiced because the job applicant had previously brought claims against him under the Act. In so far as the dictum in *Aziz* ('a motive which is consciously connected with the race relations legislation') suggests otherwise, it cannot be taken as a correct statement of the law.

This was sufficient to deal with the problem presented by the Court of Appeal in *Nagarajan*. But their Lordships went further.

Lord Steyn (with whom Lords Hutton and Hobhouse agreed):

Section 2(1) in effect provides that, in order for there to be unlawful victimisation, the protected act must constitute the 'reason' for the less favourable treatment. The contextual meaning of the words 'by reason that' is at stake. The interpretation upheld by the Court of Appeal requires that under section 2(1) a claimant must prove that the alleged discriminator had a motive which is consciously connected with the race relations legislation. On the other hand, the interpretation put forward by the applicant merely requires that a claimant must prove that the principal or at least an important or significant cause of the less favourable treatment is the fact that the alleged discriminator has done a protected act . . . If the Court of Appeal's interpretation is accepted, it would follow that motive becomes an ingredient of civil liability under section 2(1). As evidence motive is always relevant. But to make it the touchstone of civil liability would be unusual. Even in criminal law motive is only an ingredient of the offence in exceptional cases . . . the applicant's interpretation . . . contemplates that the discriminator had knowledge of the protected act and that such knowledge caused or influenced the discriminator to treat the victimised person less favourably than he would treat other persons. In other words, it postulates that the discriminator's knowledge of the protected act had a subjective impact on his mind. But, unlike the first interpretation, it is a broader construction inasmuch as it does not require the tribunal to distinguish between conscious and subconscious motivation . . . Quite sensibly in section 1(1)(a) cases the tribunal simply has to pose the question: Why did the defendant treat the employee less favourably? It does not have to consider whether a defendant was consciously motivated in his unequal treatment of an employee. That is a straightforward way of carrying out its task in a section 1(1)(a) case. Common sense suggests that the tribunal should also perform its functions in a section 2(1) case by asking the equally straightforward question: Did the defendant treat the employee less favourably because of his knowledge of a protected act? Given that it is unnecessary in section 1(1)(a) cases to distinguish between conscious and subconscious motivation, there is no sensible reason for requiring it in section 2(1) cases . . . [37]

The Court of Appeal relied strongly on an observation by Slade LJ in *Aziz v Trinity Street Taxis Ltd* [above]. The passage in *Aziz* is . . . to the effect that section 2(1) contemplates 'a motive which is consciously connected with the race relations legislation.' But as the headnote of *Aziz* makes clear the case was decided on a causative approach. In any event, the case pre-dates the decisions of the House of Lords in the *Birmingham* . . . and E*astleigh* . . . cases [above]. A contemporary reviewer of *Aziz* argued convincingly that in the light of the decision in the House of Lords in the *Birmingham* case the observation of

---

[37] Moreover, the threshold requirement laid down by the Court of Appeal in respect of s.2(1) cases would tend to complicate the task of the tribunal and would thus render the protection of the rights guaranteed by s.2(1) less effective.

Slade LJ cannot stand[38]. She said . . . that the *obiter dictum* of Slade LJ 'wrongly empha-sises the underlying motivation of the alleged discriminator rather than the immediate cause of the unfavourable treatment.' I agree.

The significance of Lord Steyn's speech is its indication that the motivation of the dis-criminator is as irrelevant to a victimisation claim as it is to a claim of direct discrimina-tion. This has, however, been called into question by the subsequent decision of the House of Lords in the *Khan* case.

Chief Constable of West Yorkshire Police v Khan [2001] ICR 1065

The case concerned a victimisation complaint brought by a police officer who, while a race discrimination claim against his employer was pending, applied for a job in another force. His race discrimination claim was made in connection with his non-promotion (this because of criticisms of his communication and leadership skills. A request for a reference in respect of Sergeant Khan was met with a refusal on the basis that, because the claimant had an outstanding tribunal application against the Chief Constable, the latter was 'unable to comment any further for fear of prejudicing his own case before the tribunal.' A request for Sergeant Khan's most recent staff appraisals was also refused.

Sergeant Khan's victimisation complaint was accepted by a tribunal (which dismissed his race discrimination claim), and the Chief Constable's appeal rejected by EAT and the Court of Appeal ([2000] IRLR 324). The House of Lords, however, overruled the tribunal's deci-sion. Having accepted that Sergeant Khan had been treated less favourably than someone who had not made the discrimination claim, their Lordships ruled that the treatment was not 'by reason that' he had brought proceedings against his employer.

Lord Nicholls (with whom Lords Hutton, Hoffmann and Scott agreed, Lord Mackay concur-ring):

Plainly, in October 1996 West Yorkshire police found themselves in a position of consider-able difficulty. The subject-matter of the request for a reference for Sergeant Khan was the very matter awaiting adjudication in the industrial tribunal. The Norfolk police force were seeking the views of the West Yorkshire force on Sergeant Khan's suitability for promotion to the rank of inspector. But the views of Sergeant Khan's supervising officers on this mat-ter, expressed as recently as June 1996, were being challenged by Sergeant Khan as racially discriminatory. Those views, he said, constituted unlawful racial discrimination. That issue remained to be decided. That being so, the Chief Constable could hardly be expected to repeat those selfsame views to another potential employer while that serious challenge against the authors of those views remained outstanding. Repetition of those views at that time could justifiably have been castigated as irresponsible behaviour by the Chief Constable, as well as possibly leading to a further allegation of direct racial discrimination. Such conduct by the Chief Constable could prejudice his case before the industrial tribunal. It would also mean that if the discrimination claim were to succeed, the Chief Constable would be at risk of being censured for his aggravation of the wrong done to Sergeant Khan by members of the West Yorkshire police, and the amount of compensation increased accordingly . . .

---

[38] EAT's decision subsequently interpreted the SDA accordingly but noted that *Adekeye v Post Office (No.2)* [1997] ICR 110, to the effect that post-employment victimisation would not constitute victimisation under the RRA, still held under that Act. *Adekeye* has subsequently been overruled by amendments of the legislation and by the decision of the House of Lords in *Rhys-Harper v Relaxion Group plc* [2003] ICR 867, discussed in Ch 4.

Victimisation occurs when, in any circumstances relevant for the purposes of any provision of the Act, a person is treated less favourably than others because he has done one of the protected acts . . . The statute is to be regarded as calling for a simple comparison between the treatment afforded to the complainant who has done a protected act and the treatment which was or would be afforded to other employees who have not done the protected act.

Applying this approach, Sergeant Khan was treated less favourably than other employees. Ordinarily West Yorkshire provides references for members of the force who are seeking new employment . . .

Contrary to views sometimes stated, the third ingredient ('by reason that') does not raise a question of causation as that expression is usually understood. Causation is a slippery word, but normally it is used to describe a legal exercise. From the many events leading up to the crucial happening, the court selects one or more of them which the law regards as causative of the happening. Sometimes the court may look for the 'operative' cause, or the 'effective' cause. Sometimes it may apply a 'but for' approach. For the reasons I sought to explain in *Nagarajan v London Regional Transport*, a causation exercise of this type is not required either by s.1(1)(a) or s.2. The phrases 'on racial grounds' and 'by reason that' denote a different exercise: why did the alleged discriminator act as he did? What, consciously or unconsciously, was his reason? Unlike causation, this is a subjective test. Causation is a legal conclusion. The reason why a person acted as he did is a question of fact . . .

Employers, acting honestly and reasonably, ought to be able to take steps to preserve their position in pending discrimination proceedings without laying themselves open to a charge of victimisation. This accords with the spirit and purpose of the Act. Moreover, the statute accommodates this approach without any straining of language. An employer who conducts himself in this way is not doing so because of the fact that the complainant has brought discrimination proceedings. He is doing so because, currently and temporarily, he needs to take steps to preserve his position in the outstanding proceedings. . . .

This is a difficult distinction to draw, but it is hard to disagree with the view that the employer in this case had no real alternative to refusing to supply Sergeant Khan with a reference while the legal proceedings were outstanding. Helpful here is Lord Hoffmann's observation that: 'A test which is likely in most cases to give the right answer is to ask whether the employer would have refused the request if the litigation had been concluded, whatever the outcome. If the answer is no, it will usually follow that the reason for refusal was the existence of the proceedings and not the fact that the employee had commenced them.'

Lord Nicholls, above, refused to categorise the 'by reason that' question as one of causation and suggested that the test applicable to direct discrimination and victimisation were the same. Lord Hoffmann's approach was somewhat different. His Lordship remarked that: 'Of course, in one sense the fact that [Sergeant Khan] had brought proceedings was a cause of his being treated less favourably. If he had not brought proceedings, he would have been given a reference.' He went on to distinguish the 'by reason that' test applicable in victimisation claims with the 'but for' test which applied in direct discrimination cases.

Lord Hoffmann:

There are parallels between the purposes of ss.1 and 2 [RRA] (and between the corresponding ss.1 and 4 [SDA]): see *Nagarajan*. But the causal questions which they raise are not identical. As Mr Hand QC, who appeared for Mr Khan, readily accepted, one cannot simply say that Mr Khan would not have been treated less favourably if he had not brought proceedings. It does not follow that his bringing proceedings was a reason (conscious or subconscious) why he was treated less favourably. In *Nagarajan*'s case Lord Steyn said that s.2:

> contemplates that the discriminator had knowledge of the protected act and that such knowledge caused or influenced the discriminator to treat the victimised person less favourably than he would treat other persons . . . But . . . it does not require the tribunal to distinguish between conscious and subconscious motivation.

This is not at all the same thing as saying that, but for the protected act, he would not have been treated in the way he was . . . once proceedings have been commenced, a new relationship is created between the parties. They are not only employer and employee but also adversaries in litigation. The existence of that adversarial relationship may reasonably cause the employer to behave in a way which treats the employee less favourably than someone who had not commenced such proceedings. But the treatment need not be, consciously or unconsciously, a response to the commencement of proceedings. It may simply be a reasonable response to the need to protect the employer's interests as a party to the litigation. It is true that an employee who had not commenced proceedings would not have been treated in the same way. Under s.1, one would have needed to go no further. Under s.2, however, the commencement of proceedings must be a reason for the treatment . . .

The other issue raised in the House of Lord's decision in *Khan* concerned the question what constitutes the 'protected act' *but for* the performance of which the victimised person would not have suffered less favourable treatment. In the previous edition of this book I posed the question whether it was (A) the act of bringing legal proceedings, giving evidence in connection with such proceedings, otherwise doing anything 'under or by reference to' legislation or alleging that the discriminator or another has contravened legislation?; or (B) bringing legal proceedings *under the relevant anti-discrimination legislation*, giving evidence in connection with proceedings *under the relevant anti-discrimination legislation*, otherwise doing anything 'under or by reference to' *the relevant anti-discrimination legislation* or alleging that the discriminator or another has contravened *the relevant anti-discrimination legislation*?

The Court of Appeal in *Aziz* demanded a connection between the specific legislation in connection with which the victimised person acted and the motivation of the discriminator. It was clear from the decision in *Nagarajan* that this *motivation* does not have to be established. It might still have been the case that the question whether the less favourable treatment was 'by reason that' the claimant acted under the particular anti-discrimination legislation. The respondent in the *Khan* case had argued that the proper comparator for Sergeant Khan was someone who had brought proceedings under different legislation, an argument rejected by EAT, and by the Court of Appeal in *Brown v TNT Worldwide (UK) Ltd* [2001] ICR 182. Lord Hoffmann, who alone of their Lordships expressly addressed this question, stated that: 'if the fact that the employee had commenced proceedings under the Act was a real reason why he received less favourable treatment, it is no answer that the employer would have behaved in the same way to an employee who had done some non-protected act, such as commencing proceedings otherwise than under the Act.'

Where do the decisions of the House of Lords in *Nagarajan* and *Khan* leave the law on victimisation? Claimants and others engaged in actual or prospective litigation will be protected by the discrimination provisions in cases in which they are less favourably treated than those who have not taken steps to enforce their or others' rights, so long as the less favourable treatment was 'by reason that' the person victimised took such steps. They will be protected even from treatment which post-dates the termination of their employment, as in a case in which an employer refuses to provide a reference to a discrimination claimant or discriminates in the context of a post-dismissal appeal. It will be no defence to a discriminator that s/he would have meted out the same treatment to someone who took similar steps under other legal provisions. An employer may, however, take steps to safeguard his or her legal position where proceedings are outstanding, so long as the steps are taken because of the fact that the proceedings are extant rather than because they have been brought. No breach of the victimisation provisions will occur even if these steps involve treating a person less favourably than one who is not involved with proceedings.

A further limitation in the victimisation provisions became apparent in *Waters v Commissioner of Police of the Metropolis*.

Waters v Commissioner of Police of the Metropolis [1997] ICR 1073

The Court of Appeal rejected a claim brought by a WPC who suffered detriment as a result of her allegation of rape and buggery by a fellow police officer while they were off-duty. Her counsel argued that the SDA: 'has to be construed in such a way as to treat as protected acts any allegations which, objectively considered, are aimed at claiming (ie, provide the basis for development of a claim for) protection under the equality legislation.' For reasons discussed in Chapter 4, the WPC's complaint relating to the assault did not amount to a claim that she had been discriminated against contrary to the SDA.

Waite LJ (for the Court of Appeal):

True it is that the legislation must be construed in a sense favourable to its important public purpose. But there is another principle involved—also essential to that same purpose. Charges of race or sex discrimination are hurtful and damaging and not always easy to refute. In justice, therefore, to those against whom they are brought, it is vital that discrimination (including victimisation) should be defined in language sufficiently precise to enable people to know where they stand before the law. Precision of language is also necessary to prevent the valuable purpose of combating discrimination from becoming frustrated or brought into disrepute through the use of language which encourages unscrupulous or vexatious recourse to the machinery provided by the Discrimination Acts. The interpretation proposed by [counsel for WPC Waters] would involve an imprecision of language leaving employers in a state of uncertainty as to how they should respond to a particular complaint, and would place the machinery of the Acts at serious risk of abuse. It is better, and safer, to give the words of the subsection their clear and literal meaning. The allegation relied on need not state explicitly that an act of discrimination has occurred—that is clear from the words in brackets in s 4(1)(d). All that is required is that the allegation relied on should have asserted facts capable of amounting in law to an act of discrimination by an employer within the terms of s 6(2)(b). The facts alleged by the complainant in this case were incapable in law of amounting to an act of discrimination by the Commissioner because they were not done by him, and they cannot (because the alleged perpetrator was not acting in the course of his employment) be treated as done by him for the purposes of s 4(1).

In his concern for the interests of those engaged in victimisation, Waite LJ perhaps exhibited too little regard for the interests of the victimised. From the point of view of the employer, and contrary to Waite LJ's view, it makes no difference whether any allegation made by an employee would, if proven, disclose a breach of the relevant legislation.

According to WPC Waters' testimony, she was subject to appalling behaviour in the wake of her rape complaint. She was aggressively treated; transferred between police stations without consultation or the normal periods of notice; her complaint improperly investigated; any semblance of confidentiality related to it breached (this in part resulting in her being ostracised by her colleagues and superior officers). She was transferred from police to civil-ian duties; denied appropriate time off; her applications for particular placements refused; her personal diary stolen and the theft never investigated. She was given unfair reports; 'harassed and unfairly treated' by her superiors; told 'that she should leave the police force before she was forced to go'; given the impression that she, rather than her alleged attacker, was under investigation and told that there would be no disciplinary proceedings against him. She was denied back-up and subjected to pornography by her fellow officers. No attempts were made by senior officers to prevent her harassment (in connection with the rape allega-tion) by her fellow officers. She was not given notice of court appearances and her complaints about this went unheeded. She was threatened with violence by her Chief Superintendent and 'quite unjustifiably and with a view to intimidating and harassing her,' was required to undergo 'psychological analysis' to see if she was 'fit for duty.' Her paperwork started to dis-appear and she was advised to leave the force by a colleague in his capacity as Police Federation representative. She eventually took sick leave.

The Court of Appeal's ruling in this case meant that WPC Waters' allegations were never proven. But, in view of their seriousness, it is difficult to comprehend Waite LJ's assertion that '[t]he interpretation proposed by [counsel for WPC Waters] would involve an impreci-sion of language leaving employers in a state of uncertainty as to how they should respond to a particular complaint, and would place the machinery of the Acts at serious risk of abuse.' The facts alleged in *Waters* are certainly at the extreme end of the spectrum. But Waite LJ's approach suggests that, in cases other than those which fall within the vic-timisation provisions, employers have a right, worthy of legal protection, to respond to complaints by subjecting the complainer to ill-treatment.

Both the CRE and the EOC have recently called for the revision of the victimisation provisions as, in the context of fair employment legislation, did the Northern Ireland's Standing Advisory Commission on Human Rights (SACHR). The EOC's 1998 reform pro-posals state that 'there is very little protection for individuals and no effective penalty that would discourage would-be victimisers' and called for a reverse in the burden of proof and the award of an automatic penalty. The CRE called for a statutory reversal of *Waters* to allow a victimisation finding where 'the initial complaint of discrimination is . . . made in good faith but . . . because of the limitations of the Act, is held not to constitute a com-plaint or proceedings under the Act.' SACHR criticised, inter alia, the failure of the provi-sions to cover victimisation of A on the grounds of B's complaint. There have been no attempts to meet these criticisms except in as much as recent changes to the burden of proof (see Chapter 5) apply to victimisation as to other forms of discrimination.

Indirect Discrimination

Indirect discrimination is intended to reflect that concept of 'disparate impact' discrimina-tion recognised by the US Supreme Court in its famous decision in *Griggs v Duke Power Co* (1971) 401 US 424.[39] There, black employees sued under Title VII of the Civil Rights Act 1964 (which, inter alia, prohibits race discrimination), claiming that the employer's practice of requiring a high school diploma or success in an IQ test as a condition of employment

[39] See R Townshend-Smith, below, 111–13.

in particular jobs discriminated against them on grounds of race, a disproportionate number of blacks being rendered ineligible by the practice. The lower courts had found that the employer's previous practice of race discrimination had ended, and that there was no evidence that the requirements had been adopted in order to discriminate on racial grounds. The Supreme Court found in favour of the plaintiffs.

Griggs v Duke Power Co (1971) 401 US 424

Chief Justice Burger, for the Court:

The objective of Congress in the enactment of Title VII is plain from the language of the statute. It was to achieve equality of employment opportunities and remove barriers that have operated in the past to favor an identifiable group of white employees over other employees. Under the Act, practices, procedures, or tests neutral on their face, and even neutral in terms of intent, cannot be maintained if they operate to 'freeze' the status quo of prior discriminatory employment practices.

The Court of Appeals' opinion, and the partial dissent, agreed that, on the record in the present case, 'whites register far better on the Company's alternative requirements' than Negroes . . . This consequence would appear to be directly traceable to race. Basic intelligence must have the means of articulation to manifest itself fairly in a testing process. Because they are Negroes, petitioners have long received inferior education in segregated schools . . . Congress did not intend by Title VII, however, to guarantee a job to every person regardless of qualifications. In short, the Act does not command that any person be hired simply because he was formerly the subject of discrimination, or because he is a member of a minority group. Discriminatory preference for any group, minority or majority, is precisely and only what Congress has proscribed. What is required by Congress is the removal of artificial, arbitrary, and unnecessary barriers to employment when the barriers operate invidiously to discriminate on the basis of racial or other impermissible classification.

Congress has now provided that tests or criteria for employment or promotion may not provide equality of opportunity merely in the sense of the fabled offer of milk to the stork and the fox. On the contrary, Congress has now required that the posture and condition of the job-seeker be taken into account. It has—to resort again to the fable—provided that the vessel in which the milk is proffered be one all seekers can use. The Act proscribes not only overt discrimination but also practices that are fair in form, but discriminatory in operation. The touchstone is business necessity. If an employment practice which operates to exclude Negroes cannot be shown to be related to job performance, the practice is prohibited.

On the record before us, neither the high school completion requirement nor the general intelligence test is shown to bear a demonstrable relationship to successful performance of the jobs for which it was used. Both were adopted, as the Court of Appeals noted, without meaningful study of their relationship to job-performance ability. Rather, a vice president of the Company testified, the requirements were instituted on the Company's judgment that they generally would improve the overall quality of the work force . . . good intent or absence of discriminatory intent does not redeem employment procedures or testing mechanisms that operate as 'built-in headwinds' for minority groups and are unrelated to measuring job capability . . .

The concept of indirect discrimination has the capacity to go beyond the formalistic approach associated with the regulation of direct discrimination (ie,, the requirement to treat like cases alike) and to challenge practices which serve to perpetuate the effects of past disadvantage and unequal life chances.

Thompson's '*Sex Discrimination and Employment*' [40]

The following requirements or conditions, with which a considerably smaller proportion of women than men can comply, may be indirectly discriminatory.

AGE BARS can indirectly discriminate against women who have taken time out of employment to bring up children.

EXPERIENCE/LENGTH OF SERVICE REQUIREMENTS can exclude women who have taken time out of employment to bring up children both in respect of the length of time actually employed and in respect of experience gained. It is too often assumed that the experience of managing a family should be discounted—presumably because men so rarely do it.

MOBILITY CONDITIONS can indirectly discriminate against women who, because of family commitments or partners' income are less likely to be able to comply with such conditions than men.

UNSOCIAL HOURS REQUIREMENTS can exclude women because of their family responsibilities. This can be particularly discriminatory—and unjustifiable—where the job requires an availability for call-out which, in practice, is likely to occur very rarely.

QUALIFICATIONS are often used to weed out applicants. Where the qualifications are such that women are less likely to be able to comply with them than men (and women have widely been excluded from training) unless they can be justified as an absolute requirement for a job, their requirement is an indirect discrimination.

HEIGHT/WEIGHT REQUIREMENTS must be justified in terms of the job to be done as men are demonstrably taller and heavier than women.[41]

CONDITIONS RELATING TO FULL-TIME WORK may be discriminatory if it can be shown that the job could be undertaken part-time or on a job-sharing basis. Separate provisions for part-time staff such as a provision that part-time staff be dismissed first in a redundancy situation or the exclusion of part-time staff from certain benefits.

Thompson's *Race Discrimination and Employment* [42]

[Discussing *Hussein v Saints Complete House Furnitures* [1979] IRLR 337].

A Liverpool furniture store refused to consider claimants from Liverpool 8 which had a high rate of unemployment because unemployed friends of staff from that district would loiter outside the premises and discourage custom. Fifty per cent of the population of Liverpool 8 was black compared with two per cent in Merseyside as a whole. The Tribunal held this to be an unlawful requirement or condition because it was one that applied to one racial group more than another. The condition could not be justified.

Selection tests have been held to constitute a requirement or condition such that the proportion of one racial group who can comply is considerably smaller than the proportion of persons who are not of that racial group. In other words, a selection test may be indirectly discriminatory.

A requirement that an applicant for a manual job should be able to read and write English where there is virtually no reading or writing required is unlikely to be justifiable. An age bar has been held indirectly to discriminate against people who had immigrated to this country as adults and therefore started their careers later than others [citing *Perera v Civil Service Commission* [1983] ICR 428, below] . . .

---

[40] This and *Race Discrimination and Employment* referred to below are available at www.thompsons.law.co.uk.

[41] Differential physical requirements would be directly discriminatory—see in the case of physical fitness teating *Allcock v Chief Constable, Hampshire Constabulary* 36 *Opportunities Review Discrimination Case Law Digest* 1. Employers must, accordingly, adopt a single standard whose disparate impact, if any, will be objectively justifiable by reference to the needs of the undertaking.

[42] Available as at n 40 above.

Any requirement for particular UK-based examinations will discriminate indirectly on grounds of nationality and, in Northern Ireland, any stipulation that job claimants come from a particular geographical area will, in most cases, disproportionately favour Catholics or Protestants. The same is true in Great Britain in relation to the racial composition of particular areas, and in both jurisdictions residence requirements will discriminate indirectly on nationality grounds. And such is the disparity in unemployment rates between the Northern Irish communities (for decades, the Catholic rate has been about twice that among the Protestant workforce) that recruiting from the unemployed will generally favour Catholics. Recognition of this, coupled with the social justice (and political) imperatives in favour of tackling disadvantage through targeted employment, resulted in the amendment of the fair employmentlegislation in 1998 specifically to permit targeted recruitment from among those not in employment (see further Chapter 9). Particular attendance requirements, holiday restrictions and dress codes will discriminate indirectly against persons of particular religious beliefs whose beliefs impose requirements as to worship and appearance, while the weighting of pension schemes and other benefits towards married persons will discriminate indirectly (at least) against gay men and lesbian women.

By contrast with direct discrimination, it is of the essence of indirect discrimination that some practices which impact unfavourably upon one or other sex, upon different racial or other groups, may nevertheless be lawful. The point is made in the extract below:

R Townshend-Smith, 'Justifying Indirect Discrimination in English and American Law: How Stringent Should the Test Be?' (1995) 1 *International Journal of Discrimination and the Law* 103, 104–5

If quotas are to be avoided an employer must be allowed as a matter of both logic and policy to explain a disparity in achievement between different groups. The task of the law is to reconcile the competing interests of the employer in efficiency and profits with those of members of the group seeking economic advancement. The assumption is that the employer must be allowed to hire, promote and pay more to those who are truly better employees, while at the same time artificial and irrational barriers to the economic advancement of protected groups can be challenged. As it will already have been shown that the challenged condition has a disparate impact, it logically follows that the burden of proof is on the employer to show that it is justified. As the rationale for permitting justification is that the employer's economic and other business objectives must be respected, it further follows that the employer's argument is only worthy of respect if it can be shown to a satisfactory level of proof that the employer's policy will indeed have the result claimed for it.

This point is the heart of the requirement for objective justification. But even if successful in proving this causal connection, the employer may still fail on the basis of what has come to be known as the principle of proportionality. First, the plaintiff may win if it can be established that there was a means of achieving the same objective which had less of a disparate impact. Secondly, the employer may also lose if the court considers that the benefit of being allowed to continue with the practice is outweighed by the discriminatory consequences to the protected group. This is problematic for two reasons. First, it is unclear whether regard should be had to the degree of adverse impact only at the defendant enterprise, or whether regard should be had to the extent the relevant practice is utilised in society generally. Secondly, the decision on this issue is at bottom an issue of competing social policy values, is a matter for the court and of course depends enormously on judicial sensitivity to the social objectives of the legislation. It is at this point that a plaintiff may argue that removal of indirectly discriminatory practices may require some positive reorganisation of workplace practices by the employer rather than merely removing barriers such as tests with an adverse impact on black people. Again, is the focus more on employer responsibility or on overall economic inequality? As Kelman puts it: '[a]n obligation to alter practices might be seen as necessary to correct historically imposed burdens, whether or not the employer . . . imposed those burdens, or to allow people to be treated in accordance with the potential that they cannot realise unless the employer restructures the work setting.' . . .

On the one hand, employers must not be permitted to utilise practices with an adverse impact which cannot be proved to achieve business objectives. On the other hand, the standard at which that proof is set must not be so stringent as to be virtually unattainable, for that would logically lead to the use of surreptitious quotas, contrary to legislative policy. It is intellectually dishonest to demand such a stringent standard because one supports quotas, in the belief that this is the likeliest way that quotas will in practice be introduced.

The task of the law is to produce a standard of justification which is sensitive to both of these policy objectives. 'The theory of disparate impact represents an uneasy compromise between the abstract and ambiguous ideal of economic equality and the means that Congress thought sufficient to achieve it.' While it is important to examine what courts have said on the matter, it is contended that too often judicial dicta have been uttered with no awareness of the practical problems of application, or of how employers are supposed to discharge the burden laid upon them.

Early UK anti-discrimination legislation (the Sex Disqualification (Removal) Act 1919,[43] and the Race Relations Acts of 1965 and 1968,[44] had concerned itself only with direct discrimination, and the Government had not originally intended to include any prohibition on indirect discrimination within the SDA (the first piece of legislation to do so). *Equality for Women* (the White Paper preceding the SDA) suggested that only intentional discrimination should be prohibited: 'to understand the meaning of unlawful discrimination, it is essential not to confuse motive with effect.'[45] But between the publication of the White Paper and that of the Sex Discrimination Bill, Secretary of State Roy Jenkins visited the United States and was familiarised with the decision in *Griggs*. On his return, Jenkins declared that 'the Bill would be too narrow if it were confined to direct and intentional discrimination.'[46] *Race Discrimination*, the White Paper preceding the RRA, instanced the failure of previous legislation to include this concept as one of the reasons for its limited success.[47]

Indirect discrimination is intended, to reiterate, to capture 'practices that are fair in form, but discriminatory in operation.' The articulation of this concept in domestic law is, however, extraordinarily problematic, no fewer than three different definitions currently being utilised in addition to the DDA's related duties of reasonable accommodation. The SDA retains its original definition for discrimination outside the context of employment (broadly defined), while applying a definition derived from the Council Directive 97/80/EC (on the Burden of Proof in Sex Discrimination) to employment-related cases. The RRA retains its original definition (which is materially identical to that originally used by the SDA) for discrimination which is not covered by the Racial Equality Directive—that is, to discrimination on grounds of nationality or colour which is not also discrimination on grounds of 'race or national or ethnic origin', and to that which falls within the RRA but

---

[43] The Act removed formal legal barriers to women's employment and holding of public office.
[44] The 1965 RRA prohibited discrimination in public places, the 1968 Act more generally.
[45] *Equality for Women* (London: Department of Employment, 1974) Cmnd 5724, para 33.
[46] 889 HC Debs (26 March 1975), col. 513.
[47] London, Department of Employment, 1975, Cmnd 6234, para 35.

not the Directive (broadly, discrimination by planning authorities, by private clubs and by public authorities other than in relation to education, social security, health care, 'social protection' and 'social advantage'—this is further considered in Chapter 7). Other forms of race discrimination are subject to the new definition derived from the Directive which is similar, but not identical, to the amended definition in the SDA. FETO applies the same definition as the SDA and the RRA originally did except in relation to employment, broadly defined, where it, in common with the SO and RB Regs, uses a definition materially identical to that in the RRA as amended. The DDA does not regulate indirect discrimination as such, but requires reasonable accommodation of the needs of disabled persons. This is further discussed in Chapter 4.

Definitions of Indirect Discrimination

Section 1(1) RRA provides as follows:

> A person discriminates against a another in any circumstances relevant for the purposes of any provision of this Act if . . .
> (b) he applies to that other a requirement or condition which he applies or would apply equally to persons not of the same racial group as that other but
>   (i) which is such that the proportion of persons of the same racial group as that other who can comply with it is considerably smaller than the proportion of persons not of that racial group who can comply with it and
>   (ii) which he cannot show to be justifiable irrespective of the colour, race, nationality or ethnic or national origins of the person to whom it is applied and
>   (iii) which is to the detriment of that other because he cannot comply with it.

This test applies to discrimination on grounds of colour or nationality which is not also discrimination on grounds of 'race or ethnic or national origin' within the scope of the Racial Equality Directive and is, as was mentioned above, materially identical to that applied by the SDA and the FETO to discrimination other than in the field of employment, broadly defined. The test applied by the SDA in relation to employment is as follows (s.1(2)):

> . . . a person discriminates against a woman if . . .
> (b) he applies to her a provision, criterion or practice which he applies or would apply equally to a man, but
>   (i) which is such that it would be to the detriment of a considerably larger proportion of women than of men, and
>   (ii) which he cannot show to be justifiable irrespective of the sex of the person to whom it is applied, and
>   (iii) which is to her detriment.

Council Directive 2002/73/EC, which came into force on 5 October 2002, amends the Equal Treatment Directive (76/207/EEC) to provide that indirect discrimination shall be taken to occur 'where an apparently neutral provision, criterion or practice would put persons of one sex at a particular disadvantage compared with persons of the other sex, unless that provision, criterion or practice is objectively justified by a legitimate aim, and the means of achieving that aim are appropriate and necessary'. This is materially identical to the definitions set out in the Racial Equality and Employment Equality directives (and in new Directive 2004/113/EC). The draft Employment Equality (Sex Discrimination) Regulations

2005 (draft SD Regs), by which the government proposes to implement the directive, define indirect discrimination in terms which are materially identical to s.1(1A) RRA, extracted immediately below. The new definition would replace that extracted immediately above and, like it, apply to discrimination in the context of employment and vocational training (broadly defined).

S.1(1A) RRA provides that:

> A person . . . discriminates against another if . . . he applies to that other a provision, criterion or practice which he applies or would apply equally to persons not of the same race or ethnic or national origins as that other, but—
>
> (a) which puts or would put persons of the same race or ethnic or national origins as that other at a particular disadvantage when compared with other persons,
>
> (b) which puts that other at that disadvantage, and
>
> (c) which he cannot show to be a proportionate means of achieving a legitimate aim.

The RB Regs and the SO Regs adopt a definition of indirect discrimination which is materially identical to that set out in the RRA (s.1(1A)) above, as does the FETO in the employment context. The new definitions (found in the SDA prior to its proposed amendment on the one hand, and FETO, the RRA and the RB and SO Regs on the other) differ from the original version in a number of ways:

1. the term 'requirement or condition' has been replaced with 'provision, criterion or practice';
2. the demand that this requirement or condition be 'such that the proportion of persons' of the claimant's group who can comply with it 'is considerably smaller than the proportion of persons not of that . . . group who can comply with it' has been replaced by one that the provision, criterion or practice 'is such that it would be to the detriment of a considerably larger proportion of women than of men' (the SDA) or (in the case of the RRA and the RB and SO Regs) 'puts or would put persons' of the claimant's group 'at a particular disadvantage when compared with other persons';
3. the requirement that the claimant in an indirect discrimination claim suffers detriment *because of his or her inability to comply* with the impugned requirement or condition has been replaced by a requirement (in the case of the SDA) that the provision, criterion or practice is to the claimant's detriment or (in the case of the RRA, the SO and RB Regs) that s/he is 'put at' the particular disadvantage referred to in the previous paragraph by the provision, criterion or practice;
4. the test for justification has not changed from the original to the amended definition of indirect discrimination in the SDA (in both cases the burden is on the discriminator to justify the impugned requirement, etc, 'irrespective of' the sex, race, etc, of the person to whom it is applied. The RRA and the SO and RB Regs, by contrast, place the obligation on the discriminator to show that the application of the impugned provision, criterion or practice is a 'proportionate means of achieving a legitimate aim.'

The significance of these changes will be considered below, in each case after we have dealt with the application by the courts of the original definition of indirect discrimination. This path is adopted because, while the amended definitions are edging out the originals, the significance of the changes cannot properly be appreciated without an understanding of the difficulties associated with the originals. In *Kidd v DRG* [1985] ICR 405, Waite J, then President of EAT, stated that '[t]he concept of indirect discrimination was one which clearly needed to be framed from the outset with the maximum flexibility if it was fully to encompass the mischief at which the anti-discrimination laws are directed.' But, as it has been interpreted by the UK courts the original test for indirect discrimination is far from flexible.

'Requirement or Condition'/'Provision, Criterion or Practice'

Early decisions applied the 'requirement or condition' provision flexibly, taking a purposive approach to ss.1(1)(b) of the SDA and RRA. In *Clarke v Eley (IMI) Kynoch Ltd* [1982] IRLR 482, for example, EAT (*per* Browne-Wilkinson J) ruled that it 'is not right to give these words a narrow construction. The purpose of the legislature in introducing the concept of indirect discrimination into the [SDA] and the [RRA] was to seek to eliminate those practices which had a disproportionate impact on women or ethnic minorities and were not justifiable for other reasons.' Browne-Wilkinson J relied on the approach of the Supreme Court in *Griggs* and concluded that: 'although such policy cannot be used to give the words any wider meaning than they naturally bear it is in our view a powerful argument against giving the words a narrower meaning thereby excluding cases which fall within the mischief which the Act was meant to deal with.'[48] A similar approach was adopted by EAT in *Watches of Switzerland Ltd v Savell* [1983] IRLR 141 but in the *Perera* case the Court Appeal adopted a narrow and restrictive reading of the 'requirement or condition' provision.

Perera v The Civil Service Commission & The Department of Customs & Excise [1983] ICR 428 [IRLR] 166

Mr Perera, who had unsuccessfully applied for a number of jobs in the Civil Service, claimed that the imposition of a number of criteria relating to nationality, experience in the United Kingdom, ability to communicate in English and an upper age preference in respect of these positions discriminated against him indirectly on grounds of his colour or national origin. The Court of Appeal agreed with EAT that Mr Perera had failed to show that a 'requirement or condition' had been applied to him.

Stephenson LJ:

. . . The matters which have to be established by an applicant who claims that he has been discriminated against indirectly are, first of all, that there has been a requirement or condition, as Mr Perera put it, a 'must'; something which has to be complied with. Here there was a requirement or condition for candidates for the post of legal assistant in the Civil Service; it was that the candidate should be either a qualified member of the English Bar or a qualified Solicitor of the Supreme Court of this country—an admitted man [sic] or a barrister; and those conditions or requirements—those 'musts'—were fulfilled by Mr Perera. But, as he admitted in his argument before the Appeal Tribunal and before this court, there is no other express requirement or condition, and he has to find a requirement or condition in the general combination of factors which he says the Interviewing Board took into account [whether the applicant had experience in the United Kingdom; whether he had a good command of the English language; whether he had British nationality or intended to apply for it, and his age]. He cannot formulate, as in my judgment he has to, what the particular requirement or condition is which he says has been applied to him and to his attempt to obtain a post of legal assistant. That is the hurdle which, as it seems to me, he is unable

---

[48] For favourable comment upon this decision see C Docksey, 'Part-time Workers, Indirect Discrimination and Redundancy' (1983) 46 *Modern Law Review* 504.

to get over . . . in my opinion none of [the four] factors could possibly be regarded as a requirement or a condition in the sense that the lack of it, whether of British nationality or even of the ability to communicate well in English, would be an absolute bar. The whole of the evidence indicates that a brilliant man [or woman?] whose personal qualities made him suitable as a legal assistant might well have been sent forward on a short list by the Interviewing Board in spite of being, perhaps, below standard on his knowledge of English and his ability to communicate in that language.

The decision in *Perera* was widely criticised. Lord Justice Stephenson's observation that 'a brilliant man' might have been shortlisted notwithstanding the employer's disparately impacting preferences relating to nationality, UK experience and age, etc, does not detract from the point that those of Mr Perera's national origin would have at least to have been better than British peers in order to be selected. Geoffrey Mead pointed out that the effect of the *Perera* decision was that 'if an advertisement states that applicants for the job of a cleaner should either have lived in the area for 20 years or have a degree of law, then although the first criterion might have a detrimental effect on certain racial groups, who might be new to the area, the fact that they could get the job if they had a law degree means that they have not been indirectly discriminated against.'[49] And Michael Connolly later complained that an employer could advertise for librarians on the basis that preference would be granted to 'those who: have a Home Counties accent; are over 6 feet tall; are under 30 years old; are willing to wear trousers to work; wear a beard; and have lived in the area all of their lives.'[50] It is inconceivable that this was the intention of the Act's framers, or of the framers of the SDA.

Despite this, when confronted with the matter once again five years later in *Meer v Tower Hamlets* [1988] IRLR 399, the Court of Appeal declared itself bound by its earlier decision. In *Jones v University of Manchester* [1992] ICR 52 the same Court approved the *Perera* approach in a sex discrimination case. And in *Brook v Haringey* EAT rejected a challenge to a redundancy scheme whose effect was to concentrate redundancies among women. Redundancies had to be made in the Council's manual and craft workforce which had been overwhelmingly male prior to recent efforts by the Council to encourage more women applicants. Redundancy selection was primarily, though not entirely, on the basis of length of service (LIFO), with the effect that women as recent employees were disproportionately selected. EAT rejected the sex discrimination challenge.

Brook v London Borough of Haringey [1992] IRLR 478

Wood J:

In the present case [LIFO] was not the sole criterion. . . it is argued that the applicants were required to obtain a preset number of points to avoid redundancy and that this in itself was a condition. It seems to us that no-one could have told what the 'cut-off' point would be in each particular trade until after the points had been calculated and there could not, in reality, be said to be any predetermined figure. A person who is rejected because he is not the best candidate on an amalgam of factors has not been subjected to any requirement or condition but he has simply failed to defeat his competitors. It is the position of the individual on the list which is the determining factor, not the amount of points scored. The cut-off is unknown until after the event.

---

[49] 'Intentions, Conditions and Pools of Comparison' (1989) 18 *Industrial Law Journal* 59, 61–2.
[50] 'How an ECJ Decision on Equal Pay May Affect British Indirect Discrimination Law' [1996] 1 *Web Journal of Current Legal Issues.*

In *Hall v Shorts* Northern Ireland's Court of Appeal relied on *Brook* in ruling that indirect discrimination could not be established under the Fair Employment Act 1989 (the precursor to FETO) where the discrimination complained of resulted from the application of a [disparately impacting] factor not itself that of religious belief, rather than 'by reason of' religious belief, overruling a tribunal's decision that the application by a company of a LIFO redundancy procedure, in circumstances where recent attempts by it to redress chronic under-representation among its workforce of Catholic employees had the result that such employees had shorter periods of service than their Protestant counterparts, would have been indirectly discriminatory under the FEA.

Hall v Shorts Missile Systems Ltd [1996] NI 214

MacDermott LJ (with whom Girvan and Pringle JJ agreed):

I do not accept that the [LIFO] agreement applied a requirement or condition. In coming to the contrary conclusion the [tribunal] does not appear to have had regard to *Brook's* case.
. . .
    I am attracted by [Wood J's] reasoning and would readily adopt it in the present case. I am satisfied that the [LIFO] agreement . . . did not apply either conditions or requirements and there was no 'must' provision in [it]. Those who were not declared redundant were those who were assessed as better than those who were made redundant—it was, and I repeat the tribunal's phrase, a competitive ranking scheme.

In *Brook* EAT also rejected a claim by the women claimants that they had been indirectly discriminated against because the redundancy selections were all made from trades in which women were concentrated, while those which were exclusively made (but the content of which did not differ significantly from that done by the women) were not put into the pool from which redundancy selections were made.

Brook v London Borough of Haringey [1992] IRLR 478

Wood J:

It is contended that because some trades were not included in the compulsory pool and that those trades were predominantly male, this constituted direct or indirect discrimination . . .
    So far as direct discrimination is relevant, it seems to us, as we think it seemed to the Industrial Tribunal, that no-one was in that pool because of a sex factor, but because of a membership of a particular trade. We do not understand that discrimination is alleged in any of those trades—save possibly in one, but there was no clear evidence of that. There is therefore no sex factor which includes or excludes any person found to be in that compulsory pool (see the test in *James* . . .)
    The alternative submission is that there was indirect discrimination because Haringey have applied a requirement or condition that unless someone was a member of one of the trades whose members were not included in the compulsory pool, they were at risk of redundancy and because there happen to have been more men than women in those other trades there is discrimination which requires justification . . . it seems to us that the Industrial Tribunal dealt with this whole subject succinctly in paragraph 208 of the decision:

    '208. In consideration of the case law, and in consideration of the evidence, the Tribunal does not find as a fact that a requirement or condition was placed upon the women with which, as women, they could not comply . . . It was an accidental happening that certain trades contained no women and it was an accidental happening

> that employees employed in certain trades were not made redundant because the needs of that particular trade were essential to [the Council] . . .'

We cannot think that what occurred constituted the erection of a rule or barrier which had the effect of discriminating against women. Those trades were open to women, in due course they might have included a preponderance of women. There are no biological or social elements concerned. . . . If this submission is well founded, namely that the mere holding of a job or position can constitute a requirement or condition, and is prima facie discriminatory requiring justification, it could be applied to whole factories.

Evelyn Ellis argued that the UK approach to indirect discrimination is, at least in the context of sex discrimination, inadequate to implement EU law.[51] And in *Falkirk Council v Whyte* [1997] IRLR 560, EAT relied on EU law to uphold a tribunal finding that a woman had been subject to unlawful indirect discrimination where she was denied a managerial post in respect of which management training and supervisory experience were stated to be 'desirable.' The *Perera* problem has, in any event, been isolated by the implementation of the new definitions of indirect discrimination in the SDA, RRA and the SO and RB Regs. But the original definition on which it rests continues to apply under the SDA and the FETO except in the context of employment[52] and to the RRA as it regulates discrimination outside the scope of the Racial Equality Directive.

Further difficulties have been generated by judicial denial that demands made by employers—even if of an absolute nature—amounted to 'requirements or conditions.' One example of this is seen in *Clymo v Wandsworth London Borough Council* [1989] ICR 250, in which EAT rejected an appeal against the dismissal by a tribunal of a claim of indirect sex discrimination by a librarian whose employers refused her application to work reduced hours after she had a child. Among the grounds relied upon by the tribunal and accepted by EAT was that no requirement had been 'applied' to Ms Clymo—full-time working was one of the terms of employment which she was initially offered and accepted when she took the job. According to the Court (*per* then President, Wood J):

> for the local authority to tell their current employees that a job continues to be 'full time' is not applying anything and that on the facts of the present case 'full time' is part of the nature of the job itself [53] . . . in many working structures . . . there will be a grade or position where the job or appointment by its very nature requires full-time attendance. At one end of the scale if a cleaner was required to work full time it would clearly be a requirement or condition. Whereas in the case of a managing director it would be part of the nature of the appointment. In between there will be many gradations but it will be for an employer, acting reasonably, to decide—a managerial decision—what is required for the purposes of running his business or his establishment.

Michael Rubenstein recently remarked (IRLR 'Highlights', October 2003) that Mr Justice Wood's 'contribution to equal pay and discrimination case law has not been viewed kindly by history.' Certainly the flawed approach taken in *Clymo* and in *Brook* has been rejected by the Court of Appeal in more recent years.

---

[51] 'The definition of discrimination in European sex equality law' (1994) 19 *European Law Review* 561, 573–4, citing the references of the ECJ in cases such as *Bilka-Kaufhaus* and *Danfoss* (below) to disparately impacting pay practices.

[52] In the case of the SDA, until amendment as required by Council Directive 2004/113/EC on equal treatment in access to goods and services, which has to be implemented in the UK by December 2007.

[53] Preferring *Francis v British Airways Engineering Overhaul Ltd* [1982] IRLR 10 to *Home Office v Holmes* [1984] ICR 678.

Allonby v Accrington & Rossendale College & Ors [2001] ICR 1189

The claimant was employed by Accrington & Rossendale College as a part-time lecturer on a succession of one-year contracts from 1990 until 1996 when the college decided to terminate or not renew the contracts of employment of part-time lecturers and instead to retain their services as subcontractors retained by ELS. Ms Allonby claimed, inter alia, that her dismissal by the college was indirectly discriminatory on grounds of sex, women lecturers being disproportionately represented amongst the part-timers. She lost her case, the tribunal ruling that the discrimination was justifiable. EAT rejected her appeal but the Court of Appeal allowed her appeal in part and remitted the case for rehearing, accepting that the college had imposed a requirement or condition that staff had to have been employed on a full-time basis[54] in order to avoid dismissal and rejecting the employer's preferred formulation that the requirement or condition imposed (if any) was that, in order to be re-engaged by the college, an hourly-paid lecturer had to be registered with ELS.

Sedley LJ (for the Court):

It is for the applicant to identify the requirement or condition which she seeks to impugn. These words are not terms of art: they are overlapping concepts and are not to be narrowly construed (*Clarke v Eley*). If the applicant can realistically identify a requirement or condition capable of supporting her case, as Ms Allonby did here to the employment tribunal's satisfaction, it is nothing to the point that her employer can with equal cogency derive from the facts a different and unobjectionable requirement or condition. . . .

The only authority which offers support to Mr Jeans's argument (for the Defendants) is the decision of the Employment Appeal Tribunal in *Brook* [cited above]. There are two reasons why Brook must be regarded as wrongly decided. One is that the reasoning in *Enderby*, on which it is explicitly founded, was overset by the European Court of Justice [Case C–127/92 [1993] ECR I–05535]. Applying Article [141] of the EEC Treaty to a national pay structure which gave a predominantly female sector of the health service lower pay than a predominantly male sector doing work of equal value (a situation in any event entirely different from the present one), the ECJ held that this was enough to require the employer to show that it was not discriminatory.

The other reason is that the decision of the EAT in *Brook* is based on an erroneous understanding of the [SDA]'s concept of indirect discrimination, an understanding which conflates it with direct discrimination. The fact—if it is a fact—that a section of a workforce facing some disadvantage 'happens to be' predominantly female may be crucial to the question of direct discrimination, but has no bearing on either the initial element of indirect discrimination under s.1(1)(b)(i) (unequal impact) or the third element under s.1(1)(b)(iii) (consequent detriment). The establishment of the requirement or condition and the evaluation of its proportional impact depend upon an exact reading of the evidence and nothing more. To say that those affected happen to be, rather than are, predominantly or exclusively men or women is to say nothing which at this stage is material. Nor does it matter that the outcome may affect a whole factory: in such cases as *Clarke v Eley (IMI) Kynoch* (above) that is exactly what happened. Where the reasons for the imbalance may become relevant, depending on the facts of the case, is in considering damages under s.66(3) or justifiability under s.1(1)(b)(ii). In the former case the employer will be relieved of liability to pay damages if he can show that there was no intention to treat the applicant unfavourably on sexual grounds in applying the requirement or condition, albeit that is what has happened. In the latter case, if the requirement or condition is objectively justified

---

[54] Or on a pro-rata rather than hourly paid part-time basis.

notwithstanding its differential impact on men and women, then it can be fairly said that those disadvantaged simply happen to be women. But that is a conclusion, not a premise.

Allonby is to be welcomed. But it has not entirely done away with the type of reasoning employed in *Brook*. In *Barry v Midland Bank plc* [1999] ICR 859, an equal pay case, the House of Lords had come close to demanding differential treatment to establish *indirect* discrimination.[55] The claimant had been employed as a full-time clerk for 11 years between 1979 and 1990 when she took maternity leave, returning in the same year on reduced hours (17.5, down from 35). Of the 16 per cent of the defendant's staff who worked part-time, 96 per cent were female. Mrs Barry was made voluntarily redundant in 1993 and received a redundancy payment calculated on the basis of her 14 years' service and her final (part-time) wage. She claimed that the bank had discriminated against her on grounds of sex by applying a requirement or condition that, in order to avoid having years of full-time service counted as part-time service for the purposes of the redundancy scheme, staff had to be working full-time at the date of redundancy. A tribunal held that the requirement or condition did not have a disparate impact on women 92.68 per cent of whom in Mrs Barry's department worked full time (99.33 per cent of men). EAT dismissed her appeal, ruling that the terms applied to Mrs Barry were no less favourable than those applied to a man and that the same rule applied to men and women, full-time and part-time workers: that is, that severance pay was calculated on the basis of their wage at the date of dismissal. (Note that an indirect discrimination claim *does not* turn on proof of disparate *treatment*, as distinct from disparate *impact*.) The Court of Appeal and House of Lords dismissed Mrs Barry's appeals, the latter ruling that, although the scheme did disadvantage workers whose hours had fluctuated downwards prior to their dismissal for redundancy, it had not been shown to treat less favourably a predominantly female group of employees to which she belonged. The scheme applied in identical terms to men and women and to full-time and part-time workers by basing redundancy payments on salary at date of termination.

Lord Slynn:

The first question which arises is whether there is a difference in treatment at all between full-time and part-time workers for the purposes of the Act and the Treaty. In that regard, it is not sufficient merely to ask whether one gets more or less money than the other. It is necessary to consider whether, taking account of the purpose of the payment, there is a difference in treatment.

With all due respect to Lord Slynn, the question posed by the case was not whether part-time and full-time workers (or, indeed, any other classifications of workers) were differently *treated* by the bank, rather whether Mrs Barry was, *as a woman*, disadvantaged by a requirement or condition applied to workers *without* discrimination on grounds of sex: that is, whether a requirement or condition had a disparate *impact* on women. The question ought to have been whether the requirement that, in order to be compensated at the higher (full-time) rate, for a past year of service, a worker had to be working full-time at the date of termination, placed women at a significant statistical disadvantage by comparison with

---

[55] *Cf* the refreshing *Whiffen v Milham Ford Girls' School* [2001] ICR 1023 in which the Court of Appeal allowed an appeal against a tribunal decision that an employer had justified an indirectly discriminatory policy by establishing that it was not *inherently* discriminatory, though it had a disproportionate impact on women. In *Kachelmann v Bankhaus Hermann Lampe KG* Case C–322/98 [2000] ECR I–07505, however, the ECJ adopted an approach very similar to that of the House of Lords in *Barry* in accepting that part-time and full-time workers were not comparably placed for the purposes of a redundancy selection scheme.

men. In assessing the impact of this requirement, regard would have to be paid not only to the part-time workers who had previously worked full-time, but also to full-time workers who had previously worked part-time but who would be compensated for those part-time years of service at the higher (full-time) rate. It may be that the impact of the requirement on men and women within the bank was, as a matter of fact, not significantly different. It may be that any disparate impact could have been justified by reference to the aims of the scheme—to cushion the effects of unemployment, as well as to compensate for loss of a job and to reward loyalty. But the House of Lords decision does exactly what the Court of Appeal in *Allonby* criticised EAT for having done in *Brook*: that is, requiring proof of less favourable treatment for *indirect* discrimination. Indirect discrimination is concerned with the *same* treatment being applied to everyone in circumstances where the *impact* of that treatment varies according to sex, race, etc.[56] This is a considerable problem, and one which may not be righted by the recent adoption of the amended definitions of indirect discrimination in the RRA, RB and SO Regs. While the replacement of 'requirement or condition' with 'provision, criterion or practice' should do away with the reasoning in cases like *Perera*, it is by no means certain that it will make any difference at all to the wrong turning recently endorsed by the House of Lords in *Barry*.[57]

Disparate Impact

In order that a complaint of indirect discrimination can succeed under the original test, the claimant has to demonstrate that the requirement of condition applied is such that a 'considerably smaller proportion' of his or her sex or racial group than of others, can comply with it. The question does not relate to the relative proportions of men and women, persons of different ethnic groups, etc within the population of those who can comply—one would not expect, absent discrimination, that 50 per cent of those complying with any particular set of job-related requirements would be black, Asian, male or female. Rather, the question relates to the representation of the relevant racial or other group in the qualifying population *relative to* their representation in the wider population or other relevant 'pool' (how this 'pool' can be determined is further discussed below). The questions which arise are: (1) how to determine the relative proportions of the claimant's group and of others who can comply with the disputed requirement or condition, and (2) what is meant by 'a considerably smaller proportion.'

Under the SDA's test, as it currently applies to employment, the claimant must establish that the provision, criterion or practice in dispute 'is such that it would be to the detriment of a considerably larger proportion of women than of men,' under the RRA as amended and the SO and RB Regs that it 'puts or would put persons' of the claimant's group 'at a particular disadvantage when compared with other persons'. The amended SDA approach is not significantly different from the original approach in terms of questions (1) and (2) above. It does however differ inasmuch as it replaces the question whether less woman *can comply* with the provision, criterion or practice with the question whether it is *to the detriment* of more of them. This could be established notwithstanding ability to comply. The

[56] See also more recently the High Court decision in *Trustees of Uppingham School Retirement Benefits Scheme for Non-Teaching Staff v Shillcock* [2002] IRLR 702 in which the Court (*per* Mr Justice Neuberger) demanded differential treatment in an indirect discrimination claim.

[57] The Equality Bill 2005, which proposes the prohibition of discrimination on grounds of religion or belief in access to goods, services and facilities, rather bizarrely adopts yet another definition of indirect discrimination which is drafted in terms of a (disparately impacting) 'requirement, condition or practice'.

difference between the original approach and that adopted by the SO and RB Regs and the amended RRA is greater, the question simply being whether 'puts or would put persons' of the claimant's group 'at a particular disadvantage when compared with other persons.' This, as we shall see below, might be established without reference to the statistics typically required in assessing 'considerably smaller' and 'considerably larger' proportions. The European Commission made it clear in the Explanatory Memorandum to the Racial Equality Directive that the definition of indirect discrimination therein was intentionally chosen to avoid the need for statistical proof.

Returning to the original definition of indirect discrimination, in order to establish the relative proportions of the plaintiff's relevant group and of others who can comply, tribunals select an appropriate 'pool for comparison', ie, a description of those who (leaving aside the disputed requirement or condition) are in the same 'relevant circumstances' as the claimant (see discussion of ss.5(3) SDA and the equivalent provisions above). The proportions of the claimant's group[58] and of others who can comply with the requirement or condition is determined by comparing those of the claimant's group and of others who are within this pool and who can[59] comply with the disputed condition.

A number of difficulties are associated with the 'pool' approach. In the first place, should the 'pool' of those who are regarded as being in the 'same relevant circumstances' as the claimant be drawn within the workplace? Should it take into account others in the relevant travel-to-work area? Or should some wider approach be taken? Secondly (and this is related), we saw above that the question of who should be regarded as being within the 'same relevant circumstances' as the claimant is not without complications.

The choice of pool made by the tribunal may well be crucial to the success or failure of a discrimination claim. The extent to which this pool may be reviewed on appeal, therefore, is a matter of some importance. In *Kidd v DRG (UK) Ltd* (EAT) [1985] ICR 405 EAT ruled that the choice of pool was a question of fact and appeals on this point would succeed only in 'exceptional cases where it can be shown that good sense has not prevailed, and the tribunal has chosen to make the proportionate comparison within an area of society so irrationally inappropriate as to put it outside the range of selection for any reasonable tribunal.'[60] This approach has however given way over recent years to a recognition that the choice of pool is both crucial to the outcome of an indirect discrimination claim and susceptible to a correct answer. It became apparent reasonably early on that the higher courts would overturn the choice of pool if it was not such that the 'relevant circumstances' of those (both of and not of the claimant's relevant group) within it were 'the same or not materially different.' In *University of Manchester v Jones* [1992] ICR 52, for example, the Court of Appeal EAT ruled that tribunals had erred in artificially restricting the category of people included in the pool. The case was brought by a 44-year-old woman who was turned down for a job limited to graduates aged 27–35. The woman had taken her degree as a mature student and she claimed that the age limit discriminated against women who had obtained their degrees as mature students. The tribunal selected, as the pool for com-

---

[58] Sex or (in Northern Ireland) religion or belief other than in the context of employment, race inasmuch as it refers to colour or nationality rather than race or ethnic or national origin (save where EEA nationals are concerned in which case *O'Flynn v Chief Adjudication Officer* Case-237/94 [1996] ECR I-02617 applies). This test, recently applied by the Court of Appeal in *Secretary of State for Work and Pensions v Bobezes* [2005] EWCA Civ 111, asks whether the disputed provision etc is intrinsically liable to impact disparately.

[59] Or, on occasion, who cannot—see decision in *London Underground v Edwards (No. 2)* and the speeches of Lord Nicholls in *ex parte Seymour Smith* and in *Barry v Midland Bank* (all discussed below).

[60] For criticism of the pool allowed by EAT in *Kidd* see K O'Donovan and E Szyszczak, 'Redundancy Selection and Sex Discrimination' (1985) 14 *Industrial Law Journal* 252.

parison, men and women who had obtained degrees at the age of 25 or over. Of these, the proportion of women aged under 35 was smaller than the proportion of male students under that age. The tribunal's finding in favour of Ms Jones was overturned on appeal and EAT's decision upheld by the Court of Appeal:

Jones v University of Manchester [1993] ICR 474

Lord Justice Evans:

If . . . the numbers of women and of men, respectively, remaining after the requirement is applied are to be compared as 'proportions' of something other than the total number of those who can comply, then the question arises, as proportions of what? One possibility is, as proportions of 'all men' and 'all women,' even of 'all humanity' subdivided in this way[61]. The other possibility is . . . 'the relevant population', meaning all persons who satisfy the relevant criteria apart from the requirement or condition which is under consideration.[62] The latter approach is supported by . . . *Perera* . . . and by *obiter dicta* in *Price v Civil Service Commission and another* (Phillips J) [extracted below]. In my judgment, it is much to be preferred. This means that the proportion of women in the 'group' (those who can comply) must not be considerably smaller than the proportion of women in the 'relevant population' or 'pool'. (Section 5(3), which requires comparisons of women with men to be such that the 'relevant circumstances' are the same, supports this construction, in my view).

It follows that the statutory concept, in my judgment, is that of a 'pool' or 'relevant population', meaning those persons, male and female, who satisfy all the relevant criteria, apart from the requirement in question. It is, in effect, the total number of all those persons, men and women, who answer the description contained in the advertisement, apart from the age requirement. Here, that means all graduates with the relevant experience.

The next question raised by this appeal is whether the number of women and men, respectively who can comply with the requirement, must be compared as proportions of the total numbers of women and men, respectively, in the whole of the relevant population (graduates with the relevant experience), or whether they may be subdivided so as to form some smaller group which then is compared with a corresponding subdivision of the larger 'pool' (mature graduates with the relevant experience) . . . I find it difficult to identify the basis on which any subdivision might be done . . . the Industrial Tribunal erred in law in having regard to a 'pool' which consisted of mature graduates with relevant experience only.[63]

In *Barry* the Court of Appeal ruled that the tribunal had erred in selecting as the pool for comparison only those within the claimant's department in circumstances in which redundancies were selected from across the bank. Since no statistics had been provided as to the impact of the scheme across the bank Ms Barry had not established even a prima facie case of disparate impact. The decision in *Barry* cast significant doubt on that in *Kidd*, which has effectively been overruled by two recent decisions of the Court of Appeal.

---

[61] Citing *R v Secretary of State for Education ex parte Schaffter* [1987] IRLR 53, *per* Schiemann J.

[62] Citing *Jones v Chief Adjudication Officer* [1990] IRLR 533, *per* Mustill LJ.

[63] See also *London Underground v Edwards* [1995] ICR 574 and the Court of Appeal in *Barry v Midland Bank* [1998] IRLR 138. Cf *Greater Manchester Police Authority v Lea* [1990] IRLR 372, in which EAT accepted a pool which was 'not statistically perfect' (in an admissions case, covering the whole population rather than those otherwise qualified for the job: 'statistical perfection is not properly to be sought in this field'—citing *Kidd*.

Allonby v Accrington & Rossendale College **[2001] ICR 1189**

Sedley LJ (for the Court):

As often happens, once the condition or requirement is identified the 'pool' within which its impact has to be gauged falls into place. So here, as the employment tribunal held, the pool was 'all persons who would qualify for . . . continuous employment if the requirement or condition had not been taken into account.' This meant not simply the dismissed hourly-paid workforce but the entire body of lecturers at the college: a total of 177 men and 292 women. The proportion of men in the pool who could comply with the condition was 67 out of the 177, about 38 per cent. The proportion of women in the pool who were able to comply was 61 out of the 292, about 21 per cent.

The EAT held that there was no error of law in the tribunal's choice of a pool. Lindsay J quoted the decision of Waite P in *Kidd* . . . 'The choice of an appropriate section of the population is in our judgment an issue of fact (or perhaps strictly a matter for discretion to be exercised in the course of discharging an exclusively fact-finding function) . . .'

I would sound a strong note of caution about this. As the EAT's excellent analysis of the possible pools shows, once the impugned requirement or condition has been defined there is likely to be only one pool which serves to test its effect. I would prefer to characterise the identification of the pool as a matter neither of discretion nor of fact-finding but of logic. This was the approach adopted by this court in *Barry v Midland Bank plc*, and endorsed by Lord Slynn on further appeal. Logic may on occasion be capable of producing more than one outcome, especially if two or more conditions or requirements are in issue. But the choice of pool is not at large.

In *Rutherford v Towncircle Ltd*, further considered below, the Court of Appeal ruled that 'the correct pool depends on the proper understanding and application of the legal principles laid down by the ECJ and the House of Lords in *R v Secretary of State for Employment ex parte Seymour-Smith*'.[64] That case involved the claim that the cut-off age (65) for entitlement to redundancy pay discriminated indirectly against men, who were more likely than women to remain in employment after the age of 65.

Rutherford v Towncircle Ltd (No.2) **[2004] ICR 119**

Mummery LJ (for the Court):

the relevant statistical comparison involves (a) taking as the pool 'the workforce' (i.e. the entire workforce) to whom the age limit is applicable, not taking just a small section of the workforce, confined to those who are adversely affected by being over 65 or within 10 years of the age of 65; (b) ascertaining the proportion of men in the workforce who are under the age of 65 and are advantaged by being able to meet the requirement, and the proportion of men who are excluded from the right and are therefore disadvantaged by being unable to meet the requirement; (c) ascertaining the proportion of women in the workforce who are under the age of 65 and are therefore advantaged by being able to meet the requirement, and the proportion of women who are excluded from the right and are therefore disadvantaged by being unable to meet the requirement; (d) comparing the results for men with the results for women in order to see whether the percentage (not the numbers) of men in the workforce who are advantaged is considerably smaller than the percentage of women who are advantaged . . .

---

[64] [1995] ICR 889, discussed further below.

Getting the pool wrong can have serious implications. In *Barry*, as we saw above, the Court of Appeal ruled that the claimant had not provided any evidence of the impact of the disputed requirement or condition on the pool of workers it regarded as appropriate.[65] In some cases proof of disparate impact will require the provision of detailed statistics.

O'Donovan and E Szyszczak, 'Redundancy Selection and Sex Discrimination' (1985) 14 Industrial Law Journal 252, 253–4

Prior to *Kidd* motherhood, especially in caring for young children, had been treated by tribunals and official discourse generally as a major factor limiting women's participation in the labour market. This 'social fact' was challenged by both the industrial tribunal and by the EAT in *Kidd v D.R.G.* Therein lies a source of uneasiness about the EAT decision. The EAT approved the tribunal's view that 'mothers of young children in the modern community are no longer conforming universally to the traditional notion that their place is in the home; and that there are plenty of couples (married or unmarried) today with young children, where the male partner stays at home for the whole or part of the time to release his female partner to undertake full-time work.' No evidence was given for this new 'social fact' despite the statutory reference to considerably smaller proportions.

The problem with looking at households with children is that this assumes that all adult members of the household are equally incapacitated by the presence of children or others who need care. In other words, this overlooks the sexual division of labour. The correct pool, we suggest, should be those at risk under the first element of the statutory definition of indirect discrimination, that is those at risk from the ostensibly neutral requirement or condition. Having identified those who are at risk, the appropriate comparison is between those who can comply with the requirement and those who are at risk under it. In the particular circumstances of *Kidd* those at risk are part-time workers and those who can comply are full-time workers. The issue of childcare commitments which was raised by the complainant is not strictly relevant. In social terms there are a number of reasons why married women work part-time. In addition to domestic responsibilities, state policies such as the tax and social security thresholds provide incentives for married women to choose part-time rather than full-time employment. In legal terms there must be a direct connection between the requirement or condition and the question of compliance. The requirement in Kidd is the ability to work full-time to avoid being 'first-out' in the redundancy procedure. Compliance by married women is the issue, not the presence of children in the household. It is enough for a complainant who alleges indirect discrimination to give statistical evidence that the numbers of persons in her class (women under s.1(1)(b); married persons under s.3(1)(b)) who can comply with the requirement are considerably less than the numbers in the comparative class.

This raises the question why there was no such statistical evidence before the tribunal and EAT. It seems that once the error of identifying the pool as households with children (instead of identifying those at risk under the requirement) was made, both tribunals wanted to hear statistical evidence about such households. But the complainant's counsel produced 'extracts from the national census figures' which were 'too broadly based' and which were held merely to confirm that more full-time jobs are held by men than are held by women. The EAT wanted figures on the effect as between the sexes, or as between married and unmarried persons, of responsibility for children as a factor potentially precluding the acceptance of a full-time job. Such figures are available in Social Trends or (now) from Martin and Roberts, *Women and Employment* (HMSO, 1984). It is submitted that the statistical evidence of women's or married persons' lesser ability to comply is enough to

---

[65] See also *Pearse v City of Bradford Metropolitan Council* [1988] IRLR 379.

show a prima facie case of indirect discrimination. The reasons for that inability rank as supplementary.

The courts will not always require statistical evidence. In *Briggs v North Eastern Education and Library Board* [1990] IRLR 181, for example, Northern Ireland's Court of Appeal accepted that a considerably smaller proportion of women than of men could comply with a requirement to work late. In *Jones v University of Manchester*, Evans LJ remarked that the wording of s.1(1)(b) 'make[s] some statistical evidence inevitable, but I have wondered throughout this appeal whether Parliament can have envisaged the kind of detail which has been produced in this case.'[66] And in *London Underground Ltd v Edwards (No. 2)*, the relevant part of which is extracted below, the Court of Appeal accepted that the tribunal was entitled to take into account 'common knowledge' of the preponderance of female over male lone parents as well as the statistical evidence relating to the ability of women in the workplace concerned to comply with the requirement in dispute.

But the *Kidd* approach is not entirely obsolete. In *Sanderson v BAA plc* (40 *Equal Opportunities Review Discrimination Case Law Digest*, 2) a tribunal refused to accept, without proof, that a requirement to work an early morning shift discriminated against women.[67] Some evidence of disparate impact will generally be necessary, and the requirement for it can make the tribunal's selection of pools crucial to the claimant's success.

Turning to the second question raised above, the question of what amounts to 'a considerably smaller proportion' was also considered by the Court of Appeal in the *London Underground* case, which concerned an indirect discrimination claim brought by a woman train driver after her employer imposed shift changes. The woman, a lone parent, claimed that a considerably smaller proportion of women (95.2 per cent) than of men (100 per cent) train drivers could comply with the new shifts. A tribunal found in her favour, taking into account 'common knowledge that females are more likely to be single parents and caring for a child than males,' the disparity in the numbers of male and female train drivers (2023 men to 21 women) and the fact that only one person (the claimant) could not comply with the employer's condition. London Underground appealed.

London Underground Ltd v Edwards (No. 2) [1999] ICR 494

Potter LJ:[68]

In my view, there is a dual statutory purpose underlying the provisions of s1(1)(b) and in particular the necessity under subparagraph (i) to show that the proportion of women who

---

[66] See also *Perera* and *Kidd*.

[67] Cf *Cowley v South African Airways* 41 *Equal Opportunities Review Discrimination Case Law Digest* 2–3 in which a tribunal ruled that using its 'knowledge of working practices there will be far less women with young children who would be able to comply with [a requirement for] back-to-back double-shift working than males.'

[68] Having acknowledged acknowledged the comment of Neill LJ in *R v Secretary of State for Employment ex p Seymour-Smith*, below, that 'before a presumption of indirect discrimination on the ground of sex arises there must be a considerable difference in the number or percentage of one sex in the advantaged or disadvantaged group as against the other sex and not simply a difference which is more than de minimis,' of Peter Gibson LJ in *Barry v Midland Bank plc*, n 63 above, that: 'the consistent approach of the European Court has been . . . to see whether the measure works to the disadvantage of far more women than men' and of Otton LJ in *R v Secretary of State ex parte Unison* [1996] IRLR 438 that a 4% disparity between the proportions of men and women able to comply with a particular requirement 'would fall within the *de minimis* exception.' He also referred to Greater *Manchester Police Authority v Lea*, n 63 above, in which EAT upheld a tribunal determination that the difference between 95.3 per cent and 99.4 per cent was 'considerable'.

can comply with a given requirement or condition is 'considerably smaller' than the proportion of men who can comply with it. The first is to prescribe as the threshold for intervention a situation in which there exists a substantial and not merely marginal discriminatory effect (disparate impact) as between men and women, so that it can be clearly demonstrated that a prima facie case of (indirect) discrimination exists, sufficient to require the employer to justify the application of the condition or requirement in question: see subparagraph (ii). The second is to ensure that a tribunal charged with deciding whether or not the requirement is discriminatory may be confident that its disparate impact is inherent in the application of the requirement or condition and is not simply the product of unreliable statistics or fortuitous circumstance. Since the disparate impact question will require to be resolved in an infinite number of different employment situations . . . an area of flexibility (or margin of appreciation), is necessarily applicable to the question of whether a particular percentage is to be regarded as 'substantially smaller' in any given case . . .

[a] tribunal does not sit in blinkers. Its members are selected in order to have a degree of knowledge and expertise in the industrial field generally. The high preponderance of single mothers having care of a child is a matter of common knowledge. Even if the 'statistic', ie the precise ratio referred to is less well known, it was in any event apparently discussed at the hearing before the industrial tribunal without doubt or reservation on either side. It thus seems clear to me that, when considering as a basis for their decision the reliability of the figures with which they were presented, the industrial tribunal were entitled to take the view that the percentage difference represented a minimum rather than a maximum so far as discriminatory effect was concerned.

Equally, I consider that the industrial tribunal was entitled to have regard to the large discrepancy in numbers between male and female operators making up the pool for its consideration. Not one of the male component of just over 2000 men was unable to comply with the rostering arrangements. On the other hand, one woman could not comply out of the female component of only 21. It seems to me that the comparatively small size of the female component indicated, again without the need for specific evidence, both that it was either difficult or unattractive for women to work as train operators in any event and that the figure of 95.2 per cent of women unable to comply was likely to be a minimum rather than a maximum figure. Further, if for any reason fortuitous error was present or comprehensive evidence lacking, an unallowed-for increase of no more than one in the women unable to comply would produce an effective figure of some 10 per cent as against the nil figure in respect of men; on the other hand, one male employee unable to comply would scarcely alter the proportional difference at all. . . .

In many respects, no doubt, it would be useful to lay down in relation to s1(1)(b) a rule of thumb or to draw a line defining the margin within, or threshold beyond, which, in relation to small percentage differences, the lower percentage should not reasonably be regarded as 'considerably smaller' than the higher percentage. However, it does not seem to me appropriate to do so. For the various reasons discussed in this judgment, and because of the wide field and variety of situations in which the provisions of the section are to be applied, the circumstances and arguments before the adjudicating tribunal are bound to differ as to what in a particular case amounts to a proportion which is 'considerably smaller' for the purposes of determining the discriminatory or potentially discriminatory nature of a particular requirement or condition. If a figure were to be selected in the field of employment, it would be likely to vary according to the context, and in particular as between a case where the requirement or condition is applied on a national scale in respect of which reliable supporting statistics are available and those where it is applied in relation to a small firm or an unbalanced workforce where the decision may have to be made on far less certain evidence and to a large degree upon the basis of the industrial tribunal's own experience and assessment as applied to such figures as are available. The difficulties are well illustrated by this case.

Plainly, a percentage difference of no more than 5 per cent or thereabouts is inherently likely to lead an industrial tribunal to the conclusion that the requirements of s 1(1)(b) have not been made out, but I am not prepared to say that such a conclusion must inevitably follow in every case.[69]

Had the Court of Appeal taken a more formulaic approach to statistical proof it would have been very difficult for the claimant to establish her case. The difference between the proportions of men and women train drivers who could comply with the condition to work the new shifts was not enormous. But the women who were employed in that capacity would have been unrepresentative of women as a whole many of whom would not have been able to comply with the working hours required of tube drivers even prior to the change to shift arrangements. Thus it was entirely appropriate of the Court of Appeal in this case to take into account wider considerations in order to balance the discrimination which was, in effect, already built into the figures.[70]

In *R v Secretary of State for Employment, ex parte Seymour-Smith & Perez* [1995] ICR 889 the Court of Appeal accepted (overruling the Divisional Court) that proportions of between 88.4 and 94.6 per cent were 'considerably smaller' than 100 per cent. The case involved a challenge to the 1985 increase in the qualifying period for unfair dismissal, in 1985, from one to two years. It was argued that women were substantially more disadvantaged than men by the increase and that, therefore, it breached the Equal Treatment Directive. The appeal Court felt constrained by the Equal Treatment Directive not to place an exaggerated emphasis on the word 'considerably.' On appeal, the House of Lords referred to the ECJ, inter alia, the question: '[w]hat is the legal test for establishing whether a measure adopted by a Member State has such a degree of disparate effect as between men and women as to amount to indirect discrimination for the purposes of Article [141] of the EC Treaty unless shown to be based upon objectively justified factors other than sex?' The ECJ ruled as follows:

R v Secretary of State for Employment, ex parte Seymour-Smith & Perez Case C–167/97 [1999] ECR I–00623

[60] . . . it must be ascertained whether the statistics available indicate that a considerably smaller percentage of women than men is able to satisfy the condition of two years' employment required by the disputed rule. That situation would be evidence of apparent sex discrimination unless the disputed rule were justified by objective factors unrelated to any discrimination based on sex.

[61] That could also be the case if the statistical evidence revealed a lesser but persistent and relatively constant disparity over a long period between men and women who satisfy the requirement of two years' employment. It would, however, be for the national court to determine the conclusions to be drawn from such statistics.

It is also for the national court to assess whether the statistics concerning the situation of the workforce are valid and can be taken into account. . . . It is, in particular, for the national court to establish whether, given that it was a matter for the national court to determine

---

[69] In *Kang v R F Brookes Ltd* 40 *Equal Opportunities Review Discrimination Case Law Digest* 2, a tribunal ruled that a requirement with which 94 per cent of Sikh and 100 per cent of non-Sikh workers could comply was not indirectly discriminatory.

[70] A similar approach was adopted by EAT In *Chief Constable of the Bedfordshire Constabulary v Graham* [2002] IRLR 239.

whether differences in ability to comply were purely fortuitous or short term phenomena, and whether, in general, they appear to be significant.

In this case, it appears from the order for reference that in 1985, the year in which the requirement of two years' employment was introduced, 77.4 per cent men and 68.9 per cent of women fulfilled that condition.

Such statistics do not appear, on the face of it, to show that a considerably smaller percentage of women than men is able to fulfil the requirement imposed by the disputed rule.

When the case returned to the House of Lords the decision of the Court of Appeal was overturned. The majority decided on the grounds that a prima facie case of discrimination had been made out but that the discrimination was justified. This aspect of the decision is considered below. Lords Slynn and Steyn concurred on the basis that no discrimination had been proven.

R v Secretary of State for Employment, ex parte Seymour-Smith & Perez (No.2) [2000] ICR 244

Lord Nicholls (with whom Lords Goff and Jauncey agreed):

In paragraph 61, unlike paragraph 60, the [ECJ] gave no guidance on the extent of statistical disparity required to establish apparent sex discrimination. Nor did the court spell out, in so many words, how these two approaches fit together.

As I see it, the reasoning underlying these paragraphs is that, in the case of indirect discrimination, the obligation to avoid discrimination . . . is to avoid applying unjustifiable requirements having a considerable disparity of impact. In this regard the European Court has adopted an approach similar to that provided in section 1(1)(b) of the [SDA]. A considerable disparity can be more readily established if the statistical evidence covers a long period and the figures show a persistent and relatively constant disparity. In such a case a lesser statistical disparity may suffice to show that the disparity is considerable than if the statistics cover only a short period or if they present an uneven picture.

Having set out the applicable principles, the European Court addressed the facts in the present case. In doing so the court focused exclusively on the 1985 statistics . . . Before your Lordships it was common ground that 1991, not 1985, was the relevant date for the purpose of the issue now being considered. The position at this later date was not considered by the European Court . . . These figures show that over the period of seven years, from 1985 up to and including 1991, the ratio of men and women who qualified was roughly 10:9 . . . This disparity was remarkably constant for the six years from 1985 to 1990, but it began to diminish in 1991. These figures are in borderline country. The question under consideration is one of degree. When the borderline is defined by reference to a criterion as imprecise as 'considerably smaller' it is inevitable that in some cases different minds may reach different conclusions. The decisions of the two courts below illustrate this . . . I find myself driven to the conclusion that a persistent and constant disparity of the order just mentioned in respect of the entire male and female labour forces of the country over a period of seven years cannot be brushed aside and dismissed as insignificant or inconsiderable. I agree with the Court of Appeal that, given the context of equality of pay or treatment, the latitude afforded by the word 'considerably' should not be exaggerated. I think these figures are adequate to demonstrate that the extension of the qualifying period had a considerably greater adverse impact on women than men . . .

Barry v Midland Bank plc [1999] ICR 859

Lord Nicholls:

A comparison must be made between, on the one hand, the respective proportions of men . . . who are not disadvantaged by the [disputed practice] and those who are disadvantaged and, on the other hand, the like proportions regarding women in the workforce . . . These proportions by themselves can be misleading, because they are affected by the comparative sizes of the non-disadvantaged group and the disadvantaged group. The smaller the disadvantaged group in proportionate terms, the narrower will be the differential. Take an employer whose workforce of 1000 comprises an equal number of men and women. Ten per cent of the staff (100 employees) work part-time, and of these 90 per cent are women. A scheme which disadvantages part-timers will disadvantage 10 men (2 per cent of the male employees) and 90 women (18 per cent of female employees). If the figures were the same save that the total workforce was 10,000 employees, the disadvantaged part-timers would comprise 10 men (0.2 per cent of male employees) and 90 women (1.8 per cent of female employees). A better guide will often be found in expressing the proportions in the disadvantaged group as a ratio of each other. In both my examples the ratio is 9:1. For every man adversely affected there are nine women. Absolute size, in terms of numbers, remains relevant, since a low ratio may be of little significance in a small company but of considerable significance in a large company.

In the present case, the figures needed to make these comparisons are not available. The allegedly disadvantaged group comprises all employees at the date of Mrs Barry's termination whose average hours of work exceeded their current hours of work. There are no statistics on the size or composition of this group. The Court of Appeal regarded this as fatal to the claim, although the court was reluctant to decide the appeal on this ground. I consider that, although unsatisfactory, the figures available are sufficient to enable an inference to be drawn regarding the composition, but not the size, of the disadvantaged group. The figures show that, in the Midland Bank as elsewhere, a disproportionately high percentage of key-time employees are women. By disproportionately high I mean that the proportion of female key-time workers is considerably higher than the proportion of women in the entire work-force. The figures also show that, in the two years (1992 and 1993) for which statistics are available, the employees whose hours of work fluctuated during the year were overwhelmingly women. It is a reasonable inference from these two facts that the disadvantaged group is composed very largely of women. A prerequisite for entry to the disadvantaged group is that the employee's hours of work have fluctuated. This characteristic appears to be confined principally to women . . .

Lord Nicholls returned to this theme in his *Seymour-Smith* speech:

R v Secretary of State for Employment, ex parte Seymour-Smith & Perez (No.2) [2000] ICR 244

Lord Nicholls:

In paragraph 59 of its judgment the European Court described the approach which should be adopted to the comparison of statistics:

'. . . the best approach to the comparison of statistics is to consider, on the one hand, the respective proportions of men in the workforce able to satisfy the requirement of two years' employment under the disputed rule and of those unable to do so, and, on the other, to compare those proportions as regards women in the workforce. It is not sufficient to consider the number of persons affected, since that depends on the number of working people in the Member State as a whole as well as the percentages of men and women employed in that State.'

This statement appears to envisage that two comparisons should be made: a comparison of the proportions of men and women able to satisfy the requirement ('the qualifiers'), and a comparison of the proportions of men and women unable to satisfy the requirement ('the non-qualifiers'). Thereafter in its judgment the court considered only the proportions of men and women who were qualifiers.

Some of the ramifications involved in looking at the composition of the disadvantaged group, as well as the composition of the advantaged group, were explored by the Divisional Court and the Court of Appeal in the present case. Suffice to say, I do not understand the European Court to have rejected use of the figures relating to the non-qualifiers in a suitable case. Indeed, the European Court has looked at the composition of the disadvantaged group in several cases, although in none of them was there an issue on this point[71] . . . Having regard to the conclusion I have expressed above on the issue of disparate impact, it is unnecessary to reach a firm conclusion on this point. I prefer to leave this question open for another occasion.

More recently, in *Rutherford v Towncircle Ltd* [2002] ICR 119, EAT set out guidelines for the determination of the question whether the proportion of (there) men who were disadvantaged by the disputed provision (there the upper age limit on unfair dismissal and redundancy claims) was 'considerably larger' than that of women. Note that the claim was brought under Article 141 TEC and that the relevant question was whether a considerably larger proportion of men could comply with the disputed provision, rather than (as in the unamended SDA) a considerably smaller proportion of women could comply. But as Linsday J pointed out: 'The apparent clarity of that provision is not . . . reflected in the language used in the cases, either domestic or in the European Court of Justice.' Thus in *Bilka-Kaufhaus* Case C-170/84 [1986] ECR 1607 (further considered below) the ECJ asked whether the occupational pension scheme at issue there excluded '*a far greater number* of women than men' while in *Nimz v Freie* Case C–184/89 [1991] ECR I–297 and *Kowalska v Freie* Case C–33/89 [1990] ECR I–02591 the Court considered whether 'a considerably smaller percentage of men than women' were disadvantaged. In *Gerster v Freistaat Bayern* Case C–1/95 [1997] ECR I–05253 and in *Gruber v Silhouette International* Case C–249/97 [1999] ECR I–05295 the ECJ asked whether a measure 'work[ed] to the disadvantage of *far more* women than men' while, as we saw above, in *Seymour-Smith* the question was whether 'a considerably smaller percentage of women than men' was disadvantaged. In that case the ECJ looked both at the relative percentages of men and women who could comply and also at the relative proportions of those who could not.

The *Rutherford* cases went up and down between EAT and the Court of Appeal on a number of points, the final decision (at present) having been reached by the latter in September 2004. In it the Court addressed the proper pool for comparison and the question whether disparate impact had been demonstrated. The claimant, who was made redundant at 67, was prevented from claiming unfair dismissal or a statutory redundancy payment by ss.109 and 156 of the Employment Rights Act, which provide that employees who have reached age 65 do not have the right either not to be unfairly dismissed or to receive redundancy payments. He argued that the upper age limit breached Article 141 TEC because it was indirectly discriminatory against men, 7.6 per cent of whom were

---

[71] Citing *Bilka-Kaufhaus*, *Nimz* (discussed below) and *Kowalska v Freie und Hansestadt Hamburg* Case C–33/89 [1990] ECR 1–2591.

economically active after age 65 by comparison with only 3.4 per cent of women. A tribunal accepted that the proportion of men disadvantaged by the upper age limit was 'considerably higher' than that of women and that the employers had failed to justify the discrimination (no evidence had been adduced in support of the assertion that the discrimination was justified on social policy grounds). EAT allowed the employer's appeal (*Harvest Town Circle Ltd v Rutherford* [2001] IRLR 599) and remitted the case for rehearing. A second tribunal ruled in favour of the claimant and EAT again ruled that the incorrect pool for comparison had been selected (the tribunal had focused on the relative proportions of men and women employees aged over 65). EAT again overturned ([2002] IRLR 768) and the Court of Appeal rejected the employee's appeal.

Rutherford v Towncircle Ltd (No. 2) [2005] ICR 119

Mummery LJ (for the Court):

The primary focus is on the proportions of men and women who can comply with the requirement of the disputed rule. Only if the statistical comparison establishes a considerable disparity of impact, must the court then consider whether the disparity is objectively justifiable.

While leaving open the question whether the proportions in the disadvantaged group, as well as in the advantaged group, should be considered, Lord Nicholls [in *Seymour-Smith*] did not suggest that it was correct to consider only the proportions in the disadvantaged group, as was done by the employment tribunal in this case. Indeed, as was pointed out in the Divisional Court in *Seymour Smith* [1995] ICR 889 . . . concentration on the proportions of men and women in the workforce, who are disadvantaged because they cannot comply with a disputed requirement, can produce seriously misleading results, as in the simple case of a requirement with which 99.5 per cent of men can comply and 99 per cent of women can comply. If the focus is then shifted to the proportions of men and women who cannot comply (ie, 1 per cent of women and 0.5 per cent of men), the result would be that twice as many women as men cannot comply with the requirement. That would not be a sound or sensible basis for holding that the disputed requirement, with which the vast majority of both men and women can comply, had a disparate adverse impact on women.

If the correct approach is taken, the statistics in evidence clearly establish that the difference in the working population between the proportion of men aged under 65 who can comply and the proportion of women aged under 65 who can comply is very small indeed. The disparities are certainly not 'considerable' in the sense required by Seymour-Smith.

Mummery LJ went on to dismiss the argument put for the claimant that the Burden of Proof Directive required the primary focus to be on the disadvantaged, rather than the advantaged, group.

The definition of indirect sex discrimination in Article 2 of the Directive focuses on an apparently neutral provision, which has unjustified disadvantages for a substantially higher proportion of the members of one sex. The definition describes when a certain state of affairs (ie, indirect discrimination) exists: it does not, however, prescribe the methodology for assessing the statistical evidence in order to determine whether or not that state of affairs exists. No methodology has been laid down in the Treaty or in any directive or in national legislation. It has been left to the national courts and tribunals, which hear and assess the evidence and find the facts, to work out from case to case a satisfactory method for assessing whether or not there is disparate adverse impact in the particular case. It is a matter of applying considerations of logic, relevance and common sense to the raw material of the statistical evidence in order to determine the existence or otherwise of the objectionable state of affairs.

As the IRLR commentary to this case pointed out ('Highlights', November 2004), the assertion that the primary focus has to be on the advantaged group is highly questionable, the ECJ having focused on the disadvantaged group in six of the seven ECJ cases reported in the IRLR post *Seymour-Smith* . . . As the IRLR commentary points out: 'The effect of focusing on the advantaged group, as was done by the Court of Appeal in *Rutherford*, is to dilute the impact of the requirement on the excluded group (if the whole of the workforce is taken into account) or to ignore it altogether (if only those under age 65 are considered)'.

Whatever criticisms may be made of the decision in *Rutherford*, it suggests that the shift (in the SDA) from the question whether a significantly smaller proportion of women can comply with a disputed requirement to the question whether a significantly larger proportion of women cannot is likely to have very substantial repercussions prior to the replacement of that test in October 2005. Perhaps of more significance will be the definition adopted by the RRA and the SO and RB Regs and, from October 2005, the SDA: whether the provision, criterion or practice 'puts or would put persons' of the claimant's group 'at a particular disadvantage when compared with other persons.' Some illustration of the potential of this change can be seen in the decision of the Court of Appeal in *Coker & Osamor v Lord Chancellor & Lord Chancellor's Department* [2002] ICR 321.

The case arose from the appointment by the Lord Chancellor of a 'Special Adviser,' a position not governed by the normal rules governing civil service appointments. These advisers, one or two of whom may be appointed by Cabinet ministers, work very closely with their respective ministers, impart political advice and play a role in policy development. The person appointed by the Lord Chancellor was Garry Hart, an old friend and godfather, incidentally, to a child of the Prime Minister with whom the Lord Chancellor himself had longstanding ties. The appointment was made without advertisement of the vacancy.

Jane Coker and Martha Osamor challenged the appointment under s.6(1)(a) of the SDA and 4(1)(a) RRA respectively, arguing that Lord Irvine had discriminated against them by denying them the opportunity to apply for the position. By restricting the potential candidates for the position to those within his predominantly white, male circle of friends, they argued that he had discriminated against otherwise qualified women and African/ Caribbean/ Afro-Caribbean people. The tribunal found in favour of Jane Coker while rejecting Martha Osamor's claim. EAT overturned the decision on Ms Coker and refused Ms Osamor's appeal, ruling that, the Lord Chancellor having intended from the outset to appoint only Mr Hart, there was no pool for comparison of the appointment as between men and women. The Court of Appeal rejected the women's appeal, ruling that the tribunal had erred in accepting that the proportion of women who could comply with the Lord Chancellor's 'requirement or condition' to be be personally known to him was 'considerably smaller' than the proportion of men within the meaning of s.1(1)(b)(i) SDA.

Lord Phillips MR (for the Court):

The test of indirect discrimination focuses on the effect that the requirement objected to has on the pool of potential candidates. It can only have a discriminatory effect within the two statutes if a significant proportion of the pool are able to satisfy the requirement. Only in that situation will it be possible for the requirement to have a disproportionate effect on the men and the women, or the racial groups, which form the pool. Where the requirement excludes almost the entirety of the pool it cannot constitute indirect discrimination within the statutes.

For this reason, making an appointment from within a circle of family, friends and personal acquaintances is seldom likely to constitute indirect discrimination. Those known to the employer are likely to represent a minute proportion of those who would otherwise be qualified to fill the post. The requirement of personal knowledge will exclude the vast proportion of the pool, be they men, women, white or another racial group.

If the above proposition will be true in most cases of appointments made on the basis of personal acquaintanceship, it was certainly true of the appointment of Mr Hart by the Lord Chancellor. This was because those members of the elite pool who were personally known to the Lord Chancellor were, on the unchallenged evidence, reduced to a single man. However many other persons there may have been who were potential candidates, whatever the proportions of men and women or racial groups in the pool, the requirement excluded the lot of them, except Mr Hart. Plainly it can have had no *disproportionate* effect on the different groupings within the pool.

This approach appears at odds with that of Lord Nicholls in *Barry* in which he accepted (see above) that precisely *because* 'the smaller the disadvantaged group in proportionate terms, the narrower will be the differential . . . A better guide will often be found in expressing the proportions in the disadvantaged group as a ratio of each other.' If it were to be asked, as it would now be under the RRA, the RB Regs or the SO Regs, whether a requirement to be personally known to the appointer 'puts or would put persons' of a claimant's relevant group 'at a particular disadvantage when compared with other persons' it may be that the answer would differ from that provided by the Court of Appeal in the questionable *Coker v Osamor* decision.

A significant difficulty may arise in establishing disparate in cases of multiple discrimination, mentioned in Chapter 1. If, for example, a woman finds herself disadvantaged by a provision, criterion or practice because she is not only female but is also, for example, Muslim and of Middle Eastern origin (as might be the case in the context of a clothing or appearance policy prohibiting the wearing of a veil, or trousers), she might only be able to establish that women of her specific group (ie, Middle Eastern Muslim women, or possibly Muslim women) would be substantially less likely to be able to comply with that rule, or be placed at a considerable disadvantage by it. If the claimant is forced to atomise herself to be *either* female (for the purposes of an SDA claim), *or* Middle Eastern (for the purposes of an RRA claim), *or* Muslim (for the purposes of an RRA claim), she may find herself quite unable to prove *collective* disparate impact as is required in order to succeed in an indirect discrimination claim. The difficulties posed by multiple discrimination are referred to in the passage below which comments upon US case law in the area. They are not significantly ameliorated by the new discrimination legislation. Whereas the hypothetical claimant can now, at least, challenge discrimination connected with her religious status under the RB Regs (this not having been previously possible—see further Chapter 7), she cannot now, any more than she could before, amalgamate the legislative provisions and be protected as a distinct, multi-faceted individual disadvantaged by virtue of her position within a number of interconnecting groups.

Detriment/Disadvantage

The original test for indirect discrimination asks whether the claimant (together with others of his or her sex or race-based group) 'can comply' with the requirement or condition imposed by the employer (and, further, whether the inability to comply disadvantages the claimant). As has been mentioned above, it has been replaced with the question whether (SDA) the provision, criterion or practice is to the claimant's detriment or (RRA, SO and RB Regs) whether it puts the claimant at a disadvantage. The requirement is made easier to fulfil, as we shall see below. But it remains the case that the claimant must be individually affected by a disparately impacting practice and that such practices cannot be challenged in the abstract. It is questionable whether this is consistent with the definition of indirect discrimination set out in the new Directives.

L Lustgarten, 'The New Meaning of Discrimination' [1978] *Public Law* 178, 190–3, footnotes omitted

s.1(1)(b)'s 'detriment' requirement presents two practical hindrances to the effectiveness of the Act that are potentially extremely serious. Virtually every suit under the American civil rights laws is brought as a class action. This procedural device enables a litigant whose claims are typical of numerous other persons to represent their interests in court. If he prevails, remedial action, including substantial compensation, may be granted to all members of the class. Class action procedure was designed and first used in commercial and corporate litigation, but it proved ideal for plaintiffs in discrimination cases, all of whom were suffering identical disabilities. Once the court approves the class action the suit goes forward on behalf of the plaintiff 'and all those similarly situated.' It is therefore not uncommon for the plaintiff to fail to establish his own case, whilst proving discrimination against the class.[72] The court may then order remedial action against the discriminatory practices, even if the named plaintiff obtains no relief.

The absence of any such procedure in Britain, coupled with the 'detriment' clause, may seriously handicap enforcement of the law. Whether even an unmistakably discriminatory practice is held illegal will depend on the more or less fortuitous occurrence that a given individual has the interest, tenacity and courage to assert his rights. He may also require an unusual degree of asceticism. An employer worried about the cost or other problems that may attend changing an entrenched practice might find it politic to make a particularly good settlement offer to the occasional black complainant. What would seem good fortune to the latter would for the employer be far cheaper than compliance with the law. This 'resist and withdraw' tactic was quite common in early American employment litigation until the courts made clear that such arrangements would not block their scrutiny of the employer's practices. But under the present statute, once the complainant withdrew his case, the tribunal would lose jurisdiction to correct the illegality of the employment practice, regardless of how severely it affected others.

Conversely if a complainant is clearly unsuitable for the position that is the subject of the claimed discrimination, the 'detriment' provision would seem to preclude further inquiry. This restriction, and the demonstrated reluctance of victims of overt discrimination in this country to seek redress, compounded by the fact that for certain kinds of jobs, notably white collar and supervisory posts, there are likely to be relatively few black applicants in the near future, may effectively insulate the discriminatory practices of many firms from correction by the law. It seems wrong that so much of the law's effectiveness should depend on the personal characteristics and qualifications of individuals . . . it seems likely that in numbers and in importance, private complaints will be the primary means of implementing the Act. It is

---

[72] See discussion of *Coker & Osamor v Lord Chancellor* [2002] ICR 321 in Ch 4. The tribunal's finding that Osamor was not qualified for the appointment and that she had not, therefore, suffered any detriment, meant that the racially discriminatory nature of the Lord Chancellor's appointment could not be challenged in that case.

therefore essential that the 'detriment' requirement does not block its central artery. Even if the complainant stays the course, an additional practical problem concerning proof of 'detriment' is that he will often be unable to establish the extent of his injury. He may, for example, have been one of 15 applicants; and whilst indirect discrimination caused him not to be hired or even short-listed, some of his competitors were in fact equally qualified or indeed preferable on legitimate grounds. If the 'detriment' clause is interpreted to require that the complainant prove that his application would have succeeded in the absence of discrimination, the Act will be eviscerated, for this will often be untrue.

These compelling practical objections apart, the imposition of such a requirement would be based on a fundamental misconception of the purpose of anti-discrimination legislation. It is not intended to ensure that a non-white (or woman) gets the job or promotion he or she wants; it insists only that the applicant be fairly considered. The new understanding of discrimination broadens the category of what will be regarded as 'unfair' criteria and practices, but—here the rejection of a pure 'fair share' approach is explicit—its focus still centres on the process of decision, not the ultimate result. Thus the minority person suffers injury, and the statute is transgressed, whenever the process of decision is tainted by discrimination, not only when he would obviously have succeeded had he been white. Practicality and principle conjoin to urge that 'detriment' be interpreted to mean simply that the process of hiring, promotion or whatever has been in any degree affected by the existence of the challenged requirement or condition.[73]

The question of the relative abilities of the claimant's group and other groups to comply with the requirement or condition has also been replaced with a question as the relative detriment (SDA) or disadvantage (RRA, SO and RB Regs) accruing to that group by virtue of the disputed provision, criterion or practice.

The ability of the group to comply appears to be measured for the most part by statistical or other evidence of actual compliance, this having been discussed above. The approach to be taken to the possibility of compliance by the individual claimant was established by EAT in *Price v Civil Service Commission*. This case arose under the SDA, and the question of 'can comply' related to the group rather than the individual plaintiff (compliance by the latter being clearly impossible on the facts). The approach taken in *Price* was, however, subsequently applied by the House of Lords in *Mandla v Dowell Lee* [1983] 2 AC 548 vis-à-vis the individual plaintiff, as well as his group. That case, which arose under the RRA, is considered further below.

The claim in *Price* was brought by a 35-year-old woman who challenged a maximum age limit of 28 imposed in relation to a Civil Service post. She argued that the age limit discriminated indirectly against women, many women being engaged in child bearing in their later twenties. Her claim was dismissed by a tribunal on the ground that the words 'can comply' had to be interpreted strictly and, given that it was theoretically possible for any woman between 17½ and 28 to apply, the proportion who were able to do so was not considerably smaller than the proportion of men also so able. Ms Price appealed to EAT.

Price v Civil Service Commission [1978] ICR 212

Phillips J:

. . . In one sense it can be said that any female applicant can comply with the condition. She is not obliged to marry, or to have children, or to mind children; she may find somebody to

---

[73] *Cf* the decision of NICA in *Gill v Northern Ireland Council for Ethnic Minorities* [2002] IRLR 74 in which it ruled that a person denied appointment could not calim to be a victim of less favourable treatment unless he or she was a better candidate than the appointee. This is almost certainly wrong.

look after them, and as a last resort she may put them into care. In this sense . . . any female applicant can comply with the condition. Such a construction appears to us to be wholly out of sympathy with the spirit and intent of the 1975 Act. Further, it should be repeated that compliance with sub-para (i) is only a preliminary step, which does not lead to a finding that an act is one of discrimination unless the person acting fails to show that it is justifiable. 'Can' is . . . a word with many shades of meaning, and we are satisfied that it should not be too narrowly, or too broadly, construed in its context in s 1(1)(b)(i). It should not be said that a person 'can' do something merely because it is theoretically possible for him to do so: it is necessary to see whether he can do so in practice. Applying this approach to the circumstances of this case, it is relevant in determining whether women can comply with the condition to take into account the current usual behaviour of women in this respect, as observed in practice, putting on one side behaviour and responses which are unusual or extreme.

Knowledge and experience suggest that a considerable number of women between the mid-twenties and the mid-thirties are engaged in bearing children and in minding children, and that while many find it possible to take up employment many others, while desiring to do so, find it impossible, and that many of the latter as their children get older find that they can follow their wish and seek employment. This knowledge and experience is confirmed by some of the statistical evidence produced . . . This demonstrates clearly that the economic activity of women with at least one A level falls off markedly about the age of 23, reaching a bottom at about the age of 33 when it climbs gradually to a plateau at about 45.

Basing ourselves on this and other evidence, we should have no hesitation in concluding that our own knowledge and experience is confirmed, and that it is safe to say that the condition is one which it is in practice harder for women to comply with than it is for men. We should be inclined to go further and say that there are undoubtedly women of whom it may be properly said in the terms of s1(1)(b)(i) that they 'cannot' comply with the condition, because they are women; that is to say because of their involvement with their children.

J Lewis 'Refusing to Allow Job Sharing' (1989) 18 *Industrial Law Journal* 244, 246–7, footnotes omitted

In *Holmes* very little evidence was needed to satisfy the EAT that the parental responsibilities of a single mother prevented her complying with a requirement of full-time work. In *Clymo*, by contrast, there were adequate child-minding facilities which the complainant could easily afford. Thus, the EAT concluded, Ms. Clymo's failure to comply was due to a mere 'personal preference' to bring up her own children. . . . While the EAT set out a workable test of ability to comply, their application of the test was inept. The EAT asserted that ultimately a question of reasonableness was involved. It must be ascertained whether Ms. Clymo could comply 'in practice,' taking into account 'the current usual behaviour of women in this respect' (see *Price v Civil Service Commission*). The need to consider social trends was thus recognised. The dominant social ideology of this country still stresses the importance of bringing up one's own children and, as recognised in Holmes, the burden still tends to fall on the mother. Of course many would prefer to take advantage of child care facilities rather than give up employment altogether. However job sharing opens the possibility of combining a continued career with personal care of one's own children. Indeed this was the motivation for Ms. Clymo's claim. In the face of this the EAT not only dismissed the pressure and influence of the dominant social ideology as mere 'personal preference,' but also dogmatically denied that job sharing allows any new choice:

A reasonable and responsible management decision has been reached and it seems clear in trying to fit society into the framework of the statute and the statute into our society that in every employment ladder from the lowliest to the highest there will come a stage at which a woman who has family responsibilities must make a choice.

Thus the employer's autonomy is again prioritised. It is mothers who must choose and not employers who must justify the denial of an adequate choice.

Readers may recall Mr Justice Wood's remarks, extracted above, on the inherently full-time nature of high status jobs. EAT further ruled in *Clymo* that there was no 'firm evidence' that the proportion of qualified women librarians who can work full-time was considerably smaller than the proportion of qualified male librarians (although '[t]here was evidence . . . that considerably fewer qualified women remained in the library service than fully qualified men. This was attributed to the child minding responsibilities of women').

The approach taken by the courts to indirect discrimination cases has improved, the standards of justification (discussed below) having tightened and the distinction drawn by the tribunal and EAT in *Clymo* between job-related 'requirements' and features regarded as part of the 'very nature' of the job having been disapproved of by the Court of Appeal in *Allonby*. But the attitude of the tribunal and EAT towards the question of whether the claimant could comply with the full-time work requirement has persisted, with women who relied on family reasons to claim that they were unable to comply with hours-related work requirements having become subject to increasingly close scrutiny prior to the amendment of the SDA in July 2001.[74]

The replacement of the 'can comply' test by the question whether the claimant (as a member of a group defined by sex, race, sexual orientation, etc) has suffered detriment or disadvantage by reason of the application of the provision, criterion or practice is to be welcomed. In cases such as the above, a woman who wishes to work reduced hours in order to accommodate her caring responsibilities will suffer a detriment is she is not permitted to do so (where, for example, this means that she has to buy in expensive childcare). What will be interesting is to see how tribunals handle the question whether 'detriment' or 'disadvantage' will be satisfied in a case in which the claimant can point to no economic loss, but rather to a denial of choice. The application of the question whether the claimant suffered a detriment by reason of discrimination is further considered in Chapter 4. The approach is not beyond criticism but the removal of the compliance test is certainly a positive step.

Justification—the Domestic Approach

The final hurdle at which an indirect discrimination claim can fall is that of justification. By contrast with the other elements discussed above, it is for the alleged discriminator to satisfy the tribunal on this matter. The original definition of indirect discrimination does not offer any guidance on the approach to be taken to justifiability, save that the justification must be 'irrespective of' the sex, race, etc, of the person to whom it is applied (by contrast, the amended RRA and the SO and RB Regs provide that the discriminator can justify the impugned provision, criterion or practice is a 'proportionate means of achieving a legitimate aim').[75] Yet the potential of a prohibition on indirect discrimination to challenge entrenched practices which serve to disadvantage groups defined by race, sex, etc, turns on how rigorous is the approach to justification.

We saw in *Griggs* that the US Supreme Court adopted 'business necessity' as the 'touchstone' of justifiability. More recently, in *Wards Cove Packing Co. v Atonio*, 490 US 642

---

[74] See, eg, *Zurich Insurance Co v Gulson* [1998] IRLR 118.
[75] This will be the test under the SDA when it is amended to comply with Council Directive 2002/73/EC (October 2005) in relation to employment and (by December 2007) to comply with Council Directive 2004/113/EC in relation to access to goods and services.

(1989), a less liberal Supreme Court set the standard rather lower than that of 'business necessity.' According to Justice White (who carried a bare majority of the Court):

the dispositive issue is whether a challenged practice serves, in a significant way, the legitimate employment goals of the employer . . . The touchstone of this inquiry is a reasoned review of the employer's justification for his use of the challenged practice. A mere insubstantial justification in this regard will not suffice, because such a low standard of review would permit discrimination to be practiced through the use of spurious, seemingly neutral employment practices. At the same time, though, there is no requirement that the challenged practice be 'essential' or 'indispensable' to the employer's business for it to pass muster: this degree of scrutiny would be almost impossible for most employers to meet, and would result in [inter alia, the imposition of racial quotas].[76]

Lustgarten, 193, footnotes omitted

Once the complainant establishes discrimination, it is open to the employer—who carries the burden of proof—to demonstrate that the practice is 'justifiable.' In a purely negative sense, this is perhaps the most important single term in the Act, for an interpretation that gave extensive deference to customary employment practices would reduce it to insignificance. It is a critical failing of the statute that it articulates no standards to direct tribunals called upon to make this judgment.

One may begin the task of interpretation by asking why this provision is in the statute. Put another way, why does it not simply proscribe any practice proven to be disadvantageous to minorities? The explanation is grounded in policy: the value of preventing the exclusion of non-whites cannot always be paramount. But in the scheme of what, for Britain, is an innovative and comprehensive enactment, this can be true for only the most compelling reasons, which may be roughly defined as the safe and efficient operation of a business. Thus no anti-discrimination law requires an employer to hire unqualified persons, but effective legislation does insist that the criteria governing qualifications truly measure competence, and do not simply express prejudice, preconception or unthinking custom.

If this analysis is correct, much of the extended Standing Committee debate over whether 'justifiable' should have been replaced by 'necessary' was misconceived, a point nicely illustrated by the confusion of the Under-Secretary for Employment, who managed to define the former by reference to the latter. He offered two main arguments against the proposed amendment. He defined necessary to mean something like 'inescapable'—a somewhat strained interpretation—and thus contended that it was too restrictive. Conversely those who favoured the substitution gave an unduly latitudinarian meaning to 'justifiable,' taking it to denote any explanation not patently specious. The Minister's second point was more cogent. He thought 'justifiable' connoted a more objective test than 'necessary.' Both sides in the debate seemed to share the same ends, whilst having conflicting understandings of each other's formulations, . . . the idea of job-relatedness first articulated in *Griggs* is not to be found in the statute; it is understood as *inherent* in the concept of discrimination itself. Bearing in mind that Britain has received the *Griggs* concept of discrimination whilst setting out in a clearer and more systematic manner the sequence in which the reviewing body must make particular legal judgments, it seems appropriate that the justifiability test should require the employer to prove that the practice in question is job-related. This interpretation gives effect to the explanation of the new concept of discrimination offered in the White Paper, which used the phrase 'substantially related to job performance' without acknowledging its origin in Griggs. It also accords quite strongly with the sense, if not the

[76] Civil Rights Act 1991.

precise language, of what both sides in the Standing Committee discussions were attempting in their disparate fashions to convey.

Job-relatedness—'a manifest relationship to the employment in question'—means above all that the requirements of the job itself, not the expressed or assumed preferences of customers or other employees must prove the guidelines. Thus it is no justification of a discriminatory practice to argue that it was agreed with trade union representatives, or that its elimination and the employment of non-whites might cause withdrawal of business, strikes or other labour trouble, or would necessitate expenditure on developing new employment criteria. Of course it is more convenient and cheaper to continue existing practices, or to pander to the prejudice of employees or customers, but acquiescence in the discriminatory status quo is precisely what laws against discrimination are designed to disturb. Though these consequences may well ensue, they are precisely the sort of considerations the statute subordinates to achieving equality of opportunity.

Only requirements inherent in the job may be regarded as justifiable. This seemingly abstract concept is in fact quite realistic, for it forces employers at first instance and then tribunals to make a practical appraisal of job content, cocking a sceptical eye at traditional restrictions and the more recent, albeit limited, vogue for credentials and testing. The result will surely be to eliminate many practices that have excluded able people and have been carried on primarily through habit and neglect. In numerical terms, more whites than non-whites will be the gainers. An effective anti-discrimination law is a powerful force for what is truly 'rationalisation' of industry—the clearing away of mythologies surrounding employment practices, and their replacement by prerequisites that demonstrably help select the most competent people. . . .

The justification provision is an integral part of the compromise of principle embodied in the Act. Had an unalloyed 'fair share' approach been taken, the mere under-representation of minorities would have been proscribed. The reason for their disadvantage would have been irrelevant. However, the statute also accepts that industrial efficiency (and fair treatment of qualified whites) are values which should not be trampled in the pursuit of racial equality. The tension between the two competing considerations can be satisfactorily resolved by a rigorous and sceptical approach towards efforts at justification. This would require firm evidence that the challenged practice actually enhanced industrial safety or efficiency. This sort of scrutiny would ensure the maximum scope for both industrial efficiency and racial equality, and achieve the greatest possible reconciliation between them where they conflict.

Notwithstanding Lustgarten's early commentary, the test of justification turned out to be rather less than rigorous. His discussion was concerned with the RRA but the SDA, whose approach to indirect discrimination is identical, has been in place for slightly longer. (Northern Ireland's fair employment regime has only prohibited indirect discrimination since 1989.) But since the mid-1970s, and prior to any rulings being made expressly in the light of EU law and its impact, in particular, on the SDA, the approach of the courts to justifiability under the SDA and RRA appeared to diverge.

In *Steel v Union of Post Office Workers*, for example, EAT considered, as a case arising under s.1(1)(b) SDA, a complaint concerning the application by the Post Office of what should have been regarded as a directly discriminatory seniority requirement in allotting 'walks' (women having, until 1975, been barred from gaining such seniority). EAT placed a heavy burden on the employer to justify disparately impacting practices, ruling (*per* Phillips J) that: 'a practice which would otherwise be discriminatory . . . is not to be licensed unless . . . its discriminatory effect is justified by the need, not the convenience, of the business or enterprise.' In *Panesar v Nestle Co Ltd* [1980] ICR 144, by contrast, the Court of

Appeal accepted the employer's argument that a 'no beards' rule which excluded Sikhs from employment was justifiable under s.1(1)(b)(ii) of the RRA on grounds of hygiene, despite the fact that the employer did not prohibit the wearing of 'moustaches, whiskers and sideburns'. According to Lord Denning MR:

> ... The scientific evidence was all in support of the practice which the Nestle company had adopted in their factory at Hayes as a matter of pure hygiene. It had nothing to do with the colour of the individual or his religious beliefs. It applied to all men of all races ... the industrial tribunal held that the rule about the wearing of beards was justifiable ... It seems to me that that finding was essentially one of fact in the circumstances of the case, against which there is no appeal except on a point of law.

The approach to justification in this case was extraordinarily lax, the tribunal and the Court of Appeal appearing to ask simply whether the alleged discriminator had been improperly motivated. It is hard to see how beards could be considered unhygienic *per se*, while other forms of facial hair were viewed as acceptable even if uncovered.[77]

In the infamous *Ojutiku* case the Court of Appeal once again ruled that the test for justification under the RRA did not, contrary to EAT in *Steel*, require that the employer prove that the requirement is necessary for the good of his business.

Ojutiku and Oburoni v Manpower Services Commission [1982] ICR 661

Eveleigh LJ:

> ... I am very hesitant to suggest another expression for that which is used in the statute, for fear that it will be picked up and quoted in other cases and then built upon thereafter, with the result that at the end of the day there is a danger of us all departing far from the meaning of the word in the statute. For myself, it would be enough simply to ask myself: is it justifiable? But if I have to give some explanation of my understanding of that word, I would turn to a dictionary definition which says 'to adduce adequate grounds for'; and it seems to me that if a person produces reasons for doing something, which would be acceptable to right-thinking people as sound and tolerable reasons for so doing, then he has justified his conduct.

At issue in *Ojutiku* was a requirement that candidates for student bursaries had managerial experience, a requirement which had a disproportionately exclusionary impact on West African applicants. Notwithstanding the evidence that the applicants' lack of experience was the result of direct discrimination on the part of would-be employers, the Court of Appeal accepted that the requirement was justified:

Eveleigh LJ:

> What the respondents have to justify is their own conduct, not that of other people. If it is justifiable to require a qualification, although it is discriminatory in the indirect sense, in my opinion it could not alter the position if the qualification were made impossible of attainment by the act of another. The latter's discrimination would be in no way the responsibility of the respondents; it would of course be deplorable, but that is another matter. Many people are without the necessary qualifications for certain pursuits—indeed, most of us are

---

[77] See also *Kang v R F Brookes Ltd* 40 n 69 above in which it was regarded as justifiable not to permit a woman wearing a Sikh bracelet to work on a sensitive part of the food production line—hygiene—no apparent thought given to covering the offending item.

without the necessary qualifications for something or another. Some lack them through their own fault; some through misfortune or lack of opportunity, but that is life; and if an employer imposed a similar qualification to that imposed in this case by the Commission, one could not expect him to waive it in the case of a person who lacked the qualification through misfortune, even if that misfortune were to be discrimination against him by another.

Kerr LJ:

. . . In *Steel* . . . [EAT] . . . put something of a gloss on the word 'justifiable' by suggesting that it was equivalent, or close to having the same meaning as 'necessary'. But that gloss was rightly shaded, to put it no higher, by another decision of [EAT] in *Singh v Rowntree MacKintosh Ltd,* [1979] IRLR 199 . . . in which the approach was in effect that 'justifiable' means 'reasonably necessary in all the circumstances' . . . I decline to put any gloss on the word 'justifiable,' which is a perfectly easily understandable ordinary word, except that I would say that it clearly applies a lower standard than the word 'necessary' . . .

Problems of consistency began to appear in the wake of the ECJ's decision in *Bilka-Kaufhaus*, Case C–170/84 [1986] ECR 1607, in which that Court, in the context of an Article 141 claim, ruled that disparately impacting pay practices were permissible only where they 'correspond to a real need on the part of the undertaking, are appropriate with a view to achieving the objectives pursued and are necessary to that end.'

The approach of the ECJ was adopted, in the context of the EqPA, by the House of Lords in *Rainey v Greater Glasgow Health Board* [1987] 1 AC 224, further discussed in chapter 10.[78] Neither *Bilka-Kaufhaus* nor *Rainey* were decisions on the meaning of s.1(1)(b)(iii) of the SDA, much less on the RRA or the FEA (as it then was). But it was accepted by the Court of Appeal in *Shields v Coomes* [1978] ICR 1159, discussed in Chapter 6) that the SDA and the EqPA should be interpreted 'as far as possible . . . so as to form a harmonious code.'[79] In *Rainey*, Lord Keith of Kinkel for the House of Lords stated that there was no 'material difference in principle' between indirect discrimination under the EqPA and SDA.

The House of Lords decision in *Hampson v Department of Education and Science* is discussed in Chapter 4. Their Lordships overturned the decision of the Court of Appeal on another point. But they expressly refrained from dealing with the issue of justifiability. The Court of Appeal had found against the Department on the justification issue after considering the effect of the decisions in *Bilka-Kaufhaus* and *Rainey*, Balcombe LJ (for the Court) categorising the approaches of Eveleigh and Kerr LJJ in *Ojutiku* as of 'little help,' neither in his view indicating 'what tests should be applied' in reaching the 'value judgment' inherent in the words '[j]ustifiable' and 'justify.'

Hampson v Department of Education and Science |1989| ICR 179

Balcombe LJ:

whatever test is to be applied it is an objective one: it is not sufficient for the employer to establish that he considered his reasons adequate. However I do derive considerable assistance from the judgment of Stephenson LJ [who] referred to:

---

[78] Their Lordships accepted that justification could be established by reference to 'administrative efficiency' as well as economic reasons.

[79] Citing Phillips J in *Steel* above.

... the comments, which I regard as sound, ... given by Phillips J in *Steel v Union of Post Office Workers* ... What Phillips J there said is valuable as rejecting justification by convenience and requiring the party applying the discriminatory condition to prove it to be justifiable in all the circumstances on balancing its discriminatory effect against the discriminator's need for it. But that need is what is reasonably needed by the party who applies the condition ...

In my judgment 'justifiable' requires an objective balance between the discriminatory effect of the condition and the reasonable needs of the party who applies the condition. This construction is supported by the recent decision of the House of Lords in *Rainey* ... The House of Lords held, applying the decision of the European Court in *Bilka-Kaufhaus* ... that to justify a material difference under s 1(3) of the [EqPA], the employer had to show a real need on the part of the undertaking, objectively justified, although that need was not confined to economic grounds; it might, for instance, include administrative efficiency in a concern not engaged in commerce or business. Clearly it may, as in the present case, be possible to justify by reference to grounds other than economic or administrative efficiency. ...

Nourse LJ agreed with Balcombe LJ that the best interpretation which could be put on the authorities was that the test: 'requires an objective balance to be struck between the discriminatory effect of the requirement or condition and the reasonable needs of the person who applies it. If, and only if, its discriminatory effect can be objectively justified by those needs will the requirement or condition be "justifiable" within s.1(1)(b)(ii) of the [RRA].'

The approach taken by the Court of Appeal in *Hampson* was not endorsed by the House of Lords in that case. While their Lordships expressly refrained from considering the justification issue, the parties not having argued it before them, Lord Lowry did remark that 'what was said in the Court of Appeal [in *Ojutiku* on the issue of justification] seems to me to merit the closest attention.' But in *Webb v EMO* [1993] ICR 175 the House of Lords approved the approach taken by Balcombe LJ for the Court of Appeal in *Hampson*.

Balcombe LJ's approach did mark a significant improvement over that taken in *Ojutiku*. Many practices which serve disproportionately to exclude women and ethnic minorities from the workforce have been practised by many employers over many years (preference for full-time employees and for those who can work 'flexibly' to suit the employer,[80] age and experience stipulations, IQ testing,[81] clothing and appearance rules)[82] and are therefore, of their very nature, capable of being explained in a manner 'acceptable to right-thinking people as sound and tolerable.' The same practices, if scrutinised in the light of their impact on those excluded by them, may appear in a different light.[83]

The ECJ in *Bilka-Kaufhaus* framed the test of 'objective justification' (by which it required that indirect sex discrimination be justified) in terms of necessity (disparately impacting practices being justifiable only where they 'correspond to a real *need* on the part of the undertaking, are appropriate with a view to achieving the objectives pursued and are *necessary* to that end'). The test established by the Court of Appeal in *Hampson* fell short

---

[80] This requires childlessness or the presence of a (usually female) support at home.

[81] Such tests are frequently culturally skewed—see *Griggs*, above.

[82] Which may impact particularly on those bound by religious obligations concerning appearance which are (see Chapter 7), race-related.

[83] This was applied by the Northern Ireland Court of Appeal in *Kennedy v Gallagher Ltd* (discussed in FEC *Review of the Fair Employment Act* (1997), para 1.22): 'in measuring the reasonable needs of the employer significant weight should be given to the fact that the majority of the workforce suffered no detriment by reason of the requirement.'

of this, replacing a requirement for business necessity with a demand for balance between the *reasonable* needs of the employer[84] and the discriminatory impact of the requirements or conditions adopted. It is likely, even under the test as it was established in *Bilka-Kaufhaus*, that the selection of the ends necessary to an undertaking would be treated as a matter in respect of which employers should be accorded a significant degree of autonomy. In this sense, the ends *necessary* to the undertaking might be interpreted as those ends which an employer could reasonably regard as necessary. By contrast, where the pursuit of those ends has a disproportionately negative impact on women, ethnic minorities, etc., the means chosen should be subjected to rigorous scrutiny.[85] Immediately below I consider the development of the test for justification in EU law before returning to consider the compatibility of the domestic approach with that of the ECJ.

Justification in EU Law

Since the decision in *Bilka-Kaufhaus* there have been a number of very significant ECJ decisions on the justification of indirect sex discrimination.

Rinner-Kühn v FWW Spezial-Gebaudereinigung GmbH Case C–171/88 [1989] ECR 2743

This claim concerned a part-time worker who challenged her employer's refusal to pay her sick-pay. National law required (and provided for the reimbursement to the employer of) such payment only for those working more than 10 hours a week. Having decided that sick pay was 'pay' within Article 141 (see above) and that its denial to part-timers amounted, prima facie, to indirect discrimination against women, the ECJ continued:

Judgment:

In the course of the procedure, the German Government stated [by way of justification]. . . that workers whose period of work amounted to less than 10 hours a week or 45 hours a month were not as integrated in, or as dependent on, the undertaking employing them as other workers.

It should, however, be stated that those considerations, in so far as they are only generalizations about certain categories of workers, do not enable criteria which are both objective and unrelated to any discrimination on grounds of sex to be identified. However, if the Member State can show that the means chosen meet a necessary aim of its social policy and that they are suitable and requisite for attaining that aim, the mere fact that the provision affects a much greater number of female workers than male workers cannot be regarded as constituting an infringement of Article [141].

Handels-og Kontorfunktionaerernes Forbund I Danmark v Dansk Arbejdsgiverforening (acting for Danfoss) Case C–109/88 [1989] ECR 3199

The claimant's challenge was, inter alia, to a practice whereby individual pay was set according to factors including adaptability, training and seniority, reliance on these factors serving to disadvantage women by comparison with men.

---

[84] In this the decision in *Hampson* echoed that of Browne-Wilkinson J (as he then was) in *Jenkins v Kingsgate (No.2)* [1981] ICR 715.

[85] Some support for this can be found in the approach taken by the ECJ in relation to social policy of member states and the means used to pursue it, see overleaf.

Judgment:

The employer may . . . justify the remuneration of [adaptability to variable hours and vary-ing places of work] by showing it is of importance for the performance of specific tasks entrusted to the employee.

In the second place, as regards the criterion of training, it is not excluded that it may work to the disadvantage of women in so far as they have had less opportunity than men for training or have taken less advantage of such opportunity. Nevertheless . . . the employer may justify remuneration of special training by showing that it is of importance for the performance of specific tasks entrusted to the employee.

In this, the *Danfoss* case, the ECJ was prepared to accept that the reward of seniority, even where it operated so as to disadvantage women: 'length of service goes hand in hand with experience and since experience generally enables the employee to perform his duties better, the employer is free to reward it without having to establish the importance it has in the performance of specific tasks entrusted to the employee.' This approach was rapidly revised in *Nimz v Freie*, in which the challenge related precisely to the reward of service where this served to disadvantage part-time workers and, accordingly, women.

Nimz v Freie und Hanse-Stadt Hamburg Case C–184/89 [1991] ECR I–297

The City of Hamburg claimed during the procedure that full-time employees or those who work for three-quarters of normal working time acquire more quickly than others the abil-ities and skills relating to their particular job. The German Government also relied on their more extensive experience.

Judgment:

It should, however, be stated that such considerations, in so far as they are no more than generalizations about certain categories of workers, do not make it possible to identify criteria which are both objective and unrelated to any discrimination on grounds of sex [citing *Rinner-Kühn*]. Although experience goes hand in hand with length of service, and experience enables the worker in principle to improve performance of the tasks allotted to him, the objectivity of such a criterion depends on all the circumstances in a particular case, and in particular on the relationship between the nature of the work performed and the experience gained from the performance of that work upon completion of a certain number of working hours . . .

Bilka-Kaufhaus concerned discrimination by employers. In cases where the discrimination is practised by the state against categories of persons (such as part-time workers), 'some-what broader considerations apply'[86] and the ECJ accepted in *Rinner-Kühn* that such discrimination may be justifiable where they 'meet a necessary aim of [a Member State's] social policy and that they are suitable and requisite for attaining that aim.' On the other hand, the ECJ ruled, in that case, that the claim that part-timers were excluded from sick-pay entitlement because they were less integrated into the workforce and therefore less in need of income during illness, was not even potentially capable of justifying the established discrimination.

In *Enderby v Frenchay* Case C–127/92 [1993] ECR I–5535 the Court ruled that pay disparities could not be justified by reference to different pay structures (there collective

---

[86] Lord Keith in *R v Secretary of State for Employment ex p EOC* [1995] 1 AC 1 discussing *Rinner-Kühn* (above).

bargaining arrangements) applicable to the male and female jobs in respect of which a comparison was made. According to the ECJ:

> the fact that the respective rates of pay of [female and male jobs of equal value] were arrived at by collective bargaining processes which, although carried out by the same parties, are distinct, and, taken separately, have in themselves no discriminatory effect, is not sufficient objective justification for the difference in pay between those two jobs . . .
>
> If . . . the national court has been able to determine precisely what proportion of the increase in pay is attributable to market forces, it must necessarily accept that the pay differential is objectively justified to the extent of that proportion . . . If that is not the case, it is for the national court to assess whether the role of market forces in determining the rate of pay was sufficiently significant to provide objective justification for part or all of the difference.

More recently, in *Jørgensen v Foreningen af Speciallæger, Sygesikringens Forhandlingsudvalg* Case C–226/98 [2000] ECR I–02447, the ECJ ruled that 'budgetary considerations cannot in themselves justify discrimination on grounds of sex.' This approach, the ECJ explains, is necessary to avoid the varying application of the principle of equal treatment with the public finances of individual Member States. This approach was applied again in *Steinicke v Bundesanstalt für Arbeit* Case C–77/02 [2003] ECR I–09027 and in *Kutz-Bauer* in which the ECJ ruled that a scheme which encouraged part-time work by those not yet entitled to a state pension (which was provided to the majority of women at 60, and the majority of men at 65) breached the Equal Treatment Directive.

Kutz-Bauer v Freie und Hansestadt Hamburg Case C–187/00 [2003] ECR I–02741

Judgment:

The German Government submits that one of the aims pursued by a scheme such as the one at issue in the main proceedings is to combat unemployment by offering the maximum incentives for workers who are not yet eligible to retire to do so and thus making posts available. To allow a worker who has already acquired entitlement to a retirement pension at the full rate to benefit from the scheme of part-time work for older employees implies, first, that a post which the scheme intends to allocate to an unemployed person would continue to be occupied and, second, that the social security scheme would bear the additional costs, which would divert certain resources from other objectives.

As regards the argument which the German Government derives from the encouragement of recruitment, it is for the Member States to choose the measures capable of achieving the aims which they pursue in employment matters. The Court has recognised that the Member States have a broad margin of discretion in exercising that power (see *Seymour-Smith and Perez*, paragraph 74).

Furthermore, as the Court stated at paragraph 71 of its judgment in *Seymour-Smith and Perez*, it cannot be disputed that the encouragement of recruitment constitutes a legitimate aim of social policy [but] . . . mere generalisations concerning the capacity of a specific measure to encourage recruitment are not enough to show that the aim of the disputed provisions is unrelated to any discrimination based on sex or to provide evidence on the basis of which it could reasonably be considered that the means chosen are or could be suitable for achieving that aim.

As regards the German Government's argument concerning the additional burden associated with allowing female workers to take advantage of the scheme at issue in the main proceedings even where they have acquired entitlement to a retirement pension at the full rate, the Court observes that although budgetary considerations may underlie a Member State's choice of social policy and influence the nature or scope of the social protection measures which it wishes to adopt, they do not in themselves constitute an aim pursued by that policy and cannot therefore justify discrimination against one of the sexes . . .

Nor can the City of Hamburg, whether as a public authority or as an employer, justify discrimination arising from a scheme of part-time work for older employees solely because avoidance of such discrimination would involve increased costs . . .

It is therefore for the City of Hamburg to prove to the national court that the difference in treatment arising from the scheme of part-time work for older employees at issue in the main proceedings is justified by objective reasons unrelated to any discrimination on grounds of sex.

Reconciling EU and Domestic Law

The application of the justification test by the domestic courts has not always been in harmony with that of the ECJ. For a time, the domestic courts appeared to demand more, rather than less, by way of justification for indirect discrimination by central government, as distinct from employers.[87] In *R v Secretary of State for Education, ex parte Schaffter* [1987] IRLR 53, in which the High Court ruled that the practice of restricting additional lone-parent student 'hardship grants' to those who had been married breached the Equal Treatment Directive because of its disparate impact on women, the Secretary of State had failed even to put forward a purported justification. But in *R v Secretary of State for Employment ex parte EOC*, in which the House of Lords struck down as contrary to Article 141 the application of differential qualifying periods in respect of unfair dismissal protection and redundancy payments to full-time and part-time workers, the justification put forward by the Secretary of State was dismissed by their Lordships.

R v Secretary of State for Employment ex parte Equal Opportunities Commission [1995] 1 AC 1

Lord Keith (for the Court):

In the *Bilka-Kaufhaus* case the European Court said . . . 'It is for the national court, which has sole jurisdiction to make findings of fact, to determine whether and to what extent the grounds put forward by an employer to explain the adoption of a pay practice which applies independently of a worker's sex but in fact affects more women than men may be regarded as objectively justified on economic grounds. If the national court finds that the measures chosen by *Bilka* correspond to a real need on the part of the undertaking, are appropriate with a view to achieving the objectives pursued and are necessary to that end, the fact that the measures affect a far greater number of women than men is not sufficient to show that they constitute an infringement of Article [141].'

Somewhat broader considerations apply where the discriminatory provisions are to be found in national legislation [citing *Rinner-Kühn*, above] . . . The original reason [for the differential qualifying periods] . . . appears to have been the view that part-time workers were less committed than full-time workers to the undertaking which employed them. In his letter of 23 April 1990 the Secretary of State stated that their purpose was to ensure that a fair balance was struck between the interests of employers and employees . . . It is now claimed that the thresholds have the effect that more part-time employment is available than would

---

[87] *Cf* the approach taken by the ECJ in *Rinner-Kühn*, discussed above.

be the case if employers were liable for redundancy pay and compensation for unfair dismissal to employees who worked for less than 8 hours a week or between 8 and 16 hours a week for under five years. It is contended that if employers were under that liability they would be inclined to employ less part-time workers and more full-time workers, to the disadvantage of the former.

The bringing about of an increase in the availability of part-time work is properly to be regarded as a beneficial social policy aim and it cannot be said that it is not a necessary aim. The question is whether the threshold provisions . . . have been shown, by reference to objective factors, to be suitable and requisite for achieving that aim. As regards suitability for achieving the aim in question, it is to be noted that the purpose of the thresholds is said to be to reduce the costs to employers of employing part-time workers. The same result, however, would follow from a situation where the basic rate of pay for part-time workers was less than the basic rate for full-time workers. No distinction in principle can properly be made between direct and indirect labour costs. While in certain circumstances an employer might be justified in paying full-time workers a higher rate than part-time workers in order to secure the more efficient use of his machinery (see *Jenkins v Kingsgate (Clothing Production) Ltd* Case C–96/80 [1981] ECR 911) that would be a special and limited state of affairs. Legislation which permitted a differential of that kind nationwide would present a very different aspect and considering that the great majority of part-time workers are women would surely constitute a gross breach of the principle of equal pay and could not possibly be regarded as a suitable means of achieving an increase in part-time employment. Similar considerations apply to legislation which reduces the indirect cost of employing part-time labour. Then, as to the threshold provisions being requisite to achieve the stated aim, the question is whether on the evidence before the Divisional Court they have been proved actually to result in greater availability of part-time work than would be the case without them. In my opinion that question must be answered in the negative. The evidence for the Secretary of State consisted principally of an affidavit by an official in the Department of Employment which set out the views of the Department but did not contain anything capable of being regarded as factual evidence demonstrating the correctness of these views. . . . no other member state of the European Community, apart from the Republic of Ireland, ha[s] legislation providing for similar thresholds . . . In the Netherlands the proportion of the workforce in part-time employment was in 1988 29.78 per cent and in Denmark 25.75 per cent, neither country having any thresholds similar to those in the 1978 Act. In France legislation was introduced in 1982 providing for part-time workers to have the same rights as full-time, yet between 1983 and 1988 part-time work in that country increased by 36.76 per cent, compared with an increase of 26.71 per cent over the same period in the United Kingdom. While various explanations were suggested on behalf of the Secretary of State for these statistics, there is no means of ascertaining whether these explanations have any validity. The fact is, however, that the proportion of part-time employees in the national workforce is much less than the proportion of full-time employees, their weekly remuneration is necessarily much lower, and the number of them made redundant or unfairly dismissed in any year is not likely to be unduly large. The conclusion must be that no objective justification for the thresholds in the 1978 Act has been established.

A similar approach was taken by the Court of Appeal in *ex parte Seymour-Smith & Perez*, in which that Court considered an argument that the increase in qualifying period for unfair dismissal in 1985 from one year to two constituted unlawful discrimination (under Article 141) against women:

R v Secretary of State for Employment, ex parte Seymour-Smith & Perez [1995] ICR 995

Neill LJ:

. . . The question for the court is whether on the evidence the threshold of two years has been proved to result in greater availability of employment than would be the case without it. . . . Before us, as before the Divisional Court, the Secretary of State relied upon a number of studies. They are examined in detail in the judgments below. That examination led the Divisional Court to the conclusion that the Secretary of State had not proved his case. No suggestion has been made in front of us by Mr Richards that the judges below had misunderstood any of the material or that their criticisms of it as proof were ill-founded. Indeed, he accepts that there is no empirical evidence directed towards the specific issue of the effect of moving from a one-year to a two-year threshold. He submits that in so far as there is evidence that unfair dismissal rights do substantially affect employment opportunities then it is reasonable to infer that the increase of the threshold from one year to two years must increase employment opportunities to some degree. His approach is similar to that adopted in argument on behalf of the Secretary of State in the EOC case.

However, we have found nothing in the evidence, either factual or opinion, which obliges or enables us to draw the inference that the increase in the threshold period has led to an increase in employment opportunities . . .

We have come to the conclusion that on the evidence before us the Secretary of State has failed to prove that the increase in the threshold has increased employment opportunities. On that evidence the threshold of two years is neither suitable nor requisite for attaining the aim of increased employment. It follows that this discriminatory measure has not been justified.

By contrast, the ECJ has tended to permit Member States a broad margin of discretion in selecting the means to further particular social policies. In *Nolte v Landesversicherungsanatalt Hannover* Case C–317/93 [1995] ECR I–4625 (a social security case), the ECJ accepted that Member States had employment of fewer than 15 hours per week which attracted less than a threshold wage. The Court noted the German Government's arguments that:

(1) 'the exclusion of persons in minor employment from compulsory insurance corresponds to a structural principle of the German social security scheme';
(2) 'there is a social demand for minor employment, that it considers that it should respond to that demand in the context of its social policy by fostering the existence and supply of such employment and that the only means of doing this within the structural framework of the German social security scheme is to exclude minor employment from compulsory insurance'; and
(3) 'the jobs lost would not be replaced by full- or part-time jobs subject to compulsory insurance. On the contrary, there would be an increase in unlawful employment . . . and a rise in circumventing devices (for instance, false self-employment) in view of the social demand for minor employment'.

The ECJ went on to rule that:

in the current state of Community law, social policy is a matter for the Member States . . . Consequently, it is for the Member States to choose the measures capable of achieving the aim of their social and employment policy. In exercising that competence, the Member States have a broad margin of discretion. . . . the social and employment policy aim relied on by the German Government is objectively unrelated to any discrimination on grounds of sex and that, in exercising its competence, the national legislature was reasonably entitled to consider that the legislation in question was necessary in order to achieve that aim.

This judgment was indicative of an apparent retrenchment on the part of an increasingly conservative court, contrasting as it did, in particular, with the earlier decision in *Rinner-Kühn* in which the court held that statements to the effect that part-time workers 'were not as integrated in, or as dependent on, the undertaking employing them as other workers' and should not, therefore, be afforded access to statutory sick pay, were 'only generalizations about certain categories of workers [which did] not enable criteria which are both objective and unrelated to any discrimination on grounds of sex to be identified.' But more recently, in *ex parte Seymour-Smith & Perez*, further discussed below, the ECJ ruled that the effect of *Nolte* was not to permit Member States to satisfy the Court as to the justification of indirectly discriminatory practices simply by showing that it was reasonably entitled to consider that the disputed measure would advance a social policy aim.

R v Secretary of State for Employment, ex parte Seymour-Smith & Perez, Case C-167/97 [1999] ECR I-00623

Judgment:

It cannot be disputed that the encouragement of recruitment constitutes a legitimate aim of social policy.

It must also be ascertained, in the light of all the relevant factors and taking into account the possibility of achieving the social policy aim in question by other means, whether such an aim appears to be unrelated to any discrimination based on sex and whether the disputed rule, as a means to its achievement, is capable of advancing that aim . . .

It is true that in . . . the *Nolte* case the Court observed that, in choosing the measures capable of achieving the aims of their social and employment policy, the Member States have a broad margin of discretion.

However, although social policy is essentially a matter for the Member States under Community law as it stands, the fact remains that the broad margin of discretion available to the Member States in that connection cannot have the effect of frustrating the implementation of a fundamental principle of Community law such as that of equal pay for men and women.

Mere generalisations concerning the capacity of a specific measure to encourage recruitment are not enough to show that the aim of the disputed rule is unrelated to any discrimination based on sex nor to provide evidence on the basis of which it could reasonably be considered that the means chosen were suitable for achieving that aim.

On its return to the domestic courts the House of Lords decided (by a majority) that the discrimination at issue in *Seymour-Smith* was justifiable:

R v Secretary of State for Employment, ex parte Seymour-Smith & Perez (No. 2) [2000] ICR 244

Lord Nicholls:

the test applied by the Court of Appeal was whether the threshold of two years had been 'proved to result' in greater availability of employment than would have been the case without it. The Court of Appeal declined to incorporate into this formulation any margin of appreciation: . . .

The answer given by the European Court to the fifth question referred to the court by this House has now shown that this test was too stringent. The burden placed on the government in this type of case is not as heavy as previously thought. Governments must be able to govern. They adopt general policies, and implement measures to carry out their policies. Governments must be able to take into account a wide range of social, economic and political factors. The European Court has recognised these practical considerations. If their aim is legitimate, governments have a discretion when choosing the method to achieve their aim. National courts, acting with hindsight, are not to impose an impracticable burden on governments which are proceeding in good faith. Generalised assumptions, lacking any factual foundation, are not good enough. But governments are to be afforded a broad measure of discretion. The onus is on the member state to show (1) that the allegedly discriminatory rule reflects a legitimate aim of its social policy, (2) that this aim is unrelated to any discrimination based on sex, and (3) that the member state could reasonably consider that the means chosen were suitable for attaining that aim.

There is no difficulty with the first two requirements. The object of the 1985 Order was to encourage recruitment by employers. This was a legitimate aim of the government's social and economic policy, and this aim was unrelated to any sex discrimination. Whether the third requirement was satisfied in 1985 is more debatable. In March 1985 the Secretary of State, Mr. Tom King, stated with regard to the proposed change in the qualifying period:

The risks of unjustified involvement with tribunals in unfair dismissal cases and the cost of such involvement are often cited as deterring employers from giving more people jobs. This change which now puts all new employees on the same basis as that already existing for those small firms should help reduce the reluctance of employers to take on more people.

The relevant question is whether the Secretary of State was reasonably entitled to consider that the extension of the qualifying period should help reduce the reluctance of employers to take on more people.

This question raises an issue of fact, to be decided on the basis of the extensive documentary evidence adduced by the parties . . . On balance, I consider the Secretary of State discharged the burden of showing his view was reasonable. It is apparent that obtaining hard evidence, including evidence of employer perceptions, is essentially a difficult task in this field. But this is not a case of a mere generalised assumption, as occurred in Rinner-Kühn . . . Here, there was some supporting factual evidence. To condemn the minister for failing to carry out further research or prepare an impact analysis . . . would be unreasonable . . .

The requirements of Community law must be complied with at all relevant times. A measure may satisfy Community law when adopted, because at that stage the minister was reasonably entitled to consider the measure was a suitable means for achieving a legitimate aim. But experience of the working of the measure may tell a different story. In course of time the measure may be found to be unsuited for its intended purpose. The benefits hoped for may not materialise. Then the retention in force of a measure having a disparately adverse impact on women may no longer be objectively justifiable. In such a case a measure, lawful when adopted, may become unlawful.

Accordingly, if the government introduces a measure which proves to have a disparately adverse impact on women, the government is under a duty to take reasonable steps to monitor the working of the measure. The government must review the position periodically. The greater the disparity of impact, the greater the diligence which can reasonably be expected of the government. Depending on the circumstances, the government may become obliged to repeal or replace the unsuccessful measure.

In the present case the 1985 Order had been in operation for six years when the two claimants were dismissed from their jobs. The Divisional Court and the Court of Appeal noted there was no evidence that the extension of the qualifying period in 1985 led to an increase in employment opportunities. Ought the government to have taken steps to repeal the 1985 Order before 1991? In other words, had the Order, lawful at its inception, become unlawful by 1991?

Here again, the matter is debatable. As time passed, the persistently adverse impact on women became apparent. But, as with the broad margin of discretion afforded to governments when adopting measures of this type, so with the duty of governments to monitor the implementation of such measures: the practicalities of government must be borne in mind. The benefits of the 1985 Order could not be expected to materialise overnight, or even in a matter of months. The government was entitled to allow a reasonable period to elapse before deciding whether the Order had achieved its objective and, if not, whether the Order should be replaced with some other measure or simply repealed. Time would then be needed to implement any decision. I do not think the government could reasonably be expected to complete all these steps in six years, failing which it was in breach of Community law. The contrary view would impose an unrealistic burden on the government in the present case. Accordingly I consider the Secretary of State discharged the burden of showing that the 1985 Order was still objectively justified in 1991.

Somewhat ironically, the decision in *Seymour-Smith* coincided with an increased willingness on the part of the ECJ to scrutinise macro-level discrimination. In *Seymour-Smith* itself the Court ruled (see above) that 'the broad margin of discretion available to the Member States in that connection cannot have the effect of frustrating the implementation of a fundamental principle of Community law such as that of equal pay for men and women' and that 'Mere generalisations concerning the capacity of a specific measure to encourage recruitment are not enough to show that the aim of the disputed rule is unrelated to any discrimination based on sex nor to provide evidence on the basis of which it could reasonably be considered that the means chosen were suitable for achieving that aim'. This approach was reiterated in *Kutz-Bauer* and again in *Steinicke*.

The cases considered above deal with macro-level discrimination—the application across the board of rules which serve to disadvantage women or men as a group. Most cases of indirect discrimination turn, however, on the application by an individual employer of employer-specific requirements, practices, etc. which impact disparately on women (or men).

London Underground Ltd v Edwards [1995] ICR 574

Mummery J (for EAT):

The tribunal referred to the 'Single Parent Link' scheme proposed . . . to assist employees in the position of the applicant and to its disbandment in September 1992 because agreement on it could not be reached with the unions . . .

> From the fact, as we have found, that a scheme for single parents was contemplated, it is clear that the employer regarded such a scheme as feasible. Provisions could have been made, without significant detriment to the savings sought to be made, for single parents like the applicant to be catered for.

> [Counsel for LUL] submitted that these statements ignored the question whether a scheme of positive discrimination in favour of a small sector of the workforce was feasible, if the workforce as a whole, through its elected representative, opposed it. There was no evidence or reasoning to support the conclusion that provision could, in those circumstances, have been made to cater for single parents. The tribunal failed to address questions as to why the law should require the employer to give single parents preference in rostering over

other categories of employees, such as those with sole responsibility for a disabled spouse or partner, or sole responsibility for an infirm parent, or those who have care of children shared with a spouse or partner who is a night security guard, or for those who experience serious strain on a marriage or relationship as a result of working unsocial hours. The tribunal failed to consider whether the [SDA] compelled the employer to require those of its workforce who are not single parents to work more night shifts than average in order to allow a privileged class of single parents to avoid night shifts altogether, and whether, if the tribunal's reasoning is correct, this in turn might give rise to sex discrimination claims by the disadvantaged majority. The adverse effect of the new rostering on the applicant had to be balanced against the reasonable needs involved in introducing the company plan with its attendant saving of £10m a year and doing so without creating anomalies and inequalities between categories of the workforce . . .

We agree with the applicant that it was for the employer to satisfy the tribunal that the requirement was justifiable. That was an issue of fact and degree which cannot be disturbed on appeal if the tribunal directed themselves, as they did, to the correct test, and came to a conclusion for which there was some evidence . . . In our view, the tribunal were entitled to come to the conclusion on that evidence that it was feasible to cater for single parents or those with primary care of children who were able to work social hours, without significant detriment to the objectives of the employer to achieve savings. The tribunal took account of the need of the employer to make savings and found that there was no significant detriment. In our view, there was no error of law in the tribunal's treatment of this issue.

When the case returned to EAT a freshly constituted tribunal having applied the correct pool for comparison, Morison J found that the second tribunal had correctly applied *Hampson* in deciding that the imposition of the disputed shift system was not justified. The tribunal had ruled that:

We have to consider the needs of the respondents and their objectives to save money and to be more efficient and on the other hand the discriminatory effect it had on the applicant and others who were single parent carers. We find from these facts that the respondents could have easily, without losing the objectives of their plan and reorganisation, have accommodated the applicant who was a long-serving employee. They were aware of her particular difficulties quite early on and after the failure of the single parent link in September 1991, she had set out her misgivings and her difficulties in writing to the management. *They did not address themselves to these issues* [my emphasis] and therefore we find that they have not justified this act of discrimination.'

London Underground Ltd v Edwards (No 2) [1997] IRLR 157

Morison J:

There was evidence to justify the conclusion that London Underground could—and, we would add, should—have accommodated Ms Edwards's personal requirements. She had been working for them for nearly ten years. Her family demands were of a temporary nature. There were no complaints about her work, which she appeared to enjoy . . . there was good evidence that London Underground could have made arrangements which would not have been damaging to their business plans but which would have accommodated the reasonable demands of their employees. It may be that London Underground would have wished to implement the single parent link but gave in to pressure from their predominantly male workforce.

We would wish to add three observations. In the first place, employers should recognise the need to take a reasonably flexible attitude to accommodating the particular needs of their employees. In a case such as this, had it been obvious that London Underground could have accommodated Ms Edwards's needs, without any difficulty or expense, there might have been a case for alleging direct discrimination. Changing the roster in a way which they must have appreciated would cause her a detriment might have justifiably led to an inference that they had treated her less well than they would have treated male train operators who had been in a similar position. In other words, the more clear it is that the employers unreasonably failed to show flexibility in their employment practices, the more willing the tribunal should be to make a finding of unlawful discrimination . . .

Second, in many cases, an employer will be able, readily, to justify a roster system, even if people with childcare responsibilities could not sensibly be accommodated within it. But the lesson from this case is that employers should carefully consider the impact which a new roster might have on a section of their workforce.

Third, nothing we have said in this judgment should be construed as favouring positive discrimination. Such discrimination is unlawful, and for what it is worth, none of the members of this court would wish the position to be otherwise.

In *London Underground* the employers failed to take a reasonable step which they had themselves identified (and which, as EAT pointed out, would have involved no 'difficulty or expense') in order to reduce the impact of the disputed requirement on the claimant. It would be difficult to argue that such a failure was justified. This is true also in cases where employers simply refuse to engage with an employee's representations in respect of an indirectly discriminatory practice. But the courts have frequently adopted a less rigorous approach to the justification question than that of the ECJ. Examples of this have occurred in *Briggs v North Eastern Education and Library Board* [1990] IRLR 181 in which Northern Ireland's Court of Appeal overturned a tribunal's decision that a school's refusal to permit a teacher to switch badminton coaching from after school to lunchtime, or to retain her scale 2 position (awarded in respect of 'additional duties' including 'assist[ing] with extra-curricular school games') without undertaking that coaching (which a tribunal found as a matter of fact comprised only a small part of these additional duties), breached Northern Ireland's equivalent of the SDA. Northern Ireland's Lord Chief Justice (subsequently Lord Hutton) cited *Hampson* but appeared to make little attempt to balance the impact on the employee of the employer's decision against its reasonable needs. A similar failure to balance in fact can be seen in *Bullock v Alice Ottley School*, in which the English Court of Appeal rejected a sex discrimination claim by a domestic worker against her mandatory retirement at 60 in circumstances in which maintenance workers and gardeners were permitted to work until 65.

The school had originally set retirement ages at 65 for men and 60 for women. When this was rendered unlawful, a retirement age of 60 was set in respect of domestic workers (who were all women) and teachers (all but two of 70 were women) while the retirement age for the (exclusively male) maintenance workers and gardeners was set at 65. A tribunal and the Court of Appeal (overruling EAT) rejected the claimant's direct discrimination claim on the basis that women were not prevented from applying for employment as gardeners or maintenance staff (all refused to draw any conclusions from the remarkable consistency between retirement ages applied in relation to individual employees prior to and after the change of rules required under the SDA). On the issue of indirect discrimination, the Court of Appeal ruled that the disparate impact by sex of the retirement ages did not prevent their being justified.

Bullock v Alice Ottley School [1993] ICR 138

Neill LJ:

It was argued on behalf of the applicant that the only reasonable conclusion that the industrial tribunal could have reached on the evidence was that she was the victim of indirect discrimination. There was no need for the school to require that the applicant should retire at 60. I am unable to accept this argument. The general retiring age adopted at the school was 60. I do not understand that this general retiring age was the subject of criticism. The later retiring age of 65 was applied for personnel who worked as gardeners or members of the maintenance staff. The question is: was this later retirement age for this group of the staff objectively justified?

Neill LJ referred to the requirement imposed by *Hampson* 'that an objective balance should be struck between the discriminatory effect of the condition and the reasonable needs of the party who applied the condition,' and cited the decision of the House of Lords in *Rainey*.

As the law stands at present, it seems to me to be clear that in order to justify a later retirement age for a group which in fact though not by design consists wholly or largely of men it is necessary for the employer to show a real and genuine need for this later retirement age. It is further clear, however, that that need is not confined to economic grounds but may include administrative efficiency and possibly other grounds . . .

In the present case the industrial tribunal accepted the bursar's evidence that a later retirement age for the gardeners and the maintenance staff was necessary because of the difficulty of recruiting such staff and the need to retain them as long as possible. As compared with a gardener the applicant was undoubtedly indirectly discriminated against. But this indirect discrimination was justified by the needs of the school . . . the industrial tribunal's acceptance of the bursar's evidence enables this court to reach a clear conclusion on indirect discrimination.

It may well have been the case that the school needed to retain maintenance staff and gardeners (though no evidence of this was apparent except for the bursar's statement). But the Court did not question why, in light of the retirement age permitted these (male) staff, the school nevertheless adopted a 'general retiring age' of 60, this retirement age applying almost exclusively to women.

It is also useful to consider the decision of the Court of Appeal in *Jones v University of Manchester* (the facts of which are set out above). The tribunal had found against the university on the justification issue, ruling that the reasons put forward by the university for imposing a maximum age limit (35) on the particular appointment were inadequate to balance the discriminatory impact of the limit on women. EAT overruled the tribunal on the basis that it had 'effectively dismissed the matters relied upon by [the university] once it was demonstrated that they were not essential.' The University had put forward two factors in support of the application of an upper age limit to the particular careers adviser post for which Ms Jones had applied, arguing that (1) it was desirable that careers advisers be not too far removed in age from the students'; (2) there was a need to achieve a better spread in the ages of advisers in the department whose staff were presently aged 62, 63, 54, 47, 45 and 42. The Court of Appeal upheld EAT's decision:

University of Manchester v Jones [1993] ICR 474

Ralph Gibson LJ (for the Court):

The test for deciding whether application of a requirement is justifiable . . . turns upon balancing the reasonable needs of the University for application of the requirement: it does not require proof of necessity.

I agree that . . . the [tribunal] was at least setting a perilously high standard of proof of reasonable need . . . On this ground alone, however, I am not confident that this Court could properly hold that the conclusion of the [tribunal] on justification could not stand. The [tribunal] had formulated the test correctly and I think that the matters complained of may properly be regarded as matters of expression rather than substance.

The second error on the part of the [tribunal] with reference to justification was, accordingly to the majority in the EAT, that the balancing of the grounds of justification put forward by the University as against the effect of the requirement was carried out subjectively instead of objectively: not objectively in relation to mature women students in general, but subjectively to the particular case of Miss Jones and other women who had suffered under her disadvantages. Further, the discrimination that was found to exist was towards only a very small proportion of the total of eligible women graduates, namely about 3 per cent of the total number of eligible women.

For my part, I cannot find any real assistance in the concept of subjective or objective assessment of the discriminatory effect of the requirement in a case of this nature. The [tribunal] is required to determine the discriminatory effect of the requirement. That seems to me to require the IT to ascertain both the quantitative effect, ie how many men and women will or are likely to suffer in consequence of the discriminatory effect; and, also, what is the qualitative effect of the requirement upon those affected by it, ie how much damage or disappointment may it do or cause and how lasting or final is that damage?

I therefore do not agree that it is improper in the balancing exercise to take into account the particular hardships which have lain in the way of the particular applicant, provided that proper attention is paid to the question of how typical they are of any other men and women adversely affected by the requirement. That, I think, is what the [tribunal] did . . .

Nevertheless, in my judgment, the [tribunal] did misdirect itself in carrying out the balancing exercise. As against the reasonable needs of the University, the [tribunal] must set the discriminatory effect of the application by the University of the requirement to Miss Jones and any others excluded by it. If, contrary to my view, the [tribunal] was entitled to hold as it did that the application of the requirement to Miss Jones was indirectly discriminatory . . . yet in carrying out the balancing exercise it was necessary, in my judgment, for the [tribunal] to keep in mind the process by which their conclusion was made out and, in particular, that the women in that small section of the total number of graduates represents a small proportion of the total of eligible women graduates . . .

For the reasons I have already stated, I consider that the [tribunal] was entitled to assess as it did the effect upon 'women like Miss Jones' of the impact of such a requirement when, after finally getting their degrees, they are excluded from suitable employment by an age bar. I share the [tribunal's] view of the nature of such an obstacle upon mature women graduates generally. It is, however, clear that the [tribunal], in carrying out the balancing exercise, was putting into the scale their assessment of the impact of such a requirement upon the 'thousands of women enrolled as mature students in English universities who will not obtain their degree until they are aged 30 or more and that many of them will come up against the obstacle of gaining the type of employment for which those qualifications make them suitable if such a requirement or condition as the one applied by the [University] to [Miss Jones] in this case is imposed.' Thus, in my judgment, the [tribunal] was placing in the balance the discriminatory effect of this requirement if permitted to be applied by employers. That was not right. This is not a case concerned with the potential effect of age requirements generally or of a university seeking to justify an age limit for general or normal recruitment of a particular class of employee. It was claiming to justify the imposition of an age requirement on this occasion of recruiting a replacement to fill one permanent post, enlarged to two permanent posts in the circumstances described, for a department which has, in addition, to the director and his deputy, seven careers advisers. The discriminatory impact is not to be measured for this purpose with reference to the impact upon the thousands of women mentioned by the [tribunal]. The indirect discrimination as established to the satisfaction of the [tribunal] was upon a small section of the total relevant number and with reference to the selection upon one occasion of two recruits to the careers advisory department of the University. There was thus, in my judgment, misdirection by the [tribunal] in the conduct by them of the balancing exercise in their consideration of the issue of justification . . .

In *Allonby* the Court of Appeal attempted to reconcile the decisions in *Bilka-Kaufhaus* and in *Hampson*. The employers had dismissed (predominantly female) part-time staff to avoid the application of the Part-time Workers Regs (see further Chapter 6). They re-employed the part-time lecturers through an intermediate agency at an estimated saving of £13,000 in total to the college, but with costs to the staff in terms of loss of benefits including sick pay and reductions in hourly pay. A tribunal decided that any indirect sex discrimination was justified: 'any decision taken for sound business reasons would inevitably affect one group more than another group.' EAT agreed but the Court of Appeal did not. The claimant had appealed on the question of justification, arguing that less discriminatory measures were available to the college and so that its action was disproportionate and therefore unjustified and that, further, the action taken by the college was itself based on discrimination and so incapable of justification.

Allonby v Accrington and Rossingdale College [2001] ICR 1189

Sedley LJ:

in *Hampson v Department of Education and Science* [1989] ICR 179, was expressly approved. Balcombe LJ said:
'In my judgment "justifiable" requires an objective balance between the discriminatory effect of the condition and the reasonable needs of the party who applies the condition.'
In *Barry* [1999] ICR 859, in their Lordships' House, Lord Nicholls ICR 179 amplified this:
'More recently, in *Enderby v Frenchay Health Authority*[88] the Court of Justice drew attention to the need for national courts to apply the principle of proportionality when they have to apply Community law. In other words, the ground relied upon as justification must be of sufficient importance for the national court to regard this as overriding the disparate impact of the difference in treatment, either in whole or in part. The more serious the disparate impact on women or men, as the case may be, the more cogent must be the objective justification. There seem to be no particular criteria to which the national court should have regard when assessing the weight of the justification relied on.'
There is further authority, on which Ms Gill [for the Applicant] relies, for the proposition that where the employer's objective is itself discriminatory, it can never justify discriminatory means [citing *ex parte EOC* (HL), *ex parte Seymour-Smith* (ECJ)].
In my judgment, the employment tribunal has failed to apply the scrutiny which the law requires when a discriminatory condition is said to be justifiable. Moreover, such reasons as it gives do not stand up in law.

[88] Case C-127/92 [1993] ECR I-05535, discussed in Ch 6.

The major error, which by itself vitiates the decision, is that nowhere, either in terms or in substance, did the tribunal seek to weigh the justification against its discriminatory effect. On the contrary, by accepting that 'any decision taken for sound business reasons would inevitably affect one group more than another group,' it fell into the same error as the EAT in *Brook* and *Enderby* and disabled itself from making the comparison.

Secondly, the tribunal accepted uncritically the college's reasons for the dismissals. They did not, for example, ask the obvious question why departments could not be prevented from overspending on part-time hourly-paid teachers without dismissing them. They did not consider other fairly obvious measures short of dismissal which had been canvassed and which could well have matched the anticipated saving of £13,000 a year. In consequence, they made no attempt to evaluate objectively whether the dismissals were reasonably necessary—a test which, while of course not demanding indispensability, requires proof of a real need.

In this situation it is not enough that the tribunal should have posed, as they did, the statutory question 'whether the decision taken by the college was justifiable irrespective of the sex of the person or persons to whom it applied.' In what are extended reasons running to 15 closely typed pages, there has to be some evidence that the tribunal understood the process by which a now formidable body of authority requires the task of answering the question to be carried out, and some evidence that it has in fact carried it out. Once a finding of a condition having a disparate and adverse impact on women had been made, what was required was at the minimum a critical evaluation of whether the college's reasons demonstrated a real need to dismiss the applicant; if there was such a need, consideration of the seriousness of the disparate impact of the dismissal on women including the applicant; and an evaluation of whether the former were sufficient to outweigh the latter. There is no sign of this process in the tribunal's extended reasons. In particular, there is no recognition that if the aim of dismissal was itself discriminatory (as the applicant contended it was, since it was to deny part-time workers, a predominantly female group, benefits which Parliament had legislated to give them) it could never afford justification.

It is conceivable that the tribunal misunderstood Lord Nicholls's remark, at the end of the passage quoted above, that 'There seem to be no particular criteria to which the national court should have regard when assessing the weight of the justification relied upon.' Lord Nicholls was not saying that the question was at large or the answer one of first impression: he was saying that, in the exercise which he had spelt out, no single factor or group of factors was of special weight.

I would therefore allow the appeal on this ground. This court is not in a position to say that the outcome of a proper approach will inevitably be in the appellant's favour, and I would therefore remit the case for a further hearing on this issue and that of proportionate impact considered above.

M Connolly, 'Discrimination Law: Justification, Alternative Measures and Defences Based on Sex' (2001) 30 *Industrial Law Journal* 311, 313–18, footnotes omitted

Sedley LJ's reconciliation of *Bilka* and *Hampson* could be interpreted in two ways. First, *Bilka* and *Hampson* were two stages of a compound definition of justification. We decide first if there was a 'real need' (*Bilka*) and second, if its discriminatory effect outweighed the College's needs (*Hampson*). This is an unlikely interpretation though. Sedley LJ quoted Lord Nicholls in *Barry v Midland Bank* . . . 'The more serious the disparate impact on women . . . the more cogent must be the objective justification.' This said Sedley LJ, 'amplified' the *Hampson* test. Although Sedley LJ failed to mention that Lord Nicholls was discussing the Community Law principle of proportionality (*Hampson* was not cited in Barry), we must assume that, Sedley LJ (and Lord Nicholls) were equating the *Hampson* 'objective balance' test with the principle of proportionality. This undermines the theory that Sedley LJ was crafting a two-stage test. This is because the principle of proportionality is inherent in the *Bilka* test, which demands that a measure must be 'suitable' and 'necessary' to achieve the goal. Proportionality, or *Hampson*, cannot work as a separate test. An employer who has shown that a practice was suitable and necessary, has at the same time shown that it was proportionate. It would be absurd to ask again, was it suitable and necessary? And in cases where an employer had failed to show that a practice was suitable and necessary, a separate question of proportionality would be pointless.

So we must accept the second interpretation, that *Hampson* merely reflects parts (b) and (c) of the Bilka test. This is the neatest integration yet of the *Bilka* and *Hampson* 'tests.'. Hitherto, British courts have done no more than treat the tests as expressing the same thing in different language . . .

However, Sedley LJ's assimilation of *Bilka*-or more precisely proportionality—and *Hampson* is not perfect. The obvious difference is in the language. The word 'necessary' appears nowhere in the *Hampson* test. But there is a difference in substance as well.

Asking if a practice is suitable and necessary is different from asking whether it is outweighed by its discriminatory effect. This becomes clear where, as Ms Allonby argued, there exists an alternative. Under *Hampson* the existence of a less discriminatory alternative practice achieving the same goal is merely an ingredient in the 'balance' test; under *Bilka* it will always defeat a justification defence . . .

Case law history also demonstrates that the British judiciary understood that there was a lower standard of justification than *Bilka*. In the early years of the British legislation, tribunals (influenced by US case law, upon which our legislation was based), spoke of 'necessity'. For example, in *Steel v Union of Post Office Workers* . . . Phillips J, President of the EAT said . . . that the practice must be inter alia 'genuine and necessary'.

In 1982, however, the Court of Appeal in *Ojutiku v Manpower Services Commission* . . . contrasted the word 'necessary' with the statutory word 'justified'; Kerr LJ stated . . . that 'justifiable . . . clearly applies a lower standard than . . . necessary.' Eveleigh LJ considered . . . it to mean 'something . . . acceptable to right-thinking people as sound and tolerable.' Balcombe LJ in *Hampson* retrieved the situation somewhat with his 'objective justification' test. However, he did not restore the standard to the pre-*Ojutiku* position. Otherwise he would have simply used the word 'necessary.' Obvious support for a lower standard lies in the legislative history. The RRA and SDA use the term 'justified' rather than 'necessary'. In Parliament, the Government resisted amendments to the Sex Discrimination Bill that would have replaced 'justifiable' with 'necessary.' Lord Harris stated that where a body offered reduced fares for pensioners, the policy might be justifiable, but not necessary (362 HL Deb, 14 July 1975, cols 10116–17).

Meanwhile, the ECJ was developing its jurisprudence on indirect discrimination. The *Bilka* test expressly demanded that any measure should be 'necessary' to achieve the goal. The existence of a less discriminatory alternative will defeat a defence of justification. However, under *Hampson*, the mere existence of a less discriminatory alternative is not enough to defeat a defence.

As *Enderby* . . . illustrates, if the discriminatory effect of the disputed measure is 'outweighed' by the employer's needs, then the defence will succeed, no matter haw many less discriminatory alternatives exist. This approach slowly permeated the British cases until the Court of Appeal in *Hampson* felt compelled to reconcile it with the British position . . .

None of this is to say that British courts will refuse to consider alternatives in the justification dcbate. Sedley's LJ judgement was not as clear-cut as that. Indeed the Court of Appeal remitted *Allonby's* case for reconsideration because, among other things, the tribunal had not considered the 'obvious' alternatives open to the College. Of course, asking a tribunal to 'consider' an alternative in the 'balance' test is different from ruling that the mere existence of an alternative will defeat the justification defence. Sedley LJ's judgement further departs from *Bilka* with his attendant comments. He noted . . . that the tribunal had failed 'to evaluate . . . whether the dismissals were reasonably necessary-a test which, while of course not demanding indispensability, requires proof of a real need.' Here Sedley LJ has diluted *Bilka* by qualifying 'necessary' with 'reasonably necessary' and not indispensable. He spoke only of obvious alternatives. This is the language of compromise. One can only conclude that he intended a broad-brush approach. Tribunals should only consider 'fairly obvious' alternatives. This deepens the impression (eg given in *Ojutiku* and *Hampson*) that the English courts will apply *Bilka* in form only, whilst actually subjecting employers to the lower *Hampson* standard of justification.

Finally, this does not mean that the difference between *Hampson* and *Bilka* is merely a matter of degree. It is a fundamental difference. The compromise in the *Hampson* test upsets the theory of indirect discrimination. Where a practice having a disparate impact is shown to be absolutely necessary to achieve a genuine non-discriminatory goal, then the cause of the disparate impact lies elsewhere. No action lies against the employer. The cause(s) of any disparate impact can only be identified if the courts impose a strict test of necessity. A lesser standard gives employers leeway to discriminate and blurs the causes of a disparate impact. As *Enderby's* case illustrates, 'excess' disparate impact amounts to discrimination. Further, a strict test of necessity forces employers to eliminate discriminatory employment practices, which by their nature, are inefficiencies. The irony is that as many men as women, and far more whites than non-whites, would benefit from that . . .

This case was remitted because the tribunal failed to apply any sort of objective test of justification. The tribunal's failure to consider an alternative was evidence of this and no more. The Court of Appeal did not recommend that the justification defence necessarily should fail because there was a 'fairly obvious' alternative. This reveals that the Court of Appeal did not apply the *Bilka* standard, only the lower *Hampson* one.

Allonby follows a series of cases in our senior courts (eg *Hampson, Barry, Webb*) where a 'balance' test has been equated with the principle of proportionality, first set out in *Bilka*. Clearly *Hampson* does not reflect fully the proportionality principle, which means no more than necessary. The effect of this is notable where there exists a less discriminatory alternative able to achieve the employer's goal. Under *Bilka*, the mere existence of one will defeat a justification defence; *Enderby* illustrates that. But according to *Allonby*, only 'obvious' alternatives qualify to be balanced against the 'reasonable' and 'not indispensable' needs of the employer. This less onerous test upsets the theory of indirect discrimination by sanctioning a certain amount of discrimination and blurring its cause(s). It also weakens the attack on business inefficiencies that benefits all.

As the law stands, the existence of less discriminatory alternative practice achieving the same goal will, under EU legislation and in the United States, defeat a defence of justification. However, under domestic legislation an alternative practice is merely an ingredient in a 'balance' test. Where the claimant can identify an alternative practice they would be well advised to bring their claim under EU legislation, where possible.

The decisions of the ECJ in *Danfoss* and in *Nimz* have been extracted above, attention having been drawn to the increasingly rigorous approach taken by that Court to the reward of seniority. Recently, however, EAT relied upon *Danfoss* in *Health & Safety Executive v Cadman* in ruling that the reward of service did not have to be objectively justified despite its disparate impact in the case. EAT overturned the decision of the employment tribunal which took the view that *Danfoss* had been overtaken on this issue by subsequent decisions of the ECJ in *Nimz* and in *Gerster v Freistaat Bayern* Case 1/95 [1997] ECR I–05253 and *Hill v Revenue Commissioners* Case C–243/95 [1998] ECR I–03739. (In both of these latter cases the ECJ ruled that favouring full-time over part-time workers on the basis that additional hours of work resulted in additional seniority breached Article 141).

Health and Safety Executive v Cadman [2004] ICR 378

Burke QC:

There is, in our judgment, an important difference between a distinction between part-time employees and full-time employees on the basis of the hours which they work and a distinction between different groups of full-time employees on the basis of their length of service. The crucial feature in *Nimz* did not lie in length of service but in the different hours worked by the two groups of employees; those who worked the same hours or whose hours fell within the same bracket would obtain the same benefit after the same length of service. We believe that that is the reason for the emphasis in paragraph 15 of the Court's judgment on the difference in hours worked. The Court should not, as we see it, be taken to have been departing from or watering down what it had very recently and very clearly stated in *Danfoss*; indeed, the court in its judgment in *Nimz* makes no express reference to *Danfoss*.

Accepting, as we do, that the European Court of Justice's approach to its past decisions does not necessarily require, if it wishes to depart from a past decision, the pattern of express reference and distinguishing so familiar in our domestic setting, nevertheless, it would be surprising if the Court had intended to depart from or to modify its own recent decision while not indicating that it was so intending and without any reference to that decision . . .

Ms Gill [for the Claimant] accepted that there has not been a decision of the European Court of Justice on length of service as a criterion in the case of full-time workers, as opposed to hours worked as a criterion where the discrimination relied upon was between full-time and part-time workers. The latter category of case appears to us to be distinct from and to raise different questions from the former. In our judgment, so far as the former category is concerned, the cases since *Nimz* do not qualify *Danfoss* any further than did *Nimz* itself; and *Danfoss* remains applicable to cases which fall within the former category.

IRLR 'Highlights' January 2004

Although undoubtedly erudite, this decision is nonetheless troubling. Understanding of how pay discrimination operates is much greater now than it was in 1989, and a mechanistic application of old case law is out of keeping with a purposive approach to European rights. There must be considerable doubt as to whether the European Court would now make such a sweeping pronouncement, especially since whether a particular defence is valid is a matter for the national courts to determine, and the Court's statement itself presupposes that experience enables the employee to perform his or her duties better, which may no longer be relevant in a particular job once a certain level of experience has been reached. This is acknowledged by the ECJ in *Nimz*, albeit in the slightly different context of pay differences between part-time and full-time workers. More fundamentally, whatever the substantive arguments in favour of allowing service-based pay (and they are highly relevant for age discrimination now as well), it is for the legislature, and not the courts, to create a general exclusion. If the UK Parliament, or the European Council of Ministers, intended to provide a blanket exemption for differences based on service, they could have done so. The US Equal Pay Act, which predates both our own Equal Pay Act and the Treaty of Rome, contains a specific defence for differences in remuneration based on a '*bona fide* seniority system,' but that model was not followed.

The Court of Appeal ([2004] IRLR 971) referred to the ECJ the question whether *Danfoss* had been overruled by subsequent caselaw of the ECJ.

The focus in this section has been on indirect sex discrimination, rather than indirect discrimination on grounds of race, disability or, in Northern Ireland, religion or political opinion. There is an abundance of appellate decisions, post-*Hampson*, dealing with the justifiability of indirect discrimination under the SDA while decisions under the RRA and FEA (now the FETO) are scarce and under the new legislation non-existent as yet. Some of the early RRA decisions on justifiability are considered above.[89] Another is *Barclays Bank v Kapur (No.2)* (App. No. EAT/92, unreported), in which EAT ruled that a pension fund rule which had been applied in order to prevent double recovery in respect of pensionable service accrued by Asians expelled in the 'Africanisation' of Tanzania and Kenya was justifiable. (The claimants had been paid off on termination of their employment, and subsequently re-employed in the UK on the basis that their African service did not count). Overruling a tribunal decision in favour of the claimants, Tucker J for EAT declared that it was 'clearly justifiable' for the bank to take steps to prevent double recovery, 'the only question' being whether the particular course adopted by the bank was justifiable (alternatives being open to it):

> There is sufficient evidence to enable us to make a finding (as we do) that the Appellants considered the alternative courses open to them and [took] the course which appeared to be the more appropriate . . . In reaching this conclusion we have applied the test formulated by Balcombe LJ in *Hampson*.

The Court of Appeal upheld EAT's decision ([1995] IRLR 87) without discussion of the appropriate test for justification. In *Board of Governors of St Matthias Church of England School v Crizzle*, EAT ruled that the restriction of a headteacher post to claimants who were communicant Christians was justified. Dealing with a race discrimination claim from an Asian woman who was, although a Christian, not a communicant,[90] Wood J accepted that the requirement operated disproportionately to exclude Asians from the post but, overruling the tribunal, declared that it was justified:

Board of Governors of St Matthias Church of England School v Crizzle [1993] ICR 401

It seems to us, on the authorities, that the approach of an industrial tribunal should be upon the following lines. (a) Was the objective of the governors [who applied the requirement] a legitimate objective? It is not for the industrial tribunal to redraft or redefine the objective. In the present case it was to have a headteacher who could lead the school in spiritual worship and in particular the administering of the sacrament at the weekly mass to those who were confirmed. The headteacher should have full membership of the Church in order to foster the Anglo-Catholic ethos of the school. (b) Were the means used to achieve the objective reasonable in themselves? (c) When balanced, on the principles of proportionality between the discriminatory effect upon the applicant's racial group and the reasonable needs of the governors, were they justified? The same tests would apply to any board of governors who restricted the headteacher to being a Jew, or a Muslim, or a Sikh, or a Buddhist or any other religion . . . in the present case the objectives of the governors related to the spiritual practices at St Matthias and its ethos. They thought it to be in the best interests of the school if it was led by a headteacher who assisted at mass and gave communion. All parents seem to have supported this view, whatever their own religious background.

[89] See, eg, *Panesar v Nestle, Ojutiku v MSC* discussed above. Cf the rigorous approach to justification taken by the House of Lords in the pre-Hampson case of *Orphanos v Queen Mary College* [1985] AC 761.

[90] It appears from this case that the claimant's own inability to comply with a disputed requirement does not have to be causally related to his or her membership of the group which is less able to comply than others.

The tribunal had ruled against the school on the basis that the governors had placed the religious ethos of the school over the need for efficient education by 'exclud[ing] the possibility of a balanced choice of the most suitable candidate for headteacher,' drawing attention in particular to the ethnic and religious mix of the pupils and 'the great difficulty in recruiting teachers generally and of appointing headteachers.' The tribunal also found as a fact that 'the assistance of the headteacher in administration of the sacrament at school mass was a convenience rather than a need, as this could be done by anyone licensed by the bishop.'

Wood J:

The test in *Hampson* . . . as approved in *Webb* . . . 'requires an objective balance between the discriminatory effect of the condition and the reasonable needs of the party who applies the condition.'

Was the objective sought to be achieved a reasonable one of the governors to take? Was the way in which it was sought to achieve it, namely, by imposing the condition, justifiable in the objective sense set out by Balcombe LJ [in *Hampson*]? . . .

We consider that this industrial tribunal did not apply the correct test in *Hampson*, namely, whether the objective of the governors was a reasonable one for them to seek, and whether the way in which they sought to achieve it was justifiable in the sense set out by Balcombe LJ. In determining the need which they assessed, they misdirected themselves and erred in law. It is in the field of worship that the governors' objective was based and it is in that context that the test of justifiability must be applied. In our view, the objective was legitimate and reasonable, the means used to achieve the objective were reasonable and, when balanced on the principles of proportionality between the discriminatory effect upon the applicant's racial group and the reasonable needs of the governors, the objective was justifiable.

In *R v Secretary of State for Social Services ex parte Nessa* the Court of Appeal considered the justifiability of the rules on funeral grants. The challenge was there brought, unsuccessfully, by a Bangladeshi woman denied reimbursement of that part of her husband's funeral expenses which was incurred in the UK, on the ground that he was buried in Bangladesh. The Court ruled against her on the basis that funeral grants did not fall within the RRA (see further Chapter 4), but went on to declare that, had the grants been so covered, their restriction to burials held within the UK would have been unjustifiable.

R v The Secretary of State for Social Services ex parte Nessa (*The Times*, 15 November 1994)

Auld J:

As recently stated by the House of Lords in *Webb* . . . the concept of justification in this context requires the court to consider: 'an objective balance between the discriminatory effect of the condition and the reasonable needs of the party who applies the condition.'

As to the extent of the discriminatory effect, the Secretary of State relies upon the ready availability in this country of Muslim burial place[s]. As to the reasonable needs for the reg 7(1)(c), the Secretary of State's case is that it would be complicated and expensive to administer a scheme to provide, and verify claims for, payments for funeral expenses incurred in this country where the burial is abroad, and that there are many other calls on the United Kingdom Government's resources.

The availability of Muslim burial places in this country does not seem to me to assist on the question of justification if, despite that availability, the requirement were discriminatory. The complications of apportionment of burial expenses between those incurred in this country and those in the place of burial do not seem to me to be of such weight as to justify discrimination if there were any. The principal candidates for payment would be the matters provided for in reg 7(2)(a) to (c), namely documentation, the cost of a coffin and transport within the United Kingdom. It is hard to see why those costs should not be equally and readily payable whether the burial takes place here or abroad.

Other Prohibited Discrimination

In addition to direct and indirect discrimination and victimisation, the legislative schemes prohibit the issue of instructions to discriminate which is defined by the Race and Employment Equality Directives (Articles 2(4)) as a form of discrimination. Section 30 RRA provides as follows:

> It is unlawful for a person—
> (a) who has authority over another person; or
> (b) in accordance with whose wishes that other person is accustomed to act,
> to instruct him to do any act which is unlawful by virtue of Part II or III, section 76ZA or, where it renders an act unlawful on grounds of race or ethnic or national origins, section 76, or procure or attempt to procure the doing by him of any such act.

This renders unlawful instructions to discriminate or commit harassment in any of the substantive areas covered by the RRA with the exception of its regulation of discriminatory advertisements (see further Chapter 4). Subsection 39 SDA is materially identical save as is s.16C(1) DDA which, however, applies only in relation to discrimination in the employment sphere. Neither the SO Regs nor the RB Regs prohibit the issue of instructions to discriminate in terms but (see *Showboat Entertainment Centre Ltd v Owens* [1982] ICR 618, discussed above) the issue of such instructions would amount to discrimination on the relevant grounds.

Section 31 RRA provides that:

> (1) It is unlawful to induce, or attempt to induce, a person to do any act which contravenes Part II or III, section 76ZA or, where it renders an act unlawful on grounds of race or ethnic or national origins, section 76.
> (2) An attempted inducement is not prevented from falling within subsection (1) because it is not made directly to the person in question, if it is made in such a way that he is likely to hear of it.

The provisions concerning instructions and pressure to discriminate may not be enforced in the normal way (through a tribunal claim) but rather only at the instance of the relevant equality commission (see further Chapter 5). The application of s.31 RRA was considered in *Commission for Racial Equality v The Imperial Society of Teachers of Dancing* [1983] ICR 473, in which EAT overruled a tribunal decision that 'induce' within s.31 did not cover a mere request to discriminate. There the respondents had suggested that the school which it had invited to send potential filing clerks for consideration did not send anyone 'coloured' as the office was exclusively white. The school was here acting as an employment agency for the purposes of the RRA. A tribunal ruled that the use of these words did not breach either s.30 or 31 (in particular, that there was no attempted 'inducement' in a mere request). EAT overturned on the basis that, although the society had no authority over the school such as to make out a s.30 claim, 'induce' meant simply 'to persuade or to prevail upon or to bring about' and was sufficiently wide to cover the subject matter of this complaint.

Section 40 SDA applies similarly but defines inducements and attempts to induce in terms of (a) 'providing or offering to provide [a person] with any benefit, or (b) subjecting or threatening to subject him to any detriment.' So too does s.16C DDA which, again, applies only in relation to discrimination in the employment context. Again, neither the SO nor the RB Regs contain express provision about pressure to discriminate.

Article 35 FETO covers both instructions and inducement to discriminate as follows:

(1) Any person who—
    (a) knowingly aids or incites; or
    (b) directs, procures or induces, another to do an act which is unlawful by virtue of any provision of Part III or IV or Article 34 shall be treated for the purposes of this Order as if he, as well as that other, had done that act. . .
(5) An inducement consisting of an offer of benefit or a threat of detriment is not prevented from falling within paragraph (1) because the offer or threat was not made directly to the person in question.

This provision, unlike those of the RRA, SDA and DDA, covers discriminatory advertisements (see further Chapter 4).

3

Equality

Introduction

This chapter considers the extent to which employers and others in the UK may or must take steps positively to improve the position of disadvantaged groups, whether those groups are defined by reference to sex, race or otherwise.

Steps taken in order to redress disadvantage, whether in the labour market or elsewhere, may be referred to as 'positive discrimination' or 'reverse discrimination' where they entail the preferential treatment of those disadvantaged by sex, race, etc. Neither of these terms has an uncontroverted meaning, and they are as politically controversial as they are linguistically indeterminate. 'Affirmative action' or 'positive action' can be taken to encompass not only such preferential forms of treatment but also the taking of steps whose impact will be to ameliorate disadvantage associated with membership of a group defined by race, sex, etc, but which are not specifically directed at those groups. Thus, for example, the European Commission defines as 'positive action' (in the field of sex equality): 'measures to eliminate the causes of the underemployment and reduced career opportunities for either sex, by intervening, in particular, when career choices are made and in vocational training'; 'measures trying to achieve a better balance between family and work responsibilities and the more even distribution of these between the two sexes, eg the development of childcare infrastructures or the introduction of career breaks'; and 'preferential treatment in favour of certain categories of persons to make up for past disadvantages.'[1]

Of all the terms mentioned, 'affirmative action,' originally embraced in the US, has the longest vintage. An Executive Order issued by President Johnson in 1965 requires private contractors and subcontractors which do business with federal government to 'take affirmative action to ensure that applicants are employed, and that employees are treated during employment, without regard to race, colour, religion, sex, or national origin.' Regulations issued under the Executive Order require that contractors examine whether their employment practices exclude, disadvantage or restrict employment opportunities for women or ethnic minorities and—if they find that any group is under-represented—that they establish goals and timetables to eliminate the under-representation. Christopher McCrudden has distinguished 'at least three different types of affirmative action':[2]

---

[1] Quoted in 'Making a Positive Difference: A Legal Guide to Positive Action' 111 *Equal Opportunities Review*.

[2] McCrudden distinguishes five different forms in 'Rethinking Positive Action' (1986) 15 *Industrial Law Journal* 219: 'eradicating discrimination' in addition to 'facially neutral but purposefully inclusionary policies' which is similar to the first of the categories distinguished above, 'outreach programmes,' 'preferential treatment' and, which will be considered further below, 'redefining merit.'

C McCrudden, 'The Constitutionality of Affirmative Action in the United States: A Note on *Adarand Constructors Inc v Pena*' (1996) 1 *International Journal of Discrimination and the Law* 369, footnotes omitted

- Needs-based programmes, such as federal assistance targeted at particular inner city areas, resulting in some racial or ethnic groups benefiting disproportionately because they are disproportionately in need. These are relatively uncontroversial ideologically, particularly if they are seen as an alternative to other (unacceptable) types of affirmative action. They do, however, cost money and at a time of budget cuts, advocating increased funding of such programmes may therefore be politically unacceptable.
- Outreach programmes have traditionally been popular across the political spectrum. These programmes are designed to attract qualified candidates from the previously under-represented group in two ways: first, by bringing employment opportunities to their attention and encouraging them to apply; second, by providing training the better to equip them for competing on equal terms when they do apply.
- Preferential treatment is the affirmative action issue which elicits the most heated debate. There are, however, considerable differences under this broad heading, relating to the type of preference accorded, and the situation in which the preference is accorded: for example, a preference where candidates are equally well qualified, as opposed to a preference where the preferred candidate is less well-qualified. There are also different aspects of the employment relationship in which preferences may be used, with some programmes involving preferences only in hiring, while others extend to promotion and layoffs.

As McCrudden makes clear, this third type of affirmative action can be divided into a number of subcategories. At one end are 'quotas' which, in their most extreme form, are used as a caricature by opponents of affirmative action. At the other end of the spectrum, arguably, is a 'tie-break' model whereby, where candidates are equally qualified, the 'disadvantaged' candidate (female; ethnic minority, etc) will generally be appointed.

McCrudden's first two types of 'affirmative action' are relatively unproblematic from a legal perspective both in the UK and in the US. Preferential treatment poses more difficulties in the US and has traditionally received scant support within the UK. The UK approach is not reflected in a number of other European states and even in the US, where there have been many successful legal challenges to programmes allowing preferential treatment of minority candidates in, for example, education, employment and contracting situations, there has generally been a significant degree of support across the political spectrum for some forms of preferential treatment.[3] And recently there have been domestic developments in relation to broader forms of 'positive action.' In the area of sex equality there have been improvements to maternity protection and statutory rights to paternity and (unpaid) parental leave have been introduced. Further, the Employment Act 2002 provided a right to request flexible working which may mature over time to an enforceable entitlement for those with dependants to achieve a better work-life balance. This is likely to benefit women in the shorter term but may in future encourage men to undertake more responsibility for hands-on childcare, a development which would have tremendous implications for equality in the workplace. The legislature has also proven willing in recent years to embrace 'goals and timetables' for the advancement of women, ethnic minority and disabled candidates in the public sphere and to impose positive obligations on some public authorities to take steps actively to combat discrimination and foster equality

---

[3] See *Women under the Law: the False Promise of Human Rights* (Harlow, Addison Wesley Longman, 1999), Ch 7.

between particular groups of people. This approach might be seen as a distinctively British 'take' on positive action—not as radical as the imposition of results-driven targets or quotas, but an approach which nevertheless goes beyond a 'first generation' prohibition on discrimination and further than the regulation of indirect discrimination which, as we saw in the previous chapter, demands an individual litigant who has personally been disadvantaged by a disparately impacting practice etc, at issue.

We will consider the goals and timetables initiatives and the positive obligations recently imposed by domestic legislation towards the end of this chapter, after we have looked at 'positive discrimination' here and elsewhere. Maternity, paternity and parental leave and other initiatives directed at the work-life balance are considered briefly in Chapter 6.

Positive Discrimination—the UK Position

'Positive discrimination' is not expressly regulated by any of the statutory provisions considered in this book (the SDA, RRA, DDA, FETO, SO or RB Regs). This does not, however, mean that it is lawful. The 'symmetrical' approach to discrimination adopted by all but the DDA has the effect that much of what could be defined as 'positive discrimination' amounts to direct discrimination and is, therefore, unlawful. The various statutory regimes protect white as well as black and Asian people from discrimination on racial grounds, men as well as women from sex discrimination, those with majority as well as minority religious beliefs from discrimination on grounds of religion or belief, etc. With a very few exceptions (discussed below), the generally accepted view is that 'positive discrimination' which consists of the preferential treatment of persons defined on grounds of sex, race, sexual orientation, religion, etc will breach the relevant anti-discrimination legislation. It was this understanding of the majority decision in *James v Eastleigh Borough Council* [1990] 2 AC 751, that Lords Lowry and Griffiths dissented from it (see further Chapter 2).[4] The question of whether 'positive discrimination' should be permitted, in what form and in what circumstances, is further addressed below. First it is useful to consider the limited extent to which UK legislation currently permits any such discrimination.

The DDA

The DDA does not adopt a symmetrical approach, prohibiting discrimination against those with disabilities (currently or in the past), rather than discrimination on grounds of (dis)ability. Private sector employers are free to discriminate in favour of disabled candidates though they may not, in so doing, discriminate against those with other disabilities unless such discrimination is justified under the Act (see further Chapter 8). Further, it was pointed out by Brian Doyle in 1996 that s.7 of the Local Government and Housing Act 1989 (LGHA) requires that all local authority workers be appointed on the basis of

---

[4] Though see L Barmes, 'Promoting Diversity and the Definition of Direct Discrimination' (2003) 32 *Industrial Law Journal* 200 for a challenge to this analysis based on the recent decisions of the House of Lords in *Nagarajan v London Regional Transport* [2000] AC 501, *West Yorkshire Police v Khan* [2001] ICR 1065 and *Shamoon v Chief Constable of the RUC* [2001] ICR 337 (all discussed in Ch 2).

'merit.'[5] The Disabled Persons (Employment) Act 1944, which was repealed by the DDA, imposed (almost universally ignored) quotas for the employment of registered disabled people, these quotas being permitted by s.7(2) of the LGHA. Some local authorities practised 'priority interviewing' whereby any registered disabled candidate who satisfied the minimum job requirements was interviewed as a matter of course. Such a course of action would not have been unlawful under s.7 of the 1989 Act.

The repeal of s.7(2) LGHA has had a 'chilling' effect on local authorities, according to a survey published in the 1998 *Industrial Relations Journal*. The two local authority employers (of six surveyed) who articulated concern over the repeal expressed regret over the removal of what they had regarded as beneficial 'priority interviewing' schemes and one was quoted to the effect that:

> The DDA wants employers to do more and be more aware in order to encourage and allow special initiatives and recruitment schemes . . . What of course it has actually done is that the one sector that has taken on this message and tried to put these schemes in place is now prohibited from doing so.[6]

Paragraph 4.66 of the Code of Practice for the elimination of discrimination in the field of employment against disabled persons or persons who have had a disability provides:

> The [DDA] does not prevent posts being advised as open only to disabled candidates. However, the requirement . . . under Section 7 . . . that every appointment to local authorities must be made on merit means that a post cannot be so advertised. Applications from disabled people can nevertheless be encouraged. However, this requirement to appoint 'on merit' does not exclude the duty under the [DDA] to make adjustments so a disabled person's 'merit' must be assessed taking into account any such adjustments which would have to be made.

The House of Lords recently decided, in *Archibald v Fife Council (Scotland)* [2004] ICR 954, that the provisions of the DDA may require the employer to treat the disabled person more favourably than others. The case is considered in detail in Chapter 8.

The SDA and RRA

The SDA and RRA (ss.47 and 48, and 37 and 38 respectively) expressly permit positive discrimination, in limited circumstances, by training bodies and employers. Section 48 SDA provides:

(1) Nothing . . . shall render unlawful any act done by an employer in relation to particular work in his employment at a particular establishment in Great Britain being an act done in or in connection with—

---

[5] 'Disabled Workers' Rights, the Disability Discrimination Act and the UN Standard Rules' (1996) 25 *Industrial Law Journal* 1.

[6] I Cunningham and P James, 'The Disability Discrimination Act—an early response of employers' (1988) 29 *Industrial Relations Journal* 304. S.729 HA does, however, provide that the duty to appoint on 'merit' is subject to the duty of reasonable adjustment imposed by ss. 5(2) and 6 DDA (see further Ch 8) as well as to the GOQ and GOR provisions of the SDA, RRA and SO and RB Regs (see Chs 6, 7, 9 and 10).

(a) affording his female employees only, or his male employees only access to facilities for training which would help to fit them for that work; or

(b) encouraging women only, or men only to take advantage of opportunities for doing that work at that establishment . . .

Section 48(2) also permits trade unions and employers' organisations, in limited circumstances, to provide single-sex training for posts within the organisation and to encourage applications for posts from men or women and s.48(3) permits sex-targeted recruitment drives in the same circumstances. Section 38 RRA is in similar terms.[7] The circumstances under which such 'positive action' is permitted are that (in the SDA context) 'at any time within the twelve months immediately preceding the doing of the act there were no persons of the sex in question among those doing that work or the number of persons of that sex doing the work was comparatively small.' The RRA (s.38(1)) permits such positive discrimination 'where any of the conditions in subsection (2) was satisfied at any time within the twelve months immediately preceding the doing of the act.' Those conditions are (s.38(2)):

(a) that there are no persons of the racial group in question among those doing that work at that establishment; or

(b) that the proportion of persons of that group among those doing that work at that establishment is small in comparison with the proportion of persons of that group—
   (i) among all those employed by that employer there; or
   (ii) among the population of the area from which that employer normally recruits persons for work in his employment at that establishment.

Section 47 SDA and s.37 RRA permit targeted training by persons other than employers along lines similar to those provided by ss.48 SDA and 38 RRA in cases of under-representation in 'particular work' either nationally or in the relevant local area. Crucially, however, ss.47(4) SDA and 37(3) RRA disapply this provision in relation to 'any discrimination which is rendered unlawful by' s.6 SDA and s.4 RRA respectively. This has the effect of prohibiting race and sex preferences in the allocation of apprenticeships, which are defined as a form of employment under the SDA and the RRA. Section 47(4) SDA and s.37(3) RRA were inserted by the Sex Discrimination Act 1986, which widened ss.47 SDA and 37 RRA by permitting training by 'any person,' as distinct from those especially accredited for the purpose. But the narrowing effect of ss.47(4) SDA and 37(3) RRA was significant. Prior to 1986, it was at least arguable that apprenticeships could be awarded under ss.47 SDA and 37 RRA.[8] More recently, the CRE has called for the express inclusion within 'training' of legal training contracts in an effort to remedy the racial imbalance in access to the legal profession.[9]

---

[7] S.38(3) and (5) RRA echo s.48 (2) and (3) SDA.

[8] Although the CRE did call in 1985 for express legislative provision to this end. This call went unheeded, the 1986 Act making it clear that apprenticeships were not subject to positive action by the inclusion of ss.37(3) and 47(4).

[9] S.35 RRA also permits any act done in affording persons of a particular racial group access to facilities or services to meet the special needs of that group in relation to their education, health, welfare or any other ancilliary benefit. This might cover special black sections in the Labour Party (note the lack of equivalent to s.33 SDA, discussed in Ch 6). As is clear from the decision in *Hughes v London Borough of Hackney*, discussed by McCrudden below, s.35 RRA does not apply in relation to employment.

In addition to the sex-specific training and advertising allowed by ss.47 and 48 SDA, s.47(3) of that Act provides that:

> Nothing . . . shall render unlawful any act done by any person in, or in connection with, affording persons access to facilities for training which would help to fit them for employment, where it reasonably appears to that person that those persons are in special need of training by reason of the period for which they have been discharging domestic or family responsibilities to the exclusion of regular full time employment.

While this section is couched in sex-neutral terms, the disproportionately female composition of those taking time out of the workforce in connection with domestic or family responsibilities means that this provision is potentially significant for women in particular.

The employment-related positive discrimination permitted by the SDA and the RRA fit McCrudden's second type of affirmative action—'outreach' programmes. It is important to note that these provisions do not in any event permit discrimination in terms of access to jobs (as distinct from encouragement to apply for them). By contrast, some of the SDA's other provisions do allow some affirmative action of McCrudden's third type. Whereas trade unions are generally prohibited by the SDA from discriminating on grounds of sex, s.49 of the Act allows them to reserve female seats on elected bodies 'where in the opinion of the organisation th[is] is in the circumstances needed to secure a reasonable lower limit to the number of members of that sex serving on that body.'[10] Section 33 SDA further provides that political parties may discriminate by making special provision for persons of one sex only in the constitution, organisation or administration of the political party. And although this section operates only in relation to s.29's prohibition on discrimination in the provision of goods, services, etc,[11] the Sex Discrimination (Election Candidates) Act 2002 inserted new section 42A SDA which provides that, until 2015 or such earlier time as the Secretary of State may provide, political parties may adopt arrangements to select election candidates for the purpose of reducing inequality in the numbers of men and women elected as candidates of the party to the relevant positions.[12] None of the other discrimination legislation contains an equivalent to ss.33 or 42A SDA. But the RRA (s.35) permits any act done in affording persons of a particular racial group access to facilities or services to meet the special needs of that group in relation to their education, health, welfare or any other ancillary benefit. This might cover special black sections in the Labour Party but does not cover employment (see further McCrudden, below).

---

[10] See *Kuttappan v PCS* discussed in 'Compensation Awards 2003' 133 *Equal Opportunities Review* for an unusual case. The tribunal did not permit the union to rely on s.49 to defend refusal to the claimant (a man) of an honorary seat on the women's committee of the union.

[11] See *Jepson v Labour Party* [1996] IRLR 116 in which an industrial tribunal ruled that single-sex short-lists, being in breach of s.13 SDA (discussed in Ch 4) were not saved by s.33. That decision was subsequently cast into doubt by the Court of Appeal's decision in *Triesman v Ali* [2002] IRLR 489 on the s.13 point (see further Ch 4) but the tribunal's conclusions on s.33 were not called into question.

[12] The Act also inserts the identical new s.43A into the Sex Discrimination (Northern Ireland) Order 1976 (SI 1976/1042 (NI 15)): see further Ch 4. The Act is discussed by N Bushy, 'Sex Equality in Political Candidature: Supply and Demand Factors and the Role of the Law' (2003) 66 *Modern Law Review* 245. Bushy remarks on the irony that the SDA's application in the election context appears only to have been to act as a break on positive discrimination while doing nothing to challenge the culture which leads to a severe under-representation of women in the political arena. She also considers the potential application in this context of EU law.

The SO Regs and RB Regs

The SO Regs and the RB Regs broadly adopt the approach taken by the RRA and the SDA to positive discrimination. Regulation 26 of the SO Regs, to which reg 25 of the RB Regs is materially identical, provides that:

> (1) Nothing in Part II or III shall render unlawful any act done in or in connection with—
>> (a) affording persons of a particular sexual orientation access to facilities for training which would help fit them for particular work; or
>> (b) encouraging persons of a particular sexual orientation to take advantage of opportunities for doing particular work,
>
> where it reasonably appears to the person doing the act that it prevents or compensates for disadvantages linked to sexual orientation suffered by persons of that sexual orientation doing that work or likely to take up that work.

Regulation 26(2) provides similarly in relation to discrimination by trade organisations in connection with training for positions within the organisation, and 'encouraging only members of the organisation who are of a particular sexual orientation to take advantage of opportunities for holding such posts in the organisation.' And reg 26(3) permits trade organisations to encourage 'persons of a particular sexual orientation to become members of the organisation.' In each case the threshold for action is set, not by statistical 'under-representation' (as is the case under the SDA and the RRA) but by the organisation's reasonable apprehension that the positive action at issue 'prevents or compensates for disadvantages linked to sexual orientation suffered by [relevant] persons of that sexual orientation.'[13] In this the Regs are not dissimilar to FETO (below), and their rubric echoes Article 7 of the Employment Equality Directive which provides that: 'With a view to ensuring full equality in practice, the principle of equal treatment shall not prevent any Member State from maintaining or adopting specific measures to prevent or compensate for disadvantages linked to' sexual orientation, religion or belief, etc).[14] The Racial Equality Directive is in materially identical terms but no amendment has been made to the RRA to reflect this despite the recommendation of Northern Ireland's CRE which pointed out 'the particular difficulty' raised by the fact that 'statistical information about the extent of minority ethnic participation in the workplace is not available to allow employers and training providers to assess the applicability of positive action provisions.'[15]

FETO

FETO appears to go far beyond the other statutory regimes in permitting positive discrimination. Article 4 defines 'affirmative action' as:

> action designed to secure fair participation [undefined] in employment by members of the Protestant, or members of the Roman Catholic, community in Northern Ireland by means including—

---

[13] That is, those who hold or are likely to hold positions in the trade organisation or who 'are, or are eligible to become, members' respectively. Again, reg 25(2) and (3) of the RB Regs are materially identical.

[14] By contrast, the Equal Treatment Directive in its unamended form permits only 'measures to promote equal opportunity for men and women, in particular by removing existing inequalities which affect women's opportunities.'

[15] The body was subsequently absorbed into the ECNI.

(a) the adoption of practices encouraging such participation; and
(b) the modification or abandonment of practices that have or may have the effect of restricting or discouraging such participation.[16]

Article 5 defines 'equality of opportunity' under FETO as 'ha[ving] the same opportunity [in terms of employment or occupation] . . . as [an]other person has or would have . . . due allowance being made for any material difference in their suitability.' Article 5 goes on to stipulate:

(3) . . . a person is not to be treated as not having the same opportunity as another person has or would have by reason only of anything lawfully done in pursuance of affirmative action.
(5) Any reference in this Order to the promotion of equality of opportunity includes a reference to the promotion of affirmative action and, accordingly, any reference to action for promoting equality of opportunity includes a reference to affirmative action.

Northern Irish employers may engage in 'affirmative action' at will, and are not constrained by the under-representation requirements imposed by the RRA and SDA. Employers are obliged to monitor their workforces (this is discussed in detail in Chapter 9) and, every three years, to 'review the composition of those employed . . . and the employment practices of the concern for the purposes of determining whether members of each community [Protestant and Catholic] are enjoying, and are likely to continue to enjoy, fair participation in employment in the concern.' Where such a review discloses an actual or anticipated lack of 'fair participation' on the part of either Catholics or Protestants, employers must (Article 55) 'determine the affirmative action (if any) which would be reasonable and appropriate.' Such action may include the establishment of goals and timetables to set out the 'progress towards fair participation in employment in the concern that can reasonably be expected to be made by members of a particular community' (Article 55(3)). Employers are under no general obligation to submit reviews to the Commission but (Article 56(4)) the Commission may require information from employers regarding such reviews and is required (Article 56(5)):

where a review discloses that members of a particular community are not enjoying, or are not likely to continue to enjoy, fair participation in employment in the concern, [to] make such recommendations as it thinks fit as to the affirmative action to be taken and, assuming the action is taken, as to the progress towards fair participation in employment in the concern, by reference to any period or periods, that can reasonably be expected to be made by members of the community.

Where the ECNI has recommended affirmative action, it is empowered to require follow-up information (not more than once every six months) as to the progress being made. And where the Commission is of the view that an employer's monitoring or review processes are not adequate, it may seek written undertakings from the employer as to changes to those

---

[16] Whereas the direct and indirect discrimination and the victimisation provisions of FETO extend protection beyond Catholic and Protestant to anyone discriminated on grounds of 'religious belief or political opinion,' those provisions dealing with 'fair participation' and 'affirmative action' concern themselves only with the 'two communities'. Such is the overriding significance of the Protestant/ Catholic divide in Northern Ireland that a very old and familiar joke concerns a Jewish person quizzed as to whether s/he is a 'Protestant Jew' or a 'Catholic Jew'.

processes and may, in the absence or breach of such undertaking, issue mandatory directions to the employer (Article 58). These may, in the final analysis, be enforced by the Fair Employment Tribunal. These powers are in addition to the ECNI's powers to carry out the 'investigations into practices' discussed in Chapter 5. Discrimination uncovered by such an investigation can be remedied either by way of undertaking or direction from the Commission.

The failure of FETO and of its predecessors to define 'fair participation' in pursuit of which affirmative action ought to be undertaken was mentioned above. The Fair Employment Commission's Code of Practice suggested (para. 3.1) that affirmative action 'should certainly be considered.' For example, if either Protestants or Roman Catholics:

> are applying in fewer numbers than might be expected for either employment, training or promotion,
> are being recruited, trained or promoted in numbers proportionately lower than their rate of application,
> hold jobs carrying higher pay, status and authority in numbers proportionately lower than their rate of application or availability,
> are, in larger undertakings, concentrated in certain branches, shifts, sections or departments,
> enjoy less attractive terms, hours or working conditions than others, are likely to be adversely affected by possible redundancies and agreed or traditional schemes such as 'last in first out.'

FETO appears to provide a much more significant role for positive discrimination than exists under either the SDA or the RRA. But Christine Bell pointed out, in 1996, that only three (now four) forms of 'affirmative action' are explicitly permitted by FETO (then the FEA):

C Bell, 'The Employment Equality Review in Northern Ireland' (1996) 2 *International Journal of Discrimination and the Law* 53, 60, footnotes omitted

* special training to enhance limited or non-existent skills among members of the under-represented group . . .
* adoption of alternative redundancy procedures designed to ensure that attempts to recruit members of the under-represented community into the workforce are not dissipated, for example by disapplying last in first out policies in redundancy situations (not to be defined with specific reference to religion or politics)
* targeted advertising to attract applicants from an under-represented group. . . .

There are several problems with affirmative action as defined by the legislation. Firstly, the fact that only three forms of affirmative action enjoy explicit protection from charges of unlawful discrimination, suggests that other forms of affirmative action are not favoured and are vulnerable to charges of discrimination. This can act to inhibit employers from taking other affirmative action measures because of fear of discrimination suits.
. . .

Since Bell's article was written the scope of lawful affirmative action under the fair employment regime has been widened. Prior to the implementation of FETO, and despite first impressions, the scope for positive action within the fair employment legislation was, despite the talk of 'affirmative action' and 'fair participation,' much narrower in some respects than that provided by the British Acts. Although the express exception covering redundancy selection was unique to the fair employment legislation,[17] the FEA did not permit any religion-specific training regardless of the degree of under-representation of one or other community in the workplace, employers being restricted in these circumstances to training which, being based in a particular geographic area or confined to a class of persons defined other than on grounds of religious belief or political opinion, was more accessible to the under-represented group.

The 1998 Order widened the scope of the training provision, Article 76 permitting employers and other training bodies to provide single-religion training:

(1) . . . in relation to employment with the employer at a particular establishment in Northern Ireland, being an act done in or in connection with affording only persons of a particular religious belief access to training which would help to fit them for that employment where the conditions in paragraph (2) are satisfied at any time within the 12 months immediately preceding the doing of that act.

(2) The conditions referred to in paragraph (1) are—
    (a) that it appears to the Commission that—
        (i) there are no persons of the religious belief in question among those engaged in that employment at the establishment; or
        (ii) that the proportion of persons of that belief among those engaged in that employment at that establishment is small in comparison with the proportion of persons of that belief among all those employed by the employer there or among the population of the area from which that employer might reasonably be expected to recruit persons for employment at that establishment . . .

But the scope for positive action in the provision of training remains considerably narrower under FETO than under the RRA and SDA in two ways. First, the ECNI must give prior approval of any such training. Second, that training may not be provided 'by an employer, or a person providing training services on behalf of an employer, in relation to any person who is employed by the employer at the time when the act is done.' It would also, of course, amount to (unlawful) direct discrimination under FETO for an employer to provide single-religion training for the under-represented community and thereafter to recruit only from that group.

Positive Action and Indirect Discrimination

Another significant amendment to the fair employment legislation was Article 75 FETO which provides:

(1) The application of any requirement or condition to any person applying to fill a vacancy for employment where the requirement or condition is one that the person applying to fill the vacancy has not been in employment for a specified period of time is not . . . by virtue of Article 3(2) unlawful . . .

[17] See *Brook v London Borough of Haringey* [1992] IRLR 478 discussed in Ch 2.

This provision was inserted to deal with the fact that, because Catholic unemployment rates in Northern Ireland have remained fairly stable at around twice the Protestant level for decades, any attempt to target the unemployed would amount, *prima facie*, to indirect discrimination the lawfulness of which would turn on the issue of justification. An employer would be permitted (even required) to alter practices which served to exclude particular groups (by, for example, opening up jobs to part-time working where the failure to do this unjustifiably disadvantages women, or permitting some flexibility over Friday afternoon working where rigid rules would disproportionately disadvantage Jews and Muslims). But where any disadvantage suffered by a group whose membership is related to sex, race, or another protected ground is societal (or not attributable, at any rate, to the particular employer); and where action to tackle it is aimed at that particular group, the prohibition on indirect discrimination can create a problem. In 1986, Christopher McCrudden wrote that:

C McCrudden, 'Rethinking Positive Action' (1986) 15 *Industrial Law J* 219, 230–2, footnotes omitted

It is arguable that an attempt by an employer to redress underrepresentation by adopting a policy which is neutral but intentionally inclusive is unlawful as a discriminatory arrangement under the SDA, the RRA and the FEA. An employer decides to give preference to those who are unemployed in order to reduce the imbalance between majority and minority groups in his workforce. This would have the effect of disproportionately including, for example, racial minorities (given the considerably greater rate of black unemployment) without explicitly or intentionally excluding whites who, if they are unemployed, would also be able to benefit. There would, however be a disparate impact on whites. That is both the intention and the problem. The decision may amount, first, to direct discrimination under the three Acts. It would, second, be for the courts to decide whether this policy was indirectly discriminatory and whether it would be 'justifiable' under the SDA and RRA.

If the approach to justifiability currently adopted by the courts in their interpretation of the SDA and RRA continues (ie one sympathetic to subjective processes) actions taken in furtherance of this second type of positive action would be lawful, given the lack of intrusiveness into employers' practices which that approach seems to imply. In this context, therefore, there is the rather ironic situation that supporters of positive action might well be arguing for an interpretation of indirect discrimination which they would otherwise be anxious to reject. This is of particular relevance should the proposal to substitute some more restrictive idea of justification, such as that proposed by the CRE, be accepted. It may be reasonable to distinguish between an interpretation of 'justifiability' when the condition or requirement is adverse to the minority group or women, from its interpretation when it is favourable to these groups. However, it may be more realistic to assume that the judiciary would be unlikely to bring these assumptions to bear in this way.

Since 1986, the narrow approach to justification adopted by the ECJ has been applied to the Equal Pay Act 1970 (and, by implication, to the SDA and RRA) by the House of Lords in *Rainey v Greater Glasgow Health Authority Board* [1987] 1 AC 224. More specifically, the possibility of justifying indirect discrimination on the part of employers by reference to wider social issues was dismissed by EAT in *Greater Manchester Police Authority v Lea*.

Greater Manchester Police Authority v Lea [1990] IRLR 372

The case concerned a police authority's policy of preferring applicants for employment who were not already in receipt of an occupational pension. The reasoning behind the policy was that occupational pension recipients were less in need of an employment-related income than were others. It was, however, demonstrated to the satisfaction of EAT that the policy impacted disadvantageously on men who were in the (un)fortunate position of being more likely than women (4.7 per cent as against 0.6 per cent) to receive such a pension. Dealing with the matter of justification, EAT ruled (applying *Hampson v Department of Education and Science* [1991] 1 AC 171, discussed in Chapter 2):

Knox J:

It is therefore now clear if it was not before that the test is, as thus stated by Lord Justice Balcombe in particular, of an objective balance being struck between the discriminatory effect of the requirement or condition and the reasonable needs of the person who applies it.

In our judgment if one applies that test the Police Authority fails to satisfy the requirement because . . . it was held and properly held by the Industrial Tribunal that there was no relevant need of the Police Authority in connection with this condition. It was of course not enough as appears from the judgments in Hampson for it to be shown, as no doubt the Police Authority did show, that the condition was imposed in pursuance of an intrinsically entirely laudable and otherwise reasonable policy of helping the unemployed. *There has in our judgment to be a nexus established between the function of the employer in this type of case and the imposition of the condition* otherwise it is impossible to carry out the objective balance that the Court of Appeal has identified as the test of justifiability in relation to the needs of the employer [my emphasis]. There was some discussion before us on the question whether or not different tests might properly be applied to public authority employers as compared with private employers. It would not in our judgment be useful or safe to seek any general principles in that field. What is appropriate to a public authority employer will, inevitably, in our view, be conditioned by the status, almost certainly statutory, of the employer in question. Generalisations would be inappropriate in that type of context because the particular framework, usually statutory, would need to be considered in any given case.

Employers will be permitted to alter indirectly discriminatory practices of their own making. But under the original SDA, RRA and FETO approach to indirect discrimination (and leaving aside specific FETO exceptions covering redundancy and the recruitment of the unemployed), an employer who acts out of altruism would have to show that a recruitment practice which was designed to favour the disadvantaged (the poor, the disaffected) but which had a disparate impact by race, sex (or, in Northern Ireland, religion or political opinion) 'correspond[ed] to a real need on the part of the undertaking, [was] appropriate with a view to achieving the objectives pursued and [was] necessary to that end.'[18] It is perhaps reasonable to make this demand in circumstances where the targeting of one disadvantaged group (for example, the unemployed) serves to exclude disproportionate numbers of another disadvantaged group (women, for example, if definition as unemployed turns on receipt of benefits);[19] or where targeting one disadvantaged (predominantly white) housing estate disproportionately excludes blacks and Asians. But where the group to whose advantage the targeting works is disadvantaged both in the sense (for example) of

---

[18] That this approach is not required as a matter of EU law, even where it is applicable, is clear from the discussion below.

[19] *Partnership for Equality* (Northern Ireland Office, March 1998), the White Paper preceding FETO, initially suggested targeting the unemployed. This was altered after representations from SACHR and the CAJ (see further Ch 9), that women would be disadvantaged by any requirement for unemployment as distinct from non-employment.

being unemployed and, further, by reason of race or sex (it being clearly demonstrable that ethnic minorities, women and, in Northern Ireland, Catholics are disadvantaged in the labour market) one has to question whether the severity of the approach adopted in *Lea* is warranted.

The *Lea* approach remains applicable under the SDA at least to its prior amendment in order to transpose Council Directive 2002/73/EC (see further Chapter 2). But the RRA's definition of indirect discrimination has been amended where the disparate impact relates to 'race, ethnic or national origin' as distinct from colour or nationality. In the former case, as under the SO Regs and the RB Regs, disparately impacting practices can be justified where the defendant can show that they are a 'proportionate means of achieving a legitimate aim.'[20] Note the absence of any requirement that the test must be made out irrespective of the prohibited ground. Though this test is modelled on that laid down by the ECJ in *Bilka-Kaufhaus GmbH v Weber von Hartz* Case C–170/84, [1986] ECR 1607 which the Court of Appeal sought to embrace in the *Hampson* case on which EAT relied in *Lea*, it is by no means certain that *Lea* would be followed in a challenge brought under the SO or RB Regs or the RRA's amended provisions.

The concept of a 'legitimate aim' might encompass aims beyond an employer's immediate workplace concerns, at any rate in a situation in which efforts are being made to ameliorate disadvantage. It should be noted, however, that any effort to favour minority groups (for example, in an attempt to ameliorate the effects of past or ongoing discrimination) may amount to direct discrimination which is not capable of justification under any of the relevant provisions (except where a specific exception to the prohibition on discrimination applies).[21] This would be the case even if the attempt was covert (a deliberate intention to favour a disadvantaged group defined by race, sex, sexual orientation, etc being pursued by targeting remedial action at an overlapping or wider group defined other than on those lines). In such circumstances, however, the intention to discriminate on the prohibited grounds might be difficult to establish.

Returning to the point made by Christine Bell, and despite the apparently generous scope of Articles 55, 56 and 5 (the latter defining 'equality of opportunity' as compatible with 'anything lawfully done in pursuance of affirmative action'), the scope afforded for positive discrimination under FETO remains almost as narrow (and in some respects is narrower) than that provided under the other statutory discrimination regimes. FETO, like the SDA, RRA, SO and RB Regs, permits such action in relation to the under-represented only to the extent that it encourages them to apply for jobs and, if necessary, provides them with training.[22] What it does not do is to permit discrimination in favour of the disadvantaged *at the point of hiring*.[23]

---

[20] FETO applies the traditional approach to discrimination on grounds of religious belief or political opinion except where discrimination on grounds of religious (or similar philosophical) belief concerns employment, broadly defined, in which case its approach mirrors that of the RB Regs. FETO is further discussed in Ch 9.

[21] For discussion of this in the US context see K Forde-Mazrui, 'Constitutional Implications of Race-Neutral Affirmative Action' University of Virginia School of Law Legal Studies Working Papers Series.

[22] Also, in the case of FETO, with *indirect* discrimination in redundancy selection.

[23] See, eg, *Jones v Chief Constable of Northamptonshire Police* 41 *Equal Opportunities Review Discrimination Case Law Digest* 6.

The Politics of Positive Discrimination

In 1986, McCrudden reported a significant degree of support for the legalisation in the UK of preferential treatment on grounds of race and sex. Such support came, inter alia, from the CRE[24] and the Council of Social Democracy of the then Social Democratic Party.[25] Since that time, however, the climate has changed. Under 'positive action' the CRE's 1998 reform proposals stated only that:

> The [RRA] recognises training as an important means of enabling members of racial groups that have been underrepresented in the past to compete on equal terms for jobs and promotion . . . the Act should clearly specify what positive action is permitted, and that it should include: training for the exclusive benefit of members of a particular racial group; reserved places on non-exclusive courses; training bursaries; on-the-job training and apprenticeship training for up to two years.

The EOC's 1998 reform proposals included the statement that '[i]n general, the EOC does not support positive discrimination,' although the Commission has, more recently, called for 'positive action measures' to remove barriers to women's full participation.[26] And even while the Government has been adopting 'goals and timetables' for increasing sex and race diversity in the public sector (see further below), it has been at pains to emphasise that this does not amount to 'positive' or 'reverse' discrimination. A study commissioned by the CRE and *SHE* magazine reported, in April 2002, that 3 in 4 women surveyed opposed positive discrimination on grounds of race, sex or age in the workplace (75 per cent, 72 per cent and 71 per cent on these grounds respectively). Ethnic minority women were more likely than others to think that race could hamper a person's career progress (75 per cent: 66 per cent), but were no more supportive of positive discrimination in the workplace (women of AB social classes and aged 25–44 were disproportionately likely to favour positive discrimination in this context).[27] The level of support for positive discrimination in politics and the police force was broadly similar (26 per cent and 30 per cent respectively).

The degree of suspicion with which 'positive discrimination' is viewed in the UK is far from universal. In *Action Travail des Femmes* v *CNR* [1987] ISCR 1114, Canada's Supreme Court accepted the imposition of quotas as a remedial measure to counter the effects of past discrimination. There the Court upheld an order that at least a quarter of those hired by the railway company for traditionally male, blue-collar jobs be women until women accounted for 13 per cent of workers in that sector (this being the average level of participation of women in such jobs across Canada). The Supreme Court accepted that 'systematic discrimination' ('discrimination that results from the simple operation of established procedures of recruitment, hiring and promotion, none of which is necessarily

[24] In its 1985 proposals for reform of the RRA, discussed in McCrudden, 'Rethinking Positive Action', above n 2.

[25] Citizens' Rights, Policy Document No. 10, 21 cited by McCrudden, *ibid*, 237. McCrudden also cites G Bindman, 'Reforming the Race Relations Act II' *New Law Journal* 22 November 1985, 1169.

[26] EOC, 'Equality in the 21st Century: A new sex equality law for Britain', available from the EOC's website at www.eoc.org.uk. See also the EOC report on women in Parliament reported in the 97 *Equal Opportunities Review* and, more generally, 'Sex and Power: Who Runs Britain?' (2004), available on the EOC's website at eoc.org.uk.

[27] *Survey on Race*, published by SHE and the CRE and available on the CRE's website at http://www.cre.gov.uk/.

designed to promote discrimination') had occurred and that the programme ordered was 'essential to combat [its] effects . . . specific hiring goals . . . are a rational attempt to impose a systemic remedy on a systemic problem.'

Section 15 of Canada's Charter of Rights now provides that: 'Every individual is equal before and under the law and has the right to the equal protection and equal benefit of the law without discrimination and, in particular, without discrimination based on race, national or ethnic origin, colour, religion, sex, age or mental or physical disability.' Section 15(2) states that the prohibition on discrimination does not apply to 'any law, program or activity that has as its object the amelioration of conditions of disadvantaged individuals or groups including those that are disadvantaged because of . . . sex.'

Some of the objections to positive discrimination are set out by Justice Stewart in his dissenting opinion in *Fullilove v Klutznick*, in which the United States Supreme Court upheld the constitutionality of a 10 per cent 'minority business enterprise' set-aside in a federal public works programme.

Fullilove v Klutznick **448 US 448 (1980)**

Justice Stewart:

> Our Constitution is color-blind, and neither knows nor tolerates classes among citizens. . . . The law regards man as man, and takes no account of his surroundings or of his color. . . .

Those words were written by a Member of this Court 84 years ago [citing Harlan J, dissenting, in *Plessy v Ferguson*, 163 US 537]. His colleagues disagreed with him, and held that a statute that required the separation of people on the basis of their race was constitutionally valid because it was a 'reasonable' exercise of legislative power and had been 'enacted in good faith for the promotion [of] the public good' . . .

Today, the Court upholds a statute that accords a preference to citizens who are 'Negroes, Spanish-speaking, Orientals, Indians, Eskimos, and Aleuts,' for much the same reasons. I think today's decision is wrong for the same reason that *Plessy v Ferguson* was wrong, and I respectfully dissent . . .

The command of the [US Constitution's] equal protection guarantee is simple but unequivocal: In the words of the Fourteenth Amendment: 'No State shall . . . deny to any person . . . the equal protection of the laws.' Nothing in this language singles out some 'persons' for more 'equal' treatment than others. Rather, as the Court made clear in *Shelley v Kraemer*, 334 US 1, 22, the benefits afforded by the Equal Protection Clause 'are, by its terms, guaranteed to the individual. [They] are personal rights.' From the perspective of a person detrimentally affected by a racially discriminatory law, the arbitrariness and unfairness is entirely the same, whatever his skin color and whatever the law's purpose, be it purportedly 'for the promotion of the public good' or otherwise . . . The Court's attempt to characterize the law as a proper remedial measure to counteract the effects of past or present racial discrimination is remarkably unconvincing. The Legislative Branch of government is not a court of equity. It has neither the dispassionate objectivity nor the flexibility that are needed to mold a race-conscious remedy around the single objective of eliminating the effects of past or present discrimination . . . since the guarantee of equal protection immunizes from capricious governmental treatment 'persons'—not 'races'—it can never countenance laws that seek racial balance as a goal in and of itself . . . Second, there are indications that the [minority business set aside] . . . may have been enacted to compensate for the effects of social, educational, and economic 'disadvantage.' No race, however, has a monopoly on social, educational, or economic disadvantage, and any law that indulges in such a presumption clearly violates the constitutional guarantee of equal protection. Since the . . . provision was in whole or in part designed to effectuate objectives other than the elimination of the effects of racial discrimination, it cannot stand as a remedy that comports with the strictures of equal protection, even if it otherwise could . . .

Laws that operate on the basis of race require definitions of race. Because of the Court's decision today, our statute books will once again have to contain laws that reflect the odious practice of delineating the qualities that make one person a Negro and make another white. Moreover, racial discrimination, even 'good faith' racial discrimination, is inevitably a two-edged sword . . . Most importantly, by making race a relevant criterion once again in its own affairs the Government implicitly teaches the public that the apportionment of rewards and penalties can legitimately be made according to race—rather than according to merit or ability—and that people can, and perhaps should, view themselves and others in terms of their racial characteristics. Notions of 'racial entitlement' will be fostered, and private discrimination will necessarily be encouraged . . .

Justice Stewart was in the dissent in *Fullilove*. In *Adarand Constructors v Pena*, Justice Thomas concurred with a majority decision finding a similar set-aside programme unconstitutional in delivering the following judgment:

Justice Thomas Adarand Constructors v Pena 515 US 2000 (1995)

I believe that there is a 'moral [and] constitutional equivalence,' between laws designed to subjugate a race and those that distribute benefits on the basis of race in order to foster some current notion of equality. Government cannot make us equal; it can only recognize, respect, and protect us as equal before the law . . .

As far as the Constitution is concerned, it is irrelevant whether a government's racial classifications are drawn by those who wish to oppress a race or by those who have a sincere desire to help those thought to be disadvantaged. There can be no doubt that the paternalism that appears to lie at the heart of this program is at war with the principle of inherent equality that underlies and infuses our Constitution. (See the Declaration of Independence 'We hold these truths to be self-evident, that all men are created equal, that they are endowed by their Creator with certain unalienable Rights, that among these are Life, Liberty, and the pursuit of Happiness') . . .

Purchased at the price of immeasurable human suffering, the equal protection principle reflects our Nation's understanding that [racial] classifications ultimately have a destructive impact on the individual and our society. Unquestionably, '[i]nvidious [racial] discrimination is an engine of oppression.' It is also true that '[r]emedial' racial preferences may reflect a desire to foster equality in society.' But there can be no doubt that racial paternalism and its unintended consequences can be as poisonous and pernicious as any other form of discrimination. So-called 'benign' discrimination teaches many that because of chronic and apparently immutable handicaps, minorities cannot compete with them without their patronizing indulgence. Inevitably, such programs engender attitudes of superiority or, alternatively, provoke resentment among those who believe that they have been wronged by the government's use of race. These programs stamp minorities with a badge of inferiority and may cause them to develop dependencies or to adopt an attitude that they are 'entitled' to preferences . . .

In my mind, government-sponsored racial discrimination based on benign prejudice is just as noxious as discrimination inspired by malicious prejudice. In each instance, it is racial discrimination, plain and simple.

The current approach of the US Supreme Court to 'affirmative action' is further discussed below, after we have considered some of the arguments in favour of positive discrimination.

B Parekh, 'The Case for Positive Discrimination' in B Hepple and E Szyszczak (eds), *Discrimination: The Limits of Law*, **272–5, footnotes omitted**

The opponents of preferential treatment for disadvantaged groups object to it on the grounds that it disregards merit and that it is unjust and violates individual rights. This is so because it introduces irrelevant and arbitrary criteria, excludes deserving candidates, and favours those with no claim to be favoured. It is unjust also because it punishes the present generation for the deeds of its predecessors, unjustly penalizes members of the dominant group, especially those superseded in specific cases, and privileges all disadvantaged groups, particularly those lucky enough to receive preferential treatment in specific cases.

The first argument makes important points. It rightly stresses that admissions and appointments should be based on clearly specified, rationally defensible and impartially applied criteria, that merit should never be disregarded, that the better qualified should not be passed over in favour of the less qualified, that patronage in all its forms must be avoided, and that efficiency is an important value. However, the definition of merit is far more problematic than its advocates realize.

When people talk about merit, whether in educational institutions or in employment, they define and determine its content in the following three rarely articulated stages. First, an organization or an area of life is abstracted from its wider social context, and its purposes are defined without reference to its place and role in the society at large. Second, a job is abstracted from its larger organizational context and treated as a self-contained unit. An organization is broken up into and viewed as an aggregate of so many separate tasks or jobs, each requiring a specific kind of competence. As a result the overall culture, ethos, ambience of the organization in question is left out of consideration and its claims are defined out of existence. Third, the complex requirements of a job are reduced to and defined almost exclusively in terms of relevant intellectual qualities as measured by examination results and, where appropriate, interview. Merit thus comes to be defined almost entirely in terms of the intellectual requirements deemed necessary to undertake an abstractly and insularly defined job.

When the critics of preferential treatment insist on the inviolability of merit, they have broadly this view of it in mind. There is no reason why we should accept this view, or agree that to depart from *this* view of merit is to depart from merit *itself*. We may question each of the three stages by which the dominant view of merit is arrived at. We might argue that no organization exists or flourishes in a vacuum, and that its purposes cannot be defined without reference to its obligations and responsibilities to the wider society. We might argue too that if the reified concept of job were to be deconstructed, we could find that it is not some independent entity with a unitary structure, but a fragment of a process, a cluster of tasks embedded in and deriving meaning from a larger structure. We might therefore conclude that the very concept of 'qualifications for a job' or of 'job-related qualifications' is misleading and even logically incoherent. Finally, we might argue that a job is not a task but a social relationship in the sense that it is done by an individual in association with other individuals and involves relating to a specific group of men and women whom it is designed to serve, and that it therefore calls for a complex range of skills and abilities of which the intellectual qualities are only a part. As a result of such a critique we might arrive at a very different conception of merit to the one currently dominant, or we might find the very concept of merit problematic, or we might arrive at some other concept of which merit as traditionally defined is an important but only one constituent.

Take admissions to medical schools. The purpose of medical schools is to produce good doctors, and our admission requirements are necessarily determined by our conception of a good doctor. By and large we define him or her as one who is competent at his or her job, and ask for good grades at public examinations as conditions of admission. But we would easily take a different and perhaps more satisfactory view of a good doctor. We could argue that a good doctor should be not only intellectually competent but also possess specific qualities of character and temperament, compassion and a sense of social concern. We could argue too that in a culturally and racially diverse society like ours, he [sic] should be able to relate to and inspire the confidence of people of different backgrounds, and be knowledgeable about their life-styles, stresses and strains, needs and approaches to health and disease. We could also argue that he should be able to appreciate that modern medicine is not the last word in scientific knowledge and that it can benefit from a dialogue with other medical traditions.

We might conclude that a man [sic] is more likely to acquire a well-rounded education and to become a better doctor if he had in his medical school students from different cultural, racial and social backgrounds, provided of course that they were reasonably bright and capable of coping with the demands of medical education. They might not have very high grades at public examinations, but they might bring with them invaluable cultural skills, intuitions and experiences necessary for creating an environment conducive to the production of better doctors overall. Judged by the criterion of narrowly defined merit, they do not deserve admission. But judged by the standards of a broadly defined 'merit' based on differently defined purposes of medical education, they do. There is no reason why, subject to certain minimum necessary qualifications, we could not trade off one set of qualities against another. We could go a step further and argue that as a highly visible and elite institution, the medical school has an obligation to set a good example to a divided society, to tap new talents and to provide them with role models. The case for admitting competent but a little less 'meritorious' black and other candidates then becomes even stronger. . . .

Our remarks about admission to medical schools apply also to other areas of education and to employment.

As for the second argument that preferential treatment is inherently unjust and violates individual rights, it is open to several objections. We have already conceded that the present generation cannot be held responsible for the deeds of its predecessors. Insofar as the case for preferential treatment rests on such a view, it is obviously untenable. However, we have shown that a different kind of case can be made out for the present generation's responsibility for the consequences of past harm, and hence preferential treatment is not without a moral basis. The other points made by its critics are equally unconvincing. Preferential treatment does introduce irrelevant criteria when a person is preferred *solely* because of his or her sex or colour, but not when he or she comes out better on a broader definition of merit or when he or she makes a distinct contribution to the culture and functions of an institution. In such cases merit in the narrow conventional sense of examination results, intelligence tests and so forth is *not* disregarded but balanced against other equally legitimate considerations. And people are not selected simply because of their colour or sex, for they do satisfy the necessary requirements of competence *and* additionally possess qualities declared and shown to be desirable. A more 'meritorious' or formally better qualified candidate has then no right to complain against his or her rejection if the criteria of selection are widely known, rationally defended and impartially applied. . . .

The advantages of preferential treatment are several. As both the American and Indian experiences show, it has a great symbolic significance. It reassures the disadvantaged that the dominant groups appreciate their predicament, accept the responsibility to do something about it, and have the political will to act decisively, including reconsidering such traditional bastions of their power as the principle of merit. Preferential treatment is also a powerful means of integrating disadvantaged groups into the mainstream of society and reducing their feeling of existential marginality. True, it benefits only a small number of men and women and its effects are necessarily limited. However, that is enough to persuade the rest that the dominant and otherwise frightening world is not inaccessible to them and that, if they were to exert themselves, the coveted prizes will not be denied to them.

As we saw, disadvantaged groups cannot overcome their handicaps without substantial help, But such help is often blocked by vested interests, or is of the wrong kind, or is subverted by those in charge of implementing it. It is here that preferential treatment becomes important. It ensures that those knowledgeable about the needs of, and committed to promoting the interests of the disadvantaged are involved in making and implementing decisions, offering advice and keeping a critical watch on the policies of the organisations in question. Such people also act as points of contact for their communities.

Preferential treatment also serves the valuable purpose of providing role models. This is a difficult area about which much remains unknown. We do not know how people are inspired and motivated, why and how they pluck up the courage to take their first tentative steps along a road they have never travelled before, and how over time they build up their confidence and cultural resources. But we do know that men and women whose pride and self-confidence have been shattered often draw their courage and strength from the struggles and achievements of those with whom they identify.

Parekh's approach has been reflected to some extent in the jurisprudence of the US Supreme Court. In *Regents of University of California v Bakke* 438 US 265 (1978) the Court accepted, by a 5:4 majority, that the university was entitled to pursue 'a diverse student body.' It ruled, however (also by a 5:4 majority), that the applicant's rights had been breached by the strict 'set-aside' policy adopted by the medical school whereby 16 places each year were reserved for disadvantaged ethnic minority students, these places being allocated on the basis of competition within that group alone. The 'reservation of a specified number of seats in each class for individuals from the preferred ethnic groups' was not the only method by which the legitimate aim of a diverse student body might be achieved and, given the particular hardship such a quota system placed on those excluded by it, it would be acceptable only if it were the only means by which such an aim could be pursued.

The US approach to strict quota systems of 'affirmative action' is further considered below. It is worth noting, however, that notwithstanding increased hostility on the part of the Supreme Court to affirmative action[28] (including, in *Adarand v Pena*, the application to race-based programmes the same 'strict scrutiny'[29] as the Court applies in other cases of race discrimination), as recently as June 2003 the Court reaffirmed the legitimacy of racial and ethnical diversity as an aim of educational establishments (see further below).[30]

The Use of Positive Action in the UK

Introduction

'Affirmative action' along the lines permitted by the FETO, previously the FEAs, has been a significant feature of Northern Irish employment for some years. The FEC's annual

---

[28] *Croson v City of Richmond* 488 US 469, *Martin v Wilks* 490 US 755, *Metro Broadcasting v FCC* (1990) 497 US 547, 490 US 755.

[29] See A McColgan, above n 3, Chs 3 and 7.

[30] *Grutter v Bollinger, Gratz et al v Bollinger et al* (23 June 2003). A desire to tackle wider societal discrimination is more problematic—see Forde-Mazrui's discussion in 'Constitutional Implications of Race-Neutral Affirmative Action', above n 21.

report for 1996/7, for example, reports that affirmative action plans had been agreed between the Commission and 110 organisations. Statements welcoming applications from under-represented groups 'are now a common feature in newspaper recruitment campaigns'campaigns.'[31] The FEC 'actively promoted community orientated affirmative action programmes, linked to goals and timetables through a programme of formal investigations [see further Chapter 5] and its work with employers on their [workforce] reviews' [see Chapter 9]. The 110 affirmative action programmes agreed in 1996–97 included undertakings regarding the development of school and community links, the inclusion of welcoming statements in advertisements and the adoption of goals and timetables for increased integration. According to the ECNI third annual report (2001–02), the Commission had in place 313 affirmative action agreements of which 214 were voluntary and the remainder legally enforceable. The Commission also reported that it had engaged in work with 186 employers to encourage the use of the FETO provision permitting preferential treatment of the long-term unemployed.

The positive action provisions of the RRA and the SDA are much less used than those of the FETO and its predecessor legislation.[32] In 1987, the EOC criticised the Training Opportunities Scheme for having made no use of its power to direct training towards women, while a study published in the same year found that only seven of the 441 employers surveyed had made any use of s.48 SDA.[33] Vera Sacks' subsequent study of the application of ss.47 and 48 concluded that:

V Sacks, 'Tackling Discrimination Positively in Britain' in B Hepple and E Szyszczak (eds), *Discrimination: The Limits of Law*, 380–1, footnotes omitted

the law in this field is little known, misunderstood, and minimally used. How has this come about?

Two related factors provide important clues. One is the symmetrical approach of the ... which, as Lacey argues, 'does not match the nature of the social problem to which sex discrimination legislation should be addressed ... The result ... of this symmetrical principle ... is to outlaw any form of reverse discrimination or affirmative action.' Yet experience over the past fifteen years has underlined the fact that men and women are running different races and that a neutral stance tends to legitimize and confirm inequality. The second fact is the obvious one that such exceptions as are presented by sections 47 to 49 are permissive and not mandatory. Experience elsewhere reveals that little is done as long as employers are not compelled to develop affirmative action measures.

In the course of this research many organizations of both employers and trainers emphasized the resource problem and the lack of commitment by those in charge. Doubtless, resources in the public sector are always subject to competing demands, and diverting resources to women's promotion and training is seen by decision-makers as controversial, expensive and unpopular, and therefore as of low priority. Commitment is essential and that is most likely to come from women, but women thus far constitute only 20 per cent of local councillors, and are in even smaller proportions in the managerial and trade union hierarchy. Thus placing a duty on employers, at least in the public sector, to provide training for women and to achieve a more balanced workforce is essential here as it has been elsewhere. To quote Marano: 'All of the systematic studies done on the issue indicate that

[31] *Annual Report* para 1.5.

[32] There is little to suggest that positive action is commonly taken on grounds of sexual orientation, religion or belief, though such action would have been legally unproblematic unless it infringed the RRA (see Ch 7) or, in Northern Ireland, FETO.

[33] EOC, 'Review of the Training Opportunities Scheme' (Manchester, EOC, 1978); EOC, 'Equality Between the Sexes in Industry: How Far Have We Come?' (Manchester, EOC, 1978).

affirmative action has had a positive effect and has resulted in increased employment opportunities and training programmes for women and minority men.' Marano also described how, in turn, this more highly trained part of the workforce continued on the same path but without compulsion. In Australia and Canada recent legislation places employers under a duty to submit a programme whose objective is to achieve tangible changes in the employment profile as it relates to women, and the same should be done in this country.

The RRA's positive action provisions appear to have been used rather more than those of the SDA. Research carried out by Welsh and others in the early 1990s, mainly in the public sector, found that 82 per cent of employers had used advertisements to encourage applications from ethnic minority workers and that 33 per cent had provided targeted training for ethnic minority workers. But these 'targeted' advertisements, however, rarely consisted of more than statements that 'all [were] welcome,' or that applicants were 'welcome regardless of race,' and Welsh concluded that the use of the provisions was generally 'patchy' and their 'overall impact . . . probably limited.'[34] In 1991 the PSI reported that 'the central aim of the race relations legislation is not what it ought to be':

> There is a need for a positive concept that is used to set in motion a programme of activity to achieve positive goals. The concept that already plays a minor role in British legislation, but which is the centrepiece of the fair employment law in Northern Ireland, is equal opportunity. There is a clear need to make much more central use of a concept such as this. Employers should have a duty to provide equality of opportunity over and above the elimination of discrimination.

Christopher McCrudden had reported, in 1986, that the positive action provisions of the RRA were being utilised, particularly in the public sector. But the extract below illustrates some of the difficulties into which attempts to increase the diversity of workforces ran:

McCrudden, 'Rethinking Positive Action', 233–4, footnotes omitted

Relatively little used until recently, the provisions have given rise to relatively little controversy. However, the increasing scrutiny by some London Boroughs of the composition of their workforces has encouraged a greater use of these provisions. Not surprisingly, it has also produced the first litigation in Britain over the permissible limits of action taken ostensibly under them, and this has demonstrated some uncertainties in their scope [discussing *Hughes v London Borough of Hackney* [1988] IRLR 55].

The London Borough of Hackney developed an equal opportunities policy in 1982 which included an element of outreach for racial minorities. This was intended to help in the recruitment and training opportunities of members of ethnic minorities. A number of posts were created as part of this programme. An advertisement appeared for two of these posts (for park apprentices) which not only described the training that would be associated with the posts but continued:

Black and ethnic minorities are heavily underrepresented in the Parks and Open Spaces Services. Where such conditions exist the RRA (section 38) allows an employer to establish

---

[34] C Welsh, J Knox and M Brett, *Acting Positively: Positive Action Under the Race Relations Act 1976* (Sheffield, Employment Department, 1994) Research Series No. 36, 37. The research found that 61 per cent of employers were influenced in their decision to take some form of positive action by the CRE.

extra training opportunities specifically for those groups. We would therefore warmly welcome applications from black and ethnic minority people for the two apprenticeships.

The three complainants, all of whom were white, applied for the posts. The application form asked for information on the candidate's ethnic group and the complainants indicated that they were white. They received a letter from the Council's personnel officer which said these posts were 'open only to black and ethnic minority people.' The three complained to an industrial tribunal which upheld their complaint . . .

The Council argued that the provision of employment of this type in these circumstances was, in accordance with section 38 of the RRA, an act done by an employer in connection with encouraging only persons of a particular racial group to take advantage of opportunities for doing particular work at a particular establishment. The proportion of persons of that group amongst those doing that work was small in comparison with the proportion of persons of that group among the population of the area from which the Council normally recruited persons for employment at that establishment. The tribunal rejected this argument, again for two reasons. The words 'in connection with' were not wide enough to cover an employer providing job opportunities restricted to racially disadvantaged members of the community. Second, the Council failed to show that the proportion of black and ethnic minority workers doing relevant work at the establishment was small within the meaning of the section. Although 9 per cent of gardeners were black or ethnic minority compared with 37 per cent of the Borough's population, since only 58 per cent of recruits came from within the Borough, there was no reason to restrict the words 'the area' to recruits from the Borough of Hackney. Since there was no evidence of where, outside the Borough the remaining recruits came from or what the percentage of black and ethnic minorities were within that population, the Council failed to satisfy the conditions set out in section 38.

Judicial discomfort with the concept of positive discrimination is also evident from the decision of the Court of Appeal in *Lambeth London Borough Council v Commission for Racial Equality* [1990] ICR 768, which is discussed in Chapter 7. The Court was concerned with the interpretation of the genuine occupational qualification defence by which the RRA permitted discrimination in favour of persons of a particular group where 'the holder of the job provides persons of that racial group with personal services promoting their welfare, and those services can most effectively be provided by a person of that racial group.' The defendant authority had advertised for African-Caribbean or Asian applicants for two positions in its housing department, this in pursuit of the council's policy of making the housing benefits system 'more sensitive to the needs and experiences of black people' who, with Asians, comprised over 50 per cent of council tenants. A tribunal ruled that, the jobs being of a managerial or administrative nature involving limited contact with the public, they did not involve 'personal services' and the council, accordingly, had failed to make out the GOQ defence. The Court of Appeal (*per* Balcombe LJ) declared itself: 'wholly unpersuaded that one of the two main purposes of the Act is to promote positive action to benefit racial groups' and went on to take a narrow approach to the personal services exception which rendered it inapplicable except in relation to 'hands-on' positions.

Goals and Timetables

We saw, above, that positive discrimination is very strictly regulated under domestic law. The recent adoption by government of widespread 'goals and timetables' projects is, therefore, of very considerable interest.

The terms 'goals and timetables' is taken from the US federal government programmes mentioned above.[35] Such 'affirmative action' has also been practised voluntarily in the US, notably by universities in relation to admissions and by public sector employers. Finally, courts have ordered employers and others to engage in 'affirmative action' where they have been found guilty of practising discrimination. The various forms such 'affirmative action' may take are discussed below.

In the UK, 'goals and timetables' are available to (and sometimes required of) Northern Irish employers under FETO. The practice was first imposed by the FEA in 1989. In July 1998 the Government established a target of 50:50 male: female appointment ratio for men and women in public life[36] and, in the *Modernising Government* White Paper (March 1999),[37] committed itself to 'pro rata representation of ethnic minority groups' among the 100,000 public appointments (those serving on NHS Trusts and advisory and executive bodies, school governors, magistrates etc). In late 1998, fewer than one third of public appointments were held by women, and only 3.6 per cent by members of the ethnic minorities.[38]

Modernising Government also stated the need to 'accelerate progress on diversity' in the public sector, expressing concern at the 'serious underrepresent[ation]' of women, ethnic minority and disabled people 'in the more senior parts of the public service.' The Government committed itself to targets, for 2004–05, of 35 per cent women in the top 3000, and 25 per cent women in the top 600 Civil Service posts;[39] and 3.2 per cent ethnic minority incumbents in the top 3000 Civil Service posts. In summer 2000 it set itself the task of doubling the proportion of disabled persons in top Civil Service jobs to 3 per cent by 2005.[40] Targets were set in summer 2000 for women and ethnic minority staff in top NHS jobs (405 and 7 per cent respectively by April 2004). And the then Director General of the BBC, Greg Dyke, committed to increase the proportion of enthnic minority staff and senior staff in the institution from 8 per cent and 2 per cent respectively in summer 2000 to 10 per cent and 4 per cent by 2003.

Perhaps most high profile of all 'goals and timetables' have been those for ethnic minority representation in the police, the fire and prison service, set in the aftermath of the McPherson enquiry into the death of Stephen Lawrence and its exposition of 'institutional racism' among the police. Subsequently, Chris Patten's report on the RUC, *Policing for Northern Ireland*, set targets of 50 per cent Catholic recruitment over the next 10 years in an attempt to redress the current position, whereby over 40 per cent of the population but only 8 per cent of RUC officers are Catholic. The Patten recommendations were accepted

---

[35] In the same year the Philadelphia Plan, adopted by President Nixon, required all those bidding for federal contracts to establish numerical goals for integration. As Attorney General, the later Chief Justice Rehnquist assured the President that the plan was in conformity with the Civil Rights Act—see R McKeever, *Raw Judicial Power?: the Supreme Court and American Society* (2nd edn, Manchester, Manchester University Press, 1995)125–6.

[36] Speech by Joan Ruddock, then Minister for Women, to a regional TUC conference on women's work 9 July 1999, press release. A publication from the Women's Unit ('Delivering for Women: the Progress so Far') reports that 1998 appointments were 39 per cent female, up from 32 per cent in 1997.

[37] (CM 4310), the forerunner to the Local Government Act 1999, further discussed in Ch 5.

[38] 81 *Equal Opportunities Review* News, 8.

[39] 17.8 per cent and 12.7 per cent respectively in 1998.

[40] A headline in the 87 *Equal Opportunities Review* (September/October 1999) read 'Middle class white men still rule Civil Service,' reporting that ethnic minorities comprise 1.6 per cent, women 16 per cent and disabled people 1.5 per cent of the senior Civil Service 'the current culture is perceived as encouraging those who are different to comply with the "norms" in order to get on.' . . . being prepared to work long and additional hours was the highest ranked enabler to career progression by two-thirds of [the 1701] respondents. Networking and patronage were also seen as too influential in assisting career development.

by Government, the then Secretary of State for Northern Ireland (Peter Mandelson) stating that he:

> attach[ed] particular importance to [the] recommendations for action to transform the composition of the police service. They are essential to gaining widespread acceptability. I endorse the proposal for 50:50 recruitment of Protestants and Catholics, from a pool of candidates, all of whom—I stress this—will have qualified on merit. We propose that the requirement for that special measure should be kept under review on a triennial basis, with rigorous safeguards to ensure that the rightly challenging targets for recruitment do not diminish the standard required of recruits.[41]

The approach taken to Northern Ireland's police service is almost unique in the UK[42] and is indicative of a recognition on the part of government that normal policing is impossible in a situation in which a large minority of the population in a jurisdiction characterised by sectarian division views the police force as the police force of the majority. The Police (Northern Ireland) Act 2000 provided for recruitment to the RUC to be done on a 50:50 Catholic: non-Catholic basis from a pool of qualified candidates. But the general approach is hostile to positive discrimination and the introduction in Great Britain of 'goals and timetables' has generally been accompanied by protestations that they, unlike 'quotas' do not entail positive discrimination which would be unlawful under the RRA and SDA.[43] In setting targets in 1999 for racial integration of the police service, then Home Secretary Jack Straw declared:

> Let me be clear about what I am not doing. I am not setting quotas and saying that you have to take somebody on because of the colour of their skin. I am setting targets that will enable the police service to more fairly represent the community [the police] serve.[44]

The *Modernising Government* White Paper, too, was at pains to emphasise that the targets in respect of women and ethnic minority representation in public sector appointments were to be 'on the basis of merit.' This indicates, perhaps, that the targets are to be achieved by the outreach methods currently permitted under the SDA and RRA provisions discussed above, or by conscious efforts to eliminate discrimination in appointment decisions together with networking initiatives directed, in particular, at ethnic minority staff. That some such activity is going on is evident from an interview published in the *Equal Opportunities Review* in January 2003 with Museji Takolia who was appointed the Government's senior adviser on diversity strategy in April 2000. Among the mechanisms adopted to increase diversity in the senior Civil Service were, he reported:

- a Cabinet Office summer development programme for ethnic minority undergraduates (this was credited with helping to increase the number of ethnic minority graduates entering the Civil Service through the fast stream from 3.4 per cent in 1998 to 7.6 per cent in 2002)

---

[41] HC Debs 19 January 2000 Col 847.

[42] Though see the discussion of the Sex Discrimination (Election Candidates) Act 2002, above and in Ch 4.

[43] See, eg, statements of Home Secretary Jack Straw quoted in Press Association Newsfile and *Equal Opportunities Review*, above n 41.

[44] Speech to a major police conference in April 1999 reproduced in 85 *Equal Opportunities Review*, above n 41.

- the 'Pathways Management Development Programme' which targets ethnic minority staff with the potential to become senior Civil Servants
- the 'Elevator Partnerships' programme which pairs junior women with senior women Civil Servants
- a bursary scheme, worth £10,000 over two years, which provides mentoring and training for disabled employees and has significantly enhanced the promotion opportunities for those who have completed it
- successful resulted in a high rate of promotion for those completing the programme.

The Commissioner for Public Appointments, whose task is 'to set the standards for recruiting and to regulate the recruitment process for appointments in public bodies,'[45] was established in the wake of the Nolan Committee's investigation into how appointments to public bodies ('Quangos') are made. The Commissioner has published a Code of Practice for ministerial appointments to public bodies and is responsible for monitoring the appointments process to ensure that such appointments are made on merit after fair and open competition. The Code, issued in July 2001 and revised in December 2003, highlights seven principles which include 'merit' and 'equal opportunities.' The annual reports published by the Commissioner track the proportions of women, people from ethnic minorities and those with declared disabilities who are appointed to public positions (as well as appointments by age), and the Code of Practice stresses that 'the principles of equal opportunity and diversity are not only socially just, but will benefit any board to which they are applied.' But in its section on 'merit (and diversity)' which provides that 'criteria for selection can take account of the need to appoint boards which include a balance of skills and background,' it warns that 'departments must guard against positive discrimination.'

In summer 2000 it was reported that the senior Civil Service had exceeded expectations in improving ethnic minority representation, though progress of women was somewhat slower than expected. At around the same time the Cabinet Office reported that women outnumbered men for the first time on the fast track Civil Service graduate scheme and that the proportion of ethnic minority staff on the scheme had doubled to 6 per cent. External experts were being used to scrutinise personnel systems for bias and secondments used to bring in people at senior level from under-represented groups. Having said this, progress was patchy in the Civil Service as a whole, the Prison Service falling behind target by early 2001. In summer 2003 the CRE reported that four central government departments and the Welsh Assembly had no senior ethnic minority staff, and that a further five departments had less than 2 per cent of ethnic minority staff in top positions. In these circumstances the question might be raised whether more radical steps ought not to be permitted—or required. And in June 2004 the *Equal Opportunities Review* reported that, while the Civil Service was becoming increasingly diverse in terms of sex and race, progress on increasing the number of disabled civil servants was 'disappointingly slow.'

In March 2002 the *Equal Opportunities Review* reported that the Fire Service in England and Wales was 'currently struggling to achieve challenging diversity targets for the recruitment of firefighters,' the actual number of ethnic minority firefighters having increased nationally by a mere 18 in 2001 to stand at 906—1.2 per cent of the total (up from 1 per cent in 1999).[46] The *Equal Opportunities Review* suggested that 'without the help of positive discrimination measures . . . some brigades cannot see how the targets will be achieved. With wastage rates at a low level, some targets are reported to make up the greater part of

---

45 See the OCPA website at http://www.ocpa.gov.uk/pages/capa.htm.
46 'Diversity in the Civil Service' reported in 'News' 92 *Equal Opportunities Review*.

a brigade's annual projected recruitment.' The article quoted one chief fire officer's belief that the targets set 'are in advance of what can be lawfully attained within the current legal framework.'[47] The failure of the police force as a whole to tackle the under-representation in their ranks of ethnic minorities is considered further in Chapter 7. It is perhaps ironic that while, on the one hand, the CRE was in the throes of Formal Investigation into the police (in part because of problems with the recruitment of ethnic minority officers), the Metropolitan Police was calling in April 2004 to be allowed to adopt positive discrimination measures in order to make London's police more representative of the capital's population.[48]

The 2003–04 Annual Report from the Office of the Commissioner for Public Appointments discloses that the proportion of women appointed to public bodies fell from 39 per cent in 2002–03 to 35.6 per cent in 2003–04. There was also a slight decrease in the proportion of ethnic minority appointees (8.4 from 8.9 per cent) while those with declared disabilities had increased their proportion from 2.7 per cent in 2002–03 to 3.2 per cent in 2003–04. Also noteworthy is the fact that, while the proportion of women members of quangos is remarkably consistent at around a third over the variety of bodies and of memberships at a wide range of remuneration or on an expenses-only basis, the proportion of women chairs, which stands at 26 per cent overall, varies very substantially according to the nature of the public body (18 per cent of the chairs of executive non-departmental public bodies, but 36 per cent of the chairs of NHS bodies, were women in 2003–04) and level of remuneration involved (10 per cent of those chairs earning in excess of £50,000 pa were women, but 26 per cent of those paid between £10,000 and £19,999 pa). Broadly similar patterns were apparent in the case of ethnic minority appointees. The success of the Government's sex equality initiatives have also been called into question by the Women's National Commission of the United Kingdom in its 2004 submission to the UN Committee on the Elimination of Discrimination Against Women. The Commission reports that, while 'Government initiatives led to an increase in women holding public appointments, from 26 per cent to 39 per cent during the 90s . . . the figure has remained constant for the past 3 years and applies to the junior, unpaid posts rather than the senior, paid ones.'

The Government's insistence that 'goals and timetables' do not amount to (and should not entail) 'positive' or 'reverse' discrimination appears to depend on a view of the latter as requiring the appointment of women/ethnic minority/other candidates, regardless of merit, until particular numerical quotas are fulfilled. This certainly corresponds to the caricature of 'affirmative action' as practised in the US. But, in truth, the distinction between (US) 'affirmative action' and (UK) 'goals and timetables' is far less clear-cut.

Strict quota-based 'affirmative action' was prohibited by the Supreme Court in *Regents of University of California v Bakke* (above). Court-ordered quotas have been upheld in the wake of judicial rulings that particular employers have themselves been guilty of discrimination. But in these cases (*Sheet Metal Workers v EEOC* (1986) 478 US 421, *US v Paradise* (1987) 480 US 149) such quotas were imposed only after 'egregious' discrimination on the part of the offender who, in both cases, consistently flouted court orders. In both of these

---

[47] 'Achieving Diversity Targets'. The report of the investigation was published 2005 and is available on the CRE website. *Equal Opportunities Review* 103.

[48] And see, more recently, 'Met considers quotas for ethnic minorities' 139 *Equal Opportunities Review* (March 2005). The Morris inquiry, which reported in 2005, found that ethnic minority officers were more likely to be disciplined than white officers ('The Case for Change: People in the Metropolitan Police Service'). It is tempting to conclude that the Met could do much more to eliminate discrimination in its ranks rather than pleading for special treatment as regards quotas.

cases the 'quotas', being flexible, were more in the nature of goals. In neither case was there any question of the unqualified being advanced. In other cases, such as the pursuit of diversity by educational establishments, race cannot be more than one of a number of factors considered in the admissions process and the Supreme Court confirmed in the recent *Grutter v Bollinger* and *Gratz vBollinger* cases (23 June 2003) that quotas were unacceptable. There (*Grutter*) the Court upheld an admissions scheme which took into account not only candidates' academic abilities but also their wider talents, experiences, and potential and ethnicity and sought to enroll a 'critical mass' of under-represented minority students (African-Americans, Hispanics, and Native-Americans) who might not otherwise have been represented in the student body in meaningful numbers. In *Gratz*, however, it struck down, a practice of awarding African-American, Hispanic, and Native American candidates 20 points of 100 required to gain admission on the basis that it was not 'narrowly tailored' to achieve diversity in that it made the factor of race a decisive factor for virtually all candidates from the under-represented racial groups.

The question was raised above whether, confronted with targets for the recruitment of women and ethnic minority candidates, employers might not be tempted to favour the woman / ethnic minority candidate at the point of recruitment (such preferential treatment being, at present, unlawful in the UK). 'Tie-break' positive discrimination occurs where a candidate from an under-represented group is favoured in the event that all else is equal between her or him and (an)other possible appointee(s). More significant still would be a requirement that an employer should, regardless of merit, appoint any candidate whose recruitment would further the goals set. It is this latter option which is sometimes conceived of (albeit wrongly) as the 'quota' method. In reality, no serious proponents of affirmative action would favour such an approach. But it is possible to support a policy of favouring the appointment of a candidate who satisfies the minimum qualifications for a job (or academic course), and whose recruitment would further the goal (a workplace integrated by sex, race or other characteristic) over a 'more' qualified candidate whose appointment would serve to undermine that goal.

This latter option appears very much more radical than a 'tie-break' approach. But the difference is one of degree rather than kind. No two candidates will ever be precisely similar, and the extent to which candidates may be regarded as 'equally qualified' depends on what qualifications are accepted as relevant to the appointment. On the one hand, it could be argued that to ignore a masters qualification or doctorate is unfair, regardless of whether or not the qualification is relevant to the job in respect of which appointment is sought. On the other hand, to the extent that appointment on the basis of particular qualifications disadvantages a group definable on protected grounds (race, religion, sexual orientation etc), reliance on those qualifications will be lawful only where they impact on the ability of the candidate to perform that particular job. This being the case, the specification of that which will be regarded as going to qualification for appointment should, arguably, be as narrow as possible.[49] In addition, when candidates are being compared, the extent of their qualifications should be measured only on the basis of the factors related to the particular job. One result of this would be to multiply the cases in which candidates can be regarded as 'equally qualified' (ie, equally fitting the 'equal opportunity-conscious' specifications).

---

[49] See the decisions of the ECJ in *Bilka-Kaufhaus GmbH v Weber von Hartz* Case–170/84, [1986] ECR 1607, *Rinner-Kühn v FWW Spezial-Gebaudereinigung GmbH* Case–171/88 [1989] ECR 2743, *Handels-og Kontorfunktionaerernes Forbund I Danmark v Dansk Arbejdsgiverforening (acting for Danfoss)* Case–109/88 [1989] ECR 3199, *Nimz v Freie und Hanse-Stadt Hamburg* Case C–184/89 [1991] ECR I–297 in Ch 2.

It is possible, despite the protestations of the Government, that the increasing commit-ment within the public sector to equal opportunities measured in numerical terms will result in a form of such discrimination, albeit not one which conforms to the caricature of appointment regardless of 'merit'. The report of the Patten commission on policing in Northern Ireland has been the only document, thus far, which has acknowledged the full implications of a 'goals and timetables' approach. While accepting that '[m]erit must remain a critical criterion for selection for the police service,' stating that 'religious or cultural identity, gender or ethnicity should [not] be regarded as a makeweight for merit', and emphasising the importance of 'outreach programmes' designed to attract applications from Catholics, the report recommended that all candidates reaching a specified standard of merit 'should then enter a pool from which the required number of recruits can be drawn . . . an equal number of Protestants and Catholics should then be drawn from the pool.'[50] The Police (Northern Ireland) Act 2000 amended FETO and Northern Ireland's race relations legislation accordingly and the Employment Equality Directive specifically pro-vides (Article 15(1)) that 'In order to tackle the under-representation of one of the major religious communities in the police service of Northern Ireland, differences in treatment regarding recruitment into that service, including its support staff, shall not constitute dis-crimination insofar as those differences in treatment are expressly authorized by national legislation.'[51]

Positive Discrimination and EC Law

The amendment of FETO to permit the adoption of the Patten recommendations relating to Northern Ireland's police force was, at the time, a matter purely for domestic govern-ment.[52] Then, prior to the adoption of the Employment Equality Directive, no issue of European law arose. The position with respect to the under-representation of women in the RUC was more complex. Although the Patten report acknowledged a severe under-representation of women in the RUC (12.6 per cent, of whom a third were part-time reservists) it made no recommendations for radical reform of recruitment practices to address the male/female imbalance, citing the advice it had 'regrettabl[y]' received that such a radical approach was precluded by EU law. This being the case, it is useful to consider the extent to which EU law is or might be compatible with any 'positive discrimination' implied in a 'goals and timetables' approach.

Until very recently the only EU provisions relevant to a discussion of positive action were Article 141 TEC, Article 2(4) of Council Directive 76/207/EEC (the Equal Treatment Directive) and Recommendation 84/635/EEC on the promotion of positive action. Article 141, being chronologically the last of these provisions, will be discussed after the Directive and the Recommendation.

[50] The *Equal Opportunities Review* (above n 1) reports *Bayoomi v British Railways Board* in which a tribunal, having found that requirements for telex operators to be proficient within six months in complex railway procedures, to learn obscure jargon and remember basic geography, where no formal training was provided, discriminated unjustifiably against persons born outside England, suggested that the Board intro-duce a proper training scheme and noted that the provision of special training facilities for members of a particular racial group would permitted by s.38 RRA.

[51] *Report of the Independent Commission on Policing*, paras 15.9–15.10.

[52] Art 15(2), which is further discussed in Ch 9, provides a rather more controversial exception relating to teachers in Northern Ireland.

Article 2(1) of Council Directive 76/207 (the Equal Treatment Directive) prohibits discrimination 'on grounds of sex either directly or indirectly by reference in particular to marital or family status' 'in the conditions, including selection criteria, for access to all jobs or posts' (Article 3), 'with regard to access to all types and to all levels, of vocational guidance, vocational training, advanced vocational training and retraining' (Article 4) and 'with regard to working conditions, including the conditions governing dismissal' (Article 5). Article 2 provides that the directive is (3) 'without prejudice to provisions concerning the protection of women, particularly as regards pregnancy and maternity' and (4) 'without prejudice to measures to promote equal opportunity for men and women, in particular by removing existing inequalities which affect women's opportunities' in access to employment, promotion, vocational training and working conditions. In addition, Recommendation 84/635/EEC on the promotion of positive action for women, passed after the failure of the Council of Ministers and the Commission to pass a directive on positive action, encourages Member States to 'adopt a positive action policy designed to eliminate existing inequalities affecting women in working life and to promote a better balance between the sexes in employment. . . .' The document recommends, inter alia, that Member States take steps to 'eliminate or counteract the prejudicial effect on women in employment or seeking employment which arise from existing attitudes'; to encourage the recruitment and promotion of women 'in sectors and professions and at levels where they are underrepresented, particularly as regards positions of responsibility'; and to adapt working conditions and adjust the organisation of work and working time. The Recommendation, which is not binding, should be taken into account in the interpretation of Article 2(4).[53]

Even in the absence of the Recommendation on positive action, the Equal Treatment Directive lacked the rigidly symmetrical approach adopted by the SDA, with its requirement for comparison (whether real or hypothetical). The ECJ might have chosen to adopt a relatively generous approach to positive discrimination by interpreting Articles 3, 4 and 5 as imposing obligations on Member States to eliminate the effects of discrimination, as well as its overt manifestations. Article 2(4), in particular, could have been applied to this end.

But in *Commission v France* Case C–312/86 [1988] ECR 6315 the ECJ took a narrow approach and ruled that France's retention of a package of rights specific to women employees amounted to a failure adequately to transpose the Equal Treatment Directive. Among the offending provisions were extended maternity leave; shortened working hours; leave to care for sick children; additional annual leave in respect of each child; one day's leave at the beginning of the school year; time off work on Mother's Day; daily breaks for women working on keyboard equipment or employed as typists or switchboard operators; additional points for pension rights in respect of the second and subsequent children and childcare allowances for mothers. Having decided that Article 2(3) did not apply to 'measures relating to the protection of women in capacities, such as those of older workers or parents, which are not specific to [women],' the Court ruled that the exception provided by Article 2(4) was 'specifically and exclusively designed to allow measures which, although discriminatory in appearance, are in fact intended to eliminate or reduce actual instances of inequality which may exist in the reality of social life. Nothing in the papers of the case, however, makes it possible to conclude that a generalized preservation of special rights for women in collective agreements may correspond to the situation envisaged in that provision.'

---

[53] *Grimaldi v Fonds de Maladies Professionnelles* Case C–322/88 [1989] ECR 4407.

D Caruso, 'Limits of the Classic Method: Positive Action in the European Union After the New Equality Directives' 44 (2003) *Harvard International Law Journal*, 331, 338–339, footnotes omitted

[T]he ECJ has conceptualized the possibility of special entitlements for women as a 'derogation from an individual right.' Such derogations, according to continental constitutional traditions, are occasionally permissible, but only if justified by legitimate goals, and only if implemented by non-disproportionate means. States, as a consequence, must design positive action policies within the narrow guidelines provided by the principle of proportionality, as developed by the ECJ in cases of indirect discrimination.

The potential conflict between individual rights and affirmative action, arising out of the Court's equality paradigm, came to a head in 1995 with *Kalanke*.

Kalanke v Freie Hansestadt Bremen Case C–450/93 [1995] ECR I–3051

The case involved a challenge to a German regional regulation whereby, in the case of equally qualified candidates, a woman would be given priority over a man where women were under-represented in the particular post. Advocate General Tesauro interpreted Article 2(4) of the Directive as a derogation from the principle established by Article 2(1), and categorised the priority given to women in the instant case as 'only too obvious[ly] . . . discrimination on grounds of sex.' He accepted that any action in favour of a disadvantaged group 'conflicts with the principle of equality in the formal sense' and declared that positive action was permissible only to the extent that it was within Article 2(4), interpreting that provision narrowly to allow only those actions 'designed to promote and achieve equal opportunities,' 'equal opportunities' being in turn defined to extend only to 'putting people in a position to attain equal results and hence restoring conditions of equality as between members of the two sexes as regards starting points,' as distinct from aiming at equality as regards results.[54]

The 'formal equality' model described by Advocate General Tesauro is similar to that 'which pertains under the SDA and the RRA.[55] But he went on to acknowledge that '[t]he principle of substantive equality,' which he defined as 'basing itself [on] . . . factors [such as sex] in order to legitimise an unequal right, which is to be used in order to achieve equality as between persons . . . complements the principle of formal equality and authorises . . . such deviations from that principle as are justified by the end which they seek to achieve, that of securing actual equality. The ultimate objective is therefore the same: securing equality as between persons.' Advocate General Tesauro took the view that Article 2(4), together with the other derogations, was based on the principle of substantive equality and authorised 'such inequalities [of treatment] as are necessary in order to achieve' equality, and that 'the rationale for the preferential treatment given to women [by Article 2(4)] lies in the general situation of disadvantage caused by past discrimination and the existing difficulties connected with playing a dual role.'

---

[54] See, however, the recent decision of the ECJ in *Abdoulaye* Case C–218/98 [1999] ECR I–05723: Advocate General Tesauro also drew the rather surprising conclusion that '[t]he very fact that two candidates of different sex have equivalent qualifications implies in fact by definition that [they] have had and continue to have equal opportunities'. This was contradicted by Advocate General Jacobs in *Marschall* who, nevertheless, shared Tesauro's conclusion.

[55] Not the DDA and, as we saw above, the position under FETO is complex.

Thus far, the Advocate-General's reasoning appears to permit formally unequal treatment under Article 2(4). But he went on to declare it 'obvious' that 'such difficulties will certainly not be resolved by means of quota systems and the like, which are even irrelevant to that end' and stated that Article 2(4) permitted only:

> measures relating to the organisation of work, in particular working hours, and structures for small children and other measures which will enable family and work commitments to be reconciled with each other . . . Positive action must therefore be directed at removing the obstacles preventing women from having equal opportunities by tackling, for example, educational guidance and vocational training. In contrast, positive action may not be directed towards guaranteeing women equal results from occupying a job, that is to say, at points of arrival, by way of compensation for historical discrimination. In sum, positive action may not be regarded, even less employed, as a means of remedying, through discriminatory measures, a situation of impaired inequality in the past.

The ECJ ruled that the granting of automatic preference to women, where candidates were equally qualified and women under-represented, breached the Equal Treatment Directive. Article 2(4), in the Court's view 'is specifically and exclusively designed to allow measures which, although discriminatory in appearance, are in fact intended to eliminate or reduce actual instances of inequality which may exist in the reality of social life . . . [citing *Commission v France*]. It thus permits national measures relating to access to employment, including promotion, which give a specific advantage to women with a view to improving their ability to compete on the labour market and to pursue a career on an equal footing with men. . . .'

The Court accepted that 'existing legal provisions on equal treatment, which are designed to afford rights to individuals, are inadequate for the elimination of all existing inequalities,' but ruled nevertheless that:

> as a derogation from an individual right laid down in the directive, Article 2(4) must be interpreted strictly[56] . . . National rules which guarantee women absolute and unconditional priority for appointment or promotion go beyond promoting equal opportunities and overstep the limits of the exception in Article 2(4) of the directive. Furthermore, in so far as it seeks to achieve equal representation of men and women in all grades and levels within a department, such a system substitutes for equality of opportunity as envisaged in Article 2(4) the result of which is only to be arrived at by providing such equality of opportunity.

The decision in *Kalanke* was greeted with a great deal of disquiet. The European Commission issued a Communication to the European Parliament and the Council on the interpretation of the judgment to the effect that the decision condemned only the granting of an 'absolute and unconditional right to appointment or promotion,' leaving it open to states to take and to permit to be taken 'all other forms of positive action including flexible quotas.'[57] The Commission also unsuccessfully proposed an amendment to the Equal Treatment Directive to the effect that 'Possible measures [permissible under Article 2(4)] shall include the giving of preference, as regards access to employment or promotion, to a

---

[56] Citing *Johnston v Chief Constable of the Royal Ulster Constabulary* Case C–222/84 [1986] ECR 1651.
[57] COM (96) 88 final 3.

member of the under represented sex, provided that such measures do not preclude the assessment of the particular circumstances of an individual case.'[58]

U O' Hare, 'Positive Action Before the European Court of Justice: Case C–450/93 *Kalank v Freie Hansestadt Bremen*' [1996] 2 *Web Journal of Current Legal Issues*, footnotes omitted

It may be argued that the interpretation given to the relevant legal provisions [by the ECJ in Kalanke] reveals a narrow vision of the principle of equality . . . the Advocate-General's analysis proceeds on the basis that the premise for [the 'tie-break'] form of positive action is compensation for past discrimination. Arguments based around the social utility of such measures are also relevant but are not addressed . . . It is now commonly accepted that the achievement of *de facto* equality is a legitimate social objective. That leads to the question what, if anything, is discriminatory, where all else is equal, about utilising objective criteria in order to achieve that de facto equality; sex here being used as a functional means of distinguishing the candidates. (At the point of the exercise of discretion, it can be argued that the exercise of management prerogative may give effect to assumptions about one group which work to their disadvantage and therefore, does not automatically proceed on the basis of the 'merit' principle.) Finally, strict quotas are, for many, unacceptable because they are deemed to offend the merit principle. Tie-break positive action schemes, on the other hand, do not. However, there is no consideration of this issue by either the Court or the Advocate-General. These arguments should at least be addressed by the Court in the context of Articles 2(1) and 2(4) and the failure to do so renders the position taken here less convincing . . .

If, as the Advocate-General contends, the objective of the directive is ultimately substantive equality, then the insistence that the legislative provisions can only bear an interpretation which permits this objective to be achieved by means of procedural equality may be unduly narrow. Although Article 2(1) is undoubtedly an anti-discrimination measure and Article 2(4) can be read narrowly to give effect to this interpretation, a more expansive interpretation of that provision may also be possible. If Article 2(4) is read in light of the Recommendation [above] then it may be possible to give a broader interpretation to that provision than has been followed here . . .

It may be argued that the fair representation of women in employment, and particularly, the presence of women in senior positions could go some way towards challenging those existing attitudes which bar women's integration in the labour market which, in turn, might encourage the appointment of more women to senior positions. The adherence by the Court and the Advocate-General to a formal vision of equality fails to recognise that the achievement of 'material equality' may ultimately require more than merely ensuring access to a 'level playing field.'

Increasingly, women do have access to the same educational opportunities and training and are entering the labour market well qualified. However, women continue to fail to achieve upper management positions ('the glass ceiling'). A number of reasons may be proffered for this failure which the Court neglects to consider; the employment culture traditionally reflects the male career-model of full-time and continuous employment with which many women are unable to comply; traditional assumptions about the role of women often work to thwart women's advancement and the absence of women from senior posts both confirms a stereotype and becomes a self-fulfilling prophecy in itself. Women remain segregated in the labour market and continue to earn proportionally less than men, notwithstanding the existence of equality laws which should have the effect of levelling the playing field . . . The exclusion of women from senior management fails to harness the full talents

---

[58] (97/C 30/19) OJ C.30/57, 30 January 1997.

of society. Furthermore, without role models in key areas, younger women are in fact dis-advantaged as compared with their male counter-parts and it becomes more difficult to break out of a cyclical pattern of disadvantage . . . For these reasons a more expansive interpretation of the principle of equal treatment could go some way to addressing these issues.

V Sacks, 'What do we think about affirmative action now?' (1996) 2 *International Journal of Discrimination and the Law* **129, 134–7, footnotes omitted**

There are those who believe that, if disadvantaged groups are to be helped to overcome existing obstacles in the competition for desirable goals, then sooner or later, underrepre-sentation of such groups will cease. To this end measures such as special training and edu-cation, relief from domestic responsibilities and the like are seen by them as sufficient and appropriate. These measures do not cause any injustice to others, do not interfere with the merit principle . . . they are hostile to preference at the selection stage. The reasons centre around the individual injustice to the person who 'loses out,' arguments about merit (or lack of it), and that the reward is misdirected 'for the beneficiaries were not themselves vic-tims of ill treatment, merely the heirs of those who were' (Lustgarten, *Legal Control of Racial Discrimination* (Basingstoke: Macmillan, 1980) at p. 21) . . . thus discriminatory selection which aims at redistributing desirable goods is too unfair to particular individu-als, and thus a denial of justice. In the words of the Advocate-General [in *Kalanke*]: 'the imposition of quotas . . . most affects the principle of equality as between individuals . . . in sum, positive action may not be regarded, even less employed, as a means of remedying, through discriminatory measures, a situation of impaired inequality in the past,'

Others believe that underrepresentation needs to be addressed directly. The reasons for desiring proportionate representation, whether in the legislature or in other spheres, are centred round ideas about compensation, and justice and has great symbolic significance. . . . In the European Union now the only help is of the kind which reinforces women's role as workers and carers, ignoring the argument advanced by Parekh (and impliedly accepted by the AG [in *Kalanke*]) that this makes the visible and invisible walls almost impossible to scale.

This is a very limited view of the difficulties faced by women especially in those areas of employment where they are most underrepresented. Attitudes and past practices are often unthinking and unconscious and the setting of goals is a small attempt to overcome this fact. The challenged legislation set a legally enforceable but very limited goal. Without such goals equality of opportunity remains elusive. . . . the reasoning of the Advocate-General that Art. 2(4) could not have been intended to confer benefits on women simply because they are women, and hence that such measures are unlawful, is by no means self-evident. Viewed in the more global context, where such measures have become quite common as a means of addressing inequality of opportunity, the rejection by the ECJ of the experience and growing understanding of the necessary mechanisms needed to remedy discrimination is very sad. . . . The Bremen law which only related to the public sector, was a minimal attempt at redress-ing imbalances at the higher and more impenetrable management level. . . . The decision in *Kalanke* is to be regretted and will have serious consequences in many member states. It seems that old democracies have something to learn from new democracies.

Within two years, the ECJ had adopted the approach advocated by the Commission in its Communication on the *Kalanke* decision. *Marschall v Land Nordrhein-Westfalen* con-cerned a challenge to a rule which provided that, where there were fewer women than men in a particular career bracket, women were to be given priority for promotion in the event of equal suitability, competence and professional performance 'unless reasons specific to an individual [male] candidate tilt the balance in his favour.' Advocate General Jacobs argued that the decision in *Kalanke* was correct, and that no distinction could properly be drawn between its facts and those in the present case, although he accepted the argument that legislative reform might well be required. The Court, however, seized upon the 'savings clause' to reach a different conclusion. Having reiterated the first paragraph of *Kalanke* reproduced above, the Court went on to acknowledge that:

Marschall v Land Nordrhein-Westfalen **Case C–409/95 [1997] ECR I–6363**

Judgment:

even where male and female candidates are equally qualified, male candidates tend to be promoted in preference to female candidates particularly because of prejudices and stereotypes concerning the role and capacities of women in working life and the fear, for example, that women will interrupt their careers more frequently, that owing to household and family duties they will be less flexible in their working hours, or that they will be absent from work more frequently because of pregnancy, childbirth and breastfeeding. For these reasons, the mere fact that a male candidate and a female candidate are equally qualified does not mean that they have the same chances.

It is at this point that the *volte-face* on the part of the Court occurs:

It follows that [my emphasis] a national rule in terms of which, subject to the application of the saving clause, female candidates for promotion who are equally as qualified as the male candidates are to be treated preferentially in sectors where they are under-represented may fall within the scope of Article 2(4) if such a rule may counteract the prejudicial effects on female candidates of the attitudes and behaviour described above and thus reduce actual instances of inequality which may exist in the real world.

While this is arguably [just] consistent with the Court's prohibition, in *Kalanke*, of the according of 'absolute and unconditional priority' to women, it is irreconcilable with the Court's demand in that case that 'as a derogation from an individual right laid down in the directive, Article 2(4) must be interpreted strictly,' and its condemnation of the rule in that case for 'substitut[ing] for equality of opportunity as envisaged in Article 2(4) the result which is only to be arrived at by providing such equality of opportunity.' The only qualification imposed by the Court in *Marschall* to its newly permissive approach to positive discrimination was that:

since Article 2(4) constitutes a derogation from an individual right laid down by the directive, such a national measure specifically favouring female candidates cannot guarantee absolute and unconditional priority for women in the event of a promotion without going beyond the limits of the exception laid down in that provision (see *Kalanke* . . .) Unlike the rules at issue in *Kalanke*, a national rule which, as in the case in point in the main proceedings, contains a saving clause does not exceed those limits if, in each individual case, it provides for male candidates who are equally as qualified as the female candidates a guarantee that the candidatures will be the subject of an objective assessment which will take account of all criteria specific to the individual candidates and will override the priority accorded to female candidates where one or more of those criteria tilts the balance in favour of the male candidate . . . It is for the national court to determine whether those conditions are fulfilled on the basis of an examination of the scope of the provision in question as it has been applied.

The ECJ seized upon the 'savings clause' in *Marschall* in order to distinguish the case from *Kalanke*. But, as Advocate General Jacobs pointed out in his opinion in *Marschall*: 'the national rule at issue in *Kalanke* was not in fact absolute and unconditional': the Court noted the national court's point that the rule had to be interpreted 'with the effect that, even if priority for promotion is to be given in principle to women, exceptions must be made in appropriate cases.' Equally, and somewhat bizarrely, it appears that the savings clause in *Marschall* permitted consideration of the very factors which, the German legislature had acknowledged in passing the preference rule, operated to women's disadvantage and necessitated the preference rule in the first place:

> where qualifications are equal, employers tend to promote men rather than women because they apply traditional promotion criteria which in practice put women at a disadvantage, such as age, seniority and the fact that a male candidate is a head of household and sole breadwinner for the household.[59]

Caruso, 'Limits of the Classic Method', 341, footnotes omitted

Underlying the Court's reasoning in *Kalanke* was a sharp distinction between equality of opportunities and equality of results, the latter being prohibited by EC law. *Marschall* brought about a major change by allowing, in the presence of adequate savings clauses, preferential treatment in actual hiring—arguably a matter of results. . . . Moreover, the *Marschall* formula still requires that male and female candidates be equally qualified for the preferential criteria to apply . . . when the two safeguard mechanisms—the savings clause and par qualifications—are not present, the ECJ does not approve of result-orientated schemes, also known as fixed-quota systems.

Caruso goes on to discuss the decision of the ECJ in *Badeck* v *Hessen*, in which the ECJ approved German provincial legislation which, inter alia, required that public administrative departments 'women's advancement plans' and take other measures to 'work towards equality of women and men in the public service and the elimination of under-representation of women and to eliminate discrimination on grounds of sex and family status.'

Part of the legislation at issue was concerned with the elimination of indirect discrimination, requiring that selection decisions were to be made on the basis of the 'requirements of the post to be filled or the office to be conferred' and, where relevant, 'capabilities and experience which have been acquired by looking after children or persons requiring care in the domestic sector (family work)' had to be taken into account 'in so far as they are of importance for the suitability, performance and capability of applicants.' Part-time work, leave and delays in completing training as a result of family commitments were to be excluded from consideration as were the applicant's family status and the income of the applicant's partner and, save where they were 'of importance for the suitability, performance and capability of applicants,' seniority, age and the date of last promotion.

But the advancement plans went beyond this to require equality of outcome to a significant degree. They were to contain binding targets for increasing the proportion of women in sectors in which they were under-represented and more than half of all positions arising during the two year duration of each plan were to be designated for women, save

---

[59] Observations of the Länder reported in the ECJ decision. Indeed the flexibility built into the preference system was such that 'the administration can always give preference to a male candidate on the basis of promotion criteria, traditional or otherwise.'

where a GOQ applied or it was 'convincingly demonstrated that not enough women with the necessary qualifications are available,' in which case a smaller proportion of posts could be designated female.

Promotions of women had, at least, to be in proportion to their relative position in the lower rung of employment and the proportion of women had to be protected in the event of redundancies. Particular measures applied to academic jobs, the appointment of women having to correspond, at least, with the proportion of women graduates, higher graduates or students in the discipline (the latter in the case of academic assistants without degrees).

Quotas were also established for training positions in occupations in which women were under-represented and, in sectors in which women were under-represented, at least as many women as men (or all the women applicants) were to be interviewed as long as they satisfied the minimum conditions for the position.

Finally, if the targets were not fulfilled in respect of each two-year plan, every further appointment or promotion of a man in a sector in which women were under represented was to require the approval of the body which had approved the advancement plan or, in some cases, the provincial government.

The ECJ ruled that measures intended to give priority to women in sectors of the public service where they are under-represented were compatible with the Equal Treatment Directive as long as (a) they did not *automatically and unconditionally* give priority to women when women and men were equally qualified, and (b) the candidatures were the subject of an objective assessment which took account of the specific personal situations of all candidates. While it was for the national courts to decide whether these conditions were satisfied, the Court went on to suggest that none of the provisions at issue breached the Directive. It ruled that the Directive 'does not preclude a national rule which:

Badeck v Hessen Case C–158/97, [2000] ECR I–01875

Judgment:

—in sectors of the public service where women are under-represented, gives priority, where male and female candidates have equal qualifications, to female candidates where that proves necessary for ensuring compliance with the objectives of the women's advancement plan, if no reasons of greater legal weight are opposed, provided that that rule guarantees that candidatures are the subject of an objective assessment which takes account of the specific personal situations of all candidates,
—prescribes that the binding targets of the women's advancement plan for temporary posts in the academic service and for academic assistants must provide for a minimum percentage of women which is at least equal to the percentage of women among graduates, holders of higher degrees and students in each discipline,
—in so far as its objective is to eliminate under-representation of women, in trained occupations in which women are under-represented and for which the State does not have a monopoly of training, allocates at least half the training places to women, unless despite appropriate measures for drawing the attention of women to the training places available there are not enough applications from women,
—where male and female candidates have equal qualifications, guarantees that qualified women who satisfy all the conditions required or laid down are called to interview, in sectors in which they are under-represented,
—relating to the composition of employees' representative bodies and administrative and supervisory bodies, recommends that the legislative provisions adopted for its implementation take into account the objective that at least half the members of those bodies must be women.

Caruso comments (at 341) that the scheme at issue in *Badeck* survived scrutiny because of its 'highly nuanced character' and, in particular, the fact that it 'required full evidence of equal qualifications prior to the triggering of gender preferences, as was riddled with exceptions. It met, in other words, the two safeguard mechanisms required by the *Marschall* ruling.' She goes on to state (at 342) that, where schemes such as those permitted under EU law have been applied:

> the proportion of women in the workforce has remained static, rather than having improved. One reason for this result may lie in these plans' most debatable feature—the need to demonstrate equivalent qualifications of male and female candidates before any preferential criterion is triggered. An expert of the German labour market, commenting on such data, has observed that '[i]t is fairly easy to evade decision quotas by simply denying the presence of equal qualifications.' If this is true, the type of positive action endorsed by the ECJ may be missing the real point.

The decision of the ECJ in *Commission v France* was noted above, as has been the increased tolerance on the part of that Court in the intervening years towards positive discrimination. The *Marschall* and *Badeck* cases concerned decisions in recruitment. But employers or states might also try to improve the position of disadvantaged groups by taking action such as that disapproved of by the ECJ in the French case. Examples of this have occurred in *Lommers v Minister van Landbouw* and in *Griesmar v Ministre de l'Economie*. One of the challenges in the former case was to a policy whereby, the Dutch Ministry of Agriculture having recognised that the existing shortage of suitable and affordable nursery facilities was likely to result in a disproportionate wastage of women staff, provided workplace nursery places for the children of women employees only, save in 'emergency' cases in which a man bringing up children on his own would be similarly eligible. The ECJ took the same approach as it did in the *Badeck* and *Marschall* cases. Having ruled that it was for the national court to determine whether women were significantly under-represented and were particularly likely to be disadvantaged by a shortage of suitable childcare facilities, and whether the 'derogation' from the right to equal treatment was 'proportionate,' the Court continued:

Lommers v Minister van Landbouw, Natuurbeheer en Visserij Case C–476/99 [2002] ECR I–02891

A measure such as that at issue in the main proceedings, whose purported aim is to abolish a de facto inequality, might nevertheless also help to perpetuate a traditional division of roles between men and women.

That fact may, admittedly, appear to lend support to the academic legal opinion to which the national court refers and which argues that, if the aim of promoting equality of opportunity between men and women pursued by the introduction of a measure benefiting working mothers can still be achieved if its scope is extended to include working fathers, the exclusion of men from its scope would not be in conformity with the principle of proportionality.

However, in the case now under consideration, account must be taken of the fact that, given the insufficiency of supply mentioned above, the number of nursery places available under the measure at issue is itself limited and that there are waiting lists for female officials working at the Ministry of Agriculture, so that they themselves have no guarantee of being able to obtain a place.

Moreover, a measure such as that at issue does not have the effect of depriving the male employees concerned, any more than other female staff who have not been able to obtain a nursery place under the nursery places scheme subsidised by the Ministry of Agriculture, of all access to nursery places for their children, since such places still remain accessible mainly on the relevant services market . . .

Next, it must also be remembered that the measure at issue does not totally exclude male officials from its scope but allows the employer to grant requests from male officials in cases of emergency, to be determined by the employer.

As far as the scope of that exception is concerned, it is to be noted that both the Minister for Agriculture, in the main proceedings and before the Commission for Equal Treatment, and the Netherlands Government, in the proceedings before this Court, have indicated that male officials who bring up their children by themselves should, on that basis, have access to the nursery scheme at issue.

In this respect, a measure which would exclude male officials who take care of their children by themselves from access to a nursery scheme subsidised by their employer would go beyond the permissible derogation provided for in Article 2(4), by interfering excessively with the individual right to equal treatment which that provision guarantees. Moreover, in relation to those officials, the argument that women are more likely to interrupt their career in order to take care of their young children no longer has the same relevance.

In the circumstances described . . . it cannot be maintained that the fact that the Circular does not guarantee access to nursery places to officials of both sexes on an equal footing is contrary to the principle of proportionality.

In *Griesmar* the Court considered the legality of a scheme whereby French civil servants who were mothers were given additional pension credits in order to address what the French Government characterised as the 'social reality,' ie, that such women were professionally disadvantaged by their unequal responsibility for children even where they continued to work.' The ECJ ruled that the arrangement breached Article 2(4) of the Equal Treatment Directive:

Griesmar v Ministre de l'Economie, des Finances et de l'Industrie Case C–366/99 [2001] ECR 09383

it should first be observed that, even if the credit at issue in the main proceedings is granted, in particular, to female civil servants in respect of their legitimate and natural children, thus their biological children, the grant of that credit is not linked to maternity leave or to the disadvantages which a female civil servant incurs in her career as a result of being absent from work during the period following the birth of a child . . . The explanations provided by the French Government in regard to the purpose served by [the disputed pension credits] not only confirm that there is no link between the credit at issue in the main proceedings and the period following childbirth, during which the mother benefits from maternity leave and is absent from work, but also, on the contrary, emphasise that this credit is linked to a separate period, namely that devoted to bringing up the children.

It appears that the national legislature used a single criterion for granting the credit at issue in the main proceedings, namely that relating to the bringing-up of the children and that, in the case of legitimate, natural or adopted children, it simply took it for granted that they were brought up at the home of their mother. It should also be noted in this connection that, as counsel for Mr Griesmar pointed out at the hearing without being contradicted, that credit dates back to 1924 and its purpose, as explained in the relevant preparatory documents, was to facilitate the female civil servant's return to her home in order for her to be better able to bring up her children.

Article 6(3) of the Agreement on Social Policy authorises national measures intended to eliminate or reduce actual instances of inequality which result from the reality of social life and affect women in their professional life. It follows that the national measures covered by that provision must, in any event, contribute to helping women conduct their professional life on an equal footing with men.

Caruso, 'Limits of the Classic Method', 347, footnotes omitted

[The *Griesmar* decision] illustrates how the supranational scrutiny of states' positive action programs may create an unwarranted legislative deficit in crucial social matters . . . Once more, there are reasons to doubt the sensibility of the Court's holding. In terms of strict logic, it may be a straightforward application of the Court's understanding of equality. Viewed in terms of European social engineering, however, Griesmar holds much less persuasive force. There are many ways in which the state, as employer, may encourage women to join the workforce. In many European states, it is thanks to employment in the public sector, and to special accommodations for the protection of the family, that women are adequately represented in the workforce. The Pensions Code's preference may well have made sense in the French design of public employment, but the Griesmar holding interferes with that design. It is de-regulatory, and very effectively so, thanks to the immediate enforceability of ECJ holdings. But it does not, and cannot, point to reconstructive suggestions, because social engineering is not within the competency of the Union. Holdings like Griesmar do not relieve member states of the task of designing optimal formulae for a diverse workplace, and yet burden them with deregulatory constraints.

Article 141, which was inserted into the Treaty after the decisions in *Kalanke, Marschall, Badeck* and *Griesmar*, provides that:

(4) With a view to ensuring full equality in practice between men and women in working life, the principle of equal treatment shall not prevent any Member State from maintaining or adopting measures providing for specific advantages to make it easier for the under-represented sex to pursue a vocational activity or to prevent or compensate for disadvantages in professional careers.

This appears to provide wider scope for positive discrimination than the relatively constrained language of Article 2(4) of the Equal Treatment Directive. Article 141(4), which applies only to sex discrimination, is echoed by the Racial Equality and Employment Equality Directives. The former provides (Article 5) that:

With a view to ensuring full equality in practice, the principle of equal treatment shall not prevent any Member State from maintaining or adopting specific measures to prevent or compensate for disadvantages linked to racial or ethnic origin.

Article 7(1) of the Employment Equality Directive is materially identical, Article 7(2) further providing that: 'With regard to disabled persons, the principle of equal treatment shall be without prejudice to the right of Member States to maintain or adopt provisions on the protection of health and safety at work or to measures aimed at creating or maintaining provisions or facilities for safeguarding or promoting their integration into the working environment.' The interpretation of Article 141(4) by the ECJ is therefore indicative of its likely approach to positive action on the newly protected grounds.

In *Abrahamsson & Anderson v Fogelqvist*, Case C–407/98 [2000] ECR–05539, the ECJ was asked to rule on the legality of Swedish regulations whereby universities which were recruiting to academic jobs in which women were under-represented were required to grant preference to a candidate from the under-represented sex. The regulations, which provided that the less qualified candidate was not to be appointed 'where the difference between the candidates' qualification is so great that such application would give rise to a breach of the requirement of objectivity in the making of appointments,' had been adopted following the failure of earlier regulations which permitted (but did not require) positive action significantly to affect the under-representation of women in the academic sphere. The ECJ ruled that the scheme breached Article 2(1) and (4) of the Equal Treatment Directive, and that it would have done so even if applied only in relation to a predetermined number of posts or to posts created as part of a specific programme of a particular higher educational institution allowing the application of positive discrimination measures. Having reiterated the *Marschall* holding that the Equal Treatment Directive was consistent with the granting of preference to a candidate of the under-represented sex where qualifications were equal and candidatures were subjected to an objective assessment taking account of their specific personal situations of all the candidates, the Court went on to rule that:

> even though Article 141(4) EC allows the Member States to maintain or adopt measures providing for special advantages intended to prevent or compensate for disadvantages in professional careers in order to ensure full equality between men and women in professional life, it cannot be inferred from this that it allows a selection method of the kind at issue in the main proceedings which appears, on any view, to be disproportionate to the aim pursued.[60]

D Caruso, 'Limits of the Classic Method', 343–344, footnotes omitted

The Commission welcomed the *Abrahamsson* decision. Interestingly, on its official web site, the Commission advertised the case as one that 'upheld Swedish measures to combat female under-representation in employment.' This is only partly true. The Court did confirm the permissibility of positive discrimination in favour of women, and explained that gender may operate as a tie-breaker once a tie is established, thereby rejecting with unprecedented clarity the logic of *Kalanke*. However, *Abrahamsson* significantly curtailed the scope of the Swedish regulation in question. The administrators of the University interpreted it to mean that, because the principle of objective assessment was not violated—the female candidate was certainly worthy of the academic post—the requirement of par qualifications could be mildly relaxed. Quite the contrary, after *Abrahamsson*, the formalistic threshold of equal qualifications must be unquestionably met. The female candidate must be just as good as her male competitor. It is only at that point that, rather than tossing a coin, the University deans can use gender as a basis for their final decision.

The case reveals a serious clash of attitude between the ECJ and a member state on affirmative action. In the view of the Swedish establishment, the *Marschall* prerequisite of par qualifications is clearly inadequate to address representational deficiencies in the academic community. Yet, it continues to control the supranational legitimacy of positive action policies.

For all of the criticisms which may be levelled at the ECJ's approach to positive discrimination, the test established in *Marschall*, *Badeck* and *Abrahammson* is far more permissive

---

[60] And see more recently the decision of the ECJ in *Briheche v Ministre de l'Interieur* Case C–319/03 [2004] ECR I–00000, OJ C 284, 20.11.2004, p. 4.

than that which prevails under domestic law. It is now for the Government to determine whether to legislate in order to further the 'goals and timetables' established by it in relation to ethnic minority recruitment and retention in the police, prison and fire service, as well as to ethnic minority and female advancement in public appointments and the senior Civil Service.[61] It is most unlikely, given the Government's hostility to intervention in the private sector, that positive action will be required other than in the public sector. But in the absence of legislative amendment to permit at least 'tie-break' reverse discrimination, goals and timetables set in respect of female and ethnic minority advancement have very little chance of being met. Every white man rejected in favour of a woman or ethnic minority candidate will have an incentive to litigate. And the fact that an employer is self-consciously in the business of seeking to appoint more women/ ethnic minority candidates will operate so as to render a judgment in favour of the aggrieved white man more likely.

The difficulties of proving discrimination are discussed in Chapter 5. Here it is useful to consider a recent EAT decision which illustrates the potential difficulties facing those employers seeking deliberately to increase the diversity of their workforces.

ACAS v Taylor, Appl No EAT/788/97, unreported (11 February 1998)

The decision concerned an appeal from a tribunal finding that Mr Taylor had been discriminated against by being refused promotion. Applications for promotion had been made by 126 ACAS officers of whom 40 per cent were female (women accounted for 38 per cent of those eligible to apply). Applications were assessed in the first place by their line managers, the grades awarded resulting either in rejection or in the case of 'A' grades, in progress to the next stage of the promotion procedure. The highest scoring 'B' grade assessed by each line manager also went forward as did, in cases where the line manager's scorings were regarded as low, the second highest ranking 'B.'

Mr Taylor was ranked fourth of the 4 'Bs' in his region, and was not put forward to the next stage. A tribunal found that he had been discriminated against on the basis that, whereas all eight of the women ranked 'B' were put forward, only six of the sixteen men so ranked were put forward. In relation to four of the six recommending officers, two 'B' candidates were put forward. In each of these cases, the second 'B' was female.

The decision of the tribunal was questionable, the fact being that, whether or not two B candidates had been put forward in relation to the applicant's region, his application would not have been put forward. Further, the fact that women in each case benefited from a judgment that their recommending officers had been parsimonious could well have reflected the common practice whereby women are undervalued by virtue of their being women. But the tribunal took the view that Mr Taylor had been the victim of a policy of positive discrimination. This decision was reached, in part, because ACAS had circulated the following recruitment guidelines to its recommending officers:

> Please remember that more needs to be done to ensure the reality of the claim that ACAS is an equal opportunity employer. For example women make up only 17 per cent of those at SEO level at present and ethnic minorities staff less than 1 per cent. All staff should be considered on their merits as individuals. Where you have any doubts about the fairness of the Annual Reports you should not hesitate to take appropriate action.

---

[61] The Metropolitan Police is considering pressurising the Government to permit it to use quotas for the recruitment of ethnic minority officers, a step which would require amendment of the RRA. See further the discussion below.

Morison J (for EAT):

It seems to us that the guidance provisions to which we have referred should be reconsidered by ACAS. The sentence 'Please remember that more needs to be done to ensure the reality of the claim that ACAS is an equal opportunity employer' is readily capable of being misconstrued. Furthermore, it begs the question as to what is to be done and by whom. It seems to us that it would have been more appropriate and quite sufficient for the guidance to have reminded the line managers that ACAS was an equal opportunity employer and to draw attention to the fact that women and ethnic minorities staff at SEO level were poorly represented. Such poor representation was itself suggestive of potentially discriminatory practices in the past and the employers were entitled to draw that to the attention of those who had the responsibility for making decisions about promotions in the future. The way the guidance was composed seems to us to be capable of leading the unwary into positive discrimination.

It would be deeply ironic if, absent legislation to extend the scope of lawful positive discrimination, even if only in certain sections of the public sector, the adoption by government of a 'goals and timetables' approach to equal opportunities served only to arm disappointed white male applicants with material from which tribunals will readily infer that they have been discriminated against. We saw, above, that EC law leaves considerable scope for an extension of the positive discrimination currently lawful in the UK.

'Mainstreaming' Equality? Positive Obligations and Public Authorities

'Mainstreaming' refers to the policy of incorporating an emphasis on equality into 'into all policies and programmes, so that, before decisions are taken, an analysis is made of the effects on' protected groups. Gender mainstreaming was adopted in the 'platform for action' by the Fourth UN World Conference on Women in September 1995 (the Beijing conference), strongly backed by the EU delegation to the conference. Mainstreaming has subsequently been incorporated into European thinking: Article 3 of the Treaty Establishing the European Community, as amended by the Treaty of Amsterdam stating that 'In all the activities [of the Community], the Community shall aim to eliminate inequalities, and to promote equality, between men and women.'

The EU

The European Commission adopted gender-mainstreaming in 1996.[62] The 1998 Third Annual Report from the European Commission on Equal Opportunities for men and women in the European Union reported that '[t]hroughout 1998, the Commission continues and consolidates its strategy of assessing all general policies and measures for their gender impact,' particular attention having been paid to the targeting of structural funds

---

[62] Communication of 21 February 1996, 'Incorporating Equal Opportunities for Women and Men into all Community Policies and Activities' COM(96)67 final.

and mainstreaming having been adopted as the 'general principle and the primary strategic objective' of the medium-term Community action programme on equal opportunities
for men and women. A gender-dimension was incorporated into educational and research
programmes, into development co-operation programmes and into the Commission input
on Member States' National Plans for Employment. The Commission's Work Programme
1998 set out for 'specific attention' policies including the promotion of equal sharing of
work and family responsibilities between women and men as part of schemes promoting
part-time work, flexibility and new forms of work organisation; the conduct of a gender
impact assessment of EMU and the EURO; and 'addressing the requirements as well as the
impact of the enlargement process on equality between women and men.'

In 2000 the Commission declared that it 'intend[ed] to operationalise and consolidate
[gender mainstreaming] through its Communications to the Council, the European
Parliament, the European Social Committee and the Committee of the Regions':

> Future Community work towards gender equality will take the form of a comprehensive
> strategy, which will embrace all Community policies in its efforts to promote gender
> equality, either by adjusting their [sic] policies (pro-active intervention: gender main-
> streaming) and/or by implementing concrete actions designed to improve the situation of
> women in society . . .
>
> This integrated approach marks an important change from the previous Community
> action on equal opportunities for women and men, mainly based on compartmental activ-
> ities and programmes funded under different specific budget headings. The Framework
> Strategy on Gender Equality aims at coordinating all the different initiatives and pro-
> grammes under a single umbrella built around clear assessment criteria, monitoring tools,
> the setting of benchmarks, gender proofing and evaluation.

The Commission expressed its commitment to promoting gender equality in economic
life using, in particular, the European Structural Funds; to promoting equal participation
and representation in decision making, gender equality in civic life and change of gender
role and stereotypes, social access and full enjoyment of social rights for women and
men:

> Equal access and full enjoyment of social rights are among the pillars of democratic
> societies. Yet, many women do not have equal access to social rights either because some of
> these rights are based on an outdated male breadwinner model or they do not take into
> account that women predominantly carry the burden of having to reconcile family and pro-
> fessional life. This is evident in many social protection systems, which in turn is one of the
> explanations of the feminization of poverty in the European Union (career-breaks, part-
> time work, lack of education and training). In many cases, women just do not access or have
> access to proper information about existing social rights. Some of these rights have already
> become European legislation. The [Commission's] actions will aim at improving the appli-
> cation of Community legislation in particular on social protection and in the areas of
> parental leave, maternity protection and working time. In addition, the actions will include
> better information dissemination.
>
> Women in developing countries often experience discrimination in access to nutrition,
> health care, education, training, decision making, and property rights. The Council
> Regulation on integrating gender issues in development cooperation underlines that
> redressing gender disparities and enhancing the role of women are crucial for both social
> justice and development.

The 2000–06 Structural Funds regulations and guidance introduced gender main-streaming as a critical goal of the funds. The Seventh Annual Report from the European Commission on Equal Opportunities for men and women in the European Union (2002) reported that, while 'the dual strategy towards gender equality, namely mainstreaming and specific actions, proved to be successful' in the employment context, 'the visibility of gender equality [having] improved even in Member States that are "lagging behind," and gender gaps hav[ing] decreased in particular for employment and unemployment rates . . . much remains to be done to achieve the Lisbon and Stockholm targets and to close gender gaps which are still too wide. . . .' The Commission went on to report that child and dependent care provision remained a problem, that reliance upon (improving) parental leave arrangements could (given the disproportionate take-up of such leave by women) further increase gender inequality and that gender mainstreaming was proving difficult to implement in Structural Fund areas such as transport, environment or rural development.

Both the Racial Equality Directive and the Employment Equality Directive note in their preambles that the EC, in implementing the principle of equal treatment therein: 'should, in accordance with Article 3(2) of the EC Treaty, aim to eliminate inequalities, and to pro-mote equality between men and women, especially since women are often the victims of multiple discrimination.' Articles 17 and 19 of the Racial Equality Directive and the Employment Equality Directive respectively require that Member States, in reporting on their implementation of the Directives, 'shall, inter alia, provide an assessment of the impact of the measures taken on women and men.'

Northern Ireland

'Mainstreaming' has also begun to find its way onto the domestic agenda. The most com-prehensive statutory provision in place is s.75 of the Northern Ireland Act 1998 which imposes upon 'public authorities' scheduled to the Act an obligation 'in carrying out [their] functions relating to Northern Ireland' to have 'due regard to the need to promote equal-ity of opportunity—

(a) between persons of different religious belief, political opinion, racial group, age, marital status or sexual orientation;
(b) between men and women generally;
(c) between persons with a disability and
(d) between persons with dependants and persons without.'

Section 75(2) provides that, without prejudice to the obligations imposed by s.75(1), pub-lic authorities shall also have regard to the desirability of promoting good relations between persons of different religious belief, political opinion or racial group.

Inasmuch as it applies to public authorities' employment functions, s.75 NIA sits somewhat uncomfortably with the Government's articulated hostility towards contract compliance (con-sidered in Chapter 5) and its continued pursuit of competition in the public sector. The pol-icy has its roots in the Policy Appraisal and Fair Treatment (PAFT) guidelines, first issued in Northern Ireland in December 1993, which in turn drew upon British guidelines launched in the 1980s by the Ministerial Group on Women's Issues. The PAFT initiative was intended 'to ensure that, in practice, issues of equality and equity condition policy-making and action in all spheres and at all levels of Government activity, whether in regulatory and administrative functions or in the delivery of services to the public.'[63] The groups to which public authorities were instructed to have regard were 'people of different gender, age, ethnic group, religious belief or political opinion; married and unmarried people; disabled and non-disabled people; people with or without dependants; and people of differing sexual orientation.'

The operation of the PAFT guidelines in Northern Ireland was heavily criticised, Christine Bell pointing out that the guidelines were not made public and, in many cases, did not even reach public authorities responsible for their implementation. Further, the first annual report on the operation of the guidelines was replete with references to issues having 'no PAFT implications' in circumstances where, as Bell points out, this conclusion was highly questionable (these included, for example, a projected intended 'to integrate and include people with a mental illness within the community').

C Bell, 'Employment Equality Review' (1996) 2 *International Journal of Discrimination and the Law* 53, 69–74, footnotes omitted

Implementation by Non Departmental Public Bodies (NDPBs)

While the implementation of PAFT guidelines at departmental level seems patchy, at the level of NDPBs it has been worse if not non-existent. This was well illustrated in a judicial review taken by UNISON against Down Lisburn Trust for refusing to suspend its decision to market test services. UNISON had argued that the decision not to suspend testing discriminated against women involved in service provision. One of the reasons given in support of suspension was the need to consider the PAFT implications of the decision. In the course of the case it was revealed that it was 6 July 1995 (that is about 18 months after their introduction) before Health Trusts received PAFT documentation.

The court found that the decision makers had not been made aware of PAFT at the time of their decision, and were therefore not at fault for not applying it. However, the court rejected the Trust's submissions that 'PAFT Guidelines were not a blueprint but more in the nature of a series of strategic objectives,' rejecting the Trust's implicit argument 'that PAFT provided no more than a lofty aspiration at which bodies such as Trusts should aim and that failure to achieve that aspiration would be a matter of little or no consequence.' While the case illustrates at best a casual approach to PAFT, the decision by the court leaves the door open for further enforcement in the future.

Contracting Out Services

The PAFT guidelines call for consideration to be given to any discriminatory effect which attaches to a particular service delivery or policy, so that alternative approaches can be assessed. Specific reference is made to the application of these principles to contracted-out services in the cover letter sent with the guidelines within departments are urged 'to use their best endeavours, consistent with legal and contractual obligations, to secure compliance with PAFT by those performing contracted-out services on their behalf.' However, according to the CCRU report, departments merely seek to encourage providers of contracted-out services to be 'consistent with the spirit of PAFT.'

Education services provides an example of the limitations of PAFT application in this area. In the case of education, article 20 of the Education and Library Boards (Northern Ireland) Order requires Boards to conduct contracting-out activities without reference to non-commercial matters. Despite the conflicts with PAFT, and the DENI clarification to Boards that the Order takes precedence, no explicit reference is made to this tension in the Department's [Central Community Relations Unit] CCRU Report entry. This not only reflects on the quality of the CCRU Report, but given that contracting out of services is a

---

[63] Central Community Relations Unit's First Annual Report on PAFT (1995).

governmental trend at present, it illustrates an important limitation of PAFT. If in practice PAFT is rendered inapplicable to this area then its usefulness is seriously diminished. Further, if legislation automatically takes precedence over PAFT, and PAFT does not require at least consideration of its amendment, then the whole operation and function of PAFT is in question.

Training in the implementation of the guidelines within government departments appeared, in 1995, to have been sketchy at best with no additional resources having been allocated to this end. Nor were resources made available for monitoring. The CCRU's second Annual Report on PAFT referred to the UNISON case, noting that:

2.13 The PAFT guidelines require Departments to use their best endeavours, consistent with legal and contractual obligations, to secure compliance with PAFT by those perform-ing contracted-out services on their behalf. The primary purpose of this reference was to seek the delivery of contracted-out services to the public on the same basis of fairness and non-discrimination which would be expected from a public body. The controversy over market testing drew attention to the . . . issue of the implications for the workforce in parts of the public sector where polices such as market testing, contracting-out and privatisation are applied. Where PAFT considerations are found to be relevant, it is, however, still entirely legitimate for a Department to conclude, on the basis of an assessment of the full range of factors at play, that greater benefit would be secured from implementation of the initiative. Furthermore, legislation predating PAFT, such as the Education and Libraries Order (NI) 1993, which introduced compulsory competitive tendering for certain functions of the Education and Library Boards, may limit the scope for the application of PAFT, since clearly statutory obligations take precedence over administrative guidance.

The report referred to the findings of a Formal Investigation conducted by the EOCNI into the impact of competitive tendering in the health and education services, the EOCNI having recommended that the gender implications of CCT in that sector were so severe that the policy should be suspended:

2.15 . . .The Government decided not to suspend the policy, pending a full examination of the evidence contained in the EOC's report. Of the report's 35 recommendations, 6 relate to the application of the PAFT guidelines. The case studies on which the report is based related to the period before the introduction of the PAFT guidance and several of the rec-ommendations would be expected to be part of current procedures. The [EOCNI's] final report was published in 1996 and is currently under consideration.'
2.16 The controversy over market testing and competitive tendering points to the potential for tensions between the philosophy of PAFT and aspects of other Government policies. Many forms of discrimination are illegal under Northern Ireland statute and clearly cannot be breached by the Government. Other forms of differential treatment are legally permissible and PAFT requires Departments to consider carefully the potential for rectify-ing them. This may sometimes involve assessing the competing claims of different policies and this may ultimately be a matter for Ministerial judgement as to public interest. PAFT seeks to ensure that issues of equality and equity are given full weight in these considera-tions, but it cannot be assumed that PAFT considerations will always predominate.

The third and final report on PAFT noted that:

2.10 . . . The Secretary of State subsequently replied to the EOC on 21 January 1997 stating that the Government was unable to accept certain of the report's recommendations, including those relating to the suspension of competitive tendering in the health and education services . . . the Secretary of State noted the need to establish an appropriate balance, consistent with statutory obligations, between achieving maximum safeguards in relation to equality issues, delivering services to the public as efficiently as practicable, setting the highest quality standards, and attaining best value for money.

In 1999 Christopher McCrudden remarked that the PAFT initiative 'proved largely unsuccessful.'[64] Criticism by McCrudden and others was not aimed at the substance of the guidelines, rather at their non-binding nature and the failures of implementation within the authorities charged with their application. One of the main criticisms made in respect of s.75 NIA, as it was originally proposed, concerned the lack of a robust 'internal mechanism' for its enforcement. Initially the Northern Ireland Bill was, according to the response from the Standing Advisory Committee on Human Rights (the forerunner to the Human Rights Commission of Northern Ireland), 'silent on the crucial issue of an internal mechanism to ensure that equality considerations are mainstreamed at the heart of government.' Voicing its criticism of the fact that Northern Ireland's separate equality commissions had been amalgamated in significant part to provide a single 'external mechanism' for the enforcement of s.75, SACHR proposed the creation of a Department of Equality headed by the Deputy First Minister of Northern Ireland's Assembly. The Northern Ireland Act did not accede to the call for a Department of Equality, but did give the Deputy First Minister responsibility for equality.

The regime eventually established by the NIA (s.75 and Schedule 9) takes into account the lessons learned from PAFT. Central to it are the 'equality schemes' which all public authorities covered by the Act were required to submit to the ECNI for approval. Schemes may be approved by the Commission or referred to the Secretary of State who may approve them, request the relevant public authority to draw up a revised scheme, or impose a scheme on the authority. Public authorities must review their schemes every five years and notify the Commission of the outcome of any such review. The ECNI can receive complaints about any failure on the part of a public authority to comply with its own equality scheme, where such complaints are brought by a person 'who claims to have been directly affected by the failure.' It can also investigate, in the absence of complaint, authorities' compliance with their equality schemes.

Each equality scheme had to set out the authority's arrangements (Schedule 9, para 4(2)):

(a) for assessing its compliance with the duties under section 75 and for consulting on matters to which a duty under that section is likely to be relevant (including details of the persons to be consulted);
(b) for assessing and consulting on the likely impact of policies adopted or proposed to be adopted by the authority on the promotion of equality of opportunity;
(c) for monitoring any adverse impact of policies adopted by the authority on the promotion of equality of opportunity;
(d) for publishing the results of such assessments as are mentioned in paragraph (b) and such monitoring as is mentioned in paragraph (c);
(e) for training staff;
(f) for ensuring, and assessing, public access to information and to services provided by the authority.

---

[64] *Equality News* available from the DGV website at http://europa.eu.int. See also the EOC's report in mainstreaming in local authorities available from its website (www.eoc.org.uk).

Schemes have to include a timetable and details of how they will be published. Before drawing up an equality scheme public authorities are required: 'in accordance with any directions given by the Commission' to consult representatives of those likely to be affected by the scheme and 'such other persons as may be specified in the [ECNI's] directions.' The Commission's guiding principles stress that '[c]onsultation can help authorities to become aware of issues and problems which policies may pose for various groups which the organisation might not otherwise discover' and provides that equality schemes must 'include the public authority's commitment to carrying out consultations in accordance' with the guiding principles which require, inter alia, requirements about the accessibility of the language and the format of information provided to prospective consultees (the provision of material, for example, in Braille, on disc and audiocassette and in minority languages), the allocation of sufficient time to allow groups to consult among themselves, and the taking of appropriate measures to ensure full participation in meetings: 'Different groups have different needs and may have different customs. Public authorities will need to consider the time of day, the appropriateness of the venue, in particular whether it can be accessed by those with disabilities, how the meeting is to be run, the use of appropriate language, whether a signer is necessary, and the provision of childcare').[65]

The ECNI's Code stresses that the 'policies' whose equality implications public authorities are required to consider cover 'all the ways in which an authority proposes to carry out its functions relating to Northern Ireland . . . employment and procurement policies are an integral aspect of the way in which an authority carries out its functions. Accordingly, the [equality] scheme must cover the arrangements for assessing the impact of such policies.' The guidance stresses the importance of reviewing the impact are not limited to those generally regarded as being concerned with 'equal opportunities.' If a preliminary 'screening' exercise such as that which public authorities are required to carry out demonstrates differential levels of uptake of a service between different groups, or different levels of participation, it suggests that an authority ought to consider carrying out a full equality impact assessment.

Public authorities must take into account any assessment and consultation carried out under the statutory obligation and must publish the results. In doing so, they are required (para 9(1)) to state the 'aims of the policy to which the assessment relates and give details of any consideration given by the authority to—

(a) measures which might mitigate any adverse impact of that policy on the promotion of equality of opportunity; and
(b) alternative policies which might better achieve the promotion of equality of opportunity.'

Some indication of the potential of the positive obligations imposed by s.75 is evident from the timetable for compliance published in March 2002 by the Northern Ireland Office as part of its equality scheme. That body is of course not typical of those covered by the obligations, being responsible for a huge range of functions in Northern Ireland ranging from human rights matters to the regulation of broadcasting and elections to policing and security, criminal justice, prisons, and the operation of statutory compensation schemes. But it is instructive to see how wide is the operation of s.75. Among the commitments made

---

[65] Guide to the Statutory Duties—A guide to the implementation of the statutory duties on public authorities arising from Section 75 of the Northern Ireland Act 1998, available from the ECNI's website at http://www.equalityni.org.

by the NIO were reviews of the 'implications for equality of opportunity' of employment-related issues such as the 'Special Bonus Pay Scheme,' the pay of part-timers and policies dealing with staff training, development, placement and transfer. The Office also committed itself to reviewing 'the implications for equality of opportunity between people of different religious beliefs and political opinions of security vetting policy and practice' and the 'implications for equality of opportunity of' the NIO's procurement policy and practice; and to carrying out 'impact assessments' of:

- the Department's functions in respect of broadcasting issues
- new measures to prevent electoral fraud
- the Strategy to tackle Violence Against Women
- the co-ordinated response to drug misuse across the criminal justice system
- the Childcare Voucher Scheme
- the policy on the supervision of juveniles in the community
- the treatment of juveniles in custody
- the arrangements for the delivery of support services to victims of crime
- the policy on working with young people in the community to divert them from the criminal justice system
- the policy for maintaining the legal framework necessary to hold elections in Northern Ireland for the European Parliament, Westminster Parliament, the Northern Ireland Assembly and local government; and
- probation policy.

It is too early to assess the impact of the statutory duty imposed on public authorities in Northern Ireland by s.75 NIA but compliance levels are high. According to the Commission's *Full Report on the Implementation of the Section 75 Equality and Good Relations Duties by Public Authorities 1 January 2000–31 March 2002*, good progress had been made on the schemes with the vast majority of public authorities obliged to draw them up having had their schemes approved by the Commission. Among the difficulties highlighted by the Commission report, however, was the difficulty in securing adequate resources for the consultee bodies.[66]

Race

Section 75 NIA was followed in Great Britain by the imposition, under the Race Relations (Amendment) Act 2000, of positive obligations on public authorities in relation to race equality. The Act amends the RRA to provide that any body specified in Schedule 1A to the Act 'shall, in carrying out its functions, have due regard to the need (s 71(1))—

(a) to eliminate unlawful racial discrimination; and
(b) to promote equality of opportunity and good relations between persons of different racial groups.'

Schedule 1A lists a long series of bodies including ministers of the Crown and government departments (though not the Security Service, the Intelligence Service or the Government Communications Headquarters), the Scottish administration and Welsh National Assembly,

---

[66] Available from the commission's website, *ibid.*

the armed forces and NHS bodies, local authorities, fire authorities, licensing boards and regional development agencies, education bodies, housing bodies and the police. In total over 43,000 bodies are covered by the positive duties. S.71 RRA provides that the Secretary of State (in Scotland, the Scottish Ministers) 'may by order impose, on such persons falling within Schedule 1A as he considers appropriate, such duties as he considers appropriate for the purpose of ensuring the better performance by those persons of their duties' under s.71(1). The Race Relations Act 1976 (Statutory Duties) Order 2001 (SI 2001/3458) required many public sector employers to publish race equality schemes by 31 May 2002.[67] Such schemes are very similar to those required under the NIA, save that they apply only in relation to race). Authorities required to publish them have to include details of those functions and existing and proposed policies which they have assessed as relevant to their performance of the duty imposed by s.71 RRA; and the authority's arrangements for:

- assessing and consulting on the likely impact of its proposed policies on the promotion of race equality
- monitoring its policies for any adverse impact on the promotion of race equality
- publishing the results of such assessments and consultation
- ensuring public access to information and services which it provides; and
- training staff in connection with the duties imposed by s.71 and the Order.

Educational institutions are not bound by these specific employment-related duties but schools have obligations to provide education authorities with specific information about employment so that the authorities can meet their monitoring obligations, and higher and further education institutions have an obligation to monitor recruitment and career progress of staff and to take reasonable steps to publish the results of such monitoring annually. Educational institutions are bound by the general positive obligation imposed by s.71 RRA.

Just as is the case in Northern Ireland, many of the policies covered by the RRA's statutory duty concern service delivery as well as employment. But public authorities covered by the amended RRA are required by the Order to undertake ethnic monitoring in relation to their workforces and to publish the results annually. The monitoring obligation extends to (a) the numbers of staff in post (b) applicants for employment, training and promotion from each racial group, and (c) where the body has 150 or more full-time staff, the numbers of staff from each racial group who receive training, benefit or suffer detriment as a result of its performance assessment procedures, are involved in grievance procedures, are the subject of disciplinary procedures, or cease employment with that body. The CRE has issued a statutory Code of Practice and four non-statutory guides to help authorities in England and Wales meet their duties under the amended RRA.

The Audit Commission reported in May 2002 (*Equality and Diversity*) that most authorities had a policy on equality and diversity but that such policies were 'rarely translated into action with specific outcomes and challenging targets' and that data collection was poor. The following year, six months after the deadline for implementation, a study of 3,338 public bodies carried out for the CRE found that almost a third of Britain's public bodies had yet to comply. Roughly one third of those surveyed were, according to an *Equal Opportunities Review* report: 'focused on delivery; a middle tier [had] laid good foundations

---

[67] The Order covers England and Wales, a materially similar Race Relations Act 1976 (Statutory Duties) (Scotland) Order 2002 (SI 2002/62) applying north of the border.

but still have some way to go; and a bottom third . . . had stumbled at the first hurdle and had not set any outcomes.'[68] Progress on employment-related issues was particularly patchy, the report found, and few authorities 'focused on furthering race equality in procurement and partnerships work.' The report recommended that the legislation be kept under review and thought given to imposing an annual reporting duty on public authorities; that practical advice and guidance be given to authorities; and that central government support and drive further progress by, for example, integrating performance measures on progress in this area into the main performance measurement and management systems that apply across the public sector.

In 2004 the Audit Commission concluded (in *The Journey to Race Equality*), that while public services were optimistic about their approaches to race equality, 'progress is not uniform.' Eight-nine per cent of chief executives surveyed said that race was a significant part of the organisation's overall objectives and 50 per cent that the organisation's priorities had changed to reflect this; 'but a gap between optimism and reality is emerging . . . many are unclear about what they are trying to achieve' and 'progress is often measured in terms of process, rather than the delivery of outcomes that will impact upon quality of life.'

Enforcement of the statutory duty is by the Commission which is empowered (s.71D RRA) to issue a compliance notice if it is satisfied that an authority has failed or is failing to comply with an order issued by the Secretary of State (see preceding page). Such a notice requires the authority to comply with the duty concerned and to inform the CRE within 28 days of the steps it has taken or is taking to do so and may, in addition, require the provision of further information to allow the CRE to verify that the duty has been complied with. If an authority fails to comply with a notice issued under s.71D the CRE may apply to a designated county court or to a sheriff court for an order requiring the authority to furnish the information required or to comply with a requirement to comply with a duty referred to therein. Enforcement of the general duty is by way of judicial review.

Disability

At the time of the RR(A)A 2000 the Government stated its intention to enact positive obligations on public authorities in relation to sex and disability as soon as parliamentary time permitted. The DDA 2005 amends the DDA by inserting new s.21B which makes it unlawful for public authorities in carrying out their functions to discriminate against the disabled (this is similar to s.19B RRA and discussed in Chapter 4). In addition, new s.49A DDA provides that:

(1) Every public authority shall in carrying out its functions have due regard to—
  (a) the need to eliminate discrimination that is unlawful under the Act;
  (b) the need to eliminate harassment of disabled persons that is related to their disabilities;
  (c) the need to promote equality of opportunity between disabled persons and other persons;
  (d) the need to take steps to take account of disabled persons' disabilities, even where that involves treating disabled persons more favourably than other persons;
  (e) the need to promote positive attitudes towards disabled persons; and
  (f) the need to encourage participation by disabled persons in public life.

---

[68] 'Race equality work needs to focus on outcomes' 120 *Equal Opportunities Review*. See also the CRE's interim report on its formal investigation into the Police, discussed in Ch 7.

Whereas the NIA and the RRA as amended list those public authorities to which their provisions apply, the DDA 2005 does not. Nor does it comprehensively define the term 'public authority' but provides instead (s.49B(1)(a)) that a public authority 'includes any person certain of whose functions are of a public nature' but does not include (s.21B(3)) either House of Parliament, 'a person exercising functions in connection with proceedings in Parliament,' the security services, Secret Intelligence Service, the GCHQ or 'a unit, or part of a unit, of any of the naval, military or air forces of the Crown which is for the time being required to assist the [GCHQ] in carrying out its functions' or (s.49B(b)) the Scottish Parliament or 'a person exercising functions in connection with proceedings in the Scottish Parliament.' The Explanatory Notes suggest that 'the definition will certainly include Government Departments, local authorities, the police and other governmental organisations', while the DRC's Code of Practice 'The Duty to promote Disability Equality' states that all those bodies listed in the RRA will be 'public authorities' for the purposes of the DDA as amended.

The approach taken by the DDA 2005 is similar to that adopted by the HRA (whose exclusions are, however, much narrower than those proposed by the Bill). Also similar to the HRA is the DDA's provision (new s.49B(2)): 'in relation to a particular act, a person is not a public authority by virtue only of subsection (1)(a) if the nature of the act is private.' Thus, for example, while Group 4 would be a public authority in relation to its handling of prisoners (this being very much in the nature of a public function) it would not be a public authority in relation to employment which is regarded as in the nature of a private relationship.[69] Section 49B(3) also provides that the Secretary of State may by regulation 'provide for a person of a prescribed description to be treated as not being a public authority for the purposes of this section' while s.49C further exempts from the obligation imposed by s.49A(1) judicial acts and primary legislation[70] and, in relation to s.49A(1)(c) alone an act done 'in connection with recruitment to any of the naval, military or air forces of the Crown' or 'in relation to any person in connection with service by him as a member of those forces.' Section 49C(4) provides that regulations may exempt further acts from the scope of the s.49A(1)(a), (b) or (c) obligations. The Explanatory Notes suggest that s.49C 'could be used, for example, to clarify the situation where there was doubt as to whether a body [or an act] was covered or not, or to exclude bodies [and types of act] altogether where there were good policy reasons as to why they should not be covered by the section 49A(1) duty.'

The amendments made to the DDA by the DDA 2005 permit the Secretary of State and Scottish Ministers to impose such specific duties on public authorities as they 'consider[ ] appropriate for the purpose of ensuring the better performance by that authority of its duty under s.49(A)(1)'. The draft Disability Discrimination (Public Authorities) (Statutory Duties) Regulations 2005 propose the imposition on bodies listed in the Appendix thereto of specific duties similar to those imposed under the RRA, that is, the obligation to draw up and implement a Disability Equality Scheme 'showing how [the body] intends to fulfil its section 49A(1) duties and its duties under these Regulations'. Public authorities would be required to 'involve in the development of the Scheme those disabled people who appear to that authority to have an interest in the way it carries out its functions' and each Scheme, which would have to be revised every three years, would be required to include information

---

[69] The Explanatory notes to the DD Bill suggested that: 'the Law Society is likely to be covered in respect of its statutory functions such as those relating to the regulation of solicitors, but not its private functions— for example the representation of the interests of the profession in dealings with Government.'

[70] Or Orders in Council which are similarly protected by the HRA as akin to primary legislation.

(draft reg 2) about that involvement and other information broadly similar to that required under the NIA (see above).

Enforcement of the general duty will be by way of judicial review and, in the case of the specific duties proposed, by compliance notices issued by the DRC and enforceable through the courts. This is similar to the enforcement scheme which applies under the RRA (above).

The Disability Rights Commission, in written evidence to the Joint Parliamentary Committee on the then draft DDB, 'applaud[ed] the government for including a Disability Equality Duty for public authorities on the face of the Bill,' stating that:

> This change will bring enormous benefits to disabled people. All the evidence tells us it is impossible to remove discrimination by relying solely on individuals one by one taking legal cases to challenge acts of discrimination. Such legal challenges almost always take place after the harm is done, and preventing discrimination is preferable to retrospective justice. This duty places the onus on public services to ensure that any systematic bias is removed from the way in which services are delivered, and from their employment practices.

The Commission pointed out the absence from the proposed amendments to the DDA of any obligation to promote 'good relations' and expressed the view that such a duty would be:

> useful, and that not to include such a duty risks being interpreted by public authorities as inappropriately signalling that the issues tackled in relation to race have no relevance for disabled people.
>
>   It is possible to distinguish four strands of activity which have been undertaken with a view to promoting good race relations:
> a. Work bringing communities together—'building community cohesion.'
> b. Addressing issues of harassment and violence outside the workplace.
> c. The promotion of general understanding/awareness in the community.
> d. Improving civic participation, combating social exclusion and deprivation.
>
>   We believe that a duty to promote good community relations, applied to disability, would be useful in respect of all these activities. It would certainly be helpful in ensuring proactive strategies at local level to tackle hate crime against disabled people—the subject of new provisions in criminal justice legislation. The duty to eliminate harassment currently in the Bill applies only to harassment unlawful under the DDA not to wider hate crime which affects 1 in 5 disabled people and 9 in 10 people with learning difficulties. It could also assist in raising awareness and encouraging respect for distinct communities such as the Deaf Community and it would ensure that local disabled people and disability groups were fully included in local community cohesion initiatives, rather than being left on the sidelines as presently tends to happen.

The Parliamentary Joint Committee which considered the draft Disability Discrimination Bill pointed out that the duty at that time proposed in relation to disability only came into play, by contrast with that imposed by the RR(A)A, where the public authority was satisfied that the 'opportunities for disabled persons are not as good as those for other persons.' The Government accepted the committee's recommendation and amended s.49A(1) accordingly. It did not, however, accede to the pressure to impose a duty to promote good relations in this context.[71]

---

[71] 'Mental illness hurdle to be scrapped' 132 *Equal Opportunities Review*.

Sex

The Equality Bill 2005 proposes the insertion into the SDA of new section 21A which would prohibit discrimination by public authorities (see further Chapter 4) and of new s.76A which would impose upon public authorities the duty 'in carrying out its functions [to] have due regard to the need (a) to eliminate unlawful discrimination, and (b) to promote equality of opportunity between women and men'. Proposed new s.76A(2)(c) provides that 'the reference to unlawful discrimination shall be treated as including a reference to contravention of terms of contracts having effect in accordance with an equality clause within the meaning of section 1 of the Equal Pay Act 1970', a provision which might provide interesting scope for challenge. The proposed coverage of the sex equality duties is similar to that of the duties proposed in relation to disability and proposed new s.76B SDA (specific duties) is in similar terms to new s.49D DDA (above). The Bill failed to become law prior to the dissolution of Parliament in April 2005, when the general election was called. The Government, however, made it clear that the passage of the Bill would be an early priority in the event of a Labour re-election and the Bill's second reading in the Commons (5 April 2005) was characterised by a remarkable degree of support across the board for its provisions.

Other Mainstreaming Measures

In addition to the equality mainstreaming approaches adopted or to be adopted by the NIA and the various equality provisions, the Government of Wales Act 1998 provides (s.120) that 'The Assembly shall make appropriate arrangements with a view to securing that its functions are exercised with due regard to the principle that there should be equality of opportunity for all people.' The Assembly is required to publish an annual report on the arrangements made for promoting equality of opportunity and the effectiveness of such arrangements, and the duty may be enforced by way of judicial review. A report commissioned by the CRE, EOC, DRC and Institute of Welsh Affairs in 2002 concluded that the obligation had made a difference to date and that 'there would be benefits in a positive duty to promote equality of opportunity across the UK,' commending the 'non-prescriptive, all-embracing' Welsh approach as a valuable complement to the more detailed and prescriptive obligations imposed by the RRA.[72] The authors list an impressive array of initiatives flowing from the 'new approach to equality matters.' These include, but are not limited to, the introduction of pay audits and formalisation of recruitment procedures to the Assembly's Civil Service, and the promotion of equal pay in the Welsh public sector, the funding of dedicated consultative equality networks for minority groups which are designed 'to promote citizen participation in the work of government,' the adoption of equality impact assessments and the adoption of contract compliance measures.

In addition to the actual and proposed powers discussed above, Schedule 5 of the Scotland Act 1998 provides that the Scottish Executive may encourage (other than by prohibition or regulation) equal opportunities and may impose upon Scottish administration office holders and public authorities the obligation to make arrangements with a view to

---

[72] P Chaney and R Fevre, *An Absolute Duty*, available at http://www.dmuracetoolkit.com/whatsnewads/Welsh.pdf.

ensuring that their functions are carried out with due regard to the need to meet equal opportunities requirements. The Executive has committed itself to the mainstreaming of equalities and the Parliament has a standing Equal Opportunities Committee. And s.33 of the Greater London Authority Act 1999 provides that the Authority shall make appropriate arrangements so that in the exercise of its powers; in the formulation of its policies and proposals; and in the implementation of its strategies 'there is due regard to the principle that there should be equality of opportunity for all people.' Section 404 of the Act also imposes the obligation on the GLA, the Metropolitan Police Authority and the London Fire and Emergency Planning Authority 'in exercising their function . . . to have regard to the need [s.404(2)]—

(a) to promote equality of opportunity for all persons irrespective of their race, sex, disability, age, sexual orientation or religion
(b) to eliminate unlawful discrimination; and
(c) to promote good relations between persons of different racial groups, religious beliefs and sexual orientation.'

The GLA is required to undertake formal equalities impact assessment in developing policies, initiatives and strategies and to report annually on the effectiveness of the pursuit of equal opportunities.

The Potential of 'Mainstreaming'

Equality mainstreaming has the potential to effect real change by centralising the needs and concerns of those groups frequently overlooked in policy making and delivery, although it is important to ensure that the rhetoric of mainstreaming does not produce a false sense that problems of inequality are being meaningfully addressed. That it is not a panacea is clear from the Audit Commission and CRE's recent reports that the mainstreaming mechanisms imposed by the RR(A)A have not produced instant revolutions in the way in which public authorities deal with racial inequalities. But it is also clear that some significant improvements have occurred, and that the implementation of positive duties in connection with sex and disability might be expected to produce similar improvements. The Government has articulated its commitment to gender mainstreaming and has been commended by the UN Committee on the Elimination of Discrimination against Women for doing so. But prior to the implementation of detailed statutory provisions such as those found in Northern Ireland and under the RR(A)A, this 'commitment' seemed at times rhetorical. Certainly the Women's National Commission of the United Kingdom, in its 2004 submission to the committee, was underwhelmed by the reality:

Women's National Commission of the United Kingdom, *Submission to the UN Committee on the Elimination of Discrimination Against Women,* **2003**

NGOs regret that there are only a handful of examples of gender mainstreaming. Most civil servants have received no training in the process and would not recognise the term . . .

The fullest possible of gender mainstreaming is essential, and although the Women and Equality Unit have produced a web-based tool for assessing the gender impact of policies and legislation on women, *there are neither means in place for ensuring that Ministries do use such a tool, nor any procedures in place to assess the impact of current policies and policy-making on women and men and girls and boys, separately*. The overwhelming majority of civil servants receive no training on gender mainstreaming and would not recognise the term [my emphasis]. . .

K Escott and D Whitfield, *Promoting Equality in the Public* Sector (EOC, 2002) 18–22, footnotes omitted

Many public organisations assume that gender mainstreaming is beneficial. In fact, mainstreaming strategies must be grounded in the structures and organisational culture for them to be of practical relevance. The research found that even in those public bodies where gender equality policies are advanced and the greatest progress is being made, gender mainstreaming is often applied in a piecemeal way. Major gaps continue to exist between corporate equalities statements and practical applications, and between mainstreaming in employment and the employer functions and mainstreaming in service delivery and policy implementation.

The research concludes that, based on the evidence from six public sector organisations, there is no coherent or strategic public sector approach to gender mainstreaming. Gender mainstreaming remains largely the province of equalities specialists, and has not become a core part of recent moves to improve public policy making.

Established structures are generally regarded as being more difficult to change. Good practice in service delivery, attuned to the needs of women and men at national and local level, is patchy and only evident where it is driven by commitment . . .

4.3 Benefits of a public sector duty

The research findings from the case study organisations revealed that the main benefits of a public sector duty include:
• Providing a statutory foundation and framework which will ensure that public authorities meet their equality obligations
• Ensuring that all public organisations are required by law directly to address inequality and tackle institutional discrimination through specific programmes, so that improvements in tackling inequality are achieved across the board
• Enhancing existing best practice approaches by integrating equalities policies into public policy making and implementation, including into funding decisions, performance management, Best Value Performance Plans, Community Strategies and wider work on diversity
• Strengthening mainstreaming, which some interviewees considered was insufficiently effective because of the length of time it took to achieve change and/or the significance of the change
• Making equality impact assessments, which the Northern Ireland experience has shown offer substantial benefits, mandatory so that they are comprehensively applied across the public sector
• Ensuring the universal implementation of the Equality Standard for Local Government, which applies to services and employment; the Gender Agenda in police services; and other similar framework documents designed to address inequality
• Removing the distinction between those authorities which are currently obliged to meet a statutory duty on equality of which gender is a part and those which are not.This would allow a greater consistency between service providers.

Interviewees in the case study organisations suggested that the other benefits of a public sector duty included:

- The faster implementation of equalities work, ie, the speeding up of the process of mainstreaming
- Providing community and equalities groups with a more powerful tool by which effective external pressure could be applied on public sector bodies to mainstream equalities in service delivery and policy making
- Imposing stronger and enforceable legal requirements to mainstream gender and equalities not only in the public sector, but also in private companies and third sector organisations (e.g. local authority arms length companies, quangos, trusts and voluntary bodies) which are involved in the delivery of public services. One of the key tests for a public sector duty will be its application to third sector organisations and the powers of public bodies to monitor and enforce it
- Assisting public sector authorities to meet their obligations to promote social and economic well-being in their communities, as well as allowing them to recover their role as model employers who set the standards for the private sector.

C O'Cinneide, 'Extending positive duties across the equality grounds' 120 *Equal Opportunities Review*, footnotes omitted

The case for extending positive duties in the public sector appears unanswerable, despite government inaction, yet it will be important that any such extension retains the potential to bring about improved outcomes for disadvantaged groups in their dealings with public authorities. A similarly strong case may exist for the private and voluntary sectors; however, rolling out a set of duties for the public sector appears to be the necessary first step.

Why positive duties?

As will be apparent to all equality practitioners, existing anti-discrimination law often proves less than adequate in dealing with complex and deeply rooted patterns of exclusion and inequality. . .The current anti-discrimination approach also results in a culture of 'negative compliance,' where being a 'good employer' or a 'progressive public authority' involves taking the necessary minimum steps to avoid liability. In the public sector, combating inequality is therefore often viewed as a reactive process that is marginalised within the concerns of public authorities.

Equality is not given its necessary place within the central objectives of public sector organisations, nor is it treated as being of crucial importance to other central objectives, such as the delivery of services to the public and strengthening social cohesion. In addition, policy is often constructed on the basis of assumptions about the needs of disadvantaged groups that may not mirror their own perceptions and needs . . .

The role of positive duties

A major problem with many existing mainstreaming policies is that they are 'soft law' initiatives that are not framed as statutory duties. In the absence of a clear statutory duty to implement mainstreaming, guidelines will not be taken seriously. Positive duties are, as a result, increasingly being used in the public sector to provide public authorities with a statutory requirement to promote equality . . .

A clear positive statutory duty to promote equality of opportunity by public authorities across all areas of government policy and activities.

The participation of affected groups in determining how this should be achieved.

An assessment of the impact of existing and future government policies on affected groups.

Consideration of alternatives which have less of an adverse impact.

The consideration of how to mitigate impacts that cannot be avoided.

Transparency and openness in the process of assessment.

The objective of positive duties is therefore to change how public authorities perform their functions, by making equality a central goal of their day-to-day activities. Duties aim to transform a reactive stance into a proactive, integrated approach, informed by the perspectives of disadvantaged groups. This can involve alterations in service delivery, employment practices, access policies, and policy formation in general.

Two key concepts that are central to both the negative and positive obligations are relevance and proportionality. Public authorities subject to positive duties are required to take action to assess and monitor the impact of policies and practices upon disadvantaged groups, as well as consulting with these groups as part of this impact assessment. The time and resources to be spent on this assessment process, and the steps that should be taken to eliminate or remedy practices or policies that have a discriminatory impact, should be proportionate to the importance of promoting equality and eliminating disadvantage, taking into account the other key functions and responsibilities of the bodies in question . . .

Illustrative of the potential of positive duties in the disability context are the following extracts from the DRC's draft Code of Practice.

DRC, 'The Duty to Promote Disability Equality' (2005)

1.10 The [general] duty will help public authorities to progress towards achieving equality of outcomes for disabled people and ultimately will require authorities to improve their existing service delivery. It also reinforces the pre-existing duties under the Act, and by ensuring that disability is 'built in' at the outset, can help public authorities avoid costly retrospective action.

For example, a local authority establishes a new recycling service and requires households to put out their collection boxes on the kerbside for collection. Some disabled residents, however, are unable to put their boxes onto the street and, as a result, and in order to meet the authority's duties under the DDA, the authority has to redesign the service to ensure collection from those households which are unable to put the boxes onto the street. This involves extra expense, time and inconvenience. Had the authority 'built in' disability equality from the outset, it would have not had to take this action.

2.2 Public authorities are expected to have 'due regard' to the four parts of the general duty . . .

For example, as a result of following its planning guidance a local authority adopts a planning policy that a maximum of one car space will be allowed per two new housing units built in their area and in some areas they are considering permitting only car free developments. All new housing will meet the basic access standards for disabled people and some new homes are wheelchair accessible.

The policy adopted on car parking and car use is in order to encourage people to use public transport but it takes no account of the inaccessibility of the public transport in the area for disabled people and the reliance of many disabled people on cars—thus due regard has not been paid to the promotion of disability equality, given the high degree of relevance which housing has for disabled people.

The result of this policy is that at least half of new homes are not appropriate for many disabled people because they cannot have a car space near their property. An alternative approach, which avoids this negative impact on disabled people, should be considered, such as dedicated parking spaces for disabled people.

4

Coverage

Introduction

None of the anti-discrimination legislation here discussed imposes a blanket prohibition on discrimination on the regulated grounds (sex, marriage, race, disability, gender reassignment, sexual orientation, religion or belief). Instead, each enactment details a number of areas: employment, facilities, goods and services, housing, etc, in respect of which discrimination is regulated. The SO Regs and the RB Regs are narrower than the other provisions, being concerned only with discrimination in the field of employment (broadly defined) and third level education, though the Equality Bill 2005 proposes the prohibition of discrimination in access to goods, facilities and services on grounds of religion or belief. Protections against discrimination on grounds of marriage and gender reassignment are narrower still, applying only to employment. And even within the areas covered by the statutory provisions, discrimination is prohibited by the various regimes only in specific instances. This does not mean that discrimination falling outside the scope of the relevant legislation is unregulated by law. Although the common law has, until very recently, been of very limited assistance in challenging discrimination (see further Chapter 1) this appears to be shifting and the implementation in the UK of the Human Rights Act 1998 has provided claimants with an additional tool in the struggle against unjust discrimination. The 1998 Act is outside the scope of this book though its shortcomings in this context are referred to briefly in Chapter 1. Nevertheless, the fact that it gives some effect to Article 14 of the European Convention on Human Rights, which provides that: 'The enjoyment of the rights and freedoms set forth in this Convention shall be secured without discrimination "on any ground such as sex, race, colour, language, religion, political or other opinion, national or social origin, association with a national minority, property, birth or other status" ' is not without significance.

Turning to the legislative provisions under consideration, it is worth noting at this stage that the RRA is broader than the other legislative provisions because it has had the benefit of amendment both by the Race Relations (Amendment) Act 2000 (which, *inter alia*, applied the prohibition on race discrimination to public authorities and placed upon them detailed positive obligations to promote race equality) and, more recently, in order to comply with the Racial Equality Directive (Directive 2000/43/EC) whose scope extends beyond employment. The DDA, whose employment-related provisions were originally narrower than those of the RRA and SDA, has been amended to comply with the Employment Equality Directive (Directive 2000/78/EC) and has also had its non-employment provisions significantly extended in recent years.[1] More amendments, mainly in the non-employment

---

[1] These amendments have been made by the Disability Discrimination Act 1995 (Amendment) Regulations 2003 (Statutory Instrument 2003 No. 1673), in Northern Ireland by the Disability Discrimination Act 1995 (Amendment) Regulations (Northern Ireland) 2004 (Statutory Rule 2004 No. 55).

context, are proposed by the Disability Discrimination Act 2005 (DDA 2005) which is discussed where relevant below. The SDA has the same broad coverage as the RRA did prior to its extension by the RR(A)A, but its application to public authorities is limited as yet and the amendment of the Equal Treatment Directive by Directive 2002/73/EC does not occur until October 2005. The Equal Treatment Directive, like the Employment Equality Directive but by contrast with the Racial Equality Directive, continues to apply only in relation to employment (broadly defined), but Council Directive 2004/113/EC, which regulates sex discrimination in goods and services, has recently been adopted. Its provisions are discussed below.

In this chapter we consider the circumstances under which discrimination is regulated by one or more of the statutory regimes and the exceptions to the prohibitions on discrimination. Differences between those regimes are highlighted here and in the individual chapters devoted to the various different regimes, and the immediately following section of this chapter considers the two exceptions to the prohibitions on discrimination which apply generally across the sphere of protection from discrimination.

General Exceptions to the Prohibition on Discrimination

The first of the two main exceptions of general application relates to national security. Typical of the exemptions is s.42 RRA which provides:

> Nothing in Parts II to IV shall render unlawful an act done for the purpose of safeguarding national security if the doing of the act was justified by that purpose.

Regs 24 of the RB and SO Regs are materially identical as is Article 79 FETO (except that the latter includes 'public safety or public order' with 'national security') and the DDA (s.59(2)) as it applies to 'employment' (broadly defined). The RRA was amended by the RR(A)A to include the reference to justification. The SDA contains no such reference, providing only (s.52 SDA) that 'Nothing in Parts II to IV shall render unlawful an act done for the purpose of safeguarding national security.' The DDA, as it applies other than to employment, is materially identical (s.59(3)) to the SDA .

Prior to its amendment by the RR(A)A the RRA contained a provision to the effect that ministerial certification that '(a) any arrangements or conditions specified in the certificate were made, approved or imposed by a Minister of the Crown and were in operation at a time or throughout a period so specified; or (b) . . . an act specified in the certificate was done for the purpose of safeguarding national security' was conclusive evidence of the matters certified. A similar provision had been removed from the SDA and the Sex Discrimination (Northern Ireland) Order 1976 in the wake of the ECJ decision in *Johnston v Chief Constable of the RUC* Case C–224/84 [1986] ECR 651 in which that Court ruled that the unavailability of judicial review to challenge a similar exemption in the SD Order breached the obligation regarding justiciability in the Equal Treatment Directive.

Prior to 2003 the RRA was not significantly affected by EU law, so no efforts were made to amend it in the wake of the *Johnston* decision. But in *Tinnelly & Sons Ltd and McElduff v United Kingdom* [1998] 27 EHRR 249, the European Court of Human Rights ruled that a materially identical provision in the fair employment legislation breached the right to a fair trial protected by Article 6 of the European Convention on Human Rights.[2] FETO was amended to permit ministerial certificates to be challenged before a special tribunal set up for that purpose under the Northern Ireland Act 1998. The RRA simply dropped the reference to ministerial certificates although it provides (s.67A) that rules may be made providing a special procedure in national security cases. No such rules have yet been made.

Section 42 RRA and its equivalents are of immensely wide reach, but, while FETO's national security provision has been relied on frequently in the courts, those of the RRA, SDA and DDA have been little used. Only one appellate decision has considered the national security provision, the question there being whether it could be relied upon by the Commonwealth of Australia in the British courts. The claimant's claim was dismissed on other grounds.[3]

The other exception of general application (though its detail varies between the legislative regimes) concerns acts done under ministerial authority. Section 41 RRA provides:

(1) Nothing in [the RRA] shall render unlawful any act of discrimination done—
   (a) in pursuance of any enactment or order in Council; or
   (b) in pursuance of any instrument made under any enactment by a Minister of the Crown; or
   (c) in order to comply with any condition or requirement imposed by a Minister of the Crown (whether before or after the passing of this Act) by virtue of any enactment.
References in this subsection to an enactment, Order in Council or instrument include an enactment, Order in Council or instrument passed or made after the passing of this Act.
(1A) Subsection (1) does not apply to an act which is unlawful, on grounds of race or ethnic or national origins, by virtue of a provision referred to in section 1(1B) [[4]].
(2) Nothing in [the RRA] shall render unlawful any act whereby a person discriminates against another on the basis of that other's nationality or place of ordinary residence or the length of time for which he has been present or resident in or outside the United Kingdom or an area within the United Kingdom, if that act is done—
   (a) in pursuance of any arrangements made (whether before or after the passing of this Act) by or with the approval of, or for the time being approved by, a Minister of the Crown or
   (b) in order to comply with any condition imposed (whether before or after the passing of this Act) by a Minister of the Crown.

Section 41(1A) was inserted to bring the RRA into line with the Racial Equality Directive which, inter alia, prohibits discrimination on grounds of racial or national origin in relation to social security, healthcare and education. Section 41 was inconsistent with this prohibition to the extent that it gave precedence to secondary legislation, hence its amendment by ss.1A in those areas (listed at s.1(1B) and discussed in Chapter 7) to which the Racial Equality Directive applies. (S.41(2) RRA is unaffected as the Directive explicitly excludes from its coverage discrimination on grounds of nationality.)

The DDA (s.59(1)) is materially identical to s.41(1) RRA. Article 78 FETO provides that, other than in relation to 'employment' broadly defined,[5] the Order does not make unlawful 'anything done in order to comply with a requirement' of primary or secondary

---

[2] See also *Devlin v UK* 34 EHRR 1029 in which the UK Government's attempt to distinguish *Tinnelly* in a case involving refusal of access to the civil service was rejected by the European Court.
[3] *Yendall v Commonwealth of Australia* EAT 515/83 (unreported) 11th October 1984.
[4] See Chapter 7.
[5] FETO was amended to this effect to give effect to the religion and belief provisions of the Employment Equality Directive.

legislation. Sections 51 and 51A SDA apply more narrowly, permitting only such discrimination as is necessary to comply with statutory provisions concerned with protecting women in connection with pregnancy or maternity or to circumstances affecting only women.[6] Section 51 SDA, as originally enacted, contained a wider statutory exception along the lines of s.41 RRA, the effect of which was to preserve 'protective' legislation. The European Commission issued a reasoned opinion in 1987 to the effect that s.51 was too broad to comply with the Equal Treatment Directive and the provision, which had been modified to some extent by the SDA 1986, was narrowed considerably by the Employment Act 1989. Neither the SO nor the RB Regs contain any equivalent to s.41 RRA but, as secondary legislation, they are subordinate to all primary legislation as well as to subsequently enacted secondary legislation to the extent of any incompatibility.

The significance of s.41(1A) RRA and its equivalents are further considered below in the context of discrimination by public authorities. But even before the RRA was amended to conform with the Racial Equality Directive, s.41 had been construed narrowly by the courts. In *Hampson v Department of Education and Science* the House of Lords considered a claim under the Act by a Hong Kong Chinese woman who was excluded from UK teaching positions by the Secretary of State's requirement that, in order to qualify for such posts, overseas-trained teachers had to have undertaken a teaching course over three consecutive years. The claimant's third year of training was completed eight years after the initial two-year course normal in Hong Kong. She had taught during the intervening years.

The Secretary of State's regulations were made under s. 27 of the Education Act 1980, which provided that:

> The Secretary of State may by regulations make provision . . . for requiring teachers at schools . . . to possess such qualification as may be determined by or under the regulations
> . . .

Ms Hampson's indirect discrimination claim was rejected by an industrial tribunal on the grounds, inter alia, that s.41(1) applied. EAT ([1988] IRLR 87) upheld this conclusion and, in the alternative, ruled that any discrimination was justifiable in accordance with the approach taken by the Court of Appeal in *Ojutiku v Manpower Services Commission* [1982] IRLR 418 (see further Chapter 2). The Court of Appeal ([1989] ICR 179) swept away the *Ojutiku* test (this aspect of the decision is discussed in Chapter 2), but upheld the tribunal and EAT on s.41. The House of Lords allowed Ms Hampson's appeal.

Hampson v Department of Education and Science [1991] 1 AC 171

Lord Lowry (who delivered the sole speech):

Balcombe J (who dissented in the Court of Appeal) framed the question clearly when he said:

> 'This argument, which succeeded below, is controvertible if the words 'in pursuance of any instrument' are apt in their context to include, not only acts done in necessary performance of an express obligation contained in the instrument (the narrow construction) but also acts done in exercise of a power or discretion conferred by the instrument (the wide construction). Both constructions are possible.' . . . I accept that the wide construction is the more natural meaning of the words used. I turn, therefore,

---

[6] Or women and others also covered.

to consider whether there is anything in the context which leads to an indication that the narrow construction is here correct.'

My Lords, I shall have occasion to refer again to Balcombe LJ's judgment, with which on the s 41 point I completely agree . . .

s 41 . . . introduces over a wide field . . . as exceptions to the [RRA's] general purpose of outlawing discrimination, five cases in which an act of discrimination shall not be unlawful and in each such case the relevant enactment, Order in Council, instrument, condition, requirement or arrangement may be either pre- or post-Act. In view of the wide sweep of these provisions, the exceptions ought therefore, I suggest, to be narrowly rather than widely construed where the language is susceptible of more than one meaning . . .

It is . . . the consideration of the wider context that demonstrates the need to adopt the narrow construction of the words 'in pursuance of,' since the wide construction is seen to be irreconcilable with the purpose and meaning of the [RRA] . . .

There is a sound argument, based on public policy, for drawing the line in this way. I refer to the need and the opportunity for parliamentary scrutiny . . . To adopt the Balcombe principle, if I may so describe it, will mean that racial discrimination is outlawed (or at least needs to be justified under s 1(1)(b)(ii)) unless it has been sanctioned by Parliament, whereas, if the respondent's argument were correct, a wide and undefined area of discrimination would exist, immune from challenge save, in very exceptional circumstances, through the medium of judicial review . . .

To sum up, the majority in the Court of Appeal rejected the wide construction but did not come down in favour of the narrow construction or, indeed, of any specific alternative interpretation of the words 'in pursuance of.' They appear, however, to have held that the Secretary of State acted, as no doubt he did, in pursuance of the 1982 regulations when he discharged the duty of considering and the further duty of deciding the appellant's application therefore, they held, his allegedly discriminatory act was protected by s.41(1)(b). It is this reasoning, my Lords, that did not commend itself to Balcombe LJ and that I find myself unable to accept. In my view it disregards, and has to disregard, the fact that, in order to decide the application one way or the other, the Secretary of State had first to set up and apply a non-statutory criterion, the setting up and application of which involved the exercise of his administrative discretion and led to the discriminatory act complained of.

What I would venture to describe as the fallacy of that approach can be recognised when one reflects that almost every discretionary decision, such as that which is involved in the appointment, promotion and dismissal of individuals in, say, local government, the police, the national health service and the public sector of the teaching profession, is taken against a statutory background which imposes a duty on someone, just as the 1982 regulations imposed a duty on the Secretary of State. It seems to me that to apply the reasoning of the majority here to the decisions I have mentioned would give them the protection of s.41 and thereby achieve results which no member of the Court of Appeal would be likely to have thought acceptable . . .

Other exceptions to the various prohibitions on discrimination are considered elsewhere in this chapter as they arise, in relation (for example) to education, employment, etc. More detailed discussion of some of the exceptions applicable to the various heads of discrimination (in particular, the genuine occupational qualification/ requirement defences) will take place in the chapters devoted to each of the head (sex, race, etc). Next, however, we consider the various contexts in which discrimination is regulated.

Employment

Scope of 'Employment'

Section 4 RRA, which is extracted below, regulates employment-related discrimination. Its provisions are echoed by s.6 SDA, s.4 DDA, Article 19 FETO and reg 6 of each the SO Regs and the RB Regs, all of which are discussed further below. Section 4 RRA and its equivalents are discussed here. It should be noted, however, that the broadly employment-related provisions of the various Acts and Regulations include not only these provisions but, in addition, provisions dealing with partners, contract workers, etc. These are considered below. To simplify the text the RRA will be discussed and attention drawn to the equivalent provisions of the other legislation only where they differ materially.

'Employment' is defined by the RRA, SDA and FETO as 'employment under a contract of service or of apprenticeship or a contract personally to *execute any work or labour*' the DDA and SO and RB Regs substituting the words 'to do any work' for those italicised.[7] These definitions[8] serve to extend the protection of the anti-discrimination provisions[8] to a wider category of workers than those entitled to claim unfair dismissal, redundancy payments, etc., under the Employment Rights Act 1996. The ERA applies only to workers employed under contracts *of service*, as distinct from contracts *for services*, the former category excluding many of the most disadvantaged workers.[9]

The boundaries of 'employment' under the anti-discrimination legislation are illustrated by the decision of the Court of Appeal in *Mirror Group Newspapers Ltd v Gunning*. Ms Gunning sought to sue MGN under the SDA when the group refused to permit her to take over her father's area distributorship on his retirement. She, like her father, was an independent newspaper wholesaler who bought papers from newspaper publishers and sold them on to newsagents. A tribunal ruled that the distributorship came within the SDA's definition of 'employment,' the contract between MGN and Ms Gunning's father requiring that he exercised day-to-day supervision over the distribution tasks, although he was not obliged to carry them out himself. The tribunal further found that MGN had discriminated unlawfully against Ms Gunning. The Court of Appeal allowed MGN's appeal on the basis that the contract at issue was not one 'personally to execute any work or labour.'

Ms Gunning's counsel had argued that 'any' should be read as applying to the *extent* as well as to the *nature* of the work or labour contracted for, so as to afford the protection of the SDA to any contract a 'material' term of which required the personal execution of work or labour by a contracting party. The Court of Appeal, however, preferred an interpretation suggested by Alexander Irvine QC, for MGN.

---

[7] Ss. 78, 82, Article 69 and s.68 of the RRA, SDA, FETO and DDA respectively, and reg 2 of the SO and RB Regs.

[8] But not, significantly, the 1992 Trade Union and Labour Relations (Consolidation) Act's prohibition of discrimination on grounds of trade union membership.

[9] The Acts and Regs, like the ERA also apply to House of Commons and House of Lords staff as if they were employees (ss.85A & 85D SDA, ss.75A & 75B RRA, 65 DDA, reg 37& 78 SO and RB Regs).

Mirror Group Newspapers Ltd v Gunning **[1986] ICR 145**

Balcombe LJ:

I cannot accept [Mr Irvine's] primary submission that the phrase 'contract personally to execute any work or labour' contemplates only a contract whose sole purpose is that the party contracting to provide services under the contract performs personally the work or labour which forms the subject matter of the contract. As was suggested during the course of argument, this would exclude from the definition a contract with a sculptor, where it was contemplated that some of the menial work might be carried out by persons other than the contracting party, a contract with a one-man builder, who might be expected to sub-contract some of the specialist work, or even a contract with a plumber, who might be expected to have his mate with him on all occasions.

However, I do accept Mr Irvine's alternative submission that the phrase in its context contemplates a contract whose dominant purpose is that the party contracting to provide services under the contract performs personally the work or labour which forms the subject matter of the contract. In the course of oral argument before us, Mr Beloff [for Ms Gunning] conceded that a single obligation to provide personal services in a contract is not of itself sufficient to bring the contract within the phrase; you have to look at the contract as a whole to see the extent to which that obligation colours the contract, which goes a long way towards accepting the 'dominant purpose' test. In my judgment, you have to look at the agreement as a whole, and provided that there is some obligation by one contracting party personally to execute any work or labour, you then have to decide whether that is the dominant purpose of the contract, or whether the contract is properly to be regarded in essence as a contract for the personal execution of work or labour, which seems to me to be the same thing in other words.

The *Gunning* case has been applied subsequently to exclude sub-postmasters from the protection of the RRA and DDA.[10] In *Kelly & Loughran v Northern Ireland Housing Executive* [1998] ICR 828, on the other hand, a majority of the House of Lords took a very generous approach to the equivalent provisions of the Fair Employment Act 1989 (as it then was). The case arose as a result of the refusal by the Housing Executive to appoint the claimants: respectively, one of two partners in a firm of solicitors and a sole practitioner, to a panel which defended public liability claims made against the Executive. The claimants sought the appointment of their firms and named themselves the designated solicitors who would be responsible for the work. The Fair Employment Tribunal ruled that neither claimant was seeking 'employment' under the FEA's wide definition, a finding upheld in respect of the first claimant only by Northern Ireland's Court of Appeal, but rejected (by a bare majority) by the House of Lords in respect of both.

Dealing first with the *Loughran* case, Lord Slynn agreed with the Court of Appeal that Mr Loughran, as a sole practitioner, was '[i]n substance . . . seeking to have himself appointed to the panel. He designated himself as the solicitor who would be mainly concerned with the work to be done for the executive.' The effect of this designation was that Loughran agreed, if appointed, to 'give priority to panel work.' This, according to Lord Slynn (with whom Lord Steyn agreed) fell within the *Gunning* test. Their Lordships regarded this test as permitting some delegation in a case, such as this, in which an individual was legally responsible for the work:

---

[10] Respectively, *Chambers v Post Office Counters Ltd* 21 February 1995, unreported (CA) and *Sheehan v Post Office Counters* EAT/417/98, 16 November 1998, unreported. See also *Commissioners of Inland Revenue v Post Office Ltd* [2003] ICR 546.

it does not cease to be a contract 'personally to execute any work' because his secretary types and posts the executive's defence to any claim or that his assistant solicitor goes along to file such a defence. The dominant purpose is that he will do the essential part of the work.

Lord Griffiths concurred on similar grounds, Lords Lloyd and Clyde dissenting as they did in *Kelly*. Lord Slynn (with Lord Steyn) took the broadest approach in *Kelly*, deciding that a contract 'personally to execute any work or labour,' could be made with a firm as well as with a natural person.[11] This conclusion rested on the Interpretation Act 1978 provision to the effect that 'unless the contrary intention appears "person" includes a body of persons unincorporated.' Lord Slynn could discern no contrary intention, the FEA's purpose being 'to outlaw discrimination on the grounds of religious or political opinion in the employ-ment sphere' and it being 'factually possible to discriminate against the partners of a firm or against the firm itself as it is against a sole practitioner':

the [FEA] clearly and deliberately adopts a wide definition of employment so as to include a contract to provide services and a firm can contract to provide services. If the definition had included only 'workman' or 'artificer' or 'a contract of service' the position might well be different but with the extended definition of employment I consider that a contract by a firm to provide services is capable of being a contract 'personally to execute any work or labour.' Is it such a contract here? In my view it is. The contract is for the firm itself, ie per-sonally, to execute work. The firm as such will be legally responsible for the doing of the work and will be liable for breach of the contract. The firm which contracts and is legally responsible consists of all the partners but clearly all the partners do not have to do all the work. It is sufficient that one or more of the partners is intended to and does execute the work subject to delegation of some activities by the firm in the same way as a sole practi-tioner can delegate. What is required is that the dominant purpose of the contract is that the firm undertakes to do, and by one of its partners is responsible for and does, the work undertaken to be done.

Although the complaint [in the *Kelly* case] could have been made, and perhaps would have been better made in the name of the firm or of both the partners, I consider that under the [FEA] it was open to one partner in the firm to complain that she, as a partner in the firm, as well as the firm itself, was subjected to discrimination when the firm was refused appointment. This is particularly so in this case, where the firm's application was based entirely on her experience and on her acceptance of responsibility for the service to be pro-vided. If, and in so far as, there is discrimination against the firm or its constituent partners, there is discrimination against her of which she can individually complain under the statu-tory provisions.

Lord Griffiths concurred with Lords Slynn and Steyn as to result, but decided the *Kelly* case on the basis that the claimant, as a partner, was a 'contracting party':

A firm of solicitors has no legal existence, independent of the partners of the firm. The con-tract . . . if it had come into existence, would have been a contract between the executive and both partners of the firm. That being so Bernadette Kelly was seeking to enter into a con-tract personally to execute work . . .

---

[11] See *Tinnelly & Sons Ltd and McElduff v United Kingdom*, discussed above and in Ch 9, where this point was not, however, argued. The approach of the House of Lords in *Loughran* should also apply to the SDA and the RRA. The DDA, however, applies only to 'disabled' *persons* as defined by the Act (see further Chapter 8).

Lord Griffiths was unable to agree with Lord Slynn's interpretation of the FEA which, in his view was 'aimed at giving protection to individuals and not to companies or unincorporated corporations. It would be a wholly unnatural use of language to say a company or corporation had personally agreed to carry out work.' In particular he declared that, had the named individual in the *Kelly* litigation been an assistant solicitor rather than a partner (who, as a constituent element of the firm, was one of the contracting parties), the arrangement would not have been a 'contract personally to execute any work or labour.' Notwithstanding this, Lord Griffith's judgment was sufficient to secure to Ms Kelly, as well as to Mr Loughran, the protection of the FEA despite the dissents of Lords Lloyd and Clyde.

Kelly and *Loughran* were unusual cases in that they permitted the application of a provision concerned with 'employment,' however broadly defined, to discrimination alleged by collective entities. There was no majority, however, to the effect that the FETO (as it now is) or the other discrimination provisions apply to 'firms' or 'companies,' as distinct from individuals. We saw above that, while Lords Slynn and Steyn took the view that the provisions did apply to firms, Lord Griffith (who concurred with them as to result) did not. The narrower premise upon which his decision was based is set out above. As to the application of the anti-discrimination provisions to companies, this would appear consistent with the last extracted paragraph of Lord Slynn, above, with which Lord Steyn agreed, although Lord Slynn declared that it was 'not necessary in this case to consider the position of a limited company.'

'Person' is defined by the Interpretation Act 1978 to include bodies corporate as well as unincorporated. On the face of it it might appear difficult to envisage a company entering into a contract 'personally to execute any work or labour.' The same objection, however, might be made in relation to a firm but this was not regarded as problematic by Lords Slynn or Steyn. Lord Clyde, dissenting, agreed that the question of corporate bodies did not arise but expressed some doubt as to whether they could be covered by the employment-related provisions of the Act, pointing out that a company 'would not readily rank as an employee under a contract of apprenticeship.' Lord Lloyd stated that, while 'A company, like an individual, can undertake to execute work or perform services . . . [it] cannot execute work personally. Nor can a partnership, or other unincorporated body of individuals.' And Lord Griffiths drew attention to the 'formidable difficulties' of requiring 'tribunals . . . to decide on the religious beliefs or political opinions of companies or corporations.' Where, however, there is evidence that a would-be contractor has been discriminated against because of the alleged discriminator's perception of its religious or political composition, the actual composition of the organisation is not relevant, all but the SDA regulating discrimination connected with *perceived* as well as actual status. As for sex, it would not be difficult for a tribunal or court to ascertain the composition of a firm or company.

The weight of authority in *Kelly & Loughran* appears to be against the proposition that a company can be covered by s.4 RRA and its equivalent provisions, although there is a majority to the effect that partners in firms can be covered when they are *both* contracting parties *and* personally liable for the work in question. The Racial Equality Directive, by contrast, applies its protections to 'persons' rather than 'individuals,' this by virtue of an amendment carried in the European Parliament. The Preamble (recital 16) states that:

> It is important to protect all natural persons against discrimination on grounds of racial or ethnic origin. Member States should also provide, where appropriate and in accordance with their national traditions and practice, protection for legal persons where they suffer discrimination on grounds of the racial or ethnic origin of their members.
>
> The Directive goes on to define discrimination as occurring 'where one person is treated less favourably than another is, has been or would be treated in a comparable situation on grounds of racial or ethnic origin,' and 'where an apparently neutral provision, criterion or practice would put persons of a racial or ethnic origin at a particular disadvantage . . .'
>
> The exhortatory tone of the preamble suggests that no prohibition on discrimination against legal persons is *required* by the Directive. Having said this, the definitions of discrimination contained in the directive appear to be broadly consistent with its application to legal as well as natural persons.
>
> Whatever the application or otherwise of the employment-related provisions to discrimination against firms and companies, there is evidence that ethnic minority who run businesses, in particular, suffer discrimination. The RRA will have to be extended to permit companies as well as natural people. The other issue of relevance here concerns the obligations imposed in Northern Ireland by s.75 of the Northern Ireland Act 1998 and in Britain by the Race Relations (Amendment) Act. The Acts impose upon public authorities obligations to 'have regard to the need to promote equality of opportunity' in carrying out their functions. (The DDA 2005 makes similar provision in relation to disabilities while the Equality Bill 2005 proposes similar provision in relation to sex.) The promotion of equality of opportunities between persons of different racial or other groups must include an obligation not to discriminate without justification between white and ethnic minority differently owned or constituted businesses, even if it is not possible to define the businesses themselves as "persons' for the purposes of the anti-discrimination provisions.

In *Patterson v Legal Services Commission* [2004] ICR 312 the Court of Appeal considered a race discrimination claim made in connection with the Legal Services Commission's franchising arrangements for legally aided work. The claimant, a black woman of African-Caribbean origin, was the sole principal in a firm of solicitors which contained five other fee-earners. The success rate among African-Caribbean applicants for legal services franchises was particularly low. The issue for the Court was whether the tribunal had had jurisdiction to entertain her complaint either under s.4 RRA (here considered) or under s.12 of the Act (considered below).

The Court of Appeal ruled that the tribunal did not have jurisdiction under s.4. The legal aid contract was not 'a contract personally to execute any work or labour.' Under the *Gunning* approach the tribunal had to ask: '(i) would the claimant have been a party to the contract she sought from the LSC? (ii) If so, was any obligation [which would have been] imposed upon her under such a contract personally to carry out work or labour? (iii) If so, was that obligation personally to carry out work and labour the dominant purpose of the contract?' The Court ruled that the contract at issue here, by contrast with those considered in *Kelly & Loughran*, did not impose obligations upon Ms Patterson as the contractor personally to carry out the work, although she would have been wholly responsible legally for it. Whereas, in the Northern Irish case, the claimants would have been 'mainly responsible for carrying out panel work . . . and [would] give priority to' it, the Court in *Patterson* concluded (*per* Clarke LJ) that 'the contract as a whole did not impose *personal* obligations upon Ms Patterson as the contractor personally to carry out the work.' In particular, it provided that the signatory to it was not prevented 'from instructing approved representatives in accordance with normal practice.' The Court ruled that the answer to the second *Gunning* question was 'No' and that, even had it been 'Yes,' the answer to the third question would have been 'No.' The contract's dominant purpose was not to ensure the personal execution of work by Ms Patterson but, rather, 'to enable [her] to provide publicly funded legal services to her clients, in accordance with standards laid down by the Commission.'

The other notable exclusion from the employment-related coverage of the discrimination legislation is ministers of religion and similar. Most of the cases concerning ministers of religion have involved unfair dismissal claims which require employment under a contract *of employment* rather than the wider rubric employed by the discrimination legislation. But the basis upon which they are almost inevitably excluded from protection is that (*President of the Methodist Conference v Parfitt* [1984] QB 368, *per* Dillon LJ) 'the relationship between a church and a minister of religion is not apt, in the absence of clear indications of a contrary intention in the document, to be regulated by a contract of service'. In *Davies v Presbyterian Church of Wales* [1986] ICR 280 the House of Lords accepted that a minister of religion (there a Presbyterian pastor) *could* be employed under a contract of employment. But it upheld the decisions of EAT and the Court of Appeal in that case, overruling a tribunal's finding that the claimant was an employee for the purposes of an unfair dismissal claim. According to their Lordships, the questions how the church's rule book was to be construed and, accordingly, whether the claimant had a contract of employment were questions of law and the tribunal had misdirected itself in ruling in favour of Mr Davies.

In subsequent decisions an Anglican curate, a Sikh priest and Muslim clerics all failed to establish that any contract existed between them and their 'employers.'[12] In any case in which a tribunal found that a contract did exist it was regarded as having misdirected itself. As long as tribunals cited *Davies* and recognised the possibility of a contractual relationship, their decisions against the claimants appeared unassailable regardless of indications of employment such as a high level of control exercised by the 'employer,' the carrying-out by the minister of religion of significant non-religious functions, the use of the term 'employee,' etc.

The reluctance of the courts to find that ministers of religion are protected by employment legislation is perhaps understandable given the unsuitability of the secular courts to intervene in disputes based on religion. We shall see, below, that the RB and SO Regs, the FETO, DDA and the RRA as it applies to discrimination other than on grounds of colour or nationality regulate discrimination against 'office-holders' very broadly defined so as, it seems to be assumed, to include most ministers of religion (though FETO provides a specific exemption in relation to such posts and the other legislative provisions include GOR defences). The implications of this are considered briefly below and in more detail in Chapter 9.

---

[12] Respectively, *Diocese of Southwark v Coker* [1998] ICR 140 (CA), *Singh v Guru Nanak Gurdwara* [1990] ICR 309 (CA), *Birmingham Mosque Trust Ltd v Alavi* [1992] ICR 435 (EAT) and *Khan v Oxford City Mosque Society* (unreported, 1998, EAT).

Geographical Scope

The DDA applies throughout the UK.[13] The RRA, SDA, DDA and SO and RB Regs apply only to employment 'at an establishment in Great Britain,' the equivalent Northern Irish provisions[14] only to 'employment in Northern Ireland.' Section 8 RRA provides that 'employment is to be regarded as being at an establishment in Great Britain if the employee does his work wholly or partly in Great Britain' and special provision is made for work on board British registered ships and within territorial waters.[15] S.8(1A) RRA further provides that, where discrimination or harassment on grounds of racial or ethnic or national origin is at issue, employment will be regarded as being at an establishment in Great Britain even if the employee works entirely *outside* Great Britain, as long as 'the employer has a place of business at an establishment in Great Britain; the work is for the purposes of the business carried on at that establishment; and the employee is ordinarily resident in Great Britain' either 'at the time when he applies for or is offered the employment' or 'at any time during the course of the employment'. The geographical applications of the DDA and the SO and RB Regs are materially identical to the RRA as it applies to discrimination and harassment on grounds of race or ethnic or national origin and the draft SD Regs propose the amendment of the SDA and Equal Pay Act 1970 to materially identical effect.[16]

DTI, 'Explanatory notes for the Employment Equality (Sexual Orientation) Regulations 2003 and Employment Equality (Religion or Belief) Regulations 2003', paras 104–06

For example, a salesman works for the French office of a large multinational computer company which has its main headquarters in Britain. The salesman operates exclusively from the French office, selling computer equipment to businesses across France; he has no dealings with his company's headquarters in Britain. The salesman could not bring a claim under the Regulations in a tribunal in Britain, because his work is not for the purposes of the business carried on at the company's headquarters in Britain. On the other hand, if the orders obtained by the salesman were sent back to the British headquarters, which then supplied the computers to the customers in France, the salesman's work would be for the purposes of the establishment in Britain.

If the first two criteria are met, the third criterion then requires, in addition, that the employee is ordinarily resident in Great Britain, either at the time of applying for or being offered the job, or at some time during the course of the employment. Ordinary residence is a question of fact, which needs to be considered on case-by-case basis, taking into account all the relevant circumstances. To be ordinarily resident in Great Britain means that a person is usually living in and based in Britain, year after year. The fact that a person goes abroad for long periods at a time may not detract from the fact that they remain ordinarily resident in Britain—for example, if the person keeps their main residence in Britain. Equally, if a person lives from year to year in another country, he is not ordinarily resident in Britain simply by virtue of working temporarily in Britain for a few weeks or months.

[13] Though responsibility for it in Northern Ireland has now devolved to the Northern Ireland Assembly with the effect that differences are being created to the Act as it applies in Northern Ireland and in Great Britain. These differences are as yet largely confined to the context of education and will be highlighted where relevant.

[14] The Sex Discrimination (Northern Ireland) Order 1976, the Race Relations (Northern Ireland) Order 1997, the Employment Equality (Sexual Orientation) Regulations (Northern Ireland) 2003 and FETO.

[15] The detail differs somewhat across the regimes, all but the RRA making special provision for hovercraft registered in the UK for example.

[16] Save only in their application to employment aboard ship—contrast s.8(3) & (5) RRA with s.68(2c)–(4A) DDA and reg 9(3) SO and RB Regs.

Prohibited Discrimination[17]

Section 4 RRA provides that:

> s.4 (1) It is unlawful for a person, in relation to employment by him at an establishment in Great Britain, to discriminate against another—
> (a) in the arrangements he makes for the purpose of determining who should be offered the employment; or
> (b) in the terms on which he offers that employment; or
> (c) by refusing or deliberately omitting to offer him that employment.
> (2) It is unlawful for a person, in the case of a person employed by him at an establishment in Great Britain, to discriminate against that employee—
> (a) in the terms of the employment which he affords him; or
> (b) in the way he affords him access to opportunities for promotion, transfer or training, or to any other benefits, facilities or services, or by refusing or deliberately omitting to afford him access to them; or
> (c) by dismissing him, or subjecting him to any other detriment.
> (2A) It is unlawful for an employer, in relation to employment by him at an establishment in Great Britain, to subject to harassment a person whom he employs or who has applied to him for employment.

Section 6 SDA is of precisely the same effect, save that it omits ss.(2)(a) and (2A). Discrimination in contractual terms is governed by the Equal Pay Act 1970 (discussed in Chapter 6), while the SDA does not as yet prohibit 'harassment' in terms (see Chapter 2 for discussion of planned amendments to the SDA by the draft Employment Equality (Sex Discrimination) Regulations 2005—the draft SD Regs. Section 4 DDA and Articles 19 and 19A FETO and reg 6 of each the SO and the RB Regs[18] are drafted in similar terms to s.4 of the RRA and cover harassment specifically. Section 4 DDA was originally subject to a small employer exemption, applying only to employers of at least 20, and from 1998 of at least 15, staff. That threshold was removed as of 1 October 2004.

Selection Arrangements

Returning to s.4 RRA and its equivalents, ss.4(1)(a) and (c) overlap to some extent, many instances of discriminatory refusals to employ arising out of discrimination in the arrangements upon which selection for employment relies. But, whereas a claimant under s.4(1)(c) and the equivalent provisions must actually have applied for and been rejected from the job in question, s.4(1)(a) is apt to cover complaints from those who have been rendered unable to apply (or, presumably, discouraged from so doing).[19]

[17] See proposed new s. to SDA, reg 11 of the draft SD Regs and note in the context of the EqPA (which requires that comparators be employed in GB) the decision in *Villalba v Merrill Lynch & Co Inc* (139 *Equal Opportunities Review*) that Article 141 requires that the claimant be allowed to use a U.S. comparator.

[18] Although reg 6 of the SO and RB Regs sub-divide the subject matter of s.6(2)(b) SDA into two provisions (reg 6(2)(b) & (c)) which deal respectively with discrimination 'in the opportunities which [an employer] affords [a relevant person] for promotion, a transfer, training, or receiving any other benefit', and 'by refusing to afford him, or deliberately not affording him, any such opportunity'.

[19] Although it does require—*London Borough of Croydon v Kuttapan* [1999] IRLR 349—that an actual vacancy existed.

Section 4(1)(a) and its equivalents prohibit discrimination 'in the arrangements [made] for the purpose of determining who should be offered . . . employment.' Such arrangements might include advertising (including questions of how any advertisements are drafted and where they are placed);[20] the use of recruitment sources such as schools, careers offices, job centres etc (including the selection of these sources and any instructions issued to them);[21] selection and training of short-listers and interviewers, and the manner in which short-listing, interviewing, and final selection is conducted.[22]

The CRE's revised draft Employment Code of Practice[23] provides detailed guidance on the avoidance of discrimination in selection drawing attention, inter alia, to the need for accurate job descriptions and person specifications and appropriately placed advertisements.

The DDA places an obligation on employers to make reasonable adjustments where (s.4A(1) DDA):

> (a) a provision, criterion or practice applied by or on behalf of an employer, or
> (b) any physical feature of premises occupied by the employer,
> places the disabled person concerned at a substantial disadvantage in comparison with persons who are not disabled, it is the duty of the employer to take such steps as it is reasonable, in all the circumstances of the case, for him to have to take in order to prevent the provision, criterion or practice, or feature, having that effect.

Employers are bound both in relation to those who have expressed an interest in applying, in the case of 'a provision, criterion or practice for determining to whom employment should be offered' and, in any other case, in relation to disabled applicants and employees, though employers are not placed under any obligation in cases in which (s.4A(3)) they did 'not know, and could not reasonably be expected to know' about the fact of disability or, in the case of an applicant, that the disabled person was or might be an applicant.

DRC, Code of Practice for the elimination of discrimination in the field of employment against disabled persons or persons who have had a disability

5.3 The inclusion of unnecessary or marginal requirements in a job specification can lead to discrimination. For example, an employer stipulates that employees must be 'energetic', when in fact the job in question is largely sedentary in nature. This requirement could unjustifiably exclude some people whose disabilities result in them getting tired more easily than others . . .

---

[20] Though EAT in *Cardiff Women's Aid v Hartup* [1994] IRLR 390 ruled that only the CRE, under s.29 RRA, could take action in respect of a discriminatory advertisement. As Michael Rubenstein pointed out in the IRLR commentary to the case ('Highlights', August 1994), the distinction drawn by EAT in that case between an act of discrimination (this being required under s.4(1)(a)) and evidence of an intention to discriminate (in respect of which only the CRE can take action), was 'unconvincing', and EAT's interpretation of s.4(1)(a) 'unduly restrictive'. *Cf Tanna v The Woods Group Ltd* reported in 130 *Equal Opportunities Review* 'Case Digest' in which the male applicant won a discrimination claim when after failing to apply for a job advertised for a 'mature lady'. The applicant rang the employers and was told he could apply but the stipulation was not actually withdrawn and he felt discouraged from applying.

[21] The CRE's draft Code of Practice states that 'it is recommended that employers should not confine recruitment unjustifiably to those agencies, job centres, careers offices and schools which, because of their particular source of applicants, provide only or mainly applicants of a particular racial group'.

[22] See *In re Ballymena Borough Council* Queen's Bench Division (Crown Side) 18 June 1993 (unreported), where selection took place by secret ballot by counsellors divided along sectarian lines. The applicant, who was rejected, succeeded in a complaint under the FEA's equivalent of s.4(1)(c) RRA. Had, for some reason, a decision been reached after the ballot to abandon the new position and not appoint, an application could still have been made under s.4(1)(a), see *Brennan v J H Dewhurst Ltd* below.

[23] The draft revised Employment Code of Practice for the Elimination of Racial Discrimination and the Promotion of Equal Opportunity in Employment.

Does an employer have to provide information about jobs in alternative formats?

5.9 In particular cases, this may be a reasonable adjustment. For example, a person whom the employer knows to be disabled asks to be given information about a job in a medium that is accessible to her (in large print, in braille, on tape or on computer disc). It is often likely to be a reasonable adjustment for the employer to comply, particularly if the employer's information systems, and the time available before the new employee is needed, mean it can easily be done.

What should an employer do when arranging interviews?

5.15 Employers should think ahead for interviews. Giving applicants the opportunity to indicate any relevant effects of a disability and to suggest adjustments to help overcome any disadvantage the disability may cause, could help the employer avoid discrimination in the interview and in considering the applicant, by clarifying whether any reasonable adjustments may be required . . .

What changes might an employer have to make to arrangements for interviews?

5.17 There are many possible reasonable adjustments, depending on the circumstances. For example, a person has difficulty attending at a particular time because of a disability. It will very likely be reasonable for the employer to have to rearrange the time. For example, a hearing impaired candidate has substantial difficulties with the interview arrangements. The interviewer may simply need to ensure he faces the applicant and speaks clearly or is prepared to repeat questions. The interviewer should make sure that his face is well lit when talking to someone with a hearing or visual impairment. It will almost always be reasonable for an employer to have to provide such help with communication support if the interviewee would otherwise be at a substantial disadvantage. For example, an employer who pays expenses to candidates who come for interview could well have to pay additional expenses to meet any special requirements of a disabled person arising from any substantial disadvantage to which she would otherwise be put by the interview arrangements. This might include paying travelling expenses for a support worker or reasonable cost of travel by taxi, rather than by bus or train, if this is necessary because of the disability. For example, a job applicant does not tell an employer (who has no knowledge of her disability) in advance that she uses a wheelchair. On arriving for the interview she discovers that the room is not accessible. The employer did not know of the disability and so could not have been expected to make changes in advance. However, it would still be a reasonable adjustment for the employer to hold the interview in an alternative accessible room, if a suitable one was easily available at the time with no, or only an acceptable level of, disruption or additional cost.

In *Coker & Osamor v Lord Chancellor* the Court of Appeal considered complaints brought under the SDA and RRA by women who challenged the then Lord Chancellor's method of appointment of an old friend to the position of his Special Adviser. The appointment was made without advertisement of the vacancy. The challenges, brought under s.6(1)(a) SDA and 4(1)(a) RRA, failed in the Court of Appeal because of a somewhat peculiar construction placed on the concept of indirect discrimination (see further Chapter 2). The case was supported by the CRE and EOC which wished to challenge appointments from a circle of family, friends or acquaintances which (like the Lord Chancellor's) was unbalanced in race and gender. The claimants, having lost their cases, were thrown the following crumbs of comfort:

Coker & Osamor v Lord Chancellor [2002] ICR 321

Lord Phillips MR (for the Court):

For the reasons that we have given, the attack advanced in these proceedings on the practice of making appointments from a circle of family, friends and acquaintances has failed. We have held that no breach of s.1(1)(b) of the statutes has been made out. It does not follow, however, that this practice is unobjectionable. It will often be open to objection for a number of reasons. It may not produce the best candidate for the post. It may be likely to result in the appointee being of a particular gender or racial group. It may infringe the principle of equal opportunities.

In conclusion, we would emphasise that this judgment is not concerned with the practice of recruiting by word of mouth. The Code of Practice issued by the Equal Opportunities Commission in 1985 under s.56A(1) [SDA], which contains valuable practical guidance for the elimination of discrimination in the field of employment and for the promotion of equality of opportunity between men and women, has this to say about that practice:

> '. . . recruitment solely or primarily by word of mouth may unnecessarily restrict the choice of applicants available. The method should be avoided in a workforce pre-dominantly of one sex, if in practice it precludes members of the opposite sex from applying.'

A Code of Practice was also issued by the Commission for Racial Equality in 1983 under s.47(1) of the 1976 Act, and nothing in this judgment detracts from the desirability of com-plying with the Codes of Practice.

A failure to observe a provision of a Code of Practice does not of itself render a person liable to any proceedings, but is admissible in evidence and, if relevant to any question aris-ing in the proceedings, shall be taken into account in determining that question: see s.56A(10) [SDA] and s.47(10) of [RRA].

It is possible that a recruitment exercise conducted by word of mouth, by personal recommendation or by other informal recruitment method will constitute indirect discrim-ination within the meaning of s.1(1)(b) of the statutes. If the arrangements made for the purpose of determining who should be offered employment or promotion involve the application of a requirement or condition to an applicant that he or she should be person-ally recommended by a member of the existing workforce that may, depending of course on all the facts, have the specified disproportionately adverse impact on one sex or on a particular ethnic group and so infringe s.1(1)(b).

It is clear from the *Coker* decision that s.4(1)(a) RRA and its equivalent provisions extend to the decision whether or not jobs will be advertised. The word-of-mouth recruit-ment method is widely acknowledged as one which perpetuates existing race and/or sex imbalances in the workforce. (In 1999 the then-Chair of the FEC attributed much of the success of the fair employment legislation in integrating private sector employment to the formalisation of recruitment methods.)[24]

The traditional paradigm of word-of-mouth recruitment is in manual work, in which recruitment frequently took place via family connections. But, as counsel for the Lord Chancellor pointed out in the employment tribunal in *Coker*, recruitment via headhunters

---

[24] In his evidence to the Northern Ireland Select Committee on Northern Ireland. See the Committee's Fourth Report of the 1998–1999 session: 'The operation of the Fair Employment (Northern Ireland) Act 1989: Ten Years On', question 160. Sir Robert Cooper's remarks are appended in the minutes of evidence for 13 January 1999 (HC 95-II). Speaking of informal methods of recruitment Sir Robert said: 'That was probably the single greatest stumbling block towards the provision of equality, not deliberate direct discrimination but those sort of practices'.

could be categorised as subject to the same failings.[25] (So, too, could current methods for appointing judges which, although they have been amended over recent years so as to rely in part on applications from interested parties, still permit the appointment of non-applicants. Having said this, the judicial appointments process is being overhauled, the Constitutional Reform Act 2005 establishing an independent judicial appointments commission). Advertisements which are themselves discriminatory can also result in action being taken by the relevant commission (the EOC, CRE or DRC) under s.29 RRA and its equivalent provisions.

Section 29 RRA provides that:

(1) It is unlawful to publish or to cause to be published an advertisement which indicates, or might reasonably be understood as indicating, an intention by a person to do an act of discrimination, whether the doing of that act by him would be lawful or, by virtue of Part II or III, unlawful.
(2) Subsection (1) does not apply to an advertisement—
  (a) if the intended act would be lawful by virtue of [the GOQ or GOR defence or the exceptions set out in ss.6, 26, 34–39 or 41 apply]; or
  (b) if the advertisement relates to the services of an employment agency . . . and the intended act only concerns employment which the employer could by virtue of section 5, 6 or 7(3) or (4) lawfully refuse to offer to persons against whom the advertisement indicates an intention to discriminate
(3) Subsection (1) does not apply to an advertisement which indicates that persons of any class defined otherwise than by reference to colour, race or ethnic or national origins are required for employment outside Great Britain.

Section 29(4) provides a defence to the publisher who proves reasonable reliance on a statement that the discrimination at issue wos not unlawful by virtue of the RRA while s.29(5) makes it a criminal offence for a person knowingly or recklessly to make such a statement 'which in a material respect is false or misleading.'

S.38 SDA is in similar terms save that it prohibits only those advertisements which 'which indicate[], or might reasonably be understood as indicating, an intention by a person to do any act which is or might be unlawful' under the SDA and contains no equivalent of s.29(3) RRA. It does, however, provide (s.38(3)) that 'For the purposes of subsection (1), use of a job description with a sexual connotation (such as 'waiter', 'salesgirl', 'postman' or 'stewardess') shall be taken to indicate an intention to discriminate, unless the advertisement contains an indication to the contrary'. Article 34 FETO is materially identical to s.38 SDA (with the obvious omission of s.38(3)). S.16B DDA, which took effect only on 1 October 2004, applies only in relation to advertisements connected with employment, and to persons placing advertisements, rather than to publishers. It provides that:

[25] The CRE's draft revised Employment Code of Practice s suggests (para 2.13) that 'if [someone] can show that . . . using head-hunters to fill senior management posts makes it more difficult for Black Caribbean people to get senior management jobs in this company, and this puts her at a disadvantage, the practice could amount to unlawful indirect discrimination. The company would have to show that using head-hunters to recruit for senior management posts is a proportionate—that is, an appropriate and necessary—means of finding suitably qualified people at this grade and that other less potentially discriminatory methods are not as effective'.

> (1) It is unlawful for a person, in relation to a relevant appointment or benefit which he intends to make or confer, to publish or cause to be published an advertisement which—
>
> (a) invites applications for that appointment or benefit; and
>
> (b) indicates, or might reasonably be understood to indicate, that an application will or may be determined to any extent by reference to—
>
> > (i) the applicant not having any disability, or any particular disability, or
> >
> > (ii) any reluctance of the person determining the application to comply with a duty to make reasonable adjustments . . .
>
> (2) Subsection (1) does not apply where it would not in fact be unlawful . . . for an application to be determined in the manner indicated (or understood to be indicated) in the advertisement.
>
> (4) In this section, 'advertisement' includes every form of advertisement or notice, whether to the public or not.[26]
>
> The DDA 2005 will amend s.16B to apply to discrimination by third parties as do the equivalent provisions of the other legislation, to create the same offence and to provide the same good faith defence as they do.

Much of the case law which has arisen under s.4(1)(a) RRA and its equivalent provisions concerns allegedly discriminatory interviews. Women frequently complain of being subjected to questioning as to their family status and, if they have children, their childcare arrangements, from which men are generally exempt. Equally, an Asian Muslim woman might be interviewed on the basis of stereotypical assumptions about familial expectations;[27] a wheelchair user subjected to the 'does she take sugar' treatment; a gay man questioned about his sexual behaviour and/or HIV status, or an appointment decision reached by means of a secret vote in circumstances where sectarian affiliations are present.[28]

The EOC's Code of Practice for the elimination of discrimination on the grounds of sex and marriage and the promotion of sex equality in employment (para 23(c)) recommends that:

> questions should relate to the requirements of the job. Where it is necessary to assess whether personal circumstances will affect performance of the job (for example, where it involves unsocial hours or extensive travel) this should be discussed objectively without detailed questions based on assumptions about marital status, children and domestic obligations . . . Questions about marriage plans or family intentions should not be asked, as they could be construed as showing bias against women.

---

[26] S.17B DDA and its equivalents provide that action can only be taken by the DRC.

[27] Though here she would have to decide—see Chs 1 and 2—whether to sue under the SDA, the RRA or the RB Regs.

[28] See *in re Ballymena BC*, above n 22. It should also be noted that, whether or not differential questioning amounts in any particular case to a breach of s.4(1)(a) RRA or its equivalent provisions, a challenge under s.4(1)(c) or equivalent to a failure to appoint would frequently be boosted by evidence of such questioning (although, as in *Saunders v Richmond upon Thames BC* [1978] ICR 75, even the most bizarrely inappropriate questioning will not necessarily result in a successful discrimination claim).

The DRC's First Review of the DDA reiterated the Commission's previous recommendation that employers should be permitted to make disability related enquiries of job applicants only in very limited circumstances. According to the Commission:

> there is a clear and pressing need for this proposal. Disabled people in [Department of Work and Pensions] research identified recruitment as the most common source of discrimination.
>
> The DDA is proving inadequate in addressing recruitment problems. Many employers still ask medical questions about applicants' disabilities prior to job interview and selection. This enables employers who wish to discriminate to simply reject disabled applicants at an early stage. It is extremely difficult to prove such discrimination. In any event some disabled applicants are discouraged by questions from even proceeding with their application. We believe that such questions prior to job selection should be prohibited . . . we are concerned at the continued prevalence amongst disabled people of the view that employers routinely discriminate in the recruitment process. For example, 39 per cent of mental health users in a MIND Survey felt that they had been denied a job because of their psychiatric history. The fear of discrimination acts as a deterrence to disabled people applying for jobs. In the same survey, 69 per cent of mental health users had been put off applying for jobs for fear of unfair treatment.

In *Brennan v J H Dewhurst Ltd* [1984] ICR 52 EAT confirmed that particular questions asked of a candidate could breach s.6(1)(a) SDA. The claimant had applied and been rejected for a job as a butcher's assistant. A tribunal accepted that the shop's manager 'both from the questions [he] asked . . . and his manner and demeanour at the interview . . . had no desire or intention to employ a woman as butcher's assistant'. In the event, the area manager, who had advertised the position, decided that there was no need to appoint. There was no suggestion that he had been guilty of discrimination. EAT accepted, *per* Browne-Wilkinson J as he then was, that s.6(1)(a) SDA could reach the *operation* of arrangements made by the employer as well as the arrangements themselves:

> If s.6(1)(a) does not cover arrangements for the purpose of determining who should be offered employment which are operated in a discriminatory way, to that extent the plain policy of the Act would not be carried out. We accept . . . that it is not our function to insert into an Act of Parliament something which the Act, on its fair reading, does not contain. But when one is faced with a doubt whether the discrimination is to be found in the operation of the arrangements or in the making of the arrangements, we think it is legitimate for us to take into account the manifest policy of the Act as stated in the long title to the Act. Therefore, we think we are entitled and, indeed, bound to hold that the provisions of s.6(1)(a) are satisfied if the arrangements made for the purpose of determining who should be offered that employment operate so as to discriminate against a woman, even though they were not made with the purpose of so discriminating.

In *Brennan* EAT agreed with the tribunal that the claimant had been discriminated against. Differential questioning does not, however, always result in this conclusion. In *Saunders v Richmond upon Thames Borough Council* [1978] ICR 75, EAT considered the s.6(1)(a) claim brought by a woman golf professional who claimed that both her interview and her non-selection for a golf position were discriminatory. The tribunal found that her non-selection was not by reason of her sex, a finding EAT upheld. Here we deal with the separate issue which arose under s.6(1)(a), the questions asked of her at interview having included the following: 'Are there any women golf professionals in clubs?'; 'So you'd be blazing the trail, would you'?; 'Do you think men respond as well to a woman golf professional as to a man?'; 'If all this is true, you are obviously a lady of great experience, but don't you think this type of job is rather unglamourous?'; 'Don't you think this is a job with rather long hours?'; 'I can see that you could probably cope with the playing and teaching side of the job, but I am rather concerned as to whether you could cope with the management side'; and 'If some of the men were causing trouble over the starting times on the tee, do you think you would be able to control this?'. According to Phillips J, whether interview questions discriminated was a question of fact in each case and, while the questions complained of 'reflect[ed], in part at least, what is now an out-of-date and proscribed attitude of mind' and while the fact that they had been asked 'may be very relevant when it comes to be determined . . . whether there has been discrimination in not appointing a woman'; 'we do not think that it is unlawful to ask such questions' or to ask questions of a woman which would not have been asked of a man (or vice versa).

The Court of Appeal in *R (on the application of European Roma Rights Centre & Ors) v Immigration Officer at Prague Airport & Ors* [2004] QB 811 ruled that differential question of Roma and other travellers coming to the UK did not amount to direct discrimination. Simon Browne LJ, with whom Mantell LJ agreed, expressed the view that an employer 'in place of the wholesale rejection of women with children as an unreliable class of employees was entitled to question them more intrusively than others,' indeed that such questioning was 'logically likely':

> Consider similarly an employer interviewing for a job involving heavy lifting. He may not be entitled to refuse to interview women at all, but is he not permitted to question a female applicant for the job more sceptically and rigorously than her male counterpart? . . . If a terrorist outrage were committed on our streets today, would the police not be entitled to question more suspiciously those in the vicinity appearing to come from an Islamic background? Similarly in the case of sectarian violence in Northern Ireland. These seem to me the relevant analogies here, not the now defunct practice of repeatedly stopping and searching black youths, clearly an unjustifiable interference with their liberty unless reasonable grounds exist for suspecting those actually stopped.

Simon Browne LJ did not elaborate as to why, in his view, the targeting of those 'appearing to come from an Islamic background' was acceptable in the aftermath of a terrorist incident whereas the targeting of black youths was 'clearly not.' The House of Lords ([2005] 2 WLR 1) allowed on appeal, ruling that the treatment of Roma 'with more suspicion' and their subjection to 'more intense and intrusive questioning' than non-Roma breached the RRA.

Failure to Appoint

Section 4(1)(a), which we have already considered, concerns discrimination in the *arrangements* made to appoint, s.4(1)(c) and its equivalents, discrimination consisting of a refusal or deliberate failure to offer an appointment.[29] They require that the aggrieved individual

---

[29] Ss.6(1)(c) SDA, 4(1)(c) DDA, Art 19(a)(iii) FETO and reg 6(1)(c) SO and RB Regs. Art 21 FETO, which has no equivalent in the other legislation, also prohibits discrimination by persons with statutory authority to select or nominate another person for employment by a third party by failing to select, discriminating in the ranking of any list, or harassment.

has actually applied for the position and been rejected. It has been noted above that differential questioning might result in inferences being drawn under this section or its equivalents even if the questioning was not accepted as being contrary to s.4(1)(a).

The CRE's original Code of Practice suggests, inter alia, that refusal to employ a Sikh by virtue of his inability to comply with uniform requirements might breach s.4(1)(c). Among the cases which have arisen under s.4(1)(c) and its equivalents have been *Martin v Marks & Spencer* (refusal to appoint by an allegedly racially biased panel); *Price v Civil Service Commission* (application of an age bar which discriminated against women) and *Meer v Tower Hamlets* (application of selection criteria which were alleged to discriminate indirectly on racial grounds).[30] Other examples include the refusal of a job as a community service supervisor to an applicant who suffered from chronic depression, on the grounds that an alternative job as a handyman was deemed less stressful by the employer's occupational health adviser (*Paul v National Probation Service*); the refusal to appoint to the police a woman who had undergone gender-reassignment—this on the basis that she would not be capable of performing intimate searches (*A v Chief Constable of the West Yorkshire Police*); and a refusal to renew an English journalist's fixed-term presenting job on BBC Scotland's 'Rugby Special' (*BBC Scotland v Souster*).[31]

The most significant difficulties which arise under s.4(1)(c) and its equivalents concern proof (see, for example, *Anya v University of Oxford* [2001] ICR 847). The issue of proof is discussed, together with enforcement more generally, in Chapter 5. One substantive legal point which has arisen in connection with them concerned the position of those discriminated against in a post-dismissal appeal procedure. In *Adekeye v Post Office (No.2)* [1997] ICR 110 the Court of Appeal ruled that such discrimination did not fall within s.4(2)'s 'a person employed by him.' This aspect of the decision is considered below. But the Court also upheld EAT's decision overturning the tribunal ruling that the refusal to reinstate the claimant on appeal from dismissal breached s.4(1)(c) RRA. The tribunal had held that '[t]o interpret s.4(1) as covering only those who are applying for employment for the first time would enable employers to discriminate against a former employee on racial grounds after that employee had been dismissed in relation to the appeal against dismissal. Given the tenor of employment legislation over the past 20 years, this tribunal cannot believe it was the intention of Parliament to facilitate such behaviour.' Both EAT and the Court of Appeal, however, took the view that s.4(1)(c) was not intended to cover the position of a dismissed ex-employee seeking reinstatement on appeal. Each provision of s.4(1) contained the words relating to 'an offer of employment,' and an ex-employee at appeal could not be regarded as seeking an offer of employment.

We shall see, below, that the decision of the Court of Appeal in *Adekeye* on s.4(2) RRA was overturned by the House of Lords in *Rhys-Harper v Relaxion Group plc* [2003] ICR 867. Their Lordships all agreed, however, that a refusal to reinstate on the order of a tribunal did not fall within s.4(1)(c). According to Lord Nicholls:

Lambeth's conduct is not readily characterised as 'deliberately omitting to offer' Mr D'Souza employment within the meaning of s.4(1)(c). The nature of Lambeth's act was different. Lambeth was not in the normal position of a prospective employer. What Lambeth did was to fail to comply with a tribunal order which required the council to restore an employee to the employment from which he had been dismissed. That characterisation, coupled with the feature that the statute itself provides remedies for non-compliance with a

[30] Respectively [1998] ICR 1005, [1977] 1 WLR 943 and, [1988] IRLR 399.
[31] Respectively [2004] IRLR 190, [2005] 1 AC 51 and [2001] IRLR 150.

reinstatement order, points strongly away from this circumstance being within s.4(1)(c) of the Race Relations Act. I would so hold.

Their Lordships did not specifically address the position of someone subject to discrimination in a post-dismissal appeal, but the tenor of Lord Nicholl's judgment is that such a claim would fall, rather, under s.4(2)(b) of the Act.

Terms of Appointment

Section 4(1)(b) RRA and its equivalents are concerned with the terms upon which employment is offered, ss.4(2)(a) with the actual terms of employment. S.6 SDA contains no equivalent of s.4(2)(a), the EqPA instead governing discrimination in contractual terms afforded to men and women. There are relatively few appellate decisions on these subsections or their equivalents. *Barclays Bank plc v Kapur* [1991] 2 AC 355 concerned alleged race discrimination in contractual terms. More recently, in *Wakeman v Quick Corporation* [1999] IRLR 424, the Court of Appeal considered a s.4(2)(a) claim made by locally-recruited staff of a Japanese firm who compared their conditions to those applied to staff seconded from Japan and in *Spicer v Government of Spain* [2004] EWCA Civ 046 the Court of Appeal considered a challenge under the RRA to the payment of expatriate allowances to Spanish civil servants but not to locally recruited UK staff.

Discrimination in Access to Promotion, Employment-related Benefits, etc

Section 4(2)(b) RRA and its equivalents apply to discrimination in access (or the refusal of access) to 'opportunities for promotion, transfer or training, or . . . any other benefits, facilities or services'. In each case the legislation provides that the 'benefits, facilities or services' to which the section applies do not include those which the employer provides to the public or a section of the public unless the provision to staff is materially different, or is regulated by the contract of employment, or is concerned with training. According to the Explanatory Notes to the SO and RB Regs, the cases excluded from s.4(2)(b) and its equivalents:

> relate to the provision of goods or services and cannot be considered discrimination in employment . . . For example, where a lesbian employee worked as a receptionist at the London airport office of a car rental company but then, while on holiday, was discriminated against on grounds of her sexual orientation when trying to hire a car from the same company's Edinburgh office, [the Regs] would prevent her from making a complaint to an employment tribunal—unless one of the three exceptions . . . applied. So if it were part of her employment package that she should receive cheap car hire while on holiday, the benefits would be regulated by her contract . . . so as to entitle her to bring employment tribunal proceedings.

In *London Borough of Southwark v Afolabi* [2003] ICR 800 the Court of Appeal upheld tribunal findings that the claimant had been discriminated against contrary to s.4(2)(b) when he was appointed on a lower grade than that of the post in respect of which he applied, and when he was treated less favourably than white colleagues in a regrading exercise. Other examples of the application of s.4(2)(b) and its equivalents include *Greenwood v British*

Airways [1999] IRLR 600, in which a senior cargo assistant who had had considerable peri-ods of sick leave associated with a psychiatric problem relied upon the DDA to challenge a refusal to promote him which was based in part on his sickness record and *O'Donoghue v Redcar & Cleveland Borough Council* [2001] IRLR 615, in which a woman whose appli-cation for a newly created post in her department was rejected relied on the SDA to challenge a decision which had been based in part on her 'strong feminist views which she had freely expressed over a period of years.' Section 4(2)(b) and its equivalents also apply in relation to the provision of non-contractual benefits such as discretionary loyalty bonuses (*GUS Home Shopping Ltd v Green*), mortgage subsidy schemes (*Calder v James Finlay Corporation Ltd*), and references (*Cornelius v University College of Swansea*).[32]

Discrimination by employers in relation to pensions, health or other forms of insurance, etc would fall within ss.4(1)(b) and 4(2)(a) and/or (b) RRA and their equivalents, or under the EqPA where the benefit was contractual and the discrimination was on grounds of sex. Prior to its amendment from 1 October 2004 the DDA excluded occupational pension schemes from the employer's duty to make reasonable adjustments. This no longer applies. In addition, the Pensions Act 1995, the DDA and the SO and RB Regs (though not the RRA) regulate discrimination by the managers and trustees of pension schemes on grounds of sex, disability, sexual orientation and religion or belief respectively.[33]

Dismissal

Turning, finally, to s.4(2)(c) RRA and its equivalent provisions, prior to recent amend-ments only the SDA expressly covered constructive dismissal, s.82(1A) providing that 'dis-missal' (and the termination of a partnership) included both the expiry of a fixed term contract and 'the termination of that person's employment or partnership by any act of his (including the giving of notice) in circumstances such that he is entitled to terminate it without notice by reason of the conduct of the employer or, as the case may be, the con-duct of the other partners.' In *Weathersfield v Sargent* [1998] ICR 198 and again in *Derby Specialist Fabrication Ltd* the EAT ruled that constructive dismissals nevertheless fell within s.4(2)(c) RRA.

Derby Specialist Fabrication Ltd v Burton [2001] ICR 833

Keene J:

There may be a number of reasons why Parliament chose to make an amendment to the [SDA], not least its wish to ensure that there could no doubt whatsoever about the Act's compliance with Community law. . . . It cannot be taken as an indication by Parliament

---

[32] Respectively, [2001] IRLR 75, [1989] IRLR 55 and [1988] ICR 735.

[33] Note also s.18 DDA which provides, essentially, that discrimination by a provider of group insurance services to employees (under an arrangement with the employer) is unlawful as a form of employment-related discrimination. The provision, which applies only in relation to insurance against 'termination of service; retirement, old age or death; accident, injury, sickness or invalidity; or any other prescribed matter,' is to be abolished, the DDA 2005 bringing such discrimination within the DDA's prohibition on discrimi-nation in the provision of goods and services (see further below). The advantage s.18 conferred on employ-ees—the ability to litigate in the employment tribunals rather than the county court—is to be preserved by new s.25(6A) which will apply in relation to all group insurance services rather than just those dealing with termination of service, etc., as at present. See *Marsh & McLennan v Pension Ombudsman* [2001] IRLR 505 for the enforcement of the Pension Act's Equal Treatment rule.

that, in other legislation with which it was not dealing, 'dismissal' was to be given a restricted meaning. We emphasise that because, if one approaches the meaning of 'dismissal' in the Race Relations Act without that extraneous influence, there is no reason why it should be so construed as to exclude constructive dismissal. Whether the employer deliberately dismisses the employee on racial grounds or he so acts as to repudiate the contract by racially discriminatory conduct, which repudiation the employee accepts, the end result is the same, namely the loss of employment by the employee. Why should Parliament be taken to have distinguished between these two situations?

In *Nottinghamshire County Council v Meikle* [2005] ICR 1 the Court of Appeal applied the *Burton* reasoning to the DDA, overruling a previous EAT decision[34] to the effect that the DDA did not apply to constructive dismissal. The implementation of the Racial Equality and Employment Equality Directives resulted in amendments being made to the DDA and the RRA to provide explicitly that dismissal, termination of partnerships and office-holdings, etc, covers the constructive form (and, where relevant, the non-renewal on expiry of a fixed term contract). So, for example (s.4 RRA):

> (4A) In subsection (2)(c) reference to the dismissal of a person from employment includes, *where the discrimination is on grounds of race or ethnic or national origins*, reference [my emphasis]—
>> (a) to the termination of that person's employment by the expiration of any period (including a period expiring by reference to an event or circumstance), not being a termination immediately after which the employment is renewed on the same terms; and
>> (b) to the termination of that person's employment by any act of his (including the giving of notice) in circumstances such that he is entitled to terminate it without notice by reason of the conduct of the employer.

The DDA, FETO, and the SO and RB Regs now contain materially identical provisions as does (see above) the SDA.[35]

Post-employment Discrimination

The decision of the Court of Appeal in *Adekeye v Post Office (No.2)* [1997] ICR 110 highlighted a significant gap in the protection afforded by the employment-related provisions of the various anti-discrimination enactments. There the Court ruled that discrimination in a post-dismissal appeal fell outwith the scope of the RRA on the grounds (*per* Peter Gibson LJ) that the 'ordinary and natural meaning' of s.4(2)'s 'a person employed by him' was restricted to present, rather than past, employees. In *Coote v Granada Hospitality Ltd* Case C–185/97 [1998] ECR I–5199 the ECJ ruled that the Equal Treatment Directive required that those complaining of sex discrimination be protected from victimisation (in the form of a refusal to supply a reference) after the termination of their employment. EAT subsequently distinguished *Adekeye* in order to rule in the claimant's favour: (*Coote v Granada Hospitality Ltd (No. 2)* [1999] ICR 942). In a series of subsequent decisions the Court

---

[34] *Commissioner of Police of the Metropolis v Harley* [2001] ICR 927.
[35] S.4(5) DDA, Art 19(3) FETO, reg 6(5) RB and SO Regs.

of Appeal preferred *Adekeye* to *Coote* in claims brought under the RRA and DDA and (*Rhys-Harper v Relaxion Group plc* [2001] ICR 1176) confined the *Coote* decision to post-employment *victimisation* claims brought under the SDA. The House of Lords overturned that decision in a judgment which dealt also with claims brought under the DDA and RRA. Their Lordships ruled ([2004] ICR 100) that *Adekeye (No.2)* had been incorrectly decided and that the term 'employed by him' in s.4(2) RRA and its equivalent provisions extended to former as well as current employees so long as there was a substantive connection between the discriminatory conduct and the employment relationship. Parliament could not, in their Lordships' view, have intended that employees would be unprotected from discrimination in a post-dismissal appeal, nor in relation to a reference given after the termination of employment.

Various of their Lordships were more or less robust in their application of the discrimination provisions to the post-employment situation, Lord Nicholls, Hobhouse and Rodger appearing more enthusiastic then Lords Scott and Hope. For most practical purposes, however, any nuances in the decision will soon be of mainly historical interest as the implementation of the Racial Equality and Employment Equality Directives has resulted in amendments to the RRA and the DDA expressly to provide that post-employment discrimination is actionable under the Acts. S.27A RRA provides that:

(1) In this section a 'relevant relationship' is a relationship during the course of which, by virtue of any provision referred to in section 1(1B), taken with section 1(1) or (1A), or (as the case may be) by virtue of section 3A—
   (a) an act of discrimination by one party to the relationship ('the relevant party') against another party to the relationship, on grounds of race or ethnic or national origins, or
   (b) harassment of another party to the relationship by the relevant party, is unlawful.
(2) Where a relevant relationship has come to an end it is unlawful for the relevant party—
   (a) to discriminate against another party, on grounds of race or ethnic or national origins, by subjecting him to a detriment, or
   (b) to subject another party to harassment;
where the discrimination or harassment arises out of and is closely connected to that relationship.
(3) In subsection (1) reference to an act of discrimination or harassment which is unlawful includes, in the case of a relationship which has come to an end before 19 July 2003, reference to such an act which would, after that date, be unlawful.
(4) For the purposes of any proceedings in respect of an unlawful act under subsection (2), that act shall be treated as falling within circumstances relevant for the purposes of such of the provisions, or Parts, referred to in subsection (1) as determine most closely the nature of the relevant relationship.

Section 27A RRA applies only to discrimination which would have been unlawful during the course of the relationship under the RRA and the Racial Equality Directive (that is, discrimination on grounds of race or ethnic or national origins in relation to those matters listed in s.1B RRA—see further Chapter 7). FETO and the SO and RB Regs provide similarly (though only in relation to 'employment', broadly defined), while the SDA was amended in July 2003 (not expressly in relation to 'harassment' and only in relation to 'employment' broadly defined, but see Chapter 2 for details of proposed amendments).[36]

---

[36] Art 33A FETO, reg 21 SO and RB Regs, and ss.20A and 35C.

The DDA's equivalent provision (s.16A) applies where the claimant has been discriminated against by being harassed or subjected to a detriment after the termination of a relationship in the field of employment, broadly defined, with the effect that the decision of the House of Lords applies only in respect of discrimination on grounds of colour or nationality and to sex and disability discrimination other than in the employment field.

The application of the post-employment provisions is explained in the Explanatory Notes to the SO and RB Regs (paras 146–7):

> For example, a university which discriminates on grounds of sexual orientation/religion or belief by refusing to provide a reference to a former student would be acting unlawfully . . . (This does not mean that a university or an employer is not entitled to refuse any request for a reference, but simply that they may not refuse in a discriminatory way on grounds of sexual orientation/religion or belief.) Also, an employer who discriminated against a former employee in the course of her internal appeal against her dismissal would be acting unlawfully . . .
>
> This regulation does not itself lay down any time limit for its application. However . . . any complaint must normally be presented to an employment tribunal within 3 months of the alleged act of discrimination or harassment. [The post-employment provision] is also restricted in its application, in that the further removed the alleged act of discrimination or harassment is from the former working relationship, in both time and context, the less likely it is that a person will be able to establish the necessary close connection to the former relationship. So an incident which takes place a number of years after the relationship has ended, or in a social context unrelated to that relationship, is unlikely to fall under [the provision].

Detriment

Turning to the 'any other detriment' element of s.4(2)(c) RRA, this serves as a 'catch all' category capable of covering most types of discrimination which might arise during employment and not otherwise covered by s.4 RRA or its equivalent provisions. This element has given rise to a considerable number of appellate decisions. The difficulty associated with it is that, whereas discrimination in respect of the other matters covered by s.4 RRA etc. is actionable *per se*, the claimant who alleges discrimination under the second head of s.4(2)(b) must convince the tribunal not only that less favourable treatment was accorded her, but also that the treatment was sufficiently disadvantageous to be regarded as an actionable 'detriment.'

The difficulties to which the 'detriment' requirement have given rise were indicated as early as 1977 in the Court of Appeal's decision in *Peake v Automotive Products Ltd* [1978] QB 233. The decision, which was discussed in Chapter 2, was reached primarily on the ground that the employer's policy of allowing women to leave work five minutes before men was not 'discrimination' against men within the meaning of s.1(1)(a) SDA. This aspect of the decision was disapproved of by the same court in the subsequent decision in *Ministry of Defence v Jeremiah* [1980] QB 87. But the alternative basis for the *Peake* ruling, which was upheld in the latter decision, was that the additional five minutes which the men were required to work was, if it amounted to a 'detriment' at all, *de minimis* and therefore outside the scope of the Act.

The *de minimis* approach has not subsequently been expressly applied to exclude discrimination complaints from the scope of s.6(2)(b) SDA and its equivalent provisions, having been called into question by the subsequent decision of the Court of Appeal in *Gill*

& Coote v El Vino Ltd.[37] But a similar outcome has been achieved by the categorisation of particular forms of discrimination (in the sense of differential or differently-impacting treatment) as 'not detrimental' to their challengers. This approach has been particularly evident in the context of alleged harassment and clothing and appearance rules (the former are discussed below, the latter in Chapter 6) but has been applied elsewhere also. In *Staffordshire County Council v Black* [1995] IRLR 234, for example, EAT rejected the claim that a factory check on all black workers entering the building, imposed in order to prevent entry by one particular man, amounted to a 'detriment' under the RRA. EAT did not accept that the claimant had been 'put under a disadvantage' by the check. And in *Clymo v Wandsworth* [1989] ICR 250 EAT ruled that a woman refused permission to return to work on a job-share basis had not been subjected to any detriment, this on the basis that (*per* Wood J) 'job sharing was not an option for branch librarians and thus the claimant was no worse off than other branch librarians. She resigned—left of her own accord—and this does not seem to us to be a 'detriment' caused by anyone but herself.'

More recently, however, the courts appear less reluctant to accept that detriment has occurred. In *Shamoon v Chief Constable of the Royal Ulster Constabulary* [2001] IRLR 520 Northern Ireland's Court of Appeal ruled, following EAT in *Lord Chancellor v Coker and Osamor* [2001] ICR 507, that 'detriment' required some 'physical or economic consequence as a result of discrimination . . . which is material and substantial.' But the House of Lords overturned NICA's decision in *Shamoon* and ruled that there could be a 'detriment' in the employment context where a reasonable worker would or might take the view that he had thereby been disadvantaged in the circumstances in which he had thereafter to work and that, although an unjustified sense of grievance could not amount to a 'detriment, it was not necessary to demonstrate any physical or economic consequence.' In that case itself, the fact that the claimant had had removed from her a responsibility which she had previously undertaken could amount to a 'detriment' even though she had no contractual entitlement to that role. And in *Jiad v Byford & Ors* [2003] IRLR 232 the Court of Appeal ruled that a tribunal had erred in striking out a race discrimination claim on the basis that the claimant had suffered no actionable detriment where he experienced psychological stress and humiliation as result of an incident with the director of BBC World Service. EAT had upheld the tribunal's decision, following NICA's decision in *Shamoon*. The Court of Appeal ruled that enduring physical or psychological injury could amount to a 'detriment' in the sense that a reasonable worker would regard it as a disadvantage, even though transitory hurt feelings might not (depending on the facts) suffice. According to the Explanatory Notes to the SO and RB Regs:

> If an employer deals with requests for prayer breaks in a discriminatory way, this may cause a detriment to employees. . . If an employer deals with requests for days off in a discriminatory way, this may also cause a detriment to employees which would be unlawful . . .

Sexual (and by implication, other forms of) harassment was recognised as falling potentially within the scope of the anti-discrimination prohibitions in *Strathclyde Regional*

---

[37] [1983] QB 425, in which the Court of Appeal refused to apply the de minimis maxim where, in a case where women were refused service in a bar unless seated at a table, men being allowed to stand at the bar. Eveleigh LJ found it: 'very difficult to invoke the maxim *de minimis non curat lex* in a situation where that which has been denied to the plaintiff is the very thing that Parliament seeks to provide, namely facilities and services on an equal basis.' The *de minimis* approach was also rejected on the facts in *R v Secretary of State for Education and Science, ex parte Keating*, *The Times* 3 December 1985. Cf, however, the decision in *Schmidt v Austicks Bookshops* [1978] ICR 85, discussed in Ch 6.

Council v Porcelli [1986] ICR 564, which case was discussed in Chapter 2. But it was remarked of the case at that time that:

J M Thompson, note on the *Porcelli* case (1985) 101 *Law Quarterly Review* 471, 471–2, footnotes omitted

discrimination was only unlawful if it fell within section 6(2)(b) of the [SDA] ie, the employer had (vicariously) unlawfully discriminated 'by dismissing her, or subjecting her to any other detriment.' Lord McDonald refused to accept the contention that 'the words 'subjecting her to any other detriment' were so universal that they covered acts of sexual harassment committed against [the complainant] during her employment, without reference to any consequence thereof so far as her employment was concerned'; . . . In other words, sexual harassment at work does not *per se* constitute unlawful sex discrimination within section 6. It is only if, as a result, the woman suffers a detriment related to her employment,eg. dismissal, or action short of dismissal, for resisting unwanted sexual advances, that section 6(2) would be satisfied. On the facts of the case, however, the complainant had suffered such an 'employment' detriment as she felt obliged to seek a transfer to another school: the request for the transfer had not been voluntary but had been forced upon her as a result of the sexual harassment.

It is thought that given the structure of the [SDA], Lord McDonald's decision is correct. But at a time of record unemployment, it is a serious limitation of the [SDA] that it is of no assistance to women who are subjected to sexual harassment at work but, for economic reasons, continue at their jobs. It remains to be seen whether either the criminal law or the law of tort will be sufficiently flexible to protect unfortunate women in these circumstances.

In *De Souza v The Automobile Association* [1986] ICR 514, the Court of Appeal accepted that harassment could be actionable within s.6(2)(b) even where its victim continued in employment, providing that 'the putative reasonable employee could justifiably complain about his or her working conditions or environment . . . whether or not these were so bad as to be able to amount to constructive dismissal, or even if the employee was prepared to work on and put up with the harassment.'[38] But the Court of Appeal in that case rejected a race discrimination claim by a woman who had overheard herself being referred to by a manager in racially derogatory terms. What was lacking, according to the court, was the necessary link between the employer and the hurt suffered by the appellant, such that the employer could be said to have '*subject[ed] her* to any other detriment' (my emphasis) within s.4(2)(c) of the RRA. The fact that the racially insulting remark was in this case made by a manager (which may have meant, according to May LJ, that the appellant 'was being considered less favourably, whether generally or in an employment context, than others'). But his Lordship did 'not think that she can properly be said to have been 'treated' less favourably by whomsoever used the word, unless he intended her to overhear the conversation in which it was used, or knew or ought reasonably to have anticipated that the person he was talking to would pass the insult on or that the appellant would become aware of it in some other way.'

More recently, in *Reed & Another v Stedman* [1999] IRLR 98 and in *Driskel v Peninsula Business Services Ltd* [2000] IRLR 151, EAT emphasised the strong subjective element in the question whether bullying, the use of sexual innuendo, etc, subjected the recipient to a 'detriment' for the purposes of the SDA. It remains the case, however, that 'detriment' will

---

[38] In *Bracebridge Engineering Ltd v Darby* [1990] IRLR 3, EAT accepted that a single incident of sexual harassment could, if it were sufficiently serious, amount to a 'detriment' (there the harassment consisted of a serious sexual assault).

not be assumed from the fact of harassment. In *Thomas v Robinson* [2003] IRLR 7 EAT overturned an employment tribunal finding that a black woman of African-Caribbean origin had been discriminated against on grounds of race contrary to the RRA when her colleague had subjected her to racist remarks to the effect that her dog was frightened of black people; that Muslim women looked like 'ninjas'; and (having been told that the claimant's parents had recently returned to the Caribbean) that Caribbeans came to the UK to 'scrounge off the system and then go back.' During the course of her evidence to the tribunal the claimant said she had been shocked and deeply offended by the remarks. The tribunal found that the last of these remarks constituted harassment, the others not having amounted to 'discrimination' because they were not addressed to her on grounds of her race and might have been made to anyone. EAT ruled that the tribunal had erred in law in finding that the claimant was racially discriminated against by 'a single remark made by a fellow junior employee' without having considered whether she had suffered detriment as a result, and in preventing the appellants from cross-examining her to show that she had not and remitted the case to a different tribunal to reconsider.

Judge JR Reid QC:

A single act of verbal sexual harassment is enough to found a complaint: see . . . *Insitu* [*Cleaning Co Ltd v Heads* [1995] IRLR 4]. There is no reason why the same should not be true of a single act of racial harassment. But a single instance of racial abuse does not nec-essarily amount to harassment. The expression 'harassment' involves two elements. The first is the targeting of the person being harassed. The second is the causing of distress to the target. The word is used in the context of discrimination proceedings as a shorthand to comprise the two elements which taken together make up actionable discrimination. Thus in the *Insitu* case Mrs Heads (a) suffered a grossly offensive remark and (b) was very dis-tressed by it. Similarly in [*Burton v*] *De Vere Hotel* Misses Burton and Rhule (a) suffered racist and sexist abuse and (b) were considerably upset and offended. Thus a tribunal which is considering whether an employee has been discriminated against by the use of racist lan-guage should consider both whether the language has been used and whether the employee has suffered detriment as a result. If both elements are established, then as a matter of shorthand it can be said that the employee has been racially harassed. In very many cases the second element will be extremely easy for the employee to establish, but this does not entitle the tribunal to assume the second element, nor (as the tribunal seems to have done here) to decide that the proof of the language created an irrebuttable presumption of detri-ment. There are some work environments in which (undesirable though it may be) racial abuse is given and taken in good part by members of different ethnic groups. In such cases the mere making of a racist remark could not be regarded as a detriment.

As a result of amendments intended to bring the domestic provisions into line with the Racial Equality Directive the RRA now provides expressly (s.4(2A)) that:

It is unlawful for an employer, in relation to employment by him at an establishment in Great Britain, to subject to harassment a person whom he employs or who has applied to him for employment.

Section 4(3) DDA is materially similar as are regs 6(3) of the SO and RB Regs. The definition of 'harassment' is considered in Chapter 2 as it is now categorised *per se* as actionable discrimination without need to prove 'detriment,' and it will be discussed here only in passing. S.3A RRA provides that:

(1) A person subjects another to harassment in any circumstances relevant for the purposes of any provision referred to in section 1(1B) where, on grounds of race or ethnic or national origins, he engages in unwanted conduct which has the purpose or effect of—

    (a) 'violating that other person's dignity, or

    (b) creating an intimidating, hostile, degrading, humiliating or offensive environment for him.'

(2) Conduct shall be regarded as having the effect specified in paragraph (a) or (b) of subsection (1) only if, having regard to all the circumstances, including in particular the perception of that other person, it should reasonably be considered as having that effect.

Note that the definition of 'harassment' does not apply in relation to colour or nationality but that, by contrast with the position under the other legislative provisions, it is not restricted to the employment context. Article 3A FETO is materially identical to s.3A(1) RRA as it applies in connection with race or ethnic or national origin, although it applies only to *employment-related* harassment in connection with 'religious belief or political opinion.' S.3B DDA is materially identical (again applying only in the context of 'employment,' broadly defined) as are reg 5 of the SO and RB Regs. The proposed amendments to the SDA, which define harassment in broadly similar terms, are considered in Chapter 2, and relate only to the employment context (prior to the implementation of Council Directive 2004/113/EC in 2007). Harassment can, however, take place in the context of housing, education, etc. and the requirement to establish 'detriment' in such cases will, like that of proving 'less favourable treatment' (see further Chapter 2) continue to prove problematic in these cases.

Under the statutory definition a claimant has to prove neither 'discrimination' other than by way of the harassment itself, or 'detriment' under s.4(2)(c) RRA or its equivalents. He or she does, however, have to establish (1) that the treatment complained of was on the relevant grounds (this is considered in Chapter 2); (2) that it had 'the purpose or effect of violating' the claimant's dignity or 'creating an intimidating, hostile, degrading, humiliating or offensive environment for' the claimant; and (3), if the treatment complained of had the *effect*, but *not* the *purpose*, of violating the claimant's dignity or 'creating an intimidating, hostile, degrading, humiliating or offensive environment for,' that 'having regard to all the circumstances, including in particular the [claimant's own] perception,' the treatment 'should reasonably be considered as having that effect.' Perhaps the most significant difference between this test and that which has developed in the domestic case law (questions of comparators having been dealt with in Chapter 2) is that where treatment is established as having had the *purpose* of violating the claimant's dignity or creating a hostile environment for him or her, no evidence will be necessary as to its effect on the claimant.

DTI, 'Explanatory notes for the Employment Equality (Sexual Orientation) Regulations 2003 and Employment Equality (Religion or Belief) Regulations 2003', paras 52–6

Calling a lesbian work colleague by an offensive nickname related to her sexual orientation would generally be prima facie evidence of intentional harassment . . . Even if the person could show that it was unintentional because he did not realise the nickname was offensive, his colleague would have the opportunity to show that it nevertheless violated her dignity or created an offensive environment for her . . .

Regulation 5(2) . . . includes a requirement to take into account the complainant's perception of the conduct. As such, the test is partly objective, and partly subjective. It is not sufficient in itself that the complainant perceives the conduct to be offensive for the conduct to constitute harassment. The test reflects the judgment . . . in *Driskel* . . . Ultimately, it will be for the court or tribunal to rule on the facts of each case as to whether conduct should reasonably be construed as having the effect of harassing the complainant.

For example, if an over-sensitive employee unreasonably took offence at a perfectly innocent comment related to his religious beliefs, it would not constitute harassment because the conduct could not reasonably be considered to have violated his dignity or created an offensive environment for him.

The fact that an employer might be unaware of an employee's sexual orientation or religious belief may be a relevant factor to be taken into account when considering the effect of the conduct in a case. However, the absence of an intention to harass is no bar to concluding that the conduct did have the effect of harassing the complainant.

For example, if an employer tells a joke which she does not deny is offensive to Muslims, then it would be reasonable to conclude that the joke offended the Muslim employee to whom she told it. The fact that the employer was unaware that the employee was Muslim makes the joke no less offensive.

Regulation 5(1)(a) and (b) require that the conduct in question had the purpose or effect of violating the employee's dignity or creating an intimidating, hostile, degrading, humiliating or offensive environment for him. There may often be overlap between the various aspects of this definition. Conduct which violates a person's dignity may also create an offensive (etc) environment for that person, and vice versa; conduct which is hostile may also be offensive and humiliating, etc. A complainant needs only to establish any one element (or more) of the definition to show that harassment has taken place.

For example, if a vocational training course provider makes a number of jokes about Christians in the course of the training, this could constitute harassment of a Christian student because it violates her dignity, and/or creates an intimidating, degrading, humiliating or offensive environment for her.

Conduct which might fall within the definition of harassment could be obviously offensive, or it could be more subtle, perhaps, reflecting a negative stereotype associated with a person of a particular sexual orientation or religious belief. It could be an isolated incident or remark, or a cumulative series of events which together amount to a degrading environment. It could be intentional or unintentional.

Wider Employment-related Provisions

Section 4 RRA, extracted above, regulates employment discrimination. The definition of 'employment' for the purposes of the anti-discrimination provisions has been considered above. But the broadly employment-related provisions of the various Acts and Regulations include not only s.4 and its equivalents but also those provisions which deal with partners, contract workers, office holders, etc. The DDA was originally narrower in this respect than the RRA and the SDA but has been amended to comply with the Employment Equality Directive's requirements. These amendments, which came into force on 1 October 2004, bring the DDA broadly into line with the SDA and RRA insofar as the broad sphere of employment-related discrimination is concerned. FETO and the SO Regs and RB Regs are also broadly similar (though the exclusively 'employment-related' focus of the Regs extends also to cover third level education). To simplify the text I will again focus on the provisions of the RRA, footnoting the equivalent provisions of the other legislation which will be discussed in the text only where it differs materially from the RRA.

Barristers, etc[39]

The anti-discrimination protections also apply to barristers (in Scotland, advocates) in relation to pupillage, tenancy and the assignment of work. Section 26A RRA provides that:

(1) It is unlawful for a barrister or barrister's clerk, in relation to any offer of a pupillage or tenancy, to discriminate against a person—
  (a) in the arrangements which are made for the purpose of determining to whom it should be offered;
  (b) in respect of any terms on which it is offered; or;
  (c) by refusing, or deliberately omitting, to offer it to him
(2) It is unlawful for a barrister or barrister's clerk, in relation to a pupil or tenant in the chambers in question, to discriminate against him—
  (a) in respect of any terms applicable to him as a pupil or tenant;
  (b) in the opportunities for training, or gaining experience which are afforded or denied to him;
  (c) in the benefits, facilities or services which are afforded or denied to him[[40]]; or
  (d) by terminating his pupillage or by subjecting him to any pressure to leave the chambers or other detriment.
(3) It is unlawful for any person, in relation to the giving, withholding or acceptance of instructions to a barrister, to discriminate against any person [or to subject any person to harassment].
(3A) It is unlawful for a barrister or barrister's clerk, in relation to a pupillage or tenancy in the set of chambers in question, to subject to harassment a person who is, or has applied to be, a pupil or tenant.

The provision and its equivalents do not apply to Scotland but s.27B and its equivalents apply to Scottish advocates in materially identical terms. The DDA and SO and RB Regs are materially identical to the RRA in their coverage of barristers and advocates, 'discrimination' under the DDA for these purposes including a failure to make reasonable adjustments as well as less favourable treatment in connection with a disabled person's disability.[41] The SDA also applies to barristers and advocates (ss.35A and B) but does not expressly deal with harassment prior to its proposed amendment by the draft SD Regs discussed in Chapter 2. Article 32 FETO is similar to s.26A RRA.[42]

Partners

Section 10 RRA prohibits discrimination by partnerships:

(1) (a) in the arrangements they make for the purpose of determining who should be offered that position; or
  (b) in the terms on which they offer [a person] that position; or

---

[39] Ss.35A & 35B SDA, Article 32 FETO, reg 12 & 13 SO and RB Regs and (from 1 October 2004) ss.7A–7C DDA.

[40] This is subject to the same qualification as discussed in relation to S.4(2)(b)RRA above.

[41] Ss.7A–D DDA, reg 12 and 13 SO and RB Regs. Prior to the amendments EAT ruled in *1 Pump Court Chambers v Horton* UKEAT/0775/03/MH (2 December 2003) that a chambers was not a 'trade organisation' for the purposes of a DDA claim by an unsuccessful applicant for pupillage.

[42] Being tailored to Northern Ireland's system which does not have chambers.

    (c) by refusing or deliberately omitting to offer him that position; or

    (d) in a case where the person already holds that position

        (i) in the way they afford him access to any benefits, facilities or services, or by refusing or deliberately omitting to afford him access to them; or

        (ii) by expelling him from that position, or subjecting him to any other detriment.

(1B) It is unlawful for a firm, in relation to a position as a partner in the firm, to subject to harassment a person who holds or has applied for that position.

(2) [Subsections (1), (1A) and (1B)] shall apply in relation to persons proposing to form themselves into a partnership as it applies in relation to a firm.

This provision applies, except where the discrimination is on grounds of race or ethnic or national origin, only to partnerships of six or more. The RRA further provides that constructive termination of a person's partnership is covered by s.10(1)(d)(ii). The amended provisions apply, however, only in relation to discrimination on grounds of 'race or ethnic or national origins'. Where the discrimination is on grounds of colour or nationality, the original provisions of the RRA apply: only partnerships of at least six are covered and no *express* provision is made for constructive termination (though see the discussion above). Further, the definition of 'harassment' within the RRA applies only in connection with 'race or ethnic or national origin'. The DDA, FETO and the SO and RB Regs are materially identical to the RRA *as amended* (ie, all sizes of partnership are included and harassment and constructive termination are expressly provided for),[43] while the SDA applies regardless of size of partnership and (because of s.82(1A)) to constructive termination, but does not, prior to its expected amendment by the currently draft SD Regs, expressly regulate harassment.

Contract Workers

Contract workers (workers who are employed by a third party who supplies them to the 'principal' under a contract) are protected from discrimination by 'principals' by s.7 RRA as if they were employed by the principal.[44]

    (2) It is unlawful for the principal, in relation to work to which this section applies, to discriminate against a contract worker—

    (a) in the terms on which he allows him to do that work; or

    (b) by not allowing him to do it or continue to do it; or in the way he affords him access to any benefits, facilities or services or

    (c) by refusing or deliberately omitting to afford him access to them; or

    (d) by subjecting him to any other detriment. . . .

    (3A) It is unlawful for the principal, in relation to work to which this section applies, to subject a contract worker to harassment.

---

[43] Ss.6A & 6B DDA—again a duty of reasonable adjustment applies. Article 26 FETO and reg 14 of the RB and SO Regs.

[44] Ss.9 SDA, 7 RRA and, from 1 October 2004, s.4B DDA; Article 20 FETO and reg 8 of the SO and RB Regs.

DTI, 'Explanatory notes for the Employment Equality (Sexual Orientation) Regulations 2003 and Employment Equality (Religion or Belief) Regulations 2003', paras 104–06

For example, if a house-building company sub-contracts some work to an electrical company, and if an electrician working for this company suffers discrimination from the foreman of the building company, she may bring a claim against the house-building company . . . [if] a nurse [who] is employed by an agency which supplies staff to a number of hospitals . . . suffers harassment from [a] hospital's manager, he may bring a complaint against the hospital and against the manager.

Reg 8 of the SO and RB Regs is materially identical as is S.4B DDA which applies to a duty to make reasonable adjustment as it applies to less favourable treatment. Section 9 SDA is also the same except that it does not, prior to the amendments proposed by the draft SD Regs, expressly deal with harassment. S.7 and its equivalents are broadly interpreted. In *BP Chemicals v Gillick & Roevin Management Services Ltd* [1995] IRLR 128, EAT accepted that s.9 SDA applied to *selection* by the principal as it did in the period after selection. The claimant there had been supplied by Roevin, an employment agency, to BP. She had worked at BP (with which she did not have a contract) for three years before having a baby, then attempted to return to her previous job with BP which refused her request but offered her alternative, lower paid work. Both the tribunal and EAT accepted that BP had discriminated against Ms Gillick contrary to s.9 SDA.[45] And in *Harrods Ltd v Renmick* [1997] IRLR 583 the Court of Appeal applied the provision to protect staff employed by concessionaires within Harrods from discrimination by Harrods (which required the employees of concessionaires to be approved by Harrods and which had withdrawn approval from the claimants on racial grounds).

In the *Allonby* case the Court of Appeal considered, inter alia, whether a woman retained as a contract worker by the respondents via ELS (an agency) could rely on s.9 SDA to challenge discrimination in terms and conditions between her and a man who was directly employed by the college. The tribunal rejected her s.9 claim on the basis that it only regulated discrimination *between* male and female contract workers. EAT dismissed her appeal but the Court of Appeal, which referred some questions to the ECJ (see Chapter 2) allowed her appeal on s.9 and remitted to the employment tribunal for reconsideration the question whether the college, by treating her less favourably than a salaried lecturer, was discriminating against her as a contract worker on the ground of her sex.

Allonby v Accrington & Rossendale College [2001] ICR 1189

Sedley LJ (for the Court):

[S.9] is there to prevent employers from avoiding the effect of the earlier provisions of that Part by bringing in workers on subcontract . . . There is no reason why it should be limited, as the employment tribunal and EAT held that it was, to discrimination between male and female contract workers supplied to a particular employer. Nothing in the wording of the section says that it is so limited. It would be remarkable if it, and equally s.7 of the Race Relations Act, permitted an employer, by bringing in black or female workers on subcontract to work alongside a predominantly white or male employed workforce, to give them inferior conditions so

---

[45] See also *Patefields v Belfast City Council* [2000] IRLR 664, in which the NICA ruled that the principals had breached Art 12 SD(NI)O (which is materially identical to s.7 RRA) by replacing the claimant (a contract worker) with a permanent employee while she was on maternity leave. While the principal could have replaced her at any other time, doing so while she was on maternity leave amounted to treating her less favourably than a man who would not have been on such leave.

long as they were all treated equally badly or (if differentially treated) were all of the same race or sex and so unable to complain. It would be particularly remarkable if this were permitted by legislation which treats the principal's own contracted labour as employees.

In my judgment, s.9 applies both as between one contract worker and another and as between one contract worker and an employee, so long as they are working for the same principal. So far, and without resistance from Mr Jeans [for the employer], Ms Gill's argument [for the claimant] succeeds. Her problem, however, is to show that in the present case the principal—that is the college—is discriminating against the appellant when it uses her services through ELS. It is ELS, says Mr Jeans, against whom the applicant's complaints lie, because it is they alone who set the terms of her employment.

This is largely but not entirely true. There are still some benefits which, Ms Gill would argue, are afforded by the college to its employed staff but not to those brought in through ELS—professional indemnity insurance, for example, and career development support. These are some way from the instances which are usually given, such as an inferior canteen or washroom for contract workers, but—while I share the doubts of Mr Justice Gage on this question—they are in my view capable of ranking under s.9(2) and ought to be considered by the employment tribunal. . . . Section 9 applies both between one contract worker and another and as between a contract worker and an employee so long as they are working for the same principal. Nothing in the section says that it is limited to discrimination between male and female contract workers. It would be remarkable if it permitted an employer, by bringing in female workers on subcontract to work alongside a predominantly male employed workforce, to give them inferior conditions so long as they were all treated equally badly or (if differentially treated) were all of the same sex and so unable to complain.

Contract workers are also protected by s.14 RRA from discrimination on the part of the supplying agency.

(1) It is unlawful for an employment agency to discriminate against a person—
    (a) in the terms on which the agency offers to provide any of its services; or
    (b) by refusing or deliberately omitting to provide any of its services; or
    (c) in the way it provides any of its services.

Section 14(4) RRA provides a good faith defence where the employment agency reasonably relies on a statement by the employer that the discrimination would not be unlawful under the Act, while s.14(5) makes it an offence for a person 'knowingly or recklessly' to make such a statement which is false or misleading 'in a material respect'. The SDA and FETO also include express prohibitions on discrimination by employment agencies, as do FETO and the SO and the RB Regs[46] but not the DDA which (s.21A), however, prohibits discrimination and harassment of disabled users and would-be users of 'employment services' by the providers of such services 'in relation to such services,' 'employment services' being defined to include 'vocational guidance; vocational training; [and] services to assist a person to obtain or retain employment, or to establish himself as self-employed.' Section 21A DDA is in Part III rather than Part II of the DDA and so is enforceable through the county courts rather than employment tribunals, but most individuals who are in prospective or actual relationships with employment agencies, other than as hiring clients, will be 'employed' by them for the purposes of the anti-discrimination legislation. So, for example, in the *BP Chemicals* case, the tribunal and EAT accepted that the claimant was employed

---

[46] Ss.15 SDA, Article 22 FETO, and reg 18 RB and SO Regs.

by the agency which had supplied her services to BP. She was not however, EAT ruled, employed by the principal (this because she had no contract with BP).[47]

Discrimination against contract workers can also be caught by ss.30, 31 and 33 RRA and their equivalent provisions, (ss.39, 40 and 42 SDA, ss.16B and 57 DDA and Article 35 FETO) which prohibit instructing, inciting or being an accessory to discrimination. Instructions and incitement to discriminate are considered in Chapter 2, assistance to discriminators below.

A significant limitation on the protection afforded to contract workers was imposed by EAT in *Lloyd v IBM (UK) Ltd* (App. No. EAT/642/94, 3 February 1995), in which the fact that the claimant supplied her services to an employment agency through a company established by her, as is common in the IT sector, excluded her from the protection of the SDA. In *MHC Consulting Services v Tansell*, however, the Court of Appeal took a different view in a case brought under the DDA.

MHC Consulting Services Ltd v Tansell [2000] ICR 789

Mummery LJ (for the Court):

The language of section 12 clearly covers the standard case in which, for example, a person makes office work available for doing by individuals employed by a temping agency. The agency enters into a contract with that person to supply individuals to do that work. That person is a principal. The individuals who are supplied are contract workers doing contract work. By section 12 they are protected from discrimination by the principal . . .

the language of the section is also reasonably capable of applying to the less common case in which an extra contract is inserted, so that there is no direct contract between the person making the work available and the employer of the individual who is supplied to do that work. . . .

This result does not involve any unconstitutional border crossing by the court. It is achieved by a conventional process of judicial construction of legislation. The normal meaning of the language of the section is capable of covering this case, as well as the standard case. An interpretation which applies the section to the less common case, as well as to the standard case, is more consistent with the object of the section and of the 1995 Act than an interpretation which does not do so. In a number of authorities the appellate courts have stressed the importance of giving the wide ranging provisions of the discrimination legislation a generous interpretation [citing, inter alia, *Jones v Tower Boot Co Ltd* [1997] ICR 254]. The general purpose of the 1995 Act is to outlaw discrimination on the ground of disability. Employment is one of the fields in which it aims to achieve that goal. In order to achieve that result Parliament decided not to confine liability for discrimination in employment to the employer who discriminates against those employed by him under a traditional contract of service. Under section 12 liability is also imposed on those who, without entering into contracts of service with individual employees, make contracts for individuals employed by others to do work made available for them to do. It would not be consistent with the legislative object to withhold protection from discrimination by a person to whom an employee, who was entitled to protection from his employer, had been

---

[47] S.4B(4) & (5) DDA impose obligations upon the employers of disabled persons to make reasonable adjustments in relation to provisions, criteria or practices 'applied by or on behalf of all or most of the principals to whom he is or might be supplied', and in relation to the physical features of their premises, where those provisions, etc, or physical features are likely to place a disabled employee 'at a substantial disadvantage in comparison with persons who are not disabled which is the same or similar in each case'. In such cases the onus falls on the employer, rather than the principal, to take reasonable steps on behalf of the disabled person.

supplied to do some work. Hence the provisions for the protection of contract workers in all the discrimination Acts. . . .

it is my view that *Lloyd v IBM* was wrongly decided . . .

Office Holders

In 1998 the CRE pointed out that the definition of employee adopted by the RRA [in common with the other discrimination provisions,] excluded most office holders (whether judges or members of commissions or authorities, etc).[48] The CRE pointed out that 'the position of office-holder, by its nature, is normally an influential one' and declared it 'particularly important that there should be no racially discriminatory barriers to access to such positions' or, indeed, be any such discrimination during or at the termination of office-holding. The Race Relations (Amendment) Act 2000 extended the provisions of the RRA as they applied to office holders (ss.76) and the Act was further amended in July 2003 to comply with the Racial Equality Directive by the inclusion of new s.76ZA.

Prior to the 2000 amendments s.76 RRA (in common with s.86 SDA as it stands today) only regulated discrimination by ministers and government departments '[in appointing office holders' and 'in making the arrangements for determining who should be offered [such] office[s] or post[s]' (s.76(3)). Post amendment, s.76 RRA also extends to discrimination in positive and negative recommendations made by ministers and government departments in relation to the appointment of office holders and the 'conferment by the Crown of a dignity or honour'; and to discrimination in 'any approval given by such a minister or department in relation to any such conferment.' It applies to unpaid as well as paid posts. Further, where an appointment to an office or post has been made by or on the recommendation or approval of a minister or government department, s.76 prohibits discrimination by the Minister or department in connection with (s.76(11)):

(a) the terms of the appointment;
(b) access for the person appointed to opportunities for promotion, transfer or training, or to any other benefits, facilities or services; or
(c) the termination of the appointment, or subjecting the person appointed to any other detriment.

Section 76ZA was inserted into the RRA to give effect to the requirements of the Racial Equality Directive. It extends the definition of office-holders protected by the Act beyond political appointees such as those covered by s.76 as amended to non-governmental appointees such as, for example, ministers of religion Neither s.76 nor 76ZA covers *political* offices or posts (that is, elected posts and political offices listed in s.76ZA(9)(b)).[49] This aside, s.76ZA applies to any office or position which does not fall within s.76 or any other provisions of the Act and which (s.76ZA) 'is an office or post to which persons are appointed to discharge functions personally under the direction of another person'; *and* 'in respect of which they are entitled to remuneration.' Section 76ZA prohibits discrimination in materially identical terms to s.4 RRA, reproduced above.

---

[48] Though see *Perceval-Price v DED & NI Civil Service* [2000] IRLR 380 in which Northern Ireland's Court of Appeal ruled that tribunal chairs were 'workers' within Article 141 and were, accordingly, entitled to protection from sex-related discrimination in relation to pay.
[49] Listed in s.76ZA(9)(b) RRA.

The amended s.76 RRA is unique to that Act, having emanated from the RR(A)A rather than directive-driven amendments to the Act. The DDA and the SO and RB Regs govern discrimination in relation to office holders but, not sharing the tortuous history of the RRA in this matter, deal with office holders in somewhat simpler terms. Section 4C–F DDA, to which Article 20 FETO and reg 10 of each the SO and the RB Regs are materially identical, apply in relation to appointment to offices or positions not otherwise covered by the legislation[50] and which (s.4C(3)) are those to which:

(a) . . . persons are appointed to discharge functions personally under the direction of another person, and in respect of which they are entitled to remuneration;
(b) . . . appointments are made by a Minister of the Crown, a government department, the National Assembly for Wales or any part of the Scottish Administration [or, in Northern Ireland, a Northern Ireland Minister or Minister of the Assembly]; or
(c) . . . appointments are made on the recommendation of, or subject to the approval of, a person referred to in paragraph (b).

The provisions protect the office holders to which they apply in similar terms to those applicable to workers covered by s.4 RRA and its equivalent (prohibiting 'harassment' as well as direct and indirect discrimination, and the DDA (s.4E) imposing a duty to make reasonable adjustments). 'Appointment' is defined to exclude election to an office or post and, while appointments covered by s.4C(3)(a) DDA and its equivalents include persons such as ministers of religion, company directors, tribunal chairs and members, judges, and the chairs and members of some non-departmental public bodies,[51] they do not apply to a range of positions including offices held by members of the House of Commons or Lords, life peerages, ministerial offices, government and political offices, etc.[52]

S.4C DDA and its equivalents regulate 'discrimination' (in the case of the DDA, both less favourable treatment and a failure to make reasonable adjustments):

• in the arrangements made for the purpose of determining who should be offered the appointment [or recommended or approved in relation to it];
• in the terms on which the appointment is offered;
• by refusing to offer the appointment, or in making or refusing to make a recommendation, or giving or refusing to give an approval, in relation to the appointment;
• in the terms of appointment;
• in the opportunities afforded for promotion, a transfer, training or receiving any other benefit, or by refusing to afford a person any such opportunity;
• in terminating an appointment (actually or constructively); or
• by subjecting a person to any other detriment in relation to the appointment.

S.4D(4) It is also unlawful for a relevant person, in relation to an office or post to which this section applies, to subject to harassment a disabled person—

(a) who has been appointed to the office or post;

---

[50] Ie, the office does not amount to 'employment' (in which case discrimination connected with it would be regulated by s.4), the holder is not regarded as a 'contract worker' within s.7 or a partner within s.10 or barrister, advocate or office holder covered by s.76.
[51] Explanatory Notes, paras 116–117.
[52] Reg 10(10) SO and RB Regs, s.4C(5) DDA. EAT confirmed in *South East Sheffield CAB v Grayson* 131 *Equal Opportunities Review* 'Law Reports' that volunteers were unprotected by s.68 DDA.

(b) who is seeking or being considered for appointment to the office or post; or
(c) who is seeking or being considered for a recommendation or approval in relation to an appointment to [a relevant] office or post.

DTI, 'Explanatory notes for the Employment Equality (Sexual Orientation) Regulations 2003 and Employment Equality (Religion or Belief) Regulations 2003', paras 112–13

in contrast to the more straight-forward employer-employee relationship, for an office-holder there may be one person who appoints her, another who sets her pay and conditions, and yet another who has the power to dismiss her. It is the relevant person with the power to act in each set of circumstances (eg making the appointment, setting pay, dismissing) who will be liable . . .

For example, a member of a tribunal is appointed by an appointments body, but once in post her terms and conditions are regulated by a tribunals body . . . the appointments body will (only) be liable for any discrimination against her relating to the appointment, and the tribunals body will (only) be liable for any discrimination against her in pay and conditions following the appointment . . .

The SDA currently provides as set out above (s.86) but the draft SD Regs propose its amendment in terms similar to the DDA and the SO and RB Regs.

Both the CRE and the EOC, in their 1998 reform proposals, called for the extension of the Acts to volunteers. The DRC's First Review of the DDA also called for an extension of the protection of the Act to all volunteers: 'Volunteering, as the Government recognises, makes a hugely important contribution to the community. Many disabled people actively engage in volunteering, for its own sake and as a step towards employment.' Section 76 RRA applies to some unremunerated offices as do the DDA, SO and RB Regs. But none of the anti-discrimination legislation applies to volunteers more generally, and the Government has not even acted on the intention it indicated to the CRE in 1999 to deal with volunteers by means of a Code of Practice. The DDA 2005, however, amends the 1995 Act to bring councillors and members of the London Assembly within its employment-related protections (new ss.15A–15C).

Trade Unions, etc

Discrimination by trade unions, employers' and trade organisations and persons concerned with vocational training is prohibited by the various anti-discrimination regimes. Section 11 RRA, which was considered in Chapter 3, prohibits discrimination against non-members (s.11(2)(a)) in the terms on which the organisation is prepared to admit them to membership, and (b) by refusals or deliberate omissions to admit to membership. The provision also prohibits discrimination against a member (s.11.3)):

(a) in the way it affords him access to any benefits, facilities or services, or by refusing or deliberately omitting to afford him access to them; or
(b) by depriving him of membership, or varying the terms on which he is a member; or
(c) by subjecting him to any other detriment.

Finally, trade unions and similar organisations are prohibited from subjecting members and applicants to harassment on grounds of 'race or ethnic or national origin'.

We saw, in Chapter 3, that the prohibition on discrimination by trade unions is subject to some 'positive action' exceptions. As before, 'harassment' as statutorily defined by the RRA applies only in connection with 'race or ethnic or national origin', rather than nationality or colour. Having said this, we saw above and in Chapter 2 that much harassment related to a protected ground will in any event amount to actionable discrimination. Reg 15 of the SO and the RB Regs are materially identical to s.11 RRA as will be s.12 SDA if it is amended, as the draft SD Regs propose, expressly to prohibit harassment. So, too, is s.13 DDA which uses the term 'trade organisation' but defines it to include workers' and employers' organisations as well as 'any other organisation whose members carry on a particular profession or trade for the purposes of which the organisation exists.' The DDA's prohibition of 'discrimination' in this context extends to the failure to make reasonable adjustments as well as less favourable treatment of a disabled person in connection with that person's disability. Article 25 FETO regulates discrimination and harassment by 'vocational organisations' in terms similar to s.12 RRA as it applies in connection with 'race and ethnic or national origins', Article 2(2) defining 'vocational organisation' as '(a) an organisation of workers; (b) an organisation of employers; (c) any other organisation of persons engaged in a particular employment or occupation, or employments or occupations of any class, for the purposes of which the organisation exists.'

The application of s.11 RRA and its equivalents has been considered in a number of cases among them *FTATU v Modgill* [1980] IRLR 142 and *Fire Brigades Union v Fraser* [1998] IRLR 697. The *Modgill* case concerned allegations that the union had discriminated against the claimants by refusing them their own shop steward and failing—on racial grounds—to support their struggles for improved wages, a better pay structure, and the same working hours as others within the same plant. EAT overturned a tribunal decision in favour of the claimants, this on the basis that race discrimination had not been proven. But the case gives some indication of the potential breadth of s.11. The same is true of the *Fraser* case in which a man accused of sexual harassment sued his union under s.12 SDA because it refused him representation in the ensuing disciplinary proceedings. The Court of Sessions overturned a tribunal decision in his favour because no discrimination was proven—the union chose not to represent him because he was accused of harassment and they were representing the accuser, not because he was a man.

Qualifications Bodies

One of the more litigated broadly employment-related provisions of the anti-discrimination legislation concerns 'qualifying authorities.' Section 12 RRA provides:

(1) It is unlawful for an authority or body which can confer an authorisation or qualification which is needed for, or facilitates, engagement in a particular profession or trade to discriminate against a person—

(a) in the terms on which it is prepared to confer on him that authorisation or qualification; or

(b) by refusing, or deliberately omitting to grant, his application for it; or

(c) by withdrawing it from him or varying the terms on which he holds it.

(1A) It is unlawful for an authority or body to which subsection (1) applies, in relation to an authorisation or qualification conferred by it, to subject to harassment a person who holds or applies for such an authorisation or qualification.

(2) In this section—
    (a) 'authorisation or qualification' includes recognition, registration, enrolment, approval and certification;
    (b) 'confer' includes renew or extend.

Reg 16 of each the SO and the RB Regs is materially identical except that it expressly excludes from its coverage educational establishments otherwise covered by the Regs, as is s.14A DDA save that it includes an additional prohibition (s.14A(1)(a)) on discrimination 'in the arrangements [made] for the purposes of determining upon whom to confer a professional or trade organisation' and renumbers the following provisions accordingly. The DDA prohibits both less favourable treatment and a failure to make reasonable adjustment in this context. Article 25 FETO applies in similar terms to s.12 RRA (covering 'harassment' as well as discrimination, but applying only to 'persons with power to confer qualifications' in respect of their conferral of qualifications.[53] Section 13 SDA is similar to s.12 RRA but it is at present silent as to harassment[54] and provides (s.13(2)) that:

> Where an authority or body is required by law to satisfy itself as to his good character before conferring on a person an authorisation or qualification which is needed for, or facilitates, his engagement in any profession or trade then, without prejudice to any other duty to which it is subject, that requirement shall be taken to impose on the authority or body a duty to have regard to any evidence tending to show that he, or any of his employees, or agents (whether past or present), has practised unlawful discrimination in, or in connection with, the carrying on of any profession or trade.

The Parliamentary Joint Committee on the then draft Disability Discrimination Bill proposed that s.14A DDA be extended explicitly to cover discrimination by those responsible for general examinations such as GCSEs which, like specialist qualifications, can facilitate engagement in particular occupations, etc. According to the Committee, 'it seems anomalous for some qualification-giving bodies to be covered by the DDA and not others. It also seems anomalous that schools, colleges and education authorities are required to make reasonable adjustments in the context of examinations but that the awarding body is not.' The government agreed to amend the legislation and the DDA 2005 amends the DDA by inserting new s31AA which regulates discrimination and harassment by 'general qualifications bodies'.[55]

Some of the litigation which has arisen under s.12 RRA and its equivalent provisions has concerned whether an alleged discriminator was a 'qualifying body'. In *Malik v Post Office Counters Ltd* [1993] ICR 93a, EAT ruled that selection for the position of post-master did not fall within s.12. Although the words of the section should not be construed narrowly, the Post Office did not have exclusive authority as to the granting or withholding of the position. In *Tattari v PPP*, the Court of Appeal ruled that the refusal by the health insurance company to add the already qualified doctor to their list of approved plastic surgeons did not fall within s.12 RRA.

---

[53] Article 27 now prohibits discrimination by establishments of higher and further education.
[54] This will have to change by October 2005 and the draft SD Regs propose the express regulation of harassment accordingly: see Ch 2.
[55] 'Mental illness hurdle to be scrapped' 132 *Equal Opportunities Review*.

Tattari v PPP Ltd [1998] ICR 106

Beldam LJ (for the Court):

. . . referring as it does to an authority or body which confers recognition or approval, [s.12 RRA] refers to a body which has the power or authority to confer on a person a professional qualification or approval needed to enable him to practice a profession, exercise a calling or take part in some other activity. It does not refer to a body which is not authorised to or empowered to confer such qualification or permission but which stipulates that for the purpose of its commercial agreements a particular qualification is required . . .

A similar decision was reached by Northern Ireland's Court of Appeal in *Kelly & Loughran v Northern Ireland Housing Executive* [1998] IRLR 70, in which that Court ruled that inclusion on the Housing Executive's panel of solicitors did not fall within s.23 FEA (now Article 25 FETO). The case proceeded to the House of Lords whose decision on the employment issue was considered above. Their Lordships relied upon *Tattari* in ruling that NICA had been correct to hold that the claimants were not discriminated against contrary to s.23 FEA (the equivalent provision to s.12 RRA) by the refusal to shortlist them for the panel. According to the House of Lords, 'qualification' did not cover the appointment of a professional to carry out paid work on behalf of a client.

In *Arthur v Attorney-General* (unreported, cited by EAT in *Sawyer v Ahsan* [2000] ICR 1, below) EAT ruled that non-selection by the Attorney-General as a lay magistrate did not come within s.12 RRA. According to the appeal tribunal in that case, s.12 was 'directed to circumstances in which A confers on B a qualification which will enable B to render services for C. A and C are the same entity, the section would appear to be inapplicable, otherwise it would apply to every selection panel.' In *Patterson v Legal Services Commission*, by contrast, the Court of Appeal accepted that the award of a franchise by the Legal Services Commission did fall within s.12 RRA. According to that Court, the award of such a franchise amounted to the conferment of an 'authorisation' to perform publicly funded legal work and 'facilitat[ing]' engagement in the solicitors' profession by making it easier or less difficult to carry on the profession. Further, the award of a franchise was sufficiently personal to the claimant to come within s.12 because, although the franchise certificate is issued for a solicitor's office, some of its requirements related to the Commission and the individual partner or partners within a firm.

It is clear from the decision in *Patterson* that 'profession' within s.12 RRA and its equivalents was not restricted to 'employment' (that being the subject heading of Part II of the Act within which s.13 appears). That it was so restricted was argued by the Labour Party in *Jepson & Dyas-Elliott v The Labour Party* [1996] IRLR 116, in which the legality of all-women shortlists for parliamentary elections was at issue. This would have served to disqualify membership of Parliament as a 'profession,' MPs being office-holders and therefore outside the employment-related provisions of the Act. The tribunal rejected this argument as a matter of construction: 'It soon becomes apparent from the wording of s.13 that more than employment as defined in s.82 [SDA] is intended to be covered by that section. It would have been quite easy for s.13 to have been drafted in such a way as to have restricted its operation just to employment as so defined.' Nor did it matter that councillors were not paid. In *Triesman*, however, the Court of Appeal took a different approach:

Triesman v Ali [2002] IRLR 489

Peter Gibson LJ (for the Court):

At first sight, [s.12 RRA] is an unlikely candidate for application to the suspension by a political party of a member wanting to be selected as a party candidate for local government elections. That has nothing to do with employment and, while s.12 is in a portion of Part II which covers discrimination in particular circumstances extending beyond employment, it is far from obvious that it was intended to cover a circumstance which does not appear to relate to the employment field even in a wide or loose sense. The obvious application of the section is to cases where a body has among its functions that of granting some qualification to, or authorising, a person who has satisfied appropriate standards of competence, to practise a profession, calling or trade. There are many such bodies, for example, in the medical field . . .

We own to having doubts as to whether being a local government councillor is being engaged in a profession or occupation within the meaning of the section, still more so if the profession or occupation is limited to being a Labour Party councillor. To our minds it is certainly not being engaged in a profession and, while being a councillor occupies some of the time of the councillor who is entitled to receive allowances, it is not an activity from which the councillor will earn his living or receive a salary, and we question whether it is within the intendment of the section.

The Council of Legal Education has been recognised as a 'qualifying body' under s.12 RRA (*Bohon-Mitchell v Common Professional Examination Board and Council of Legal Education* [1978] IRLR 526 (IT)), the issue concerning discrimination against overseas applicants in terms of access to the Common Professional Examination course. In *Jepson* and in the later *Sawyer v Ahsan* the Labour Party was accepted as being a 'qualifying body' in relation, respectively, to Labour MPs and Labour councillors. *Sawyer* concerned a complaint against the de-selection of an Asian councillor in favour of a centrally-imposed white man. The decision in *Jepson* resulted, some years later, in the Sex Discrimination (Election Candidates) Act 2002 which amended the SDA to allow political parties to adopt arrangements to select election candidates for the purpose of reducing inequality in the numbers of men and women elected as candidates of the party. This provision is discussed below. In *Triesman v Ali* the Court of Appeal overruled the earlier decision in *Sawyer* and ruled that the Labour Party was not acting as a 'qualifying body' within the RRA when it selected candidates for local government elections or allowed persons to be nominated to the pool from which prospective candidates were to be selected. According to the Court, even if being a Labour councillor amounted to being engaged in a profession for the purposes of s.12 RRA, the Labour Party was not conferring an 'authorisation or qualification' for the purposes of that section when it selected a candidate or accepted a nomination because its activities were for its own political purposes.

Triesman v Ali [2002] IRLR 489

Peter Gibson LJ (for the Court):

[In] *Sawyer v Ahsan* [EAT ruled] that the Labour Party when undertaking its selection functions in relation to the nomination of candidates for local elections was acting as an authority or body able to confer an authorisation or qualification which is needed for or facilitates engagement in the particular occupation of being a Labour councillor for the purposes of s.12 . . .

In *Sawyer*, Lindsay J, giving the judgment of the EAT, referred to the familiar dictum of Templeman LJ in *Savjani v IRC* [1981] QB 458, 466–7: 'the [1976] Act was brought in to remedy a very great evil. It is expressed in very wide terms, and I should be very slow to find that the effect of something which is humiliatingly discriminating in racial matters falls outside the ambit of the Act.' It was common ground in *Sawyer* that if s.12 did not outlaw racial discrimination in the circumstances of that case, then nothing else in domestic English law did so either. That was an important factor in the EAT's conclusion in that case.

The tribunal in the present case found that there were three principal requirements for individuals to be qualified for nomination for local government office, viz:

'(a) Membership of the Labour Party
(b) Payment of party membership and subscription
(c) Membership for a continuous period of 12 months (other than in exceptional circumstances)' . . .

It said that once an individual had fulfilled those requirements the Labour Party had effectively conferred on that person an authorisation or qualification which was needed for nomination as a candidate for local government office, and that the decision to suspend both the respondents withdrew from them the authorisation or qualification which had been conferred on them by virtue of their length of membership and their payment of the subscription. That, it said, constituted a potential breach of s.12(1)(c) . . .

The EAT proceeded on the basis that *Sawyer* was rightly decided and that the Labour Party was a 'body', that representation of the Labour Party as a councillor on a local authority amounted to engagement in a particular occupation, and that a party can confer an approval or recognition which is needed for engagement in that particular occupation . . .

In the present case, adopting the approach of the court in *Tattari* and construing s.12 as a whole, we are unable to agree with the EAT in *Sawyer* or the EAT in the present case that the Labour Party in selecting a candidate for local government elections or allowing a person to be nominated to the pool from which prospective candidates are to be selected is a body which can confer an authorisation or qualification which is needed for or facilitates engagement in a particular profession . . . we cannot see that the Labour Party in selecting a candidate or accepting a nomination for such candidacy is conferring an authorisation or qualification such as is within the contemplation of . . . section [12]. It is not the type of qualifying body to which the section is intended to apply, its activities being for its own political purposes just as PPP's activities were for its commercial purposes. In the present case, we cannot accept that there is any conferment of approval by the Labour Party when a member who has nominated himself or been nominated as a local government candidate has his name go forward to the pool available for selection. No status in any meaningful sense is thereby conferred. We have to say that it seems to us wholly artificial to treat s.12 as applying to such a case.

We would add that in any event, if the respondents are right, the scope of the application of s.12 is limited to discriminatory actions in relation to a member's candidacy for election. On their argument, which treats s.25 as inapplicable, the Labour Party would be free under the [RRA] to discriminate against those ordinary members or those applying to become members who have no ambitions to represent the Labour Party. That would be a very narrow basis for the application of the [RRA] to complaints about discrimination in respect of membership of a political party.

For these reasons, therefore, we would hold that *Sawyer* was wrongly decided and that s.12 has no application to the present case.

The claimants were not left without a remedy in any event, being able to bring their claims under s.25 RRA (considered below) which regulates discrimination by associations not covered by s.11.

The Court of Appeal in *Triesman* did not mention the decision in *Jepson*. The facts there could be distinguished on the basis that the position of MP to which the claimants sought election was a remunerated post, unlike that of councillor. But this does not deal with the main plank of the Court of Appeal's decision in *Triesman*: that the Labour Party was not conferring an 'authorisation or qualification' on the claimants when it selected a candidate, because its activities were for its own political purposes.

Discrimination by political parties will be returned to below. But many of the cases brought under s.12 RRA its equivalents have related to proceedings of the General Medical Council which licenses doctors in the UK.[56] In *Rovenska v GMC* [1998] ICR 85, for example, a Czechoslovakian-qualified doctor challenged, as indirectly discriminatory under the ss.1(1)(b) and 12 RRA, the Council's language-related qualifying criteria for full registration in the UK. A complicating feature of such claims is often s.54(2) RRA[57] which provides that s.54(1) RRA, which allows for the enforcement of the employment-related provisions of the Acts in the employment tribunals, 'do[es] not apply to a complaint under section 12(1) [RRA] of an act in respect of which an appeal, or proceedings in the nature of an appeal, may be brought under any enactment . . .'[58]

The impact of s.54 was felt in *Khan v General Medical Council* [1993] ICR 627, in which the claimant challenged, as indirectly discriminatory, the GMC's requirements for full registration of overseas practitioners after twice being refused such registration. His application, pursuant to s.29 Medical Act 1983, to the Review Board for Overseas Qualified Practitioners for review of the Council's decision had been unsuccessful. The issue for the Court of Appeal was whether the Review Board procedure was 'in the nature of an appeal' under s.54(2) despite the fact that the Board had no power to reverse the decision of the Council, its role being restricted to providing an opinion to the President of the Council.[59] What the case illustrates, however, is that s.54(2) can operate to prevent challenge to alleged discrimination. Further, according to the Court of Appeal in *Khan*, the appeal procedure could not, if it were alleged itself to be discriminatory, found a claim under s.12. It was argued in *Khan* that s.54(2) ought to be given the same construction as s.63(2) of the SDA which would have to be interpreted so as to provide an 'effective remedy' under the Equal Treatment Directive. But, according to (then) Hoffmann LJ:[60]

I do not see why it should not be regarded as an effective remedy against sex or race discrimination in the kind of case with which s. 12(1) of the [RRA] deals. That concerns qualifications for professions and trades. Parliament appears to have thought that,

---

[56] See also *Trivedi v General Medical Council* App. No. EAT/544/96 (unreported, 1st July 1996), *Jeffrey-Shaw v Shropshire County Premier Football League & Shropshire County Football Association* App. No. EAT/0320/04/TM, 16 September 2004 and, on a related issue, *Chaudhary v BMA* [2003] ICR 1510.

[57] See similarly s.63(2) SDA, s.17A(1A) DDA, reg 28(2)(a) SO and RB Regs.

[58] Complaints could not be made under the RRA or the EqPA in relation to service in the armed forces until the amendment of those Acts by the Armed Forces Act 1997. The SDA provides (s.85) that '(4) Nothing in this Act shall render unlawful an act done for the purposes of ensuring the combat effectiveness of the naval, military or air forces of the Crown. (5) Nothing in this Act shall render unlawful discrimination in admission to the Army Cadet Force, Air Training Corps, Sea Cadet Corps or Combined Cadet Force, or to any other cadet training corps for the time being administered by the Ministry of Defence.' These provisions must be read subject to the decision of the ECJ in *Sirdar v Army Board & Secretary of State for Defence* Case C–273/97 [1999] ECR I-07403.

[59] *Cf Zaidi v FIMBRA* [1995] ICR 836.

[60] Concurring with Neill LJ with both of whose speeches Waite LJ agreed. In *Heath v Commissioner of Police for the Metropolis* [2005] ICR 329 the Court of Appeal ruled that absolute judicial immunity applied in relation to police disciplinary proceedings in a case in which the complainant alleged that she had been subjected to sex discrimination in disciplinary proceedings against a fellow officer whom she had accused of sexual harassment.

although the industrial tribunal is often called a specialist tribunal and has undoubted expertise in matters of sex and racial discrimination, its advantages in providing an effective remedy were outweighed by the even greater specialisation in a particular field or trade or professional qualification of statutory tribunals such as the Review Board, since the Review Board undoubtedly has a duty to give effect to the provisions of s.12 [this having been established by the Divisional Court in *R v Department of Health ex p Gandhi* [1991] ICR 805] . . . This seems to me a perfectly legitimate view for Parliament to have taken. Furthermore, s.54(2) makes it clear that decisions of the Review Board would themselves be open to judicial review on the ground that it failed to have proper regard to the provisions of the [RRA]. In my view, it cannot be said that the Medical Act 1983 does not provide the effective remedy required by European law.

In the *Gandhi* case the Divisional Court had ruled that the Secretary of State, in exercising an appellate function in respect of the Medical Practices Committee of the NHS,[61] was bound to consider the allegation of race discrimination upon which the appeal rested (the Secretary of State had resisted this conclusion). The Secretary of State was not required, however, to make a specific finding in relation to the allegation in dismissing the appeal. Further, the appeal being 'nearer the administrative end of the spectrum than the judicial end,' the requirements of natural justice were not onerous. In that case Dr Gandhi had not received an oral hearing.

An additional complication in the application of s.12 RRA was threatened in *General Medical Council v Goba* [1988] ICR 885, in which case the GMC argued that any discrimination under s.12 RRA was rendered lawful by s.41 RRA. The complaint in that case, as in *Rovenska*, concerned the Council's qualifying criteria for registration of overseas doctors. The Council sought to rely on s.41(1)(a) RRA (above), arguing that the section provided 'an umbrella protection' for any act done in pursuance of its statutory registration duty, the duty having been imposed on it by s.22 of the Medical Act 1983. EAT ruled that s.41(1) provided a defence only in respect of those acts that were 'reasonably necessary' in order to comply with any condition or requirement imposed.' It is now clear, from the decision of the House of Lords in *Hampson v Department of Education and Science* [1991] 1 AC 171 that s.41 covers only those acts done in the necessary performance of an express obligation contained in the instrument (see, further above).

Vocational Training

We also came across s.13 RRA and its equivalents in Chapter 3, this being another of the provisions in relation to which some positive action is permitted. This aside, s.13 provides that:

(1) It is unlawful, in the case of an individual seeking or undergoing training which would help fit him for any employment, for any person who provides, or makes arrangements for the provision of, facilities for such training to discriminate against him—

---

[61] Under the National Health Service Act 1977 and the National Health Service (General Medical and Pharmaceutical Services) Regulations 1974.

(a) in the terms on which that person affords him access to any training course or other facilities concerned with such training; or
(b) by refusing or deliberately omitting to afford him such access; or
(c) by terminating his training; or
(d) by subjecting him to any detriment during the course of his training . . .
(3) It is unlawful for any person who provides, or makes arrangements for the provision of, facilities for training to which subsection (1) applies, in relation to such facilities or training, to subject to harassment a person to whom he provides such training or who is seeking to undergo such training.

Reg 17 of each the SO and the RB Regs are materially similar as will be s.14 SDA if it is amended as proposed by the draft SD Regs. The Explanatory Notes to the SO and RB Regs provide that 'regulation 17 would apply to a company which provides courses to train people to be plumbers or hairdressers. It would also apply to an engineering employer who takes on (or refuses to take on) an engineering student for a 3 month period of work experience as part of her degree course which helps fit her for employment.'

The application of s.14 SDA was considered in *Lana v Positive Training in Housing (London) Ltd* [2001] IRLR 501, which is dealt with below in relation to principals' liability for discrimination by their agents. The DDA applies somewhat differently, s.14C and D prohibiting less favourable treatment of and an unjustified failure to make reasonable adjustments in relation to a disabled person in connection with 'practical work experience.' The provision covers discrimination in relation to such placements in very similar terms to s.6 of the Act, which covers employment. So, for example, discrimination in the arrangements made 'for the purpose of determining who should be offered a work placement,' in access to, the terms of and facilities provided in relation to the placement, in termination of the placement, etc are all regulated by s.14C DDA while s.14D imposes an obligation to make reasonable adjustments.

Exceptions to the Prohibitions on Employment-related Discrimination

Exceptions to the prohibitions on discrimination in the field of employment and elsewhere will be considered in some detail in the chapters dealing with the various heads of discrimination, and will be little more than listed here. It is useful, however, to note that all of the statutory regimes recognise that there will be cases in which sex, race, etc may amount to a 'genuine occupational qualification' or a 'genuine occupational requirement' for the job. The difference between these terms and the detail of the various GOQs and GORs provided for will be considered in the relevant chapters. Where they apply they do so not only in relation to 'employment' itself but also to discrimination by principals against contract workers, to discrimination by employment agencies, partnerships and providers of vocational training, and to discrimination against office holders.

All the statutory regimes provide exceptions relating to national security (above) and positive action (see further Chapter 3), and each has its own particular exceptions also considered in detail in the specific chapters. So, for example, the DDA does not apply to discrimination by charities and other bodies under charitable instruments aimed at providing benefits for categories of person 'determined by reference to any physical or mental capacity'; or to discrimination in favour of particular categories of disabled persons by the providers of supported employment (s.18C). The DDA's previous exemption of employers of fewer than 15 (originally 20) employees from its employment-related provisions has been removed from 1 October 2004 in order to comply with the Employment Equality Directive, and the Act now applies to a wide variety of previously uncovered employment-related discrimination (including, for example, employment on ships, planes and hovercraft, discrimination against disabled actual or prospective fire-fighters, prison officers, police, barristers, advocates and office holders; discrimination by qualifying bodies and in relation to practical work experience). The Act continues, however, to have no application to the armed forces (s.64(7)).

The RRA (s.41) does not apply to discriminatory acts done under statutory authority (see above) or (s.75(5)) to 'rules . . . restricting employment in the service of the Crown or by any public body prescribed for the purposes of this subsection by regulations made by the Minister for the Civil Service to persons of particular birth, nationality, descent or residence.' Nor does it apply (s.9) to discrimination on grounds of *nationality* in connection with pay (broadly defined) against a person employed (or engaged as a contract worker) on a ship who applied or was engaged for that employment outside Great Britain, or who was brought to Great Britain in order to enter into an agreement to be employed on any ship. Previous exceptions covering small partnerships and employment in private households were removed to achieve compliance with the Racial Equality Directive as has been a previous exception covering employment by charities.

The SDA permits (s.17) discrimination as regards height, uniform and equipment requirements and allowances in lieu of uniform or equipment between male and female police officers, and pensions 'to or in respect of special constables or police cadets'; (s.18) discrimination between male and female prison staff in relation to height requirements; (s.19) discrimination in relation to ministers of religion; as well as providing a limited exception for acts done under statutory authority (discussed above). The Act, in its original form, also provided wide exceptions under s.6 in relation to discrimination in retirement provisions. These exceptions have been removed as a result of the ECJ's decision in *Marshall v Southampton and South-West Hampshire Area Health Authority* Case C–152/84 [1986] ECR 723 and successive decisions on equality in relation to pensions and redundancy pay (see Chapter 6).[62] Section 12, which applies to discrimination by trade unions and employers' organisations, 'does not apply to provision made in relation to the death or retirement from work of a member' but the draft SD Regs propose to remove this exception by October 2005.

Articles 70–79 FETO exclude from the provisions of the Order (Article 70) 'employment or occupation as a clergymen or minister of a religious denomination' or in relation to which a GOQ applies; (Article 71) much employment of schoolteachers (see further Chapter 9); and a variety of other situations considered in that chapter.

The SO Regs contain a very wide exception for benefits dependent on marital status. The legality of this provision has been challenged in the Administrative Court whose decision is considered in Chapter 10. And the RB Regs provide (reg 26(2)) that any special treatment afforded to a Sikh by virtue of s.11(1) or (2) of the Employment Act 1989 (which exempt Sikhs from requirements as to wearing of safety helmets on construction sites) shall not amount to discrimination contrary to the Regs.

---

[62] Equal state pensionable ages will be phased in between 2010 and 2020.

Establishing Liability for Discrimination

A breach of the anti-discrimination legislation requires that a nexus be established between the employer and the injury suffered by the person discriminated against. This is the case whether the discrimination at issue is in the field of employment or not (an educational establishment, for example, may be liable for unlawful discrimination in the education context by its staff, equally a shop for discrimination by its staff against customers).

There are three ways in which employers can be pinned with responsibility for the actions of others. In the first place, ss.32 and its equivalent provisions[63] impose vicarious liability upon employers for '[a]nything done by a person in the course of his employment . . . whether or not it was done with the employer's knowledge or approval'. This, in turn, is subject to a 'due diligence' defence whereby employers can escape liability by proving that they 'took such steps as were reasonably practicable to prevent the employee from doing that act, or from doing in the course of his employment acts of that description.' Employers may also be liable for the actions of their agents, and may incur direct or personal liability where they themselves harass or subject the harassed employee to a detriment by failing to deal with past harassment about which the employer has, or to harassment by others over whom the employer has control.

Vicarious Liability

Establishing vicarious liability for discrimination rarely gives rise to difficulties where the alleged discrimination takes the form of arrangements made for recruitment, decisions about recruitment and terms of employment, etc, and dismissals, as in these cases it will generally be easy to attribute the acts of the individual discriminator to the employer. Cases of alleged 'detriment' consisting of harassment have, however, been more problematic. In *Irving and Anor v The Post Office* [1987] IRLR 289 the Court of Appeal applied the common law test of vicarious liability to find the Post Office not liable in respect of racist remarks scrawled upon the post delivered to the home of a black couple. According to the Court, an employer was liable under the RRA only (*per* Fox (LJ)) for:

> acts actually authorised by him . . . [and] acts which he has not authorised, provided they are so connected with acts which he has authorised that they may rightly be regarded as modes—although improper modes—of doing them . . . if the unauthorised and wrongful act of the servant is not so connected with the authorised act as to be a mode of doing it, but is an independent act, the master is not responsible: for in such a case the servant is not acting in the course of his employment, but has gone outside of it.[64]

In the instant case the Post Office authorised employees to write on mail only 'for the purpose of ensuring that they were properly dealt with in the course of the post,' and 'wholly improper' scrawlings unrelated to this purpose were outside the sphere of the employment.

The difficulty with the common law test was that (1) it tended to restrict employers' vicarious liability for acts of harassment to those employees who were in some type of managerial

---

[63] Ss.41, 58 and Article 36 of the SDA and DDA and FETO, reg 22 of the SO and RB Regs.

[64] Citing the 9th edition of *Salmond on Torts*, and approved by the Privy Council, in *Canadian Pacific Railway v Lockhart* (1942) AC 591, 599.

position vis-à-vis the harassee[65] and (2) the more egregious the conduct of the harasser, the more likely it was to be considered outside the course of his/her employment. In *Tower Boot Co Ltd v Jones* [1995] IRLR 529, for example, EAT applied the *Irving* approach to reject a race discrimination complaint made by a man who had been repeatedly called 'chimp', 'monkey' and 'baboon', had been attacked and burnt with a hot screwdriver, had metal bolts thrown at his head, been whipped and had a notice pinned on his back reading 'Chipmonks are go.' An industrial tribunal found in his favour, but EAT ruled that the acts complained of could not be described, by any stretch of the imagination, as an improper mode of performing authorised tasks and that the employers were not, accordingly, liable under s.32(1) RRA.

The Court of Appeal ([1997] ICR 254) allowed Mr Jones' appeal, pointing out that the Court of Appeal in *Irving* had not taken into account the wording of s.32(1) RRA in adopting the common law test of vicarious liability. 'Free of authority,' the Court in the current instance declined to follow *Irving*.[66] Adopting, instead, a purposive approach, Waite LJ cited the words of Templeman J (as he then was) in *Savjani v IRC* [1981] 1 QB 458 (discussed below) 'the [RRA] was brought in to remedy a very great evil. It is expressed in very wide terms, and I should be slow to find that the effect of something which is humiliatingly discriminatory in racial matters falls outside the ambit of the Act' and interpreted 'course of employment' in s.32 RRA (and, correspondingly, in the other Acts) broadly, in an everyday rather than a legalistic fashion.[67] The alternative, as Waite LJ recognised, was that:

> the more heinous the act of discrimination, the less likely it will be that the employer would be liable . . . [This would] cut[] across the whole legislative scheme and underlying policy of s.32 (and its counterpart in sex discrimination), which is to deter racial and sexual harassment in the workplace through a widening of the net of responsibility beyond the guilty employees themselves, by making all employers additionally liable for such harassment, and then supplying them with the reasonable steps defence under s.32(3) which will exonerate the conscientious employer who has used his best endeavours to prevent such harassment, and will encourage all employers who have not yet undertaken such endeavours to take the steps necessary to make the same defence available in their own workplace.

The difficulties associated with establishing vicarious liability have been eased by the decision of the Court of Appeal in *Tower Boot*, although the decision in *Waters v Commissioner of Police of the Metropolis* [1997] ICR 1073 (also discussed in Chapter 2) indicates that legal protection from harassment is not absolute. According to Lord Justice Waite, who was considering the alleged rape and buggery of a WPC by a fellow officer in the bedroom of a police 'section house' while both were off-duty:

---

[65] See, for example, *Bracebridge*, n 38 above, where vicarious liability for a serious indecent assaulted rested upon the fact that the assaulters were at the time 'engaged in disciplinary supervision' of the complainant. Even then, according to EAT in *Tower Boot*: '*Bracebridge* seems to stretch the [Irving] test to its limit'.

[66] More recently, in *Lister v Helsey Hall Ltd* [2002] 1 AC 215 the House of Lords moved away from the common law test of authorisation as the basis for vicarious liability (i.e., whether the act complained of was an unauthorized way of doing an authorized act) and considered instead the closeness of the connection between the nature of the employment and the employee's wrongdoing. This brings the common law test close to that established in *Jones v Tower Boot*. See also *Majrowski v Guy's & St Thomas's NHS Trust* [2005] EWCA Civ 251 in which the Court of Appeal accepted that an employer could be vicariously liable for torts committed by one employee against another contrary to the Protection from Harassment Act 1997.

[67] *Cf Sidhu v Aerospace Composite Technology Ltd* [2001] ICR 167 in which the Court of Appeal reinstated a tribunal's decision that harassment which occurred on an 'away day' was not within the scope of the employer's liability.

He lived elsewhere, and was a visitor to her room in the section house at a time and in circumstances which placed him and her in no different position from that which would have applied if they had been social acquaintances only, with no working connection at all. In those circumstances it is inconceivable, in my view, that any tribunal applying the *Tower Boot* test could find that the alleged assault was committed in the course of [his] employment.

In *Chief Constable of the Lincolnshire Police v Stubbs* [1999] ICR 547, EAT accepted that sexual harassment which took place at a social gathering which could be regarded as 'an extension of the employment' of those involved could be 'within the course of' the harasser's employment as understood post-*Tower Boot*. In *Chief Constable of Bedfordshire Police v Liversidge* [2002] ICR 1135 the Court of Appeal held that a Chief Constable was not vicariously liable under the RRA for discrimination by one police officer towards another. Whereas that Act provided (s.16) that 'For the purposes of this Part, the holding of the office of constable shall be treated as employment (a) by the chief officer of police as respects any act done by him in relation to a constable or that office, that provision simply served to make the Chief Constable liable for his or her acts of discrimination against a police officer and did not for other purposes render police offices 'employees' of the Chief Constable (rather than office holders) so as to make the latter vicariously liable for their own discriminatory acts.

Liability for Agents

The RR(A)A amended the RRA to provide that Chief Constables are vicariously liable for race discrimination by police officers. Similar amendments have been made to the SDA and the DDA.[68] Even before that provision came into effect, the Court of Appeal in *Baskerville v Chief Constable of Kent* [2003] ICR 1463 found that a tribunal had been correct to refuse to strike out a claim against a Chief Constable relating to the sexual harassment of a woman officer by male colleagues. The Court of Appeal distinguished *Liversidge* and on the basis that the officers could be regarded as having acted as agents of the Chief Constable, albeit not as his employees. Section 41(2) SDA (which is materially identical to s.32(2) RRA, Article 36(2) FETO, s.58(2) DDA and reg 22(2) of the SO and RB Regs) provides that:

Anything done by a person as agent for another person with the authority (whether express or implied, and whether precedent or subsequent) of that other person shall be treated for the purposes of this Act (except as regards offences thereunder) as done by that other person as well as by him.

The Court of Appeal returned the case to the tribunal to determine whether, on the particular facts, the police officers were acting as the Chief Constable's agents.[69]

In the *Lana* case EAT adopted a wide approach to s.41(2) SDA to hold a training body liable for discrimination on the part of the organisation with which it had placed a trainee. Ms Lana had been placed by Positive Action with Walker Management as a trainee quantity surveyor. Walker Management agreed to pay Positive Action £10,000 towards the claimant's training allowance over the period of a year. When, five months into the year, the claimant informed Walker (with whom she did not have a contract) that she was

---

[68] See now s.76A RRA, s.64A DDA, s.17 SDA and reg 11 SO and RB Regs.
[69] In *Kimberley v Metropolitan Police Commissioner* 16 December 2003 EAT followed this in a race discrimination claim.

pregnant, they terminated the placement contract between themselves and Positive Action. Positive Action then terminated their training contract with Ms Lana on the basis that, through circumstances beyond their control, they had neither a training placement nor the means to pay her. Her s.14 SDA claim against Positive Action was dismissed by a tribunal which ruled that the respondents had not themselves discriminated against her. EAT overturned this decision and ruled that Walker Management had been acting as the Respondent's agent for the purposes of s.41(2) when it discriminated against the claimant.

Lana v Positive Training in Housing (London) Ltd [2001] IRLR 501

Mr Recorder Langstaff QC:

authority to commit discrimination was, [the respondent's counsel] rightly observed, not something which the employment tribunal here found that the respondent had conferred on Walker Management.

However, to read this subsection in that way would be to place an almost impossible restriction upon its utility. It is difficult if not impossible to conceive any situation in which a contract could lawfully provide an agent with the authority to discriminate. It seems to us that the proper construction of s.41(2) is that the authority referred to must be the authority to do an act which is capable of being done in a discriminatory manner just as it is capable of being done in a lawful manner.

It was within the authority of Walker Management to terminate the engagement of the appellant under the provisions to which we have already referred. If that act was done in circumstances in which it constituted discrimination then it seems to us to fall full-square within the scope of s.41(2). . . . The inevitable consequence is that s.14 provides that where a person who agrees to provide or make arrangements for the provision of facilities for training discharges any obligation to make those arrangements by using another agency he will be liable for any act of discrimination which falls within the scope of that agency. . . . we simply note that there would be a lacuna in the protection to which we have referred if it were the case that an individual selected by another to provide training might discriminate. The lacuna would not necessarily be that that individual himself or itself could not be sued but there are or may be rather difficulties in enforcement . . . it may perhaps be only natural for someone in the position as was the appellant here of having a contract with a training provider to look to the training provider for redress if the training provided fell short of her entitlement.

Taking the view that we do on the statute as a whole and in particular of the interaction of s.14 and s.41(2) we think that the relevant question which the employment tribunal should have addressed was why it was that the engagement of the appellant was terminated by Walker Management. If they had asked and answered that question they might well have concluded that it was terminated for a reason which by inference fell foul of the [SDA]. Have they done so then they would inevitably have been bound to find the respondent liable, however well meaning the respondent itself might have been when viewed in isolation.

The Employer's Defence

Even where an act of harassment or other discrimination is found to be within s.32(1) RRA or its equivalent provisions, employers can escape liability by proving that they 'took such steps as were reasonably practicable to prevent the employee from doing that act, or from doing in the course of his employment acts of that description.'[70] (This defence is not

---

[70] S.41(3) SDA, s.32(3)RRA, s.58(5) DDA and Article 36(4)FETO, reg 22(3) SO and RB Regs.

available where liability is incurred for the actions of an agent within s.32(2) RRA and equivalent, as this provision applies only where the actions of the agent are 'authorised' by the principal).

Almost invariably where employers plead the 'due diligence' defence, the issue is one of harassment. *Martin v Marks & Spencer* is an unusual case. There the employers disputed liability for alleged discrimination by their own interviewing panel. A tribunal made an inference of racial discrimination from an interviewing panel's 'bias' and ruled against the employer's on the s.32(3) issue. Both EAT and the Court of Appeal, however, ruled in favour of the employer on both issues. That part of the decision concerned with the tribunal's finding of discrimination is discussed in Chapter 2. Here we consider the s.32(3) RRA point.

Martin v Marks & Spencer [1998] ICR 1005

Mummery LJ (for the Court):

s. 32(3) is directed to providing a defence for an employer who has taken, in advance of the alleged discriminatory treatment, all reasonable and practicable steps to prevent discrimination from occurring . . . It is relevant for the purposes of s.32(3) to have regard to what was done by Marks & Spencer in advance of and prior to the interview to determine whether they had taken reasonably practicable steps to prevent discrimination by the employees in the interview, which inevitably led to the decision of Marks & Spencer not to offer employment to Ms Martin . . . there can be no doubt that Marks & Spencer made out the defence on the findings of fact about . . . their equal opportunities policy; their compliance with the Code of Practice issued by the Commission for Racial Equality in relation to selection procedures, criteria and interviewing; and their selection of the interviewing panel to include a person with an interest in recruiting from ethnic minorities.

In *Canniffe v East Riding of Yorkshire*, EAT allowed an appeal against a tribunal decision that an employer had made out the s.41(3) defence in a sexual harassment claim. The claimant had been repeatedly harassed by a work colleague who, on one particular occasion, was alleged to have committed a very serious sexual assault on her. The tribunal ruled that the employers had taken such steps as were reasonably practicable to prevent the harassment, this on the basis that:

While the applicant has levelled complaints about the culture within which she worked and about the steps taken by the respondent to draw its employees' attention to matters such as the personal harassment policy and equal opportunities, we fail to see that those sorts of steps would have made any difference in the type of acts about which complaint is made. We failed to see that any better implementation of such policies would have any effect in relation to the very serious criminal behaviour perpetrated upon the applicant. It is almost superfluous to have a Code of Conduct and to train employees not to indecently expose themselves or to carry out indecent assaults upon their colleagues, any more than it may be necessary to advise them not to steal from their colleagues or to assault their colleagues in any other way.

EAT ruled, on appeal, that the tribunal should not have focused entirely on whether anything that the employers did or could have done would have made any difference. The questions it should have asked were (1) whether the respondents took steps to prevent the employee from doing the act or acts complained of in the course of his employment; and (2) whether there were any further steps the employers could have taken which were reasonably practicable.

Canniffe v East Riding of Yorkshire Council [2000] IRLR 555

Burton J:

The question as to whether the doing of any such acts would in fact have been successful in preventing the acts of discrimination in question may be worth addressing, and may be interesting to address, but are not determinative either way. On the one hand, the employer, if he takes steps which are reasonably practicable, will not be inculpated if those steps are not successful; indeed, the matter would not be before the court if the steps had been successful, and so the whole availability of the defence suggests the necessity that someone will have committed the act of discrimination, notwithstanding the taking of reasonable steps; but on the other hand, the employer will not be exculpated if it has not taken reasonable steps simply because if he had taken those reasonable steps they would not have led anywhere or achieved anything or in fact prevented anything from occurring . . .

It appears to us that the tribunal has found that the respondent took some steps and was satisfied that those steps that the respondent had taken were reasonable. The tribunal has not however asked itself the missing question, which is: were there any other steps which could reasonably have been taken which the respondent did not take? It appears to us that there is or could be a very substantial difference between the two different scenarios at the workplace. One is where there is no knowledge on the part of employers or managers of risk of any harassment or inappropriate sexual behaviour by an employee, or indeed in particular by one employee towards another particular employee or employees. In those circumstances it may well be sufficient for there to be adequately promulgated a sexual harassment policy, particularly where it can be said that when a one-off incident occurs of a seriousness of the kind that occurred in this case, it must in any event have been known to any employee, never mind a reasonable or honest employee, that the conduct could not possibly be condoned or encouraged by employers. In those circumstances, it may be sufficient for the question simply to be addressed as to whether there was a policy and whether it was promulgated without more. There may, however, be an entirely different situation in which there was knowledge or suspicion in relation to a particular employee of his own predilections or temperament, and certainly of a risk that he might commit inappropriate acts towards a particular employee or particular employees. In this case, there was such a possibility, but the tribunal did not, in our view, adequately address that possibility or ask itself the right questions. It may well be that on a proper consideration of the position of [employees who had been made aware of the harassment], it could be concluded that there was nothing more that those gentlemen could or should have done that was reasonably practicable to do. On the other hand it may well be that on a proper consideration it would be concluded that, because of the failure of those gentlemen to take any further steps, the respondent, who is vicariously liable for them, should be held not to have taken such steps that were reasonably practicable to prevent the kind of conduct which eventually occurred.[71]

The Harasser's Personal Liability

Section 33 RRA and its equivalent provisions render it unlawful to assist the discriminatory act of another.[72] This enables harassers to be found liable for aiding the discriminatory acts

---

[71] In *Peden v Specialist Photoprinters (Liverpool) Ltd* ('Case Digest', 126 *Equal Opportunities Review*) a tribunal rejected the employer's attempt to rely on the defence where, although it had a harassment policy, it had taken no steps to train an employee who sexually harassed the claimant.

[72] 42 SDA, 57 DDA and Article 35 FETO, reg 23 SO and RB Regs.

of their employers who are vicariously liable for the acts of the harassers. In this circular way, the perpetrators of harassment or other forms of discrimination can personally be held accountable for their actions, and damages awarded against them. These damages are not generally of a very high order (in *Thomas v Robinson* the employee who made the racist remarks was ordered by the tribunal to pay £500, the employers £2,000). This award was quashed by EAT which, as we saw above, remitted the case for reconsideration but it was not atypical. In *Yeboah v Crofton* [2002] IRLR 634, by contrast, the respondent had been ordered to pay no less than £45,000 to the claimant for injury to feelings after a sustained campaign of racial harassment during which he made very serious allegations against the claimant. The employers were found to have made out the s.32(3) defence (although they paid Mr Yeboah over £400,000 in respect of related claims). The respondent appealed against the award on the basis that he could not be liable for 'aiding' the employer in committing an unlawful discriminatory act, when the employer had been found not to have committed such an act. The Court of Appeal gave this argument short shrift, Mummery LJ (with whom Brooke LJ and Sir Christopher Slade agreed) accepting the claimant's argument that even if the council did make out the due diligence defence: 'the employment tribunal was entitled to hold that Mr Crofton was personally liable under s.33(1) of the [RRA] for "knowingly" aiding the unlawful act of discrimination by the council.'[73]

Remedies for discrimination are considered in detail in Chapter 5. In *Hallam v Avery* [1999] ICR 547 the Court of Appeal ruled (*per* Judge LJ) that liability under s.33 RRA required the aider to know 'that the party from whom his liability is alleged to derive is treating, or is about to treat, or is contemplating treating someone less favourably on racial grounds, and with that knowledge, or knowing that such treatment would be the likely result of doing so, he provides him with aid.' This will rarely cause any difficulties in harassment cases.[74] Nor will s.32(3) which provides that 'A person does not under this section knowingly aid another to do an unlawful act if (a) he acts in reliance on a statement made to him by that other person that, by reason of any provision of this Act, the act which he aids would not be unlawful; and (b) it is reasonable for him to rely on the statement."

More problematic was the decision of the Court of Appeal in *Anyanwu v South Bank University* [2000] ICR 221 in which that Court, by a majority, ruled that s.33 RRA was not applicable to those who could properly be described as 'prime movers.' According to Laws LJ, with whom Butler-Sloss concurred (Pill LJ dissenting), the use of the term 'aid' by s.33 RRA 'contemplates a state of affairs in which one party, being a free agent in the matter, sets out to do an act or achieve a result, and another party helps him to do it.' Applied to harassment cases the decision risked precluding the possibility of harassers themselves being found liable under the anti-discrimination provisions. The House of Lords, however, allowed an appeal, adopting a purposive approach to s.33(1) RRA and ruling that the term 'aids' did not have any technical or special meaning under the RRA. Lord Bingham, declared that an alleged discriminator could 'aid' under the Act 'whether his help is substantial and productive or whether it is not, provided the help is not so insignificant as to be negligible . . . it does not matter who instigates or initiates the relationship . . . It is not helpful to introduce "free agents" and "prime movers." ' Section 33(1) did require the identification of an act of some kind done by the university which helped the union to do the alleged act of race discrimination and the decision of the lower courts to strike out the case would be overturned.

---

[73] 33(2) RRA provides that 'For the purposes of subsection (1) an employee or agent for whose act the employer or principal is liable under section 32 (or would be so liable but for section 32(3)) shall be deemed to aid the doing of the act by the employer or principal'.

[74] Though see *Hallam* for the difficulties created by that requirement on the facts there.

Direct Liability

The concept of *direct*, as distinct from *vicarious* liability on the part of employers is best illustrated by EAT's decision in *Burton and Rhule v De Vere Hotels* [1997] ICR 1, a case in which no vicarious liability could have been incurred by the employer in circumstances where the harassers were neither employed by it nor acting under its authorisation. *Burton* involved a race discrimination claim brought by two black waitresses after they had been exposed to racist jokes made by Bernard Manning, and associated racial and sexual abuse, at a police function at which they served. A tribunal dismissed the women's race discrimination claims on the grounds that, while the claimants had suffered a 'detriment' within the meaning of the RRA, '[i]t was not . . . the respondent which subjected them to it.' The tribunal further ruled that the manager's failure to ensure that staff were not offended by the act did not amount to 'less favourable treatment on racial grounds' because his failure to address his mind to what the act might contain was not related to the employees' ethnic origins. EAT overruled the tribunal's decision, ruling that (1) 'An employer subjects an employee to the detriment of racial harassment if he causes or permits the racial harassment to occur in circumstances in which he can control whether it happens or not' and (2) where the treatment to which the employer had permitted the employees to be subject was race specific, there was no need for the claimants to prove that the employers treated them less favourably than they did or would treat employees of a different racial group.

The decision in *Burton* was relied upon in a number of cases in which employers were pinned with direct liability for harassment which they culpably failed to control.[75] In *Pearce v Mayfield School* however, the House of Lords ruled that it had been wrongly decided in two respects. First, race-specific treatment did not necessarily amount to less favourable treatment on grounds of race (this aspect of the decision is considered in Chapter 2). Secondly, the employer would only have been liable for treating the waitresses less favourably on racial grounds if its failure to protect them from the treatment they received was itself connected with their race. The employment tribunal had found that this was not the case and EAT, accordingly, was not entitled to find that the employer had discriminated on grounds of race.

Pearce v Governing Body of Mayfield School [2003] ICR 937

Lord Nicholls:

Viewed in the broadest terms, the *Burton* decision has much to commend it. There is, surely, everything to be said in favour of a conclusion which requires employers to take reasonable steps to protect employees from racial or sexual abuse by third parties. But is a failure to do so 'discrimination' by the employer? Where the *Burton* decision is, indeed, vulnerable is that it treats an employer's inadvertent failure to take such steps as discrimination even though the failure had nothing to do with the sex or race of the employees. . . . the harassment in *Burton* was committed by third parties for whose conduct the employer was not vicariously

---

[75] *Chessington World of Adventures v Reed* [1998] ICR 97—this dealt with employees but the decision of the tribunal predated Jones and EAT affirmed that direct liability would have been satisfied in any event. In *Sidhu*, n67 above, by contrast, the Court of Appeal ruled that an employer did not directly discriminate against an employee in a case in which it dealt in a non-discriminatory manner with an incident in which he had been racially abused. (there having been no vicarious liability for the abuse). A similar conclusion was reached by the Court of Appeal in *Home Office v Coyne* [2000] ICR 1443, although Sedley LJ dissented on the grounds that the tribunal had been entitled to (and in his view did) find that the employer had treated the claimant less favourably on grounds of sex.

responsible. Despite this, [EAT] seems to have proceeded on the basis that the racial harassment of the waitresses by the speaker and some of the guests constituted discrimination on the part of the employer, and that the only issue left outstanding on the appeal, if the discrimination claim were to succeed, was whether the employers had by active or passive conduct subjected the waitresses to racial harassment by the speaker and the offending guests. This cannot be right. In order to succeed the two Caribbean waitresses had to prove discrimination by their employer.

Smith J said . . .

'The [employment] tribunal should ask themselves whether the event in question was something which was sufficiently under the control of the employer that he could, *by the application of good employment practice*, have prevented the harassment or reduced the extent of it. If such is their finding, then the employer has subjected the employee to the harassment' [emphasis added].'

This decision, I have to say, seems to have proceeded on altogether the wrong footing. 'Subjecting' an employee to 'detriment' is one of the circumstances in which it is unlawful for an employer to 'discriminate' against an employee: s.4(2)(c) of the Race Relations Act 1976. Thus s.4(2)(c) is not satisfied unless the conduct constituted 'discrimination' . . . The hotel's failure to plan ahead properly may have fallen short of the standards required by good employment practice, but it was not racial discrimination . . .

Had the factual position been otherwise, and had the employer permitted exposure of the black waitresses to racist remarks by a third party when it would not have treated white employees similarly in a corresponding situation, this would have been a case of racial discrimination. This conclusion would follow from the difference in treatment afforded to black waitresses on the one hand and the treatment which would have been afforded to white waitresses on the other hand . . .

Lords Hobhouse and Rodger agreed with Lord Nicholls on *Burton* and Lord Hope's remarks on the issue echoed those of Lord Nicholls. Lord Scott agreed that *Burton* was wrongly decided because it overlooked the need to establish discrimination by the employer.

The decision of the House of Lords in *Pearce* overruled *Burton*, but does not do away with the concept of direct liability. An employer will be liable for any action which amounts to less favourable treatment of a worker and which is on a protected ground. Thus, for example, had the manager in *Burton* exhibited less concern for the claimants there than he would have for white waitresses or waiters subjected to equally offensive treatment, he (and through him the hotel) would have been liable for discriminating against them.[76]

Education

Discrimination in education is regulated by the RRA, SDA and FETO in similar terms, considered below. Until recently the DDA did not prohibit discrimination in education,

---

[76] This was accepted by the Court of Appeal in *Sidhu* (*ibid*) and in *Home Office v Coyne* (*ibid*). In *Waters v Commissioner of Police of the Metropolis* [2000] ICR 1064 the House of Lords accepted that one respondent could be liable in negligence for injuries arising from the harassment of the claimant by her fellow officers.

ss.29–31 being concerned only with rights to information about provision made for the disabled by educational establishments. This position has been altered with the passage of the Special Education Needs and Disability Act 2001 (SENDA) which seeks to 'mainstream' pupils with special educational needs (SEN) into ordinary schools where possible. SENDA also removed the DDA's exemption of education from its goods and services provisions (discussed below), and amended Part IV of the Act to regulate discrimination in the context of education more comprehensively. SENDA began to come into force on 1 September 2002 and will be fully implemented by 1 September 2005. Its provisions do not apply to Northern Ireland where responsibility for equal opportunities issues has been devolved to the Assembly (by contrast, jurisdiction over equal opportunities is reserved to the UK Parliament under the Scottish and Welsh settlements). 'The Special Education Needs and Disability Bill—Consultation Document' was published in November 2002 by Northern Ireland's Departments of Education and Employment and Learning with a view to the production of draft legislation in early 2004 to bring the DDA as it applies in relation to education in Northern Ireland broadly into line with the position elsewhere. The draft SEND Regulations were published in April 2004 and it is intended that the final Regulations will come into force on 1 September 2005.

The SO and RB Regs do not generally apply to education (or, indeed, outside the context of employment). They do, however, apply to third level education in order to comply with the Employment Equality Directive's provisions relating to vocational education. It is, of course, too soon after the implementation of the SO and RB Regs and the amendments to the DDA for any case law to have developed under them. Even where the provisions have been in place for decades, as is the case with the SDA and RRA, it is noteworthy that the volume of litigation they generate is very considerably less than that which has occurred in the employment context. The same is true for all the other non-employment provisions we consider, below. This may in part be because discrimination in employment is particularly rife. It may also be because the economic implications of employment-related discrimination are especially obvious to its victims. In addition, however, while employment-related discrimination is challenged through the employment tribunals which are relatively accessible by comparison with the ordinary courts, and in which costs are very rarely awarded against unsuccessful claimants, non-employment cases are litigated in the county courts which are more formal and intimidating for inexperienced claimants and in which the normal 'loser pays' approach to costs applies.

The SDA, RRA and DDA: Application to Schools and Other Educational Bodies

Questions of costs and the accessibility of justice will be returned to in Chapter 5. Here we begin our consideration of the education provisions with ss.17(1) and 22 of the RRA and SDA which, respectively, prohibit race and sex discrimination by an educational establishment:[77]

    (a) in the terms on which it offers to admit . . . [pupils] to the establishment, or

    (b) by refusing or deliberately omitting to accept an application for . . . admission to the establishment, or

    (c) . . . [in relation to existing pupils]:

---

[77] The establishments are listed and orders may be made under s.24(1) SDA to alter these from time to time.

(i) in the way it affords . . . access to any benefits, facilities or services, or by deliberately omitting to afford . . . access to them, or

(ii) by excluding [them] . . . from the establishment or subjecting [them] . . . to any other detriment.

The educational establishments covered by ss.17 RRA and 22 SDA include all those maintained by local education authorities in England and Wales or by education authorities in Scotland, independent schools, Scottish grant aided schools, universities and bodies providing further and higher education.[78] The SDA is in materially similar terms save that it contains no equivalent to s.17(2) RRA, which further prohibits harassment by educational establishments of: (a) a person who applies for admission to the establishment as a pupil; or (b) a pupil at the establishment. The draft SD Regs propose to prohibit harassment in further and higher education by amending s.22 SDA.

Article 27 FETO is in similar terms to s.22 SDA, although it applies only to further and higher educational establishments, religion-specific schooling being the norm in Northern Ireland. Section 28A DDA is also similar to s.22 SDA but it only covers schools, institutions of further and higher education being dealt with separately. Section 28A DDA applies also (s.28A(1)(a)) to discrimination 'in the arrangements [a school] makes for determining admission to the school as a pupil'; (s.28A(2)) discrimination 'against a disabled pupil in the education or associated services provided for, or offered to, pupils at the school by that body'; and (s.28A(4)) discrimination 'against a disabled pupil by excluding him from the school, whether permanently or temporarily.' The Employment Equality Directive not extending to first and second level education, the DDA does not in this context expressly prohibit 'harassment'. The DRC's Code of Practice for Schools suggests (paras 4.23–4.24) that 'Education and associated services' include (but are not limited to) 'preparation for entry to the school, the curriculum, teaching and learning, classroom organisation, timetabling, grouping of pupils, homework, access to school facilities, activities to supplement the curriculum, for example, a drama group visiting the school, school sports, school policies, breaks and lunchtimes, the serving of school meals, interaction with peers, assessment and exam arrangements, school discipline and sanctions, exclusion procedures, school clubs and activities, school trips, the school's arrangements for working with other agencies [and] preparation of pupils for the next phase of education.'

The obligations imposed by the DDA on institutions of further and higher education are set out at ss.28R–28X DDA (Part 4, Chapter 2). Whereas enforcement proceedings in relation to discrimination against school pupils must be taken in the Special Educational Needs and Disability Tribunal (in Wales the Special Educational Needs Tribunal), the FE and HE provisions are enforceable only in the county courts. They are broadly similar to those applicable to schools except that students are protected (s.28R(2)) from discrimination in relation to 'student services' rather than (s.28A(2)) 'education [and] associated services.' Schools are covered by the FE and HE provisions to the extent that they provide FE services. FE and HE institutions may be obliged to comply with their duty not to place disabled students at particular disadvantage in relation to admissions and student services by removing or altering a physical feature or by providing an auxiliary aid or services (see further Chapter 8). The DDA as amended does not as yet expressly prohibit harassment in relation to education at any level. The Explanatory Notes to the draft DDA 1995 (Amendment) Regulations stated that 'where any minor changes are required [in relation to] discrimination against disabled students and prospective students in Further and

---

[78] See ss.22 & 24 SDA, 17 RRA.

Higher Education, these will be dealt with separately and to a different timescale.' No further draft Regs have yet been published but the DDA ought to be amended to this effect by October 2005.[79]

Harassment of pupils is covered expressly by s.17(2) RRA and, as was mentioned above, may also amount to unlawful discrimination on grounds of sex or disability contrary to the relevant provisions of the SDA and DDA. It is worth noting that schools may not be vicariously liable for harassment of pupils by their peers—any liability will be direct and subject to the limitations considered in the discussion of *Pearce* above.

The CRE's Code of Practice for the elimination of discrimination in education suggests that schools might discriminate on grounds of race by privileging claimants whose siblings are already at the school where there is a racial imbalance at the school; or pupils from a particular catchment area which is racially imbalanced. *Mandla v Dowell Lee* [1983] 2 AC 548 illustrates that the imposition of uniform requirements as a precondition for entry into a school may discriminate contrary to s.17 RRA and its equivalents. A school might breach s.17(1)(c)(i) or its equivalent by segregating ethnic minority or disabled students or by treating them less favourably than others in terms of special educational support, subject choice, exam entry and so on. And school exclusions, where they fall disproportionately by sex or race, may breach s.17(1)(c)(ii) RRA or its equivalents. Perhaps the most infamous case came to light as a result of a Formal Investigation by the CRE (see further Chapters 5 and 7). In *Medical School Admissions: A CRE Investigation*, the Commission found that the computer programme utilised by St George's Medical School to sift applications included a (deliberate) bias against women and non-white claimants. The programme had been designed to replicate academic decision-making.[80]

Exceptions

Section 26 SDA provides that s.22(a) and (b) of that Act do not apply in relation to admissions to single-sex schools, to schools which admit students other than of a single sex only exceptionally or to particular classes or courses. Such schools can lawfully discriminate in relation to admissions, but are bound not to discriminate in relation to students they have 'exceptionally' admitted once they are at the school (s.26). The same is true of discrimination by single-sex boarding schools in relation to boarding facilities and access thereto, and ss.27 and 28 SDA provide further exceptions for single sex schools which are in the process of becoming co-educational and in relation to physical education courses. There are, unsurprisingly, no equivalent provisions in the RRA (which, as we saw in Chapter 2, expressly defines segregation as a form of race discrimination). That Act does not, however, apply (s.36) to discrimination on grounds of colour or nationality in the provision of education or training for persons not ordinarily resident in Great Britain 'where it appears to [the provider] that the persons in question do not intend to remain in Great Britain after their period of education or training there.' Further, s.35 RRA provides that:

> Nothing in Parts II to IV shall render unlawful any act done in affording persons of a particular racial group access to facilities or services to meet the special needs of persons of that group in regard to their education, training or welfare, or any ancillary benefits.

[79] This being the date by which the Government has undertaken to amend the Act.
[80] C Bourn and J Whitmore, *Anti-discrimination Law in Britain* (3rd ed, London: Sweet and Maxwell, 1996), para 7.07.

This provision would ensure the lawfulness of (say) Jewish or Sikh schools, restricted admission to which would otherwise breach the education provisions of the RRA (this on the basis that discrimination on grounds of these religions amounts to discrimination on grounds of race—see further Chapter 9).

Education Authorities

Local education authorities are liable under s.17 RRA , s.22 SDA and s.28A and Schedule 4 DDA for discrimination by maintained schools in relation to the authority's functions (the governing bodies of the schools being similarly responsible for discrimination in their own functions). LEAs are also prohibited from discriminating in relation to any of their statutory functions by ss.18, 23 and 28F of the RRA, SDA and DDA respectively. Discrimination which arises *between* rather than *within* institutions (such as where, for example, pupils at a boys' school are treated more favourably than those at a girls' school) falls under ss.18 RRA and its equivalent provisions.[81] Thus, for example, while *Mandla v Dowell Lee* was brought under s.17 RRA, the challenge in *EOC v Birmingham City Council* [1989] AC 1155 was brought under s.23 SDA. Both cases are considered in detail in Chapter 2. Sections 18A, 18B and 18D RRA regulate discrimination and harassment by Further Education and Higher Education Funding Councils, Scottish Further and Higher Education Funding Councils and the Teacher Training Agency in carrying out their respective functions while ss.23A, 23B and 23D SDA apply similarly (but without express reference to harassment) in relation to sex discrimination. The DDA contains no equivalent provisions, though discrimination by these bodies in the provision of 'goods, services and facilities' is actionable under s.19 of that Act (see further below).

There have, as was mentioned above, been relatively few appellate decisions on the education-related provisions of the SDA, RRA, DDA and FETO.[82] Of great practical significance have been decisions relating to the '11 Plus' exam by which students in various parts of the UK are streamed into grammar and non-grammar schools at 11. The *EOC v Birmingham City Council* case concerned the setting of different pass marks for girls and boys by the council to accommodate the fact that it had available more boys' than girls' grammar school places. In the 1980s the practice in Northern Ireland was to set different pass marks for boys and girls to ensure that equal numbers of the sexes passed (this because boys tend to lag behind girls educationally at 11 but catch up somewhat in later years). Northern Ireland's High Court, in an unreported case, allowed a claim for judicial review by Northern Ireland's EOC and declared the practice contrary to Northern Ireland's equivalent of s.23 SDA. Papers for the '11 Plus' then had to be marked and places awarded irrespective of the sex of the pupils.[83] Intriguingly, a BBC News report on 21 November 2003 reported that, while fewer boys than girls in Northern Ireland now sat the '11 Plus' (only two thirds of pupils took it in 2003), boys outdid girls in terms of pass rate in 2003 for the third consecutive year. In January 2004 the Northern Ireland Education Minister announced that the examination was to be scrapped from 2008. The decision was made

---

[81] See, for example, *R v Secretary of State for Education and Science, ex p. Keating* [1985] LGR 469.

[82] In *R v Cleveland County Council ex p. CRE* (1992) 91 LGR 139, [1993] 1 FCR 597 the Court of Appeal ruled that the parental choice provisions of the Education Act 1988 overrode those of the RRA to the effect that a local authority which be obliged to accommodate even racially discriminatory parental preferences. The CRE argued that the apparently unqualified nature of the EA should be read in the light of s.18 RRA.

[83] The case is discussed in the subsequent decision in *Re Equal Opportunities Commission for Northern Ireland's Application* [1989] IRLR 64.

significantly because of concerns that the system benefited economically privileged children at the expense of the disadvantaged, and perpetuated inequalities accordingly.

The SO Regs and RB Regs

Turning, finally, to the application to education of the SO and RB Regs, reg 20 of each provides that:

(1) It is unlawful, in relation to an educational establishment to which this regulation applies, for the governing body of that establishment to discriminate against a person—
    (a) in the terms on which it offers to admit him to the establishment as a student
    (b) by refusing or deliberately not accepting an application for his admission to the establishment as a student; or
    (c) where he is a student of the establishment—
        (i)   in the way it affords him access to any benefits,
        (ii) by refusing or deliberately not affording him access to them, or
        (iii) by excluding him from the establishment or subjecting him to any other detriment.
(2) It is unlawful, in relation to an educational establishment to which this regulation applies, for the governing body of that establishment to subject to harassment a person who is a student at the establishment, or who has applied for admission to the establishment as a student.

The educational establishments covered by reg 20 are those in England and Wales within the FE sector, universities and other bodies in the HE sector and, in Scotland, FE colleges, institutes of HE and similar. The Equality Bill 2005, which failed to become law prior to the 2005 general election, proposed the regulation of religion and belief discrimination in education more generally, albeit subject to generous exceptions for religious schools and the curriculum etc.

It is too early to comment upon the impact in this context of the RB and SO Regs. What is noteworthy is that, by contrast with the generally minimalist approach taken by the Government to implementation of the Racial Equality and Employment Equality Directives (and most EC Directives), the SO and RB Regs appear to go beyond what was strictly required by the Employment Equality Directive by covering third level education in general, rather than only that which could truly be said to entail 'vocational training.' It remains the case, however, that pupils of primary and secondary schools are unprotected by the Regs from discrimination connected with their own or others' sexual orientation, religion or belief. So, for example, while the Sikh pupil in the *Mandla* case was protected from discrimination in education because Sikhs were regarded as an 'ethnic group' for the purposes of the RRA, similar protection is very unlikely to apply to a scarf-wearing Muslim pupil for the reasons discussed in Chapter 9.[84]

---

[84] Also, see *R (on the application of Williamson) v Secretary of State for Education* [2005] UKHL 15, discrimination in relation to education may be the subject of challenge (albeit there unsuccessful) under the Human Rights Act 1998. See also the decision of the Court of Appeal in *R (Begum) v Denbigh High School* [2005] EWCA Civ 199, discussed in Ch 9.

Positive Obligations Imposed by the RRA, SDA and DDA

The positive obligations imposed upon public authorities by the RRA as amended by the Race Relations (Amendment) Act 2000 are discussed in Chapter 3. Among the bodies listed in Schedule 1A to the RRA are local authorities, the governing bodies of educational establishments maintained by local education authorities and institutions within the further and higher education sectors, the managers of grant-aided Scottish schools and the boards of management of self-governing school and colleges of further education. These bodies are all subject to statutory duties to eliminate unlawful race discrimination and to publish and apply race equality schemes. The CRE has produced a Code of Practice on the Duty to Promote Race Equality, together with guides on the application of the duty for schools in England and Wales and in Scotland, and for Institutions of Further and Higher Education, and Framework Race Equality Policies for FE and HE institutions and for schools, and Performance Guidelines for Colleges and Universities, local authorities and schools. It stresses the need for schools to, inter alia, prioritise the promotion of racial equality, ensure ethnic minority representation on governing bodies, have strategic action plans with targets for achieving race equality, which plans are reviewed annually, and monitor and publish the effects of their policies.

The SDA does not as yet contain any equivalent to s.19B RRA or to the race equality obligations imposed upon public authorities. Meanwhile, ss.25 and 25A SDA, which have no equivalent in the RRA or DDA, provide that:

(1) Without prejudice to its obligation to comply with any other provision of this Act, a body to which this subsection applies shall be under a general duty to secure that facilities for education provided by it, and any ancillary benefits or services, are provided without sex discrimination.

The obligation imposed by s.25(1) applies to local education authorities in England and Wales and to education authorities in Scotland, as well as to (broadly) state schools and the Teacher Training Agency. Section 25A imposes an obligation on the Learning and Skills Council for England and the National Council for Education and Training for Wales to secure that facilities for education, training and 'organised leisure-time occupation connected with such education or training' which they secure the provision of are provided without sex discrimination. The obligations imposed by ss.25 and 25A are not enforceable under the SDA, but rather by the Secretary of State for Education exercising powers under the Education Act 1996 or the Education (Scotland) Act 1980 to prevent the unreasonable exercise of their powers by local education authorities, schools, etc.

The DDA (s.28D) imposes obligations upon LEAs and the governing bodies of maintained, independent and special schools[85] respectively to draw up 'accessibility strategies' and 'accessibility plans' respectively in relation to schools for which they are the responsible body. The obligation is an ongoing one, and an 'accessibility strategy' is defined (s.28D(2)) as 'a strategy for, over a prescribed period—

(a) increasing the extent to which disabled pupils can participate in the schools' curriculums;

---

[85] Where those special schools are not maintained special schools but are approved by the Secretary of State, or by the National Assembly, under section 342 of the Education Act 1996.

(b) improving the physical environment of the schools for the purpose of increasing the extent to which disabled pupils are able to take advantage of education and associated services provided or offered by the schools; and

(c) improving the delivery to disabled pupils—

    (i) within a reasonable time, and

    (ii) in ways which are determined after taking account of their disabilities and any preferences expressed by them or their parents of information which is provided in writing for pupils who are not disabled.

An accessibility plan is similarly defined save that it relates to a single school. Accessibility strategies and plans must be in writing, must be kept under review and revised if necessary during the period of their operation, and must be implemented by the LEA or the responsible body as relevant. Inspections of LEAs or schools may extend to the performance by them of their functions in relation to the preparation, publication, review, revision and implementation of accessibility strategies and plans. Section 28E DDA further provides that LEAs and governing bodies must have regard, inter alia, to the need to allocate adequate resources for implementing accessibility strategies and plans and to any guidance issued by the Secretary of State (in Wales by the Welsh National Assembly). The Secretary of State (in Wales the Welsh National Assembly) is entitled, on request, to a copy of any accessibility strategy or plan.

The Disability Discrimination Act amends the DDA in order to impose on public authorities, including education authorities, an obligation (proposed s.49A(1) DDA) 'in carrying out [their] functions [,to] have due regard to (a) the need to eliminate discrimination that is unlawful under this Act; (b) the need to eliminate harassment that is unlawful under this Act; and (c) the need, where opportunities for disabled people are not as good as those for other persons, to promote equality of opportunity between disabled persons and other persons by improving opportunities for disabled persons.' This duty, which is similar to that imposed upon specified public authorities by the RR(A)A, is considered in Chapter 5.

Discrimination in Housing/Premises

The RRA, SDA, DDA and FETO all regulate discrimination in connection with housing and premises (and, in the case of the RRA alone, planning). Neither the SO nor the RB Regs apply in this context. Some housing-related discrimination on grounds of sexual orientation, religion or belief will, however, breach one or more provisions of the European Convention on Human Rights and, in some cases, the Human Rights Act 1998. Detailed consideration of the application of the Convention and HRA are beyond the scope of this book but a broad outline of the provisions is set out in Chapter 1 and the decision of the House of Lords in *Mendoza v Ghaidan* [2004] 2 AC 557 illustrates the possible application of the Convention and HRA to sexual orientation discrimination in the housing context. It should also be noted that public authorities are covered by the positive obligations discussed in Chapter 3 in the performance of their functions in relation to housing and premises, as elsewhere.

Sections 21–24 RRA and 30–31 SDA regulate discrimination in relation to the disposal of premises within the UK. The equivalent provisions of FETO and the DDA are Articles

29–30 of the former and ss.22 and 23 of the latter. The provisions cover commercial as well as domestic lettings but do not cover the hire of hotel rooms and the like, or of premises (for example for the purposes of having a party in a pub), discrimination in connection with which is covered by the goods and services provisions considered below.

Section 30 SDA, which does not apply to discrimination falling within the employment or education provisions of the Acts, provides that:

(1) It is unlawful for a person in relation to premises in Great Britain of which he has power to dispose, to discriminate against a woman—
    (a) in the terms on which he offers her those premises, or
    (b) by refusing her application for those premises, or
    (c) in his treatment of her in relation to any list of persons in need of premises of that description.
(2) It is unlawful for a person, in relation to premises managed by him, to discriminate against a woman occupying the premises —
    (a) in the way he affords her access to any benefits or facilities, or by refusing or deliberately omitting to afford her access to them, or
    (b) by evicting her, or subjecting her to any other detriment.
(3) Subsection (1) does not apply to a person who owns an estate or interest in the premises and wholly occupies them unless he uses the services of an estate agent for the purposes of the disposal of the premises, or publishes or causes to be published an advertisement in connection with the disposal.[86]

Section 31 SDA provides that:

(1) Where the licence or consent of the landlord or of any other person is required for the disposal to any person of premises in Great Britain comprised in a tenancy, it is unlawful for the landlord or other person to discriminate against a woman by withholding the licence or consent for disposal of the premises to her.

Sections 32 and 31(2) provide that the prohibitions on discrimination in ss.30 and 31(1) respectively do not apply if the discriminator:

(a) . . . or a near relative of his ('the relevant occupier') resides, and intends to continue to reside, on the premises, and
(b) there is on the premises, in addition to the accommodation occupied by the relevant occupier, accommodation (not being storage accommodation or means of access) shared by the relevant occupier with other persons residing on the premises who are not members of his household, and
(c) the premises are small premises . . .

'Small premises' are (s.32(2) SDA):

(a) in the case of premises comprising residential accommodation for one or more households (under separate letting or similar agreements) in addition to the accommodation occupied by the relevant occupier, there is not normally residential accommodation for more than two such households and only the relevant occupier and any member of his household reside in the accommodation occupied by him;

---

86 Even if it does not amount to a breach of one of those provisions because a defence applies (ss.35 SDA, s.23(1) RRA, s.19(5A) DDA.

(b) in the case of premises not falling within paragraph (a), there is not normally residential accommodation on the premises for more than six persons in addition to the relevant occupier and any members of his household.

Sections 21–24 RRA are materially similar with the important distinctions that (1) 'harassment' as well as discrimination are expressly prohibited and (2) the exceptions provided by s.30(3) SDA in relation to owner-occupied premises, and by ss.31(2) and 32, do not apply where the discrimination is on grounds of race or ethnic or national origin. Article 29 FETO and ss.22–23 DDA are materially similar to ss.30–32 SDA. The Equality Bill 2005 proposed similar regulation of discrimination on grounds of religion or belief.

Relatively few cases have been litigated under the premises sections of the anti-discrimination legislation. The CRE has carried out a number of Formal Investigations (see further Chapter 5) into race discrimination by local authorities in the provision of housing. In 1984 it found that the London Borough of Hackney had been guilty of 'direct discrimination against black applicants and tenants who had been allocated housing from the waiting list . . . in that whites had received better-quality allocations of housing than blacks.[87]

> Although there were almost as many black applicants on the council waiting list as whites (45 per cent compared with 49 per cent), among white applicants 16 per cent were allocated houses, 19 per cent maisonettes and 65 per cent flats, whereas 4 per cent of blacks received houses, 11 per cent maisonettes and 85 per cent flats. Whites were more likely to be allocated new property than blacks (25 per cent compared with 4 per cent) moreover, a higher proportion of white tenants were awarded ground or first floor accommodation.[88]

Discrimination in the provision of accommodation by Hackney was regarded by the CRE as discrimination in access to services under s.20 RRA (see below); discrimination in relation to waiting lists as discrimination under s.21(1)(c).[89] The Commission's 1978 *Annual Report* also records that the London Borough of Islington complied with CRE pressure to change a rule whereby dependants were recognised for the purpose of its waiting list only if they were resident in the UK.[90] And the Formal Investigation at issue in *Hillingdon London Borough Council v Commission for Racial Equality* [1982] AC 779 (see Chapter 5) also concerned housing.

The CRE has issued codes of practice on rented and non-rented (owner-occupied) housing (1991 and 1992 respectively). Among the examples of potentially unlawful practices detailed therein are the imposition by a local authority of a lengthy residence qualification for accommodation with which persons of one racial group are less able to comply than others, the operation of a rule prioritising the offspring of by current tenants for rehousing, and reliance on word-of-mouth recommendations from existing tenants, where this serves to advantage one or more racial groups over others.

'Discrimination' in this context, by contrast with the general position under the DDA, applies *only* to less favourable treatment of a disabled person for a reason connected with her disability. Here, as elsewhere in the non-employment provisions of the DDA, discrimination can be justified if it is for a 'material and substantial reason' (see further Chapter 2).

---

[87] Bourn and Whitmore, n80 above, para 7.48. See also M Bryan, 'Discrimination in the Public Provision of Housing: the Commission for Racial Equality Report on Housing in Hackney' [1984] *Public Law* 194.

[88] Bryan, *ibid*, p.196.

[89] S.35(3) SDA, s.23(1) RRA.

[90] This was altered to permit consideration of those entitled to live in the UK.

The DDA 2005, however, inserts new ss.24A–24L DDA which impose in this context also a duty to make reasonable adjustments. This duty, which extends to alterations in policies and practices, etc, and in the provision to disabled persons of auxiliary aids, will not apply in relation to the sale (as distinct from letting-out) of premises. Nor does it impose any duty to make alterations to the premises themselves (as distinct, for example, from allowing a visually impaired person to keep a guide-dog in a flat in which dogs are not generally permitted, reading a tenancy agreement to a visually impaired prospective tenant, or exempting a wheelchair user from an obligation to place their rubbish in the usual (inaccessible) place. The DDA 2005 also provides a power for the Secretary of State to amend or repeal the small dwellings exemption (which applies also in relation to the new duty to make reasonable adjustments) by regulation.

Discrimination in Planning

Section 19A RRA prohibits discrimination by planning authorities in relation to their planning functions, such authorities being defined to include counties, county boroughs, district and London borough councils, the Broads Authority, National Park authorities, and joint planning boards in England & Wales (in Scotland, planning authorities, regional planning authorities), together with urban development corporations and bodies having functions (whether as enterprise zone authorities or bodies invited to prepare a scheme) under Schedule 32 to the Local Government, Planning and Land Act 1980. Section 19A has no equivalents in the other discrimination legislation and had generated little case law, though in *Davis v Bath and North East Somerset District Council* a county court awarded £750 000 plus costs to a claimant whose applications for planning permission had been repeatedly obstructed by the Council's staff.[91]

Discrimination in the Provision of Goods, Facilities and Services

The SDA, RRA, DDA and FETO (but neither the SO nor the RB Regs) prohibit discrimination in connection with access to goods, facilities and services. These provisions were adopted in Northern Ireland's fair employment legislation only in 1998 with the implementation of FETO, the Order's predecessors having been concerned only with employment. Discrimination which falls within the scope of the employment or education provisions of the SDA or RRA cannot be challenged under their goods and services provisions. The same is true, in the DDA context, for discrimination which falls within the scope of that Act's education provisions. Discrimination in the provision of goods and services has been affected by EC law only very recently with the implementation of the Racial Equality Directive. Council Directive 2004/113/EC regulates sex discrimination in access to goods and services and may result in significant changes to the SDA in particular in relation to insurance (see below).

[91] The RRA alone prohibits discrimination by planning authorities, s.19A having been inserted after the *Amin* case in order to deal with pressure to discriminate upon planning authorities (see below).

The goods, facilities and services provisions do not apply (s.36 SDA, s.27 RRA, Article 33 FETO) to goods, facilities or services outside Britain (or Northern Ireland as the case may be) or to 'facilities by way of banking or insurance or for grants, loans, credit or finance, where the facilities are for a purpose to be carried out, or in connection with risks wholly or mainly arising, outside Great Britain' except where the goods, facilities or services are on 'any ship registered at a port of registry in Great Britain', 'any aircraft or hovercraft registered in the United Kingdom and operated by a person who has his principal place of business, or is ordinarily resident, in Great Britain' or 'any ship, aircraft or hovercraft belonging to or possessed by Her Majesty in right of the Government of the United Kingdom' or, in the case of facilities for travel outside Britain, the refusal or omission occurs in Britain or on such a ship, aircraft or hovercraft.

We will see, below, that the application of the goods, facilities and services provisions to the public sector has been severely curtailed by judicial interpretation—in particular the decision of the House of Lords in *Amin v Entry Clearance Officer, Bombay* [1983] 2 AC 818, which restricted their application to those activities of the Crown which resembled those carried out by private actors. That decision and others in a similar vein are considered further below. Very significantly, however, the RR(A)A largely removed the impact of these cases on the RRA by rendering unlawful race discrimination by a 'public authority in carrying out any functions of the authority' (s.19B RRA). The Act also imposed upon public authorities specific duties, considered in Chapter 3, to promote equality. S.19B radically extends the operation of the RRA. The DDA 2005 amends the DDA by inserting new s.21B DDA, further discussed below. The SDA does not as yet contain any similar provision, though the Equality Bill 2005 proposes the insertion of equivalent provisions while s.76 of the Northern Ireland Act makes it 'unlawful for a public authority carrying out functions relating to Northern Ireland to discriminate, or to aid or incite another person to discriminate, against a person or class of person on the ground of religious belief or political opinion.' The prohibitions on discrimination by public authorities are considered in the following section and the positive obligations in Chapter 3.

The goods and services provisions of the DDA were introduced gradually, discrimination in the form of less favourable treatment being regulated from December 1996 and duties of reasonable adjustment being imposed first in October 1999 to the extent that they consisted of obligations on service providers to provide additional help to disabled service users and to make changes to the way in which the services were provided. As of 1 October 2004 service providers are also under an obligation to make reasonable adjustments to the physical features of their premises where those features make it 'impossible or unreasonably difficult for disabled persons' to access those services. The duties of reasonable adjustment placed on service providers and others by the DDA are further explored in Chapter 8 and are mentioned here only in passing.

Section 29 SDA, to which s.20 RRA and Article 28 FETO are materially identical, provides:

(1) It is unlawful for any person concerned with the provision (for payment or not) of goods, facilities or services to the public or a section of the public to discriminate against a woman who seeks to obtain or use those goods facilities or services—
   (a) by refusing or deliberately omitting to provide her with any of them, or
   (b) by refusing or deliberately omitting to provide her with goods, facilities or services of the like quality, in the like manner and on the like terms as are normal in his case in relation to male members of the public or (where she belongs to a section of the public) to male members of that section.

(2) The following are examples of the facilities and services mentioned in subsection (1)—
   (a) access to and use of any place which members of the public or a section of the public are permitted to enter;
   (b) accommodation in a hotel, boarding house or other similar establishment;
   (c) facilities by way of banking or insurance or for grants, loans, credit or finance;
   (d) facilities for education;
   (e) facilities for entertainment, recreation or refreshment;
   (f) facilities for transport or travel;
   (g) services of any profession or trade, or any local or other public authority.

Section 29 SDA has been applied by the Court of Appeal in *Gill v El Vino Co Ltd* [1983] QB 425 to cover a wine bar's refusal to serve women unless they were seated; and, in *Quinn v Williams Furniture Ltd* [1981] ICR 328, a shop's refusal to extend credit facilities to a woman unless her husband stood as a guarantor. The Northern Irish equivalent has been applied by Northern Ireland's High Court in *McConomy v Croft Inns Ltd* [1992] IRLR 561 to cover discriminatory clothing and appearance rules applied by a pub (men were not allowed to wear earrings).[92] In *Bain v Bowles* [1991] IRLR 356 the Court of Appeal ruled that s.29 was infringed by a refusal on the part of *The Lady* magazine to accept an advertisement for a housekeeper/cook from a man; and, as we saw above, the House of Lords in *James v Eastleigh* [1990] 2 AC 751 applied the provision to discriminatory charges for access to a public swimming pool. Section 20 RRA has been applied by the Court of Appeal to race discrimination in access to prison work (*Alexander v The Home Office* [1988] ICR 685); in affording tax relief (*Savjani v Inland Revenue Commissioners* [1981] QB 458— see below) and in the issue of marriage licences (*Tejani v The Superintendent Registrar for the District of Peterborough* [1986] IRLR 502). And the High Court accepted in *R v Commission for Racial Equality ex parte Cottrell & Rothon* [1980] 1 WLR 1580 that the Act applied to race discrimination by estate agents. Having said this, litigation under the goods and services provisions of the anti-discrimination legislation is much less common than that in the employment field. Some of the reasons behind this were mentioned above and there are few reasons to suppose that the relative absence of litigation is indicative of a lack of discrimination. The Explanatory Memorandum to the European Commission's proposal for a directive regulating sex discrimination in access to goods and services contained the following statement:

Commission of the European Communities, 'Explanatory Memorandum accompanying the Proposal for a Council Directive implementing the principle of equal treatment between women and men in the access to and supply of goods and services'

Just as with the Directive on Racial Discrimination, the proposal addresses a serious inequality which is faced by millions of European citizens in their everyday lives . . . it is clear from the experience of existing independent bodies promoting equal treatment for men and women in the Member States that, where they deal with questions linked to goods and services, they are faced with a wide variety of cases [examples given include [r]efusal to provide mortgages to pregnant women; refusal to allow a woman's name to be put first on joint accounts (with resulting discrimination in entitlement to benefits such as share options, which are frequently restricted to the first named member); refusal to offer loans to people working part-time (indirectly discriminatory in the light of standing ECJ case law as the

---

[92] This is an unusual case—see Ch 2 for a full discussion of clothing and appearance rules.

majority of part-time workers are women; requirement for a woman to have a guarantor for a loan, where a man with a similar credit rating would not face a similar requirement; sexual harassment by landlords; different treatment of men and women in insurance schemes]. In a Eurobarometer survey carried out in 2002, people saying that they had personally experienced discrimination on grounds of sex in the area of goods and services made up just under one quarter of the discrimination reported in this area on all grounds covered by the survey. In Member States where legislation does exist, it can be seen that complaints in this area make up a significant proportion of those dealt with by the specialised bodies concerned. In Ireland, for example, approximately 25 per cent of the cases of sex discrimination cases dealt with so far in 2003 by the Office for the Director of Equality Investigations have concerned goods and services (with the remaining 75 per cent concerning various aspects of employment). In the Netherlands, complaints about unequal treatment based on sex in the area of goods and services made up just over 10 per cent of the cases dealt with by the Equal Treatment Commission in 2002. It is clear, therefore, that European legislation in this field will meet a previously unmet need in Member States which do not presently have specific legislation on equal treatment in access to goods and services.

Certainly, in the UK the goods, facilities and services provisions of the discrimination legislation are much less frequently litigated than the employment provisions. In summer 2003 the DRC's Director of Legal Services Nick O'Brien contrasted the 7,000 employment-related DDA cases which had been begun in the period 1995–2000 with the 51 county or sheriff court cases commenced:

> The paucity of Part 3 cases led one informed commentator to conclude that 'in reality, it seems that disabled people have rights that are virtually unenforceable and that, on order for the DDA to be effective, its enforcement mechanisms must be changed. Hence, calls from the [Royal National Institute for the Blind], and more recently in its first legislative review from the DRC, for the removal of all Part 3 cases from the civil courts to the employment tribunals.[93]

County courts (in Scotland Sheriff courts) are far less experienced in discrimination cases, and subject to the normal rules on costs. These factors may go some way to explain why so much less litigation has been generated by the goods, facilities and services provisions of the discrimination legislation (and by the other non-employment provisions) by contrast with the position regarding employment.

Section 19 DDA is materially similar to s.29 SDA save that the prohibition on discrimination consisting in a failure 'to provide [a woman] with goods, facilities or services of the like quality, in the like manner and on the like terms as are normal in his case in relation to' men (s.29(1)(b) SDA) is replaced by a prohibition (s.19(c)–(d) DDA) on discrimination 'in the standard of service which he provides to the disabled person or the manner in which he provides it to him; or in the terms on which he provides a service to the disabled person.' Further, 'discrimination' is defined here to include an unjustified failure to comply with a duty to make reasonable adjustment, where the failure makes it 'impossible or or unreasonably difficult for the disabled person to make use of any such service,' as well as less favourable treatment of a disabled person for a reason connected with his or her disability. The duty of reasonable adjustment comes into operation in the employment context only

---

[93] 'The DRC's Strategic Enforcement Powers and its Experience of their Use', Disability Rights in Europe conference (Leeds, September 2003).

in relation to specific disabled persons (applicants or staff) who are disadvantaged by the employer's practices etc, or by a physical feature of the employer's premises. By contrast, the DRC's Code of Practice: Rights of Access Goods, Facilities, Services and Premises warns that:

> 4.14 Service providers should not wait until a disabled person wants to use a service which they provide before they give consideration to their duty to make reasonable adjustments. They should be thinking now about the accessibility of their services to disabled people. Service providers should be planning continually for the reasonable adjustments they need to make, whether or not they already have disabled customers. They should anticipate the requirements of disabled people and the adjustments that may have to be made for them. In many cases, it is appropriate to ask customers to identify whether they have any particular requirements and, if so, what adjustments may need to be made. Failure to anticipate the need for an adjustment may render it too late to comply with the duty to make the adjustment. Furthermore, it may not of itself provide a defence to a claim that it was reasonable to have provided one . . .

Section 19(3) DDA lists the same examples as does s.29(2) SDA, with the addition of '(b) access to and use of means of communication; (c) access to and use of information services' and '(g) facilities provided by employment agencies or under section 2 of the Employment and Training Act 1973.' 'The use of any means of transport' is expressly excluded from the application of the DDA's goods and services provisions though (see below) the DDA does have some application to transport. The DDA 2005 narrows the exclusion from s.19 DDA to apply only (new s.21ZA) to transport services consisting of the provision and use of vehicles or provided while a person is travelling in a vehicle. Meanwhile, the exclusion of 'the use of any means of transport' does not exclude from the DDA's goods and services provisions:

Palmer et al, *Discrimination Law Handbook* (Legal Action Group, 2002) 901

> all the infrastructure related to the means of transport which do not themselves involve the use of the mode of transport itself . . . So, for example, a café on a railway platform clearly falls within the service provisions but the on-train buffet car does not. Transport infrastructure such as bus or tram stops, stations and termini fall within the [DDA's] service provisions as do airport facilities. Timetables, ticketing arrangements, booking facilities and waiting areas for example would also be covered by Part III DDA.

In *Ross v Ryanair* [2004] EWCA Civ 1751 the Court of Appeal ruled that both Ryanair and Stansted Airport had discriminated against the claimant by failing to provide him with a wheelchair free of charge where he needed the facility to access a flight.[94]

> The goods and services provisions do not apply to the manufacture of goods. This is of little consequence other than in the disability context where its effect is explained by the DRC's Code of Practice on Rights of Access: Goods, Facilities, Services and Premises.

---

[94] See also *Roads v Central Trains Ltd* [2004] EWCA Civ 1541 which concerned access to a station platform.

2.40 The manufacture and design of products are not in themselves covered by Part III of the Act because they do not involve the provision of services direct to the public. Nothing in the Act requires manufacturers or designers to make changes to their products, packaging or instructions. However, it makes good business sense for manufacturers and designers to make their goods (and user information) more accessible to disabled customers and they should consider doing so as a matter of good practice.

—A food processing company produces tinned food which it supplies to a supermarket chain. Whether the tins are branded with the supermarket's own label or with that of the producer, the food processing company is not supplying goods to the public and so does not have duties under the Act. The supermarket is likely to have duties under the Act because it is supplying goods to the public, but these duties do not extend to the labelling or packaging of the tinned food. . .

2.41 However, if a manufacturer does provide services direct to the public, then it may have duties under the Act as a service provider.

—A manufacturer of electrical goods provides a free guarantee. A purchaser of the goods is then entitled to have the goods replaced by the manufacturer if they are faulty within 6 months of purchase. For a fixed sum the manufacturer also provides an optional extended guarantee covering the goods against defects for up to 2 years after purchase. In both cases, the manufacturer is providing a service to the public (the guarantee) and is subject to the Act in relation to the provision of that service (but not in relation to the goods themselves).

Part V DDA deals with transport, providing a statutory basis for the imposition of specific obligations on transport providers. These obligations for the most part relate to accessibility standards and have yet to be appointed as they apply to taxis, although both taxis and private hire vehicles are regulated as regards the carriage of guide and hearing dogs. Accessibility standards have been imposed in relation to public service vehicles and rail vehicles but, except in the case of guide and hearing dogs, the DDA imposes no obligations on transport providers to carry those with disabilities (or otherwise not to discriminate against them). The DDA 2005 inserts new s.21ZA which replaces the current exemption of transport from the goods and services provisions with a much narrower one:

(1) Section 19(1)(a), (c) and (d) do not apply in relation to a case where the service is a transport service and, as provider of that service, the provider of services discriminates against a disabled person—
    (a) in not providing, or in providing, him with a vehicle; or
    (b) in not providing, or in providing, him with services when he is travelling in a vehicle provided in the course of the transport service.

New s.21ZA(2) regulates the duty of adjustment in transport-related service cases while s.21ZA(3) provides a basis for regulations to be passed modifying or disapplying s.21ZA(1) and (2) 'in relation to vehicles of a prescribed description.' Thus, for example, train, coach, bus and/or taxi services could be brought within the full protection of s.19 as the Secretary of State saw fit.

The DRC Code of Practice points out that the obligations imposed by the DRC apply to each service provided. Thus, for example, a 24 hour/ 7 day cash machine is likely to be considered a service provided by a bank, as (separately) is the bank's counter service, though both are concerned with facilitating customers' access to their cash. An airline, although not covered (as yet) by the DDA in relation to its transport functions (s.19(5)(b)), provides a service covered by s.19 DDA when it hosts a website through which customers can reserve and book flights.

DRC, Disability Discrimination Act 1995 Code of Practice: Rights of Access: Goods, Facilities, Services and Premises

2.14 Among the services which are covered are those provided to the public by local councils, Government departments and agencies, the emergency services, charities, voluntary organisations, hotels, restaurants, pubs, post offices, banks, building societies, solicitors, accountants, telecommunications and broadcasting organisations, public utilities (such as gas, electricity and water suppliers), national parks, sports stadia, leisure centres, advice agencies, theatres, cinemas, hairdressers, shops, market stalls, petrol stations, telesales businesses, places of worship, courts, hospitals and clinics. This list is for illustration only and does not cover all the services falling under the Act. . . .

2.18 A wide range of services are covered by the Act so as to include access to and use of any place which members of the public are permitted to enter. For example, toilet facilities and in–store restaurants open to the public are covered and a service provider might have to make changes to entrances, fire exits and emergency escape procedures which make it impossible or unreasonably difficult for disabled people to use its service

— A service provider converts a large building for use as retail premises. It recognises that it must take reasonable steps to provide a means of escape in an emergency, accessible for disabled people, which might include adjustments to the premises

2.19 The Act says that 'services' include 'access to and use of any place which members of the public are permitted to enter'. Thus, a person who permits 'members of the public' to enter such a place is providing a service to those people consisting of access to and use of that place . . .

It is important to note that it is the *provision* of services to the disabled, rather than the nature of the services provided, which is covered by s.19 DDA. The DRC's Code of Practive states that:

4.28 . . . a service provider does not have to comply with a duty to make reasonable adjustments in a way which would so alter the nature of its business that the service provider would effectively be providing a completely different kind of service.

— A restaurant refuses to deliver a meal to the home of a disabled person with severe agoraphobia (a fear of public or open spaces) on the grounds that this would result in the provision of a different kind of service. This is unlikely to be against the law. However, if the restaurant already provides a home delivery service, it is likely to be discriminatory to refuse to serve the disabled person in this way.

— A night club with low level lighting is not required to adjust the lighting to accommodate customers who are partially sighted if this would fundamentally change the atmosphere or ambience of the club.

— A hair and beauty salon provides appointments to clients at its premises in a town centre. A disabled person with a respiratory impairment is unable to travel into town because this exacerbates her disability. She asks the salon to provide her with an appointment at home. The salon refuses as it does not provide a home appointment service to any of its clients. This is likely to be within the law.

4.29 However, there might be an alternative reasonable adjustment which would ensure the accessibility of the services. If this can be provided without fundamentally altering the nature of the services or business, it would be a reasonable step for the service provider to have to take.

The DRC's First Review of the DDA had the following to say about the application of the Act's goods and services provisions:

DRC, *Disability Equality: Making it Happen* (2003), 34–35

The research which has so far been conducted on this part of the Act indicates that whilst progress has been made, there is considerable work to be done to make services accessible to disabled customers.

A 'mystery shopping' exercise by Grassroots found a pattern of poor provision such as 83 per cent of companies being unable to provide specific information in an alternative format, 61 per cent of loop systems tested by the deaf or hard of hearing networking properly and 44 per cent of disabled customers finding counters at the cash points or customer service desks an unsuitable height. In July 2000, Scope published its report 'Left Out' which considered how businesses and organisations were facing up to the challenge of the DDA. Its findings included that: 76 per cent of respondents could find no evidence that parking bays for disabled people were being checked by staff; 37 per cent of designated parking bays were being used by non-disabled drivers; that only 30 per cent of the businesses surveyed had customer information available in a format other than standard print; and that only 21 per cent of facilities had hearing loops.

Despite the evidence as to the failure by many organisations to address their practices under the DDA, there remains a paucity of cases brought under this part of the Act—a total of only 53 goods and services cases were known to have been issued in the courts by February 2001, according to the latest research.

Exceptions to the Prohibition on Discrimination in the Provision of Goods and Services

'Private Associations'

Above we considered the general exceptions provided by the various legislative regimes in relation to national security and acts done under statutory authority. We will see, below, that the goods, facilities and services provisions of the anti-discrimination legislation only apply where the provider of goods, etc, is concerned 'with the provision [of them] . . . to the public or a section of the public.' This has the effect that private associations are exempted from the regulation of discrimination in relation to their provisions of goods, services and facilities to their members (*Race Relations Board v Charter* [1973] AC 868, *Dockers' Labour Club and Institute Ltd v Race Relations Board* [1976] AC 285, in which the House of Lords ruled that the RRA 1968 Act's equivalent of s.20 RRA did not apply to discrimination in access to a Conservative club and by a working men's club to a member of an associated club).[95]

[95] The EOC's annual report for 1999–2000 reports (8) a county court ruling that the Professional Football Players' Annual Awards Dinner was not 'private' and that, therefore, the exclusion from it in 1997 and 1998 of a woman agent on the ground of her sex was actionable as a breach of the SDA. She was awarded £7,500.

The decisions in *Charter* and *Dockers' Labour Club* resulted in the incorporation into the RRA 1976 of s.25 which provides:

(1) This section applies to any association of persons (however described, whether corporate or unincorporate, and whether or not its activities are carried on for profit) if—
    (a) it has twenty-five or more members; and
    (b) admission to membership is regulated by its constitution and is so conducted that the members do not constitute a section of the public within the meaning of section 20(1); and
    (c) it is not an organisation to which section 11 applies [a trade union or similar].
(2) It is unlawful for an association to which this section applies, in the case of a person who is not a member of the association, to discriminate against him—
    (a) in the terms on which it is prepared to admit him to membership; or
    (b) by refusing or deliberately omitting to accept his application for membership.
(3) It is unlawful for an association to which this section applies, in the case of a person who is a member or associate of the association, to discriminate against him—
    (a) in the way it affords him access to any benefits, facilities or services, or by refusing or deliberately omitting to afford him access to them; or
in the case of a member, by depriving him of membership, or varying the terms on which he is a member; or
    (c) in the case of an associate, by depriving him of his rights as an associate, or varying those rights; or
    (d) in either case, by subjecting him to any other detriment.

Section 26 RRA provides that s.25 does not make unlawful any discrimination otherwise within s.25 whose 'main object . . . is to enable the benefits of membership (whatever they may be) to be enjoyed by persons of a particular racial group defined otherwise than by reference to colour.'

The application of this provision was considered in *Triesman* in which the Court of Appeal dealt with alleged discrimination by the Labour Party in the selection of candidates for election to positions as Labour councillors. The ruling of that Court that the selection did not fall within s.12 RRA was considered above. Here we consider the application of s.25.

Triesman v Ali [2002] IRLR 489

Peter Gibson LJ (for the Court):

The only question is whether admission to membership [of the Labour Party] is so conducted that the members do not constitute a section of the public within the meaning of s.20(1). Section 20(1) does not in fact directly assist in explaining the meaning of a section of the public, containing as it does no definition of the words in question, but indirectly it does assist because of the meaning given by the House of Lords in *Charter* and *Dockers* to the words.

The test for members not constituting a section of the public appears to be therefore of genuine personal selection and it is to the rules of the club or association to which it is appropriate to turn in the first place. If the rules so provide, then a factual question arises whether admission is conducted in accordance with the rules . . .

Mr Cavanagh criticises the EAT for holding that joining the Labour Party was a 'rubber-stamp' process and that membership did not depend on anything more selective than a willingness to join and pay the subscription. He submits that the Rules require an applicant for membership to have a real and genuine commitment to the substantive political aims and objectives of the Labour Party and no other party and he points in particular to rules 2A.6(a), 2A.3(c) and 2A.4. He argues that the provision enabling objections to the applicant for membership to be made by the constituency Labour Party (rule 2B.2(f)) and the provision giving a power of rejection of an application to the general secretary for any reason he thinks fit (rule 2B.2(h)) provide a sufficient filtering process so that it cannot be said that the members of the Labour Party are no more than a section of the public.

Mr Allen argues to the contrary. He points to the fact that there is no automatic pre-membership screening and that an applicant for membership automatically becomes a member after eight weeks in the absence of objection by the constituency Labour Party or a ruling by the general secretary. He relies on what appears to have been a common acceptance by counsel and the members of the House of Lords in *Charter* that members of the Conservative party were members of the public . . . and he submits that similarly members of the Labour Party are a section of the public.

We confess that we find the question a difficult one, not least because of the narrowness of the test suggested in *Charter* and apparently adopted by Parliament in s.25(1) by reason of the reference to s.20. It is easy enough to see why a Soho club, seeking to evade licensing or other regulations by claiming to be a private members' club when in reality allowing entry to anyone willing to pay the entry fee, should be treated as a club whose members remain members of the public. It is harder to see why a society with a serious purpose limited to members interested in that purpose should not be an association whose members are not a section of the public. In the present case, not only are the members of the Labour Party limited to persons accepting and conforming to the constitution, programme, principles and policy of the Labour Party and no other party, but admission to the Labour Party is subject to the procedure allowing objections to be made by the constituency Labour Party and to the general secretary's veto . . . We must proceed on the limited evidence before us, and on that material we would hold that s.25 is capable of application to the Labour Party. If the respondents were to pursue proceedings in the County Court that court would have to consider whether in reality admission to membership of the Labour Party was so conducted that s.25(1)(b) was not satisfied

This conclusion renders it unnecessary for us to consider the applicability of s.20 to the particular circumstances of the present case. We will only say that, whilst it may well be that a political party like the Labour Party can and does provide goods, facilities or services to its members not being a section of the public, it is far from obvious that it does so relevantly in the present case. But we express no concluded view on the point.

If, indeed, political parties are caught by the provisions of s.25 RRA then that provision plugs the gap in protection from discrimination highlighted by the Court of Appeal's decision in *Triesman* on the application of s.13 RRA. The downside is that s.25 RRA does not, at present, have any equivalent provisions in the SDA, the DDA or FETO. The DDA 2005 includes in the DDA new s.21F which applies in similar terms to s.25 RRA. But neither the SDA nor FETO contain any similar provisions despite almost annual attempts to amend the former to like effect. So if political parties are accepted as 'private associations' so as to render their members *not* a section of the public for the purposes of s.29 SDA and its equivalents, sex discrimination against election candidates would in any event fall outwith the SDA.

If, on the other hand, s.25 RRA is not applicable on the basis that the members of political parties are to be considered a 'section of the public' within s.20 RRA and its equivalent provisions, Peter Gibson LJ's expressions of doubt as to whether the selection of election candidates could be considered as falling within s.20's 'provision of goods, facilities or services' gives cause for concern. It is perhaps ironic that the legislature felt it necessary to include within the SDA s.33 (which creates an exception from that Act's prohibition on discrimination in goods and services in respect of political parties, permitting 'special provision' and acts done to give effect to such provision, 'for persons of one sex only in the constitution, organisation or administration of the political party') and, more recently (in the wake of the *Jepson* case) new s.42A SDA which excludes from the reach of the SDA 'arrangements made by a registered political party (s.42(2)): 'which (a) regulate the selection of the party's candidates in a relevant election, and (b) are adopted for the purpose of reducing inequality in the numbers of men and women elected, as candidates of the party, to be members of the body concerned'.

Insurance

Neither the RRA nor FETO contain any provisions dealing specifically with insurance which falls under the goods, services and facilities provisions considered above (or, to the extent that it is offered as a benefit by an employer), under the provisions dealing with employment. Discrimination on grounds of sexual orientation, religion or belief would be covered by the SO and RB Regs only in the employment context. But the DDA and SDA make particular provision in relation to insurance.

Insurance falls within the DDA's goods, services and facilities provisions as it does also under the RRA and FETO. But the DDA, which permits discrimination in relation to insurance, as elsewhere, where it is 'justifiable'—see further Chapter 2—makes special provision in relation to insurance. In addition to the special provisions relating to 'group insurance,' which are considered above, the Disability Discrimination (Services and Premises) Regulations 1996 allow an insurance services provider to treat a disabled person less favourably for a reason connected with his or her disability where (reg 2(2)) the less favourable treatment is:

(a) in connection with insurance business carried on by the provider of services;
(b) based upon information (for example, actuarial or statistical data or a medical report) which is relevant to the assessment of the risk to be insured and is from a source on which it is reasonable to rely; and
   reasonable having regard to the information relied upon and any other relevant factors.

According to the DRC's Code of Practice *Rights of Access: Goods, Facilities, Services and Premises*:

8.5 Information which might be relevant to the assessment of the risk to be insured includes actuarial or statistical data or a medical report. The information must also be current and from a source on which it is reasonable to rely. An insurer cannot rely on untested assumptions or stereotypes or generalisations in respect of a disabled person . . .
8.6 An insurer should not adopt a general policy or practice of refusing to insure disabled people or people with particular disabilities unless this can be justified by reference to the [conditions set out] above. Similarly, unless justifiable in this way, an insurer should not adopt a general policy or practice of only insuring disabled people or people with particular disabilities on additional or adverse terms or conditions.
8.7 The special rules on insurance services recognise that insurers may need to distinguish between individuals when assessing the risks which are the subject of an insurance proposal or insurance policy. However, it is for the insurer to show that there is an additional risk

associated with a disabled person which arises from his or her disability. Blanket assumptions should be avoided.

Section 45 SDA permits sex discrimination in relation to annuities, life assurance policies, accident insurance policies or similar matters concerning the assessment of risk where the discrimination results from reasonable reliance upon actuarial or other statistical material, and is reasonable in the light of the statistical and other factors. The test of reasonableness is not onerous, the County Court accepting in *Pinder v Friends Provident*, *The Times*, 16 February 1985 that a practice of charging women 50 per cent more than men for health insurance on the basis of 1953 statistics fell within s.45.[96]

The insurance-related exception was criticised by David Pannick:

D Pannick, *Sex Discrimination Law* (Oxford, OUP, 1985) 189–95

Sex discrimination is a common feature of insurance policies. Because of a belief that women are more prone to illness than men, women tend to be charged higher premiums than men in order to receive the same benefits in permanent health insurance and in many other forms of cover. Because women tend to live longer than men, they often pay lower premiums than men for life assurance and receive lower annuity rates.

It is strongly arguable that, as a matter of principle, the 1975 Act should not exempt insurance policies. The criterion of sex is an unreliable, unnecessary, and unfair one to use in the assessment of risk in insurance policies. In any event, it is doubtful whether many of the insurance policies which currently discriminate on the ground of sex would satisfy the criteria of section 45.

The practice of charging women more for equal benefits, or giving women lesser benefits for the same premium, is justified by insurance companies on the basis that statistics show that women, as a group, are more frequently ill than men, as a group, and that women tend to live longer than men. Sex discrimination in insurance cannot be defended unless this statistical basis is a reliable one. The problem for insurance companies is that '[i]nsurance rates are calculated from mortality tables based on persons already dead, and charged to persons who will live far into the future. Thus there is no reason to expect sex differences among current insureds to match those reflected in the tables.' Insurance companies use old, sometimes antiquated, statistics which are based on the behaviour of previous generations of men and women whose occupational and social experiences were vitally different from those of the current generation of insured persons. Because sex differences in the statistics are largely due to behavioural rather than genetic factors, the relevance of the statistics will crtically depend on whether women (and men) have similar occupational and social patterns today. Changes in such patterns since the time to which the statistics relate will obviously have an impact on sickness and death rates for men and women. Often, the statistics will tell us little or nothing about sickness and mortality rates today because of important changes in society since the period to which the statistics relate. Furthermore, the sickness statistics may merely reflect occupational segregation between men and women: since women tend to do less responsible work, they are likely to take more time off work.

Even if the statistical information relied on by an insurance company shows that there are differences between the sickness and mortality rates which can be predicted for men and women working today, it may be unnecessary for insurers to discriminate between men and women in this way. Other factors, such as a person's age, class, occupation, family medical history, and whether the person smokes, may be far better predictors of illness and death than sex. In *Los Angeles Department of Water and Power v Manhart* [435 US 702], the US

---

[96] Bourn and Whitmore, fn 80 above, para 777.41.

Supreme Court held that it was unlawful sex discrimination contrary to Title VII of the Civil Rights Act 1964 for an employer to require female employees to make larger contributions than male employees to a pension fund in order to receive the same benefit. The employers argued that their practice was valid because women tend to live longer than men and so the average woman will tend to receive more out of the fund than the average man. One reason for the decision of the Court to reject this argument was that '[s]eparate mortality tables are easily interpreted as reflecting innate differences between the sexes; but a significant part of the longevity differential may be explained by the social fact that men are heavier smokers than women.' Often, insurance companies give no weight, or inadequate weight, to these other statistically valid factors; they merely charge one premium (or allow one payment) for women and a different premium (or payment) for men. Such policies take insufficient note of the fact that '[w]hile actuarial tables may be relatively accurate in predicting the average longevity of men and women respectively, quite a substantial deviation occurs within either sex,' for many non-sex based reasons.

A third reason for questioning sex discrimination in insurance is that it is unfair to individual men and women. Assume that sex-based differentials in health insurance or pension plans are statistically valid: that they are based on valid material and ignore no other relevant classifications, so that an insurance company can accurately predict significantly different risks for relevant men and for relevant women. In such circumstances, it may well be that the scheme treats men (as a group) equally with women (as a group), allocating roughly equal amounts of benefits to, and taking approximately equal contributions from, each sex when there are equal numbers of men and women who participate in the scheme. All women who belong to the scheme will be charged a higher premium for health insurance or for a pension than all men because of an assumption that, by reason of their sex, they will tend to become ill more frequently than, and to die later than, comparable men. This is irrespective of the characteristics of an individual woman, who may in fact be a good health risk or may die much sooner than a man of her age doing a similar job. The question is whether it is fair to impose this detriment on any woman because she is a woman, irrespective of her own individual attributes.

It is a general principle of anti-discrimination law that people should not be treated by reference to a stereotyped assumption based on their race or sex. They are entitled to treatment by reference to their individual characteristics irrespective of their race or sex. Two arguments are used to defend the use of stereotyped assumptions in the context of insurance. First, that here the assumption is a true one: women do live longer than men. Secondly, that insurance is concerned with the assessment of risk and so it is here permissible to treat people by reference to the risk associated with persons of their sex.

In *Manhart*, the US Supreme Court recognised that the case before it did not 'involve a fictional difference between men and women. It involves a generalisation that the parties accept as unquestionably true: women, as a class, do live longer than men.' But, said the Court, it is improper to act on a stereotyped assumption unless it is true of all women so treated. It may well be true that women tend to be less able than men to lift heavy weights. Still it would be unlawful sex discrimination for an employer to reject a woman for a job involving the lifting of such weights simply because she is a woman: she is entitled to be considered on her individual ability to do the job, not to be rejected because of an assumption true of most women. The concept of direct discrimination under the 1975 Act is concerned with the individual. Like Title VII of the US Civil Rights Act, it 'precludes treatment of individuals as simply components of a . . . sexual . . . class . . . Even a true generalisation about the class is an insufficient reason for disqualifying an individual to whom the generalisation does not apply.' Those women who do not live as long as the average man will pay higher contributions to the pension fund while working, yet they will receive no compensating advantage when they retire. The fact that the erroneous assumption made about them was true of some other women—that those others would live longer than the average man—does not alter the fact that they have been classified according to their sex and that this has resulted in them suffering a disadvantage compared with similar men. Such treatment is particularly unfair because it penalizes a person for a factor outside her control and offers her no opportunity to decrease the relevant risk. Conversely, there will be many men who live longer than the average woman. They will pay lower pension premiums during their working lives, yet will receive considerable benefits during their prolonged retirement. They will receive these benefits, by comparison with comparable women, not because of their individual characteristics, but simply because of their sex. Since anti-discrimination law is primarily designed to entitle individuals to be treated by reference to their individual characteristics, it is as discriminatory to treat people by reference to a stereotyped assumption true of most women (or men) as it is to treat them according to an assumption true of few women (or men).

Nor is it a convincing defence of sex-based insurance policies that insurance is fundamentally concerned with the assessment of risk for people defined by reference to class characteristics. As the US Supreme Court emphasised in *Manhart*, '[i]t is true that insurance is concerned with events that are individually unpredictable, but that is characteristic of many employment decisions.' When deciding whether to appoint, promote, or dismiss a worker, employers need to weigh risks and to assess future potential. But employers are prohibited from doing this by reference to stereotyped assumptions. No doubt it is more expensive for employers to undertake an individual assessment of whether a woman applicant is capable of lifting the heavy weights, which is part of the job, rather than merely refusing the application of all women because most women could not lift such weights. Why should different principles apply to insurance practices? Indeed,

> when insurance risks are grouped, the better risks always subsidise the poorer risks. Healthy persons subsidise medical benefits for the less healthy; unmarried workers subsidise the pensions of married workers; persons who eat, drink or smoke to excess may subsidise pension benefits for persons whose habits are more temperate. Treating different classes of risk as though they were the same for purposes of group insurance is a common practice that has never been considered inherently unfair. To insure the flabby and the fit as though they were equivalent riks may be more common than treating men and women alike; but nothing more than habit makes one 'subsidy' seem less fair than the other.

One further factor suggests that insurance companies are capable of avoiding discriminatory policies even when those policies could be justified statistically. The US Supreme Court noted in Manhart that '[a]ctuarial studies could unquestionably identify differences in life expectancy based on race or national origin, as well as sex.' Insurers did, at one time, use race-segregated insurance tables. Yet the Race Relations Act 1976 does not allow insurance companies to treat persons of different races in a disparate manner by reference to actuarial data on which it is reasonable to rely. As the US Supreme Court said in *Arizona Governing Committee v Norris* [463 US 1073 (1983)] (applying the *Manhart* principle of equality between the sexes so as to find it unlawful sex discrimination for an employer to pay out lower monthly annuity payments to women than to men who had made equal contributions prior to retirement), it is impossible to see any difference of principle between race classifications and sex classifications in this context.

The objective of securing equal treatment for men and women, irrespective of sex, requires the avoidance of different insurance terms for each sex. A woman may be charged a higher premium than a man because of her individual characteristics, but not because she is a woman and he is a man. In insurance, as elsewhere, '[p]ractices that classify [persons] in terms of . . . sex tend to preserve traditional assumptions about groups rather than thoughtful scrutiny of individuals.' To impose higher premiums on persons, or to give them lower benefits, because of their sex and because of assumptions based on sexual stereotypes is to use unreliable, unnecessary, and unfair criteria.

Section 45 of the 1975 Act, by including references to whether it is 'reasonable' to rely on the actuarial data in all the relevant circumstances, no doubt offers courts the opportunity to limit the amount of sex discrimination which may lawfully be practised by insurance companies. But even the references to reasonableness cannot excuse section 45 and its approval of some such sex discrimination. The existence of section 45 owes much to the lobbying powers of the insurance industry in 1975. It is time for section 45 to be repealed.

Despite these and other criticisms, s.45 remains intact and was given implied approval by the decision of the ECJ in *Neath v Hugh Steeper Ltd* Case C–152/91[1993] ECR I–6935, in which that court permitted some pension-related actuarial discrimination. More recently, the European Commission's Proposal for a Council Directive implementing the principle of equal treatment between women and men in the access to and supply of goods and services[97] would have prohibited sex discrimination in insurance. This proposal was significantly watered down in the final Directive (2004/113/EC), which is notably narrower in its scope than the Racial Equality Directive (see further Chapter 7). It regulates sex discrimination in 'access to and the supply of goods and services which are available to the public, including housing, as regards both the public and private sectors, including public bodies,' but omits from its scope discrimination in relation to social protection including health care, social advantages and taxation (which was lobbied for and included in an early draft) and expressly excludes from its scope discrimination in the field of education, media and advertising. Within the scope of its application it will prohibit direct and indirect discrimination and harassment and victimisation on grounds of sex (including pregnancy). One of the most important aspects of the Directive, in its originally proposed form, was (at least from the domestic perspective) its proposed regulation of sex discrimination in the insurance context.

Commission of the European Communities, 'Explanatory Memorandum accompanying the Proposal for a Council Directive implementing the principle of equal treatment between women and men in the access to and supply of goods and services'

. . . It is common for insurance to be offered on different terms to women and to men. Actuarial factors are broken down by sex in order to evaluate the risk of insuring men and women separately in various parts of the insurance market, but especially in life, health and car insurance and in the calculation of annuities. The factors taken into consideration include variations in average life expectancy, but also different patterns of behaviour (particularly in car insurance) and consumption (in health insurance).

However, insurance companies in different Member States use a wide variety of tables which are updated more or less regularly and which, in certain cases, lead to different results for men and women. In France, for example, it is common practice to apply unisex tariffs for men and women in private health insurance. The same is true in the United Kingdom (though sex differences are applied in critical illness insurance). In Germany, however, insurers differentiate between men and women. Similar differences of approach arise in the areas of term life insurance and pensions annuities, where insurers in France use unisex tables, whereas others tend to calculate contributions and annuity payments on the basis of tables showing life expectancy according to sex. In the area of car insurance, insurers in

---

[97] COM(2003) 657 final.

some Member States apply a strong differentiation in the rates applied to (especially young) men and women (eg the United Kingdom and Ireland), whereas others (in eg Sweden) do not. Both approaches are therefore possible without affecting the financial viability of the companies.

Studies show that sex is not the main determining factor for life expectancy. Other factors have been shown to be more relevant, such as marital status, socio-economic factors, employment/unemployment, regional area, smoking and nutrition habits . . .

Insurance companies enjoy freedom to set their tariffs within the limits of Community law as laid down in the Treaty and in the various Council and European Parliament Directives on life and non-life insurance. All insurance is based on the pooling of risk and the solidarity which is created between the insured. Currently, insurers decide for themselves how they wish to define the pool of risk. Many have concluded that men and women should be divided into separate pools and that the risks they face should not be shared.

However, equal treatment for women and men is a fundamental right and the Commission believes that the freedom to set tariffs must be subject to that right. The separation of men and women into different pools leads to an unjustified difference of treatment and a resulting disadvantage for one sex or the other. The practice must be judged to be discriminatory and the legislator should therefore take action to prohibit it. An equivalent situation was at one time frequently found in the field of employment: in the past, it was not uncommon for employers to argue that they were reluctant to employ women of child-bearing age as there was a risk that they would be absent from work for periods of maternity leave, thus increasing their exposure to risks and resulting costs. While this is statistically true, it is clearly morally unacceptable as a reason for a difference of treatment of women and men in the labour market and the legislator has acted to prohibit such behaviour. The same argument holds true in the field of insurance.

The Commission concludes therefore that differences of treatment based on actuarial factors directly related to sex are not compatible with the principle of equal treatment and should be abolished. This position is in line with the ruling of the European Court of Justice in *Coloroll* [Case C–200/91], to the effect that different contributions for men and women to an occupational pension scheme are discriminatory.

The Commission's view is reinforced by the trend in Member States to replace or supplement state provision in the field of pensions by private insurance, and especially by annuity-based pensions. In many cases, Governments are encouraging the move to private provision through tax incentives or equivalent arrangements. The legislator has decided that, in the case of statutory social insurance, the principle of equal treatment must be respected. However, the move towards private provision is undermining this principle: sex-neutrality in state social insurance schemes is being gradually replaced by sex differentiation in the private market, in both the second and third pillars of pension provision. This is all the more important because arrangements which compensate (in the main) women for various disadvantages they face on the labour market—such as recognition of periods of absence from the labour market for reasons of child care, or survivor's benefits—are less common or less generous in second and third pillar schemes. Moreover, self-employed workers frequently have no option but to resort to the private market for pension coverage. The numbers of people in self-employment—and among them the proportion of women—are steadily increasing.

As the European Court of Justice made clear in the *Defrenne II* case [Case C–43/75], the proper implementation of equal treatment requires not only that the law should conform to the principle but that rules found in collective agreements and private contracts should also be brought into line. The developments in the nature of pension provision make action to require the equal treatment of women and men in the private provision of pensions all the more urgent and a necessary corollary of action in the state sector . . .

The EOC argued in favour of limiting the circumstances in which insurers could still set different rates for women and men, rather than banning it entirely as the Directive originally proposed.[98] This approach was preferred because research commissioned by the EOC suggested that, although women's rates in a unisex market could improve by 10 per cent, men's rates were likely to decrease by 3 per cent with the result that 'three-quarters of pensioners with annuities are likely to see a drop in retirement income. This would include some wives and widows who were dependent on their husband's annuity. The introduction of unisex annuities is therefore unlikely to be of widespread or significant benefit.'[99] In the event, Article 5 of the Directive allows Member States to 'permit proportionate differences in individuals' premiums and benefits where the use of sex is a determining factor based on relevant and accurate actuarial and statistical data'. Any policy of permitting such discrimination must be reviewed by December 2012.

Public Bodies

The most significant exception to the prohibition on discrimination in the provision of goods and services concerns the public sector. In *Kassam v Immigration Appeal Tribunal* the Court of Appeal ruled that s.29 SDA did not apply to the Secretary of State for the Home Department in the exercise of his immigration function.

Kassam v Immigration Appeal Tribunal [1980] 1 WLR 1037

Stephenson LJ:

Counsel for the appeal tribunal . . . submits that the Secretary of State does not provide facilities and the immigrant does not obtain or use them when he or she obtains leave from him or his immigration officers. Section 29 is concerned with what he called marketplace activities. The Secretary of State is exercising statutory powers to control immigration and any facilities he may be said in the course of their exercise to provide or to be concerned in providing are not within the aim or purview of the section.

I am of the opinion that the Secretary of State is not a person concerned with the provisions of facilities to a section of the public. Subsections (1) and (2) of s 29 repeat *mutatis mutandis* s 2(1) and (2) of the [RRA] 1968 (now repealed and reenacted in s 20(1) and (2) of the 1976 Act) and so are not free from judicial interpretation. But read in their natural and ordinary meaning they are not aimed at and do not hit the Secretary of State concerned with giving leave to enter or remain in the exercise of his powers under the 1971 Act. The kind of facilities with which the sections of the [RRA] are concerned is of the same order as goods and services, and though it may not always be easy to say whether a particular person (or body of persons) is a person concerned with the provision of any of those three things to the public or a section of the public and although a minister of the Crown or a government department might be such a person (for instance, in former days the Postmaster General, as Sir David Cairns suggested in argument), I am clearly of the opinion that the Secretary of State in acting under the Immigration Act and rules is not such a person, and he cannot be held to have unlawfully discriminated against the appellant . . . He is operating in a field outside the fields in which Parliament has forbidden sex discrimination.

---

[98] http://www.eoc.org.uk/cseng/news/30_june_annuities.asp.
[99] C Curry and A O'Connell, 'An analysis of unisex annuity rates' (EOC and Pensions Policy Institute).

In *Savjani v Inland Revenue Commissioners* the Court of Appeal applied s.20 RRA to the activities of the Inland Revenue. According to Lord Denning MR:

> the Revenue are entrusted with the care and management of taxes. They provide a service to the public in collecting tax. They also provide a service to a section of the public in so far as they give relief from tax or make repayments of tax or, I would add, give advice about tax. Those are all most valuable services which the Revenue authorities provide to the public as a whole and to sections of the public. It seems to me that the provisions for granting relief, giving advice, and the advice which is given, are the provision of services.

Lord Denning distinguished *Kassam* on the ground that, while in that case the Court of Appeal: 'held that, in dealing with people coming in under the immigration rules, the immigration authorities were not providing 'services' within the meaning of the [SDA, t]his case is very different. The Revenue are providing 'services' in regard to relief from tax or repayment of tax. Those services come within the provisions of the Act. If there is discrimination in the carrying out of those services, it is unlawful.'

Savjani v Inland Revenue Commissioners [1981] 1 QB 458

Templeman LJ:

the board and the inspector are performing duties, those duties laid on them by [statute] . . . but, in my judgment, it does not necessarily follow that the board and the inspector are not voluntarily or in order to carry out their duty also performing services for the taxpayer. The duty is to collect the right amount of revenue; but, in my judgment, there is a service to the taxpayer provided by the board and the inspector by the provision, dissemination and implementation of regulations which will enable the taxpayer to know that he is entitled to a deduction or a repayment, which will entitle him to know how he is to satisfy the inspector or the board if he is so entitled, and which will enable him to obtain the actual deduction or repayment which Parliament said he is to have. For present purposes, in my judgment, the inspector and the board provide the inestimable services of enabling a taxpayer to obtain that relief which Parliament intended he should be able to obtain as a matter of right subject only to proof . . .

Counsel for the commissioners submitted that the [RRA] does not apply to the Inland Revenue at all, but he naturally and wisely recoiled from the suggestion that the inspector of taxes might decline to interview a taxpayer if the taxpayer were coloured. He made forcibly the submission that, when the board decides for sensible reasons that a higher standard of proof is required from taxpayers who come from the Indian subcontinent, the board are not providing a service to that taxpayer; they are carrying out their duty to the Crown. As I have already indicated, it does not seem to me that the two concepts are mutually exclusive. The board and the inspectors perform their duty and carry out a service and, in my judgment, it is a service within the meaning of s 20 [RRA].

Counsel for the commissioners relied on *Kassam*, where this court had to consider the very different case of the powers of the Secretary of State under the Immigration Act 1971. In relation to those powers, wide discretions are conferred on the Secretary of State. Ackner LJ said in that case . . .

> In my judgment, when the Secretary of State is exercising his discretion in relation to powers granted to him by the Immigration Act 1971, he is not providing a 'facility' within the meaning of [the similar, almost identical, SDA].

In the present case, as I have indicated, subject to the question of proof, the taxpayer is absolutely entitled to the relief which he prays; and the Inland Revenue performs the service of enabling him to get the relief to which he is absolutely entitled. Accordingly, I do not think the *Kassam* case stands in the way of our reaching the conclusion which I have mentioned.[100]

J Gardner, 'Section 20 of the Race Relations Act: Facilities and Services' (1987) 50 *Modern Law Review* 345, 346, footnotes omitted

Savjani makes it clear that a person who has a primary statutory function which does *not* amount to the provision of a 'facility or service' to the complainant may nevertheless have some other function which *does*. There is nothing inconsistent in saying that HM Inspector has, apart from the (detrimental) function of collecting taxes, a further (advantageous) function which falls within section 20, since section 20 is 'not particularly concerned with the nature of the body which discriminates . . . it is concerned with what the body does in the course of which it discriminates.'

This could be applied with equal force to the case of a Prison Officer, who, it could be claimed, is predominantly concerned with ensuring the detention of a prisoner, but might still 'provide facilities' to prisoners, for example by allocating work or privileges to them [see *Alexander v Home Office*].

A related point which arises from *Savjani* is this: there is no conceptual reason why, in the course of subjecting someone to a detriment, a person cannot provide that other with a 'facility' for lightening the burden of the detriment. The point was made by Templeman LJ in *Savjani*: HM Inspector might 'voluntarily, or in order to carry out [his] duty, also perform . . . services for the taxpayer.' The example which *Savjani* itself suggests is that of advice on income tax liabilities; another would be the optional 'facility' of Television Licence Stamps offered by the Home Office, which renders less onerous the obligation of paying for a television licence.

These observations reveal that there is no necessary relationship between a person's primary function under statute and his subjection or non-subjection to section 20. Nor is there any necessary relationship between public conceptions of his role and his subjection or non-subjection to section 20. A government officer may conceive of himself as primarily an agent of control. The general public (even those who are successful in extracting some favourable decision from him) may also view him as an agent of control. Nevertheless, he may provide 'facilities' to the public for the purpose of section 20 if, for example, he accepts applications for some advantage or concession; he also provides 'services' by advertising the facility, advising on it, and considering applications.

Shortly after the decision of the Court of Appeal in *Savjani*, the House of Lords considered a challenge under the SDA to discriminatory immigration practices in *Amin v Entry Clearance Officer, Bombay*. The facts of the case are set out in Chapter 1. Their Lordships took the narrow view of the 'goods and services' provisions, restricting the application of s.29 SDA to those activities of the Crown which resembled those carried out by private actors.[101]

---

[100] Dunn LJ, albeit reluctantly, agreed with Lord Denning and Templeman LJ. Similarly, in *Alexander v Home Office* which went to the Court of Appeal on damages (see Ch 5 the Court of Appeal decision is at [1988] ICR 685), the county court ruled that the allocation of work to prisoners was within s.20 and in *Farah* below the Court of Appeal accepted that police services, as distinct from police powers, came within s.20 RRA.

[101] See also *Home Office v Commission for Racial Equality* [1982] QB 385. The decision in *CRE v Riley*, CRE *Annual Report* 1982, p18, in which a county court judge had ruled that the granting of planning permission fell outwith s.20 RRA, resulted in the insertion of s.19A RRA which reverses that decision in the planning sphere.

Amin v Entry Clearance Officer, Bombay **|1983| 2 AC 818**

Lord Fraser, with whom Lords Keith and Brightman agreed:

It was said that the granting of special vouchers for entry into the United Kingdom was provision of facilities or services to a section of the public, and that the wide general words of subsection (1) of section 29 were not cut down by the examples given in subsection (2) which are only 'examples' and are not an exhaustive list of the circumstances in which the section applies. Reliance was also placed on paragraph (g) of section 29(2) which expressly refers to services of a public authority and which has been held to apply to the Inland Revenue . . .

My Lords, I accept that the examples in section 29(2) are not exhaustive, but they are, in my opinion, useful pointers to aid in the construction of subsection (1). Section 29 as a whole seems to me to apply to the direct provision of facilities or services, and not to the mere grant of permission to use facilities. That is in accordance with the words of subsection (1), and it is reinforced by some of the examples in subsection (2). Example (*a*) is 'access to and use of any place' and the words that I have emphasised indicate that the paragraph contemplates actual provision of facilities which the person will use. Example (*d*) refers, in my view, to the actual provision of schools and other facilities for education, but not to the mere grant of an entry certificate or a special voucher to enable a student to enter the United Kingdom in order to study here. Example (*g*) seems to me to be contemplating things such as medical services, or library facilities, which can be directly provided by local or other public authorities. So in *Savjani*, Templeman L.J. took the view that the Inland Revenue performed two separate functions—first a duty of collecting revenue and secondly a service of providing taxpayers with information. He said:

> As [counsel] on behalf of the revenue submitted, the board and the inspector are performing duties—those duties laid upon them by the Act which I have mentioned— but, in my judgment, it does not necessarily follow that the board and the inspector are not voluntarily, or in order to carry out their duty, also performing services for the taxpayer. The duty is to collect the right amount of revenue; but, in my judgment, there is a service to the taxpayer provided by the board and the inspector by the provision, dissemination and implementation of regulations which will enable the taxpayer to know that he is entitled to a deduction or a repayment, which will [enable] him to know how he is to satisfy the inspector or the board if he is so entitled, and which will enable him to obtain the actual deduction or repayment which Parliament said he is to have.

In so far as that passage states the ground of the Court of Appeal's decision in that case I agree with it. . . . In the present case the entry clearance officer in Bombay was in my opinion not providing a service for would-be immigrants; rather he was performing his duty of controlling them.

Counsel for the appellant sought to draw support for his contention from section 85(1) of the [SDA] which provides:

> This Act applies—(*a*) to an act done by or for purposes of a Minister of the Crown or government department, or (*b*) to an act done on behalf of the Crown by a statutory body, or a person holding a statutory office, as it applies to an act done by a private person.

That section puts an act done on behalf of the Crown on a par with an act done by a private person, and it does not in terms restrict the comparison to an act *of the same kind* done by a private person. But in my opinion it applies only to acts done on behalf of the Crown which are of a kind similar to acts that might be done by a private person. It does not mean that the Act is to apply to any act of any kind done on behalf of the Crown by a person holding statutory office. There must be acts (which include deliberate omissions—see section 82(1)), done in the course of formulating or carrying out government policy, which are quite different in kind from any act that would ever be done by a private person, and to which the Act does not apply [citing Woolf J. in *Home Office v Commission for Racial Equality* [1982] QB 385] Part V of the SDA makes exceptions for certain acts including acts done for the purpose of national security (section 52) and for acts which are 'necessary' in order to comply with certain statutory requirements: section 51. These exceptions will no doubt be effective to protect acts which are of a kind that would otherwise be unlawful under the Act. But they do not in my view obviate the necessity for construing section 29 as applying only to acts which are at least similar to acts that could be done by private persons.

Lords Scarman and Brandon dissented from the conclusion of the majority:

Lord Scarman:

Entry into the United Kingdom for study, a visit, or settlement is certainly a facility which many value and seek to obtain. And it is one which the Secretary of State has it in his power under the Immigration Act to provide: section 3(2) of that Act. The special voucher scheme which he has introduced does provide to some this very valuable facility, namely the opportunity to settle in this country. It is a facility offered within Great Britain, albeit to persons outside: the exception in section 36 of the SDA does not apply.

Upon the literal meaning of the language of section 29(1), I would, therefore, construe the subsection as covering the facility provided by the Secretary of State.

It is, however, said that the kind of facilities within the meaning of the subsection are essentially 'market-place activities' or activities akin to the provision of goods and services, but not to the grant of leave to enter under the Immigration Act. Reliance is placed upon section 29(2) as an indication that this was the legislative intention of the section and upon the decision of the Court of Appeal which interpreted the section in this way in *Kassam*'s case.

In *Kassam's* case, Stephenson L.J. found the submission, which is now made to the House in this case, namely that in giving leave to immigrants to enter the country and to remain here the Secretary of State provides a facility to a section of the public, so plausible that he was tempted to accede to it . . . I agree with him. But I have yielded to the temptation, if that is a fair description of selecting a sensible interpretation of a statutory provision. He, however, did not. He appears to have accepted the submission that section 29 was concerned with 'market-place activities.' If he did not restrict the section to the full extent of that submission, he certainly took the view, which was also expressed by Ackner LJ and concurred in by Sir David Cairns, that the section applies only to facilities which are akin to the provision of goods and services. Ackner LJ . . . held that 'facilities' because of its juxtaposition to goods and services must not be given a wholly unrestricted meaning but must be so confined.

I reject this reasoning. I derive no assistance from subsection (2) in construing subsection (1) of section 29. I can find no trace of this House accepting any such assistance when in . . . *Applin* . . . this House had to consider the directly comparable provision in section 2(1) and (2) of the Race Relations Act 1968. Section 29(2) does no more than give examples of facilities and services. It is certainly not intended to be exhaustive. If some of its examples are 'market-place activities' or facilities akin to the provision of goods and services, others are not: I refer, in particular, to examples (*a*), (*d*), and (*g*). And, if the subsection cannot, as I think it cannot, be relied on as a guide to the construction of subsection (1), one is left only with Ackner LJ's point as to the juxtaposition of goods, facilities and services in subsection (1).

This is too slight an indication to stand up to the undoubted intention of Parliament that the Act is to bind the Crown. Section 85(1) provides:

> This Act applies—(a) to an act done by or for purposes of a Minister of the Crown or government department, or (b) to an act done on behalf of the Crown by a statutory body, or a person holding a statutory office, as it applies to an act done by a private person.

An attempt was made in reliance upon the concluding three words of the subsection to argue that in its application to the Crown the Act is limited to the sort of acts which could be done by a private person, eg 'marketplace activities' or the provision of facilities akin to the provision of goods and services. I do not so read the subsection. It means, in my judgment, no more and no less than that the Act applies to the public acts of Ministers, government departments and other statutory bodies on behalf of the Crown as it applies to acts of private persons. It would be inconceivable that the generality of subsection (1)(a) and (b) could be restricted by words which in drawing a distinction between two classes of act are intended to show that the distinction is immaterial. I cannot accept that so short a tail can wag so large a dog.

Section 52 also is consistent with the view that the Act has a wide cover in respect of acts of the Crown. It is designed to ensure that nothing in Parts II to IV of the Act (which include section 29) shall render unlawful an act done for the purpose of safeguarding national security.

Accordingly I think that on this point *Kassam* was wrongly decided. In my view, the granting of leave to enter the country by provision of a special voucher or otherwise is the provision of a facility to a section of the public. Indeed, I have no doubt that some see it as a very valuable facility. It is certainly much sought after. Section 29(1) is wide enough, therefore, to cover the special voucher scheme which, in my judgment, is properly described as offering a facility to some members of the public, ie, United Kingdom passport holders, who seek access to this country for the purpose of settlement but have no lawful means of entering other than by leave.

In the course of argument, your Lordships' attention was drawn to the Court of Appeal's decision in *Savjani* in which it was held that by putting the plaintiff because of his ethnic origin to a higher standard of proof of his entitlement to a tax relief than is normally required of a claimant the revenue had unlawfully discriminated against him in the provision of services to the public within the meaning of section 20(1)(b) [RRA]. The decision was, I am satisfied, correct and is certainly consistent with the approach which I would hold that the courts should adopt to section 29(1) [SDA]. But it was a different case on its facts from this case in that the revenue did provide, however informally, an advisory service to taxpayers seeking guidance on their problems.

The majority decision in *Amin* has been widely criticised:

D Pannick, *Sex Discrimination Law*, footnotes omitted

Lord Fraser said that section 29 applies 'to the direct provision of facilities or services and not to the mere grant of permission to use facilities.' That is rather a fine distinction on the facts of the case. The voucher is itself a facility: if it is not, then any shop or restaurant can escape the effect of section 29 (and the similar provision in the Race Relations Act 1976) by admitting people only if they have a voucher and by refusing to distribute such vouchers to women (or blacks). In any event, section 50(1) of the 1975 Act (to which none of their Lordships referred) states that indirect access to benefits is covered by section 29.

Secondly, the majority opinion of Lord Fraser contended that section 29 only applies to acts by the Government which 'are at least similar to acts that could be done by private persons.' But, as Lord Scarman pointed out in his dissenting opinion, the examples of facilities and services given in section 29(2)—in particular the services of any local or public authority—are hardly confined to 'market-place activities.' Section 29(1) applies to provision 'for payment or not.' Moreover, the special exemption from liability under section 29 for sex discrimination relating to political parties and religious bodies shows that section 29 covers more than market-place activities. The majority opinion placed reliance on section 85(1) of the 1975 Act. This states that the Act covers State action 'as it applies to an act done by a private person.' However, it would not seem that this takes the matter any further. Lord Fraser acknowledged that it 'does not in terms restrict the comparison to an act *of the same kind* done by a private person.' The crucial issue is the nature of the benefits provided, not their source, public or private. All that section 85(1) does, as Lord Scarman argued, is to ensure that 'the Act applies to the public acts of Ministers, Government departments and other statutory bodies on behalf of the Crown as it applies to acts of private persons.'

The House of Lords has in *Amin*, without any justification from the language or purpose of the 1975 Act, denied much of the statute's application to State action even though that action discriminates against women, even though the action concerns the provision of facilities to the public and even though the 1975 Act contains an express exception for acts done under statutory authority (suggesting that State action is covered by section 29). The decision of the House of Lords in *Amin* is particularly unfortunate when so much sex discrimination in immigration, social security, and tax law directly results from Government conduct. The decision in *Amin* adopted a similar approach to the earlier Court of Appeal decision in *Kassam*.

J Gardner (1987) 50 *Modern Law Review* 345, 349–51, footnotes omitted

In order to reach this conclusion, Lord Fraser examined some of the examples in section 29(2), which he considered to be 'useful pointers to aid in the construction of subsection (1).' He thought that some of the examples excluded mere passive permissions, 'Access to and use of any place' seemed to him to suggest not a simple permission to enter a place, but the active provision of something there; 'the services of any profession or trade, or any local or other public authority' seemed to him to cover 'things such as medical services, or library facilities, which can be directly provided . . .'

There is nothing in subsection (2) to suggest that it is designed to place any restrictions on the meaning of 'facilities or services' in subsection (1), which, as we have seen, prima facie bears its ordinary meaning. If this is wrong, however, it does not seem likely that the restriction is the one which Lord Fraser suggested. There is no implication in any of the examples that 'facility' to which they refer need to be a 'directly provided' (active) facility. Indeed, the action of an Entry Clearance Officer is *precisely* that of facilitating 'access to and use of' a place.

Moreover, an 'active facility' cannot be anything other than a 'service,' so that Lord Fraser's view entails that the word 'facility' in subsection (1) is redundant . . .

Lord Fraser also approved the distinction drawn by Templeman L.J. in *Savjani*, between 'services' and 'duties.'

. . . the more plausible basis for *Savjani* is the distinction between benefits and detriments. In some respects the Entry Clearance Officer in *Amin* does seem to belong to the same category as a tax collector: for it was a decision *not* to grant a special voucher that was challenged, a decision which appears detrimental. To this degree the distinction between 'controlling' immigrants and 'providing a service for' them does have some attraction.

It is probably true to say that a *decision not to grant* a special voucher is not a 'facility or service' within the ordinary meaning of those words. On the other hand, this does not mean that an Entry Clearance Officer does not, or did not in *Amin*, 'provide . . . facilities or services' to would-be immigrants. Both the [SDA] and the [RRA] are concerned with 'what [someone] does, in the course of which [he] discriminates.' What the Entry Clearance Officer in Bombay did, in the course of which he discriminated against Mrs Amin, was to *consider her application* for a special voucher. The activity of considering applications is not detrimental, but is a 'facility or service' within the ordinary meanings of those words. The Officer (whether acting out of duty to Parliament or otherwise) provides a 'facility' by entertaining applications for leave to settle, and a 'service' by considering the merits of such applications, Lord Fraser's second reason is thus misconceived. . . .

Quite apart from the absence of any express limitation on Crown liability, example (g) of subsection (2) makes Lord Fraser's restriction appear extremely implausible: 'the services of . . . any . . . public authority' clearly aims at encompassing more than just those 'services' which could also be provided by individuals.

However, even if it were plausible to claim that the [SDA] and the [RRA] only bind the Crown in respect of actions which are 'similar' to those of private persons, we need to provide a criterion of similarity. In some respects the process of considering an application for leave to settle is very similar to the process of considering whether to grant a gratuitous licence to another to reside on one's land. In other respects the process of considering whether to grant leave does seem peculiar to governments. Unless the criterion of similarity is spelled out, we cannot tell whether Lord Fraser is right to treat the grant of a clearance voucher as being a peculiarly governmental power. It is really only peculiarly governmental in the obvious sense in which all statutory powers of the Crown are peculiarly governmental. So even if it were cogent as a general principle, Lord Fraser's third argument would not apply comfortably to the case of a refused special voucher. . . .

As long as the House of Lords' decision in *Amin* represents the law, the words 'facilities or services' in section 20 [RRA] do not bear their ordinary meanings.

More recently, in *Farah v Commissioner of Police of the Metropolis* the Court of Appeal considered the application of s.20 RRA to the police. The case arose from an incident in which the Applicant, who was Somali, was subject to a racial attack. When she sought assistance from the police she was arrested, detained, and charged with a number of offences of which she was eventually acquitted. She claimed that the police had deliberately omitted to provide her with services, or with services of a like quality or in like manner or on the like terms to those normally provided by the officers to other members of the public, under s.20 RRA. The police sought to strike her claim out as disclosing no cause of action, a tactic rejected both at first instance court and by the Court of Appeal:

Farah v Commissioner of the Police of the Metropolis [1998] QB 65

Hutchinson LJ (for the Court):

As a matter of construction, Mr Seabrook [for the Police Commissioner] submits, s 20 does not apply to police officers performing the duties of their office—they are not providing services. The acts alleged against them all entail the exercise of discretion and judgment. What they were engaged on, from the moment the 999 call was received, was the exercise of their powers of investigation, detection and the bringing of offenders to justice . . .

Mr Seabrook relies on the passage from Lord Fraser's speech cited above as authority that the relevant act must be similar to an act done by a private person—and certainly that is what Lord Fraser says, though it might be argued that his observations are obiter.

Mr Nicol, while not accepting that what Lord Fraser said is applicable to the present case, argues that the assistance and protection that the plaintiff sought from the police were similar to acts which might have been performed by a private person—for example a security firm—and that accordingly Lord Fraser's test is satisfied in this case . . .

my conclusion is that it is arguable that the limited service for which the plaintiff looked to the police comes within Lord Fraser's test. As to Mr Nicol's second submission, I agree that it is strained and I consider that the most that can be said is that section 75(3) shows that section 75(1) and (2) might easily apply to the police, not that they do so apply . . .

In my view Mr Nicol is correct when he argues that, prima facie, section 20 is wide enough to apply to at least some of the acts undertaken by police officers in the performance of the duties of their office. The crucial words—to be interpreted of course in the light of the examples given, but not on the basis that the examples are definitive of the circumstances to which the section can apply—are 'any person concerned with the provision (for payment or not) of . . . services to the public.'

I accept Mr Nicol's contention that these words are entirely apt to cover those parts of a police officer's duties involving assistance to or protection of members of the public. Mr Nicol emphasised that it is in regard to that aspect of the officers' duties that the claim in the present case is advanced; it is not suggested that pursuing and arresting or charging alleged criminals is the provision of a service. What is said is that the service sought by the plaintiff was that of protection and that she did not, because of her race, obtain the protection that others would have been afforded. It seems to me that that is no less the provision of a service than is the giving of directions or other information to a member of the public who seeks them.

Turning to the examples in subsection (2) I find nothing expressly or impliedly to exclude police officers; and in my view they can properly be regarded as falling within paragraph (g)—'the services of any profession or trade, or any local or other public authority.'

Furthermore, I find in Savjani's case support for the conclusion that the police, in some aspects of their activities, fall within the Act. The passage in Templeman LJ's judgment approved in *ex parte Amin* shows that there is no reason why a person performing a public duty may not also be providing a service, and strongly supports the plaintiff's arguments. The first paragraph of his judgment helpfully states and contrasts some of the conflicting policy considerations and emphasises the necessity, notwithstanding those matters, to construe the Act. The last of the paragraphs I have cited from his judgment could easily be adapted to pose an example in as stark terms but concerning a member of the public and police officers.

The s.20 aspect of the *Farah* decision was favourable to the plaintiff in the instant case,[102] but fell far short of declaring that the provisions of the RRA applied to all aspects of policing.[103] Further, the Court of Appeal also ruled in *Farah* that the Commissioner was not vicariously liable for the discriminatory actions of police officers. This ruling was particularly controversial given its coincidence in time with the public unrest which followed the bungled investigation into the Stephen Lawrence case. We shall see, below, that the implementation of the RR(A)A removed the effect of *Amin* and *Kassam* in the context

[102] See also *Conwell v Newham* [2000] ICR 42 in which EAT (*per* Charles J) ruled that the provision of care to children by a local authority came within s.20—this with the result that a worker victimised for protesting the authority's refusal, on racial grounds, to let a black child holiday with a white family fell within the RRA.

[103] See, more recently, *Brooks v Commissioner of Police of the Metropolis* [2002] EWCA Civ 407 (26th March 2002) in which, in a race discrimination claim brought by Stephen Lawrence's companion on the night of his death against the police, the Court of Appeal accepted a concession to the effect that investigatory services requested of the police by a member of the public could fall within s.20 RRA.

of race. The DDA 2005 makes similar amendments to the DDA. And in Northern Ireland the NIA provides (s.76(1)) that 'It shall be unlawful for a public authority carrying out functions relating to Northern Ireland to discriminate, or to aid or incite another person to discriminate, against a person or class of person on the ground of religious belief or political opinion.' The Equality Bill 2005, whose passage was frustrated by the announcement of the May 2005 general election, proposes similar amendments to the SDA.

Further difficulties arise in relation to the application of the anti-discrimination legislation in connection with social security. The RRA specifically prohibits discrimination on grounds of race or ethnic or national origin in this context, this as a result of amendment to implement the provisions of the Racial Equality Directive. The application of that Act to social security will be considered briefly below. But the decision in *Amin* served to exclude from the reach of ss.29 SDA and its equivalents most social security related decisions.[104]

Sex discrimination in social security and related areas is far from uncommon and, although the SDA itself provides very limited tools for challenges to it, the position in relation to sex discrimination has always been complicated as a result of EU law, in particular, by Council Directive 79/7/EEC on the progressive implementation of equal treatment in social security schemes relating to sickness, invalidity, old age, accident and unemployment. This Directive is less radical than Article 141 (discussed in Chapter 6) which prohibits virtually all discrimination on grounds of sex in relation to 'pay' including occupational pension schemes. It does, however, provide that:

4(1). The principle of equal treatment means that there shall be no discrimination whatsoever on ground of sex either directly, or indirectly by reference in particular to marital or family status, in particular as concerns:
— the scope of the schemes and the conditions of access thereto,
— the obligation to contribute and the calculation of contributions,
— the calculation of benefits including increases due in respect of a spouse and for dependants and the conditions governing the duration and retention of entitlement to benefits.
4(2). The principle of equal treatment shall be without prejudice to the provisions relating to the protection of women on the grounds of maternity.

The Directive does not prohibit all sex discrimination in the context of social security:

7(1). This Directive shall be without prejudice to the right of Member States to exclude from its scope:
(a) the determination of personable age for the purposes of granting old-age and retirement pensions and the possible consequences thereof for other benefits;
(b) advantages in respect of old-age pension schemes granted to persons who have brought up children; the acquisition of benefit entitlements following periods of interruption of employment due to the bringing up of children;
(c) the granting of old-age or invalidity benefit entitlements by accidents at work and occupational disease benefits for a dependent wife;
(d) the consequences of the exercise, before the adoption of this Directive, of a right of option not to acquire rights or incur obligations under a statutory scheme.

---

[104] And social security is in any event beyond the scope of the RB and SO Regs which deal only with employment-related discrimination.

E Collins and E Meehan, 'Women's Rights in Employment' in C McCrudden and G Chambers (eds), *Individual Rights and the Law in Britain* (Oxford, Clarendon, 1994) 383–8, footnotes omitted

The social security system was not affected by the introduction of the equal pay and sex discrimination legislation in 1975, although changes were introduced in both the Social Security Act and the Social Security Pensions Act of 1975 to provide for equal treatment in some areas, such as the right to unemployment benefit and sickness pay for married women on the same basis as men. The same legislation, however, also introduced new discriminatory elements into the system, such as invalid care allowance and the non-contributory invalidity pension, for which married and cohabiting women were ineligible. A 'housewives' version' of the non-contributory invalidity pension was introduced in 1977, giving these women an entitlement to the pension if they could prove that they were incapable of carrying out normal household duties, a test which did not apply to the general invalidity pension.

In general terms, however, the main changes which have been introduced since the 1970s have been as a result of Community directives applying the principle of equal treatment to both statutory and occupational social security schemes. The former, adopted in 1979, aimed to ensure the application of the principle of equal treatment to statutory social security schemes, and member states were obliged to implement any necessary changes by 23 December 1984. The Directive is designed primarily to cover the main employment-related risks, such as sickness, invalidity, old age, accidents at work, and unemployment, and it applies to the 'working population' which is defined to cover those in work and seeking work, as well as those whose employment is interrupted by accident, sickness, or involuntary unemployment.

A series of changes was implemented from the end of 1983 to bring the United Kingdom into compliance with the provisions of the Directive. This included changes to the discriminatory rules relating to adult and child dependency additions, for which a variety of approaches was adopted, involving both levelling up (extending benefit to previously excluded groups) and levelling down (taking benefits away from previously included groups). The rules regarding eligibility for supplementary benefit were amended at this time, to allow married and cohabiting women to claim for the first time—but only if they could establish themselves as the 'breadwinner' rather than a 'dependant,' a concept which has remained problematic for women under social security rules. Changes were also made to family income supplement and the non-contributory invalidity pension and its housewives' equivalent were repealed. Invalid care allowance was not repealed at this time, however, and it was not until the judgment of the European Court in the *Drake* case [Case C–150/85 [1986] ECR 01995], which challenged the allowance, was pending that the Government took steps to provide the entitlement on the same basis as men and single women to married and cohabiting women.

Despite these changes, there has been a significant amount of litigation about the scope of European obligations since the Directive came into force. For example, the European Court ruled in *Johnson v Chief Adjudication Officer* [Case C–31/90 [1991] ECR I–3723], a case concerning eligibility for severe disablement allowance, the successor to non-contributory invalidity pension, that the personal scope of Article 2 of Directive 79/7 does not apply to a person who had interrupted her occupational activity for child-caring purposes and who is prevented from returning to work because of illness *unless* the person was seeking employment and her search was interrupted by the onset of one of the risks set out in Article 3 of the Directive, the reason for previously leaving employment being irrelevant. It also held that the Directive could be relied on to set aside national legislation which makes entitlement to a benefit subject to rules for eligibility to a preceding benefit which contained discriminatory conditions. In the absence of appropriate measures implementing

Article 4 of the Directive, women placed at a disadvantage by the maintenance of discriminatory conditions are entitled to be treated in the same manner as men.

Questions concerning the requirement on a man to pay national insurance contributions for five years longer than women in order to be entitled to the same basic pension and the requirement that, should a man continue to work between the ages of 60 and 65, he still has to pay national insurance contributions when women over 60 years of age do not, whether they are working or not, were also considered by the European Court in a case in the name of the Equal Opportunities Commission. The Court ruled in 1992, that the United Kingdom is not in breach of Directive 79/7 by imposing this requirement. Cases concerning eligibility for supplementary benefit and income support were also decided by the European Court in 1992. It held that Directive 79/7 does not apply to such benefits.

National courts themselves of course have to apply the provisions of the Directive and, in respect of social security, a 1990 judgment of the Court of Appeal augurs well. In *Thomas v Adjudication Officer and Secretary of State for Social Security* [Case C–328/91 [1993] ECR I–01247], it held that the female claimants, who were over 60 years of age, were entitled to rely on the 1979 Directive to claim severe disablement allowance or invalid care allowance, despite the fact that these benefits were restricted to those under the state retirement age. The Court held that the Secretary of State had failed to prove that the restriction properly fell within the scope of the exclusion in the Directive relating to the determination of pensionable age for the purposes of old-age and retirement pensions and the possible consequences thereof for other benefits. The House of Lords referred questions arising from this case to the European Court in November 1991.

Much of the case law under Council Directive 79/76/EEC is concerned with whether particular public sector pension schemes fall within its scope or within the scope of Article 141.[105] But in joined cases C–377/96—C–384/96, *De Vrient v Rijksdienst voor Pensionenen* [1998] ECR I–2105 the ECJ ruled that the derogation permitted by Article 7 applied only in respect of matters 'necessarily and objectively related to the difference in pensionable age.' If a Member State abolished discriminatory retirement ages, it could not retain differential methods of calculating pensions by reference to the earlier, discriminatory pensionable ages. In *Taylor v Secretary of State for Social Security* Case C–382/98 [1999] ECR I–08955 the Court ruled that the Directive was breached by the UK's restriction of winter fuel payment to those of pensionable age—ie, to women of 60, men of 65. Ruling that the benefit was 'directly and effectively linked to . . . the risk of old age' (this on the grounds that it was payable even to elderly people 'without financial or material difficulties'), the ECJ rejected the argument put forward by the UK that the aim of the payment was to protect against a lack of financial means. On this ground, and on the ground that 'if the benefit is designed to provide protection against the risk of old age . . . it does not follow that the [qualifying age for receipt] . . . must necessarily coincide with the statutory age of retirement,' the ECJ ruled that differential access to the benefit breached the directive and was not saved by the derogation permitted by Article 7. In *Hepple v Adjudication Officer* Case C–196/98 [2000] ECR I–03701, on the other hand, the ECJ ruled that a reduced earnings allowance which discriminated between men and women in relation to age conditions did fall within Article 7's derogation because 'the allowance is designed to compensate for a decrease in income from work [and] there is a coherence between that scheme and the

[105] See recently *Schönheit v Stadt Frankfurt am Main* Case C–4/02 [2003] ECR I–0000, OJ C 304, 13.12.2003, p. 6, joined with *Becker v Land Hessen* Case C–5/02; *Neimi* Case 351/00 [2002] ECR I–07007; and *Mouflin v Recteur de l'Academie de Reims* Case C–206/00 [2002] ECR I–10201.

old-age pension scheme and, accordingly, such discrimination is objectively and necessarily linked to the difference between the retirement age for men and that for women.'[106]

Of greater significance both in relation to sex and to other forms of discrimination in social security is the European Convention on Human Rights, especially after the implementation in the UK of the Human Rights Act 1998. Discrimination on a variety of grounds in connection with social security may breach Article 14 of the Convention read either with Article 8 (which concerns family life) or Article 1 of Protocol 1 to the Convention (which concerns property). Litigation in this field has been relatively rare until recently, but an increasing willingness on the part of the ECtHR to apply Article 1 of Protocol 1 to social security payments, coupled with the partial implementation of the Convention in domestic law by the HRA, has resulted in a recent wave of litigation. This litigation is outside the scope of this text book but the relevance of the HRA and the Convention in this context ought not to be overlooked.[107]

Miscellaneous Other Exceptions

Section 34 SDA allows non-statutory, non-profit making bodies to restrict membership wholly or mainly to one sex, and the provision of benefits, facilities or services to members of such bodies. Section 35 also allows the provision of single-sex facilities or services in hospitals and 'other establishment[s] for persons requiring special care, supervision or attention'; in sex-segregated places 'occupied or used for the purposes of an organised religion [where] the facilities or service are restricted to men so as to comply with the doctrines of that religion or avoid offending the religious susceptibilities of a significant number of its followers'; and in circumstances where:

(c) the facilities or services are provided for, or are likely to be used by, two or more persons at the same time, and
   (i) the facilities or services are such, or those persons are such, that male users are likely to suffer serious embarrassment at the presence of a woman, or
   (ii) the facilities or service are such that a user is likely to be in a state of undress and a male user might reasonably object to the presence of a female user.
(2) A person who provides facilities or services restricted to men does not for that reason contravene section 29(1) if the services or facilities are such that physical contact between the user and any other person is likely, and that other person might reasonably object if the user were a woman.

Like the other provisions of the SDA, 'woman' and 'male' here include 'man' and 'female' respectively. S.29(3) SDA further provides that:

For the avoidance of doubt it is hereby declared that where a particular skill is commonly exercised in a different way for men and for women it does not contravene subsection (1) for a person who does not normally exercise it for women to insist on exercising it for a woman only in accordance with his normal practice or, if he reasonably considers it impracticable to do that in her case, to refuse or deliberately omit to exercise it.

---

[106] See also *Haackert v Pensionsversicherungsanstaldt der Angestellten* Case C–303/02 [2004] ECR I–00000, OJ C 94, 17.04.2004, p. 8.

[107] See, for example, the recent decisions of the Court of Appeal in *R (on the application of Hooper v Secretary of State for Work & Pensions* [2003] 1 WLR 2623. An appeal from the decision of the CA was heard by the HL in March 2005.

Section 46 SDA permits discrimination in admission to communal accommodation and associated benefits, as long as the treatment of each sex is 'fair and equitable.' This provision, unsurprisingly, has no equivalent in the RRA. Section 43 SDA permits charitable instruments to confer benefits (disregarding exceptional or insignificant benefit) entirely on persons of one sex, ss.78 and 79 providing for the alteration of such instruments connected with education. And s.44 SDA provides that the Act shall not:

> In relation to any sport, game or other activity of a competitive nature where the physical strength, stamina or physique of the average woman puts her at a disadvantage to the average man, render unlawful any act related to the participation of a person as a competitor in events involving that activity which are confined to competitors of one sex.

This exception does not permit all sex discrimination in sport. In April 1998, Jane Couch won a tribunal case brought against the British Boxing Board of Control over that body's refusal to grant her a boxing licence. The board sought to defend its decision on the grounds that:

The Times, 28 April 1998

> ... women were more prone to accidents than men because of pre-menstrual tension; they were more susceptible to bruising and therefore to brain damage; and monthly hormonal changes resulted in fluid retention and weight gain, making weight categorisation harder ... [the] tribunal ... held that the decision was prompted solely by 'gender-based stereotypes and assumptions' ... Ms Couch was never examined by a board doctor, and that there was no evidence that 'boxing poses a higher risk to women than to men or vice versa.' In a damning decision, it criticised the board for not obtaining any medical evidence about Ms Couch ... 'No male boxer would have been rejected on medical grounds without having had a medical investigation.'

Section 23(2) RRA provides that s.20(1) of that Act 'does not apply to anything done by a person as a participant in arrangements under which he (for reward or not) takes into his home, and treats as if they were members of his family, children, elderly persons, or persons requiring a special degree of care and attention.' This provision was considered by EAT in *Conwell* in which that Court ruled that s.23(2) did not provide a defence to the local authority in respect of its discrimination against a child for which it had parental responsibility—the authority did not have a 'family' or a 'home' within s.23(2) RRA and so s.20 was not excluded in the circumstances of the case.

Section 26 RRA provides an exception from s.25 (see above) for associations whose 'main object . . . is to enable the benefits of membership (whatever they may be) to be enjoyed by persons of a particular racial group defined otherwise than by reference to colour.' It is this exception which is reflected in the proposed non-application of the various legislative provisions which would extend the application of s.29 SDA to private clubs to single-sex clubs.

Section 34 RRA permits some discrimination by charitable instruments. Any provision in such an instrument:

> (1) ... which provides for conferring benefits on persons of a class defined by reference to colour shall have effect for all purposes as if it provided for conferring the like benefits—
>   (a) on persons of the class which results if the restriction by reference to colour is disregarded; or
> where the original class is defined by reference to colour only, on persons generally.

But s.34(2) provides that the RRA shall not otherwise affect any charitable instrument, or any act to give effect to such an instrument, 'which provides for conferring benefits on persons of a class defined otherwise than by reference to colour,' unless the act is unlawful as employment-related discrimination on grounds of race or ethnic or national origins.

Section 39 RRA permits discrimination on grounds of nationality, birthplace or length of residence in the selection of persons to represent areas, places or countries in any sport, or in competition rules regarding eligibility. Section 35 RRA, which concerns access to facilities or services to meet the special needs of persons of a particular racial group 'in regard to their education, training or welfare, or any ancillary benefits,' has been mentioned above in the context of education.

The DDA permits discrimination in this context where it is 'justifiable'—see further Chapter 8. It also, with the Disability Discrimination (Services and Premises) Regulations 1996[108] contains special rules dealing with insurance, guarantees and deposits. The rules relating to insurance have been considered above. The Regs also provide that, where a disabled person's disability results in heavier than average wear and tear, the guarantor may (reg 5) refuse to honour the guarantee where this is reasonable in all the circumstances of the case. The DRC's Code of Practice gives an example of a person with a mobility impairment who wears out the left shoe of a pair after a few months because his left foot has to bear most of his weight. The Regs further permit (reg 6) discrimination by way of a refusal to return a deposit (or to return it in full) where damage has been sustained to goods borrowed or hired for a reason connected with a customer's disability. Such less favourable treatment 'shall be taken to be justified' when 'it is reasonable in all the circumstances of the case for the provider to refuse to refund the deposit in full'. The Code goes on to state that the service provider is not permitted to discriminate by treating a disabled person less favourably than others in relation to the amount of the deposit charged, or buy charging him or her a deposit in circumstances where this amounts to less favourable treatment (para 8.17). Nor (para 8.18) is the service provider entitled to penalise a disabled person for damage at a level at which the deposit would normally be returned in full.

Discrimination by Public Authorities

The CRE's 1998 *Annual Report* began with the words:

> In years to come 1998 will be seen as a watershed for race relations in Britain. No one will ever forget that it was the year of the MacPherson Inquiry into the racist murder of the black teenager, Stephen Lawrence.[109]

The report, which concluded that: 'institutional racism . . . exists both in the Metropolitan Police Service and in other Police Services and other institutions countrywide',[110] recommended that:

> the full force of the Race Relations legislation should apply to all police officers, and that Chief Officers of Police should be made vicariously liable for the acts and omissions of their officers relevant to that legislation.

[108] In Northern Ireland see the Disability Discrimination (Services and Premises) Regulations (Northern Ireland) 1996 Statutory Rule 1996 No.557.
[109] P.3, available from www.cre.gov.uk.
[110] Report of an Inquiry by Sir William MacPherson of Cluny, February 1999 Cm 4262–I, para 6.39.

'Institutional racism' was defined by the MacPherson report, as:

> The collective failure of an organisation to provide an appropriate and professional service to people because of their colour, culture, or ethnic origin. It can be seen or detected in processes, attitudes and behaviour which amount to discrimination through unwitting prejudice, ignorance, thoughtlessness and racist stereotyping which disadvantage minority ethnic people.
>
> It persists because of the failure of the organisation openly and adequately to recognise and address its existence and causes by policy, example and leadership. Without recognition and action to eliminate such racism it can prevail as part of the ethos or culture of the organisation. It is a corrosive disease.

Almost twenty years before, Lord Scarman's inquiry into the Brixton riot contained the following passage:

> If by [institutionally racist] it is meant that [Britain] is a society which knowingly, as a matter of policy, discriminates against black people, I reject that allegation. If, however, the suggestion being made is that practices may be adopted by public bodies as well as private individuals which are unwittingly discriminatory against black people, then this is an allegation which deserves serious consideration, and where proved, swift remedy.[111]

Publication of the MacPherson report led to a lemming-like rush on the part of all manner of institutions to declare themselves guilty of 'institutional racism,' apparently on the basis that this form of racism was rather less reprehensible than the raw version. In July 1999, the National Officer of the Fire Brigades Union 'acknowledged that the service suffered from the institutional racism that affected many public bodies, and had its share of 'bigoted, racist staff.'[112] In August, the firemaster of Lothian and Borders 'admitted . . . that his force was guilty of institutionalised racism under the definition set out in the MacPherson report' and reported that only two of 1000 firefighters were of ethnic minority background.[113] 'Institutional racism' has also been acknowledged within the NHS[114] and, as a problem for her union, by the General Secretary of the Royal College of Nursing.[115] And in June, Scotland's Lord Advocate accepted that there was 'institutional racism' within the Scottish criminal justice system.[116]

It is easy to be cynical about the rush to confess. But the focus on racism which has followed the MacPherson report has served to highlight the extent of the problem. In July, a letter to the *Glasgow Herald* pointed out that: '[d]espite consistent lobbying, the body politic has successfully manufactured an all-white Scottish Parliament. This defines [sic] structured and institutionalised racism and maybe cultural racism too . . . How was it possible to structure in (white) women to the Scottish Parliament and not parallel that action for black people?'[117] In the same month, an Asian woman barrister won her claim of 'insti-

---

[111] Cited by Baronness Howells, HL Debs 14th Dec 1999, col. 149.

[112] Press Association *Newsfile*, 28 July 1999.

[113] *Guardian*, 10 August 1999.

[114] Director of Nursing Nottingham Healthcare Trust, *Nottingham Evening Post*, 10 July 1999.

[115] *Guardian*, 12 March 1999.

[116] *Daily Record*, 16 June 1999. The newspaper reports that the same Lord Hardie had castigated as 'uninformed and ill-advised' a trial judge's anger that only one of three men arrested in respect of the racist murder of Surjit Chhokar ('Scotland's Stephen Lawrence') faced trial—he was convicted only of assault. The Press Association *Newsfile* 28 July 1999 reports that targets have been set also for the fire service and for Home Office civil service staff.

[117] July 28, letter from Andrew Johnson, Director, Equality and Discrimination Centre, University of Strathclyde.

tutional racism' against the CPS—she had been denied promotion for 12 years.[118] In March 1999, Ofsted had accused 'virtually all schools' of the same failing.[119] Defining as 'institutional racism,' the 'collective failure of an organisation to provide an appropriate and professional service to people because of their colour, culture or ethnic origin . . . It could be detected in processes, attitudes and behaviour that amounted to discrimination through "unwitting prejudice" that disadvantaged ethnic minority people,' the chief inspector of secondary schools, Jim Rose, stated that 'the poor performance of black pupils, the fact that they often achieved more than their teachers expected and the disproportionate number who were excluded from school' made it 'difficult . . . to imagine a school not being guilty of "institutional racism." '[120]

The Government's response to the apparently newly discovered problem of 'institutional racism' came in the form of the Race Relations (Amendment) Act 2000. The original version of the Bill proposed only to outlaw *direct* discrimination by public authorities (this on the rather specious reasoning that a prohibition on indirect race discrimination 'would have uncertain and potentially far-reaching effects on the Government's ability to make policy').[121] But the Government was eventually shamed by Lord Lester and others into including indirect discrimination (which had accounted for most of the 'institutional racism' identified by the MacPherson report). The Government's preferred option for dealing with indirect discrimination by public authorities (save that which fell within s.20 RRA and equivalent provisions) lay in the imposition of an obligation on such authorities to promote equality.[122] This obligation is discussed in Chapter 3. But the weight of pressure caused a rethink between the second reading and the report stage in the House of Lords, the Bill being amended to prohibit indirect discrimination.[123] The result of this is to fill the gap left by the *Amin* decision in the RRA. More recently, s.19B has been amended to comply with the Racial Equality Directive whose provisions (alone of the EU directives) extend to 'social protection, including social security and healthcare, social advantages; and education.'

Section 19B RRA, which applies only to discrimination not otherwise covered by the Act, provides:

(1) It is unlawful for a public authority in carrying out any functions of the authority to do any act which constitutes discrimination.

(1A) It is unlawful for a public authority to subject a person to harassment in the course of carrying out any functions of the authority which consist of the provision of—

(a) any form of social security;
(b) healthcare;
(c) any other form of social protection; or
(d) any form of social advantage,

which does not fall within section 20.

'Public authority' is defined (s.19B(2)–(4)) to include 'any person certain of whose functions are functions of a public nature,' though only in relation to those public functions, but to exclude 'either House of Parliament,' 'a person exercising functions in connection with

---

[118] *Daily Mail*, 10 June 1999.
[119] *Daily Telegraph*, 11 March 1999.
[120] *Ibid*. See more recently LDA Education Commission, 'Rampton Revisited, the Educational Experiences and Achievements of Black Boys in London Schools' (2004).
[121] Lord Bassam, for the Government: HL Debs Vol 608 14 Dec 1999, cols. 129–130.
[122] *Ibid*.
[123] Announcement by Jack Straw, 26th January 2000 (Home Office press release 012/2000).

proceedings in Parliament,' 'the Security Service,' 'the Secret Intelligence Service,' 'the Government Communications Headquarters,' and 'any unit or part of a unit of any of the naval, military or air forces of the Crown which is for the time being required by the Secretary of State to assist the Government Communications Headquarters in carrying out its functions.'

Section 19C and F RRA exempt from the scope of s.19B:

- judicial acts and 'acts done on the instructions, or on behalf, of a person acting in a judicial capacity,'
- 'act[s] of, or relating to, making, confirming or approving any enactment or Order in Council or any instrument made by a Minister of the Crown under an enactment';
- decisions not to institute/ continue criminal proceedings and related decisions and acts
- act[s] of, or relating to, imposing a requirement, or giving an express authorisation, of a kind permitted by the Act (s.19D) in relation to the carrying out of [immigration functions].

Section 19D RRA exempts discrimination 'on grounds of nationality or ethnic or national origins' in carrying out immigration functions by a minister of the Crown acting personally, or by any other person acting in accordance with an authorisation given 'with respect to a particular case or class of case,' by a minister of the Crown acting personally or, 'with respect to a particular class of case' by the Immigration Acts, the Special Immigration Appeals Commission Act 1997, provision made under s.2(2) of the European Communities Act 1972 (c 68) which relates to immigration or asylum, or any provision of Community law which relates to immigration or asylum, or by any instrument made under or by virtue of any of those enactments.

Section 19D generated controversy during the passage of the RR(A)A, Lord Lester declaring that:

Unlike discrimination on grounds of nationality or place of residence, discrimination based on ethnic or national origins is as much racial discrimination as is discrimination based on colour or race, as the definition of racial discrimination in Article 1 of the United Nations Convention on the Elimination of All Forms of Discrimination 1966 makes crystal clear. Such discrimination involves treating one individual less favourably than another for what is not chosen by them but for what is innate in them at birth—their genetic inheritance— whether as ethnic Jews, Roma gypsies or Hong Kong Indians. It is as invidious and unfair as is discrimination based on the colour of a person's skin . . .

The sweepingly broad exception in Section 19[D] is incompatible with the very principle of non-discrimination which the legislation is intended to secure. If the Home Office wishes to make special arrangements aimed at providing protection to particular groups seeking shelter in the United Kingdom, such as the Bosnians and Kosovars who were granted exceptional leave to remain during the recent crisis in the Balkans, it is difficult to understand how that would require an exception. The reason for affording favourable treatment to some of those groups is surely not their ethnic or national origins but their well-founded fear of persecution, the urgency of their humanitarian needs and the need to comply with the UK's obligations under the refugee convention. The policy is not based upon or caused by their ethnicity. It does not involve discriminating against anyone on the grounds of their ethnic or national origins . . . Even if it were appropriate, for the avoidance of doubt, to include an exception to cover situations of that kind, the exception to the fundamental right to equal treatment without discrimination would need to be prescribed in legislation in a way carefully tailored to what is necessary to give effect to the Government's legitimate aims, with adequate judicial safeguards against the abuse of this extraordinary power, to ensure that the doing of a discriminatory act is justified by its purpose, as with national security.

The functions covered by s.19[D] include decisions to deport, exclusion directions, leave to enter or remain, the grant of asylum, exceptional leave to remain, and even naturalisation as a British citizen. Section 44 of the British Nationality Act 1981 provides that any discretion vested by that Act in the Secretary of State, a governor or lieutenant governor, must be exercised, 'without regard to the race, colour or religion of any person who may be affected by its exercise.'

Yet Section 19[D] would allow the discretion to be exercised on the basis of ethnic or national origins which are part of the international legal definition of what constitutes 'racial discrimination.'

As it stands, Section 19[D] authorises breaches by a future populist illiberal Home Secretary, or by a prejudiced administration, of the various international human rights conventions by which the UK is bound: notably, Articles 2, 5 and 6 of the Convention on the Elimination of Racial Discrimination and Articles 2 and 26 of the International Covenant on Civil and Political Rights . . .

In 1975 the previous Labour government's White Paper, *Racial Discrimination*, observed that legislation was the essential pre-condition for an effective policy to combat discrimination and promote equality of opportunity and treatment. I quote that White Paper:

Where unfair discrimination is involved, the necessity of a legal remedy is universally accepted. To fail to provide a remedy against an injustice strikes at the rule of law. To abandon a whole group of people in society without legal redress against unfair discrimination is to leave them with no option but to find their own redress. It is no longer necessary to recite the immense damage, material as well as moral, which ensues when a minority loses faith in the capacity of social institutions to be impartial and fair.[124]

Lord Bassam, for the Government, sought to justify s.19D (as it became) on the basis (Col 131) that:

The existing safeguards in the Race Relations Act for covering acts of discrimination done in pursuance to other statutory provisions are insufficient to allow the immigration system to continue to operate as it should. If consequential provisions were not made. Ministers would, for example, be unable to authorise special compassionate exercises where necessary for particular ethnic or national groups and immigration staff would be unable to exercise the operational discretion necessary to carry out their duties in accordance with ministerial instructions. That is why the Bill provides in new Section 19[D] that acts of discrimination by immigration staff will not be unlawful if such acts are required or authorised by specified immigration and nationality laws, or expressly authorised by ministers who of course are themselves accountable to Parliament.

Overall, therefore, it will be unlawful for immigration staff to discriminate on the grounds of race or colour, or, in the case of nationality and ethnic and national origins, where they go beyond what is specified in immigration and nationality laws or what is expressly authorised by ministers. The personal decisions of ministers in individual immigration and asylum cases will also be exempt, as such decisions may make legitimate distinctions on the grounds of nationality not covered by existing approved arrangements.

---

[124] Fn 121 above, Cols 144–146.

And Parliamentary Under-Secretary of State for the Home Office, Mr Mike O' Brien, made the following statement in the House of Commons:

> . . . (the Member for Leyton and Wanstead) . . . asks whether junior civil servants have the ability to take unto themselves the exemption. The answer is no: a junior civil servant has no ability to say, 'I have decided that, in that case, such a course of action is no longer discriminatory,' nor does a senior civil servant, or the chief immigration officer. Immigration officers will operate under the guidance issued by ministers, which is, by and large, in the public arena. My hon. Friend will be able to ascertain the criteria by which such decisions are made and the way in which they are reached.
>
> In no sense does the Bill create an exemption that gives a civil servant broad discretion to discriminate. Civil servants will be able to discriminate properly and lawfully only when there is a clear instruction from the Minister to do so in specific circumstances, and those circumstances are mainly in the public arena. . . . We do not accept that any official is entitled to discriminate in a way that is unacceptable to the Government.[125]

Notwithstanding these assurances, the first ministerial authorisation for discrimination in grounds of national or ethnic origins (which came into force on 2 April 2001) provided that immigration officers could discriminate, on grounds of nationality, in a variety of immigration-related decisions on grounds of nationality where either 'there is statistical evidence showing a pattern or trend of breach of the immigration laws by persons of that nationality' or 'there is specific intelligence or information which has been received and processed in accordance with the [Immigration and Nationality Directorate's] Code of Practice for the recording and dissemination of intelligence material and which suggests that a significant number of persons of that nationality have breached or will attempt to breach the immigration laws.'

In the *Tamil Information Centre* case Forbes J allowed an application for judicial review of this authorisation, ruling that the Secretary of State was empowered under s.19D RRA only himself to list those groups against which discrimination on grounds of national or ethnic origin was acceptable, rather than (as he had done here) to delegate the decision-making power to immigration officers with what was described as guidance which was 'wholly uncertain in meaning and unclear on its face, because it is not possible to say from its terms how and/or when either condition is or will be satisfied.'

R (Tamil Information Centre) v Secretary of State for the Home Department [2002] EWHC 2155 Admin

Forbes J:

It was . . . Mr Allen's submission [for the Applicants] that, in order to constitute a valid 'relevant authorisation' within the meaning of section 19D(3)(a) of the 1976 Act, the purported 'licence to discriminate' must satisfy the following conditions:

> (i) the authorisation in question must be given by the Minister, acting personally; and
> (ii) it must be clear from the terms of the authorisation in question what act or acts in respect of what case or class of case are rendered lawful, despite constituting discrimination against another person on the grounds of nationality or ethnic or national origins.

. . . Mr Allen submitted (correctly, in my view) that, although the general nature of the material and/or intelligence considered to be relevant [under the Authorisation] is referred

---

[125] HC Debs, 30 October 2000, col 542.

to in Mr Woodhouse's evidence . . . there is nothing in that evidence which gives any indication as to the appropriate threshold or standard (if any) that has to be met before either of the conditions is satisfied and the discrimination in question. . . made permissible.

Mr Allen pointed out that . . . the first Authorisation did not actually specify who is to determine the trend or evaluate the relevant evidence/information, to which reference is made in the conditions, for the purposes of deciding whether, in any particular case or class of case, either of the . . . conditions has been satisfied, except to the extent that there is no suggestion that this important aspect of the matter is to be decided by the Secretary of State. Mr Allen emphasised that it was not any part of the Secretary of State's case that he was the person who has to make that decision—a decision of fundamental importance, because it is that decision that triggers the Authorisation and thus makes the discrimination in question permissible. In this regard, Mr Allen also pointed out that. . . the Secretary of State has '*delegated the assessment of the statistical evidence or intelligence of breaches of the immigration laws to officials.*'

Mr Allen pointed out that, in order to bring the relevant act or acts of discrimination within the scope of the first Authorisation, it is necessary to decide whether one or other of the conditions in paragraph 6 has been satisfied, because only then are the various acts of discrimination set out in paragraphs 3, 4 and 5 of the Authorisation duly authorised. Mr Allen submitted that . . . in practice this will be done by an immigration officer making an assessment of the statistical evidence and/or intelligence material and deciding whether, in respect of persons of a particular nationality, one or other of the conditions specified . . . is, in fact, satisfied.

Mr Allen suggested (correctly, in my view) that this necessarily means that the effective decision to authorise discriminatory acts in respect of persons of a particular nationality will actually be made by a person other than the minister, albeit that such a person will make that judgment within the limits of the Secretary of State's broadly defined criteria. Mr Allen submitted that such must be the case, because it will be the immigration official who actually decides whether either of the . . . conditions has been satisfied in respect of persons of a particular nationality and, most importantly, he will do so by applying to the evidence and/or information such standard and/or threshold as he considers to be appropriate in the circumstances of the case and not by reference to any standard or threshold that is defined and/or specified in [the authorisation] (and, thus, specified by the minister). In my opinion, that submission is correct.

Mr Allen therefore suggested that the effect of the first Authorisation is to give authority to persons other than the Minister to set and apply the standards and/or the threshold for compliance with the . . . conditions and thus to empower them to decide whether the discrimination in respect of persons of a particular nationality comes within . . . the first Authorisation. Mr Allen submitted that, when analysed in this way, it can be seen . . . the first Authorisation, in effect, involves an impermissible delegation of the Secretary of State's power to authorise when discriminatory acts will be lawful, and is therefore ultra vires and invalid . . .

I have come to the firm conclusion that Mr Allen's submissions on this aspect of the matter are correct. . . . In the present case, as it seems to me, although he has given some widely defined criteria for the identification of appropriate cases or classes of case, the Secretary of State has delegated the essential task of actually identifying and defining any such case or class of case entirely to the decision-making of immigration officials and, what is more, by reference to their standards and/or thresholds rather than his own. In my view, this approach is clearly ultra vires section 19D of the 1976 Act, as amended. I agree with Mr Allen that a licence to discriminate, such as that envisaged by section 19D, can be expected to be subject to strict control and that, in the present case, Parliament has made it clear by the express terms of the section that the necessary control is to be by the democratic process, namely by every essential aspect of the power being clearly exercised personally by a minister accountable to Parliament.

The *Roma* case, discussed in Chapter 2, involved a claim under s.19B RRA in respect of discrimination by a public authority (there the immigration officers at Prague airport). The Secretary of State had in fact issued a ministerial authorisation under s.19B RRA which provided for discrimination on grounds of ethnic or national origin against listed groups, the groups including Roma, but the case was decided on the basis that the Authorisation had not been used and was not relied upon by the Government. It was revoked in June 2002.

The limited application of the SDA to social security was mentioned above. We have seen, however, that the impact of the decision in *Amin* has been removed from the RRA and that s.41(1A) disapplies the exclusion from the Act of discrimination done under statutory authority (see above) 'to an act which is unlawful, on grounds of race or ethnic or national origins, by virtue of a provision referred to in section 1(1B).' Section 1(1B) lists employment (widely defined); education, ss.20–24 (goods and services, etc), and section 19B, so far as it relates to 'any form of social security, health care; any other form of social protection; and any form of social advantage' which does not fall within s.20. Thus, discrimination on grounds of race or ethnic or national origin in relation to social security and similar matters, like most other instances of discrimination on these grounds, is caught by the provisions of the RRA.

Overt discrimination in the area of social security on grounds of ethnic, national or racial origins is likely to be unusual (though it is possible that indirect discrimination might result from the application of rules relating to family composition, etc, and its impact on entitlement to payment. Equally, while overt discrimination is unlikely in healthcare, rationing of treatment for conditions experiences unevenly by different racial groups could now be challenged under the amended RRA. To the extent that such discrimination would have been actionable under the RRA prior to 2000 (ie, to the extent that it falls within s.20 as applied by the House of Lords in *Amin*), it must be challenged under s.20. To the extent that it falls outwith this provision but is, nevertheless, discrimination by a public authority, it can be challenged under s.19 RRA.

The prohibition of discrimination on grounds of race or ethnic or national origin (albeit not colour or nationality) in this context is to be welcomed. Given the difficulties of proof associated with proving discrimination (in particular, indirect discrimination) it is likely that, in the long term, the imposition by the RRA on public authorities of positive obligations to promote race equality is likely to have more profound effects in areas such as health and social care.

The RRA is alone at present in prohibiting discrimination by public authorities other than as it falls within the employment, goods and services, housing, etc, provisions of the anti-discrimination regimes. But the DDA 2005 inserts new ss.21B to 21D into the DDA which broadly reflects the RRA as it applies to discrimination by public authorities not otherwise covered by the Act. The provisions extend to a duty to make reasonable adjustments (this where a 'practice, policy or procedure' makes it 'impossible or unreasonably difficult' for the disabled person to receive a benefit or to be subjected to any detriment) as well as regulating 'less favourable treatment' of disabled persons by public authorities. 'Public authorities' are defined as in the HRA 1998 and new s.21B(5) provides that 'Regulations may provide for a person of a prescribed description to be treated as not being a public authority' in this context. The Equality Bill 2005 proposes the insertion of new s.21A SDA which would prohibit sex discrimination by public authorities in similar terms to s.19 RRA.

5

Enforcement

Introduction

The approach adopted by domestic discrimination legislation is, for the most part, a highly individualistic one. Consideration of 'group' characteristics (such as women's childcare responsibilities, or the needs of adherents of particular religions for time off) can be taken into consideration in an indirect discrimination claim. But most legal challenges to discrimination take the form of legal cases brought by individuals, whose outcomes apply only to those individuals. Trade unions and the equality commissions support 'test cases' whose outcome may, in practical terms, reach beyond the individual. And 'sample cases' can be selected where many litigants are involved in similar claims.[1] But the focus of the law is on the individual, and legal success turns on the demonstration of detriment suffered by the individual as a result of discrimination.

The details of individual enforcement are dealt with below, as are the (limited) circumstances in which the anti-discrimination provisions may or must be enforced other than by individual action. Extremely important in this context are the equality commissions which currently have statutory functions in relation to sex, race and disability discrimination (and, in Northern Ireland, to discrimination on grounds of religious and political belief). At present there are three equality commissions in Great Britain: the EOC, CRE and DRC. These bodies have responsibilities in relation, respectively, to sex (including gender reassignment), race and disability. The single Equality Commission for Northern Ireland has responsibility for these grounds of discrimination and also for religious and political belief, as well as for the broader positive obligations imposed by the Northern Ireland Act 1998 (see further Chapter 3) and, albeit in more limited form, for sexual orientation. The ECNI was the result of s.75 of the NIA which imposed on public authorities the duty to promote equality on grounds, inter alia, of sex, sexual orientation, disability, race and religion (see further Chapter 3). Section 75 was a significant element in the peace process, and the creation of a single Equality Commission (together with the Northern Ireland Human Rights Commission, unique in the UK, and the Commission on Policing), was promised in the pivotal Good Friday Agreement of 1998. In Britain the extension of anti-discrimination provision to sexual orientation, religion and belief and the impending inclusion of age among the protected grounds triggered a debate about the roles of the various commissions: in particular, whether responsibility for the various grounds should be distributed between the various commissions or all of the commissions amalgamated and responsibility for the newly regulated grounds transferred to the resulting single body. The proposed Commission

---

[1] See, eg, *Ashmore v British Coal* [1990] 2 QB 338, in which the Court of Appeal stayed as abusive cases brought after the dismissal of 12 sample cases of 1500.

for Equality and Human Rights (which will, as its name suggests, absorb some responsibility also for human rights issues) is considered below.

The EOC came into existence in December 1975 and the CRE in June 1977. Their duties and powers are set out in the SDA and RRA (ss.43–8 and 66 RRA, ss.53–7 and 75 SDA) and include duties to work towards the elimination of discrimination, to promote equality of opportunity (and, in the case of the CRE, 'good relations, between persons of different racial groups generally'), to keep under review the working of the relevant legislation, and to issue annual reports. The commissions are empowered to promote equality, to conduct formal investigations 'for any purpose connected with the carrying out of those duties,' to provide assistance to claimants, to issue codes of practice and (in the case of the CRE) to provide financial or other assistance to other organisations. Codes of practice should be taken into consideration by employment tribunals and courts where relevant. Their significance is touched upon in cases considered throughout the book. The DDA, which was passed in 1995, did not create a commission on the lines of the EOC and the CRE. Rather, and until August 1999, it established a National Disability Council whose role was purely advisory, and whose remit did not extend to the provision of employment advice until mid-1998. Nor did the Council have the power to issue codes of practice, this falling to the Secretary of State for Education and Employment. The Disability Rights Commission Act 1999 created the DRC broadly along the lines of the EOC and the CRE, but with a number of differences discussed below.

The Fair Employment Agency (FEA) was established in Northern Ireland by the FEA 1976. Its powers were wider than those of the EOC and the CRE, extending to conciliation (carried out in Britain by ACAS in the case of sex and race discrimination and by the DRC in non-employment cases) and to the policing of the monitoring obligations imposed by the fair employment legislation. The FEA also acted as the tribunal dealing with fair employment cases. Northern Ireland also had its own EOC while the implementation of the RRA and the creation of the Northern Irish CRE had to wait until 1997, by which stage the FEA had been replaced by the Fair Employment Commission (FEC) which retained the FEA's conciliation role but did not itself function as a tribunal. Sex and race discrimination claims went to industrial tribunals as in Britain (where they are now called employment tribunals), with appeal directly to the Northern Ireland Court of Appeal. In the case of fair employment complaints, however, a special Fair Employment Tribunal was established by the FEA 1989. Appeals from this tribunal, too, went direct to NICA. The FET has been retained under the Fair Employment and Treatment Order (FETO), but the FEC was absorbed in October 1999 into the ECNI which has also been provided with the powers granted to the DRC in Britain and whose rights and obligations vary with the legislation at issue.

The amalgamation of the various Northern Irish equality commissions took place in the face of very considerable opposition. The creation of the ECNI appears to have been particularly important in the view of nationalist political parties, but Northern Ireland's EOC, CRE and Disability Council all expressed fears that the new Commission would concentrate on sectarian discrimination at the expense of the other grounds.

C O'Cinneide, *A Single Equality Body: Lessons from Abroad* (EOC, 2002)

The single Northern Irish Commission has had a troubled gestation, partially due to the fact that the inevitable challenge of establishing a single commission was amplified by the relatively recent extension of the race relations legislation to Northern Ireland, and the newness of the Disability Discrimination Act. This meant that in Northern Ireland the

CRE was just beginning to establish itself, while no body apart from the advisory National Disability Council was exercising commission-style functions in respect of disability. In addition to this, the timetable for establishing the Equality Commission was excessively rushed. As a result, the Commission was set up in difficult circumstances, with a high level of initial scepticism reflected in the consultation exercise and considerable discontent generated by the government-imposed speed of the transition process. Fears were expressed in particular that the size, cuture and political importance of the Fair Employment Commission would overshadow the other strands, especially the fledgling race and disability strands. In addition, the lack of single equality legislation was identified as a major stumbling block.

However, the benefits of a cross-strand approach are beginning to be reflected in the Commission's work, despite the transition difficulties. In media, political and access terms, a single commission provides a definite access point, enhanced influence and clout and a clearly identifiable agency: the less the degree of multiplicity of equality agencies, the greater the profile of equality within the population at large. In the context of Northern Ireland, its cross-strand, inclusive agenda also makes the concepts of equality and diversity easier to convey and promote across the different political and religious communities, where specific strands such as fair employment are frequently seen as 'loaded' in favour of one community over the other.

Providing integrated, cross-strand advice and support to individual complainants, public authorities and employers is also proving to be easier and more effective with a single commission, and inevitably allows more effective use of resources in enforcing the section 75 public sector equality duty [see Chapter 3] and in encouraging effective public sector mainstreaming. General information and questionnaires are easier to prepare and circulate, and the cross-strand approach also has benefits in encouraging employers to extend their required monitoring (and positive action mechanisms) under the fair employment legislation across the other equality strands, even without a legislative requirement.

The Commission has however experienced certain problems with a perceived loss of focus on gender, which has lead to immediate corrective steps, and disquiet still exists as to its structure. However . . . many of these problems do not relate to the unified nature of the commission itself, but to the structural and functional issues relating to how such a commission is established. Stakeholder opinion in all the countries surveyed remains strongly supportive of single commissions, and sees their benefits as considerably outweighing the drawbacks.

. . . if age, sexual orientation and religion anti-discrimination legislation is confined in scope to employment, this will create considerable difficulties in respect of enforcement and promotion, and will raise difficult questions of funding allocation. The same applies if a positive duty to promote equality is confined within its current application in Britain to race, or even if it is extended to disability and gender. This will create an immediate hierarchy of equalities, which Northern Ireland has been able to avoid . . . The [US] EEOC Task Force Report on Best EEOC Practice published in December 1997 clearly identified the myriad nature of US anti-discrimination law as being a major factor impeding the efficacy of the Commission and employers' understanding of the law.

Nevertheless, the experience of NI and other countries with variegated equality legislation such as the US shows that a single commission can operate without a single act, if necessary. It should also be borne in mind that single legislation, while closing the more egregious gaps between the different strands, will be unable to establish a fully uniform equality code, given the different exceptions that come into play across the different strands. There is a danger that single legislation will be seen as a panacea for any future strand differences and tensions, whereas in comparative experience promoting and enforcing the different strands inevitably requires a number of different approaches.

... Nevertheless, unified legislation, while perhaps not a necessary precondition for a single equality commission to work, is still necessary if it is to fulfil its potential and to achieve consistency of approach and fairness across the strands. Its absence may not hole a single equality commission below the waterline, but it will hinder its plain sailing.

The proposal for a single equality commission for Britain was put forward by the Government in *Towards Equality and Diversity; Making it Happen* (October 2002) which was the outcome of what its sponsoring minister, Barbara Roche MP, hailed as 'the most significant review of equality in over quarter of a century.' The CRE and EOC were supportive of the proposal to create a single equality body:

EOC, 'Towards Equality And Diversity—Making It Happen: A Response From The Equal Opportunities Commission'

3 The EOC supports creation of a single equality body (SEB) because:
• An SEB will have the best chance of delivering effective work across all areas of equality on all the necessary levels, ie single strand issues, generic equality issues and inter-sectional or multiple discrimination issues
• Recent EOC research demonstrates that sex equality is an increasingly subtle and complex issue that cannot be effectively tackled using a simple model of what it is about
• An SEB is the best option for supporting all the equality strands equally effectively, including the new strands of age, sexual orientation and religion or belief.
4 However, the effectiveness of an SEB would depend to a substantial degree on a number of other factors being in place including a compelling and substantial vision of equality and further reform of equality legislation. The EOC is therefore very disappointed that the Government's plans to reform equality institutions do not reflect this wider vision by further reform of Britain's equality law.
5 The case for wider reform is strong:
• To reap the enormous benefits that equality could bring to Britain's economy and society, we need modern legislation that actively promotes equality rather than focusing on acts of unlawful discrimination
• Legislation needs to be consistent across the equality strands both to promote genuinely equal rights for all people and to enable employers, service providers and individuals to understand it and use it effectively
• The effectiveness of a single equality body would be significantly limited if it were working within the existing confusing and hierarchical framework.
6 We recognise that implementation of the Employment Framework Directive will be a major step forward and that the pace of reform needs to be manageable for those with the main responsibility for implementing it. Nonetheless we believe the case for further reform is very strong and we give a very high priority to the Government coming forward with plans for legislative reform that could be implemented alongside changes to institutions.

The DRC was equally critical of the substantive legal issues raised by the EOC, stating that 'getting the right framework of rights is a higher priority than changes in institutional arrangements,' criticising the limited application of the DDA to transport and housing, the low threshold for justification (see further Chapters 2 and 3) and the 'lack of reference to a Single Equalities Act in the document or indeed any discussion of means to secure consistent, strong legislation across all strands,' and calling for 'a guaranteed, effective programme of resources, leadership and time to ensure successful preparation for and implementation of the legislation throughout Britain.' By contrast with the EOC and CRE, however, it was less than enthusiastic about the prospects of amalgamation, expressing its concern about the lack of additional powers proposed for the commission and, in particular, the danger of disruption to the programme of work begun by the recently established DRC.[2] On 12 May 2004 the Government published a White Paper, *Fairness for All: A New Commission for Equality and Human Rights*. The document set out detailed proposals for the creation of the new Commission and asserted that the new body would bring benefits, inter alia, as a single 'strong and authoritative champion for equality and human rights,' that it would 'incorporate a depth of expertise on specific areas of discrimination, while also being able to cast a wide net across all equality and human rights issues,' that it would, as a single body, be more user-friendly both to potential claimants and to employers and service providers, and 'be better equipped to address the reality of the many dimensions of an individual's identity, and therefore tackle discrimination on multiple grounds.' The proposals were given effect in the Equality Bill 2005 which failed, however, to become law as a result of the calling of a May 2005 general election. Secretary of State for Trade and Industry, Patricia Hewitt, stated that the Bill would be given priority in the event of a Labour victory.

The Government did not take the opportunity presented by the White Paper to strengthen the enforcement powers of the existing commissions (discussed below), initially adopting a tone which strongly favoured 'light touch' and 'promotional' activities over enforcement. The DRC's concerns were, to a significant extent, addressed by the proposed structure of the CEHR (which is to have at least one disabled member on its board, and a 'disability committee' comprising at least 50 per cent disabled members). But the DRC, like the EOC and CRE, expressed concerns about, inter alia, the 'light touch' emphasis of the White Paper,[3] the adequacy of resources intended to be made available to the CEHR, the absence of commitment to harmonised equality legislation and the apparent narrowing of the commissions' powers to conduct formal investigations and to support litigation (see further below). And the CRE, which had supported the proposal for a single commission in principle, was trenchant in its root and branch criticism of the White Paper and initially rejected the proposed commission.

CRE, 'Fairness for All: A new Commission for Equality and Human Rights, A response' (August 2004)

what [the White Paper] is proposing is less a single champion enforcing strong legislation, and more a hopeful chorus of voices, which [Fairness for All] speculates can be made to sing in tune. This may be a worthy aim for a body whose job is just about spreading goodwill. It may even be a way of allowing those who suffer from inequality to make common cause, in reminding the privileged that we are still far from being an equal society. Yet, there is no suggestion as to how the conflicts of rights and expectations that already exist might be resolved *in practice*. But there has to be more to cooperation than a common declaration of victimhood, and these tasks are but a small part of the mandate of a serious, statutory equality regulator . . . we regard equality enforcement as too important a task to be carried out in name only. As well as in principle, this proposal would have to work in practice, offer more to the nation than the current arrangements, and not detract from the urgent tasks we face today. Unfortunately, the blueprint sketched out in FFA does not meet the challenge.

---

[2] Disability Rights Commission Briefing on *Equality and Diversity: Making It Happen*.
[3] See the DRC, 'Government White Paper 'Fairness for All . . .', Response from the DRC'.

The CRE went on to express its 'main concerns' with the White Paper: listing no fewer than 18 perceived 'downgrading [of commission] powers or direct legal detriment'; and 10 'instances of clear detriment to equality, including unclear or unworkable proposals.' In particular, the Commission was extremely concerned about the change in emphasis from enforcement: whereas, under the current provisions, 'the law enforcement duty, to work towards the elimination of discrimination' is the first for each of the commissions, the White Paper listed it as fourth of five duties all the rest of which are concerned with promotion. According to the CRE 'This reversal suggests a downgrading of the duty' while the CRE's powers to enforce were in its views downgraded by the White Paper's categorisation of law enforcement as 'complementary and secondary,' to be 'used sparingly and in the last resort, rather than strategically as at present.'

The CRE was also very critical, as were the other commissions, of the proposed tightening of the criteria for direct support of litigation. That body's opposition wrung concessions from the Government on this as well as in relation to FIs, and an agreement that the CEHR would have a phased introduction with the CRE remaining autonomous until 2008–09. Some of these issues are returned to below where we consider the powers of the commissions in relation to enforcement. First, however, the question of individual enforcement will be addressed after a brief discussion of the enforcement in the domestic courts of EC law.

Enforcement of EU Legislation

Some of the detail of the EC equality legislation (Articles 39 and 141 of the Treaty of Rome, Council Directives 75/117, 76/207, 79/7, 86/378, 92/85, and 97/80 on, respectively, equal pay, equal treatment in employment, the progressive implementation of equal treatment in social security and in occupational social security schemes, pregnant workers and the burden of proof in cases of sex discrimination), together with new directives 2000/43/EC, 2000/78/EC, 2002/73/EC and 2004/113/EC, is considered throughout the book. Here the focus is on the relevance and application of EU law in the UK.

Article 141 of the Treaty has both horizontal and vertical direct effect in domestic law. This means that plaintiffs can rely on it in the UK courts regardless of any UK provisions to the contrary, and can do so regardless of whether the legal action is taken against the state or another individual. The difficulty which arises in this context, however, concerns the manner in which Article 141 may be relied upon in the domestic courts.

In the normal course of events, individuals rely on Article 141 through the mechanisms of the EqPA. Where these are inadequate fully to implement Article 141, they can be subjected to whatever violence is necessary to give effect to the rights guaranteed by it. In *Worringham v Lloyds Bank plc* Case C–69/80 [1981] ECR 767, for example, the claimant challenged the employer's differential contributions to male and female pensions. The ECJ ruled that the contributions were 'pay' within Article 141. When the case returned to the Court of Appeal ([1982] ICR 199), the Court simply ignored that provision of the EqPA which excluded claims in relations to pensions and declared in favour of the claimant.[4] A similar approach was taken by EAT in *Bossa v Nordstress & Anor* [1998] ICR 694 to Article 39.

---

[4] The claimants in *Gillespie v Eastern Health and Social Services Board* Case C–342/93 [1996] ECR I–0475 brought their claims in part under the EqPA, claiming (unsuccessfully) that their contracts should be amended to include more favourable terms relating to maternity pay. See also *Levez v Jennings (Harlow Pools) Ltd (No.2)* [2000] ICR 58, discussed below.

In other cases, for example where the EqPA's restriction to contractual terms precludes an Article 141-based claim in respect of a gratuitous benefit, claimants can bring their claims under the SDA. This was the case in *Garland v British Rail* Case C–12/81 [1982] ECR 359, in which the claimant challenged the discriminatory provision of gratuitous travel benefits. Again, the ECJ ruled that the benefits constituted 'pay' within Article 141 and the claim succeeded despite the exclusion from the SDA of (s.6(4)) 'provision in relation to death or retirement.'

In some cases, claims based on Article 141 fall entirely outside UK legislation concerned with discrimination. The most notable example of this arose in the wake of the House of Lords decision, in *R v Secretary of State for Employment ex parte EOC* [1995] 1 AC 1, that discrimination against part-timers in terms of access to redundancy payments and unfair dismissal protection breached EC law. (It also appeared from the decision that unfair dismissal compensation might and redundancy payments did qualify as 'pay' within Article 141—suggestions later confirmed by the House of Lords in *R v Secretary of State for Employment, ex parte Seymour-Smith & Perez (No. 2)* [2000] 1 WLR 235. The post-*EOC* claims (*Biggs v Somerset County Council* [1996] ICR 364 and *Barber v Staffordshire County Council* [1996] ICR 379, discussed below) were made under the unfair dismissal and redundancy provisions currently found in the Employment Rights Act 1996 [ERA].

It is clear that, to the extent that the ERA (or its successor legislation) failed to give effect to Article 141, the national courts would be under an obligation to do whatever violence to its provisions was required to implement the rights guaranteed by that Article. The same is true where an Article 141 claim is brought under the SDA or the EqPA itself. But attempts have been made to circumvent national provisions barring actions by claimants who have argued that they should be permitted to rely on 'freestanding' Article 141 rights. In *Shields v Coomes* [1978] ICR 1159 Lord Denning suggested that: 'a married woman could bring an action in the High Court to enforce the right to equal pay given to her by article [141].' But the remark was made *obiter* and, while the 'freestanding right' approach has found intermittent support both in the Court of Appeal (*Macarthys v Smith (No 2)* [1981] QB 180 and *Pickstone v Freemans* [1988] 1 AC 66)[5] and in EAT,[6] it has recently been rejected by the Court of Appeal in *Biggs v Somerset* and in *Barber v Staffordshire County*. In *Biggs* Neill LJ, for the Court of Appeal, declared that Article 141:

> does not confer a right to compensation for unfair dismissal where there is no sex discrimination . . . Article [141] does not provide a separate claim for compensation for unfair dismissal. Moreover, even if such a separate basis of claim existed, it would not fall within the jurisdiction of an industrial tribunal.[7]

And in *Barber v Staffordshire*, which was decided on the same day as *Biggs*, Neill LJ adopted the reasoning of Mummery J for EAT in *Biggs v Somerset*:

> (a) The industrial tribunal has no inherent jurisdiction. Its statutory jurisdiction is confined to complaints that may be made to it under specific statutes, such as the [ERA, the SDA, the RRA, the EqPA] . . . and any other relevant statute. We are not able to

---

[5] The House of Lords reached their decision on different grounds. See also Lord Denning's speech in *Worringham*, above.

[6] *Amies v Inner London Education Authority* [1977] ICR 308 and most recently *Scullard v Knowles & Southern Regional Council for Education & Training* [1996] ICR 3994.

[7] Auld LJ and Sir Iain Glidewell agreed, the latter adding that 'Article [141] does not . . . provide any remedy for breach of th[e] right [not to be discriminated against in redundancy pay or unfair dismissal compensation]. . . The remedy is provided by national law in this country by the [ERA].'

identify the legal source of any jurisdiction in the tribunal to hear and determine disputes about Community law generally.

(b) In the exercise of its jurisdiction the tribunal may apply Community law. The application of Community law may have the effect of displacing provisions in domestic law statutes which preclude a remedy claimed by the applicant. In the present case the remedy claimed by the applicant is unfair dismissal. That is a right conferred on an employee by the [ERA] and earlier legislation. If a particular applicant finds that the Act contains a barrier which prevents the claim from succeeding but that barrier is incompatible with Community law, it is displaced in consequence of superior and directly effective Community rights.

(c) In applying Community law the tribunal is not assuming or exercising jurisdiction in relation to a 'free-standing' Community right separate from rights under domestic law. In our view, some confusion is inherent in or caused by the mesmeric metaphor, 'free-standing.' 'Free-standing' means not supported by a structural framework, not attached or connected to another structure. This is not a correct description of the claim asserted by the applicant. She is not complaining of an infringement of a 'free-standing' right in the sense of an independent right of action created by Community law, unsupported by any legal framework or not attached or connected to any other legal structure. Her claim is within the structural framework of the employment protection legislation, subject to the disapplication of the threshold qualifying provisions in accordance with the EOC case . . .

Having adopted this approach, Neill LJ continued:

Article [141] can be relied upon by an applicant to disapply barriers to a claim which are incompatible with Community law. The statutory conditions which have to be satisfied before compensation can be obtained can therefore be disapplied if they are discriminatory and contrary to Community law . . . But, as I understand the matter, the impact of Community law on claims brought before industrial tribunals is that Community law can be used to remove or circumvent barriers against or restrictions on a claim but that Community law does not create rights of action which have an existence apart from domestic law. We are not of course concerned in this case with a claim for compensation such as that which was considered by the ECJ in *Francovich v Italian Republic* [joined cases C–6/90 and C–9/90 [1991] ECR I–5357, [1992] IRLR 84] . . . But, unless parliament otherwise decided, such a claim would not come within the jurisdiction of an industrial tribunal.

The position with respect to Article 39 TEC is a little less clear. The Article provides that:

1. Freedom of movement for workers shall be secured within the Community.
2. Such freedom of movement shall entail the abolition of any discrimination based on nationality between workers of the Member States as regards employment, remuneration and other conditions of work and employment . . .

The horizontal direct effect of Article 39 was implied by the ECJ in *Bosman*, Case C–415/93 [1994] ECR I–04921 and expressly confirmed in *Roman Angonese v Cassa di Risparmio di Bolzano SpA*, Case C–281/98 [2000] ECR I–04139.

Article 39 does not merely prohibit *discrimination* connected with nationality but regulates all measures which interfere with the free movement of workers within the Community. The measure impugned in *Bosman* was the rule which required payment between football clubs in connection with the transfer of players after the completion of their contracts. There was no question that this rule discriminated as between players of different EU nationality. It was clear, on the other hand, that it had the potential to interfere with their freedom of movement between the Member States.

Article 39 is limited in that, despite its reference to 'workers,' it has been interpreted to apply only to those having nationality of one of the Member States. The final point to make about Article 39 is its non-application in 'wholly internal' situations. In *R v Saunders* Case C–175/78 [1979] ECR 1129 a Northern Irish woman claimed that a sentence whereby she was bound over to return from Bristol to Northern Ireland and to remain there for three years restricted her right to free movement under Article 39 (this provision, as was pointed out above, not being restricted to discriminatory restrictions). Her claim was rejected on the grounds that it had no extra-British element such as to bring it within the scope of Article 39. In *Knoors v Secretary of State for Economic Affairs*, Case C–115/78 [1979] ECR 399, the fact that a Dutch plumber was refused permission to work as a plumber in the Netherlands, his qualifications having been gained in Belgium, did provide such an external element as to bring his claim within Article 39. More recently the ECJ has become increasingly reluctant to define any situation as 'wholly internal' (see, most recently, the decision in *Avello v Belgian State* Case C–148/02 [2003] ECR I–11613).

By contrast with Article 141 and Article 39, directives have only *vertical* direct effect.[8] This means that, assuming that their terms are sufficiently clear, precise and unconditional to be enforceable at all,[9] directives can be directly enforced only against Member States. This can occur where, as in *Marshall v Southampton and South West Hampshire Area Health Authority (Teaching)* Case C–152/84 [1986] 2 ECR 723, an individual employed by the state (widely defined)[10] relies on the terms of a directive against her employer. Secondly, an individual may sue the state, other than as his or her employer, for failure to implement the terms of directives in national legislation. (This is the so-called *Francovich* claim, after the decision of the ECJ in *Francovich*, above[11]). Organisations such as the EOC and, on occasion, individuals may also seek judicial review of UK legislation on the grounds of its failure to conform with EC law.[12]

Directives may not be relied upon directly against private individuals. But, increasingly, they are giving rise to *indirect* vertical and horizontal effect by the interpretative obligation imposed upon national courts by the Treaty of Rome and by s.2(4) of the European Communities Act 1972 (ECA).

The Directive in respect of which most relevant litigation has arisen is the Equal Treatment Directive, whose provisions are given effect in Britain through the SDA (which, however, predates the Directive). In *Duke v GEC Reliance* [1988] AC 618 the House of Lords took a narrow approach to the interpretive obligation, ruling that it did not apply as between the SDA and the Directive because the former (*per* Lord Templeman, with whom their Lordships agreed):

> was not intended to give effect to the Equal Treatment Directive . . . Section 2(4) of the [ECA] does not . . . enable or constrain a British court to distort the meaning of a British statute in order to enforce against an individual a Community Directive which has no direct effect between individuals.

---

[8] *Marshall*, Case C–152/84 [1986] ECR 723 discussed below.
[9] *Van Gend en Loos* Case C–26/62 [1963] ECR 1.
[10] *Foster v British Gas* Case C–188/89 [1990] ECR I–3313 and (House of Lords) [1991] AC 306.
[11] Referred to by Neill LJ in *Biggs*.
[12] See, eg, *R v Secretary of State for Employment, ex p. Seymour-Smith & Perez (No.2)* [2000] ICR 244. Both cases are discussed in Ch 2.

In *Marleasing SA v Comercial Internacional de Alimentacion SA* Case C–106/89 [1990] ECR I–4135, the ECJ ruled that national courts were obliged to interpret domestic legislation '*so far as possible*, in the light of the wording and the purpose of [any related] directive in order to achieve the result pursued by the latter' (my emphasis), this obligation not being restricted to legislation passed in order to give effect to the directive.

In *Webb v EMO Air Cargo (UK) Ltd (No 2)* [1995] ICR 1021, which is discussed in Chapter 2, the House of Lords took a more generous approach to the interpretive obligations imposed by the Equal Treatment Directive than it had previously been prepared to do. Prior to referring the case to the ECJ Lord Keith, for the Court, had taken the view that the SDA was unambiguously unfavourable to the claimant but allowed that, if the ECJ ruled that her treatment breached the terms of the Directive: 'it would be necessary for this House to consider whether it is possible to construe the relevant provisions of the [SDA] in such a way as to accord with such a decision' ([1993] ICR 175). When the case returned to the House of Lords, their Lordships appeared to have no difficulty in construing the relevant provisions to this effect and made no complaint about interpreting the SDA in a way which they had previously apparently regarded as impossible.[13] We shall return to questions of EC law below in relation to challenges to domestic time limits.

Individual Enforcement

It was mentioned above that the enforcement of discrimination law in the UK relies in the main upon actions taken by individuals. In order to win discrimination cases, individuals have to bring their claims to employment tribunals (or, in non-employment cases, the county court). Legal aid (now 'legal assistance') is generally unavailable to them except in Scotland. Those who regard themselves as the victims of discrimination can apply to the relevant commission for financial and other assistance. But the demand for such assistance far outweighs the available resources. In 2002, for example, according to its *Annual Report*, the CRE granted full representation in 6 per cent and limited representation in a further 4 per cent of the 1300 cases in which it received formal applications. It also gave 50 per cent of such applicants either full or limited legal advice and assistance not including representation. The following year these figures dropped by 65 per cent and 84 per cent respectively (28 applicants receiving full representation and a further 9 more limited representation) as the CRE pursued a new policy of assisting only strategically important cases. A further 55 applicants were assisted by racial equality councils but the overall number of those receiving assistance fell by 32 per cent. The EOC's 1999/2000 *Annual Report* discloses that the Commission granted legal assistance in 101 of the 246 cases it received applications in respect of.

The various commissions have petitioned for the extension of legal aid/ assistance to tribunals, in which the vast majority of discrimination cases are litigated.[14] Legal aid is available in some employment cases in Scotland but is generally unavailable except at the appellate level elsewhere, although the Green Form scheme does permit the provision of

---

[13] And see more recently the decision of the House of Lords in *Rhys-Harper v Relaxion Group plc* [2003] ICR 167.

[14] See, eg, the FEC, *Review of the Fair Employment Acts* (1997), and the CRE's 1998 proposals, *Reform of the Race Relations Act 1976*.

basic preliminary advice in some cases. Legal assistance is available in theory for county court cases but means testing applies and, since costs are awarded in the county court on the usual ('loser pays') basis, litigation is risky. Employment tribunals do not generally have power to award costs, but may do so when, in the opinion of the tribunal (2001 Rules, rule 14(1)):

(i) a party has in bringing the proceedings, or a party or a party's representative has in conducting the proceedings, acted vexatiously, abusively, disruptively or otherwise unreasonably; or

(ii) the bringing or conducting of the proceedings by a party has been misconceived.[15]

Tribunals also have a new power to strike out at any stage an application or response with no real prospect of success and may demand deposits of up to £500 (£150 prior to 2001) at pre-hearing reviews. Where a tribunal considers it appropriate to award costs it may assess costs up to £10,000 (prior to 2001 this figure was £500), may order the payment of a sum agreed by the parties, or may order that the whole or part of the costs be assessed in the county court. The 2001 Rules also permitted claimants to be subject to costs for the first time for the way in which their *representatives* conduct proceedings, and imposed upon tribunals for the first time an *obligation* to consider (though not to award) costs once they determine that any of the criteria in rule 14(1) has been met.

A claimant will act 'vexatiously' or otherwise unreasonably where s/he is 'motivated by resentment and spite in bringing the proceedings,' and there is 'virtually nothing to support [the] allegations of . . . discrimination.' Of more concern is rule 14(1)(b). Prior to 2001 costs could only be awarded against a claimant who had some degree of fault. But the inclusion of 'misconceived' cases allows the award of costs where a case had 'no reasonable prospect of success.' In *Gee v Shell (UK) Ltd* [2003] IRLR 82, Scott Baker LJ stated that this had 'lowered the threshold' for the award of costs. Under the old rules the Court of Appeal took the view that the chances of a costs award against a claimant whose case was arguable were extremely low. It ruled, accordingly, that the tribunal has erred in issuing a costs warning to the claimant who had, as a result, withdrawn her claim. The danger with increased chances of costs is not only that tribunals will more frequently award costs, but also that they may be more inclined to issue costs warnings which will frequently result in the abandonment of even arguable claims by unrepresented and/or unfunded claimants. It is worth noting here that only a very small fraction of discrimination claims which reach tribunals are upheld. In 1997–99 (the last period for which detailed statistics are available) one third of sex discrimination claims, fewer than one in five race discrimination claims and a mere 2 per cent of equal pay claims heard by tribunals were successful.[16]

A further hurdle has been placed in the path of discrimination claimants by the Employment Act 2002 and the Employment Act 2002 (Dispute Resolution) Regulations

[15] The rules governing tribunal procedures are in schedules to the Employment Tribunals (Constitution and Rules of Procedure) Regulations 2001 (SI 2001/1171) and the Employment Tribunals (Constitution and Rules of Procedure) (Scotland) Regulations 2001 (SI 2001/1170) respectively, which came into force on 16 July 2001. The English and Scottish versions are virtually identical. See *Keskar v Governors of All Saints Church of England School* [1991] ICR 493.

[16] *Labour Force Trends* 1999. See *Sahota v Birmingham City Council* ('Case Digest' 125 *Equal Opportunities Review*) for a case in which a tribunal refused to award costs against an unrepresented claimant whose DDA claim it struck out as misconceived. In *Roach v AOG Advisory Services Ltd*, reported in 127 *Equal Opportunities Review*, on the other hand, a tribunal ordered that the claimant pay £1,500 costs because her representative's conduct of the case was vexatious, disruptive and unreasonable. He was unprepared for a directions hearing, late for the substantive hearing and, inter alia, accused one witness of perjury in her absence without substantiation.

2004 which came into force on 1 October 2004. The Act requires employee to set out his or her grievance in writing to the employer before being permitted to present a discrimination claim to a tribunal. A three stage grievance procedure must be followed unless the employee is no longer employed, and has agreed in writing with the employer to use a two-stage procedure. If the grievance relates to the employee's actual or contemplated dismissal the Act's provisions on dismissal and disciplinary procedure must be complied with (these similarly require that the claimant follow internal procedures before bringing a legal claim). A failure to begin grievance procedures can result in the claimant being denied access to the tribunal, a failure to complete them in the reduction (or, where the employer is at fault) increase of compensation. The time limit for tribunal cases is extended to six months once the grievance procedure has been started and the Regulations provide exceptions relating to collective complaints which may be raised by a union or workplace representative and (reg 11) where:

(a) the party has reasonable grounds to believe that commencing the procedure or complying with the subsequent requirement would result in a significant threat to himself, his property, any other person or the property of any other person;
(b) the party has been subjected to harassment and has reasonable grounds to believe that commencing the procedure or complying with the subsequent requirement would result in his being subjected to further harassment; or
(c) it is not practicable for the party to commence the procedure or comply with the subsequent requirement within a reasonable period.

Note that even a claimant subjected to harassment by an employer is not relieved of the obligation to follow the internal route unless (reg 11(b)) he or she 'has reasonable grounds to believe that commencing the procedure or complying with the subsequent requirement would result in his being subjected to further harassment'.

Burden of Proof

The burden of proof in discrimination cases is on the applicant. The protected factor need not be established as the sole cause of the less favourable treatment, but must be proven to have been 'the principal or at least an important or significant cause of the less favourable treatment.'[17] The various codes of practice issued by the equality commissions provide good practice guidance in relation to discrimination and, although they are not legally binding, any failure to observe their provisions may be taken into account by a tribunal or court. The provisions of various of the codes of practice are referred to in a number of cases below, as is the relevance of their breach to the proof of discrimination.

The domestic courts have recognised the difficulties associated with proving discrimination—in particular, the fact that direct evidence of such discrimination is only rarely available. It is one thing to demonstrate that an applicant has been treated less favourably than someone of a different sex, racial group, etc, and to demonstrate that s/he has suffered a detriment thereby. But only in the rarest cases will a discriminator admit that the less favourable treatment was 'by reason of' the applicant's sex, race, etc; in other words, that s/he would not have been so treated 'but for' the protected reason. Courts and tribunals have, therefore, to *infer* unlawful discrimination from primary facts (ie, to conclude that the reason for proven less favourable treatment was a prohibited one). Such inference might also be necessary in a case

---

[17] See Ch 2 n8.

which turns on a hypothetical, rather than an actual, comparator, in order to establish the very fact of less favourable treatment.[18]

The leading authority in this area is the decision of the Court of Appeal in *King v The Great Britain-China Centre*, as affirmed by the House of Lords in *Glasgow City Council v Zafar*. Below we consider recent legislative amendments to the burden of proof, but the *King/ Zafar* approach is still binding in relation to the SDA, DDA and FETO as they apply outside the employment sphere, and to the RRA as it applies to discrimination on grounds of colour and nationality.

The *King* case was brought by a woman of Chinese origin who claimed that she had been subject to race discrimination in a job application. Her claim succeeded at tribunal, a majority finding that the employers 'had failed to demonstrate that the applicant had not been treated unfavourably [in not being shortlisted], or that such unfavourable treatment was not because of her race.' EAT allowed the employers' appeal, ruling that the tribunal had incorrectly placed the burden of proof on them. The Court of Appeal, however, reinstated the tribunal's decision, Neill LJ for the Court summarising the existing authorities as follows:

King v The Great Britain-China Centre [1992] ICR 516

(1) It is for the applicant who complains of racial discrimination to make out his or her case. Thus if the applicant does not prove the case on the balance of probabilities he or she will fail.

(2) It is important to bear in mind that it is unusual to find direct evidence of racial discrimination. Few employers will be prepared to admit such discrimination even to themselves. In some cases the discrimination will not be ill-intentioned but merely based on an assumption 'he or she would not have fitted in.'

(3) The outcome of the case will therefore usually depend on what inferences it is proper to draw from the primary facts found by the Tribunal. These inferences can include, in appropriate cases, any inferences that it is just and equitable to draw in accordance with s.65(2)(b) [RRA] from an evasive or equivocal reply to a questionnaire [discussed below].

(4) Though there will be some cases where, for example, the non-selection of the applicant for a post or for promotion is clearly not on racial grounds, a finding of discrimination and a finding of a difference in race will often point to the possibility of racial discrimination. In such circumstances the Tribunal will look to the employer for an explanation. If no explanation is then put forward or if the Tribunal considers the explanation to be inadequate or unsatisfactory it will be legitimate for the Tribunal to infer that the discrimination was on racial grounds. This is not a matter of law but, as May LJ put it in [*North West Thames Regional Health Authority v Noone* [1988] ICR 813], 'almost common sense.'

(5) It is unnecessary and unhelpful to introduce the concept of a shifting evidential burden of proof. At the conclusion of all the evidence the Tribunal should make findings as to the primary facts and draw such inferences as they consider proper from those facts. They should then reach a conclusion on the balance of probabilities, bearing in mind both the difficulties which face a person who complains of unlawful discrimination and the fact that it is for the complainant to prove his or her case . . .

---

[18] See *Balamoody v UK Central Council for Nursing, Midwifery and Health Visiting* [2002] ICR 646— where there is no suitable real comparator the tribunal must, according to the Court of Appeal, construct a hypothetical comparator against whose treatment that of the claimant can be considered.

Miss King is an ethnic Chinese. So were four other of the 30 candidates. Eight candidates were called for interview. None of these eight candidates was an ethnic Chinese. The majority of the Tribunal were satisfied that Miss King's paper qualifications fulfilled the requirements set out in the advertisement and in the job specification, and that she had been treated less favourably than the candidates called for interview . . . The majority were also impressed by the fact that no ethnic Chinese had ever been employed by the centre.

In these circumstances the Tribunal were clearly entitled to look to the centre for an explanation of the fact that Miss King was not even called for an interview. The majority, however, found the explanation unsatisfactory and were also dissatisfied with the reply to the questionnaire. They therefore concluded that Miss King had made out her case . . . reading the relevant parts of the [tribunal's] reasons as a whole the majority's decision was not flawed by an error of law. They clearly had in mind that it was for Miss King to make out her case . . . They were entitled to look to the centre for an explanation of the fact that Miss King was not selected for interview. They were not satisfied with the explanation and they were entitled to say no. It was therefore legitimate for them to draw an inference that the discrimination was on racial grounds. This process of reasoning did not involve a reversal of the burden of proof but merely a proper balancing of the factors which could be placed in the scales for and against a finding of unlawful discrimination.

The question whether an applicant has proven his or her claim of discrimination is one of fact and, as such, cannot be appealed unless the tribunal has applied the wrong legal test or otherwise reached a perverse decision. In *King* the Court of Appeal took the view that the tribunal had been entitled to draw an inference of discrimination. Similarly, in *The Belfast Port Employer's Association v Fair Employment Commission*, Northern Ireland's Court of Appeal ruled that the FET had been entitled to infer discrimination, in the absence of a satisfactory explanation from the employer, where 'there were 167 applicants for 15 posts, 29 from Roman Catholics. No Roman Catholics were shortlisted, although it was established that the complainants were experienced dockers and at least as well qualified for consideration as a number of those included in the short list.'[19] And in *In re Ballymena Borough Council* Northern Ireland's High Court accepted that a tribunal had been entitled to infer discrimination where a Catholic's application for employment was rejected after a secret ballot among councillors who were divided along religious lines.[20] Having drawn attention to a number of procedural irregularities, and failures on the part of the appointing councillors to follow the relevant Code of Practice, Carswell J, as he then was, continued:

One of the major factors was that set out by the Tribunal . . . [for its decision was t]hat very little evidence was forthcoming from those councillors who voted for the successful candidate in preference to the applicant . . . As the Tribunal also observed, the assessment forms, to which it might have turned in default of direct personal evidence, were not all completed, returned or marked consistently. In these circumstances there appears to me to be force in the Tribunal's remarks . . . [that]:

We do not know precisely who voted for whom. If we are asked not to draw an inference of unlawful discrimination from our finding of less favourable treatment, the method of appointment by secret ballot as adopted by the respondent, and the failure to record assessments of the candidates, obviously makes the task of the Tribunal

[19] Court of Appeal 29 June 1994, unreported, *per* Carswell LJ, approving the Fair Employment Tribunal's application of *King*.
[20] Queen's Bench Division 18 June 1993, unreported.

extremely difficult if not impossible. The use of a secret ballot does not reconcile with the recommendation in the Fair Employment Code of Practice that recruitment should be systematic and objective so that it can be tested if a complaint is made. If there is anonymity in appointments, as well as absence of records of assessment, it makes the respondent's explanation for selection of candidates much more difficult to defend.

This test, as Geoffrey Bindman wrote in 1992 was still:

> Far from satisfactory. It still means that a respondent will be able to avoid a finding of racial [or other prohibited] discrimination by producing *plausible* explanation other than race [etc.] for an act of discrimination (ie. less favourable treatment . . .) without being under a positive obligation to prove that the alternative explanation was the *true* one . . . it is all too easy to find a plausible subjective ground, especially in recruitment or promotion cases, for choosing one candidate rather than another.[21]

Further, a tribunal which considered itself *bound* to infer unlawful discrimination from a finding of less favourable treatment, coupled with an unsatisfactory explanation from an employer, would err as a matter of law. Neill LJ stated in *King* that 'a finding of discrimination [in the sense of less favourable treatment] and a finding of a difference in race [or sex] will often point to the possibility of racial discrimination . . . If no explanation is then put forward or if the Tribunal considers the explanation to be inadequate or unsatisfactory *it will be legitimate* for the Tribunal to infer that the discrimination was on racial grounds' (my emphasis). In a number of subsequent cases[22] the courts suggested that inferences of discrimination *ought* to be drawn in cases in which apparent discrimination was not adequately explained. The issue was resolved in *Glasgow City Council v Zafar*, in which the House of Lords ruled that a tribunal had erred in regarding itself as *bound* to infer unlawful discrimination from the employer's unsatisfactory explanation of the disputed treatment and, further, that the tribunal had erred in inferring *less favourable* (ie, prima facie discriminatory) treatment from *bad* treatment.

Glasgow City Council v Zafar [1998] ICR 120

Lord Browne-Wilkinson (for the Court):

The [RRA] requires it to be shown that the complainant has been treated by the person against whom the discrimination is alleged less favourably than that person treats or would have treated another. In deciding that issue, the conduct of a hypothetical reasonable employer is irrelevant. The alleged discriminator may or may not be a reasonable employer. If he is not a reasonable employer he might well have treated another employee in just the same unsatisfactory way as he treated the complainant in which case he would not have treated the complainant 'less favourably' for the purposes of the [RRA]. The fact that, for the purposes of the law of unfair dismissal, an employer has acted unreasonably casts no light whatsoever on the question whether he has treated the employee 'less favourably' for the purposes of the [RRA]. . . .

The industrial tribunal, having wrongly drawn the inference of less favourable treatment, then held that, in the absence of any satisfactory non-racial explanation for such treatment,

---

[21] 'Proof and Evidence of Discrimination' in B Hepple and E Szyszczak, *Discrimination: the Limits of Law* (London, Mansell, 1992) 57–8.
[22] *Khanna v Ministry of Defence* [1981] ICR 653, *Chattopadhyay v Headmaster of Holloway School* [1982] ICR 132, *Baker v Cornwall County Council* [1990] ICR 452 and *West Midlands Passenger Transport Executive v Singh* [1988] ICR 614.

it was bound by authority to draw the inference that such less favourable treatment was on the grounds of the applicant's race . . .

Claims brought under the [RRA] and the [SDA] present special problems of proof for complainants since those who discriminate on grounds of race or gender do not in general advertise their prejudices: indeed they may not even be aware of them . . . The best guidance if that given by Neill LJ in *King* [citing principles 1–5 extracted above] . . .

In my judgment that is the guidance which should in future be applied in these cases. In particular, certain remarks of mine in the Employment Appeal Tribunal in *Khanna v Ministry of Defence and Chattopadhyay v Headmaster of Holloway School* to the effect that such inference 'should' be drawn put the matter too high, are inconsistent with later Court of Appeal authority and should not be followed.

A commentary in the *Equal Opportunities Review* warned that, although the Lord Browne-Wilkinson's approach was:

> logically indisputable . . . Whether the employer was reasonable is not relevant to whether the employee was treated less favourably . . . there is a danger that Lord Browne-Wilkinson's dictum will be taken out of context and misapplied . . . like the statement in Qureshi v London Borough of Newham [1991] IRLR 264 . . . that incompetence by an employer does not equate to discrimination, as indicating that it is for the applicant to prove that the unexplained treatment was on racial grounds rather than because the employer was simply unreasonable or incompetent.[23]

The CRE's 1998 proposals for reform of the RRA, suggested that the decision in *Zafar* had rendered 'courts and tribunals . . . less willing to . . . draw an inference of racial discrimination.' The Commission suggested that such an inference might be permitted on the basis of unreasonable treatment, where that treatment was contrary to employment legislation and codes of practice and where there was no evidence that an employer had taken steps to prevent discrimination of the type alleged and protested that:

> employers . . . must not be allowed to hide behind poor or unreasonable practices or decisions to avoid inferences of discrimination being drawn. Implicitly this was the policy which Parliament sought to establish in the [RRA], since they made employers responsible for the discriminatory acts of their employees unless . . an employer could prove that he or she had taken such steps as were reasonably practicable to prevent such acts. Where . . . the employer not only took no positive steps to avoid race discrimination but permitted poor employment practice, which may well either include or conceal race discrimination, then courts or tribunals should not be prohibited from drawing an inference of discrimination where there is evidence of unreasonable treatment of a person from a racial group which constitutes a minority within the whole, or a relevant section, of that employer's workforce.

In *Martin v Marks & Spencer* [1998] ICR 1005, however, the Court of Appeal ruled that a tribunal had been 'perverse' in inferring race discrimination from its finding that an interview panel had been 'biased' against an applicant.[24] Michael Rubenstein's commentary to

---

[23] 77 *Equal Opportunities Review* 44, 45–6.

[24] Somewhat bizarrely, the Court also ruled that, even had the panel discriminated against the claimant, the employer would not have been liable because, under s.32(3), it had taken 'such steps as were reasonably practicable to prevent' discrimination by the interviewers—ie, 'the employers' equal opportunity policy; their compliance with the Code of Practice issued by the [CRE] in relation to selection procedures, criteria and interviewing and their selection of the interviewing panel to include . . . a person with an interest in recruiting from ethnic minorities.' This aspect of the decision was touched upon in Ch 4.

the IRLR report of the case remarked on 'a disturbing trend in higher court decisions on allegations of race discrimination' (this trend including the decision of the House of Lords in *Zafar*): 'Why should the tribunal's finding of bias be displaced by the speculative, rather implausible thesis that the interviewer would also have acted in a biased way towards someone from a different racial group? And how is the applicant to prove that there was no bias in someone else's interview while the tribunal at the same time avoids investigating the process in such detail as to render itself liable to being accused of "usurping the functions of the interviewers"?'

The *Zafar* approach also encourages employers to run the so-called 'bastard' defence: 'yes I treated the applicant badly/ unfairly/ unreasonably/ appallingly. But I would have treated someone of a different sex/ race/ etc equally badly . . . Recognition of this resulted in the decision of the Court of Appeal in *Anya v University of Oxford* [2001] ICR 847. The claimant, a black Nigerian permanently resident in the UK, claimed he had been subject to race discrimination when he was rejected for a post-doctoral research position. The interview was conducted by a panel of three which included Dr Anya's PhD supervisor, who disclosed to another panel member prior to the interview his view that Dr Anya was unsuitable for the post. An employment tribunal found that the university had failed to comply with its own recruitment policies (which, inter alia, required that applicants be given a full 'person specification' prior to interview and that references were to be taken up), and that there were inconsistencies in the evidence of the claimant's supervisor, but that his reasons for deciding against Dr Anya were untainted by race discrimination. The claimant appealed unsuccessfully to EAT but then successfully to the Court of Appeal which ruled that an employer who wished to assert that s/he treated *everyone* equally badly (so that his or her bad treatment of a claimant was not *less favourable* treatment on any actionable grounds) would have to provide evidence of this, and that it did not fall to the claimant to prove that the employer had singled him or her out.

The *Anya* approach has been called into question by the recent decision of the Court of Appeal in *Bahl v Law Society*. The claimant, a former Chair of the EOC, brought her discrimination claim after being accused of bullying staff in her position as Vice President of the Law Society. A tribunal found that she had been the victim of race and sex discrimination, a finding which was successfully appealed by the Law Society and EAT's decision upheld by the Court of Appeal. Mr Justice Elias, for EAT, stated that a tribunal could only infer discrimination from a finding of less favourable treatment which was explained by an alleged discriminator if the 'explanation . . . was inadequate or unsatisfactory in the sense that the tribunal did not accept it as genuine, not in the sense that it was a genuine, non-racial explanation, albeit that it was unreasonable because it resulted in unreasonable treatment.' He went on:

The Law Society v Bahl [2003] IRLR 640

Elias J:

Employers often act unreasonably, as the volume of unfair dismissal cases demonstrates. Indeed, it is the human condition that we all at times act foolishly, inconsiderately, unsympathetically and selfishly and in other ways which we regret with hindsight. It is, however, a wholly unacceptable leap to conclude that whenever the victim of such conduct is black or a woman then it is legitimate to infer that our unreasonable treatment was because the person was black or a woman. All unlawful discriminatory treatment is unreasonable, but not all unreasonable treatment is discriminatory, and it is not shown to be so merely because the victim is either a woman or of a minority race or colour. In order to establish unlawful discrimination, it is necessary to show that the particular employer's reason for acting was one of the proscribed grounds. Simply to say that the conduct was unreasonable tells us nothing about the grounds for acting in that way. The fact that the victim is black or a woman does no more than raise the possibility that the employer could have been influenced by unlawful discriminatory considerations. *Absent some independent evidence supporting the conclusion that this was indeed the reason, no finding of discrimination can possibly be made.* The inference cannot be drawn from the fact that other employers sometimes discriminate in such circumstances; it cannot be inferred that A discriminates merely because B, C and D have been known to do so in similar circumstances. That is a plainly deficient basis for inferring discrimination. It would be wholly unjust to make a finding of such serious import on such a flawed basis. *Nor does it help to say that it is a finding which is open to a tribunal but which it is not obliged to make. It is unjustifiable to make it in any circumstances* . . .

Mr de Mello [for Dr Bahl] submitted that the analysis in *Zafar* should now be read together with certain comments of Sedley LJ in *Anya* . . . Mr de Mello says that these comments demonstrate that it is open to a tribunal to infer discrimination from unreasonable treatment, at least if the employer does not show that equally unreasonable treatment would have been meted out to a white person or man, as the case may be. We recognise that read broadly the passage could indeed justify such an interpretation, not least because the tribunal's comments in *Anya* which Sedley LJ referred to as 'arguably' incorrect seem to us, with respect, faithfully to reflect the principle established by the House of Lords in the *Zafar* case. However, we do not think that they could have been intended to be read in that manner. We do, however, respectfully accept that Sedley LJ was right to say that racial bias may be inferred if there is no explanation for the unreasonable behaviour. But *it is not then the mere fact of unreasonable behaviour which entitles the tribunal to infer discrimination; it is not, to use the tribunal's language, unreasonable conduct 'without more,' but rather the fact that there is no reason advanced for it.* Nor in our view can Sedley LJ be taken to be saying that the employer can only establish a proper explanation if he shows that in fact he behaves equally badly to members of all minority groups. The fact that he does so will be one way of rebutting an inference of unlawful discrimination, even if there are pointers which would otherwise justify that inference. For example, an employer may have unreasonable disciplinary procedures which are regularly applied to all staff. Plainly there is no unlawful discrimination simply because the employee subjected to them happens to be black or female. The employer has not adequately explained, in the sense of justified, his conduct, because he has applied an unreasonable disciplinary procedure; however, he has shown that, whatever the reason, it is not discriminatory. No doubt the mere assertion by an employer that he would treat others in the same manifestly unreasonable way, but with no evidence that he has in fact done so, would not carry any weight with a tribunal which is minded to draw the inference on *proper and sufficient grounds* that the cause of the treatment has been an act of unlawful discrimination.

However, demonstrating the similar treatment of others of a different race or sex is clearly not the only way in which an employer who has acted unreasonably can rebut the finding of discrimination. Were it so, the employer could never do so where the situation he was dealing with was a novel one, as in this case. The inference may also be rebutted—and indeed this will, we suspect, be far more common—by the employer leading evidence of a genuine reason which is not discriminatory and which was the ground of his conduct. Employers will often have unjustified, albeit genuine, reasons for acting as they have. If these are accepted and show no discrimination, there is generally no basis for the inference of unlawful discrimination to be made. Even if they are not accepted, the tribunal's own findings of fact may identify an obvious reason for the treatment in issue, other than a discriminatory reason. We return to this point below.

Accordingly, to the extent that the tribunal found discriminatory treatment from unreasonable treatment alone, their reasoning would be flawed and the finding of discrimination could not stand. That is the clear ratio of *Zafar* and that decision remains unaffected by *Anya*.

That is not to say that the fact that an employer has acted unreasonably is of no relevance whatsoever. The fundamental question is why the alleged discriminator acted as he did. If what he does is reasonable, then the reason is likely to be non-discriminatory. In general, a person has good non-discriminatory reasons for doing what is reasonable. This is not inevitably so since sometimes there is a choice between a range of reasonable conduct, and it is of course logically possible the discriminator might take the less favourable option for someone who is, say, black or a female and the more favourable for someone who is white or male. But the tribunal would need to have very cogent evidence before inferring that someone who has acted in a reasonable way is guilty of unlawful discrimination.

By contrast, where the alleged discriminator acts unreasonably then a tribunal will want to know why he has acted in that way. If he gives a non-discriminatory explanation which the tribunal considers to be honestly given, then that is likely to be a full answer to any discrimination claim. It need not be, because it is possible that he is subconsciously influenced by unlawful discriminatory considerations. But again, there should be proper evidence from which such an inference can be drawn. It cannot be enough merely that the victim is a member of a minority group. This would be to commit the error identified above in connection with the *Zafar* case: the inference of discrimination would be based on no more than the fact that others sometimes discriminate unlawfully against minority groups.

The significance of the fact that the treatment is unreasonable is that a tribunal will more readily in practice reject the explanation given than it would if the treatment were reasonable. In short, it goes to credibility. If the tribunal does not accept the reason given by the alleged discriminator, it may be open to it to infer discrimination. But it will depend upon why it has rejected the reason that he has given, and whether the primary facts it finds provide another and cogent explanation for the conduct. Persons who have not in fact discriminated on the proscribed grounds may nonetheless sometimes give a false reason for the behaviour. They may rightly consider, for example, that the true reason casts them in a less favourable light, perhaps because it discloses incompetence or insensitivity. If the findings of the tribunal suggest that there is such an explanation, then the fact that the alleged discriminator has been less than frank in the witness box when giving evidence will provide little, if any, evidence to support a finding of unlawful discrimination itself [my emphasis throughout].

This approach appears to increase, rather than decrease, the difficulties for claimants by insisting that a difference in sex or race, coupled with less favourable treatment, are not *sufficient* grounds upon which an inference of discrimination may be drawn. Dr Bahl's appeal did not, however, succeed.

Bahl v Law Society v Bahl [2004] IRLR 799

Peter Gibson LJ (for the Court):

. . . [the] ratio [of *Anya*] takes matters no further than *King* and *Zafar*, both of which are cited in the judgment of the Court given by Sedley L.J. However, the judgment contains an *obiter* passage which has attracted debate in a number of cases including the present appeal [citing the final paragraph extracted above] . . .

It has been suggested, not least by Mr de Mello in the present case, that Sedley L.J. was there placing an important gloss on *Zafar* to the effect that it is open to a tribunal to infer discrimination from unreasonable treatment, at least if the alleged discriminator does not show by evidence that equally unreasonable treatment would have been applied to a white person or a man.

In our judgment, the answer to this submission is that contained in the judgment of Elias J. in the present case. It is correct, as Sedley L.J. said, that racial or sex discrimination may be inferred if there is no explanation for unreasonable treatment. This is not an inference from unreasonable treatment itself but from the absence of any explanation for it. However, the final words in the passage which we have quoted from *Anya* are not to be construed in the manner that Mr. de Mello submits. That would be inconsistent with *Zafar*. It is not the case that an alleged discriminator can only avoid an adverse inference by proving that he behaves equally unreasonably to everybody. As Elias J observed (para. 97): 'Were it so, the employer could never do so where the situation he was dealing with was a novel one, as in this case.' Accordingly, proof of equally unreasonable treatment of all is merely one way of avoiding an inference of unlawful discrimination. It is not the only way. He added (*ibid*):

'The inference may also be rebutted—and indeed this will, we suspect, be far more common—by the employer leading evidence of a genuine reason which is not discriminatory and which was the ground of his conduct. Employers will often have unjustified albeit genuine reasons for acting as they have. If these are accepted and show no discrimination, there is generally no basis for the inference of unlawful discrimination to be made. Even if they are not accepted, the tribunal's own findings of fact may identify an obvious reason for the treatment in issue, other than a discriminatory reason.'

We entirely agree with that impressive analysis. As we shall see, it resonates in this appeal . . .

Mr de Mello challenged the view taken by the EAT that unreasonable treatment of a complainant alleging discrimination by an employer, if there is nothing else to explain it, cannot in itself lead to an inference of discrimination in the absence of evidence from the employer that equally unreasonable treatment would have been meted out to the comparator. The basis of that challenge was the remarks made by Sedley LJ in *Anya*.

For the reasons which we have given . . . above, we do not accept the validity of that challenge. The principle laid down in *Zafar* is clear . . . If Mr de Mello was right, in *Zafar*, where there was no evidence from the employer of unreasonable treatment of comparators, the House of Lords should not have concluded that the appeal from the Court of Session should be dismissed as it would have been open to the ET to draw the inference which it did.

The *Bahl* decision illustrates the particular difficulties experienced by those who regard themselves as having been the victim of multiple discrimination. The claimant there, an Asian woman, alleged that she had been discriminated against as a black woman. A tribunal, finding in her favour, declared that:

We do not distinguish between the race or sex of the applicant in reaching this conclusion . . . The claim was advanced on the basis that Kamlesh Bahl was treated in the way she was because she is a black woman. Kamlesh Bahl was the first office holder that the Law Society had ever had who was not both white and male . . . We do not know what was in the minds of [the alleged discriminators] at any particular point. It is sufficient for our purposes to find, where appropriate, that in each case they would not have treated a white person or a man less favourably.

EAT overturned. Having made the observations set out above, Elias J continued:

The reason for the tribunal not approaching the matter in that way appears to be because of the tribunal's observations that 'there was no basis in the evidence for comparing her treatment with that of a white female or black male office holder.' We confess to having some difficulty in understanding what this sentence means. It may be that the tribunal was intending to indicate that there was no actual comparator with whom any comparison could be made. That is plainly correct, although in those circumstances the tribunal was entitled to consider how the hypothetical comparator would have been treated in that situation. In the case of sex discrimination that would have involved considering how a male (white or black) would have been treated in otherwise like circumstances, and in the case of race discrimination how a white person (male or female) would have been treated in such circumstances. Alternatively, the tribunal may have meant simply that it could not disentangle the two elements and reach a clear conclusion on either.

Plainly it is possible for a tribunal to infer that there may be discrimination both on grounds of race and sex after considering the evidence in respect of each. But if the evidence does not satisfy the tribunal that there is discrimination on grounds of race or on grounds of sex, considered independently, then it is not open to a tribunal to find either claim satisfied on the basis that there is nonetheless discrimination on grounds of race and sex when both are taken together. That would fail to give effect to the fact that the burden of proof is on the applicant. Nor can the tribunal properly conclude, if it is uncertain about whether it is race or sex, that it will find both.

Mr de Mello submits that the tribunal was entitled to adopt this approach. It was not obliged to separate out the two strands of race and sex from the mix. The applicant had put her case before the tribunal on the basis that she was a black woman, and it was entitled to treat the two elements together. It was a unique case and the tribunal was justified in treating the evidence in the round without identifying those aspects which it considered justified the inference of race discrimination and those which justified a finding of sex discrimination.

We do not accept that submission. In our view the tribunal did err in law in failing to distinguish between the elements of alleged race and sex discrimination. The result was that it failed to reach properly reasoned findings on the question whether Dr Bahl had satisfied the tribunal—the burden being on her—that discrimination had occurred in respect of either ground. This would, in our view, be a sufficient basis for upholding these appeals even in the absence of any other error of law.[25]

Dr Bahl's appeal against this aspect of EAT's decision failed, the Court of Appeal characterising the passage of the tribunal's judgment set out above as 'puzzling' and continuing:

It says that there was no basis in the evidence for comparing the treatment of Dr. Bahl with that of a white female, or a black male office holder, and yet the ET had to make a comparison on the evidence between her treatment and that of an appropriate comparator. It is not disputed that to find discrimination on the ground of race or sex the ET must find that subjectively racial or sexual considerations were in the mind of the discriminator, but here the ET says that it does not know what was in the minds of [the alleged discriminators] at any particular point . . .

[25] See however *Baker v Lennox*, discussed in 'Compensation Awards 2002' 124 *Equal Opportunities Review* in which a tribunal categorised as both racial and sexual harassment the treatment accorded to a claimant who was, inter alia, questioned as to whether her husband was circumcised (she was black, her husband white and the abuse levelled at the fact of her mixed-race relationship) and called a 'bitch.'

What the ET has plainly omitted to do is to identify what evidence goes to support a finding of race discrimination and what evidence goes to support a finding of sex discrimination. It would be surprising if the evidence for each form of discrimination was the same . . . In our judgment, it was necessary for the ET to find the primary facts in relation to each type of discrimination against each alleged discriminator and then to explain why it was making the inference which it did in favour of Dr Bahl on whom lay the burden of proving her case. It failed to do so, and thereby, as the EAT correctly found, erred in law.

The logic of the Court of Appeal's approach is perhaps unassailable. The decision does, nevertheless, indicate some of the difficulties experienced by discrimination claimants who differ from the apparent 'norm' (i.e., white, male, non-disabled, heterosexual, of mainstream Christian or indeterminate faith) by reference to more than one characteristic. These particular difficulties raised by multiple discrimination are further considered in Chapters 1 and 2, but recognition of the problems experienced more generally by those attempting to prove discrimination resulted at the European level in the adoption in 1997 of Council Directive 97/80 (the Burden of Proof Directive), which provides (Article 4(1)) that:

Member States shall take such measures as are necessary, in accordance with their national judicial systems, to ensure that, when persons who consider themselves wronged because the principle of equal treatment has not been applied to them establish, before a court or other competent authority, facts from which it may be presumed that there has been direct or indirect discrimination, *it shall be for the respondent to prove that there has been no breach of the principle of equal treatment* (my emphasis).

At the time, European legislation only applied to sex discrimination and so the Burden of Proof Regulations amended only the SDA (and then only in its application to 'employment', broadly defined). Section 63A(2) SDA provides:

Where, on the hearing of the complaint, the complainant proves facts from which the tribunal could, apart from this section, conclude in the absence of an adequate explanation that the respondent—

(a) has committed an act of discrimination against the complainant which is unlawful by virtue of Part 2 [the employment-related provisions] . . .
the tribunal shall uphold the complaint unless the respondent proves that he did not commit, or, as the case may be, is not to be treated as having committed, that act.

Section 66A makes similar provision for claims brought in the county or sheriff court in relation to discrimination against barristers or pupil barristers or in relation to vocational training (these being regarded as employment-related for the purposes of EU law). The CRE called, in 1998, for primary legislation to bring the RRA into line with the Burden of Proof Directive. This did not, in the event, happen until 2003 when it was required as part of the implementation of the Racial Equality Directive which, with the Employment Equality Directive, applies the same rule to the proof of discrimination on grounds of race or ethnic or national origin, sexual orientation, religion and belief, disability and age[26] as the Burden of Proof Directive does to discrimination on grounds of sex. The RRA has, accordingly, been amended in its application to discrimination on grounds of 'race or

---

[26] The latter from October 2006.

ethnic or national origin' (but neither colour nor nationality) and provides (ss.54A and 57ZA) that, where it is alleged that a respondent has committed an act of discrimination or harassment, on grounds of 'race or ethnic or national origin':

(2) Where, on the hearing of the complaint, the complainant proves facts from which the tribunal [or county court] could, apart from this section, conclude in the absence of an adequate explanation that the respondent—
    (a) has committed such an act of discrimination or harassment against the complainant . . .[27]
the tribunal [or county court] shall uphold the complaint unless the respondent proves that he did not commit or, as the case may be, is not to be treated as having committed, that act.

The SO and RB Regs (reg 29) are materially identical as is s.17A DDA and Articles 38A and 40A FETO[28] (which apply only in relation to employment, broadly defined). The *King/Zafar* approach is applicable to non-employment related discrimination under that Act, under the SDA and under FETO, as well as to discrimination on grounds of nationality and colour under the RRA.

The SO and RB Regs, and the amendments to the RRA, have been in place for too short a time to be tested in litigation. But there are encouraging early indications from the application of the SDA as amended that the change in the rules on proof of discrimination may have a significant impact on claimants.

In *Barton v Investec* EAT considered the application of the burden of proof in the SDA post amendment. The case concerned allegations both under the EqPA and the SDA by an analyst who had been paid less and granted less favourable non-contractual bonuses than a male comparator.

Barton v Investec Henderson Crosthwaite Securities Ltd [2003] ICR 1205

Judge Ansell:

Mr Allen [for the Applicant] argues that [s.63A SDA] clearly introduces a new approach to sex discrimination cases, requiring, effectively, an amendment to the guidelines in *King* . . . and he highlights the words 'could . . . conclude in the absence of an adequate explanation.' Thus he submits that the first stage of the procedure is for the tribunal to consider primary facts proved by the applicant to see what inferences of secondary fact could be drawn from them from which they could conclude that an act of sexual discrimination had been committed absent any explanation from the employers. He submits further that these inferences could include, in appropriate cases, inferences that it is just and equitable to draw in accordance with s.74 [SDA], eg from an evasive or equivocal reply to a questionnaire [see further below], and also any inferences that it is proper to draw from a failure to comply with any relevant code of practice under s.56A [SDA]. He submits that at this stage the tribunal does not have to reach a definitive determination that such facts would lead it to the conclusion that there was an act of unlawful discrimination but only that the facts could lead to that conclusion.

In those circumstances he submits that the burden of proof will then move to the respondents to prove that he did not commit, or as the case may be, is not to be treated as having

---

[27] Or is to be treated as having done so by virtue of vicarious liability, agency or assistance provided to a discriminator.
[28] Articles 38A and 40A deal respectively with cases brought to the Fair Employment Tribunal and non employment-related cases.

committed that act. To discharge that burden, it would be necessary for the respondents to prove on the balance of probabilities that the treatment in question was in no sense whatsoever on the grounds of sex, since he argues 'no discrimination whatsoever' is compatible with the Equal Treatment Directive or the Burden of Proof Directive. In other words, the burden of proof is upon the employer to show that sex was not any part of the reasons for the treatment in question.

Mr Lemon, for the respondents . . . submits that if the tribunal, having considered all the evidence, are unable to decide where the balance of probabilities lies and the employee has proved facts from which the tribunal could conclude that the employer had committed an act of unlawful discrimination, it would then uphold the complaint, unless the employer proves that it did not commit or is not to be treated as having committed the act of discrimination. We cannot agree with this submission, which does not appear to accord with the proper approach, as set out in both the Council Directives and s.63A [SDA].

We therefore consider it necessary to set out fresh guidance in the light of the statutory changes:

(1) Pursuant to s.63A [SDA], it is for the applicant who complains of sex discrimination to prove on the balance of probabilities facts from which the tribunal could conclude, in the absence of an adequate explanation, that the respondents have committed an act of discrimination against the applicant which is unlawful by virtue of Part II or which by virtue of s.41 or 42 SDA is to be treated as having been committed against the applicant. These are referred to below as 'such facts.'

(2) If the applicant does not prove such facts he or she will fail.

(3) It is important to bear in mind in deciding whether the applicant has proved such facts that it is unusual to find direct evidence of sex discrimination. Few employers would be prepared to admit such discrimination, even to themselves. In some cases the discrimination will not be an intention but merely based on the assumption that 'he or she would not have fitted in'.

(4) In deciding whether the applicant has proved such facts, it is important to remember that the outcome at this stage of the analysis by the tribunal will therefore usually depend on what inferences it is proper to draw from the primary facts found by the tribunal.

(5) It is important to note the word is 'could'. At this stage the tribunal does not have to reach a definitive determination that such facts would lead it to the conclusion that there was an act of unlawful discrimination. At this stage a tribunal is looking at the primary facts proved by the applicant to see what inferences of secondary fact could be drawn from them.

(6) These inferences can include, in appropriate cases, any inferences that it is just and equitable to draw in accordance with s.74(2)(b) [SDA] from an evasive or equivocal reply to a questionnaire or any other questions that fall within s.74(2) [SDA]: see *Hinks v Riva Systems* EAT/501/96.

(7) Likewise, the tribunal must decide whether any provision of any relevant code of practice is relevant and if so, take it into account in determining such facts pursuant to s.56A(10) SDA. This means that inferences may also be drawn from any failure to comply with any relevant code of practice.

(8) Where the applicant has proved facts from which inferences could be drawn that the respondents have treated the applicant less favourably on the grounds of sex, then the burden of proof moves to the respondent.

(9) It is then for the respondent to prove that he did not commit, or as the case may be, is not to be treated as having committed that act.

(10) To discharge that burden it is necessary for the respondent to prove, on the balance of probabilities, that the treatment was in no sense whatsoever on the grounds of sex, since 'no discrimination whatsoever' is compatible with the Burden of Proof Directive.

(11) That requires a tribunal to assess not merely whether the respondent has proved an explanation for the facts from which such inferences can be drawn, but further that it is adequate to discharge the burden of proof on the balance of probabilities that sex was not any part of the reasons for the treatment in question.

(12) Since the facts necessary to prove an explanation would normally be in the possession of the respondent, a tribunal would normally expect cogent evidence to discharge that burden of proof. In particular, the tribunal will need to examine carefully explanations for failure to deal with the questionnaire procedure and/or code of practice.

IRLR 'Highlights' June 2003

Contrary to the view that was consistently put forward by the Government, as reflected in the Cabinet Office guidance—'we do not think it will make any significant difference to the outcome of cases'—the Regulations clearly go further than *King* and *Zafar*. They compel a tribunal, once a prima facie case has been established, to find unlawful sex discrimination unless the employer proves that there has been no discrimination—'the tribunal shall uphold the complaint unless the respondent proves that he did not commit . . . that act.' The same language will apply in race discrimination cases from July and in religious and sexual orientation discrimination cases from December. The most important part of the guidance offered by Judge Ansell [in *Barton*] is the emphasis that in order to discharge the burden of proof, 'it is necessary for the respondent to prove, on the balance of probabilities, that the treatment was in no sense whatsoever on the grounds of sex, since 'no discrimination whatsoever' is compatible with the Burden of Proof Directive . . . That requires a tribunal to assess not merely whether the respondent has proved an explanation for the facts from which such inferences can be drawn, but further that it is adequate to discharge the burden of proof on the balance of probabilities that sex was not any part of the reasons for the treatment in question.' *Barton* is interesting also because of the EAT's holding on transparency and its unequivocal rejection of the City culture of secrecy about individual pay. This is particularly apposite with the recent introduction of statutory equal pay questionnaires. The employment tribunal regarded secrecy as 'a vital component of the City bonus culture,' but the EAT declares that 'no tribunal should be seen to condone a City bonus culture involving secrecy and/or lack of transparency because of the potentially large amounts involved, as a reason for avoiding equal pay obligations.'

The decision in *Barton* left open the question at which point the shift in the burden of proof takes place under the new regime. This question was addressed in *University of Huddersfield v Wolff* [2004] ICR 828 in which a senior lecturer challenged a refusal to promote her in circumstances in which a male comparator was promoted. The question for the tribunal was whether the fact of a difference in sex, coupled with a disparity in treatment between the claimant and her comparator, was *itself* sufficient to shift the burden of proof (note in *Bahl* above this was not even sufficient without more to *permit*, much less require, an inference of discrimination). EAT ruled that it was not and that, in addition to the fact of a difference in sex and less favourable treatment, a claimant had to establish a causal link between the two in order to benefit from the shift in the burden of proof.

Barton was approved by the Court of Appeal in *Igen Ltd v Wong* [2005] EWCA Civ 142 in which Peter Gibson LJ, for the Court, expressed the view that the amendments to the SDA altered rather than consolidated the previous position,[29] and ruled that the failure by a respondent to provide an adequate explanation for a prima facie case required, rather

---

[29] Dismissing as *obiter* comments to the contrary by Simon Brown LJ, as he then was, in *Nelson v Carillion Services Ltd* [2003] ICR 1256.

than permitted, a tribunal to find that discrimination had occurred. The court accepted the argument put forward for the claimant that 'it may be helpful for the *Barton* guidance to include a paragraph stating that the ET must assume no adequate explanation at the first stage'. The Court of Appeal expressly rejected the ruling by EAT in *Chamberlin v Emokpae* [2004] IRLR 592 that in order for discrimination to breach the SDA it had to have a 'significant influence' on the decision. The decision in *Chamberlin* was one of several joined cases dealt with by the Court of Appeal with *Wong*.

The Questionnaire Procedure

The anti-discrimination provisions set out a questionnaire procedure which was intended to ameliorate some of the difficulties of proving discrimination. Section 65 RRA provides that:

(1) With a view to helping a person ('the person aggrieved') who considers he may have been discriminated against [or subjected to harassment] in contravention of this Act to decide whether to institute proceedings and, if he does so, to formulate and present his case in the most effective manner, the Secretary of State shall by order prescribe—

(a) forms by which the person aggrieved may question the respondent on his reasons for doing any relevant act, or on any other matter which is or may be relevant; and

(b) forms by which the respondent may if he so wishes reply to any questions

(2) Where the person aggrieved questions the respondent (whether in accordance with an order under subsection (1) or not)—

(a) the question, and any reply by the respondent (whether in accordance with such an order or not) shall, subject to the following provisions of this section, be admissible as evidence in the proceedings;

(b) if it appears to the court or tribunal that the respondent deliberately, and without reasonable excuse, omitted to reply within a reasonable period [or, where the question relates to discrimination on grounds of race or ethnic or national origins, or to harassment, the period of eight weeks beginning with the day on which the question was served on him] or that his reply is evasive or equivocal, the court or tribunal may draw any inference from that fact that it considers it just and equitable to draw, including an inference that he committed an unlawful act.

Section 56 DDA is materially identical as is s.76 SDA except that the latter makes no reference as yet to harassment. The EqPA has recently been amended to provide for the service of questionnaires (new s.7B). So, too, are Article 44 FETO and reg 33 of the SO and the RB Regs.

> The form of the questionnaire is prescribed by statutory instrument under the relevant legislation, the race questionnaire, for example, being set out in the Race Relations (Questions and Replies) Order 1977 (SI 1977 No 842), Schedule 1, as follows:
>
> To (*name of person to be questioned*) of (*address*)
> 1. (1) I (*name of questioner*) of (*address*) consider that you may have discriminated against me contrary to the [RRA].

(2) (*Give date, approximate time and a factual description of the treatment received and of the circumstances leading up to the treatment.*)

(3) I consider that this treatment may have been unlawful (because (*complete if you wish to give reasons, otherwise delete*)).

2. Do you agree that the statement in paragraph 1(2) above is an accurate description of what happened? If not, in what respect do you disagree or what is your version of what happened?

3. Do you accept that your treatment of me was unlawful discrimination by you against me? If not—

(a) why not,

(b) for what reason did I receive the treatment accorded to me, and

(c) how far did considerations of colour, race, nationality (including citizenship) or ethnic or national origins affect your treatment of me?

4. (*Any other questions you wish to ask.*)

5. My address for any reply you may wish to give to the questions raised above is (that set out in paragraph 1(1) above) (*the following address*).

(*signature of questioner*) (*date*).

N.B.—By virtue of section 65 of the Act this questionnaire and any reply are (subject to the provisions of the section) admissible in proceedings under the Act and a court or tribunal may draw any such inference as is just and equitable from a failure without reasonable excuse to reply within a reasonable period, or from an evasive or equivocal reply, including an inference that the person questioned has discriminated unlawfully.

The same statutory instrument prescribes the form of response (Schedule 2): To (name of questioner) of (address).

1. I (*name of person questioned*) of (*address*) hereby acknowledge receipt of the questionnaire signed by you and dated .... which was served on me on (date).

2. [I agree that the statement in paragraph 1 (2) of the questionnaire is an accurate description of what happened.] [I disagree with the statement in paragraph 1 (2) of the questionnaire in that ....]3. I accept/dispute that my treatment of you was unlawful discrimination by me against you. [My reasons for so disputing are .... The reason why you received the treatment accorded to you and the answers to the other questions in paragraph 3 of the questionnaire are ....]

4. (*Replies to questions in paragraph 4 of the questionnaire.*)

[5. I have deleted (in whole or in part) the paragraph(s) numbered .... above, since I am unable/unwilling to reply to the relevant questions in the correspondingly numbered paragraph(s) of the questionnaire for the following reasons............................]

Similar forms are set down by the Sex Discrimination (Questions and Replies) Order 1975 (SI 1975 No.2048), the Disability Discrimination (Questions and Replies) Order 1996 (SI 1996 No.2793), the Fair Employment (Questions and Replies) Order 1999 (Statutory Rule 1999 No. 463) and Schedules 2 and 3 to the SO and the RB Regs. The questionnaires set out in the SO and RB Rules make specific reference to harassment but those applicable to FETO and RRA claims do not as yet. The Equal

Pay (Questions and Replies) Order 2003 (SI 2003 No.722), Schedules 1 and 2, are materially similar except that the questions are specifically directed towards pay and include the following (Schedule 1):

2. (b) Do you agree that I have received less pay than my comparator(s)?
(c) If you agree that I have received less pay, please explain the reasons for this difference?
(d) If you do not agree that I have received less pay, please explain why you disagree(a) Do you agree that my work is equal to that of my comparator(s)?(b) If you do not think that I am doing equal work, please give your reasons.

The employer is provided with the opportunity to explain any difference in pay between the applicant and her comparator(s), and/or to deny that the chosen comparator is suitable for the purposes of the EqPA.

As is noted on the face of the questionnaires, any deliberate failure 'without reasonable excuse' on the part of the respondent to reply within a reasonable time in full or in part, or an 'evasive or equivocal' reply, will permit a court or tribunal to draw an inference of discrimination as in *King*, above (see also the discussion in *Barton*). The period has been set at eight weeks in the case of the SO and RB Regs, the DDA and (insofar as it applies to discrimination on grounds of 'race or ethnic or national origin') the RRA. The DDA and RRA were amended in 2003 to comply with the Racial and Employment Equality Directives and the draft SD Regs propose similar amendment to the SDA. This provision was objected to in the strongest terms by some Conservative politicians on the ground that it compelled 'self-incrimination', and 'smack[ed] of the Star Chamber.'[30] But its impact has been less than dramatic. Respondents can refuse to answer questions on the grounds of irrelevance, or because to do so would impose an onerous and undue burden, and an explanation by the respondent of any refusal to answer will prevent any adverse inferences being drawn. Evasiveness or a refusal to respond can assist an applicant to persuade a court or tribunal to draw inferences of discrimination,[31] but will not of itself suffice for such an inference.[32] The CRE's 1998 proposals suggested that tribunals ought to be obliged to draw unfavourable inferences from failure of refusal to reply but no such change has been made as yet, although the approach of the Court of Appeal in *Wong* is perhaps a development in this direction.

Statistical Evidence

Among the most powerful evidence from which discrimination may be inferred is statistical evidence relating to an employer's past or current practice. (The relevance of statistics to indirect discrimination is considered in Chapter 2 as it goes to questions of substance

---

[30] Leon Brittan MP, 893 HC Debs (18 June 1975), col. 1602. See also Ian Percival MP at col. 1598.

[31] In *Clarke v Kay & Co Ltd* 41 *Equal Opportunities Review* Discrimination Case Law Digest 7 inferences were drawn from unsatisfactory replies but the case was strong in any event.

[32] See also *Gamble & Anor v Nadal & Anor* Appl No. EAT/350/98, unreported, 16 October 1998, in which EAT overturned a decision in favour of a claimant who alleged race discrimination in spite both of refusal to answer the questionnaire and evidence of racism on the part of the manager.

rather than proof. Here we are concerned with the proof of direct discrimination). In *Jalota v Imperial Metal Industries* [1979] IRLR 313 EAT rejected statistical evidence as 'irrelevant' to the question whether a claimant had been discriminated against, and voiced disapproval (*per* Talbot J) of the collection of statistics on race: 'how do you define colour? What is the precise definition that would have to be applied? But much worse than that, what could be more undesirable, and . . . more divisive than requiring the respondents to go around their thousands of employees; to check on the colour; to try to make a decision as to that?' The decision in *Jalota* was condemned at the time.

J Bowers, 'More Bonds for the Fettered Runner' (1980) 43 *Modern Law Review* 215–19

A complainant on the grounds of race or sex discrimination is like a fettered runner, shackled by bonds at the starting line. The onus of proof rests on the applicant in all discrimination cases, and it is a most difficult burden to discharge. Outside the most blatant forms of discrimination, inferences have to be drawn as to an employer's actions and motives. What can be gleaned from discovery of documents is thus a vital issue, recently considered by the House of Lords in *Science Research Council v Nassé* [[1979] ICR 921].

In consolidated appeals, Mrs. Nassé and Mr. Vyas sought discovery of confidential assessment reports from their employers to assist in their sex and race discrimination actions. The House of Lords rejected the employers' contentions that confidentiality alone is a ground of privilege from disclosure. The general test to be applied by the court or tribunal is whether discovery of each document is necessary for disposing fairly of the proceedings. The relevance of the document is an important ingredient in this decision, but not sufficient in itself. This makes the case of *Jalota v Imperial Metal Industries (Kynoch) Limited* all the more significant. In this case the door was closed on the creative use of statistics in employment discrimination cases, in marked contrast to the position in the United States. . . .

The decision in *Jalota* is against logic and principle, which suggest that the racial make up of the employers' work force is indeed relevant. In direct discrimination actions tribunals have sown themselves willing to draw inferences from the fact that minorities are employed in a particular workplace. This has been used to rebut discrimination. To hold the converse has proved anathema. For instance, in *Balkaran v City of London Corporation* an Industrial Tribunal was invited to infer that the absence of coloured people [sic] in supervisory jobs showed an anti-colour policy. It refused to do so. In *Downer v Liebig Meat*, the chairman poured scorn on the very idea: 'One can no more read from the statistics that there has been discrimination than one can infer from the fact that of the High Court judiciary only two are females, while 10 per cent of the Bar are of that sex, that there is a policy of sex discrimination in the office of the Lord Chancellor.' [!]

It is suggested that, by a skilful use of statistics, inferences can indeed be drawn as to the occurrence of discrimination. This is supported by American experience. 'Statistics speak loudly, and the courts listen' is there an oft repeated dictum. They are accepted as of great significance in both class and individual actions brought under Title VII of the Civil Rights Act 1964, which is in terms very similar to Britain's race and sex discrimination legislation. The demonstration of a large disparity between the number of females or members of minority groups in a work force, and the local or national population establishes a prima facie case, while in some cases, statistics have been held 'dispositive' of the whole case. The rationale is important; as enunciated in *Hazelwood School District v U.S.P* [534 JF (2d) 805], it runs 'absent explanation, it is ordinarily to be expected that non-discriminatory hiring practices will in time result in a workplace more or less representative of the racial and ethnic population in the community from which the employees are hired.' . . .

Talbot J.'s second reason against ordering discovery in the instant case would deny any of this development, and is more fundamental than the first. The claim to be shown a racial profile of the work force was 'wholly unreasonable, irrelevant, and should not be answered.' He instead commends the respondents for not categorising the colour of their employees and asks 'What could be more undesirable and more divisive' than keeping such records?

The judgment comes at time when many previously sceptical employers, government departments and civil liberties lobbies are taking the view that ethnic statistics are an essential element in monitoring the Race Relations and Sex Discrimination Acts, and that they should be applauded as providing a springboard for new voluntary initiatives. . . .

Civil liberties and immigrant associations have long been particularly concerned about the use of statistics in an unexplained way by those opposed to integration. Controversy has surrounded, in particular, the ethnic question in the census. The Runnymede Trust, and the National Council for Civil Liberties now advocate the keeping of figures in the employment area, with adequate safeguards. Moreover, the last government 'considered that a vital part of our equal opportunities policy is a regular system of monitoring.' It proposed, on the lines of the American experience, that the Department of Employment should be given power to request from government contractors details of employment practices, including statistical information.

It would be outrageous to analogise Britain's race problems with those of the United States, but in the use of statistics, both as evidence in court cases, and as a basis for monitoring employment practices, the Americans appear to have more of the answers. Talbot J's judgment in *Jalota*, if it is followed, will not permit the questions to be formulated.

As Bowers pointed out, the horror with which Talbot J viewed the collection of race statistics by employers sat uncomfortably with the emphasis placed by the CRE on the importance of their collection.

CRE, 'Race Relations Code of Practice for the elimination of racial discrimination and the promotion of equality of opportunity in employment' (1980)

employers should regularly monitor the effects of selection decisions and personnel practices and procedures in order to assess whether equal opportunity is being achieved. The information needed for effective monitoring . . . will best be provided by records showing the ethnic origins of existing employees and job applicants. . . . the need for detailed information and the methods of collecting it will vary according to the circumstances of individual establishments . . . in small firms or in firms in areas with little or no racial minority settlement it will often be adequate to assess the distribution of employees from personal knowledge and visual identification.

It is open to employers to adopt the method of monitoring which is best suited to their needs and circumstances. but whichever method is adopted, they should be able to show hat it is effective . . . Analyses should be carried out of:

> The ethnic composition of the workforce of each plant, department, section, shift and job category, and changes in distribution over periods of time.
> Selection decisions for recruitment, promotion, transfer and training, according to the racial group of candidates, and reasons for these decisions.
> Except in cases where there are large numbers of applicants and the burden on resources would be excessive, reasons for selection and rejection should be recorded at each sage of the selection process, e.g. initial shortlisting and final decisions. Simple categories of reason for rejection should be adequate for the early sifting stages.

. . . in order to identify areas which may need particular attention, a number of key questions should be asked.

Is there evidence that individuals from any particular racial group:
Do not apply for employment or promotion, or that fewer apply than might be expected?
Are not recruited or promoted at all, or are appointed in a significantly lower proportion than their rate of application?
Are underrepresented in training or in jobs carrying higher pay, status or authority?
Are concentrated in certain shifts, sections or departments?

The Code of Practice is not binding but, as with the other statutory codes, failure to observe its recommendations may (para 2):

> result in breaches of the law where the act or omission falls within any of the specific prohibitions of the Act. Moreover, its provisions are admissible in evidence in any proceedings under the [RRA] before an industrial tribunal and if any provision appears to the tribunal to be relevant to a question arising in the proceedings it must be taken into account in determining that question. If employers take the steps that are set out in the Code to prevent their employees from doing acts of unlawful discrimination they may avoid liability for such acts in any legal proceedings brought against them.

It was not until 1987 that EAT accepted the relevance of statistical evidence in *West Midlands Passenger Transport Executive v Singh*, a decision upheld by the Court of Appeal.

The *Singh* case involved a race discrimination claimant who applied for discovery of the ethnic origins of all applicants for senior inspector posts with the employer over a particular period, which post he had unsuccessfully applied for.[33] This information was collected by the employer in pursuit of its equal opportunities policy. The Transport Executive resisted the application and appealed against an industrial tribunal order which was subsequently upheld by EAT. EAT ruled that the statistics sought were logically probative as evidence from which an inference might be drawn that the employers had adopted a racially discriminatory policy. The Court of Appeal also rejected the employer's appeal, overruling *Jalota*.

West Midlands Passenger Transport Executive v Singh [1988] ICR 614

Balcombe LJ (for the Court):

The issue is whether evidence that a particular employer has or has not appointed any or many coloured [sic] applicants in the past is material to the question whether he has discriminated on racial grounds against a particular complainant; and whether discovery devoted to ascertaining the percentage of successful coloured applicants with successful white applicants should be ordered . . .

[Balcombe LJ remarked on the special difficulties of proving discrimination, and the need for inferences to be drawn from primary facts] . . . Statistical evidence may establish a discernible pattern in the treatment of a particular group: if that pattern demonstrates a

---

[33] Rule 4(1)(b)(ii) of the Industrial Tribunals Rules of Procedure 1985 (now replaced by the 2001 Rules, see above) provided that discovery was available in the industrial tribunals as in the county courts, this in turn being governed by Order 14, Rule 8(1) of the County Court Rules 1981 which provides that 'On hearing of an application [for discovery or disclosure of particular documents] the court . . . shall in any case refuse to make an order if and so far it is of opinion that discovery [or] disclosure . . . as the case may be, is not necessary either for disposing fairly of the action or matter or for saving costs.' Rule 4(5) now provides that 'a tribunal may, on the application of a party or of its own motion—(b) require one party to grant to another such disclosure or inspection (including the taking of copies) of documents as might be granted by a court under rule 31 of the Civil Procedure Rules 1998.'

regular failure of members of the group to obtain promotion to particular jobs and to under-representation in such jobs, it may give rise to an inference of discrimination against the group. That is the reason why the Race Relations Code of Practice . . . recommends ethnic monitoring of the workforce and of applications for promotion and recruitment, a practice adopted by the appellants in their own organisation. Statistics obtained through monitoring are not conclusive in themselves, but if they show racial or ethnic imbalance or disparities, then they may indicate areas of racial discrimination . . .

If a practice is being operated against a group then, in the absence of a satisfactory explanation in a particular case, it is reasonable to infer that the complainant, as a member of the group, has himself been treated less favourably on grounds of race. Indeed, evidence of discriminatory treatment against the group in relation to promotion may be more persuasive of discrimination in the particular case than previous treatment of the applicant, which may be indicative of personal factors peculiar to the applicant and not necessarily racially motivated . . .[34]

The suitability of candidates can rarely be measured objectively; often subjective judgments will be made. If there is evidence of a high percentage rate of failure to achieve promotion at particular levels by members of a particular racial group, this may indicate that the real reason for refusal is a conscious or unconscious racial attitude which involves stereotyped assumptions about members of that group . . .

[referring to *Jalota*] if and insofar as the case purported to lay down any general principles as to the probative effect of statistical evidence in racial discrimination cases, then it is inconsistent with the principles we have endeavoured to state above and should no longer be followed. In particular, the passage in the judgment . . . that it is unreasonable to expect employers to maintain records of the colour or ethnic origins of their employees, is inconsistent with the provisions as to monitoring contained in the Race Relations Code of Practice . . .

Balcombe LJ pointed out that an order for discovery did not follow automatically upon a finding of relevance, the question being whether such an order was necessary for the fair disposal of the proceedings[35] and, in particular, whether the party seeking the request was 'fishing' or the request 'oppressive' in the sense that: '(1) It may require the provision of material not readily to hand, which can only be made available with difficulty and at great expense [or] . . . (2) It . . . may . . . require the party ordered to make discovery to embark on a course which will add unreasonably to the length and cost of the hearing.' It was for the tribunal to decide, as it had done here, whether the discovery order ought to be granted.

The limits of the *Singh* decision became apparent in *Carrington v Helix Lighting Ltd* which involved an employer which, unlike the West Midlands Transport Executive, did not conform to the CRE's Code of Practice in respect of ethnic monitoring. Ms Carrington, who had applied for a light assembly job, was interviewed for only a couple of minutes and was rejected without notification, advertisements for the jobs in question continuing to appear in the local press. She sought discovery of statistical material relating to the ethnic composition of the respondents' workforce, an application refused by the tribunal on the grounds that, the documents sought not already being in existence, discovery of them could not be ordered. EAT rejected her appeal, Wood J stating that legislative provision had been

---

[34] 'If evidence of a non-discriminatory attitude on the part of an employer is accepted as having probative force, as being likely to have governed his behaviour in the particular case [as was the case in *Owen & Briggs*, above n18], then evidence of a discriminatory attitude on his part may also have probative effect . . .'

[35] Citing *Science Research Council v Nassé* [1979] QB 144.

made, in respect of the difficulties of proving discrimination, by the questionnaire procedure and by the power given to tribunals to draw adverse inferences in relation thereto.

Carrington v Helix Lighting Ltd [1990] ICR 125

Wood J MC (P):

... There are always two sides to an issue, and whilst the elimination of discrimination—
unfairness—whether of race or sex is the object of the legislation, it is important to remember that it is the function of the Industrial Tribunal, just like any other judicial body, to
maintain the balance—doing that which is fair, just and reasonable between the parties.

Whilst the Tribunal in each case will adopt its own approach to the problems facing it, it
seems to us that an order for discovery of documents may be a useful first step before considering any second or subsequent questionnaire, and that in any event it may be possible
for the parties to agree to draft a schedule of facts. However, in our judgment, it is
not within the power of a Tribunal to order such a schedule—at least where there is no
documentation upon which the schedule is to be based and where the production of the
schedule is in the nature of creating evidence.

The CRE['s] ... Code of Practice encourages the keeping of records in order to monitor
possible elements of unfairness ... failure to comply with the provisions and spirit of the
Code of Practice can be taken into account by a Tribunal and when it considers the whole
of the case an adverse inference may be drawn.

Finally, the learned chairman in the present case decided that to make an order would be
oppressive. This is essentially a matter within his discretion. In the present case there were
only some 155 employees, but he may very well have had in mind the fact that the only relevant employees were those in employment on 26 May 1988; that there was a considerable
turnover in the workforce, and that he had been assured there was no documentation which
was relevant to the issue. It would therefore have meant an investigation throughout the
workforce, and in considering oppression he might have taken into account the possibility
of exacerbating relationships in the factory.

The potential usefulness of racial monitoring (and, by implication, the monitoring of
other employee characteristics such as sex, etc) is clear from the decisions in *Singh* and in
Carrington, above.[36] Relatively few employers comply with the CRE's recommendation
regarding monitoring and the tribunals do not appear in practice to use their power to draw
unfavourable inferences from such failure.

Both the EOC and the CRE called, in their 1998 reform proposals, for the imposition of
'positive obligations' on employers to conduct sex and race monitoring and to pass such
information to the relevant statutory bodies.[37] These recommendations have been implemented to some extent, the RR(A)A having amended the RRA to impose positive obligations, including workforce monitoring obligations, on many 'public authority' employers.
These obligations, with the others imposed by the RRA, are considered in Chapters 2 and
3 as are similar duties imposed in relation to disability by the Disability Discrimination Act
2005 (DDA 2005) and proposed in relation to sex by the Equality Bill 2005. The EOC have
called for some time for the imposition of monitoring obligations with respect to gender
gaps in pay, the Code of Practice on Equal Pay (December 2003) most recently suggesting
that employers carry out pay reviews as an aspect of good practice. The Government has

---

[36] Though, as Bindman's article goes on to consider, no such inference was actually drawn in *Singh*.
[37] The CRE proposes this, in relation to private sector employers, only in relation to those having at least
250 employees (the EOC to all save private households).

thus far insisted on a voluntary approach (though Government departments have been obliged to carry out such reviews—see further Chapter 3). In summer 2004, however, it announced the creation of a commission to investigate equal pay. It is not impossible that the commission will herald some change of heart in this matter.

Time Limits

A further significant difficulty which discrimination complainants frequently encounter relates to the time limits imposed by legislation. Section 76 SDA provides that:

(1) An [employment] tribunal shall not consider a complaint . . . unless it is presented to the tribunal before the end of the period of three months beginning when the act complained of was done . . .
(2) A county court or a sheriff court shall not consider a claim under section 66 unless proceedings in respect of the claim are instituted before the end of—
    (a) the period of six months beginning when the act complained of was done . . .
(5) A court or tribunal may nevertheless consider any such complaint . . . which is out of time if, in all the circumstances of the case, it considers that it is just and equitable to do so.

The time limit applicable in employment-related armed services cases and in cases in which the statutory grievance procedures are used is six months, that in some education cases eight months.[38] S.68 RRA is materially identical as is schedule 3, para 3 DDA and reg 34 of each the SO and the RB Regs. The EqPA generally imposes a time limit of six months (further discussed below) and Article 46(1) FETO requires that claims are brought by: 'whichever is the earlier of (a) the end of the period of three months beginning with the day on which the complainant first had knowledge, or might reasonably be expected first to have had had knowledge, of the act complained of, or (b) the end of the period of six months beginning with the day on which the act was done.' All but the EqPA provide, like s.76(5) SDA, for complaints to be considered out of time where a court or tribunal considers it 'just and equitable' so to do.[39]

Subsection 76(6) SDA goes on to provide that:

For the purposes of this section
    (a) when the inclusion of any term in a contract renders the making of the contract an unlawful act, that act shall be treated as extending throughout the duration of the contract; and
    (b) any act extending over a period shall be treated as done at the end of that period; and
    (c) a deliberate omission shall be treated as done when the person in question decided upon it; and in the absence of evidence establishing the contrary a person shall be taken for the purposes of this section to decide upon an omission when he does an

---

[38] Ss.22 and 23 SDA, but more general extensions are provided by the Higher Education Act 2004 which amends all three discrimination Acts. Note that extensions are permitted in cases in which application has been made to the CRE for assistance or a reference made to the DRC for conciliation.

[39] RRA, s.68(6); DDA, sch 3, para 3(2)); FETO Article 46(5)); reg 34(3) SO and RB regs.

act inconsistent with doing the omitted act or, if he has done no such inconsistent act, when the period expires within which he might reasonably have been expected to do the omitted act if it was to be done.

Section 68(7) RRA, schedule 3 DDA, Article 46(6) FETO and reg 34(4) of the SO and RB Regs are all materially identical. The EqPA, whose provisions differ, is considered in Chapter 6 below. Leaving aside, for the moment, the significance of ss.76(5) SDA and its equivalents, it is clear from ss.76(6) that, where the discrimination relates to a contractual term, the three month time limit applies only from the end date of the claimant's employment or, where this is sooner, from the removal of the offending term.[40] Of rather more controversial import is ss.(b), by virtue of which a doctrine of 'continuing discrimination' has been developed which has permitted workers, on occasion, to sidestep the three month limitation period.

The courts have been at pains to distinguish 'continuing acts' from 'continuing consequences.'[41] Whereas any act of discrimination will have consequences which persist over time (a discriminatory dismissal or refusal to employ may result in a period of unemployment, a discriminatory refusal to promote may give rise to continuing financial losses), EAT ruled in *Owusu v London Fire & Civil Defence Authority* [1995] IRLR 574 (*per* Mummery J as he then was) that a 'continuing act' refers to 'some policy, rule or practice, in accordance with which decisions are taken from time to time'. In that case, a fire safety caseworker complained of a persistent failure on the part of his employers to promote, regrade, or shortlist him for promotion. The effect of EAT's acceptance that the 'continuing act' complained of was the practice of discriminatorily excluding the claimant from regrading was that a race discrimination complaint which specified a number of failures on the part of the employer to regrade the claimant was within the three month time limit, despite the fact that more than three months had elapsed since the last act alleged.

A similar approach was taken by the Court of Appeal in *Cast v Croydon College* which concerned a woman denied permission to transfer from full-time to part-time work after her return from maternity leave. The employer's written policy was one of 'receptiveness to proposals for jobsharing at all levels', but Ms Cast was informed that it was essential for the holder of her post (information centre manager) to work full-time in order properly to coordinate the work of the centre's part-time employees. The claimant resigned a month after her return to work and made her sex discrimination claim two months later. The claim was rejected by an industrial tribunal and EAT on the grounds that the act of discrimination (if it was such an act) took place prior to the claimant's return from maternity leave (the date of her first request).[42] The complaint, accordingly, was long out-of-time. Further, both the tribunal and EAT denied that the employer's refusal (despite repeated requests on Ms Cast's part) amounted to a policy. According to EAT (per Judge Hargrove):

[t]he mere repetition of a request . . . cannot convert a single managerial decision into a policy, practice or rule. In the *Owusu* case, it does not hold that a series of refusals must amount to a practice. In our view, the tribunal was forced to the view that this was a single act and

---

[40] Attempts by the employer in *Barclays Bank plc v Kapur* to argue that the (allegedly discriminatory) refusal of the bank to credit, for pension purposes, the East African service of Asian employees who moved to Britain in the 1970s as a result of the 'Africanisation' policies in that region, was a 'deliberate omission' within s.68(7)(c) were dismissed by the House of Lords [1991] 2 AC 355.

[41] See *Sougrin v Haringey Health Authority* [1992] IRLR 416 (CA), for example, and *Owusu v London Fire & Civil Defence Authority* [1995] ICR 650.

[42] See also *Commissioner of the Police for the Metropolis v Harley* [2001] ICR 927 in which EAT ruled that the time limit in a constructive dismissal case under the DDA ran from the repudiatory act rather than its acceptance.

being a finding of fact after considering correctly the question of law, it cannot be impeached.

The Court of Appeal allowed Ms Cast's appeal.

Cast v Croydon College [1998] ICR 500

Auld LJ (for the Court):

The fact that a specific act out of time may have continuing consequences within time does not make it an act extending over a period . . [43]

As to an act extending over a period, the authorities make clear—at least in the case of discrimination in the field of employment under s 6 of the 1975 Act and s 4 of the 1976 Act[44] . . . that it is the existence of a policy or regime, not a specific act of an employer triggering its application to the complainant, that matters. A moment's consideration of the concluding words of s 76(6)(b) 'any act extending over a period shall be treated as done at the end of that period' (my emphasis)—shows that that must be so. If the 'act extending over a period' required a specific act by an employer to give it effect there would be no need or room to 'treat . . . it as done at the end of the period' . . .

There may be a policy or regime for this purpose even though it is not of a formal nature or expressed in writing; and it may be confined to a particular post or role[45] . . .

The passage from . . . Judge Hargrove's judgment [above] confuses the question whether the repetition of requests, and it would seem corresponding refusals, can convert a single decision into a policy with the question whether there was a single decision or several decisions. His conclusions that the industrial tribunal had been 'forced to the view that this was a single act' and, implicitly, that it had so found are not, in my judgment, justified on the material before the tribunal or evident from the way it expressed its findings . . .

To acknowledge that there may be successive acts of discrimination in this way does not negate the time bar provided by s.76, provided that decision-makers make clear in responding to further requests whether they have reconsidered the matter. If they have, time begins to run again; if they have not, and merely refer the complainant to their previous decision, no new period of limitation arises. However, where the successive acts are such as to indicate and/or are pursuant to a policy or regime, different considerations arise . . .

In *Tyagi v World Service* [2001] IRLR 465 the Court of Appeal ruled that a job applicant could not bring a discrimination complaint under the RRA in relation to 'continuing discrimination'. According to the Court, a discrimination claim by a job applicant turns on the selection arrangements for a particular job, or to a particular refusal to offer employment. Claims had to be brought by reference to individual refusals to employ or by the

---

[43] Citing *Amies v Inner London Education Authority* [1977] ICR 308 EAT—failure to appoint to a position; and *Sougrin v Haringey Health Authority* [1992] ICR 650 (CA)—refusal to upgrade an employee. For a decision on this issue under the FEA (as it then was) see *Kearney v Northern Irish Civil Service Commission* [1996] NI 415.

[44] *Cf* Brooke LJ in *Rovenska v General Medical Council* [1998] ICR 85 on s.12 of the RRA, which deals with professional qualifications. Auld LJ in Cast appeared to doubt this which was, in any event, obiter, no discriminatory policy being required where the complaint follows within three months of the last act alleged.

[45] Citing *Owusu* and Lord Griffiths in *Barclays Bank v Kapur*, fn 40 above who, in turn, cited with approval a passage from the judgment of Bristow J in *Amies*: 'So, if the employers operated a rule that the position of head of department was open to men only, for as long as the rule was in operation there would be a continuing discrimination and anyone considering herself to have been discriminated against because of the rule would have three months from the time when the rule was abrogated within which to bring the complaint.'

relevant commission pursuing its powers to take action against 'persistent discrimination' (see further below).

Tribunals may extend time in any event (see further below). And since the decisions in *Owusu* and *Tyagi* there appears to have been some softening of judicial approach. Mummery J (now LJ) had himself, in *Owusu*, referred to a 'continuing act' as a 'policy, rule or practice, in accordance with which decisions are taken from time to time'. But he adopted a more flexible approach for the Court of Appeal in the *Hendricks* case.[46] The claimant complained of more than one hundred acts of race and sex discrimination over the course of her 11 years' service in the police. Most had taken place in the first five years of her service but she alleged that discrimination had continued up to the date of her claim notwithstanding that in the year immediately prior to it she had been on long-term stress related sick leave. A tribunal ruled as a preliminary matter that complaints related to a 'continuing act' and were therefore to be treated as done at the end of the period over which the act extended: 'In our view, on the basis of the applicant's as yet untested allegations, a policy, rule or practice could be detected as result of which female officers and officers from ethnic minorities were treated less favourably than white male officers.' EAT overturned on the basis that the claimant's allegations could not support findings of a generalised discriminatory policy so as to amount to a 'continuing act'—this on the basis that she did not allege a 'policy' as such or claim that others had been the victims of it. The Court of Appeal reinstated her claim.

Hendricks v Commissioner of Police for the Metropolis [2003] ICR 530

Mummery LJ:

On the 'continuing act' point it was made clear by the counsel then appearing for Miss Hendricks that, although the acts complained of appeared on their face to be separate incidents, they in fact constituted a 'seamless whole of continual and continuing less favourable treatment by the respondent's officers.' . . .

On the crucial issue whether this is a case of 'an act extending over a period' within the meaning of the time limits provisions of the [SDA] and the [RRA], I am satisfied that there was no error of law on the part of the employment tribunal.

On the evidential material before it, the tribunal was entitled to make a preliminary decision that it has jurisdiction to consider the allegations of discrimination made by Miss Hendricks. The fact that she was off sick from March 1999 and was absent from the working environment does not necessarily rule out the possibility of continuing discrimination against her, for which the Commissioner may be held legally responsible . . . She is, in my view, entitled to pursue her claim beyond this preliminary stage on the basis that the burden is on her to prove, either by direct evidence or by inference from primary facts, that the numerous alleged incidents of discrimination are linked to one another and that they are evidence of a continuing discriminatory state of affairs covered by the concept of 'an act extending over a period.' I regard this as a legally more precise way of characterising her case than the use of expressions such as 'institutionalised racism,' 'a prevailing way of life,' a 'generalised policy of discrimination,' or 'climate' or 'culture' of unlawful discrimination.

At the end of the day Miss Hendricks may not succeed in proving that the alleged incidents actually occurred or that, if they did, they add up to more than isolated and unconnected acts of less favourable treatment by different people in different places over a long period and that there was no 'act extending over a period' for which the Commissioner can

---

[46] See also *Kells v Pilkington plc* [2002] IRLR 693.

be held legally responsible as a result of what he has done, or omitted to do, in the direction and control of the Service in matters of race and sex discrimination. It is, however, too soon to say that the complaints have been brought too late.

I appreciate the concern expressed about the practical difficulties that may well arise in having to deal with so many incidents alleged to have occurred so long ago; but this problem often occurs in discrimination cases, even where the only acts complained of are very recent. Evidence can still be brought of long-past incidents of less favourable treatment in order to raise or reinforce an inference that the ground of the less favourable treatment is race or sex.

In my judgment, the approach of both the employment tribunal and the Appeal Tribunal to the language of the authorities on 'continuing acts' was too literal. They concentrated on whether the concepts of a policy, rule, scheme, regime or practice, in accordance with which decisions affecting the treatment of workers are taken, fitted the facts of this case . . . The concepts of policy, rule, practice, scheme or regime in the authorities were given as examples of when an act extends over a period. They should not be treated as a complete and constricting statement of the indicia of 'an act extending over a period.' I agree with the observation made by Sedley LJ, in his decision on the paper application for permission to appeal, that the Appeal Tribunal allowed itself to be sidetracked by focusing on whether a 'policy' could be discerned. Instead, the focus should be on the substance of the complaints that the Commissioner was responsible for an ongoing situation or a continuing state of affairs in which female ethnic minority officers in the Service were treated less favourably. The question is whether that is 'an act extending over a period' as distinct from a succession of unconnected or isolated specific acts, for which time would begin to run from the date when each specific act was committed.[47]

The discretion open to courts and tribunals to disapply time limits where it is just and equitable so to do is much wider than that afforded under the ERA s.111(2) of which provides that a tribunal 'shall not consider' a claim made out-of-time unless made 'within such further period as the tribunal considers reasonable in a case where it is satisfied that it was not reasonably practicable' for the complaint to be presented in time. Nor will EAT readily overturn the exercise of such discretion. In *Director of Public Prosecutions v Marshall*, a tribunal exercised its powers under s.76(5) SDA to allow an out-of-time sex discrimination claim brought in the wake of *P v S & Cornwall*, Case C–13/94 [1996] ECR I–2143 (see Chapter 10).[48] The claim was brought by a transitioning male to female trans person whose job offer was withdrawn when he announced that he would take up his position as a woman. It was filed within three months of the decision in *P v S*. The respondents claimed that the interests of legal certainty were against such an extension of the time limit.

Director of Public Prosecutions v Marshall [1998] ICR 518

Morison J:

. . . The proposition that to allow the applicant to present her complaint offends against the principle of legal certainty begs the question: what is the nature and extent of the principle? There are, as it seems to us, a number of general factors which suggest that every mature

---

[47] See also *Spender v HM Prison Service* ('In the Courts' 132 *Equal Opportunities Review*) in which EAT ruled that absence from work (there on maternity and parental leave) did not prevent discrimination continuing for the purpose of extending time.

[48] See also *British Coal Corporation v Keeble* [1997] IRLR 336. In *Aniagwu v London Borough of Hackney* [1999] IRLR 303 EAT ruled that a tribunal ought to have allowed an extension of time where one day over was due in part to the respondent's delay in processing the appeal.

legal system should adopt limitation provisions, of which legal certainty is but one. The state has an interest in avoiding trials of actions which are so stale that justice cannot be seen to have been done. If all the evidence is so stale that it is inherently unreliable, then the parties' rights cannot be judicially determined. Further, the citizens of the state have an interest in not being troubled by proceedings brought long after the event people are entitled to arrange their affairs on the basis that what happened in the past is, after a defined period, over and done with. But, equally, citizens are to be allowed a reasonable opportunity to bring their legitimate grievances to the court . . . legal certainty does not require that a person's perception of his rights to bring a valid complaint cannot be taken into account in every case . . . Some discretionary provisions will permit the court to take that factor into account; some will not. It is a question of construction of the words used which determines the answer.

In this legislation, the [SDA], the court's power to extend time is on the basis of what is just and equitable. These words could not be wider or more general. The question is whether it would be just or equitable to deny a person the right to bring proceedings when they were reasonably unaware of the fact that they had the right to bring them until shortly before the complaint was filed. That unawareness might stem from a failure by the lawyers to appreciate that such a claim lay, or because the law 'changed' or was differently perceived after a particular decision of another court. The answer is that in some cases it will be fair to extend time and in others it will not. The industrial tribunal must balance all the factors which are relevant, including, importantly and perhaps crucially, whether it is now possible to have a fair trial of the issues raised by the complaint. Reasonable awareness of the right to sue is but one factor . . .

It is arguably the case that EAT was obliged under the terms of the Equal Treatment Directive to exercise its discretion in favour of Ms Marshall (see further the discussion below). The discretion accorded to tribunals in this context is broad. In *London Borough of Southwark v Afolabi* [2003] ICR 800 the Court of Appeal ruled that a tribunal had not erred in hearing a race discrimination complaint which concerned the terms of his appointment to a position some nine years before. It was not until shortly prior to the issue of the complaint that the claimant had seen his personnel file which revealed that the employer's refusal to appoint him to the position he had originally sought (as distinct from the more junior one in which he was taken on) was made notwithstanding very high ratings he had received at his interview. The tribunal ruled that it was just and equitable to consider his complaint, there having been no reason for him to inspect his personal file before he did, and Mr Afolabi having brought his claim within three months of seeing the file. The tribunal, which decided the time limits issue as a preliminary matter, took the view that the elapse in time would be no more prejudicial to the respondent than it was to the claimant himself. EAT and the Court of Appeal upheld the tribunal's exercise of discretion, although Peter Gibson LJ (with whom Rix LJ expressly agreed on this point) suggested that:

it can only be in a wholly exceptional case that the [tribunal] could properly conclude that despite a delay of a magnitude anywhere approaching nine years it was just and equitable to extend time. The policy of the Act is made clear by the brevity of the limitation period; that period of three months is in marked contrast to the limitation periods in ordinary litigation.' Parliament having envisaged that complaints within the jurisdiction of the [tribunal] will be determined within a short space of time after the events complained of, it will be an extremely rare case where the [tribunal] can properly decide that there can be a fair trial so long after those events. Had Southwark duly applied itself to what it needed to prove and submitted appropriate evidence, the result may well have been different. As it is, I am compelled to conclude that, on the findings which it was open for the [tribunal] to make, the decision to extend time cannot be impugned.

Sedley and Rix LJJ stressed the discretion of the tribunal as to when the decision on time limits should be made, as well as to the substantive exercise of discretion. Having said this, a tribunal which directs itself incorrectly on the law will step outside the limits of its discretion. In *Apelogun-Gabriels v London Borough of Lambeth* [2002] ICR 713 the Court of Appeal ruled that the fact that an employee deferred tribunal proceedings while awaiting the outcome of domestic proceedings was only one factor to be taken into account in determining whether it was 'just and equitable' to extend time limits.[49] According to Peter Gibson LJ, there was no 'general principle that one should always await the outcome of internal grievance procedures before embarking on litigation.' Where, as in this case, a tribunal extended time to give effect to such a non-existent principle, EAT had been correct to allow the employer's appeal and remit the case to a differently constituted tribunal for redecision.

A rather alarming example of a refusal to extend time is reported in the EOC's Interim Report into its 2004 Formal Investigation into pregnancy discrimination. In *O'Herlihy v The Passionate Pub Co Ltd* the claimant, who was sacked during pregnancy, was hospitalized for a pregnancy-related illness and, having lived in tied accommodation, also had to find somewhere to live as a result of her dismissal. A tribunal refused to extend time when she missed the deadline by two days.

The ECJ has accepted that Member States may impose time limits in respect of claims based on Community law provided (*Rewe-Zentralfinanz eG v Landwirtschaftskammer fur das Saarland* Case C–33/76 [1976] ECR 1989) that they are no less favourable for such actions than for similar rights of a domestic nature, and that they do not render the exercise of rights conferred by Community law impossible in practice. The difficulty which arises relates to claims in respect of which the relevant national time limit has expired before a Member State has properly implemented the EU legislation. In *Emmott v Minister for Social Welfare and Attorney General*, Case C–208/90 [1991] ECR I–04269 the ECJ ruled that, while time limits were acceptable within the provisos established by *Rewe*, the obligation on Member States to implement EU law must be taken to provide that, until a Directive had been properly transposed, Member States could not rely on delay against an individual seeking to exercise rights granted by that Directive.

The approach taken by the ECJ in *Emmott* would appear to indicate that no time limits could be applied in respect of European-related claims until after the relevant EU law has been properly implemented by Member States. Thus, where inadequacies of transposition become apparent in future years, the three month time limit would not begin to run until after further amendments. But the result of this application of *Emmott* would be such as to do away, in practice, with the principle, discussed above, that directives, as distinct from a number of Treaty provisions and other EU legislation, do not have horizontal direct effect.

If *Emmott* were to be applied in all its logic by the ECJ, private actors (in this case, employers) would be rendered liable, perhaps long after the event, for breaches of EU law of which they were unaware and could not have been aware at the time of the breach. The rationale behind *Marshall* and *Francovich* has been, in part, to encourage compliance with EU law by Member States otherwise tardy in the transposition of directives. But no such

---

[49] Preferring the approach taken by Lindsay J in *Robinson v Post Office* [2000] IRLR 804 to that in *Aniagwu, ibid.*

logic applies in relation to private sector actors such as employers who would be caught by any wide application of the *Emmott* principle. It was perhaps the recognition of this dilemma which caused the about-turn taken by the ECJ in *Steenhorst-Neerings v Bestuur van de Bedrijfsvereniging voor Detailhandel, Ambachten en Huisvrouwen* Case C–338/91 [1993] ECR I–4575 and *Johnson v Chief Adjudication Officer (No. 2)* Case C–410/92 [1994] ECR I–5483. Both concerned Council Directive 79/7 (the Social Security Directive) and, in particular, national rules which limited the back-dating of benefits to one year prior to any claim made. In both cases, the claimants sought to avoid the domestic time limits on the grounds that the social security legislation in question had not previously provided for equal treatment as required by the Directive. Both claimants argued that their claims should be back-dated to the end of 1984, the date when the Netherlands and the UK should properly have transposed the Directive so as to provide for equality in respect of the benefits at issue. But, while Advocate General Damon took the view, in *Steenhorst-Neerings*, that *Emmott* mandated a decision favourable to the claimant in the instant case, the Court distinguished the earlier case on the grounds that, while it related to time-limits, *Steenhorst-Neerings* concerned back-dating. Time limits, according to the ECJ, served to ensure that the legality of administrative decisions could not be challenged indefinitely. Limitations on backdating of benefit claims, on the other hand, served the interests of sound administration and financial balance. The Court did not, however, explain why the latter, but not the former, trumped the principle of equality.[50]

In *Denkavit Internationaal BV v Kamer van Hopophandel en Fabrieken voor Middengelderland*, Case C–2/94 [1996] ECR I–2827, Advocate-General Jacobs suggested that *Emmott* was properly understood, in the light of the intervening decisions:

> as establishing the principle that a Member State may not rely on a limitation period where a Member State is in default both in falling to implement a directive and in obstructing the exercise of a judicial remedy in reliance upon it, or perhaps where the delay in exercising remedy and hence the failure to meet the time limit—is in some other way due to the con-duct of the national authority. In *Emmott*, the delay had been caused by the state itself, the administrative authorities refusing to adjudicate the applicant's social security claim until litigation in a relevant case had been concluded.[51] A further factor in *Emmott* was that the applicant was in the particularly unprotected position of an individual dependent on social welfare.
>
> Seen in those terms, the *Emmott* judgment may be regarded as an application of the well-established principle that the exercise of Community rights must not be rendered 'exces-sively difficult' . . . That view is consistent with the Court's remark in *Johnson* that the time bar in *Emmott* 'had the result of depriving the applicant of any opportunity whatever to rely on her right to equal treatment under the Directive,' whereas the application of the rules in *Steenhorst-Neerings* and *Johnson* did not 'make it impossible to exercise rights based on the Directive.' . . .
>
> The *Emmott* judgment may nevertheless be seen as a new application of that principle in so far as it demonstrates that a national court may be obliged to set aside a limitation period which is in principle unobjectionable where the special circumstances of the particular case so demand. It seems to me, in the interests of legal certainty the obligation to set aside time limits should be confined to wholly exceptional circumstances such as those in *Emmott*.

---

[50] In *Johnson* the ECJ relied on *Steenhorst*.
[51] *McDermott v Minister for Social Welfare* Case C–286/85 [1987] ECR 1453.

Particular problems have arisen concerning the time limits applicable in respect of claims related to Article 141 TEC. In *Biggs v Somerset County Council* and in *Barber v Staffordshire County Council* [1996] ICR 379 the claimants sought to argue that the time-limit in respect of claims based on Article 141 could not begin to run until the provision had been implemented in UK law. Both cases arose in the wake of the House of Lords decision in *EOC v Secretary of State for Employment* [1995] 1 AC 1 and were brought by women who, having been dismissed from part-time employment with less than the five years' service then required for redundancy pay/unfair dismissal claims, sought to make their claims years after dismissal. Their claims were rejected and their appeals dismissed by both EAT and the Court of Appeal. Above we considered whether Article 141 gave rise to 'free-standing' rights enforceable in the tribunal system (the Court of Appeal in *Biggs* and *Barber* declared that it does not). Here we consider the issued raised in relation to time limits only. Neill LJ considered a number of ECJ cases.[52] From *Rewe* he cited the following extract before going on to consider the case before him:

Biggs v Somerset County Council [1996] ICR 364

Neill LJ:

> In the absence of Community rules on this subject, it is for the domestic legal system of each Member State to designate courts having jurisdiction and to determine the procedural conditions governing actions at law intended to ensure the protection of the rights which citizens have from the direct effect of Community law, it being understood that such conditions cannot be less favourable than those relating to similar actions of a domestic nature . . . The position would be different only if the conditions and time limits made it impossible in practice to exercise the rights which the national courts are obliged to protect.

> It was . . . argued on behalf of Mrs Biggs that the statutory time limit should be disapplied because its application would run counter to the principle that it must not be impossible or extremely difficult to present a claim . . .

> In reliance on the decision in *Emmott* . . . it was argued . . . that the council could not rely on any time limit until UK law had been brought into conformity with Community law. It is necessary to consider this argument first in relation to Article [141]. It is clear from the decision of the ECJ in *Francovich* . . . that even where a Directive is capable of having direct effect, an individual cannot rely on its terms while the Directive is unimplemented. Until implemented it has no force of law in the relevant jurisdiction, though the fact that it has not been implemented may give rights to compensation. . . . But a provision in the Treaty itself which has direct effect stands on a different basis. Thus the validity of Article [141] in UK law does not depend on any implementation by the UK Parliament; it is part of UK law. It follows therefore in my view that the principle set out in *Emmott, supra*, has no application to a claim involving Article [141]. Indeed, it is to be noted that in paragraph 17 of the judgment in *Emmott* attention was drawn to the 'particular nature of Directives.'[53]

Biggs and *Barber v Staffordshire* fell at the time-limits imposed by the ERA, the claims relating to unfair dismissal and redundancy (albeit interpreted in light of Article 141's

---

[52] Including those in *Amministrazione Delle Finanze Dello Stato v San Giorgio* Case C–199/82 [1983] ECR 3595, *Johnson v Chief Adjudication Officer*, *Francovich* and *Rewe*.

[53] Nor did the Court of Appeal accept that Ms Biggs could rely on the non-conformity of UK law at the time of her dismissal to bring an *Emmott* claim under the Equal Pay Directive: 'The Equal Pay Directive was adopted in order to implement the principle in Article 141. In these circumstances it does not seem to me that the Equal Pay Directive conferred any new or separate right.'

equality guarantee). In *Preston v Wolverhampton NHS Trust*, the time limit at issue was the six month period at the time imposed by s.2(4) EqPA. That section, subsequently amended as detailed below, at the time provided that claims had to be brought within six months of the end of the employment to which the claim related. In *National Power plc v Young* [2001] ICR 328 the Court of Appeal ruled that 'employment' in s.2(4) did not refer to the partic- ular job done by the *claimant*, but the overall period of employment with her employer. The provision appears more generous than the position under the SDA, RRA, DDA or the SO or RB Regs (three months) but, whereas the other anti-discrimination provisions permit the time limit to be extended where such extension is 'just and equitable' (and the ERA where an earlier claim was not 'reasonably practicable'), the six month period imposed by the EqPA was absolute, and remains so except in the circumstances outlined below.

In *Preston v Wolverhampton Healthcare NHS Trust* Case C–78/98 [2000] ECR I–03201, the ECJ considered the compatibility of s.2(4) with Community law. The claimants had been denied access to occupational pension schemes by virtue of their part-time status. The ECJ had ruled, in the *Vroege* case,[54] that Article 141 entitled women and men to equal access to membership of pension schemes (as well as to payments thereunder). *Barber v Guardian Royal Exchange* Case C–262/88 [1990] ECR I–1889 imposed a time constraint on equal pay claims relating to pension *payments* (the ECJ permitting claims in relation to pension payments in respect of service prior to the date of judgment only where the claims were filed before the date of the *Barber* judgment). But, according to the Court in *Vroege*, that time limit did not apply to claims relating to the denial of *membership* on grounds of sex.

Ms Preston was among the tens of thousands of women who launched equal pay claims in the wake of the *Vroege* decision. A number of cases were selected in order that prelimi- nary issues such as time limits could be resolved. These claims, of which Ms Preston's was one, were rejected by a tribunal, EAT and the Court of Appeal. One of the stumbling blocks concerned the six month time limit imposed by the EqPA. Many of the women had left employment years before commencing their actions. Others had been employed on a succession of fixed term contracts. Of this group, even those who had filed their claims while they were still working were met with the ruling that the six month period flowed from the end of each successive contract of employment, with the result that their claims in rela- tion to earlier periods of employment were out of time.

All arguments advanced to the effect that the EqPA's six month limit conflicted with EU law were rejected. In response to the argument that the limit made it impossible in practice for claimants to press their Article 141 claims, the courts followed the approach taken by the Court of Appeal in *Biggs* and said that, Article 141 being directly enforceable by indi- viduals in the national courts, the claimants could have challenged their exclusion from the pension schemes at the time. Nor did the courts accept that the time limits imposed by the EqPA were less favourable than those which applied elsewhere (such as the RRA, whose three month time limit could be extended). In the first place, the courts ruled that the EqPA's limits applied whether cases were based solely on national law or whether they emanated from Article 141. On this basis, there was no discrimination against European law claims. Secondly, even if it was appropriate to look beyond the EqPA, the *Rewe* decision did not oblige the courts (Court of Appeal [1997] ICR 899, *per* Schiemann J):

> to cast around the whole of domestic law in order to discover some other legislation . . . which is concerned with some other sort of equality in order to see whether the limitation periods in that Statute are in certain circumstances more generous than those in the [EqPA].

---

[54] *Vroege v NCIV Institut voor Volkshuisvesting BV* Case C–57/93 [1994] ECR I–4541.

Our domestic law as no doubt the domestic law of other Member States, has innumerable different time limits in relation to innumerable different situations. Some of those time limits incorporate a certain degree of flexibility, (I accept that in the employment field no other claim has a completely rigid time limit which cannot be disapplied by the court) others do not. It is not, and could not be, suggested that this in itself is contrary to Community law. What is objectionable is discrimination in the treatment of similar claims as between claims based on domestic law and claims based on Community law. That does not exist in the present cases.[55]

Preston was appealed to the House of Lords which referred to the ECJ the question whether the six month time limit imposed by the EqPA rendered it 'impossible' or 'excessively difficult' for claimants to exercise their Article 141 rights, and whether the different time limits which applied to equal pay and other claims (including contractual claims) breached European law. Their Lordships referred similar questions dealing with the then two year limit on compensation. The ECJ ruled that the six month time limit did not render impossible or excessively difficult the exercise of rights conferred by the Community legal order and is not therefore liable to strike at the very essence of those rights'. That Court did not accept, however (as the Court of Appeal had) that the appropriate comparison was between those equal pay claims which did and those which did not rely on Community law, both being governed by the EqPA's limitation. It was for the domestic courts to determine the question of discrimination of discrimination as between Community and domestic claims. But 'the [EqPA] constitutes the legislation by means of which the United Kingdom discharges its obligations under Article [141] of the Treaty and . . . cannot therefore provide an appropriate ground of comparison against which to measure compliance with the principle of equivalence.' The ECJ ruled that national courts, in determining the appropriate comparison, 'must consider whether the actions concerned are similar as regards their purpose, cause of action and essential characteristics' and 'in order to decide whether procedural rules are equivalent, the national court must verify objectively, in the abstract, whether the rules at issue are similar taking into account the role played by those rules in the procedure as a whole, as well as the operation of that procedure and any special features of those rules.'

Finally, the ECJ dealt with the question of how the six month time limit should apply in the case of successive fixed term contracts, ruling that 'setting the starting point of the limitation period [in respect of successive short-term contracts] at the end of each contract renders the exercise of the right conferred by Article [141] of the Treaty excessively difficult' and that Article 141 required that the time limit in such cases began to run from the end of the 'stable employment relationship.'

On its return the House of Lords accepted that claims for breach of contract were sufficiently similar to Article 141 claims to permit comparison of the time limits applicable thereto, but that the limits, considered in the round, were no less favourable:

---

[55] Between the date of reference and that of the ECJ's decision, the latter had handed down judgment in *Levez v Jennings (Harlow Pools) Ltd* Case C–326/96 [1998] ECR I–07835 in which, dealing with s.2(5) EqPA, that Court ruled that the comparison required by *Rewe* could not be made between Article 141 claims, on the one hand, and EqPA claims, on the other: 'the [EqPA] is the domestic legislation which gives effect to the Community principle of non-discrimination on grounds of sex in relation to pay, pursuant to Article [141] of the Treaty and the [Equal Pay] Directive. Accordingly . . . the fact that the same procedural rules [there s.2(5) EqPA] apply to two comparable claims, one relying on a right conferred by Community law, the other on a right acquired under domestic law, is not enough to ensure compliance with the principle of equivalence, as the United Kingdom Government maintains, since one and the same form of action is involved.'

Preston v Wolverhampton Healthcare NHS Trust [2001] 2 AC 455

Lord Slynn (for their Lordships):

There is . . . a six-year period for contract claims rather than a six-month claim for infringement of Article [141]. This, however, is not the end of the inquiry. Merely to look at the limitation periods is not sufficient. It is necessary to have regard to the role played by that provision in the procedure as a whole, as well as the operation and any special features of that procedure before the different national courts'.

In *Levez v T H Jennings (Harlow Pools) Ltd* the Court of Justice said:

'51. On that point, it is appropriate to consider whether, in order fully to assert rights conferred by Community law before the county court, an employee in circumstances such as those of the applicant will incur additional costs and delay by comparison with an applicant who, because he is relying on what may be regarded as a similar right under domestic law, may bring an action before the industrial tribunal, which is simpler and, in principle, less costly.'

There are thus factors to be set against the difference in limitation periods. As has already been seen, the claim under a contract can only go back six years from the date of the claim whereas a claim brought within six months of the termination of employment can go back to the beginning of employment or 8 April 1976 (the date of the judgment in *Defrenne v Sabena* Case C–43/75 [1976] ECR I–00455), whichever is the later. Moreover, the applicant can wait until the employment is over, thus avoiding the possibility of friction with the employer if proceedings to protect her position are brought during the period of employment, as will be necessary since the six-year limitation runs from the accrual of a completed cause of action. It is in my view also relevant to have regard to the lower costs involved in the claim before an employment tribunal and if proceedings finish there the shorter time-scale involved. The period of six months itself is not an unreasonably short period for a claim to be referred to an employment tribunal. The informality of the proceedings is also a relevant factor.

I am not satisfied that in these cases it can be said that the rules of procedure for a claim under s.2(4) are less favourable than those applying to a claim in contract. I therefore hold that s.2(4) does not breach the principle of equivalence.

Lord Slynn went on to rule, in compliance with the ECJ's approach, that the time limits applicable to successive short-term contracts could not begin to run until the employment relationship had come to an end, although 'where there are intermittent contracts of service without a stable employment relationship, the period of six months runs from the end of each contract of service.' The EqPA has been amended to give effect to *Preston* and the earlier decision of the ECJ in *Levez* (in which that court ruled that the six month limit breached Article 141 in a case in which the employer had actively concealed the pay difference at issue from the claimant). Subsection 2(4) and new 2ZA EqPA now provide that the six month time limit applies:

• In the case of a 'stable employment relationship from the day on which the stable employment relationship ended (unless the case is also a 'disability'and/ or 'concealment' case);
• In a 'concealment case' (see s.2ZA(2)), from the day on which the woman discovered the qualifying fact in question, or could with reasonable diligence have discovered it (unless the case is also a 'disability' case);
• In a 'disability case', from the on which the woman ceased to be under a disability (unless the case is also a 'concealment' case);
• In a case which is both a concealment and a disability case from the later of the dates referred to in in the two paragraphs immediately above;

- In a 'standard case' (not being a 'stable employment relationship', 'concealment' and/or 'disability' case), six months after the last day on which the woman was employed in the employment.

Individual Remedies

The SDA, RRA, DDA, FETO and Regs

There are significant differences in this area between the SDA, RRA, SO and RB Regs, on the one hand, and FETO and, to a lesser extent, the DDA, on the other (the remedies under the EqPA are considered below).

Section 56(1) RRA provides that employment tribunals may award the following remedies:

(a) an order declaring the rights of the complainant and the respondent in relation to the act to which the complaint relates;
(b) an order requiring the respondent to pay to the complainant compensation of an amount corresponding to any damages he could have been ordered by a county court or by a sheriff court to pay to the complainant . . .
(c) a recommendation that the respondent take within a specified period action appearing to the tribunal to be practicable for the purpose of obviating or reducing the adverse effect on the complainant of any act of discrimination to which the complaint relates.

The relevant provisions of the other legislation[56] are materially identical to s.56(1) RRA save that s.17A(2) DDA substitutes the words 'reasonable, in all the circumstances of the case' for the word 'practicable' and the word 'matter' for the words 'act of discrimination' in s.56(1)(c) RRA, while Article 39(1)(d) FETO provides an additional remedy by permitting the Fair Employment Tribunal to recommend:

> that the respondent take within a specified period action appearing to the Tribunal to be practicable for the purpose of obviating or reducing the adverse effect on a person *other than the complainant* of any unlawful discrimination to which the complaint relates [my emphasis].

This power to make recommendations was amended to this effect only in 1998. In the same year the CRE criticised the individualistic focus of s.56(c) RRA and proposed that it be widened to allow tribunals to make recommendations 'regarding the future conduct of the respondent to prevent further acts of discrimination,' including recommendations 'regarding any of the respondent's practices or procedures which have been at issue and future treatment of the applicant by the respondent . . . whether or not she or he remains in employment.' The EOC also criticised the narrow range of remedies available and called for powers to be given to tribunals to order 'reinstatement, re-engagement, appointment, or promotion as appropriate' as well as 'action needed to end the discrimination [against] the person bringing the complaint *and anyone else who might be affected*' (my emphasis).

---

[56] Ss. 65 SDA, 17A DDA, Art 39 FETO and reg 30 of the SO and RB Regs.

Section 56(3) RRA and its equivalent provisions provide that, where 'without reasonable justification the respondent to a complaint fails to comply with a recommendation' made by a tribunal under s.65(1)(c), the tribunal may make an award of compensation or increase the amount of compensation awarded if it regards it as 'just and equitable' so to do. But despite their availability in employment tribunal claims, declarations and recommendations are almost never made in discrimination cases.[57]

The power to make recommendations is limited both by the statutory provisions themselves and by their judicial application. The first limitation is that discussed above, i.e., that (save in the case of FETO) the recommendation must relate to the *complainant* rather than the wider workforce and must be remedial rather than aimed at preventing future acts of discrimination. Having said this, in *London Borough of Southwark v Ayton* (2004, discussed in 'In the Courts' 127 *Equal Opportunities Review*) EAT accepted that a recommendation that the person who had discriminated against the claimant undergo race awareness training was one within the power of the tribunal to make. This type of recommendation can obviously have implications for workers other than the complainant him or herself.

The second limitation on the power to make recommendations is found in the decisions of the Court of Appeal in *Noone v North West Thames Regional Health Authority (No 2)* [1988] ICR 813, and EAT in *British Gas plc v Sharma* [1991] ICR 19. The courts there ruled that tribunals were not entitled to recommend that the claimants respectively be appointed to the next suitable job and promoted to the next suitable vacancy, this on the basis that the RRA (and its equivalents) did not permit 'positive' discrimination (see further Chapter 3). This limitation should not, however, be too rigidly applied. As *Harvey* points out (para 405): 'If the tribunal merely finds that, but for an act of unlawful discrimination, the complainant *might* have been given the relevant job, then it is indeed fair that he should be allowed to join the next queue but not jump it; but if the finding is that, but for the unlawful act, he *would* definitely have got the job, then surely it is right that he should be allowed to jump in ahead of the next queue?'

The discrimination provisions do not provide any express power to order reinstatement or re-engagement (*cf* ERA on an unfair dismissal claim). The approach of the courts to recommendations has been described by Deakin and Morris 'highly restrictive' (this in a comment on the decision in *Noone*). But in *Chief Constable of West Yorkshire Police v Vento (No.2)* [2003] ICR 318 Wall J characterised the discretion given to tribunals by s.65(1)(c) SDA as 'extremely wide,' and there seems to be no reason in principle why a tribunal could not recommend reinstatement or re-engagement. In *Smith v Ingram Motoring Group Ltd* (2004, reported in 'Case Digest' 126 *Equal Opportunities Review*) a tribunal recommended that the claimant, who had won a claim relating to a refusal to permit her to return part-time after maternity leave, be permitted to return on that basis.

Where claims are brought in the county court (in Scotland, the sheriff court), s.57 RRA and its equivalents provide that the remedies obtainable shall be all those which 'would be obtainable in the High Court or the Court of Session, as the case may be,' s.57(4) providing that '[f]or the avoidance of doubt it is hereby declared that damages in respect of an unlawful act of discrimination may include compensation for injury to feelings whether or not they include compensation under any other head.'[58]

Settlements account, in Northern Ireland, for many more fair employment cases than do tribunal determinations in favour of claimants. The same is true under the SDA, RRA and

[57] Ss.65(1) SDA, 17A(2) DDA, Art 39(1) FETO, reg 30 RB and SO Regs.
[58] The amendment of the RRA to regulate discrimination by public authorities resulted in the inclusion within it of special provisions dealing with remedies in such cases.

DDA in Great Britain (the SO and RB Regs have not been in place for long enough to comment on their enforcement). But, whereas pre-tribunal hearing conciliation is attempted in employment-related discrimination cases by ACAS, conciliation in fair employment cases falls within the remit of the ECNI (previously the FEC) in Northern Ireland (and, in non-employment disability discrimination cases, within the remit of the DRC in Britain). Whereas information about the settlements reached under the auspices of ACAS and otherwise is hard to access, the FEC in Northern Ireland published details of settlements reached under the fair employment legislation. Such settlements almost invariably included apologies and undertakings on the part of the employer. Undertakings commonly made included agreements to liaise with the FEC to ensure an 'adequate and effective' equal opportunities policy, to create 'a harmonious working environment,' or to take 'pro-active action on sectarian harassment,' together with a review of equal opportunities policies.[59] Information has become more sparse since the amalgamation of the FEC into the ECNI in 2000 but a news release on 17 May 2001 provided details of financial settlements reached with the Commission's assistance in the previous 12 months (56 cases involving payouts of over a third of a million pounds in total, with individual payments varying between £25,000 in two cases and £1,500 in another) and the ECNI's annual reports contain details of settlements reached across the protected grounds.

By far the most common remedy under the SDA, RRA and DDA is compensation which, until 1993 and 1994 in sex and race cases respectively, was capped (most recently at £11,000). The SDA cap was removed in the wake of the decision in *Marshall v Southampton and South-West Hampshire Area Health Authority (No.2)*, Case C–271/91 [1993] ECR I–04367, [1993] IRLR 445, in which the ECJ ruled that it contravened the Equal Treatment Directive, and a Private Member's Bill amended the RRA similarly.[60] The FEA's £30,000 cap was removed in 1994 while compensation payable under the DDA, passed after the removal of the other caps in respect of the other forms of discrimination, was never subject to a statutory maximum. (Note that the Employment Act 2002 and related regulations provides for the reduction of compensation by a minimum 10 per cent and maximum 50 per cent in cases in which a claimant has not completed internal statutory grievance procedures (unless the failure to complete is because of the employer's behaviour in which case mandatory increases of minimum 10 per cent and maximum 50 per cent apply.)

Respondents could avoid the award of compensation in indirect discrimination claims (ss.66(3) SDA, 57(3) RRA and 26(2) FEA) by proving 'that the requirement or condition in question was not applied with the intention of treating the claimant unfavourably on the ground of' sex, race, married status, religious belief or political opinion. Quite what was meant by 'intentional' as distinct from 'unintentional' discrimination was not clear until 1995, when EAT reached its decision in *London Underground v Edwards* [1995] ICR 574. EAT ruled that an intention to apply the disputed requirement or condition, coupled with the knowledge of its impact on the claimant as a member of the group upon which it impacted disadvantageously, sufficed.[61]

The *London Underground* case was brought under the SDA, but a similar decision was reached under the RRA the following year in *JH Walker Ltd v Hussain* [1996] ICR 291. There, EAT upheld an award of damages made to a number of Muslims who were disci-

[59] These from four settlements reported 11 March 1997, press report on FEC's website at www.fec-ni.org.
[60] Sex Discrimination and Equal Pay (Remedies) Regulations 1993 SI 1993/2798; Race Relations (Remedies) Act 1994.
[61] Cf *Orphanos v Queen Mary College* [1985] ICR 761. See also *Hussain v Streamline Taxis* 10 November 1997 36. *Equal Opportunities Review Discrimination Case Law Digest* 12, cf *Lane v London Metropolitan University*, EAT, 28 October 2004.

plined for taking time off during Eid contrary to their employer's recently adopted rule that non-statutory holidays could not be taken during the summer months. According to Mummery J, for the Court:

> as a matter of ordinary English, 'intention' in this context signifies the state of mind of a person who, at the time when he does the relevant act (ie the application of the requirement or condition resulting in indirect discrimination),
> (a) wants to bring about the state of affairs which constitutes the prohibited result of unfavourable treatment on racial grounds; and
> (b) knows that that prohibited result will follow from his acts . . .
> Depending on the circumstances, a tribunal may infer that a person wants to produce certain consequences from the fact that he acted knowing what those consequences would be
> . . .

In the period between *London Underground* and *Walker*, the SDA was amended to permit compensation for employment-related unintentional indirect discrimination in employment cases in which the tribunal regarded such compensation as 'just and equitable.' This action was prompted, it seems, by the Government's fear that it would be subject to legal action under *Francovich* (discussed above),[62] in the wake of a number of tribunal decisions that the SDA did not comply with the Equal Treatment Directive and the decision of EAT in *Macmillan v Edinburgh Voluntary Organisations Council* (unreported, App No. EAT/1995/ 536) that the SDA's 'unambiguous' provisions could not be interpreted so as to permit an award in respect of unintentional discrimination). When the fair employment legislation was amended and consolidated into FETO, a similar change was made as regards employment-related discrimination and regs 30(2) of the SO and RB Regs are materially identical to the SDA as it now applies to employment-related discrimination. The amendment of the RRA in 2003 to give effect to the provisions of the Racial Equality Directive resulted in the simple removal of s.56(3) but s.57(3), which applies to cases brought in the county or sheriff court, continues (like the SDA and FETO as they apply other than to employment) to provide that no compensation may be awarded for 'unintentional' indirect discrimination on grounds of nationality or colour or which otherwise falls outwith the Race Directive (see further Chapter 7).

Where compensation is available in discrimination cases, the heads under which it may be awarded (whether by a tribunal or a court) were set out by the Court of Appeal in the following case:

Alexander v Home Office [1988] ICR 685

May LJ (for the Court):

> . . . damages for this relatively new tort of unlawful racial discrimination are at large, that is to say that they are not limited to the pecuniary loss that can be specifically proved . . . compensatory damages may and in some instances should include an element of aggravated damages where, for example, the defendant may have behaved in a high-handed,

---

[62] S.65(1B)(b), as inserted by the Sex Discrimination and Equal Pay (Miscellaneous Amendments) Regulations 1996 SI 1996 No 438. See more recently *BMA v Chaudhary* (EAT, 24 March 2003, App. Nos UK/EAT/1351/01/DA and UK/EAT/0804/02/DA) in which the tribunal ruled that the BMA could not avoid an award of compensation in respect of indirect race discrimination in its refusal to support race discrimination claims. According to the report of the case in the EOR '2002 Compensation Awards', the BMA 'knew, if it cared to consider it, that more Asian members would be affected by that attitude, but it did not want to consider it expressly'. This issue is one of a number which has been appealed by the BMA.

malicious, insulting or oppressive manner in committing the act of discrimination.[63] . . .
The material passage from Lord Diplock's speech in *Cassell & Co Ltd v Broome* [[1972] 1
AC 1136] is in these terms:

The three heads under which damages are recoverable for those torts for which damages
are 'at large' are classified under the following heads. (1) Compensation for the harm caused
to the plaintiff by the wrongful physical act of the defendant in respect of which the action
is brought. In addition to any pecuniary loss specifically proved the assessment of this
compensation may itself involve putting a money value upon physical hurt, as in assault on
curtailment of liberty, as in false imprisonment or malicious prosecution on injury to reputation, as in defamation, false imprisonment and malicious prosecution on inconvenience
or disturbance of the even tenor of life, as in many torts, including intimidation.
(2) Additional compensation for the injured feelings of the plaintiff where his sense of
injury resulting from the wrongful physical act is justifiably heightened by the manner in
which or motive for which the defendant did it. This Lord Devlin calls 'aggravated damages.' (3) Punishment of the defendant for his anti-social behaviour to the plaintiff. This
Lord Devlin calls 'exemplary damages.'

Although damages for racial discrimination will in many cases be analogous to those
for defamation, they are not necessarily the same. In the latter the principal injury to be
compensated is that to the plaintiff's reputation I doubt whether this will play a large part
in the former. On the other hand, if the plaintiff knows of the racial discrimination and that
he has thereby been held up to 'hatred, ridicule or contempt', then the injury to his feelings
will be an important element in the damages . . . in the substantial majority of discrimination cases the unlawful conduct will cause personal hurt in the sense of injury to feelings
. . . I do not think that this must 'inevitably' follow. A proper inference to draw in a case such
as this may be that the discrimination will cause a plaintiff 'hurt' of a particular kind. But,
unless the court can and feels it right to draw that inference, then the mere fact that a
defendant is guilty of racial discrimination is not in my opinion in itself a factor affecting
damages . . .

Claimants, then, can recover compensation for pecuniary losses flowing from the discrimination, and for non-pecuniary losses subject to the duty to mitigate.[64] Such losses are com-
pensable as future losses as well as in the case of losses and/or damage already incurred at
the date of the tribunal hearing (in disability cases in 2002, damages for future loss of earnings comprised half of the compensation awarded). Interest is also available in respect of
pecuniary losses prior to the date on which damages are awarded, and in respect of compensation for injury to feelings.

In *Gibbons v South West Water Services Ltd* [1993] 2 WLR 507 the Court of Appeal ruled
that exemplary damages were available in respect only of those torts, whether statutory or
common law, which existed prior to the decision of the House of Lords in *Rookes v Barnard*
[1964] AC 1129. On this view, such damages were not available in respect of sex or race discrimination.[65] Nor, according to Northern Ireland's Court of Appeal in *McConnell v Police
Authority for Northern Ireland*, were they available under the FEA.[66] Claimants could still
recover damages for pecuniary and non-pecuniary damages (the latter consisting for the
most part of injury to feeling, further discussed below).

---

[63] Citing *Rookes v Barnard* [1964] AC 1129 *per* Lord Devlin, *Cassell & Co Ltd v Broome* [1972] AC 1027.
[64] This may require that a claimant accept an offer of reinstatement even after egregious discrimination—
see *Stephens v The Foundation Training Co* 138 *Equal Opportunities Review* 'Case Digest' but *cf Skelton v
Stuart Walker* also reported in the same 'Case Digest'.
[65] See *Deane v Ealing London Borough Council and Anor* [1993] ICR 329, [1993] IRLR 209, EAT.
[66] (1997) CARF 2410.

The FEC called, in 1998, for exemplary damages to be awardable under the FEA (as it then was)[67] and for the FET to have the power to order continuing financial payments until a stipulated event such as a promotion occurred. Neither request was acceded to by government, this despite much criticism of the *Gibbons* decision.[68]

But in *Kuddus v Chief Constable of Leicester Constabulary* [2002] 2 AC 122, the House of Lords held that the availability of exemplary damages depended on the conduct of the public authority rather than the cause of action sued upon, and that such damages were available in that case on a complaint of misfeasance in public office notwithstanding the fact that the tort had not been accepted as a cause of action before 1964.

In *Kuddus* Lord Mackay stated that exemplary damages would be available 'only if the legislation expressly authorises exemplary damages in relation to any particular breach' while Lord Hutton reserved his opinion 'until the matter arises directly for decision.' In *Virgo Fidelis Senior School v Boyle* [2004] IRLR 268, EAT considered whether exemplary damages were available under the public interest disclosure provisions of the ERA. According to Judge Ansell, for the Court:

> we would venture to suggest that once the cause of action test no longer exists and the *Rookes v Barnard* test becomes fact sensitive rather than cause of action sensitive we see no reason why in principle exemplary damages could not be awarded, provided that the other conditions are made out. Clearly in the majority of cases aggravated damages would be sufficient to mark the employer's conduct.

The appellate courts have yet to consider the availability of exemplary damages, post *Kuddus*, under the discrimination legislation but there seems no reason to doubt their availability in a suitable case.

The level of compensation traditionally awarded in discrimination cases has been far from high.[69] Whereas, in the US, discrimination awards can run to millions of dollars, in the period between the removal of the statutory caps on compensation (November 1993 and March 1994 in sex and race cases respectively) and the end of 1995, over 20 per cent of both sex and race discrimination awards in employment cases were for less than £1,000 and about 75 per cent of each were for less than £5,000. Only 10 per cent of race discrimination awards, and 8 per cent of sex discrimination awards, were in excess of £10,000 and only 6 per cent of sex awards and 10 per cent of race awards made in 1994–95 exceeded the caps which had previously applied.[70] Further, as a commentary in the *Equal Opportunity Review* pointed out in 1995,[71] the vast majority of discrimination cases which reach tribunals do not result in the award of any damages at all. In 1996, for example, of 7500 race and sex cases completed (1934 of which reached a tribunal), compensation was awarded in only 10 per cent). Figures for awards made in the county court are not collated but the same principles apply (although because loss of earnings comprises a significant element in many

[67] Above n 15, para 1.87. The FEC also recommended, para 1.93, that interim orders should be available in FE cases to maintain the *status quo*.

[68] See, for example, the Law Commission in *Aggravated, Exemplary and Restitutionary Damages* (Consultation Paper No. 132): 'To assert that the role of the law of civil wrongs is only to provide compensation, or less restrictively does not at least include punitive aims [this being the basis for the decision in *Gibbons*], is to assume what is at issue and fails to address the question of policy involved.'

[69] The significant exceptions to this rule involved servicewomen dismissed for pregnancy—see Lord Lester, HL Debs, 16 February 1995, col. 855; and, more generally, A Arnull, 'EC Law and the Dismissal of Pregnant Servicewomen' (1995) 24 *Industrial Law Journal* 215—also discussed below.

[70] '1994–5 Compensation Awards: The Rising Cost of Discrimination' 67 *Equal Opportunities Review*.

[71] *Ibid.*

employment cases, county court awards are generally lower). *Alexander v Home Office* was a services and facilities case and the Sheriff Principal recently confirmed in *Purves v Joydisc* [2003] IRLR 420 that the measure of compensation recoverable under the DDA in a goods, services and facilities case was the same as that which would apply under the employment provisions of that Act.[72]

Levels of compensation have increased gradually since the mid 1990s and a few cases have generated huge awards (see further below). By 2003 just 7 per cent and 5 per cent of awards in sex and race discrimination employment cases were of less than £1,000 and just over 21 per cent (almost 33 per cent of race cases) were of £10,000 or more. And, whereas average payouts in 1995 were £3,617 and £5,032 in sex and race respectively, and median payments £3,000 in each, by 2003 the average figures for sex and race respectively were £7,960 and £12,225, although median figures were a more modest £5,677 and £5,100 respectively.[73] In 2003, average and median awards in employment disability cases ran at at £15,634 and £5,310 respectively while in 2003 just under 8 per cent of awards in disability cases were for £1,000 or less and almost 34 per cent for £10,000 or more. The average awards in each category are inflated significantly above the median awards by some (exceptional) very large payouts (these included awards of over £130,000, £74,000 and £216,000 in sex, race and disability cases respectively). But despite the increases over time, in 2003 only £4.2 million was paid in total in discrimination claims by order of a tribunal (369 cases in all). Bearing in mind that in excess of 10,000 discrimination claims are filed annually, this is not an especially large amount.

A significant proportion of discrimination compensation generally consists of an award for injury to feelings (this being the largest factor, frequently, in harassment claims and accounting for 39 per cent of the total awarded in 2003, 48 per cent of that in sex and race cases). Only rarely will such compensation not be awarded.[74] Typically, race discrimination claims attach the largest awards for injury to feelings (in recent years, pregnancy claims have attracted the lowest awards in respect of injury to feelings of sex discrimination cases).

Prior to EAT's decision in *Prison Service v Johnson* [1997] ICR 275, and even after the abolition of the compensation limits in 1993–94, tribunals continued to apply the decision of the Court of Appeal in *North West Thames Regional Health Authority v Noone* that, taking into account the then overall limit of £7,500 compensation in discrimination cases and the amount of damages typically awarded under this heading, £3,000 should be regarded as the upper limit for injury to feelings compensation. The level of such awards did not significantly change in the years immediately after the removal of the caps for sex and race discrimination compensation (increasing only from £1,825 to £2,823 and £1,239 to £1,398 respectively, with the median award in sex cases falling from £1,750 to £1,000 in the year immediately after the removal of the cap. But a cultural shift appeared to occur in the early to mid-1990s, most notably perhaps in the multiple cases arising out of the Ministry of Defence's policy of dismissing pregnant servicewomen.[75] In July 1994 EAT ruled, in

---

[72] The same principles apply in trade union cases—*Adams v London Borough of Hackney* [2003] IRLR 402 though EAT accepted in that case that injury to feelings were not as inevitable in trade union cases as they would be in cases of discrimination based on personal characteristics.

[73] All figures in this section taken from *Equal Opportunities Review*.

[74] Although injury to feelings must be established by the claimant, in *Murray v Fowertech (Scotland) Ltd* 44 *Equal Opportunities Review* EAT accepted that a claim for injury to feelings is 'so fundamental' to a discrimination case that 'it is almost inevitable.' In *Ministry of Defence v Cannock* EAT accepted that injury to feelings 'will often be easy to prove, in the sense that no tribunal will take much persuasion that the anger, distress and affront caused by the act of discrimination has injured the applicant's feelings.'

[75] Judicial review action was brought against this policy in 1990. The policy was ended in August of that year and the MOD conceded its unlawfulness in December 1991. 5,000 service women had been dismissed

Ministry of Defence v Cannock [1994] ICR 918, that many of the MOD awards were 'massively excessive and wrong,' and imposed guidelines which reduced the levels of compensation payable for injury to feelings in these cases, as well as the level of damages for future loss (average awards fell from £33,846 to £16,009 and median awards from £23,161 to £10,000 in the twelve months subsequent to this decision, by comparison with a similar period prior to it). And in November 1995 EAT ruled, in *Orlando v Didcot Power Station Sports and Social Club* [1996] IRLR 262, that *Noone* continued to apply in respect of injury to feelings awards: 'We are not persuaded that the Court of Appeal was so linking the amount of an award for injury to feelings to the then limit on compensation that it can be legitimately argued that without the limit the award would thereby have been higher.' But in *Prison Service v Johnson* (considered below) EAT upheld an award of £21,000 for injury to feelings (and a further £7,500 aggravated damages) to a black prison officer who sued in respect of racial harassment.[76] The award was the highest made by any industrial tribunal at the time, although much larger overall awards (by far the largest proportions of which were in respect of pecuniary loss) have been made since.

In 1997, in *D'Souza v London Borough of Lambeth* [1997] IRLR 677 (a race discrimination case) EAT increased from £8,925 to £358,289 an award in respect of the 'worst case of discrimination it ever had to encounter.'[77] The award was reduced on appeal ([1999] IRLR 241), but on the grounds only that the EAT had not had the power to award an uncapped sum at the relevant time.

An award of over £234,000 was made under the SDA against the London Borough of Southwark in respect of the discriminatory down-grading and dismissal of a senior council employee. £15,500 of the award was for injury to feelings, the rest for past and future loss of earnings including over £45,000 for loss of pension rights.[78] At that point it was the highest ever in a sex discrimination case. The London Borough of Hackney was ordered to pay £113,964 (including £25,000 in respect of injury to feelings) in *Chan v Hackney* and this award was upheld by EAT.[79] More recently, an employment tribunal awarded £131,000 including £20,000 in respect of injury to feelings to an Asian machinist who was 'severely traumatised' as a result of racial abuse[80] and another awarded £35,000 for injury to feelings with £10,000 aggravated damages and £12,500 for psychiatric injury to a woman subject to appalling victimization by her employers after she alleged racial discrimination against them.[81] Even these have been dwarfed by the recent awards of over £800,000 in *Chaudhary v British Medical Association* to a doctor whose career was damaged by race discrimination[82] and an eye-watering £1.4 million in *Bower v Schroder Securities Ltd*. In 1998, after

---

or forced to resign between 1978 (when the policy became unlawful with the entry into force of the Equal Treatment Directive) and August 1990. The MOD reached settlements with the vast majority of those affected, but not before a number had won very significant payouts in the tribunals.

[76] See also *Sheriff v Klyne Tugs (Lowestoft) Ltd* [1999] ICR 1170, discussed below, and *A v B* 40 *Equal Opportunities Review Discrimination Case Law Digest* 1, in which £23,000 was awarded for injury to feelings including symptoms akin to PTSD, in respect of which the judicial studies board currently recommends between £10,000 and £20,000: 'The injury extended beyond the more usual humiliation and embarrassment to severe emotional distress.' The respondents in *Stubbs* appealed unsuccessfully (see Ch 4) but did not dispute the quantum of damages.

[77] 'Compensation Awards 1997' 81 *Equal Opportunities Review*.

[78] *McLoughlin v London Borough of Southwark* 36 *Equal Opportunities Review Discrimination Case Law Digest* 12.

[79] 36 *Equal Opportunities Review Discrimination Case Law Digest* 19.

[80] 'Compensation Awards 2002', above n 25, discussing *Eccles v The General Conference of the Seventh Day Adventist Church*.

[81] *Mustafa v Ancon Clark Ltd & McNally* 40 *Equal Opportunities Review Discrimination Case Law Digest* 6.

[82] This was upheld by EAT in March 2004 n 62 above.

a finding of race discrimination against it, Hackney received the dubious honour of reaching the largest settlement ever to be made public at that time—£380,000, which included £40,000 paid in respect of injury to feelings.[83] This has been dwarfed by the reported £5 to £10 million settlement (the details of which remain confidential) between Goldman Sachs and a black bond dealer in respect of his race discrimination claim and, more recently, a reported £2.2 million paid in settlement of a sex discrimination claim brought by a former nurse in relation to discrimination by the chairman of a recruitment firm started by her and subject to a management buy-out after which she was asked to resign (112 *Equal Opportunities Review*).

The perspective taken by EAT in *Prison Service v Johnson* and subsequently on the injuries inflicted by discrimination and, in particular, by racial (and, by implication, sexual) harassment, is new. Previous decisions showed a tendency to play down the emotional impact of discrimination, even of harassment. In *Orlando v Didcot Power Station* [1996] IRLR 262, for example, EAT suggested that:

> an admission, or a finding in the complainant's favour, together with an appropriate award [there £750 for injury to feelings, £637 compensatory and £753 basic award for a woman dismissed for pregnancy after 14 years' part-time employment], may put an end to any continuing or further sense of hurt and outrage.[84]

The average award for injury to feelings in sexual and racial harassment cases respectively in 1995–6 was £2,501 and £2,127. In *Johnson*, by contrast, the appeal tribunal both accepted that the level of compensation for injury to feelings should be fixed with regard to damages in personal injury claims, and stated with equanimity that:

> [t]he most severe cases [of post-traumatic stress disorder], resulting in an inability to work, attract awards in the region of £25,000–£35,000. Moderately severe cases where some recovery has occurred or is anticipated attract damages between £10,000 and £20,000. Cases described as 'moderate' attract awards in the region of £3,000–£7,500.

Despite some very large awards such as those mentioned above, average awards for injury to feelings remained low after *Johnson*, falling 5 per cent in 1997 in sex cases to £2,441 (the median remained at £1,500 from 1996), although both average and median awards in respect of racial harassment increased (11 per cent to £4,632 and 25 per cent to £2,500 respectively). In *ICTS v Tchoula* EAT set out guidelines for compensation, in particular in relation to injury to feelings, in response to concern about a significant degree of variation between regions in relation to the level of such awards. The case concerned an appeal from an award for injury to feelings of £27,000 (including £5,000 aggravated damages) made to a man who was dismissed after alleging race discrimination. EAT reduced the award in respect of injury to feelings to £10,000 (including £2,500 aggravated damages) and set out the following guidelines for tribunals to follow when assessing the level of damages for injury to feelings in discrimination cases.

---

[83] *Yeboah v Hackney* reported 82 *Equal Opportunities Review*, 2. The *Guardian,* 28 January 2000, reported that a settlement had been reached in *Coote v Granada* (see Ch 4) of £200,000.

[84] See also *Wileman v Minilec Engineering Ltd* [1988] ICR 318, EAT upheld an award of £50 nominal damages made to a woman who had been sexually harassed for four years by a director of the company for which she worked.

ICTS (UK) Ltd v Tchoula [2000] ICR 1191

Judge Peter Clark:

In [*Johnson*], Smith J set out useful guidance on the principles to be applied in assessing compensation under this head, borrowing in part from the judgment of Sir Thomas Bingham MR in the libel case of *Elton John v Mirror Group Newspapers* [1996] 3 WLR 593, and the Court of Appeal decision in *Alexander v Home Office* . . .

Awards for injury to feelings are compensatory, not punitive. Awards should not be so low as to diminish respect for the policy of anti-discrimination legislation; nor so high as to be perceived as a way to untaxed riches. They should have a broad general similarity to the range of awards in personal injury cases. Employment tribunals should remind themselves of the value in everyday life of the sum they have in mind. Awards should command public respect.

Mr Martin [for the employers] submits that this tribunal failed to apply those principles in the award which they made.

We begin with the level of awards in personal injury cases. We have noted the recent decision of a five-member Court of Appeal in *Heil v Rankin* [2000] 2 WLR 1173, in which the court held that awards of damages for pain, suffering and loss of amenity over £10,000 ought to be increased by a tapering amount up to one-third in order to produce compensation which is fair, reasonable and just.

Mr Martin has taken us to the JSB guidelines on awards for damages under this head, reproduced in *Kemp & Kemp on Damages*. He invited us to compare and contrast the type of injury which would attract an award of £27,000 (the combined total of awards for injury to feelings and aggravated damages in this case). They include moderate brain damage, affecting concentration and memory, reduced ability to work, possible risk of epilepsy, limited dependence on others; moderately severe psychiatric damage at the top end of the scale, involving a significant impact on most of these factors, ability to cope with life and work, effect on relationships with the family, extent to which treatment will be successful, and future vulnerability, with a reasonably optimistic prognosis for the future; moderately severe post-traumatic stress disorder, with significant disability for the foreseeable future; loss of sight in one eye; particularly severe facial scarring in a male under 30 years of age with permanent disfigurement even after plastic surgery.

He submits that the facts of the present case do not begin to equate with the type of injury referred to above. A closer analogy is to cases of moderate post-traumatic stress disorder, where the range is said to be £3,500–£9,500.

Whilst considering awards in the personal injury field, it is worth noting this analogy with the total award of £112,000 contended for by the applicant in his letter to the tribunal dated 23 June 1999 and rejected by the tribunal.

In one of the cases considered by the Court of Appeal with *Heil v Rankin* . . . that of *Ramsey v Rivers*, the court increased general damages for brain injury and fractures suffered by the applicant from £112,000 to £138,000. In the JSB guidelines the top of the bracket for moderately severe brain damage is put at £110,000 (plus a small inflation increase). That condition is described as amounting to severe disability, substantial dependency and requiring constant care. Disabilities may be physical, such as limb paralysis or cognitive, with marked intellectual impairment.

It is plain, applying an analogy with that type of injury, that the award contended for by Mr Tchoula is well wide of the mark. The tribunal were right to reject that claim. In considering these appeals we have had recourse also to the recently published *Butterworth's Discrimination Law*, up to date as at 1 August 1999 . . . We bear in mind . . . that we should not interfere with this tribunal's award unless satisfied that it is a wholly erroneous estimate of the damage suffered by the applicant. In short, does it fall outside the permissible bracket?

Personal injury litigation has produced a vast body of reported awards. They are collected in *Kemp & Kemp on Damages* and *Current Law* to the extent that it has been possible for discernible brackets to be formulated in the JSB guidelines. Awards in the field of discrimination have not reached that level. It is thus not yet possible for tribunals to turn to similar guidelines. Quantification in this field remains an even less precise exercise than in the personal injury field. Nevertheless, we have been referred by Mr Martin and Mr Tchoula to a number of cases both at EAT and employment tribunal level, which has allowed us to group those cases into broadly two categories (the high and lower categories).

Judge Peter Clark went on to suggest that the more serious type of case would include one like *Johnson* which involved 18 months of very severe racial harassment which affected the claimant's home life and which resulted in an award of £28,500 for injury to feelings and aggravated damages (also *Chan*, mentioned above, in which the claimant had been subjected to months of sustained and continued pressure before being dismissed). In the lower category he placed cases such as *IBC v Khanum* in which £8,000 injury to feelings and aggravated damages was awarded in a case in which the claimant, 'who suffered a great deal of stress, suffered from depression and lost her chosen career at a critical point, aggravated by the arrogant manner in which the respondents brushed aside her complaints of discrimination'; *Tesco Stores Ltd v Wilson*, in which a claimant, a contract worker, was awarded £6,500 after being stopped by a security officer who referred to 'you lot' (this a reference to his race) and was subsequently dismissed as a result; and *Singh v London Borough of Ealing*, in which the claimant was awarded £10,000 for injury to feelings after his job application was rejected despite his 'being the outstanding candidate for a job vacancy tailor-made for him.' Returning to the case in hand, Judge Clark continued:

We accept, again from experience in the personal injury field, that no two cases are precisely the same. However, in determining the bracket in which the instant case falls we have found it helpful to group the sample cases referred to above in higher and lower categories. We also draw a parallel between the type of personal injury cases attracting a similar award to the overall figure of £27,000 in this case and the higher-category discrimination cases.

The question is whether this case, on its own facts, falls into the higher category, in which case we shall not interfere, or the lower category, in which event we are satisfied that the overall award was manifestly excessive and must be set aside.

We have no hesitation in finding that it does fall within the lower category and as such was wrong in principle. It would be otherwise had the applicant proved most if not all of his complaints of discrimination; but he did not. This is therefore not a case of an employer subjecting the applicant to a campaign of harassment over a period of several months or more. The tribunal expressly found that the unlawful acts found proved did not cause the applicant to suffer from depression nor did they contribute to his marriage breakdown. Those acts continued over a short period from 5 to 15 August 1997. Although he lost his employment and the opportunity to continue in the security industry, he plainly saw that work as a means to an end. He wished to better himself. It was a 'poxy job'.

EAT's approach has not gone uncriticised.

IRLR 'Highlights' September 2000

One can sympathise with the desire to have greater precision in quantifying awards for injury to feelings, but there is a major limitation in the approach adopted in this case. Whereas the cases reported by the PI damages services are attempting to identify a typical tariff, awards noted in *Discrimination Case Law Digest* are selected because they have some special (ie atypical), newsworthy feature of interest—either in respect of the nature of the discrimination, or the issues of law involved, or the award itself. It follows that there is not much validity in identifying brackets from these cases, and it is likely that a different mix of cases would produce very different brackets.

In *Vento v Chief Constable of West Yorkshire Police (No.2)* the Court of Appeal developed the approach taken by EAT in the *ICTS* case. The claim was brought by a police officer who was sexually harassed and eventually dismissed. A tribunal awarded her £257,844 including £65,000 for injury to feelings including £15,000 by way of aggravated damages and £9,000 for personal injury. The award for injury to feelings reflected the tribunal's finding that the claimant had been bullied by her superiors following the breakdown of her marriage, that this had contributed to her suffering clinical depression, that she had then suffered shock and disappointment and lost a 'satisfying and genial career' because of her dismissal, and that she had been subject to a tribunal hearing at which her private life had been subjected to minute scrutiny. The additional award for aggravated damages reflected the tribunal's finding that the employers had 'throughout acted in a high-handed manner' and that their attitude was one of 'institutional denial.'

EAT ([2002] IRLR 177) reduced the award for injury to feelings, including aggravated damages, from £65,000 to £30,000 on the basis that the tribunal's award was well outside the range which any tribunal properly directing itself to the cited authorities would have made. The Court of Appeal allowed the respondent's appeal against EAT's failure to substitute a lower figure than £30,000 as compensation for injury to feelings, taking into account the award of an additional £9,000 by the tribunal for psychiatric injury. The Court reduced to £18,000 and £5000 the awards for injury to feelings and aggravated damages, leaving the award for psychiatric injury at £9,000.

Vento v Chief Constable of West Yorkshire Police (No.2) [2003] ICR 318

Mummery LJ (for the Court):

This is the first time for many years that the Court of Appeal has had the opportunity to consider the appropriate level of compensation for injury to feelings in discrimination cases. Some decisions in the employment tribunal and in the Appeal Tribunal have resulted in awards of substantial sums for injury to feelings, sometimes supplemented by compensation for psychiatric damage and aggravated damages. Cases were cited to the court in which employment tribunals had, as in this case, awarded compensation for injury to feelings (plus aggravated damages) larger than the damages separately awarded for psychiatric injury, and totalling well in excess of £20,000. The court was shown the decision of an employment tribunal in a race discrimination case awarding the sum of £100,000 for injury to feelings, plus aggravated damages of £25,000: *Virdi v Commissioner of Police of the Metropolis*. (This pales into insignificance in comparison with the reported award in 1994 by a Californian jury of $7.1m to a legal secretary for sexual harassment, and even with the subsequent halving of that sum on appeal).

Compensation of the magnitude of £125,000 for non-pecuniary damage creates concern as to whether some recent tribunal awards in discrimination cases are in line with general levels of compensation recovered in other cases of non-pecuniary loss, such as general damages for personal injuries, malicious prosecution and defamation. In the interests of justice (social and individual), and of predictability of outcome and consistency of treatment of like cases (an important ingredient of justice) this court should indicate to employment tribunals and practitioners general guidance on the proper level of award for injury to feelings and other forms of non-pecuniary damage.

It is self-evident that the assessment of compensation for an injury or loss, which is neither physical nor financial, presents special problems for the judicial process, which aims to produce results objectively justified by evidence, reason and precedent. Subjective feelings of upset, frustration, worry, anxiety, mental distress, fear, grief, anguish, humiliation, unhappiness, stress, depression and so on and the degree of their intensity are incapable of objective proof or of measurement in monetary terms. Translating hurt feelings into hard currency is bound to be an artificial exercise. As Dickson J said in *Andrews v Grand & Toy Alberta Ltd* (1978) 83 DLR (3d) 452 at 475–476, (cited by this court in *Heil v Rankin* [2000] 2 WLR 1173) there is no medium of exchange or market for non-pecuniary losses and their monetary evaluation:

> is a philosophical and policy exercise more than a legal or logical one. The award must be fair and reasonable, fairness being gauged by earlier decisions; but the award must also of necessity be arbitrary or conventional. No money can provide true restitution.

Although they are incapable of objective proof or measurement in monetary terms, hurt feelings are none the less real in human terms. The courts and tribunals have to do the best they can on the available material to make a sensible assessment, accepting that it is impossible to justify or explain a particular sum with the same kind of solid evidential foundation and persuasive practical reasoning available in the calculation of financial loss or compensation for bodily injury. In these circumstances an appellate body is not entitled to interfere with the assessment of the employment tribunal simply because it would have awarded more or less than the tribunal has done. It has to be established that the tribunal has acted on a wrong principle of law or has misapprehended the facts or made a wholly erroneous estimate of the loss suffered. Striking the right balance between awarding too much and too little is obviously not easy.

[Mummery LJ referred to *Johnson* and *ICTS*, as well as to the decisions of EAT in *Gbaja-Bianila v DHL International (UK) Ltd* [2000] ICR 730 and *HM Prison Service v Salmon* [2001] IRLR 425), and continued] At the end of the day this court must first ask itself whether the award by the employment tribunal in this case was so excessive as to constitute an error of law. That was the conclusion of the Appeal Tribunal and it is clearly right. The totality of the award for non-pecuniary loss is seriously out of line with the majority of those made and approved on appeal in reported Employment Appeal Tribunal cases. It is also seriously out of line with the guidelines compiled for the Judicial Studies Board and with the cases reported in the personal injury field where general damages have been awarded for pain, suffering, disability and loss of amenity. The total award of £74,000 for non-pecuniary loss is, for example, in excess of the JSB Guidelines for the award of general damages for moderate brain damage, involving epilepsy, for severe post-traumatic stress disorder having permanent effects and badly affecting all aspects of the life of the injured person, for loss of sight in one eye, with reduced vision in the remaining eye, and for total deafness and loss of speech. No reasonable person would think that that excess was a sensible result. The patent extravagance of the global sum is unjustifiable as an award of compensation. It is probably explicable by the understandable strength of feeling in the tribunal and as an expression of its condemnation of, and punishment for, the discriminatory treatment of Ms Vento . . .

Employment tribunals and those who practise in them might find it helpful if this court were to identify three broad bands of compensation for injury to feelings, as distinct from compensation for psychiatric or similar personal injury:

(i) The top band should normally be between £15,000 and £25,000. Sums in this range should be awarded in the most serious cases, such as where there has been a lengthy campaign of discriminatory harassment on the ground of sex or race. This case falls within that band. Only in the most exceptional case should an award of compensation for injury to feelings exceed £25,000.

(ii) The middle band of between £5,000 and £15,000 should be used for serious cases, which do not merit an award in the highest band.

(iii) Awards of between £500 and £5,000 are appropriate for less serious cases, such as where the act of discrimination is an isolated or one-off occurrence. In general, awards of less than £500 are to be avoided altogether, as they risk being regarded as so low as not to be a proper recognition of injury to feelings.

There is, of course, within each band considerable flexibility, allowing tribunals to fix what is considered to be fair, reasonable and just compensation in the particular circumstances of the case.

The decision whether or not to award aggravated damages and, if so, in what amount must depend on the particular circumstances of the discrimination and on the way in which the complaint of discrimination has been handled.

Common sense requires that regard should also be had to the overall magnitude of the sum total of the awards of compensation for non-pecuniary loss made under the various headings of injury to feelings, psychiatric damage and aggravated damage. In particular, double recovery should be avoided by taking appropriate account of the overlap between the individual heads of damage. The extent of overlap will depend on the facts of each particular case.

The *Equal Opportunities Review* reported in September 2004 that average and median awards for injury to feelings were higher in those cases in which employment tribunals took into account the *Vento* guidelines.

'Aggravated damages' featured in the *ICTS* and *Vento* cases extracted above. Injury to feelings compensation may include such damages (which are sometimes subsumed within injury to feelings compensation though the Court of Appeal ruled in *Scott v Commissioners of the Inland Revenue* [2004] ICR 1410 that aggravated damages should not be amalgamated into the award for injury to feelings). Aggravated damages, which are intended to compensate for 'high-handed, malicious, insulting or oppressive' behaviour by the discriminator, may be awarded for the discriminator's conduct after the act of discrimination, including in its conduct of the tribunal proceedings, as well as for the behaviour at the time of the initial act of discrimination. An example of this is provided by *Baker v Lennox Thompson*. The respondents there (in a sexual and racial harassment case) not only replied to a race discrimination questionnaire to the effect that the allegations were 'a creative fabrication to which we are unable to offer any kind of clarification', but cross-examined the claimant in a grossly offensive manner at tribunal. The tribunal awarded £10,000 injury to feelings plus £8,500 aggravated damages.[85] Equally in *Franklin v Pectel Ltd* (discussed in 'Compensation Awards 2003' 133 *Equal Opportunities Review*) a tribunal awarded

---

[85] '2002 Compensation Awards', above n 25. The award of aggravated damages in respect of the conduct of the hearing was approved by EAT in *Zaiwalla v Walia* [2002] IRLR 697, while in *BT plc v Reid* [2004] IRLR 327 the Court of Appeal approved an award of aggravated damages in respect of the promotion of the claimant's harasser when her complaints against him were outstanding.

£5,000 on top of £17,000 compensation for injury to feelings to a woman subject to sexual harassment, 'malicious and insulting behaviour' and tribunal proceedings during which her harasser had sought 'to belittle . . . the hurt and anguish caused to her' by stating, for example, that she had been denied a pay rise due to her incompetence (rather than, as the tribunal found as a fact, because she was pregnant), and had questioned her truthfulness. 16 of a total 219 sex discrimination awards made in 2003 included aggravated damages which varied between £500 and £5,000 (down from a maximum £8,500 in 2002). Eleven of 61 race discrimination awards and three of 89 disability awards made in 2003 also included aggravated damages.

Unlike exemplary damages, whose express purpose is to punish the discriminator, aggravated damages are meant to compensate the victim of the wrongdoing. In 1991–2 and 1994–5 only 5 per cent and 3 per cent of cases respectively in which compensation was awarded included a figure for aggravated damages but this appears to have become more common since. So, for example, in 2001 aggravated damages were awarded in 6 per cent and 12 per cent of sex and race cases respectively in which compensation was awarded (8 per cent of race and sex cases in total), and in 2002 in 10 per cent of sex cases, 17 per cent of race cases and 9 per cent of disability cases (11 per cent cases overall).

In the *ICTS* case EAT upheld a tribunal award of aggravated damages.

ICTS (UK) Ltd v Tchoula [2000] ICR 1191

Judge Peter Clark:

Mr Martin [for the employers] submits that the tribunal failed to apply the correct principles in making an extra award of aggravated damages to the applicant over and above that for injury to feelings. There was no finding by the tribunal that the respondent had acted maliciously towards the applicant. Following *McConnell* [1997] IRLR 625, paragraph 26, it cannot be said, at the highest, that the respondent had conducted the tribunal proceedings in other than an honest, if unfounded or even misguided, advancement of its case. There is no explanation in the tribunal's reasons as to why the respondent has been ordered to pay £5,000 aggravated damages: *Meek v City of Birmingham District Council* [1987] IRLR 250.

Dealing with those points, it is of interest to note that tribunals sometimes include an element of aggravated damages in their award for injury to feelings (see, eg *Williams* and *Chan* above); sometimes the awards are expressed separately. In our view, that is a matter of form rather than substance. However expressed, the principle stated by Carswell LCJ at paragraph 19 of *McConnell* is correct. We do not understand Smith J to have been saying anything different in *Johnson*. The first question must always be, do the facts disclose the essential requirements for an award of aggravated damages?

In this present case we are satisfied that on their findings of fact this tribunal was entitled to answer that case in the affirmative. In the liability decision the tribunal found that Mr Dewane was 'going after' the applicant in the hope of finding him in dereliction of his duty, consciously motivated by the applicant's claims of racial discrimination made against him (complaints which, although dismissed, we infer the tribunal found were made in good faith: [RRA] s.2(2)). Mr Lewis carried out a disciplinary procedure which was seriously flawed, again consciously motivated by the applicant's original complaint of unlawful discrimination, culminating in his dismissal. Further, the tribunal conducted these proceedings over 22 days. They are the best judges of whether the proceedings were improperly conducted to any extent as they found at paragraph 20 of the remedies reasons. Without spelling it out, it is clear to us that the tribunal regarded that combination of factors as amounting to high-handed, malicious, insulting or oppressive behaviour directed towards the applicant, to borrow the words of May LJ in *Alexander*. In these circumstances we are satisfied that the tribunal was entitled to make an award of aggravated damages.

The availability of personal injury awards in discrimination cases was mentioned above. In 1997, for example, in *Stubbs v Chief Constable of Lincolnshire Police & Walker* (41 *Equal Opportunities Review Discrimination Case Law Digest* 8), a tribunal awarded £41,500 in respect of injury to feelings and personal injury to a woman who suffered symptoms akin to Post Traumatic Stress Disorder and was forced to retire on medical grounds after 14 months of severe harassment by her line manager. In *Salmon* (referred to in the *ICTS* case above), a prison officer received £11,250 for 'moderately severe' psychiatric damage (reduced by 25 per cent from £15,000 to take account of other causal factors involved). Smaller awards were also made in a number of cases for 'minor psychiatric injuries' arising from discrimination[86] and 2002 saw an award of £24,000 to a woman who suffered anxiety, depression and mood disorder after a sexually discriminatory demotion.[87]

The availability of personal injury damages under the RRA (and, by implication, the other discrimination legislation) was confirmed by the Court of Appeal in *Sheriff v Klyne Tugs (Lowestoft)* [1999] ICR 1170, in which it ruled that the county court was correct to strike out a claim in negligence seeking damages for personal injury arising out alleged racial harassment. According to the Court Mr Sheriff, who had brought and compromised a claim in the employment tribunal arising from the same incident, ought to have made his personal injury claim then and so was estopped from bringing his action in the county court. According to the Court of Appeal, the victim of discrimination is entitled to be compensated for all loss and damage sustained as a result of the discrimination.

In the *Sheriff* case Lord Justice Stuart-Smith declared that: 'all that needs to be established is the causal link' between the act of discrimination and the injury in respect of which damages are sought. In *Essa v Laing Ltd* [2004] ICR 746, in which all three equality commissions intervened in support of the claimant, the Court of Appeal ruled that damages were recoverable under the RRA for financial losses resulting from psychiatric injury arising from a single episode of racial harassment. The claimant had suffered depression and had not been able to seek work after his constructive dismissal. A tribunal limited his damages in respect of loss of wages to three weeks, this being the period in which he would otherwise have been expected to gain alternative work. EAT ([2003] IRLR 346) allowed his appeal on the basis that, once the claimant proved a causal link between the act of discrimination and his loss, compensation was not limited to losses that were reasonably foreseeable. EAT remitted the case to the employment tribunal to reconsider the question of compensation and the Court of Appeal rejected the employer's appeal. Having decided that psychiatric injury (although not the extent of it) was foreseeable in any event, and that recovery could be made even on a forseeability test, the Court of Appeal went on to decide (by a majority) that mere causation was sufficient to establish liability for personal injury and that no requirement of forseeability applied under the discrimination provisions: 23 awards in respect of personal injury were made by tribunals in discrimination cases in 2003 (up from 17 the previous year). These awards varied between £750 and £24,000 and frequently related to depressive illnesses resulting from harassment.

Before leaving our consideration of compensation it is worth reiterating that successful claimants are entitled to recover all pecuniary losses flowing from unlawful discrimination.

---

[86] See, eg, *Martin v Unilever UK Central Resources Ltd* and *Stringer v First Leisure Corporation*, discussed in '1999 Compensation Awards', 93 *Equal Opportunities Review*.

[87] *Brozek v F & R Dunlop Ltd*, discussed in '2002 Compensation Awards', above n 25.

Thus, for example, a significant portion of the damages at issue in *Essa* were pecuniary losses associated with unemployment. As mentioned above, tribunals can award damages in respect not only of past losses but also of future losses, subject to consideration of mitigation and the exigencies of life. It follows that, where significant losses are established, awards such as some of the more spectacular mentioned in this section are available to the small proportion of discrimination claimants who succeed at tribunal or in the county courts.

One of the grounds of appeal in *Vento* concerned pecuniary losses. The tribunal had awarded the claimant £257,844 in total, £165,829 of which was in respect of future loss of earnings. EAT set aside the award for loss of earnings on the basis that there were no proper grounds upon which the tribunal could justify departing from the statistical evidence that only 9 per cent of women who had left the West Yorkshire police force had served for more than 18 years (the tribunal having calculated the claimant's loss of future earnings on the basis that there was a 75 per cent she would have served 21 years). The Court of Appeal allowed Ms Vento's appeal on this point, and reinstated the original sum for loss of earnings.

Vento v Chief Constable of West Yorkshire Police (No.2) [2003] ICR 318

Mummery LJ (for the Court):

The decision of the employment tribunal on this point ought only to be overturned if it is shown to be a perverse conclusion, that is a decision which no reasonable tribunal, properly directing itself on the law and on the materials before it, could reasonably have reached. An appellate tribunal or court is not entitled to interfere with such a conclusion simply on the basis that it would itself have reached a different conclusion on the same materials.

It has to be accepted that the figure of a 75 per cent chance of a full career is certainly on the high side. We doubt whether we would have estimated Ms Vento's chances as high as that had we been sitting in the employment tribunal. It was, however, an option reasonably open to the employment tribunal. The decision on that point ought not to have been interfered with by the Appeal Tribunal. We would allow Ms Vento's appeal.

We accept the basic submission made by Mr Christopher Jeans QC that the employment tribunal's conclusion on this point was plainly and properly influenced by the impression gained by it in seeing her give evidence at the lengthy liability and remedies hearings. It concluded that she had a lifelong ambition to become a police officer. Her determination to achieve her ambition was demonstrated by her persistence with her probation in the face of the appalling discriminatory treatment described in the extended reasons. The employment tribunal was entitled to place considerable weight on the view it had formed of Ms Vento's determination to pursue her career and of the way she had dealt with the problems confronting her in her probationary period, as well as having to cope with the break-up of her marriage and the demands on a single parent with three children. These matters weighed heavily with the tribunal in estimating her chances of achieving a full period of service down to retirement.

The statistical evidence produced by the police on the respective percentages of men and women leaving the service between 1989 and 1999 before completing anything like a full career in it was relevant to the assessment of Ms Vento's chances of a full career. It could not, of course, be determinative of Ms Vento's future prospects in the police force and Mr Bean did not, in his moderate submissions, contend that it was. The real question is whether much more weight should have been given by the tribunal to the statistics and whether the tribunal was justified in departing from the general indications of past experience of average length of service demonstrated by the statistics.

In our judgment, the employment tribunal was entitled to approach the statistics with cir-cumspection. Quite apart from its findings on the special factors of Ms Vento's career ambi-tion, dedication and determination in the face of adversity and its predictions of her future career based on those factors, the tribunal had relevant evidence that the future situation in the police force would be different from the social and working conditions prevailing in the decade covered by the statistics. Recent and continuing social changes affecting women in society and in the workplace are reflected in the adjustments now being made to working conditions in the police force. There was evidence about the anticipated need to retain officers and to maintain resource levels. The introduction of 'family friendly policies' is aimed at retaining more women officers in the future. Ms Vento's inability to have any more children was important in decid-ing what weight to place on the statistics in her case, as the high incidence of women officers not completing police careers was attributable to leaving in order to have children.

As Mr Jeans pointed out, the Appeal Tribunal regarded the statistics as a governing con-sideration from which departure had to be strictly justified. That was not the right approach when there were a number of special factors affecting Ms Vento's situation, which consid-erably lessened the impact of the statistics on her particular case.

In our judgment, the employment tribunal did not apply any wrong principle of law or reach a perverse decision in the difficult and imprecise exercise of assessing the relative future chances. There was material on which its evaluation could be justified. It explained its conclusion sufficiently to comply with its duty to give sufficient reasons for its decision. The parties were able to tell in broad terms why they had won or lost on that issue. It is difficult to see what further reasons or explanation could reasonably be expected of the tri-bunal on a point such as this. It referred to the statistics on which the police relied. It also referred to the factors casting doubt on the applicability of past statistics to the future prospects of this particular police officer . . .

In *Instant Muscle Ltd v Kharwaja* (reported in 'Case Digest' 128 *Equal Opportunities Review*) EAT applied the reasoning in *Vento (No.2)* to a DDA claim, reducing an award of £6,000 for injury to feelings to £2,500 in the case of a claimant whose employers had failed to make reasonable adjustments to his needs as a wheelchair user. According to Judge Richardson, for EAT:

it would be rare indeed for an award in a disability discrimination case to fall within the top band. We observe that it is thankfully rare in our society for there to be lengthy campaigns of harassment on the grounds of disability, but in the rare case of such a campaign, an award in this bracket will be appropriate . . . The middle band will occur more frequently in a disability discrimination case . . . Such an award is likely to be appropriate where an employee has been dismissed on grounds which amount to disability discrimination; it may be appropriate where over many months or years an employee has had to put up with work-ing conditions which plainly call for amelioration and affected his work substantially, but in our view it is plain that there are lesser cases of failure to make an adjustment which are likely to fall within the lower band.

This award seems low in view of the decision in *Hill v Farmstar Ltd,* reported by the *Equal Opportunities Review* in the same month, in which a woman excluded, because of her sex, from a single social event (a 'gentleman's evening' designed as a thank-you to staff for their hard work), was awarded £3,000 for injury to feelings.

The Equal Pay Act

The EqPA operates by inserting an 'equality clause' into the successful claimant's contract of "employment. The remedy to which claimants become entitled consists both of this, with its impact on subsequent wages, etc and, where relevant, of damages in respect of the under-payment of past services. Until July 2003 these damages are limited by s.2(5), which provides that:

> A woman shall not be entitled, in proceedings brought in respect of a failure to comply with an equality clause . . . to be awarded any payment by way of arrears of remuneration or damages in respect of a time earlier than two years before the date on which the proceedings were instituted'.

We saw above that procedural limitations are acceptable under EU law only where (*Rewe-Zentralfinanz eG v Landwirtschaftskammer für das Saarland* Case C–33/76 [1976] ECR I–01989 they neither render the Community right impossible or excessively difficult to secure, nor are less favourable than the rules regulating actions in respect of similar rights of a domestic nature.

In *Levez v Jennings (Harlow Pools) Ltd, Hicking v Basford Group Ltd (No.2)* [1999] ICR 58, EAT ruled that s.2(5) was unenforceable. The decisions followed that of the ECJ in *Levez v Jennings* Case C–326/96 [1999] ECR I–07835 in which that Court had ruled that s.2(5) could not be applied in a case in which the delay in bringing proceedings flowed from the employer's deceit, any such application rendering impossible or excessively difficult the exercise of the claimant's rights under Article 141. Similarly, in *Magorrian and Cunningham v Eastern Health and Social Services Board and Department of Health and Social Services* Case C–246/96 [1997] ECR I–7153, the two-year rule was found in breach of Article 141 on the facts of the particular case (there concerning access to pension rights).

Neither the decision of the ECJ in *Levez* nor that in *Magorrian* excluded the possibility that s.2(5) might, in the general run of cases, be compatible with Community law or that, in any event, the imposition of such a rule coupled with a degree of flexibility in particular cases would be so compatible. In *Levez*, the ECJ went so far as to state that: 'a national rule under which entitlement to arrears of remuneration is restricted to the two years preceding the date on which the proceedings were instituted is not in itself open to criticism'. But in *Levez* the ECJ accepted EAT's invitation to consider the second limb of *Rewe*—the principle of equivalence as between procedural rules governing domestic and Community causes of action.

Having stated the principle that it was for 'the national court—which alone has direct knowledge of the procedural rules governing actions in the field of employment law' to determine this question having considered 'both the purpose and the essential characteristics of allegedly similar domestic actions' and taking into account 'the role played by that provision in the procedure as a whole, as well as the operation and any special features of that procedure before the different national courts' the judgment in *Levez* went on to dismiss the UK Government's argument that, the EqPA having predated the accession of the UK to the EC and the application in domestic law of Article 141, the appropriate comparison was between the (identical) restrictions imposed by the EqPA on claims arising under domestic and EC law:

> Following the accession of the United Kingdom to the Communities, the Act constitutes the legislation by means of which the United Kingdom discharges its obligations under

Article [141] of the Treaty and, subsequently, under the [Equal Pay] Directive. The Act cannot therefore provide an appropriate ground of comparison against which to measure compliance with the principle of equivalence.

It is . . . suggested that claims to those based on the Act may include those linked to breach of a contract of employment, to discrimination in terms of pay on grounds of race, to unlawful deductions from wages or to sex discrimination in matters other than pay.

When *Levez* returned for decision by EAT, it was heard together with a case in which no allegation of deceit on the part of the employer was made. Morison J, for EAT, refused to distinguish between the two cases: 'Either section 2(5) is in conflict with European principles or it is not . . . there will be many cases where an employee does not know the true facts about the salaries of the alleged comparators . . . It seems to us inherently improbable that the decision of the ECJ is contingent upon fraud being found . . .'. EAT accepted the arguments put forward on behalf of the claimants that the appropriate comparison was between the EqPA's limitation and that—six years—which was imposed by the Limitation Act 1980 in respect of other contract-based claims. Section 2(5) and 2ZB EqPA now provide that damages may be backdated to (in England and Wales) six years prior to the point of claim (or, in a concealment or disability case—see above, six years prior to the discovery (constructive or otherwise) or the removal of the disability respectively). In Scotland the general limit is five years with special provision also being made (s.2(5) and 2ZC for cases of fraud and disability.

'Collective' Enforcement

The individualistic mechanisms put in place by the SDA, the RRA and the DDA account for the bulk of activity associated with the Acts. But they do not stand entirely alone, by contrast with the position under the SO and RB Regs. The sex, race and disability discrimination regimes each come with an enforcement commission—the EOC, CRE and DRC respectively (in Northern Ireland, the ECNI). These bodies, as we shall see below, have limited but significant enforcement powers which they can wield either in support of, or independent from, individual discrimination claimants. One major criticism of the new regulation in Britain of discrimination on grounds of sexual orientation, religion and belief is that no enforcement body has as yet been charged with responsibilities akin to those currently borne by the EOC (which is responsible for the EqPA as well as the SDA), the CRE and the DRC. (Northern Ireland's Equality Commission does have responsibility for sexual orientation discrimination under the new regime[88] and has from its outset had responsibility for discrimination connected with religious belief.) We saw, above, that the equality commissions are to be replaced by an *uber* 'Commission for Equality and Human Rights'

---

[88] Although it has not been granted power to provide legal assistamce to complainants or to undertake formal investigations, it can issue codes of practice, conduct research and education and has a duty (a) to work towards the elimination of discrimination;(b) to promote equality of opportunity between persons of differing sexual orientations; and (c) to keep under review the working of the [NISO Regs] . . . and, when it is so required by the Department or otherwise thinks it necessary, draw up and submit to the department proposals for amending these Regulations (Employment Equality (Sexual Orientation) Regulations (Northern Ireland) 2003, Statutory Rule 2003 No. 497), regs 30–32 (which have no counterpart in the British legislation).

whose remit will, in common with that of the ECNI, extend to all the the regulated grounds of discrimination. Here we will consider the purpose and impact of collective enforcement and its operation to date in the UK.

The EqPA, as it was originally enacted, provided (s.3) that discriminatory collective agreements or pay structures could be referred to the Central Arbitration Committee (CAC) which had the power to amend the offending terms.[89] This provision was to prove very significant, early commentators on the Act attributing much of the initial hike in women's relative wages to s.3. Zabalza and Tzannatos, for example, who studied the impact of the EqPA on the employment and wages of women, found:

> evidence that collective agreements started to move towards equalisation quite early in the decade, that these increases in relative rates resulted in corresponding and contemporaneous increases in relative earnings, and that the effect on average earnings was not confined to the covered sector but also spilled over to non-covered employees.[90]

And one Australian study attributed the success of the UK legislation, relative to that in the US, precisely to this factor:

> in terms of institutional mechanisms a comparatively centralised wage-fixing system is a more efficient vehicle for implementing equal pay initiatives . . . across the board . . . initiatives such as those seen in Great Britain . . . are the most effective in reducing sex-based differentials.[91]

Section 3 was capable of providing the benefits of 'equal pay' even to women in exclusively female workplaces, in cases where those workplaces were covered by multi-employer collective agreements. And even where women were not covered by collective agreements, 'female rates' within workplaces had to be raised to the level of the lowest 'male rate' regardless, again, of the content of the jobs performed by the men and women respectively. But the powers of the Committee were narrowly defined—in particular, they could revise only those provisions which explicitly applied 'to men only or to women only.' And the CAC's liberal approach to these powers—it was prepared to amend agreements and pay structures in which, in the committee's view, insufficient steps had been taken fully to eradicate the effects of past discrimination[92]—was blocked by the Divisional Court in *R v CAC ex parte Hy-Mac Ltd* [1979] IRLR 461, in which it ruled that the Committee had exceeded its jurisdiction in interfering with a collective agreement which did not contain overtly discriminatory 'male' and 'female' payscales.

The *Hy-Mac* decision rendered s.3 obsolete. Whereas, between 1976 and 1979 the CAC had ruled on about 50 equal pay cases, between 1981 and 1986 not one case was decided. The SDA 1986 stripped the CAC of its powers under the EqPA, s.3 of that Act being replaced by s.6 SDA 1986, which provided that discriminatory terms in collective agree-

---

[89] The provisions of the EqPA extend beyond pay to cover all contractual terms.

[90] A Zabalza and Z Tzannatos, *Women and Equal Pay: The Effects of Legislation on Female Employment and Wages* (Cambridge, Cambridge University Press, 1985) 9. See also Z Tzannatos and A Zabalza, 'The Anatomy of the Rise of British Female Relative Wages in the 1970s: Evidence from the New Earnings Survey' (1984) 22(2) *British Journal of Industrial Relations* 177, J Rubery, 'Structured Labour Markets, Worker Organisation and Low Pay' in A Amsden (ed), *The Economics of Women and Work* (Harmondsworth, Penguin, 1980) 120.

[91] K MacDermott, *Pay Equity: A Survey of 7 OECD Countries* (Canberra, Australian Government Publishing Service, 1987), Women's Bureau, Information Paper No.5, 77.

[92] *See, eg, Prestcold & APECCS* (1978) CAC 78/830, reported in EOC *Annual Report* 1978, 50.

ments and pay structures, were void.[93] But s.6 contained no enforcement mechanism—in particular, no means by which women could demand that their terms be improved to match those enjoyed by men.

The Trade Union Reform and Employment Rights Act 1993 amended s.6 to provide individuals the right of complaint to a tribunal in respect of discriminatory terms of collective agreements and 'rules of undertakings.'[94] Although pursued as an individual remedy, s.6 SDA 1986 should be regarded as a collective measure in the sense that, once successfully challenged, the offending provision is struck down in its application across the board. By contrast, ss.77 SDA, which provides for a declaration that unlawfully discriminatory contractual terms are unenforceable, permits such a declaration *only* vis-à-vis the complainant herself, where s/he is a party to the disputed contract. The same is true for the materially identical s.72 RRA, reg 35 and Schedule 4, Part I, SO and RB Regs and s.17C and Schedule 3A Part II DDA.[95] But s.72A RRA, introduced into the Act in order to give effect to the Racial Equality Directive, permits a tribunal to declare void any collectively agreed term, or rule or an employer, trade organisation or qualifying body, which discriminates on grounds of racial, ethnic or national origin. S.72B provides that a tribunal may hear a complaint under s.72A from anyone who (broadly) 'has reason to believe . . . that the term or rule may at some future time have effect in relation to him'. A complaint may be made by someone who is 'genuinely and actively seeking' to become an employee or member of the relevant organisation, or to have an authorisation or qualification conferred by it, as well as existing employees/ members/ persons authorised of or by it. Section 72B(4) provides that 'When an employment tribunal finds that a complaint presented to it under subsection (1) is well-founded the tribunal shall make an order declaring that the term or rule is void.' Reg 35 and Schedule 4, Part II of the SO and RB Regs are in materially identical terms to ss.72A and 72B RRA as is s.17C and Schedule 3A Part II DDA.

In *Meade-Hill v British Council* [1995] ICR 847 it was accepted that s.77 SDA applied to indirectly, as well as directly, discriminatory terms.[96] The same would apply in respect of s.6 SDA 1986 and its equivalent provisions but, by contrast with the position which prevailed under s.3 EqPA, that provision does not permit the extension of benefits to those to whom they are at present (discriminatorily) denied.[97] This would not pose a problem in a case where, as in *Meade-Hill*, the disputed term consisted of a wide contractual mobility clause with which women were less likely than men to be able to comply. A successful application under s.6 SDA 1986 or its equivalents would result in the striking-out of the term from the collective agreement or rules of the employer's undertaking as the case may be. But it would

[93] This despite the suggestion by the AG in *Commission v United Kingdom* Case C–165/82 [1983] ECR I–03431 44 [1984] IRLR 29 at 3453–5 that the CAC was the most appropriate body to deal with collective cases—B. Fitzpatrick 'The Sex Discrimination Act 1986' (1987) 50 *Modern Law Review* 934, 945. Fitzpatrick also points out that, s.77 permitting only parties to collective agreements or contractual terms to challenge them, someone covered by discriminatory collectively agreed term had no power to challenge them. Ss.77 SDA and 72 RRA provided for declarations that unlawful terms be unenforceable against the complainant.

[94] The relevant provisions are now to be found in s.77 SDA 1975 and s.6 SDA 1986 (dealing, respectively, with contracts and collective agreements), as amended by the Trade Union Reform and Employment Rights Act 1993.

[95] This is more akin therefore to s.6 SDA/ 2.RRA.

[96] *Cf* doubts expressed by Fitzpatrick, above n 93, 943–4.

[97] It is arguable that, in this respect, British law falls short of the requirements of Article 141. In *Kowalska v Freie und Hansestadt Hamburg* Case C–33/89 [1990] ECR I–259 the European Court of Justice ruled that, in the absence of any national legislation providing for the equalisation of collectively agreed terms as between men and women, the disadvantaged sex would be entitled to be granted the benefits enjoyed by the advantaged sex.

not permit, for example, the extension of collectively agreed benefits from full-time to part-time workers where it was established that the non-entitlement of the latter to them amounted to indirect sex discrimination. The aggrieved part-timers would be required to present individual claims under the EqPA or SDA.

The power of individuals to challenge discrimination, other than exclusively as it impacts on them, is very limited.[98] But the EOC, CRE and DRC and the ECNI may in some cases act on their own behalf, as well as in support of individuals. Their action can take the form of litigation or the pursuit of 'Formal Investigations.' The commissions' powers of Formal Investigation (FI) are considered first, their various powers to litigate below. The CRE and EOC will be considered first, the other bodies being of much more recent vintage and, in the case of the ECNI in particular, being subject to special rules, considered below. What is said in respect of the CRE, EOC and DRC, however, applied equally to their sibling organisations in Northern Ireland during the period (however brief) of their existence. It applies today to the ECNI in its role vis-à-vis the Sex Discrimination (Northern Ireland) Order 1976, the Race Relations (Northern Ireland) Order 1997 and the DDA. The changes recently proposed by the Government in relation to FIs are considered below.

Formal Investigations

The investigative powers of the EOC and the CRE are set out in ss.57–70 SDA and ss.48–64 RRA respectively. These powers were intended to play a very significant role in the enforcement of the early anti-discrimination legislation.[99] Vera Sacks and Judith Maxwell pointed out, in 1984, that the power granted to the Commissions to carry out Formal Investigations (FIs):

V Sacks and J Maxwell, 'Unnatural Justice for Discriminators' (1984) 47 *Modern Law Review* **334, 334–5, footnotes omitted**

was identified in two Government White Papers which preceded the [SDA] and [RRA] as strategic in identifying and eliminating discriminatory practices: 'The Commission's *main tasks* will be . . . to identify and deal with discriminatory practices by industries, firms or institutions' and this could be 'on its own initiative' and 'whether or not there had been individual complaints about the organisation investigated.' Extensive investigatory powers were conferred on the Commission for this purpose for it was recognised that the individual would usually lack the resources to finance and compile proof, and that what was needed was an independent body acting in the public interest who could undertake a thorough appraisal of practices, policies and procedures which, although apparently neutral, might have a discriminatory impact . . . established business practices often excluded minorities, albeit unintentionally, and it was therefore essential that recruitment, selection and promotion policies be scrutinised as a whole within the context of the entire organisational structure.

The investigative powers of the CRE are set out in ss.48–50 RRA, ss.57–9 of the SDA being in similar terms:

---

[98] The inclusion of a detriment requirement in indirect discrimination is discussed in Ch 2. In cases of direct discrimination the claimant must have been less favourably treated.

[99] *Race Discrimination* (London: Department of Employment, 1975), Cmnd 6234, the White Paper which preceded the RRA, envisaged that the CRE's investigative powers would account for much of the legislative enforcement of the new Act.

s.48 (1) Without prejudice to their general power to do anything requisite for the performance of their duties under section 43(1) the Commission may if they think fit, and shall
if required by the Secretary of State, conduct a formal investigation for any purpose
connected with the carrying out of those duties.

s.49 ... (2) Terms of reference for the investigation shall be drawn up by the Commission
or, if the Commission were required by the Secretary of State to conduct the investigation, by the Secretary of State after consulting the Commission.

(3) It shall be the duty of the Commission to give general notice of the holding of the
investigation unless the terms of reference confine it to activities of persons named in
them, but in such a case the Commission shall in the prescribed manner give those persons notice of the holding of the investigation.

(4) Where the terms of reference of the investigation confine it to activities of persons
named in them and the Commission in the course of it propose to investigate any act
made unlawful by this Act which they believe that a person so named may have done,
the Commission shall—

(a) inform that person of their belief and of their proposal to investigate the act in
question; and

(b) offer him an opportunity of making oral or written representations with regard to
it (or both oral and written representations if he thinks fit) ...

s. 50 (1) For the purposes of a formal investigation the Commission ...

(a) may require any person to furnish such written information as may be described in
the notice, and may specify the time at which, and the manner and form in which,
the information is to be furnished;

(b) may require any person to attend at such time and place as is specified in the notice
and give oral information about, and produce all documents in his possession or
control relating to, any matter specified in the notice.

(2) Except as provided by section 60, a notice shall be served under subsection (1) only
where—

(a) service of the notice was authorised by an order made by the Secretary of State; or

(b) the terms of reference of the investigation state that the Commission believe that a
person named in them may have done or may be doing ...

(i) unlawful discriminatory acts;[100] ...

and confine the investigation to those acts.

Sacks and Maxwell point out, of s.49(4) RRA,[101] that it was (336):

added at the latest possible stage when the Race Relations Act was going through
Parliament—the third reading in the House of Lords. Proposed by Lord Hailsham in committee as a protection for respondents during the *course of the investigation*, in addition to
their right to be heard at the conclusion of the investigation, it was resisted by the
Government on the grounds that the C.R.E. should be free to investigate 'with a minimum
of procedural requirements.' But the Government eventually gave way and apparently by
mistake the section was added to other amendments as subsection (4) instead of appearing
as a new and separate clause 50.

The cost of the Government's mistake will become apparent below, allowing as it did
the commissions' FI powers to be 'emasculated by a judiciary which, being apparently

---

[100] (ii) and (iii) expressly list discriminatory practices, discriminatory advertisements and instructions and
pressure to discriminate.

[101] The RRA also applied this provision to the SDA (s.58(3A)).

uncommitted to the objectives of the law, have emphasised the narrow letter of the statute and upheld the rights of discriminators in preference to those of the potential victims.'[102]

The EOC appeared reluctant from the start to utilise its powers and has, until recently, conducted only a handful of FIs.[103] The first dealt with the allocation of grammar school places by Tameside Education Authority ('a somewhat idiosyncratic first use by the EOC of its enforcement powers since the factual issue was so specialised and unlikely to recur');[104] the second into discrimination in employment by Electrolux, this on the suggestion of Phillips J, (then President of EAT), who was faced with 600 individual claims relating to the company. An investigation into the credit practices of Debenhams stores was threatened in 1978 and resulted in a co-operative exercise which produced recommendations of general application in the retail credit industry. Two of the four FIs begun in 1979 dealt with employment-related discrimination at individual educational establishments; one was into discrimination vis-à-vis its members by the SOGAT trade union; and the other into discrimination in employment practices by Leeds Permanent Building Society. In 1980 the Commission investigated redundancy provisions applied in one British Steel Corporation works. The Provincial Building Society headed off a mortgage FI in the same year with a successful allegation of bias to the Divisional Court and by 1984 the FI agreed in 1983 into the provision of craft, design and technology courses in FE colleges had not yet begun.[105]

More recently the EOC has been more enthusiastic in carrying out FIs. 2003 saw the first FI for 10 years by the commission—a 'named investigation' (see further below) into sexual harassment in the Post Office. In the same year the EOC launched a 'general investigation' into occupational segregation (this with a particular focus on modern apprenticeships in construction, plumbing, engineering, ICT and childcare) and in 2004 followed this up with general investigations into pregnancy discrimination, working carers, and part-time and flexible work. The general investigations are ongoing while that into the Post Office was suspended in August 2003 when the Royal Mail agreed an action plan with the EOC to stamp out sexual harassment.

The CRE made full use of its FI powers in the early years, launching no less than 17 such investigations in its first eighteen months of operation (June 1977–January 1979), and a total of 63 to the end of 1999.[106] The CRE displayed considerably more relish for its investigative powers than did the EOC though, as Ellis and Appleby pointed out, it did have the benefit of years of experience on the part of the Race Relations Board (whose, albeit considerably expanded, remit it inherited).[107] Having said this, the pace of FI slowed considerably after 1984 in the wake of the *Hillingdon* and *Prestige* cases (discussed below) half of the FIs being concluded in the 7.5 years to the end of 1984, the other 50% taking an additional 15 years. The early approach of the CRE to FIs is discussed by Mary Coussey:

---

[102] Sacks and Maxwell, 334.

[103] Only four of the 13 FIs to 1991 led to the issue of NDNs (see below). CRE investigations tended to relate to broader areas than those conducted by the EOC—typical of the former were investigations into Cardiff employers, the hotel industry and chartered accountancy training: investigations into Dan Air's failure to recruit male cabin staff and into allegations of discrimination in promotion at a number of individual schools were more typical of those carried out by the EOC. See C McCrudden, D Smith and C Brown, *Racial Justice at Work* (London, Policy Studies Institute, 1991) ch 3 for details of the CRE's record.

[104] E Ellis and G Appleby, 'Formal Investigations: the CRE and the EOC as Law Enforcement Agencies' (1984) *Public Law* 236, 256.

[105] Ellis and Appleby, *ibid*, 255–9.

[106] McCrudden *et al*, *ibid*, 452.

[107] Above n 104. The Board was established under the RRA 1965.

M Coussey, 'The Effectiveness of Strategic Enforcement of the Race Relations Act 1976', in B Hepple and E Szyszczak (eds), *Discrimination: The Limits of Law*, footnotes omitted

The strategic investigations carried out by the CRE before the *Prestige* decision in 1984 were chosen with reference to the broad labour market position. It was decided to carry out a rolling programme of general enquiries into the extent of inequality in a number of representative industries located in areas of significant ethnic minority population. In this way, it would be possible to build up a range of models, demonstrating in practical terms how discrimination operates. Over a dozen such enquiries were started. By selecting large companies in industrial sectors in which ethnic minorities were concentrated, it was anticipated that the findings of the investigations would be relevant to other employers in the same industry.

These enquiries combined a strategic and inspectorial approach. However, their aims were not fulfilled because many of the early strategic investigations had to be abandoned after the *Prestige* decision. But the experience gained was the basis for many of the recommendations in the Code of Practice, as these enquiries identified most of the potentially discriminatory practices and other barriers caused by disadvantage in the labour market.

For example, there were five reports published of general investigations, started before the *Prestige* decision, into named organizations. The enquiries covered a wide range of personnel decision-making and practices at different job levels. Many potentially discriminatory practices were identified. These included informal word-of-mouth recruitment, which effectively excluded ethnic minority applicants from access to jobs, and the application of geographical preferences, which in some circumstances disproportionately excluded ethnic minorities (e.g. applicants should not live in Liverpool 8). Discriminatory selection criteria were also found, such as informal oral or written English tests which had little relation to the standards needed for the work, and which screened out a large majority of Asian candidates. Subjective criteria, acceptability criteria and stereotypical judgments were widespread. The use of sponsorship as a qualification for a hackney cab licence was found to be a discriminatory practice. One enquiry was restarted as a 'belief' investigation, and focused more narrowly on promotion procedures, identifying the interview as a discriminatory practice because it rejected ethnic minority candidates for lack of communication skills. This was found to be unjustifiable because the interview did not test the more direct work-related communication require for the job.

Other early investigations published before 1984 (and therefore unaffected by *Prestige*) uncovered a similar array of discriminatory practices. These included direct discrimination and pressure to discriminate by shop stewards, and indirect discrimination by Massey Ferguson in the use of unsolicited letters for recruitment. The latter practice favoured applicants with links with the workforce. As the workforce was overwhelmingly white, the letters of application also came mainly from white people. Inside knowledge also meant that applicants wrote to apply for a specific vacancy as it arose. Ethnic minority applicants had no such networks at the plant, and tended to call at the factory gates. When this occurred, they may have been advised to 'write in,' but few did so. Many had no confidence that their letters would be successful. The company argued that this recruitment practice was not a 'requirement' (which is one of the criteria in the statutory definition of indirect discrimination [see further Chapter 2]) because applicants who applied in other ways were sometimes considered. Had this early case come to the courts, it would have been an interesting test of the meaning of 'requirement or condition' in Section 1(1)(b) of the Race Relations Act, demonstrating as it does the ease with which employers can point to one or two exceptions to challenge the existence of a practice or 'requirement.'

This investigation also showed the powerful effect of a poor company image: the chill factor. It was known among the ethnic minority communities in Coventry, the site of the plant, that it was a 'waste of time' applying to Massey Ferguson for a job if you were black or Asian, because 'no one like me' was employed there. The 'chill factor' is still an important deterrent to ethnic minority candidates, as several recent surveys by employers have shown. See, for example, the recent survey 'Ethnic Minority Recruitment to the Armed Services,' published by the Ministry of Defence in January 1990. According to this research, one-third of Asians and half of Afro-Caribbeans in the survey expected to find racial discrimination when applying to the armed services.

None of the companies involved in these pre-1984 investigations had taken steps to implement equal opportunities policies. The discriminatory practices could flourish unchecked, as there were no records of the ethnic origin of applicants or employees. Ironically; in the absence of such data, it was difficult for the commission to find sufficient evidence of discriminatory practices. The alternative was to rely on employers' records of reasons for rejection or their accounts of selection practices. Not surprisingly, the evidence gleaned from this was often too weak to justify the use of the enforcement powers.

One significant problem faced by the EOC and the CRE—in particular by the latter, given its more aggressive investigative stance, came from the courts. The disapproval with which much of the judiciary regarded the investigative powers of the Commissions was evident from the start. Lord Hailsham, who, in his legislative capacity, was responsible for the insertion of s.49(4), likened the CRE's powers to those of the Star Chamber in the House of Lords debate on the Bill.[108] In *Science Research Council v Nassé* [1979] QB 144, Lord Denning declared that the Commission's investigative powers enabled it to 'interrogate employers . . . up to the hilt and compel disclosure of documents on a massive scale . . . You might think that we were back in the days of the inquisition.'

Sacks and Maxwell, 338, footnotes omitted

Lord Oliver in *Mandla v Dowell Lee* [1983] 2 AC 548 has accused the CRE of using the Race Relations Act as an 'engine of oppression,' Lord Denning has likened an investigation to a criminal charge, while Lord Diplock voiced an implied criticism against the C.R.E. for wasting public money—when the waste was in fact occasioned by the courts' interpretation of their powers. . . . The courts have found in favour of respondents and their multiplicity of challenges to the CRE on procedural grounds.

The bulk of judicial disapproval was reserved for the CRE, probably because, as we saw above, it was less backward about utilising its powers than was the EOC. In *Hillingdon London Borough Council v CRE* [1982] AC 779 the House of Lords took its first substantial step towards curbing what it evidently saw as the excessive powers of the Commission.

The case concerned a challenge brought by the council to the CRE's decision to launch an FI into possible race discrimination by it in the provision of housing. The CRE believed that the council might be discriminating in providing housing for homeless immigrants. This belief was based, in part, on the contrasting approach of the council to an Asian and a white family who had, respectively, immigrated from Kenya and from (now) Zimbabwe. The council took the view that the former were intentionally but the latter were unintentionally homeless, and a council member dumped the Asian family at the Foreign Office, by way of protest that responsibility for housing immigrants who arrived at Heathrow airport fell on the council, rather than on national government.

---

[108] 373 HL Debs 20 July 1976, col. 745.

The House of Lords interpreted ss.49(4) and 50(2)(b) RRA to require that, before it began a named investigation, the CRE must have formed a belief that the persons being investigated might be or have been engaged in unlawful discrimination *of the type* (narrowly defined) which was to be investigated. Unless the instances relied upon by the CRE caused them to form a belief that the council was engaged in a wider policy of discrimination (which, on the CRE's own evidence, was not the case), they were entitled only to investigate the possibility of discrimination in the provision of housing to homeless immigrants.[109] Further, the House of Lords agreed with the Court of Appeal's (*obiter*) view that s.49(4) required the CRE to carry out a preliminary inquiry prior to any FI during which the subject of the planned FI would have an opportunity to argue against the launch of such an investigation.

The decision of the House of Lords in *Hillingdon* was followed by that in *ex parte Prestige*, in which their Lordships rejected the argument put forward by the CRE that it could carry out 'named investigations' without suspicion of unlawful action by the person named, and that in such cases s.49(4) did not apply. The terms of reference of the *Prestige* FI had been 'to inquire into the employment of persons of different racial groups by the Prestige Group . . . with particular reference to the promotion of equality of opportunity between such persons as regards [*inter alia*] recruitment [and] access to promotion.' The company challenged the FI after the CRE, having uncovered unlawful action by it in the course of the FI, had issued a non-discrimination notice. According to Lord Diplock, who delivered the sole speech in *Prestige* (as he had in *Hillingdon*):

R v CRE ex parte Prestige Group plc [1984] ICR 472

The requirements of section 49(3) as to the notice to be given of the holding of a general investigation is to be contrasted with the limited notice to be given of a named-person investigation [s.49(4)]. Of the holding of an investigation of the latter type, notice of the holding of it (which obviously must include a statement of its terms of reference) need be, and in practice is, given only to the persons named in it whose 'activities' are the subject of the formal investigation. The fact that Parliament has thought fit to limit in this manner the notice to be given of a formal investigation of a particular kind, (viz. a named-person investigation) that the CRE is minded to conduct, provides in my view a strong indication of a Parliamentary intention that the nature of such an investigation should not be purely exploratory, as in the case of a general investigation, but should be accusatory in the sense that it is directed to determining whether or not there is justification for pre-existing suspicions of the CRE that the persons to whose activities the named-person investigation is confined had in the course of those activities committed acts made unlawful by the [RRA]. The most likely source of such suspicions before any formal investigation starts is complaints received by the CRE from members of racial groups who claim to have been victims of unlawful discriminatory acts committed by the named persons. In the absence of any belief by the CRE that the named persons may have committed unlawful acts why should those persons alone be picked upon to have their activities investigated to the exclusion of the activities of other employers engaged in the same industries as the persons named? And why, except on the assumption not only that the CRE already had suspicions but also that such suspicions were derived from the most likely source, should Parliament have treated it as unnecessary that the holding of the investigation should be brought to the notice of

---

[109] This, as Ellis and Appleby point out (244), appears at odds with the wording of s.49(4). Although the test was drawn quite widely by the HL: (246) 'the prudent course for the Commission to take will . . . be the minimalist one, resulting in narrow terms of reference and putting a serious practical brake upon the Commission's enforcement powers.'

members of those groups of persons which are likely to include victims or potential victims of unlawful acts committed by the named persons in the course of their activities that are to be investigated?

Lord Diplock's interpretation of parliamentary intention is in striking contrast to the extract from the White Paper cited by Sacks and Maxwell above and fails to take account of the role of such FIs as outlined by Coussey, also above. The decision in *Prestige*, of course, predated *Pepper v Hart* [1993] AC 593, in which their Lordships relaxed the strict rule by which Parliamentary materials could not be referred to in attempting to determine the parliamentary intent behind legislation.[110] Its impact was to render all but unuseable the commissions' powers to carry out FIs.

G Appleby and E Ellis, 'Formal Investigations: the CRE and the EOC as Law Enforcement Agencies' (1984) *Public Law* 236, 247, footnotes omitted

It was far from a foregone conclusion that the legislation would have to be interpreted this way. Section 49(4) refers to the situation where the investigation is into named persons and the Commission in the course of it propose to investigate those persons' suspected unlawful discrimination. This wording would appear to suggest that a named-person investigation need not be directed to uncovering discrimination, and the CRE argued in Prestige that it was empowered to conduct a general investigation into a named person. In such a case, it would have no coercive powers. Lord Diplock, however, repeated his earlier remarks and held that it is a 'condition precedent to the exercise by the CRE of its power to conduct named-person investigations that the CRE should in fact have already formed a suspicion that the persons named may have committed some unlawful act of discrimination . . .

Nor is the judicial approach taken in *Hillingdon* and in *Prestige* on all fours with that adopted in respect of other investigative bodies. Whereas, in *Hillingdon*, Lord Diplock declared that the 'first rule of natural justice—*audi alteram partem* is expressly required to be observed at this stage':

Sacks and Maxwell, 339, footnotes omitted

. . . the courts' treatment of other investigative bodies exercising similar powers suggest that the issue is not as definite as Lord Diplock would have us believe. It appears from the authority of earlier cases not concerning the C.R.E. that, in preliminary proceedings to establish the necessity of undertaking further investigations, there is no right to be heard at this stage. In *Wiseman v Borneman* [1971] AC 297 for example, the House of Lords held that there was nothing inherently unfair in refusing the taxpayer an oral hearing before a tribunal that was concerned only to establish whether there was a prima facie case for an investigation by the Commissioners of Inland Revenue. The Law Lords made it quite clear that at this preliminary stage the requirements of natural justice were minimal. Lord Reid said, 'It is, I think, not entirely irrelevant to have in mind that it is very unusual for there to be a judicial determination of the question whether there is a prima facie case. Every public officer who has to decide whether to prosecute or raise proceedings ought first to decide whether there is a prima facie case, but no one supposes that justice requires that he should first seek

---

[110] In *Pepper*, the House of Lords by a majority of 6:1 (Lord Mackay LC dissenting) ruled that such reference could be made where (a) the legislation was 'ambiguous or obscure, or led to an absurdity'; (b) the material relied on consisted of one or more statements by a Minister or other promoter of the Bill together if necessary with such other parliamentary material as was necessary to understand such statements and their effects; and (c) the statements relied on were clear.

the comments of the accused or the defendant on the material before him. *So there is nothing inherently unjust in reaching such a decision in the absence of the other party.*' This passage was cited with approval in both *Re Pergamon Press Ltd* [1970] 3 WLR 729, where Lord Denning applied it to inspectors investigating a company's affairs, and *Pearlberg v Varty* [1972] IWLR 524, where Lord Pearson said that 'If there were too much elaboration of procedural safeguards, nothing could be done simply and quickly and cheaply. Administrative or executive efficiency and economy should not be too readily sacrificed.' It is clear from these and other cases, that the courts have not invoked *audi alteram partem* at preliminary stages and have not previously thought it necessary to invoke the *audi alteram partem* rule for preliminary hearings designed to establish a prima facie case for proceeding with an investigation.

Indeed the courts have warned against allowing natural justice to be oppressive in its requirements. In a slightly different context of a tribunal exercising licensing functions, Sir Robert Megarry VC warned that 'the concepts of natural justice and the duty to be fair must not be allowed to discredit themselves by making unreasonable requirements and imposing undue burdens.' But this is exactly the situation in which the CRE have now found themselves.

Ellis and Appleby point out some of the difficulties raised by the *Prestige* decision:

E Ellis and G Appleby 'Blackening the *Prestige* Pot? Formal Investigations and the CRE' (1984) 100 *Law Quarterly Review* 349, 354, footnotes omitted

For example, what is the Commission to do when minded to begin an investigation into a field of activity exclusively occupied by one individual who, even if not actually named in the terms of reference, is identifiable? An instance would be provided by a Government department (such as in the case of the current C.R.E. investigation into the administration of the immigration service by the Home Office) or a nationalised industry. Perhaps even more intractable is the difficulty that, if a 'non-belief' investigation cannot take place into the activities of one named person, neither presumably can such an investigation be concerned with the activities of any finite number of named persons. Assuming that the courts would not be satisfied by the mere subterfuge of not naming those involved where is the line to be drawn between an investigation into a number of individuals and a general investigation? Such an argument eventually leads to the conclusion that there may never be able to be a valid general investigation, but this obviously flies in the face of the legislative provisions already cited.

. . . *Prestige* . . . enhances the importance of section 49(4), which in turn gives more scope for respondents seeking judicial review. The House of Commons Home Affairs Committee recommended in 1981 that the subsection be repealed, and the CRE itself has echoed this . . . Whilst not for a moment suggesting that individuals should be denied the right to challenge a statutory body's exercise of its powers, the effectiveness of the CRE's role as a law enforcement agency has certainly been undermined by respondents seizing every opportunity open to them of delaying investigations by seeking judicial review. It is therefore unfortunate if an effect of this judgment has been to provide them with yet more such opportunities.

The latter fear proved well-founded. Subsequent to the *Hillingdon* and *Prestige* decisions, attempts by the CRE to instigate formal investigations became mired in 'lengthy and rarely productive challenges before a formal investigation is begun.'[111] It took 13 years for the

---

[111] CRE, *Annual Report* 1988.

commission to be in a position to launch its formal investigation into the army in 1994, and the number of investigations instigated by the CRE has been drastically reduced. The requirements in respect of FIs were listed by Vera Sacks, in an article dealing with the EOC:

V Sacks, 'The Equal Opportunities Commission—Ten Years On' (1986) 49 *Modern Law Review* **560, 581–2, footnotes omitted**

. . . those who are to be investigated must be informed by way of terms of reference served upon them of the situation which the E.O.C. intend to investigate. Before the investigation begins that party has the right to make representations to the Commission, both oral and in writing if desired, in the hope that the Commission will not proceed with the investigation. If the EOC should revise its terms of reference (as a result usually of representations) then the respondent may make representations again. The Act then provides that, at the conclusion of the investigation, if the Commission is 'minded' to serve a non-discrimination notice on them, the other party has the right to make further representations. A right of appeal against the non-discrimination notice is also available. Such is the procedure laid down by the Act in outline.

However, further requirements have been added by judicial exegesis. The terms of reference must specify the grounds for the suspicion that unlawful acts have been committed, and the Commission may not go beyond them in their investigations unless they revise the terms of reference or the respondent agrees. On appeal all the facts on which the notice was based can be reopened by the appellant in front of a court or tribunal, and are subject to cross-examination—usually years after the events have occurred. at all stages of the investigation the Commission must act in accordance with the principles of natural justice, and here the *Hillingdon* case indicates that the respondent has rights of reply other than those laid down in the Act. Finally it seems that there may be other matters, as yet unexplored, which may be capable of being reviewed—for example, whether an investigation can continue when the factual situation has changed, ie whether it can refer only to past practices.

The additional rights of reply to which Sacks refers consist, presumably, of the right to reply to a specific charge levelled by the Commission prior to any FI. The significance of this in narrowing the terms of reference of any investigation, and of precluding any departure from those terms as an FI uncovers wider discrimination, is enormous, and would not have arisen had the right to be heard been incorporated in the course of the FI itself, rather than at the preliminary stage. It is the preliminary nature of the right to be heard, too, which underlies the doubts expressed by Sacks in relation to changed circumstances.

Sacks attributes the low number of FIs conducted by the EOC in part both to the technicality of the legal provisions, and to their judicial interpretation. Discussing a number of the investigations begun by the EOC:

Sacks, 582–5, footnotes omitted

The delay consequent upon stringent legalism can be illustrated by the Ebbw Vale inquiry. The EOC was threatened with judicial review because it appointed a new Commissioner after the warrant of the existing two had expired. Ebbw Vale College argued that the appointment of the new Commissioner part-way through the investigation was unfair (although the existing Commissioners had been re-appointed as additional Commissioners under section 57). This threat was withdrawn after a long delay but by then, in the words of the CRE, 'It does not matter whether the respondent succeeds; the damage caused by repeated delays is enormous, and all this without touching on the fundamental question whether discrimination has occurred and what should be done about it.' The impact has also been devastating on morale, and needed resources are spent obtaining legal opinions to avoid further challenges. Although it would be improper to deny protection to those under investigation, the current situation is neither what was intended by Parliament nor in the interests of victims of discrimination.

Apart from cost and delay the main legal difficulty which now confronts the EOC is that they cannot go on 'fishing expeditions' but must confine their investigations to the narrow factual issue which was reported to them. For example both in the Leeds and Barclays investigations the Commission would have liked to extend their investigations into other matters, but since new terms of reference would have had to have been drawn up and new representations made, were understandably deterred. Another current example of this situation is whether statistical evidence showing an imbalance between the sexes in the workforce would provide sufficient suspicion to justify an investigation. The White Paper which preceded the [SDA] did not envisage these difficulties; the Commission was to invest-igate discriminatory practices 'on its own initiative' and 'whether or not there had been indi-vidual complaints about the organisation investigated.' Given the fact of widespread inequalities the piecemeal approach to its eradication dictated by case law presents a gloomy prognosis. The way ahead lies in repeal of section 58(3A) and its equivalent in the [RRA] . . .

The legal challenges outlined above are the result of strong hostility by those under inves-tigation. As time has progressed, investigatees have developed more and different avoidance tactics. Recently an important institution responded to the EOC's initial inquiries by swamping them with information, then made long oral and written submissions repre-sented by senior counsel, while conducting their own internal investigation. Having estab-lished in this way that the complaints were justified, they indulged in a 'pincer' movement: on the one hand they agreed to co-operate with the Commission on new recruitment prac-tices while on the other their legal advisers insisted on further clarification of the Commission's findings and threatening judicial review. Either the Commission continued the investigation or settled. It chose the latter course, although wisely only agreed to sus-pend the investigation pending monitoring. The adversarial stance adopted by the institu-tion and its delaying tactics, especially given the fact that they knew its practices to be wrong, typify many other cases. The Leeds Permanent investigation timetable illustrates all that has been described here and is worth considering:

1977 Complaint received from a woman applicant that much stress was placed on mobility in her interview for management trainee. EOC request application forms so that analysis can be made of other factors which might account for the total lack of female man-agement trainees although a quarter of the applicants are female.

1978 Commission decides to investigate—Leeds seek clarification of complaints; formal terms of reference sent to Society after Counsel's opinion sought.

1979 Written and oral representations received; as a result terms of reference revised, fur-ther correspondence on these, further representations promised but none received. Application forms analysed and counsel's opinion sought on whether formal investigation could be undertaken.

1980 Questionnaire drafted and sent to applicants whose forms have been analysed. This done in order to obtain information about interviews. Society consider trying to stop use of questionnaire but do not. Further discussions with Society on current practices and Counsel's advice sought on these relative to whether formal investigation could proceed.

1981 Report on findings drafted and redrafted.

1982 Preliminary report sent to Society (June) who request further representations which are not received until December. Counsel's advice sought.

1983 Final report sent to Society who reject it—more representations made as a result of which Part 3 (containing the Society's representations and the Commission's findings) is redrafted. Further correspondence—EOC agrees to confine its findings to 1978 because practices have changed.

1984 Counsel's opinion sought on redrafting report; Part 3 re-written and sent to Society.

1985 Society's comments received and report considered by Commissioners.

1985 (June) Report published.

The CRE has long campaigned for a reversal of the *Prestige* decision. Even prior to the House of Lords' decision in that case, the Commission's first review (published in 1983), highlighted difficulties it had experienced in carrying out FIs.

CRE, *The Race Relations Act 1976—Time for a Change?* (1983), para 5

. . . the rate at which legal challenges are mounted to head off an investigation or its results is very high. . . . if enforcement is to be effective the scope for legal challenges must be reduced both by the introduction of greater flexibility and by a shortening of the whole investigative process. The following are some suggestions relating to this:

There have been legal challenges over investigations on such highly *technical procedural matters* as whether terms of reference are too wide; whether the Commission can investigate named persons without a belief that they are acting unlawfully; whether it is reasonable to embark on an investigation; whether natural justice applies as well as the statutory requirements to hear representations; whether the right to make representations under s.49(4) of the Act applies during the course of an investigation if the Commission forms a belief as to unlawful acts; whether it is reasonable to change from a strategic investigation to one based on a belief that unlawful acts have occurred; whether in drawing conclusions after representations pursuant to s.58(5) of the Act the Commission has acted reasonably.

None of these matters actually touch on the fundamental question whether discrimination has occurred and what should be done about it. . . . The *Amari* case dealing with appeals against non-discrimination notices [discussed below] permits the whole factual basis of the non-discrimination notice to be re-opened in an appeal.

Yet, all this has happened in a system which was itself designed to give the person investigated every opportunity to make representation. The result is that they have those opportunities and the right of re-hearing on appeal and plentiful opportunities for requesting a judicial review. In a sense it does not matter whether the respondent succeeds; the damage caused by repeated delays is enormous. In some ways, the possibility of delay on procedural grounds must be reduced.

It may be that the judges will never be able to accept the fact that Parliament has entrusted the CRE with sweeping investigative powers to work towards the eradication of a great social evil being carried out covertly. It may also be that those investigated see the CRE as too partisan for them to be able to accept the conclusions of the CRE administratively reached even after proper hearings. This combination of factors suggests powerfully that a new approach is called for.

The CRE must have wide investigative *powers for any purpose connected with their functions* and should on notifying the terms of reference be able to require the production of information. The only alternative would be a system where legal proceedings subject to wide discovery powers are commenced very early in the day with little or no preliminaries. Yet at the same time the CRE should have power to accept, from persons investigated, binding undertakings to change their practices. (It would have to be established that a judicial review is not possible if the CRE declines to accept such an undertaking—because otherwise this again would hold up work.) there may be many instances where persons will be willing to make changes in practices and procedures to avoid discrimination occurring in future and, if binding undertakings include sanctions against breach, the CRE's public duty may be satisfied by accepting them.

The present system of investigations is designed to have formal investigations directed at large general problems. This makes investigations slow and proceedings complex and, as we have noted, with many opportunities for challenges in the courts as well as the possibility of appeal at the end. A substantial improvement could be effected if the Commission could apply in the course of an investigation to a court or tribunal for a finding that an individual act or practice is discriminatory and for appropriate remedies. (Once again, it would have to be established that the decision to take the matter to court or tribunal was not itself subject to judicial review).

Commenting upon the Divisional Court's decision in *Prestige*, which the House of Lords was later to uphold, the CRE protested that the restriction of named investigations to cases where unlawful behaviour was suspected would be 'a severe, and in our view wrong, constraint on the discretion of the Commission,' pointing out in particular that FIs could be used 'to highlight and illustrate a particularly desirable practice.' The CRE called for the removal of s.49(4), the need for a preliminary hearing at which the person being investigated had a right to be heard being identified by the Commission as a 'major delaying factor' in FIs.[112]

CRE (1983), para 49

... the hope of the respondent is raised and as as result representations are frequently made at very great length and by very senior Counsel, at considerable expense and by respondents with high expectations. The expectation is frequently dashed and the expense is unnecessary; the standard of proof at this stage of an investigation has been defined by the House of Lords in the Hillingdon case and is a very low one. It is no more than 'to raise in the minds of reasonable men, possessed of the experience of covert racial discrimination that has been acquired by the Commission, a suspicion that there may have been acts by the person named of racial discrimination of the kind which it is proposed to investigate.' A mere suspicion is remarkably difficult to dispel and a respondent would, in our view, suffer no disadvantage if we endorsed the recommendations of the Select Committee and *recommended that s.49(4) be repealed.*

The 1983 review by the CRE, and the various reforms it suggested, was ignored by a hostile Conservative Government.[113] The CRE's second review, published nine years later, reiterated the call for statutory reversal of *Prestige* (this call had also been made by the EOC in its 1988 reform proposals), citing in support the view of the White Paper on Racial Discrimination that the CRE's predecessor, the Race Relations Board 'has been hampered by its dependence on receiving significant complaints in pursuing the crucial strategic role of identifying and dealing with discriminatory practices and encouraging positive action to secure equal opportunity.' According to the CRE:

---

[112] A view shared by the Employment Select Committee discussed by L Lustgarten, 'The New Meaning of Discrimination' [1978] *Public Law* 178.

[113] Post-consultation the document was sent as the *Review of the Race Relations Act 1976: Proposals for Change* (1985).

CRE, *Second Review of the Race Relations Act,* **1992, para 12**

Paragraph 111 of the White Paper preceding the RRA said that under the new legislation the successor body would be able to conduct formal investigations on its own initiative into a specific organisation for any purpose connected with the carrying out of its functions. The new body would also be able to compel the production of information/attendance of witnesses, without the sanction of the Secretary of State where the investigation was confined to unlawful conduct which it believed was occurring . . .

Until Section 49(4) was added to the legislation there was no doubt that the Government understood that the power of the new Commission to investigate the affairs of an individual or particular organisation was not limited to a situation where there was some initial evidence of unlawful activity.

When the Government accepted the House of Lords amendment which became Section 49(4) the effect was stated as being 'to give a person against whom a complaint is made a right to information' (House of Commons Debates 918 c.603). Nothing was said which indicated any belief on the part of Government that it had now accepted a restriction on the Commission's powers to conduct investigations.

A strategic approach to formal investigations is needed. Named person investigations, with or without a suspicion of unlawful acts, should form part of this strategy. Direct discrimination is generally covert. Indirect discrimination is often not recognised as unlawful by those operating the practices involved. Indeed they may not even be applied to any particular member of an ethnic minority, as Section 28 of the Act acknowledges. For example, word of mouth recruiting may be indirectly discriminatory precisely because no one outside the organisation knows the jobs exist. In these circumstances information as to discrimination is unlikely to be brought to the Commission's attention.

The Commission, therefore, needs to be able to look at selected major employers to enable it to identify what practices may be disadvantaging ethnic minorities. In this respect the Commission should be thought of as an inspectorate, bringing technical expertise to bear on identifying the causes of major social problems. We recommend that against this background the intended power taken away by *Prestige* be restored.

As the Policy Studies Institute researchers concluded in their Home Office sponsored research:

> The decision in the *Prestige* case seems to have frustrated the intentions of the legislators. A particularly unfortunate consequence is that formal investigations of specified organisations are bound to be confrontational., since there must be prior belief of unlawful discrimination . . . Investigations of specified organisations which do not allege unlawful discrimination should be available to the Commission in future, as they are by the Fair Employment Commission.

Once again, the 1992 reform proposals were ignored by the Conservative Government and the CRE's 1998 proposals called, yet again, for the statutory reversal of *Prestige*:

> It should be unambiguously stated in the Act that the Commission may conduct a formal investigation—either wide-ranging or confined to a particular organisation or individual— on its own initiative for any purpose connected with the carrying out of its functions. Specifically, the Commission should not be required to obtain and produce evidence of unlawful racial discrimination before embarking on an investigation of a named person . . . The Commission would still be expected to have sufficient information about the respondent to formulate relevant terms of reference for the investigation, and terms of reference which exceeded the Commission's powers could be challenged by judicial review. Where a respondent considers that the terms of reference are ill- or misconceived, the respondent would be able to make representations as at present.

Notwithstanding the difficulties associated with FIs the CRE has continued to make use of its powers in this area. In 2000, for example, it began an FI into race discrimination in the Crown Prosecution Service at its Croydon branch. The FI was closed in 2002 with the CPS, which had accepted the CRE's recommendations, entering into a partnership agreement with the Commission for a four-year period. An investigation into the Ford motor company was suspended in 2001 after an action plan had been agreed between the company and the Commission. At the same time an FI was being carried out into the Prison Service. This concluded in late 2003 with the CRE having found race discrimination. According to Trevor Phillips, chair of the Commission:

> What's most shocking about this report is that, despite numerous wake-up calls, Prison Service managers persistently failed to tackle racism in their institutions and that very often they also failed to implement their own policies on racial discrimination, abuse and harassment.
>
> ... I'm pleased to announce that we have reached an agreement with the Prison Service, whereby they have committed themselves to implementing a detailed action plan in order to deliver race equality throughout the service.[114]

The CRE made no fewer than 17 findings of race discrimination in its report on the Prison Service FI. Most related to individual cases such as that of Zahid Mubarek, who was stabbed to death in Feltham Young Offenders Institution in March 2000 by his racist cell mate. The CRE found that the Prison Service had failed to provide equivalent protection to all prisoners in its care and to deliver race equality in the way it employed staff and treated prisoners. The report further identified 14 'failure areas' which included the general atmosphere in prisons; the treatment of prison staff and prisoners; prisoners' access to goods, facilities, services and work; the control of the use of discretion; prison transfers and allocations; discipline, incentives and earned privileges for prisoners and the treatment of race complaints by prisoners. An action plan was drawn up by the CRE and the prison service to address the many failings highlighted by the FI.

The DRCA 1999 establishes the DRC's investigative powers in terms which, while they are not precisely the same as ss.49(4) and 58(3A) of the RRA and SDA respectively, fall far short of explicitly excluding *Prestige* even in the disability context. The Government in 1999 indicated its intention to amend the powers of the CRE and the EOC consistent with those of the DRC,[115] a move which the CRE welcomed as a 'first step' towards permitting the strategic use of FIs.[116] Developments under the Equality Bill 2005 are considered further below.

Section 2 DRCA requires that the DRC draw up terms of reference prior to any FI and give notice, in the case of a named person investigation, to the named person(s) or, in the case of a general investigation, that it 'publish a notice . . . in such manner as appears to the Commission appropriate to bring it to the attention of persons likely to be affected by it.' Sections 3 and 4 deal expressly with the investigation of unlawful acts, and provide:

> S.3(1) This paragraph applies where the Commission proposes to investigate in the course of a formal investigation (whether or not the investigation has already begun) whether—

---

114 CRE News Release 16 December 2003, 'CRE finds prison service guilty of racial discrimination'.
115 Ian McCartney, Minister of State for the Cabinet Office, in an equality statement 30 November 1999.
116 According to the CRE's briefing on the Government's response to the 1998 proposals.

    (a) a person has committed or is committing any unlawful act . . .[117]

(2) The Commission may not investigate any such matter unless the terms of reference of the investigation confine it to the activities of one or more named persons (and the person concerned is one of those persons).

(3) The Commission may not investigate whether a person has committed or is committing any unlawful act unless—

    (a) it has reason to believe that the person concerned may have committed or may be committing the act in question,[118] or . . .

(4) The Commission shall serve a notice on the person concerned offering him the opportunity to make written and oral representations about the matters being investigated.

(5) If the Commission is investigating whether the person concerned has committed or is committing any unlawful act the Commission shall include in the notice required by sub-paragraph (4) a statement informing that person that the Commission has reason to believe that he may have committed or may be committing any unlawful act.

(6) The Commission shall not make any findings in relation to any matter mentioned in sub-paragraph (1) without giving the person concerned or his representative a reasonable opportunity to make written and oral representations . . .

S.4(1) For the purposes of a formal investigation the Commission may serve a notice on any person requiring him—

    (a) to give such written information as may be described in the notice; or

    (b) to attend and give oral information about any matter specified in the notice, and to produce all documents in his possession or control relating to any such matter.

(2) A notice under this paragraph may only be served on the written authority of the Secretary of State unless the terms of reference confine the investigation to the activities of one or more named persons and the person being served is one of those persons.

Section 3(1) appears, *contra* the approach taken to the RRA (and, by implication, the SDA) by the House of Lords in *Prestige*, to countenance a named-person FI which is not directed at investigating whether a person has committed an unlawful act, s.3(2) then providing that if, in the course of such an investigation or otherwise, the Commission decides to investigate whether a person is committing an unlawful act, it must (other than in a follow-up investigation, see further below) not do so without (a) having reason to believe that the unlawful act may have been/ be being committed *and* (b) having complied with the requisite procedures. Crucially, the requirement in s.49(4), as it was interpreted by the courts, that the right to be heard was exercised at a *preliminary* hearing (at which stage, therefore, the terms of reference had to be set in stone), appears not to apply to the DRC— this because of s.3(1)'s express provision that a named person FI can become an *accusatory* named person FI during the course of the investigation.

It appears that the intention of s.3 is to disapply the *Prestige* decision in the context of the DDA. But its contemplation of non-accusatory named person FIs is not much more explicit than was s.49(4) itself, which, by using the conjunctive: '*[w]here* the terms of reference of the investigation confine it to activities of persons named in them *and* the Commission in the course of it propose to investigate any act made unlawful by this Act

---

[117] 'Or (b) any requirement imposed by a non-discrimination notice served on a person (including a requirement to take action specified in an action plan [discussed below]) has been or is being complied with; (c) any undertaking given by a person in an agreement made with the Commission under section 5 [discussed below] is being or has been complied with.'

[118] 'Or (b) that matter is to be investigated in the course of a formal investigation into his compliance with any requirement or undertaking mentioned in sub-paragraph (1)(b) or (c).'

which they believe that a person so named may have done' (my emphasis); quite clearly contemplated a named person investigation other than one based on a belief in unlawful action. It is possible, therefore, that s.3 will not be sufficient to prevent the judiciary from encasing the DRC in the same straitjacket as it applied to the CRE and, by implication, the EOC.

The DRC has, to date, carried out only one FI (concluded in 2004) into the access to and inclusion of disabled people within the worldwide web. The FI concluded that 82 per cent of websites failed to satisfy the most basic accessibility standards and had 'characteristics that make it very difficult, if not impossible, for people with certain impairments, especially those who are blind, to make use of the services provided. This results both from lack of interest and knowledge on the part of website developers, and from perceived commercial obstacles to accessibility on the part of website commissioners, notwithstanding that anecdotal evidence suggests that this concern is misplaced.' The Commission made a number of recommendations including the involvement of disabled users in website design and government action in the public sector. In February 2004, following consultation about its future operations, it announced its intention to concentrate its efforts in FIs and supporting strategic litigation.

FIs generate huge problems for the investigating commissions and, despite a recent spate of them on the part of both the CRE and EOC, that they are not fully performing the functions originally envisaged for them. It appeared from *Fairness for All* that the Government was content to exacerbate existing difficulties by making general investigations subject to a 'public interest' test which does not apply at present and by prohibiting the conduct of general investigations into named organisations. (The CRE points out that some FIs, 'like the CRE's general investigation of immigration procedures, which was aimed at the Immigration and Nationality Department of the Home Office, can only be conducted into a specific body'.) The CRE's view was that the bulk of the changes proposed by *Fairness for All* would downgrade the powers of investigation further by making named investigations 'a tool for occasional use to allow suspected cases of serious discrimination to be explored' and by further restricting the criteria for embarking upon such investigations by permitting them only in relation to acts of *unlawful* discrimination or harassment. The Commission points out that it had carried out about 65 named investigations of which the:

CRE, 'Fairness for All: A New Commission for Equality and Human Rights, A Response' (August 2004)

principal function [has been to] to uncover or discover discrimination and to use the finding to negotiate the introduction, or improvement, of equal opportunity policies, or to enforce the policies through a non-discrimination notice. The CRE has never used named investigations simply to enforce the law, but to secure wider policy and procedural changes. The power of investigation is an invaluable tool, which should not be restricted to 'occasional use' only . . . Indeed, it should be widened to include named investigations of the way a public authority carries out any of its functions . . . [The White Paper] appears to have accepted the limitations imposed on the CRE's investigation powers as a result of legal challenges in the early 1980s, and codified these into future legislation. This would constitute regression, preventing any opportunity for the rulings to be overturned. This is especially important, given the widely held view that the House of Lords' judgements of the early 1980s did not reflect the intention of Parliament in passing the Act.

We have always recommended that the CRE should be able to: . . . conduct a formal investigation—either wide-ranging or confined to a particular organisation or individual—on its own initiative for any purpose connected with the carrying out of its functions.

Specifically, the Commission should not be required to obtain and produce evidence of unlawful racial discrimination before embarking on an investigation of a named person or before exercising its powers to require attendance and/or the production of documents. (Reform of the Race Relations Act 1976, 1998).

[*Fairness for All*] appears to overlook the fact that the Disability Rights Commission's investigation powers to some extent reflect the views of the CRE and EOC, who were consulted at the time, on how investigations could be made more effective. The power in the Disability Discrimination Act should have been the starting point for developing investigation powers for a new equality body.

In the event, however, the Equality Bill 2005 proposes that the CEHR has powers to conduct *both* 'inquiries' (clause 17) and 'investigations' (clause 22). The former may not concern alleged unlawful discrimination by any particular person but the latter, which provide procedural protections similar to those applicable under the DRCA for those under investigation, may. Clause 17 appears quite clearly to contemplate named person inquiries as long as they are not concerned with discrimination which would be unlawful. Significantly, the Equality Bill also contemplates wider coercive powers or the CEHR. At present the EOC and CRE can only require attendance and evidence from witnesses when they are conducting a 'belief' investigation, or by order of the Secretary of State (s.50(2) RRA, extracted above (the equivalent provision of the SDA is s.59(2)), and the DRC only when it is conducting a 'named person' investigation or on the written authority of the Secretary of State (s.4(1) DRCA, also extracted above). By contrast, Schedule 2 to the Equality Bill 2005 proposes (paras 10–14) that the CEHR can use coercive powers in any inquiry or investigation, as well as in any assessment of whether a public authority is complying with its proposed positive obligations (see further Chapter 3). The provision of these new powers was a significant factor which caused the CRE to end its opposition to the establishment of the Commission.

The ECNI's powers in relation to FIs vary according to the ground of discrimination, the same rules applying to it in relation to race, sex and disability investigations as apply to the EOC, the CRE and the DRC respectively while different and more liberal rules apply in relation to FETO. Not only does FETO impose monitoring obligations on employers, which obligations are policed by the ECNI (see further above); but Article 11 permits the Commission to conduct investigations into, inter alia:

(a) 'the composition, by reference to religious beliefs' of
  (i) employees of or applicants to any particular employer or class of employers; [and]
  (ii) 'persons who have applied for or obtained the services of any employment agency' . . . and
(b) into practices—
  (i) affecting the recruitment, admission to membership or access to benefits of persons belonging to any class referred to in sub-paragraph (a) or the terms of employment or membership or provision of benefits applicable to such persons;
  (ii) involving any detriment to such persons . . . including practices discontinued before the time of the investigation so far as relevant for explaining the composition of the class of persons in question at that time.'

There is no requirement for any suspicion of unlawful action prior to the launch of an investigation by the Commission which can, however, conduct Article 11 investigations only in relation to employment. The differences between the ECNI's powers of investigation under FETO and under the Northern Irish equivalents of the SDA and RRA are commented upon in the following extract.

Equality Commission for Northern Ireland, 'Legislative Reform: Commission Powers/ Judicial Process' (August 2003)

In relation to investigative powers, the Commission, in common with other agencies, has encountered great difficulties in its use of its powers of formal investigation in gender and race cases . . . Due in part to early interpretation of these powers in relation to the [RRA], a highly adversarial model of formal investigation has developed. On the other hand, the FETO contains a different model which does include a range of powers to obtain necessary evidence and documentation etc but is based on a less adversarial, more cooperative approach . . . these significant powers were devised with issues of labour market composition largely (but not exclusively) in mind and have, in fact, rarely been used (but still frequently threatened) for over a decade. Nonetheless, this consideration of the potential extent of the Commission's powers provides an opportunity to examine how powers of formal investigation may be reformed and adapted in relation to both grounds and scope and the extent to which the FETO model could, if suitably reformed, either replace or coexist with a reformed formal investigation model. The Commission's powers of general investigation should also be considered in this exercise.

The Commission is particularly attracted to the potential value of 'Article 11' investigations across the full range and scope of SEA grounds. Article 11 applies both to issues primarily of labour market composition but also of discriminatory practices. There is a low threshold entitling the Commission to initiate an investigation 'for the purpose of assisting it in considering what, if any, action for promoting equality of opportunity ought to be taken by [various categories of] persons.' The investigative power is supported by undertakings under Article 12, voluntary undertakings under Article 13 and directions under Article 14. The focus throughout is on 'equality of opportunity' rather than 'fair participation,' upon which Article 5 reviews are largely based. Nonetheless, in the absence of a 'belief' that an unlawful act of discrimination has been committed, as in 'named person' formal investigations, both the letter and spirit of Article 11 investigations are less confrontational than in the former and yet a significant array of enforcement powers are available. At present, Article 11 investigations cannot involve findings of discriminatory practices and hence the Commission would require a reconsideration of enforcement powers under the FETO model and consideration of its applicability to GFS cases . . .

The Commission has come to the view that the emphasis in a future investigative model should be with a reformed Article 11-type investigative procedure. Such a procedure would need to be on the basis of a broad agenda of discriminatory practices and the enforcement powers of an Article 11 investigation should be carefully examined, particularly with aspects of the DDA model in mind. Given that formal investigation powers apply across the scope of the relevant statutes, the Commission is of the view that a suitably reformed Article 11-type investigative power should apply across the full scope of the SEA.

Preventing Further Discrimination

The EOC and CRE may, during the course of and after the completion of FIs, issue recommendations including recommendations to the Secretary of State for changes to the law. They are obliged, at the close of FIs, to issue reports on them[119] and, if in the course

---

[119] Ss.60 SDA, 51 RRA.

of an FI the relevant commission is satisfied that the person under investigation is committing or has committed an unlawful act, may issue a non-discrimination notice.[120]

Where discriminators are recalcitrant it may be necessary for NDNs to be issued. Such notices have been issued, *inter alia*, by the CRE after its investigation into Hackney's housing practices (see Chapter 4) and, more recently, in respect of the same borough's employment practices (some of the recent awards against the council having been mentioned above). The issue of the later NDN followed the failure of the council to comply with an action programme agreed with the CRE under threat of an NDN.

The contents of NDNs are prescribed by legislation, s.58 RRA (s.67 SDA) providing that the NDN may require its recipient:

(2) (a) not to commit any such acts; and
    (b) where compliance with paragraph (a) involves changes in any of his practices or other arrangements—
        (i) to inform the Commission that he has effected those changes and what those changes are; and
        (ii) to take such steps as may be reasonably required by the notice for the purpose of affording that information to other persons concerned.
(3) A non-discrimination notice may also require the person on whom it is served to furnish the Commission with such other information as may be reasonably required by the notice in order to verify that the notice has been complied with.[121]

Sections 58(5) RRA and 67(5) SDA provides that the relevant Commission will not issue an NDN until it has given the proposed recipient notice of its intention and the grounds for it, has given them an opportunity to make representations and has taken such representations into account. Ss.59 RRA and 68 SDA provide a right of appeal against an NDN, the appeal going to an employment tribunal in employment-related cases, to the county or (in Scotland) sheriff court in other cases. Sections 59(2) RRA and 68(2) SDA provide that:

(2) Where the tribunal or court considers a requirement in respect of which an appeal is brought . . . to be unreasonable because it is based on an incorrect finding of fact or for any other reason, the tribunal or court shall quash the requirement.

This provision was interpreted by the Court of Appeal in *R v CRE ex parte Amari Plastics* [1982] QB 1194, to require a reopening of all the findings of fact, rather than simply the NDN requirements themselves. This approach, defended by Browne-Wilkinson J on the basis that 'a requirement 'to stop beating your wife' is unreasonable if you have never beaten your wife',[122] had the effect that:

Sacks and Maxwell, 337–8, footnotes omitted

. . . despite two hearings having already taken place, another hearing is available, this time before the court to examine all the findings of fact. This is so despite the fact that 'the

---

[120] Unlawful discrimination in this context includes pressure, instructions to discriminate, discriminatory advertisements and discriminatory practices. It appears, from Lord Diplock's speeches in *Hillingdon* and *Prestige*, that such notices may only be issued after named investigations.

[121] (4) . . . the time at which any information is to be furnished in compliance with the notice shall not be later than five years after the notice has become final.

[122] [1982] 1 QB 265, 272 (EAT). This approach suggests a degree of judicial arrogance as to the fact-finding capabilities of administrative enforcement bodies such as, in this case, the CRE.

Commission have carried out a searching inquisitorial inquiry to satisfy themselves of the truth of the facts on which the notice is based, and have given at least two and probably three opportunities to the person to put his case, whether orally or in writing, either by himself, through solicitors, counsel or any other person of his choice,' only to find that the 'Act requires that their findings of fact are liable to be re-opened and reversed on appeal.' None of the judges felt that section 59(2) could be read any other way, and advised the Commission to seek legislative reform to extricate themselves from the 'spider's web spun by Parliament from which there is little hope of their escaping.' The effect of the case is to permit the whole factual basis of the non-discrimination notice to be re-opened on appeal . . . the cost of these proceedings will disable the CRE from doing other and more valuable work and respondents are aware of them.

The other significant difficulty with NDNs relates to their scope.

CRE, *Time for a Change?* (1983)

The most serious gap in the non-discrimination notice provisions is the absence of any power to postulate what changes, in the Commission's view, are necessary to avoid a repetition of the discriminatory act. On this the CRE has power to make recommendations only (see s.51, p30). This has proved, in practice, a very serious constraint and *we recommend that the CRE is given power to state in a non-discrimination notice what changes in the respondents practice are the minimum necessary.* We feel confirmed in this proposal by the very extensive powers of appeal the respondent has against a s.58 notice, which would ensure the avoidance of any unnecessary hardship, which the Notice might inadvertently cause.

Doubts have been raised whether a notice resultant in an unlawful discriminatory act or practice at one particular site of an organisation can give rise to a notice affecting the whole of the organisation or merely its operation at the location investigated. We have always taken the view that as the s.58 notice affects a person (whether human or corporate) it affects the whole of his activity in the particular field covered. However, because it has seriously been questioned, clarification is needed and *we recommend an added provision to make it clear that a non-discrimination notice resultant in an unlawful act or practice makes unlawful the act or practice concerned wherever the respondent may perform it.*

By contrast, the DRCA, which establishes the DRC and sets out its powers, including the powers of FI, not only requires (s.4) that an NDN gives details of the unlawful act which the DRC has found the recipient to be committing or have committed, and ((1)(b)) 'requires him not to commit any further unlawful acts of the same kind (and, if the finding is that he is committing an unlawful act, to cease doing so).' In addition, s.4 DRCA provides that:

(2) The notice may include recommendations to the person concerned as to action which the Commission considers he could reasonably be expected to take with a view to complying with the requirement mentioned in subsection (1)(b).
(3) The notice may require the person concerned—
    (a) to propose an adequate action plan (subject to and in accordance with Part III of Schedule 3) with a view to securing compliance with the requirement mentioned in subsection (1)(b); and
    (b) once an action plan proposed by him has become final, to take any action which—
        (i) is specified in the plan; and
        (ii) he has not already taken, at the time or times specified in the plan.

(4) For the purposes of subsection (3)—
- (a) an action plan is a document drawn up by the person concerned specifying action (including action he has already taken) intended to change anything in his practices, policies, procedures or other arrangements which—
  - (i) caused or contributed to the commission of the unlawful act concerned; or
  - (ii) is liable to cause or contribute to a failure to comply with the requirement mentioned in subsection (1)(b); and
- (b) an action plan is adequate if the action specified in it would be sufficient to ensure, within a reasonable time, that he is not prevented from complying with that requirement by anything in his practices, policies, procedures or other arrangements; and the action specified in an action plan may include ceasing an activity or taking continuing action over a period.

Schedule 3, part 3 DRCA provides that the action plan must be served on the DRC within the time specified in the NDN.[123] If the DRC is not satisfied with the action plan it may request its revision, and make 'recommendations as to action which the Commission considers might be included in an adequate action plan' (para 16(2)). If the second plan is inadequate, or if it is not served, the DRC may seek a court order declaring that the plan is inadequate, requiring a revised plan and (para 17(3)(c)) 'containing such directions (if any) as the court considers appropriate as to the action which should be specified in the adequate action plan required by the order.' Clauses 23 and 24 of the Equality Bill 2005 propose powers relating to 'unlawful act notices' and 'action plans' which are broadly similar to those currently enjoyed by the DRC.

The DRC has a further power sought by the CRE since 1983, ie, the power to enter into 'voluntary undertakings,' binding agreements with suspected discriminators whereby, in exchange for the Commission's undertaking either not to begin[124] or to continue an FI, or (at the completion of an FI) not to issue a non-discrimination notice, the suspected discriminator undertakes (s.5(2)(b) DRCA):

(i) not to commit any further unlawful acts of the same kind (and, where appropriate, to cease committing the act in question); and

(ii) to take such action (which may include ceasing an activity or taking continuing action over any period) as may be specified in the agreement.

Subsection 5(5) goes on to provide that:

The action specified in an undertaking under subsection (2)(b)(ii) must be action intended to change anything in the practices, policies, procedures or other arrangements of the person concerned which—
- (a) caused or contributed to the commission of the unlawful act in question; or
- (b) is liable to cause or contribute to a failure to comply with his undertaking under subsection (2)(b)(i).

---

[123] Failure to do so may result in the issue of an injunction ordering compliance.

[124] This provision was, presumably, inserted after Roger Berry's complaint (22 April 1999 col 1087–8) that agreements couldn't be made early enough 'According to the CRE, the key time for a written agreement is following the preliminary written inquiry before the start of the formal investigation. It is then that organisations suspected of being discriminatory start getting a little nervous and want to avoid bad publicity.' Berry also called (as the CRE and EOC had) for NDNs to 'specify the nature of the changes required and the time frame for their implementation' and complained over the DRC's lack of power to take action over discriminatory practices, persistent discrimination and instructions to discriminate. The power to enter voluntary legally binding written undertakings.

'Agreements in lieu of enforcement action' may be varied or revoked by agreement of the parties. Enforcement by the DRC is by way of application to the county or sheriff court. In addition, it is common for the EOC and CRE to enter into voluntary agreements with the subjects of FIs either during the course of the investigation, or after the report has been issued.[125] Such plans typically include binding commitments to the achievement of specified outcomes by particular dates. So, for example, the CPS investigation mentioned above resulted in the adoption of a programme of action by the CPS as a result of which the FI was suspended in September 2001. Review of progress followed in March and September 2002 and the progress made by the CPS resulted in the closure of the investigation. Notwithstanding the termination of the investigation, however, the CRE entered into a formal partnership with the CPS designed to ensure further progress on recruitment and selection, and to 'achieve deeper, more long-lasting change in the culture of the organisation.' A partnership agreement was also reached with the MOD/ Household Cavalry after a FI by the CRE disclosed serious cause for concern. The agreement, which came to an end in 2003, was directed at improving the recruitment and retention of ethnic minority staff and the creation of 'an environment free from discrimination and racial abuse.' And the EOC's recent FI into sexual harassment in the Post Office was suspended on the conclusion of an agreement with the Royal Mail about the adoption of steps to eradicate this form of discrimination.

The Equality Bill 2005 proposes the provision of powers to the CEHR to enter into agreements with persons it suspects of unlawful discrimination. The powers are similar to those currently enjoyed by the DRC. The ECNI has powers similar to those of the DRC (and of the ECNI itself in relation to disability discrimination) in relation to FETO, Article 13 providing that the Commission may accept written undertakings 'in such terms as appear satisfactory to the Commission for the purpose of ensuring that the person giving it takes such action for promoting equality of opportunity as is, in all the circumstances, reasonable and appropriate.' The undertakings may be given in response to notice by the Commission that the latter 'in exercising its functions under this Order . . . has formed the opinion that he ought to take action for promoting equality of opportunity' or 'from any [FETO-related tribunal] decision . . . or from any evidence given in such proceedings is of the opinion that such action ought to be taken.' Enforcement is by way of notice served by the Commission[126] or by order of the FET on application from the Commission.

The FEC's review of the FEAs suggested that the power to enter into Voluntary Undertakings was unduly narrow:

[t]he Commission would prefer to work with employers rather than to enter into an investigatory procedure . . . the Commission has a statutory function to fulfil and it cannot embark on courses of action which would not ultimately be enforceable. Voluntary Undertakings provide the opportunity for meeting the objectives of a co-operative approach combined with enforcement if necessary. The current requirement that 'In exercising its functions under this Order the Commission has formed the opinion that he ought to take action for promoting equality of opportunity' means that Voluntary Undertakings may only be obtained in those circumstances where the Commission has specific power 'to form an opinion' . . . Although a bona fide employer may wish to co-operate with the Commission and be able to refer to a public statement of commitment to working with the Commission he/she may not be in a position to conclude a voluntary undertaking.[127]

---

[125] Details of recent such agreements can be found in the CRE's *Annual Reports* (most recently, the 2002 report).

[126] Appealable to the FET.

[127] FEC *Review*, above n 14, paras 3.19 and 3.20.

FETO did not address the point raised by the FEC. Nor did the DRCA or the Equality Bill, both of which limit statutory agreements to situations in which the Commission has reason to believe that discrimination has occurred.

Returning to the formally-issued NDNs, the various commissions are given the power to follow up the issue of such notices. Sections 60 and 69 of the SDA and RRA respectively permit such investigations absent any belief in unlawful discrimination within five years of the issue of a NDN. Section 59(2) DRCA is in similar terms.

The Commissions as Litigants

The various commissions are given exclusive power to litigate in respect of a number of provisions of the RRA and SDA. These consist of 'discriminatory practices,' such a practice being defined as 'the application of a requirement or condition which results in . . . [unlawful indirect sex or race discrimination] . . . *or which would be likely to result in such an act of discrimination*' if those to whom it applied were not all of one sex or if they included people of any particular racial group (my emphasis).[128]

The discriminatory practices provision (SDA s.37, RRA s.28) was aimed at 'unintended discrimination [which is] . . . so deeply entrenched or so overwhelmingly effective that it is practically invisible and, therefore, may not give rise to any single individual complaint.'[129] Its enforcement is by way of an NDN which, as noted above, can be issued only after an FI with all the difficulties attendant thereon.[130]

Neither the DDA nor FETO contains any provision relating to discriminatory practices. The DRCA 1999 does contain, as do the SDA, RRA and FETO, a provision prohibiting 'persistent discrimination' (SDA ss.71 and 72, RRA ss.62 and 63). These, again, are enforceable only by the commissions which are permitted to apply to the county (in Scotland, the sheriff) court for an injunction restraining a respondent from engaging in discriminatory practices or otherwise contravening the relevant Act where 'it appears to the commission that unless restrained [the respondent] is likely to engage in discriminatory practices or otherwise contravene the relevant Act.'[131] Such an application can only be made within five years of a tribunal finding of unlawful discrimination against the respondent, or the service by the same commission of an NDN upon that respondent. Where the action for persistent discrimination follows the issue of an NDN, the commission must first apply to the tribunal for a declaration that the respondent was guilty of unlawful discrimination. In the period 1977–92, the EOC's *Annual Reports* record only two cases relating to persistent discrimination by employers. One such case was *CRE v Precision Manufacturing Services Ltd* COIT 4106/91, discussed in Chapter 2.

The powers to enforce the provisions relating to persistent discrimination and, where available, discriminatory practices, vest solely in the relevant commissions. In addition, the EOC, CRE and DDA have sole power (ss.72, 63 and 17B SDA, RRA and DDA respectively), to take action against discriminatory advertisements, instructions to discriminate and pressure to discriminate. Such action may consist of a complaint to a tribunal which may decide that the alleged contravention of the relevant Act occurred. Alternatively, and

---

[128] SDA, ss. 38, 39, 40, 42 & 37(10) and RRA, ss. 29, 30, 31, 33 & 28 respectively.

[129] John Fraser, Under-Secretary of State for Employment 906 HC Debs (4 March 1976) col. 1430. See cols. 1431–3 and 1434–5 for opposition.

[130] Discriminatory practices can subsequently be challenged as 'persistent discrimination' in the manner discussed below.

[131] S.71 SDA, s.62 RRA, s.6 DRCA, art 41 FETO.

where 'it appears to the Commission . . . that unless restrained [a person] is likely' to continue to breach the relevant section, the Commission may apply for an injunction from a designated county court.[132]

Again, the utilisation of these powers has not been significant. Between 1977 and 1992 the EOC's took action in two cases each against employers who persistently instructed job centres to discriminate and who placed discriminatory advertisements, and a handful of cases in which employers capitulated to EOC demands in the face of action relating to instructions to discriminate.[133] More recently, a smattering of cases relating to discriminatory advertisements and inducement and/or pressure to discriminate have passed through the tribunals. The EOC's inaction in relation to discriminatory advertisements was criticised in 1986:

V Sacks, 'The Equal Opportunities Commission—Ten Years On' (1986) 49 *Modern Law Review* **560, 566–7, footnotes omitted**

. . . it appears that in 1984 there were more inquiries relating to advertising than any other topic (2186 compared to 1625 on employment), but all the Annual report has to say on this is that there:

> has been an increase in the number of complaints to the Commission about apparently unlawful advertisements. The vast majority of such complaints are resolved without recourse to the tribunals or courts; and there has been no deterioration in the generally high level of compliance by publishers with the requirements of section 38 of the Act. The Commission's Advertising Unit has continued to devote any time possible, after dealing with complaints and enquiries, to developing a strategy of prevention by speaking to seminars of publishers and advertisers.

No details of the kind of discriminatory advertising, the places where it occurs, nor any other information is contained in these paragraphs. The only clue to trouble is contained in two sentences:

> Discussions took place with the Employment Services Division of the Manpower Services Commission following a Survey of Job Centres' advertising practice. This had indicated that the indirect discrimination provisions of the [SDA] needed clarification in respect of recruitment advertising . . .

At the end of that paragraph on what is clearly a serious source of discrimination all that is known is that discriminatory advertisements are appearing at Job Centres and that the EOC has 'surveyed' these practices and 'discussed' them with the MSC Considering that this is an area in which only the EOC can litigate (individuals must refer complaints to them) the public is entitled to know in more detail about discriminatory advertising and the results which the Commission has achieved 'without recourse to the tribunals or courts.' The conclusion is that despite 10 years' experience of the Act, there is a growing tide of discriminatory advertisements about which something is being done *informally*. Yet the EOC has only once litigated in respect of an advertisement. Further use of law enforcement powers, perhaps by a formal investigation into job centres, suggests itself most forcibly.

What has been described here in regard to advertising is true of other activities of the Commission. The Commission is possibly doing itself a grave injustice by the use of anodyne phraseology and lack of hard information. It points out, and this is a comment

[132] Ss.72 and 63 SDA and RRA respectively and s.6(2) DRCA.
[133] *Annual Report* 1988, 1986 and 1988 respectively. In 1985, action relating to instructions to discriminate was taken against Barclays, in 1988 against Clarks and in 1986 a further three were threatened and agreement reached.

made repeatedly in regard to other spheres of its work, that it can do more by keeping the identity of offenders anonymous and by persuasion and education. But the lack of real information to the reader seems pointless and unjustifiable. The Annual Report is a clear indication that the Commission has failed to evaluate its work.

As with FIs, the CRE appear to have been rather more active—the *Annual Reports* 1990–94, for example, each refer to a number of proceedings started, as well as to agreements reached, in respect of discriminatory advertisements and instructions or pressure to discriminate.[134] The 2001 *Annual Report* states that 83 written complaints were received in that year about advertisements, and a further 14 complaints about 'no travellers' signs. In addition, it received 22 complaints about pressure or instructions to discriminate. The following year the Commission reported 100 complaints about advertisements, 14 complaints about 'no travellers' and 3 about 'no asylum seeker' notices, and 14 complaints about pressure or instructions to discriminate. Neither report mentions any proceedings taken by the CRE in response to these complaints and the EOC's latest annual report is silent as to complaints received, much less action taken, on these issues.

The ECNI is empowered to take action against advertisements which discriminate on grounds of sex, race, disability, religious belief or political opinion.

In addition to those powers specifically vested in the various commissions by the relevant legislation, the commissions may make judicial review applications according to where the ordinary rules on standing permit. *EOC v Birmingham City Council* [1989] AC 1155, which was discussed in Chapter 2, was one such case. There the EOC challenged the council's discriminatory provision of grammar school places. In 1990, the EOC's application for judicial review of the Queen's Regulations for the Army and the Royal Air Force, which provided for the dismissal of women who became pregnant, resulted in the abandonment of the policy. As Lord Lester has pointed out, the 'good grace' with which the Defence Secretary surrendered to the judicial review application was not matched by the Ministry of Defence's response to the flood of compensation claims which followed: 'no doubt because of the very large sums at stake.'[135]

In the *Birmingham* case the EOC's standing was not challenged. In *EOC v Secretary of State for Employment*, on the other hand, the Government (as respondent) argued that the EOC had no right to challenge its imposition of differential qualifying periods (two and five years respectively) for employment protection on full-time and part-time workers. The House of Lords rejected the Government's argument and issued a declaration that the discriminatory periods were contrary to Article 141.

EOC v Secretary of State for Employment [1995] 1 AC 1

Lord Keith (Lord Jauncey dissenting on this issue):

RSC Ord 53, r 3(7) provides that the court shall not grant leave to apply for judicial review 'unless it considers that the applicant has a sufficient interest in the matter to which the application relates' . . . Has the EOC a sufficient interest in that matter? Under s.53(1) of the [SDA] the duties of the EOC include: '(a) to work towards the elimination of discrimination; (b) to promote equality of opportunity between men

---

[134] Ironically, the CRE became the first and only body required to submit its advertisements, pre-publication, to the Advertising Standards Authority after allegations of racism were made in connection with a CRE campaign designed to raise awareness of racism.

[135] A Lester, 'Discrimination: What Can Lawyers Learn From History?' [1994] *Public Law* 224, 233.

and women generally . . .' If the admittedly discriminatory [qualifying periods] . . . are not objectively justified, then steps taken by the EOC towards securing that these provisions are changed may very reasonably be regarded as taken in the course of working towards the elimination of discrimination. The present proceedings are clearly such a step. In a number of cases the EOC has been the initiating party to proceedings designed to secure the elimination of discrimination. The prime example is *EOC v Birmingham* . . . in which it was not suggested at any stage that the EOC lacked *locus standi*.[136] In my opinion it would be a very retrograde step now to hold that the EOC has no *locus standi* to agitate in judicial review proceedings questions related to sex discrimination which are of public importance and affect a large section of the population. The determination of this issue turns essentially upon a consideration of the statutory duties and public law role of the EOC as regards which no helpful guidance is to be gathered from decided cases. I would hold that the EOC has sufficient interest to bring these proceedings and hence the necessary *locus standi*.[137]

The potential impact of proceedings such as those in the *EOC* case is difficult to overestimate. Whereas an individual challenge to the qualifying periods would have to be brought by a claimant against her employer under the relevant legislation and would result, if successful, only in the non-application of the period to her alone, action by the EOC resulted in the removal at the national level of the discriminatory provisions.

One question which has recently become of increased significance (particularly with the implementation of the HRA) has concerned the power of the various equality commissions to intervene in litigation between other parties. In the *Northern Ireland Human Rights Commission* case Northern Ireland's Court of Appeal ruled that the Commission had no power to intervene in litigation commenced by individuals. The case concerned an inquest into the deaths of victims of the Omagh bomb in 1998. The Commission wished to make a formal submission on human rights issues but was refused by the coroner on the basis that it had no statutory power so to do. The Commission's application for judicial review failed as did its appeal to Northern Ireland's Court of Appeal but the House of Lords (*In re Northern Ireland Human Rights Commission* [2002] UKHL 25, *Times Law Reports* 25 June 2002) allowed its further appeal (Lord Hobhouse dissenting). According to the majority of their Lordships, although the Commission's powers did not explicitly include any power to intervene, such a power was 'reasonably incidental' to express duties such as, in particular, duties to 'keep under review the adequacy and effectiveness of law and practice relating to the protection of human rights' and to 'promote [understanding] and [awareness of the importance] of human rights in Northern Ireland'). The similarities between that Commission's powers and those of the British and Northern Irish equality commissions are such that the case has clear implications for them and the British commissions have become noticeably more willing to intervene in litigation in recent years (all three, for example, intervening in *Essa v Laing*, considered above).

---

[136] His Lordship also relied on *R v Secretary of State for Defence, ex p Equal Opportunities Commission* (20th December 1991, unreported) in which it was common ground that the EOC had *locus standi*. Another instance is *R v Secretary of State for Social Security, ex p Equal Opportunities Commission* Case C–9/91 [1992] ECR I–04297, which went to the European Court.

[137] Lord Jauncey dissented on the basis that: 'the fact that the commission may properly initiate judicial review proceedings in pursuance of their duties against local authorities or other ministers is not, in my view, conclusive of its ability so to do in relation to the Secretary of State. . . .

If Parliament had intended that the commission should be empowered to challenge decisions of the Secretary of State and impose its will upon him it is quite remarkable that Pt VI of the Act which sets out in some detail the powers and duties of the commission, both at large and in relation to the Secretary of State, should have remained totally silent upon this particular matter'.

Contract Compliance

The Use of Contract Compliance

Thus far in this chapter we have considered the ways in which discrimination and equality provisions are enforced in the UK. In this final section I want to concentrate instead on one very important mechanism which is largely not used in the UK, and to explore its potential as a mechanism for challenging discrimination.

One of the most significant methods by which anti-discrimination legislation and guidelines are enforced in the United States consists of contract compliance, ie, the practice of conditioning access to government contracts, grants, etc, on compliance with particular criteria. In the United States, for example, an Executive Order was issued by President Roosevelt in 1914 to prohibit discrimination by defence contractors.[138] The US federal government has used contract compliance since 1968 in order to require government contractors, more generally, to adopt 'affirmative action' (first race-based, then also sex-based) in an attempt to assimilate the racial and sexual balance of workforces to those of locally available workforces.[139]

Executive Order 11246 binds federal contractors and subcontractors whose US-based government contracts are worth in excess of $10,000. Such contractors are required to monitor and report on the racial and sexual composition of their workforces. Those whose federal contracts are worth in excess of $50,000 and who employ at least 50 staff must, in addition, produce written affirmative action plans. It is estimated that the contract compliance programme covers over 20 per cent of the civilian workforce.[140]

In Canada, federally regulated employers and contractors bidding for goods and services contracts with the federal government are required to provide 'employment equity,' defined as 'an action-oriented approach that identifies under-representation or concentration of, and employment barriers to, certain groups of people, and provides a number of practical and creative remedies.[141] The Employment Equity Act 1995 and accompanying regulations require employers, in consultation with their workforces to:

- conduct a workforce survey to ascertain the proportion and position of women, aboriginal, disabled and 'visible minority' workers;
- undertake a 'workforce analysis' to determine the degree of under-representation, if any, of the groups within the workforce;
- undertake an 'employment systems review' to determine what, if any, barriers 'prohibit the full participation of designated group members within the employer's workforce';

---

[138] In the same year the Philadelphia Plan, adopted by President Nixon, required all those bidding for federal contracts to establish numerical goals for integration. As Attorney General, the later Chief Justice Rehnquist assured the President that the plan was in conformity with the Civil Rights Act—see R McKeever, 'Raw Judicial Power? The Supreme Court and American Society' (2nd edn, Manchester, Manchester University Press, 1995) *ibid*, 125–6.

[139] Paras 99–100 Fourth Report of the Select Committee on N Ireland, 1998–99, HC 95–I.

[140] Human Resources Development Canada, Introduction to Employment Equity.

[141] The 1946 Resolution was, in addition to being administered by the executive in the allocation and content of government contracts, incorporated into a number of statutes (see further A. McColgan, *Just Wages for Women* (Oxford, OUP, 1997 Ch 9)) although, as in the case of the Resolution itself, the obligations were not directly enforceable by the employees concerned. See also *Simpson v Kodak Ltd* [1948] 2 KB 184.

- develop and implement an 'employment equity plan' which 'must include . . .
  — positive policies and practices to accelerate the integration of designated group members in employers' workforces;
  — elimination of employment barriers pinpointed during the employment systems review;
  — a timetable for implementation;
  — short term numerical goals;
  — and longer term goals';
- monitor the implementation of the plan, reviewing and revising it as necessary.

The Canadian rules apply to contractors with at least 100 employees wishing to bid for contracts worth at least $200, 000. Failure to comply with the rules can result in ineligibility to bid for further contracts. Those concerned with the efficacy of the various anti-discrimination statutes (and, in the case of Northern Ireland, FETO) have long called for contract compliance to be utilised as an enforcement method. The CRE's 1992 reform proposals included the statement (para 9) that:

Without any new legislation, a Government could bring its economic power in Britain to bear on the whole question of equal opportunities. Indeed, by not doing so it may be criticised on the moral ground that that power is inevitably being used in many instances to support firms which are not providing equal opportunities, as well as on the practical ground that it is throwing away a chance to influence change for the better.

We believe the economic power of government, both national and local, should be used in support of equal opportunity.

The CRE's call for the adoption of contract compliance was reiterated by that body and by the EOC, in their 1998 reform proposals and by Justice in its 1997 report, *Improving Equality Law: the Options*. But until very recently, much contract compliance was actually prohibited in the UK. Prior to the implementation of the LGA 1988, a number of local authorities (and, in particular, the GLC and the Inner London Education Authority) had adopted policies of contract compliance.. Christopher McCrudden wrote of that period:

C McCrudden, 'Codes in a Cold Climate' (1988) 51 *Modern Law Review* 409, 429, footnotes omitted

Local authorities have basically the same powers to contract as others, including the power to seek to have firms with which they contract accept conditions on how the contract is to be carried out. In all cases, however, these powers are subject to public law requirements, including the duties to act reasonably, not ultra vires, and in compliance with the fiduciary duty to the ratepayers. The Greater London Council (GLC) in drawing up its contract compliance policy in 1983, sought counsel's opinion on how best to satisfy these public law duties. As a result of that advice, the GLC relied on section 71 of the Race Relations Act, which imposes on councils a duty to seek to eliminate racial discrimination and promote equality of opportunity, as a primary legal support for its contract compliance policy. Though there was no specific legal obligation for other areas of discrimination, it was considered justifiable on moral grounds for public bodies to seek positively to promote the laws against sex discrimination in equivalent ways. Furthermore, it decided that the detail of any compliance sought 'should relate as closely as possible to officially recognised standards . . . using the Codes of Practice of the CRE and the EOC' Indeed, one of the architects of the policy has written that, '[b]ecause of the clear legal advice the GLC received, the operational core of the policy turned on the Codes of Practice.' An equivalent policy was also adopted by the Inner London Education Authority. Most importantly, ethnic monitoring and the submission of statistics became standard elements in contract compliance policy.

Although it was open for those subject to local authority contract compliance policies to challenge them by way of judicial review, the Government eventually acceded to requests from the CBI and the construction and civil engineering employers to introduce legislation restricting local authority powers to impose contract compliance policies on those with whom they contracted.

Section 17 of the Local Government Act 1988 prohibited local and other public authorities from taking into account, in their contracting functions: 'non-commercial matters,' these matters being defined to include 'the terms and conditions of employment by contractors of their workers or the composition of, the arrangements for the promotion, transfer or training of or the other opportunities afforded to, their workforces.' The only exception to this prohibition was provided by s.18 (2) LGA, which permitted only that local authorities 'ask . . . approved questions seeking information or undertakings relating to workforce matters and consider . . . the responses to them' and/or 'include[e] in a draft contract or draft tender for a contract terms or provisions relating to workforce matters and consider . . . the responses to them . . . if, as the case may be, consideration of the information, the giving of the undertaking or the inclusion of the term is reasonably necessary to secure compliance with [RRA s 71].' S.71 RRA imposed upon local authorities an obligation to 'to make appropriate arrangements with a view to securing that their various functions are carried out with due regard to the need (a) to eliminate unlawful racial discrimination; and (b) to promote equality of opportunity and good relations, between persons of different racial groups.' The LGA permitted local authorities to ask six 'approved questions' of prospective contractors concerning, inter alia, their arrangements for complying with the RRA and the existence of any findings of unlawful race discrimination against them in the previous three years. But according to the CRE's second (1992) report on the RRA (41–2):

> . . . we were disappointed by Government action in relation to the local government legislation of 1988. If it had not been for the existence of [s.71 RRA], the probability is that Government would have banned local authorities altogether from considering equal opportunities in their contracting processes. . . . The [SDA] contains no similar provision and Government did ban local authorities from considering equal opportunities between men and women in their contracting processes.
>
> Because of Section 71 the Government felt it had to permit some local government action in the area of race, but restricted it. By use of the Approved Questions under the legislation, Government has stopped local authorities obtaining ethnic monitoring data from those they might wish to contract for the supply of goods and services. Yet, in *West Midlands Passenger Transport Executive v Singh* . . . and in the Commission's *Code of Practice in Employment*, the value of that data in determining whether equal opportunities is being provided is recognised.

Recent amendments to s.71 RRA and the corresponding provisions are considered below. The prohibition on contract compliance was particularly problematic given the widespread contracting-out of services previously provided by the public sector. Compulsory competitive tendering was introduced in 1980 and had a devastating impact on the terms and conditions of former public sector jobs.

L Dickens, 'Gender, race and employment equality in Britain: inadequate strategies and the role of industrial relations actors' (1997) 28 *Industrial Relations Journal* 282, footnotes omitted

There has been a disproportionate adverse effect on women and ethnic minorities (in particular black women) who tend to be over-represented in those sectors and jobs which have been effected. Some predominantly male areas, such as refuse collection have been affected, although the stronger union and bargaining position of male workers helped reduce some of the adverse consequences of CCT for them. The major impact has been on women who have lost jobs, had hours reduced and work intensified, experienced pay reductions and loss of benefits . . . The government policy shift in the public sector towards sub-contracting could have been harnessed for equality through a strategy of contract compliance . . . [which] had been used to some effect by local authorities in the past. Instead a contrary path was taken with contract compliance being curtailed by [the LGA 1988]

. . . Nor was there any equality-proofing of the CCT process. Rather than disseminating good practice out from the public sector (which traditionally provides the model of a 'good employer'), increased commercialism within a deregulated framework has weakened the good practice itself.

Dickens states that 'some protection of existing terms and conditions was provided by the need for the UK to conform to European requirements relating to transfers of undertakings.' But, as she points out, this protection was 'belated,' the Transfer of Undertakings Regulations 1981 only being amended in 1993 clearly to apply to public sector contracting-out. In any event, their imperfect protection applies only to existing workers, rather than to jobs, so they have little long-term impact on terms and conditions in contracted-out sectors. Research in 1995 by Escott and Whitfield for the EOC further demonstrated that women in particular had suffered as a result of CCT.[142]

FETO embraces a form, albeit an extremely limited form, of contract compliance, Article 64 providing that public authorities 'shall not enter into [relevant] contract[s] with' an unqualified person, and 'shall take all such steps as are reasonable to secure that no work is executed or goods or services supplied for the purposes of [a relevant] contract by any unqualified person.'[143] An 'unqualified person' is one declared as such by the Equality Commission (Article 62) on the grounds either of failure to register with the Commission (a prerequisite to the monitoring obligations discussed in Chapter 3) or to submit a monitoring return, or of failure to comply with an order issued by the ECNI.

Article 64(6) FETO provides that '(6) Nothing in this Article affects the validity of any contract.' Writing in 1996, Christine Bell remarked that:

C Bell, 'The Employment Equality Review and Fair Employment in Northern Ireland' (1996) 2 *International Journal of Discrimination and Law* 53, 63, footnotes omitted

Since the legislation was introduced in 1989 the disqualification provisions have only been applied on one occasion and then only for a short period. This occurred after an employer failed to register. However, the employer registered quickly thereafter and the disqualification was lifted. As no non-compliance findings have been made by the FET no

---

[142] *The impact of CCT in Local Government* (Manchester, EOC, 1995).
[143] Such a contract is either (Art.64(2)): 'a contract made by the public authority accepting an offer to execute any work or supply any goods or services where the offer is made . . . (b) in response to an invitation by the public authority to submit offers' or (Art.64(3)) 'a contract falling within a class or description for the time being specified in an order made by the Department, where work is to be executed or goods or services supplied by any unqualified person.'

opportunity has arisen to utilize that route of disqualification. The fact that recourse has only been made to the disqualification provisions on one occasion does not mean that these provisions have had no impact. Contract compliance does much of its work as a deterrent and the threat of disqualification may have been one factor which led so many companies to register and send in monitoring returns.

There are several ways in which this regime could be strengthened. Under the present system the contract compliance requirements operate as a penalty mechanism where grants and contracts are removed after evidence of discriminatory practice. They could operate as an incentive scheme whereby to be eligible for a grant or contract one must demonstrate compliance with equality goals or good practice. Incentive operated schemes as utilized in the U.S. and by some local authorities in England (prior to the [LGA]), have proved a successful tool for increasing the proportion of an under-represented group in the workforce.

Even if the present scheme is not amended SACHR's Employment Equality Review should examine to what extent equality considerations are taken into account by public entities . . . which exercise significant powers to make grants or award contracts. Have pressures towards greater 'value for money' and cost reduction in the public sector led to the marginalization of equality concerns when grants or contracts are awarded? Further, the penalty scheme model could be extended. The possibility of disqualification could be added to enforce the present remedy available in an individual complaint, whereby the FET can order the employer to take action to reduce the effect of discrimination on the complainant, within a specified period. An employer who fails to do this could be disqualified. This would make the deterrent of disqualification for maintenance of discriminatory practices a more visible one than it is under the present provisions.

The Standing Advisory Commission on Human Rights proposed, in 1997, that the then-FEA be amended to require that prospective contractors provide information on their 'policies, procedures and practices in relation to fair employment and equal opportunities,' and that contracts could specify terms which contractors would be obliged to meet. But *Partnership for Equality*, the White Paper which preceded FETO, made clear the Government's general disapproval of the CC mechanism: (paras 5.25–7):

Partnership for Equality 1998 (Northern Ireland Office, 1998)

[C]ontract compliance . . . runs counter to the spirit of market liberalisation in public procurement which has been promoted by the European Union and the UK Government. The Government's policy has been that value for money is central to public sector procurement policy . . . The [fair employment legislation] includes a form of contract compliance [which] . . . stand[s] as a significant modification of general government policy on contract compliance and an acknowledgement that the particular circumstances of fair employment in Northern Ireland might warrant sanctions of a different magnitude from those applying to other types of discrimination . . . the Government does not propose to extend contract compliance to achieve fair employment objectives.

The only significant contract compliance model currently operating in the UK is that discussed immediately below.

P Chaney and R Fevre, 'An Absolute Duty: Equal Opportunities and the National Assembly for Wales' (Institute of Welsh Affairs, 2002)

Contract Compliance

In promoting equality of opportunity, the National Assembly Government is developing the use of contractual terms or 'contract compliance' in relation to its annual budget of £10 billion. These reforms have the potential to impact upon two areas: in respect of the goods and services that the Assembly (including all public sector organisations that come under its remit) procures, and in the employment practices of those that the legislature does business with . . .

the Assembly executive has launched a voluntary code of equality practice supported by a dedicated website. In accordance with EC law, most contracts are still awarded on the basis of open competition, but suppliers who support the new voluntary Code will be assisted with positive action such as guidance on ways to improve their practices, and constructive feedback on unsuccessful tenders. In this way they will be able to improve their competitive advantage and be better placed to win future Assembly Government contracts. In the first months following its introduction seventy new suppliers signed-up to the new Voluntary Code.

In addition, a supplier database is presently being compiled that records the 'level of progress' in promoting equality of opportunity attained by those doing business with the Assembly (and its sponsored public bodies). The use of contract compliance is to be extended to those applying for grants and funding awarded by the National Assembly. As a result, all applicants for social housing maintenance grants are now required to sign a declaration stating both that they are implementing equality of opportunity policies and that these are open to inspection by Assembly officials. The voluntary equality code has also been circulated to ASPBs in order that it will be used in the conduct of their business.

The Assembly Government is considering the use of contract compliance in Welsh local government where consultation is being carried out on a new Best Value Order. This will enable local authorities, when awarding contracts, to take account of contractors' ability to deliver services to different communities and the extent to which they provide equality awareness training to staff.

In relation to its provision of primary healthcare, NHS Wales has set out detailed plans to ensure that independent contractors' employment practices promote equality of opportunity. The Assembly Government's strategic Health Plan aims to ensure that by early 2002 all health organisations will have scrutinised existing and future contracts. They will be held accountable for progress in these areas on an annual basis.

Contract Compliance and EU Law

The Public Procurement Directives (Council Directives 93/37, 93/36, 92/50 and 93/38) regulate the contracting process in relation, respectively, to works, supplies, services and utilities. They apply to contracts which exceed specified financial thresholds and require that the tendering process be transparent and that the selection of candidates in the award of tenders be based on objective criteria.[144] In March 2004 the Council of Ministers adopted new Directives 2004/17/EC and 2004/18/EC dealing with procurement in, respectively, the water, energy, transport and postal services sectors, and public works contracts,

---

[144] Transposed into UK law, respectively, by The Public Works Contracts Regulations 1991 (SI 1991/2678), The Public Supply Contracts Regulations 1995 (SI 1995/2010); The Public Service Contracts Regulations 1993 (SI 1993/3228), and The Utility Supply and Works Contracts Regulations 1992 (SI 1992/3279).

public supply contracts and public service contracts. These new Directives, which come into force in January 2006, will be discussed below insofar as they alter the legality of contract compliance. They will replace the current Directives.

The Directives currently in force permit the tendering authorities to advise prospective contractors as to the national employment regulations and in the view of the FEC appear to permit authorities 'to request tenderers to provide a guarantee that their future compliance with national anti-discrimination requirements had been included in their tender price . . . The fundamental principle applied is that the method adopted by the contracting authorities in satisfying themselves of future conformity must not directly or indirectly discriminate against contractors from other member states.'[145]

It was established, in *Commission v Italy* Case C–360/89 [1992] ECR 3401, that the only criteria upon which tendering authorities could assess the *suitability* of prospective contractors were those set out in the Directives themselves. The suitability criteria imposed by the Public Procurement Directives provide little scope for enforcing anti-discrimination provisions, the only potentially relevant criteria included in the Works Directive, for example, being a legal finding of professional misconduct or a finding of 'grave professional misconduct proved by any means which the contracting authority can justify.' Northern Ireland's Fair Employment Commission took the view, in its *Review of the Fair Employment Act* (1997) that this provision would permit the rejection at the 'suitability' stage of contractors who had been found to have discriminated on grounds of religion and/or p[olitical opinion.[146] There is, in addition, more scope for consideration of non-economic factors in the *award* criteria, that is, the determination of who actually *gets* the contract (rather than merely being eligible to tender). The Directives require that the contract be awarded to the lowest-priced or 'economically most advantageous tender.' In the *Beentjes* case the ECJ considered the lawfulness of *award* criteria concerning the employment of the long-term unemployed. The ECJ took the view that, the Public Procurement Directives not being intended exhaustively to regulate procurement, such factors could be taken into account as long as they did not operate in a discriminatory manner.

The FEC expressed the view in 1997 that EC law permitted the specification of equal opportunity requirements in tender documents produced by contracting authorities, though 'in assessing contracting responses [public authorities should] not discriminate between contractors from different member states.' Finally, the FEC proposed that, consistent with the requirements of the various public procurement directives, contracting authorities could include a range of equality conditions in contracts including:

FEC, *Review of the Fair Employment Act* (1997)

3.97 a) The contractor shall adopt a policy to comply with statutory obligations under the Fair Employment Acts.
   b) The contractor shall take all reasonable steps to ensure that all its staff or agents employed in the performance of the contract will comply with the policy. These steps shall include the issue of written instructions to staff, the appointment of a senior manager with responsibility for equal opportunities, and the provision of information to staff on availability of support from staff and from the Commission.
   c) The contractor shall take all reasonable steps to observe the Fair Employment Code of Practice.

---

[145] FEC *Review*, above n 14, para 3.64.
[146] *Ibid*, para 3.96.

d) In the event of any finding of unlawful religious or political discrimination being made against the contractor during the period of the contract by any court or Fair Employment Tribunal the contractor shall inform the contracting authority and take such steps as the contracting authority directs and seek the advice of the Commission in order to prevent repetition of the unlawful discrimination.

e) The contractor shall monitor the religious composition of applicants and of its workforce under the contact, it shall review the composition of those employed under the contract and the employment practices for the purposes of determining whether there is more which could be done to promote fair participation in employment in the contractors workforce.

f) If the contractor determines that there is more which could be done to promote fair participation in employment in the contractor's workforce then he/she shall take reasonable and appropriate affirmative action which will include setting goals and timetables.

g) In the event that a contractor during the period of the contract is found to have committed a summary offence under the Fair Employment Acts the contractor shall inform the contracting authority and take such steps as the contracting authority directs and seek advice from the Commission to prevent further offences.

h) In the event that a contractor during the period of the contract is served with notices, directions, orders or recommendations or provides a written undertaking under the Fair Employment Acts, the contractor shall inform the contracting authority, take such steps as the contracting authority directs and seek the advice of the Commission i order to comply with its statutory obligations under the Fair Employment Acts.

i) The contractor shall provide such information as contracting authority may reasonably request for the purpose of assessing contractor compliance with the equal opportunities terms of the contract.

3.98 *As the contracting authority has no direct relationship with sub-contractors, the Commission recommends that a clause in the contract should make the contractor responsible for ensuring that sub-contractors comply with the equality conditions in the contract.*

3.99 *The Commission is of the opinion that the contract compliance provisions should operate on contracts above a specified financial threshold and suggests a threshold of £100,000.*[147]

In September 2000 the ECJ handed down judgment in *Commission v France* in which, although it ruled against France on other grounds, the Court accepted criteria for the award of public sector contracts covered by the procurement directives could include a social clause designed to combat unemployment. According to the Court, the reference in the procurement directives to criterion 'such as price, period for completion, running costs, profitability, technical merit'.

Commission of the European Communities v French Republic Case C–225/98 [2003] ECR I–07445

Judgment:

does not preclude all possibility for the contracting authorities to use as a criterion a condition linked to the campaign against unemployment provided that that condition is

---

[147] The FEC *Review,* above n 14, points out, further, that EC law permits the grant of state aid, even in cases where this distorts the competitive position of firms, where inter alia, the aid is to promote the economic development of areas where the standard of living is abnormally low or where there is serious under-employment or the execution of an important project of common European interest. The FEC points out the obvious relevance of these criteria to fair employment in Northern Ireland. They could also be applied to cover sex discrimination and, since the adoption of Article 13 TEC, discrimination on the other listed grounds.

consistent with all the fundamental principles of Community law, in particular the principle of non-discrimination flowing from the provisions of the Treaty on the right of establishment and the freedom to provide services . . .

Furthermore, even if such a criterion is not in itself incompatible with Directive 93/37, it must be applied in conformity with all the procedural rules laid down in that directive, in particular the rules on advertising (see, to that effect, on Directive 71/305, *Beentjes*, paragraph 31). It follows that an award criterion linked to the campaign against unemployment must be expressly mentioned in the contract notice so that contractors may become aware of its existence . . .

In 2001 the European Commission issued an 'Interpretive Communication' which suggested that the permissive approach taken by the ECJ in *Bentjees* and *Commission v France* applied only to 'additional criteria' ie, where there was otherwise a 'tie-break' situation involving two or more tenderers, or where a tender was 'abnormally low.'[148] It is worth noting, however, the Commission's confirmation that contracting authorities may impose contractual clauses relating to the manner in which a contract will be executed as long as the clauses do not discriminate directly or indirectly against non-national tenderers and are otherwise in compliance with EU law:

> In addition, such clauses or conditions must be implemented in compliance with all the procedural rules in the directives, and in particular with the rules on advertising of tenders . . . "Transparency must also be ensured by mentioning such conditions in the contract notice, so they are known to all candidates or tenderers.
>
> Finally, a public procurement contract should, in any event, be executed in compliance with all applicable rules, including those in the social and health fields. Contract conditions are obligations which must be accepted by the successful tenderer and which relate to the performance of the contract. It is therefore sufficient, in principle, for tenderers to undertake, when submitting their bids, to meet such conditions if the contract is awarded to them. A bid from a tenderer who has not accepted such conditions would not comply with the contract documents and could not therefore be accepted. However, the contract conditions need not be met at the time of submitting the tender.
>
> Contracting authorities have a wide range of possibilities for determining the contractual clauses on social considerations. Listed below are some examples of additional specific conditions which a contracting authority might impose on the successful tenderer while complying with the requirements set out above, and which allow social objectives to be taken into account:
>
> - the obligation to recruit unemployed persons, and in particular long-term unemployed persons, or to set up training programmes for the unemployed or for young people during the performance of the contract;
> - the obligation to implement, during the execution of the contract, measures that are designed to promote equality between men and women or ethnic or racial diversity;
> - the obligation to comply with the substance of the provisions of the ILO core conventions during the execution of the contract, in so far as these provisions have not already been implemented in national law;
> - the obligation to recruit, for the execution of the contract, a number of disabled persons over and above what is laid down by the national legislation in the Member State where the contract is executed or in the Member State of the successful tenderer . . .

[148] 15 October 2001 COM(2001)566 final.

The problem with the Commission's approach is that it appear to prevent contracting authorities from assessing the *conduct*, as distinct from the *promises*, of contracting parties. Having said this, it certainly provides wide scope for the imposition of conditions on contractors. The Commission's relatively parsimonious approach to social conditions formed the basis of its initial proposal for the amended public procurement directives (see further below), but was recently rejected by the ECJ in *Concordia Bus Finland Oy Ab, formerly Stagecoach Finland Oy Ab v Helsingin kaupunki and HKL-Bussiliikenne* Case C–513/99 [2003] ECR I–07213. There the Court ruled that, in considering which tender for the provision of urban bus transport services was the most economically advantageous, a public authority could properly 'take into consideration ecological criteria such as the level of nitrogen oxide emissions or the noise level of the buses, provided that they are linked to the subject-matter of the contract, do not confer an unrestricted freedom of choice on the authority, are expressly mentioned in the contract documents or the tender notice, and comply with all the fundamental principles of Community law, in particular the principle of non-discrimination.' Nor did the principle of equal treatment preclude the taking into consideration of these criteria 'solely because the contracting entity's own transport undertaking is one of the few undertakings able to offer a bus fleet satisfying those criteria.' The Commission had argued that the criteria for the award of public contracts which may be taken into consideration when assessing the economically most advantageous tender had to (a) be objective, (b) apply to all the tenders, (c) be strictly linked to the subject-matter of the contract in question, and (d) be of direct economic advantage to the contracting authority. The ECJ disagreed in a decision widely regarded as liberalising the EC position on contract compliance, ruling that the Directive could not be interpteted to restrict award criteria to those of a 'purely economic nature,' although those criteria had to relate, according to the Court, to 'identifying the economically most advantageous tender' and had, therefore to 'be linked to the subject-matter of the contract.' The impact of the decision is commented upon in the extract below. (Note that environmental and social considerations are strongly linked and the points made in relation to the former below are equally applicable to the latter.)

Coalition for Green and Social Procurement, 'Whose money is it anyway?—European Court Decision confirms EU Public Procurement Rules must reflect Public Interest'

Today, 17 September 2002, the European Court of Justice confirmed that people matter when local, regional and national contracting authorities spend taxpayers' money. The Court found that the City of Helsinki was correct to award a call for tender for buses to a company whose buses emitted less air pollutants and noise, and not simply to the tender which provided the lowest cost offer. This decision supports the call of the Coalition for Green and Social Procurement that, when authorities spend taxpayers' money, the economic benefit must reflect the wider public interest and not just that of the contracting authority alone. Moreover, the Court's decision builds upon a long-term trend of interpretative cases, and is in line with many local authorities' initiatives to promote fair and Eco-procurements.

'This decision is a welcome and timely reminder to the European Commission and certain European Governments that contracting authorities are the trustees and not the owners of public money. If economic advantage is seen solely on behalf of the contracting authority, this ignores the wider health and social costs of pollution—costs that often come back to the local authorities,' said Jan Willem Goudriaan, Deputy General Secretary of EPSU and member of the Coalition. 'Any authority has an obligation to protect the public interest, and the court decision states clearly that benefit should be for 'society as a whole.'

The implications of this landmark decision go beyond environmental considerations, and confirm the need for social, employment and ethical considerations to be more firmly reflected in the current revision of the directives on Public Procurement.'

British Labour MEP, Stephen Hughes, who drafted the Opinion of the European Parliament's Employment and Social Affairs Committee on the Proposals [for the revised procurement Directives], praised the European Court's decision;

'This judgement confirms the validity of the position that we held during the first reading of these proposals. I am looking forward to seeing a more positive approach from the European Commission and the Council on the wider inclusion of social, environmental and ethical aspects relating to how public authorities spend money when the proposals come back to the European Parliament later this year.'

Prior to the decision in the *Concordia* case the Commission had put forward proposals for an amended Procurement Directive which would have required contracts to be awarded to the lowest priced tenderer and which would have expressly prohibited criteria relating to the environment, social policy or ethical considerations. This proposal was fiercely contested, the European Parliament's Legal Affairs and Internal Market Committee supporting the freedom of public authorities to take into account public concerns when awarding contracts. Social and environmental issues were ping-ponged between the various parties over a period and the resulting Directives, though not as explicitly permissive as many would have preferred, are certainly clearer as to the acceptability of social (and, to a greater extent, environmental) criteria then their predecessors. The Public Sector Directive in its adopted form includes the following in its preamble:

Council Directive 2004/18/EC

Recital 1
This Directive is based on Court of Justice case-law, in particular case-law on award criteria, which clarifies the possibilities for the contracting authorities to meet the needs of the public concerned, including in the environmental and/or social area, provided that such criteria are linked to the subject-matter of the contract, do not confer an unrestricted freedom of choice on the contracting authority, are expressly mentioned and comply with the fundamental principles mentioned in recital 2 [freedom of establishment, freedom to provide services, equal treatment, non-discrimination, etc].

Recital 6
Nothing in this Directive should prevent the imposition or enforcement of measures necessary to protect public policy, public morality, public security, health, human and animal life or the preservation of plant life, in particular with a view to sustainable development, provided that these measures are in conformity with the Treaty.

Recital 46
Contracts should be awarded on the basis of objective criteria which ensure compliance with the principles of transparency, non-discrimination and equal treatment and which guarantee that tenders are assessed in conditions of effective competition. As a result, it is appropriate to allow the application of two award criteria only: 'the lowest price' and 'the most economically advantageous tender' . . .

Where the contracting authorities choose to award a contract to the most economically advantageous tender, they shall assess the tenders in order to determine which one offers the best value for money. In order to do this, they shall determine the economic and quality criteria which, taken as a whole, must make it possible to determine the most economically advantageous tender for the contracting authority. The determination of these criteria depends on the object of the contract since they must allow the level of performance offered by each tender to be assessed in the light of the object of the contract, as defined in the technical specifications, and the value for money of each tender to be measured.

In order to guarantee equal treatment, the criteria for the award of the contract should enable tenders to be compared and assessed objectively. If these conditions are fulfilled, economic and qualitative criteria for the award of the contract, such as meeting environmental requirements, may enable the contracting authority to meet the needs of the public concerned, as expressed in the specifications of the contract. Under the same conditions, a contracting authority may use criteria aiming to meet social requirements, in response in particular to the needs—defined in the specifications of the contract—of particularly disadvantaged groups of people to which those receiving/using the works, supplies or services which are the object of the contract belong.

Article 19 of the Directive permits Member States to reserve contract award procedures to sheltered workshops and similar and Article 26 permits contracting authorities to:

lay down special conditions relating to the performance of a contract, provided that these are compatible with Community law and are indicated in the contract notice or in the specifications. The conditions governing the performance of a contract may, in particular, concern social and environmental considerations.

Article 45 provides that tenderers may be excluded by reason, inter alia, of having been found guilty of 'grave professional misconduct' which is explicitly defined in the preamble to include breach of the Equal Treatment and Equal Treatment Amendment Directives (though, oddly, not the other equality Directives), and Article 55 provides that contracting authorities can seek information relating, inter alia, to a tenderer's 'compliance with the provisions relating to employment protection and working conditions in force at the place where the work, service or supply is to be performed' in the event of an 'abnormally low tender.' But Article 53, which provides that awards may be made to the 'most economically advantageous' rather than the lowest tender, lists 'various criteria linked to the subject-matter of the public contract in question,' which might be taken into account in assessing the tenders, to include 'quality, price, technical merit, aesthetic and functional characteristics, environmental characteristics, running costs, cost-effectiveness, after-sales service and technical assistance, delivery date and delivery period or period of completion' and is silent as to social issues despite the preamble's explicit acknowledgment that such factors might properly be taken into account.

'Time for European action', (2002) 73 *Thompson's Labour and European Law Review*

[Commenting on a materially similar earlier draft of the directive.] In sum, the Council's proposal is a recipe for future conflict. A commitment to labour standards on public contracts is just about visible, but it is hidden away in options which Member States and contracting authorities can choose. These include (i) observance of labour standards as contract performance conditions, (ii) information on labour standards for tenderers, (iii) exclusion of tenderers for violations of labour standards (grave misconduct), and (iv) labour standards as secondary award criteria. All these are couched in ambiguous language.

It would have been simple to formulate a commitment in unambiguous language to mandatory labour standards. There are a number of provisions in the Council proposal which clearly accept environmental standards . . . Perhaps most frustrating is the explicit inclusion of 'environmental characteristics' among possible contract award criteria . . . while labour standards and social criteria are not mentioned, although both environmental and social requirements are specified in Recital [33].

The Council's proposed directive could easily be adapted to labour standards. Instead, contracting authorities, tenderers and contractors are left in doubt and the European Court will have to tidy up the mess on a case-by-case basis. This may be better than nothing, but it does no credit to the Council.

UNICE ('The Voice of Business in Europe'), by contrast, was trenchant in its criticism of the introduction into the new Public Procurement Directives of express references to social policy. Having characterised social contract performance conditions as 'introducing unrelated political requirements' it continued:

UNICE, 'Public Procurement EU Legislative Package: No Longer Acceptable' 9 October 2002

There is enough evidence that using the award of public contracts as a vehicle for the pursuit of general political objectives is detrimental to competition and transparent procurement procedures. Once again, it becomes clear that [small and medium size enterprises] in particular, who depend on their competitiveness to survive, will be adversely affected. Furthermore, one must bear in mind that muddy elements in public procurement procedures foster manipulation and corruption and are therefore in conflict with the objectives and measures necessary to fight corruption . . .

Notwithstanding all the criticism and uncertainty, it is possible to say with some assurance that EU law permits a degree of contract compliance which is not currently practised in the UK, and which could radically improve compliance with equality standards as well as with employment legislation more generally. The CRE's and EOC's lobbying on contract compliance was mentioned above as was that carried out by SACHR in Northern Ireland and the Government's response thereto which was criticised by the Northern Ireland Affairs Select Committee in 1999. Having cited the passage from the White Paper reproduced above, the report went on to state that:

The Operation of The Fair Employment (Northern Ireland) Act 1989—Ten Years On, HC 95–I, paras 97–105

We . . . received evidence which indicated that, provided adequate advice was given by Government to ensure that the criteria did not discriminate against tenderers in other EU Member States, European Community law was a less significant barrier to the use of public procurement than Ministers indicated in evidence. Our view on this was strengthened by the fact that, in a recent Communication on public procurement, the European Commission 'encourages the Member States to use their procurement powers to pursue' a range of social objectives, including equality, 'providing the limits laid down by Community law are respected.'[149] The Secretary of State, subsequent to her oral evidence, has commented that no practical guidance has yet been given by the Commission as to the circumstances in which compliance with conditions of social character could lawfully be included in a contract. The Secretary of State considered that the ambiguity of the Commission's present guidance raised the possibility of legal challenge by an unsuccessful tenderer, should contract compliance be applied.

---

[149] Commission Communication, Public Procurement in the European Union, COM (98) 143 (March 1998), desposited in Parliament as European Community Document No. 6927/98.

Another objection raised by Ministers was that the use of public procurement for social policy objectives was likely to run counter to the principle of value for money. We take the view that this need not be the case: it can be argued that a definition of best value which excluded the beneficial results of the achievement of the social policy objective at issue would not be supportable, a point which, in evidence, [the Northern Ireland Minister] appeared not to dissent from . . .

We were impressed with the use of contract compliance in the United States.

We recommend that the Government look again at the potential contribution of contract compliance to achieving fair employment objectives, taking account of the full extent to which this may be compatible with EU law and drawing fully on the experience of the United States Federal Government. The Government has acknowledged, in the White Paper, the principle that contract compliance has a part to play in the particular circumstances of fair employment in Northern Ireland. This is, as the Government says, a significant modification of general Government policy on contract compliance. We believe that the present limited provisions can, and should, be developed into a more effective mechanism for helping to deliver fair employment policy objectives . . .

Government and public bodies award public contracts on behalf of the communities that they serve. It is not therefore, in our view, unreasonable that these communities might expect that public contracts should, all other things being equal, go to contractors who further such a basic policy aim as fair employment. We do not consider the award of public contracts as simply an economic activity by the Administration, in which the Administration can consider itself as equivalent to a private sector organisation.

We find it difficult to see how public purchasing activity can in principle be regarded as a separate area of state activity in which equality criteria are ignored that are considered self-evident in other areas of state activity, such as public sector employment. This consideration is strengthened if a company tendering for a contract is able to tender at a lower price for that contract because it does not engage in good employment practices which other tenderers do and is thus able to cut costs. Public bodies might reasonably be expected to take account of, and discount, any unfair competitive advantage acquired as a result. Unfortunately, the existing limited linkage between Government contracts and fair employment in Northern Ireland does not encompass this approach.

A new dimension to the debate about contract compliance has been added by the existence of the equality duty under the Northern Ireland Act 1998. As [one]witness commented: 'It would seem only fair and reasonable that public authorities should be free to examine how contractors are fulfilling their legal obligations under the existing legislation before deciding whether or not they may be breaching their statutory duty. They have to consider these matters in terms of fulfilling their statutory duty.'[150] We recommend that Government Departments and public bodies review the position they have taken with regard to public procurement in the context of the preparation of their equality schemes under section 75 of the Northern Ireland Act 1998.

Compulsory Competitive Tendering and Best Value

Linda Dickens suggested, in the article extracted above, that the election of the (New) Labour Government in May 1997 'heralds the end of CCT.' In the event, CCT has been replaced, as from April 2000, by 'best value' which requires public bodies to engage in a rolling programme of review to ensure the achievement of 'best value' whether in-house or

---

[150] SACHR evidence to the Select Committee on N. Ireland, appended to the fourth report, 1998–1999, n 140 above.

contracted-out, in all their services.[151] Just as was the case with CCT, contracts must exclude 'non-commercial matters.'[152] *Implementing Best Value—A Consultation Document on Draft Guidance* (1999, Department of the Environment, Transport and the Regions) stated that the Government 'recognises that it is important that employees have confidence in the fairness of the competitive process. It intends to amend [s.17 LGA] in such a way as to enable local authorities to take into account appropriate workforce matters in the selection of tenderers and the award of contracts, consistent with its EC obligations and the achievement of value for money.'[153]

Section 19 of the Local Government Act 1999, which established the new 'best value' regime, provides that:

(1) The Secretary of State may by order provide, in relation to best value authorities, for a specified matter to cease to be a non-commercial matter for the purposes of [s.17 LGA 1988] . . .

The Local Government Best Value (Exclusion of Non-commercial Considerations) Order 2001 (SI 2001/909) was passed under the 1999 Act and came into force in March 2001. It provides (reg 3) that:

The matters specified in section 17(5)(a) ['the terms and conditions of employment by contractors of their workers or the composition of, the arrangements for the promotion, transfer or training of or the other opportunities afforded to, their workforces'] and the conduct of contractors or workers in industrial disputes between them as specified in section 17(5)(d) [LGA] . . . shall cease to be non-commercial matters for the purposes of section 17 of that Act—

(a) to the extent that a best value authority considers it necessary or expedient, in order to permit or facilitate compliance with the requirements of Part I of the 1999 Act (Best Value), to exercise the functions regulated by that section in relation to its public supply or works contracts with reference to those matters; or

(b) for the purposes of any functions regulated by that section in relation to a public supply or works contract which involves a transfer of staff to which the provisions of the Transfer of Undertakings (Protection of Employment) Regulations 1981 may apply.

Section 18 LGA, as amended by the RR(A)A, now provides that:

(1) Except to the extent permitted by subsection (2) below, section [71(1) RRA and any duty imposed by an order under section 71(2) of that Act . . . shall not require or authorise a [public authority to which section 17 above applies] to exercise any function regulated by section 17 above by reference to a non-commercial matter.

(2) Subject to subsection (3) below, nothing in section 17 above shall preclude a [public authority to which that section applies] from—

(a) asking approved questions seeking information or undertakings relating to workforce matters and considering the responses to them, or—

(b) including in a draft contract or draft tender for a contract terms or provisions relating to workforce matters and considering the responses to them,

---

[151] Local Government Act 1999.

[152] Para 19 of the White Paper.

[153] See also clarification of the TUPE application, *Staff Transfers in the Public Sector: Statement of Practice: A Consultation Document* July 1999, Cabinet Office.

if, as the case may be, consideration of the information, the giving of the undertaking or the inclusion of the term is reasonably necessary to secure compliance with . . . section [71(1) or any duty imposed by an order under section 71(2)].

(3) Subsection (2) above does not apply to the function of terminating a subsisting contract and, in relation to functions as respects approved lists or proposed contracts, does not authorise questions in other than written form . . .

(5) The Secretary of State may specify—

(a) questions which are to be approved questions for the purposes of this section; and

(b) descriptions of evidence which, in relation to approved questions, are to be approved descriptions of evidence for those purposes;and the powers conferred by this subsection shall be exercised in writing.

UNISON's Guide to the Code of Practice on Workforce Matters in Local Authority Service Contracts in England suggests that councils may 'consider a range of issues when selecting and awarding contracts including the contractor's policy and practice for its own workforce' on basic and bonus pay and pensions, equal pay, unsocial hours payments, pay related benefits, working patterns, health and safety, training, trade union recognition, part-time workers' rights, race, sex, disability and lesbian and gay equality, family friendly policies and job security.

Best Value, coupled with the amendments made to the LGA 1988, provide a climate less hostile to contract compliance than did CCT. But it is not at all clear that the new regime will result in enhanced equal opportunities outcomes. Higgins and Roper argue that the application of Best Value across the range of local authority activities (by contrast with CCT which only ever applied to specific local authority functions), coupled with the requirement that authorities subject 'all of their services to a fundamental [Best Value] review process over five years and in so doing . . . address each of the 'four C's" (challenge, consultation, comparison and competition), is likely to result in more, rather than less, outsourcing than took place under CCT.

P Higgins and I Roper, *Does Best Value Offer a Better Deal for Local Government Workers than Compulsory Competitive Tendering?* **(Middlesex University), references omitted**

Not only has the 'competition' requirement been supplemented with three additional principles previously absent from CCT but, in addition, the actual definition of competition itself has been opened up to traverse beyond that of the rather linear definition contained within competitive tendering. In particular, post-legislative statutory guidance outlined seven options that authorities should consider when conducting the competition element of the BV review process. The first of these requires local authorities to consider whether certain activities ought to be provided by the council and ultimately the taxpayer at all. In arriving at this decision, local authorities have been instructed to consult with a range of interests to identify the relative need for and extent of service provision. Local authorities must then use the competition element to decide exactly who shall provide services.

. . . It is true that there remains scope within BV for local authorities to continue to provide services by direct labour, provided that they first 'restructure their in-house service.' In practice 'restructuring' requires the authority to prove via the regulatory domains of performance management and BV inspection that continued direct services provision is fully justified, ensures value for money and will deliver continuous improvements. It is noticeable that the Labour Party's emphasis has shifted between 1997 and 2001 in this respect. In place of 'what matters is what works' . . . from 1997, the 2001 general election manifesto pledged that 'where the quality is not improving quickly enough [in public services], alternative providers should be brought in. Where private sector providers can support public endeavour, we should use them.' It is in this regard that the Labour Government has taken forward its performance programme. The performance programme includes not only a suite of performance indicators but also an audit regime and a far-reaching BV inspection process. Section 10 of the 1999 Local Government Act provides for the Audit Commission to undertake BV inspections. The purpose of the BV inspection service is to check the validity of each local authority's BV review process and to make two judgements concerning the 'current' and 'likely future' performance of the activities contained within. The latter of the two judgements tends to carry more weight for it is the ability of the authority to 'continuously improve' that is the substance of BV.

Higgins and Roper go on to detail the implications for local authorities of being seen to fail in their Best Value obligations and conclude that:

BV poses a greater threat to workers and unions who wish to remain council employees than was the case under CCT. While CCT created a process that was explicitly geared towards transferring work to the private sector, it was at least, a transparent process. Councils could attempt to—and succeed in—keeping a service in-house. In contrast, the provisions for BV are far more wide-ranging and ambiguous. In particular, the notion of retaining services in-house is less clear cut under BV and its provisions extend far beyond a one-off tendering exercise. Thus even if, as part of the BV review process, local authorities decide to restructure services in-house, post inspection findings could signal failure and enact one of a number of the laid down remedial options . . .

Whilst it is true that *transferred* staff now receive much better employment protection by virtue of the Transfer of Undertakings: Protection of Employment (TUPE) regulations, the situation for new recruits is less clear and the emergence of a 'two-tier workforce' is now envisaged. The absence of any real safeguards for new employees taken on after the service has been contracted out has been at the forefront of union efforts. Research by Unison (2002) amongst 116 branches in England enquiring about 190 local government service contracts awarded to private companies or voluntary organisations during 2000/2001, a period capturing the operation of BV, investigated the differences in pay and conditions between transferred staff and new starters. From this it was found that pay levels for new employees were worse than those for transferred staff; that most companies offered inferior occupational sick pay, maternity leave, special leave and holiday entitlements to new staff; that one in five organisations specified a longer working week for new staff; that there was not a single example of a defined benefit pension scheme being open to new employees; and that generally there were more than two sets of terms and conditions in existence . . .

Meanwhile, even if the exact terms and conditions for both transferred and new staff are maintained, the demands of BV are such that reductions in the numbers of staff employed and the intensification of workplace practices of those retained is likely to continue. The relative success of Labour's pursuit of better employment regulation therefore must be questioned in the context of a policy that signals continued de-unionisation and by implication an increased absence of collective bargaining . . . Despite movements towards new codes of employment practice therefore, the very substantive issues of job security, sick pay, workplace practices and training remain far from resolved and over time shall increasingly become the responsibility of arms-length contractors operating in an environment of 'continuous performance improvements' . . .

Escott and Whitfield found that only a minority of local authorities took gender considerations into account in Best Value. Forty-four per cent took gender into account in consultation, 45 per cent in Best Value reviews, 22 per cent in setting improvement targets and plans and only 12 per cent in contract or partnership arrangements.[154]

K Escott and D Whitfield, *Promoting Equality in the Public* Sector (EOC, 2002) 18–22

The findings show that less than half of authorities look at gender equality issues as part of Best Value reviews, and only a fifth of those surveyed had considered gender equality in the setting of improvement targets. Only 12 per cent took gender issues into consideration in contract and partnership arrangements involving external bodies . . . It is of interest to note that the picture for disability, race and age was similar, but far fewer (32 per cent) local authorities took sexuality into account in Best Value reviews.

The five national Best Value Performance Indicators[155] (BVPI) on equality include only one specifically aimed at addressing gender issues: BVPI 11 (the percentage of senior management posts filled by women). This excludes any focus on the vast majority of women who deliver public services, for example, police support staff, care services, school cleaning and catering—all services subject to Best Value . . .

Increasing pressure is being applied under Best Value for public sector authorities (local government, the police and the fire service) to [outsource service provision]. For example, the Audit Commission's latest management paper, *Competitive Procurement* places councils in four categories according to their enthusiasm and capacity to make use of competition. This ranged from 'high performing' councils, which demonstrated enthusiasm to use competition to drive improvement and innovation with the capacity to do this effectively, to 'poor performing' councils, which had no real enthusiasm for competition and tended to retain services in-house following review. Authorities with the most developed approaches had generally received high star ratings from inspectors for quality of service . . .

An analysis of the Government's initiatives to promote better public policy making reveals that gender has not been effectively mainstreamed; this is also true for other equality issues, although the position on race is changing as a result of the [RR(A)A], and work being carried out across the public sector directly to address the findings of the MacPherson Report . . . Moreover, the modernisation agenda to improve the provision of public services has not taken sufficient account of an equality dimension. The government has recently increased the role of competition in Best Value . . . and launched a national taskforce to promote strategic service-delivery partnerships, in effect large outsourcing contracts. The wider use of competitive tendering with larger contracts than those under CCT is almost certain to produce similar, if not more serious, consequences for the gender and equality agenda. This aspect of the government's modernisation programme conflicts with its equality policy statements. The inclusion of equality policies and public duty responsibilities in contract documents between the public and private sectors is unlikely to prove adequate protection given the historical difficulties of ensuring that equality policies are applied and implemented. Gender mainstreaming is rarely implemented in private and third sector organisations. Further research is required which assesses the most appropriate methods for achieving the desired change in reducing inequalities and social exclusion promoted through the modernisation agenda and how the application of a public sector equality duty would assist in this.

The authors mention the 'Equality Standard for Local Government' which was developed in conjunction with the EOC, CRE and DRC and is included as a 'Best Value Performance

---

[154] Citing the Improvement and Development Agency, 'Best Value Database' 2002, unpublished.
[155] By which authorities' compliance with their Best Value obligations are measured.

Indicator' (by which local authorities' performance is assessed) for 2003/4. The Standard at present covers sex, race and disability but is capable of being extended to cover age, sexual orientation, class and religious beliefs. In that local authorities can assess their progress on five levels (1) commitment to a comprehensive equality policy; (2) asssessment and consultation; (3) setting equality objectives and targets; (4) information systems and monitoring against targets, (5) achieving and reviewing outcomes. The development of a standard which previously applied only to race is welcome, though it should be noted that five years after the introduction of the race standard a 2002 Audit Commission report (*Equality and Diversity: Learning from Audit, Inspection and Research*) found that only two fifths of English authorities had assessed themselves as having reached even the first level of the five stage process, with only one in five English and one in eight Welsh authorities self-assessing as having reached level two.

On 13 March 2003 the Government published a statutory Code of Practice on Workforce Matters in Local Authority Service Contracts. The Code, product of prolonged negotiations between government and the public sector unions, is intended to extend the benefits of TUPE to new staff employed by private sector firms which contract with local authorities. TUPE provides that staff transferred into the private sector in the process of contracting-out ought to have their terms and conditions of employment (though not their pensions) preserved. The application of these provisions was very slow in the public sector, which in part explains the devastating effect of contracting-out on staff terms and conditions. It has been established for a number of years now that TUPE does apply to transferring staff, but concern has grown as to the creation of a 'two-tier' workforce with new staff being employed by private contractors on inferior terms in an effort to cut costs. The Code must be incorporated in all local authority contracts advertised after 13 March 2003. It states that:

> Service providers who intend to cut costs by driving down the terms and conditions for staff, whether for transferees or for new joiners taken on to work beside them, will not provide best value and will not be selected to provide services for the council. However, nothing in this Code should discourage local authorities or service providers from addressing productivity issues by working with their workforces in a positive manner to achieve continuous improvement in the services they deliver.
>
> In its contracting-out of services, the local authority will apply the principles set out in the Cabinet Office Statement of Practice on Staff Transfers in the Public Sector and the annex to it, A Fair Deal for Staff Pensions. The service provider will be required to demonstrate its support for these principles and its willingness to work with the local authority fully to implement them.
>
> The intention of the Statement is that staff will transfer and that TUPE should apply, and that in circumstances where TUPE does not apply in strict legal terms, the principles of TUPE should be followed and the staff involved should be treated no less favourably than had the Regulations applied. The Government has now indicated an intention to legislate to make statutory within local government the provisions in the Cabinet Office Statement.
>
> The annex to the Statement requires the terms of a business transfer specifically to protect the pensions of transferees [which are not protected by TUPE]. Staff must have ongoing access to the Local Government Pension Scheme or be offered an alternative good quality occupational pension scheme, as defined in the annex to the Cabinet Office Statement, under which they can continue to earn pension benefits through their future service. There must also be arrangements for handling the accrued benefits which staff have already earned.
>
> Where the service provider recruits new staff to work on a local authority contract alongside staff transferred from the local authority, it will offer employment on fair and reason-

able terms and conditions which are, overall, no less favourable than those of transferred employees. The service provider will also offer reasonable pension arrangements . . .

The principle underpinning the provisions of paragraph 7 is to consider employees' terms and conditions (other than pensions arrangements . . .) in the round—as a 'package.' This Code does not prevent service providers from offering new recruits a package of non-pension terms and conditions which differs from that of transferred staff, so long as the overall impact of the changes to this package meets the conditions in paragraph 7. The aim is to provide a flexible framework under which the provider can design a package best suited to the delivery of the service, but which will exclude changes which would undermine the integrated nature of the team or the quality of the workforce.

The service provider will consult representatives of a trade union where one is recognised, or other elected representatives of the employees where there is no recognised trade union, on the terms and conditions to be offered to such new recruits. [References to 'trade unions' throughout this code should be read to refer to other elected representatives of the employees where there is no recognised trade union.] The arrangements for consultation will involve a genuine dialogue. The precise nature of the arrangements for consultation is for agreement between the service provider and the recognised trade unions. The intention is that contractors and recognised trade unions should be able to agree on a particular package of terms and conditions, in keeping with the terms of this Code, to be offered to new joiners.

The service provider will be required to offer new recruits taken on to work on the contract beside transferees one of the following pension provision arrangements:
- membership of the local government pension scheme, where the employer has admitted body status within the scheme and makes the requisite contributions;
- membership of a good quality employer pension scheme, either being a contracted out, final-salary based defined benefit scheme, or a defined contribution scheme. For defined contribution schemes the employer must match employee contributions up to 6 per cent, although either could pay more if they wished;
- a stakeholder pension scheme, under which the employer will match employee contributions up to 6%, although either could pay more if they wished.

On a retender of a contract to which this Code applies the new service provider will be required to offer one of these pensions options to any staff who transfer to it and who had prior to the transfer a right under the Code to one of these pension options.

Throughout the length of the contract, the service provider will provide the local authority with information as requested which is necessary to allow the local authority to monitor compliance with the conditions set out in this Code. This information will include the terms and conditions for transferred staff and the terms and conditions for employees recruited to work on the contract after the transfer.

Such requests for information will be restricted to that required for the purpose of monitoring compliance, will be designed to place the minimum burden on the service provider commensurate with this, and will respect commercial confidentiality. The service provider and the local authority will also support a central Government sponsored review and monitoring programme on the impact of the Code, drawn up in consultation with representatives of local government, contractors, trade unions and the Audit Commission and will provide information as requested for this purpose. Such requests will follow the same principles of proportionality and confidentiality.

The local authority will enforce the obligations on the service provider created under this Code. Employees and recognised trade unions should, in the first instance, seek to resolve any complaints they have about how the obligations under this Code are being met, directly with the service provider. Where it appears to the local authority that the service provider is not meeting its obligations, or where an employee of the service provider or a recognised trade union writes to the authority to say that it has been unable to resolve a complaint directly with the service provider, the local authority will first seek an explanation from the service provider. If the service provider's response satisfies the local authority that the Code is being followed, the local authority will inform any complainant of this. If the response does not satisfy the local authority, it will ask the service provider to take immediate action to remedy this. If, following such a request, the service provider still appears to the local authority not to be complying with the Code, the local authority will seek to enforce the terms of the contract, which will incorporate this Code. In addition, where a service provider has not complied with this Code, the local authority will not be bound to consider that provider for future work.

The contract shall include a provision for resolving disputes about the application of this Code in a fast, efficient and cost-effective way as an alternative to litigation, and which is designed to achieve a resolution to which all the parties are committed. The service provider, local authority and recognised trade unions or other staff representatives, shall all have access to this 'alternative dispute resolution' (ADR) process. The Government has asked local authorities, trade unions and contractors to come forward with an ADR mechanism which is consistent with this Code, for inclusion in contracts. In the event that within a specified timescale the parties are unable to agree, the government will publish as an annex to this Code its proposed ADR mechanism.

Local authorities will be required to certify in their Performance Plans that individual contracts comply with best value requirements, including workforce requirements in this Code and the accompanying statutory guidance. The Audit Commission's appointed auditor will through the audit of the Performance Plan:
- provide assurance that local authorities are meeting their statutory duty of certifying their compliance with the Code and that they have put in place adequate arrangements to ensure compliance;
- receive information from third parties about any concerns with the authority's compliance;
- consider the information received and decide how to deal with those concerns;
- where the subject of any concern is of material significance (e.g. large contracts or where a major breach of this Code is alleged) the auditor will decide on a proportionate response to investigate the concerns.

If, as a result of investigations, the auditor has concerns about an authority's compliance with this Code, they may exercise their appropriate statutory powers, which include:
- requiring the authority to respond publicly to a written recommendation;
- recommending that the Secretary of State should give a direction under Section 15 of the Local Government Act 1999.

The Code of Practice applies only in England but a similar Code was applied to Welsh local authorities from April 2003 and a year previously the Scottish Executive had agreed with the Scottish TUC a protocol on Public Private Partnerships which, again, was in similar terms. The Local Government Act 1999, which sets out the Best Value regime for England and Wales, does not apply to Scotland. Instead, s.1 of the Local Government in Scotland Act 2003, which applies 'best value' there, provides that:

(1) It is the duty of a local authority to make arrangements which secure best value.
(2) Best value is continuous improvement in the performance of the authority's functions
(3) In securing best value, the local authority shall maintain an appropriate balance among

  (a) the quality of its performance of its functions
  (b) the cost to the authority of that performance; and
  (c) the cost to persons of any service provided by it for them on a wholly or partly rechargeable basis

(4) In maintaining that balance, the local authority shall have regard to—
  (a) efficiency;
  (b) effectiveness;
  (c) economy; and
  (d) the need to meet the equal opportunity requirements [i.e., the requirements imposed by the EqPA, SDA, RRA and DDA].

It is too early as yet to determine the impact of the new regime on workplace equality. As Higgins and Roper point out, the Code of Practice does not prevent the intensification of work and is unlikely to counteract the pressure towards de-recognition associated with privatisation of service provision. But it appears that some authorities are already taking steps towards using contract compliance as a way of resisting economic pressures towards a 'race to the bottom.' The *Equal Opportunities Review* reported in September 2004 that the GLA is including fair employment clauses into a number of its cleaning and catering contracts in particular. And a consortium of West Midlands authorities have drawn up a 'Common Standard' for assessing the compliance of service providers with the RRA, and are extending this to cover the other discrimination provisions. It may prove to be the case—particularly as a result of the imposition of positive obligations upon public authorities to promote equality on the various grounds—that contract compliance will increasingly be used as a mechanism for enforcing anti-discrimination law (see further Chapter 3).

6

Sex

Introduction

In 2002, women accounted for 45 per cent of those in employment and 70 per cent of women (84 per cent men) of working age were economically active; 54 per cent of British mothers of dependent children were engaged in paid work in 2003,[1] 28 per cent of these (15 per cent of all women) as sole breadwinners. The female employment rate increased from 47 per cent to 69 per cent in 40 years as the male rate fell from 94 per cent to 79 per cent, while even in the last 25 years the model of working husband and full-time housewife declined from 43 per cent of two-adult households with dependent children to 24 per cent.[2]

Women have made enormous strides in the working sphere over the thirty years . The headline 'gender pay gap' has decreased from around 30 per cent to 18 per cent (full-time women workers earning an average 82 per cent of full-time male hourly wages in 2003). And women have increased significantly their share of management, administration and professional jobs. Girls have been out-performing boys at school for a number of years, doing better than boys in all GCSE/CSE subjects and being out-performed by them only marginally at A Level in English Literature and French.[3] In higher education institutions women outnumber men in every subject area except physical, mathematical and computer sciences and engineering and technology and architecture, building and planning, the over-all numbers of women (473,100 full-time and 59,100 part time) outstripping men (419,500 full-time and 39,100 part-time) to a significant extent.[4] Nor is women's numerical strength confined to traditionally female areas of study. Women outnumber men in medicine, veterinary science, law, agriculture and related science, political and economic studies and business and administrative studies as well as in subjects allied to medicine, biological science, social studies, education and other traditionally female areas.

For all of this, women remain significantly disadvantaged. Despite huge increases in the number of women MPs following the 1997 general election, the proportion of women in the House of Commons fell (marginally) following the 2001 elections (from 18.2 per cent to 17.9 per cent) for the first time in 20 years. Women accounted, in 2002, for only 24 per cent of British MEPs, though they comprised 37 per cent of SMPs and 40 per cent of

---

[1] 121 *Equal Opportunities Review*.

[2] 99 *Equal Opportunities Review*. The economically active rate includes the unemployed.

[3] EOC, 'Facts about women and men in Britain', 1999, available on the EOC website at http://www.eoc. org.uk/. The EOC analysed results for 11 popular GSCE and 10 popular A level subjects. per cent per cent. For more detailed analysis see S Dench *et al*, 'Key indicators of women's position in Britain', and S Walby *et al*, 'The impact of women's position in the labour market on pay and implications for UK productivity' (both 2002, DTI and Women & Equality Unit).

[4] *Ibid.*

Members of the Welsh Assembly.[5] The EOC's 'Sex and power: who runs Britain?' discloses that only 17 per cent of those in the House of Lords in 2003 were women, 12 per cent of local authority council leaders and university vice chancellors, 9 per cent of national newspaper editors and 0 per cent of chairs of national arts companies. Less than 9 per cent of the FTSE 100 companies' board members are women[6] and in 2004 the Fawcett Society reported that the criminal justice system excludes women from top jobs.[7] According to the *Equal Opportunities Review*, the 2000 Office for National Statistics Report 'Men and Women in the Workforce' 'demonstrates that [the very significant changes in employment patterns] have yet to have a real impact on female equality at work.'[8]

G James, 'Pregnancy Discrimination at Work: A Review'[9]

Overall, women are far more likely than men to be in part-time employment: 42 per cent of female employees compared with only 9 per cent of males.

Women's employment status . . . varies according to age. Their employment rate increases by age up to the age band of 35 to 49 then falls to retirement age. The difference between the employment rate of men and women is greatest for those aged 25–34 (88 and 72 per cent respectively). In addition, women in ethnic minority groups have lower employment rates than white women. Around three in five Indian women compared with one in five Bangladeshi women are in employment, while almost two thirds of Black Caribbean and just under half of Black African women are employed.

A number of factors impact on the rate of female employment. These include marital status, partnered women are more likely to be employed than single women, and qualifications, women with higher qualifications are most likely to be in employment. Women with dependent children are less likely than those without to be employed. This is particularly true for those with children under school age; the employment rate for women with children under four is 53 per cent, compared with 73 per cent for those with dependent children aged five and over. The number of economically inactive women fell from 17 per cent in 1992 to 12 per cent in 2002 and those that do become economically inactive do so for a shorter period of time than was previously the case.

In 1998, the 45 per cent of working women who worked part-time earned around 60 per cent of men's average hourly rate' per cent. This gap had barely changed over the preceding twenty-five years. Part-time women workers, who account for two-thirds of mothers with children under five in paid work, are concentrated in 'low paid, low status work with fewer prospects for career advancement than in higher paid occupations,'[10] very often because of employers' reluctance to open up higher-status work to part-time or flexible work patterns. In the adult population taken as a whole, women's incomes were only 51 per cent of men's in 2000/1. Women are almost invariably the lower earners in their households and are radically less likely than men to belong to pension schemes (in 1998, 72 per cent of men working full-time belonged to occupational pension schemes in comparison with 64

---

[5] J Squires and M Wickham-Jones, 'Women in parliament: a comparative analysis' (EOC, 2001). See also 'Man enough for the job? A study of Parliamentary candidates' (EOC, 2002).

[6] According to research reported in 130 *Equal Opportunities Review*.

[7] H Dustin (ed), Commission on Women and the Criminal Justice System 'Women and the Criminal Justice System', March 2004.

[8] 99 *Equal Opportunities Review*. See also M Thewlis *et al*, 'Advancing Women in the Workplace: Statistical Analysis' (Women and Equality Unit, EOC & IRS), Working Paper Series No.12, 2004.

[9] Available from the EOC website, above n 3.

[10] EOC, 'The lifecycle of Inequality' (2001).

per cent of full-time and 34 per cent of part-time women workers).[11] In the late 1990s, men in pension-aged couples received an average £88.00 per week from occupational pensions compared with women's average £16.00.[12]

Women comprise the large majority of those who benefited from the implementation of the National Minimum Wage and the 1.2 million homeworkers in Britain[13] who are for the most part denied employment rights altogether are women (homeworkers are entitled to a minimum wage but this was, until October 2004, set at 80 per cent of the norm). Women, particularly those who work part-time, are very badly hit by the lower earnings limit (LEL) for National Insurance (£82 per week from April 2005). Some efforts have recently been made to ameliorate the impact of the LEL (in particular, by introducing an employee's earnings threshold, £94 per week as of April 2005) at which the worker's obligation to pay NI £94 per week as of April 2004 cuts in, whereas those earning between the LEL and the employee earnings threshold (EET) are assessed as having a nil rate of *payment* of NI, while being eligible for benefits dependent on earning in excess of the LEL. Nevertheless, in March 2004 the *Equal Opportunities Review* estimated that that 0.5 million men and 1.4 million women earned less than this threshold. Workers who dip into and out of employment may well pay NI contributions for years, but fail to build up sufficient years of contributions to be eligible for state pensions.[14] These workers—the large majority of them women—effectively subsidise those (predominantly male) workers whose working lives are less interrupted. Half a million women in 2003 had no entitlement to state pension. The EOC has recently been highly critical of government plans for pension reform (which consist in the main of encouraging workers to save for retirement).[15] According to the EOC Chair, Julie Mellor, the proposals were a 'wasted opportunity' to ameliorate the current position under which women have an average retirement income of only 56 pence in the male pound, and only 30 per cent of women pensioners have their own private pension.[16] State and occupational pension schemes are based on the male earner model—this despite (or because of?) the fact that two of every three pensioners are women.[17]

The disadvantage suffered by women in the workplace and, in particular, the pay inequalities resulting therefrom, impact profoundly upon their lives. While some women earn sufficient to maintain themselves and their children, many more do not. Women's economic dependency traps many in abusive relationships, and (as we saw above) poverty in old age is a predominantly female state. Women have, since the implementation of the SDA, been entitled not to be discriminated against in terms of their access to mortgages, etc. But the level of women's earnings, relative to those of men, results in precisely that effect. And while women continue to be relatively disadvantaged at work, they continue to shoulder the bulk of childcare responsibility which, in turn, serves to perpetuate their workplace disadvantage.

---

[11] Industrial Society Survey 1993 discussed in the TUC Women's Conference Report, 'No Excuse—No Harassment at Work' (1999), available from the TUC's website at www.tuc.org.uk. The TUC's own survey showed 27 per cent women reporting personal experience of sexual harassment.

[12] EOC, 'Pensions and Social Security' (2001).

[13] According to a report in 130 *Equal Opportunity Review*, citing a campaign by Oxfam, the TUC and the National Group on Homeworking. For discussion of women and pensions see D Kingsford Smith, 'Superannuating the second sex; law, Privatisation and retirement income' (2001) 64 *Modern Law Review* 519.

[14] Above n 12.

[15] Work and Pensions Select Committee, 'Working and Saving for Retirement' (2003). See also Age Concern and the Fawcett Society, 'One in Four' (2003).

[16] 117 *Equal Opportunities Review*.

[17] *Ibid.*

According to the *Equal Opportunities Review* in September 2003, 43 per cent of lone parent households with dependent children were workless by comparison with 5 per cent of couple households including dependent children.[18] The vast majority of lone parents are women. The introduction of tax credits has served to alleviate some of the poverty experienced by the working poor, and ought to alleviate some of the poverty experienced by working lone parents. But they act as a disincentive to second earners in couple households, with significant implications for women's poverty.[19]

J Bradshaw, N Finch, P Kemp, E Mayhew and J Williams, 'Gender and Poverty in Britain' (EOC Working Paper No. 6, 2003)

The Poverty and Social Exclusion Survey shows that women are more likely to be lacking two or more socially perceived necessities, that women are more likely to feel poor, more likely to be dependent on Income Support and more likely to be poor on all four dimensions of poverty (namely: lacking two or more necessities; earning below 60 per cent median income; subjective poverty; and receiving income support).

There are other factors as well as gender associated with the prevalence of poverty, for example: labour market status, household composition, age and number of children, but having controlled for the impact of these there is still a clear gender dimension. Women who are single pensioners, unemployed, Pakistani or Bangladeshi, teenage heads of household and tenants are more likely to be poor than men with the same characteristics. In some dimensions women are also more likely to be socially excluded—labour market excluded, excluded from services, from social activities and restricted in going out . . .

The reasons why women are more likely than men to be poor are clear from the existing literature. There is still a gender pay gap which is explained by continued occupational segregation and the fact that jobs which are predominantly done by women tend to be lower paid; child-birth and caring responsibilities result in many women, especially those with low education qualifications, having an interrupted profile of labour market activity, and much higher rates of part-time work than men. In addition, the pay gap between full-time and part-time workers is widening.

Investment in human capital, especially education, is closely linked to employment. However, social class affects educational experience and working class children obtain lower qualifications, which translate into greater disadvantage in the labour market. In addition, far from taking low status part-time work out of choice, many poorly qualified women have no other option because of the lack of available and affordable childcare and limited employment opportunities in their area.[20]

Lone mothers and older single women are most likely to experience poverty. Lone mothers find it very difficult to access employment, partly because of childcare problems, but also because of their concentration in areas of high unemployment. Women's disadvantages in the labour market continue to have an impact in retirement. Their entitlement to the basic pension is lower than men's in every age band, and they are less likely to have an occupational pension.

Three other elements which reveal the gender dimension of poverty remain largely hidden. First, the distribution of money within households is not always fair. Where men are the sole breadwinners, their partners may not get equal access to earnings entering the

---

[18] 109 *Equal Opportunities Review* reported that lone parents stayed out of work longer (90 per cent of lone parents are mothers).

[19] *Ibid*, citing R Blundell, J McCrae and C Meghir, 'The Labour Market Impact of the Working Families Tax Credit' (Institute for Fiscal Studies, 1999).

[20] 122 *Equal Opportunities Review* reported a study which suggested that the provision of universal childcare in the UK could generate an additional £40 billion over 65 years at 2003 prices.

household, which appears to be the case in some low-income households. Second, women tend to be the money managers, particularly in low-income households. They are more likely to experience the stresses involved in managing on low incomes and having to manage debts. Third, in some low-income households parents, but especially mothers, forego their own consumption to meet the demands of their children.

Underpinning the above causes of poverty is the assumption that women are, or should be, financially dependent upon men and that their role within the family is as carer, rather than earner. Ending women's poverty and deprivation will, to some extent, rely on reducing their economic dependence on men . . .

Despite some significant improvements in the position of women relative to men, poverty in Britain is much more of a female experience than a male one. Women are generally poorer than men and more women than men are poor. In other words, poverty in Britain is highly gendered . . .

Much of women's poverty is associated—directly or indirectly—with their workplace position. Many women drop out of the workforce for extended periods because of the low-paid, low-status jobs into which they are segregated. Such jobs may not be paid sufficiently to pay for the necessary childcare (upon which, according to research carried out recently by the Labour Research Department, two-thirds of working women's wages is spent).[21] It is hardly surprising that many women 'choose' to forego paid work, or to opt for part-time work which can be structured around children's schooling hours. But the low-paid and low-status of much part-time work means that this is a high-cost option in terms of women's lifetime earnings.

Women are segregated into the lower-paying service sector and, in significant numbers, in only three of the nine major occupational groups.[22] Women also remain concentrated at the lower rungs of occupational hierarchies. In 2004–5 for example, women comprised 59 per cent of graduates, 50 per cent of lay magistrates, 40 per cent of solicitors, 30 per cent of barristers, 28 per cent district judges, 12 per cent recorders, 11 per cent circuit judges, 7 per cent High Court Justices, 8 per cent Lords Justices of Appeal and (as of the appointment of the first woman top the House of Lords in 2004) 8 per cent (1 in 12) law lords. The pattern is similar in medicine which is, in addition, heavily gendered by specialism.[23] The persistence of male domination at the top of the professions, and in the earnings leagues, appears to escape the attention of over-excited journalists who declare, from time to time, that it truly is now a 'women's world' (see, for example, Gaby Hinsliff whose article ('So, it's a woman's world,' the *Observer* 15 August 2004) begins: 'They were the first generation of girls to beat the boys in their school exams—and then outstrip them at university. Now they are storming the last bastions of male-dominated professions. For today's young women, it seems the future really is female'). A cynic might be tempted to contrast this rosy view with the recent report of an accountant sacked by City firm Goldenberg Hehmeyer while she was on maternity leave, who was instructed by job centre staff to delete any mention of her one year old daughter from her CV if she hoped to succeed in obtaining other work.[24]

---

[21] Research carried out for the TGWU union and reported in 115 *Equal Opportunities Review*.

[22] *Labour Market Trends* 1998, reported in 85 *Equal Opportunities Review*, 35.

[23] EOC, above n 3. See also 'Women and Men in Britain: Professional Occupations' (EOC, 2002) and 78 *Equal Opportunities Review* 4, Bristol Business School, 'Room at the Top' (2001) on problems for women in local government.

[24] *Evening Standard*, 10 August 2004 'City worker "told to lie about daughter."' For the similarly bleak European picture see 'Advancing women in the workplace: statistical analysis' and 'Advancing women in the workplace' (EOC and Women and Equality Unit, 2004) available from the EOC's website.

Women's workplace disadvantage is at least in part the result of discrimination. Sexual harassment, which is endemic, serves to exclude women from male-dominated working environments and to underline their frequently subordinate position at work (whether that subordination is job-related or the product of physical and sexual intimidation). Fifty-four per cent of working women have experienced such harassment (as against 15 per cent of men).[25] The levels of harassment and direct discrimination reported by ethnic minority women are particularly high. And the legal regulation of this problem is patently inadequate. Over 90 per cent of those who win sexual harassment claims resign or are dismissed from their jobs.[26]

Research published by Cranfield School of Business in 2000 suggested that the commitment of women managers was systematically underestimated.[27] Male and female senior managers alike cite women's family responsibilities as the major barrier to their advancement, and senior women employed in companies with flexible work policies generally think that taking the opportunity to put their families first will have a detrimental impact on their careers.[28] Small wonder, then, that women managers are much less likely than male managers to be married and much less likely to have dependent children.[29] In 2000, the *Equal Opportunities Review* reported the results of a survey of managers which found that 'mothers continue to feel under most pressure in the workplace'; that 34 per cent of mothers (but only 20 per cent of fathers) were uncomfortable about asking for time off to care for a sick child and that 40 per cent of women as against 29 per cent of men found it difficult to ask for a family-related change in working patterns.[30]

E Collins and E Meehan, 'Women's Rights in Employment' in C McCrudden and G Chambers (eds), *Individual Rights and the Law in Britain* (Oxford, Clarendon, 1994) 403, 405, footnotes omitted

One test of the effectiveness of the [SDA] might be a reduction in occupational and industrial segregation but on the basis of official statistics there has been little change since the mid-1970s. We have shown that the development of the right to equal treatment under the [SDA] since 1975 has not always been straightforward. The indirect discrimination provisions particularly should have enabled the courts and tribunals to take a purposive approach to tackling the structural discrimination which is embedded deeply in the labour market. Instead, they have focused on technicalities and procedures and there is evidence of 'a judicial reluctance to widen the ambit of the debate over equality.'

[25] Industrial Society Survey 1993 discussed in the TUC Women's Conference Report, 'No Excuse—No Harassment at Work' (1999). The TUC's own survey showed 27 per cent women reporting personal experience of sexual harassment.

[26] 100 *Equal Opportunities Review*, citing EOC research.

[27] Opportunity Now, 'Breaking the Barriers: Women in Senior Management' (2000) and Institute of Management, 'A Woman's Place' (2001). See also Opportunity Now, 'Sticky floors and cement ceilings' (2002) which cited family commitments and managers' attitudes as the biggest barriers to women managers' career advancement.

[28] See also Ceridian Performance Partners, 'Work-life balance: whose move is it next?' which found that women managers were particularly likely to take the view that any flexible working on their part would result in damage to their careers. The Joseph Rowntree Foundation made similar findings more recently amongst employees (see report in 125 *Equal Opportunities Review*).

[29] According to the *Equal Opportunities Review* report (March 2002) of Office for National Statistics figures for 2001, 71 per cent male managers (as against 58 per cent of male workers generally) were married and 47 per cent had dependent children (20 per cent children under five). The figures for women were 58 per cent, 54 per cent, 35 per cent and 12 per cent.

[30] Ceridian Performance Partners, 'Time to Choose' reported in 93 *Equal Opportunities Review*. See also Institute for Employment Studies, 'Work-life balance: beyond the rhetoric' (2002).

The industrial tribunal system has also been found to be a disappointment as a mechanism for dealing with individual complaints and ensuring the more widespread adoption of non-discriminatory employment practices. Leonard concluded, for example, from her analysis of successful claimants in the period 1980–4, that compensation awarded to individual applicants was inadequate; that often claimants were out of pocket themselves, despite winning their cases; that there were often real difficulties in collecting the compensation; and that the costs for complainants in terms of emotional stress and damaged future employment prospects were extremely high. Also, the fact of winning a case seemed to have little impact on the conditions of co-workers, in that it led to little change in the organisation. Gregory, in her analysis of unsuccessful applicants in the 1985–6 period painted a similar, dismal picture. Gregory and Leonard both recorded problems with lack of specialised knowledge of discrimination law in the tribunal system, often due to problems such as the allocation of cases widely across membership and the absence of compulsory formal training. Chambers and Horton looked at the impact of tribunal decisions on employers and their conclusions are also an indictment of a mechanism which had the potential to effect change in the workplace. It is clear that changes are necessary not only to the legislation but also to the systems of advice, assistance and representation; to the tribunal procedure itself; and to the remedies and sanctions which can be applied, to ensure that they impact on employers both as a deterrent and as an incentive to introduce changes.

Comparison between the UK and other countries regarding the scope of rights available and the effectiveness of any equal treatment laws is difficult without a full discussion of the different legal systems, the different laws, and the different social and economic contexts within which the countries operate. Formally, all Community countries have, for example, fulfilled their obligation to implement the equality directives in their jurisdiction, but as directives leave it open to member states to decide the means to do this, the approaches have been different and it is difficult to say which is 'better' or 'worse.' While a significant number of references to the European Court have come from the United Kingdom, for example, it cannot be said that it is the worst in the Community. The references are as likely to be as a result of the fact there are larger independent equality Commissions here then elsewhere, which have strategically used Community law as a means of forcing change nationally. On some counts, however, particularly in respect of child-care provision and parental leave, it is clear that the United Kingdom ranks among the lowest (with Ireland) in the Community.

Equal pay legislation has been in place in the UK since 1975, in which year the Equal Pay Act 1970 (EqPA) was implemented. Despite this, very significant disparities remain between men's and women's pay. Women are paid less than men whether their wages are measured hourly or weekly.[31] They are paid less than men both at the top of the hierarchy and at the bottom. In 1998, taking only those women who worked full-time, women doctors and financial managers earned 80 per cent and 64 per cent respectively of their male colleagues' hourly rate, women bar staff and petrol pump forecourt attendants 88 per cent and 91 per cent. Women who do 'women's jobs' are paid less than men who do 'men's jobs'—in 1998, full-time female nurses, for example, earned 85 per cent of male engineering technicians' hourly rate'. Women who do 'women's jobs' are paid less than men who do 'women's jobs'—full-time women financial clerks and nurses earned only 85 per cent and 96 per cent of their male colleagues' rates. And women who do 'men's jobs' are paid less than men who do 'men's jobs' —full-time women police officers and women machine tool operatives earned 91 per cent[32] and 69 per cent of the male rate. However the information

---

[31] See, eg, ESRC 'Seven Ages of Man and Woman' (2004) available from the EOC's website, above n 3.
[32] These figures apply only in respect of sergeants and below.

is categorised, however large or small the occupational categories examined, women earn less than men.[33] Women and, in particular, ethnic minority women and those who work part-time, have been the main beneficiaries of the National Minimum Wage.

Even when women's jobs have been assessed as being of equal value to those of their male colleagues, women still find themselves paid less. Local authority workers have for years had their jobs evaluated and basic wages pinned to these evaluations. It is still the case that men, but not women, workers receive considerable supplements by way of bonuses which are payable only in respect of 'male' jobs. In 1999, the *Equal Opportunities Review* reported that 'bonus payments represent 15 per cent of average male earnings [for local authority workers] compared with just over 1 per cent of female earnings':

> . . . There is a growing acceptance that most of the schemes in operation are indefensible in terms of equal pay, but the total cost of equalisation could run into many millions of pounds. In the West Midlands alone, employers have put the annual cost of equalising bonus payments . . . at over £20 million . . . At the beginning of 1997, 1,500 schools meals workers employed by the former Cleveland County Council settled their equal pay claim based on bonuses for £4 million . . .[34]

In 2000 the same publication reported findings by the higher education union NATHFE that women academics in the UK were being paid up to £8 000 less than men doing the same jobs in the same subject areas.

'Gender and ethnic pay gap in academia' 97 *Equal Opportunities Review*

Although women are being discriminated against at all grades and in almost all subject areas, some areas are worse than others, according to the research. Top of the list is anatomy and physiology, with an £8,000 difference in male and female professors' pay, closely followed by veterinary science with a £7,000 gap. Nursing and paramedical studies is one of only two subject areas where female professors earn more—just over £1,000 ahead of men, although male nursing lecturers and senior lecturers still earn more than their female counterparts, the research shows.

Even in subjects with a comparatively high proportion of women, there is still a big difference between male and female lecturers' pay. For example, at lecturer grade in health and community studies, comprising 38 per cent women, there is a £1,960 pay gap; in general sciences, where a quarter of lecturers are women, there is a £4,169 gap; and in nursing, where 70 per cent of lecturers are women, male lecturers earn £1,558 more than their female counterparts.

A high proportion of women in a subject area appears to depress the average salary. At lecturer grade, subjects with approximately 10 per cent women, such as physics, civil engineering, chemistry, electrical, electronic and computer engineering, had an overall average salary of £27,064. In comparison, subjects with over 30 per cent women lecturers, including nursing and paramedical studies, language-based studies and health and community studies, had an average salary of £24,924—a difference of about 8 per cent.

Orthodox economists sometimes attempt to explain the gender-wage gap in terms of 'human capital'—the skills, training and education, etc, in which workers invest. It is often argued that women have lower human capital then men—that they are less well educated, trained, motivated, and/or skilled than men. But these arguments have been countered by

---

[33] All figures are taken from the NES 1998.
[34] 84 *Equal Opportunities Review* 4.

research (much of it conducted in Britain) which has shown that women are paid less not *because* they were concentrated in jobs requiring less skill, but *despite* their working in jobs very similar to those performed by men in different organisations;[35] and that women's jobs are frequently ungraded:

> firms would often recognise differences in skill between the women workers . . . but nevertheless pay all of them at the same rate, justifying the practice on the basis that any differentiation would cause resentment amongst the other women workers. The fact of women's pay being less than men's cannot therefore simply be explained on the grounds that women's work is less skilled, for even within women's work there is little or no differentiation of reward by skill . . . the predominant influence on the shape and structure of the pay and employment system was the sex of the workers.[36]

The differences in education between men and women workers are narrow and closing fast, well-educated women also being more likely than their counterparts to remain in the workforce after having children. A recent Workplace Industrial Relations Survey found that 'establishment performance is not significantly affected by the level of female concentration. We therefore find no support for the hypothesis that higher female concentration is an indicator of lower human capital.'[37] And Jan Waldfogel found that:

> only a small proportion of the gender gap . . . is due to differences in characteristics between young men and women . . . if women had the same characteristics they do now but received the same returns as men in the labour market, the gender gap at age 23 would fall 84 per cent (from 19 per cent to 3 per cent) and at age 33 would fall 70 per cent (from 30 per cent to 7 per cent). This means that the much greater part (84 per cent at age 23 and 70 per cent at age 33) of the gender gap is due to differential treatment (my emphasis).[38]

Other recent estimates of the relationship between 'human capital' and the gender-wage gap in Britain suggest that: '[t]he primary reason for women's lower pay is smaller

---

[35] S Horrell, J Ruberry and B Burchell, 'Unequal Jobs or Unequal Pay?' (1990) 20 *Industrial Relations Journal* 176. Job skills were compared using index allocating points for responsibility, degree of supervision, autonomy, training and education.

[36] C Craig, J Rubery, R Tarling and F Wilkinson, *Labour Market Structure, Industrial Organisation and Low Pay* (Cambridge, CUP, 1982) 84.

[37] N Millward and S Woodland, 'Gender Segregation and Male/Female Wage Differences' (London, LSE, 1995) 21. As interesting as their findings on the human capital issue were Millward and Woodland's comments on their fellow economists. Noting that analysts of the Workplace Industrial Relations Survey (WIRS) data tended not to remark on the wage premium associated with working in a predominantly male workplaces, 'save to cast female concentration in the role of a proxy measure of low labour quality,' they declared the contrast between this assumption and the recognition that the negative wage impact of concentrations of ethnic minority workers could be attributed to discrimination 'difficult to understand' (8–9). Certainly, the economists who attributed lower female wages to lower human capital accumulation appeared to do so simply on the basis that 'one would expect that a higher quality workforce would result in a higher gross weekly pay of the '"typical" employee,' and that women's wages were lower (at 8, citing D Blanchflower, 'Union Relative Wage Effects: a Cross-section Analysis using Establishment Data' (1984) 22(3) *British Journal of Industrial Relations* 311).

[38] 'Women Working For Less: A Longitudinal Analysis of the Family Gap' (London, LSE, 1993) 47. P Sloane, 'The Gender Wage Differential' in A. Scott (ed), *Gender Segregation and Social Change: Men and Women in Changing Labour Markets* (Oxford, OUP, 1994) 191, found that discrimination accounted for approximately one third of the wage gap between single men and women, one quarter of that between married men and women. It should be noted, however, that Sloane included as factors distinct from 'sex' (the latter being the measure of discrimination) some, such as marriage and experience, which might be considered themselves to be discriminatory.

remuneration for human capital attributes in their jobs: if women's human capital was remunerated at the same rate as men's, their hourly pay would be substantially—of the order of one fifth—higher'.[39] And Waldfogel's research has been supported very recently by the Government Women's Unit which reported in 1999 that:

K Rake et al, 'Women's Incomes over the Lifetime'

having children is possibly the most significant factor affecting women's income and earnings opportunities. For many working women, having children means a drop in personal income, a loss of momentum on the career ladder and often leaving employment for several years.

There has been a dramatic increase in recent years in the number of women who work during pregnancy and are back in work within nine to eleven months of the birth of their child. But most commonly, women who return to work after having children do so on a part-time basis. Working mothers still bear the primary responsibility for care of their children . . .

A working life fragmented by caring responsibilities and low earnings, together with the lack of pensions provision, combine to make women more likely to be reliant on means-tested benefits in old age. They are more likely to be frail or ill, and to need professional care.

For many women, the point at which work-related disadvantage bites hardest is after childbirth. Many jobs at the top of the economic hierarchy are structured on the assumption not only that the holder has no caring obligations, but also that he does not even have to look after himself. Women face an almost impossible task in attempting to reconcile such jobs with motherhood no matter how comprehensive and high quality their childcare arrangements. Further down the scale, relatively few jobs pay sufficient to buy good quality childcare so women are dependent on informal arrangements which require a significant degree of flexibility on their part. Many women 'choose' part-time work as part of this balancing act, only to find themselves denied promotion, downgraded or having to accept work for which they are over-qualified.[40]

The problems faced by black and other ethnic minority women are particularly acute. Women from all ethnic minority groups account for just under 5 per cent of all women in formal employment, but these figures exclude substantial proportions of women employed in the informal economy. Of those ethnic minority women whose employment is recorded Indians form the largest single group (164,000 or 1.5 per cent of all women workers), followed by Black Caribbeans (118,000 or 1 per cent), women of mixed and other origins (92,000), Chinese and other Asian (70,000), Black African (47,000) and Pakistani and Bangladeshi (45,000).[41] Research by the Women and Equality Unit of the Cabinet Office in 2002 found that ethnic minority women, like ethnic minority men, were considerably more likely than their white counterparts to be unemployed (4 per cent of white women, 15 per cent of African women and Pakistani/Bangladeshi women, 13 per cent of women of mixed background, 11 per cent black and black British women, 8 per cent Caribbean and Asian/ Asian British woman and 6.8 per cent Indian women). 17 per cent of white women but 40 per cent of Pakistani/Bangladeshi women, 26 per cent Asian/ British women and 20 per cent African women had no qualifications but mixed race, black/ black British and

---

[39] J Ermisch and R Wright, 'Differential Returns to Human Capital in Full-time and Part-time Employment' in N Folbre, B Bergmann, B Agarwal and M Floro (eds), *Issues in Contemporary Economics: Volume 4, Women's Work in the World Economy* (New York, New York University Press, 1992) 208.

[40] See further, A McColgan, *Just Wages for Women* (Oxford, OUP, 1997) Chs 2 and 6.

[41] EOC, above n 3, 9, citing the Labour Force Survey, Spring 1998.

Caribbean women were less likely than their white counterparts to have no qualifications (14 per cent, 15 per cent and 11 per cent respectively). The average age of women differed very significantly by ethnic background, from 40 in the case of white women to 34, 33, 31, 30, 29, 27, 24 and 20 for Caribbean, Indian, Chinese, black/black British, Asian/Asian British, African, Pakistani/Bangladeshi and mixed race women.

In this chapter we consider the EqPA, which permits challenge to sex discrimination in contractual terms of employment, and the SDA which applies more broadly to discrimination on grounds of sex (and, in the employment context, discrimination against married people and in connection with gender reassignment). These legislative provisions cannot be considered in isolation from the relevant European provisions: Article 141 TEC and the Equal Treatment Directive as amended by Directive 2002/73/EC from October 2005. The Equal Pay Directive is of less significance given the direct effect (both vertical and horizontal) of Article 141 and the express application of that provision (by contrast with the predecessor Article 119) to work of equal value. Mention will also be made of Council Directive 2004/113/EC which regulates sex discrimination in access to goods and services and which has been considered in Chapter 4. That Directive must be implemented by December 2007. Its limited scope means that its implications for domestic law are relatively slight. Finally, the European Commission in 2004 issued a proposal for a 'super equality directive' which would amalgamate and simplify the various directives which deal with equal treatment between women and men. It will not be further considered as anything that might be said about it at this stage is highly speculative.[42]

In Chapters 1, 2 and 3 we considered those aspects of the SDA that it shares with some or all of the other legislation under discussion—the definitions of discrimination it employs, problems of proof and procedural issues such as time limits. In Chapter 4 we discussed the sphere within which anti-discrimination legislation operates, ie, those aspects of employment, housing, the provision of services, etc, in respect of which discrimination is prohibited by this and other legislation. But it is worth stressing here that much of the discrimination from which women suffer ('domestic' violence, sexual assault, the dual burden of paid and unpaid work, the impact of actuarial discrimination on pension schemes and insurance), is untouched by the provisions of the SDA and the EqPA. The Government has finally taken steps to extend the SDA to cover discrimination by public bodies such as the police, immigration and prison authorities which was excluded from the Act's coverage by the decision of the House of Lords in *Amin v Entry Clearance Officer, Bombay* [1983] 2 AC 818 (see further Chapter 4). Some six years after the commitment was first made, the Equality Bill 2005 finally proposed to bring the SDA into line with the RRA. The Bill was not passed prior to the 2005 General Election but the outgoing Government indicated an intention to reintroduce it as a matter of priority if it was re-elected. Meanwhile, and subject to possible developments under the Human Rights Act, discrimination which takes the form of police downgrading of 'domestic' violence, sexist assumptions about rape victims which permeate the legal system, or the operation of the immigration system which threatens recently arrived women with deportation if they attempt to leave abusive partners, is outside the scope of the SDA. Equally, unless and until the proposed extension to sex of the positive obligations imposed by the RRA on public authorities in relation to race, the SDA does not reach the kind of problem discussed in the YWCA's recent report 'Young, Urban and Female'. According to the EOC's recent publication, 'Promoting Gender Equality in the Public Sector', the report:

---

[42] COM/2004/0279/final.

Found the near absence of reference to the specific needs of women of all ages in the Social Exclusion Unit's national strategy for urban renewal and a lack of recognition that women experience disadvantage differently from men. The research findings from four case studies revealed a male dominance in regeneration structures and a lack of women in the decision making structures. The study concluded that regeneration planning had not addressed many of the issues specifically affecting young women. Young women cited the lack of affordable and adequate childcare, poor play facilities, infrequent and inefficient transport, and fears about personal safety as key areas which had been overlooked by regeneration planners. A public duty to promote gender equality which included the commission and contracting of aspects of regeneration programmes to trusts, development agencies, management consultants and private contractors could ensure an improved gender balance in . . . decision making. It would also be a mechanism for improving the gender balance of beneficiaries from such projects. . .

the modernization agenda to improve the provision of public services has not taken sufficient account of an equality dimension. The government has recently increased the role of competition in Best Value . . . and launched a national taskforce to promote strategic service delivery partnerships, in effect large outsourcing contracts. The wider use of competitive tendering with larger contracts than those under CCT is almost certain to produce similar, if not more serious, consequences for the gender and equality agenda . . This aspect of the government's modernisation programme conflicts with its equality policy statements. The inclusion of equality policies and public duty responsibilities in contract documents between the public and private sectors is unlikely to prove adequate protection given the historical difficulties of ensuring that equality policies are applied and implemented.

The extension of the SDA to impose positive obligations on public authorities could revolutionise the way in which domestic violence is dealt with by the authorities, the funding of rape crisis centres, the approach taken to foreign sex workers who have been brought to the UK against their will and who currently, if they approach the authorities, risk deportation as illegal immigrants.[43] Northern Ireland's Equality Commission, in its 2003 submissions to the CEDAW Committee, remarked that s.75 of the Northern Ireland Act, which imposes positive obligations on public authorities in relation to, inter alia, sex: 'can impact on a range of public sector policies including the full range of employment policies, policies relating to Private Finance Initiatives, Public Private Partnerships, access to public sector resources such as education, social welfare and health.'[44]

The SDA has been discussed at some length in the preceding chapters. Here we turn to those issues which are unique to the regulation of sex discrimination. Most concern employment, the Act being differentiated from the RRA at present mainly by the continuing operation in relation to it of the *Amin* decision. Discrimination in goods and services is covered in Chapter 4. The main focus of the chapter will be on the EqPA. We will also

---

[43] The Women's National Commission has recently commented unfavourably on this in its shadow report to the UN Committee on the Elimination of Violence Against Women on the UK's implementation of its obligations under CEDAW. The Commission notes that, according to the Conventions and its Protocols; 'victims should be referred to a specialist agency for support, including secure accommodation; information in a language they can understand; medical and psychological assistance; legal assistance; and the ability to communicate with family. However, no organisation exists in the UK to which the police, immigration services, or local authorities can refer victims. . . . Victims who are returned home may be subject to torture, rape, held in slavery or servitude, or even killed by traffickers; their family may be threatened to gain the victim's cooperation, or the victims may face reprisals from their families, especially if they have been involved in the sex industry.'

[44] Available on the Commission's website (www.equalityni.org).

consider pregnancy and its coverage by the SDA, dress codes and 'family friendly' working. The legality of dress codes arises also in relation the RRA but the issues differ between the Acts and will be considered both here and in Chapter 7. Finally we will consider the GOQ (genuine occupational qualification) defence as it applies under the SDA.

The Equal Pay Act and Article 141

The EqPA deals only with discrimination connected with sex. Like all the other legislative provisions with the exception of the DDA the Act adopts a symmetrical approach and permits claims by men as well as women. The similarities between the EqPA, on the one hand, and the other discrimination provisions considered in this book, on the other, do not extend far beyond their shared symmetry of approach. The other legislation prohibits 'discrimination,' direct or indirect, in a number of situations. While originally (and in some cases still) the SDA, RRA and DDA placed the burden of proof on the claimant, hypothetical comparators may be used to establish discrimination. The EqPA, on the other hand, does not actually use the term 'discrimination,' much less distinguish its direct and indirect varieties. Instead, it sets out three situations in which there is a de facto right to the same contractual terms (including pay) as another. The claimant must prove that she (or he) falls within one of these three situations—ie, that she does the same work, work which has been rated by the employer as equivalent (in value) or work which a tribunal has determined to be of equal value, to that done by someone of the opposite sex in the 'same employment' as her. Where the claimant does this she is entitled, subject to the employer's defence, to have an 'equality clause' inserted into her contract which gives her the same contractual term(s) as that (those) enjoyed by her comparator and sought by her.

Before we turn to the detail of the EqPA it is necessary to mention Article 141 TEC (originally Article 119 of the Treaty of Rome) which provides a right as between men and women to equal pay for work of equal value. The EqPA, which was passed some five and a half years prior to its implementation in 1975, predated the UK's accession to the EEC (as it then was). The right to equal pay which it established (ie, the right to equal pay for like work or for work which had been rated as equivalent by the employer) was thought by the government of the time to be more generous than that required by Article 119 which stipulated merely that: 'Each Member State shall during the first stage ensure and subsequently maintain the application of the principle that men and women should receive equal pay for equal work. . . .' This was understood by many to require only that men and women were paid equally in respect of the *same* work. The UK acceded to the EEC in 1973, and with this accepted the supremacy of Community (now EU) law. In 1975, Council Directive 75/117 (the Equal Pay Directive) defined the 'principle of equal pay' to require the elimination of sex-related pay differentials in respect of 'the same work *or . . . work to which equal value is attributed*' (Article 1, my emphasis). Article 2 of the Equal Pay Directive required Member States to:

> introduce into their national legal systems such measures as are necessary to enable all employees who consider themselves wronged by failure to apply the principle of equal pay to pursue their claims by judicial process after possible recourse to other competent authorities.

Council Directive 117/75 proved to be a Trojan horse. Having agreed to it on the understanding that it was already adequately implemented by the EqPA, the UK found itself pursued by the Commission on the grounds that it was not. The Commission eventually took enforcement action against the UK on the grounds that, the evaluation of dissimilar jobs being entirely at the discretion of the employer, the latter had not implemented 'equal pay for work of equal value' as required by Article 141 and the Directive. In *Commission v United Kingdom*, Case C–61/81 [1982] ECR 2601 the ECJ ruled that: 'where there is disagreement as to the application of the concept of "work to which equal value is attributed" . . . the worker must be entitled to claim before an appropriate authority that his work has the same value as other work.' The Equal Pay (Amendment) Regulations 1983, presented to the Commons by a drunk and derisive Alan Clark (then Under-Secretary of State for Employment),[45] amended the EqPA to provide for an equal value claim.

In *Defrenne v Sabena (No.2)* Case C–43/75 [1976] ECR 455, the ECJ accepted that Article 141 was directly effective.[46] Since that date individuals within the various Member States have been able to rely on Article 141 to claim equal pay in their national courts. Article 141 now provides, so far as is relevant, that:

(1) Each Member State shall ensure that the principle of equal pay for male and female workers for equal work or work of equal value is applied.
(2) For the purposes of this Article, 'pay' means the ordinary basic or minimum wage or salary and any other consideration, whether in cash or in kind, which the worker receives, directly or indirectly, in respect of his employment from his employer.
Equal pay without discrimination based on sex means:
   (a) that pay for the same work at piece rates shall be calculated on the basis of the same unit of measurement;
   (b) that pay for work at time rates shall be the same for the same job. . . .

This provision is, for the most part, given effect in domestic law by the EqPA, s.1(2) of which provides that:

An equality clause is a provision which relates to terms (whether concerned with pay or not) of a contract under which a woman is employed (the 'woman's contract'), and has the effect that [(s.2(a) (b) and (c))] . . .
(i) if (apart from the equality clause) any term of the woman's contract is or becomes less favourable to the woman than a term of a similar kind in the contract under which that man is employed, that term of the woman's contract shall be treated as so modified as not to be less favourable, and
(ii) if (apart from the equality clause) at any time the woman's contract does not include a term corresponding to a term benefiting that man included in the contract under which he is employed, the woman's contract shall be treated as including such a term.

The majority of claims brought under the EqPA concern pay. But it is clear from s.1(2) that the Act's scope is wider than this.

The EqPA does not permit a hypothetical comparator, s.1(2) referring to an actual comparator ('that man') with whose contract the claimant's must be compared. The com-

---

[45] SI 1983/1794.
[46] The effect of the decision was 'backstopped' at the date of the judgment, 8 April 1976.

parator, further discussed below, must be engaged in 'like work,' 'work rated as equivalent' or work of equal value to the claimant's, and must be 'in the same employment' as her. These requirements are considered further below. But the EqPA must be read to permit comparison with a woman's predecessor, according to the Court of Appeal in *Macarthys Ltd v Smith (No.2)* [1980] ICR 672. The Court's decision followed that of the ECJ that such comparators must be permitted to be made under Article 141 of the Treaty Establishing the European Community. Accordingly, the Court of Appeal ruled that the EqPA must be read, however inelegantly, to give effect to this. More recently, in *Diocese of Hallam Trustees v Connaughton* [1996] ICR 860, EAT ruled that Article 141 required the possibility of comparison with a successor in employment.

The equal pay claimant does not have to prove that she has been discriminated against, simply that she has been less favourably treated in some contractual term than a suitable comparator.[47] In these circumstances, one might say that a presumption of discrimination arises. The employer can displace that presumption, and escape the imposition of an equality clause, by proving that the difference in pay (or other contractual term) is due to a 'material factor' which is 'not the difference of sex.' This is called the 'GMF' (genuine material factor) or s.1(3) defence (being laid down by s.1(3) EqPA). It is considered further below. A 'material factor' which is 'not the difference of sex' does not discriminate directly between men and women and, if it is indirectly discriminatory (in the sense that reliance upon it disfavours women as a matter of fact), reliance upon it must be justified in line with the test established under Article 141.

It is clear that Article 141 may be relied upon in the UK courts, generally by way of having the EqPA (or, in the case of non-contractual 'pay', the SDA) interpreted (however contrary to their express terms) so as to give effect to the European provision.[48] The question of what is 'pay' is not significant to the EqPA itself. But its scope within Article 141 is crucial to the wider picture: to the extent that work-related discrimination falls outwith the scope of the SDA and the EqPA, it can be challenged most effectively where it falls within Article 141. The strength of the provision lies, as we saw above, in its application *horizontally*—between individuals—as well as *vertically*—between the individual and the state (this is not true of the equal treatment which regulates employments related discrimination other than in relation to pay). In addition, the equality provisions which relate to 'pay' are considerably stronger that those which deal with 'social security' in respect of which Member States have traditionally been given more discretion.

---

[47] Ie, like work, work rated as equivalent or work of equal value.

[48] Article 141 does not (*Biggs v Somerset County Council* [1996] ICR 364) give rise to any 'free-standing' cause of action but must be applied through the domestic provisions (see further Ch 5. As McMullan J put it in *Preston v Wolverhampton Healthcare NHS Trust (No.3)* [2004] IRLR 96, citing with approval the tribunal's decision: 'Community provisions which are of direct effect, such as Article 141, are given effect to by disapplying provisions of domestic law which conflict with them. . . . UK domestic law must therefore be interpreted in conformity with Article 141 (by disapplying it to the extent necessary to allow it to be so interpreted) and be deemed to extend to cases where the inequality of pay is consequent upon indirect discrimination. That is the extent of an claimant's Article 141 right.'

We saw, above, that Article 141 categorises as 'pay' all benefits, contractual or otherwise, 'receive[d], directly or indirectly, in respect of . . . employment from [the] employer.' Early decisions on the scope of 'pay' tended to be restrictively decided (*Defrenne v State of Belgium (No.1)* Case C–80/70 [1971] ECR 445, *Burton v British Railway Board* Case C–19/91 [1982] ECR 554, *Newstead v Department of Transport* Case C–192/85 [1987] ECR 4753). But in *Bilka-Kaufhaus GmbH v Weber von Hartz* Case C–170/84 [1986] ECR 1607, the ECJ accepted that an occupational pension which supplemented the state scheme was 'pay' for the purposes of the then Article 119. And in *Barber v Guardian Royal Exchange Assurance Group* Case C–262/88 [1990] ECR 1889 the ECJ extended the reasoning in *Bilka* to cover a non-contributory 'contracted-out' pension scheme (ie., one which replaced, in part, the state pension). This decision was regarded as sufficiently momentous that the court agreed to block retrospective reliance upon it—only those workers who had already instituted claims at the date of the decision (17 May 1990) could challenge pension payments based on service prior to that date. The exact meaning of the temporal restriction was established over a succession of cases discussed and the Maastricht Treaty was subject to the 'Barber protocol' which restricted the impact of the decision to pension payments relating to service after the date (note the recent decision in *Quirk v Burton Hospitals NHS Trust* [2002] IRLR 353). The Pensions Act 1995 now contains provisions which are materially identical to those in the EqPA. The ECJ also ruled in *Barber* that statutory, as well as contractual, redundancy payments fell within Article 141.

In *Bestuur van het Algemeen Burgerlijk Pensioenfonds v Beune* Case C–7/93 [1993] ECR I–0131 Article 141 was interpreted to include Civil Service pensions paid by the state as employer. And in *Vroege v NCIV Institut voor Volkshuisvesting BV* Case C–57/93 [1994] ECR I–4541, the ECJ categorised as 'pay' access to membership of a pension scheme, as distinct from payments thereunder. In addition to all of the above, the ECJ has accepted as 'pay' within Article 141: gratuitous (and, *ipso facto*, contractual) travel concessions (*Garland v British Rail* Case C–12/81 [1982] ECR 359, *Grant v South West Trains* Case C–249/96 [1998] ECR I–00621); paid leave and overtime pay paid in respect of attendance at trade union training, etc. (*Arbeiterwohlfhart der Stadt Berlin eV v Bötel* Case C–360/90 [1982] ECR I–3589); rules governing the accrual of seniority, where seniority is directly related to pay (*Hill & Stapleton v Revenue Commissioners* Case C–243/95 [1998] ECR I–3739); and the provision of subsidized nursery places (*Lommers v Minister van Landbouw* Case C–476/99 [2002] ECR I–02891). Also arguably in the nature of 'social security', though embraced by the ECJ as 'pay', have been sick pay (*Rinner-Kühn v FWW Spezial-Gebaudereiningung GmbH & Co KG* Case C–171/88 [1989] ECR 2743), unemployment payments made by an employee's last employer on a periodic basis (*European Commission v Kingdom of Belgium* Case C–173/91 [1993] ECR I–0673), unfair dismissal compensation (*Seymour-Smith & Perez* Case C–167/97 [1999] ECR I–00623) and, in the domestic courts *R v Secretary of State for Employment ex parte Equal Opportunities Commission* [1994] IRLR 176 (HL)) and maternity pay (*Gillespie v Northern Health and Social Security Board* Case C–342/93 [1996] ECR I–0475). As far as the latter is concerned, however, the ECJ ruled (in *Gillespie*) that:

> . . . discrimination involves the application of different rules to comparable situations or the application of the same rule to different situations. . . women taking maternity

> leave provided for by national legislation . . . are in a special position which requires them to be afforded special protection, but which is not comparable either with that of a man or with that of a woman actually at work . . . neither Article [141] . . . not Article 1 of Directive 117/75 [the equal treatment directive] require[s] that women should continue to receive full pay during maternity leave.
>
> Pay during maternity leave, and the issue of pregnancy more generally, is considered further below

The EqPA establishes three types of claim. Section 1 provides for the inclusion of an equality clause into a woman's contract in respect of 'any term of [her] . . . contract [which] is or becomes less favourable to [her] than a term of a similar kind in the contract under which [her comparator] is employed,' that comparator being employed on (s.1(2)(a)) 'like work', (s.1(2)(b)) 'work rated as equivalent or (s.1(2)(c)) 'work . . . of equal value' to hers. The comparator must be 'in the same employment' as the woman (this is further discussed below) and the effect of the 'equality clause' is to modify the offending contractual term so 'as not to be less favourable'. Section 1(4) goes on to define as 'like work':

work . . . of the same or a broadly similar nature . . . the differences (if any) . . . not [being] of practical importance in relation to terms and condition of employment; and accordingly in comparing her work with theirs regard shall be had to the frequency or otherwise with which any such differences occur in practice as well as to the nature and extent of the differences.

Section 1(5) defines as 'work rated as equivalent' work which has:

been given an equal value, in terms of the demand made on a worker under various headings (for instance effort, skill, decision), on a study undertaken with a view to evaluating in those terms the jobs to be done by all or any of the employees in an undertaking or group of undertakings, or would have been given an equal value but for the evaluation being made on a system setting different values for men and women on the same demand under any heading.

As was noted above, employers cannot be obliged to carry out job evaluation schemes such as would found equal pay claims under s.1(1)(b) (such schemes are discussed further below). S.1(2)(c) states that an 'equal value' claim may be made by a woman:

employed on work which, not being work in relation to which paragraph (a) or (b) above applies, is, in terms of the demands made on her (for instance under such headings as effort, skill and decision), of equal value to that of a man in the same employment.

We consider the various types of equal pay claim in some detail below. First it is useful to deal with an issue which arises by virtue of the particular 'equalising' mechanism employed by the EqPA—ie, the insertion of an 'equality clause' to modify 'any term of the woman's contract [which] is or becomes less favourable to [her] than a term of a similar kind in the contract under which [her comparator] is employed.'

On the face of it, this approach would appear to allow 'leap-frogging,' ie, attempting to 'cherry pick' any particularly favourable terms of a comparator's contract which may, in theory or practice, be balanced by terms which are more favourable to the claimant than her comparator's equivalent are to him. It was argued by the employers in *Hayward v Cammell Laird*, that the EqPA did not permit such an approach.

Hayward was brought by a canteen worker who named, as her comparators, a painter, a joiner and an insulation engineer. By way of defence her employers claimed that, although her basic and overtime rates of pay were lower than those of her comparators, her sickness benefits and meal breaks were better than theirs with the effect that, taken as a whole, her contractual terms were no less favourable to her than theirs were to them. A tribunal, EAT and the Court of Appeal all agreed that the claimant would not have been entitled to relief if, as the respondent employer argued, her contract, taken as a whole, was no less favourable than those of her comparators.[49] The House of Lords allowed her appeal, unanimously deciding that s.1(2) of the EqPA meant what it said.

Hayward v Cammell Laird Shipbuilders Ltd (No.2) [1988] 1 AC 894

Lord Goff (with whom Lords Griffiths, Bridge and Brandon agreed, Lord Mackay delivering a concurring judgment):

. . . If I look at the words used [in s.1(2)(c)(ii), this being an equal value claim], and give them their natural and ordinary meaning, they mean quite simply that one looks at the man's contract and at the woman's contract, and if one finds in the man's contract a term benefiting him which is not included in the woman's contract, then that term is treated as included in hers. On this simple and literal approach, the words 'benefiting that man' mean precisely what they say, that the term must be one which is beneficial to him, as opposed to being burdensome. So if, for example, the man's contract contains a term that he is to be provided with the use of a car, and the woman's contract does not include such a term, then her contract is to be treated as including such a term.

The respondents, and the lower courts, had made much of the 'absurd and unreal consequences' which would follow a literal interpretation of s.1(2), the former using an example of a woman with a salary of £7,500 and a car worth £3,500 pa who sought to compare her wages with those of a man paid £11,000 but without a company car. Lord Mackay accepted that 'one can envisage difficult examples' but 'in the ordinary case such as the present . . . it would be wrong to depart from the natural meaning of the words Parliament has used because of the difficulty in their application to particular examples especially when those examples do not arise in actual cases.' Neither Lord Mackay nor Lord Goff found it necessary to examine the European legislation in view of their conclusion on the clarity of the UK provisions. Nevertheless, both took the view that it supported their approach. In the event, the ECJ decisions in *Brunhofer*, discussed below, and in *Jämställdhetsombudsmannen v Örebro Läns Landsting* Case C–236/98 [2000] ECR I–02189 confirm that the approach under Article 141 is the same, the principle of transparency requiring equivalence in each aspect of pay in the absence of objective justification.

Dealing with the concern of the lower courts as to the potential of their interpretation to lead to 'mutual enhancement or leap-frogging, as terms of the woman's contract and the man's contract are both, so to speak, upgraded to bring them into line with each other,' Lord Goff expressed the opinion that s.1(3) might provide a defence in relation to 'compensating' terms such as those upon which the employer in the present case sought to rely.

---

[49] [1988] QB 12 (CA) and [1987] 1 All ER 503 (EAT).

Lord Mackay was not convinced of this, suggesting 'at the very least' that s.1(3) required the establishment of a causal link between the woman's unfavourable term and that which claimed to balance it.

This question has never really been resolved, but Lord Goff's provisional view was supported by Lord Bridge in *Leverton v Clwyd County Council* [1989] 1 AC 706. The decision is considered further below. On the question, however, whether a woman's unfavourable pay could be balanced against her shorter hours, Lord Bridge concluded, perhaps not surprisingly, that:

> Where a woman's and a man's regular annual working hours, unaffected by any significant additional hours of work, can be translated into a notional hourly rate which yields no significant difference, it is surely a legitimate, if not a necessary, inference that the difference in their annual salaries is both due to and justified by the difference in the hours they work in the course of a year and has nothing to do with the difference in sex.

The decision of the House of Lords in *Hayward* denied employers *carte blanche* to decide on their workers' behalf the manner in which they should be paid, to the extent that the manner discriminated between men and women.[50]

'Like Work'

Turning to consider the various equal pay claims in more detail, s.1(2)(a)'s 'like work' claim was regarded by the framers of the EqPA as quite a broad and generous provision. The Government's view of the breadth of s.1(2)(a) turned out to have been optimistic indeed as the courts adopted an extraordinarily narrow approach to the provision from the start. In *Eaton Ltd v Nuttall*, EAT overturned a tribunal decision in favour of a woman production scheduler who, being responsible for ordering 2,400 units per week of a value up to £2.50, received 85 per cent of the salary of a male production scheduler who was responsible for ordering 1,200 units per week of a value ranging between £5 and £1,000. The employers argued that the woman's work involved a lower degree of responsibility than that of the man, an argument rejected by a tribunal on the grounds that both performed the same function with the same degree of competence.

Eaton Ltd v Nuttall [1977] ICR 272

Phillips J:

Several decisions of the appeal tribunal have said that in applying s 1(4) of the Act [like work] the most important point to consider is what the woman does and what the man does, but we do not think that it is right to disregard the circumstances in which they do it . . . Thus in *Waddington v Leicester Council for Voluntary Service* [[1977] 1 WLR 544], when considering s.1(4), we said that it was wrong to ignore the responsibility for supervision taken by the woman and not by the man albeit that in the circumstances of that case it was difficult to pin-point particular acts done in performance of the duty to supervise. In

---

[50] See also *Matthews v Kent & Medway Towns Fire Authority* [2004] ICR 257 in which EAT declared, *obiter*, that an employment tribunal had correctly insisted on comparing each individual term enjoyed by part-time and full-time firefighters for the purposes of a claim under the Part-time Workers Regulations, see below. The Court of Appeal ([2005] ICR 84) did not comment on this appropriate method of comparison.

earlier cases we have tried to discourage industrial tribunals from applying s.1(4) too narrowly, and this we strongly endorse; and we should expect them to act in that way when considering such matters as responsibility. Nonetheless this is a job aspect highly regarded by all groups of employers and employees alike, and we would think it not only unacceptable, but also wrong, to ignore it as a factor properly to be taken into account ... For example, suppose two bookkeepers working side by side doing, so far as actions were concerned, almost identical work, where on an examination of the importance of the work done it could be seen that one was a senior bookkeeper and another a junior bookkeeper. Such distinctions between two employees are often easy to spot in practice but difficult to distinguish only in the terms of what each of them does. That is the sort of case where we think that the existence of the factor of responsibility might be crucial.

EAT's decision might appear reasonable. But its effect was to preclude consideration of the fact that the only other female production scheduler in employment, who was paid the same rate as the claimant, had replaced a man who had been paid on the same (higher) rate as that paid to the only male production scheduler whose rate of pay was known. It is also worth noting that the decision in *Waddington*, to which Mr Justice Phillips referred, was to the effect that, a woman being paid less than a man in respect of a job which was determined to be *more* responsible than his, she could not claim equal pay under s.1(4).

In *Capper Pass Ltd v Lawton* [1977] QB 852 EAT adopted a broad approach to s.1(3), ruling that no account should be taken, in determining the question of 'like work,' of 'trivial differences or differences not likely in the real world to be reflected in the terms and conditions of employment.' And in *Shields v Coomes* the Court of Appeal approved of this approach. The claimant, who worked in a betting shop, was paid less than her male colleague who, in addition to those duties he shared with her, was required to work longer hours, to open the shop, and to carry cash to and from it. The employers, who usually staffed their shop with women, had a policy of employing one man in each of their shops which they considered to be in 'rough' areas. The employers took the view that these men, who were all paid at the higher rate, functioned 'as a cover or precaution against illegal entry.'

A tribunal took the view that the man's security and cash-carrying duties constituted a difference 'of practical importance in relation to terms and conditions of employment' so as to defeat a s.1(4) claim. EAT disagreed, a ruling upheld by the Court of Appeal.

Shields v E Coomes (Holdings) Ltd [1978] ICR 1159

Lord Denning MR:

When a woman claims equal pay with a man in the same employment, she has first to show that she is employed on 'like work' with him ... her work and that of the men must be 'of the same or a broadly similar nature.' Instances of the 'same nature' are men and women bank cashiers at the same counter; or men and women serving meals in the same restaurant. Instances of a 'broadly similar nature' are men and women shop assistants in different sections of the same department store; or a woman cook who prepares lunches for the directors and the men chefs who cook breakfast, lunch and teas for the employees in the canteen: see *Capper Pass Ltd v Lawton*. ...

Second, there must be an enquiry in to (i) the 'differences ... between the things [that the woman] does and the things [that the men do],' and (ii) a comparison of them so as to see 'the nature and extent of the differences' and 'the frequency or otherwise with which such differences occur in practice' and (iii) a decision as to whether these differences are or are not 'of practical importance in regard to terms and conditions of employment.'

This involves a comparison of the two jobs, the woman's job and the man's job, and making an evaluation of each job as a job irrespective of the sex of the worker and of any special personal skill or merit that he or she may have. This evaluation should be made in terms of the 'rate for the job,' usually a payment of so much per hour. The rate should represent the value of each job in terms of the demand made on a worker under such headings as effort, skill, responsibility and decision. If the value of the man's job is worth more than the value of the woman's job, it is legitimate that the man should receive a higher 'rate for the job' than the woman. For instance, a man who is dealing with production schedules may deal with far more important items than the woman, entailing far more serious consequences from a wrong decision. So his job should be rated higher than hers: see *Eaton Ltd v Nuttall*. But, if the value of the woman's job is equal to the man's job, each should receive the same rate for the job. This principle of 'equal value' is so important that you should ignore differences between the two jobs which are 'not of practical importance.' The employer should not be able to avoid the principle by introducing comparatively small differences in 'job content' between men and women; nor by giving the work a different 'job description' . . .

Nor should the employer be able to avoid the principle of 'equal value' by having the work (at the same job) done by night or for longer hours. The only legitimate way of dealing with night work or for longer hours is by paying a night shift premium or overtime rate assessed at a reasonable figure . . .

In this case the woman and the man were employed on work of a broadly similar nature. They were both counterhands. There were several differences between the things she did and the things which he did. For instance, he started at opening time and worked longer hours; but this did not, by itself, warrant a difference in the 'rate for the job.' He carried cash from shop to shop or to head office. But this difference was, by itself, 'not of practical importance.' The one difference of any significance between them was that the man filled a protective role. He was a watchdog ready to bark and scare off intruders. This difference, when taken with the others, amounted to differences which the majority of the industrial tribunal found were 'real and existing and of practical importance.' Accepting this finding, I do not think these differences could or did affect the 'rate for the job.' Both the woman and the man worked alongside one another hour after hour, doing precisely the same work. She should, therefore, receive the same hourly rate as he. It is rather like the difference between a barman and a barmaid. They do the same work as one another in serving drinks. Each has his or her own way of dealing with awkward customers. Each is subject to the same risk of abuse or unpleasantness. But, whichever way each adopts in dealing with awkward customers, the job of each, as a job, is of equivalent rating. Each should, therefore, receive the same 'rate for the job.' It comes within s 1(4) as 'like work.'

It would be otherwise if the difference was based on any special personal qualification that he had; as, for instance, if he was a fierce and formidable figure, trained to tackle intruders, then there might be a variation such as to warrant a 'wage differential' under s.1(3). But no such special personal qualification is suggested. The only difference between the two jobs is on the ground of sex. He may have been a small nervous man, who could not say boo to a goose. She may have been as fierce and formidable as a battle-axe. Such differences, whatever they were, did not have any relation to the terms and conditions of employment. They did not affect the 'rate for the job.'

I confess, however, that I have felt great difficulty in overcoming the finding of the industrial tribunal that the differences, especially the protective role of the man, were 'real and existing and of practical importance.' I thought for some time that this protective role should be rewarded by some additional bonus or premium. But my difficulties on this score have been resolved by giving supremacy to Community law. Under that law it is imperative that 'pay for work at time rates shall be the same for the same job'; and that 'all discrimination on the ground of sex shall be eliminated with regard to all aspects and conditions of remuneration.' The differences found by the majority of the industrial tribunal are all based on sex. They are because he is a man. He only gets the higher hourly rate because he is a man. In order to eliminate all discrimination, there should be an equality clause written into the woman's contract . . .

With the advent of the equal value pay claim in 1984, the significance of the 'like work' claim and, in particular, of the narrow approach generally taken to it, was reduced. The type of claim which Lord Denning had, in *Shields v Coomes*, thought should be accommodated within a stretched s.1(2)(a) in order to give effect to Article 141's 'equal pay for work of equal value' could, after that date, be dealt with instead under s.1(2)(c). And, whereas in *Waddington*, 'added value' in the woman's job served to block a s.1(2)(a) claim, it is not conceivable today that an equal value claim would be denied on the ground that the woman's work was more valuable than that done by the man.[51] Equal value claims are further considered below. It is worth noting here, however, the decision of the ECJ in *Angestelltenbetriebsrat der Wiener Gebietskrankenkasse v Wiener Gebietskrankenkasse,* Case C–309/97 [1999] ECR I–02865 in which that Court ruled that psychotherapists engaged in the same work were not to be regarded as being employed in 'the same work' for the purposes of Article 141 where they were differently qualified (the comparators, but not the claimants, having medical degrees). The decision is questionable and Lord Nicholls, who was invited to apply it in *Glasgow v Marshall*, showed little enthusiasm for it. That case is considered further below but, briefly, it was argued before the House of Lords that the claimant instructors and their teacher comparators, although engaged in very similar work, ought not to be regarded as doing 'like work' for the purposes of the EqPA because, as in the *Wiener* case, their qualifications were different. Lord Nicholls declined to reopen the issue of comparability, ruling that the decision 'must, of course, be read in the context of the facts under consideration [and] will be better explored in a case where the fact-finding tribunal have these particular issues before them when making their findings on the 'like-work' issue.'

Work Rated as Equivalent

Section 1(2)(b) allowed comparisons between the wages of women and those of men, working in the same employment, whose jobs had been rated as equivalent by a job evaluation scheme (JES). Had such schemes been designed to 'capture' the undervaluation of women's work, and had employees and/or trade unions been able to force job evaluation on employers. Section 1(2)(b) might have been a significant tool in the battle against unequal pay. But job evaluation schemes are, for the most part, designed to justify existing wage hierarchies, rather than to subvert them. And the EqPA's five-year phase-in period gave employers ample time, if their schemes had indicated the underpayment of female jobs, to change the schemes or to change the content of male and female jobs therein so as to render them 'unequal.' Further, the question whether or not to conduct a JES was one for the employer alone.

The EqPA did allow for challenge to blatantly discriminatory job evaluation schemes, s.1(5) providing that:

---

[51] *Murphy v Bord Telecom Eireann* Case C–157/86 [1988] ECR 0673.

A woman is to be regarded as employed on work rated as equivalent with that of any men if . . . her job and their job . . . would have been given an equal value but for the evaluation being made on a system setting different values for men and women on the same demand under any heading;

In order to qualify as a JES for the purposes of s.1(2)(b), the scheme had to satisfy s.1(5)'s requirement that it evaluate jobs 'in terms of the demand made on a worker under various headings (for instance effort, skill, decision).' In *Eaton Ltd v Nuttall*, EAT declared that, in order to found a claim under the scheme must be:

thorough in analysis and capable of impartial application. It should be possible by apply-ing the study to arrive at the position of a particular employee at a particular point in a par-ticular salary grade without taking other matters into account except those unconnected with the nature of the work. It will be in order to take into account such matters as merit or seniority etc, but any matters concerning the work (eg responsibility) one would expect to find taken care of in the evaluation study. One which does not satisfy that test, and requires the management to make a subjective judgment concerning the nature of the work before the employee can be fitted into the appropriate place in the appropriate salary grade, would seem to us not to be a valid study for the purpose of s 1(5).[52]

In *Springboard Sunderland Trust v Robson* [1992] ICR 554 a question arose as to whether the claimant's job and that of her comparator had, as a matter of fact, been rated as equiv-alent under the scheme in question. The claimant's job had been awarded 410 points and that of her comparator 429 points on a scheme which placed jobs rated between 360 and 409 points on grade 3, and those rated 410 to 449 points on grade 4. The employers did not pay the claimant a grade 4 salary and, in response to her s.1(2)(b) claim, argued that s.1(2)(b) assisted only those claimants whose jobs had been awarded precisely equal point scores on a job evaluation scheme, rather than those whose point scores placed them within the same grade as that of their comparators. Both the tribunal and EAT ruled in the claimant's favour.[53]

Work of Equal Value

We saw, above, that the gender-pay gap is associated with occupational sex segregation. If a woman has to prove that she is doing the same job as a man in order to be entitled to receive the same pay, that part of the gender-pay gap which results from this type of segregation goes unchallenged. Under the EqPA as it was first enacted, this aspect of the pay gap could be challenged only through the collective mechanism (discussed above), or in cases in which 'female' jobs had been acknowledged by the employer to be equivalent in value to higher paid 'male' jobs. The establishment in 1984 of the 'equal pay for work of equal value claim' opened the possibility of real challenge to this part of the pay gap.

---

[52] At 74, *per* Phillips J. This approach was approved by the Court of Appeal in *Bromley v Quick*, below.
[53] In *Dibro Ltd v Hore and others* [1990] ICR 370, EAT ruled that an industrial tribunal had erred in refus-ing to accept, as a defence to an equal value claim, the results of a job evaluation scheme carried out after the claimants' equal value claims had been made. See however *Avon County Council v Foxall* [1989] ICR 407 (EAT)—a tribunal did not err in refusing to stay equal value cases pending the outcome of an employer's subsequently implemented JES. For a recent example of a work rated as equivalent claim see *Diageo plc v Thomson* (29 April 2004, ET) reported in 131 *Equal Opportunity Review*.

D Pannick, *Sex Discrimination Law* (Oxford, OUP, 1985) 102

Equal pay for work of equal value is an essential element of anti-discrimination law in a society in which occupational segregation of men and women persists. The anthropologist Margaret Mead explained that all societies tend to undervalue work done by women:

> Men may cook or weave or dress dolls or hunt humming-birds, but if such activities are appropriate occupations of men, then the whole society, men and women alike, votes them as important. When the same occupations are performed by women, they are regarded as less important.

In *Pickstone v Freemans plc* [1988] 1 AC 66 the House of Lords confirmed that equal value claims could be brought notwithstanding the presence of a man in the same job as the claimant (or one which has been rated as equivalent). According to Lord Keith, the alternative: 'would leave a large gap in the equal pay provision, enabling an employer to evade it by employing one token man on the same work as a group of potential women claimants who were deliberately paid less than a group of men employed on work of equal value with that of the women. This would mean that the United Kingdom had failed yet again fully to implement its obligations under art [141] of the Treaty and the Equal Pay Directive.'[54]

One interesting result of the decision in *Pickstone* was seen in *Milligan v South Ayrshire Council* [2003] IRLR 153. In *South Ayrshire Council v Morton* [2002] IRLR 256, further considered below, the Court of Session had held that a female primary school headteacher employed by South Ayrshire Council could claim equal pay with a male secondary school headteacher working for Highland Council. This decision is considered further below. But in Applicant in *Milligan* was a male primary school teacher who wished to use as his comparator a female primary school headteacher whose wages would, as a result of the *Morton* litigation, be increased to match those of a male secondary school teacher (all such teachers were male so the applicant in *Milligan* could not use this direct method of comparison for the pourposes of an equal pay claim). The Court of Session permitted Mr Milligan to make a 'contingent' claim and, further, to have this claim stayed until the resolution of his comparator's equal pay claim. The Court took the view that the applicant would suffer 'real prejudice in relation to back pay' if he was required to await the outcome of his comparator's pay claim prior to launching his claim (see further Chapter 5 for the limits on back-dating in equal pay claims).

In cases of like work and work rated as equivalent, the task of deciding whether the claimant has established her case (subject to the employer's defence) is a fairly straightforward one. In equal value claims, on the other hand, a tribunal has to consider the relative value of the woman's job and that of her male comparator in terms of (s.1(3)) 'the demands made on her (under such headings as effort, skill and decision)'.

---

[54] Lord Keith's particular reasons for taking into account parliamentary statements: 'The draft regulations of 1983 were presented to Parliament as giving full effect to the decision in question. The draft regulations were not subject to the parliamentary process of consideration and amendment in committee, as a Bill would have been. In these circumstances and in the context of s.2 of the European Communities Act 1972, I consider it to be entirely legitimate for the purpose of ascertaining the intention of Parliament to take into account the terms in which the draft was presented by the responsible minister and which formed the basis of its acceptance.'

The EqPA, having made provision for the dismissal of 'hopeless' cases (see below), provided for the appointment of 'independent experts' to advise tribunals on the issue of value. These experts, appointed by the tribunal at a preliminary hearing,[55] would go to the relevant workplace and draw up a report and a recommendation on the relative value of the claimant's job and that (those) of her comparator(s). Until 1996, a tribunal was not entitled to determine the issue of value in favour of the equal pay claimant until it had received the report of the independent expert. The tribunal did not have to agree with the recommendation of the expert (although in general tribunals did).

The Sex Discrimination and Equal Pay (Miscellaneous Amendments) Regulations 1996 amended the EqPA to permit tribunals to determine the question of value without the report of an independent expert. More recently, the Employment Tribunals (Constitution and Rules of Procedure) (Amendment) Regulations 2004, which became law in October 2004, amend the Employment Tribunals (Constitution and Rules of Procedure) Regulations 2004[56] in relation to equal pay claims by providing power to appoint tribunal panels with specialist knowledge of equal value cases, by making procedures more 'user friendly,' by imposing time limits and other procedural steps designed to improve case management and by encouraging the early exchange of information between the parties. Limits will be imposed on the use of experts by the parties. The Annex to the Regulations suggests that equal value claims not involving independent experts should take 25 weeks to determine, those involving independent experts no more than 37 weeks.

The normal procedure for equal value claims has altered very recently as a result of the 2004 amending regulations. Under the new regime a tribunal has to hold an initial hearing to determine whether the claimant's job and that of her comparator have been rated as unequal by a job evaluation scheme and, if so, whether there are reasonable grounds for determining that the scheme can be shown to be discriminatory on grounds of sex or otherwise unsuitable. Assuming the claim is not blocked by a valid JES, the tribunal has to decide whether to appoint an independent expert or to determine the question of value itself. The residual 'no reasonable grounds' provision, under which a tribunal could dismiss a claim without determining the question of value where there were 'no reasonable grounds for determining that the work is of equal value' was removed by the Equal Pay Act 1970 (Amendment) Regulations 2004.[57] If the tribunal decides to appoint an expert the second hearing will deal with that expert's report and those of any other experts the tribunal permits. Strict time limits are imposed. The final hearing (whether or not an independent expert is appointed) will consider whether the jobs are of equal value and whether a GMF defence applies, and determine any remedy.

There have been very few appellate decisions on s.2A(2). The provision was criticised in 1985 on the grounds that the low burden of proof imposed upon the claimant who wishes to challenge an existing job evaluation scheme is 'from a personnel and industrial relations standpoint . . . patently absurd' and that the provision would permit challenge to job evaluation schemes which did not discriminate on grounds of sex.[58] But in the few reported cases in which s.2A(2) has featured, the courts have allowed job evaluation schemes of very dubious merit to block equal value claims.

EAT's decision in *Eaton v Nutall* was mentioned above. In it, that tribunal ruled that an equal pay claim could not succeed under s.1(2)(b) unless the job evaluation scheme on the

---

[55] From an ACAS list.
[56] Respectively SI 2004 No. 2351 and SI 2004 No. 1861.
[57] SI 2004 No. 2352.
[58] M Rubenstein, 'Discriminatory Job Evaluation and the Law' (1985–86) 7 *Comparative Labour Law* 172, 178.

basis of which it was made was 'analytical, in the sense of being 'thorough in analysis and capable of impartial application'. On the one hand, this restriction might be thought unnecessary—if an employer accepts that a man's job and a woman's job are of equivalent value, s/he should perhaps be estopped from deciding to pay the man more unless a s.1(3) defence operates. But, EAT having decided in *Eaton* to restrict job evaluation schemes under s.1(2)(b) and s.1(5) to those which were 'analytical', it would seem obvious that the same restriction should apply to s.2A(2) which refers, after all, to 'a study such as is mentioned in section 1(5) above.'[59] In *Bromley v Quick* [1987] ICR 47, however, EAT characterised as a 'gloss upon the words' of s.1(5) the suggestion that only an analytical scheme could block an equal value claim. The job evaluation scheme at issue in the case had ranked 'benchmark' jobs by comparing them on the basis of a number of factors. These jobs were then re-ranked on a 'felt fair' basis before the remaining jobs (the demands made by which had never been scrutinised in accordance with the chosen factors) were slotted into the established hierarchy. The claimant's job, together with those of her comparators, had been among these unscrutinised jobs, their places in the hierarchy had been determined without benefit even of full job descriptions.

The Court of Appeal overturned EAT's decision, citing the decision of the European Court in *Rummler v Dato Druck GmbH* Case C–237/85 [1986] ECR 2101 in support of its conclusion that, while the evaluation of jobs entailed a degree of subjective judgment:

Bromley v H & J Quick Ltd [1988] ICR 623

. . . the consideration of any job, and of the qualities required to perform that job, under a job evaluation study must be objective [to the extent that this was possible. S.1(5) required, therefore] . . . a study undertaken with a view to evaluating jobs in terms of the demand made on a worker under various headings (for instance effort, skill, decision). To apply that to s.2A(2)(a) it is necessary, in my judgment, that both the work of the woman who had made application to the Industrial Tribunal and the work of the man who is her chosen comparator should have been valued in such terms of demand made on the worker under various headings . . . the word 'analytical' . . . is not a gloss, but indicates conveniently the general nature of what is required by the section, viz that the jobs of each worker covered by the study must have been valued in terms of the demand made on the worker under various headings. The original application of s.1(5) to women within subheading (b) in s.1(2) of the Act (women employed on work rated equivalent to that of a man) necessarily required that the woman's work and the man's should each have been valued in terms of the demand made on the worker under appropriate headings; the wording of s.2A(2)(a), read with that of s.1(5), necessarily shows that the same applies to the present appellants who claim to be within subheading (c), and their male comparators. . . .

It is to be noted that the procedure which the respondent company has invoked under s.2A is a procedure which if successfully invoked would put, as the Industrial Tribunal held it did, a summary end to the appellants' applications without the otherwise mandatory reference of the questions raised by those applications to an independent expert under s.2A(1)(b). S.2A(2)(b) puts the onus on the employer to show that there are no reasonable grounds for determining that the evaluation contained in a job evaluation study such as is mentioned in s.1(5) was made on a system which discriminates on grounds of sex. If in the view of the Industrial Tribunal there are reasonable grounds for so determining, the Industrial Tribunal cannot summarily dismiss an application, but must refer the relevant question to an independent expert for report . . .

[59] See also *Neil v Ford Motor Co Ltd* [1984] IRLR 339.

In common with those who would seek equal pay for like work and for work rated as equivalent, those wishing to claim equal pay for work of equal value must first discover what comparable men earn. This may not pose insuperable problems in a unionised workplace. But in many non-unionised workplaces, employees are not in a position readily to find out what others earn. Not until 2003 was a questionnaire procedure provided under the EqPA (see further Chapter 5). It is too early to assess the impact of the equal pay questionnaire, although a report in the *Evening Standard* ('City faces flood of sex case tribunals,' 19 July 2004) suggested that the introduction of the questionnaire, coupled with the 43 per cent pay-gap in the City, a massive US pay-out that month by Morgan Stanley and a recent spate of high profile cases in which awards amounted to millions of pounds were paid, was likely to result in a large increase in equal pay challenges to the banking and related institutions. Whether or not this occurs, equal value claims remain subject to significant difficulties associated with assessing the relative value of jobs. Even if there were established criteria for assessing value, and claimants were able accurately to evaluate their own jobs, they would have enormous problems in determining the value of potential comparators' jobs. But there are no such criteria. And even if prospective claimants were in possession of all possible information relating to their own jobs and those of their comparators, there is simply no way of knowing how the relative value of those jobs will be assessed.

Anne-Marie Plummer's 1991 study of independent experts' reports found 'remarkably little consistency' in the approach taken to the assessment of value,[60] the reports studied (40 per cent of those commissioned by that year) showing great variety in the choice of factors analysed, methods of scoring, weighting of factors and interpretation of equal value. The question whether or not a claimant's job was regarded as of equal value to that of her comparator turned, to a large extent, on the method of evaluation. Yet there was no consensus between 'experts' on the methodology. A potential claimant may be able to decide, with a fair degree of certainty, that her job is the same as that done by a man. She may also be able to make an informed decision that her job and that of a man have been rated as equivalent by her employer. But she simply cannot know whether or not her job will be regarded as 'equal' to that done by a male comparator. This being the case, the only reasonable chances of success in equal pay for work of equal value cases lie with women who select as their comparators men who are paid more for jobs which are apparently much less demanding, and with women whose pay claims are organised (as in the *Enderby*, *Ratcliffe*, and *British Coal* cases, all discussed below) by well informed and well financed unions committed to improving the wages of their women members.

A prudent claimant would, if only one comparator were permitted, use one whose job seemed self-evidently less valuable than hers, in order to maximise the chances of a favourable decision on this issue. But such a comparator would probably be less well paid than one whose job was closer in 'value' to that performed by the claimant. It might be thought that the claimant should name a range of comparators. But this tactic was not approved of by the House of Lords in *Leverton*. According to Lord Bridge, with whom the other Lords agreed:

---

[60] A Plummer, 'Equal Value Judgements: Objective Assessment or Lottery?' Industrial Research Unit, School of Business Studies, University of Warwick.

I think that industrial tribunals should, so far as possible, be alert to prevent abuse of the equal value claims procedure by applicants who cast their net over too wide a spread of comparators. To take an extreme case, an applicant who claimed equality with A who earns £X and also with B who earns £2X could hardly complain if an industrial tribunal concluded that her claim of equality with A itself demonstrated that there were no reasonable grounds for her claim of equality with B.

Cross-establishment comparisons

It is clear from the foregoing that the equal value claim is not an easy one to bring. Having said this, the EqPA is capable—at least in theory—of permitting challenge to that part of the gender-pay gap which results from occupational sex segregation (this through the equal value pay claim). We have seen some of the problems associated with that claim—complexity, delay, etc. But it is possible to imagine that, properly revised, the equal pay for work of equal value claim could prove effective in tackling this aspect of the gender-pay gap. But part of the gender-pay gap is associated with women's industrial and workplace segregation—that is, their concentration in predominantly female workplaces. This, by contrast, is largely outwith the scope of the EqPA which applies only in relation to differentials between men and women employed essentially by the same employer. Under the EqPA, the successful claimant's comparator must (as we saw above) be engaged in 'like work,' 'work rated as equivalent' or 'work of equal value' to that done by the equal pay claimant. He must also be 'in the same employment' as her. Section 1(6) EqPA defines, as being in 'the same employment' as an equal pay claimant, a person who is employed 'by the same or any associated employer at the same establishment or at establishments in Great Britain which include that one and at which common terms and conditions of employment are observed either generally or for employees of the relevant classes.' We shall see, below, that the House of Lords has adopted a reasonably generous approach to the question whether 'common terms and conditions' apply between establishments. But the 'same or any associated employer' has proven much more restrictive of equal pay claims.

The 'common terms and conditions' provision was first explored in *Leverton v Clwyd County Council* which culminated with the House of Lord's decision extracted below. Ms Leverton was a nursery nurse. Her comparators occupied a variety of posts the terms of which were, like hers, determined by a collective agreement covering local authority administrative, professional, technical and clerical staff. All were employed by Clwyd County Council, but they worked in a variety of establishments. In response to her claim her employers argued that she was not in the 'same employment' as her comparators. This argument failed at tribunal but won favour with the Court of Appeal which ruled, somewhat bizarrely ([1988] IRLR 239), that s.1(6) assisted only those claimants who were employed on the same terms and conditions as their comparators. (Such women would, of course, have little need of an equal pay claim.) The House of Lords allowed her appeal, ruling ([1989] 1 AC 706, *per* Lord Bridge) that 'Terms and conditions of employment governed by the same collective agreement . . . represent the paradigm, though not necessarily the only example, of the common terms and conditions of employment contemplated by the subsection.' His Lordship went on to declare his rejection of a construction of s.1(6) which 'frustrates rather than serves the manifest purpose of the legislation. . . . it cannot, in my opinion, possibly have been the intention of Parliament to require a woman claiming equality with a man in another establishment to prove an undefined substratum of similarity between the particular terms of her contract and his as the basis of her entitlement to eliminate any discriminatory differences between those terms.'

Notwithstanding the strong terms adopted by the House of Lords in *Leverton* the Court of Appeal once again adopted a very narrow approach to s.1(6) in *British Coal Corp v Smith & Ors*, [1994] ICR 810, requiring that the woman and her comparator(s) were employed in establishments in which the prevailing terms and conditions were, not merely 'broadly similar' or 'essentially similar' but were (exactly) 'the same.' The House of Lords ([1996] ICR 515) once again overruled, adopting a purposive approach and characterised the Court of Appeal's demand for identical terms and conditions as 'far too restrictive' (*per* Lord Slynn).

Cross-employer comparisons

Subsection 1(6) EqPA clearly allows cross-establishment comparisons. But comparators must be employed by the same employer as the claimant, or by an 'associated employer.' An employer is only 'associated' for the purposes of the EqPA if (s.1(6)(c)) where 'one [employer] is a company of which the other (directly or indirectly) has control or if both are companies of which a third person (directly or indirectly) has control.'

The narrow scope of the equal pay claim under the EqPA has been the subject of adverse comment. One particular area where problems arise is in the contracting-out context. The term 'contracting-out' refers to the 'hiving-off' of discrete functions from the central employer to contractors. In the public sector, as we saw in Chapter 5, this has been driven until very recently by 'compulsory competitive tendering' (CCT), local authorities being required to put cleaning, waste disposal, catering and other functions out to tender at regular intervals, and being allowed to retain these functions only where they were won, in competition, by separately administered Direct Services Organisations (DSOs). These DSOs had to be financially separate from the local authority and run as commercial enterprises.

CCT brought huge deterioration in the terms and conditions of the workers, in particular the women workers, affected by it. Part of that deterioration resulted from the failure of the Transfer of Undertakings Regulations 1981 adequately to give effect to the Acquired Rights Directive—the Regulations originally excluded 'non commercial' undertakings, such as most public authority functions, from their protection. The consequence of this was that most contractors competing for public functions did so on the basis of radically reduced labour costs. In many cases low paid workers were brought into the authority from outside. In others, workers were made redundant and re-employed by the private contractors at reduced wages. The reduced working conditions were felt particularly by women workers whose wages had been protected by collective bargaining in the public sector, and had been pegged considerably higher (often as a result of job evaluation) than the rates prevalent in the private sector.

Even where workers managed to retain their jobs, they did so frequently because DSOs, in preparing 'in house' bids, slashed labour costs in order to compete with the market. One example of this resulted in *Ratcliffe v North Yorkshire County Council*, the House of Lords decision which is discussed at some length below. For our current purposes the point of interest is that, whereas the 'dinner ladies' DSO had to reduce labour costs by 25 per cent in order to compete with outside tenders, the DSOs employing their comparators did not. According to the tribunal:

> It was clear to [the DSO manager] that he had to have regard to the market forces and, in particular, that because of low pay in the catering industry in general, and particularly in those areas where women were exclusively employed, he could not afford to continue to engage staff on [National Joint Council] terms, conditions and pay . . .

[the DSO manager] . . . perceived that it was necessary to [reduce those terms from the NJC terms] in order to be able to compete in the open market, that is to say due to his perception of market forces in a market which is virtually exclusively female doing work which is convenient to that female workforce and which, but for the particular hours and times of work, that workforce would not be able to do . . . It was clear to [him] that it was a workforce that would, by and large, continue to do the work, even at a reduced rate of pay, when the alternative was no work or ceasing to have the advantages of remaining a county council employee and becoming an employee of a commercial catering organisation doing the same work for less favourable terms in any event.

It is clear that both the DSO and the employees were over the proverbial 'barrel' due to the fact that competitors only employed women and, because of that, employed them on less favourable terms than the council did previously under the NJC agreement.

In *Ratcliffe*, as we shall see below, the women eventually won their equal pay claim. (Prior to the CCT exercise, their jobs had been rated as equivalent in value to those done by their comparators.) The issue of the employer's defence, with which that case was primarily concerned, is discussed below. But their claim succeeded only because they were, in fact, employed by the DSO which, like their comparators' DSO, was still part of the local authority. By contrast, women whose terms and conditions suffered when their jobs were contracted out (as many were), would be able to use, as comparators, only those men employed by the same contractor. This would remain the case even (see *Lawrence v Regent Office Care*, below) where they continued to do precisely the same job in the same workplace as their former colleagues, with whose jobs theirs had (prior to contracting-out) been rated as equivalent.

The TUPE Regulations were amended in 1995 to give effect to the fact that 'non-commercial' undertakings are included within the Acquired Rights Directive, to which the Regulations were supposed to give effect. Even where workers are transferred on the same terms and conditions, however, there is nothing to prevent those terms and conditions from falling behind those which apply in respect of former comparators' jobs which have remained in the public sector. Nor have DSOs been able to ignore this potential for private-sector cost cutting in determining their own pay and conditions. CCT, as such, is now at an end. But local authorities and other public bodies remain obliged to achieve 'Best Value' in all their services (see further Chapter 5). The formal requirement to tender at particular intervals has been replaced with a rolling obligation to assess whether services could be better performed other than by the authority itself. It is probable that women workers will continue to shoulder the burden of cost-cutting.

It is clear that the EqPA does not permit cross-employer comparisons save between 'associated employers' this concept being very narrowly defined. But it was not clear that Article 141 adopts so narrow an approach. In *Defrenne (No.2)* Case C–43/75 [1976] ECR 455 the ECJ ruled that Article 141 requires equal pay 'for equal work which is carried out in the same establishment or service, whether private or public.' In *Scullard v Knowles*, EAT accepted that the approach required under Article 141 was wider than that set out under the EqPA.[61] There, a unit manager employed by a Regional Advisory Council sought to name, as her comparators, male unit managers employed by other such bodies, all of which were independent and of the Secretary of State for Employment, but funded by the Department of Employment.

---

[61] See also *Hasley v Fair Employment Agency* [1989] IRLR 106 (NICA).

Scullard v Knowles & Southern Regional Council for Education & Training [1996] ICR 399

Mummery J:

. . . s 1(6) . . . excludes, for example, employees of different employers who, though not companies, are all under the direct or indirect control of a third party and have common terms and conditions of employment. The crucial point is that the class of comparators defined in s.1(6) is more restricted than that available on the application of Article [141], as interpreted by the European Court of Justice. Article [141] is not, for example, confined to employment in undertakings which have a particular legal form, such as a limited company
. . .

In *Defrenne* no distinction is drawn between work carried out in the same establishment or service of limited companies and of other employers, whether incorporated or not . . .

The crucial question for the purposes of Article [141] is, therefore, whether Mrs Scullard and the male unit managers of the other councils were employed 'in the same establishment or service.' The tribunal did not ask or answer that question. To the extent that that is a wider class of comparators than is contained in s 1(6) of the [EqPA], s 1(6), which is confined to 'associated employers,' is displaced and must yield to the paramount force of Article [141] . . .

Scullard went some way towards addressing the shortcomings of s.1(6). But the gaping hole in the protection offered by the EqPA was exposed by EAT in *Lawrence v Regent Office Care*. The case was brought by 'dinner ladies' who had, like the claimants in *Ratcliffe*, been employed by North Yorkshire County Council. During the course of the *Ratcliffe* litigation the county council lost some tenders for school meal provision to the private sector. The women in the Lawrence case were among those whose jobs were transferred into the private sector. Some were transferred on the understanding that TUPE applied, others on the assumption that it did not. Nevertheless (and this is testament to the ineffective nature of TUPE), all women ended up working on less favourable terms and conditions than had applied during their employment by the council. They sought to rely on Article 141 to compare themselves with men still employed by the council whose jobs had, pre-contracting out, been rated as equivalent to those of the claimants. Their claims were dismissed both by the tribunal and by EAT.

Lawrence v Regent Office Care Ltd [1999] ICR 654

Morison J:

. . . are the rights conferred by Article [141] wide enough to permit an employee of company A to make a comparison with the work done by an employee of company B, and claim unlawful discrimination? The appellants say that either the answer to that question is 'yes' or alternatively we should refer it to the European Court of Justice for them to give guidance
. . .

[For the respondents] Mr Elias makes the valid point that an employer not only has to prove that the factors which he alleges have caused the disparity were genuine but also 'causally relevant' to the disparity in pay complained of. It would be difficult, if not impossible, for an employer to run a justification defence if he was not the employer of the comparator because he would not know precisely what the factors were that gave rise to the pay of that person. Furthermore, it would be difficult to understand how the applicant's employer could say that any factor was causally connected to the disparity when their pay was most likely determined quite independently of one another, and in ignorance of the differential . . .

There are two general principles of note from the authorities:

(1) The purpose of Article [141], like s 1 of the Equal Pay Act, is not to achieve fair wages but to eliminate discrimination on grounds of sex.

(2) Whilst it is the policy of Article [141] eventually to eliminate all such discrimination across industries (for example, catering and cleaning have traditionally been regarded as 'women's work' and probably thereby been poorly paid), a radical assault across industries will require further agreement between Member States, and detailed in domestic laws (see paragraph 19 of the judgment in *Defrenne*). The precise ambit of the Article, as it stands and without further agreement or direction, is not precisely defined. Case law of the Court will assist on a case-by-case basis. Technical limitations, such as the dates when the comparator and applicant were employed, will not be allowed to defeat the application of the Article. But there must be a line to be drawn somewhere, as the ECJ recognised in the *Defrenne* case, as we read it.

The ECJ [in *Defrenne*] distinguished between 'individual undertakings' on the one hand and 'entire branches of industry' and even of the economic system as a whole' on the other. We agree with Mr Elias that a feature of this distinction is that in the one case there is a single employer and in the other a multiplicity of employers, but that may not be the only distinction. Sometimes the identity of the employer is different from the entity which controls the work and fixes the pay, for example, where a person's services are 'assigned' to subsidiary companies within a group, but where the parent is formally the employer. In such a case the subsidiaries would clearly be associated and fall within s 1(6). But what if the employers were different, such as the Northern Ireland EOC and FEA [referring to the facts in *Hasley*. Not in every case where Article [141] applies will the same entity be employer of both applicant and comparator, nor will they necessarily be associated employers within the meaning of the section. But it does not follow that the Article applies whenever the employers are unconnected other than by the nature of the industry to which they belong. There must be something other than common identity or direct association which provides the boundary line.

. . . the ECJ ha[s] not confined the principle of Article [141] to 'work carried out in the same establishment or service' as the words 'even more' and 'at least' in paragraphs 22 and 24 of the judgment in *Defrenne* make clear. It seems to us that, absent any further agreement between Member States or a Directive, we cannot say more precisely where the boundary line lies save that the applicant and comparator must be 'in a loose and non-technical sense in the same establishment or service.' By 'loose and non-technical sense,' we mean to embrace within the definition such cases as *Hasley* and *Scullard* and any other similar cases.

It follows, therefore, that we reject Mr Langstaff's argument [for the applicants] that Article [141] is to be given a much wider range of application. Such a construction would be likely to create a substantial economic effect of the sort which, no doubt, the Court had in mind in the *Defrenne* case and which would need 'legislation.'

Further, without such legislation, a wide interpretation would deny the respondent any effective opportunity for a defence of justification. Again, no doubt, the ECJ had in mind the need for progressive implementation of any industry-wide application, with proper safeguards built in to accommodate some kind of a justification defence.

It seems to us that Mr Langstaff's submission that the line would be drawn naturally on the basis of what an applicant could prove was unrealistic. He cannot escape from the fact that there is nothing about this case which would distinguish it from any other case where an applicant claimed equal pay with a comparator employed by another company, not necessarily even engaged in the same industry.

The Court of Appeal ([2002] IRLR 822), referred to the ECJ the following questions:

'1. Is Article 141 directly applicable in the circumstances of this case . . . that it can be relied upon by the applicants in national proceedings to enable them to compare their pay with that of men in the employment of the North Yorkshire County Council who are performing work of equal value to that done by the applicants?
2. Can an applicant who seeks to place reliance on the direct effect of Article 141 do so only if the respondent employer is in a position where he is able to explain why the employer of the chosen comparator pays his employees as he does?'

Prior to the decision of the ECJ in *Lawrence* the Court of Sessions reached what was described in the IRLR commentary as a 'remarkable decision' in *South Ayrshire Council v Morton* [2002] IRLR 256. The claimant was a female headteacher who was employed by a local education authority in Scotland. The Court of Session ruled that she could choose as her comparator a male headteacher employed by a different Scottish education authority. According to the Court, the use by the ECJ in *Defrenne* of the term 'same establishment or service' was merely a description of specific examples of cases which fell within Article 141 and was not to be taken as requiring, for an Article 141 claim to be made out, that the claimant's comparator be in the same 'service.' In the instant case the Court took the view that pay was determined under statutory authority and overall governmental control, and that this amounted to the type of national collective agreement contemplated by the ECJ in *Defrenne (No.2)* when it ruled that:

among the forms of direct discrimination which may be identified solely by reference to the criteria laid down by Article [141] must be included in particular those which have their origin in legislative provisions or in collective labour agreements and which may be detected on the basis of a purely legal analysis of the situation.

Shortly after the decision of the Court of Sessions in *Morton* the ECJ delivered its judgment in *Lawrence*.

Lawrence v Regent Office Care Ltd Case C–320/00 [2002] ECR I–07325

There is . . . nothing in the wording of Article 141(1) EC to suggest that the applicability of that provision is limited to situations in which men and women work for the same employer. The Court has held that the principle established by that article may be invoked before national courts, in particular in cases of discrimination arising directly from legislative provisions or collective labour agreements, as well as in cases in which work is carried out in the same establishment or service, whether private or public . . .

However, where, as in the main proceedings here, the differences identified in the pay conditions of workers performing equal work or work of equal value cannot be attributed to a single source, there is no body which is responsible for the inequality and which could restore equal treatment. Such a situation does not come within the scope of Article 141(1) EC. The work and the pay of those workers cannot therefore be compared on the basis of that provision.

In view of all of the foregoing, the answer to the first question must be that a situation such as that in the main proceedings, in which the differences identified in the pay conditions of workers of different sex performing equal work or work of equal value cannot be attributed to a single source, does not come within the scope of Article 141(1) EC.

Regard being had to the answer to the first question, it is unnecessary to reply to the second question.

It is not clear that the decision of the Court of Sessions in *Morton* would have been any different had it been delivered after *Lawrence*. The salary scales of primary and secondary school teachers in Scotland were set at the relevant by the Scottish Joint Negotiating Committee which was a quasi-autonomous body set up by the Education (Scotland) Act under the general control of the Secretary of State. The Act provided that individual education authorities were obliged to implement the SJNC settlement and that its terms were incorporated into the every teacher's contract of employment. Each education authority had autonomy over the employment terms of its own employees and the way in which salary scales were implemented in relation to individual employees. But the Court of Sessions noted the tribunal's finding that 'in reality there is very little scope for individual local authorities to vary, either by increasing or decreasing, an individual teacher's salary. In effect, councils are regulated by what is known as the "Yellow Book" and any attempt to depart from the terms of that scheme of terms and conditions is likely to be subject to judicial review.'

The replacement of CCT by 'Best Value' has been mentioned above and is discussed in Chapter 5 in which a Code of Practice issued by the Government (the Two Tier Workforce Agreement) is considered. The Code obliges local authorities to enter into binding agreements with incoming contractors requiring the latter to guarantee the terms and conditions of transferring and subsequently employed workers. It remains to be seen whether this will be sufficient to bring contractors and local authorities within the *Lawrence* rubric so as to permit equal pay claims spanning both.

Hypothetical comparators

Article 141 requires the possibility of comparison beyond (although not very far beyond) the narrow confines of s.1(6) EqPA. What is unclear is whether it also requires that women (or, indeed, men) can challenge pay discrimination other than in the narrow circumstances provided for by s.1(2). In the first place, there is no provision for increasing women's wages where they are shown to be disproportionately underpaid by comparison with, for example, a man whose job is 120 per cent as valuable but whose wages are 150 per cent higher. Secondly (and the resolution of this would in large part also solve the first problem), the EqPA does not permit an equal pay claim based on a hypothetical comparator.

D Pannick, *Sex Discrimination Law* (Oxford, OUP, 1985) 96, footnotes omitted

Can a woman claim equal pay to that of a hypothetical male worker by showing that, if she were a man, she would be paid more by her employer? In *Macarthys* the ECJ suggested that a comparison with 'a hypothetical male worker' could not be made as it would be 'indirect and disguised discrimination, the identification of which' would require 'comparative studies of entire branches of industry.' Therefore, the direct application of Article [141] is 'confined to parallels which may be drawn on the basis of concrete appraisals of the work actually performed by employees of different sex within the same establishment or service.' The ECJ here seems to have confused two different concepts. It is understandable that Article [141] should not entitle a woman to compare her pay with that of a man in a different industry. But the practical difficulties there involved are not raised where the woman is able to prove that her employer would pay her more if she were male. The reference to the hypothetical male worker is merely one means of proving that she has been less favourably treated on the ground of her sex.

The notion of the hypothetical male comparison is central to the concept of discrimination in the Sex Discrimination Act 1975. Direct discrimination is there defined as treating the complainant, on the ground of her sex, less favourably than one treats, or would treat, a man. The absence of this express concept in the Equal Pay Act is one indication of its lack of sophistication. Since the 1970 and 1975 Acts form an interlocking code and since the mischief aimed at by the 1970 Act cannot be removed unless the statute prohibits an obvious form of sex discrimination, it may well be that the 1970 Act can be interpreted as covering this case. US courts have had similar difficulties as to whether the US Equal Pay Act 1963 entitles a woman to a remedy if she can prove that a hypothetical male employee would receive higher pay. In *County of Washington, Oregon v Gunther* [425 US 161 (1981)], the majority of the US Supreme Court held that Title VII of the US Civil Rights Act 1964 allows a claim for sex-based wage discrimination by reference to the pay of a hypothetical male worker. The majority opinion of Brennan J explained that any other view of the scope of Title VII would render lawful discriminatory wage policies which could not be brought under the Equal Pay Act. He said that if Title VII gave no remedy, there would be no redress where 'an employer hired a woman for a unique position in the company and then admitted that her salary would have been higher had she been male . . .' The dissenting opinion of Rehnquist J (joined by Burger CJ, Powell and Stewart JJ) argued that there was no need for such a remedy under Title VII since the Equal Pay Act already covered the situation: 'However unlikely such an admission might be in the bullpen of litigation, an employer's statement that "if my female employees performing a particular job were males, I would pay them more simply because they are males" would be' sufficient to establish a claim under the US Equal Pay Act since '[o]vert discrimination does not go unremedied' by that Act.

In *Allonby v Accrington & Rossendale College* Case C–256/01 the ECJ ruled that the claimants, whose teaching jobs had been contracted out to a private sector provider, could not rely as their comparators on men still employed by the state (see relying on *Lawrence v Regent Office Care*, above, notwithstanding the Court's acceptance that the contracting-out in this case had been designed deliberately to evade the consequences of Article 141). But the ECJ went on to decide that Article 141 claims could be made in cases in which discrimination arises directly from legislative provisions or collective agreements, as long as a single source determines the pay and conditions of men and women between whom inequality arose. In the instant case the women claimants complained that, as contracted-out workers, they were no longer eligible for membership of the Teachers' Superannuation Scheme.

Ms Allonby relied on the decisions of the ECJ in cases including *Rinner-Kühn*, in which that Court had ruled that part-timers could not lawfully be excluded from an employer's sick pay scheme in the absence of objective justification (which the Court found was lacking in that case); *Seymour-Smith and Perez* (in which the Court accepted that access to statutory compensation in the event of unfair dismissal fell within the scope of Article 141) and *Fisscher v Voorhuis Hengelo*, Case C–128/93 [1994] ECR I–4583 in which the Court held that the trustees of a pension scheme were bound by Article 141 EC although not the employers of the claimant. Noting that the part-time workers whose jobs had been contracted out were disproportionately female, the ECJ ruled that Article 141 extended to 'workers' rather than to 'employees' alone (a 'worker' being defined for EC purposes as 'a person who, for a certain period of time, performs services for and under the direction of another person in return for which he receives remuneration') and that the discriminatory exclusion of these contracted-out workers had to be disapplied by the domestic courts:

Allonby v Accrington & Rossendale College, Case C-256/01 [2004] ECR 1-00000, OJ C 47, 21.02.2004, p. 4

Judgment:

the national court seeks in essence to ascertain whether the requirement of being employed under a contract of employment as a precondition for membership of a pension scheme for teachers, set up by State legislation, must be disapplied where it is shown that, among the teachers who fulfil the other conditions for membership, a clearly lower percentage of women than of men are able to satisfy that condition and it is established that that condition is not objectively justified . . .

According to Article 2 EC, the Community is to have as its task to promote, among other things, equality between men and women. Article 141(1) EC constitutes a specific expression of the principle of equality for men and women, which forms part of the fundamental principles protected by the Community legal order . . As the Court held in *Defrenne (No.2)* the principle of equal pay forms part of the foundations of the Community. Accordingly, the term worker used in Article 141(1) EC cannot be defined by reference to the legislation of the Member States but has a Community meaning. Moreover, it cannot be interpreted restrictively. For the purposes of that provision, there must be considered as a worker a person who, for a certain period of time, performs services for and under the direction of another person in return for which he receives remuneration . . . The question whether such a relationship exists must be answered in each particular case having regard to all the factors and circumstances by which the relationship between the parties is characterised. . . . The formal classification of a self-employed person under national law does not exclude the possibility that a person must be classified as a worker within the meaning of Article 141(1) EC if his independence is merely notional, thereby disguising an employment relationship within the meaning of that article.

In the case of teachers who are, vis-à-vis an intermediary undertaking, under an obligation to undertake an assignment at a college, it is necessary in particular to consider the extent of any limitation on their freedom to choose their timetable, and the place and content of their work. The fact that no obligation is imposed on them to accept an assignment is of no consequence in that context . . .

in the case of company pension schemes which are limited to the undertaking in question, the Court has held that a worker cannot rely on Article [141] . . . in order to claim pay to which he could be entitled if he belonged to the other sex in the absence, now or in the past, in the undertaking concerned of workers of the other sex who perform or performed comparable work (case C–200/91 *Coloroll Pension Trustees* [1994] ECR I-04389). On the other hand, in the case of national legislation, in case 171/88 *Rinner-Kühn*, the Court based its reasoning on statistics for the numbers of male and female workers at national level.

In order to show that the requirement of being employed under a contract of employment as a precondition for membership of the TSS—a condition deriving from State rules—constitutes a breach of the principle of equal pay for men and women in the form of indirect discrimination against women, a female worker may rely on statistics showing that, among the teachers who are workers within the meaning of Article 141(1) EC and fulfil all the conditions for membership of the pension scheme except that of being employed under a contract of employment as defined by national law, there is a much higher percentage of women than of men.

If that is the case, the difference of treatment concerning membership of the pension scheme at issue must be objectively justified. In that regard, no justification can be inferred from the formal classification of a self-employed person under national law . . .

Where it is found that the requirement of being employed under a contract of employment as a precondition for membership of a pension scheme is not in conformity with

Article 141(1) EC, the condition concerned must be disapplied, in view of the primacy of Community law . . .

Article 141(1) EC must be interpreted as meaning that, where State legislation is at issue, the applicability of that provision vis-à-vis an undertaking is not subject to the condition that the worker concerned can be compared with a worker of the other sex who is or has been employed by the same employer and who has received higher pay for equal work or work of equal value.

S Fredman, 'Marginalising Equal Pay Laws' (2004) 33 *Industrial Law Journal* 281, 282–3 footnotes omitted

To what extent can equal pay buttress workers against the downward slide of terms and conditions accompanying the move to flexibility? Or can employers sidestep equal pay laws by changing the structure of the organisation or the status of the worker? Alternatively, might these issues be better dealt with by giving rights directly to flexible workers or by new ways of characterising the employment contract? In *Allonby*, the ECJ faced in two directions. On the one hand, its inability to see beyond the formal boundaries of the employing enterprise rendered equal pay law impotent in the face of employers who deliberately fragment the supervisory and the remunerative dimensions of the managerial function. On the other hand, the Court opened up new possibilities for challenging discrimination in legislative schemes by introducing an autonomous, EU level definition of 'worker' for the purposes of gender equality, and by moving from an individualised comparator to an indirect discrimination approach. . . . Underlying [the ECJ's] conclusion [on the identity of the suitable comparator] is a particular model of the employer, and, derivatively, of the function of equal pay laws. On this model, the employing institution is a 'given', not to be scrutinised by the court. Yet, as Kahn-Freund showed, management is an abstraction: managerial powers can be exercised by many. . . . In the case of agency workers, the managerial function is triangulated, so that the entity which has control over the worker is different from the entity which is responsible for remuneration. Thus, in *Allonby*, the managerial function was deliberately manipulated to achieve this result. Ms Allonby continued to operate under the direction and responsibility of the College, which organised her activities and was liable to the students for the quality of her teaching. The duty to remunerate her, however, lay with the ELS, which in turn was contractually bound to the College to deliver the service.

It was this fragmentation of managerial power which the Court found impossible to address. Despite the contractual nexus between the agency and the ultimate user, the Court refused to see beyond the formal boundaries of each enterprise. The fact that the level of pay received by Ms Allonby was 'influenced' by the amount paid by the college to ELS was not, in the court's view, a sufficient basis for concluding that there was a single source for the purposes of the *Lawrence* test. This rigid view of the demarcation of each enterprise leaves the Court wholly deferent to the employer's self-definition of the boundaries of its responsibility. Yet the clear contractual nexus between ELS and the College meant that it could not only easily ascertain the level of pay of the appropriate comparator, but also pass on the extra cost to the College.

This formal and deferent view of the employing enterprise was reinforced by the fault-oriented model of equal pay law inherent in *Lawrence*. In insisting that a body must be found which is responsible for the inequality, the ECJ in both *Lawrence* and *Allonby* assumes that liability only arises if fault an be established . It is now widely recognised that inequality of pay is frequently a consequence of institutional arrangements for which no single actor is 'to blame'. In *Allonby* itself, the Court demonstrated a disturbingly narrow understanding of fault, a direct result of the refusal to acknowledge the nexus between the

College and ELS. This emerges strikingly from the opinion of the Advocate General where he stated: 'On any other view, ELS would have to bear the consequence attributable to another employer without there being any connection between the body responsible for the inequality and the body required to restore equal treatment'. This meant that the Court was unable to locate fault despite the acknowledgement by both the Advocate General and the Commission that the institutional arrangements had been deliberately manipulated. What is not explained is why the loss should fall on those who are least at fault, the part-time lecturers themselves.

Such a focus on fault has meant that, far from extending the reach of equal pay laws beyond the single employer, *Lawrence* and *Allonby* have had the effect of casting doubt on the applicability of equal pay laws even within the same employment. This is because, if an employer delegates control over pay to managers of subdivisions, it may be argued that there is no single source of terms and conditions and therefore no body capable of restoring equality. The result is to prevent an equal pay claim based on a comparison between workers in different sub-divisions. This is precisely what occurred in *Robertson v DEFRA* (UKEAT/0273/03/DM, 10 December 2003), in which the EAT held that the *Lawrence* test applied even when all the employees were employed by the same employer. The result of that case is that, even without creating a new employing entity, an employer can insulate workers in one department from equal pay claims by those in another department by delegating control over terms and conditions to different department heads. The legitimacy of this extension of the principle to such cases of 'internal disintegration' is dubious, as is the finding in *Robertson* that delegation by the Crown is equivalent to a transfer of power. Both aspects of the decision may yet be overturned on appeal. But the dangers of the focus on fault and responsibility inherent in the *Lawrence* test are clear.

Allonby clearly raises the question as to whether equal pay laws are the appropriate mechanism for addressing the detrimental effect of transfers from direct to agency employment. Both the Commission and the Advocate General took the view that any protection to be offered to agency workers should come through the legislative process and could not be developed judicially. Although they acknowledged the seriousness of the potential abuse when an employer reconfigured its operations to evade equal pay laws, both were clearly reluctant to pre-empt the stalled directive on agency workers.

Yet this ignores both the gendered dimension of the move to flexibility and the Court's own record in developing sex discrimination law in this field. Statisitics show that the detriments attached to flexible working are largely borne by women. Those most at risk of transfer along *Allonby* lines are part-time workers and in 2003, 43% of female employees worked part-time compared with only 9% of male employees, most of whom were under 25. Women working part-time earn only 59% of the average hourly earnings of men working full-time, a pay-gap which has hardly changed since 1975 (Equal Opportunities Commission *Facts about Men and Women in Great Britain* 2003). The Court has a strong record of adapting sex discrimination law to recognise and address the gendered nature of part-time work (*Bilka Kaufhaus*). Far from impeding legislative progress in this field, the case law on part-time work constituted a major impetus to such legislation. Both avenues of redress now co-exist happily.

This is not to say that discrimination law is the optimal approach. Because proof of disproportionate impact remains a major stumbling block, the absence of a need to prove a link between gender and marginal work makes legislation giving rights directly to the worker far more attractive. Nevertheless, in refusing to address the gender inequalities, the Court was abdicating its responsibilities and ignoring the position of gender equality as a fundamental right in EU law. Nor would an opposite conclusion have undermined the injunction in *Defrenne* (Case 43/75 [1976] ECR 455) against cross-industry comparisons. The contractual link between the agency and the end-user means that the comparison is closely confined.

The Equal Treatment Directive as amended by Council Directive 2002/73/EC provides (Article 3) that its prohibition on discrimination applies, inter alia, to pay. Previously discrimination in relation to pay was regulated at the EU level exclusively by Article 141 and the Equal Pay Directive (Council Directive 75/117/EC), the largely comparator-driven approach to which was set out by the ECJ in the *Lawrence* and *Allonby* cases. We saw above that even under the Equal Pay Directive and Article 141 the ECJ allowed some scope for a claim in the absence of a comparator. Not only was this explicitly stated in *Allonby* but *Bilka-Kaufhaus, Rinner-Kuhn Kowalska v Freie und Hansestadt Hamburg*, Case C-33/89 [1990] ECR I-02591, to name but a few cases, concerned rules of general application, and in none of them did the ECJ require demonstration of less favourable treatment than a specific (male) other engaged in equivalent work. The inclusion of pay within Directive 2002/73/EC was a deliberate move on the part of the European Parliament and it is distinctly arguable that the UK Government will have to amend domestic legislation to permit pay and other contractual claims to be made under the SDA, as it is difficult to envisage how the EqPA could operate in anything like its current form other than by reference to an actual male comparator. Meanwhile a claimant could bring a suitable pay-related claim under the SDA and press for a reference to the ECJ on the appropriate construction of that Act.

The Employer's Defence

Introduction

Section 1(3) EPA provides that:

> An equality clause shall not operate in relation to a variation between the woman's contract and the man's contract if the employer proves that the variation is genuinely due to a material factor which is not the difference of sex and that factor–
> (a) in the case of an equality clause falling within subsection (2)(a) or (b) above, must be a material difference between the woman's case and the man's; and
> (b) in the case of an equality clause falling within subsection (2)(c) above, may be such a material difference.

Section 1(3)(b) was added by the Equal Pay (Amendment) Regulations 1983, which introduced the equal pay for work of equal value claim. The section was meant to by-pass the decision of the Court of Appeal in *Clay Cross v Fletcher* that only 'personal' factors could be considered under s.1(3). The employer had put forward, as a GMF defence, 'market forces,' ie, the argument that he had had to match the comparator's previous salary in order to attract him to the job. This had been accepted by EAT on the assumption, as Lord Denning put it, that 'the issue depended on the employer's state of mind, on the reason why he paid the man more than the woman. If the reason had nothing to do with sex, they could pay him more.' Lord Denning went on to proscribe what he saw as the appropriate limits of s.1(3):

Clay Cross (Quarry Services) Ltd v Fletcher [1979] ICR 47

The issue does not depend on the employer's state of mind. It does not depend on his reasons for paying the man more. The employer may not intend to discriminate against the woman by paying her less; but, if the result of his actions is that she is discriminated against, then his conduct is unlawful, whether he intended it or not . . .

The issue depends on whether there is a material difference (other than sex) between her case and his. Take heed to those words, 'between her case and his.' They show that the tribunal is to have regard to her and to him, to the personal equation of the woman as compared to that of the man, irrespective of any extrinsic forces which led to the variation in pay. As I said in *Shields v Coomes* [above] . . . the subsection applies when 'the personal equation of the man is such that he deserves to be paid at a higher rate than the woman.' Thus the personal equation of the man may warrant a wage differential if he has much longer length of service; or has superior skill or qualifications; or gives bigger output or productivity; or has been placed, owing to down-grading, in a protected pay category, vividly described as 'red circled'; or to other circumstances personal to him in doing his job.

But the tribunal is not to have regard to any extrinsic forces which have led to the man being paid more. An employer cannot avoid his obligations under the [EqPA] by saying: 'I paid him more because he asked for more,' or 'I paid her less because she was willing to come for less.' If any such excuse were permitted, the Act would be a dead letter. Those are the very reasons why there was unequal pay before the statute. They were the very circumstances in which the statute was intended to operate.

Nor can the employer avoid his obligations by giving the reasons why he submitted to the extrinsic forces. As for instance by saying: 'He asked for that sum because it was what he was getting in his previous job,' or 'He was the only applicant for the job, so I had no option.' In such cases the employer may beat his breast, and say: 'I did not pay him more because he was a man. I paid it because he was the only suitable person who applied for the job. Man or woman made no difference to me.' Those are reasons personal to the employer. If any such reasons were permitted as an excuse, the door would be wide open. Every employer who wished to avoid the statute would walk straight through it . . .[62]

In *Rainey v Greater Glasgow Health Board* [1987] 1 AC 224, the House of Lords disapproved of the approach taken by both Lord Denning and Lord Lawton (concurring) in *Clay Cross*, Lord Keith for the Court declaring that the decision was:

unduly restrictive of the proper interpretation of section 1(3). The difference must be 'material,' which I would construe as meaning 'significant and relevant,' and it must be between 'her case and his.' Consideration of a person's case must necessarily involve consideration of all the circumstances of that case. These may well go beyond what is not very happily described as 'the personal equation,' ie the personal qualities by way of skill, experience or training which the individual brings to the job. Some circumstances may on examination prove to be not significant or not relevant, but others may do so, though not relating to the personal qualities of the employee. In particular, where there is no question of intentional sex discrimination whether direct or indirect (and there is none here) a difference which is connected with economic factors affecting the efficient carrying on of the employer's business or other activity may well be relevant.

The decision in *Rainey* will be considered further below. But the difference of approach between the Court of Appeal in *Clay Cross* and the House of Lords in *Rainey* does indicate some of the difficulties to which s.1(3) gave rise. On its face, the section allows any pay

---

[62] Citing in support, inter alia, Phillips J in *National Coal Board v Sherwin* [1978] ICR 700, 710 'The general principle [is] that it is no justification for a refusal to pay the same wages to women doing the same work as a man to say that the man could not have been recruited for less.' Lawton and Browne LJJ concurred on similar grounds.

difference which is due (1) to a 'material factor/ difference' which is (2) 'not the difference of sex.' Whether a factor is 'material,' and whether it is or is not 'the difference' of sex should, presumably, be judged on the facts of the particular case (this is further explained below). But what appears frequently to happen in practice is that employers (and, indeed, the courts) grasp particular categories of reasons to explain pay differences on the assumption that the categories themselves, rather than their application in any particular case, constitute 'GMFs' (or, in the *Clay Cross* decision, do not). This approach was perhaps understandable in *Clay Cross*, which predated EAT's decision in *Jenkins v Kingsgate* (see below). But it has proven a blight on the application of s.1(3), engendering whole lines of cases in which 'market forces' (post *Rainey*), 'separate collective bargaining structures,' 'administrative reasons,' and so on, have been accepted per se, as justifying pay disparities.

At the outset (and prior to anyone in the UK considering the concept of indirect discrimination), the GMF defence was intended to permit differentials based on 'length of service, merit, output and so on . . . provided that the payments are available to any person who qualifies regardless of sex.'[63] It did not appear, at this stage, that regard would be had to the actual impact by sex of any such factors, as distinct from the question whether both men and women could qualify for them. But, as we shall see below, the ECJ gradually developed an understanding of indirect discrimination and applied it, in the equal pay context, to permit only such differentials as were either unrelated to sex, in the sense that they did not impact disparately between men and women or which, although they did have such an (unintended) impact, were nevertheless justifiable in line with the test discussed below.

In *Snoxell v Vauxhall Motors Ltd* [1978] QB 11 EAT set out a more rigorous approach to s.1(3) than had previously prevailed. The case was brought by female machine inspectors who named, as their comparators, male machine inspectors whose salaries had been 'red-circled' when their exclusively male grade had been assimilated into a new unisex pay structure. It seems from the headnote to the EAT decision that the tribunal had dismissed the case without analysis: 'the variation was genuinely due to . . . red-circling and . . . the requirements of s.1(3) were therefore satisfied'.

Phillips J, for EAT, stated that 'it cannot be right to justify the variation in pay by another variation between the man's and the woman's contract [the fact that the man used to have staff status] which itself requires to be justified as being genuinely due to a material difference (other than the difference of sex).'[64] Rejecting the employer's argument that the difference in pay between female machine parts inspectors and male inspectors resulted from the 'red-circling' of the latter after their previously exclusively male grade had been assimilated into the, unisex, pay structure, Phillips J pointed out that women had not been eligible for the grade in respect of which the men's wages were red-circled and continued:

---

[63] Barbara Castle, 795 HC Debs, 9 February 1970, col. 920.

[64] [1977] IRLR 123, 128. Having said this, even the Court of Appeal, in *Farthing v Ministry of Defence* [1980] IRLR 402 accepted, as a material factor 'not the difference of sex' the fact that the employers had, in the process of eliminating directly discriminatory pay scales, first moved the women from grade 4 to grade 6 of the women's pay scale (which entitled them to roughly equal pay with men on grade 4 of the male pay scale) then, in response to the women's complaints at being moved down to the unisex grade 4 (where they continued to receive the same wages as they had on grade 6 of the women's pay scale), transferred them up to grade 6 on the unisex scale 'on a personal basis'. The men employed on grade 4 made an equal pay claim but Lord Denning, in the Court of Appeal, ruled that both the tribunal and EAT had erred in finding that the variation was due to sex: it came about, rather: 'because of the system which had been adopted to eliminate the difference in pay between men and women.' Waller and Dunn LJJ agreed.

Snoxell v Vauxhall Motors **[1978] QB 11**

Phillips J (for EAT):

The onus of proof under s.1(3) is on the employer and it is a heavy one. Intention, and motive, are irrelevant; and we would say that an employer can never establish in the terms of s.1(3) that the variation between the woman's contract and the man's contract is genuinely due to a material difference (other than the difference of sex) between her case and his when it can be seen that past sex discrimination has contributed to the variation. To allow such an answer would, we think, be contrary to the spirit and intent of the [EqPA], construed and interpreted in the manner we have already explained. It is true that the original discrimination occurred before 29 December 1975, and accordingly was not then unlawful; nonetheless it cannot have been the intention of the [EqPA] to permit the perpetuation of the effects of earlier discrimination.[65]

In *Snoxell*, Phillips J had sought out (direct) discrimination which was disguised behind the 'red-circling' GMF. But it was a long time before this rigour was extended to 'GMF' defences which were tainted by discrimination of the indirect variety. One byproduct of this can be seen in the popularity of the 'grading' and 'separate pay structure' GMFs. Indeed, so popular were these defences that they continued to be relied upon even after EAT accepted, in *Jenkins v Kingsgate (No. 2)* [1981] 1 WLR 1485, that indirectly discriminatory factors could not be relied on under s.1(3) unless such reliance was 'justified'. The issue of justification, and the *Jenkins* case itself, are considered below and in Chapter 2.

In *Davies v McCartneys* [1989] ICR 705 EAT accepted that, even had the claimant been able to establish equivalence with her chosen comparator, the employer would have been able to make out the GMF defence on the basis of factors which went to the value of the jobs (there working conditions and responsibility). This aspect of the decision is highly questionable. As the IRLR 'Highlights' (October 2003) point out: 'It is illogical that a difference in effort (or skill or responsibility) should not be sufficiently important to make two jobs of unequal value and yet the same difference should be treated as sufficient to negate the equal pay claim of claimants employed on work of equal value.' Nevertheless, in *Christie v John E Haith Ltd* [2003] IRLR 670, EAT reached the same conclusion as it had in *Davies*. The claimants were bird seed packers who worked in one packing room with packages of up to 12 kg in weight, and whose male comparators worked in a different room with packages of up to 30 kg, loaded and unloaded delivery vehicles and wheeled and emptied rubbish trolleys. A tribunal assessed the work as being of equal value, but went on to find that these differences (which went to the value of the jobs) provided the employer with a GMF defence.

The GMF and Indirect Discrimination

In *Jenkins v Kingsgate* Case C–96/80 [1981] ECR I–00911 the ECJ was asked to consider whether Article 141 was breached by lower payments to (predominantly female) part-time workers than to (predominantly male) workers. That Court ruled that the purpose of Article 141 was: 'to ensure the application of the principle of equal pay for men and women . . . The differences in pay prohibited by that provision are therefore exclusively those based on the difference of the sex of the workers.'

---

[65] Citing, in support, the US decision in *Corning Glassworks v Brennan* (1974) 417 US 188.

This, on the face of it, suggested that only direct discrimination was prohibited under Article 141. But the ECJ had gone on to muddy the waters by ruling that:

> the fact that work paid at time rates is remunerated at an hourly rate which varies according to the number of hours worked per week does not offend against the principle of equal pay laid down in Article [141] of the Treaty in so far as the difference in pay between part-time work and full-time work is attributable to factors which are objectively justified and are in no way related to any discrimination based on sex . . . By contrast, if it is established that a considerably smaller percentage of women than of men perform the minimum number of weekly working hours required in order to be able to claim the full-time hourly rate of pay, the inequality in pay will be contrary to Article [141] of the Treaty where, regard being had to the difficulties encountered by women in arranging to work that minimum number of hours per week, the pay policy of the undertaking in question cannot be explained by factors other than discrimination based on sex.

The effect of the ECJ's decision was to leave unclear the question whether indirect pay discrimination was or was not prohibited under Article 141. On the case's return to EAT (*Jenkins v Kingsgate (No. 2)* [1981] 1 WLR 1485), however, that Court ruled that, whatever the position under European law, s.1(3) EqPA permitted reliance upon indirectly discriminatory factors (here the fact that the woman was engaged in part-time and her comparator in full-time work) only where that reliance was justified. According to Browne-Wilkinson J:

> If the industrial tribunal finds that the employer intended to discriminate against women by paying part-time workers less, the employer cannot succeed under section 1(3). Even if the employer had no such intention, for section 1(3) to apply the employer must show that the difference in pay between full-time and part-time workers is reasonably necessary in order to obtain some result (other than cheap female labour) which the employer desires for economic or other reasons.

The ECJ had, in *Jenkins*, taken a cautious approach to Article 141. But within a few years it had developed a much more radical line. Most significant for our purposes was the decision in *Bilka-Kaufhaus GmbH v Weber von Hartz* Case C–170/84 [1986] ECR 1607, which made it clear that Article 141 permitted indirect pay discrimination only where it was 'justified.' The same decision marked the beginning, in the equal opportunities context, of a line of authority on the meaning of 'justifiable'—there the court ruled that disparately impacting pay practices were permissible under Article 141 only where they 'correspond to a real need on the part of the undertaking, are appropriate with a view to achieving the objectives pursued and are necessary to that end.'

Subsequently, the decisions of the ECJ in *Rinner-Kühn*, *Danfoss* and *Nimz*[66] set ever more challenging tests for the justification of indirect discrimination in pay. The decisions in these and other cases require a rigorous approach to the application of the GMF defence. In particular it is clear that, in determining the justifiability of indirect pay discrimination, the domestic courts must accept only such factors as are demonstrably related to the requirements of the jobs under consideration.

The decision in *Bilka* was embraced by the House of Lords in *Rainey v Greater Glasgow Health Board*, in which their Lordships incorporated the ruling of the ECJ in that case into s.1(3) EqPA. The background to the case was a decision taken by the board to establish an

---

[66] See further Ch 2.

NHS prosthetics service, prosthetic services always previously having been 'bought in' from the private sector. The board decided that, in order to recruit from the private sector, it would have to offer 'indirect applicants' (ie, those recruited from the private sector) the opportunity to retain their private sector terms and conditions indefinitely. This policy was retained for one year, after which both direct and 'indirect' applicants (those recruited other than from private sector employment) were employed on the normal NHS rates. Every one of the 20 indirect recruits was male. Directly recruited prosthetists included one man who subsequently left. No attempts were made to phase out the disparities between direct and indirect applicants and, at the time of the hearing, the applicant was paid £7,295 pa, her comparator (whose qualifications and experience were broadly similar), £10,085.

We saw above that the House of Lords overruled the approach taken by the Court of Appeal in *Clay Cross* and accepted that the GMF defence could extend beyond factors personal to the claimant and her comparator. Lord Keith interpreted the decision in *Bilka* as permitting objectively justified economic grounds and 'objectively justified grounds which are other than economic, such as administrative efficiency in a concern not engaged in commerce or business.' In the instant case their Lordships took the view that:

Rainey v Greater Glasgow Health Board [1987] 1 AC 224

Lord Keith (for their Lordships):

the difference between the case of the appellant and that of [her comparator] is that the former is a person who entered the National Health Service . . . directly while the latter is a person who entered it from employment with a private contractor. The fact that one is a woman and the other a man is an accident . . . the new prosthetic service could never have been established within a reasonable time if [the comparator] and others like him had not been offered a scale of remuneration no less favourable than that which they were then enjoying . . .

[I]t was argued for the appellant that it did not constitute a good and objectively justified reason for paying the appellant and other direct entrants a lower scale of remuneration . . . from the administrative point of view it would have been highly anomalous and inconvenient if prosthetists alone, over the whole tract of future time for which the prosthetic service would endure, were to have been subject to a different salary scale and different negotiating machinery . . . there were sound objectively justified administrative reasons, in my view, for placing prosthetists in general, men and women alike, on the Whitley Council scale and subjecting them to its negotiating machinery . . . It was not a question of the appellant being paid less than the norm but of Mr Crumlin being paid more. He was paid more because of the necessity to attract him and other privately employed prosthetists into forming the nucleus of the new service . . .

Counsel for the appellant put forward an argument based on section 1(1)(b) of the Sex Discrimination Act 1975 (with which the [EqPA] to be read as one: *Shields v E Coomes* . . .) This provision has the effect of prohibiting indirect discrimination between women and men. In my opinion it does not, for present purposes, add anything to section 1(3) of the [EqPA] since, upon the view which I have taken as to the proper construction of the latter, a difference which demonstrated unjustified indirect discrimination would not discharge the onus placed on the employer. Further, there would not appear to be any material distinction in principle between the need to demonstrate objectively justified grounds of difference for purposes of section 1(3) and the need to justify a requirement or condition under section 1(1)(b)(ii) of the Act of 1975. It is therefore unnecessary to consider the argument further.

The decision of the House of Lords in *Rainey* was, on the one hand, to be welcomed because of its incorporation of the ECJ's decision in *Bilka*, and therefore of a rigorous approach to the justification of indirect discrimination, into UK law. But in applying the test to the facts before it, the House of Lords fell into the trap of failing to take into account the impact, on men and women, of the factor relied on by the employer in determining whether it was (indirectly) discriminatory. Instead, their Lordships just looked at the abstracted factor—here the need to attract indirect applicants while making some effort to control labour costs—and decided that it fitted into the 'category' of 'administrative efficiency,' which category they took to be within *Bilka*. The House of Lords characterised as 'accident' the composition by sex of the groups of indirect and direct applicants. But this may not have been the case. And given the disparate impact by sex of the factor, the retention of the enhanced rates payable to private sector prosthetists, coupled with the payment of lower rates to directly recruited staff, at least raised a requirement of objective justification which would, in turn, have had to be made out taking into account its discriminatory impact. The failure of the House of Lords in Rainey to consider the disparate impact by sex of the 'market forces' defence had the effect of permitting the employer to say: 'I paid him more because he asked for more,' or 'I paid her less because she was willing to come for less.'[67] These, as Lord Denning pointed out in *Shields*, 'are the very reasons why there was unequal pay before the statute . . . the very circumstances in which the statute was intended to operate.'[68]

The impact of *Rainey* was to be felt for a long time, its interpretation by the lower courts sometimes having the effect that *Bilka* served to widen, rather than to control, the scope of the GMF. In *Reed v Boozer* [1988] ICR 391, for example, EAT regarded itself as fortified by the House of Lords' decision in *Rainey* in allowing an appeal from an employer. The tribunal had rejected the employer's attempt to block an equal pay claim, prior to the assessment of value, on the grounds that the claimants (women dispatch clerks) were graded on the employer's 'staff' pay structure and received a weekly wage, but their comparator (a male dispatch clerk) was paid according to the employer's pay scheme for hourly workers. According to the tribunal:

> Despite [the employer's] hint that shock waves would be sent through the system if the two women applicants were allowed to compare themselves with [the man], it seems to the tribunal that the principal difficulty for [the employers] is that the principles of equal pay, now that they are with us, do not take kindly to the somewhat artificial differences between staff and hourly paid workers which are the product of historical development. It is accepted by the [employers] that there is no internal machinery to allow a staff employee to compare herself with an hourly paid worker, or for that matter vice versa. If the tribunal were to allow this defence at this stage, it would mean that these particular women would not be able to break through the artificial barrier which, so far as the internal machinery is concerned, denies them the opportunity of pursuing claims to equal pay with a selected male employee. If there was a single structure they would, of course, be able to do so.

The approach taken by the tribunal was patently correct. The employers had certainly not shown that the difference in pay was 'not the difference of sex.' They had, rather, merely given an historical account of how that difference had developed. The claimants were

---

[67] *Per* Lord Denning in *Clay Cross*, above.

[68] Equally, according to Lawton LJ: 'an exception based on such a vague conception as economic factors or market pressures . . . would strike at the object of the article. In the labour market women have always been in a worse position than men. Under both Article 141 and the EqPA 1970 that was no longer to be so.'

represented by the Association of Clerical Workers, the comparators by the Transport and General Workers' Union. No explanation was given as to why the two groups, whose work was very similar indeed, were represented by different unions. Further, the very title of the claimants' union suggested that it was a predominantly female organisation whose industrial strength would, by reason of that, be considerably less than that of the T&G. But EAT took a different view:

Reed Packaging Ltd v Boozer [1988] ICR 391

There is no suggestion that either of the pay structures contains any element of discrimination based upon sex, whether direct or indirect. Two questions therefore remain. Is the variation due to a material factor, namely, the separate pay structures? And is the operation of these structures genuine? . . .

No one suggests that the variation here was due to a difference of sex. No one has suggested that these pay structures are not genuinely operated. Therefore, can the separate pay structures constitute a material factor? We can see no reason why not—a single grading scheme is clearly capable of being such a factor . . . We are also re-inforced in our view by the recent case of *Rainey* . . . [in which the House of Lords held] that . . . section 1(3) might apply where a difference in pay was reasonably necessary in order to obtain some result, other than cheap female labour, that the employer desired to achieve for economic reasons or for other reasons such as administrative efficiency in a concern not engaged in commerce or business . . .

The present case, in our judgment, shows an objectively justified administrative reason and therefore a material factor which was genuine or sound. We have therefore reached the conclusion that the only decision which the industrial tribunal could have reached was that the employers had made out this defence under section 1(3) and that the claim should have been dismissed . . .

Post-*Bilka* developments (specifically, the decisions in *Rinner-Kühn*, *Danfoss*, and *Nimz v Freie*) were mentioned above. Given the direct effect of Article 141 (discussed in Chapter 5), these developments have been incorporated, as a matter of European law, into the GMF defence. But there is an ongoing difficulty in the domestic courts about getting to the point at which justification for disparately impacting pay factors is required from the employer. The first clash of approach between the ECJ and the domestic courts, illustrated in *Reed v Boozer*, came to a head in *Enderby v Frenchay*, in which EAT accepted collective bargaining arrangements as a defence to an equal value pay claim. The ECJ, however, took a different view.

Enderby v Frenchay Health Authority Case C–127/92 [1993] ECR I–5535

The fact that the rates of pay at issue are decided by collective bargaining processes conducted separately for each of the two professional groups concerned, without any discriminatory effect within each group, does not preclude a finding of prima facie discrimination where the results of those processes show that two groups with the same employer and the same trade union are treated differently. If the employer could rely on the absence of discrimination within each of the collective bargaining processes taken separately as sufficient justification for the difference in pay, he could . . . easily circumvent the principle of equal pay by using separate bargaining processes. Accordingly . . . the fact that the respective rates of pay of two jobs of equal value, one carried out almost exclusively by women and the other predominantly by men, were arrived at by collective bargaining processes which, although carried out by the same parties, are distinct, and, taken separately, have in themselves no discriminatory effect, is not sufficient objective justification for the difference in pay between those two jobs . . .

The decision of the ECJ in *Enderby* places beyond argument the unacceptability of the 'category' approach to the GMF defence. It is not sufficient for an employer, faced with an equal pay claim, to explain the difference in pay by reference to some factor such as 'market forces,' 'different pay structures or collective agreements,' 'red-circling' etc. He or she must go further and establish to the satisfaction of the tribunal either that, as the House of Lords accepted (albeit controversially) in the *Rainey* decision, that the factor is neutral as regards sex or, to the extent that it serves to disadvantage either sex (as distinct merely from the claimant(s)[69]), that reliance upon it is nevertheless justified consistent with European law.

A factor which is 'not the difference of sex' within s.1(3) must be one which is neither directly discriminatory nor, in the absence of adequate justification, indirectly discriminatory. But in the *Enderby* case EAT ruled ([1991] IRLR 44) that a mere difference in pay, in a case where a woman and her comparator were employed on like work, work rated as equivalent or work of equal value, was not sufficient to found an allegation of unintentional indirect discrimination without the identification of a barrier, requirement or condition causing disparate impact.

The Court of Appeal (*per* Neill LJ), saw 'force in the argument that . . . discrimination by employers means or involves the application of some test or standard by employers whereby one individual is differentiated from another [and that therefore] before one considers whether there may be some justification for alleged unintentional indirect discrimination one has first to examine whether the employer applies any test or standard or erects any barrier based on sex at all' adopting the approach of the SDA discussed in Chapter 2. Nevertheless, it referred to the ECJ the question whether the employer's reliance on the separate negotiating structures which governed the pay, respectively, of the claimant and her comparators, was objectively justifiable within Article 141. The employers (and the UK Government) argued that objective justification could only be required in cases which fitted within the SDA's definition of indirect discrimination—where the claimant could point to criteria which a considerably smaller proportion of women than men could comply with and which had discriminatory effects because of the sex of the worker concerned.[70] Again the ECJ took a different view:

Enderby v Frenchay Health Authority Case C–127/92 [1993] ECR I–5535

Judgment:

It is normally for the person alleging facts in support of a claim to adduce proof of such facts. Thus, in principle, the burden of proving the existence of sex discrimination as to pay lies with the worker who, believing himself to be the victim of such discrimination, brings legal proceedings against his employer with a view to removing the discrimination.

---

[69] The inherent tendency of a pay-determining factor to disadvantage women might be established, as in *Enderby*, by evidence of the outcome of collective bargaining by sex or, as in *Rinner-Kühn*, by the disproportionately female nature of the part-time workers adversely affected. If, on the other hand, pay is determined according to a factor by which the female claimant is disadvantaged, but women in general are not, no justification ought to be required. See, further, the discussions of *Loughran* and *Enderby* below. For a recent example of the approach to grading systems see *Ruff v Hannant Cleaning Services* (29 April 2002, ET) reported in 107 *Equal Opportunities Review*.

[70] This, as the Court of Appeal in *Enderby* pointed out, appears contrary to the dicta of Lord Bridge in *Leverton*: 'the appellant, if she could establish that she was employed on work of equal value to that of "a man in the same employment,"' would prima facie be entitled under s.1(2)(c) to have the terms of her contract treated as modified as provided by the section to bring them into line with the terms of his contract.

However, it is clear from the case law of the Court that the onus may shift when that is necessary to avoid depriving workers who appear to be the victims of discrimination of any effective means of enforcing the principle of equal pay. Accordingly, when a measure distinguishing between employees on the basis of their hours of work has in practice an adverse impact on substantially more members of one or other sex, that measure must be regarded as contrary to the objective pursued by Article 141 of the Treaty, unless the employer shows that it is based on objectively justified factors unrelated to any discrimination on grounds of sex [citing *Bilka-Kaufhaus, Kowalska* and *Nimz*]. Similarly, where an undertaking applies a system of pay which is wholly lacking in transparency, it is for the employer to prove that his practice in the matter of wages is not discriminatory, if a female worker establishes, in relation to a relatively large number of employees, that the average pay for women is less than that for men [citing *Danfoss*[71]] . . .

Enderby fell to be considered once again by the Northern Ireland Court of Appeal in *British Road Services Ltd v Loughran*, the issue concerning whether the decision could be relied upon by women whose job was only 75 per cent, rather than almost exclusively, female. The employers put forward, in support of their argument that the ECJ's decision did not apply, its reference, in paragraphs 4 and 6 of the extract above, to jobs 'almost exclusively carried out by women.' This argument convinced neither the tribunal nor the majority of the Court of Appeal.

British Road Services Ltd v Loughran [1997] IRLR 92

MacDermott LJ (for the majority):

. . . the mischief at which the legislation is aimed is women being paid less than men for performing work of equal value. Where the women are members of an exclusively female group it is fair to assume that there is discrimination—an assumption could not easily be made if that group were a mixed group. It seems to me that the more women there are in the group the easier it would be to draw an assumption in their favour—conversely, if there were more men in the group it is unlikely that such an assumption could be fairly drawn—indeed it probably could not be drawn at least without convincing evidence. I would also add that the composition of a group may lead to a presumption one way or the other and in the light of relevant evidence that presumption will be revealed as sound or unsound and a final determination will be reached having regard to all the evidence . .

Paragraph [2 of the *Enderby* extract immediately above] makes it clear that the existence of two non-discriminatory wage agreements do not 'preclude a finding of prima facie discrimination': that reservation being necessary to prevent circumvention of the equal pay principle. In turn, paragraph [3] seems to be saying that where the claimant group is almost exclusively female and the other predominantly male such agreements are not ipso facto sufficient objective justification for the difference in pay between the two groups . . . paragraph [3] . . . recognises that a s.1(3) Stage 1 defence will not arise on the mere production of a non-discriminatory wage agreement where the applicant group is almost exclusively female. It does not say that where an applicant group contains fewer women than would exist in an 'almost exclusively' situation that the working agreements viewed in the light of all the relevant circumstances may not show objective justification because the more men there are in an applicant group the greater is the chance of the wage differential not being sex-related.

---

[71] Discussed in Ch 2 and below, in which the ECJ also ruled that, where a pay system lacked transparency and resulted in lower wages for women than for men, the burden passed to the employer to disprove discrimination.

It follows from this that if you get a group such as the present which is predominantly female the tribunal should at Stage 1 examine the facts to ascertain why a wage differential exists and whether or not it is due to sex discrimination.[72]

The Northern Ireland Court of Appeal demanded, in *British Road Services*, that the employer establish that the factor relied upon under s.1(3) was non-discriminatory. That court, on that occasion, broke ranks with the 'category' approach which has so often been applied to s.1(3) and took into account the impact of the factor on male and female wages respectively. This is the only correct approach, given that the obligation is on the employer to prove, under s.1(3), that the disputed pay difference 'is genuinely due to a material factor which is not the difference of sex.' In order to be 'not the difference of sex,' the factor which gives rise to the pay difference must be one which discriminates either directly or (without justification) indirectly between women and men.

The decision in *British Road Services* was echoed by that of the House of Lords in *Ratcliffe v North Yorkshire County Council*. The facts of the case have been mentioned above. The claimants initially won their claim, a tribunal ruling that the 'market forces' relied upon by the council in this case could not be said to be 'not the difference of sex.' EAT allowed the employer's appeal, and the Court of Appeal ([1994] ICR 810) rejected the women's appeal on the ground that they, the claimants, had failed to prove that the 'market forces' relied on in this instance were indirectly discriminatory. The House of Lords allowed the women's appeal.

Ratcliffe & Ors v North Yorkshire County Council [1995] ICR 833

Lord Slynn of Hadley:

. . . the three appellants . . . like some 1,300 other women, worked in different schools in the council's area serving school dinners, work which was done almost exclusively by women, who found that the hours of work fitted in well with their family responsibilities and who in the area where they lived might have found it difficult to obtain other work compatible with those responsibilities . .

There has been much argument in this case as to the relationship between s.1 of the [EqPA] and s.1 of the [SDA]. The latter distinguishes between . . . 'direct' . . . [and] 'indirect' discrimination. It is submitted that this distinction must be introduced equally into the [EqPA]. For my part I do not accept that this is so . . . In my opinion the [EqPA] must be interpreted . . . without bringing in the distinction between so-called 'direct' and 'indirect' discrimination. The relevant question under the [EqPA] is whether equal treatment has been accorded for men and women employed on like work or for men and women employed on work rated as equivalent . . . In the present case . . . the women were found to be engaged on work rated as equivalent to work done by men. That is sufficient for the women to be entitled to a declaration by the industrial tribunal in their favour unless s.1(3) of the [EqPA], as set out previously, is satisfied.

This was the question for the industrial tribunal to consider. By a majority they were satisfied that the employers had failed to show that the variation between the appellants'

---

[72] The decision of the majority is consistent with the approach of the ECJ in *R v Secretary of State for Employment ex p Seymour-Smith*, above, in which that court took a flexible view to relative proportions of men and women affected by a practice in order that discriminatory impact be established. Its limits were established by EAT in *Home Office v Bailey* [2004] IRLR 921 in which that Court ruled that no justification had to be put forward in a case in which the disadvantaged group was evenly balanced in terms of sex although the comparator group was predominantly male. The decision is to be appealed.

contracts and those of their male comparators was due to a material factor which was not the difference of sex.

In my opinion it is impossible to say that they were not entitled on the evidence to come to that conclusion. It is obvious that the employers reduced the appellants' wages in order to obtain the area contracts and that to obtain the area contracts they had to compete with CCG who, the tribunal found, employed only women and 'because of that, employed them on less favourable terms than the Council did previously under the NJC agreement'. . . . The fact, if it be a fact, that CCG discriminated against women in respect of pay and that the DSO had to pay no more than CCG in order to be competitive does not, however, conclude the issue. The basic question is whether the DSO paid women less than men for work rated as equivalent. The reason they did so is certainly that they had to compete with CCG. The fact, however, is that they did pay women less than men engaged on work rated as equivalent. The industrial tribunal found and was entitled to find that the employers had not shown that this was genuinely due to a material difference other than the difference of sex.

The women could not have found other suitable work and were obliged to take the wages offered if they were to continue with this work. The fact that two men were employed on the same work at the same rate of pay does not detract from the conclusion that there was discrimination between the women involved and their male comparators. It means no more than that the two men were underpaid compared with other men doing jobs rated as equivalent . . .

The fact that they paid women less than their male comparators because they were women constitutes direct discrimination and ex hypothesi cannot be shown to be justified on grounds 'irrespective of the sex of the person' concerned . . .

Lord Slynn's refusal, in this case, to distinguish between direct and indirect discrimination in the s.1(3) context, did not survive the subsequent decision of the House in *Strathclyde v Wallace*, considered below. It is very unlikely, in any event, that his intention was to preclude justification of an indirectly discriminatory GMF (if this was the case, employers could never pay more for seniority, overtime, flexibility, experience, or any other factor which tends to favour men). It is almost certainly the case that Lord Slynn was seeking simply to rule out the possibility that another court could, as the Court of Appeal did in this case, impose the burden of proving pay discrimination under s.1(3) upon the claimant. In *Strathclyde v Wallace*, Lord Browne-Wilkinson hastened to label that part of the earlier decision obiter and to state that:

Strathclyde Regional Council v Wallace [1998] ICR 205

Whilst there is no need to apply to the [EqPA] the hard and fast statutory distinction between the two types of discrimination drawn in the [SDA], this House did not intend, and had no power, to sweep away all the law on equal pay under article [141] laid down by the European Court of Justice, including the concept of justifying, on *Bilka* grounds, practices which have a discriminatory effect on pay and conditions of service.[73]

---

[73] 'The law on Article [141], while recognising that in many cases there is a *de facto* distinction between direct and indirect discrimination, does not draw the same firm legal demarcation between the two as does the [SDA] which permits justification of indirect discrimination but not of direct discrimination. The correct position under s.1(3) of the [EqPA] is that even where the variation is genuinely due to a factor which involves the difference of sex, the employer can still establish a valid defence under sub-s (3) if he can justify such differentiation on the grounds of sex, whether the differentiation is direct or indirect. I am not aware as yet of any case in which the European Court of Justice has held that a directly discriminatory practice

Lord Browne-Wilkinson went on to suggest, in *Strathclyde*, that:

article [141] . . . does not draw the same firm legal demarcation between [direct and indirect discrimination] as does the [SDA] . . . [t]he correct position under s.1(3) of the [EqPA] is that even where the variation is genuinely due to a factor which involves the difference of sex, the employer can still establish a valid defence under sub-s (3) if he can justify such differentiation on the grounds of sex, *whether the differentiation is direct or indirect* (my emphasis).

Not only is this entirely at odds with the wording of s.1(3) which requires that the factor relied upon by the employer be 'not the difference of sex', but it is also inconsistent with the approach taken to discrimination by the ECJ. The European Commission, in its submissions to the ECJ, has argued on a number of occasions for the recognition of a defence of justification to direct discrimination (see, for example, *Birds Eye Walls* Case C–132/92 [1993] ECR I–05579 and *Webb v EMO* Case C–32/93 [1994] ECR I–03567). So, too, has Advocate-General Van Gerven (*Birds Eye Walls* and *Neath v Hugh Steeper* Case C–152/91 [1993] ECR I–06935).But the ECJ has consistently refused to accept that direct discrimination can be justified—relying, occasionally, on sleight of hand to avoid what would otherwise be regarded as an unacceptable outcome. In *Grant v South West Trains* Case C–249/96 [1998] ECR I–00621, Advocate General Elmer declared that:

in its assessment of whether discrimination based on sex might be justified, the court has traditionally drawn a distinction between direct and indirect discrimination [citing *Dekker v Stichting Vormingscentrum voor Jong Volwassenen* (Case C–177/88 [1990] ECR I–3941), *Nimz* and *Enderby*] . . . Only where discrimination is indirect does the court appear to accept the possibility that it might be justified by reference to objective circumstances . . . In the present case, gender discrimination [is direct] . . .

The ECJ declined to follow the opinion of Advocate General Elmer, but did so on the grounds that no discrimination on the grounds of sex had occurred, rather than because any such discrimination was justified.

Explaining Part of the Pay Gap

In *National Coal Board v Sherwin* [1978] ICR 700, EAT decided that the GMF put forward by the employer—the fact that the comparator worked on nightshift, explained just over half the pay difference between his pay and that of the claimants. This being the case, the tribunal 'without falling into the error of setting itself up as a wage-fixing body may adjust the woman's remuneration . . . so that it is at the same rate as the man's, discounting for the fact that he works at inconvenient hours and she does not.' In *Thomas v National Coal Board* [1987] IRLR 451, in a case involving different (similarly situated) claimants and the same comparator, a differently constituted EAT ruled that the employers had established that 'a variation in . . . pay is genuinely due to a material factor other than the difference of sex' without considering the fact that the factor did not explain all of the difference in pay.

---

can be justified in the *Bilka* sense. However, such a position cannot be ruled out since, in the United States, experience has shown that the hard and fast demarcation between direct and indirect discrimination is difficult to maintain.'

In *Enderby* EAT accepted, as a GMF, a factor which explained only 10 per cent of the pay differential at issue, ruling that: 'where market forces are genuinely material, it is the whole of the difference which is justified,' the alternative being to 'involve the Tribunal in a wage-fixing role [which] would be an unreal approach.' The Court of Appeal specifically referred to the ECJ the question whether this satisfied Article 141, the response of that Court being to the effect that 'if . . . the national court has been able to determine precisely what proportion of the [difference] is due to [there,] market forces [and, it must be presumed, free of sex discrimination], it must necessarily accept that the pay differential is objectively justified to the extent of that proportion. When national authorities have to apply Community law, they must apply the principle of proportionality.' If, on the other hand, it is not possible to determine precisely the extent to which the factor relied upon explains the pay differential 'it is for the national court to assess whether the role of the [factor] in determining the rate of pay was sufficiently significant to provide objective justification for part or all of the difference.'

This appears to ignore the ruling of the ECJ in *Danfoss* that:

Handels-og Kontorfunktionaerernes Forbund I Danmark v Dansk Arbejdsgiverforening (acting for Danfoss) Case 109/88 [1989] ECR I–3199

. . where a system of individual pay supplements which is completely lacking in transparency is at issue, female employees . . . would be deprived of any effective means of enforcing the principle of equal pay before the national courts if the effect of adducing such evidence was not to impose upon the employer the burden of proving that his practice in the matter of wages is not in fact discriminatory. . .

under Article 6 of the Equal Pay Directive Member States must, in accordance with their national circumstances and legal systems, take the measures necessary to ensure that the principle of equal pay is applied and that effective means are available to ensure that it is observed. The concern for effectiveness which thus underlies the directive means that it must be interpreted as implying adjustments to national rules on the burden of proof in special cases where such adjustments are necessary for the effective implementation of the principle of equality.

To show that his practice in the matter of wages does not systematically work to the disadvantage of female employees the employer will . . . be forced to make his system of pay transparent. . .

The Equal Pay Directive must be interpreted as meaning that where an undertaking applies a system of pay which is totally lacking in transparency, it is for the employer to prove that his practice in the matter of wages is not discriminatory, if a female worker establishes, in relation to a relatively large number of employees, that the average pay for women is less than that for men.

It could be argued that *Enderby* and *Danfoss*, read together, ought to require that employers explain at least the bulk of any pay difference by reference to the factors relied upon. This conclusion is strengthened by the general principle of proportionality in EC law. Where a pay difference impacts disadvantageously on one sex and is significantly unjustified by the factor put forward in its defence, it is counter-intuitive to regard that difference as justified. This was recognised by Lord Nicholls in *Barry v Midland Bank* [1991] ICR 859 where he stated that the ECJ in *Enderby* 'drew attention to the need for the national courts to apply the principle of proportionality where they have to apply Community law.' In other words, the ground relied upon as justification must be of sufficient importance for the national court to regard this as overriding the disparate impact of the difference in treatment, either in whole or in part. The more serious the disparate impact on women or men, as the case may be, the more cogent must be the objective justification'. On the other hand, as Michael Connolly has pointed out: the 'objective balance' approach adopted in *Hampson* might result in a finding that disproportionate pay difference was justifiable. Referring to the facts in *Enderby* itself: 'On the one hand there is the 40 per cent difference in pay, on the other the need for sufficient pharmacists. Given that stark choice, a tribunal could easily hold that the difference in pay was justified.'[74]

'Material Factors' and the GMF Defence

In *Tyldesley v TML Plastics*, EAT ruled that 'a difference in pay explained by a factor not itself a factor of sex, or tainted by sex discrimination, should, in principle, constitute a valid defence' to an equal pay claim. There, the employer had appointed the claimant's comparator at a higher wage on the mistaken view that he was in possession of a particular qualification. A tribunal had ruled in the claimant's favour on the basis, inter alia, that 'the employer had not established a good and objectively justified ground' for the pay differential. EAT allowed the employer's appeal, ruling that (per Mummery J) the tribunal had 'erred in law in requiring the employer to satisfy a test of objective justification, apparently in addition to the matter specified expressly in s.1(3).'

It is true that s.1(3) requires the objective justification, in line with *Bilka* and subsequent decisions of the ECJ, only in cases where the factor relied upon by the employer was tainted by sex. It is also true that the tribunal had run together the 'material factor' issue with that concerning the justification of indirect discrimination in appearing to require 'objective justification' of the factor put forward by the employer as the GMF, absent any finding that it was tainted by sex. But it is entirely possible that the tribunal had done no more than to express, albeit imperfectly, a finding that the factor relied upon by the employer was not 'material' and that, therefore, the s.1(3) defence failed even prior to the consideration of discrimination. But EAT entirely failed to advert to the need for a 'material factor' in ruling in favour of the employers.

Tyldesley v TML Plastics Ltd [1996] ICR 356

Mummery J (for EAT):

The [EqPA, Art 141] . . . and the Equal Pay Directive . . . have as their purpose the elimination of sex discrimination, not that of achieving 'fair wages.' Their detailed provisions are to be construed in the light of that purpose.

A difference in pay explained by a factor not itself a factor of sex, or tainted by sex discrimination, should, in principle, constitute a valid defence . . .

In the absence of evidence or a suggestion that the factor relied on to explain the differential was itself tainted by gender, because indirectly discriminatory or because it adversely impacted on women as a group in the sense indicated in *Enderby*, no requirement of objective justification arises. Thus, even if a differential is explained by careless mistake, which could not possibly be objectively justified, that would amount to a defence . . . provided that the tribunal is satisfied that the mistkae was either the sole reason for it or of sufficient influence to be significant or relevant. If a genuine mistake suffices, so must a genuine

---

[74] 'The Sex Discrimination (Indirect Discrimination and Burden of Proof) Regulations 2001 (SI 2001 No 2260)' (2001) 30 *Industrial; Law Journal* 375, 379.

perception, whether reasonable or not, about the need to engage an individual with particular experience, commitment and skills.[75]

Tyldesley was approved by the House of Lords in *Strathclyde v Wallace* in which their Lordships posed for themselves the question whether any and all factors relied upon by the employer under s.1(3) had to be 'objectively justified.'

The equal pay claim was brought by a number of women teachers who named, as their comparators, male principal teachers with whom they were doing the same work while 'acting up' without pay or appointment. A tribunal found that none of the factors relied upon by the employer were related to sex (most of the 'acting up' teachers were male) but ruled in favour of the claimants on the ground that the employer's reliance upon these (albeit non-discriminatory) factors was not objectively justified. EAT overturned the decision of the tribunal, and was upheld in turn by the Court of Sessions and the House of Lords.

Strathclyde Regional Council v Wallace [1998] ICR 205

Lord Browne-Wilkinson:

. . . Of the 134 unpromoted teachers who claimed to be carrying out the duties of principal teachers, 81 were men and 53 women. The selection by the appellants in this case of male principal teachers as comparators was purely the result of a tactical selection by these appellants: there are male and female principal teachers employed by the respondents without discrimination. Therefore the objective sought by the appellants is to achieve equal pay for like work regardless of sex, not to eliminate any inequalities due to sex discrimination. There is no such discrimination in the present case. To my mind it would be very surprising if a differential pay structure which had no disparate effect or impact as between the sexes should prove to be unlawful under the [EqPA] . . .

To establish a sub-s (3) defence, the employer has to prove that the disparity in pay is due to a factor 'which is not the difference of sex,' ie is not sexually discriminatory. The question then arises 'what is sexually discriminatory?' Both the [SDA] and Article [141] of the EEC Treaty recognise [direct and indirect discrimination] . . . Under the SDA, direct sexual discrimination is always unlawful. But, both under the SDA and under Article [141], indirect discrimination is not unlawful if it is 'justified' [citing Bilka-Kaufhaus]. Indirect discrimination can be 'justified' if it is shown that the measures adopted by the employers which cause the adverse impact on women 'correspond to a real need on the part of the [employers], are appropriate with a view to achieving the objectives pursued and are necessary to that end' [citing *Rainey*].

The cases establish that the [EqPA] has to be construed so far as possible to work harmoniously both with the [SDA] and Article [141]. All three sources of law are part of a code dealing with unlawful sex discrimination: see *Shields v Coomes* . . . and *Garland v British Rail Engineering Ltd.* . . . It follows that the words 'not the difference of sex' where they appear in s 1(3) of the [EqPA] must be construed so as to accord with the SDA and Article [141], ie an employer will not be able to demonstrate that a factor is 'not the difference of sex' if the factor relied upon is sexually discriminatory whether directly or indirectly. Further, a sexually discriminatory practice will not be fatal to a sub-s (3) defence if the employer can 'justify' it applying the test in the *Bilka-Kaufhaus* case . . .

There is no question of the employer having to 'justify' (in the *Bilka* sense) all disparities of pay. Provided that there is no element of sexual discrimination, the employer establishes

75 Cf *McPherson v Rathgael* [1991] IRLR 206 (NICA), overruled by the House of Lords in *Strathclyde v Wallace*.

a sub-s (3) defence by identifying the factors which he alleges have caused the disparity, proving that those factors are genuine and proving further that they were causally relevant to the disparity in pay complained of . . .[76]

It appeared, on the facts in *Wallace*, that s.1(3)'s requirement that the pay difference at issue result from 'a material factor' was met. But the failure of the House of Lords to advert to that fact, in stressing that only discriminatory factors require to be justified, is unfortunate. Further, their Lordships once again failed adequately to address the question whether the pay-related factor put forward in *Wallace* was in fact untainted by sex.

Lord Browne-Wilkinson did, it is true, state that most of the 'acting up' teachers were male. But he did not divulge whether an even greater proportion of principal teachers were men. If this was the case (as is likely), the denial of the disputed payments to 'acting up' teachers would have constituted prima facie pay discrimination. And if this had been established, the employers should have been required to justify the practice whereby women performing the duties of a principal teacher were considerably less likely than men performing those duties to be accredited and rewarded as a principal teacher. It may have been demonstrable that this situation was unavoidable in the absence of an (unlawful) decision on the part of employers to restrict the proportion of women 'acting up.' But, had their Lordships taken account of the sex composition of principal teachers, the justifiability of the employer's pay practices would, at least, have been open to scrutiny.

In *Glasgow City Council v Marshall* the House of Lords again considered the operation of the GMF. The case was brought by seven women and a man who were employed as instructors in special schools in Scotland for children with severe or profound learning disabilities. They named as their comparators teachers of the opposite sex, also employed in special schools, who were paid under settlements agreed by the Scottish Joint Negotiating Committee for Teaching Staff in School Education, instructors (whether qualified as teachers or not) being paid according to the NJC for Local Authorities' APT&C scale.

The employment tribunal accepted that there was no sex discrimination (having considered statistics on the breakdown by sex of instructors and teachers), but held that the employers had failed to establish a defence under s.1(3) in that all that they had done was to point to a historical basis for the disparity. In effect, the tribunal concluded that s.1(3) requires a good and sufficient reason for the variation in pay, even where the absence of sex discrimination has been demonstrated. EAT dismissed the Council's appeal but the Court of Session allowed it and the House of Lords rejected the claimants' appeal.

Glasgow City Council v Marshall [2000] ICR 196

Lord Nicholls (with whom their Lordships agreed):

. . . the effect of the industrial tribunal's decision was that, even in a case where the absence of sex discrimination was demonstrated, some good and sufficient reason must exist for the variation in pay. If none was proved, the claim succeeded. The question for your Lordships' House is whether this was a proper interpretation of s.1(3) . . .

I can well understand that an instructor in a special school, whether a woman or a man, may feel aggrieved that a teacher in the same school is being paid more for doing the same

---

[76] Approving the decision of EAT in *Tyldesley v TML Plastics Ltd* and overruling that of the NICA in *McPherson v Rathgael* n75.

or broadly similar work. I have more difficulty in understanding how, in the absence of sex discrimination, this perceived unfairness is said to be caught and cured by a statute whose object, according to its preamble, is to prevent discrimination between men and women as regards terms and conditions of employment. The instructors' contention is that this conclusion follows from the clear wording of s.1. Further, they contend that this conclusion is not surprising. Proof that women are being paid less than men for like work is prima facie evidence of sex discrimination. Part of the purpose of the [EqPA] was to ensure that discrimination does not arise through accident or inertia. If an employer fails to rebut the presumption of sex discrimination because he is unable to show a proper reason for the disparity in pay, the case falls within the mischief the Act was intended to remedy. This conclusion may go further than the provision regarding equal pay for equal work in Article 119 (now renumbered Article 141) of the EC Treaty. But there is no reason why the equality of pay legislation in a Member State should be confined in its scope to that of Article 119.

I am unable to agree with the main thrust of this submission or with the approach adopted by the industrial tribunal. This approach would mean that in a case where there is no suggestion of sex discrimination, the equality clause would still operate. That would be difficult to reconcile with the gender-related elements of the statutory equality clause. The equality clause is concerned with variations in pay or conditions between a woman doing like work with a man and vice versa. But if the equality clause were to operate where no sex discrimination is involved, the statutory starting point of a gender-based comparison would become largely meaningless. On this interpretation of the Act, what matters is not sex discrimination. What matters is whether, within one establishment, there is a variation in pay or conditions between one employee doing like work with another employee. The sex of the employees would be neither here nor there, save that to get the claim off the ground the chosen comparator must be of the opposite sex. On this interpretation the Act could be called into operation whenever mixed groups of workers are paid differently but are engaged on work of equal value. In such a case the statutory equality clause would operate even when the pay differences are demonstratively free from any taint of sex discrimination. Indeed, a notable feature of the industrial tribunal's decision in the present case is that a male instructor succeeded as well as seven female instructors. It is a curious result in a sex discrimination case that, on the same facts, claims by women and a claim by a man all succeed.

I do not believe the Equal Pay Act 1970 was intended to have this effect. Nor does the statutory language compel this result. The scheme of the Act is that a rebuttable presumption of sex discrimination arises once the gender-based comparison shows that a woman, doing like work or work rated as equivalent or work of equal value to that of a man, is being paid or treated less favourably than the man. The variation between her contract and the man's contract is presumed to be due to the difference of sex. The burden passes to the employer to show that the explanation for the variation is not tainted with sex. In order to discharge this burden the employer must satisfy the tribunal on several matters. First, that the proffered explanation, or reason, is genuine, and not a sham or pretence. Second, that the less favourable treatment is due to this reason. The factor relied upon must be the cause of the disparity. In this regard, and in this sense, the factor must be a 'material' factor, that is, a significant and relevant factor. Third, that the reason is not 'the difference of sex.' This phrase is apt to embrace any form of sex discrimination, whether direct or indirect. Fourth, that the factor relied upon is or, in a case within s.1(2)(c), may be a 'material' difference, that is, a significant and relevant difference, between the woman's case and the man's case.

When s.1 is thus analysed, it is apparent that an employer who satisfies the third of these requirements is under no obligation to prove a 'good' reason for the pay disparity. In order to fulfil the third requirement he must prove the absence of sex discrimination, direct or indirect. If there is any evidence of sex discrimination, such as evidence that the difference in pay has a disparately adverse impact on women, the employer will be called upon to satisfy the tribunal that the difference in pay is objectively justifiable. But if the employer proves the absence of sex discrimination he is not obliged to justify the pay disparity.

Some of the confusion which has arisen on this point stems from an ambiguity in the expression 'material factor.' A material factor is to be contrasted with an immaterial factor. Following the observations of Lord Keith of Kinkel in *Rainey v Greater Glasgow Health Board*, the accepted synonym for 'material' is 'significant and relevant.' This leaves open the question of what is the yardstick to be used in measuring materiality, or significance and relevance. One possibility is that the factor must be material in a causative sense. The factor relied on must have been the cause of the pay disparity. Another possibility is that the factor must be material in a justificatory sense. The factor must be one which justifies the pay disparity. As already indicated, I prefer the former of these two interpretations. It accords better with the purpose of the Act. The distinction may not greatly matter in practice when an employer is having to justify the disparity in pay. But the matter stands differently when sex discrimination is not under consideration. Then the distinction may be of crucial importance, as the present case exemplifies. The industrial tribunal, in the course of its self-direction on the applicable law, held that a purely historic explanation of the pay difference between sexes is insufficient. That is correct, when justification is in point. It is not correct when, as in the present case, the absence of sex discrimination was not in issue.

The analysis set out above does not lack supporting authority. A clear exposition is to be found in the judgment of Mummery J, giving the judgment of the Employment Appeal Tribunal, in *Tyldesley v TML Plastics Ltd*. However, a survey of the various decisions and dicta bearing on this point is now unnecessary, in the light of the recent decision of your Lordships' House in *Strathclyde Regional Council v Wallace*. . . .

In the present case the education authorities identified the factor which caused the pay disparity: teachers and instructors were remunerated according to two different nationally negotiated pay scales. This was so, even though the education authorities themselves decided how many spinal column points on the APT&C scale should be attributed to instructors in special schools. As the Lord President observed, it would be wrong to conclude that the causal connection was broken simply because the education authorities could have chosen to pay the instructors more. No one questioned the genuineness of the explanation. Most importantly, no one suggested that the pay disparity was tainted with sex discrimination. Accordingly, the education authorities made good their defence under s.1(3).

Mr Underhill QC, on behalf of the applicant instructors . . . sought to distinguish [*Wallace* on the basis that] in the present case, unlike the *Wallace* case, no specific reason was ever adduced by the education authorities for paying instructors less than teachers. This was an historic practice, of unexplained origin, which had been continued through inertia. Such a 'non-explanation' could not satisfy s.1(3).

My Lords, this beguiling submission invites your Lordships to fall into the same trap as the industrial tribunal. The tribunal rejected the education authorities' explanation for the pay disparity not because they disbelieved the explanation but because they applied a wrong test. This is apparent from the importance the tribunal attached to the education authorities' failure to address themselves to a reassessment of the duties and responsibilities of instructors in special schools. The gist of the tribunal's reasoning was that the authorities could, and should, have done something about the pay disparity and, because they had not done so, could not bring themselves within s.1(3). For the reasons stated above, I take the view that this was an erroneous approach to the application of the statute in the present case. There is here no ground on which to conclude that the reasoning in the *Wallace* is inapplicable to the present case . . .

IRLR 'Highlights', April 2000

The policy expressed by this decision is that the [EqPA] is a sex discrimination statute, not a fair wages law. A finding of equal work creates a presumption that the difference in pay is due to sex discrimination, but an employer who shows that there was no taint of sex discrimination has rebutted the presumption. This is compelling reasoning in a case like *Marshall*, where it was accepted by the applicants that there was no sex discrimination, where the gender composition of the groups concerned—instructors and teachers—was not markedly dissimilar, and where there were both male and female complainants. In that sense, *Marshall*, like *Strathclyde Regional Council v Wallace* before it, was a notably unattractive case to push forward to the House of Lords to test the correct construction of s.1(3). By interpreting the requirement that the reason for the difference must be due to a 'material' factor as meaning that it merely needs to be causally relevant rather than having objective substance, the House of Lords has robbed the word of its function. The use of the words 'due to' provide a causative test and s.1(3), as it has now been interpreted, would read no differently if the word 'material' was removed. Without the word 'material,' the test is subjective; with the word 'material,' the test is also objective. If any reason suffices, so long as it is genuine and not discriminatory, an employer may be able to satisfy s.1(3) by showing that it genuinely thought that one job was worth more than the other and paid the two jobs accordingly. If a good faith defence discharges the burden of proof under s.1(3), it will place a major constraint on the future potential of the [EqPA].

In *Brunnhofer* the ECJ appeared to rule that all material factor defences had to be justified within *Bilka Kaufhaus* and the line of authorities following it, rather than only those factors which by their nature indirectly discriminated on grounds of sex. There the claimant, a bank employee, claimed equal pay with a male colleague who was classified under the applicable collective agreement as being in the same category and who received the same basic salary, but who from his recruitment had been paid a higher supplement than her.

Brunnhofer v Bank der Österreichischen Postsparkasse AG, Case C–381/99 [2001] ECR I–04961

a difference in the remuneration paid to women in relation to that paid to men for the same work or work of equal value must, in principle, be considered contrary to Article [141] . . .
It would be otherwise only if the difference in treatment were justified by objective factors unrelated to any discrimination based on sex . . .
Furthermore, the grounds put forward by the employer to explain the inequality must correspond to a real need of the undertaking, be appropriate to achieving the objectives pursued and necessary to that end . . .
As regards . . . possible justifications for unequal treatment . . . the employer may validly explain the difference in pay, in particular by circumstances not taken into consideration under the collective agreement applicable to the employees concerned, in so far as they constitute objectively justified reasons unrelated to any discrimination based on sex and in conformity with the principle of proportionality.
It is for the national court to make such an assessment of the facts in each case before it, in the light of all the evidence . . .
— as a general rule, it is for employees who consider themselves to be the victims of discrimination to prove that they are receiving lower pay than that paid by the employer to a colleague of the other sex and that they are in fact performing the same work or work of equal value, comparable to that performed by the chosen comparator; the employer may

then not only dispute the fact that the conditions for the application of the principle of equal pay for men and women are met in the case but also put forward objective grounds, unrelated to any discrimination based on sex, to justify the difference in pay . . .
— in the case of work paid at time rates, a difference in pay awarded, at the time of their appointment, to two employees of different sex for the same job or work of equal value cannot be justified by factors which become known only after the employees concerned take up their duties and which can be assessed only once the employment contract is being performed, such as a difference in the individual work capacity of the persons sconcerned or in the effectiveness of the work of a specific employee compared with that of a colleague.

In *Barton v Investec Henderson Crosthwaite Securities Ltd* [2003] IRLR 332 EAT considered the application of the burden of proof in the context of the GMF. The case is considered in some detail in Chapter 5, constituting as it did the first appellate decision on the application of the SDA's amended burden of proof. Here we consider only the EqPA aspects of the case. The claimant alleged breaches of the SDA and EqPA in connection with bonus payments, a male colleague having been paid a significantly higher salary and bonuses after other firms attempted to poach him. An employment tribunal accepted the employer's concern about the comparator being head-hunted as satisfying the GMF defence. EAT allowed the appeal and remitted the case to a different tribunal. Applying the decision of the ECJ in *Brunnhofer*, EAT ruled that the burden was on the employer to prove (1) that there were objective reasons for the difference in pay, (2) which were unrelated to sex, (3) which corresponded to a real need on the part of the undertaking, (4) were appropriate to achieving that objective (5) and necessary to that end, (6) that the difference conformed to the principle of proportionality, and (7) that that was the case throughout the period during which the differential existed.

> The tribunal in *Barton* had accepted that it was a 'vital component of the City bonus culture that bonuses are discretionary, scheme rules are unwritten and individuals' bonuses are not revealed,' this because 'invidious comparisons would become inevitable. If such comparisons were generally possible the bonus system would collapse.' EAT ruled that the tribunal had erred in appearing to condone the lack of transparency in the employers' bonus system.
>
> *Judge Ansell:*
>
> The Equal Opportunities Commission Code of Practice on Equal Pay was issued on 26 March 1997 and was brought into force on that date.
>   Under the heading 'Transparency' the code provided as follows:
>   '19. It is important that the pay system is clear and easy to understand; this has become known as transparency. A transparent pay system is one where employees understand not only their rate of pay but also the components of their individual pay packets and how each component contributes to total earnings in any pay period. Transparency is an advantage to the employer as it will avoid uncertainty and perceptions of unfairness and reduce the possibility of individual claims.
>   20. The ECJ has held that where the organisation concerned applies a system of pay which is wholly lacking in transparency and which appears to operate to the substantial disadvantage of one sex, then the onus is on the employer to show that the

> pay differential is not in fact discriminatory. An employer should therefore ensure that any elements of a pay system which could contribute to pay differences between employees are readily understood and free of sex bias.'
>
> Paragraphs 25 onwards in the Code set out a suggested review of pay systems for sex bias and in paragraph 29 bonuses were highlighted as an area of potential difficulty. Finally, paragraph 39 provided as follows:
>
> > 'It is good employment practice for employees to understand how their rate of pay is determined. Information about priorities and proposed action could be communicated to employees as part of the process of informing them about how the pay systems affect them individually. This will serve to assure employees that any sex bias in the payment system is being addressed' . . .
>
> Dealing with transparency, the appellant's substantial complaint was in relation to certain paragraphs of the decision . . . wherein the tribunal found and appeared to condone, in part relying on their 'industrial knowledge', that the City 'bonus culture' was one of secrecy and lack of transparency. The tribunal's alleged 'industrial knowledge' of this culture certainly conflicted with the lay members of this court, who had experience of many large institutions operating transparent bonus systems, including formal end-of-year appraisals, followed by a properly documented bonus setting procedure. This court would certainly wish to make it clear that no tribunal should be seen to condone a City bonus culture involving secrecy and/or lack of transparency because of the potentially large amounts involved, as a reason for avoiding equal pay obligations.

In *Parliamentary Commissioner for Administration v Fernandez* EAT ruled that a tribunal had erred in placing the burden of proof on an employer to justify pay differentiation based on factors which were not indirectly discriminatory.

Parliamentary Commissioner for Administration v Fernandez [2004] IRLR 22

Judge Peter Clark (for the majority):

This appeal raises directly for determination the question as to whether the European Court of Justice judgment in *Brunnhofer* . . . alters the approach to be taken by employment tribunals, following the House of Lords guidance in *Strathclyde Regional Council v Wallace* and *Glasgow City Council v Marshall*, when considering an employer's genuine material factor defence raised under s.1(3) [EqPA] . . .

Mr Paines QC [for the employer] submits that the employment tribunal has misdirected itself in law in requiring the respondent to objectively justify the differences in pay in circumstances where it was not suggested on behalf of the applicant that the skills factors relied upon by the respondent were indirectly discriminatory. He prays in aid the House of Lords authorities of *Wallace* and *Marshall*, the latter case expressly approving the approach of Mummery P in *Tyldesley* . . .

Mr Allen QC [for the employee], to the contrary, submits that the employment tribunal was merely applying the well established principle, to be found consistently in ECJ jurisprudence, that Article 141 (formerly Article 119) of the Treaty of Rome requires that similar situations shall not be treated differently unless the differentiation is objectively justified. *Brunnhofer* applies that principle in a way particularly relevant to the issue in this case and in a way inconsistent with the reasoning in *Tyldesley*. We should follow the ECJ guidance . . .

Mr Allen points out that in *Wallace*, by the time that case reached the House of Lords it had been conceded on behalf of the applicants that the factor put forward by the respondent was genuine and not tainted by discrimination. In these circumstances, said the House of Lords, no further burden lay on the respondent to objectively justify the pay disparity. In the present case no such concession has been made on behalf of Mr Fernandez. In *Marshall* the House was not invited to depart from its reasoning in *Wallace* . . .

In *Marshall*, Lord Nicholls set out those matters on which the employer must satisfy the tribunal in order to show that the pay variation is not tainted by sex . . .

Mr Allen submits that the approach of the Employment Appeal Tribunal in *Tyldesley* and the earlier case of *Plaskitt* is inconsistent with European law principles in general and *Brunnhofer* in particular . . . It is at this point that this tribunal finds itself divided. The majority accept that general proposition, however, as the Court went on to say in *Brunnhofer*, paragraph 40:

'. . . the differences in treatment prohibited by Article 119 are exclusively those based in the difference in sex of the employees concerned.'

We paraphrase that observation to mean, using the expression to be found in the domestic cases, that the variation in pay is tainted by sex . . . where a prima facie case of indirect discrimination is made out in relation to the factor relied upon by the employer to establish the s.1(3) defence then that factor is tainted by sex discrimination unless it can be objectively justified. That, we think, is the effect of *Bilka*, itself a case of alleged indirect sex discrimination.Which brings us to *Brunnhofer*. It is important to note the relevant question posed by the national court. Question 2(b) reads: 'Are Article 119 (now Article 141) of the Treaty and Article 1 of [the Equal Treatment] Directive 75/117/EEC to be interpreted as meaning that the fixing of different pay may be objectively justified by circumstances which can be established only ex post facto, such as in particular a specific employee's work performance?'It is that question which is addressed in paragraph 63 and following of the judgment. Thus, the reference to the *Bilka*-test at paragraph 67, on which Mr Allen relies, must be seen in the context of the specific question posed to the Court. We do not understand the Court to be laying down, in that case, any requirement that in a case where the factor relied on by the employer is not tainted by direct sex discrimination, and where no suggestion of prima facie indirect sex discrimination is raised, that it is nevertheless necessary for the employer to objectively justify the pay difference in the *Bilka* sense.

In these circumstances the majority are not persuaded that the European jurisprudence requires us to depart from the approach set out in the domestic jurisprudence to which we have referred . . .

The decision in the *Parliamentary Commissioner* case is perhaps not surprising in light of the aim of Article 141: the elimination of gender-based pay disparities, rather than of irrational pay distinctions in general. A similar decision was reached by EAT in *Home Office v Bailey* [2004] IRLR 921. More problematic, however, is the decision of the Court of Appeal in *Nelson v Carillion Services* in which that Court ruled that the burden of proof was on the employee to prove that a GMF put forward by an employer was indirectly discriminatory, rather than it being on the employer to prove that it was not. This claim was brought by a steward employed by Carillion Services at Chelsea and Westminster Hospital who compared their pay to stewards who had originally been employed by Initial Health Care but whose jobs had been transferred to Carillion, their wages protected by TUPE. The claimant alleged that the factor relied upon by the employer to explain the difference in pay was indirectly discriminatory inasmuch but did not establish this statistically to the satisfaction of the tribunal. EAT rejected her appeal. On appeal to the Court of Appeal the claimant argued that she needed to do no more than put forward a credible suggestion about disparate impact, the burden of proof to establish the GMF being placed on the employer by s.1(3) EqPA. The Court of Appeal ruled, however, that the burden of proof in every claim of indirect discrimination was on the claimant to establish disparate impact.[77]

Nelson v Carillion Services Ltd [2003] ICR 1256

Simon Brown LJ (for the Court):

Enderby establishes that the burden of proving sex discrimination lies initially on the employee (paragraph 13). To shift that burden to the employers, the employee (depending upon the particular nature of the case) must establish that the measure 'has in practice an adverse impact on substantially more members of one or other sex' (the first limb of paragraph 14) or, where the system lacks transparency, must 'establish . . . in relation to a relatively large number of employees, that the average pay for women is less than that for men' (the second limb of paragraph 14). Or, as is described in paragraphs 16–18, the complainant must establish 'a prima facie case of sex discrimination' (the phrase used in paragraphs 16 and 18), on statistics which are 'valid' (paragraph 16) and 'appear to be significant' (paragraph 17), at which point 'it is for the employer to show that there are objective reasons for the difference in pay' (paragraph 18). Or, as summarised in paragraph 19, it is for the employee to establish 'an appreciable difference in pay' by 'significant statistics,' at which point the onus shifts to the employer to show that that difference is justified.

That decision was subsequently applied by the ECJ in *Specialarbejderforbundet i Danmark v Dansk Industri* Case C–400/93 [1995] ECR I–1275, where at paragraph 24 the Court said:

> Similarly, where significant statistics disclose an appreciable difference in pay between two jobs of equal value, one of which is carried out almost exclusively by women and the other predominantly by men, so that there is a prima facie case of sex discrimination, Article 119 of the EEC Treaty requires the employer to show that that difference is based on objectively justified factors unrelated to any discrimination on grounds of sex: see *Enderby*, paragraphs 16 and 19.

In the light of those judgments, Mr Langstaff [for the claimant] recognises that, if an unequal pay claim which depends on indirect sexual discrimination is made in the employment tribunal directly under Article 141 of the Treaty (as, of course, it can be), then the burden rests on the applicant to establish disproportionate adverse impact. If he or she were to discharge that burden, the onus would then shift to the employer to prove that his practice is not in truth discriminatory but rather is justifiable . . .

The burden of proving indirect discrimination under the [SDA] was, as Mr Langstaff accepts, always on the complainant, and there pursuant to s.63A [see further Chapter 5] it remains, the complainant still having to prove facts from which the tribunal could conclude

---

[77] *Cf* the decision of EAT (Mrs Justice Cox) in *Ministry of Defence v Armstrong* [2004] IRLR 672, in which EAT relied on the decision of the ECJ in *Enderby* and that of EAT in *Bhudi v IMI Refiners Ltd* [1994] ICR 307 to rule that 'the concept of indirect discrimination is not the same in relation to inequality of pay as to inequality of treatment,' and that 'What matters is whether, in any particular case, a Tribunal is satisfied on the evidence before them and the facts found that the pay difference is caused by a factor or factors which are related to the difference in sex.' Cox J distinguished *Nelson* as a case in which the claimants had only 'raised a "credible suggestion" that relevant, valid and significant statistics might establish disproportionate impact . . . In the present case, for the purposes of the preliminary issue, this Tribunal were asked to assume that the Applicants were doing like work or work of equal value to that of their comparators. The variation between the Applicants' pay and that of their comparators was therefore, in the clear words of Lord Nicholls in *Marshall* "presumed to be due to the difference of sex" and the burden therefore passed to the Appellants to show that the explanation for the pay difference was not tainted by sex, or to seek objectively to justify it if it was.'

that he or she has been unlawfully discriminated against 'in the absence of an adequate explanation' from the employer. Unless and until the complainant establishes that the condition in question has had a disproportionate adverse impact upon his/her sex the tribunal could not in my judgment, even without explanation from the employer, conclude that he or she has been unlawfully discriminated against.

This to my mind accurately reflects the position laid down by the ECJ in *Enderby* and that, indeed, is hardly surprising. True it is, as Mr Langstaff points out, that the Burden of Proof Directive expressly provides that, '[T]his Directive shall not prevent Member States from introducing rules of evidence which are more favourable to plaintiffs.' It is difficult to see, however, why the UK should have wished to introduce a rule more favourable to applicants (a) than had earlier been established by the domestic authorities, or (b) than the ECJ thought appropriate for a claim directly brought under Article 119.

All these considerations notwithstanding, it is the appellant's submission that when one comes to a claim brought under the [EqPA] the burden lies throughout on the respondent employer, the applicant in an indirect discrimination case having to advance no more than 'a credible suggestion' of disproportionate adverse impact.

This somewhat surprising conclusion, Mr Langstaff submits, is justified, indeed required, by the plain language of s.1(3) itself, a provision differently framed from anything in the [SDA]. Section 1(3) in terms puts the burden of proof on the employer. And support for this approach, he argues, is to be found in Lord Nicholls's speech in *Glasgow Corporation v Marshall* . . . He relies in particular upon Lord Nicholls's statement, in the second of the two paragraphs I have cited, that:

> In order to fulfil the third requirement [that the reason for the less favourable treatment is not 'the difference of sex', a phrase 'apt to embrace any form of sex discrimination, whether direct or indirect'] he must prove the absence of sex discrimination, direct or indirect.

The argument is in my judgment unsustainable. In the first place, it overlooks the very next sentence in Lord Nicholls's speech:

> If there is any evidence of sex discrimination, such as evidence that the difference in pay has a disparately adverse impact on women, the employer will be called upon to satisfy the tribunal that the difference in pay is objectively justifiable.

This seems to me to recognise that it is for the complainant initially to establish that the matter complained of has indeed had 'a disparately adverse impact on women'. Secondly, however, it should be appreciated that *Glasgow Corporation v Marshall* was not concerned with the burden of proof at all; that simply was not an issue in the case.

There seems to me every reason for approaching the burden of proof in indirect discrimination cases in the same way irrespective of whether they are brought under Article 119 (141), under the [SDA], or under the [EqPA]. As Lord Browne-Wilkinson said in *Strathclyde Regional Council v Wallace*:

> The cases establish that the [EqPA] has to be construed so far as possible to work harmoniously both with the [SDA] and Article 119. All three sources of law are part of a code dealing with unlawful sex discrimination: see *Shields v E Coomes (Holdings) Ltd* and *Garland v British Rail Engineering Ltd*. It follows that the words 'not the difference of sex' where they appear in s.1(3) of the [EqPA] must be construed so as to accord with the [SDA] and Article 119 of the EC Treaty, ie an employer will not be able to demonstrate that a factor is 'not the difference of sex' if the factor relied upon is sexually discriminatory whether directly or indirectly. Further, a sexually discriminatory practice will not be fatal to a subsection (3) defence if the employer can 'justify' it applying the test in the *Bilka-Kaufhaus* case.

Mr Langstaff's argument furthermore seems to me irreconcilable with at least one of the authorities relied upon by Mr Linden: *Barry v Midland Bank plc* [1999] ICR 319 (Court of Appeal); [1999] ICR 859 (House of Lords). I shall content myself with a brief citation from a judgment at each level. In the Court of Appeal, Peter Gibson LJ said at:

> In our opinion it would be necessary to look at all part-time workers at the time of Mrs Barry's termination of employment and the average of their hours of work throughout their service and to compare the men and the women in the advantaged and disadvantaged groups. But there are no such statistics available, as we understand the position. It was an agreed fact that 12 out of the 33 part-time staff who were female employees (of unspecified grades throughout the bank) made redundant in April 1993 had previous full-time service. But we have no more details and it is unsafe to base any conclusion on that bare statistic. The bank as the employer is likely to have the relevant information though it may well be that it would not be readily to hand. But it was for Mrs Barry to prove her case of indirect discrimination, seeking, if necessary with the industrial tribunal's assistance, the relevant information from the bank.

Lord Slynn in the House of Lords said this:

> The question is thus whether Mrs Barry can establish indirect discrimination by showing (a) that she belongs to a group of employees which is differently and less well treated than others, and (b) that that difference affects considerably more women than men and, if she can, whether (c) the bank can show that the difference in treatment is objectively justified . . .

Mr Langstaff submits that *Barry*, properly understood, does not assist the respondents. The issue there, he contends, was not where the burden lay for the purposes of establishing the s.1(3) defence, but rather whether Mrs Barry had surmounted the initial hurdle of demonstrating a breach of the equality clause under s.1(2), something in the event she was found not to have done. This, however, to my mind involves too narrow and technical an analysis of the judgments in that case. It would, I think, be bizarre to require an applicant to establish her prima facie case of indirect discrimination for the purpose of establishing that a term of her contract 'is . . . less favourable to [her] than a term of a similar kind in the contract under which [a man in the same employment] is employed,' but not when her case of indirect discrimination is advanced to counter the employer's explanation for her less favourable term, an explanation which is apparently genuine and attributable to reasons other than sex.

I have in short come to the clear conclusion that in an indirect discrimination case the burden of proving disproportionate adverse impact lies on the complainant, and that merely to raise 'a credible suggestion' that, were the relevant (valid and significant) statistics provided, these might establish disproportionate impact is not sufficient for the applicant's purposes and imposes no further burden of explanation upon the employer.

Coverage of the SDA and Exceptions Thereto

Exceptions and the Equal Treatment Directive

The SDA is frequently regarded as an Act which prohibits discrimination against women. Its terms, however, apply equally to men. Further, the SDA prohibits discrimination against married persons as well as discrimination on grounds of sex, although this prohibition applies only in relation to employment and the definition of indirect discrimination is that which applies to sex *outside* the employment field (that is, the original definition set out in the Act—see further Chapter 2). As of 1999, the SDA also applies expressly to discrimination in connection with gender-reassignment, although this prohibition extends only to direct discrimination in the employment sphere and is otherwise more qualified than is the case with discrimination on grounds of sex or married status.[78] Discrimination connected with gender reassignment is dealt with further in Chapter 10.

A number of the exceptions to the SDA (sports, charities and insurance, height requirements for prison and police officers, etc) have been mentioned in Chapter 4. We saw there that the Act does not apply in relation to employment outside Britain, and we considered the exceptions set out in ss.51 and 51A SDA (acts done under statutory authority). In Chapter 3 we considered the scope of positive action permissible under the SDA.

The exceptions to the SDA must be considered in light of the Equal Treatment Directive whose provisions are directly effective as regards public sector employers and impose interpretive obligations on the courts regardless of the public or private sector nature of the employer. That Directive prohibits discrimination on grounds of sex (Article 2) 'either directly or indirectly by reference in particular to marital or family status.' Prior to their amendment by Council Directive 2002/73/EC from October 2005, Articles 2(2)–(4) set out limited exceptions to the scope of the prohibition on discrimination:

> (2) This Directive shall be without prejudice to the right of Member States to exclude from its field of application those occupational activities and, where appropriate, the training leading thereto, for which, by reason of their nature and of the context in which they are carried out, the sex of the worker constitutes a determining factor.
>
> (3) This Directive shall be without prejudice to provisions concerning the protection of women, particularly as regards pregnancy and maternity.
>
> (4) This Directive shall be without prejudice to measures to promote equal opportunity for men and women, in particular by removing existing inequalities which affect women's opportunities in [employment, broadly defined].

In Chapter 4 we also considered s.52(1) SDA which provides that 'Nothing in Parts II to IV shall render unlawful an act done for the purpose of safeguarding national security.' This provision is of potentially wide application, and was relied upon by the Secretary of State for Northern Ireland in *Johnston* to block substantive consideration by a tribunal of a challenge under the Sex Discrimination (Northern Ireland) Order 1976 to a prohibition imposed upon the handling and use of firearms by women police officers. The impact of this ban, in a police force which was generally armed, was to deny the claimant continued full-time employment. The effect of the national security certificate issued by the Secretary of State at the time was to dispose of the claim, s.52 providing that ministerial certification that 'an act specified in the certificate was done for the purpose of safeguarding national security' was conclusive evidence of the matters certified. Ms Johnston appealed to the ECJ which ruled that the conclusive nature of the ministerial certificate was incompatible with the right imposed by the Equal Treatment Directive of access to judicial determination of a discrimination complaint. It then went on to consider the substantive claim under the Directive. The decision, and the others considered below, give an indication of the approach taken by the Court to Article 2(2).

---

[78] The SDA does not prohibit discrimination against single people.

Johnston v Chief Constable of the Royal Ulster Constabulary **Case C–222/84 [1986] ECR 1651**

The policy towards women in the RUC full-time reserve was adopted by the chief constable because he considered that if women were armed they might become a more frequent target for assassination and their fire-arms could fall into the hands of their assailants, that the public would not welcome the carrying of fire-arms by women, which would conflict too much with the ideal of an unarmed police force, and that armed policewomen would be less effective in police work in the social field with families and children in which the services of policewomen are particularly appreciated. The reasons which the chief constable thus gave for his policy were related to the special conditions in which the police must work in the situation existing in Northern Ireland, having regard to the requirements of the protection of public safety in a context of serious internal disturbances.

As regards the question whether such reasons may be covered by Article 2(2) of the Directive, it should first be observed that that provision, being a derogation from an individual right laid down in the Directive, must be interpreted strictly. However, it must be recognized that the context in which the occupational activity of members of an armed police force are carried out is determined by the environment in which that activity is carried out. In this regard, the possibility cannot be excluded that in a situation characterized by serious internal disturbances the carrying of fire-arms by policewomen might create additional risks of their being assassinated and might therefore be contrary to the requirements of public safety.

In such circumstances, the context of certain policing activities may be such that the sex of police officers constitutes a determining factor for carrying them out. If that is so, a Member State may therefore restrict such tasks, and the training leading thereto, to men . . . it is for the national court to say whether the reasons on which the chief constable based his decision are in fact well founded and justify the specific measure taken in Mrs Johnston's case. It is also for the national court to ensure that the principle of proportionality is observed . . .

The scope of Article 2(2) was considered more recently by the ECJ in *Sirdar v Secretary of State for Defence*, a claim brought by a woman denied a position in the marines. Women are prohibited from serving in the marines by virtue of that organisation's principle of 'interoperability'—that is, the rule that all marines must be capable of operating in a commando unit. Women are prohibited from active combat service[79] with the effect that Ms Sirdar, who had applied for transfer as a chef to the marines in order to avoid redundancy, was ineligible for the position. Her claim could not be brought under the SDA, s.85(4) of which provides that '[n]othing in this Act shall render unlawful an act done for the purpose of ensuring the combat effectiveness of the naval, military or air forces.'

The UK Government sought to argue that 'decisions concerning the organisation and administration of the armed forces, particularly those taken for the purpose of ensuring combat effectiveness in preparation for war, fall outside the scope of EC law.' The ECJ rejected this argument, ruling instead that the case turned on Article 2(2) of the Equal Treatment Directive.

---

[79] This rule was maintained after an MOD review—see 'Women in the Armed Forces' (May 2002), available at http://www.mod.uk/linked_files/women_af_summary.pdf.

Sirdar v Secretary of State for Defence Case C–273/97 [1999] ECR I–07403

it must be noted . . . that, as a derogation from an individual right laid down in the Directive, [Article 2(2)] must be interpreted strictly . . .

The Court has thus recognised, for example, that sex may be a determining factor for posts such as those of prison warders and head prison warders (Case 318/86 *Commission v France* [1988] ECR 3559), or for certain activities such as policing activities where there are serious internal disturbances (*Johnston*).

A Member State may restrict such activities and the relevant professional training to men or to women, as appropriate. In such a case, as is clear from Article 9(2) of the Directive, Member States have a duty to assess periodically the activities concerned in order to decide whether, in the light of social developments, the derogation from the general scheme of the Directive may still be maintained . . .

In determining the scope of any derogation from an individual right such as the equal treatment of men and women, the principle of proportionality . . . must also be observed, as the Court pointed out in paragraph 38 of *Johnston*. That principle requires that derogations remain within the limits of what is appropriate and necessary in order to achieve the aim in view and requires the principle of equal treatment to be reconciled as far as possible with the requirements of public security which determine the context in which the activities in question are to be performed.

However, depending on the circumstances, national authorities have a certain degree of discretion when adopting measures which they consider to be necessary in order to guarantee public security in a Member State . . .

The question is therefore whether, in the circumstances of the present case, the measures taken by the national authorities, in the exercise of the discretion which they are recognised to enjoy, do in fact have the purpose of guaranteeing public security and whether they are appropriate and necessary to achieve that aim.

In *Kreil v Germany* Case C–285/98 [2000] ECR I–69 the ECJ ruled that, although it was for Member States to make decisions on the organisation of their armed forces, such decisions were subject to the Equal Treatment Directive and their lawfulness fell to be assessed under Article 2(2). A complete prohibition on women in the armed services was disproportionate since Article 2(2) permitted exceptions to the prohibition on sex discrimination only in relation to specific activities. Nor could such a complete ban be permitted under Article 2(3).[80]

Genuine Occupational Qualifications

The SDA recognises (s.7(2)) a number of situations in which sex is a 'genuine occupational qualification' (GOQ) for a job. Where this is the case, discrimination is not prohibited in relation to appointments to the job under s.6(1)(a) and (c) SDA, or in relation to 'opportunities for promotion or transfer to, or training for, such employment' under s.6(2)(a) SDA. Section 67(2), which must be interpreted so far as possible in conformity with Article 2 of the Equal Treatment Directive[81] provides that 'being a man [or a woman] is a genuine occupational qualification for a job only where':

[80] More recently, in *Dory v Germany* Case C–186/01 [2003] ECR I–02479 the ECJ ruled that the German requirement for men (but not women) to perform national service did not fall within the scope of the Equal Treatment Directive. The ECJ categorised the exclusively male obligation as a 'choice[] of military organisation for the defence of their territory or of their essential interests.'

[81] See *Webb v EMO*, discussed below.

(a) the essential nature of the job calls for a man for reasons of physiology (excluding physical strength or stamina) or, in dramatic performances or other entertainment, for reasons of authenticity, so that the essential nature of the job would be materially different if carried out by a woman; or

(b) the job needs to be held by a man to preserve decency or privacy because—
  (i) it is likely to involve physical contact with men in circumstances where they might reasonably object to its being carried out by a woman, or
  (ii) the holder of the job is likely to do his work in circumstances where men might reasonably object to the presence of a woman because they are in a state of undress or are using sanitary facilities; or

(ba) the job is likely to involve the holder of the job doing his work, or living, in a private home and needs to be held by a man because objection might reasonably be taken to allowing to a woman—
  (i) the degree of physical or social contact with a person living in the home, or
  (ii) the knowledge of intimate details of such a person's life, which is likely, because of the nature or circumstances of the job or of the home, to be allowed to, or available to, the holder of the job; or

(c) the nature or location of the establishment makes it impracticable for the holder of the job to live elsewhere than in premises provided by the employer, and—
  (i) the only such premises which are available for persons holding that kind of job are lived in, or normally lived in, by men and are not equipped with separate sleeping accommodation for women and sanitary facilities which could be used by women in privacy from men, and
  (ii) it is not reasonable to expect the employer either to equip those premises with such accommodation and facilities or to provide other premises for women; or

(d) the nature of the establishment, or of the part of it within which the work is done, requires the job to be held by a man because—
  (i) it is, or is part of, a hospital, prison or other establishment for persons requiring special care, supervision or attention, and
  (ii) those persons are all men (disregarding any woman whose presence is exceptional), and
  (iii) it is reasonable, having regard to the essential character of the establishment or that part, that the job should not be held by a woman; or

(e) the holder of the job provides individuals with personal services promoting their welfare or education, or similar personal services, and those services can most effectively be provided by a man, or

(g) the job needs to be held by a man because it is likely to involve the performance of duties outside the United Kingdom in a country whose laws or customs are such that the duties could not, or could not effectively, be performed by a woman, or

(h) the job is one of two to be held by a married couple.

The 'personal services' GOQ is considered in some detail in Chapter 7 (see, in particular, the discussions of the *Lambeth* and *Tottenham Green* cases—the holdings in which are equally applicable here). The absence of any GOQ permitting the operation of, for example, women-only taxi services is of note, given the widespread perception on the part of women that the use of minicabs renders them vulnerable to sexual assault. But many consider that the GOQ defence is too widely drawn in the context of the SDA.

D Pannick, *Sex Discrimination Law*, 250–71, footnotes omitted

Part of the difficulty with section 7 is that it attempts to deal with three separate types of cases, those of physical, functional, and social differences between the sexes. The physical differences concern cases where, by reason of his or her sex, a person is simply unable to perform the job. The functional differences concern cases where Parliament has recognised that, by reason of her sex, a person is less able effectively to perform the job. Such cases are hard to reconcile with the fundamental premiss of the 1975 Act that one should consider persons as individuals irrespective of the qualities commonly possessed by or associated with their sex. Section 7(2)(d) and section 7(2)(e) also seem inconsistent with the principle that sex is not a GOQ merely because of customer preference. The social differences between men and women recognised by section 7 include those concerned with privacy and decency. Clearly it is a matter of social policy to what extent privacy and decency should limit the employment opportunities of one sex. Different societies adopt different values relating to the sharing of sleeping accommodation by men and women at work or relating to states of undress at work. . . .

Once one moves away from the obvious examples of cases where the essential nature of the job calls for a person of a particular sex for reasons of 'physiology,' difficult questions are raised of what is 'the essential nature' of a job and when is its performance 'materially different' because carried out by a man (or a woman)? Suppose a company which manufactures motor cars wishes to advertise its product by hiring attractive models to be photographed in a state of undress lying on the bonnet. Although it wants to employ women, and not men, for reasons of physiology, it is unclear whether the essential nature of the job would be materially different if performed by a male model. Even if the company is correct in assuming that it will sell more cars by employing *female* models, this is insufficient to make sex a GOQ for the job. There is a thin, but important, line between sex as a GOQ where the essential nature of the job requires a woman, and the case where the job can more effectively be performed by a woman because of customer reaction. A publican cannot refuse to employ men behind the bar because he believes (rightly or wrongly) that a barmaid attracts more custom. The essential nature of the job, that is serving alcohol, would not be materially different if performed by a man. The reference in section 7(2)(a) to 'the essential nature of the job' and to whether it would be 'materially different' if carried out by a man requires the court to look objectively at the job in its context. If a men's club employs topless waitresses, sex may be a GOQ even though in other circumstances the essential nature of the job (serving customers) is not materially different when performed by a man. The court is required to look at the essence of the job and to reject an employer's attempt to add sex appeal to the job definition unless that is part of the essential nature of the job. . . .

The vague criterion of reasonableness in section 7(2)(c)(ii) gives courts and tribunals the unenviable task of deciding how to balance a person's right not to be discriminated against on the ground of their sex and an employer's plea that it should not have to incur a financial burden in employing that person.

In deciding what is 'reasonable' under section 7(2)(c)(ii) it is unfortunately not relevant that, as Baroness Seear emphasised in Parliament, in other European countries 'it is far more common for men and women to share certain premises and conveniences' (for example, train couchettes). The question under section 7(2)(c)(ii) is whether it is reasonable to expect the employer to provide separate sleeping accommodation and private sanitary facilities for each sex, not whether it is reasonable to refuse to employ women because there are no such facilities provided. Section 7(2)(c) adopts a very conservative approach to this question, allowing employers to refuse jobs to women even if women are prepared to share facilities with men, and even if those men are prepared to share the facilities with the women. It is not a precondition for the applicability of section 7(2)(c), as it is for the applicability of section

7(2)(b), that relevant men (or women) 'might reasonably object' to the employment of members of the other sex. Section 7(2)(c) needs amendment to include such a precondition. . . .

The difficulty with section 7(2)(d) is to understand why it is necessary. Why should sex be a GOQ in jobs done in special establishments where the privacy and decency GOQ in section 7(2)(b) does not apply, when the communal accommodation GOQ of section 7(2)(c) does not apply, and where the personal services GOQ of section 7(2)(e) does not apply? If any of these other bases for a GOQ supply the rationale for section 7(2)(d), then section 7(2)(d) is otiose. If these other factors are not relevant, what is the rationale for section 7(2)(d)? No rationale different from those presented in section 7(2)(b) and section 7(2)(e) was suggested by the Government during the parliamentary debates on the Bill. The argument that prisoners, or patients, or persons in other institutions need to be dealt with by a person of their own sex (even though this is neither to preserve decency or privacy nor because persons of that sex can most effectively provide personal services) badly smells of the offensive sex stereotyping that the 1975 Act aims to eradicate. . . .

Two objections were raised to section 7(2)(g) during parliamentary debates. Neither of them received a satisfactory answer. First, which countries have laws or customs which prevent the performance (or effective performance) of which jobs by women (or men)? It is difficult to assess the propriety of an exception to the general anti-discrimination principle unless one knows precisely what one is validating.

The second objection to the existence of section 7(2)(g) was that we should not 'enshrine in our legislation a concession to the prejudices of other countries . . .'. It was emphasisd by those unhappy about section 7(2)(g) that the 1975 Act would be a model for amended legislation prohibiting race discrimination: surely we would not allow employers to discriminate against blacks or Jews in filling jobs whose partial duties were performed in Great Britain, on the ground that some duties were to be performed in a less enlightened country where such individuals would, by reason of that country's laws or customs, be unable to perform the duties adequately or at all. Indeed, the Race Relations Act 1976 does not make membership of a particular racial group a GOQ in circumstances similar to those defined in section 7(2)(g). In *American Jewish Congress v Carter, Aramco*, an oil company with interests in Saudi Arabia, were accused of acting contrary to the New York State Law against discrimination by refusing to employ Jews for work which might involve travel to Saudi Arabia. They discriminated in this way because the King of Saudi Arabia not only prohibited the employment of Jews there but also 'strenuously objects to the employment of Jews in any part of Aramco's operation'. The judge in the Supreme Court of New York rejected the claim that being a non-Jew was a BFOQ [bona fide occupational qualification] for the job. He declared that:

> This court does not pretend to assert that Saudi Arabia may not do as it pleases with regard to whom it will employ within the borders of Saudi Arabia . . . What this court does say is that Aramco cannot defy the declared public policy of New York State and violate its statute within New York State, No matter what the King of Saudi Arabia says. New York State is not a province of Saudi Arabia, nor is the constitution and statute of New York State to be cast aside to protect the oil profits of Aramco.

He said that if Aramco cannot employ Jews because of the orders of the King, 'the answer of New York State is simply—Go elsewhere to serve your Arab master—but not in New York State.'

The rationale of section 7(2)(h) is difficult to comprehend. If by section 7(2)(h) Parliament merely wished to allow employers to continue to require a married couple to perform the two jobs, then the subsection is otiose. A single person applying for one of the jobs, or an unmarried couple applying for the jobs, would have no legal complaint. There would be no sex discrimination, and section 3 prohibits discrimination on the ground of marital status only when it is against married persons. Presumably, therefore, Parliament intended to allow an employer, taking on a married couple for two jobs, to specify which job should be done by which spouse. Why is it unlawful for an employer to require that, in its offices, its caretaker must be male or to require that its cleaner must be female, but lawful for the employer to require a married couple to act as caretaker and cleaner and to specify that the husband must be the caretaker and the wife must be the cleaner? One hopes that courts and tribunals would interpret section 7(2)(h) to prevent employers abusing this exemption by requiring a married couple as a pretext for sex discrimination . . .

The late Sir Ronald Bell MP vigorously opposed the 1975 Bill in Parliament. However, he welcomed the clause which became section 7. He described it as 'a good, old clause about the authentic male characteristics. It is the lavatory clause—and all that. Nothing would help the Bill to make sense, but if we did not have Clause 7 the Bill would be such manifest nonsense that it would have been laughed out on Second Reading.' Section 7 indeed more often furthers the objectives of those who opposed the 1975 Act than the objectives of those who supported the legislation . . .

In *Sisley v Brittania Security Systems Ltd* [1983] ICR 628 EAT accepted, as falling within s.7(2)(b), a job in which the state of undress was incidental to, rather than required by, the job. The case was brought by a man refused a job in a security control room because the women working shifts there were in the habit of removing their uniforms so as to avoid creasing them when they took rests during long shifts. A tribunal found that the rest periods were necessary and accepted that the state of undress was reasonably incidental thereto. Both the tribunal and EAT ruled in favour of the employer. The decision was doubted by Pannick.

D Pannick, *Sex Discrimination Law*, 250, footnotes omitted

Section 7(3) suggests that sex is a GOQ only where the job 'duties' so require. Section 7(2)(b)(ii) refers to the 'needs' of the job. The reference to 'sanitary facilities' in section 7(2)(b)(ii) does not, as the EAT suggested, show that the subsection extends further than job duties. When men might reasonably object to the presence of a woman because the men are using sanitary facilities, it is the job *duties* of the lavatory attendant which made sex a GOQ for the job. The attendant *needs*, by reason of the essence of the job, to be present where the sanitary facilities are being used.

Section 7(2) and the EEC Directive 76/207 [the Equal Treatment Directive] demand a compelling justification before sex discrimination is validated in employment. *Sisley* does not appear to present such a justification since there was no need for women employees to take off their clothes; in any event, there was no reason why they should not change into leisure clothes in the lavatory area and rest on the bed in those clothes rather than in their underwear. If there is a clash between the desire of female employees not to crumple their uniforms and the desire of Mr Sisley to be considered for a job vacancy irrespective of his sex, the former must give way to the latter. The policy of the 1975 Act and the EEC Directive admits of no other solution.

Section 17(2)(d) of the Irish Employment Equality Act 1977 provided that sex was an occupational qualification 'where either the nature of or the duties attached to a post justify on grounds of privacy or decency the employment of persons of a particular sex.' After receiving an indication from the European Commission that this body considered section 17(2)(d) to be inconsistent with EEC Directive 76/207/EEC [the Equal Treatment Directive], the Irish Government repealed section 17(2)(d) . . . This action, expressly carried out 'for the purpose of giving effect to Council Directive 76/207/EEC,' strongly suggests that section 7(2)(b) of the 1975 Act should be given a narrow construction whenever possible so as to ensure consistency with the Directive. Section 7(2)(b), like the other parts of section 7(2) of the 1975 Act, should be held to make sex a GOQ for a job only where there is 'justification for so doing under the EEC Directive.

Among the cases which have arisen under s.7 are *Etam v Rowan* [1989] IRLR 150 in which EAT accepted that a job in a women's clothing shop could come within s.7(2)(b) where it involved assisting in a changing area. In that case the GOQ defence was defeated under s.7(4), see below. And in *Buckinghamshire County Council v Ahmed*, EAT allowed an appeal against a finding of unlawful discrimination in respect of a man who had not been given work as a Punjabi interpreter. His name had been entered on a list of Punjabi and other interpreters, most of the Punjabi interpreters being women, but only female interpreters had actually been used by the Council. EAT ruled that the tribunal had erred in rejecting as a GOQ the Council's evidence that:

Buckinghamshire County Council v Admed App. No. EAT/124/98, 18 June 1998 (unreported)

Hull J:

in a number of the ethnic communities with which they dealt and in particular the Punjabi Muslim community, there was great delicacy in dealing with women who were concerned in various social or medical or other problems. It was said that if an interpreter were to go into one of the homes, or to see women collectively at perhaps a 'well woman' session, or women's health session or something of that sort, it would be regarded generally in the community and by the woman concerned as inappropriate that the interpreter should be a man. It was said that although if (say) a white social worker went to a house that might be in order, if a person who was a Punjabi went there it were better, it said, that it should be a woman than a man, out of feelings of delicacy and tact.

It was not said, of course, that it was essential that it should be a woman interpreter but what was said was that the services could be provided more effectively: it would be easier for a Punjabi Muslim woman, on many occasions, to explain in such matters as the case perhaps where her children had been involved in matters which had attracted the attention of the Police, or where she herself had medico-social problems or something like that. It would be easier for her to speak to a woman and would not attract the sort of comment that might happen if a male Punjabi-speaker, particularly a Punjabi himself, were to go to the house.[82]

It should be noted that s.7(3) provides that discrimination in access to employment is permitted 'where only some of the duties of the job fall within paragraphs (a)–(g),[83] as well as where all of them do' and s.7(4) generally precludes the operation of the GOQ defence in relation to vacancies 'when the employer already has male [female] employees:

(a) who are capable of carrying out the duties falling within [the relevant] paragraph; and
(b) whom it would be reasonable to employ on those duties; and
(c) whose numbers are sufficient to meet the employer's likely requirements in respect of those duties without undue inconvenience'.[84]

---

[82] The case was remitted to a different tribunal for rehearing, the original tribunal having placed undue evidence on the opinion of its Sikh member.

[83] S.7(2)(h) relating to jobs to be held by married couples.

[84] In *Lasertop Ltd v Webster* [1997] ICR 828 EAT ruled that s.7(4) had no application in a case in which such employees had not yet been recruited—the job refusal occurred at pre-opening recruitment for a health club and was based on the argument that a man could not show potential clients around the changing facilities.

In *Timex Corporation v Hodgson* [1982] ICR 63, the first GOQ case to reach EAT, that tribunal failed to take account of s.7(4) in finding in favour of an employer who had selected a woman rather than a man for a supervisory position on the basis that, there being no other women supervisors at the factory, it was necessary to have one woman supervisor to deal with the personal problems of women staff, to keep the women's toilets stocked and to take urine samples from women staff working with toxic substances when the woman whose job this was was unavailable. A tribunal rejected the employer's argument that the duties at issue brought the job within s.7(2)(b), ruling that other non-supervisory staff were available for this purpose. EAT overruled (without referring to s.7(4)), stating that the tribunal 'cannot tell the employers how to manage their business and that they need not have included the additional duties in the . . . job.'

The relationship between the SDA's GOQ defence and the provisions of the Equal Treatment Directive has been mentioned above. That Directive is to be amended by Council Directive 2002/73 whose provisions must be implemented in domestic law by October 2005. It replaces Article 2(2)–(3) as follows (Article 2):

6. Member States may provide, as regards access to employment including the training leading thereto, that a difference of treatment which is based on a characteristic related to sex shall not constitute discrimination where, by reason of the nature of the particular occupational activities concerned or of the context in which they are carried out, such a characteristic constitutes a genuine and determining occupational requirement, provided that the objective is legitimate and the requirement is proportionate.
7. This Directive shall be without prejudice to provisions concerning the protection of women, particularly as regards pregnancy and maternity. A woman on maternity leave shall be entitled, after the end of her period of maternity leave, to return to her job or to an equivalent post on terms and conditions which are no less favourable to her and to benefit from any improvement in working conditions to which she would be entitled during her absence.

Less favourable treatment of a woman related to pregnancy or maternity leave within the meaning of Directive 92/85/EEC shall constitute discrimination within the meaning of this Directive.

This Directive shall also be without prejudice to the provisions of [the parental leave directive]. It is also without prejudice to the right of Member States to recognise distinct rights to paternity and/or adoption leave. Those Member States which recognize such rights shall take the necessary measures to protect working men and women against dismissal due to exercising those rights and ensure that, at the end of such leave, they shall be entitled to return to their jobs or to equivalent posts on terms and conditions which are no less favourable to them, and to benefit from any improvement in working conditions to which they would have been entitled during their absence.

Article 2(7) is considered below. But Article 2(6) replaces the original Article 2(2)'s sex as a 'determining factor' with sex as a 'genuine and determining occupational requirement, provided that the objective is legitimate and the requirement is proportionate'. This on its face is a higher threshold. It, like the original Article 2(2), may apply because of the context in which occupational acts are carried out, as well as the activities themselves. But the onus will be on the employer to demonstrate that the is not only legitimate, but that its pursuit is proportionate to the discrimination resulting from it. A similar provision in the Race Equality Directive has resulted in the inclusion in the RRA, where discrimination on grounds of racial, ethnic or national origin is at issue, of the following (s.4A(2) RRA):

(2) This subsection applies where, having regard to the nature of the employment or the context in which it is carried out—
  (a) being of a particular race or of particular ethnic or national origins is a genuine and determining occupational requirement;
  (b) it is proportionate to apply that requirement in the particular case; and
  (c) either—
    (i) the person to whom that requirement is applied does not meet it, or
    (ii) the employer is not satisfied, and in all the circumstances it is reasonable for him not to be satisfied, that that person meets it.

Section.4A RRA is discussed in Chapter 7. The draft SD Regs do not propose any equivalent amendment to the SDA but, given the shortcomings of S7 SDA highlighted above, it is unlikely that such inaction will satisfy the requirements of the amended Directive.

Clothing and Appearance Rules

It is very common indeed for employers (and, indeed, schools), to impose regulations concerning clothing and appearance. In the employment field these rules are generally regarded as falling within the sphere of managerial discretion. A number of challenges have, however, been mounted against the operation of clothing and appearance rules. Such challenges have been made under the SDA, generally in cases where differential rules are imposed on men and women. They have also been made, as we shall see in Chapter 7, under the RRA. These latter claims tend to be quite different from those considered here, the alleged discrimination consisting in the disparate impact of the rules on persons of different race-related religious groups.

If a very straightforward approach is taken, it might be thought that any application of different rules to men and to women should be regarded, in the absence of express provision to the contrary, as breaching s.1(1)(a) SDA. Thus, for example, employers should not be permitted to require that women wear skirts or, indeed, that men wear trousers (unless the same requirement exactly is applied to both sexes). This type of interpretation was rejected by the Court of Appeal in the recent *Smith v Safeway plc* decision ([1996] ICR 868). In this case, which is further discussed below, Phillips LJ declared that:

a code which made identical provisions for men and women, but which resulted in one or other having an unconventional appearance, would have an unfavourable impact on that sex being compelled to appear in an unconventional mode. Can there be any doubt that a code which required all employees to have 18-inch hair, earrings and lipstick would treat men unfavourably by requiring them to adopt an appearance at odds with conventional standards?

This statement is difficult to dispute. But what it overlooks is that any code which applied those standards of appearance to women forces them to conform with a particular model of 'appropriate' femininity. It is damaging to women in a different and less obvious way than it is damaging to men. But it is damaging nonetheless. And, whereas Phillips LJ used his argument to support the imposition of what were regarded by the court as 'sex appropriate' sex-specific appearance codes, it is equally consistent with a different approach.

If dress codes were to be permitted only where they applied, in identical form, to men and women, the imposition of any code which, in practice, presented more difficulties to either men or women would be indirectly discriminatory. This being the case, it could be upheld only to the extent that it was justifiable. It is difficult to picture any circumstances, outside the performing arts, where it would be justifiable for an employer to require that men wore long hair, earrings and lipstick. But it is also difficult to see many circumstances in which an employer could justify the application of such a rule to women. And the beauty of adopting the approach set out above is that, once the code has been declared to discriminate indirectly against men, its use in respect of women would also have to stop. What employers would still be permitted to do would be to require that employees conform to particular standards of hygiene, neatness and smartness.

The weakness which might be identified with the alternative approach set out above is that it would not, for example, allow an employer to permit women to wear skirts or trousers, while prohibiting men from wearing skirts. Few employers would, perhaps, object to men wearing kilts (which are, after all, the favoured apparel of conventional royal males). But 'appalling vistas' might be conjured up regarding mini-skirted lumberjacks and stiletto-clad postmen.

Assuming that cross-dressing is regarded as a matter over which employers are entitled to have control (an argument which might become more difficult to sustain in view of the SDA's gender reassignment provisions, particularly given the early, pre-medical intervention—point at which protection begins), one could argue that employers be permitted to require that employees adopt 'conventional' dress codes. This would permit women to wear trousers (garb which has been widely regarded as acceptable for sixty years), while permitting control over more eccentric forms of dress. This approach is not conceptually very far removed from that which has found favour in the British courts. The difference of degree involved, however, has proven very significant in allowing employers to enforce such 'sex appropriate' dress codes as they see fit.

The judicial approach which prevails to this day was established by EAT in *Schmidt v Austicks Bookshops*. The claimant complained that she was prohibited from wearing trousers to work and, in addition, required to wear overalls while serving customers. Men, by contrast, were subject to the sole restriction that they were not permitted to wear t-shirts at work. Her claim failed before the tribunal and EAT. Phillips J, for the Court, disregarded the matter of the overalls (which, presumably, gave female staff a subordinate appearance by comparison with men) as too trivial to amount to a 'detriment' (see further Chapter 4) before going on to establish the general approach to clothing rules:

Schmdt v Austicks Bookshops [1978] ICR 85

Phillips J:

. . . although there was less scope for positive rules [ie, 'no skirts'] in the case of the men, in that the choice of wearing apparel was more limited, there were restrictions in their case, too. For example, they were not allowed to wear [tee] shirts; and it is quite certain, on a reasonable examination of the evidence, that they would not have been allowed to wear, had they sought to do so, any out-of-the-way clothing. And so they were subjected to restrictions, too, albeit different ones—because, as we have already said, the restrictions to which the women were subjected were not appropriate to the men. Experience shows that under the [SDA] a lot depends on how one phrases or formulates the matter of which complaint is made. Here it has been formulated in the terms of skirts and overalls. As has been pointed out, in another case it might be in terms of ear-rings for men, long hair, all sorts of possibilities. But it seems to us that the realistic and better way of formulating it is to say that there were in force rules restricting wearing apparel and governing appearance which applied to men and also applied to women, although obviously, women and men being different, the rules in the two cases were not the same. We should be prepared to accept . . . an alternative contention . . . 'that in any event, in so far as a comparison is possible, the employers treated both female and male staff alike in that both sexes were restricted in the choice of clothing for wear whilst at work and were both informed that a certain garment should not be worn during working hours.'

It seems to us, if there are to be other cases on these lines, that an approach of that sort is a better approach and more likely to lead to a sensible result, than an approach which examines the situation point by point and garment by garment . . .

The *Schmidt* approach operates, within the structure of the SDA, by accepting that a 'sex appropriate dress code' can be a 'relevant circumstance' within s.5(3) (see further Chapter 2), and by finding discrimination only if the terms of the code, as they apply to one sex, are significantly less favourable than those which apply to the other. The approach entails (1) accepting that a 'sex appropriate dress code' can be a 'relevant circumstance' within s.5(3) of the SDA, and (2) finding discrimination only if the terms of the code, as govern employees of the claimant's sex, are significantly less favourable than those which govern employees of the opposite sex.

Such less favourable treatment has, on occasion, been found by tribunals. In January 2000, for example, Judy Owen's success in an SDA claim against the Professional Golfers' Association, which had required her to wear trousers at work, was widely publicised. Such decisions are, however, rare. In *Schmidt*, as we saw above, a dress code forbidding women from wearing trousers and requiring them to wear overalls was regarded as not significantly less favourable than that forbidding men from wearing T-shirts. In *Burrett v West Birmingham Health Authority* (unreported, but noted in the *Industrial Law Journal* (1995) 24, 177), a uniform which required, in respect of female nurses, that a linen cap be worn was not regarded as imposing upon them significantly less favourable treatment than in the case of men, who had no obligation in respect of headgear. Finally, in *Smith v Safeway plc* [1996] ICR 868 the Court of Appeal ruled that the prohibition, in the case of male employees, of long hair (female employees were permitted to wear their hair long and tied back) was not discriminatory. In doing so, the Court overruled EAT which had ([1995] ICR 472) distinguished the code, bearing as it did on the employee's appearance outside employment, from those upheld in *Schmidt* and in *Burrett*.

Schmidt permits employers to reinforce, through dress codes, the very stereotypes of 'male' (serious, responsible, mature) and 'female' (decorative handmaidens) which disadvantage women at work. Because they are in line with stereotyped notions of what is appropriate to men and women respectively, these dress codes are not seen 'objectively' to 'demean' women even where they serve to mark them out as 'second class.' The other difficulty with *Schmidt*, upheld as it has been by the Court of Appeal in *Smith*, is that its approach to discrimination has more in common with that of the Court of Appeal in *Peake* [[1978] QB 233] (subsequently disapproved of in this regard in *Farthing* ([1980] QB 87]) than it does with the decision of the House of Lords in *James v Eastleigh* [1990] 2 AC 751] in which their Lordships refused to accept, as a 'relevant circumstance' within s.5(3), the attainment of retirement age on the grounds that this was, itself, gender-based (see further Chapter 2).

It is true that the Court of Appeal in *Dhatt v McDonald Hamburgers* [[1991] ICR 238] accepted a nationality-related factor as a 'relevant circumstance' under s.5(3) (see further Chapter 2), but neither this decision nor those in *Schmidt* and *Smith* can properly be viewed as consistent with *James*.

The approach of the British courts to appearance codes has been widely criticised.

L Flynn, 'Gender Equality Law and Employer's Dress Codes' (1995) 25 *Industrial Law Journal* 255, 256–60, footnotes omitted

It is important to clarify the distinction between 'sex' and 'gender.' Sex means those irreducible, biological differentiations between those members of the human species who have XX and those who have XY chromosomes which include more or less marked dimorphisms of genital formation, hair growth, fat distribution, hormonal function, and reproductive capacity. *Gender*, the assumptions, expectations habits and usages which identify a particular individual to themselves and to others as being a man or a woman, is socially constructed. The precise form and content of those elements constituting social gender vary greatly over time and from one place to another; historical and anthropological studies show that the signals indicating that a given individual is 'really' a man or a woman are contingent and historically situated. In short, gender is a system of categories constructed on the site of the body but lacks any essential, given link with the (sexed) body.

There is an expectation that gender and sex should coincide so that gender, which is socially constructed, acquires an air of inevitability while sex is perceived as being inextricably linked with a range of behaviour which is taken as appropriate even though it lacks any intrinsic connection with biological sex. A demand for coincidence between superficially 'feminine' (or 'masculine') dress and the sexed reality of the body has been applied and enforced in our society, save in a few socially sanctioned situations, throughout the modern period. Thus dress difference (which is gendered) is assumed to . . .

As a result of its dual function, identifying both what the subject is and what she should be, dress has a significance beyond the conventional; aspects of personal appearance which are regarded as feminine, such as long hair, earrings and make-up, not only indicate that, in general, one is looking at a woman but also serve to identify a deviation from social norms if one knows that the person one is observing is male. This equation of the habitual with the normal means that any move by some members of one sex to take up the elements of dress associated with the other sex are initially treated as a major transgression. That spectre of cross-dressing may, in turn, provoke a panicked defence of masculinity (or femininity) which sometimes spills over into the courts. . . .

Although *Schmidt* stands as the leading English case on this matter, it can be criticized at two key points. The reasoning of the EAT rests on a questionable assumption, namely, that it is not open to men to wear certain items of apparel which are available to women. This premise removes the possibility of strict comparability between the sexes in matters of dress and necessitates the use of a modified, equivalence analysis of the situation. Neither of these elements in the EAT's reasoning—the impossibility of a skirt-wearing male, and the necessity of an identical comparator—stands up to scrutiny. To say that something is not usual or normal is not to say that it is not possible. The starting point produced by the EAT in *Schmidt* was ill-founded and is not convincing. The boundaries of acceptable male and female dress can, and have, shifted significantly over the centuries and have altered with dramatic speed in the past few decades. Efforts to fix this process through an ascription of natural limits to 'female' and 'male' apparel cannot be reconciled with the basic philosophy of anti-discrimination legislation. It is true that if one did accept the argument that this requirement, not to wear trousers and to wear skirts or dresses, could never be applicable to men, then a similarly situated male comparator would be absent. However, in the wake of European Court of Justice cases, such as *Dekker* and *Webb*, dealing with pregnancy, a genuinely sex-unique characteristic, this gap need not be fatal to a successful direct discrimination claim. Nonetheless, rather than indulge this fantasy of the impossibility of a man in a dress, one must return to the basic point that *Schmidt* forces an inappropriate inevitability onto the gender of apparel.

Paul Skidmore wrote of the *Smith v Safeway* case:

P Skidmore, 'Sex, Gender and Comparators in Employment Discrimination Law' (1997) 26 *Industrial Law Journal* 51, 54–6, footnotes omitted

Phillips LJ considered the proposition put to the Court by counsel for Nicholas Smith 'that conditions of employment which place restrictions on men which do not apply to women, or vice versa, are unlawful.' This proposition is in accordance with existing case-law: *R v Birmingham CC ex p EOC* [[1989] 1 AC 1155] and *James v Eastleigh BC* which interpreted s.1(1)(a) SDA strictly, holding that the motive of the discriminator is irrelevant. Safeway did not however argue that there was discrimination, albeit with a benign motive, for example, to protect its business reputation and so as not to frighten or offend customers. It argued in line with the decision in *Schmidt* that Smith had not suffered less favourable treatment and that different treatment of men and women could be non-discriminatory. Phillips LJ accepted this by placing an unacceptable gloss on 'less favourable treatment' (as had been done in *Schmidt*). He chose firstly to look at the dress code as a whole, rather than item by item, and assumed secondly that any overall package which reinforces conventional gender stereotypes (or as he put it 'a conventional standard of appearance') does not give rise to less favourable treatment. He refused to accept the reasoning of the industrial tribunal in *Rewcastle v Safeway* (a case with very similar facts). There the tribunal held that the rationale of the SDA, that is to say challenging traditional assumptions about the sexes, extended to assumptions about dress and appearance.

This gloss on 'less favourable treatment' cannot be justified. A restriction on hair length which applies to men and not to women is less favourable treatment of men. In the light of *James*, this should be the full extent of the analysis. All the surrounding factors are totally irrelevant. Thus Peter Gibson LJ's discussion of the employer's motives or rationale should have had no place in this judgment. He also suggests that it is a matter of fact and degree whether the employee has been subjected to less favourable treatment. This seems to be allowing the tribunal too great a degree of discretion—the comparison he makes with *Boychuk v Symons* [[1977] IRLR 395] is inappropriate—the unfair dismissal legislation gives the tribunal considerable discretion, which is not present under s.1(1)(a) SDA. For a man to lose his job for having long hair when a woman with hair of the same length would not have done so, should on any interpretation constitute less favourable treatment. . . .

The misunderstanding of the judges, clearly evident in *Nicholas Smith*, is that they think that those challenging conventional gender roles and assumptions want so to disrupt conventionality that it itself becomes unconventional, with compulsory cross-dressing as a rule. For many workers and campaigners, the aim is to have sufficient freedom in law for all workers to have autonomy and control over their gendered appearance and relationships, without this infringing the autonomy to others. Using sex discrimination legislation to the full is one way of attempting this. . . . the prospects for gays and lesbians at least to achieve this autonomy through the traditional political processes of the EC/EU remain remarkably slim, thus litigation is likely to remain high on the agenda.

A number of cases decided post *Smith v Safeway* suggested that the tide might have turned. Judy Owen's sucess in *Owen v Professional Golf Association* (2000) was mentioned above. Her employers had instructed her to go home and change from a smart trouser suit into a skirt. Female Eurostar guards persuaded their employer to allow them to wear trousers at work after a dispute. And the EOC won a settlement in a well-publicised case involving a challenge brought by a school girl to a uniform requirement that girls wore skirts rather than trousers.[85] The orthodox approach was recently restated by EAT in *Department for Work and Pensions v Thompson*, however. The case concerned a challenge to a dress code imposed on Jobcentre Plus staff which required all staff to dress 'in a professional and businesslike way,' but which (as of April 2002 only) stipulated that men were required to wear a collar and tie while women had 'to dress appropriately and to a similar standard.' The claimant, an administrative assistant whose job did not involve public contact, refused to wear a collar and tie and received a formal warning. An employment tribunal ruled that the dress code breached the SDA, this on the basis that women had greater choice than their male colleagues as to what they could wear. EAT overruled, applying the classic *Schmidt* approach. According to the Court, the fact that different rules applied to men and women did not amount to sex discrimination.

Department for Work & Pensions v Thompson [2004] IRLR 248

Keith J:

It is unquestionably the case that the requirement on male members of staff to wear a collar and tie meant that female members of staff had a far greater choice in what they could wear than men. But the employment tribunal acknowledged Jobcentre Plus's right to introduce and enforce a dress code whose aim was to achieve a uniform level of smartness on the part of all its staff. Thus, in the context of the overarching requirement for its staff to dress in a professional and businesslike way, the question for the employment tribunal was whether, applying contemporary standards of conventional dresswear, the level of smartness which Jobcentre Plus required of all its staff could only be achieved for men by requiring them to wear a collar and tie. The level of smartness which Jobcentre Plus thought appropriate for women can be seen from the photographs of Mr Thompson's five women colleagues. If, for example, a level of smartness for men which equates to dressing in a professional and businesslike way which is appropriate for an undertaking like Jobcentre Plus can be achieved by men dressing otherwise than in a collar and tie, then the lack of flexibility in the dress code introduced by Jobcentre Plus would suggest that male members of staff are being treated less favourably than female members of staff because it would not have been necessary to restrict men's choice of what to wear in order to achieve the standard of smartness required. The issue is not resolved by asking whether the requirement on men to wear a collar and tie meant that a higher level of smartness was being required of men rather than women. It is resolved by asking whether an equivalent level of smartness to that required of the female members of staff could only be achieved, in the case of men, by requiring them to wear a collar and tie . . .

---

[85] See discussion at http://www.eoc.org.uk/cseng/advice/school_uniformsfaqs.asp.

It is not for the Employment Appeal Tribunal to decide whether men have to wear a collar and tie in order to achieve the level of smartness which Jobcentre Plus required of both sexes. That is for the employment tribunal to decide. Mr Thompson's case will therefore have to be remitted to the employment tribunal for that issue to be addressed.

The IRLR commentary stated ('Highlights', May 2004) that 'This emphasis on overall even-handedness does have the advantage of avoiding item-by-item clothing comparisons. However, it raises the intriguing issue of whether members of employment tribunals should be regarded as the appropriate arbiters of smart dresswear.'

Pregnancy

Pregnancy and Equality

It is clear from Chapter 2 that one of the major applications of the SDA has been to women *as mothers*. Whereas complaints of direct discrimination are concerned with the conscious application of less favourable treatment to women *as women*, many indirect discrimination claims have challenged practices which disadvantage women who have taken time out of the labour market (*Price v Civil Service Commission* [1978] ICR 27, *Jones v University of Manchester* [1992] ICR 52, *Falkirk Council v Whyte* [1997] IRLR 560), or those whose childcare commitments preclude full-time or other particular patterns of work (*Clymo v Wandsworth* [1989] ICR 250, *Cast v Croydon* [1998] ICR 500, *London Underground v Edwards* [1995] ICR 574).

Motherhood poses very significant challenges to women in the labour market. Many jobs, certainly most high status jobs, are shaped around workers who are not responsible for the physical care of others. But even more fundamental, in terms of the hurdles to labour market equality, is the discrimination frequently associated with pregnancy itself:

[p]regnant women workers are still seen as 'invalids' who are not physically or emotionally capable of fulfilling the demands of their employment. Two other traditional attitudes to emerge were that pregnant women who were already mothers should be at home, and that pregnant workers were placing themselves, their child, fellow workers and clients in 'danger' and selfishly using employers' and taxpayers' resources.[86]

Traditionally, many women left the paid labour market in order to have children. As more women have continued in work through pregnancy—generally with a view to returning relatively shortly after childbirth—the discrimination they face appears to have intensified. The National Association of Citizens Advice Bureaux recently found very high levels of discrimination associated with pregnancy.[87] And the EOC's recent publication 'Pregnancy Discrimination at Work: A Review' reported that 'most [pregnancy-related] dismissals take place prior to maternity leave, some [25 per cent of those reaching a tribunal] within days,

---

[86] 81 *Equal Opportunities Review* 10–11, citing H Gross, 'Pregnancy and Employment: the perceptions and beliefs of fellow workers', Department of Human Sciences, Loughborough University.
[87] 'Birthrights' available from NACAB's website at nacab.org.uk.

even hours, of [women] informing employers of their pregnancy.' An average of over 1000 pregnancy-related unfair dismissal cases were registered each year between 1996 and 2002 (these in addition to complaints relating to terms and conditions and to non-recruitment). According to the EOC's interim report on the pregnancy FI, 'Tip of the Iceberg' (2004), on average, tribunals award £2,000 less in pregnancy-related than in other sex discrimination dismissal claims. The report cited OECD evidence that concern about the career implications of childbearing is depressing the birth rate[88] and reported that, while some 80 per cent of women return to work within 17 months of child birth, only 47 per cent return to their original employer.

G James, 'Pregnancy Discrimination at Work: A Review', footnotes omitted

Calls to the EOC Helpline since the launch of the [pregnancy] investigation in September 2003 provide anecdotal evidence of a multitude of problems experienced by pregnant women at work, as follows:

- A university lecturer, employed for 12 years in the same department on a series of fixed term contracts (all of one year or less) reported how she had had to 'grovel' for a contract extension for benefits because her contract was due to expire the day she started maternity leave.
- An accountant reported how, when she told her employer she was pregnant, she was accused of under performing and told that 'people' had complained about her conduct. When she returned to work with another employer following a second pregnancy, she was given a pay rise which was substantially less than that given to her colleagues.
- A shop worker at a national retailer was refused time off for an antenatal appointment. When absent due to pregnancy related illness she was told that they were 'starting to lose compassion for her' and wanted her to come in as they 'had a shop to run.' She did not have adequate breaks during a shift and was made to sit on a backless chair that caused her back problems. She was eventually made redundant . . .

Examples of discriminatory treatment can also be read in the tribunal decisions. There is evidence of women being pressurised into resigning when they inform their employer of their pregnancy, or being given the ultimatum of either resigning or aborting the baby. Others are verbally abused, ignored or ha[ve] their working conditions altered as a result of pregnancy or childbirth, including drastic reductions in their working hours or increased workloads . . . Particular examples of derogatory treatment include [a claimant] . . . who was told to accept a 'lesser' position or be dismissed [, another who] . . . was asked to sign a letter of resignation when she insisted that she wanted to continue with the pregnancy and [another] . . . who was simply handed her P45 in an envelope and her job was soon advertised in the local paper. The applicant's supervisor in [one case] . . . told her, in the presence of witnesses (including the Managing Director who, incidentally, took no action), that they did not want a 'pregnant split arsed cow' working in their office . . .

When seeking to explain the reasons for pregnancy related discrimination in the workplace it is useful to consider employers' experiences of employing pregnant women employees and female staff with dependent children. The latter is important not least because it highlights employers' potential fears and assumptions about the impact of pregnancy on their business in the long term. A MORI survey of Britain's big employers found [in 2002], for example, that employers of working parents experience a variety of problems:

---

[88] The OECD report cited is 'Babies And Bosses: reconciling work and family life. Austria, Ireland and Japan'. Vol 2 (2003, OECD).

- 70 per cent reported that childcare problems meant staff were unable to work extra hours or work late when needed
- 66 per cent reported absenteeism due to childcare problems
- 55 per cent found that childcare problems resulted in late attendance or leaving work early
- 44 per cent had difficulties recruiting and retaining the staff they need
- 42 per cent felt that childcare problems meant their staff were tired, irritable or stressed, and
- 40 per cent said that childcare problems lead to female staff not returning to work after maternity leave

EOC, 'Tip of the Iceberg' (2004) 10, 25

In Britain today, pregnancy is still seen as an issue for women. The role of fathers in supporting partners during pregnancy and in looking after their own children once they are born is hardly recognised. EOC research shows that, 30 years ago, fathers spent around 15 minutes a day looking after their children. They now spend around two hours a day, a major social change.

The position in Sweden provides a good contrast. There the policy focus is on parents rather than mothers. Both parents can split 480 days' leave up to the child's eighth birthday, and claim a high level of state parental benefit while they are off work. What we term pregnancy discrimination is seen there not as sex discrimination, but as a broader, non-gender-specific discrimination. In Sweden only 2 per cent of women are economically inactive because of family responsibilities, compared with 14 per cent in the UK. The flexible provisions in Sweden are grounded upon a policy which seeks to advance the well-being of the child, to promote women's economic independence and encourage fathers' involvement in childcare and family life . . .

The current system is failing to protect women from pregnancy discrimination, much of which is going unchallenged and unmonitored. It relies on individuals, and their families, to gamble their health, income and well being in order to take action against their employers. Individual litigation is not the most effective way to combat systemic discrimination.

Many women who return to work after childbirth do so on a part-time basis (almost 50 per cent of all working women working part-time). The problems associated with this practice are considered further below. Here we deal exclusively with the issues of pregnancy and maternity.

Pregnancy and Maternity Rights

The Employment Rights Act 1996 [ERA] provides some protection against pregnancy-related discrimination.

S. 99(1) An employee who is dismissed shall be regarded . . . as unfairly dismissed if—
    (a) the reason (or, if more than one, the principle reason) for the dismissal is that she is pregnant or any other reason connected with her pregnancy,
    (b) her maternity leave period is ended by dismissal and the reason (or, if there is more than one, the principle reason) for the dismissal is that she has given birth to a child or any other reason connected with her having given birth to a child,
    (c) her contract of employment is terminated after the end of her maternity leave period and the reason (or, if more than one, the principle reason) for the dismissal is that she took, or availed herself of the benefits of, maternity leave . . .

Special provision is made (s.77) for redundancy arising during the course of maternity leave, the employer being obliged to offer the woman any suitable alternative employment which is available and failure so to do being regarded as automatically unfair dismissal within s.99. No qualifying period of employment applies in respect of s.99.

In addition to the right not to be dismissed, all women are entitled under ss.71–85 ERA to maternity leave of 26 weeks (this right was introduced only in 1996 and between then and April 2000 was for a period of only 14 weeks, between then and April 2003 18 weeks).[91] Women who have been continuously employed for at least 26 weeks have additional rights to absence for a period of six months after the birth. Failure on the part of an employer to permit a woman to return will amount to a dismissal and shall, if it falls within s.99 above, be automatically unfair.

Some provision is made for maternity pay, though this is not generous (being restricted, at best, to 90 per cent of salary for six weeks and £106 a week (from April 2005) for a further twenty—though this is a significant improvement from the previous levels.[92] In September 2004 the Trade and Industry Secretary Patricia Hewitt proposed the extension of paid leave to twelve months. But women earning less than the National Insurance threshold (£82 per week from April 2005) during a particular eight week period of their pregnancy are not entitled to any maternity pay. The *Equal Opportunities Review* pointed out in 1998 that 25,000 women were affected by this rule. Such women are entitled to a Sure Start Maternity Grant of £500 from the Social Fund (previously a Maternity Payment which was for ten years frozen at £100 before being increased to £200 in 1999 and replaced with the Sure Start Grant in 2000).

The position in Britain does not compare favourably with that elsewhere. In 2003 (prior to the April increase in that year) it was third from bottom in the EU. According to 114 *Equal Opportunities Review* a British woman earning £15,000 pa would have been entitled to £2,458 over the course of six months' maternity leave (this figure would now stand at £3,658) by comparison with a Greek figure of £1,250 and one in Luxembourg of £1,845. The EU average, however, stood at £4,198 while Danish and Italian women were entitled to £6,756 and £6,058 respectively. The best maternity provision in this respect, both in Europe and globally, was made by Norway where a similarly paid women would receive full pay— £7500—over six months' leave. Even the relatively cash-strapped former Eastern-bloc Hungary and Poland managed £4,846 and £5,615 respectively.

Had the protection afforded by the ERA and its successors against pregnancy-related discrimination been comprehensive, no issue might have arisen as to the inclusion or otherwise of pregnancy discrimination within the SDA's prohibition on 'sex' discrimination. But the provisions discussed above are of relatively recent vintage. Prior to 1996, dismissal on grounds of pregnancy was only prohibited in the case of women having at least two years qualifying service (five in the case of those working for under 16 hours a week). The ERA protections apply only to 'employees' rather than to the broader category protected under the SDA and other discrimination-related legislation.[93] Further the right to return was, in respect of babies expected prior to 30 April 2000, subject to fulfilment of technical

---

[91] Two weeks leave after the birth is compulsory on pain of criminal sanctions for the employer.

[92] £59.55 in 1999 increased to £70 from April 2002 and £100 from April 2003. From that date one adoptive parent per child is entitled to maternity-length adoptive leave at the flat rate. Those who have been employed for less than about nine months at the time of the birth are entitled only to Maternity Allowance at the lower rate.

[93] To the extent that this continues to deny the right to maternity leave to other women workers it appears to be inconsistent with Article 2.7 of the Equal Treatment Directive (as amended). This has not been acknowledged in the draft SD Regs which make no proposal to extend the right to maternity leave to 'workers'.

requirements of mind-numbing complexity. The notice requirements have been simplified by the Maternity and Parental Leave, etc, Regulations 1999 and the Maternity and Parental Leave (Amendment) Regulations 2002.[94] Finally, whereas the compensation which may be awarded under the SDA has, since 1993, been uncapped, unfair dismissal compensation under the ERA is subject to a maximum limit which stands at £56,800 from 2005 but which, until 2000, was a mere £12,000. (By contrast, women who relied on the SDA to challenge their pregnancy-related dismissals from the armed forces (which, until 1990, operated a blanket policy of dismissing pregnant women), proved losses, and secured awards, of up to around £300,000).

Pregnancy and Sex Discrimination

Such were the shortcomings of legislation expressly dealing with pregnancy that women began to argue that pregnancy-related discrimination fell within the prohibitions of the SDA. Whether 'pregnancy' equates with 'sex' in this context has been one of the long-running debates associated with the legislation. That there should have been some disagreement as to whether or not pregnancy discrimination could be regarded as direct sex discrimination is not surprising. Most employers who discriminate against pregnant women do not do so because they disapprove of pregnancy as such, rather because of its actual or anticipated impact of attendance, flexibility, etc, and the ensuing requirement for maternity leave. Challenging pregnancy-related discrimination as sex discrimination has been problematic because of the formal approach to equality adopted by the SDA.

S Fredman, 'A Difference with Distinction: Pregnancy and Parenthood Reassessed' (1994) 110 *Law Quarterly Review* 106, 106–9, footnotes omitted

In many areas, such as that of the suffrage, equality has been a useful tool. It has, moreover, had an important influence on anti-discrimination law. In this context, the policy that gender alone should not be a sufficient ground for differentiation translates into the equal treatment principle, namely, that those who, apart from their gender, are alike, should be treated alike. However, in the pregnancy context, the equal treatment principle presents some intractable problems. Five central limitations will be dealt with here. First, the equal treatment principle requires an answer to the question 'Equal to whom?' The answer supplied by anti-discrimination law is, generally, 'equal to a man.' For example, under the [SDA], it is unlawful for an employer to treat a woman less favourably on grounds of her sex or marital status than a man would have been treated. In the pregnancy context, this central reliance on a male norm leads straight into the awkward question of who the relevant male comparator should be. Secondly, the reach of the equal treatment principle is necessarily restricted to those who are held to be similarly situated. It requires no explanation for the type of treatment meted out to those who are not equal in the relevant ways. Thus, no justification is required for detrimental treatment of women in cases in which there is no similarly situated male. In the pregnancy context, if no relevant comparator can be found, detrimental treatment is in effect legitimated. The third limitation of the equality principle is that it requires only consistency of treatment between men and women, not

---

[94] Respectively SI 1999 No. 3312 and SI 2002 No. 2789. The Regs are discussed in more detail by the author at (2000) 29 *Industrial Law Journal* 125, 'Family Friendly Frolics.' One significant improvement resulting from the Employment Relations Act 1999, under which the Regulations were passed, is that the contract of employment is declared to subsist throughout maternity leave. For the previous position and the implications thereof see *Kelly v Liverpool Maritime Terminals* [1988] IRLR 310 (CA), *Crees v Royal London* [1998] ICR 848 (CA) and *Halfpenny v IGE* [1999] ICR 834 (CA).

minimum standards. In the pregnancy context, this means that a women's rights are entirely dependent on the extent to which comparable rights are afforded to comparable men. For example, if it is accepted that a pregnant woman is similarly situated to an ill man, then she is entitled only to the rights he has. If he has no protection against dismissal or sick leave, then she has correspondingly no protection against dismissal on grounds of her pregnancy or rights to maternity leave. Fourthly, the equal treatment principle leads to an inadequate consideration of the question of who should bear the social cost of pregnancy and child-bearing. Because the principle translates into an obligation placed on the individual employer, the courts are prompted to require justification for placing the cost of pregnancy on that employer. But this ignores the fact that sparing an 'innocent' employer leaves the whole cost with the woman and prevents any consideration of the potential cost-spreading role of the State. Finally, the equal treatment principle tends to operate symmetrically, striking down inequalities between men and women regardless of whether the differential treatment favours women or men. One implication is that, in the absence of specific legislative exceptions, maternity leave policies might be challenged on the grounds that they constitute a benefit which is not available to men.

Traditional assumptions that pregnancy and maternity belonged to the home, or the 'private sphere,' are increasingly challenged by the great increase in women working in the market-place, or 'public sphere.' Indeed, the pregnant worker forces the law to confront the breakdown in traditional divisions between public and private.

In facing this challenge, however, legislatures and courts have become ensnared in another of the dichotomies which bedevil analysis of women's rights: that between equality and difference. Most anti-discrimination legislation follows a well-trodden path: those who are equal deserve equal treatment, and, conversely, those who differ may be treated differently. Unpacking this apparently straightforward formula reveals unsuspected complexity. For example, the principle itself gives no guidance as to which of the myriad differences and similarities between individuals are relevant for the purpose at hand. As Finley argues, 'the outcome of the analysis which asks whether someone is different or the same . . . depends entirely on the characteristic or factor selected for emphasis. This selection is a highly political, value-laden choice.' Yet too often no attempt is made to articulate or justify the underlying values. This approach generates particular difficulties when applied to pregnancy: clearly a woman is different from a man when she is pregnant, but how significant is this difference, and what legal consequences should follow from it?

If it were the case that women were discriminated against by virtue simply of the fact that they were pregnant, the SDA could quite readily be construed so as to offer protection. This was recognised by David Pannick in 1985, in a commentary on the decision in *Turley v Allders Department Stores Ltd*, which is discussed below.

D Pannick, *Sex Discrimination Law*, 147–50, footnotes omitted

Because only women can become pregnant, the complainant who is dismissed because she is pregnant can argue that she would not have been less favourably treated but for her sex. It requires a very narrow construction of the statute to exclude less favourable treatment on the ground of a characteristic unique to one sex. It is quite true that not all women are (or become) pregnant. But it is important to note that direct discrimination exists not merely where the defendant applies a criterion that less favourably treats all women. It also exists where special, less favourable, treatment is accorded to a class consisting only of women, albeit not all women. Suppose an employer announces that it will employ any man with stated qualifications but only a woman who has those qualifications and who is over six feet tall. Albeit not all women are excluded, the employer has directly discriminated against women because it has imposed a criterion which less favourably treats a class composed entirely of women. That such treatment must constitute direct discrimination is emphasized by the fact that it would not give rise to a claim of indirect discrimination: the employer has not applied a condition or requirement equally to members of both sexes. There can be no doubt that Parliament intended to proscribe such conduct.

Less favourable treatment by reference to a criterion which affects only women, albeit not all women, has been considered by the US Federal courts in applying Title VII of the Civil Rights Act 1964. Section 703(a) of Title VII makes it unlawful for an employer 'to fail or refuse to hire or to discharge any individual or otherwise to discriminate against any individual with respect to his compensation, terms, conditions or privileges of employment, because of such individual's . . . sex . . .' The US courts have held that 'sex-plus' criteria, those less favourably treating only women, but not all women, violate Title VII. In *Sprogis v United Air Lines*, [444 F 2d 1194 (1971)] (the US Court of Appeals found that the defendants had breached Title VII by requiring female flight attendants to be unmarried. The court held that:

> The scope of [the statute] is not confined to explicit discrimination based 'solely' on sex. In forbidding employers to discriminate against individuals because of their sex, Congress intended to strike at the entire spectrum of disparate treatment of men and women resulting from sex stereotypes. . . . The effect of the statute is not to be diluted because discrimination adversely affects only a portion of the protected class. Discrimination is not to be tolerated under the guise of physical properties possessed by one sex . . .

In *Hurley v Mustoe* [1981] ICR 490, the EAT had no doubt that an employer who refused to employ women with young children was directly discriminating on the ground of sex contrary to the 1975 Act.

It is true that in *Hurley* the less favourable treatment was expressly pointed at women who had stated attributes. The employer who dismisses an employee because she is pregnant does not expressly direct his policy at women. But the distinction is meaningless in this context. Whether the less favourable treatment is 'on the ground of her sex' must depend on whether it can, in practice, affect only women, and not on how the employer labels the disadvantaged class. Because only women can become pregnant, the employer who dismisses a woman for reasons connected with pregnancy has treated her on the ground of a characteristic unique to her sex. It has applied special treatment to a class consisting only of women, albeit that class does not consist of all women. The less favourable treatment (if any) is therefore 'on the ground of her sex.'

Pannick is clearly of the view that treatment by reason of pregnancy is treatment by reason of sex. But a breach of the SDA requires *discrimination*, that is, *less* favourable treatment, by reason of sex. In *Turley v Allders* (EAT's first engagement with pregnancy-as-sex discrimination), this was to prove the claimant's undoing. She claimed that she had been discriminated against when she was dismissed by reason, she claimed, of her pregnancy. A tribunal rejected her claim having decided, as a preliminary issue, that pregnancy-related dismissal was not prohibited by the SDA. Her appeal failed.

Turley v Allders Department Stores Ltd [1980] ICR 66

Bristow J (for the majority):

Section 1(1) [SDA] provides: 'A person discriminates against a woman in any circumstances relevant for the purposes of any provision of this Act if—(a) on the ground of her sex he treats her less favourably than he treats or would treat a man, or (b) he applies to her a requirement or condition which he applies or would apply equally to a man but—(i) which is such that the proportion of women who can comply with it is considerably smaller than the proportion of men who can comply with it, and (ii) which he cannot show to be justifiable irrespective of the sex of the person to whom it is applied, and (iii) which is to her detriment because she cannot comply with it.'

Section 1 (2) underlines the intention which underlies subsection (1). You are to look at men and women, and see that they are not treated unequally simply because they are men and women. You have to compare like with like. So, in the case of the pregnant woman there is an added difficulty in the application of subsection (1). Suppose that to dismiss her for pregnancy is to dismiss her on the ground of her sex. In order to see if she has been treated less favourably than a man the sense of the section is that you must compare like with like, and you cannot. When she is pregnant a woman is no longer just a woman. She is a woman, as the Authorised Version of the Bible accurately puts it, with child, and there is no masculine equivalent.

So, in our judgment, to dismiss a woman because she is pregnant is not within the definition of discrimination against women in section 1 of the [SDA] . . .

Like Pannick, EAT here accepted that pregnancy-based treatment was 'by reason of' sex. But the majority ruled that the claimant had not been *less favourably* treated than a man, this on the ground that no comparison was possible between a pregnant woman and a man. This approach was criticised by Pannick who advocated an approach similar to that taken by the dissenting member in *Turley*.

Pannick states (160) that the conceptual problem with pregnancy is 'in its essence an irreconcilable theoretical conflict between those who believe that the gender equality principle can only be applied where men and women are treated differently with respect to a shared characteristic (which pregnancy is not) and those who believe that discrimination on the basis of physical characteristics inextricably linked to one sex must be sex discrimination.'

Pannick goes on to assert that 'Neither of the suggested approaches is . . . correct. A third, preferable solution is that classification by reference to a characteristic unique to one sex . . . is treatment on the ground of sex. Whether it is less favourable treatment . . . is . . . dependent on how the other sex is treated in "not materially different" circumstances.' It was this 'third way' which found favour with EAT in the subsequent case of *Hayes v Malleable Working Men's Club* [1985] ICR 703. The claimants were dismissed after they informed their employers that they were pregnant, neither having sufficient qualifying service for a claim under the EP(C)A 1978 (which statute then governed unfair dismissal). Their claims were dismissed in line with *Turley*, but their appeals to EAT were successful and their cases were remitted for rehearing, Waite J ruling that a comparison had to be made between the treatment afforded the claimants and that which was or would have been received by men who needed comparable periods of time off or whose circumstances were otherwise relevantly similar to those of the claimants. Waite P restricted *Turley* to its narrow facts (which he took to be discrimination on the basis of pregnancy *itself*, rather than any work-related consequences of it, and in the alternative took the view that it was wrongly decided

Hayes permitted women to argue that pregnancy-related discriminations breached the SDA, but its protection was far from comprehensive. To return to the argument made by Sandra Fredman, above, it afforded the protection of the SDA only to women who behaved like men—like those men to whom their employers would have afforded equivalent periods of sick leave to the maternity leave they required. The shortcomings of the *Hayes* approach were further illustrated by the decision in *Berrisford v Woodard Schools* [1991] ICR 564, in which EAT rejected an appeal by a woman dismissed because her pregnancy, coupled as it was with a refusal to marry, manifested her participation in extra-marital sex. A different approach from that adopted by EAT in either *Turley* or in *Webb* was taken by the European Court of Justice in *Dekker v Stichting Vormingscentrum Voor Jonge Volwassen Plus* Case C–177/88 [1990] ECR I–3941.

E Ellis, 'The Definition of Discrimination in European Sex Equality Law' (1994) 19 *European Law Review* **561, 567–8, footnotes omitted**

Dekker concerned a refusal to employ a pregnant woman who would otherwise have been appointed to a job of training instructor in a youth centre. The employers explained that, as Ms Dekker was already pregnant when she applied for the job, the employer's insurers would not reimburse the sickness benefits paid to Ms Dekker during her maternity leave. It would therefore be impossible for the employers to employ a replacement during Ms Dekker's absence, which would mean in the end that they would lose some of their training places. The first question which the Court of Justice had to answer was whether or not this situation amounted to direct sex discrimination. They held that this depended on whether the most important reason for the refusal to recruit Ms Dekker was a reason which applied without distinction to employees of both sexes or whether it applied exclusively to one sex. Since employment can only be refused because of pregnancy to a woman, such a refusal, the Court held, must be direct discrimination on the ground of sex. And a refusal to employ because of the financial consequences of pregnancy *must* be deemed to be based principally on the fact of the pregnancy. In other words, the Court was saying that, *but for* Ms Dekker's sex, she would have been appointed, so that her adverse treatment must be grounded on her sex; there was no need to prove any subjective consideration of Ms Dekker's sex on the part of the employers. The Court of Justice's conclusion here thus seems to be substantially the same in theory as that of the House of Lords in the *James* case.

However, the Court of Justice added a further point in *Dekker*, which indicates its fundamental grasp of what the law in this area is seeking to achieve. It had been urged to hold that the employers could escape liability if they could establish a 'legal justification' for their action. This it refused to do, saying that the only defences to unlawful sex discrimination were those contained in Article 2 of the Equal Treatment Directive. It is highly significant that the Court did not allow itself to be muddled by the introduction of a notion of justification into *direct* discrimination (as distinct from *indirect* discrimination where, as will be explained below, it plays a vital role in relation to causation). In effect it took a very clear-sighted view of direct discrimination, accepting that Ms Dekker would win her case if she could show simply that she had suffered detrimental treatment and that that treatment was grounded on her sex; if the employers could not rely on one of the listed defences, that was the end of the matter for them. Once causation had been established, the discrimination could only be excused for one of the specific reasons articulated by the directive. Looking at this from a different angle, the Court is focusing here on the *effect* of the impugned treatment, rather than being diverted by subjective inquiries into *why* the employers behaved as they did. The important thing which the Court keeps uppermost in its mind is the *remedial* function of the anti-discrimination law, and it is not thrown off course by arguments about culpability which would be appropriate in a criminal law context.

At about the same time that the ECJ decided *Dekker*, the pregnancy-as-sex argument came before EAT once again in *Webb v EMO*. There, EAT rejected an appeal from a woman who, having been employed, on an indefinite contract, to cover for another employee who was to take maternity leave, was dismissed when she subsequently discovered and announced that she was pregnant her baby due at the same time as that of the employee she was hired to cover. The Court ruled ([1990] ICR 442, *per* Woods J) that the appropriate comparator under s.5(3) was a man who was or would be absent from work. The Court of Appeal rejected Ms Webb's appeal ([1992] ICR 445), agreeing with EAT as to the proper comparator for a pregnant woman. The House of Lords ([1993] ICR 175) found it necessary to refer the case to the ECJ for a preliminary ruling on the position under the Equal Treatment Directive. The ECJ (Case C–32/93 [1994] ECR I–03567) ruled that the dismissal, by reason of pregnancy, of a woman from indefinite employment breached the Equal Treatment Directive. Again, the ECJ ruled that discrimination on the grounds of a characteristic unique to one sex is necessarily direct sex discrimination, there being no need for a comparator. The House of Lords interpreted the SDA accordingly.

Webb v EMO Air Cargo (UK) Ltd (No 2) [1994] QB 718

Lord Keith of Kinkel (for their Lordships):

. . . The reasoning in my speech in the earlier proceedings was to the effect that the relevant circumstance which existed in the present case and which should be taken to be present in the case of the hypothetical man was unavailability for work at the time when the worker was particularly required, and that the reason for the unavailability was not a relevant circumstance . . . So it was not relevant that the reason for the woman's unavailability was pregnancy, a condition which could not be present in a man.

The ruling of the European Court proceeds on an interpretation of the broad principles dealt with in articles 2(1) and 5(1) of Directive 76/207. Sections 1(1)(a) and 5(3) of the [SDA] set out a more precise test of unlawful discrimination, and the problem is how to fit the terms of that test into the ruling. It seems to me that the only way of doing so is to hold that, in a case where a woman is engaged for an indefinite period, the fact that the reason why she will be temporarily unavailable for work at a time when to her knowledge her services will be particularly required is pregnancy is a circumstance relevant to her case, being a circumstance which could not be present in the case of the hypothetical man. It does not necessarily follow that pregnancy would be a relevant circumstance in the situation where the woman is denied employment for a fixed period in the future during the whole of which her pregnancy would make her unavailable for work, nor in the situation where after engagement for such a period the discovery of her pregnancy leads to cancellation of the engagement.[95]

In *Webb* the House of Lords took a more generous approach to the interpretive obligations imposed by the Equal Treatment Directive than it had previously been prepared to do. The House of Lords decision in *Duke v GEC Reliance* [1988] 1 All ER 626, [1988] AC 618, upon which the Court of Appeal in *Webb* relied, was to the effect that the SDA should not be 'distorted' to give effect to the directive.[96] In *Webb* the House of Lords appeared to find it impossible to construe the SDA in the claimant's favour. Yet in *Webb (No.2)* their Lordships did precisely that, and without apparent difficulty.

---

[95] More recently, in *Jones v William Monk Ltd* 38 *Equal Opportunities Review Discrimination Case Law Digest* 6, a tribunal found that a woman dismissed for abortion-related absence was discriminated against on grounds of sex without need for a comparator.

[96] Compare the willingness of the House of Lords in this case to revise its previous construction of the Act with its earlier decision in *Duke v GEC Reliance Ltd*, *per* Lord Templeman: 'Section 2(4) of the European Communities Act 1972 does not in my opinion enable or constrain a British court to distort the meaning of a British statute in order to enforce against an individual a Community directive which has no direct effect between individuals. Section 2(4) applies and only applies where Community provisions are directly applicable. . . .'

It is now clear, as a matter of English as well as European law, that discrimination on grounds of pregnancy will invariably amount to sex discrimination (whether the discrimination is subjectively motivated by the pregnancy itself, or the woman's anticipated absence or, presumably, any other reason).[97] The doubts expressed by Lord Keith in *Webb* as to the position of women on temporary contracts have been put to rest by the decisions of the ECJ in *Tele Danmark* and *Jiménez Melgar v Ayuntamiento de Los Barrios*.[98] The first of these cases concerned a claim brought under the Equal Treatment Directive by a woman who took a temporary fixed-term job knowing that she was pregnant, and that she would be unable to perform the job for a significant period as a result, but did not notify the employer of her situation. The ECJ ruled that her subsequent dismissal breached the Equal Treatment Directive:

> Since the dismissal of a worker on account of pregnancy constitutes direct discrimination on grounds of sex, whatever the nature and extent of the economic loss incurred by the employer as a result of her absence because of pregnancy, whether the contract of employment was concluded for a fixed or an indefinite period has no bearing on the discriminatory character of the dismissal. In either case the employee's inability to perform her contract of employment is due to pregnancy.

Jiménez Melgar involved a challenge to a refusal to renew a woman's fixed term contract, which refusal was by reason of pregnancy. The ECJ ruled that the refusal breached the Equal Treatment Directive. And in *Mahlburg v Land Mecklenburg-Vorpommern* Case C–207/98 [2000] ECR I–00549 the ECJ ruled that the Directive prohibited a refusal to appoint a pregnant woman to an indefinite post on the ground that a statutory prohibition on employment attaching to the condition of pregnancy prevented her from being employed in that post from the outset and for the duration of the pregnancy. According to the Court:

> dismissal of a pregnant woman recruited for an indefinite period cannot be justified on grounds relating to her inability to fulfil a fundamental condition of her employment contract. The availability of an employee is necessarily, for the employer, a precondition for the proper performance of the employment contract. However, the protection afforded by Community law to a woman during pregnancy and after childbirth cannot be dependent on whether her presence at work during maternity is essential to the proper functioning of the undertaking in which she is employed. Any contrary interpretation would render ineffective the provisions of the Directive . . .
> the application of provisions concerning the protection of pregnant women cannot result in unfavourable treatment regarding their access to employment, so that it is not permissible for an employer to refuse to take on a pregnant woman on the ground that a prohibition on employment arising on account of the pregnancy would prevent her being employed from the outset and for the duration of the pregnancy in the post of unlimited duration to be filled.[99]

---

[97] *Cf* the approach taken by Manitoba's Court of Appeal in *Janzen v Platy Enterprises Ltd* and overturned by Canada's Supreme Court ([1989] ISCR 1284). The decisions are discussed in Ch 2.

[98] Respectively Case C-109/00 [2001] ECR I-6693 and Case C-438/99 [2001] ECR I-06915.

[99] See also the recent decision of the ECJ in *Gómez v Continental Industrias del Cauco SA* Case C–342/01 [2004] ECR I–0000 in which that Court ruled that a woman who was on maternity leave during a fixed period of annual leave had to be permitted to take that leave at another time.

The ECJ in the *Tele Danmark* did not accept that the employee was at fault for failing to notify the employer of her pregnancy. A similar approach was taken in *Busch v Klinikum Neustadt* [2003] ECR I–02041 in which the ECJ ruled that a woman was entitled to shorten her maternity leave and return to work while pregnant again (this in order to avail herself of maternity leave in relation to the second pregnancy). She could not be required to inform the employer of the fact of her second pregnancy (in order that the employer could refuse to permit her early return to work). According to the ECJ, the fact that the claimant would be unable to carry out all her job functions on her return—or, indeed, that she returned solely to qualify for enhanced payment in respect of the second maternity leave—could not justify an exception to the prohibition under the Equal Treatment Directive of pregnancy-related discrimination.

Shortcomings of the Current Approach

But the protection afforded even by EC law in relation to pregnancy is not comprehensive. The ECJ ruled in *Brown v Rentokil Ltd* Case C–394/96, [1998] ECR I–04185 that the Equal Treatment Directive prohibited discrimination on grounds of pregnancy (or pregnancy-related illness):

> throughout the period of pregnancy . . . dismissal of a female worker during pregnancy for absences due to incapacity for work resulting from her pregnancy is linked to the occurrence of risks inherent in pregnancy and must therefore be regarded as essentially based on the fact of pregnancy. Such a dismissal can affect only women and therefore constitutes direct discrimination on grounds of sex.

This was a more generous approach than that which had previously prevailed.[100] *Brown* was subsequently applied by EAT in *Abbey National v Formosa* [1999] IRLR 222 to find that the dismissal of a woman prevented the opportunity to defend herself at a disciplinary hearing because she was on maternity leave amounted to sex discrimination under the SDA.[101] And in *Caisse Nationale D'assurance Jiménez Vieillesse des Travailleurs Salariés (CNAVTS) v Evelyne Thibault* Case C–136/95 [1998] ECR I–2011 the Court ruled that a woman on maternity leave could not be denied access to a performance assessment, where the results of that assessment determined a subsequent pay review.

In *GUS Home Shopping Ltd v Green* [2001] IRLR 75 EAT ruled that employers discriminated on grounds of sex when they denied women loyalty payments because they were absent from work during the relevant period due to pregnancy-related illness or maternity leave. But *Brown* leaves unregulated discrimination on grounds of pregnancy-related sickness absence which takes place after the period of maternity leave. Also unaffected by EU law is the employer's right to trigger maternity leave where a woman requires sick leave (however unrelated to pregnancy) in the four weeks before the due date[102] and, perhaps most fundamentally, the matter of maternity pay.

The extension in 1995 of maternity leave in the UK from women with at least two years' qualifying employment to all women came about as a result of Council Directive 92/85/EC

---

[100] *Handels-og Kontorfunktionaerer-nes Forbund i Danmark (acting for Hertz) v Dansk Arbejdsgiverforening (acting for Aldi Marked K/S)* Case C–179/88 [1990] ECR I–03979, which was handed down on the same day as *Dekker* Case C–400/95 [1997] ECR I–02757.

[101] See also *Healy v William B Morrison* (EAT/172/99, 30 June 1999) in which EAT ruled that an absence-related selection for redundancy during the period of maternity leave breached the SDA without need for comparison with the treatment of a sick man.

[102] This was accepted by the ECJ in *Boyle v EOC*, below.

(the Pregnant Workers Directive). The Directive prohibits pregnancy-related dismissals and provides for payment at no less than the rate of statutory sick pay.[103] The Directive has proven beneficial to some women in the UK, if only by extending existing protections to women without the qualifying periods previously required. But the Directive's provisions relating to payment have, it seems, operated against the interests of women.

In *Gillespie v Northern Health and Social Services Board* Case C–342/93 [1996] ECR I–0475 the claimants argued that Article 141 [ex 119] entitled them to full pay during maternity leave. If discrimination against women during the period of maternity leave is discrimination on grounds of sex, the argument went, then non-payment of wages during this period was contrary to Article 141. The ECJ accepted that maternity pay was 'pay' within Article 141. But:

> [t]he principle of equal pay laid down in Article [141] . . . and set out in detail in Council Directive 75/117/EEC [the equal pay directive] . . . neither requires that women should continue to receive full pay during maternity leave, nor lays down specific criteria for determining the amount of benefit payable to them during that period, provided that the amount is not set so low as to jeopardise the purpose of maternity leave.

When that case returned to the Northern Ireland Court of Appeal (*Gillespie v Northern Health and Social Services Board (No. 2)* [1997] IRLR 410), it was considered together with *Todd v Eastern Health and Social Services Board*, in which a pregnant woman challenged, as discriminatory, the setting of maternity pay at 90 per cent of salary for six weeks followed by 50 per cent for 12 weeks, where contractual sick pay was set at five months' full pay followed by five months' half pay. Dealing with the questions (1) whether statutory maternity pay was 'set so low as to jeopardise the purpose of maternity leave,' and (2) whether a tribunal was entitled to rule in favour of Ms Todd on the grounds that maternity pay was less favourable than sick pay, the Court ruled that maternity pay was adequate so long as it was at least equivalent to statutory sick pay (this being the approach adopted by the Pregnant Workers Directive). In relation to Ms Todd's claim, the Court of Appeal rejected the argument that contractual maternity pay had to be set at the same level as contractual sick pay:

> the only requirement imposed by the ECJ [in *Gillespie*] was that . . . the amount of maternity pay must not be so low as to undermine the purpose of maternity leave . . . Article 11(3) [of the pregnant workers directive] deems [maternity pay] to be adequate if it is at least equivalent to the amount of statutory sickness benefit. It need hardly be said that this is by no means the same thing as saying that maternity pay must always be fixed at the same level as sickness pay in order to be adequate. It follows necessarily from what we have already held in this judgment that it does not have to be payable at the same level as contractual sickness benefit.[104]

[103] Save (see Art 11(4) of the Pregnant Workers Directive, applied by EAT in *Banks v Tesco & Secretary of State for Employment* [1999] ICR 1141), where the claimant has not satisfied the statutory qualifying criteria.

[104] See also *BA (European Operations at Gatwick) Ltd v Botterill* [2000] IRLR 296. An additional question posed by the *Gillespie* case related to whether the calculation of maternity pay had to take into account a backdated pay increase awarded during the period of maternity leave. The ECJ ruled that it did. In *Abdoulaye v Regie Nationale de Usines Renault SA* Case C–218/98 [1999] ECR I–05723 the ECJ permitted payment of a maternity bonus on top of full pay during maternity leave in recognition of the occupational disadvantages inherent in maternity leave 'a woman on maternity leave may not be proposed for promotion . . . her period of service will be reduced . . [she] may not claim performance-related salary increases. . . may not take part in training [and] . . . the adaptation of a female worker returning from maternity leave becomes complicated.'

Any doubt as to the correctness, of this decision as a matter of EC law, was laid to rest by the decision of the ECJ in *Boyle v Equal Opportunities Commission* Case C–411/96, [1998] ECR I–06401 in which that Court took a precisely similar approach. In that case the ECJ rejected, inter alia, a challenge brought by EOC employees to the practice whereby, if they failed to return to work after maternity leave, they were required to repay any contractual maternity pay which they had received in excess of the statutory requirement.[105]

M Wynn, 'Pregnancy Discrimination: Equality, Protection or Reconciliation?' (1999) 62 *Modern Law Review* 435, 441–5, footnotes omitted

Despite the injunction in Article 2 of Directive 92/85/EC that the protection of the health and safety of such workers should not jeopardise equal treatment, the Court of Justice has firmly rejected the possibility of any equality comparison between women on maternity leave and other workers on the basis that such women are in a special position, but are not actually at work; thus the usual obligations deriving from the contract of employment do not arise. Furthermore, the delineation of women on maternity leave as dependant mothers as opposed to productive workers has allowed the Court to by-pass notions of equality and locate the problem in the realm of social protection where economic justifications are more likely to gain recognition. Protected status has thus resulted in a regime which has penal consequences for women in that entitlement to adequate income and immunity from dismissal during maternity leave without the need for inappropriate male comparisons has been substituted for substantive equality. . . .

The logic of *Gillespie* was reiterated in *Boyle v Equal Opportunities Commission*, where the Court of Justice again rejected a comparative approach . . .

The result of *Boyle* and *Gillespie* is that women on maternity leave are left without effective recourse where employers exploit the modicum of protection provided by Directive 92/85/EC. Financial detriments will continue to be incurred by women who choose to combine work and childbearing and employers will not be penalised for minimising their costs as long as the threshold of adequacy of income is not undermined. These cases indicate that the limits of maternity protection are determined by the European Court's perception of national autonomy in matters of social welfare. The result of balancing competing interests on the social plane is that the cost of applying the principle of equal treatment militates against the vindication of individual rights. As Advocate General Iglesias noted in *Gillespie*, to give full protection to pregnant mothers 'would threaten to upset the balance of the entire social welfare system'.

By contrast with these decisions on maternity rights, recent cases concerning pregnant workers indicate that a more favourable regime applies to the pregnant woman *qua* worker. In *Thibault* the Court of Justice stated that pregnancy and maternity require substantive, not merely formal rights. Here it was the woman's capacity as a worker which the Court emphasised as the factor which triggered the operation of discrimination law, as pregnancy itself could not act as the cause for any adverse treatment in working conditions. Thus the deprival of the right to an annual performance assessment as a result of absence on maternity leave was regarded as unfavourable treatment.[106] Notably, *Gillespie* was referred to in order to support the conclusion that the taking of maternity leave should not deprive a woman of any benefits from pay rises due to her as a worker.

---

[105] In *Alabaster v Woolwich plc and Secretary of State for Social Security* Case C–147/02 [2004] ECR I–00000 the ECJ rejected the suggestion made by Advocate General Légere that the Court overrule *Gillespie* and rule that maternity pay fell exclusively within the scope of the Pregnant Workers Directive rather than Art 141.

[106] See more recently *Lewen v Denda* Case C–333/97 [1999] ECR I–07243.

The bifurcation in the Court's jurisprudence on pregnancy and maternity rights has received more specific confirmation in *Hoj Pedersen* Case C–66/96 [1998] ECR I–7327. The applicants were deprived of full pay when they became unfit for work because of pregnancy-related illness before the beginning of their maternity leave. According to Danish national legislation, pregnancy-related incapacity for work entitled the worker to half pay, whereas incapacity for other illness resulted in full benefits. The Court of Justice held that it was contrary to Article 119 [now 141] of the Treaty of Rome and Directive 75/117/EEC to withhold full pay from a pregnant woman who became unfit for work before the commencement of maternity leave by reason of a pathological condition connected with pregnancy.

The importance of this case lies in the explicit comparison made between pregnancy and maternity rights. Advocate General Colomer had made clear in *Boyle* that there is no basis for comparison between a woman on maternity leave and a man on sick leave because the man's contractual obligations are only suspended for so long as he undergoes treatment for a sickness, whereas maternity leave is a special 'block' period granted to protect specific pregnancy and maternity needs, ie to protect the biological condition of pregnancy and the relationship between mother and child. This distinction was developed in *Pedersen* where the Advocate General rejected the view that unfitness for work caused by pregnancy before maternity leave began amounted to 'pre-maternity' leave. He stated that maternity leave differs from pregnancy-related sickness absence in a number of respects: first, maternity leave has a finite duration; secondly, entitlement is not linked to illness; thirdly, a woman is released from all employment obligations including work. This reasoning focuses on differences in employment rights: whereas pregnant workers must prove unfitness for work in order to be released from employment obligations, workers on maternity leave acquire rights independently of any such obligations. The dichotomy between maternity leave as social protection and pregnancy unfitness as worker incapacity allows the 'sick-mate comparison' to operate only in cases of pregnancy. Gender specific rights attaching to maternity leave are diluted because they are welfare rights; pregnancy rights as equal rights emphasise the point of similarity with men and are thus conditioned by factors shaping the rights of male workers . . .

There is an implied acceptance in the judgments in *Gillespie* and *Brown* of economic justifications for inferior treatment of pregnant women. In *Pedersen*, the European Court was faced with an explicit argument based on loss distribution in relation to the costs of pregnancy and firmly rejected this on the premise that discrimination cannot be justified on such grounds. The employers had argued that the discriminatory treatment was justified on the grounds that Danish legislation reflected a sharing of risks and costs of pregnancy between the pregnant worker, the employer and society as a whole. The Court stated that the aim of loss-sharing was not an objective factor within the meaning of previous case law:

> The discrimination cannot be justified by the aim of sharing the risks and economic costs connected with pregnancy . . . That goal cannot be regarded as an objective factor unrelated to any discrimination based on sex . . .

The interests of the employer, in contrast with the interests of the State, require more specific economic justification than broad loss-sharing goals.[107]

---

[107] NB the recent decision of the ECJ in *Land Brandenburg v Sass* Case C–284/02 [2004] ECR I-00000 in which the Court appears to adopt a more radical approach, requiring the protection of women on maternity leave from disadvantage associated with, for example, accrual of seniority during the entire period of statutory leave rather than, as in *Boyle*, only in relation to the minimum period of leave required by the Pregnant Workers Directive.

Combining Work and Family Life

Introduction

EOC, 'Women and Men in Britain: the Work-Life Balance' (2000)

In the past men usually went out to work and were the sole breadwinners while women stayed at home to look after the family and home. This has now changed radically as more women have entered the work force. There is now a mismatch between people's caring and parental responsibilities and the demands of inflexible employment patterns. For mothers, these are lower than for women without children. For fathers the opposite applies—men with children are more likely to be working and working longer hours than men without children . . .

The proportion of 'traditional' households comprising a couple with at least one dependent child fell from 38 per cent in 1961 to 23 per cent in 1998 whereas the percentage of one person households increased from 11 to 28 per cent . . .

The hours of work of mothers and fathers differ greatly. In 1999, 38 per cent of all working mothers with dependent children worked for 20 hours or less, compared with only two per cent of fathers. Fathers are more likely to work and to work longer hours than men who are not fathers: 65 per cent of fathers worked in excess of 40 hours a week [in 1999] compared with 53 per cent of men who did not have dependent children . . . the long hours culture is criticised by women and men alike for interfering with home life. Fathers who work for long hours are less involved in family life than those who work shorter hours. Nearly two-thirds of male full-time employees in Britain work in excess of 40 hours per week, by far the highest proportion in the European Union . . .

In England, there is now one registered childcare place for every 7.5 children under eight. The percentage of three and four year olds in maintained nursery and primary schools in England has increased from 44 per cent in 1987 to 56 per cent in 1997. However, childcare is often not available for severely disabled children and, when it is, is generally far more expensive than for children without a disability . . .

In 1995, 14 per cent of women and 11 per cent of men aged 16 and over were carers, ie, looking after or providing a regular service to help someone who was sick, disabled or elderly. As there are more women than men in the adult population, there are considerably more female carers than male: 3.3 million compared with 2.4 million . . .

To encourage parents and carers into work and enable them to stay there, work-life policies are essential . . . Yet access to flexible and family-friendly policies is not widely available, nor is it widely spread between the sexes . . . Flexible work is more prevalent in the public than private sector and in general, women are more likely than men to have access to these arrangements.

Employees with access to flexible and family-friendly working arrangements, 1998
Per cent

Sector	Private		Public	
	Women	Men	Women	Men
Flexitime	36	24	39	37
Job sharing	15	6	34	23
Parental leave	30	21	33	35
Working at/from home	6	10	9	13
Workplace nursery/ childcare subsidy	3	2	9	6
None of these	42	57	34	40

'Flexibility,' together with 'prudence' and 'joined-up government' has been one of the mantras of the New Labour government. The emphasis on labour market flexibility is one of those which it shares with its predecessors. And 'flexibility' is very fashionable in the European Union whose push towards maximising employment is associated with moves to dismantle 'unnecessary' and 'inflexible' labour market regulation.

The flexibility which is the rallying call of those on the economic right is concerned with the needs of employers and the perceived needs of the wider economy. By contrast, the flexibility with which we are concerned here is the flexibility which permits workers to combine work and family life. Whether this means a phased return to work after maternity leave (part-time, term-time, job-share or flexi-time work) or the ability to take time off without retaliation in the event of family illness, a degree of flexibility is crucial unless motherhood (or, less commonly, fatherhood) is to be home-based. Some employers have made significant steps towards accommodating the needs of working parents. Many more have not. The obligation on employers to permit a degree of flexibility rested almost entirely, until very recently, on the SDA. In the last few years, however, the Part-time Workers Regulations have entered the arena as has the right to request flexible working which was introduced by the Employment Rights Act 2002. Both the Regulations and the right to request flexible working are further considered below, although the SDA remains the main focus of this chapter.

Prior to the implementation of the Employment Act 2002 women who wished to work other than the employer's preferred hours had to rely on the indirect discrimination provisions of the SDA. The concept of indirect discrimination turning on the statistical relationship between the complainant's needs and her sex, the indirect discrimination route to flexible working was closed to men. Men could, however, claim direct discrimination if refused access to flexible working in circumstances where women were or would have been permitted such access.

The difficulties associated with indirect discrimination claims were discussed in Chapters 2 and 4, many of the cases considered therein dealing precisely with the issue of flexible working. Most of those cases concerned employees' needs for flexibility—*Clymo v Wandsworth*, for example, *Cast v Croydon College, Briggs v North Eastern Education and Library Board, Eley v Huntleigh Diagnostics Ltd*.[108] One—*London Underground v Edwards*—concerned the employee's inability to comply with the employer's need for 'flexibility.'[109] We considered the difficulties associated with establishing that the employer's refusal of request for flexible working amounted to a 'requirement or condition' (*Clymo*), the problems associated with pools (*Edwards, Kidd v DRG*) and with establishing an inability to comply (*Clymo*) and, finally, the ease with which employers can justify indirect discrimination (*Kidd, Clymo, Briggs*).[110]

A number of these difficulties have been reduced by the adoption in 2001 of the revised definition of indirect sex discrimination in the employment context as a result of the Burden of Proof Directive and its implementing regulations. And these changes have to a degree been overtaken by the Part-time Workers Regulations and the right to request flexible working. But the difficulties associated with changing working conditions after maternity leave, and, for women seeking to change jobs or to return to work after time out of the labour market, of finding flexible jobs of equivalent status to previously-held full-time jobs,

[108] Respectively, [1989] ICR 250, [1998] ICR 500, [1990] IRLR 181.
[109] [1985] ICR 405.
[110] In *British Telecommunications plc v Roberts* [1996] ICR 625 EAT rejected the argument that *Webb* protected a flexible return to work.

means that the inability to perform an 'inflexible'[111] full-time job has for many years forced some women into jobs in respect of which they are over-qualified, others into jobs which are under-rewarded relative to the demands made by them.[112]

The Part-time Workers Regulations

Discrimination against part-timers has been recognised as usually unlawful for almost twenty years[113] and women do successfully take action against employers who refuse access to part-time work, job-sharing or other flexible work after maternity leave.[114] But most discrimination against part-time workers takes place unchallenged, as does most employer intransigence in the face of attempts to engage in flexible work. Council Directive 96/34/EC (the Part-time Workers Directive) marked the culmination of almost twenty years' efforts to regulate 'atypical' work at the European level. The Directive was adopted under the Social Chapter, the UK having vetoed attempts to pass it under the Article 137 TEC. The social partners concluded an agreement on part-time work in accordance with the procedure established by the Social Chapter and the agreement was adopted as Directive 96/34/EC. It in turn has been implemented in UK law by the Part-time Workers (Prevention of Less Favourable Treatment) Regulations 2000 (SI 2000 No 1551) which came into force on 1 July of that year. They provide (reg 5) that 'A part-time worker has the right not to be treated less favourably by his employer than the employer treats a comparable full-time worker' where the less favourable treatment is 'on the ground that the worker is a part-time worker' and 'is not justified on objective grounds.' A 'comparable worker' is (reg 2(4)) one who is 'engaged in the same or in broadly similar work [to that done by the part-time worker] having regard, where relevant, to whether they have a similar level of qualification, skills and experience.' The comparator must be employed by the same employer as the claimant and must work at the same establishment unless there is no comparator at that establishment. Finally, the comparator must be employed under the same type of contract as the claimant, reg 1 distinguishing between contracts applicable to indefinitely retained employees, indefinitely retained workers, apprentices and 'any other description of worker that it is reasonable for the employer to treat differently from other workers on the ground that workers of that description have a different type of contract.'

Claims can be brought under the PTW Regs without such a narrowly defined comparator only where claimants have transferred within their employment from full-time to part-time work or have returned after an absence of less than one year 'to the same job or to a job on the same level,' whether on the same or a different type of contract. In either of these

---

[111] Flexibility being assessed from the worker's perspective.

[112] Though see Diamond Ashiaghor, extracted above, on the race-specific characteristics of female part-time work.

[113] Since *Bilka-Kaufhaus GmbH v Weber von Hartz* Case–170/84, [1986] ECR 1607, arguably since *Jenkins v Kingsgate (Clothing Production) Ltd* (Case–96/80) [1981] ECR 911. K O'Donovan and E Szyszczak note, in a commentary to *Kidd v DRG* [1985] ICR 405 ((1985) 14 *Industrial Law Journal* 252, 252) that '[d]espite the close correlation between female participation and part-time work, industrial tribunals and EAT have been reluctant to conclude that the concept of sex discrimination may be generally applied to the differential treatment of full-time and part-time workers.'

[114] 84 *Equal Opportunities Review* 3, for example, reports a £22,500 settlement between Royal & Sun Alliance and a woman manager refused permission to job-share on the basis that such an arrangement was not possible in her managerial position, and a £45,000 settlement between the Solicitors Indemnity Fund and a solicitor refused permission to work on a part-time or job share basis in order that she could care for three under-fives. See also the decisions in *Home Office v Holmes* [1984] ICR 678 (*cf* more recently, *British Telecommunications v Roberts*, above n 110). See also *Greater Glasgow Health Board v Carey* [1987] IRLR 484.

cases, the claimants may choose instead (regs 3 and 4) to compare their treatment with that of a notional full-time worker employed on the terms and conditions s/he enjoyed prior to the transfer or the period of absence or, in the latter case, to the treatment of a notional full-time worker employed on the terms and conditions which would have applied to the worker had s/he continued to be employed full-time during her period of absence. The Regs provide that the *pro-rata* principle shall be applied unless inappropriate, and also that part-timers need not be paid over-time rates until they have worked the normal full-time hours.[115] They are accompanied by 'guidance notes' and a 'programme of information' which advise on compliance and best practice.

The Government's regulatory impact assessment estimated that the PTW Regs would 'directly' benefit only 7 per cent of the six million part-time workers in the UK, most of the rest being excluded from protection by the absence of a comparator. This aspect of the Regs has been severely criticised. The protection afforded by the Regs is further reduced by their failure to prohibit dismissals in connection with a refusal to transfer between part-time and full-time work. Compensation in respect of injury to feelings is generally precluded by the Regs.

The PTW Regs provide additional protections to some part-time workers (including male part-timers who, unless treated less favourably than female workers, could not previously challenge discrimination against them as part-time workers). But the failure of the Regulations to regulate the most significant source of the disadvantage experienced by part-time workers—their very denial of access to the same jobs in the same workplaces as full-time workers—means that, for the most part, they will continue to have to rely on the SDA, which Act has proved its inadequacies in this respect over the past twenty-five years.

Parental Leave, etc

The PTW Regs are not the only legislative changes in recent years which have implications for those attempting to combine work and family life. The Parental Leave and Maternity etc Regulations 1999 (Parental Leave Regs) which were passed in order to implement the Parental Leave Directive in the UK in the wake of its acceptance of the 'Social Protocol' of the Maastricht Treaty (now incorporated within the Treaty Establishing the European Community), came into force in December 1999.[116] Prior to their implementation, workers in the UK had no entitlement to parental or family leave. By contrast, workers in every other EU Member State with the exceptions only of Belgium, Ireland and Luxembourg were entitled to parental leave even prior to the adoption of the Parental Leave Directive (the details which follow were correct in 1995). The period of leave varied between three years in Spain (unpaid), France and Germany (paid at around £380 and £267 monthly respectively); and three months (unpaid) in Greece. Six months leave was available in both Italy and Netherlands (the former at 30 per cent of salary and the latter unpaid) and two years in Austria and Portugal (the former paid at between £344 and £510 monthly, the latter unpaid). Sweden afforded its workers 18 months leave (12 months of which were paid at 75 per cent,[117] three months at a flat rate of around £165 monthly); Denmark between

[115] This approach was accepted by the ECJ in *Stadt Lengerich v Angelika Helmig*, (joined cases C–399/92, C–409/92, C–425/92, C–34/93, C–50/93 and C–78/93) [1994] ECR I–5727, [1995] IRLR 216 but is problematic in failing to mark the inconvenience associated with working in excess of a worker's own normal hours.

[116] SI 1999, No. 3312. The Regs should be read with the ERA 1999, Sch 4 part 1.

[117] Reduced from 90 per cent in 1994 and 80 per cent in 1995—figures from 'Parental and Family Leave in Europe' 66 *Equal Opportunities Review*.

23 and 62 weeks with some remuneration and Finland six months on two-thirds of salary plus child-care leave until the child's third birthday at between £282 and £507 monthly. In addition, all other Member States with the exception of Denmark, Ireland and Italy afforded workers a period of family leave, generally paid and varying in length between one and four days in France to 60 days per year in Sweden.

The Parental Leave Regs provide an entitlement to three months' (unpaid) parental leave to be taken by everyone having responsibility for a child during the first five years' of the child's life.[118] This is in addition to maternity leave and the new right accorded under the ERA (s.57A) to: a reasonable amount of time off . . . in order to take action which is necessary—

(a) to provide assistance on an occasion when a dependant falls ill, gives birth or is injured or assaulted,
(b) to make arrangements for the provision of care for a dependant who is ill or injured,
(c) in consequence of the death of a dependant,
(d) because of the unexpected disruption or termination of arrangements for the care of a dependant, or
(e) to deal with an incident which involves a child of the employee and which occurs unexpectedly in a period during which an educational establishment which the child attends is responsible for him.

Section 57A(2) ERA provides that the employee must inform the employer as to the reason for absence 'as soon as reasonably practicable', and, save where no notice could practically be given, of the likely period of absence. The application of the ERA's 'emergency leave' provisions of the ERA has been comprehensively explained by EAT in *Qua v John Ford Morrison Solicitors* [2003] IRLR 184 in which that Court, in the first appellate decision on the provisions.

Section 57A is not subject to any qualifying period of employment. Parental leave rights, by contrast, apply only in respect of employees with at least one year's qualifying service. The Regulations provide for the continuation of specified contractual terms (entitlement to notice, redundancy pay and disciplinary procedures; obligations in respect of notice, confidentiality and loyalty).

In respect of parental leave taken in blocks of less than 4 weeks, and of a period of additional maternity leave of similar length,[119] employees are entitled to return to their job, in other cases to that job 'or, if it is not reasonable practicable for the employer to permit her to return to that job, to another job which is both suitable for her and appropriate for her to do in the circumstances.'[120] The terms and conditions to which employees return must be no less favourable than had no leave been taken, and continuous employment unbroken by (but not accumulated) during the leave period. Protection against detriment is accorded to those exercising their rights under the Regs and a dismissal in connection with the exercise of such rights is automatically unfair for the purposes of the ERA.

The primary method by which the regulations are intended to be implemented is through the mechanism of a 'workforce agreement', the statutory detail below being by way of a

---

[118] In respect of children in receipt of Disability Living Allowance, 18 years and five years after adoption or until 18 if sooner or where employer has postponed leave.

[119] Additional maternity leave being in addition to the now basic 26 weeks.

[120] The Directive provides for alternative job where return to original is not 'possible' rather than 'reasonably practicable.' There is no entitlement to return where redundancy provisions apply. In the case of a woman taking parental leave of less than four weeks directly after additional maternity leave, original job unless not reasonably practicable applies both to end date of maternity leave and of parental leave.

default arrangement. Workforce agreements can be reached between the employer and recognised unions or, where no such union exists, between the employer and elected representatives of the workforce. In the absence of such an agreement, the Parental Leave Regs establish detailed conditions to which the right to parental leave is subject. No more than four weeks' leave may be taken in any year in respect of a single child. Employees who wish to avail of their right to take parental leave must provide evidence of the child's birth or adoption and of parental responsibility for the child, together with notice of their intention to take leave. The notice must be given at least 21 days in advance except where the timing of leave turns on the date of birth or adoption, and must specify the start and end date of the leave requested.[121] Employers may postpone the taking of any such leave, except where it is connected with birth or adoption, where s/he 'considers that the operation of his [sic] business would be unduly disrupted if the employee took leave during the period identified in his [sic] notice,' and where the employer agrees to permit the employee the same period of leave within six months of the requested period. The employer must give the employee written notice of postponement with the reasons for it and the alternative period of leave permitted within seven days of the employee's original request.

The Parental Leave Regs have been criticised for permitting employers to postpone parental leave, as well as for their adoption of a five-year rather than eight-year cut-off point; their application only to 'employees'[122] the lack of a clear right to return to the same job for those taking additional maternity leave and lengthy blocks of parental leave ; the fact that the parental leave is to be unpaid;[123] and the minimum one-week period of leave permitted under the default arrangements. In addition, the TUC argued that employers should be permitted to postpone leave only for objectively justified reasons and after consultation with workers or their representatives.

In those EU Member States in which parental leave is already available (see above), its popularity, according to the *Equal Opportunities Review*:[124]

is more often than not dependent upon whether leave is paid or not. The number of parents taking parental leave in countries where no benefit is available, such as Greece, Portugal, Spain and the Netherlands, is believed to be correspondingly low, even though there are no precise figures available . . . In Germany, where flat-rate payments are available, the vast majority of mothers take parental leave, although men account for only 1 per cent of all leave-takers . . . In Denmark, where an additional entitlement to leave was introduced in 1992, take-up . . . was initially low, due mainly to the fall in income that this would cause . . .

Take-up rates of parental leave are highest in countries paying earnings-related benefit, such as Finland, Norway and Sweden. In Finland, virtually all mothers take parental leave, although fathers account for only 2 per cent of takers . . . Sweden is unusual in that, in addition to nearly all mothers taking leave, a high percentage of fathers—around 50 per cent— also take up their option to parental leave. This may be due to the fact that leave arrangements are very flexible, with parents being able to take short or long periods of full- or part-time leave. In addition, the law stipulates that at least one month of earnings-related leave must be taken by either parent.

---

[121] In these cases specification of EWC and duration of leave or expected week of placement and period of leave. In the latter case 21 days' notice or as soon as practicable.

[122] The Directive refers to those in 'an employment relationship' which is probably wider.

[123] See, eg, the TUC's and EOC's submissions to the Social Security Select Committee, appended to the Ninth Report of the Committee, 1998–99 Session, 'Social Security Implications of Parental Leave' HC 543.

[124] N 120, 23–24.

The Government's own figures projected that only 2 per cent men and 35 per cent women with children would take advantage of the right to parental leave over the five year period, the low take-up rate being in large part due to the lack of payment available.[125] Having lost the argument for paid leave, the TUC lobbied for parental leave to be available 'in principle, flexibly, in months, weeks or shorter periods or on a reduced hours basis, subject to objective justification by employers[126] in small chunks' in order to encourage uptake, questioning the government's categorisation of parental leave as a major contribution to its 'family friendly' employment strategy on its own projected take-up rates. The availability of such flexible leave was seen as particularly important in encouraging its uptake by men.

TUC, Submissions to the House of Commons Social Security Committee, June 1999

In order to promote gender equality . . . there are wider arguments for not instituting a parental leave system where it is only women who take up unpaid leave. In particular, women taking unpaid parental leave will become almost entirely economically dependent on men which research shows may result in less family income being spent on children. In the long term, periods of unpaid leave for women are likely to result in lesser pension and other social security entitlements and more disparity in lifetime earnings with men. This can lead to poverty for women in old age, particularly following relationship breakdown. In addition, as acknowledged by the objectives behind the Parental Leave Directive, take-up by men of parental leave should encourage greater gender equality, by facilitating more sharing of childcare and other family responsibilities between women and men. The most recent British Social Attitudes Survey shows that in 80 per cent of households, women still do most of the domestic tasks apart from small repairs around the home.

More recently, payment (£106 per week from April 2005) has been introduced for the two-week period of paternity leave—this at a time at which maternity leave (paid at a similar rate) was extended from 18 to 26 weeks and unpaid maternity leave to an additional 26 weeks. The upshot of this is to provide a mother earning £15,000 with £3,658 over six month's leave (or a year if she choose to take her full leave allowance) while a father who took a similar period off work would be entitled to £205.60 pay (and, indeed, would not be entitled to return to work). The Industrial Society recently warned that increasing maternity rights would damage women's career prospects.[127] It is difficult to disagree. While some imbalance in the rights afforded in relation to maternity and paternity is probably unavoidable, given the demands of late pregnancy and post-partum recovery, and while many opposite-sex couples would, given a choice, assign most or all birth-related leave to the women (whether to facilitate breast-feeding or given the fact that she is likely to be paid less than him, or for any of a variety of other reasons) it is difficult to justify a position which denies parents the right to choose who, if anyone, will be the primary carer. From an equality perspective the denial of choice is all the worse given its perpetuation of the uneven distribution of childcare between men and women and the implications of this for women in the workplace. Recognition of this caused the EOC in the Interim Report on its Pregnancy FI to recommend that maternity leave be reduced to six months and the second six months of what is currently maternity leave be made available to either parent. The Government's 2005 consultation paper, *Work and Families*, floats a number of options to permit the transfer of between six months and virtually all the proposed twelve month leave to fathers at the same rate of pay as the mother would receive.

---

[125] TUCs submissions to the Committee, *ibid.*
[126] TUC's response to the DTI consultation on parental leave.
[127] 'Mothers versus men: why women lose at work' (2000).

Flexible Working

One of the significant weaknesses of the PTW Regs is their failure to provide any right to transfer to part-time or reduced hours working. This gap has been partially addressed by the Employment Act 2002 which provides a right to request flexible working. Section 80F of the Employment Rights Act 1996, inserted by the 2002 Act, provides that an employee may apply to have his or her terms relating to hours, timing and/or place of work varied in order to care for a child under the age of six (18 if the child is disabled). Where the employer receives an application in the appropriate form he or she must consider it in accordance with a procedure which requires that a meeting be held between employer and employee, reasons for the employer's decision given and an appeal provided for. But the employer may reject a request for flexible working on grounds of (1) cost; (2) 'detrimental effect on ability to meet customer demand'; (3) 'inability to re-organise work among existing staff' or (4)'to recruit additional staff'; (5) 'detrimental impact on quality' or (6) 'performance'; (7) 'insufficiency of work during the periods the employee proposes to work' or (8) 'planned structural changes' (the Secretary of State may add additional grounds). An employee whose request is refused may complain to an employment tribunal that the appropriate procedure was not followed or that the employer's refusal was based on 'incorrect facts.' But the tribunal will not scrutinise whether, in the absence of factual mistakes, an employer's refusal of a request for contractual change is justified on the grounds given by the employer.

It would be easy to be scathing about the new rights created by the 2002 Act which provides employees only with a right to make request flexible working (and not to be subject to detriment for so doing) rather than a right to work flexibly. But it appears that employers who are required at least to go through the motions of giving such requests serious consideration actually find that they can be accommodated without undue strain.[128] So, for example, whereas the *Equal Opportunities Review* reported in 2000 (May/June) that 54 per cent of those who asked for changes to their working patterns in order to improve their work-life balances had their requests refused or unacceptable alternatives offered them. In April 2004, in a survey by the Office for National Statistics found that no less than 80 per cent of those requesting changes to their patterns of work under the EA 2002 had had their requests granted.[129] Interestingly, the second work-life balance survey, carried out in 2003 for the DTI, found that there was little employee resistance to flexible working by parents. Contrary to the oft-cited suggestion that other employees (in particular childless women) are aggrieved by the special needs of working parents, the survey found that 85 per cent of employees agreed that employers should make a special effort to accommodate the particular needs of parents of young and disabled children. It also reported that one in six parents had approached their employers about flexible working, that:

National Centre for Social Research, 'The Second Work-Life Balance Study' (DTI Employment Research Series No. 22)

- . . . [t]hese requests were most likely to be made by women, mothers, parents whose youngest child was under two years old and those in services and sales, and least likely by older employees (45+) and full-time workers.

---

[128] S Dex and C Smith, 'The nature and extent of family friendly employment policies in Britain' found that family friendly (ie, flexible) working policies were associated with improved financial performance by firms.

[129] This may in part be due to awareness on the part of employees that refusal may trigger a sex discrimination claim.

- Nearly three in ten employees who made a request to change how they regularly work (29 per cent) wanted to reduce their hours (including working part-time). A further 23 per cent wanted to change when they worked including the number of days they worked (such as a compressed working week or changing shifts). One in eight wanted to work flexi-time, and less than 10 per cent wanted to work longer hours (nine per cent) or take some form of time off (eight per cent).
- Nearly half (48 per cent) of requests were dealt with by a line manager or supervisor rather than by the managing director (21 per cent), the head of department (14 per cent) or the personnel department (12 per cent). Just over a quarter of employees who made a request (27 per cent) put their request in writing, whereas three-quarters had a meeting to discuss the request (with their employer or line manager/ supervisor).
- Of those employees who made a request to change the way they regularly work, over three quarters (77 per cent) said their request had been agreed. Agreement to such requests did not vary significantly by the size of the establishment that the employee worked in, an employee's occupation or their length of service, or by whether they were a parent.

The Executive Summary to the results from the survey of employers concluded that the results 'support the business case for the provision of work-life balance practices. Despite some concerns about staff shortages, the majority of employers who provided flexible working practices and leave arrangements found them to be cost effective, with a positive impact on labour turnover, motivation and commitment and employee relations.' So successful was the initiative regarded as being that *Work and Families* floats the possibility of extending the right to parents of older children and other carers. A note of caution, however, is struck by the director of the Maternity Alliance in the following article:

Kendall, 'Life's Off Balance', *The Guardian*, 5 April 2004

The Maternity Alliance has conducted a detailed survey of parents' experiences of flexible work. We found that while two-thirds of parents had their request agreed or reached a compromise, a quarter of these have accepted worse conditions, such as a cut in their salary or job status.

And only a quarter say their new arrangement is going well in practice. The most common problem is increased workloads. A typical example is a woman who asked to work four extended days a week instead of five. Her employer agreed, but said she had to take a cut in pay and holiday entitlement. She had to check her emails when she wasn't in the office and take on new areas of work. As a result, she ended up going back to full-time work.

A quarter of parents have had their request for flexible work refused, often for reasons disallowed by the law. Some employers fail to give reasons for their refusal. Others say they 'don't do part-time work' or 'don't want to open the floodgates' to requests from other staff. Its not just employees of small businesses who experience these problems—similar cases can be found in high-street chains, hospitals and local councils. Few parents are willing to challenge decisions because they're worried about losing their jobs or harming future career prospects. While many parents suffer in silence, others feel there is no option but to give up work.

Why is the law failing to deliver for many parents? Lack of awareness is partly to blame. A quarter of parents don't know they have a 'right' to request flexible work and almost half say their employers don't know or don't follow the correct procedure when considering requests.

The law also lacks 'bite.' Employers can refuse requests for a range of reasons open to broad interpretation. And employers' reasons for refusal cannot be challenged by tribunals:

parents can only challenge on the grounds their employer failed to follow the correct procedure for considering a request. Parents who mount a challenge and win only receive a maximum of £270 compensation a week for eight weeks.

Other factors also prevent the shift towards flexible work. The long-hours work culture is still rife in Britain, despite the lack of evidence that this makes us more economically productive. It is overwhelmingly women who are seeking flexible work.

This is partly because many fathers don't know that the law also applies to them, but also because women still do the lion's share of caring. Fathers are becoming more involved in bringing up their children, but until they demand flexible work in similar numbers to mothers, many employers will continue to ignore or downplay the issue . . .

A new right to work fewer hours when children are less than one year old would help many parents at a crucial stage in their child's development. Introducing a code of practice for employers to assess employees' requests for flexible work; giving parents the right to challenge a refusal; and raising compensation levels, would all help ensure flexible work becomes a reality for more parents.

Liz Kendall challenges the level of success of requests for flexible working suggested by the ONS data. Her concerns chime with those of the *Equal Opportunities Review* in a headline (October 2003) 'Slow-progress on work-life balance.' The article reported evidence of 'pockets of resistance to flexible working and a narrow approach among many employers,' prompting calls for an end to the long-hours culture and the extension of the legal right to request flexible working to include all workers.' The TUC's recent report, 'More time for families: tackling the long hours crisis in UK workplaces' similarly reports problems experienced by parents requesting flexible work and, alarmingly, a very narrow approach on the part of tribunals to the application of the Regulations.

TUC, More time for families: tackling the long hours crisis in UK workplaces

. . . the TUC undertook a detailed analysis of recorded employment tribunal decisions since the flexible working legislation came into force in April 2003. We discovered that there were 313 cases in total relating to the legislation, which had been registered since April 2003. However, there were only five decisions that set out in detail the significant issues involved. The other cases concerned preliminary legal points, were still pending or had been settled or withdrawn. The five cases examined revealed all too clearly the weaknesses of the legislation, including difficulties experienced by applicants who are unrepresented, the burdensome procedural hurdles for applicants, and the unfairness of the maximum limit on compensation of eight weeks' pay.

Employment Tribunal Case 1: *Allison v First Chevin Housing Group*, Case No 1804591/03, 21 May 2004, Leeds

Ms Allison had a mobility clause in her contract requiring her to change workplaces at the direction of her employer, the First Chevin Housing Group. For childcare reasons, Ms Allison put in an application under the flexible working regulations in order to try and resist a change in her place of work. The employment tribunal held that an application seeking to resist a change in working arrangements could in theory fall within the regulations, as she was effectively seeking to vary a clause in her contract. However, the regulations did not include changes to a place of work as one of the specific issues which could be raised by applicants, in contrast for example to a request to work at home. Ms Allison's application was therefore dismissed.

Employment Tribunal Case 2: *Kilby v Anything Left Handed Limited*, Case No 2300721/2004, 6 May 2004, London South

Ms Kilby applied under the flexible working regulations to start work half and hour later in the mornings. She was responsible for processing orders. The company said that it was vital to process orders and queries promptly, and insisted that orders should be processed by noon each day. It stated that neither the directors nor a more junior member of staff could cover for the extra half an hour in the mornings. The employment tribunal, in dismissing Ms Kilby's application, held that it was satisfied that the company had given proper consideration to the application and had refused it for sound business reasons.

Employment Tribunal Case 3: *King v St Martin's Property Corporation Limited*, Case No 2301107/2004, 27 May 2004, London South

Mr King was an administrator for St Martin's, a property management company. He applied under the flexible working regulations to start work at 7.30 am rather than 6.30 am, so that he could look after his young daughter. His intention was that his employers should count the hour between 6.30 am and 7.30 am as his lunch break, so that he did not have any pay deducted. Unfortunately for him, he failed to make this clear in the letter of application under the regulations. The company granted his application, but told him that his pay would be deducted and that they would not hold a meeting to discuss it. The tribunal held that they had no jurisdiction to consider the merits on either side, and that the company did not have to hold a meeting to discuss the application since it had apparently agreed to a written proposal by the applicant.

Employment Tribunal Case 4: *Pickering v ASDA Stores Limited*, Case Nos. 1201643/2003 and 1202315/2003, 11 March 2004, Bedford

Mr Pickering was a team leader at the ASDA Bedford depot, and a non-residential parent. He applied to work a fixed Sunday to Thursday shift pattern, and said that he did not want to work on Saturdays for childcare reasons. He was not given notice of the meeting to discuss his application nor was he told of his right to be accompanied at the hearing. Nevertheless, the tribunal held that the meeting was valid since Mr Pickering had agreed to it. The company maintained that other team leaders could not have weekends off if the request was granted, that Mr Pickering's proposals would require him to work across their shifts and that it would set a precedent. The tribunal dismissed the application, holding that the reasons were not a sham, despite the reference to 'setting a precedent.'

Employment Tribunal Case 5: *Snelling v Tates Ltd t/a Spar*, Case No 1502720/2003, 30 January 2004, Norwich

Ms Snelling, who worked for a branch of Spar supermarkets, had sole responsibility for her three-year-old daughter. She applied under the flexible working regulations to change her working hours. Spar had trained their Area Managers in the new regulations but had failed to 'cascade' this training to store managers. As a result, Spar failed to comply with the requirements of the regulations, including failing to hold a meeting. They also refused Ms Snelling's request in writing, over a month after she made her formal request. The tribunal therefore found in favour of Ms Snelling and ordered a reconsideration of the application. They awarded her a mere £500 in compensation, despite the fact that the tribunal hearing took place in January 2004, over five months after Ms Snelling had put in a valid application under the regulations and regardless of the fact that, as a large employer with a central human resources department, Spar should have been more than able to deal with her application.

Kendall makes the point that the existence of a right to work flexibly can serve further to entrench gendered working arrangements. Even where entitlement to family-related leave and work-related flexibility is equal between parents, men are radically less likely to take advantage of (particularly unpaid) leave than are women. Jane Pillinger warns that:

> Across Europe, some experiments in making working time more flexible have had the consequence of legitimising women's exit from the labour market, and therefore further undermining their position within it. For example, working time experiments in Finnish municipalities and health services, to introduce a six-hour day, part-time work, part-time benefits and work rotation—the bulk of which have been taken up by women—have had this negative consequence associated with them. Parental leave schemes in Sweden have had such a low take-up from fathers that a father's month is now included in the 12-month leave entitlement for parents [ie, it can be transferred to the mother rather than simply lost].[130]

Pillinger reports that, as a result of the problems of take-up associated with parental leave: 'in a growing number of countries, the collective reduction and reorganisation of working time has become strategically more important to achieving equality and the sharing of work and family life.' It is interesting to note in this context the TUC's 2002 report that more than three quarters of a million women worked in excess of 48 hours a week (a quarter of all those working these hours) and that the implementation of the Working Time Regulations 1998 (WT Regs) had had little impact on this. The UK remained at the top of the EU working hours league with an average 43.6-hour week to the EU. In October 2002 the *Equal Opportunities Review* reported DTI figures showing that 13 per cent of women (up from 6 per cent in 2000) worked in excess of 60 hours per week and that 86 per cent of employees were stressed by their current work-life balance. In 2003 the Mental Health Foundation reported research which showed that a poor work-life balance damages mental health.[131] And in October 2003 the *Equal Opportunities Review* reported that over 50 per cent of fathers worked in excess of 40 hours per week, 30 per cent more than 48 per cent. One in eight mothers worked in excess of 40 hours per week (this not including household work) and 6 per cent in excess of 48 hours.

There have been significant moves in a number of EU Member States to impose 35 hour maximum working weeks—this in part to permit the reconciliation of work and family life by all workers, in part to encourage job creation.[132] By contrast, the British approach to working time still leaves much to be desired. The long hours culture has been mentioned above. The WT Regs were passed in 1998 to comply with the Working Time Directive (Council Directive 93/104/EC). They impose a general maximum 48 hour week and provide for daily and weekly rest periods as well as in-work breaks. They also provide an entitlement to all workers of four weeks' annual paid holiday.

The general regulation of working time could, as Pillinger implies, have significant implications for greater gender equality at work. But the WT Regs are deeply flawed as an instrument of equalisation. Not only are the maximum weekly hours provided for (48) themselves incompatible with the exercise of any significant domestic or other extra-workplace responsibility, but the Regs permit individual 'opt-outs' in respect of the maximum 48-hour week and disapply the 48-hour maximum in respect of workers who control their own hours (such control is more often theoretical than practical). Worse, they

---

[130] *Equal Opportunities Review* 107.
[131] The *Equal Opportunities Review* August 2003 reported that workplace stress resulting from poor work–life balance cost the economy £370 million pa.
[132] See EIRS, 'Working time developments and the quality of work'.

provide that additional hours 'voluntarily' worked overtime by other workers do not count towards the 48-hour maximum week. The result is that the WT Regs have had little perceptible impact on working hours in the United Kingdom.

In February 2004 the European Commission started proceedings against the UK in the ECJ, alleging that the UK's transposition of the working time directive was inadequate. The proceedings, which resulted from a complaint to the Commission by the Amicus trade union, will challenge the Regulations' exclusion of additional hours 'voluntarily' worked overtime, as well as employers' responsibility in relation to workers' rest periods. A report on the proceedings by the European Industrial Relations Observatory on-line makes the point, however, that 'the significance of a ruling by the ECJ against the UK's provisions on partly unmeasured working time will remain limited for as long as the UK can continue to allow employees to opt out of the 48-hour ceiling on weekly working hours altogether.'

The individual opt-out was reviewed by the European Commission in January 2004 with particular reference to the UK's individual opt-out. The Commission's proposal for an amending directive did not, however, advocate removal of the opt-out (although it would prohibit work in excess of 65 hours per week and tighten the procedural requirement for opted-out workers).[133] In May 2004 the Commission launched the second stage of its review, urging the social partners to negotiate an agreement. It remains to be seen what the content of any amended Working Time Directive will be, the question of the opt-out being a politically controversial one. It is hard to avoid the conclusion, however, that working hours in the UK are unlikely to reduce significantly in the forseeable future and that workers, women workers in particular, will continue to struggle in order to reconcile the competing demands of home and workplace.

[133] COM/2004/0607.

7

Race

Introduction

Legislative prohibitions on race discrimination have been in place in Britain for almost 40 years (though in Northern Ireland only since 1997).[1] Despite this, people from ethnic minority groups suffer discrimination and disadvantage. This experience differs between ethnic minority groups and even within groups, this on the basis of factors such as sex, educational attainment and economic activity. But for all the heterogeneity of experience of people from ethnic minority groups, there is for many a shared experience of relative disadvantage.

The spotlight in recent years has been on racism in the criminal justice system, this as a result of the bungled police investigation and prosecutions brought in connection with the racist murder of black south London teenager Stephen Lawrence in 1993, and the widespread 'institutionalised racism' disclosed by the subsequent *Macpherson* report. That race influences experience of the criminal justice system is clear. In 1992, for example, Roger Hood reported (*Race and Sentencing, a Study in the Crown Court*) that black defendants stood between 5 per cent and 8 per cent greater overall chance of an immediate prison sentence than white defendants (this with over 100 possible variables held constant) and that in cases of medium gravity, in which judges had more discretion than in the more serious cases, the difference was 13 per cent.[2] In 1998 Phillips *et al* surveyed 4250 people held in 10 police stations in 1993/94, and concluded that:

> Members of ethnic minority groups–and black suspects in particular–appeared to be dealt with differently or responded differently from white suspects at a number of points between arrest and conviction. For example, they were on average: more likely to request legal advice; less likely to provide confessions; less likely to be cautioned and more likely to have no further action taken against them by the police; less likely to be bailed after charge; less likely (where the suspect was a juvenile) to have their cases referred for inter-agency consultation; and much more likely to have their cases terminated by the CPS.

---

[1] The correlation between the provisions of the RRA and the almost materially identical Race Relations (Northern Ireland) Order 1997 are set out in a table available at www.legal-island.com/Tablerd.htm.

[2] See 'Probation service fails ethnic minorities' 92 *Equal Opportunities Review*, reporting under-representation in management grades and 'a lack of confidence in the service's ability to deliver racial equality for its own staff' and (127 *Equal Opportunities Review*) 'Although racism faced by black and Asian probation officers from offenders had fallen sharply [since 2000] . . . the proportion of ethnic minority staff experiencing racism from their own colleagues and external organisations was "depressingly unchanged." '

Judicial Studies Board, *Equal Treatment Benchbook*

The [Phillips] research study found differences in the use of stop and search powers: black suspects were less likely to be charged or cautioned when arrested following a stop and search, and those arrested after a stop and search for stolen property were more likely to be 'NFAed'—to have no further action taken against them . . .

The police's 'stop and search' practices have been studied in at least two recent surveys. In 1999, Home Office statistics showed that black people were on average five times more likely than white people to be stopped and searched by the police. In 1995 the British Crime Survey showed that in the 16–25 age group, 47 per cent of young white men and 53 per cent of young African Caribbean men had been stopped by the police in the previous year.

This 1995 survey also showed that although about a third of all respondents had experienced some form of police-initiated contact that year, this proportion rose to 44 per cent among unemployed people, and to 56 per cent among young men.

Of the 108 deaths in police custody between 1990 and 1996, 23 per cent were of people from racial minorities [ethnic minorities account for around 8 per cent of the population]. Of the 69 people who died in police custody between April 1997 and March 1998, eight (12 per cent) were black, four were Asian, and one was from another minority ethnic group.

Young People and Crime, a 1995 Home Office study of self-reported offending among young people, found little difference between patterns of offending among young white and young black people (lower rates of offending among Asian young people) and slightly higher drug use by white than black youths. In 1998, another Home Office Report—*Statistics on Race and Criminal Justice*—found that 61 per cent of the adult black male prison population was serving sentences of over four years, compared with 59 per cent of Asians and 47 per cent of white prisoners, that 58 per cent of black women prisoners and 31 per cent of white women prisoners were serving over four years, and that, excluding foreign nationals, black men and women respectively accounted for 10 per cent and 13 per cent of prisoners—per cent of people aged over 10 in the general population. Yet the 1998 Home Office study found *no evidence* that black people committed more crimes than white people.

Formal investigations carried out by the CRE have found evidence of unlawful race discrimination in the CPS and prison service. Ethnic minority probation staff report that they suffer high levels of discrimination from their colleagues and organisations with which they come into professional contact. And racism in the police service would appear to be endemic. Despite the imposition, post-*Macpherson*, of targets for the recruitment of ethnic minority police officers the pace of change appears to be very slow. The recently published 'Thematic review of race and diversity in the Metropolitan Police Services' (Metropolitan Police, March 2004) disclosed that, although the number of visible ethnic minority recruits to the MPS increased from 60 in 1998 and around 95 in 2001 to around 375 in 2003, failure rates for ethnic minority candidates in the selection process were disproportionately high and the retention rates for visible minority police officers were significantly lower than those for whites. In 2001/2, for example, 70 per cent per cent of white leavers had been in the force for more than five years, by comparison with only 45 per cent per cent of ethnic minority staff: in 2003/4 these figures stood at about 63 per cent per cent and 26 per cent per cent respectively. During 2001/2, 26 per cent of ethnic minority staff and 9 per cent of white staff left during the initial 18-week training period. By 2003/4 these figures were around 43 per cent and 11 per cent respectively. The thematic review also commented on the 'acute under-representation of visible ethnic minorities at all ranks but particularly in middle and senior ranks,' coupled with 'insufficient throughput of visible ethnic minority officers to meet future needs' and the disproportionate subjection of black and Asian officers to internal investigations and written warnings.[3]

In November 2003 the BBC screened 'The Secret Policeman' which showed white recruits to the Greater Manchester Police explaining how they discriminated against black and Asian members of the public and engaging in the most extraordinarily racist behaviour. According to Daly, writing for the BBC magazine (21 October 2003):

> What I found was a police service trying very hard—and failing—to put its house in order . . . It was at the Police National Training Centre in Warrington, where trainees from 10 forces in the North West and Wales spend 15 weeks, that much of my material was garnered. The extremity of some of the racism I encountered from these recruits beggared belief. The majority of the officers I met will undoubtedly turn out to be good, non-prejudiced ones intent on doing the job properly. But the next generation of officers from one of Britain's top police colleges contains a significant minority of people who are holding the progress of the police service back. Racist abuse like 'Paki' and 'Nigger' were commonplace for these PCs. The idea that white and Asian members of the public should be treated differently because of their colour was not only acceptable for some, but preferable. I had become a friend to these men. They trusted me with their views. And they believed I was one of them. I operated under strict guidelines. I was not allowed to make racist comments or incite anyone to do or say anything which they wouldn't have otherwise said or done. But I had to laugh at their jokes and behave like a dumb apprentice. I said I was eager to hear other people's views in order to form my own. And they didn't hold back.

The initial response of the Greater Manchester force was to shoot the messenger: to arrest the reporter (who had successfully applied to join the force for the purposes of making the programme) on dishonesty offences and to threaten to withdraw cooperation from the BBC if it screened the programme. Nor is it easy to miss the extraordinarily high rate of attrition of the few high-profile black Metropolitan Police officers. Iranain born superintendent Ali Dizaei, for example, was subject to intense investigation by the Met for four years, during two years of which he was suspended from the force, before all charges against him were dropped in September 2003. Dizaei, then vice chair of the newly established National Black Police Association and tipped as the UK's first black chief constable, had called at its launch for the imposition of sanctions on police forces who fail to reach government targets for ethnic minorities. He alleged that black and Asian officers were subject to racism on a daily basis and that they were experiencing a 'post-Lawrence backlash.' He also claimed that ethnic minority police officers were trapped under a 'chicken mesh', unable to reach the more senior posts because of promotion tests which included questions, for example, about a 1970s TV advertisement, rather than police competence. Within a year Dizaei was suspended, the investigation into his alleged activities as a drug-taker, a threat to national security, and a friend of drug-traffickers involving 100 officers, MI5, the Inland Revenue and police in the US and Canada at a cost to the taxpayer of £4 million. Dizaei was cleared of perverting the course of justice and a second trial over an accusation of fiddling £270 of expenses was dropped. He was reinstated after the NBPA called for a boycott by black and Asian applicants of the Met on the basis that the force was guilty of persistent discrimination and in June 2004 the Independent Police

---

[3] See on a similar note the findings of the Morris inquiry into the Metropolitan Police: 'The Case for Change: People in the Metropolitan Police' (2005) and the report of the CRE's formal investigation into the Police Service (2005).

Complaints Commission found that the Dizaei investigation, after which the Met paid £80,000 in settlement of race discrimination proceedings, was 'seriously flawed' and mishandled 'from start to finish,' and ordered that outstanding disciplinary proceedings threated against Dizaei be dropped.

Dizaei claimed he had been subject to a 'witch hunt' because of his outspoken views on racism in the police. Nor is he an isolated example. Gurpal Virdi, an Asian officer, was sacked on charges of sending racist hatemail to himself. The Metropolitan Police subsequently paid him £150,000 in compensation for race discrimination. He later told the *Guardian* (18 January 2001): 'The tendency in the Met, if you speak out, is that you either get suspended or you get accused of some sort of crime. The Met can't investigate allegations against black or Asian officers properly. I have no faith in them.'

The Met launched an inquiry into 'the case against' Gurpal Virdi after he won his discrimination case in August 2000. The inquiry, which reported in January 2002, made wide-ranging recommendations for reforms of procedure and, having noted the fact that Virdi had not yet been permitted to return to work, called for the Met to provide progress reports on his return to duty. PS Virdi did eventually return to work in February 2002, 18 months after he had established his innocence of the charges brought against him by the Met and won his race discrimination claim. The Dizaei fiasco resulted in the appointment in January 2004 of former TGWU General Secretary Sir Bill Morris to head an official inquiry into racism in the Met—in particular, into how internal complaints about ethnic minority officers are investigated and how black officers' grievances are treated. The inquiry concluded that ethnic minority officers were disproportionately subjected to formal disciplinary procedures, partly because managers 'lacked confidence' in dealing with complaints against ethnic minority officers and tended to formalise them accordingly. The inquiry also found that some efforts made to further diversity had been 'counterproductive'. Public hearings are now complete but the report has not been published at the time of writing though the *Observer* reported (22 August 2004) that the inquiry 'is understood to be considering a range of potential measures, including an independent ombudsman for internal police discipline, and case managers to speed up the handling of complaints.' . . .

Concern about racism in the police force resulted in the announcement by the CRE in 2004 of a Formal Investigation into the police (for discussion of FIs see Chapter 5). The CRE's interim report into the police FI showed that 90 per cent of the police race equality schemes (see further Chapter 3) were so poor they breached the RRA. Steps taken by the police to weed out racist applicants had resulted in the exclusion of more ethnic minority than white applicants–this in the name of increasing racial equality and diversity! Ethnic minority recruits felt bullied by sometimes racist white instructors and there was widespread denial of the existence of racism within the police, and hostility to equality and anti-racist training.[4] The CRE threatened enforcement action against 14 chief constables and the heads of eight police authorities (ironically, at about the same time as Tory leader Michael Howard was promising to scrap 'politically correct' requirements on the police to record stop-and-search activity by ethnicity). Meanwhile, the *Observer* reported (22 August 2004) that 'Record numbers of white police officers are launching legal actions claiming they have been victimised because of the colour of their skin . . . convinced they are [now] the ones being overlooked for promotion.' The promotion of an Asian sergeant in

---

[4] See also S Holdaway, 'Black Police Associations: the organisation of ethnicity within the workforce' (2004: ESRC) which showed that the police still failed to understand the concept of 'institutionalised racism', that open racism has given way to covert racism post-MacPherson, that most ethnic minority police officers regarded their police forces as racist and that the workplace culture of the police is exclusionary of minority ethnic officers and staff.

Nottinghamshire led to complaints of race discrimination by six white officers. The final report of the FI (2005) concluded that the police service had a long way to go in eliminating race discrimination. Notwithstanding the threats of legal action (and some compliance action taken by the CRE in June 2004), the service was still generally failing to comply with the positive obligations imposed by the RR(A)A 2000. The report also found that a number of forces had taken it upon themselves to engage in unlawful positive discrimination in favour of ethnic minority candidates.

The effects of racism are not confined to the criminal justice system.[5] In early 1998, for example, an independent inquiry by barrister Lincoln Crawford found some of the 'worst manifestations of race discrimination' in Hackney's employment practices. The Council had succeeded in transforming itself from an almost exclusively white employer in the mid 1980s (itself a remarkable feat for a predominantly non-white borough)[6] but, the report found, had failed to give ethnic minority staff support and career development.

[M]ediocre performance from white staff was ignored, but managers came down 'like a tonne of bricks' on the heads of visible minority staff for similar performance.' More disciplinary actions were taken against ethnic minority staff for misconduct than against white staff whose conduct 'appeared to be excused . . . many ethnic minority staff remained in the posts into which they were recruited, and were never promoted; very few were given the opportunity to perform higher level duties or to 'act-up' to more senior positions; and more of them than of white staff were displaced through the process of restructuring. The result was that the confidence of many ethnic minority staff was regularly undermined, and 'psychological damage may have been done to many visible minority staff though their experience of working for the council.'[7]

Hackney agreed an action programme with the CRE under threat of a statutory Non Discrimination Notice arising out of the investigation but was issued with an NDN (see further Chapter 5) after its failure to comply with the action plan.

Hackney may provide a particularly egregious example of race discrimination at work. But it is far from an isolated one. In Spring 1997 the Office of Public Management reported that racism was a 'pervasive, long-running and deeply entrenched problem' within the armed services (in which ethnic minorities, comprising 8 per cent of the population, account for 1.4 per cent of personnel). And in November/ December 2000 the *Equal Opportunities Review* reported CRE condemnation of the armed services which had failed to meet targets set in 1998 for the recruitment of ethnic minority applicants and which continued to be the subject of harassing allegations relating to racist abuse and harassment.

A survey by the European Commission, published in December 1997, found that a third of adults in the UK admitted to being 'very' (8 per cent) or 'quite' (24 per cent) racist. Two-thirds of those interviewed in the UK thought that 'minority groups are being discriminated against in the job market.'[8] Even among firms which include an equal opportunities statement in their annual reports, 42 per cent responded less favourably to an apparently

---

[5] In *Commissioners of the Inland Revenue v Morgan* [2002] IRLR 776 the EAT ruled that there was no statutory or other offence of 'institutionalised racism'—is a body was found to be institutionally racist, this would only be a step towards establishing discrimination rendered unlawful by the RRA.

[6] See C McCrudden, 'Rethinking Positive Action' (1986) 15 *Industrial Law Journal* 219, extracted in Ch 3.

[7] 77 *Equal Opportunities Review* 7.

[8] 78 *Equal Opportunities Review* 6–7. This compares with 55 per cent in Belgium, 48 per cent in France and 42 per cent in Austria.

Asian job applicant than to one who was apparently white and similarly qualified.[9] The findings of this 1998 study were consistent with those of the CRE in 1996.[10]

A recent study of 56,000 job applications found that white graduates were almost twice as likely as ethnic minority graduates to be recruited. The study, presented to the British Psychological Society's Annual Conference in 1998 by researchers from the University of East London, found that ethnic minority candidates were disproportionately likely to be weeded out at the initial sifting stage and at the final stage, generally an 'assessment centre' exercise. Unemployment rates for ethnic minority workers have run at double those of whites for 20 years despite similar levels of qualification[11] and the fact that ethnic minority students are more likely overall than whites to continue in post-compulsory education (African-Caribbean men aged 20–24 were twice as likely as their white peers to be in full-time education, according to the Judicial *Equal Treatment Benchbook* 1999, and African-Caribbean women also better qualified than their white peers):

> Nevertheless, the return for this investment in training was considerably less, both in terms of employment rates and average earnings. Many ethnic minority employees work unsocial hours, or longer hours, in order to maintain their incomes. The industrial and occupational sectors in which ethnic minority employees are most likely to be found remain the least secure or worst paid. In particular, ethnic minorities are still disproportionately employed in poorly paid 'service', retail and transport occupations, and within such professions as nursing. These patterns, which may have been accepted by the first generation of post-war immigrants as part of the price for the opportunities gained in migration, have persisted among the UK-born and educated ethnic minority population.[12]

Even where ethnic minority workers avoid ghettoisation into traditional sectors of employment they continue to suffer disadvantage. In May/ June 2000 the *Equal Opportunities Review* reported a study of 516 economics lecturers which found that, after adjusting for age and research records, ethnic minority staff were paid 8 per cent less than whites. Two-fifths of ethnic minority staff surveyed reported that they felt they had suffered discrimination on grounds of racial or ethnic origin or nationality, 61 per cent of these in relation to career advancement and 20 per cent in relation to salary. The next edition of the *Equal Opportunities Review* carried the headline 'NHS pay scheme "riddled with racism"' above the report of a study carried out by the MSF union and the Community Practitioners' and Health Visitors' Association (CPHVA). The report found that black health visitors and community nurses were only one third as likely to receive a pay rise under the discretionary points scheme introduced by the Government in 1998 as their white colleagues, this despite the fact that 'there is nothing in the regional, age, full-time status or grades of black staff to provide any explanation of this disproportionate impact.' The report, which was based on the responses of 1210 health visitors and community nurses, was rubbished by the Department of Health (on the basis that its survey sample was too small to make meaningful deductions on the overall operation of the discretionary points scheme).[13] In 2004 the BMA accepted, at the start of its annual conference, that racism,

---

[9] The study was carried out by the Employment Policy Institute among *The Times* Top 100 companies.
[10] 81 *Equal Opportunities Review* 11.
[11] A TUC report published in June 2004, 'Moving on . . . how Britain's unions are tackling racism' shows that the picture has worsened recently, black and Asian unemployment running, at 11.3 per cent, at 2.5 times white unemployment.
[12] See also TUC, 'Black and Excluded' (2000), 'Qualifying for Racism' (2000) and 'Black Workers Deserve Better' (2001), available from the TUC website at tuc.org.uk.
[13] 91 *Equal Opportunities Review*.

sexism and homophobia were endemic among the medical profession. The association had commissioned research which found that, at the top of the medical profession, 78 per cent of consultants were white, but a majority of senior doctors without consultant status were black or Asian. Doctors who qualified outside Europe were frequently sidelined with little opportunity to advance their careers and ethnic minority doctors were more likely than whites to be disciplined.[14]

In 2002 the TUC called for action to tackle race discrimination in pay, publishing research which showed a pay gap of up to £150 per week between black and Asian men on the one hand and white men on the other. The report, 'Black and Underpaid,' showed disparities of between this level in the case of Pakistani and Bangladeshi men compared with white men, this gap reducing to £115 in the case of Caribbean men and 5 per cent for Indian men. The figures for women were complicated by the fact that black women are far more likely to work full-time than white women thus avoiding the significant downward impact of part-time work on wages (see further Chapter 6).

A 2000 survey by the Runnymede Trust found that race equality was not high on the agenda of many FTSE 100 companies and that little progress had been made despite almost a quarter century of the RRA.[15] There was a general lack of awareness of race issues, little monitoring of race, and virtually no organisations had targets for the representation of ethnic minorities. Ethnic minority workers were under-represented, particularly at the higher grades (only 3.2 per cent of junior managers and 1 per cent of senior managers were from ethnic minorities), with black Caribbeans particularly under represented at managerial and profession levels and Bangladeshis at all levels. While the 2000 report suggested that the race issue was at least moving up the agenda, the Trust's 2001 survey, reported in 2002, found a diminishing interest on the part of FTSE 100 companies.[16] And in 2000 the Office for National Statistics reported racial bias in the operation of the New Deal whereby young people are trained for work. According to the *Equal Opportunities Review*, April/May 2000:

> Ethnic minority participants . . . are less likely to find jobs despite making more attempts to secure jobs than white participants, and being better qualified . . . the report concludes that race discrimination by employers could be one of the reasons for this . . . the report finds that ethnic minority groups are less likely to leave the programme for a known subsidised or unsubsidised job. For example, one-fifth of white participants go on to subsidised employment when they leave New Deal, compared with just one in ten (12 per cent) ethnic minority leavers. By contrast, almost three-fifths (59 per cent) of ethnic minority participants take up the option of full-time education and training on leaving the programme, compared with just over two-fifths (43 per cent) of white leavers.
>
> In relation to unsubsidised jobs, more than two out of five (43.6 per cent) white leavers move into such jobs on leaving the New Deal, compared with just over one-third (35.5 per cent) of ethnic minority leavers. The national ratio between ethnic minority and white participants' known rates of going into unsubsidised jobs is 81 per cent.
>
> However, the report calculates that much of this difference is the result of incomplete destination data for ethnic minority leavers and from variation in performance between

[14] Reported in 132 *Equal Opportunities Review* (August 2004). 130 *Equal Opportunities Review* reports a case in which a reported £635,000 settlement was reached after an employment tribunal finding that arrangements for the qualification of medical consultants discriminated on grounds of race (*Jadhav v Secretary of State for Health*).

[15] 'Moving on up? Racial equality and the corporate agenda. A study of FTSE 100 companies.'

[16] See also Race for Opportunity, 'Race: Creating Business Value' (2003) and 'Top 100 Report' (2003).

local areas. It is argued that a significant part of the disparity between white and ethnic performance nationally, is not the result of ethnicity or race per se, but is the effect of poorer outcomes generally from the New Deal in areas, usually urban or inner city, where many ethnic minority participants live.

When these differences are taken into account, ethnic minority participants achieve, on average, 97 per cent of the job outcomes of the white participants in their local delivery areas—leaving a 3 per cent discrepancy. However, as the report points out, if higher levels of qualifications are an indicator of better employability, then ethnic minority participants should actually do better than whites.

Whereas only a quarter of white entrants to the programme have NVQ level 2 qualifications or above, more than a third (34 per cent) of ethnic minorities have such qualifications. Indian (46 per cent) and Chinese (43 per cent) have the highest qualifications, although every ethnic minority group is better qualified than white entrants.

In addition, when ethnic minority participants secure jobs, it takes them more attempts to do so. Nationally, ethnic minority participants are submitted to as many jobs while they are on New Deal as are white participants. However, within the same locality, the report indicates, ethnic minority participants actually get submitted to more jobs than their white counterparts.

It is clear that ethnic minority participants make more attempts to secure employment, the report concludes, given that ethnic minority participants have higher submission rates and lower job outcomes. It is suggested that race discrimination in the wider labour market may be one of the reasons for this.

The Cabinet Office commissioned research on the position of ethnic minorities in the labour market the objective of which was to increase the participation and achievement of black and Asian ethnic minorities in the UK labour market through a better and shared understanding of the current differentials between and within ethnic groups and the causes of these differentials; assessment of the effectiveness of different approaches for increasing the achievement of ethnic groups; the drawing up of clear policy recommendations for building on existing work and adopting new approaches to address the causes of the differentials in labour market achievement; and a 'fresh intellectual and policy approach to the issue of ethnic minority differential performance in the labour market.' The Executive Summary, extracted below, demonstrates both the lack of homogeneity across ethnic minority groups and the shared experience of their members of disproportionate disadvantage.

The Prime Minister's Strategy Unit, 'Ethnic Minorities and The Labour Market: Final report' (2003)[17]

Ethnic minorities currently make up 8 per cent of the UK population. Between 1999 and 2009 they will account for half the growth in the working-age population . . .

Currently, there are wide variations in the labour market achievements of different ethnic minority groups.

Indians and Chinese are, on average, doing well, and often out-performing Whites in schools and in the labour market. Their success shows that there are no insuperable barriers to successful economic and social integration.

However, other groups are doing less well. Pakistanis, Bangladeshis and Black Caribbeans experience, on average, significantly higher unemployment and lower earnings than Whites. This brings not only economic costs but also potential threats to social cohe-

---

[17] http://www.number10.gov.uk/su/ethnicper cent20minorities/report/downloads/ethnic_minorities.pdf.

sion. Improving performance in schools and in the labour market for these groups is a major priority for Government.

Significantly, the evidence in this report shows that all ethnic minority groups—even those enjoying relative success, such as the Indians and Chinese—are not doing as well as they should be, given their education and other characteristics . . .

On average, ethnic minorities are disadvantaged in the labour market relative to their White counterparts

Employment rates amongst almost all ethnic minority groups are lower than those of the White population. With the important exception of Indians, earnings and progression in work are also persistently lower. Critically, these gaps are not closing.

However, this hides enormous variations: the old picture of White success and ethnic minority underachievement is now out of date

Over the last three decades, some ethnic minorities in the UK have done very well. On the measures of employment, earnings and progression within work, there is a clear pattern of Indians on a par with, or outperforming, not just other ethnic minorities, but often Whites as well. This pattern is also reflected in educational achievement, strengthening chances of long-term labour market success.

Nonetheless, all ethnic minorities, including these 'successful' groups, are not doing as well as they could be

There are important and worrying disparities in the labour market performance of ethnic minorities and Whites that are not attributable to different levels of education and skills. The persistence of workplace discrimination is an important reason for this. Limited access to job and social networks is also critical, and subtle in its impact.

Failure to make the most of the potential of ethnic minorities has an impact on the UK's economic performance

With ethnic minorities set to account for more than half of the growth of the working age population over the next decade, failure to tackle the problems of labour market underachievement will have increasingly serious economic consequences.

Low employment rates for particular ethnic minority groups hold back economic growth, particularly in the context of full employment and skills shortages. For example, if the employment rates of Pakistanis matched those of their Indian counterparts, the proportion of male and female workers in this group would rise by 24 and 136 per cent respectively, an increase of some 96,000 people in work. Similarly, if the employment rates of the Black, Pakistani and Bangladeshi groups matched those of their Indian counterparts, the British workforce would grow by over 180,000 people.

Labour market disadvantage also has potential social costs. Lack of achievement in the labour market feeds social exclusion, damaging relations between ethnic groups in Britain and putting social cohesion at risk.

However, the nature and extent of this disadvantage varies widely, between and within different ethnic minority groups

The position of ethnic minorities is now much more complex than in previous decades, going back to the 1960s. There are significant differences, for example, between the different Asian groups, with Indians having higher employment rates and occupational achievement than Pakistanis and Bangladeshis, as well as much higher participation rates amongst women. The patterns of disadvantage amongst the Black population are different again. Whilst there are only small differences in average pay and occupational achievement between the Black African group and Whites, the Black Caribbean group is significantly disadvantaged in comparison.

Distinctions within ethnic minority groups also shape outcomes in the labour market. Gender, generation and geography play key roles. In the case of gender, many Asian groups are characterised by low participation rates among women, something that is reversed in the case of the Black Caribbean population. First-generation immigrants among ethnic minorities often do less well in the labour market than their children. Finally, settlement patterns that have taken some groups to certain parts of the country, for example, heavy Pakistani concentrations in the Midlands and the North, have also influenced employment outcomes.

The reasons for labour market disadvantage are no less varied

There is no single cause of this pattern of labour market disadvantage. The class backgrounds of different ethnic minorities, culture and family patterns all play a part. Educational underachievement is both a symptom of these factors and an important cause factor in its own right. The proportion of pupils who get five or more GCSE grades at A*–C is much lower amongst Black, Pakistani and Bangladeshi pupils, especially boys, than amongst Whites—although Indian attainment at GCSE level is actually higher than the White population. However, even when differences in educational attainment are accounted for, ethnic minorities still experience significant labour market disadvantages.

In general, ethnic minorities, including Indians, do not get the jobs that their qualification levels justify.

There are various reasons for this. In some cases, ethnic minority groups are concentrated in areas of deprivation. These areas contain barriers, such as poor public transport and isolation in areas with high proportions of workless households, that may disproportionately affect ethnic minorities.

However, there is also strong evidence that discrimination plays a significant role. Whilst equal opportunities legislation has had some success in combating overt discrimination and harassment, indirect discrimination, where policies or practices have the inadvertent result of systematically disadvantaging ethnic minorities, remains a problem . . .

The CRE has drawn attention to the disproportionate exclusion of ethnic minority pupils from schools.

CRE, 'Exclusion from School and Racial Equality: A Good Practice Guide' (1997)

Pupils from ethnic minorities are significantly overrepresented among those excluded from school. 1994/5 was the first year that ethnic monitoring of permanent exclusions formed part of the DfEE's national schools census. Data from that census . . . confirm previous research findings that black boys and girls are four to six times more likely to be permanently excluded than their white counterparts.

As long ago as 1985, a CRE investigation of exclusions from Birmingham schools showed that black boys were four times more likely than white boys to be excluded, and for behaviour that did not result in exclusion for white boys. In 1996, two important reports from OFSTED, the schools inspectorate, *Exclusions from Schools* and *Recent Research on the Achievements of Ethnic Minority Pupils*, highlighted and confirmed the problem. The latter pointed out that: 'On average, Caribbean young men . . . appear to be achieving considerably below their potential . . . A combination of gender and racial stereotypes may make it more difficult for young black men to avoid being caught up in cycles of increasingly severe criticism and control.'

High exclusion rates are not just an issue for black pupils. A 1996 OFSTED report on *The Education of Travelling Children* notes that pupils from Gypsy and travelling families are also disproportionately excluded, despite the behaviour of travelling pupils being generally good. Children assessed as requiring support for special educational needs (particularly emotional and behavioural difficulties) and children looked after by social services, are also disproportionately liable to be excluded. A 1996 Audit Commission report, *Misspent Youth* emphasises the social consequences of exclusion from school, suggesting that nationally only 15 per cent of permanently excluded pupils return to mainstream schooling.

In addition to the direct race discrimination experienced by many, those belonging to ethnic minority groups also suffer disadvantage because of characteristics disproportionately shared by particular of those groups. In Chapter 6 we considered the labour market difficulties experienced by single parents, 90 per cent of whom are women. According to the 1991 census, single-parent households accounted for 18.8 per cent of white households, but no less than 54.7 per cent of African-Caribbean households. In 1998, economic activity rates for men varied between 84 per cent for white and 81 per cent for black Caribbean men, and 72 per cent for Bangladeshi men, while those for women varied between 76 per cent and 72 per cent for black Caribbean and white women, and 32 per cent and 22 per cent respectively for Pakistani and Bangladeshi women.[18] The Department of the Environment's English Housing Survey 1994–95 showed that 19 per cent of white households, but 42 per cent of black and 63 per cent of Pakistani/Bangladeshi households, were located in council estates or low income areas, while 73 per cent of white but only 3 per cent of each black and Pakistani/Bangladeshi households were in affluent suburban or rural areas. Almost 50 per cent of Bangladeshi and 30 per cent of Pakistani households were overcrowded, and 40 per cent of Bangladeshi households, 20 per cent of Pakistani households, just over 20 per cent of black households and 7 per cent of white households were dissatisfied with their housing.[19] Figures for 2004 in Scotland were not dissimiliar.

'Census data confirms disadvantage of ethnic minorities in Scotland' 128 *Equal Opportunities Review*

Data from the 2001 Census illustrate the extent of disadvantage faced by ethnic minority groups in Scotland.

Some of the key findings to emerge from analysis carried out by the Scottish Executive are that:

- unemployment among all ethnic minorities is higher than for white Scots—black Scots (15 per cent) and Africans (15 per cent) are twice as likely as whites (7 per cent) to be unemployed;
- overcrowding is much more prevalent among ethnic minorities—30 per cent of the Pakistani, Bangladeshi and African communities live in overcrowded accommodation compared with 7 per cent of white British people;
- self-employment among Pakistanis (32 per cent) is three times higher than for white Scots (10 per cent);
- some 27 per cent of Pakistanis work more than 49 hours a week in their main job, compared with 14 per cent of all people in Scotland; and
- of those aged over 60, Pakistanis are most likely to describe themselves as having poor health (41 per cent) compared with 22 per cent of white Scots.

The imposition of positive obligations upon public authorities by the RRA as a result of its amendment in 2000 by the RR(A)A may prove significant over time in tackling some of the disadvantages disproportionately experienced by those belonging to ethnic minority groups although the Audit Commission's 2002 report, *Equality and Diversity: Learning from Audit, Inspection and Research* suggests that progress has been slow. In November/ December 2000 the *Equal Opportunities Review* reported that almost half the councils in England and Wales had made no plans to address institutional racism in the wake of the *Macphearson* report[20] and in March/April 2001 it reported that only 5 per cent of NHS

---

[18] Office for National Statistics, Labour Force Survey winter 1998.
[19] *Ibid.*
[20] See the LGA, 'Paved with good intentions? a survey of local authority responses to the Stephen Lawrence Inquiry'.

Trusts had fully implemented racial equality action plans. These plans had been recommended by the NHS Executive in 1993, the same year in which the CRE had reported the results of a Formal Investigation into race discrimination in the NHS (the FI found 'glaring inconsistencies between equal opportunities policies and practice [and] . . . questionable employment procedures in many NHS trusts and health authorities.')[21] Progress made under the RR(A)A is considered further in Chapter 3. But in May 2003 the CRE chairman Trevor Phillips condemned the lack of progress made by public authorities in eradicating institutionalised racism:

'CRE condemns authorities' slow progress on tackling institutional racism' 117 *Equal Opportunities Review*

'Levels of consciousness around racial discrimination in the public sector have risen,' acknowledged Philips. But, he said, 'that has not translated to real change on the ground. Ethnic minorities are still underrepresented in employment and many public bodies may be found wanting in the way they service their customers. Across the board people are looking at the problem but simply not changing anywhere near fast enough.'

The Metropolitan Police, described in the Macpherson report as institutionally racist, admits that it still has a long way to go, but says it is proud of the progress made in the past four years. 'No organisation can claim to have completely eradicated institutional racism,' said a Metropolitan Police spokesperson, 'and we are not complacent, we are continually reassessing and re-evaluating how we do things.'

Numbers of ethnic minority recruits to the Met, although still nowhere near representative of the local population, are rising. Non-white recruits now make up 10.5 per cent of the total, twice the number of serving police officers (5.4 per cent). In addition, more than a quarter (27.4 per cent) of Community Support Officers (CSOs) are from non-white groups.

Although CSOs have less training and do not have the power to arrest, 'they are the eyes and ears on the street and are a good source of reassurance for the public,' says the Met. Their experience can act as a useful stepping stone while they find out what kind of organisation the police force is and whether a career as a police officer is something that they want to pursue.

By January 2004, almost three years after the positive obligations imposed by the RR(A)A came into force, the *Equal Opportunities Review* reported that one third of Scottish public bodies were not in compliance with the Act.

The positive duties imposed by the RRA have been considered in Chapter 3, its prohibition of discrimination by public authorities in Chapter 4. Those features shared by the RRA with other discrimination legislation (its prohibition of direct and indirect discrimination, victimisation, etc; questions relating to its scope) have been dealt with in Chapters 2 and 4 while its provision for positive discrimination and questions of enforcement have been considered in Chapters 3 and 5. Here we turn our attention to a number of issues which are unique to the RRA. These include the meaning of 'racial group' and its genuine occupational qualification (GOQ) and genuine occupational requirement (GOR) defences. Before we consider the RRA itself, however, it is useful briefly to deal with the relevance in this area of EC law and its recent impact on the substance of the RRA itself.

---

[21] According to the CRE report of the 2001 survey, 'Racial Equality and NHS Trusts'.

Race Discrimination and EU Law

For many years now, it has been impossible adequately to understand sex discrimination law without taking into account the relevant provisions of European law. The same has recently become true of race discrimination law with the implementation of Council Directive 200/43/EC (the Racial Equality Directive). Prior to July 2003, the only direct impact of EC law on domestic race discrimination law was by virtue of Article 39 of the Treaty Establishing the European Community, which provides:

1 Freedom of movement for workers shall be secured within the Community.
2 Such freedom of movement shall entail the abolition of any discrimination based on nationality between workers of Member States as regards employment, remuneration and other conditions of work and employment.

Article 39 generated scant litigation in the UK context, its protections being considerably weaker for most purposes than those provided by the RRA. The disadvantages, from a race equality perspective, of the EU dimension are discussed in the extract below.

E Szyszczak, 'Race Discrimination: The Limits of Market Equality' in B Hepple and E Szyszczak (eds), _Discrimination: The Limits of Law_, 125, 126–9, footnotes omitted

It is felt that many black and ethnic minorities, particularly when they are only 'guest workers' in the European economy, will be adversely affected by the consequences of the Internal Market. Wong vividly describes the future Europe as a '. . . landscape for increasing problems of social polarisation and exacerbation of racial tensions and uprisings.' The fears of black and ethnic minority communities may be separated into three recognized issues for the purposes of analysis, although obviously the three areas overlap and interrelate to form a web of what could be classified as institutionalized discrimination.

The first fear is the invisibility of black and ethnic minority rights in the Social Charter and in Community law generally. . . . A second fear is that indirect discrimination may occur as a result of the operation of the Internal Market. Freedom of movement is an illusory right to a non-Community national. Equally, discrimination at the national level may lead to black and ethnic minorities having difficulty in obtaining the transportable Euro-skills.

Examples of the kind of indirect discrimination which may occur are given by the Commission for Racial Equality. In analyzing the implications of Council Directive 89/48/EEC on a 'general system for recognition of higher education diplomas awarded on completion of professional education and training of at least three years' duration,' several issues of indirect discrimination emerge. The Directive requires member states to recognize Community professional qualifications subject to the completion of one of the adaption procedures provided where the qualifications are lower than those of the host state. Article 1 of the Directive states that a diploma must show:

. . . that the education and training attested . . . were received mainly in the Community, or the holder thereof has three years' professional experience certified by the Member State which recognises a third country diploma . . .

There is nothing in the Directive to allow a challenge by an individual alleging that a decision by a competent authority is racially discriminatory. . . .

Another example of the indirect discrimination consequences of the Internal Market is in the area of public procurement. Community law has already been used by the

Conservative government as an excuse not to introduce local labour contracts as a way of alleviating local unemployment after the Broadwater Farm and Handsworth disturbances. Anxieties are now expressed about the decision in *Gebroeders Beentjes BV v State (Netherlands)* [Case C–31/87] [1998] ECR I–04635 discussed in Chapter 5]. . . . A third fear of the consequences of the Internal Market is that by promoting a common European identity, even further alienation of black and ethnic minority groups will occur, fuelled by the lack of legal protection in national and Community law, the indirect discrimination consequences of the Internal Market and the growth of rightwing fascist groups in Europe. Even Mrs Thatcher, not the greatest supporter of the Internal Market, alluded to this in her famous speech at Bruges in 1988:

> From our perspective today, surely what strikes us most is our common experience. For instance the story of how Europeans colonised and (yes, without apology) civilised much of the world, is an extraordinary tale of talent, skill and courage.

The fostering of a common European identity may prevent the acceptance of different 'non-European' forms of religion, languages, cultural ideas and education. Sivanandan has warned: 'We are moving from an ethnocentric racism to a Eurocentric racism, from the different racisms of the different member states to a common, market racism.'

Issues have already arisen in Europe over multi-racial schooling and the wearing of traditional clothes at school and at work. These are indicative of some of the features of alienation already experienced. With cutbacks in public expenditure it is felt that even fewer resources will be available to finance projects relating to the education of black and ethnic minorities and that more attention will be paid to the teaching of European languages, history, policies and culture.

Article 39 has been supplemented, since the Treaty of Amsterdam, by Article 13 which provides:

> Without prejudice to the other provisions of the Treaty and within the limits of the powers conferred by it upon the Community, the Council, acting unanimously on a proposal from the Commission and after consulting the European Parliament, may take appropriate action to combat discrimination based on sex, racial or ethnic origin, religion, belief, disability, age or sexual orientations.

The Racial Equality Directive, like the Employment Equality Directive, was adopted under Article 13 TEC. Its adoption has improved the protection afforded in relation to race discrimination at the European level. But the overall picture remains far from satisfactory.

B Hepple, 'Race and Law in Fortress Europe' 67 (2004) *Modern Law Review* 1, 3–13, footnotes omitted

The [Race Equality] Directive extends 'hard' EC anti-discrimination law from the existing narrow focus on gender to cover discrimination on grounds of racial and ethnic origin (terms which are left undefined). The material scope of the Race Directive goes beyond employment and covers social protection including social security and healthcare, social advantages, education, access to and supply of goods and services available to the public including housing . . . Other innovations in the Race Directive are the requirements for member states to designate bodies for the promotion of racial equality, to promote social dialogue between the two sides of industry with a view to promoting equal treatment, and to encourage dialogue with NGOs in the fight against racial discrimination.

I intend to examine two features of these important legal instruments [the Racial Equality Directive and the European Convention on Human Rights] which, in my view, prevent them from being as effective as they might be in promoting a pluralistic culture of human rights in Europe. The first is that the universality of human rights is undermined by being restricted to those who are nationals of the EU states. The second is that these instruments are incapable of redressing collective racial disadvantage because they do not provide for the enforcement of positive social, economic and cultural obligations . . .

discrimination on grounds of nationality is altogether excluded from [the] scope [of the Racial Equality Directive]. The member states were worried that their immigration controls might be susceptible to challenge. So they secured changes to the draft in order to limit its application. The Preamble makes it clear that the Directive does not apply to provisions governing the entry and residence of third-country nationals and their access to employment and occupation. Article 3(2) goes beyond the exclusion of national discretion in relation to immigration controls by also excluding 'any treatment arising from the legal status of third-country nationals.' There is nothing to prevent member states granting more extensive protection against discrimination, but in many of their legal systems there are extensive distinctions between citizens and third country nationals (TCNs). So far as the UK is concerned, the Race Relations Act does cover discrimination on grounds of nationality. Since the amending Act of 2000 this extends to the exercise of immigration functions. However, a controversial ministerial authorisation under the 2000 Act permits discrimination on the basis of nationality in relation to the examination of a claim, detention and conditions of temporary admission . . .

The Race Directive is aimed at securing equal treatment in respect of a range of social and economic rights, and it permits but does not require positive action. At present no member state requires positive action, apart from the UK in respect of Northern Ireland and in respect of racial discrimination in Great Britain. Article 5 of the Directive provides that 'the principle of equal treatment shall not prevent any Member State from maintaining or adopting specific measures to prevent or compensate for disadvantages linked to racial or ethnic origin.' In its case law on positive action for women in the field of employment, the ECJ has excluded schemes giving women automatic preferment in respect of engagement or promotion. If that case law is followed in the interpretation of Article 5, then some existing schemes such as those in the Netherlands which give preference to members of disadvantaged ethnic minorities may be vulnerable to legal challenge.

The concept of indirect discrimination is not redistributive in the sense of requiring equality of outcomes for all racial or ethnic groups. The essential feature of indirect discrimination is that an apparently neutral provision, criterion or practice has an unjustifiable adverse disparate impact upon the group to which the individual belongs. The wording of Article 2(2)(b) of the Race Directive speaks of a provision which 'would put persons of a racial or ethnic origin at a particular disadvantage compared with other persons.' This builds on the ECJ's case law on nationality discrimination (rather than that relating to gender discrimination) and avoids the need to rely on statistical evidence of disparate impact. However there is no violation if there is no exclusionary provision, or if a 'particular disadvantage' cannot be shown, or if the practice can be objectively justified by a legitimate aim and the means adopted for achieving that aim are appropriate and necessary.

Indirect discrimination thus only partially captures the various interacting factors which cause racial inequality. These include: racism, that is beliefs of biological superiority; cultural beliefs about the incompatibility of certain lifestyles and traditions; divisions of social class and gender; and social space, that is the structure of opportunities which is moulded by the geographical location in which communities live. Indirect discrimination is also not the same as 'institutional racism.' The Macpherson inquiry into the death of Stephen Lawrence defined this in relation to the police as 'the collective failure of an organisation to provide an appropriate and professional service to people because of their colour, culture or ethnic origin. It can be seen or detected in processes, attitudes and behaviour which amount to discrimination through unwitting prejudice, ignorance, thoughtlessness and racist stereotyping which disadvantages minority ethnic people.' For Sir William Macpherson the death of Stephen Lawrence was attributable not to individual acts of overt discrimination by police officers, but stemmed instead from the occupational culture of the police in which 'both negative racial categorisations of black youth and the apparent irrelevance of race to incidents that require its recognition are features.' Yet, unless a specific 'provision criterion or practice' can be identified, such an occupational culture will not fall within the scope of the law on indirect discrimination. Even if direct or indirect discrimination can be established, the outcome is usually compensation for an individual, not positive measures to ensure the full participation of disadvantaged groups in the workforce and fair access for them to education, training, goods, facilities and services.

The Race Directive is based on a British model of the 1970s rather than what is required in the 21st century in Europe in order to achieve racial equality. While the British Race Relations Acts have succeeded in breaking down many barriers for individuals in their search for jobs, housing and services and there are far fewer overt expressions of discrimination than there once were, members of ethnic minorities still suffer from stereotypes about their abilities . . .

The British model was designed to deal largely with organisations with hierarchical, vertically integrated and centralised bureaucracies. This is not appropriate for modern, flatter, organisational structures in which the achievement of equality depends not simply on avoiding negative discrimination, but on the active participation of all stakeholders, on training and improving skills, and developing wider social networks and encouraging adaptability. [A] . . . duty of public authorities to have regard to the need to promote equality of opportunity has now been implemented in the Race Relations (Amendment) Act 2002 . . . The campaign for positive duties gained further momentum when 246 MPs signed an early day motion calling on the government to introduce a single equality bill. Other member states will need to follow this 'fourth generation' equality legislation if a real impact is to be made on racial disadvantage

The Racial Equality Directive has been mentioned throughout the book but it is useful here to recap the major amendments which have been made to the RRA as a result. The first point which ought to be made about the RRA as amended is that it now contains a fault line dividing discrimination on grounds of 'race or ethnic or national origins' on the one hand from discrimination on grounds of colour or nationality on the other. All the amendments made to comply with the Racial Equality Directive apply only to discrimination on the former grounds, the Act's original provisions continuing to apply to discrimination on grounds of colour and nationality. As Bell points out the interpretation by the UK Government of the Racial Equality Directive not to apply to discrimination on grounds of 'colour' is 'without any clear explanation'.[22] The ossification of 'colour' discrimination may not be significant given that such discrimination is likely also to qualify as 'race', if not ethnic or national origin, discrimination. It remains to be seen how the courts will approach this issue. Discrimination on grounds of nationality against citizens of EU Member States will be caught by Article 29 and all the rules on free movement of citizens in any event, but discrimination against non-EU citizens on grounds of nationality may be challenged only on the basis of the unamended Act.

---

[22] M Bell, 'A Patchwork of Protection: the New Anti-discrimination Law Framework' 67 (2004) *Modern Law Review* 465, 467.

The existence of this fault line, and other shortcomings of the RRA, have recently been the subject of trenchant international criticism.

'UN condemns UK race laws' 122 *Equal Opportunities Review*

A United Nations committee has called for major changes to UK race laws to ensure compliance with international law. The committee's report follows a review of the state of race relations in a number of countries. Areas the UN considers need addressing include:

- comprehensive race legislation: current UK race discrimination laws are complex and fail to give full coverage to discrimination on grounds of colour and nationality. It calls for the introduction of 'a single comprehensive law consolidating primary and secondary legislation, to provide for the same protection from all forms of racial discrimination' so as to comply with international law;
- legislation against incitement to religious hatred: 'Islamophobia' following the September 11 attacks is a cause for concern, and the UN called for 'the extension of the crime of incitement to racial hatred to cover offences motivated by religious hatred against immigrant communities'; and
- an end to the Home Secretary's licence to discriminate in immigration control: section 19D of the Race Relations Act enables the Home Secretary to write his own licence to discriminate against persons of a specific nationality or ethnicity in immigration control.

The limited application of the RRA to immigration has been considered in Chapter 4, the issue of Islamophobia is dealt with below. As for the first point made by the UN committee, this structural criticism echoes that made in Chapter 1: the distinction, recently created in the RRA, between discrimination on grounds of 'race' or ethnic or national origin, on the one hand, and between discrimination on grounds of colour or nationality, on the other, is just the most topical example of the incoherence and inconsistency which characterises domestic discrimination law.

Returning to some of the detail of the RRA, the Act (s.1A) contains a new definition of indirect discrimination which is consistent with the definitions in the new SO and RB Regs, and broadly in line with that which applies to sex discrimination in employment (this as a result of the 2001 amendments to comply with the Burden of Proof Directive). Unlike the position under SDA, the new definition of indirect discrimination (in common with the express prohibition of harassment and the changes in the burden of proof, etc) apply to discrimination other than in the field of employment. It was noted above that the definitions apply only to discrimination on grounds of 'race' or ethnic or national origin. Bearing this in mind, s.1B RRA provides that the various amendments apply to discrimination regulated by:

(a) Part II [RRA, which deals with 'employment' broadly defined]
(b) sections 17 to 18D [education]
(c) section 19B [discrimination by public authorities], so far as relating to—any form of social security
   (ii) health care
   (iii) any other form of social protection; and
   (iv) any form of social advantage which does not fall within section 20
(d) sections 20 to 24 [goods, facilities and services; premises]
(e) sections 26A and 26B; [barristers and advocates and]
(f) sections 76 and 76ZA [public appointments]

Section 27 RRA provides that the prohibitions on discrimination and harassment on grounds of 'race' or ethnic or national origins shall apply in respect of relationships which have come to an end (see further Chapter 4) and s.4A changes the GOQ (now genuine occupational *requirement*) applicable to such discrimination. Other miscellaneous amendments include the extension of the prohibitions on discrimination and harassment on grounds of race or ethnic or national origins to private households and to small partnerships, the removal of a number of exceptions to the prohibitions on such discrimination in relation to premises, the extension of the geographical extension of the RRA and the inclusion of provisions permitting the voiding of discriminatory provisions in collective agreements. All of these amendments are considered in Chapters 4 and 5 and are mentioned here only to give a flavour of the amendments to the RRA made by virtue of the Racial Equality Directive.

Coverage of the RRA

The first very significant issue which arises under the RRA concerns the people to whom it applies. In one sense the RRA, adopting a formal approach, applies to all people. But the concern of the Act is with discrimination *on racial grounds* (s.1(1)(a)) and, in the context of indirect discrimination, treatment which disadvantages particular *racial groups*. Section 3 of the RRA defines these terms as follows:

(1) In this Act, unless the context otherwise requires—
   'racial grounds' means any of the following grounds, namely colour, race, nationality or ethnic or national origins;
   'racial group' means a group of persons defined by reference to colour, race, nationality or ethnic or national origins, and references to a person's racial group refer to any racial group into which he falls.
(2) The fact that a racial group comprises two or more distinct racial groups does not prevent it from constituting a particular racial group for the purposes of this Act.

In Chapter 2 we considered the significance of the terms 'on racial grounds' as distinct from, for example, 'on grounds of his (or her) race'—see, in particular, the discussion of *Showboat Entertainment Centre Ltd v Owens* [1984] 1 WLR 384 and *Weathersfield (trading as Van & Truck Rentals) v Sargent* [1999] ICR 425. Before we turn to consider the meaning of 'racial grounds' it is useful to note that the RRA, by contrast with the other anti-discrimination legislation, expressly defines segregation as discrimination. Section 1(2) of the Act provides that 'for the purposes of this Act, segregating a person from other persons on racial grounds is treating him less favourably than they are treated.'

Only one appellate decision has been reached on this provision—that of EAT in *FTATU v Modgill*. The case was brought by a number of African Asians who were employed by PEL in the paint shop. They complained, *inter alia*, that the employers had discriminated against them by segregating them contrary to s.1(2). EAT overturned a tribunal decision in their favour.

FTATU v Modgill [1980] IRLR 142

Slynn J:

There is no doubt that if an employer does keep apart one person from others on the grounds of his race, that amounts to discrimination on the part of the employer. If it can be shown that it is the policy of the company to keep a man of one colour apart from others, and that it does in fact happen, then a Tribunal clearly is entitled to find that there has been discrimination contrary to the provisions of the Act . . .

Had it here been clear that there was this policy of the company, and had the facts been that through the personnel department only Asians had been sent to this particular section of the factory, it seems to us that there would have been evidence upon which the Tribunal could have reached the conclusion which it did in fact reach. But that is not the way that the Tribunal, at the end of the day, put it. They had evidence which they appear to have accepted, in the body of their decision, that when vacancies arose in the paint shop they were filled by persons introduced by those who were already working there or those who were leaving . . . Indeed, the evidence was that, in a significant number of cases, people had applied for employment even before the company know that there was either a vacancy or was about to be a vacancy because one of the Asian workers was to leave . . . for a period of something like two years, the personnel department of the company had not had to select or interview persons for employment in this particular area. Those who worked there had produced candidates for appointment to [the manager] and he had found men who were able and willing to take on the job. It seems to us that the Tribunal accepted that there arose a situation, really by the acts of those working in the paint shop itself, that all the workers were in fact Asian . . .

The Tribunal, as we read their decision, really decided the case on the basis that there had been what they called 'indirect' or 'secondary' discrimination because the company had not had a more positive employment policy which would have removed any element of factual segregation, or suspicion of it, arising in the paint shop. This appears to suggest that it was the opinion of the Industrial Tribunal, not so much that the company had by its own acts segregated these men in this particular area away from others, but that it had not prevented the men themselves from coming together in this way. What appears to be suggested is that the company ought to have taken steps to ensure that for some of these jobs, white or non-Asian or coloured men were put in, and that Asians were not allowed to take on these jobs on the grounds of their colour, in order to prevent this segregation in fact arising . . . We do not consider that the failure of the company to intervene and to insist on white or non-Asian workers going into the shop, contrary to the wishes of the men to introduce their friends, itself constituted the act of segregating persons on racial grounds within the meaning of s.1(2) of the Act. A refusal to appoint other applicants because of their colour, or because they were Asians, might in itself indeed have amounted to discrimination within the meaning of the Act.

JM Thompson (1981) 97 *Law Quarterly Review* 10, 11–12, footnotes omitted

While it is perhaps understandable that the EAT was reluctant to compel an employer to ensure that his workforce was racially balanced, nevertheless the decision is open to criticism. Throughout his judgment, Slynn J. emphasised that there would have been discrimination if an intention to segregate on the part of the company could have been established. But why should intention be relevant? The Act simply states that 'segregating a person' is treating him less favourably: Slynn J's construction in effect adds the restrictive gloss '*intentionally or deliberately* segregating a person.' In the parallel field of equal pay, the Court of Appeal has held that an employer has no defence to a claim merely because he had no intention to discriminate. Thus in *Clay Cross (Quarry Services) Ltd. v Fletcher* [1978] I.C.R. 1, 5 Lord Denning M.R. maintained that 'The issue does not depend on the employer's state of mind. It does not depend on his reasons for paying the man more. The employer may not intend to discriminate against a woman by paying her less; but, if the result of his actions is that she is discriminated against, then his conduct is unlawful whether he intended it or not.'

The EAT's decision in *Modgill* would seem to ignore this important principle. Instead, it is submitted that the EAT should have adopted the approach of an industrial tribunal in *Hussein v Saints Complete House Furnishers* [1979] IRLR 337, where an employer was held guilty of indirect racial discrimination as a result of his policy of not employing youths from the 'City Centre' of Liverpool. Since a large proportion of the population living there was coloured, the effect of this policy was to treat coloured youths less favourably than their white counterparts who lived in the suburbs and the tribunal held that it was irrelevant that the employer had not intended to discriminate on the grounds of race. Similarly, it is thought that the issue of intention to discriminate is out of place when considering whether there was segregation for the purpose of section 1(2). There can be few better examples than *Modgill* of a hard case making bad law.[23]

'Racial Grounds', 'Racial Group'

Turning to the meaning of 'racial grounds' and 'racial group,' 'ethnic origins' has proven the most problematic subcategory and has given rise to substantial case law. The leading decision is that of the House of Lords in *Mandla v Dowell Lee* [1983] 2 AC 548, in which case their Lordships considered whether Sikhs were properly considered a racial group. Prior to this decision EAT had accepted, in *Seide v Gillette* [1980] IRLR 427, that Jews were properly regarded as a racial group, with the result that anti-Jewish discrimination was caught by the provisions of the RRA. The question of the extent to which the RRA applies to discrimination associated with various religious affiliations is still very important despite the implementation of the RB Regs which apply only in the context of employment.

I McKenna (1983) 46 *Modern Law Review* 759, 759–60, footnotes omitted

In a number of cases it appeared to have been taken for granted that Sikhs were a racial group for the purposes of the Race Relations Act 1976. In *Singh v Rowntree Mackintosh Ltd.* [1979] ICR 504 and *Panesar v Nestlé Co. Ltd.* [1980] ICR 144 the Scottish and the English EATs respectively appeared to accept this implicitly. The issue was more explicitly dealt with in *CRE. v Genture Restaurants Ltd* [unreported] where the County Court judge held that Sikhs were a 'group of persons defined by reference to . . . ethnic origins' within the meaning of section 3(1). Thereafter, judicial doubt began to creep in. When the *Genture* case went to the Court of Appeal on a different point, two members expressed reservations *obiter*.

This scepticism was taken a step further by Judge Gosling in *Mandla v Lee* when he ruled that Sikhs were not a racial group. In confirming this, the Court of Appeal had to find that Sikhs did not constitute a group capable of classification by reference to 'colour, race, nationality or ethnic or national origins.' The appellants contended that Sikhs were a group

---

[23] Note the discussion in Ch 5 of the CRE investigation into discrimination in the Crown Prosecution Service in which it applied the ratio of *Modgill* that racial segregation was unlawful under the RRA only if deliberately produced, rather than permitted.

defined by reference to 'ethnic origins' relying, in part, on a definition of 'ethnic' in the 1972 Supplement to the *Oxford English Dictionary*: '. . . pertaining to or having common racial, cultural, religious or linguistic characteristics especially designating a racial or other group within a larger system. . . .' The Sikhs, the appellant contended, are a classic example of an 'ethnic' group because of their distinctive cultural traditions.

Lord Denning preferred the definition of 'ethnic' in the 1934 edition of the *Concise Oxford Dictionary*: 'pertaining to race.' Thus, 'ethnic origins' meant 'racial origins.' Both Lord Denning and Kerr LJ indicated clearly that they considered the term 'race' (embracing the notion 'ethnic') as used in the Act to refer, as Kerr LJ put it, to 'characteristics or attributes which are, by their nature, unalterable.'

There are difficulties with this. First, if the term 'race' as used in section 3(1) does indeed refer to immutable characteristics, it is difficult to explain why Parliament should have included both the terms 'race' and 'ethnic' origins (meaning 'racial origins' according to the Court of Appeal). The Court's literal interpretation thus made one of the statutory terms redundant.

A second difficulty is the attempt to distinguish Sikhs and Jews. Lord Denning considered Jews definable by 'ethnic origins' not by virtue of any cultural or religious bonds but by the common 'racial' characteristic of being descended, however remotely, from a common ancestor. In contrast, Sikhs were not definable by 'race' but by religion and culture.
. . .

So spurious was this distinction that the Jewish Employment Action group urged action by the House of Lords or Parliament to ensure that the protection of Jews under the Act had not been jeopardised.

As McKenna points put, the early assumption that Sikhs were protected by the RRA was not, perhaps, surprising, given that this was the very firm intention of its drafters.

I McKenna, 760–1, footnotes omitted

In the Standing Committee debates on the Race Relations Bill, the Opposition spokesman sought to introduce 'religion' for the express purpose of protecting Sikhs. The amendment was withdrawn on the Government's express assurance that they would be protected. Mr Brynmor John stated 'I hope to be able to show . . . that the Bill is a considerable advance in protecting the religions of people in its concept of indirect discrimination. . . . Where any requirements laid down by an employer are notionally equal but, in fact, discriminatory against *the Sikhs* because of their religion, they would be caught, where it is unjustifiable, by indirect discrimination.' Withdrawing his support for the amendment, Mr Frederick Willey said 'I accept . . . that the minorities on whose behalf we are expressing disquiet will have all the protection within the present definition that they would probably obtain even from an extended definition.'

In the House of Lords a similar amendment was again withdrawn upon identical Government assurances. The Lords also debated an amendment to delete the term 'ethnic origins' from the list of prohibited grounds of discrimination. The Government spokesman argued that the term 'ethnic origin' was essential to ensure the protection for a group such as, *inter alia*, the Sikhs which was not definable by race, colour, nationality or national origin. He contended that the term 'ethnic origin' 'gets away from the idea of physical characteristics which inform the words "colour" and "race" and introduces the idea of groups defined by references to cultural characteristics geographic location, social organisation and so on.' In withdrawing his proposed amendment, Lord O'Hagan accepted that the word 'ethnic' was part of the whole formula of protection against discrimination and not merely a redundant term that meant the same as 'race.'

Debates in both Chambers leave no doubt that it was explicit Government, Opposition and back-bench opinion that the enacted statute both should and did protect Sikhs on grounds of their ethnic origin.

As McKenna accepts, convention at the time prevented judges from looking officially at statements made in Parliament in interpreting the meaning of legislation. This position was altered by the decision of the House of Lords in *Pepper v Hart* [1993] AC 593.

The *Mandla* case was brought on behalf of a schoolboy who was refused access to a private school on the grounds that he, consistent with the requirements of his Sikh religion, wore a turban. The school's argument was that the turban would draw attention to the boy's origins and 'accentuate religious and social distinctions in the school which, being a multiracial school based on the Christian faith, the headmaster desired to minimise'.[24]

The House of Lords decided unanimously, and contrary to the county court and the Court of Appeal, that Sikhs comprised a 'racial group' within s.3(1). The effect of this was that the application of a 'no turban' rule amounted, subject to its justifiability, to indirect discrimination against the boy.

Mandla v Dowell Lee [1983] 2 AC 548

Lord Fraser:

It is suggested that Sikhs are a group defined by reference to colour, race, nationality or national origins. In none of these respects are they distinguishable from many other groups, especially those living, like most Sikhs, in the Punjab. The argument turns entirely on whether they are a group defined by 'ethnic origins.' It is therefore necessary to ascertain the sense in which the words 'ethnic' is used in the 1976 Act . . . an ethnic group in the sense of the 1976 Act . . . must . . . regard itself, and be regarded by others, as a distinct community by virtue of certain characteristics. Some of these characteristics are essential others are not essential but one or more of them will commonly be found and will help to distinguish the group from the surrounding community. The conditions which appear to me to be essential are these: (1) a long shared history, of which the group is conscious as distinguishing it from other groups, and the memory of which it keeps alive (2) a cultural tradition of its own, including family and social customs and manners, often but not necessarily associated with religious observance. In addition to those two essential characteristics the following characteristics are, in my opinion, relevant: (3) either a common geographical origin, or descent from a small number of common ancestors (4) a common language, not necessarily peculiar to the group (5) a common literature peculiar to the group (6) a common religion different from that of neighbouring groups or from the general community surrounding it (7) being a minority or being an oppressed or a dominant group within a larger community, for example a conquered people (say, the inhabitants of England shortly after the Norman conquest) and their conquerors might both be ethnic groups.

A group defined by reference to enough of these characteristics would be capable of including converts, for example, persons who marry into the group, and of excluding apostates. Provided a person who joins the group feels himself or herself to be a member of it, and is accepted by other members, then he is, for the purpose of the 1976 Act, a member. That appears to be consistent with the words at the end of sub-s (1) of s 3: 'references to a person's racial group refer to any racial group into which he falls.' In my opinion, it is possible for a person to fall into a particular racial group either by birth or by adherence, and

---

[24] By denying the manifestation of difference, the school just assimilated all racial groups to the presumably white 'norm.'

it makes no difference, so far as the 1976 Act is concerned, by which route he finds his way
into the group . . .

Sikhs . . . were originally a religious community founded about the end of the fifteenth
century in the Punjab by Guru Nanak, who was born in 1469. But the community is no
longer purely religious in character. Their present position is summarised sufficiently for
present purposes in the opinion of the county court judge in the following passage:

> The evidence in my judgment shows that Sikhs are a distinctive and self-conscious
> community. They have a history going back to the fifteenth century. They have a writ-
> ten language which a small proportion of Sikhs can read but which can be read by a
> much higher proportion of Sikhs than of Hindus. They were at one time politically
> supreme in the Punjab.

> The result is, in my opinion, that Sikhs are a group defined by a reference to ethnic ori-
> gins for the purpose of the 1976 Act, although they are not biologically distinguishable
> from the other peoples living in the Punjab.

Lord Templeman pointed out that the RRA did not prohibit discrimination on grounds
of religion and ruled that, for the purposes of the Act:

a group of persons defined by reference to ethnic origins must possess some of the characteristics of a race, namely group descent, a group of geographical origin and a group history.
The evidence shows that the Sikhs satisfy these tests. They are more than a religious sect,
they are almost a race and almost a nation. As a race, the Sikhs share a common colour, and
a common physique based on common ancestors from that part of the Punjab which is centred on Amritsar. They fail to qualify as a separate race because in racial origin prior to the
inception of Sikhism they cannot be distinguished from other inhabitants of the Punjab. As
a nation the Sikhs defeated the Moghuls, and established a kingdom in the Punjab which
they lost as a result of the first and second Sikh wars they fail to qualify as a separate nation
or as a separate nationality because their kingdom never achieved a sufficient degree of
recognition or permanence. The Sikhs qualify as a group defined by ethnic origins because
they constitute a separate and distinct community derived from the racial characteristics I
have mentioned. They also justify the conditions enumerated by my noble and learned friend
Lord Fraser. The Sikh community has accepted converts who do not comply with those
conditions. Some persons who have the same ethnic origins as the Sikhs have ceased to be
members of the Sikh community. But the Sikhs remain a group of persons forming a
community recognisable by ethnic origins within the meaning of the 1976 Act.

The approach taken by the House of Lords in *Mandla* has not gone uncriticised:

**GT Pagone, 'The Lawyer's Hunt for Snarks, Religion and Races' [1984] *Cambridge Law
Journal* 218, 218–22, footnotes omitted**

To the social scientist . . . the lawyer's attempt at definition must seem like the famous hunt
for Snarks described by Lewis Carroll and the object of the hunt as dangerous as the
Boojum, for if you ever catch sight of a Boojum you 'will softly and suddenly vanish away.'
So too with 'race,' 'ethnicity' and 'religion,' since the closer the definition approaches the
concept the less it appears as a definition at all . . .

Lord Fraser . . . considered the competing senses in which 'ethnic' is used and attempted
to strike a balance between (a) the need of lower courts and public officials for guidance and
certainty in the administration of the law and (b) an awareness that a rigid legal definition
of such concepts would be inappropriate . . . in deciding that Sikhs were an 'ethnic' group

and hence a 'racial group' for the purposes of the Act, the House of Lords has adopted a definition which seeks to contain the elusiveness of the concept under discussion by allowing for future changes and variation in the nature of the concept . . .

It could be argued that there is no compelling reason why the House of Lords . . . needed to provide any definition at all. The court[] could, for example, have taken the view that what is a 'race' is a question of fact to be determined by the trier of fact . . .

In the final analysis, however, [the] court[] provide[d a] solution[] which g[a]ve recognition to the impossibility of fixed and certain meanings. Ultimately, whether any group of people can be called an 'ethnic group' or 'race' . . . requires a judgment for which no amount of legal training can assist. The lawyer is neither equipped nor entitled to give fixed legal definitions for such important social phenomena and at best the law can do little more than point to the general direction of what seems an elusive concept. It is thus not surprising that in the end the approach[] of . . . the House of Lords should be to list what appear to be some relevant factors and leave additions, weightings and orderings of importance in each case as, and when, it arises.

Pagone takes issue with the very attempt to define 'ethnic group'. Benyon and Lore, whose article is extracted below, comment on the disparities between Lord Fraser's judgment and that of Lord Templeman who, while setting out a substantially different test, appeared also to agree with Lord Fraser. (The three remaining Law Lords expressed their agreement with both speeches.)

H Benyon and N Love, 'Mandla and the Meaning of "Racial Group"' (1984) 100 *Law Quarterly Review* 120, 121–3, footnotes omitted

A very cursory reading of *Mandla* might suggest that Lord Fraser gave the leading speech, which Lord Templeman merely repeated in an abbreviated form. But closer inspection reveals important discrepancies between the two speeches. They both regard a sense of history (a 'long shared history' (Lord Fraser) or a 'group history' (Lord Templeman)) as an essential characteristic of a group of persons defined by reference to ethnic origins. But there the similarity ends. The second of Lord Fraser's two essential characteristics (ie, a 'cultural tradition,' etc,) and the last four of his five relevant characteristics (ie, 'language,' 'literature,' 'religion' and 'oppressed or dominant group') do not feature in Lord Templeman's definition at all; whilst Lord Templeman's two other essential characteristics (ie, 'group descent' and 'group of geographical origin') only appear in Lord Fraser's speech in the alternative, as the first of his five non-essential but relevant characteristics. This creates a difficulty in identifying the *ratio* of the case, in view of the fact that the remaining Law Lords concurred in *both* speeches. Is the true *ratio* to be found in Lord Fraser's speech, in Lord Templeman's, or perhaps in both?

No doubt, one should strive as hard as possible to avoid finding any inconsistency between the two formulations, so that one true ratio emerges. Is this possible here? It scarcely seems so. Granted, towards the end of his speech Lord Templeman remarked that 'they [the Sikhs] also justify the conditions enumerated by [Lord Fraser],' and this might conceivably be taken as indicating his concurrence in anything in Lord Fraser's speech that went beyond his own. The difficulty arises in establishing Lord Fraser's agreement with those parts of Lord Templeman's speech which different from his. Can such a consensus be found if conditions which Lord Templeman states 'must' exist ('group descent' and 'geographical origin') Lord Fraser merely regards as 'relevant'? Surely not. There is surely a crucial difference between 'must' and 'may,' of between a necessary condition and a contingent characteristic, even if, as will shortly be shown, other aspects of Lord Fraser's speech suggest that in other respects he attached little importance to the distinction he was here at pains to draw. So, at the very least, even if (a dubious point) Lord Fraser and Lord Templeman concurred in requiring a 'cultural tradition' as well as a 'group history' (lengthy or otherwise), they did not concur as to whether or not 'group descent' and 'geographical origin' were essential (Lord Templeman) or merely relevant (Lord Fraser). It is true that sentences and phrases in judgements should not *normally* be treated as if they were provisions in an Act of Parliament, because it is not *normally*—at common law—the function of judges to frame definitions so much as to enunciate principles. But when judges are interpreting an Act of Parliament—are, in other words, performing their function as constitutionally-appointed semasiologists—then the case is rather different. Some conceptual and verbal precision can be expected. . . . Lord Fraser's interpretation of 'racial group' might well embrace gipsies as nomads and itinerants, even though Lord Templeman's clearly would not, since nomads and itinerant as such would fall foul of Lord Templeman's second requirement of 'geographical origin.' In fact, Lord Fraser's definition would seem to embrace many groups quite outside the intended scope of the Race Relations Act, such as the British Royal Family, or the working class. Do they not each possess, in their different ways, 'long shared histories' and 'cultural traditions, including family and social customs and manners . . .'? One response to this might be that although both the Royal Family and the working class possess Lord Fraser's characteristics, they are not 'defined by reference to' them. They are instead probably 'defined by reference to' consanguinity or affinity with a reigning monarch, and occupation, respectively. A perfectly sensible response, indeed, but not one open to anyone supporting Lord Fraser's interpretation of the Act, since he himself, as will be shown, did not use 'defined by reference to' in this limiting sense. So, another possible response might be that, however distinctive the family and social customs of the Royal Family and the working classes, they do not amount to a 'cultural tradition,' but only to a 'sub-cultural' tradition. But if so, the infinite regress towards which that tends is another argument against Lord Fraser's interpretation. The law should try, if it can, to offer clearer criteria for recognising what practices might be unlawfully discriminatory, and on that ground Lord Templeman's formulation is possibly preferable to Lord Fraser's— irrespective of any greater narrowness it may possess.

W McLeod, 'Autochthonous language communities and the Race Relations Act' (1998) 1 *Web Journal of Current Legal Issues*, footnotes omitted

Lord Fraser's . . . initial observation that 'the word 'ethnic' still retains a racial flavour' . . . received undue emphasis in *Dawkins* . . .

The 'racial flavour' required for 'ethnic group' status is not . . . coterminous with the broader term 'race'. The inquiry appears to be somewhat more specific. Lord Fraser amplified his reference to 'racial flavour' by noting that 'the word 'ethnic'. . . is used nowadays in an extended sense to include other characteristics which may be commonly thought of as being associated with common racial origin'. . . Lord Fraser cited with approval the decision of the New Zealand Court of Appeal in *King-Ansell v Police* . . . 'a group is identifiable in terms of its ethnic origins if it is a segment of the population distinguished from others by a sufficient combination of shared customs, beliefs, traditions and characteristics derived from a common or presumed common past even if not drawn from what in biological terms is a common racial stock' . . . This nuanced approach to the concept of 'racial flavour' means that traits based on a relatively recent shared tradition can be sufficient even in the absence of a common racial stock; Lord Fraser concluded in *Mandla* that Sikhs constitute an ethnic group for RRA purposes 'although they are not biologically distinguishable from the other peoples living in the Punjab' . . . It should be noted, however, that Lord Templeman's speech in *Mandla* appeared to emphasise the racial dimension to a rather greater degree, arguing that 'a group of persons defined by reference to ethnic origins must possess some of the characteristics of a race, namely group descent, a group of geographical origin and a group history' . . .

Gypsies (but not 'travellers') were accepted as a 'racial group' by the Court of Appeal in *Commission for Racial Equality v Dutton*. The case concerned a 'no travellers' sign displayed in a pub, 'traveller' being defined by the landlord as a 'person who travels around in a caravan and parks on illegal sites and gives him "hassle." '

Commission for Racial Equality v Dutton [1989] QB 783

Nicholls LJ: .

The [CRE's] case was that in these notices 'travellers' is synonymous with gipsies . . .

the judge rejected the view that the words are synonymous. I agree with him. But before proceeding further it is necessary for me to comment on the word 'gipsy.' One of the difficulties in the present case, in my view, is that the word 'gipsy' has itself more than one meaning. The classic 'dictionary' meaning can be found as the primary meaning given in the Oxford English Dictionary (1933):

> A member of a wandering race (by themselves called Romany), of Hindu origin, which first appeared in England about the beginning of the 16th century and was then believed to have come from Egypt.

Hence the word 'gipsy,' also spelled as 'gypsy.' It is a corruption of the word Egyptian . . . Alongside this meaning, the word 'gipsy' also has a more colloquial, looser meaning. This is expressed in the Longman Dictionary of Contemporary English (1987) . . . 'a person who habitually wanders or who has the habits of someone who does not stay for long in one place.' In short, a nomad.

I can anticipate here by noting that if the word 'gipsy' is used in this second, colloquial sense it is not definitive of a racial group within the Act. To discriminate against such a group would not be on racial grounds, namely, on the ground of ethnic origins. As the judge observed, there are many people who travel around the country in caravans, vans converted buses, trailers, lorries and motor vehicles, leading a peripatetic or nomadic way of life. They include didicois, mumpers, peace people, new age travellers, hippies, tinkers, hawkers, self-styled 'anarchists,' and others, as well as (Romany) gipsies. They may all be loosely referred to as 'gipsies,' but as a group they do not have the characteristics requisite of a racial group within the Act . . .

In this judgment, save where I indicate otherwise, I shall henceforth use the word 'gipsy' in the narrower sense, of the first of the two means mentioned above . . .

In my view, [in the circumstances] . . . 'No travellers' will be understood by those to whom it is directed, namely, potential customers, as meaning persons who are currently leading a nomadic way of life, living in tents or caravans or other vehicles. Thus the notices embrace gipsies who are living in that way. But the class of persons excluded from the Cat and Mutton is not confined to gipsies. The prohibited class includes all those of a nomadic way of life mentioned above. As the judge said, they all come under the umbrella expression 'travellers,' as this accurately describes their way of life.

It is estimated that nowadays between one-half and two-thirds of gipsies in this country have wholly or largely abandoned a nomadic way of life, in favour of living in houses. I do not think that the notices could reasonably be understood as applying to them, that is, to gipsies who are currently living in houses. Gipsies may prefer to be described as 'travellers' as they believe this is a less derogatory expression. But, in the context of a notice displayed in the windows of a public house near a common on which nomads encamp from time to time, I do not think 'No travellers' can reasonably be understood as other than 'No nomads.' It would not embrace house-dwellers, of any race or origin.

For this reason I cannot accept that the defendant's notices indicate, or might reasonably be understood as indicating, an intention by him to do an act of discrimination within section 1(1)(a). Excluded from the Cat and Mutton are all 'travellers,' whether or not they are gipsies. All 'travellers,' all nomads, are treated equally, whatever their race. They are not being discriminated against on racial grounds . . .

Nicholls LJ went on to consider whether 'gipsies' were a 'racial group' for the purposes of deciding whether the notice amounted to unlawful indirect discrimination against them.

On the evidence it is clear that such gipsies are a minority, with a long-shared history and a common geographical origin. They are a people who originated in northern India. They migrated thence to Europe through Persia in medieval times. They have certain, albeit limited, customs of their own, regarding cooking and the manner of washing. They have a distinctive, traditional style of dressing, with heavy jewellery worn by the women, although this dress is not worn all the time. They also furnish their caravans in a distinctive manner. They have a language or dialect, known as 'pogadi chib,' spoken by English gipsies (Romany chals) and Welsh gipsies (Kale) which consists of up to one-fifth of Romany words in pace of English words. They do not have a common religion, nor a peculiar, common literature of their own, but they have a repertoire of folktales and music passed on from one generation to the next. No doubt, after all the centuries which have passed since the first gipsies left the Punjab, gipsies are no longer derived from what, in biological terms, is a common racial stock, but that of itself does not prevent them from being a racial group as widely defined in the Act.

I come now to the part of the case which has caused me most difficulty. Gipsies prefer to be called 'travellers' as they think that term is less derogatory. This might suggest a wish to lose their separate, distinctive identity so far as the general public is concerned. Half or more of them now live in houses, like most other people. Have gipsies now lost their separate, group identify, so that they are no longer a community recognisable by ethnic origins within the meaning of the Act? The judge held that they had. This is a finding of fact.

Nevertheless, with respect of the judge, I do not think that there was before him any evidence justifying his conclusion that gipsies have been absorbed into a larger group, if by that he meant that substantially all gipsies have been so absorbed. The fact that some have been so absorbed and are indistinguishable from any ordinary member of the public, is not sufficient in itself to establish loss of what Richardson J, in *King-Ansell v Police* . . . referred to as 'an historically determined social identity in [the group's] own eyes and in the eyes of those outside the group.' There was some evidence to the contrary from Mr Mercer, on whose testimony the judge expressed no adverse comment. He gave evidence that 'we know who are members of our community' and that 'we know we are different.' In my view the evidence was sufficient to establish that, despite their long presence in England, gipsies have not merged wholly in the population, as have the Saxons and the Danes, and altogether lost their separate identity. They, or many of them, have retained a separateness, a self-awareness, of still being gipsies.

Nicholls LJ ruled that the 'no travellers' rule amounted to indirect discrimination against Gypsies, subject to the question of justification which he referred back to the county court for decision. Taylor and Stocker LJJ concurred, though the latter expressed reservations about the qualification as an 'ethnic group' of Gypsies given what he saw as the degree of their absorption into the wider population. Concern over the level of discrimination against Gypsies has grown in recent years as sections of the media have whipped up alarm that the implementation of the Human Rights Act 1998 has given Gypsies 'carte blanche' to ignore planning regulations. Sarah Spencer (deputy Chair of the CRE) stated in April 2004 that 'Discrimination against Gypsies and Travellers appears to be the last "respectable" form of racism' and highlighted serious difficulties experienced by Gypsies in relation to education, health and accommodation. Of particular concern is the fact that local authorities are under no obligation to provide sufficient sites for Gypsies since the repeal in 1994 of the Caravan Sites Act 1968 which used to impose this duty. Accordingly, Gypsies have real difficulty finding places where they may lawfully park their caravans and some accordingly resort to parking them on land (frequently bought for the purpose) which does not have the appropriate planning permission.

In 2003 the Committee on the Elimination of Race Discrimination (which is responsible for enforcing the UN's Convention on the elimination of all Forms of Race Discrimination) expressed its 'concern about the discrimination faced by Roma/Gypsies/ Travellers that is reflected, inter alia, in their higher child mortality rate, exclusion from schools, shorter life expectancy, poor housing conditions, lack of available camping sites, high unemployment rate and limited access to health services'. The committee recommended that the UK develop appropriate means communication and dialogue between Roma/Gypsy/Traveller communities and central authorities and adopt national strategies and programmes 'with a view to improving the situation of the Roma/Gypsies/Travellers against discrimination by State bodies, persons or organizations'.

We saw, above, that the 'Irish Traveller Community' is expressly recognised as a racial group by the Race Relations (Northern Ireland) Order 1997. Complaints about such discrimination figure heavily in the race discrimination case load there, the first two cases on goods and services, for example, involving discrimination against travellers.[25] And in *O'Leary v Allied Domecq* (unreported, 2000), the Central London County Court accepted that Irish Travellers were an ethnic group for the purposes of the RRA despite their lack of express inclusion in the statute. According to Judge Goldstein, who ruled in favour of a number of Irish Travellers denied access to a pub: 'Modern Irish Travellers are guided by culture and traditions which have been handed down by generations.'

Two of the very significant gaps in the coverage of the RRA, as interpreted by the House of Lords in *Mandla*, have become apparent in recent years. The first concerns discrimination, whether direct or indirect, against Muslims. This is considered in Chapter 9. The second, which will become an increasingly important issue in light of the devolution of power to Scotland, Wales and Northern Ireland, concerns discrimination in relation to 'autochthonous' languages—that is, indigenous minority languages such as Scots Gaelic and Welsh.[26]

Nyazi v Rymans Ltd EAT/6/88 (unreported) concerned a complaint from a Muslim woman who had been denied leave to celebrate Eid. The tribunal found itself:

> unable to conclude that Muslims . . . come within the meaning of 'ethnic group'. All we can say is that Muslims profess a common religion in a belief in the Oneness of God and the prophethood of Muhammed. No doubt there is a profound cultural and historical background and there are traditions of dress, family life and social behaviour. There is a common literature in the sense that the Holy Quaran is a sacred book. Even so, many of the other relevant characteristics would seem to be missing.
>
> The Muslim faith is widespread, covering many nations, indeed many colours and languages, and it seems to us that the common denominator is religion and a religious culture.

---

[25] See ECNI First Annual Report, 1999–2000.
[26] The issue under the FETO would be religion/ political opinion and Irish language.

In other words we believe Muslims are a group defined mainly by reference to religion and that being so we must find that we have no jurisdiction under the Act.

The autochthonous languages issue relates to the wider question whether, for example, discrimination between English and Scots people, or between Irish and Welsh, offends the RRA.

CRE, *The Irish in Britain*

The Irish are Britain's largest ethnic minority group . . . Since the Commission was established in 1977, Irish people have been coming to it with complaints of unlawful discrimination. Academic research and official statistics have revealed inequalities in Irish people's experience of the labour and housing markets, the health service and the benefits system. Many Irish people in Britain have also objected to being made the butt of humour and remarks which they find offensive . . . There has been a failure, both at an official level and in general discussions of race relations, to recognise the difficulties that many Irish people experience in Britain . . . 'Irish people are constantly reminded that they are not entitled to an equal place in British society. On the other hand they are not seen as sufficiently distinct for this racism to be acknowledged and to be afforded some measure of protection.'[27]

There is no doubt that anti-Irish discrimination comes within the RRA, such discrimination having successfully been challenged on a number of occasions. Among the cases cited by the Commission were *O'Driscoll v Post Office* (1990) in which an Irish applicant was questioned as to whether he had a drink problem; *Nicholl v London Staff Bureau* (1991) in which an woman was refused a job interview because she was Irish and therefore unreliable; and *Bryans v Northumberland College* (1995) in which an Irish man was victimised for complaining about his abuse in front of colleagues and visiting professionals.

Discrimination against the Irish is discrimination on grounds of nationality or national origin. More problematic, however, is the Scots/ Welsh/ English/ Northern Irish distinction. Neither colour nor, presumably, race would be implicated. As far as nationality is concerned, it could be argued that all are British. The questions which remain concern whether these groups could be distinguished either in terms of their national or their ethnic origins.

In *Ealing London Borough Council v Race Relations Board*, a case which arose under the RRA 1965, the House of Lords considered the meaning of 'national origins.'

Ealing London Borough Council v Race Relations Board [1972] AC 342

Lord Simon of Glaisdale:

[The] words ['national origins'] are part of a passage of vague terminology in which the words seem to be used in a popular sense. 'Origin,' in its ordinary sense, signifies a source, someone or something from which someone or something else has descended. 'Nation' and 'national,' in their popular, in contrast to their legal, sense, are also vague terms. They do not necessarily imply statehood. For example, there were many submerged nations in the former Hapsburg Empire. Scotland is not a nation in the eye of international law, but Scotsmen constitute a nation by reason of those most powerful elements in the creation of national spirit—tradition, folk memory, a sentiment of community. The Scots are a nation because of Bannockburn and Flodden, Culloden and the pipes of Lucknow, because of Jenny Geddes and Flora MacDonald, because of frugal living and respect for learning,

---

[27] Citing *Discrimination and the Irish Community in Britain*, a national research project commissioned by the CRE in 1994.

because of Robert Burns and Walter Scott. So, too, the English are a nation—because Norman, Angevin and Tudor monarchs forged them together, because their land is mostly sea-girt, because of the common law and of gifts for poetry and parliamentary government,[!] because (despite the Wars of the Roses and Old Trafford and Headingley) Yorkshireman and Lancastrian feel more in common than in difference and are even prepared at a pinch to extend their sense of community to southern folk. By the Act of Union English and Scots lost their separate nationalities, but they retained their separate nationhoods, and their descendants have thereby retained their national origins. So, again, the Welsh are a nation—in the popular, though not in the legal, sense—by reason of Offa's Dyke, by recollection of battles long ago and pride in the present valour of their regiments, because of musical gifts and religious dissent, because of fortitude in the face of economic adversity, because of the satisfaction of all Wales that Lloyd George became an architect of the welfare state and prime minister of victory. To discriminate against Englishmen, Scots and Welsh, as such, would, in my opinion, be to discriminate against them on the ground of their national origins . . .

In *Boyce v British Airways plc*, EAT ruled that the Scots and the English could not be distinguished on the grounds of ethnic origins. The claimants appealed to EAT against a tribunal finding that anti-Scots discrimination fell outwith the RRA. The appeal was rejected. On the question whether the Scots were a group identified by reference to their ethnic origins, EAT ruled:

Boyce v British Airways plc **App. No EAT/385/97, unreported**

Lord Johnston (for EAT):

In determining the guidance afford by the House of Lords in *Mandla*, we consider it essential to have regard (1) to all that was said in that case, and not simply to those parts of Lord Fraser's speech dealing with the tests to be applied, in determining whether a given group was an ethnic group and (2) the facts of that case . . .

As we understand the matter, the House of Lords insisted (as did the Court of Appeal) that the word 'ethnic' had a strong racial flavour, and it is against that background that the factors, specified by Lord Fraser, fall to be considered.

Turning to the facts of *Mandla*, it is clear that there was a strong racial flavour. . . .

Turning to the facts of this case, we can find no racial flavour, and, indeed, none was ever suggested, and, in these circumstances, in the total absence of any racial flavour or element, we are satisfied that the applicants cannot claim that they have been discriminated against on the grounds of their ethnic origins. . . .

We would add that, even if we were not satisfied that the racial flavour, insisted upon by the House of Lords, were absent in this case, we would have some doubt about the wisdom of our proceeding to consider the factors mentioned by Lord Fraser . . . We were urged, for example, to find that the Scots have a cultural tradition of their own, including family and social customs and manners often, but not necessarily, associated with religious observance. We were urged to hold that the Scots had a cultural tradition of their own, and reference was made to the works of Scott, Burns and McGonigle. In our view, it would not be appropriate for us to attempt to determine whether or not Scott and Burns were peculiarly Scottish writers, and thus evidence of, or constitutive of a Scottish cultural tradition, as opposed to being merely part of—say—a wider European movement.

We do not see how we could even begin to address the third factor mentioned by Lord Fraser. Lord Fraser said that either a common geographical origin or descent from a small number of common ancestors was a relevant factor. Given the waves of immigration to Scotland, and emigration from it to England, we do not see how we could answer that question unaided. As already noted, we have some doubt as to whether or not we could determine whether or not 'Scottish literature' is peculiar to Scotland or part of a wider cultural movement. Always assuming that we were prepared to hold that Scotland did have a religion, it would be again difficult for us to determine whether the Church of Scotland was a peculiarly Scottish institution, or part of a wider European religious movement . . .

It will be noted that the decision in *Boyce* was restricted, expressly, to the question whether Scots could be regarded as a racial group by virtue of their *ethnic* origins. In *Northern Joint Police Board v Power* [1997] IRLR 610, EAT considered whether a Scots/English distinction could be drawn, for the purposes of the RRA, on grounds of *national origin*.[28]

Mr Power claimed that the failure of the respondents to shortlist him was because he was English rather than Scots. A tribunal accepted that discrimination between English and Scots was on 'racial grounds,' 'racial' being defined by reference to 'national origins.' The tribunal based its decision on the reasoning of the House of Lords in *Ealing*, above.

It seemed to the tribunal sufficient in applying the ratio of the decision in *Ealing* to ask itself the question whether England and Scotland are nations in the popular or non-legal sense and to try to answer the question objectively.

In the unanimous opinion of the tribunal, they are separate nations in that sense. That they are is attributable principally to the fact that prior to the Act of Union the two countries were separate nations in the legal sense, that is to say, they were each formerly sovereign states in their own right. The two countries have since the Act of Union continued to be separated geographically.

They have retained their separate names. There was preserved to Scotland under the Act of Union its legal system, its church and its education system. In the words of Lord Simon [above], 'By the Act of Union, English and Scots lost their separate nationalities, but they retained their separate nationhoods.' Each country has thus retained a separate status and identity notwithstanding having been absorbed into what is the United Kingdom. Although the circumstances are wholly different, England and Scotland as part of the United Kingdom are in this context 'nations' in the same way that Poland was a 'nation' as part of the Russian Empire before it became a sovereign state. There are many manifestations of the separate status of the two countries in present-day life. It is not something which is merely historical. It is continuing. There is no difficulty in saying now . . . that the Scots and the English are each a group of people who can be described as a 'nation.'

EAT rejected the employer's appeal. Having expressed the view that the speech of Lord Simon in *Ealing*, extracted above, was 'not particularly helpful, other than to point to the nature of the elements which may enter the equation determining whether or not, in a particular context of England and Scotland, there are national attributes,' Lord Johnston continued:

Nationality, we consider, has a juridical basis pointing to citizenship, which, in turn, points to the existence of a recognised state at the material time. Within the context of England, Scotland, Northern Ireland and Wales the proper approach to nationality is to categorise

---

[28] See also *BBC Scotland v Souster* [2001] IRLR 150 in which the Court of Sessions confirmed that discrimination against an English journalist amounted to discrimination on grounds of national origins, rather than nationality. A subsequent attempt by the claimant in *Boyce* to re-argue his claim as one of discrimination on grounds of *national origins* was dismissed by the Court of Sessions [2001] IRLR 157 as res judicata.

all of them as falling under the umbrella of British, and to regard the population as citizens of the United Kingdom. Against that background, what context, therefore, should be given to the phrase 'national origins'? It seems to us, so far as there needs to be an exhaustive definition, what has to be ascertained are identifiable elements, both historically and geographically, which at least at some point in time reveals the existence of a nation. Whatever may be difficult fringe questions to this issue, what cannot be in doubt is that both England and Scotland were once separate nations. That, in our opinion, is effectively sufficient to dispose of the matter, since thereafter we agree with the proposition that it is for each individual to show that his origins are embedded in such a nation, and how he chooses to do so requires scrutiny by the tribunal hearing the application. In our opinion, whatever factors are put forward to satisfy the relevant criteria will be self-evidently relevant or irrelevant as the case may be. There is, therefore, no need for the tests such as enunciated by Lord Fraser in *Mandla*, with regard to the question of groups based on ethnic origins in relation to the issue of national origins, since the former by definition need not have, although it might have, a defined historical and geographical base. It is perfectly possible that the two defined groups may overlap, but that does not affect the issue which is required to be approached in each context from a different direction. The existence of a nation, whether in the present or past, is determined by factors quite separate from an individual's origins, and those factors are easily established in any given case by reference to history and geography. That the same cannot be said in relation to groups based on ethnic origins creates the need for Lord Fraser's test.

We are also entirely satisfied that it is legitimate, assuming there is any doubt in the matter as to whether Parliament intended to include the constituents within the United Kingdom as part of the 'races' to be considered within the legislation, to examine the surrounding materials in order to determine the intention, and indeed the mischief being addressed. On doing so, it is manifest that Parliament's intention was to include the constituent races, so-called, within the United Kingdom under the umbrella of the legislation. The matter is, therefore, put beyond doubt.

The legal status of language requirements designed to encourage, for example, the continued and expanded use of Welsh or Scots Gallic is problematic. This is likely to become an issue of increasing importance in the wake of devolution. It could be argued that any requirement that an employee be conversant with Welsh or Scots Gallic would amount to race-based discrimination. On the reasoning in *Power*, such a requirement might, depending on its justifiability, amount to unlawful indirect discrimination on grounds of national origin against, for example, English Irish and Scots (in Wales), Welsh Irish and English (in Scotland).[29] It might also, subject to questions of justification, amount to indirect discrimination under Article 39 of the Treaty of Rome.[30] A non-Welsh-speaking Welsh person who wishes to challenge the application of a Welsh language requirement, or a non-Gallic-speaking Scot who wishes to challenge the application of a Gallic language requirement, can rely neither on any claim of discrimination on grounds of national origins nor, generally, on Art 39.[31] In *Gwynedd County Council v Jones*, however, two non-Welsh-speaking Welsh

---

[29] Justification would have to relate to operational needs of the business—see *Greater Manchester Police Authority v Lea* [1990] IRLR 372, discussed in Ch 2.

[30] Justification is not difficult in this area—In *Groener v Minister for Education* Case C–397/87 [1989] 2 ECR 3967 the ECJ permitted the imposition of an Irish language requirement in a teaching job in which it was not required in practice, although there it was because the language had constitutionally guaranteed official status. For discussion of this see McLeod, above.

[31] Art 39 does not apply in 'wholly internal' situations and could protect nationals from discrimination within their Member State only to the extent that, as in *Knoors* Case C–115/78 [1979] ECR 399, some external element was present. But more recently—see *Avello v Belgian State* Case C–148/02 [2003] ECR I–41613—the ECJ has become increasingly reluctant to define any situation as 'wholly internal'.

complainants sought to argue that they had been discriminated against on grounds of their ethnic origin by the application of a Welsh language requirement. A tribunal accepted their claims, ruling that the Welsh could be divided into two ethnic groups—English-speaking-Welsh and Welsh-speaking-Welsh. EAT allowed the employers' appeal.

Gwynedd County Council v Jones [1986] ICR 833

Sir Ralph Kilner Brown:

. . . it was wrong in law to use the language factor alone and in isolation as creating a racial group. Even if . . . this approach is said to be a question of fact, the decision is wholly unreasonable . . . We cannot believe that, for example, a Mrs Jones from Holyhead who speaks Welsh as well as English is to be regarded as belonging to a different racial group from her dear friend, a Mrs Thomas from Colwyn Bay who speaks only English. This concept seems to us to be as artificial as the proposition that 5,000 or so spectators at Cardiff Arms Park who are fluent in Welsh are a different racial group from the 45,000 or so whose command of the Welsh tongue is limited to the rendering of the Welsh national anthem, or 'Sospan fach.' An Englishman who dared to suggest this would be in danger of his life!

W McLeod, 'Autochthonous language communities and the Race Relations Act' (1998) 1 *Web Journal of Current Legal Issues*, footnotes omitted

How are Gaelic speakers in Scotland and Welsh speakers in Wales to be classified within the framework of the [RRA], and how are their rights—if any—to be measured against those of other protected groups?

These questions have scarcely been considered at all by industrial tribunals or by the courts, and the little treatment they have received has been problematic and unsatisfactory . . . The analysis in *Jones* was superficial, indeed cryptic, and a range of important sociological and legal questions were ignored. These questions have become all the more critical in light of changing policies and increasing attention at the UK and European levels to the rights and needs of autochthonous linguistic groups. If carefully and sensitively construed, the RRA may serve as a mechanism to reinforce these policies and solidify the position of the autochthonous languages . . .

the critical question with respect to the Gaels and to Welsh speakers must be whether they properly constitute an 'ethnic group'—'a group of persons defined by reference to . . . ethnic origins'—since it would seem clear that none of the other enumerated categories applies . . .

Although Lord Fraser's speech in *Mandla* emphasised the need to construe the word 'ethnic' 'relatively widely, in a broad, cultural/historic sense,' his initial observation that 'the word 'ethnic' still retains a racial flavour' . . . has received undue emphasis in subsequent decisions. . . [citing *Dawkins* and *Boyce*] . . .

In concluding that English-monoglot Welsh people did not constitute a protected racial group, the EAT [in *Jones*] adopted a view of the Welsh as an undifferentiated unit and thus implicitly determined that Welsh speakers were also not a protected group. Noting the criteria identified in *Mandla, Jones* opined that language, standing alone, is not an essential factor in the determination, and that the analytic emphasis should be on the combination of factors . . .

Although its decision may ultimately have been correct in light of the overall position of the Welsh language in Wales and the nature of the Welsh-speaking community, the EAT in *Jones* clearly failed to consider the question with any serious analysis. Language cannot properly be considered something that stands alone; in particular, it very often tends to create among its speakers 'a cultural tradition of [their] own' (*Mandla* . . .), and it is certainly arguable that such a distinct tradition can be discerned among Welsh speakers. It is unfortunate that the status of the Welsh language community was determined in this essentially negative context; a much more vigorous and culturally sensitive case could have been mounted within the *Mandla* framework if the question affirmatively presented had been the status of the Welsh-speaking minority community, rather than the English-monoglot majority.

The analysis in *Jones* was also distorted to some extent by the unhelpful terminology of the RRA, with its reliance on the term 'racial group' as the unit of analytic currency. Although *Mandla* took the proper analytic approach and spoke of 'ethnic groups'—the pertinent subset of the 'racial group' under the statute—the EAT's reasoning in *Jones* seems to have been confused by the 'racial group' terminology. The EAT's evident difficulty in seeing Welsh-speakers and English-monoglots as separate 'racial groups' in the ordinary lay sense led it to explain its decision with peculiar images [Mrs Jones and Mrs Thomas] . . .

Although the principal factor differentiating the Gaels from other Scots is the use of the Gaelic language itself, it can well be argued that the language is actually the medium of a distinct and separate culture, manifested in a variety of ways including deep-rooted traditions of poetry, song and music, and unique forms of religious worship. To some extent at least, this distinctiveness extends to material existence as well, the present-day crofting communities remaining substantially different in their way of life from the highly urbanised Scottish mainstream. The claim of Gaelic speakers to recognition as an ethnic group is also strengthened by the fact that a very high proportion of Gaelic speakers, relative to the UK's other autochthonous language communities, are native speakers born and brought up in Gaelic-speaking communities in the Hebrides and West Highlands. It would be safe to say that at least 90per cent of Gaelic speakers come from such backgrounds, whereas the Welsh language community contains significant proportions of learners and non-traditional speakers. In the case of Gaelic, then, there is a very significant link between the ability to speak the language and a distinct culture and way of life, and the language is the badge of a community that has long been outside the societal mainstream.

Significantly from a legal standpoint, this 'combination of shared customs, beliefs, traditions and characteristics' is largely 'derived from a common . . . past,' distinct from the social institutions and practices of Lowland Britain . . . Although Gaelic was once the language of almost all Scotland, language shift and cultural divergence began as early as 1100, and already by 1380 the Gaels were identified as an entirely distinct and separate group. Marginalised by geography and outsiders' hostility, the Gaels have without question emerged from a common history and experience not shared by others . . .

Genuine Occupational Qualifications and Other Exceptions

Miscellaneous Exceptions

A number of the exceptions to the RRA's provisions are considered in Chapter 4. The discussion there of the Act's geographical scope should be noted. The RRA does not apply, unless discrimination is on grounds of 'race or ethnic or national origin', to employment in private households (save in respect of victimisation),[32] or to discrimination in respect of

[32] This exception was removed from the SDA as a result of *Commission v UK* Case C–165/82 [1983] ECR 3431.

partners in firms with less than six partners. The most significant exceptions provided to the RRA's prohibition of discrimination are found in ss.41 and 42 (discussed in Chapter 4), and in s.75 and the 'genuine occupational qualifications' (s.5) and 'genuine occupational requirement' (s.4A) defences (discussed below) after a number of other exceptions and/or qualifications to the RRA's prohibitions on discrimination.

Section 75 RRA provides that:

> (5) Nothing in this Act shall—
>> (a) invalidate any rules (whether made before or after the passing of this Act) restricting employment in the service of the Crown or by any public body prescribed for the purposes of this subsection by regulations made by the Minister for the Civil Service to persons of particular birth, nationality, descent or residence.

This provision appears to be consistent with Article 39 TEC whose prohibition of discrimination on grounds of nationality does not apply to employment 'in the public service' (para 4). The Government has, nevertheless, agreed that civil service rules ought to be changed in order to allow non-EEA and non-Commonwealth citizens, who are currently ineligible for positions in that service, to be eligible and to minimise the number of posts reserved for UK nationals.[33]

Asylum and Immigration

Before we turn to the GOQ defence, s.8 of the Asylum and Immigration Act 1996 should be mentioned. It provides that it is an offence to employ someone 'subject to immigration control' where ((1)(a)) that person has not been granted leave to enter or remain in the UK; ((1)(b)) that person's leave is either 'no longer valid and subsisting' or is 'subject to a condition precluding the taking up of employment.' Section 8(2) provides a defence to an employer who either retained 'a document which appeared . . . to relate' to the worker (or a copy thereof), that document being one of several listed in the Immigration (Restrictions on Employment) Order 1996,[34] unless the employer knew that the employment was in breach of immigration law. A fine of up to £5,000 may be imposed on offenders

Section 8 has been widely criticised, not least because it is at once under- and over-inclusive:

B Ryan, 'Employer Enforcement of Immigration Law after S.8 of the Asylum and Immigration Act 1996' (1997) 26 *Industrial Law Journal* 136, 140–1, footnotes omitted

On the one hand, notwithstanding the comprehensiveness of the 1996 Order, some individuals may still find it difficult to prove their right to take up employment. It seems likely that most employers will give priority to the possession of a national insurance number as evidence of a right to work. National insurance numbers are issued automatically at sixteen to British residents in respect of whom child benefit has been claimed. But many individuals do not have a national insurance number when they first look for employment. This category includes nationals of other states, British nationals who have lived abroad, British residents who reached sixteen before national insurance numbers were issued automatically, and others for whom child benefit has not been claimed. Until they acquire a national

---

[33] Government Response to the CRE's *Reform of the Race Relations Act 1976* (1998), Home Office press release 219/99 14 July 1999.

[34] SI 1996 No. 3225.

insurance number, the practical result of section 8 may be to make it harder for these individuals to find employment . . .

On the other hand, the comprehensiveness of the 1996 Order means that many individuals without a right to work will be able to produce one of the listed documents. In some circumstances, they may possess the document legitimately. For example, they may have a national insurance number even though they have no right to work, where they have worked on a work permit for a particular employer or have previously lived and worked in the United Kingdom. It was partly for this reason that, in the consultation paper which preceded the introduction of the employer offence, the Government admitted that national insurance numbers were 'limited as an indicator of entitlement to work' (Home Office, *Prevention of Illegal Working: Consultation Document*, para 31). Similarly, individuals may have a British birth certificate without British citizenship: since the coming into force of the section 1 of the British Nationality Act 1981 on 1 January 1983, children born in the United Kingdom acquire British citizenship only if they have a parent who is a British citizen or settled in the United Kingdom.

Alternatively, reliance upon one of the permitted documents may be entirely fraudulent. In particular, the absence of a photograph on birth certificates or on documents bearing national insurance numbers makes personation a substantial possibility. The possibility of personation is itself enhanced by the existence of many unused national insurance numbers. (A Social Security Select Committee report in November 1995 found that there were up to 20 million more numbers in existence (over 65 million on one estimate) than the United Kingdom population over 16 (roughly 45 million): see *The Work of the Department of Social Security and its Agencies*, (1994–95) HC Papers 382, pp. ix–x.) Remarkably however the Home Office guidance to employers states that 'you do not need to worry about whether National Insurance numbers are genuine or belong to the person if you have seen an appropriate document' (*Guidance*, p 15). It may be thought surprising that a system which is supposed to discourage illegal working should leave open so many possibilities for it to occur.

Perhaps of more concern here is the potential for increased discrimination. The CRE argued that the section imposed on employers an immigration control function :

which should rightly and properly be carried out by the [state, whose staff] are trained specifically to carry out this function and are publicly accountable for the performance of this duty. Individual employers . . . will not be accountable for their performance of their public control function . . . many employers are likely to avoid both the administrative burden of making checks and the risk of prosecution by simply not offering employment to any person whose immigration status might in their view be uncertain. This may include, for example, people with names which are not of UK origin; people of visible ethnic minority origin; and people with accents which identify them as being not of UK origin.[35]

Ryan (1997) 26 *Industrial Law Journal*, 141–3, footnotes omitted

If Section 8 does make it harder for some workers to take up employment, then it is likely to have its greatest impact upon workers from abroad and from ethnic minorities. There is already substantial evidence of discrimination in the British labour market, with official surveys finding that workers from ethnic minorities have a significantly higher rate of unemployment than other workers at every level of qualifications. (See F Sly, 'Ethnic Groups and the Labour Market,' *Employment Gazette*, May 1994, 147.) Against this

---

[35] Reported in 66 *Equal Opportunities Review* 8.

background, it is not unreasonable to suspect that employer checks following section 8 will lead to greater discrimination. To quote from the Commission for Racial Equality's response to the *Consultation Document* which preceded the introduction of section 8, 'an inevitable result will be the creation of additional barriers to the employment of people from ethnic minorities.' . . .

Litigation on the application of equal treatment law to employer checks of immigration status is to be anticipated. It will raise difficult questions as to the definition of unlawful discrimination in this area. These are examined here by looking first at the implications for employer checks of the Race Relations Act 1976, which prohibits discrimination . . .

The coming into force of section 8 adds to the uncertainty as to the authority of *Dhatt*. If the Court of Appeal was correct to conclude [in *Dhatt*, Chapter 2] that it was not inherently discriminatory to treat EEC and non-EEC nationals differently, then its reasoning is strengthened by the distinction drawn in section 8 between 'persons subject to immigration control,' in relation to whom the offence may be committed, and others. Alternatively, if *Dhatt* was wrongly decided, and the result turns on section 41, then a court might conclude that at least some discrimination against non-EEA job applicants has been made 'necessary' by section 8. . . .

If *some* distinctions between job applicants are to be allowed, the question remains— which ones? The most straightforward case would be where an employer asked all applicants their nationality, and then required proof of a right to work only from those who did not declare an EEA nationality. That kind of distinction was permitted in *Dhatt*. It might also be defensible under section 41, in that there would be a broad correspondence between the offence in section 8 and the distinction drawn. But what if an employer questioned the nationality and immigration status of only the applicants about whom there were doubts? Or what if, having asked all applicants their nationality, the employer required proof of EEA nationality of only some applicants? In those circumstances, an employer would probably be distinguishing between applicants on the basis of their ethnic background, or accent, or possible nationality. That would be a prima facie case of discrimination—but one which might nevertheless be allowed under the *Dhatt* principle or the section 41 exception.

A second situation to examine under the Race Relations Act is where an employer declines to hire a worker because of doubts as to their immigration status. This was considered by the Scottish EAT in *Grampian Health Board v Cole*. That case concerned a South African national who was denied employment out of a mistaken belief that she would require a work permit. The industrial tribunal had held this to be direct discrimination under the Race Relations Act, and the result was accepted by the EAT.

The main issue is whether there are any limits to the principle. What if an employer refused to hire someone because of the difficulty of establishing that they had a right to work? Or what if, having investigated the applicant's status, the employer genuinely reached the wrong conclusion? Each of these outcomes would undermine an individual's right to work. Nevertheless, a court might decide that it was too much to require employers to have a full investigation, or to require them to reach the right answer in every case. This conclusion is supported in particular by the defence set out in section 8(2), which gives statutory recognition to the undesirability of imposing a strict requirement upon employers. Here too, it is possible that the impact of section 8 will be to weaken a claim of discrimination under the Race Relations Act.

The Better Regulation Task Force, which reported on anti-discrimination legislation in 1999, at the Government's request, recommended the repeal of s.8 on the basis that it:

Has caused particular concerns in placing a blanket duty on all employers to identify job applicants who may be illegal immigrants. The problem of illegal working appears largely confined to racketeers operating in a few specific sectors but a lack of targeting has created the potential for well-intentioned employers across all employment sectors to discriminate against ethnic minority applicants.[36]

Somewhat surprisingly the Government, which had opposed s.8 in opposition, rejected the Task Force's recommendation:

Illegal working is a growing problem . . . Illegal employment leads not only to abuse of vulnerable employees who will not have the full protection of the law but also serves to deny job opportunities to those who are lawfully entitled to work here . . . controls on employers are needed . . . in order to deal with the problem comprehensively.

Experience suggests that Section 8 can be a valuable tool if targeted against unscrupulous or exploitative employers. Having looked very carefully at the way in which it is operating in practice, the Government has decided to retain Section 8 to test its effectiveness in dealing with those who are engaging in systematic abuse.

The Immigration (Restrictions on Employment) Code of Practice Order 2001 brought into force a Code of Practice on s.8 which stresses employer obligations under the RRA, and states that it is lawful for employers to employ asylum seekers and others subject to immigration control as long as their leave to enter has not expired and the workers have written permission to work in the former case, no restrictions on working in the latter. It stresses that employers are obliged only to check entitlement to work on *appointment*: 'There is no requirement to do anything else, even if the person's permission to be in the United Kingdom is not yet permanent. You should not ask existing employees to demonstrate that they have permission to work'. It goes on to advise that the best way for employers to comply with s.8 without breaching the RRA is for them to treat all applicants for employment the same at each stage of the recruitment process. It further stresses that all the documents listed in the Immigration (Restrictions on Employment) Order 1996 are of equal status and that 'Rejecting a candidate who does not have a particular document even though they have one of the [others listed] could be unlawful discrimination.'

'Employing refugees' 126 *Equal Opportunities Review*

Section 8, which was opposed by the Confederation of British Industry and the Trades Union Congress at the consultation stage, puts the onus on employers to investigate applicants' eligibility for employment in the UK or face the prospect of significant fines. Expecting employers to police immigration legislation in this way has made some wary of employing refugees for fear that they might fall foul of the law. Recent announcements of a Home Office crackdown on illegal working have added to employers' concerns.

Compliance with the law is not helped by the fact that many refugees do not have passports, birth certificates or the usual set of documentation possessed by most European Union nationals, such as national insurance numbers. They may also lack corroborative paperwork to verify their professional or academic qualifications and experience. Those wishing to work with children or in sensitive occupations also face the problem of having their background checked—something that may not be possible if, for example, they have fled a war zone.

The paper documents that refugees currently receive from the Home Office can quickly become tatty and are easily forged. Most employers are also unfamiliar with these

---

[36] Better Regulation Task Force 'Report on Anti-discrimination Legislation', 10.

documents, making them reluctant to employ refugees, even though they have permission to work.

Research carried out by the Institute of Employment Studies for the Employability Forum has found that the complexity of procedures and the lack of clarity about correct documentation make employers worried that they will inadvertently take on someone who is not allowed to work . . .

Asylum seekers are currently issued with an asylum registration card that carries biometric information—fingerprints and a photograph. These cards state that employment is prohibited. If an individual is granted refugee status and permission to work, the card is withdrawn. The Employability Forum believes that once an asylum seeker is given permission to stay they should be issued with a similar card that states that employment is allowed.

The *Equal Opportunities Review* article points out that refugees are disproportionately highly qualified, their non-employment a real loss to the domestic economy.

The GOQ Defence

Turning finally to the RRA's GOQ and GOR defences, s.5 provides that the RRA's prohibitions on discrimination in relation to appointments, promotion, transfer or training do not apply where (s.5(1)(a)) 'being of a particular racial group is a genuine occupational qualification for the job'. S.5 applies only to discrimination on grounds of colour or nationality. Where discrimination is on grounds of 'race' or ethnic or national origins s.4A RRA, discussed below, applies. S.5(2) RRA goes on provide that the GOQ defence may apply only where:

(a) the job involves participation in a dramatic performance or other entertainment in a capacity for which a person of that racial group is required for reasons of authenticity; or
(b) the job involves participation as an artist's or photographic model in the production of a work of art, visual image or sequence of visual images for which a person of that racial group is required for reasons of authenticity; or
(c) the job involves working in a place where food or drink is (for payment or not) provided to and consumed by members of the public or a section of the public in a particular setting for which, in that job, a person of that racial group is required for reasons of authenticity; or
(d) the holder of the job provides persons of that racial group with personal services promoting their welfare, and those services can most effectively be provided by a person of that racial group.

Sections 5(3) and 5(4) are in similar terms to ss. 7(3) and 7(4) SDA, discussed in Chapter 6. The CRE suggested that s.5(2)(a)–(c) RRA, which has not really been litigated, are flawed:

'Return of the Race Relations Act 1976: Proposals for Change', submitted by the CRE to Jack Straw MP, Home Secretary, 30 April 1998

The current criterion of 'authenticity' is too wide. It enables the unjustifiable underrepresentation of ethnic minorities in theatre, opera, cinema, television drama etc to continue indefinitely. The new formulation would enable actors to be selected on racial grounds where the race or colour of the character to be portrayed is central to the portrayal, for example to select a black actor to appear in a drama about Nelson Mandela, but would not enable only white actors to be recruited for a production of Hamlet. The Commission also advises that the criterion of racial 'authenticity' should not be relevant to future employment patterns in the catering industry in Britain. The new formulation would also enable people to be selected on racial grounds where the purpose of the job is to test for racial discrimination, and for the tests to have validity it is essential to employ people from particular racial groups.

Section 5(2)(d) RRA provides that a genuine occupational qualification (GOQ) will apply where 'the holder of the job provides persons of that racial group with personal services promoting their welfare, and those services can most effectively be provided by a person of that racial group.' The interpretation of this section by the courts is discussed below.

Turning to the operation of s.5(2)(d), the leading case is *Lambeth London Borough Council v CRE* [1990] ICR 768, in which the CRE challenged advertisements placed by the Council which stipulated African-Caribbean or Asian applicants for jobs in the Council's housing department.[37] The advertisements were placed in line with the Council's policy of making the housing benefits system 'more sensitive to the needs and experiences of black people' who, with Asians, comprised over 50 per cent of Council tenants. In pursuit of this aim the Council had reserved two positions in the housing benefits section for black workers. A tribunal ruled that, the jobs being of a managerial or administrative nature involving limited contact with the public, they did not involve 'personal services' and the Council, accordingly, had failed to make out the s.5(2)(d) defence. The tribunal further ruled that the racial groups of the post holder and the recipient of his services were not sufficiently identified so as to establish that the holder and the recipient were of the same racial group. Both EAT ([1989] ICR 641) and the Court of Appeal rejected the Council's appeal. Having rejected the idea that s.5(2) permitted positive discrimination, Balcombe LJ continued:

Lambeth London Borough Council v CRE [1990] ICR 768

The services provided by the local authority's housing benefits department undoubtedly promote the welfare of the recipients to those benefits, but the rest of the phrase is qualified by the word 'personal.' 'Personal' is defined by the Oxford English Dictionary as 'Of, pertaining to, concerning or affecting the individual or self (as opposed, variously, to other persons, the general community, etc . . .); individual; private; one's own.'

The use of the word 'personal' indicates that the identity of the giver and the recipient of the services is important. I agree with the appeal tribunal when they say that the Act appears to contemplate direct contact between the giver and the recipient—mainly face-to-face or where there could be susceptibility in personal, physical contact. Where language or a knowledge and understanding of cultural and religious background are of importance, then those services may be most effectively provided by a person of a particular racial group
. . .

the decision in any particular case whether the holder of a particular job provides persons of a particular group with personal services promoting their welfare is a question of mixed law and fact, and . . . unless the industrial tribunal have come to a decision which is wrong in law, neither the appeal tribunal nor this court can interfere. The industrial

---

[37] S.63(2)(a) RRA gives the CRE the power to bring claims in respect of discriminatory advertisements, themselves prohibited under s.29 of the Act '[I]t is unlawful to publish or to cause to be published an advertisement which indicates, or might reasonably be understood as indicating, an intention by a person to do an act of discrimination, whether the doing of that act by him would be unlawful or, by virtue of Part II ['Discrimination in the Employment Field'] or III ['Discrimination in Other Fields'], unlawful.' To this, there is an exception under subsection (2) if, inter alia, the intended act would be lawful by virtue of section 5 (which establishes the GOQs).

tribunal held that the holders of the jobs advertised, being managerial positions, did not provide personal services promoting the welfare of persons of a particular racial group. I can find no error of law in that decision. On this ground alone I would dismiss this appeal.

. . .

If a person is providing persons of a racial group defined by colour (eg black people) with personal services promoting their welfare (eg a health visitor), it will be open to an industrial tribunal on the particular facts of the case to find that those services can be most effectively provided by a person of that colour, from whatever ethnic group she (or he) comes, and even though some of her (or his) clients may belong to other ethnic groups.[38]

The approach laid down by the Court of Appeal in *Lambeth* is narrow, but the approach to GOQs is wide in two respects, both of which are illustrated by *Tottenham Green Under Fives Centre v Marshall* [1989] ICR 214, a decision approved by the Court of Appeal in the *Lambeth* case. The case involved a challenge brought by a white man to a GOQ put forward by a nursery which had advertised for an 'Afro-Caribbean worker.' The nursery had a policy of maintaining an ethnic balance both for children and for staff, but had four white, one Greek-Cypriot and one African-Caribbean worker. In addition to specifying racial group, the advertisement placed by the nursery stipulated that the applicant would need 'a personal awareness of Afro-Caribbean culture' and 'an understanding of the importance of anti-racist and anti-sexist child care.' An industrial tribunal took the view, contrary to the nursery's contention, that the 'personal services' exception would relate only to reading and talking where necessary in dialect and not, in addition, to maintaining the cultural background link for children of African-Caribbean background; dealing with the parents and discussing those matters with them and generally looking after their skin and health, including plaiting their hair. This decision rested on the finding that workers of other ethnic origins would be able to perform the same functions. EAT allowed the nursery's appeal on the grounds, *inter alia*, that s.5(2)(d) required only that the services at issue (*per* Wood J):

can most effectively be provided by a person of that racial group' [rather than that they] 'can only be provided' [by that group]. The Act assumes that the personal services could be provided by others, but can they be 'most effectively provided?' Would they be less effective if provided by others? Welfare of a child will include the broad understanding and handling of the child, and in the present circumstances an understanding of the background of the culture and the ways of the family. This issue is a matter of fact for the Tribunal, and in so deciding the Tribunal will need to carry out a delicate balancing exercise bearing in mind the need to guard against discrimination, and the desirability of promoting racial integration. However, it seems to us that if a Tribunal accepts that the conscious decision of a responsible employer to commit an act of discrimination and to rely upon s 5(2)(d) is founded upon a genuinely held and reasonably based opinion that a genuine occupational requirement will best promote the welfare of the recipient, then considerable weight should be given to that decision when reaching a conclusion whether or not the defence succeeds.

The tribunal reached a second decision unfavourable to the nursery, which again resulted in a successful appeal to EAT. The issue this time related to s.5(3), the tribunal having rejected the s.5 defence on the grounds that the reading requirement was 'the least emphasised of the four' and was 'in the nature of a desirable extra and no more'.

---

[38] Mann LJ concurred on the basis that the question was one of fact for the tribunal, and Mustill LJ agreed with both judgments.

Tottenham Green Under Fives' Centre v Marshall (No.2) **[1991] ICR 320**

Knox LJ:

The issue before us . . . is: whether it is open to an Industrial Tribunal to disregard a duty in coming to the conclusion that it does not figure for the purposes of deciding whether s 5(2)(d) applies. One can set on one side two particular categories which it was common ground between the parties did not apply in this case . . . The first of those two categories is what lawyers call matters which are *de minimis* . . . The other category which would clearly very properly be disregarded in any case, is one where the duty in question is included as a sham or a smokescreen to avoid the requirement that there should be no racial discrimination or indeed for any other purposes. It is common ground that this is not relevant in this particular case . . .

What remains is a relatively unimportant but not trivial duty and we have reached the conclusion that it is not the correct view of the meaning of this paragraph that the Industrial Tribunal can make an evaluation of the importance of the duty in question and disregard it although it is satisfied that it is something that is not so trivial that it can properly be disregarded altogether. It seems to us that subsection (3) indicates clearly that one of the duties of the job if it falls within any of the relevant paragraphs, in our case paragraph (d) of the preceding subsection, will operate to make the exception available. That is what one can discern that Parliament intended to provide.

The GOR Defence

Section 4A RRA provides a new GOR defence which applies where discrimination on grounds of race or ethnic or national origins is at stake. It provides:

(1) In relation to discrimination on grounds of race or ethnic or national origins—
 (a) section 4(1)(a) or (c) does not apply to any employment; and
 (c) section 4(2)(b) does not apply to promotion or transfer to, or training for, any employment; and
 (d) section 4(2)(c) does not apply to dismissal from any employment;
 where subsection (2) applies.
(2) This subsection applies where, having regard to the nature of the employment or the context in which it is carried out—
 (a) being of a particular race or of particular ethnic or national origins is a genuine and determining occupational requirement;
 (c) it is proportionate to apply that requirement in the particular case; and
 (d) either—
  (i) the person to whom that requirement is applied does not meet it, or
  (iii) the employer is not satisfied, and in all the circumstances it is reasonable for him not to be satisfied, that that person meets it.

The new GOR defence, consisting as it does of a principled test rather than a list of situations in which race discrimination is permitted, meets some of the criticisms made by the CRE in 1998 of the GOQ. But the GOR, which has been in force only since December 2003, raises some interesting questions. Article 6(2) of the Racial Equality Directive provides that:

The implementation of this Directive shall under no circumstances constitute grounds for a reduction in the level of protection against discrimination already afforded by Member States in the fields covered by this Directive.

In some respects the new GOR is narrower than the old GOQ inasmuch as it applies only where race is a 'genuine and determining occupational requirement,' and where its application in a particular case is *proportionate*. On the other hand:

- the new GOR covers dismissal as well as refusal to appoint or promote;
- it would permit a GOR to be established in a factual situation falling outside the list contained in s.5 RRA;
- it applies where the context in which a job is carried out, rather than the job itself, requires someone to be of a particular ethnic, racial or national origin. The CRE draft Code of Practice on Employment suggests (para. 2.38 b) that this would cover 'the post of a manager of a sexual health clinic for Pakistani women as well as the post of a counsellor'. To the extent that this is accurate it suggests a reduction (however desirable) in the protection from discrimination from the test established in the Lambeth case;
- it applies where 'the employer is not satisfied, and in all the circumstances it is reasonable for him not to be satisfied, that' the person to whom the GOR is applied does not meets it, as well as where this is actually the case.

Of even greater concern is the fact that the new GOR defence appears to *supplement*, rather than to *replace* the GOQ defence in relation to discrimination on grounds of 'race or ethnic or national origin'. The draft Race Relations Act 1976 (Amendment) Regulations had proposed the amendment of s.5 RRA to apply to 'racial discrimination other than that which is referred to in section 4A', that is, discrimination on grounds of colour or nationality, but *not* discrimination on grounds of 'race or ethnic or national origins'. The RRA as amended, however, does not contain that provision, s.5 instead providing that it applies 'in cases where section 4A does not apply' and the explanatory notes describing s.4A as 'a new exception (from the discrimination in employment provisions)'. On its ordinary reading this appears to suggest that discrimination on grounds of 'race or ethnic or national origins' is subject both to the GOR defence provided by s.4A and also (where the discrimination at issue does not fall within s.4A) to the GOQ defence provided by s.5. If this is the case, the UK is almost certainly in breach of the principle of non-regression given that protection provided in relation to discrimination on grounds covered by the Racial Equality Directive has actually been subject to more, rather than fewer, exceptions.

8

Disability

Introduction

According to the Department of Education and Employment (DfEE) 'Disability Briefing' (November 1999):

- Disabled people account for nearly a fifth of the working-age population in Great Britain, but for only about one eighth of all in employment. There are over 6.5 million people with a current long-term disability or health problem which has a substantial adverse impact on their day-to-day activities or limits the work they can do.
- The level of disability increases with age: only 11 per cent of those aged 20–29 years have a current long-term disability or health problem compared with 31 per cent of those aged 50–59 years . . .
- Disabled people are over six times as likely as non-disabled people to be out of work and claiming benefits. There are over 2.6 million disabled people out of work and on benefits: over a million of them want to work . . .
- Disabled people are more than twice as likely as non-disabled people to have no qualifications.
- Disabled people are only half as likely as non-disabled people to be in employment. There are currently around 3.1 million disabled people in employment; they make up 12 per cent of all people in employment. When employed, they are more likely to work part-time or be self-employed.[1]
- Around three quarters of those with mental illness and two thirds of those with learning difficulties are out of work and on state benefits.
- ILO unemployment rates for long-term disabled people are nearly twice as high as those for non-disabled people, 10.1 per cent compared with 5.7 per cent. Their likelihood to be long-term unemployed is also higher: 38 per cent of unemployed disabled people have been unemployed for a year or more compared with 24 per cent of non-disabled unemployed.

Of the long-term disabled analysed by the DfEE, 19 per cent (the largest group) had back or neck trouble, 14 per cent chest or breathing difficulties, 11 per cent each problems with legs and feet or heart and blood pressure, 8 per cent mental illness, 6 per cent problems with hands or arms, 5 per cent problems with stomach, liver, kidney or digestion, 5 per cent diabetes and 2 per cent each learning difficulties, epilepsy, skin or allergy, sight and

---

[1] Employment rates vary greatly between types of disability. Some types of disability are associated with relatively high employment rates for those affected (these include diabetes, skin conditions and hearing problems) while other groups (such as those with mental illness and learning disabilities) have much lower employment rates.

hearing problems. The stereotypical picture of the disabled person as a wheelchair user is inaccurate. In 2003, the *Equal Opportunities Review* reported that there were by then 6.9 million disabled people of working age in Great Britain of whom 42 per cent were in employment (by comparison with 81 per cent of those without disabilities) and of whom fewer than 8 per cent used wheelchairs.[2]

TUC, 'Civil Rights or a Discriminating Law?' (1996)

Sixty-nine per cent of adult disabled people are unemployed . . . Employers are six times more likely to turn down a disabled person for interview than a non-disabled applicant with the same qualifications.

Most public transport is inaccessible:

— Only one in eight long-distance National Express coaches is accessible.
— Only 130 British Rail stations are fully accessible.
— Wheelchair users wishing to use the London Underground are advised to give 24 hours' notice of their intention to travel, to go with a non-disabled companion and to avoid the rush hour.
— There are 4–5 million people with mobility impairments but only 80,000 accessible houses.
— Public information is rarely given in ways that are accessible to people with sensory impairments and to people with learning difficulties.

Public meetings and TV are rarely accessible to deaf people.

Because of lack of information, based on figures for October 1992, the proportion of deaf people who have died of AIDS-related illnesses is one in 3,200, compared to one in 68,000 of the total population.

Shops, pubs, restaurants, theatres, cinemas, sports stadia, town halls, law courts and churches are inaccessible to many disabled people.

If disabled people cost more than £500 a week to support, they are forced into institutions.

At the last general election, 88 per cent of polling stations were inaccessible to disabled people . . .

Some of the problems faced by the disabled (in particular, unequal access to employment) bear some similarities to the difficulties encountered by women and ethnic minority groups. But the attempt to provide equality for the disabled is immensely more complicated, in legal terms, than is the case with gender, race, sexual orientation and the like. This complexity arises both in the concept of 'equality' and in the nature of its absence.

The Disability Rights Task Force, which was established in 1997 to 'to look at the full range of issues that affect disabled people's lives and to advise the Government on what further action it should take to promote comprehensive and enforceable civil rights for disabled people,' drew attention to the weight of discrimination against some disabled people. Among the case studies included by the Task Force in its final report, *From Exclusion to Inclusion*,[3] were the following:

A company director with spinal muscular atrophy . . . was admitted to hospital with a chest infection. To her horror she found a doctor had placed a 'Do Not Resuscitate' notice on her medical notes because it was considered that her quality of life did not warrant such intervention.

[2] 'Managing diversity at work' 114 *Equal Opportunities Review*.
[3] Available at http://www.disability.gov.uk/.

An adult man and woman who lived in a residential care home were prevented by staff from becoming engaged to marry and denied the privacy to form a close and loving relationship. The staff refused to take them to a jeweller's shop to buy a ring and used various methods to keep the couple apart. After three years, the couple persuaded some friends outside of the home to help them leave for a day; they married in a registry office in 1997. They are now in a supported living flat, employing personal assistants.

The Task Force also cited Department of Health statistics showing that '[p]eople with schizophrenia have standardised mortality ratios two and a half times the national average.' 'One reason for this is that they often receive late, or inadequate, physical investigations. The complaints of psychiatric service users are all too readily put down to their 'anxiety, or delusions, or other psychiatric symptoms.' People with disabilities frequently find themselves under significant pressure not to reproduce and, in the event of having children, some have to work hard to counter the presumption that their parenting skills will be inadequate.

In *R (Burke) v General Medical Council* [2005] 2 WLR 431 (Admin) the Administrative Court accepted a challenge to the lawfulness of the General Medical Council's Guidance 'Withholding and withdrawing life-prolonging treatments: good practice in decision making' on the basis that it failed to give effect to the European Convention on Human Rights by making the wishes of patients (expressed at the time, if competent, or by advanced directive if no longer competent) determinative in the case of refusal to accept treatment, but not where the patient wished to continue with treatment. The emphasis throughout the guidance was on the right of a patient to *refuse* rather than to *require* treatment and this, together with its failure to acknowledge 'that it is the duty of a doctor who is unable or unwilling to carry out the wishes of his patient to go on providing the treatment until he can find another doctor who will do so' and 'sufficiently to acknowledge the heavy presumption in favour of life-prolonging treatment' (that is, that the patient's best interests, in cases in which they have not expressed a competent view on the matter, are served by such treatment unless it is intolerable), meant that the claimant was entitled to a declaration that aspects of the guidance were unlawful. The case illustrates the potential of the Human Rights Act 1998, by which the Convention is given effect to in domestic law, to supplement the provisions of the DDA. The HRA is considered briefly in Chapter 1 but the emphasis of this book is on the legislative provisions dealing specifically with discrimination.

The debates about equality on grounds of sex, sexual orientation and race have, to a very significant extent, been shaped by a notion of formal equality which, concerned as it is with treating like alike, has resulted in a failure fully to grapple with the accommodation of difference. This has been seen particularly in the pregnancy-as-sex discrimination saga (Chapter 6) and, more generally, in the integration of work with (at present predominantly female) family responsibilities. The SDA and the RRA (and, more recently, the SO and RB Regs) prohibit unjustified 'indirect discrimination,' which concept has the potential to promote substantive equality by requiring the removal of rules, etc, which serve to disadvantage particular groups, by reason of characteristics common to the group. But indirect discrimination has been dogged by the rigidity of its legislative expression (see Chapter 2) and by the reluctance of the courts to challenge (through the concept of justification) the detached white maleness of the stereotypical worker.[4] Thus, for example, indirectly

---

[4] See the extract from B Hepple, 'Race and Law in Fortress Europe' 67 (2004) *Modern Law Review* 1, in Chapter 7 on the need (in the race discrimination context) of positive obligations. Similar arguments are applicable in the context of disability.

discriminatory policies and practices have not, until recently, been capable of challenge unless they amounted to 'complete bars.'

In the case of disability, adherence to a formal equality approach is untenable. Part of the difficulty faced by disabled people is the result of stereotyping (the 'does he take sugar?' approach frequently cited by wheelchair users). In this context the prohibition of direct discrimination against real or perceived disability will, properly enforced, be effective in promoting equality. But much of the difficulty faced by disabled people relates to their denial of access to a world shaped for those who are not disabled (a point taken up below in the context of the medical model/ social model debate). Without the imposition of a duty to accommodate the needs of disabled people, any formal guarantee of equality would be a cynical exercise.[5]

The DDA differs markedly from the other discrimination legislation in eschewing the normal symmetrical approach to discrimination and confining its protections instead to those who are regarded as 'disabled' for the purposes of the Act (except in the case of victimisation, see further Chapter 2). This definition, as we shall see below, is narrow and unsatisfactory in many ways, and serves to deny the Act's protection to many who are discriminated against in connection with their actual or perceived health status, although the non-symmetrical approach at least avoids the possibility of challenges from non-disabled persons to action intended to ameliorate the disadvantages associated with many forms of disability. It is questionable, however, whether the restriction of the Act's employment-related protections to discrimination 'for a reason which relates to the disabled person's disability' or 'on the ground of the disabled person's disability' is adequate to comply with the requirements of the Employment Equality Directive. The Directive, which came into force in this context in October 2004, provides (Article 1) that:

1. For the purposes of this Directive, the 'principle of equal treatment' shall mean that there shall be no direct or indirect discrimination whatsoever *on any of the grounds* referred to in Article 1 [my emphasis—these grounds include 'disability'].

2. For the purposes of paragraph 1:

    direct discrimination shall be taken to occur where one person is treated less favourably than another is, has been or would be treated in a comparable situation, *on any of the grounds* referred to in Article 1 . . .

It is strongly arguable that the Directive's prohibition on discrimination 'on grounds of disability' ought to extend to discrimination on grounds of someone *else's* disability and discrimination on grounds of *perceived* disability. Ireland's Equal Status Act expressly extends protection to those who are discriminated against because of perceived status or association (this on any of the grounds regulated by the Act). And while domestic legislation does not expressly address this point, we saw in Chapters 2 and 7 that 'racial grounds' under the RRA has been interpreted to extend to discrimination on grounds of another person's race. This approach has been adopted in relation to sexual orientation and religion or belief, the SO and RB Regs regulating discrimination 'on grounds of sexual orientation' and 'on grounds of religion or belief' respectively. It is fairly clear that this rubric would cover discrimination on grounds of a person's *perceived* religion, belief or sexual

---

[5] This is not to say that formal equality is not also important. The mentally ill, in particular, face enormous stigma discrimination. 71 *Equal Opportunities Review* 7 cites a MIND survey which found that almost 40 per cent had been harassed and one third dismissed or forced to resign. Forty per cent had been denied jobs because of their history and over half concealed their history of mental illness.

orientation. The non-symmetrical approach adopted by the DDA can be expected to give rise to some differences between it and the other anti-discrimination legislation. But this approach is not inconsistent with the extension of protection to those who are perceived to be disabled, or are discriminated against because of an association with a disabled person. Despite this, recent proposals to amend the Act so as to regulate discrimination on grounds of perceived disability have been rejected by the Government on the ground (see further below) that the DDA 'is 'one-way' in nature . . . because it does not generally prohibit discrimination against non-disabled people.'[6]

The DDA prohibits victimisation, harassment of disabled persons, the issue of instructions to discriminate and the provisions of assistance to discriminators. These aspects of discrimination, the coverage of which by the DDA does not differ materially from that of the other discrimination legislation, are considered in Chapters 2 and 4. Uniquely, the Act does not employ the concept of indirect discrimination, but defines 'disability-related discrimination' (a term coined by the Disability Rights Commission) in some ways more widely than 'direct discrimination' as less favourable (and unjustified) treatment *for a reason which relates to* the disabled person's disability,' as distinct from less favourable treatment *'on the grounds of'* sex etc. This form of discrimination being subject to justification, the DDA has been amended from October 2004 to bring it into line with the Employment Equality Directive by prohibiting 'direct' disability discrimination in the employment context without a general justification defence. 'Direct' discrimination occurs (s 3A(5) DDA) where 'on the ground of [a] disabled person's disability, [someone] treats the disabled person less favourably than he treats or would treat a person not having that particular disability whose relevant circumstances, including his abilities, are the same as, or not materially different from, those of the disabled person.' In addition, the DDA imposes duties of reasonable adjustment in relation to employment, the provision of goods and services, etc, and defines discrimination to include any unjustified failure (in the context of employment, any failure) to comply with such a duty.

The failure of the DDA to prohibit indirect discrimination in terms appears to be consistent with the Employment Equality Directive which provides (Article 2) that:

(b) indirect discrimination shall be taken to occur where an apparently neutral provision, criterion or practice would put persons having a particular religion or belief, a particular disability, a particular age, or a particular sexual orientation at a particular disadvantage compared with other persons unless:

(i) that provision, criterion or practice is objectively justified by a legitimate aim and the means of achieving that aim are appropriate and necessary, or [my emphasis]

(ii) as regards persons with a particular disability, the employer or any person or organisation to whom this Directive applies, is obliged, under national legislation, to take appropriate measures in line with the principles contained in Article 5 in order to eliminate disadvantages entailed by such provision, criterion or practice.

The DDA was amended to ensure, in the employment context, that a duty to adjust would apply in every case in which 'an apparently neutral provision, criterion or practice would put persons having a particular . . . disability . . . at a particular disadvantage compared with other persons.' Prior to this the duty was framed more narrowly (see further below). It is possible, however, that the UK approach is flawed inasmuch as the duty to adjust applies only where the disabled person is placed at a '*substantial* disadvantage in comparison with

---

[6] See 'Mental illness hurdle to be scrapped' 132 *Equal Opportunities Review.*

persons who are not disabled' (s.4A(1)) and requires an employer to take only '*such steps as it is reasonable*, in all the circumstances of the case, for him to have to take in order to prevent the provision, criterion or practice, or feature, having that effect.' The Directive uses the term 'particular' rather than 'substantial' and disapplies the prohibition on indirect discrimination only in cases in which 'as regards persons with a particular disability, *the employer . . . is obliged*, under national legislation, *to take appropriate measures* in line with the principles contained in Article 5 in order to eliminate disadvantages entailed by such provision, criterion or practice.' Article 5 provides that:

> In order to guarantee compliance with the principle of equal treatment in relation to persons with disabilities, reasonable accommodation shall be provided. This means that employers shall take appropriate measures, where needed in a particular case, to enable a person with a disability to have access to, participate in, or advance in employment, or to undergo training, unless such measures would impose a disproportionate burden on the employer. This burden shall not be disproportionate when it is sufficiently remedied by measures existing within the framework of the disability policy of the Member State concerned.

It is arguable that, in a case in which no steps could reasonably be taken under the DDA, the Directive requires indirect discrimination to be prohibited in the sense that the operation of the provision, criterion, practice or the existence of the feature of the premises would have to justified in order for compliance with the Directive. This is further considered in the following extract.

K Wells, 'The Impact of the Framework Employment Directive on UK Disability Discrimination Law' (2003) 32 *Industrial Law Journal* 253, 272, footnotes omitted

Th[e DDA's] framework is problematic for situations of indirect discrimination, as the following scenario seeks to illustrate. An employer imposes an indistinctly applicable measure which has an adverse effect on a disabled person. An example of such a measure would be a requirement that all employees start work at 9am. Employee B has mobility problems and public transport is such that travel during rush hour is extremely difficult. Thus the requirement to start work at 9am places B at a particular disadvantage compared with employees who have no mobility problems. The reason for requiring all employees to start at 9am is due to operational exigencies and has nothing to do with B's disability. Thus the requirement of a 9am start is neither direct discrimination nor less favourable treatment for a reason related to the disability. B can only base a DDA claim on a failure to make a reasonable adjustment.

To defend the claim, the employer is likely to argue that there is no duty to make reasonable adjustments for B. To some extent, this seems to distort the situation envisaged in the Framework Employment Directive, which allows a defence to the indirect discrimination if the employer establishes that there is a duty to accommodate that particular person: thus the 9am start which places all people with mobility problems at a disadvantage is allowed if an accommodation is made in order to remove the discriminatory effect for B. However, the end result is the same: in the second case the employer could only, under the . . . Directive, defend a claim of indirect discrimination if he had complied with the duty to accommodate B, otherwise he would face a claim of a failure to comply with this duty. And this takes us back to the situation under the DDA where B's only claim against the employer is a failure to make adjustments.

In striving to preserve the 'familiar' reasonable adjustments approach, the Government may well have made the DDA more obscure. The amended DDA model is convoluted and messy in comparison with the . . . Employment Directive's three concepts of direct and indirect discrimination and reasonable accommodation, and the Government's avoidance of replicating the Directive's model seems rather counter-productive. From this confusion though, one thing seems clear. The 'reasonable adjustments' approach proposed for the DDA and the removal of the justification defence for failure to adjust will result in an intensification of disputes over the reasonableness of an adjustment. Tribunals will need to be vigilant over employer's arguments on this point, to ensure that conventional and ill-held views about the employment of disabled people are challenged.

The ECNI has also criticised the failure of the DDA to regulate indirect discrimination in terms.

Equality Commission for Northern Ireland, 'Response to "Promoting Equality of Opportunity Implementing EU Equality Obligations in Northern Ireland"', A Consultation by the Office of the First and Deputy First Minister' (2003)

we believe that indirect discrimination should apply to disability, in addition to the duty to make reasonable adjustments. This will harmonise the DDA with other anti-discrimination legislation and help prepare it for eventual integration into single equality legislation. Moreover, we feel that it is potentially a useful—and arguably more powerful—measure to tackle institutionalised discrimination, which continues to exist. An example of how this might help concerns taxis. Once the transport exemption has been removed from the DDA, it could still be possible for taxi operators to justify charging a higher fare to wheelchair users, because they use a larger taxi. Taxi operators could argue that non-disabled people who use that same taxi are charged the same higher rate and therefore the policy does not constitute discrimination. However, in terms of outcomes, non-disabled people have a choice of taxis and, therefore, would generally pay the lower rate. Similar examples exist in respect of blanket requirements (eg driving licences, educational qualifications), which may not easily be tackled through the reasonable adjustment duty.

History and Development of the DDA

It is clear from the above both that disability affects a considerable number of people in the UK and that its impact on employment and other areas of life is significant. Yet the passage of legislation in this area required a prolonged battle. In 1982 Peter Large's Committee of Inquiry into Restrictions Against Disabled People, 'stressed and documented the urgent need to make unjustified discrimination unlawful by means of a commission with powers and duties to conciliate and, where necessary, to take enforcement action.'[7] The then Conservative Government took the view that 'education and persuasion' were preferable to legislation, a view that persisted through thirteen successive attempts to introduce backbench disability rights legislation in the House of Commons. Alf Morris MP (now Lord Morris) introduced the Civil Rights (Disabled Persons) Bill in November 1991, this Bill being blocked then and in three successive years when it was introduced by Roger Berry and

---

[7] Lord Morris of Manchester (who, in 1979, had as Minister for the Disabled set up the inquiry) speaking in the House of Lords Second Reading of the Disability Rights Commission Bill, HL Debs 17 December 1998, col. 1475.

Harry Barnes MP. In 1994–5 the Bill achieved an almost unopposed second reading, at which stage the Government was 'shamed into introducing their own Bill.'[8] The much more radical Civil Rights Bill was talked out.

Given the background to the DDA it was not surprising that the DDA was not as ambitious a piece of legislation as had been the SDA and the RRA in their time. The Act was characterised by Brian Doyle at the time as 'at best, half measures and reluctant reform.' He pointed out that, 'within a few months of [its] Royal Assent, [the] same government was voicing its opposition to the extension of disability rights across the European Union where the DDA . . . has been viewed with great interest' (and, ironically, formed the basis of the Employment Equality Directive's disability-related provisions).[9]

The DDA was passed in 1995. Its employment-related provisions came into effect in December 1996 and its other provisions in staggered form from that date. Whereas the EOC and CRE were established by the SDA and the RRA respectively, the DDA provided only for the establishment of a National Disability Council which, unlike the EOC and CRE, had an advisory capacity only. Even this was limited, until mid-1998, to the non-employment area. The failure of the DDA to establish a commission was put right by the Disability Rights Commission Act 1999, which established the DRC from early 2000. We saw in Chapter 5 that, although similar to those of the CRE and the EOC, the DRC's powers differ somewhat from those of the older commissions in order to avoid a number of their shortcomings. In Northern Ireland, the Disability Council was subsumed within the new ECNI (discussed in Chapters 5 and 9) in 1999.

The transposition of the Employment Equality Directive's provisions took place in October 2004. The Disability Discrimination Act 1995 (Amendment) Regulations 2003 (SI 2003 No 1673) bring the employment-related provisions of the Act broadly into line with those of the SDA, RRA and SO and RB Regs (by, for example, removing the small employer exemption[10] and extending the coverage of the Act to the police and fire services etc, though not to the military). A new Code of Practice on Employment and Occupation has been adopted which replaced the 1996 Employment Code of Practice as of October 2004. Both old and new Codes are referred to below. Nor do developments stop there. The Disability Discrimination Act 2005 incorporates a number of the recommendations made by the Disability Rights Task Force. It broadens the definition of 'disability', prohibits disability discrimination by public authorities, and imposes positive obligations on them in relation to disability equality. It also extends to application of the DDA to private clubs and the policing function, and extends the DDA's application in the context of transport and premises. Many of these amendments have been discussed in Chapters 3 and 4. They will be also touched upon below.

---

[8] *Ibid.*

[9] B Doyle, 'Enabling Legislation or Dissembling Law? The Disability Discrimination Act 1995' (1997) *Modern Law Review* 64, 64–5, 78.

[10] Prior to October 2004 the employment-related provisions of the DDA applied only to employers having at least 15 employees (until the end of 1998 this figure was 20).

'Disability'

Social and Medical Models of Disability

Section 1(1) DDA provides that '[s]ubject to the provisions of Schedule 1, a person has a disability for the purposes of this Act if he has a physical or mental impairment which has a substantial and long-term adverse effect on his ability to carry out normal day-to-day activities.' Section 2 states that the Act applies equally to 'a person who *has had* a disability' (my emphasis), but not to someone who will have one in the future. It is, in every case, for the complainant to establish that s/he has or has had a disability.

The model of disability adopted by the DDA is a medical, rather than a social, one. The 'social' model of disability recognises 'the close connection between the limitation experienced by individuals with disabilities, the design and structure of their environments and the attitude of the general population.'[11] It identifies social barriers and the infrastructure of society as the cause of disability; preventing participation on equal terms and denying equality of opportunity. Thus, for example (and in an interesting illustration of an absence of joined-up thinking on the part of government) the interim analytical report of the Prime Minister's Strategy Unit in the Cabinet Office, *Improving the Life Chances of Disabled People* (June 2004) recognises that: '*Disability* is the disadvantage or restriction of activity caused by a society which takes little or no account of people who have impairments and thus excludes them from mainstream activity. *Impairment* is a characteristic, feature of attribute within an individual. . . .'[12] The 'medical model' by contrast locates the problem of disability in the disabled person, regarding disability as an individual impairment and referring solely to physical conditions or impairments.[13]

The medical approach to disability rights has long been criticised by the disability community. Anne Begg MP expressed a common view in the House of Commons Second Reading debate on the Disability Rights Commission Act: 'It's not my disability that stops me playing an equal part in society, it's the fact that some people put steps in buildings that I can't get into. I have no limitations in what I can do in a fully accessible building . . . It is society that has built the physical barriers and it is people in society who have the attitudes that cause the problem—not the disability.'

The conformity of the medical model of discrimination upon which the DDA is based with EU provisions has been called into question.

Wells, (2003) 32 *Industrial Law Journal* 253, 261–2, footnotes omitted

The social model of disability was first acknowledged by the European Commission in 1996, when the Commission announced a new Community strategy based on equal opportunities for disabled people. Inspired by the 1993 UN Standard Rules for the Equalisation

---

[11] See United Nations Standard Rules on the Equalization of Opportunities for Persons with Disabilities, para 5, cited by B Doyle, Disabled Workers' Rights, the Disability Discrimination Act and the UN Standard Rules (1996) 25 *Industrial Law Journal* 1, 11.

[12] At 12, citing *British Council Of Disabled People*. The project seeks to adopt a holistic approach to the problems faced by disabled people and to determine how these might best be addressed. The interim analysis contains a wealth of information about the disadvantages currently experienced by disabled people.

[13] Initially, New Labour seemed willing to dismantle much of what they inherited from the Tories, and was keen to promote the concept of active citizenship and equality of opportunity. One example of this was indicated in their manifesto, heralded by the promise of 'comprehensive and enforceable civil rights' for disabled people—*The Journal* (Newcastle, UK) 21 June 1999.

of Opportunities for Persons with Disabilities, this rights-based strategy endorsed an emphasis on identifying and removing barriers to full participation faced by disabled people, and aimed at placing equality and the valuing of human diversity at the core of Community disability policy. The Communication was politically endorsed by the Council and the Member States in a Resolution on equality of opportunity for people with disabilities. The Commission has since termed this the 'social approach to disability,' which 'recognises that the circumstances of people with disabilities and the discrimination they face, are socially created phenomena which are not directly related to their impairments per se.' The move away from the medical model of disability is a 'critical reorientation of perspective', and henceforth 'the problem is not in the impairment itself but rather is one which results from the structures, practices and attitudes that prevent the person from exercising his or her capabilities.'

The Commission's Proposal for the Framework Employment Directive did not define disability . . . But absent any express designation of disability, the . . . Directive still lends itself to a reading that is consistent with the social model . . . There is nothing in the Directive or other Community materials that supports a definition of disability which limits the scope of the Directive to considerations of medical impairment rather than disability in the wider social sense. However, anti-discrimination legislation based on the social model does not necessarily require a definition of disability with no reference to medical impairment at all. Indeed, some reference to impairment is required for the sake of identifying this issue specifically as one of disability, as opposed to disadvantage through belonging (or a perception of belonging) to a discriminated group. In considering the definition of disability in the European context, Whittle writes that the concept of impairment is a necessary basis for the definition, but goes on to make two points. First, 'it is crucial that the legislative concept of impairment does not (a) incorporate the phraseology that will encourage an assessment as to the extent of an individual's functional limitations and (b) ignore the social dimension to disability.' Second, 'the concept of impairment must be defined in a comprehensive manner to ensure that the question for the judiciary is more to do with whether an individual's past, present future or perceived impairment constitutes an appropriate disability for the purposes of the law.' Essentially, the key focus of an anti-discrimination law should be the occurrence of disability discrimination itself; such a law should not exclude victims of discrimination through its definition of disability.

The current UK system falls down on all these counts, and may be vulnerable to challenge on the basis that these failings frustrate the objectives of the Framework Employment Directive. The DDA's focus is on individual functional impairment, and not on impairments created by society. Even though the DDA contains a duty on employers to make adjustments for disabled people, it nonetheless fails to support a social construction of disability: the basis of the definition of disability on medical factors, and the tendency of tribunals to interpret this definition in a rigid and formal way, seriously undermines the potential of the legislation to address the systemic and social factors that prevent disabled people from enjoying equal employment opportunities. The DDA definition of disability may not be enough to combat discrimination 'on grounds of disability,' and the formal approach taken by tribunals in interpreting the definition may be inconsistent with the purposive approach required by Community law.

Further, the restrictiveness of the UK definition in comparison to the way other Member States define beneficiaries may offend against the general principles of uniform application of Community law throughout the EU and its effectiveness, as well as the maintenance of equal conditions for competition. Thus in the future, claimants who face difficulties in establishing that the DDA applies to them may see questions being referred to the Court of Justice for a preliminary ruling on the lawfulness, at Community level, of the DDA definition. In addition, the Court of Justice may make preliminary rulings in respect of the national disability discrimination legislation of other Member States, which could impact on the UK system. The Court of Justice could well take a proactive approach and seek to develop the Community law on equality for disabled people, rather than respecting the integrity of the Member States' national legal systems . . .

Even as a medical model of disability, the approach taken by the DDA is very narrow, excluding protection on grounds of perceived, rather than actual disability[14] and adopting a functional approach which requires actual, substantial, impairment in relation to normal, day-to-day activities. This latter aspect of the DDA echoes the approach taken by the Americans with Disabilities Act 1990, upon which the DDA is modelled in many respects. The ADA prohibits discrimination against those who are 'disabled' in the sense that they have: (a) a physical or mental impairment that substantially limits one or more of the[ir] major life activities . . . or (b) a record of having such an impairment; or (c) [that they are] . . . regarded as having such an impairment'. Australia's Disability Discrimination Act 1992, by contrast, defines as 'disability':

(a) total or partial loss of the person's bodily or mental functions; or
(b) total or partial loss of a part of the body; or
(c) the presence in the body of organisms causing . . . or
(d) . . . capable of causing disease or illness; or
(e) the malfunction, malformation or disfigurement of a part of the person's body; or
(f) a disorder or malfunction that results in the person learning differently from a person without the disorder or malfunction; or
(g) a disorder, illness or disease that affects a person's thought processes, perception of reality, emotions or judgement or that results in disturbed behaviour.

The Australian definition of 'disability' requires no limitation of activities (as in the case of the ADA) or 'effect on' the disabled person's 'ability to carry out . . . activities' (as is required by the DDA) over and above the medical conditions listed.

M McDonagh, 'Disability Discrimination in Australia', in G Quinn, M McDonagh and C Kimber (eds), _Disability Discrimination Law in the US, Australia & Canada_ (Dublin, Oak Tree Press, 1993) 128, footnotes omitted

The definition of disability in the [Australian] DDA follows closely the recommendations of the HREOC's (Human Rights & Equal Opportunities Commissions) Draft Position Paper. It is interesting to note therefore that the HREOC in that document expressly rejected the definition of disability set out in the . . . (ADA).

The HREOC argued that the requirement that a person's impairment substantially limits major life activities is a source of unnecessary legal difficulties or complexities. In particular, it saw such a definition as posing difficulties for people whose condition has disabling effects only intermittently rather than continuously or whose condition is controlled by medication and/or other treatments (for example many people with epilepsy, some forms of mental illness or asthma). In addition there are those people whose disability relates to physical disfigurement, rather than loss of any functional capacity and who are not limited in any major life activities but who are nonetheless discriminated against because of prejudice. Finally, there are people who have overcome any loss of capacity (through their own efforts, with or without any assistance and the use of aids or appliances), for example, many hearing impaired people who would deny that they are limited in their ability to lead a full

---

[14] This omission was quite deliberate, the government of the day resisting every attempt to amend the Bill to include perceived disabilities—79 _Equal Opportunities Review_, 'Interpreting the DDA—Part 1'.

and active life, other than by prejudice and discrimination. As the HREOC argues 'the need for protection against discrimination does not disappear as a person becomes more able to participate in the community.' Apart from the legal difficulties raised by such definitions, it is also questionable whether a person in seeking the assistance of anti-discrimination law in asserting their ability and entitlement to participate equally may paradoxically find it necessary to argue that their ability to participate fully is in fact limited by their impairment in order to qualify for the protection of the law.

Approaching the Disability Question

The general approach to determining whether a claimant is disabled within the meaning of the DDA was set out by EAT in *Goodwin v Patent Office*.[15] There, EAT stressed the importance of the Guidance issued by the Secretary of State about the 'matters to be taken into account in determining whether an impairment has a substantial adverse effect on a person's ability to carry out normal day-to-day activities; and whether such an impairment has a long-term effect.' As is the case with statutory codes of practice issued by the discrimination commissions and other bodies, the provisions of the Guidance must be taken into account, where they appear relevant, by any tribunal or court 'which is determining . . . whether a person's impairment has a substantial and long-term adverse effect on his or her ability to carry out normal day-to-day activities' under s.1. EAT also emphasised the importance of the Employment Code of Practice to which tribunals should have reference in determining whether a complainant satisfied s.1. Morison J accepted that: 'in many cases the question whether a person is disabled within the meaning of the Act can admit of only one answer. In these cases it would be wrong to search the Guide and use what it says as some kind of extra hurdle over which the applicant must jump.' But here the tribunal had erred in failing to make reference to the Guidance in reaching what he characterised as a 'surprising' decision 'that a person admittedly diagnosed as suffering from paranoid schizophrenia and who had been dismissed partly because of what one might call bizarre behaviour, consistent with that diagnosis, fell outside the definition in s 1 of the Act.'

The tribunal had decided that the claimant's normal day-to-day activities were not substantially adversely affected by his condition, which resulted in paranoia, 'thought broadcasting' when he imagined that other people could access his thoughts, and auditory hallucinations which, in turn, affected his ability to concentrate on his work and to watch television. According to the majority, the claimant 'must have been able to remember, to organise his thoughts and plan a course of action and execute it, in order to carry out his day-to-day activities of looking after himself at home, getting to and from work and carrying out his work.' EAT ruled that the tribunal had erred in concluding 'from the finding that the claimant was able to cope at home . . . that, therefore, he fell outwith the provisions of the Act'. Rather than remit to a tribunal the question whether or not the claimant fell within s.1, EAT concluded that he did: 'It seems to us that in this case the question whether the applicant was, at the relevant time, disabled within the meaning of the Act admitted only one conclusion: he was.'

Morison J, for the Court, interpreted the Guidance as establishing four 'conditions' which had to be satisfied before a complainant could be regarded as 'disabled.'

[15] [1999] ICR 302.

Goodwin v Patent Office **[1999] ICR 302**

Morison J:

(1) The impairment condition

The applicant must have either a physical or mental impairment. Mental impairment includes an impairment which results from or consists of a mental illness provided that the mental illness is 'a clinically well-recognised illness' . . .

If there is doubt as to whether the impairment condition is fulfilled in an alleged mental illness case, it would be advisable to ascertain whether the illness described or referred to in the medical evidence is mentioned in the WHO's International Classification of Diseases. That Classification would very likely determine the issue one way or the other . . .

(2) The adverse effect condition

In many ways, this may be the most difficult of the four conditions to judge . . . The fact that a person can carry out such activities does not mean that his ability to carry them out has not been impaired . . . Furthermore, disabled persons are likely, habitually, to 'play down' the effect that their disabilities have on their daily lives. If asked whether they are able to cope at home, the answer may well be 'yes,' even though, on analysis, many of the ordinary day-to-day tasks were done with great difficulty due to the person's impaired ability to carry them out . . .'

(3) The substantial condition

'Substantial' might mean 'very large' or it might mean 'more than minor or trivial.' Reference to the Guide shows that the word has been used in the latter sense . . . The tribunal will wish to examine how the applicant's abilities had actually been affected at the material time, whilst on medication, and then to address their minds to the difficult question as to the effects which they think there would have been but for the medication: the deduced effects. The question is then whether the actual and deduced effects on the applicant's abilities to carry out normal day-to-day activities is clearly more than trivial.

In many cases, the tribunal will be able to reach a conclusion on these matters without reference to the statutory Guidance (which is there to illuminate what is not reasonably clear . . . Although Parliament has linked the effect of medication to the 'substantial condition,' as we have already said, splitting the statutory words into conditions should not divert attention from the definition as a whole, and in determining whether the adverse effect condition is fulfilled the tribunal will take into account deduced effects.

(4) The long-term condition

Paragraph 2 of Schedule 1 applies, as does paragraph B of the Guidance, where reference to it is necessary. The provisions appear to be straightforward and we have nothing useful to say about them.

In *Ridout v TC Group* [1998] IRLR 628 EAT had suggested that a tribunal which failed to refer to the Code of Practice on employment would err as a matter of law:

It seems to us that as the case law develops in relation to the Disability Discrimination Act, industrial tribunals will build up a knowledge of how the Act should be applied in practice. At this period of development it is particularly important, in my judgment, that industrial tribunals should always refer to the relevant provisions of the Code of Practice as they are required to do under s.53. The code will help them in resolving questions at issue since the code sets out the standards to be expected, in relatively straightforward language. In this case, there is nothing in the code, in our judgment, which is of particular assistance to the appellant. The passages which we have quoted in this judgment do not seem to us to throw light on the real question at issue, which was: what should the employers reasonably have done when she appeared at the interview room, it being clear, in our judgment, that they could not reasonably have been expected to anticipate any problems as a result of them simply looking at the application forms? In relation to what happened at the interview room, that was a matter of evidence and we cannot interfere with the tribunal's conclusions which seems to us, if I might respectfully say so, to be sensible and well reasoned.

In *Fu v London Borough of Camden* [2001] IRLR 186, EAT overturned a tribunal decision to the effect that no duty to adjust arose in a case in which the employer's occupational health unit was unable to say when the applicant might return to work (the Applicant's position being that she could return to work is appropriate adjustments were made). Judge Altman, for the appeal tribunal, had the following to say about the Code of Practice:

> Mr Martin [for the Applicant] suggested, following *Ridout* . . . that the employment tribunal should have referred specifically to the code. Whilst it is true that, sitting two-and-a-half half years ago, the Employment Appeal Tribunal considered that at that stage of the development of the law it was important to do so, it seems to us that there is no rule of law as to what must appear, word for word, in the decision of an employment tribunal. Indeed the history of case law on the contents of the reasons for a tribunal's decision leaves it very much to the discretion of the individual chairman. Of course, s.53 of the Act imposes an obligation on the tribunal to in fact consider the code and whilst something could have been said about certain of the propositions within it in this particular case, we are not satisfied that the tribunal failed to consider it. The same goes for the need to set out word for word the terms of the statute. Some chairmen may find it very helpful to do so, but we hold back from suggesting that there is some rule of law to that effect.

EAT did, however, rule that the tribunal had erred inasmuch as it was not possible to determine from its decision whether it viewed the applicant's 'underlying medical condition [as] so serious that no adjustments could be made [or whether] the respondents, in consulting [the medical adviser], did not engage with him, nor he with them, as to the very question as to the extent to which any adjustments could assist the appellant back to work apart from the removal of home visits to which specific reference was made.' In *Archibald v Fife Council* [2004] IRLR 197, Lord Hamilton (with whom the rest of the Court of Session appeared to agree) downplayed the significance of the Code in a duty to adjust case in which the Court of Session's preferred reading of the statutory provisions did not accord with examples given in the Code: According to his Lordship, the Code could not be 'prayed in aid' in interpreting the statute

> The Code is admissible in evidence (s.53(5)); under s.53(6) if any provision of it 'appears to a court or tribunal to be relevant to any question arising in any proceedings under this Act, it shall be taken into account in determining that question'. However, it is plain from s.53(1) that the Secretary of State is empowered to issue codes of practice for the purpose of giving 'practical guidance'. Notwithstanding the apparent breadth of s.53(6) I am unable to accept that it requires this court in interpreting s.6 as a matter of law to have regard to the terms or examples found in the Code. The Code itself (rightly, in my view) recognises in paragraph 1.3 that authoritative interpretation of the Act is for the courts and tribunals.

> The House of Lords ruled ([2004] ICR 954) that the approach taken by the Court of Session had failed adequately to take into account the Code of Practice.

The ADA's definition of 'disability' is wider than that adopted by the DDA, extending as it does to perceived rather than actual disability and accepting HIV infection as 'inherently substantially limiting.'[16] In the UK, by contrast, someone sacked for being (or thought to be) HIV positive, in circumstances where, as is usual, s/he is perfectly capable of living a normal life, is outside the protection of the Act. The Disability Discrimination Act 2005 brings within the definition of 'disability' anyone with 'cancer, HIV infection or multiple sclerosis', subject to the power of the Secretary of State to make regulations excluding from the definition certain types of cancer. The Act does not, however, alter the position as regards perceived disability so the person sacked because he is wrongly suspected of being HIV positive will remain unprotected by the Act, as will someone refused a job because her employer wrongly assumes that a condition (such as, for example, controlled diabetes) will have an impact on her attendance record. The recommendation by the Parliamentary Committee which scrutinised the Disability Discrimination Bill in its draft form, that the DDA be amended to protect those associated with a disabled person or who were perceived to be disabled,[17] was rejected by the Government:

> It is important to recognise that disability discrimination differs from other forms of discrimination. It is 'one-way' in nature and this is reflected in legislation. The DDA is unique because it does not generally prohibit discrimination against non-disabled people. Indeed, it actively requires positive action to be taken to ensure a disabled person has equality of access or outcome. This contrasts with the approach taken in other anti-discrimination legislation, where discrimination against people of either gender or any race, for example, is prohibited. Extending the Act to cover people who associate with disabled people, or who are perceived to be disabled, would fundamentally alter the approach taken in the DDA. This would also significantly change and extend the responsibilities of those with duties under the Act. We consider it is inappropriate to legislate at a time when a wide range of new rights need effective implementation.[18]

The Disability Discrimination (Meaning of Disability) Regulations 1996[19] exclude from 'impairment' within s.1 'addiction to or dependency on alcohol, nicotine, or any other [non-prescribed] substance,'[20] although the results of such addiction (cirrhosis, emphysema, lung cancer, psychosis) are covered by the DDA. So, for example, in *Power v Panasonic UK Ltd* [2003] IRLR 151, EAT overruled a tribunal which had dismissed a claim on the basis that the claimant's unchallenged depression might have been a symptom or manifestation of alcohol addiction and abuse.

---

[16] Guidance issued by the US Equal Employment Opportunity Commission, available at www.eeoc.gov.

[17] Similar proposals were made in 2003 by the ECNI. The report of the Joint Scrutiny Committee was published in May 2004, HL 82–I/HC 352–I, 'Draft Disability Discrimination Bill'.

[18] 'Mental illness hurdle to be scrapped', above n 6.

[19] SI 1996 No 1455.

[20] In Northern Ireland, the materially identical Statutory Rule 1996 No.421 (The Disability Discrimination (Meaning of Disability) Regulations (Northern Ireland) 1996). Note that 'liver disease' resulting from alcoholism would amount to an impairment, according to para 10 which provides that 'It is not necessary to consider how an impairment was caused, even if the cause is a consequence of a condition which is excluded.'

Notwithstanding this decision, the DDA's exclusion of addictions means that it takes a comparatively narrow approach to disability. In the US, although the ADA excludes current illegal drug users and 'current' alcoholics, its provisions do protect non-using addicts.[21] In Canada, by contrast, human rights legislation recognises addiction as a disability. The DDA also excludes from its definition of 'impairment' hayfever ('except where it aggravates the effect of another condition'); exhibitionism; voyeurism; a tendency to steal, to set fires, or to abuse others either physically or sexually. In *Murray v Newham Citizens Advice Bureau (No. 2)* [2003] ICR 643 EAT ruled that the claimant, who was discriminated against in connection with a conviction for violence as a result of which he had been diagnosed as a paranoid schizophrenic, was 'disabled' for the purposes of the DDA. A tribunal had rejected his claim on the basis that he had a tendency to violence ('physical abuse' within the Regs). EAT overturned on the basis (*per* Judge Serota QC) that the conditions set out in the Regs are 'freestanding' rather than 'the direct consequence of a physical or mental impairment, within the meaning of s.1(1).' The claimant's physical violence was a consequence of his paranoid schizophrenia and, accordingly, a manifestation of his disability.

The decision of EAT in *Murray* has been strongly criticised:

IRLR, 'Highlights' June 2003

Many people who have a tendency to set fires, steal, physical or sexual abuse of other persons, exhibitionism, or voyeurism will also be mentally disordered. Indeed, logically, the more severe the tendency, the more likely it is that it will not be 'freestanding.' Thus, the EAT's reasoning undermines the utility of excluding these conditions via the Regulations from the definition of disabled person. It gets worse. On the holding in *Murray*, it is not just that discrimination by reason of these tendencies needs to be justified by the employer. It follows that the employer has a duty of reasonable adjustment to those with a tendency to set fires, steal, physical or sexual abuse of other persons, exhibitionism, or voyeurism, so long as those tendencies are a result of a mental illness. This aspect of the decision casts a shadow on the rest of the judgment, which contains some interesting guidance on carrying out an adequate investigation. An alternative approach to the Regulations is that, as an exclusion, they should be construed strictly, so that on the facts of this case, a one-off incident of violence that has been successfully treated and controlled would not be regarded as amounting to a 'tendency.'

Mental impairment' includes, for the purposes of s.1(1)DDA, 'a wide range of impairments relating to mental functioning, including what are often known as learning disabilities.' Prior to the implementation of the DDA 2005, however, mental illnesses are excluded by the Act (schedule 1) save where they are 'clinically well-recognised'.[22] This restriction, which is to be removed by the 2005 Act, has given rise to significant problems of both a conceptual and evidential nature.

In *Rugamer v Sony Music Entertainment UK Ltd and McNicol v Balfour Beatty Rail Maintenance* [2001] IRLR 644, EAT ruled that the question whether an impairment was mental or physical turned on the nature of the impairment itself, rather than the activities or functions it affected. In that case, for example, the claimant suffered shoulder pain (which could not be organically explained and which was attributed by the medical evidence to psychological factors). The effect of this was to render such conditions less likely to

---

[21] ADA s.104(c)(4).

[22] Para 13. Para 14, which is to be removed by the DDA 2005, goes on to provide that 'A clinically well-recognised illness is a mental illness which is recognised by a respected body of medical opinion. It is very likely that this would include those specifically mentioned in publications such as the World Health Organisation's International Classification of Diseases.'

qualify as 'disabilities' under the DDA, any mental condition giving rise to them having to be 'clinically well recognised.' The Court of Appeal ([2002] IRLR 711) ruled (*per* Mummery LJ) that 'impairment' bears its ordinary and natural meaning and that it 'may result from an illness or it may consist of an illness,' and stressed the Secretary of State's Guidance which emphasises (para 10) that 'it is not necessary to consider how an impairment was caused.'[23] Notwithstanding this, the Court of Appeal rejected the appeal on the basis that the claimant had not established that his condition (severe back pain) was the result of either a physical or a mental impairment.

EAT ruled in *Morgan v Staffordshire University* [2002] ICR 475 that references in the claimant's medical notes to 'anxiety,' 'stress' and 'depression' were insufficient to establish a 'clinically well recognised' condition. In order to establish such a condition a claimant had to prove that he or she suffered from: (i) 'a mental illness specifically mentioned as such in the World Health Organisation's International Classification of Diseases (WHOICD)'; (ii) 'a mental illness specifically mentioned as such in a publication "such as" that classification, presumably therefore referring to some other classification of very wide professional acceptance'; or (iii) a medical illness recognised by a respected body of medical opinion.' EAT accepted the possibility of a state 'recognisable as mental impairment yet which neither results from nor consists of a mental illness' but took the view that such a state would 'likely . . . rarely if ever [be] invoked and could be expected to require substantial and very specific medical evidence to support its existence.' As the IRLR 'Highlights' (March 2002) pointed out: 'this overlooks the range of mental impairments relating to mental functioning, such as learning disabilities, which cannot be regarded as an "illness".'

Functional Impairment

Section 1 DDA defines disability in terms of 'physical or mental impairment *which has a substantial and long-term adverse effect on [the person's] ability to carry out normal day-to-day activities*' (my emphasis).[24] Except in the case of severe disfigurement this requires (schedule 1) the impairment of 'mobility; manual dexterity; physical co-ordination; continence; ability to lift, carry or otherwise move everyday objects; speech, hearing or eyesight; memory or ability to concentrate, learn or understand; or perception of the risk of physical danger'. In August 2004 the Government rejected the recommendation made by the Parliamentary Scrutiny Committee on the then draft Disability Discrimination Bill that 'ability to care for oneself,' 'ability to communicate and interact with others' and 'perception of reality' should be added to this list (this would have made it easier for those with severe depression to qualify for the protection of the Act).[25] The Guidance issued by the Secretary of State provides, however, that 'disfigurements which consist of a tattoo (which has not been removed), non-medical body piercing, or something attached through such piercing, are to be treated as not having a substantial adverse effect on the person's ability to carry out normal day-to-day activities.'

[23] See also *College of Ripon & York St John v Hobbs* [2002] IRLR 185 in which EAT accepted that the claimant, who experienced muscle cramps, twitching and muscle weakness the organic cause of which (if any) could not be determined was suffering from a 'physical impairment' since the effects of her impairment could be described as 'physical.'

[24] According to EAT in *Vicary v British Telecommunications plc* [1999] IRLR 680 it is for the tribunal (rather than any medical witness) to decide what is a 'normal day-to-day activity' and a 'substantial effect.'

[25] 'Mental illness hurdle to be scrapped' above n 6. The Government's refusal to accept a House of Lords amendment to the effect that anyone who suffered from depression for at least six months should be recognised as disabled was the final sticking point for the Bill.

Genetic Testing

Employees are not protected either in the UK or in the US where a relatively minor medical condition has some real or perceived impact on their ability to do their particular job; or where their employer's pre-employment screening has disclosed a genetic predisposition to cancer or some other condition. Such screening, which was already used by 6 per cent of US employers in 1997, is likely to become ever more common.

The Independent on Sunday 16 November 1997

Weeding out employees who are shown to have a predisposition to an illness associated with particular industrial conditions, such as asthma, eczema or cancer, could have a significant impact on insurance, compensation and re-recruitment costs, while testing potential employees for predispositions to conditions such as heart disease, cancer, arthritis or mental illness could reduce sickness absence costs, identify potential poor performers, prevent the drain of early retirements on pension funds, and reduce premiums on corporate health insurances. Some go as far as suggesting that employers might even find it useful to know whether a potential recruit has a high risk of having a child with a serious genetic illness which could detract their attention, time and energy from work.

And even if the company you work for, or want to work for, isn't keen on genetic spying, insurance companies, who see genetics as another way to load the risk dice, are likely to start applying pressure, increasing premiums or refusing compensation claims to employers they see as neglecting to minimise health risks . . . employees have no legal right to refuse to take a genetic test, nor to claim discrimination or unfair dismissal as a result of refusing. And since taking a genetic test for any reason is now insurance-form declarable . . . the genetic test you have been forced to undergo in order to get a job could jeopardise your ability to secure life insurance, pension or a mortgage.

In the UK, the Human Genetics Advisory Commission's 1999 Report, *The Implications of Genetic Testing for Employment* reported that 'with one exception [the Ministry of Defence] employers in the UK are not currently using genetic test results' and that '[i]t will take major developments both in our understanding of common diseases and in genetic testing itself before genetic testing becomes a serious issue for employment practice.' The report contrasted the position in the UK and Europe with the greater prevalence of testing in the US but warned that 'In view of the rapid pace of developments in human genetics and the possible development of cheaper multi-tests, it might become attractive for employers to make use of genetic test results to predict future health and illness in a cost effective way.' The HGAC advised that genetic testing would not be justified in the employment context except in 'exceptional circumstances . . . where there is strong evidence of a clear connection between the working environment and the development of 'a serious health' condition for which genetic testing can be conducted', the condition being one 'for which the dangers cannot be eliminated or significantly reduced by reasonable measures taken by the employer to modify or respond to the environmental risks'. The HGAC went on to recommend that 'if and when genetic testing in employment becomes a real possibility', individuals should not be required 'to take a genetic test for employment purposes,' or 'to disclose the results of a previous genetic test unless there is clear evidence that the information it provides is needed to assess either current ability to perform a job safely or susceptibility to harm from doing a certain job.'The Disability Rights Task Force's final report, *From Exclusion to Inclusion* (1999), recommended that '[a]t this time, genetic pre-dispositions to impairments should not be considered a disability under the DDA.' The Task Force suggested, however, that:

> [d]isability or disability-related questions before a job is offered should only be permitted in limited circumstances, such as where it is necessary to establish the need for a reasonable adjustment to the interview or selection process or thereafter to do the job and for certain monitoring purposes.

The pressure for genetic testing of employees and others, when it does come, is likely to emanate from the insurance industry. Liberal Democrat health spokesman Nick Harvey has warned of a 'new "underclass" of people unable to get health or life insurance, mortgages, loans or jobs and thereby financially excluded from society.' His Genetic Testing (Consent and Confidentiality) Bill, which was introduced in the Commons on in 25 May 2000, did not is unlikely to become law and the Government has thus far failed to take action in line with the banning recommendation of the HGAC. It did, however, establish the Human Genetics Commission under Baroness Helena Kennedy QC to advise on the ethical and social implications of genetic testing. In April 2000, the German Government declared its intention to ban compulsory genetic testing on staff and customers after insurers suggested that such testing could reduce insurance premiums. The US Government acted similarly in relation to Federal employees in February 2000. In May 2001 the HGC made interim recommendations on the use of genetic information in insurance. These included an 'immediate moratorium on the use by insurance companies of the results of genetic tests' in relation to policies of up to £500,000. The moratorium, which was proposed to last for three years or such longer period as required to review the regulatory options, collect necessary data and resolve the issues satisfactorily, would have prohibited insurance companies from requiring disclosure of adverse results of any genetic tests, or using such results in determining the availability or terms of all classes of insurance, except in relation to policies in excess of £500,000 in relation to which only genetic tests approved by the Genetics and Insurance Committee (GAIC) would be taken into account. In October 2001 the Government and the Association of British Insurers reached agreement on a five-year moratorium on the use of genetic test results by insurers. It applies to life insurance policies of up to £500,000 of life insurance and critical illness, income protection and long-term care insurance policies of up to £300,000. In March 2005 it was announced that the moratorium, which had been due to expire in October 2006, had been extended by agreement to 2011.

Whether any particular impairment should be considered 'substantial' ('more than 'minor' or 'trivial') requires consideration of: the time taken by the person 'to carry out a normal day-to-day activity'; the way in which such an activity is carried out; the 'cumulative effects' where more than a single day-to-day activity is affected; the extent to which the person has or ought to have developed 'coping strategies'; and the effects of the environment on the impairment. The Guidance provides examples of what may and might not be regarded as a significant adverse effect on normal day-to-day activities. These examples, which are described as 'indicators and not tests,' suggest 'what it would, and what it would not, be reasonable to regard as substantial adverse effects.' Among the former category are:

- 'difficulty in going up or down steps, stairs or gradients'
- 'inability to use one or more forms of public transport'
- 'inability to handle a knife and fork at the same time'
- 'ability to pour liquid into another vessel only with unusual slowness or concentration'
- 'even infrequent loss of control of the bowels'
- 'loss of control of the bladder while asleep at least once a month'
- 'inability to carry a moderately loaded tray steadily'
- 'inability to ask specific questions to clarify instructions'
- taking significantly longer than average to say things'
- 'inability to hear and understand another person speaking clearly over the voice telephone'
- 'inability to see to pass the eyesight test for a standard driving test'
- 'total inability to distinguish colours'
- 'intermittent loss of consciousness and associated confused behaviour'
- persistent inability to remember the names of familiar people such as family or friends'
- inability to adapt after a reasonable period to minor change in work routine'
- 'inability to operate safely properly-maintained equipment'
- 'inability to nourish oneself (assuming nourishment is available)'
- 'inability to tell by touch that an object is very hot or cold'.

Regarded by the Guidance as not capable, *considered alone*, of amounting to a 'substantial adverse effect' are:

- 'difficulty walking unaided a distance of about 1.5 kilometres or a mile without discomfort or having to stop'
- 'inability to undertake activities requiring delicate hand movements, such as threading a small needle'
- 'inability to reach typing speeds standardised for secretarial work'
- 'mere clumsiness'
- 'infrequent minor leakage from the bladder'
- 'inability to carry heavy luggage without assistance'
- 'inability to articulate fluently due to a minor stutter, lisp or speech impediment'
- 'inability to speak in front of an audience'
- 'having a strong regional or foreign accent'
- inability to hold a conversation in a very noisy place'
- 'inability to read very small or indistinct print without the aid of a magnifying glass'
- 'inability to distinguish between red and green'
- 'occasionally forgetting the name of a familiar person, such as a colleague'
- 'inability to fill in a long, detailed, technical document without assistance'
- 'minor problems with writing or spelling'
- 'fear of significant heights'
- 'underestimating the risk associated with dangerous hobbies, such as mountain climbing'.

We saw above that the Disability Discrimination Act 2005 provides that those with HIV, muscular dystrophy or multiple sclerosis will be regarded as disabled for the purposes of the DDA regardless of functional impairment (save in the case of any forms of cancer exempted by regulation). Prior to the implementation of the amending Act, people with these conditions are regarded as having suffered substantial adverse effect under s.1 'from the moment any impairment resulting from that condition first has some effect on ability to carry out normal day-to-day activities. The effect need not be continuous and need not be substantial. Further, it may result from treatment for the condition rather than the condition itself. But medical diagnosis of the condition is not by itself enough.'[26] Thus, for example, in *Mowat-Brown v University of Surrey* [2002] IRLR 235 the claimant, who had been diagnosed with multiple sclerosis, failed to establish that he was disabled for the purposes of the Act where the medical evidence was that his condition was 'quiescent.'

The Parliamentary Scrutiny Committee on the then draft Bill recommended that 'all progressive conditions which are currently covered under the DDA when they begin to have an effect should be included from the point of diagnosis,' this on the basis that it was 'inequitable and wrong to cover some progressive conditions from the point of diagnosis and some from the point that they have an effect on a person's ability to carry out day-to-day activities.'[27] The Government accepted 'the principle of this recommendation, but [was] not persuaded that there are any additional progressive conditions where protection would be inadequate once the Bill is enacted.' It stated that it would reserve power to amend the definition of disability by regulation 'if and when the need arises, and it will provide flexibility in the event that case law emerges which shows that the definition is not working in the way intended.'

In *Law Hospital NHS Trust v Rush* [2001] IRLR 611 the Court of Session ruled that the effect of an impairment on work activities was not irrelevant, as work might well include normal day-to-day activities. And in *Cruickshank v VAW Motorcast Ltd* [2002] IRLR 24 EAT ruled that, where the impact of an impairment fluctuates according to whether an employee is at work or not (as here, in which working conditions exacerbated the claimant's asthma), the question whether the condition had a substantial and long-term adverse effect on the employee's ability to perform normal day-to-day activities had to be assessed taking into account both the work and non-work situations. According to EAT, *per* Judge Altman: 'If, whilst at work, an applicant's symptoms are such as to have a significant and long-term effect on his ability to perform day-to-day tasks, such symptoms are not to be ignored simply because the work itself may be specialised and unusual, so long as the disability and its consequences can be measured in terms of the ability of an applicant to undertake day-to-day tasks.' The importance of this decision is that it overturns the prevailing view which was to the effect that a person was not disabled if she could carry out day-to-day activities in all circumstances save the particular circumstances of her particular employment. According to EAT: 'it would risk turning the Act on its head if the employer were able to avoid any liability [to make reasonable adjustments] by dismissing the employee.'

In *Leonard v Southern Derbyshire Chamber of Commerce* [2001] IRLR 19 EAT emphasised that tribunals ought not to balance what a claimant could against what she could not do for the purposes of determining whether her condition substantially impaired her ability to carry out normal day-to-day activities. In that case the claimant, who was clinically depressed, was able to eat and drink and catch a ball, but could not negotiate pavement edges safely. EAT ruled that the tribunal had erred in balancing the former abilities against the latter disability as her ability to catch a ball did not assist the claimant in negotiating pavements. The tribunal ought to concentrate on what a claimant cannot do or can do only with difficulty. And in *Ekpe v Commissioner of Police of the Metropolis* [2001] ICR 1084

---

[26] Sch 1, para 8 and *Kirton v Tetrosyl Ltd* [2003] ICR 1237 (CA).
[27] N 17 above and similarly see the ECNI, 'Enabled? Review of the DDA in Northern Ireland' (2003) available at http://www.equalityni.org.

EAT ruled that, if any of the abilities listed in para 4(1) has been affected 'it must be almost inevitable that there will be some adverse effect upon normal day-to-day activities.' There a tribunal had reached the conclusion that the claimant's inability to put rollers in her hair or to use her right hand to apply makeup did not impair her 'normal day-to-day activities,' as these activities were carried on almost exclusively by women and were therefore not to be considered 'normal'(!). EAT ruled that 'normal' under the DDA is anything not abnormal or unusual, rather than something the majority of people do.

Long-term Effects

In order to qualify as 'disabled' under the DDA, the 'substantial . . . adverse effect' of the claimant's impairment 'on his or her ability to carry out normal day-to-day activities' has to be 'long-term' (s.1), a 'long-term' effect being defined as one which has lasted or is likely to last for at least 12 months from onset, or which is likely to last for the remainder of the disabled person's life.[28]

In *Cruickshank v Motorcast* EAT ruled that the point in time at which it has to be determined whether the effect of an impairment is 'likely' to last for at least 12 months is at the time of the alleged discriminatory act.[29] And in *Swift v Chief Constable of Wiltshire Constabulary* EAT considered the meaning of 'recurring.'[30] The claimant, a civilian communications officer, was absent from work from February to April 2001 and February to July 2002 with what her employers conceded was a recognised psychiatric condition (a 'moderately severe adjustment reaction with predominate symptoms of low mood and anxiety'). She claimed that she had been harassed and bullied by two colleagues and, on her return to work, requested that she should not have to work with them. She was, however, rostered in such a way that she would overlap with them from time to time and claimed that, in failing to comply with her request, her employers had failed to make reasonable adjustments to her shift pattern. The question therefore arose whether she continued to be disabled for the purposes of the DDA. (Note that the question here was whether the employer was under a duty to make reasonable adjustments to the claimant's needs: had the employer treated her less favourably for a reason connected with her condition this would have fallen within the DDA as discrimination relating to a past disability (s.2).)

A consultant psychiatrist reported that between January 2001 and mid-2002 the condition produced a substantial and long-term adverse effect on her ability to carry out normal day-to-day activities but found that those substantial adverse effects were not present after she returned to work, although she continued to have intermittent panic attacks and although he took the view that her symptoms would return to the point of 'impairment' if she had to work with the alleged perpetrators of the harassment. The claimant accepted that the impairment resulting from her illness no longer had a substantial adverse effect on her ability to carry out normal day-to-day activities in July 2002, but argued that she continued to be disabled for the purposes of the DDA because the illness was recurrent. The question which arose was whether it was the *substantial adverse effect of illness on normal day-to-day activities* which had to be likely to recur for Ms Swift to be qualified as disabled for the purposes of the Act, or whether it was sufficient that the *illness* itself was likely to recur. According to EAT (*per* Judge Richardson), it was the former, and a substantial adverse effect was 'likely to recur' if it was more probable than not that the effect would

---

[28] Sch 1, para 2.
[29] [2002] IRLR 24.
[30] [2004] ICR 909.

recur. An illness might result in an impairment which might recur without the illness itself so doing. Conversely, as here, an illness might be likely to recur without the impairment being so likely. The question here, which the tribunal had correctly identified, was whether the claimant was likely to re-experience the original impairment caused by her mental illness—one which affected memory or ability to concentrate to the extent that it had a substantial effect on her ability to carry out normal day-to-day activities, and the tribunal was entitled to conclude that an occasional panic attack or consequent sleepless night did not necessarily have such an effect.

The Effect of Medical Treatment

Save in relation to the correction of sight defects by glasses or contact lenses, no account should be taken by a tribunal or court, in assessing the question of disability, of the effects of treatment upon it. 'This applies even if the measures result in the effects being completely under control or not at all apparent' (Secretary of State's Guidance on disability, para A12).[31] Thus (para A13):

> if a person with a hearing impairment wears a hearing aid the question whether his or her impairment has a substantial adverse effect is to be decided by reference to what the hearing level would be without the hearing aid. And in the case of someone with diabetes, whether or not the effect is substantial should be decided by reference to what the condition would be if he or she was not taking medication.

In *Kapadia v London Borough of Lambeth* [2000] IRLR 14, EAT accepted that counselling being received by a claimant who had suffered from reactive depression was 'treatment' for the purposes of the DDA, despite the fact that it was directed at the alleviation of symptoms of the illness rather than at its cause. Thus the claimant was entitled to have his claim to disability assessed on the basis of what his condition would have been absent the counselling (there being uncontested medical evidence that without the counselling there was a strong likelihood that he would have had a mental breakdown). In *Abadeh v British Telecommunications* [2001] ICR 156 EAT distinguished between continuing and concluded medical treatment ruling that, in the latter case, the 'deduced effect' provisions had no application and the claimant had to be assessed as he or she presented. EAT further distinguished between continuing medical treatment which has resulted in a permanent improvement, and that which has not. As in the case of concluded medical treatment, continuing treatment whose impact is permanent (or, more precisely, which was permanent at the time of the discrimination) ought not to be disregarded for the purposes of determining whether the claimant is 'disabled' for the purposes of the DDA. Tribunals ought, however, to bear in mind that a claimant who is discriminated against on the basis that he or she has been disabled in the past is also protected by the DDA.

In *Woodrup v London Borough of Southwark* [2003] IRLR 52 the Court of Appeal took a very narrow approach to the 'deduced effects' provisions of the DDA and ruled that, where someone sought to rely on the effects a condition *would have had* in the absence of treatment (but did *not in fact have*, because of the treatment being received), the claimant 'should be required to prove his or her alleged disability with some particularity.' The Court

---

[31] Similarly under the ADA 'The determination of whether an individual is substantially limited in a major life activity must be made on a case by case basis, without regard to mitigating measures such as medicines, or assistive or prosthetic devices. . .'

there dismissed an appeal by a claimant who had failed to provide medical evidence in support of her argument that, if her psychotherapy treatment for anxiety neurosis had been discontinued, her impairment would have had a substantial adverse effect on her ability to carry out normal day-to-day activities. According to Simon Brown LJ, who delivered the leading judgment: 'Those seeking to invoke this peculiarly benign doctrine . . . should not readily expect to be indulged by the tribunal of fact' and an employment tribunal should not have to 'pretend that the applicant is in fact disabled when it knows that he or she is not.'

Direct Discrimination

In this part of the chapter we consider only 'discrimination' as it is defined in the DDA and to the extent that it differs from the concepts of discrimination employed in the other anti-discrimination legislation. The more general approach to discrimination is considered in Chapter 2, while Chapter 4 considers those areas in which discrimination is regulated under the DDA and other legislation.

The DDA's approach to discrimination differs significantly from that of the other discrimination legislation in a number of respects. In the first place, the Act contains no prohibition of indirect discrimination). Secondly, discrimination is not unlawful if the employer shows that it is 'justifiable' although, as a result of amendments designed to bring the Act into line with the Employment Equality Directive, no such defence is permitted in relation to employment-related 'direct' disability discrimination or failure to make reasonable adjustment (see below). 'Justifiability' differs according to the context in which the alleged discrimination occurs and is discussed in the final section of this chapter.

In Chapter 2 we came across the requirement set out in s.5(3) SDA and its equivalents[32] that comparison for the purposes of determining whether discrimination has occurred should be between persons (real or hypothetical) in the same 'relevant circumstances.' Post-amendment, the DDA defines 'direct discrimination' in employment as occurring (s.3A(5)) if 'on the ground of the disabled person's disability, [a person] treats the disabled person less favourably than he treats or would treat a person not having that particular disability whose relevant circumstances, including his abilities, are the same as, or not materially different from, those of the disabled person.' This is broadly similar to the normal model of direct discrimination, though its application by the courts has yet to be tested. Some examples are, however, provided in the new Code of Practice on Employment and Occupation.

DRC, 'Code of Practice on Employment and Occupation', paras 4.8–4.13

. . . if the less favourable treatment occurs because of the employer's generalised, or stereo-typical, assumptions about the disability or its effects, it is likely to be direct discrimination. This is because an employer would not normally make such assumptions about a non-disabled person, but would instead consider his individual abilities.

---

[32] S. 3(4) RRA, reg 3(2) SO Regs and RB Regs.

- A blind woman is not short-listed for a job involving computers because the employer wrongly assumes that blind people cannot use them. The employer makes no attempt to look at the individual circumstances. The employer has treated the woman less favourably than other people by not short-listing her for the job. The treatment was on the ground of the woman's disability (because assumptions would not have been made about a non-disabled person).

In addition, less favourable treatment which is disability-specific, or which arises out of prejudice about disability (or about a particular type of disability), is also likely to amount to direct discrimination.

- An employer seeking a shop assistant turns down a disabled applicant with a severe facial disfigurement solely on the ground that other employees would be uncomfortable working alongside him. This would amount to direct discrimination and would be unlawful.

Direct discrimination will often occur where the employer is aware that the disabled person has a disability, and this is the reason for the employer's treatment of him. Direct discrimination need not be conscious—people may hold prejudices that they do not admit, even to themselves. Thus, a person may behave in a discriminatory way while believing that he would never do so. Moreover, direct discrimination may sometimes occur even though the employer is unaware of a person's disability.

- An employer advertises a promotion internally to its workforce. The job description states that people with a history of mental illness would not be suitable for the post. An employee who would otherwise be eligible for the promotion has a history of schizophrenia, but the employer is unaware of this. The employee would, nevertheless, have a good claim for unlawful direct discrimination in relation to the promotion opportunities afforded to him by his employer. The act of direct discrimination in this case is the blanket ban on anyone who has had a mental illness, effectively rejecting whole categories of people with no consideration of their individual abilities . . .

In determining whether a disabled person has been treated less favourably in the context of direct discrimination, his treatment must be compared with that of an appropriate comparator. This must be someone who does not have the same disability. It could be a non-disabled person or a person with other disabilities.

- A person who becomes disabled takes six months' sick leave because of his disability, and is dismissed by his employer. A non-disabled fellow employee also takes six months' sick leave (because he has broken his leg) but is not dismissed. The difference in treatment is attributable to the employer's unwillingness to employ disabled staff and the treatment is therefore on the ground of disability. The non-disabled employee is an appropriate comparator in the context of direct discrimination because his relevant circumstances are the same as those of the disabled person. It is the fact of having taken six months' sick leave which is relevant in these circumstances. As the disabled person has been treated less favourably than the comparator, this is direct discrimination.

Disability-related Discrimination

'Direct' discrimination is expressly regulated by the DDA only in relation to employment (Part II of the Act), but 'disability-related' discrimination is prohibited also in relation to Parts II (goods, facilities and services and premises) and Part IV (education). Section 3A(1) DDA provides (in the employment context) that:

. . . a person discriminates against a disabled person if—

(a) for a reason which relates to the disabled person's disability, he treats him less favourably than he treats or would treat others to whom that reason does not or would not apply, and

(b) he cannot show that the treatment in question is justified.

Section 3A(1) is concerned with employment, but the definition of disability-related discrimination does not differ across the various areas regulated by the DDA. The test for justification does, however, vary with the context (see further below). As far as employment (broadly defined) is concerned, disability-related discrimination falling outside new s.3A(5) ('direct discrimination') is capable of being justified under the DDA 'if, but only if, the reason for it is both material to the circumstances of the particular case and substantial.' The application of this test is considered in detail below.

The breadth of this form of 'discrimination,' which is unique to the DDA, is clear from the Court of Appeal's decision in *Clark v TDG Ltd (t/a Novacold)* [1999] ICR 951.[33] An employment tribunal had rejected a claim that a man dismissed for disability-related absence from work had been discriminated against contrary to the then equivalent of s.3A(1) DDA. According to the tribunal, and to EAT, the treatment meted out to Mr Clark had to be compared with that which a non-disabled employee who was absent for a similar period of time had or would have received (this, the reader will recognise, is the approach taken by the UK courts, pre-*Webb v EMO Air Cargo (UK) Ltd (No.2)* [1995] ICR 1021, to pregnancy dismissal).

The tribunal dismissed the DDA claim on the basis that a comparable non-disabled employee would also have been dismissed. The Court of Appeal disagreed. Having pointed out that the differences between the RRA and SDA, on the one hand, and the DDA, on the other, were such that the interpretation of the latter 'is not facilitated by familiarity' with the former, Mummery LJ (for the Court) relied both on statements made by the Minister for Social Security and Disabled People during the second reading of the Bill (below)[34] and upon the Code of Practice on Rights of Access to Goods, Facilities and Services to lay down the following principles:

(1) Less favourable treatment of a disabled person is only discriminatory under s 5(1) if it is unjustified.

(2) Treatment is less favourable if the reason for it does not or would not apply to others.

(3) In deciding whether that reason does not or would not apply to others, it is not appropriate to make a comparison of the cases in the same way as in the [SDA] and the [RRA]. It is simply a case of identifying others to whom the reason for the treatment does not or would not apply. The test of less favourable treatment is based on the reason for the treatment of the disabled person and not on the fact of his disability. It does not turn on a like-for-like comparison of the treatment of the disabled person and of others in similar circumstances . . .

The DDA does not expressly regulate indirect discrimination as such. But it was recognised by the Court of Appeal in *Clark v Novacold* that the definition of discrimination adopted—in particular, the omission of any section equivalent to s.5(3) SDA—was such as

[33] A similar decision was reached by EAT in *British Sugar v Kirker* [1998] IRLR 624.
[34] 'The Bill is drafted in such a way that indirect as well as direct discrimination can be dealt with . . . A situation where dogs are not admitted to a cafe, with the effect that blind people would he unable to enter it, would be a prima facie case of indirect discrimination against blind people and would be unlawful' HC Debs vol 253, 24 January 1995, col.150.

to include that which would be characterised as indirect discrimination under the RRA or SDA. The Court drew attention to the comments made by the minister responsible for the Act and the examples of unlawful discrimination given in the Code of Practice:

> On the second reading of the Bill for this Act the Minister for Social Security and Disabled People stated: 'The Bill is drafted in such a way that indirect as well as direct discrimination can be dealt with . . . A situation where dogs are not admitted to a cafe, with the effect that blind people would he unable to enter it, would be a prima facie case of indirect discrimination against blind people and would be unlawful'[35] . . .
>
> The same point can be made on the example given in the Code of Practice on Rights of Access issued by the Secretary of State at para 2.12: 'A waiter asks a disabled customer to leave the restaurant because she has difficulty eating as a result of her disability. He serves other customers who have no difficulty eating. The waiter has therefore treated her less favourably than other customers. The treatment was for a reason related to her disability— her difficulty when eating. And the reason for her less favourable treatment did not apply to other customers. If the waiter could not justify the less favourable treatment, he would have discriminated unlawfully.'

Both of these cases would be characterised as indirect discrimination under the other discrimination legislation—the café and restaurant customers were subject to conditions (respectively, being without a dog and eating without difficulty) with which they, as disabled persons, were less able to comply with than non-disabled persons would be. Further, the approach taken by the DDA avoids the technical difficulties 'associated with the definitions of indirect discrimination adopted by these Acts (see Chapter 2). Certainly, the Under-Secretary of State for Employment, in Standing Committee, stated that the DDA: 'firmly cover[s]—and [is] intended to cover—the use of standards, administrative methods, work practices or procedures that adversely affect a disabled person.'[36]

Examples of disability-related discrimination outside the employment context are provided by the Code of Practice on Rights of Access to Goods, Facilities, Services and Premises, and the Codes of Practice on Schools and on Post 16 Education.

Disability Rights Commission, 'Code of Practice for Schools', paras 5.7–5.10

A father seeks admission to a primary school for his son, who has epilepsy. The school tells him that they cannot take the boy unless he stops having fits.

In effect, the school is placing conditions on the boy's admission because he might have fits. Having fits is an intrinsic part of the boy's epilepsy. The reason for the less favourable treatment is one that relates to the boy's disability . . . the comparison has to be made between the treatment that he got and the treatment someone else got, or would get, if they did not have fits. In this case, other children did not have this condition placed on their admission, nor would they have. So, for a reason that relates to his disability, this boy is being treated less favourably than another child to whom that reason does not apply . . .

A pupil with Tourette's Syndrome is stopped from going on a school visit because he has used abusive language in class. The school has a policy of banning pupils from trips and after-school activities if they swear or are abusive to staff.

The reason for not allowing the pupil to go on the school visit is his use of abusive language. His involuntary swearing is a symptom of his Tourette's Syndrome. This is less favourable treatment for a reason that relates to the pupil's disability . . . The comparison

---

[35] *Ibid.*
[36] HC Standing Committee E, col. 142, cited by Doyle, above n 11, 6.

has to be made with others who had not used abusive language. In this case, the pupil who used abusive language, which is directly related to his disability, was treated less favourably than pupils who had not used abusive language. So, for a reason that relates to his disability, this boy is being treated less favourably than another child to whom that reason does not apply.

The 'less favourable treatment' duty does not mean that disabled pupils have an excuse for disruptive or antisocial behaviour. There has to be a direct relationship between the reason for the less favourable treatment and the child's disability.

The claimant in *Edwards v Mid Suffolk District Council*, who suffered from chronic anxiety disorder, was dismissed as a result of his inability to work with his assistant.[37] There was conflicting medical evidence. His GP had suggested that, although the claimant's 'most recent difficulties have been largely associated with stresses arising in his workplace, in particular his working relationship with his allocated assistant,' he was 'medically fit for all his contracted duties [and] . . . interpersonal difficulties rather than illness' were the reason why he was unable to undertake his normal duties. Another doctor, Dr Helps, had provided evidence that, had the employers recognised the claimant's disability: 'it would have helped him considerably. The problems encountered with his assistant exacerbated his anxiety state and he was unable to cope. If the council had made reasonable adjustments to [the Claimant's] working arrangements, his stress levels would have been reduced and performance would have improved significantly.' The claimant's DDA claim was dismissed by a tribunal which concluded that:

> the cause of the breakdown in the relationship between employer and employee was nothing whatsoever to do with the applicant's disability. The applicant deliberately, selfishly, consistently and obdurately set his face against working with Mrs Batchelor. It is right that he has suffered from ME in the past and that he has a chronic anxiety state. It may well be the case that his conduct has exacerbated his illness. We are satisfied, however, that he has not established that his conduct towards Mrs Batchelor and Mr Chilton was caused by his illness. We are satisfied that, with the benefit of hindsight and having visited solicitors, that he is using his mental illness as a stick with which to beat the employer. We are therefore satisfied that the disability claim is a complete red herring and that the applicant was well capable of performing his duties at all relevant times in accordance with the report of Dr Duncan and that there is nothing in this case, other than the applicant's evidence which we do not accept, to gainsay that medical opinion.

EAT allowed Mr Edwards' appeal on the basis that the tribunal had erred in law by failing to make a finding on the impact of the claimant's disability on his behaviour and ability to carry out his work, and remitted the case to a differently constituted employment tribunal.

Edwards v Mid Suffolk District Council [2001] ICR 616

Judge Levy QC:

It is clear . . . that the tribunal's sympathy on the facts as found was entirely with the council and that theirs was a clear holding that the appellant was the author of his own misfortunes and that the DDA claim was 'entirely spurious'. . . .

Ms Moor [for the employers] submitted that from the finding that the disability claim was a red herring and that the report of Dr Duncan, found to be an impressive witness, each

---

37 [2001] ICR 616.

supported a finding that the appellant was 'well capable of performing his duties.' In those circumstances she submitted we could be satisfied that other medical evidence to that of Dr Duncan had been considered and rejected.

We are unable to accept Ms Moor's submission. If a tribunal is to reach a conclusion that there is no connection between disability and an appellant's work behaviour, we agree with Mr Carr's submission [for the claimant] that it is necessary for the tribunal to explain why. It is not sufficient simply to state that there is no connection . . .

Where dismissal under the provisions of the DDA is a ground of complaint, in our judgment it is jejune of the tribunal to state, without more, why conduct and disability are unconnected and why the possibility of adjustment being made to benefit a person under a DDA disability is not to be considered. In our judgment it is essential in a case such as this for a tribunal, first, to make findings of the nature and extent of an applicant's disability, and then to consider its impact in terms of his ability to carry out his allotted work. We think Mr Carr is right in submitting that in order to consider whether an employer fails to make reasonable adjustments to a disabled employee's work, it is essential to consider the nature and extent of disability in the context of his work. We cannot find such analysis here and this fatally flaws the tribunal's decision . . .

We have referred already to the evidence of Dr Helps . . . We appreciate, as Ms Moor submitted, that the tribunal accepted the evidence of Dr Duncan that the appellant's anxiety symptoms were not the *cause* of the difficulties with Mrs Batchelor . . . We accept, as Ms Moor submits, that . . . the tribunal rejects the submission that illness *caused* his inappropriate behaviour to Mrs Batchelor and Mr Chilton. However, it is clear that Dr Helps expressed the view that his disability contributed to that behaviour. The tribunal may have been entitled to reject, as they did, the *appellant*'s own evidence as to what caused the breakdown. However, there is no analysis of why Dr Helps's evidence was rejected, as it appears to have been . . .

In a case where a disability claim is put forward by a litigant who has disabilities coming within the DDA, in our judgment a tribunal is not entitled to sidestep the medical issues raised. It is under a duty to summarise and take into account medical evidence adduced on behalf of the applicant; if it rejects that evidence, it is under a duty to explain why. The other findings on which Ms Moor relied, all findings of the tribunal as to the effect of the appellant's ability to work, are, in our judgment, flawed because of the failure to examine and make findings on medical evidence put forward.

For the respondent, Ms Moor also submitted that dismissal of the appellant was inevitable in any event, given the findings of fact of the tribunal. She sought to support the decision on that ground. Mr Carr submitted that Ms Moor's submission ignored the fact that the tribunal appear not to have considered the nature and extent of the appellant's disability and the requirement placed upon the council by the DDA. Had the tribunal concluded that the nature of his disability was such that there was a connection between the appellant's behaviour in relation to Mrs Batchelor and/or that the council should have made reasonable adjustments by removing her from contacts with him, their conclusion that the dismissal was nevertheless fair might not have followed. We accept Mr Carr's submission that if the breakdown in a working relationship had arisen substantially out of an employer's failure to comply with the provisions of the DDA by making adjustments, a claim by the employee of unfair dismissal might succeed in the light of the failure by the tribunal to make sufficient findings as to the extent of the appellant's impairment and the effect of this on his work behaviour. We cannot accept Ms Moor's submission that dismissal was inevitable in any event.

The decision in *Edwards* was reached under Part II of the Act. But the definition of disability-related discrimination which applies there is the same as that which applies in relation to Parts III and IV DDA so EAT's approach ought to be followed by county courts and by Special Educational Needs and Disability Tribunals (and, in Wales the Special Educational Needs Tribunal).

In *O'Neill v Symm & Co Ltd* [1998] ICR 481, EAT ruled that an employer could not discriminate 'by reason of' disability unless he knew or ought reasonably to have known of the complainant's disability. We shall see, below, that specific statutory provision is made in the employment context in relation to the duty to make reasonable adjustments (s.4A(3)) provides that no such duty is imposed 'on an employer in relation to a disabled person if the employer does not know, and could not reasonably be expected to know—(a) in the case of an applicant or potential applicant, that the disabled person concerned is, or may be, an applicant for the employment; or (b) in any case, that that person has a disability and is likely to be affected in the way mentioned in subsection (1).' Part IV DDA (education) provides defences in relation both to less favourable treatment and the duty to make adjustments where the alleged discriminator 'did not know and could not reasonably have been expected to know, that he was disabled' (s.28B). No such express provision is made, however, in relation to less favourable treatment under Part II or III DDA (employment and goods, services, etc).

The claimant in *O'Neill* had not informed her employers that she had been diagnosed as having ME, although she did inform them that she had suffered (and recovered) from viral pneumonia a number of months before her appointment. She was dismissed for absence (15.5 days in her first three months) having, contrary to her contractual obligations, failed to provide sick notes. A tribunal accepted that Ms O'Neill came within s.1 of the Act, but ruled that the employer's ignorance of her condition, coupled with the fact that her dismissal was because of her uncertified absences, meant that she was not discriminated against because she had a disability. On the face of it, this was inconsistent with the decision of the Court of Appeal in *Clark*. EAT (prior to the Court of Appeal decision in *Clark*) upheld the tribunal's ruling, Kirkwood J for the Court rejecting the appellant's argument that s.5(1) was satisfied on proof: '(a) that the employee is a disabled person; (b) [of] less favourable treatment; [and] (c) for a reason that relates to the disabled person's disability.' In *Heinz Co Ltd v Kendrick*, however, EAT took a different approach. The case concerned a man who had been dismissed after a period of a year's absence but before he received a confirmed diagnosis to the effect that he was suffering from ME. Having pointed out that the tribunal's decision pre-dated reports of the Court of Appeal, the appeal tribunal rejected the argument that the reason for the less favourable treatment had to be judged, subjectively, from the employer's point of view.

Heinz Co Ltd v Kendrick [2000] ICR 419

Lindsay J:

Among the points made by *Clark v Novacold* in the Court of Appeal is that a textual comparison between the disability discrimination legislation and that relating to sex or race discrimination is not helpful and may even be misleading . . .

O'Neill . . . appears to conclude that there cannot be some less favourable treatment of a person by an employer within Section 5(1)(a) of the 1995 Act being properly held to be for a reason that relates to that person's disability unless the employer has knowledge of the disability 'or at least the material features of it as set out in Schedule I of the Act' . . .

We would hesitate before adopting that view. Firstly, its adoption, if Mr Linden's argument on behalf of Heinz in this case is a guide, would, we fear, lead in many cases to hair-splitting medical evidence. We were addressed on whether CFS was a physical or mental condition or some combination of the two, was it psychosomatic, was it clinically well-recognised, was it long-term? One can readily imagine cases in which, if detailed knowledge were to be relevant as *O'Neill* was argued to require, there would need to be medical evidence as to the labels which could be attached to this or that symptom or aggregation of symptoms as a person's condition deteriorated or improved. We cannot think such an approach was within the legislature's broad intendment.

Secondly, the conclusion arrived at in *O'Neill* was based partly on a comparison between the legislative provisions relating to disability discrimination and those relating to other forms of discrimination, a comparison which, as *Clark v Novacold* has since held, can be misleading.[38] . . .

one can imagine, for example, a postman or messenger who, at his engagement and for a while afterwards, successfully conceals the fact that he has an artificial leg and can walk only for short distances at a time. He may later be dismissed for a conduct or capability ground, namely that he had proved to be unacceptably slow in making his rounds, but still without his disability being spotted. His slowness could have been taken by the employer to have been by reason of idleness or absenteeism. If, however, the employee were then able to show that his slowness was by reason of his having an artificial leg then, as it seems to us, he would, in such a case, have been treated less favourably 'than others to whom that reason does not apply' (namely, as *Clark v Novacold* requires, less favourably than other employees who did their rounds at an acceptable pace).

Moreover he would have been so treated for a reason—unacceptable slowness—which related to his disability. That, it seems to us, would be the case whether or not the employer ever knew before the dismissal that the reason for the slowness was that the employee was disabled. The employee would, as it seems to us, have been discriminated against within the Act even if the employer had assumed that the slowness was attributable only to laziness or absenteeism. As another example, one might imagine a secretary dismissed because he or she, despite repeated training, persisted in typing hopelessly misspelt letters, yet without the employer or, perhaps, even the employee knowing that the reason for the errors was not ignorance or carelessness but dyslexia . . .

there is no language in section 5(1) that requires that the relationship between the disability and the treatment should be adjudged subjectively, through the eyes of the employer, so that the applicable test should be the objective one of whether the relationship exists, not whether the employer knew of it. Indeed, unless the test is objective there will be difficulties with credible and honest yet ignorant or obtuse employers who fail to recognise or acknowledge the obvious . . .

The phrase, 'which relates to' in the expression, in Section 5(1)(a), of 'for a reason which relates to the disabled person's disability' widens the description of the reasons which may be relevant beyond what the case would have been had the Act said 'by reason of . . . the disability.' As we see it, the expression may include a reason deriving from how the disability manifests itself even where there is no knowledge of the disability as such. This, we think, opens no floodgates but it does require employers to pause to consider whether the reason for some dismissal that they have in mind might relate to disability and, if it might, to reflect on the Act and the Code before dismissing. There is, in our judgment, no need to imply into the statute a requirement not expressly present, namely that the employer should know of the disability as such or as to whether its material features fell within or without Schedule 1 of the 1995 Act. It may be that *O'Neill* does not, in any case, go that far. This is not to say, though, that such knowledge or its absence may not be highly material to justifiability under Section 5(1)(b) or Section 5(2)(b) or as to the steps to be considered or taken under Section 6—see also Section 6(6)(b).

---

[38] EAT further suggested that the decision of EAT in *Del Monte Foods v Mundon* [1980] ICR 694 to the effect that a woman can be dismissed 'in connection with' pregnancy only where an employer knows that she is pregnant was incorrect.

In *Quinn v Schwarzkopf Ltd* [2002] IRLR 602 the Court of Sessions ruled that an employer could discharge the onus of justifying a failure to make reasonable accommodation where it did not apply its mind to the issue because of its ignorance about the fact of the claimant's disability. The claimant had been dismissed for absence related to a condition which, it later transpired, was rheumatoid arthritis. The issue of justification is considered below. Here it is sufficient to state yet again that, whereas 'discrimination' as defined by s.3A(1) DDA can be justified, 'direct' discrimination as newly defined by s.3A(5) DDA cannot.

Duty to Make Adjustments

B Doyle, 'Enabling legislation or dissembling law? The Disability Discrimination Act 1995' (1997) 60 *Modern Law Review* 64, 74, footnotes omitted

The duty to make reasonable adjustments will assume . . . great[ ] importance as a means to prevent (or to require the adjustment of) unjustifiable practices, rules, policies, requirements or conditions which have a harsh or adverse impact upon access by disabled persons and to compensate for the absence of an explicit prohibition on indirect disability discrimination. The concept of a reasonable accommodation or adjustment is at the heart of disability discrimination statutes in other jurisdictions. It is an example of legally mandated positive action rather than a requirement of reverse or positive discrimination. A failure without justification to comply with a duty to make reasonable adjustments will amount to an act of discrimination.

The issue of justification is further considered below, though it is worth noting here that recent amendments to the DDA have removed the possibility, in the employment context, of justifying a failure to make reasonable adjustments. Across the DDA, in addition, service providers and educational institutions, etc, cannot justify disability-related discrimination unless they establish that the discrimination would have been justified even if the discriminator had complied with any duty of reasonable adjustment imposed upon them by the DDA.[39]

The imposition upon employers and others of duties to make adjustments to accommodate the needs of disabled people are, in one sense, radical, none of the other discrimination legislation imposing, *in express terms*, any duty of adjustment. It is true that the concept of indirect discrimination can, on occasion, impose an obligation to adjust (by, for example, permitting mothers to work part-time). But under the DDA, by contrast with the position under the other legislation, the expectation is that the employer or service provider will adjust. Under the other legislative provisions, a complaint about a failure to adjust currently requires that the claimant proves the ingredients of indirect discrimination. These have been simplified as a result of the application of the Burden of Proof Directive to the employment-related provisions of the SDA, the application of the Racial Equality Directive to the race and ethnic or national origins provisions of the RRA, and the application of the Employment Equality Directive to FETO, but complexities remain (not least because of the proliferation of different definitions of indirect discrimination—see further Chapter 2). The exact nature of the duty varies across the different context in which the

---

[39] Or, other than in an employment-related case, justifiably failed to do so.

DDA regulates disability discrimination, and will be considered separately in relation to each.

The first point to note about the duty to adjust as it applies in the employment field is that it is not a free-standing obligation, but arises in connection with specific disabled individuals. In this, Part II of the DDA[40] differs from Parts III and IV (goods, services, facilities and premises, and education) which impose *anticipatory* duties (see below). Employers and others covered by Part II DDA are under no obligations to make adjustments prior to being confronted with a particular individual whose disability results in the need for such an adjustment although, as the new employment Code of Practice points out (para 2.13): 'it is a good idea for employers to keep all their policies under review, and to consider the needs of disabled people as part of this process. It is advisable for employers to do this in addition to having a specific policy to prevent discrimination.'

Prior to its amendment in October 2004 the duty to make reasonable adjustments was set out in s.6(1) DDA. Ss.5(2) DDA provided that 'an employer . . . discriminates against a disabled person if (a) he fails to comply with a s.6 duty imposed on him in relation to the disabled person; and (b) he cannot show that his failure to comply with that duty is justified.' Section 6 DDA then went on to provide that the duty to adjust arose where '(a) any arrangements made by or on behalf of an employer, or (b) any physical feature of premises occupied by an employer, place[d] the disabled person concerned at a substantial disadvantage in comparison with persons who are not disabled,' in which case the employer was required to 'take such steps as are reasonable, in all the circumstances of the case, for him to have to take in order to prevent the arrangements or feature having that effect.'[41] The duty to adjust was qualified by s.6(2) which provided that s.6(1) 'applies only in relation to—(a) arrangements for determining to whom employment should be offered; (b) any term, condition or arrangements on which employment, promotion, a transfer, training or any other benefit is offered or afforded.'[42]

The limitations of the duty to make reasonable adjustments, as it was originally couched, were made apparent in a number of cases. In *Kenny v Hampshire Constabulary* [1999] ICR 27, for example, EAT ruled that the duty of reasonable adjustment did not extend to the provision of personal assistance to enable a cerebral palsy sufferer to use the toilet (this because not every 'arrangement which could be made to facilitate the disabled person's employment falls within the definition in section 6(2)'). In *Clark v Novacold* [1999] ICR 951 the Court of Appeal ruled that the duty to adjust did not apply to dismissals (though it could apply to pre-dismissal arrangements such as selection for redundancy). And in *Archibald v Fife Council* [2004] IRLR 197 the Court of Sessions ruled that s.6 applied only to changes in a particular position rather than, as the claimant argued here, to a transfer between jobs of a worker who could no longer fulfil the basic functions of her job even with any adjustments which might be made to it. This approach, which was curiously reminiscent of that taken by Mr Justice Wood in *Clymo v Wandsworth London Borough Council* [1989] ICR 250 (see Chapter 2) was overruled by the House of Lords but illustrates the difficulties caused by the non-comprehensive nature of s.6.

---

[40] Which covers discrimination not only in relation to 'employment' strictly so-called but also in relation to contract workers, partners, office holders, police and prison officers, barristers and advocates, people undertaking practical work experience, and applies to the trustees and managers of occupational pension schemes, insurers providing group insurance, landlords of employer premises, employees and agents, Ministers of the Crown.

[41] S.15 provides a duty of reasonable adjustment by trade organisations in similar terms.

[42] In relation to discrimination by trade organisations (s.15(2)), to 'arrangements for determining who should become or remain a member . . . [and] any term, condition or arrangements on which membership or any benefit is offered or afforded.'

In *Archibald v Fife Council (Scotland)* [2004] ICR 954 the House of Lords ruled that the terms, conditions and arrangements relating to the essential functions of a person's job were 'arrangements made by the employer' for the purposes of s.6(1) DDA, as is the liability of a person to be dismissed if he or she becomes incapable of fulfilling the job description, and that this liability would place a disabled person at a 'substantial disadvantage' compared with a non-disabled person. Their Lordships further ruled that the duty to make reasonable adjustments may require an employer to treat a disabled person more favourably than a non-disabled person, for example, by transferring him or her to a suitable vacant post. Section 6(7) DDA, which provides that 'nothing in this Part is to be taken to require an employer to treat a disabled person more favourably than he treats or would treat others' is qualified by the phrase 'subject to the provisions of this section' (s.6) which may require the employer to treat the disabled person more favourably than others.

'Reasonable adjustment duty may require transfer to another job' 132 *Equal Opportunities Review*

This decision recognises that the DDA is concerned with addressing the special needs of people with disabilities, and that the approach taken to this is different from that in other discrimination legislation. As [Baroness] Hale points out, under the [SDA] and [RRA] everyone is to be treated equally: 'men and women, black or white, as the case may be, are opposite sides of the same coin . . . Treating men more favourably than women discriminates against women. Treating women more favourably than men discriminates against men.' The DDA does not expect disabled and non-disabled people to be treated in the same way. It makes provision for 'reasonable adjustments' to be made to meet the special needs of disabled people. It is made clear that the DDA 'entails a measure of positive discrimination, in the sense that employers are required to take steps to help disabled people which they are not required to take for others.' However, it is also the case that employers are required to take only those steps 'which in all the circumstances it is reasonable for them to have to take.' So, in discussing how far the duty goes, it is established that the scope of the duty is to be determined by what is reasonable 'considered in the light of the factors set out in s.6(4) [now s.18B].' That section sets out factors that should be taken into account in determining what steps are reasonable, including the extent to which the step would prevent the disadvantage, the extent to which it is practicable for the employer and the financial costs incurred.

It was also recognised that underlying the debate in this case was 'a fundamental philosophical difference about the permissible limits of positive discrimination which the duty to make reasonable adjustments inevitably entails.' The fundamental difference here was when the duty to make reasonable adjustments is 'triggered' to use Hale LJ's [sic] phraseology. The council argued that the duty arises only in relation to the removal of obstacles in the way of a disabled person doing the job they are employed to do (eg adapting premises, modifying equipment, etc), which will then enable a disabled person to compete with others on a 'level playing field.' The duty does not arise, it was argued, where a person cannot do the job at all. The Disability Rights Commission argued, on the contrary, that the duty is triggered in such circumstances, and that the control mechanism lies in the fact that the employer is required to take such steps as it is reasonable for it to have taken.

The House of Lords' decision has returned common sense to the interpretation of the s.6 duty to make adjustments. As Lord Hope states: 'it is not simply a duty to make adjustments. The making of adjustments is not an end in itself. The end is reached when the disabled person is no longer at a substantial disadvantage, in comparison with persons who are not disabled.'

The question remaining is whether or not the council acted reasonably in its application of its redeployment policy. The House of Lords commends the council on the considerable care taken to help Ms Archibald find an alternative post—for example, it arranged retraining and automatically short-listed her for available posts. It went beyond its normal redeployment policies. But it drew the line at transferring her to a 'slightly higher grade' without undergoing a competitive interview.

One reason considered by the court for the council sticking to its policy on redeployment is s.7 of the Local Government and Housing Act 1989, which requires that all staff engaged by a local authority must be appointed 'on merit.' Although recognising this as an 'extremely important principle,' it is pointed out that it is subject to the provisions of the DDA, as expressly stated in s.7(2)(f) of the Local Government and Housing Act.

The case has been remitted to the employment tribunal to consider whether the council fulfilled its s.6(1) duty to take such steps as was reasonable in all the circumstances. Although leaving the decision on reasonableness to the employment tribunal, the judges did comment on the circumstances. For example, Hale LJ [sic] says that it might (with the emphasis on 'might') 'be reasonable to expect a small modification either in general or in the particular case to meet the needs of a well-qualified and well-motivated employee who has become disabled.' She goes on to say: 'We are not talking here of high-grade positions where it is not only possible but important to make fine judgments about who will be best for the job. We are talking of positions which a great many people could fill and for which no one candidate may be obviously "the best."' She poses the question 'whether this case should have been seen as a sideways rather than an upwards move.'

Clearly this decision does not mean that a disabled person should be given preferential treatment for any post for which they are qualified. However, it does make clear that the scope of the s.6 duty to make reasonable adjustments is much wider than the lower courts believed, and that employers are going to have to consider carefully what positive measures they can take to remove the disadvantages that disabled employees, or prospective employees, may face.

The decision of the House of Lords in *Archibald* is to be welcomed for its purposive and progressive approach to the duty to adjust. Its practical significance, however, is limited as s.6 DDA has been replaced, as of October 2004, with s.4A DDA which provides as follows:

(1) Where—
    (a) a provision, criterion or practice applied by or on behalf of an employer, or
    (b) any physical feature of premises occupied by the employer
    places the disabled person concerned at a substantial disadvantage in comparison with persons who are not disabled, it is the duty of the employer to take such steps as it is reasonable, in all the circumstances of the case, for him to have to take in order to prevent the provision, criterion or practice, or feature, having that effect.
(2) In subsection (1), 'the disabled person concerned' means—
    (a) in the case of a provision, criterion or practice for determining to whom employment should be offered, any disabled person who is, or has notified the employer that he may be, an applicant for that employment;
    (b) in any other case, a disabled person who is—
        (i) an applicant for the employment concerned, or
        (ii) an employee of the employer concerned.
(3) Nothing in this section imposes any duty on an employer in relation to a disabled person if the employer does not know, and could not reasonably be expected to know—
    (a) in the case of an applicant or potential applicant, that the disabled person concerned is, or may be, an applicant for the employment; or
    (b) in any case, that that person has a disability and is likely to be affected in the way mentioned in subsection (1).

Section 3A(2) DDA now provides that:

'For the purposes of this Part, a person . . . discriminates against a disabled person if he fails to comply with a duty to make reasonable adjustments imposed on him in relation to the disabled person.'

The Duty to Adjust: Employment

Materially identical duties of reasonable adjustment are imposed in relation to office holders (see Chapter 4), the duty inhering in the person with control over the provision, criterion, practice or premises concerned; on the trustees of occupational pension schemes; on barristers and clerks in relation to barristers and pupil barristers (in Scotland, on advocates in relation to other advocates and trainees); on qualifications bodies and on placement providers in relation to practical work experience.[43] A new Code of Practice on Trade Unions and Qualifying Bodies came into effect in October 2004. It is very similar in content to the new Employment Code but draws its examples from the relevant contexts.

The new duty to adjust is considerably wider than the old. Not only does it remove the much-criticised justification defence from an employer who has failed to make a reasonable adjustment, but it replaces 'arrangements made' with 'provision, criterion or practice applied' by or on behalf of the employer, and removes the restrictive s.6(2).

In order to benefit from the duty to make reasonable adjustment the disabled employee must show that he or she has been placed at a substantial disadvantage by the disputed provision, criterion or practice. (Duties to adjust in contexts other than employment is considered below). In *London Clubs Management Ltd v Hood* [2001] IRLR 719, which concerned the application of the then s.6(1) DDA), EAT overruled a tribunal which found that the claimant had been discriminated against contrary to the DDA when he was denied sick pay in respect of disability-related absence. EAT criticised the tribunal's failure to give due weight to the fact that the employer had exercised its discretion to deny sick pay to *all* staff (this as a result of concern about the levels of absenteeism). Further, the tribunal had not sufficiently:

considered the question of whether Mr Hood was placed at a substantial disadvantage by the non-payment of sick pay in comparison with persons who were not disabled. If the tribunal is to be taken to have concluded that Mr Hood suffered a substantial disadvantage because of the sick pay arrangements, the reason for that conclusion is not evident from the decision. We consider that if such a conclusion were reached, it was particularly important to give the reasons for doing so in the circumstances of this case where the evidence appears to have indicated that non-disabled employees in common with Mr Hood had significant periods of unpaid sickness absence. Thus in our judgment insufficient reasons were given for the tribunal's conclusion that there had been discrimination.

In each case where an employment-related duty to adjust is alleged it is a defence for the person on whom the obligation is placed that he or she 'd[id] not know, and could not reasonably be expected to know' that the particular disabled person was disabled and was likely to be placed at a substantial disadvantage by the provision, criterion, practice or physical feature of the premises. The application of this defence has been considered in a

---

[43] Ss. 4E, 4H, 7B, 7D, 14B and 14D respectively.

number of cases. In *Foord v JA Johnstone & Sons* it was applied by a tribunal in finding that there was no duty of adjustment in a case in which the employer did not know and, according to the tribunal, 'could not reasonably be expected to know of' the claimant's fallen arches, 'given the absence of any medical certificate, signs of disability or complaint by the claimant'.[44] This seems reasonable. But in *Ridout v TC Group* [1998] IRLR 628, EAT rejected an appeal from a complainant who, having brought her (medically controlled) photosensitive epilepsy to the attention of her prospective employers and remarked, on being shown into an interview room with 'bright fluorescent lighting without diffusers or baffles,' that she might be disadvantaged by the lighting, was nevertheless interviewed in the room. The basis of her claim was that her prospective employers failed to make reasonable adjustments to their interview arrangements to prevent them from substantially disadvantaging her.

Ms Ridout was wearing sunglasses around her neck at the time, and the tribunal accepted the employers' contention that they took her remark as an explanation of the glasses (which she did not wear during the interview). EAT took the view that the employers were not, having been told that the applicant's epilepsy was medically controlled, under any duty to make further inquiry. Nor could they be criticised for not taking Ms Ridout's remark when she entered the room as a suggestion that the room was unsuitable: 'it would have been possible for the applicant to be much more forthcoming about what she regarded as being required.' The tribunal did not accept that, once the applicant had mentioned that she had epilepsy, the onus passed to the employers to do everything which was necessary to be done:

> The Act is phrased in such a way that the respondent must react in the appropriate way to that which it knows and to that which it could reasonably be expected to know. There is an onus on the employers to make 'reasonable inquiry based upon information given to it' but there is no 'absolute onus to make every inquiry possible.'

EAT upheld the tribunal's decision, ruling that s.6(6) (now s.4A(3) DDA):

> requires a tribunal to measure the extent of the duty, if any, against the actual or assumed knowledge of the employer both as to the disability and its likelihood of causing the individual a substantial disadvantage in comparison with persons who are not disabled. Tribunals should be careful not to impose upon disabled people a duty to give a long detailed explanation as to the effects of their disability merely to cause the employer to make adjustments which it probably should have made in the first place. On the other hand, it is equally undesirable that an employer should be required to ask a number of questions as to whether a person with a disability feels disadvantaged merely to protect themselves from liability.

Here EAT accepted that, given the very rare form of epilepsy suffered by the claimant, 'the tribunal was entitled to conclude that no reasonable employer could be expected to know, without being told in terms by the claimant, that the arrangements which were made for the interview might disadvantage her . . . Whether the employers should have taken any other steps as a result of what was said at the interview was a matter of fact and evidence for the tribunal.'

---

[44] Reported in 'Interpreting the DDA: Part 2', 80 *Equal Opportunities Review*.

Thompson's *Labour and European Law Review* commented that:

As with other recently reported disability decisions, [the decision in *Ridout*] flags up the difficulty that disabled people face, in having to decide whether to alert employers to a disability so running the risk of potential discrimination, or saying nothing and then losing the protection of the legislation.[45]

It would not, perhaps, have been requiring a great deal from employers to place the onus on them to enquire as to the suitability of the interview arrangements in a situation in which the claimant had (1) notified them of her disability, albeit in general terms and (2) given some indication that the arrangements made by them were such as to place her at a disadvantage. But the *Equal Opportunities Review* suggests that:

'Interpreting the Disability Discrimination Act—Part 2' 80 *Equal Opportunities Review*

Although the outcome of some of the decisions relying upon s.6(6) may appear somewhat harsh, it must be borne in mind that the alternative to emphasising the employee's responsibility to request an adjustment is to intensify the employer's duty to inquire. Where the disabled employee is already doing the job adequately, it is arguable that the law should not encourage an employer to be too proactive, since the line between inquiry and intrusion may be a thin one. In *Davies v Toys R Us*, the applicant was missing part of his arm and wore an artificial limb. Part of his duties involved climbing a ladder and handling goods. After his dismissal, an issue arose as to whether an adjustment to his duties should have been made in this respect. A Leicester industrial tribunal . . . said that: 'Even if the applicant was placed at a substantial disadvantage . . . he covered that up. He was asked on a number of occasions if he had problems and said he did not. On the facts of this case we do not consider that the respondent should have gone beyond the applicant's assertion that he did not have a problem. It would be contrary to the general intention of the Disability Discrimination Act if employers were to determine that a disabled person, who apparently can do the work and maintains when asked that he is capable of doing the work, should be denied that work on a contrary assumption made by the employer.'

In *Callaghan v Glasgow City Council* [2001] IRLR 724 EAT ruled that an employer had not failed to comply with the duty to make reasonable adjustments in a case in which it had not offered part-time work to an employee who, because of a disability not known at the time to the employers, was on prolonged sick leave. The claimant was dismissed and his DDA claim rejected by a tribunal and EAT. According to Lord Johnstone, for the appeal tribunal:

the nub of the appellant's position before us [was that] the employer should have offered part-time work to accommodate the appellant and by failure to do so they had not complied with s.6 . . .

the issue of part-time working had never arisen. On that basis we do not consider, against the particular facts of this case, that there was any duty on the part of the employer, ex proprio motu, to offer part-time working against the background of the sickness record and absence record and also the fact that the appellant was not fit for any form of working at the relevant time. It is also highly significant to our mind that if the appellant had cooperated properly with the various efforts made by the employer to accommodate him, the question of part-time working might well have arisen and might, for all we know, have been

[45] Issue 30, available at http://www.thompsons.law.co.uk/ltext/libindex.htm.

the solution. In this respect, therefore, we consider the appellant was to some extent the author of his own misfortune and certainly the circumstances do not in this particular case create a duty on the part of the employer in relation to the question of part-time working in the context of reasonable adjustments . . .

Callaghan involved a claimant whose failure to cooperate with her employer cost her her DDA claim. But the duty in relation to adjustments is placed firmly on the employer in a case in which the employee's (or prospective employee's) disability was known or ought to have been known about. In the following case, for example, EAT ruled that a tribunal had erred in law in finding against the claimant because 'neither [she] nor her medical witness were able to state what adjustments the respondents could have made to improve her situation and to facilitate an eventual return.'

Cosgrove v Caesar & Howie [2001] IRLR 653

Lindsay J (P):

At several points the tribunal states that neither Ms Cosgrove nor her general practitioner could think of anything that would have represented a satisfactory adjustment, being, for this purpose, one which would have been reasonable for the employer to take in order to prevent the arrangements it made placing Ms Cosgrove at a substantial disadvantage in comparison with a person who was not disabled . . . But the duty to make adjustments under s.6 is upon the employer. The employer, consistently with its view that there was no disability, had said in its particulars: 'The respondents did not consider any steps or adjustments could be made as in their view the applicant was not suffering from a disability.'
  And a little later in the same particulars: 'The respondents did not consider any further adjustments as in their view the applicant was not suffering from a disability.' That was confirmed in evidence. The tribunal held:

> 'Mr Borrowman (a partner in the firm) confirmed in evidence that he was aware of the terms of the Act as staff partner, although he did not consider that the Act applied in connection with the applicant's condition. He therefore did not consider what steps he might be able to take to assist her.'

The tribunal jumped from the evidence given at the employment tribunal that Ms Cosgrove's general practitioner and she herself could not think of any useful adjustment to the conclusion that no useful adjustment could be made . . .
  But whether *the employer* could, had it considered s.6 and the duty thereby imposed upon it, have thought up any useful adjustment was not a question as to which, as far as one can tell, evidence on the employer's part was adduced. The employer, as Mr Borrowman's evidence made clear, never turned its mind to adjustments or their possibilities.
  There will, no doubt, be cases where the evidence given on the applicant's side alone will establish a total unavailability of reasonable and effective adjustments. But it does not seem to us to follow that because a former secretary, long absent from the firm and clinically depressed to the point of disability and her general practitioner also (the latter, at least, being unlikely to know what office or other practicabilities were open to the employer) could postulate no useful adjustment, that the s.6 duty on the employer should, without more, be taken to have been satisfied. Indeed, in the course of argument before us, Mr Millar accepted that the doctor and the applicant were not the most appropriate persons to be asked as to what adjustments could be made. The tribunal said:

> 'Perhaps most importantly both the applicant and Dr Brook stated in evidence that the applicant's condition could not have responded to any adjustments to the workplace.

She could not think of anything that the respondents could have done which would have improved the situation.'

That relates only to Ms Cosgrove's ability to discern some adjustment and to the possibility of adjustment to the workplace (and not, be it noted, *at* the workplace). But if the employer had turned its mind to adjustments, might a transfer to another office of the firm have been a possibility? Would it have so reduced the stress which she had suffered at, and could well have suffered on return to, the Bathgate office and upon her working with the partners and staff at that office that a return to work similar to the work she had undertaken earlier or at least a return to some work would become possible?—see s.6(3)(c) or (e). She was under a degree of stress by reason of her having to look after her mother, who was found to have Alzheimer's disease; would an alteration of her working hours– sees.6(3)(d)—to allow her the better to cope with her mother's needs have so reduced Ms Cosgrove's symptoms that a return to her erstwhile work or to some work would have become possible? Would a very gradual return, building slowly from part-time working in gentle duties to full-time working on her erstwhile duties, have materially facilitated a return? The heading 'altering the person's working hours' in para. 4.20 and the passage at para. 6.21 in the Disability Discrimination Code of Practice seem to suggest that the working of shorter hours is a form of alteration of working hours that needs to be considered within the range of appropriate possible adjustments. We do not suggest that there would necessarily have been a positive answer to such questions, but there can be no assurance at all that there would not have been since, unfortunately, such questions were not asked at or around the time of dismissal, or indeed, as it would seem, even at the tribunal. It cannot, it seems to us, be as *decisive* as the tribunal took it to be on the issue of whether any reasonable adjustments were available that might have prevented Ms Cosgrove's inability to work by reason of her medical condition that neither she, a mentally disabled person, could, at the tribunal itself, suggest any, nor that her doctor, who, as far as we can tell, had no such questions posed to him and could not, presumably, in any event be expected to know what office possibilities the employer could offer, had, at the tribunal, not been able to suggest any either.

In the circumstances there was, in our judgment, a second material error of law, namely in regarding Ms Cosgrove's views and those of her general practitioner as decisive on the issue of adjustments, where the employer himself had given no thought to the matter whatsoever.

'Reasonable' Adjustments

We turn now to consider when a particular employment-related adjustment will be regarded as 'reasonable' for the purposes of the DDA. S.18B provides that:

(1) In determining whether it is reasonable for a person to have to take a particular step in order to comply with a duty to make reasonable adjustments, regard shall be had, in particular, to—
   (a) the extent to which taking the step would prevent the effect in relation to which the duty is imposed;
   (b) the extent to which it is practicable for him to take the step;
   (c) the financial and other costs which would be incurred by him in taking the step and the extent to which taking it would disrupt any of his activities;
   (d) the extent of his financial and other resources;
   (e) the availability to him of financial or other assistance with respect to taking the step;
   (f) the nature of his activities and the size of his undertaking;

    (g) where the step would be taken in relation to a private household, the extent to which taking it would—
       (i) disrupt that household, or
      (ii) disturb any person residing there.
(2) The following are examples of steps which a person may need to take in relation to a disabled person in order to comply with a duty to make reasonable adjustments—
    (a) making adjustments to premises;
    (b) allocating some of the disabled person's duties to another person;
    (c) transferring him to fill an existing vacancy;
    (d) altering his hours of working or training;
    (e) assigning him to a different place of work or training;
    (f) allowing him to be absent during working or training hours for rehabilitation, assessment or treatment;
    (g) giving, or arranging for, training or mentoring (whether for the disabled person or any other person);
    (h) acquiring or modifying equipment;
    (i) modifying instructions or reference manuals;
    (j) modifying procedures for testing or assessment;
    (k) providing a reader or interpreter;
    (l) providing supervision or other support. . .
(3) For the purposes of a duty to make reasonable adjustments, where under any binding obligation a person is required to obtain the consent of another person to any alteration of the premises occupied by him—
    (a) it is always reasonable for him to have to take steps to obtain that consent; and
    (b) it is never reasonable for him to have to make that alteration before that consent is obtained.
(6) A provision of this Part imposing a duty to make reasonable adjustments applies only for the purpose of determining whether a person has discriminated against a disabled person; and accordingly a breach of any such duty is not actionable as such.

The new Employment Code of Practice fleshes out these factors. In addition, it suggests that:

DRC, 'Code of Practice on Employment and Occupation', paras 5.20–5.24

. . . it might be reasonable for employers to have to take other steps, which are not given as examples in the Act. These steps could include:
• conducting a proper assessment of what reasonable adjustments may be required
• permitting flexible working
• allowing a disabled employee to take a period of disability leave . . .
• participating in supported employment schemes, such as Workstep
• employing a support worker to assist a disabled employee
• modifying disciplinary or grievance procedures
• adjusting redundancy selection criteria
• modifying performance-related pay arrangements . . .
    In some cases a reasonable adjustment will not work without the co-operation of other employees. Employees may therefore have an important role in helping to ensure that a reasonable adjustment is carried out in practice. Subject to considerations about confidentiality (explained at paragraphs 8.21–8.23), employers must ensure that this happens. It is unlikely to be a valid defence to a claim under the Act that staff were obstructive or unhelpful when the employer tried to make reasonable adjustments. An employer would at least need to be able to show that it took such behaviour seriously and dealt with it appropriately.

Employers will be more likely to be able to do this if they establish and implement the type of policies and practices described at paragraph 2.12.

Section 18B(1)(f) and (g) are new, the remaining factors having been listed previously in s.6(4) of the Act. The Code notes the extension of the DDA as of October 2004 to small employers and private households and suggests (at para 5.40) that particular steps which might be reasonable for a large employer to take might not reasonably be expected of a very small employer. It further suggests (para 5.41) that: 'even if the financial cost would be minimal, it might not be reasonable to take a particular step if doing so would entail disruption to [a private] household or disturbance to people who live there.' So, to use two examples from the Code, while it might be reasonable to communicate with a deaf cleaner by using written notes, it is 'unlikely' to be reasonable for a family to have to accommodate a nanny with a severe dust allergy by ensuring a dust-free house. The Code suggests that other factors may be relevant to whether an adjustment is reasonable, among them the effect on other employees, adjustments already made for other disabled employees and the extent to which the disabled person is willing to cooperate (paras 5.40–5.42).

Section 18A makes provision, in the employment context, for a person placed under a duty to make reasonable adjustment to seek permission to make any necessary alterations to premises occupies under a lease. S.18A implies into the terms of such a lease—except where the lease expressly provides otherwise—a provision to the effect that occupiers shall be entitled to make alterations in order to comply with the duty to adjust with the written consent of the lessor, such consent not to be unreasonably withheld where the lessee applies in writing for permission to make the alteration. Consent may be granted subject to reasonable conditions.

In *Mid Staffordshire v Cambridge* EAT ruled that the proactive nature of the duty to adjust required the employer to take steps to put itself in a position properly to decide what steps would be reasonable in a case in which an employee's disability was or ought to have been known to it.

Mid Staffordshire General Hospital NHS Trust v Cambridge [2003] IRLR 566

Keith J:

The tribunal, in effect, construed the words 'to take such steps as . . . is reasonable . . . to prevent' Mrs Cambridge from being at such a disadvantage as including taking such steps as would enable the Trust to decide what steps would be reasonable to prevent her from being at such a disadvantage. Those steps included obtaining a proper assessment of
(a) Mrs Cambridge's condition and prognosis;
(b) the effect of her disability on her;
(c) the effect of her disability on her ability to perform the duties of her post;
(d) the effect of the physical features of her workplace on her and her ability to perform the duties of her post; and
(e) the steps which might be taken to reduce or remove the disadvantages to which she was subjected.
Only then would the Trust be able to come to an informed view about what steps it would be reasonable for the Trust to take to prevent Mrs Cambridge from being substantially disadvantaged. The tribunal found that the Trust did not do that . . .

The principal criticism of the tribunal at this stage of its reasoning is that the gloss which the tribunal put on s.[4A] is unjustified. It is not warranted by the statutory language, and the effect of the gloss is to impose on the employer an antecedent duty which, once it has been performed, may establish that there are no steps which can reasonably be taken to ameliorate the disabled person's disadvantage. If the duty imposed by s.[4A] is to take such steps as are reasonable to ameliorate a disabled person's disadvantage, how can there be, so it is said, an antecedent duty which once carried out may show that no duty has in fact arisen because there are no steps which can reasonably be taken to ameliorate the disabled person's disadvantage? And if those antecedent enquiries reveal that there are no steps which can reasonably be taken to ameliorate the disabled person's disadvantage, all that the disabled person will have lost by the employer's breach of the antecedent duty (which the tribunal identified) would be the prospect that those enquiries might have produced a different result. Although the tribunal recognised that that was the logical consequence of its approach, the fact that the tribunal concluded that Mrs Cambridge's loss had to be assessed by reference to the loss of that prospect, shows, so it is said, the flaw in its approach, because the law only recognises the assessment of loss by reference to the loss of a chance when liability has already been established.

We are not persuaded by this argument. If it were correct, it would deny s.[4A] practical application in very many cases. There must be many cases in which the disabled person has been placed at a substantial disadvantage in the workplace, but in which the employer does not know what it ought to do to ameliorate that disadvantage without making enquiries. To say that a failure to make those enquiries would not amount to a breach of the duty imposed on employers by s.[4A] would render s.[4A]) practicably unworkable in many cases. We do not believe that that could have been Parliament's intention. The fact that the preliminary steps which the tribunal had in mind are not referred to in s.[18B(1)] is not decisive since the list of steps in s.[18B(1)] is not exhaustive, and although s.[18B(2)] is, in terms of language, difficult to link in with preliminary steps of the kind which the tribunal had in mind, s.[18B(2)] was only a consideration which the tribunal had to have regard to, and it was not one which was to be treated as decisive. A proper assessment of what is required to eliminate the disabled person's disadvantage is therefore a necessary part of the duty imposed by s.[4A] since that duty cannot be complied with unless the employer makes a proper assessment of what needs to be done. As the tribunal said in paragraph 36 of its extended reasons:

'in the absence of such an assessment it will often be impossible for an employer to know what adjustments might be reasonable, possible or effective.'

The making of that assessment cannot, in our judgment, be separated from the duty imposed by s.[4A] because it is a necessary precondition to the fulfilment of that duty and therefore a part of it.

The Employment Code of Practice provides concrete examples of the types of steps which might be required under each of s.18B(2)(a)–(l). It suggests, for example, that 'making adjustments to premises' might include: 'widening a doorway, providing a ramp or moving furniture for a wheelchair user; relocating light switches, door handles or shelves for someone who has difficulty in reaching; providing appropriate contrast in décor to help the safe mobility of a visually impaired person.' Failure to make adjustments, which have been accepted by tribunals as breaching the DDA, include the following:

- retraining, in the case of a schizophrenic software engineer selected for redundancy after extended periods of absence reduced his IT skills
- considering whether a security guard with multiple sclerosis could have been provided with alternative work at a new store being opened by the employers
- allowing a magistrates' clerk suffering from depression to work a four day week
- considering the provision of alternative equipment to a legal secretary prevented by leg pain from operating the foot pedal on her audio typing equipment

- considering the swapping of postal rounds on a temporary basis in the case of a post woman who was unable, because of post-traumatic stress disorder, to travel by vehicle or bicycle
- promptly taking adequate initiatives to secure equipment appropriate to the needs of an IT worker with a serious wrist condition who was left to struggle with inadequate equipment for almost four years
- actively seeking to redeploy a woman whose diabetes and obesity made her unfit to continue with a physically strenuous job. The employers had temporarily reassigned her but then placed her in a redeployment pool and instructed her that she would be made redundant within a specified period if she did not obtain another position within the council.[46]

Research carried out in the early days of the DDA's implementation found that the following were the most common forms of adjustment considered by tribunals:

S Leverton, *Monitoring the Disability Discrimination Act 1995*[47]

Table 13—Cases by nature of adjustment considered by tribunal, where known*

Adjustment	Number	Percentage
Transfer to existing vacancy	61	33.9
Assignment to different place of work	29	16.1
Alteration to working hours	28	15.6
Acquiring or modifying equipment	28	15.6
Reallocation of duties	27	6.7
Leave of absence for rehabilitation, assessment or treatment	12	6.7
Adjustments to premises	10	5.6
Providing a carer or support worker	10	5.6
Giving or arranging training	9	5
Providing supervision	9	5
Modifying procedures for testing or assessment	5	2.8
Modifying instructions or reference manuals	2	1.1
Providing a reader or interpreter	2	1.1
Other	12	6.7

* In many cases more than one type of adjustment was considered. The sum of the percentages in the right hand column exceeds 100 per cent because the percentage figures are based on the 180 cases in which the issue of reasonable adjustments arose.

Duties to Adjust Outside the Employment Sphere

The foregoing discussion of the duty to make reasonable adjustments relates to employment (broadly defined). But duties of reasonable adjustment under the DDA are not unique to the employment context. They apply, in addition, in relation to the provision of goods, facilities and services and the letting of premises (Part III) and education (Part IV).

[46] Respectively, *Electronic Data Systems Ltd v Travis*, cited in 'In the Courts' 130 *Equal Opportunities Review*; *Whitrid v Next Retail Ltd*, *Smith v Humberside Magistrates Courts Committee* and *Chadwick v Redfern Stigant Solicitors*, all reported in 'Case Digest' 125 *Equal Opportunities Review*; *Hibberd v Royal Mail Group plc* and *Roberts v Fisher Gauge Ltd*, both reported in 'Case Digest' 132 *Equal Opportunities Review*; and *Kelly v London Borough of Southwark* reported in 'Case Digest' 127 *Equal Opportunities Review*.
[47] Phase 2, First Interim Report to the Department for Education and Employment (March 2000).

The duties differ across these areas and will be considered in turn. It is important to bear in mind, however, that, while a failure to comply with an employment-related duty to adjust cannot be justified, general justification defences are provided in relation to failure to adjust under Parts II and IV DDA.

Part V of the Act, which deals with transport, is very different from Parts II–IV and operates by providing a statutory basis for the imposition of specific obligations on transport providers in relation to accessibility and (in the case of taxis and private hire vehicles) the carriage of guide and hearing dogs. At present, Part III of the DDA contains a broad exclusion of 'any service so far as it consists of the use of any means of transport' (s.19(5)(b), see further Chapter 4). The Disability Discrimination Act 2005 repeals s.19(5)(b) and introduces a new s.21ZA which makes it clear that the exclusion applies only to discrimination which consists (new (s.21ZA(1)) in the provision of or failure to provide a disabled person with a vehicle or the provision or failure to provide a disabled person 'with services when he is travelling in a vehicle provided in the course of the transport service'. Further, new s.21ZA(3) would provide a basis for Regulations incrementally to bring within the scope of s.19 'vehicles of a prescribed description.' New s.21ZA(2) would, in turn, make special provision for the duty to adjust in the transport field. This is further discussed below.

Section 21 DDA provides that:

(1) Where a provider of services has a practice, policy or procedure which makes it impossible or unreasonably difficult for disabled persons to make use of a service which he provides, or is prepared to provide, to other members of the public, it is his duty to take such steps as it is reasonable, in all the circumstances of the case, for him to have to take in order to change that practice, policy or procedure so that it no longer has that effect.

(2) Where a physical feature (for example, one arising from the design or construction of a building or the approach or access to premises) makes it impossible or unreasonably difficult for disabled persons to make use of such a service, it is the duty of the provider of that service to take such steps as it is reasonable, in all the circumstances of the case, for him to have to take in order to—
(a) remove the feature;
(b) alter it so that it no longer has that effect;
(c) provide a reasonable means of avoiding the feature; or
(d) provide a reasonable alternative method of making the service in question available to disabled persons.

Section 20(2) DDA provides that an unjustified failure to comply with a duty imposed by s.21 amount to discrimination for the purposes of Part III DDA. The duties imposed by s.21 are anticipatory in the sense that they are owed to disabled persons at large. They are enforceable, however, only by particular disabled persons who are discriminated against by an unjustified failure to comply on the part of the service provided (s.21(10) which provides that, in common with all the other DDA provisions which impose duties to adjust, s.21 'imposes duties only for the purpose of determining whether a provider of services has discriminated against a disabled person; and accordingly a breach of any such duty is not actionable as such').

DRC, 'Code of Practice on Rights of Access to Goods, Facilities, Services and Premises', paras 4.13–4.14

A service provider's duty to make reasonable adjustments is a duty owed to disabled people at large. It is not simply a duty that is weighed up in relation to each individual disabled person who wants to access a service provider's services. Disabled people are a diverse group with different requirements which service providers need to consider.

Service providers should not wait until a disabled person wants to use a service which they provide before they give consideration to their duty to make reasonable adjustments. They should be thinking now about the accessibility of their services to disabled people. Service providers should be planning continually for the reasonable adjustments they need to make, whether or not they already have disabled customers. They should anticipate the requirements of disabled people and the adjustments that may have to be made for them. In many cases, it is appropriate to ask customers to identify whether they have any particular requirements and, if so, what adjustments may need to be made. Failure to anticipate the need for an adjustment may render it too late to comply with the duty to make the adjustment. Furthermore, it may not of itself provide a defence to a claim that it was reasonable to have provided one.

C Gooding and C Casserley, 'Disability Discrimination Laws in Europe Relating to Goods and Services', Disability Rights in Europe conference (Leeds, September 2003), footnotes omitted

Because the wording of the s.21 provisions refers specifically to 'disabled persons,' the duty is, as indicated thus framed as an anticipatory one: service providers are said to owe duties to disabled people as a whole and, as a result, they should ensure that they have considered and taken steps to ensure, the accessibility of their services. This has been seen as immensely significant in Britain, a major driver in encouraging service providers to think in advance about removing barriers experienced by disabled customers—or would be customers. It help avoid the situation where a providers says that because they did not know in advance that an adjustment was required it is not reasonable to provide one. Because of the anticipatory duty, for example, a conference provider should ask delegates in advance about what adjustments they need.

On the other hand, the legislation is somewhat confusing in adopting different triggers, depending upon what adjustment is required. This confusion is compounded by the fact that in order to bring a claim of discrimination on the basis that an adjustment has not been made, the failure must result in it being impossible or unreasonably difficult for the disabled person to use the service– a failure to comply with the duty per se is not actionable.

The trigger of 'impossible or unreasonably difficult' is a potentially high one to meet: it means that, in effect, a service can be reasonably difficult to use and a disabled person may have no remedy . . . The concerns appear to be substantiated by some negative decisions by county courts. In the case of *Baggley v Kingston-upon-Hull Council* Mr Baggley, who is a wheelchair user, had been required to sit at the back of a concert hall for health and safety reasons. As everyone else at the concert was standing Mr Baggley was unable to see the performer, Mel C aka *Sporty Spice*. A District Judge had held that there had not been a failure to provide reasonable adjustments by failing to provide a viewing platform, although he had given leave to appeal. Although it was not a point argued by the concert hosts, or relevant to the original judgement, the Judge on appeal expressed doubt as to whether Mr Baggley was entitled even to have adjustments considered under the DDA: 'I understand that Ms Chisholm is an energetic performer and that the theatrical aspect of her concert is important. Mr Baggley could not see the stage show, but that is not to say that it made it 'impossible or unreasonably difficult to make use of the service.'

The case of *Alistair Appleby and Department for Work and Pensions* also raised the question of interpretation of this trigger. It concerned a man who has a hearing impairment. He wears binaural hearing aids but has to supplement his hearing with visual clues. As a New Zealand national, he had to attend at the Benefits Agency Office to obtain a National Insurance number on 13 November 1999. The office operated a numbered ticket queuing system for interviews. A visual display monitor system was installed which was intended to display the ticket number of the person whose next turn it was. There was also a tannoy system which called out the number. Both of these, the District Judge hearing the case found, were intended to address the needs of those with hearing and visual disabilities, but on the day on which the applicant attended, they were out of operation. The applicant asked the security guard to inform him when it was his turn. He was eventually called, and, as he could not hear what was being said to him because the staff member was behind a glass screen, he asked for, and was given, an interview room without a glass screen.

The following week, the applicant received a telephone message that he had to return to the office to provide his passport and should ask for someone called David. When he returned to the office, the systems were still out of order and he explained that he was deaf and asked to be notified when it was his turn. This request was refused and he was told that he would have to ask another member of the public as to when his turn came up. The applicant said that this would not address this problem, as all those in the room would have already had their turn before he had to go in, but he managed to determine when it was his turn by the process of elimination of the penultimate ticket holder and with the help of a young boy who told him the room number. He was shown to a screened interview room where he had an interview with David, but found it hard to understand what was being said. He asked for an unscreened room but this was not given. He said that the interviewer became frustrated with his inability to understand what was being asked of him. At no stage, did he recall seeing a sign that indicated that there was an induction loop fitted.

Mr Appleby claimed breach of the s.21(1) duty in relation to policies procedures and practices in relation to: the waiting room practice, the monitor practice, the security screen policy.

The District Judge (DJ) dealt with the waiting room and monitor practice together; he held that the practice of having to ask a member of the public to notify him of when it was his turn did not make it 'unreasonably difficult' for Mr Appleby to use the service. The DJ stated 'Indeed with commendable imagination and improvisation he enlisted without apparent difficulty the help of two members of the public who, it would appear, were more than willing to assist, and he was thus able to ascertain when it was his turn.'

The case did succeed on other grounds, however. The DJ did take a robust approach to the policy of interviewing people, including the hearing impaired applicant, behind a screen. He held that there had been a breach of the Act. The defendant was relying upon its installation of induction loops to meet their obligations under the Act, but the DJ found that there were no signs either in the reception area or the screened interview rooms indicating the presence of such a system. The DJ also stated in his judgement that 'Failure to make its (the induction loop) existence known is tantamount to a failure to have such a system in the first place.'

Adjustments are only required where they are 'reasonable'; the legislation provides no guidance on what might be reasonable, but the Code of Practice indicates that essentially the same factors as those relating to reasonable adjustments in employment will affect the reasonableness or otherwise of an adjustment: effectiveness, practicability, cost, disruption, resources, amount already spent on adjustments, availability of other sources of assistance.

Other reasonable adjustments upheld by the courts have included: permitting a motorised golf cart to be used on a golf course in dry weather [for further details of this and other cases see www.drc-gb.org].[47]

Section 21(1) DDA was brought into force throughout the UK in October 1999, as was s.21(2)(d). Section 21(2)(a)–(c) are effective as of October 2004. The Code of Practice on Rights of Access to Goods, Facilities, Services and Premises suggests that examples of

[47] See also the recent decisions of the Court of Appeal in *Ross v Ryanair* [2004] EWCA Civ 1751 and *Roads v Central Trains Ltd* [2004] EWCA Civ 1541, mentioned in Ch 4, both of which concerned the s.21 DDA duty to adjust.

adjustments to premises might include (para 4.8) 'widening a doorway; providing a permanent ramp for a wheelchair user; relocating light switches, door handles or shelves for someone who has difficulty in reaching; providing appropriate contrast in decor to assist the safe mobility of a visually impaired person; installing a permanent induction loop system; providing tactile buttons in lifts.' Whereas, prior to October 2004, no duty to make adjustments to premises arose if a service provider was unable to provide a 'reasonable alternative method of making the service in question available to disabled people,' now the service provider will have to consider, in the alternative, removing the problematic feature, altering it, and providing a reasonable means of avoiding it.

DRC, 'Code of Practice on Rights of Access to Goods, Facilities, Services and Premises', para 5.34

A public inquiry point is located on the second floor of a government office building and is accessed by a flight of stairs. This makes it impossible or unreasonably difficult for some disabled people to get to it. People with a mobility disability or a mental health disability (like anxiety related depression) may find using the stairs difficult.

Since 1 October 1999 the government department has had to consider what it could do to provide a reasonable alternative method of making its inquiry service accessible to disabled members of the public. For example, it might provide the service in the form of a telephone inquiry line. This may be a reasonable alternative method of providing the service if it effectively delivers the service in another way.

However, if it does not do so (for instance, if staff at the inquiry point also help people to complete forms and that cannot be done by telephone), the provision of a telephone service may not be a reasonable alternative. The department will then have to consider whether there are other reasonable steps it can take to provide the same service. For example, it might provide a courtesy telephone on the ground floor to enable disabled people to call staff down to help them.

Despite this, if the service is still not accessible to all disabled people, from 1 October 2004 further reasonable steps may involve a physical alteration of some kind. For example, it might be reasonable to install a lift or to move the inquiry point to the ground floor. Although there is no requirement to make physical alterations before 1 October 2004, it may be sensible to consider and give effect to such possibilities before then, especially if refurbishment of the building is being planned . . .

The Act does not require a service provider to adopt one way of meeting its obligations rather than another. The focus of the Act is on results. Where there is a physical barrier, the service provider's aim should be to make its services accessible to disabled people. What is important is that this aim is achieved, rather than how it is achieved. If a service remains inaccessible, a service provider may have to defend its decisions.

For example, a service provider may decide to provide a service by the option of an alternative method. If the result is that disabled people are then able to access the service without unreasonable difficulty, that will satisfy the service provider's obligations under the Act. If, on the other hand, it is still unreasonably difficult for a disabled person to make use of the service, the service provider would then have to show that it could not have reasonably removed or altered the physical feature, or provided a reasonable means of avoiding it. The cost of taking such action may be a relevant consideration. Similarly, if the service provider takes no action, it will have to show that there were no steps which it could reasonably have taken.[48]

---

[48] In Roads, *ibid*, the Court of Appeal ruled that the policy of the DDA was 'to provide access to a service as close as it is reasonably possible to get to the standard normally offered to the public at large', so that service providers did not have an unrestricted choice between accessibility solutions where one was significantly more attractive than another to the disabled service user.

Section 21(4) DDA provides that:

Where an auxiliary aid or service (for example, the provision of information on audio tape or of a sign language interpreter) would—

(a) enable disabled persons to make use of a service which a provider of services provides, or is prepared to provide, to members of the public, or

(b) facilitate the use by disabled persons of such a service,

it is the duty of the provider of that service to take such steps as it is reasonable, in all the circumstances of the case, for him to have to take in order to provide that auxiliary aid or service.

Section 21(6) DDA provides that s.21 does not require 'a provider of services to take any steps which would fundamentally alter the nature of the service in question or the nature of his trade, profession or business.' The duties of reasonable adjustment are further restricted by s.21(7) which limits the expenditure which can be required of a service provider to a prescribed maximum to be set out by regulation (no such regulations have been published as of April 2005). Section 27 DDA makes similar provision in relation to service providers occupying premises under a lease as does s.18A in the employment context, the Disability Discrimination (Providers of Services) (Adjustment of Premises) Regulations 2001,[48a] which came into force in October 2004, providing that service providers are not obliged by the DDA to make alterations to premises without permission from the lessors, or to alter or remove accessibility features which conform to the relevant building design standard. The partial exemption from the duty to adjust for service providers whose premises comply with the relevant requirements of the building regulations (see extract below) does *not* apply in relation to *employers* regulated under Part II DDA.

DRC, 'Code of Practice on Access', paras 6.4–6.11

Since 1985 building regulations in England and Wales have required reasonable provisions to be made for disabled people to gain access to and to use new buildings (and some extensions). Part M of the Building Regulations (Access and facilities for disabled people), was extended in 1992 and again in 1999. It now applies to [n]ew buildings, and [g]round floor extensions to existing buildings but not the existing buildings themselves.

Buildings to which Part M applies should make reasonable provision for access and use by disabled people . . . Guidance is issued to accompany the Building Regulations. For Part M of the Building Regulations in England and Wales this is the Approved Document M. This sets out a number of 'objectives' to be met, 'design considerations' and technical details of design solutions (called 'provisions'). These provisions suggest one way in which the requirements of the regulations might be met but there is no obligation to adopt any of them. Most buildings will have followed the guidance in the Approved Document, but some will have adopted other acceptable design solutions.

Some disabled people might find it impossible or unreasonably difficult to use services provided at a building even though the building meets the requirements of Part M. In this situation, if a physical feature accords with the 1992 or 1999 Approved Documents to Part M, an exemption provided by The Disability Discrimination (Providers of Services)

[48a] SI 2001 No 3253.

(Adjustment of Premises) Regulations 2001 (the '2001 Regulations') means that the service provider will not have to make adjustments to that feature if 10 years or less have passed since it was constructed or installed . . .

A building with features which do not accord with the effective edition of the Approved Document . . . may have been accepted as meeting the requirements of Part M. If the feature is one which is covered by the Approved Document (for example, a lift) then, provided it enables any disabled person to access and use the building with the same degree of ease as would have been the case had the feature accorded with the Approved Document, it is unlikely to be reasonable for a service provider to have to make adjustments to that feature if 10 years or less have passed since its installation or construction. This is because the 2001 Regulations are not intended to deter people from adopting effective innovative or alternative design. Where a feature is one which is not covered by the Approved Document (for example, lighting) then under the DDA the service provider may still have to make adjustments to that feature . . .

Similar provisions to those in England and Wales were also introduced in Scotland in 1985 when 'facilities for disabled persons' were added to the Building Standards (Scotland) Regulations . . . An exemption from the duty to make reasonable adjustments to physical features applies where those features accord with the relevant version of Part T or the corresponding requirements in the Technical Standards introduced [under the Building Standards (Scotland) Regulations] in April 2000 and March 2002 . . .

The Disability Rights Commission recommended ('Disability Equality: Making it Happen') that the DDA be clarified to require that when service providers make reasonable adjustments to their premises they must first consider removing or altering the physical barriers, and only if this is not reasonable consider providing the service by an alternative means, and that the factors determining what is 'reasonable' by way of adjustment, which are presently listed in the Code of Practice, should be stated in the DDA. It also recommended that the DDA be amended to require reasonable adjustments where a disabled customer would otherwise be at a 'substantial disadvantage' in accessing a service (rather than, as at present, where the service is 'impossible or unreasonably difficult' for the disabled person to access). This would bring the goods and services provisions of the DDA more into line with the Act's other provisions. The Government has not acted on these recommendations.

The premises provisions of Part 3 DDA are considered in Chapter 4. At present, no duty of reasonable adjustment applies in relation to these provisions. But the DDA 2005 will insert new ss.24A–24J into the DDA to impose duties to adjust on landlords and managers of premises in relation to premises they let or wish to let. New s.24C will provide that a 'controller of let premises [who] . . . receives a request made by or on behalf of a person to whom the premises are let,' where 'it is reasonable to regard the request as a request that the controller take reasonable steps in order to provide an auxiliary aid or service,' is under a duty 'to take such steps as it is reasonable, in all the circumstances of the case for him to have to take in order to provide the auxiliary aid or service,' where that service (s.24C(3)(a)):

will allow a disabled person to enjoy the premises or facilitate her enjoyment of them in circumstances such that, if the auxiliary aid were not provided, her enjoyment of the premises would be 'impossible or unreasonably difficult'. The duty to provide an auxiliary aid also arises where it enables or facilitates the use by the disabled person of a 'benefit, or facility, which by reason of the letting is one of which he is entitled to make use' *as an occupier or tenant of the premises*, and where the use of that benefit or facility would otherwise be 'impossible or unreasonably difficult'.

New s.24(D)(3)–(5) impose upon controllers of premises an obligation 'to take such steps as it is reasonable, in all the circumstances of the case, for [them] to have to take in order to change' any term of the letting or 'practice, policy or procedure which has the effect of making it impossible, or unreasonable difficult, for a relevant disabled person (i) to enjoy the premises, or (ii) to make use of any benefit, or facility, which by reason of the letting is one of which he is entitled to make use.' This applies only (s.24D(2)) to terms, practices, policies or procedures which 'would not have that effect if the relevant disabled person concerned did not have a disability,' where the controller has received a request by or on behalf of the person to whom the premises are let and where 'it is reasonable to regard the request as a request that the controller take steps in order to change the practice, policy, procedure or term so as to stop it having that effect.' Section 24E(1) provides that 'For the purposes of this section, it is never reasonable for a controller of let premises to have to take steps which would involve the removal or alteration of a physical feature.' Section 24G sets out relevantly similar duties in respect of premises to be let. In each case, as in relation to every duty of reasonable adjustment arising outside Part II DDA, a justification defence is available in relation to a failure to make reasonable adjustments. This is considered below.

Turning to the transport provisions contained in the DDA 2005, we noted above that the current application of the DDA to transport consists mainly in the creation of a statutory base for the issue of specific accessibility regulations covering various means of transport (though note *Ross v Ryanair*, discussed in Chapter 4). If the Bill is passed in its present form s.19 would apply to transport except where the discrimination consists (new s.21ZA(1) DDA) of the provision of or failure to provide a vehicle or the provision of or failure to provide services when the disabled person is travelling in a vehicle provided in the course of a transport service. Insofar as s.19 DDA applies to transport, new s.21ZA(2) DDA provides that:

> . . . it is never reasonable for a provider of services, as a provider of a transport service—
> (a) to have to take steps which would involve the alteration or removal of a physical feature of a vehicle used in providing services,
> (b) to have to take steps which would
>   (i) affect whether vehicles are provided in the course of the service or what vehicles are so provided, or
>   (ii) where a vehicle is provided in the course of the service, affect what happens in it while someone is travelling in it.

Part IV of the DDA is concerned with education. We noted above that Part IV prohibits the less favourable treatment of disabled students and pupils in the normal way. But Part IV operates in conjunction with the Special Educational Needs and Disability Act (SENDA), which imposes specific obligations on education authorities and schools in relation to pupils with special educational needs, and the duty to make reasonable adjustments differs. Section 28C provides that (subject to the justification defence, discussed below):

> (1) The responsible body for a school must take such steps as it is reasonable for it to have to take to ensure that—
>   (a) in relation to the arrangements it makes for determining the admission of pupils to the school, disabled persons are not placed at a substantial disadvantage in comparison with persons who are not disabled; and
>   (b) in relation to education and associated services provided for, or offered to, pupils at the school by it, disabled pupils are not placed at a substantial disadvantage in comparison with pupils who are not disabled.
> (2) That does not require the responsible body to—

(a) remove or alter a physical feature (for example, one arising from the design or con-struction of the school premises or the location of resources); or

(b) provide auxiliary aids or services.

The provision has been in place since September 2002. It is supplemented by the Code of Practice for Schools issued by the Disability Rights Commission.[49] The Code explains that the duty imposed by s.28C does not extend to the provision of auxiliary aids or services or the removal or alteration of physical features because the Special Educational Needs (SEN) framework, rather than the DDA, 'is designed to identify, assess and make provision for chil-dren's special educational needs. Special educational provision should include any educational aids and services where these are necessary to meet the child's identified needs. The disability discrimination duties are designed to sit alongside the SEN framework and do not provide an additional route of access to auxiliary aids and services.' The use of auxiliary aids provided under the SEN framework is, however, covered by the DDA: to use an example given in the Code, the refusal by a teacher to use a radio aid provided to a hearing impaired pupil would likely breach the DDA. Physical alterations to schools are similarly excluded from the duty to make reasonable adjustments, being subject instead to the obligations imposed on schools and education authorities to draw up accessibility plans and strategies (see Chapter 4).[50]

The Code of Practice gives guidance, *inter alia*, on the kinds of adjustments schools might reasonably be expected to make. Having pointed out the width of the pupil-related activities covered by the DDA (see Chapter 4) the Code sets out some examples of less favourable treatment (see above) and goes on to consider the question of reasonable adjust-ments.

Disability Rights Commission, 'Code of Practice for Schools', para 6.11

In considering what might constitute a substantial disadvantage, the school will need to take account of a number of factors. These may include: the time and effort that might need to be expended by a disabled child; the inconvenience, indignity or discomfort a disabled child might suffer; the loss of opportunity or the diminished progress that a disabled child may make in comparison with his or her peers who are not disabled.

A secondary school with a number of disabled pupils fails to negotiate the special arrangements for disabled pupils who are taking public exams. This is likely to place disabled pupils at a substantial disadvantage and may be unlawful.

A secondary school hosts a special unit for pupils with a visual impairment. The school is already appropriately equipped for enlarging text and providing Braille versions of doc-uments for pupils who use Braille. When the pupils are working in the unit all information is provided at the beginning of the lesson by the school in the range of formats they need. When they are working in mainstream classes in the school, the school regularly fails to provide information in time to be transferred into different formats for the lesson. Not providing the information in time leaves the disabled pupils unable to refer to written infor-mation during the lesson, whilst their non-disabled peers can. This is likely to constitute a substantial disadvantage in comparison with non-disabled pupils. The failure to take rea-sonable steps to prevent this disadvantage is likely to be unlawful.

---

[49] Available at www.drc.gb.org.

[50] In Scotland, physical access to schools is a devolved issue relating to the planning and the provision of education. The Scottish Executive has brought forward draft legislation that introduces planning duties in Scotland.

The duties of reasonable adjustment applicable in the context of education, as in the context of goods and services, are 'anticipatory.' They arise, in other words, wherever there is the *potential* for a substantial disadvantage to pupils or prospective pupils. According to the Code of Practice: 'Schools cannot, in general, wait until a disabled pupil has arrived before making reasonable adjustments. This may be too late and it may not be possible to take reasonable steps before the pupil is placed at a substantial disadvantage.' Further, the duty to make reasonable adjustments is owed to disabled pupils in general rather than (as is the case in the context of employment), only to a particular person. 'This means,' according to the Code, 'that schools will need to review their policies, practices and procedures, as a matter of course, to ensure that they do not discriminate against disabled children. It means that schools should not wait until a disabled child seeks admission to the school or is admitted as a pupil to consider what reasonable adjustments it might make generally to meet the needs of disabled pupils.' The Code goes on to suggest that schools should take steps such as making sure that policies on bullying address disability-related incidents; that contractual arrangements for (for example) annual residential visits ought to anticipate the possibility that disabled students might be among those participating; that (in the case of selective schools) disabled students are facilitated in terms of access to exams (this by, for example, arranging early 'admissions meetings' with parents of such students to discuss arrangements); and that policies are adopted to permit staff to administer medicines to pupils after appropriate training, and with proper indemnification arrangements in place.

Disability Rights Commission, 'Code of Practice for Schools', paras 6.14–6.35

In these examples anticipatory changes are made to policies so that disabled pupils would not be placed at a substantial disadvantage. The changes that were made in these examples were of a general nature, although anticipatory changes may be prompted by thinking about groups of children or individual children who might come to the school.

A large secondary school is opening a special unit for pupils with speech and language impairments. They plan to include the pupils from the unit in mainstream lessons. One of the challenges is how to enable the children from the unit to follow the timetable. They might otherwise be at a substantial disadvantage. The school has an established 'buddy system' as part of its anti-bullying policy. After discussions with pupils, parents and the speech and language specialist teacher, the school extends its buddy system. It provides training for additional volunteer buddies to guide the disabled pupils from class to class. This is likely to be a reasonable step that the school should take.

A boy with a spinal injury who uses a wheelchair wants to attend his local primary school. The teachers are concerned as they do not know what he should do in PE lessons. The boy might be at a substantial disadvantage if he did not do PE. The physiotherapist is asked to help the school to adjust the PE curriculum appropriately. Amongst other things the school includes:
• an exercise routine to carry out on the mat which other pupils will also do and benefit from;
• ball work sitting on chairs in a circle.
These are likely to be reasonable steps that the school should take.

It should be recognised that not every school will need to adopt the same approach as the schools in these examples. Other schools might have identified different steps to be taken. The important point about the steps is that they need to ensure that disabled pupils are not at a substantial disadvantage. There may be many different ways of doing this . . . For all schools, discussions with parents and pupils themselves will be important in informing the responsible body more precisely about the nature of the adjustments that may be needed in anticipation of a particular pupil being admitted. There is no onus on pupils and parents to share such information but, to the extent that information is shared, schools will be better able to make appropriate adjustments for the individual pupil . . . Schools will need to keep their policies, practices and procedures under continuous review. The need for good information continues after children have been admitted to the school. Schools need to consider on a continuing basis whether disabled pupils may be at a substantial disadvantage.

Considering whether it is reasonable to have to take a particular step

To comply with the reasonable adjustments duty responsible bodies will need to consider what they might do to ensure that disabled pupils are not at a substantial disadvantage. There may be a variety of ways in which adjustments might be made. In considering whether it is reasonable to have to take a particular step, responsible bodies must have regard to any relevant provisions of this Code of Practice [s 28C(4)].

The reasonable adjustments duty assumes the involvement of disabled pupils in every aspect of the life of the school. A careful consideration of how that participation is best facilitated will help the responsible body to determine what a reasonable step might be. Any relevant factors need to be explored and balanced. They need to be weighed against the potential for a disabled pupil being placed at a substantial disadvantage. Some of the factors below may be relevant to this consideration. Where any of these factors is relevant it may be taken into account:

- the need to maintain academic, musical, sporting and other standards;
- the financial resources available to the responsible body;
- the cost of taking a particular step;
- the extent to which it is practicable to take a particular step;
- the extent to which aids and services will be provided to disabled pupils at the school under Part IV of the Education Act 1996 or Sections 60–65G of the Education (Scotland) Act 1980;
- health and safety requirements;
- the interests of other pupils and persons who may be admitted to the school as pupils.

Where a factor is relevant it needs to be considered. It should be used to help determine whether and how a reasonable step might be taken in order to ensure that a disabled pupil is not at a substantial disadvantage.

A consideration of the factors may lead to the adoption of certain reasonable adjustments rather than others, for example on the grounds of cost or practicability. On other occasions a consideration of the factors may mean that there is no adjustment that it would be reasonable to make, for example, where a disabled pupil did not meet an objective standard required to participate in a particular activity.

A school may choose its best footballers, singers or mathematicians where a consideration of standards is relevant; for example in an inter-school competition. However, it should not be assumed that a consideration of standards will mean that a disabled pupil will be barred from an activity . . .

Justification for a material and substantial reason

Failing to make reasonable adjustments can only be justified if there is a reason which is both material to the circumstances of the particular case and substantial. This is the same as the second ground for justification of less favourable treatment.

The duty to adjust does not arise in the education context where (s.28B(3) DDA) the governing body 'it did not know and could not reasonably have been expected to know' at the relevant time that the pupil or prospective pupil was disabled, and where 'its failure to take the step was attributable to that lack of knowledge.' The Code sets out when that defence might be available (and when schools will be regarded as having actual or constructive knowledge of disability). Special provision is made where parents request a school to keep confidential the fact of their child's disability.

Section 28T DDA makes similar provision in relation to students in third level education and the DRC has issued a Code of Practice for providers of post-16 education and related services which is materially similar to the Code discussed above.[51] Some of its provisions are extracted below in relation to the justification of discrimination. Unlike the duty to adjust as it applies to schools, providers of post-16 education may be obliged to provide auxiliary aids and to make adjustments to premises (the SEN arrangements applying only to pre-16 education). The duty to adjust is anticipatory as it is in the case of schools, and the Code of Practice suggests that institutions will have to make advance provision to finance reasonable adjustments that may be required over a budget period. It also suggests, by way of example of the anticipatory duty, that teaching materials on an institution's intranet facility ought to be prepared so as to be consistent with software which is likely to be used by dyslexic students. Other adjustments which the Code of Practice suggests might be required include the taking of steps to ensure that feedback on coursework is in suitable form to be accessible to, for example, visually impaired students, and that the timing of work placements is, where possible, adjusted to students' health-related needs. As in the case of compulsory education, a lack of information on the part of the institution as to the student's disability provides a defence to claims both of disability-related discrimination and failure to adjust. But the Code points out that the anticipatory nature of the duty to adjust may on occasion render knowledge irrelevant, and suggests that institutions have to be proactive to encourage students and prospective students to disclose disabilities.

DRC, 'Code of Practice for Providers of Post-16 Education,' paras 5.12–5.15

A man with a visual impairment asks for information about courses at a college. He does not tell the college that he has a visual impairment. He can read type if it is of a reasonable size. He is sent a prospectus for the college, which is printed in very small type that he cannot read. The college does not produce information in any other format or even in reasonably sized type. The college's failure to make an adjustment for the enquirer with the visual impairment is not related to lack of knowledge about his disability, it is due to the college's failure to make anticipatory adjustments for disabled people. This is likely to be unlawful . . .

A responsible body needs to be proactive to encourage people to disclose a disability. This might involve asking people to declare their disabilities on application and enrolment forms. It may mean publicising the provision that is made for disabled people, and then providing opportunities for people to tell tutors, teachers or other staff in confidence. It might involve asking students when they apply for examinations whether they need any specific arrangements because of a disability. It means ensuring that the atmosphere and culture are open and welcoming so that disabled people feel safe to disclose a disability . . .

The Code goes on to provide guidance as to when particular adjustments might be regarded as reasonable (paras 6.1–6.2).

What steps are reasonable for a particular responsible body to take depends on all the circumstances of the case. For example, they will vary according to:

[51] Available at www.drc.gb.org.

- the type of services being provided
- the nature of the institution or service and its size and resources
- the effect of the disability on the individual disabled person or student.

Under the Act, responsible bodies must have regard to relevant provisions of this Code. [s 28T(2)] Without attempting to be exhaustive, the following are some of the factors that might be taken into account when considering what is reasonable:

- the need to maintain academic and other prescribed standards
- the financial resources available to the responsible body
- grants or loans likely to be available to disabled students (and only disabled students) for the purpose of enabling them to receive student services, such as Disabled Students' Allowances
- the cost of taking a particular step
- the extent to which it is practicable to take a particular step
- the extent to which aids or services will otherwise be provided to disabled people or students
- health and safety requirements
- the relevant interests of other people including other students.

Special provision is made in relation to adjustments to buildings by the Disability Discrimination (Educational Institutions) (Alteration of Leasehold Premises) Regulations 2002. These bring the education-related provisions in this context broadly into line with Part II of the Act as it applies to employment (see above).

The DDA 2005 has been mentioned above. In Chapter 4 we considered its prohibition of disability discrimination by public authorities and, in Chapter 3, its imposition of a duty on public authorities to take positive measures so as to promote equality between disabled and non-disabled persons. Here it is useful to note that the 'discrimination' which will be regulated would extend beyond the less favourable treatment of persons with disabilities to an unjustified failure to make reasonable adjustments. The duty to adjust is similar to that which applies in relation to goods and services, discussed above.

The DDA 2005 will also amend the DDA to regulate discrimination by private clubs and associations (new s.21F). 'Discrimination' for these purposes includes less favourable treatment and the failure to make reasonable adjustments, in each case subject to a justification defence (see below). The duty to adjust is not given flesh in new s.21H which provides, instead, that regulations may make provision imposing on relevant associations:

(1) (a) a duty to take steps for a purpose relating to a policy, practice or procedure of the association, or a physical feature, which adversely affects disabled persons who (i) are, or might wish to become, members or associates of the association; or (ii) are, or are likely to become guests of the association,
   (b) a duty to take steps for the purpose of making an auxiliary aid or service available to any such disabled persons.

Justification

Employment

The DDA generally permits the justification of discrimination, though this is no longer the case in the employment context in relation to a failure to make reasonable adjustments. Nor does it apply in relation to 'direct' discrimination which is regulated only in that context. The test for justification differs across the various contexts in which the DDA applies. Here we consider its operation in the employment sphere and below we turn to look at the justification of discrimination in the other areas covered by the Act.

Section 3A(3) DDA provides that, disability-related discrimination in the context of employment (broadly defined): 'is justified if, but only if, the reason for it is both *material* to the circumstances of the case and *substantial*' (my emphasis). Section 3A(6) further provides that:

> If, in a case falling within subsection (1), the employer is under a duty to make reasonable adjustments in relation to the disabled person but fails to comply with that duty, his treatment of that person cannot be justified under subsection (3) unless it would have been justified even if he had complied with that duty.

Prior to the development of case law on the justification defence, Brian Doyle remarked that '[h]ow [it] . . . works in practice will be the making or breaking' of the DDA. This is particularly the case in view of the generous approach adopted to 'less favourable treatment' by the Court of Appeal in *Clark*. The easier it is to prove less favourable treatment (ie, the fewer hurdles are erected in terms of the appropriate comparator—*Clark*, and any requirement for knowledge of disability on the part of the employer, etc),[52] the greater the significance of the justification defence.

In *Clark v Novacold* (the first DDA case to reach EAT), the appeal tribunal emphasised the importance of the Code of Practice in this matter. So, too, did the Court of Appeal.

The original Code of Practice addressed the issue of justification by asserting that 'less favourable treatment will be justified only if the reason for it . . . relate[s] to the individual circumstances in question and [is] not just . . . trivial or minor' (para 4.6). It went on to suggest that '[a] general assumption that blind people cannot use computers would not in itself be a material reason—it is not related to the particular circumstances'; that the fact that clerical worker with a learning disability 'cannot sort papers quite as quickly as some of his colleagues [where t]here is very little difference in productivity . . . is very unlikely to be a substantial reason' for his dismissal; that the muttering of a mentally ill worker, where other workers make similar levels of noise of a mentally ill person who mutters to himself at a level accepted in relation to other employees 'is unlikely to be a substantial reason' for his transfer. By contrast, the rejection of someone with 'psoriasis (a skin condition) . . . for a job involving modelling cosmetics on a part of the body which in his case is severely disfigured by the condition . . . would be lawful if his appearance would be incompatible with the purpose of the work. This is a substantial reason which is clearly related—material—to the individual circumstance.' Equally, the rejection of a blind applicant for a job 'which requires a significant amount of driving' is likely to be justified (para 4.7) '[I]f it is not reasonable for the employer to adjust the job so that the driving duties are given to someone else.'

In *Heinz v Kendrick* EAT upheld the tribunal's decision that the claimant's dismissal was unjustified where the employer had not considered whether the claimant, who was on long-term sick leave, could be found alternative employment, and had not followed fully its own procedures for medical dismissals. But Lindsay J stressed the low threshold of justification as did the Court of Appeal in *Jones v Post Office*. The claimant in *Jones* had been removed from driving duties after he became insulin dependent as a result of diabetes. A tribunal

---

[52] See *Heinz v Kendrick*, above.

took the view that the discrimination, which was conceded by the employer, was unjustified, this on the grounds that a correct appraisal of the claimant's medical condition would have led the Post Office to conclude that he was fit to continue driving duties. EAT overruled on the grounds that the employers were entitled to prefer their medical evidence to that out forward by the claimant. The employee's appeal was dismissed, the Court of Appeal ruling that the tribunal was not entitled to find against the employer on the justification issue on the basis that the medical evidence relied upon was incorrect. The Court ruled that s.5(3) DDA confined tribunals to considering whether the reason given for less favourable treatment could properly be described as material to the circumstances of the particular case and substantial. The tribunal was entitled to investigate facts and to assess the employer's decision by determining whether there was evidence on the basis of which a decision could properly be taken. So, for example, if the employer had not carried out any risk assessment, or had made a decision other than on the basis of appropriate medical evidence, or had acted irrationally, the tribunal could find the treatment unjustified.

Jones v Post Office [2001] ICR 805

Pill LJ:

. . . The 1995 Act is plainly intended to create rights for the disabled and to protect their position as employees, but those intentions must be considered in the context of the employer's duties to employees generally and to the general public. I cannot accept, in a case such as the present, involving an assessment of risk, that Parliament intended in the wording adopted to confer on employment tribunals a general power and duty to decide whether the employer's assessment of risk is correct. The issue is a different one from whether a person has a disability, within the meaning of s.1 of the Act, which is to be determined by the employment tribunal [citing *Goodwin*].

Upon a consideration of the wording of s.5(3) in context, I conclude that the employment tribunal are confined to considering whether the reason given for the less favourable treatment can properly be described as both material to the circumstances of the particular case and substantial. The less favourable treatment in the present case is the limit upon the hours of driving. The reason given for it is the risk arising from longer periods of driving. The respondent obtained what are admitted to be suitably qualified and expert medical opinions. Upon the basis of those opinions, the respondent decided that the risk was such as to require the less favourable treatment. In order to rely on s.5(3) it is not enough for the employer to assert that his conduct was reasonable in a general way; he has to establish that the reason given satisfies the statutory criteria. The respondent asserts in this case that the risk arising from the presence of diabetes is material to the circumstance of the particular case and is substantial. Where a properly conducted risk assessment provides a reason which is on its face both material and substantial, and is not irrational, the tribunal cannot substitute its own appraisal. The employment tribunal must consider whether the reason meets the statutory criteria; it does not have the more general power to make its own appraisal of the medical evidence and conclude that the evidence from admittedly competent medical witnesses was incorrect or make its own risk assessment.

The present problem will typically arise when a risk assessment is involved. I am not doubting that the employment tribunal is permitted to investigate facts, for example as to the time-keeping record of the disabled person or as to his rate of productivity, matters which would arise upon some of the illustrations given in the Code of Practice. Consideration of the statutory criteria may also involve an assessment of the employer's decision to the extent of considering whether there was evidence on the basis of which a decision could properly be taken. Thus if no risk assessment was made or a decision was taken otherwise than on the basis of appropriate medical evidence, or was an irrational decision as being beyond the range of responses open to a reasonable decision-maker (a test approved by Sir Thomas Bingham MR in a different context in *R v Ministry of Defence ex parte Smith* [1996] 1 QB 517), the employment tribunal could hold the reason insufficient and the treatment unjustified.

The tribunal cannot, however, in my judgment, conclude that the reason is not material or substantial because the suitably qualified and competently expressed medical opinion, on the basis of which the employer's decision was made, was thought by them to be inferior to a different medical opinion expressed to them. Moreover, a reason may be material and substantial within the meaning of the section even if the employment tribunal would have come to a different decision as to the extent of the risk. An investigation of the facts by the tribunal will often be required, but it cannot go to the extent of disagreeing with a risk assessment which is properly conducted, based on the properly formed opinion of suitably qualified doctors and produces an answer which is not irrational. This constraint limits the power of tribunals to provide relief to disabled employees, but in my view it follows from the wording of the section, which requires consideration of the reason given by the employer, and recognises the importance of the employer's responsibility for working practices.

Arden LJ:

An example may help throw light on the function of the word 'material' in s.5(3). Suppose that it is shown that diabetes (of either type) leads to diminished night-time vision and the employer of an employee with diabetes prohibits that employee from doing night-time shifts for the reason that he has diabetes. In this example there would be a material connection between the employer's reason and the circumstances of the particular case. Miss Tether [for the claimant] sought to argue that materiality also involved correctness. However, in my judgment, if the employer in the example last given believed that diabetes diminished night-time vision but was entirely wrong in that belief, the requirement for materiality in the example which I have given would still be met. However, there would be difficulty in the employer meeting the second requirement of substantiality, to which I now turn.

The second requirement in s.5(3) is that the reason should be 'substantial.' This means, in my judgment, that the reason which the employer adopted as his ground for discrimination must carry real weight and thus be of substance. However, the word 'substantial' does not mean that the employer must necessarily have reached the best conclusion that could be reached in the light of all known medical science. Employers are not obliged to search for the Holy Grail. It is sufficient if their conclusion is one which on a critical examination is found to have substance. Thus a reason which on analysis is meretricious would not be a 'substantial' reason. It would fail to meet the test in s.5(3).

A tribunal faced with a claim of justification may well find it helpful to proceed by asking the following questions:

What was the employee's disability?

What was the discrimination by the employer in respect of the employee's disability?

What was the employer's reason for treating the employee in this way?

Is there a sufficient connection between the employer's reason for discrimination and the circumstances of the particular case (including those of the employer)?

Is that reason on examination a substantial reason?

The first three of those questions involve pure questions of fact. The fourth and fifth questions, however, involve questions of judgment. The latter questions may involve hearing expert evidence, but the employment tribunal should not conduct an enquiry into what is the best course of action to take in all the circumstances of the case. Nor are the tribunal required to be persuaded themselves. They are not entitled to find that the employer's reason for the discrimination was not justified simply because they take the view that some conclusion, other than that to which the employer came, would have been preferable. Nor can they conclude that justification has not been shown simply because they entertain doubts as to the correctness of the employer's conclusion. If credible arguments exist to support the employer's decision, the employment tribunal may not hold that the reason for the discrimination is not 'substantial.' If, however, the employer's reason is outside the band of responses which a reasonable employer might have adopted, the reason would not be substantial. (This test was applied by the Court of Appeal in the different context of unfair dismissal in *Post Office v Foley* [2000] IRLR 827.) In short, so far as the second limb of s.5(3) of the 1995 Act is concerned, justification is shown provided that the employer's reason is supportable.

Statute can provide different levels of protection for employees in different situations depending on the meaning of the language which Parliament has used. The scale ranges from 'de novo', or complete retrial of the issue which the employer had to decide at one end of the scale—which is the test which the employment tribunal applied in this case—to absolute deference to the employer's decision provided he acts in good faith, at the other end of the scale. There are many intermediate points on this scale. The test in this case of sufficient connection and supportable grounds represents one of these intermediate points.

The fact that the true construction of a particular statutory provision indicates that the protection given to an employee in one respect is not the maximum protection that could have been conferred or as great as the protection conferred in other areas of statute law is not of itself a reason for rejecting that construction. The right level is a matter for Parliament. It may be that in the case of disability discrimination Parliament had in mind that an employer has to balance the interests of the employee with a disability with those of fellow employees and indeed also of members of the public. Accordingly, I reject Miss Tether's submission that it would be surprising if the criteria for review under s.5(3) [DDA] were less rigorous than, for instance, under the [RRA] or [SDA].

J Davies, 'A Cuckoo in the Nest? A "Range of Reasonable Responses", Justification and the Disability Discrimination Act 1995' (2003) 32 *Industrial Law Journal* 164, 170–1, footnotes omitted

On Pill LJ's reasoning, the quality of the investigative process will be a crucial factor in determining the reasonableness of the resulting response. In stipulating that only decisions based on 'proper' risk assessments or 'properly formed' opinion of 'suitably qualified' medical experts are capable of falling within a range of reasonable responses, Pill LJ effectively establishes a lower boundary of the range as applied within the DDA. 'Proper' investigation acts as the gatekeeper to the range of reasonable responses. Only once this threshold has been crossed, may an otherwise discriminatory decision fall within the range and so be justified.

A standard of 'proper' investigation, if rigorously applied by employment tribunals, offers a basis for objective assessment of employers' reasons for their discriminatory decisions. However, objectivity is likely to be undermined both by the realities of tribunal adjudication, and by application of the range of reasonable responses test to employers' decisions. On a practical level, what are 'proper' investigations? How are tribunals to identify them? Do they have the expertise to do so? In attempting to find a workable way forward, Pill LJ's reasoning creates new complexities of adjudication for tribunals . . .

Although neither of the other two judges in *Jones* considers explicitly the subtle distinctions in Pill LJ's reasoning between the investigative process and decisions, Kay LJ endorses 'entirely' the reasoning and conclusions of his colleague, while Arden LJ agrees with both the other judgements. On her analysis, however, 'proper' risk assessment or medical evidence is relevant only to whether a reason is substantial, not to whether it is material.

Pill LJ's approach is clearly fuelled by the need, on the facts of *Jones*, to balance employers' protective duties to meet health and safety requirements with Parliament's intention to create equality of employment opportunity for disabled persons. The range of reasonable responses formula offered the neat solution of an apparently objective test of employers' decisions. However, the test has a chequered history even in its home environment . . .

Davies goes on to challenge the approach of the Court in *Jones*, arguing that the decision 'fails to recognize the conceptual mismatch between discrimination law and unfair dismissal.'

Davies (2003) 32 *Industrial Law Journal* 178–81, footnotes omitted

Practical application of the range test to disability discrimination law may confuse the concept of reasonable responses with the range of reasons on which a response may be based, despite Pill LJ's best efforts to distinguish between the two. A reasonable response is simply one which falls within a reasonable, or 'normal' range. Whether or not it arises from material and substantial reasons is another matter entirely. We should remember that reasonableness reflects standards of normal behaviour. Normal behaviour for many employers includes prejudice and stereotyping—indeed, the DDA Part II was enacted to tackle precisely this truism. Introduction of the range test risks giving the green light to 'normal' discriminatory attitudes should tribunals subconsciously mirror them by 'thinking into the shoes of employers' when applying the standard of the hypothetical reasonable employer to decisions. If this happens, *Jones* will have failed to apply the 'red light' to an area of employment practice ear-marked by Parliament for intervention.

Regrettably, Arden LJ's judgement in *Jones* opens the door for 'normal' discriminatory attitudes to prevail. In her view, misconceived health and safety fears establish a causal link between an employer's reason and the circumstances of the case sufficient to show materiality. This is worrying, as a reason based on error, stereotypes or misconception can only be regarded as material to a decision where materiality is assessed from the subjective perspective of the employer. Admittedly, she continues that such a reason is unlikely to be substantial. However, as substantial means nothing more demanding than 'having substance,' Lady Justice Arden's reasoning firmly endorses green light theory. Her reasoning on this point fails to take account of the standard of 'proper' risk assessment and medical evidence that Pill LJ has been at pains to establish as the test of materiality, as well as of substantiality.

Arden LJ's oversight of Pill LJ's emphasis on 'proper' investigative processes and of his limited application of the range test to employers' decisions, suggests that his reasoning may be too finely tuned for the realities of tribunal practice. If an appeal court judge, and one who 'agrees' his reasoning, fails to appreciate this crucial conceptual distinction, what hope that tribunals will recognise it?

Pill LJ's reasoning places a heavy burden on tribunals called upon to define the lower boundary of the range of reasonable responses by reference to 'proper' investigation of employers' reasons. If they fail in this task, either because the conceptual distinction drawn by Pill LJ eludes them, or because the task is too complex practically, then the range of reasonable responses test will be as vulnerable to charges of covert subjectivity within disability discrimination law as it is within its home environment. Even if they succeed, the test may still endorse subjective decisions by including them within the reasonable range.

Assuming for the sake of argument that tribunals do recognise the nature of the task, what problems do they face? First, they must identify the characteristics of a 'proper' investigative process. Pill LJ offers no guidance here. Tribunals are left to search for an elusive boundary to the range of reasonable responses recognisable only by the absence of 'proper' risk assessment and expert advice. It is tempting to speculate that they will fall back on the test as one of employers' 'normal' investigative behaviour, thereby perpetuating traditionally discriminatory attitudes to disability in the workplace. Of course, 'normal' behaviour for an employer should encompass risk assessments meeting statutory requirements as set out in the Management of Health and Safety at Work Regulations. Whether or not it does is another matter.

A second problem relates to tribunal expertise. Have tribunal panels, as currently constituted, the expertise necessary to scrutinise employers' investigations into whether material and substantial reasons exist for less favourable treatment? In relation to unfair dismissals, the investigative process will be familiar territory for industrial juries who will have been selected for their knowledge of the industrial workplace. They may, however, be less well equipped to assess investigations involving the complexities of risk assessments and medical evidence which frequently present in disability discrimination cases . . .

Third, in addition to potential deficiencies of expertise, jurisdictional limitations restrict the ability of tribunals to ensure that employers' investigations meet the 'proper' standard. Jones precludes tribunals from assessing the merits of expert medical evidence. Their role is restricted to ensuring that it is appropriate in the sense of emanating from suitably qualified sources. Of course, the question of what is 'suitably qualified' medical evidence raises its own difficulties. Where expert opinions conflict, the tribunal cannot find that an employer's decision is not justified simply because it finds the employee's medical evidence more persuasive. If it is based on 'suitably qualified' medical opinion, the employer's response will fall within the reasonable range even in the face of patently better evidence. This renders the tribunal's function as reviewer of materiality and substantiality largely an empty exercise. It smacks of green light theory where red light interventionism is necessary in order to change the norm.

Jones places an unwarranted degree of trust in the notion that 'suitably qualified' medical evidence will necessarily be material to the circumstances of the particular case and give rise to a substantial reason for employer's actions. Medical evidence is proving to be of crucial importance in many disability discrimination cases. Evidence to date suggests that it is not always material in the sense of relating to the individual circumstances of each case. It is regrettable that Jones denies tribunals a power to scrutinise it beyond satisfying themselves that it comes from a 'suitably qualified' source. This may be in tacit recognition of the limited ability of tribunal panels, as presently constituted, to deal with the medical issues arising in disability discrimination cases. A better approach must be to select specialist panels empowered to reject medical evidence insufficient to found objectively material and substantial reasons.

Jones imposes a very low threshold for the justification of discrimination. There are, however, two very important provisos. In the first place, s.3A(6) DDA (extracted above) provides that an employer cannot justify less favourable treatment unless, in a case in which a duty to adjust applied, the less favourable treatment would have been justified even if the employer had complied with the duty. An example of the application of this provision is provided by the Code of Practice on Employment which suggests that: '[if] an employee who uses a wheelchair is not promoted, solely because the work station for the higher post is inaccessible to wheelchairs—though it could readily be made so by rearrangement of the furniture . . . [t]he refusal of promotion would . . . not be justified.'

Section 3A(6) was successfully relied on on appeal by the claimant in *Paul v National Probation Service* [2004] IRLR 190. Mr Paul, who suffered from a chronic depressive illness, was rejected for a position with the respondents because of the assessment of the employer's occupational health adviser that the job would be unduly stressful for him given his medical history. The adviser reached this conclusion without having discussed the claimant's case with his consultant psychiatrist, relying instead on a medical report from his GP (who did not know the claimant well and had not been involved in the treatment of his depression). The GP's report did not, further, deal with the claimant's fitness for the position sought or his ability to deal with stress. An employment tribunal dismissed the claimant's DDA challenge on the grounds that the discrimination involved in denying him the position was justified within the DDA, applying the Court of Appeal's decision in *Jones v Post Office* below. EAT overruled, in part on the basis that the tribunal had not considered the employers' duty to adjust. The occupational health adviser's assessments, which were part of the employers' appointment arrangements, placed the claimant at a substantial disadvantage, and reasonable steps might have included the obtaining of specialist advice from the claimant's consultant, discussions with the claimant himself, a reference back to the occupational health adviser and possible adjustments to the job itself.

Secondly, the *Jones* test does not apply in relation to the justification of a failure to make reasonable adjustments. We saw, above, that the justification defence has been removed in cases in which *employers* fail to comply with duties to make reasonable adjustments in line with the DDA. It remains available outside the employment context. But much of its sting has been removed by the decision of the Court of Appeal in *Collins v Royal National Theatre Board Ltd* [2004] IRLR 395 in which the Court ruled that a failure to make reasonable adjustments could not be justified by reference to factors which had already been taken into account in deciding whether an adjustment was reasonable. The decision appears to signal a retreat on the part of the Court from the very permissive approach in *Jones*.[53]

Jones has also been narrowed in its application to disability-related discrimination. In *Paul v National Probation Service* EAT distinguished *Jones* (on which the tribunal had purported to rely). According to EAT, the Court of Appeal in *Jones* decided that 'a tribunal is not permitted to make up its own mind on justification on the basis of its own appraisal of an employer's medical evidence, when there has been a *properly conducted risk assessment by reference to competent and suitably qualified medical opinion* [my emphasis]. In the present case, the nature and quality of the general practitioner's evidence was plainly in issue before the tribunal, since the GP had never treated the claimant for his condition, did not know him well and said nothing in his report about his fitness for the post in question or his ability to cope with stress.'

There is a degree of uncertainty as to the relevance, to the justification defence, of medical evidence obtained after the dismissal. To the extent that *Jones* mirrors the approach taken to unfair dismissal prior to the Employment Act 2002, the focus is on the reasonableness of the employer's actions *at the time of dismissal*. In *Jones* the Court of Appeal accepted that an employer's failure to carry out a risk assessment, or irrational or medically unsupported decision making, could result in a finding that disability related discrimination was not justified under the DDA. The respondents in *Surrey Police v Marshall* [2002] IRLR 843 withdrew their offer of employment to the claimant, who had bipolar affective disorder, because their medical officer took the view that she did not meet the required medical standard. The tribunal, claiming to direct itself in accordance with *Jones*, ruled that the employers 'did not obtain suitably qualified and expert medical opinions about the particular circumstances of the applicant's case in advance of reaching a decision not to appoint her. It was not a properly conducted risk assessment.' The tribunal refused, further, to take into account subsequently obtained evidence from a

---

[53] See also *Law v Pace Micro Technology plc* [2004] EWCA Civ 923.

consultant psychiatrist to the effect that there was a significant risk of further episodes. EAT overturned, ruling that *Jones* did not prevent a tribunal from making findings of fact on medical evidence which post-dated the discrimination complained of. Parts of that evidence in this case were material as to whether there was evidence in the medical officer's hands at the time of the discrimination on which the rejection of the claimant could properly have been based, and as to whether it was a decision open to a reasonable decision-maker on the material before her. On the facts of the particular case the subsequently obtained evidence supported the employer's decision. In a different case, it could go the other way.

The limits of reliance on medical evidence obtained after the fact are illustrated by the decision of EAT in *Murray v Newham Citizens' Advice Bureau* in which the court considered whether the discrimination against the claimant, a paranoid schizophrenic with a prison sentence for stabbing a neighbour who was rejected for a volunteer position with the respondents, was justified within the *Jones* test. The tribunal had taken the view that any discrimination against the claimant was justified. EAT disagreed.

Murray v Newham Citizens Advice Bureau [2003] ICR 643

Judge D Serota QC:

There was significant medical evidence available to the employment tribunal, but not referred to . . . Dr McIver prepared a report for the employment tribunal and gave oral evidence. Dr McIver's opinion was that the risk of recurrence of a violent incident was 'very low indeed,' although there was a possibility of a relapse if Mr Murray were to cease taking his medication.

It is possible that . . . evidence [from the claimant's GP] did play some part in the employment tribunal's decision, but no reference is made at all to the matters which we have just referred to. Some of this evidence might clearly be regarded as controversial. We do not know how the employment tribunal view the risks to the respondent of employing Mr Murray on the basis of the factual information that was before the respondent when it took its decision not to offer him a place on the induction course. Neither do we know what level of risk the employment tribunal concluded the respondent considered Mr Murray to pose at the time his application was rejected . . .

It is clear that an employment tribunal is not permitted to substitute its views as to the merits of the decision of a prospective employer for those of the prospective employer. However, an employer must make such inquiries as are appropriate in the circumstances of the case. These circumstances are bound to vary infinitely. However, it must be borne in mind, in particular, that a prospective employer cannot be expected to carry out the rigorous investigation that might be expected of an employer who already employs a disabled person. It should also be borne in mind that a prospective employer may have to deal with numerous applications and clearly cannot be expected to carry out any form of detailed checks or seek medical evidence in respect of every applicant.

In our opinion, having regard to the authorities which we have cited [*Heinz, Jones, Marshall*], it is insufficient for an employer who has to justify less favourable treatment to say, 'This is the reason for the less favourable treatment. It is justified on the evidence before the tribunal.' A prospective employer must, if he seeks to rely upon the defence of justification, show that the justification was based on material that it had before it at the time it took the relevant decision. An employment tribunal should only interfere where the prospective employer's investigations are outside the reasonable range of responses by a reasonable prospective employer, in the circumstances. In the case of an employer who has failed to carry out reasonable investigations, an employment tribunal may hold that the reason was insufficient and the less favourable treatment unjustified. In a case where the employer failed to obtain the appropriate information which may, in the event, have justified its decision, that evidence cannot provide ex post facto justification, but might be relevant to the question of compensation. It might be open to the respondent to show that the applicant would, had a proper inquiry been carried out, have never been appointed, or that his chances of appointment would have been problematical . . .

We agree with the conclusion of the employment tribunal [that] 'In the case of a Citizens Advice Bureau in inner London attended by vulnerable and worried members of society, the issue of whether a potential volunteer had a propensity to inflict violence is material to the circumstances of the particular case and, in the context, substantial.'

The issue in the case is however, not whether the reason is capable of being material and substantial, but whether or not the respondent had sufficient material and had carried out adequate inquiries to justify its decision. The employment tribunal should firstly consider what material the respondent had at the time of the interview to justify its decision. It should then consider whether on the basis we have mentioned, the respondent should properly have sought additional information from Mr Murray's GP and medical advisers. If the employment tribunal comes to the conclusion that the decision not to seek further information was within the reasonable band of responses it should consider whether upon the information that the respondent had, the decision not to offer Mr Murray a post was for a reason that was both material and substantial. So far as concerns Mr Murray that information would need to show that Mr Murray was reasonably considered to pose a real, as opposed to a fanciful, threat to clients. In determining this issue the employment tribunal would be entitled to have regard to material not before Ms Young at the time of the interview, in so far as it throws light on the credibility and rationality of Ms Young. It may assist in determining whether the decision not to offer a post to Mr Murray because of his supposed risk was one that could properly have been made by Ms Young on the material before her and whether it was a decision open to her as a reasonable decision-taker on that material.

Should the employment tribunal conclude that inadequate inquiries were made and that the failure to seek further information from Mr Murray's medical advisers was outwith the reasonable band of responses of a responsible employer, then it may find the reason for the decision not to offer Mr Murray a post to be insufficient and unjustified. In the circumstances we remit the matter to be considered by a differently constituted employment tribunal to consider whether the defence of justification has been made out in accordance with our decision.

Justification Outside the Employment Context

The justification of non-employment related discrimination is dealt with somewhat differently under the DDA. Turning first to discrimination in the provision of goods, services, etc, s.20 DDA provides that this is justified only where:

(3) (a) in the opinion of the provider of services, one or more of the conditions mentioned in subsection (4) are satisfied; and

   (a) it is reasonable, in all the circumstances of the case, for him to hold that opinion.

(4) (a) . . . the treatment is necessary in order not to endanger the health or safety of any person (which may include that of the disabled person);

   (b) . . . the disabled person is incapable of entering into an enforceable agreement, or of giving an informed consent, and for that reason the treatment is reasonable in that case; [or]

    (c) in a case falling within section 19(1)(a), the treatment is necessary because the provider of services would otherwise be unable to provide the service to members of the public;

    (d) in a case falling within section 19(1)(c) or (d), the treatment is necessary in order for the provider of services to be able to provide the service to the disabled person or to other members of the public;

    (e) in a case falling within section 19(1)(d), the difference in the terms on which the service is provided to the disabled person and those on which it is provided to other members of the public reflects the greater cost to the provider of services in providing the service to the disabled person.

(5) Any increase in the cost of providing a service to a disabled person which results from compliance by a provider of services with a section 21 duty shall be disregarded for the purposes of subsection (4)(e).

This test for justification applies to discrimination consisting both of 'less favourable treatment' and a duty to make reasonable adjustments. Because the factors upon which a discriminator may rely are listed in s.20(4) there is no room for the application of the decision in *Jones* nor of that in *Collins*.

Similarly, s.22's regulation of discrimination in relation to premises provides that less favourable treatment in this context is justified only if (s.24):

(2)(a) in A's opinion, one or more of the conditions mentioned in subsection (3) are satisfied; and

    (b) it is reasonable, in all the circumstances of the case, for him to hold that opinion.

(3) (a) . . . the treatment is necessary in order not to endanger the health or safety of any person (which may include that of the disabled person);

    (b) . . . the disabled person is incapable of entering into an enforceable agreement, or of giving an informed consent, and for that reason the treatment is reasonable in that case;

    (c) in a case falling within section 22(3)(a), the treatment is necessary in order for the disabled person or the occupiers of other premises forming part of the building to make use of the benefit or facility;

    (d) in a case falling within section 22(3)(b), the treatment is necessary in order for the occupiers of other premises forming part of the building to make use of the benefit or facility.

Section 22(4), like s.20(6) DDA, provides that 'Regulations may make provision, for purposes of this section, as to circumstances in which—(a) it is reasonable for a person to hold the opinion mentioned in subsection 2(a).' The amendments to the premises provisions in the DDA 2005 provide that discrimination consisting of a failure to comply with the proposed new duty to adjust can be justified only where the controller of premises might be taken reasonably to hold the opinion (s.24K(2)):

(a) that it is necessary to refrain from complying with the duty in order not to endanger the health or safety of any person (which may include that of the disabled person concerned); or

(b) that the disabled person concerned is incapable of entering into an enforceable agreement, or of giving informed consent, and for that reason the treatment is reasonable.

New s.24K(3) provides a duty to make regulations making further provision in relation to the justification defence. Again there is no room for the application of *Jones* or *Collins* in the context of discrimination in relation to premises.

The structure of the justification defence as it applies to Part II DDA has proved controversial, critics objecting to the scope it provides for prejudicial assumptions about the disabled.[54] The only reported example to date of its application has been in the case of *Rose v Bouchet* [1999] IRLR 463 in which a visually impaired man challenged the refusal of the defender (this being a Scottish case) to let him a flat access to which was up five steps from the pavement to reach a landing.[55] At the time there was no handrail to the steps from which there were drops of two-and-a-half feet on one side, one-and-a-half feet on the other. A sheriff accepted the defender's argument that his less favourable treatment of the pursuer (Mr Rose) was justified within s.24 DDA and the Principal Sheriff Court refused his appeal:

Rose v Bouchet [1999] IRLR 463

Sheriff Principal Nicholson QC:

Looking first at subsection 2(a) along with subsection (3), we find that the defender's discriminatory treatment of the pursuer would be justified if, in the defender's opinion, the treatment was necessary in order not to endanger the pursuer's safety. So far as that part of the test is concerned, there can be little doubt in my view that it is subjective, in the sense that what is in issue is the opinion of the person carrying out the discriminatory act. I should also say that, contrary to what was submitted by counsel for the pursuer, I do not construe the statute as meaning that, as an objective fact, the treatment in question should have been necessary for the pursuer's safety. What the subsections require is that in the opinion of the defender the treatment was necessary. Subsequent evidence might well reveal that the treatment was in fact not necessary, but what matters at the time when the treatment took place was what the defender considered to be necessary at that time.

Now that does not mean, of course, that a defender can get over the hurdle presented by this part of the statute simply by saying that in his opinion it was necessary for the pursuer's safety to act as he did. His evidence in that regard must be accepted by the court as being truthful and not simply a fabrication concocted after the event. In the present case, however, (and this is where issues of credibility are, in my view, of relevance) the sheriff has accepted that the defender's refusal to let the flat to the pursuer was motivated by concern for the pursuer's safety in view of the absence of a handrail alongside the steps leading to the flat's front door. In that situation, and on the basis of what I consider to be a correct construction of this part of the Act, I consider that the sheriff was entitled to hold that the defender had satisfied the requirements of subsections (2)(a) and (3)(a) of s.24.

However, that is not the end of the matter for a person in the position of the defender. In terms of subsection (2)(b), he must go on to establish that it was reasonable, in all the circumstances of the case, for him to hold the opinion in question. In my opinion, that part of the test requires an objective assessment of all the relevant circumstances. But that, of course, raises a question as to what circumstances are relevant for this purpose; and in particular it raises the question of whether a person in the defender's position is under some sort of obligation to make inquiries of a disabled person before forming any opinion.

In considering this aspect of the case, it may be helpful at the outset to make clear that 'the relevant circumstances' do not extend to include all of the facts which may be

---

[54] See, eg, C Gooding and C Casserley, 'Disability Discrimination Laws in Europe relating to Goods and services,' extracted above and below.

[55] In neither *Ross v Ryanair* nor in *Roads v Central Trains* was justification argued.

established at a much later stage, for example during proof in a litigation. Counsel for the pursuer did not suggest that the reasonableness of an opinion should be tested, ex post facto as it were, by objective reference to all of the facts which might come to light at a later stage, and I am of opinion that counsel was correct to adopt that position. However, as I have noted earlier, he founded strongly on the submission that the defender should have engaged in dialogue with the pursuer so as to obtain more relevant facts than were immediately available to him. That submission bore, of course, to be founded on the Code of Practice . . .

In my opinion, counsel's submission on this point is crucial if the pursuer is to succeed because, like the sheriff, I consider that the opinion reached by the defender, *on the facts as then known to him*, was a reasonable one for him to reach. He knew that the pursuer is blind and uses a guide dog; he knew that the steps leading up to the flat had no handrail, with the result that there was an unguarded drop on each side; he considered that that posed a threat to safety (the reasonableness of which view was subsequently confirmed by the inspector from the Environmental Health Department); and he had the view of a second person, namely his wife, which confirmed his own opinion as to the risk which the steps might pose to the pursuer. Looking objectively at the foregoing facts, I am of opinion that the sheriff was fully entitled to hold that, in terms of subsection (2)(b) of s.24, it was reasonable for the defender to hold the opinion which he did.

The question then is whether the defender should have endeavoured to obtain more information before finalising his opinion. The Act itself does not impose any such duty, but I accept that the Code contains a suggestion that some inquiry may be desirable. In my opinion, however, the need for further inquiry will depend very much on the facts and circumstances of a particular case. If the owner of a flat which is available for letting receives an inquiry from a person who uses a wheelchair, and the owner is unsure whether certain doors in the flat will be wide enough to let the wheelchair pass through, then it is probably reasonable to expect some inquiry to be made as to the measurements of the wheelchair before declining to let the flat. That, it seems to me, is just the sort of situation where the closing words of paragraph 1.7 of the Code ('When in doubt, ask the disabled person'), would be of relevance. In the present case, however, the facts as found by the sheriff appear to me to demonstrate that the pursuer himself gave the defender no opportunity to pursue any further inquiries. The sheriff's findings, which I have mentioned earlier, are that, as soon as the defender advised the pursuer that he thought the flat would be unsafe for him, the pursuer shouted, accused the defender of refusing to take his guide dog, and brought the telephone conversation to a conclusion. I agree with the solicitor for the defender that in a situation such as this one it is not unreasonable to expect the disabled person himself to offer some further information which might influence the other person's opinion. The pursuer in this case did not do that, and in my view that failure, coupled with the abrupt and angry ending of the telephone conversation, must mean that the defender cannot be open to any criticism for not making further inquiry of the pursuer.

C Gooding and C Casserley, 'Disability Discrimination Laws in Europe Relating to Goods and Services', Disability Rights in Europe conference (Leeds, September 2003)

Subsequent to this decision, a revised Code of Practice was issued which referred specifically to 'all the circumstances of the case' including seeking advice and the opinion of the disabled person.

More recently, the Queens Bench Division, in another housing case, considered the test of justification under the premises provisions. *North Devon Homes Ltd. and Christine Brazier* concerned an order for possession which had been granted in respect of a tenant with a psychiatric disorder, despite the District Judge having found that the local authority had acted contrary to the DDA in seeking possession . . . Ms. Brazier had admitted to persistent anti-social behaviour, including shouting at neighbouring tenants, keeping them awake, using foul language etc. The District Judge found that the eviction was not necessary in order not to endanger the health and safety of any person, as, *inter alia*, although the neighbours underwent a great deal of uncomfortableness, and were still experiencing such difficulties, 'they are not such as to endanger the health or safety of any person.' This aspect of the decision was upheld by the Queens Bench, whilst the eviction order was quashed.

In the *Glover* case, involving a refusal to admit a disabled person with their guide dog, the District Judge considered the justification put forward by the café owner for refusing to let Mr. Glover in with his guide dog (he defended the claim on the basis that he had an incident with a guide dog some years previously when the dog had been sick in the café and had caused £1,000 of loss. He also indicated that there was not enough room in the café for the dog to be [in]—in essence, a health and safety justification). The District Judge found that to the extent that the 'no dogs in the eating area' policy was implemented in response to this incident, it was primarily out of financial rather than health and safety considerations. 'In any event, adults and children may become ill when using a restaurant; events of this nature will always be a possibility and this is not a reason for excluding them.' In relation to the size of the premises, the district judge preferred the evidence of the applicant's witnesses as to the availability of tables and the ability of the dog to sit under them. In addition, the defendant made no attempt to make an objective assessment of the policy he adopted in relation to the incident, and did not assess the situation when the applicant presented at the café. It was held that the defendant's opinion that guide dogs present a danger to health and safety was not a reasonable one for him to hold in all the circumstances of the case.

Concerns remain, however, about the operation of the justification—in particular the fact that essentially prejudicial views, which society may ascribe to, can be held to justify discriminatory treatment. The Commission has recommended that the wording of the justification provision be amended to provide an objective test for justifying potential discrimination in goods and services matters. The Commission has also invited the government to work with it in researching the use and efficacy of the present justifications, and in particular to consider the barriers to service provision of the health and safety justification.

The DRC's Code of Practice on Rights of Access to Goods, etc, provides examples of cases in which the justification defence may and may not be made out, drawing attention to the need for the discriminator's opinion to be reasonably held if it is to constitute a defence to discrimination under Part II of the Act (ie, in relation to goods, services, facilities and premises). In *Council of the City of Manchester v Romano & Samari* [2004] EWCA Civ 834 the Court of Appeal took into account the respondent's obligations under the DDA in determining whether it had acted 'reasonably' for the purposes of possession proceedings taken under Housing Act 1985 for causing nuisance, annoyance and harassment to neighbours.

Turning to the justification of discrimination in the context of education, s.28B (see above) provides as follows:

(6) Less favourable treatment of a person is justified if it is the result of a permitted form of selection.
(7) Otherwise, less favourable treatment, or a failure to comply with section 28C, is justified only if the reason for it is both material to the circumstances of the particular case and substantial.

Section 8S, which applies to post 16 education, provides that:

(6) Less favourable treatment of a person is justified if it is necessary in order to maintain—
    (a) academic standards; or
    (b) standards of any other prescribed kind.
(7) Less favourable treatment is also justified if—
    (a) it is of a prescribed kind;
    (b) it occurs in prescribed circumstances; or
    (c) it is of a prescribed kind and it occurs in prescribed circumstances [no Regulations have been made under this section].
(8) Otherwise less favourable treatment, or a failure to comply with section 28T, is justified only if the reason for it is both material to the circumstances of the particular case and substantial.

The Disability Rights Commission's Code of Practice for Schools suggests (para 5.15) that the treatment accorded to the pupils in the examples set out above would not be justified. In the first case this is because the governing body has not sought to justify the treatment. In relation to the second example (the pupil with Tourette's syndrome) the Code suggests that: 'the responsible body might argue that the inclusion of the disabled pupil on the visit would make the maintenance of discipline impossible. This may constitute a material and substantial reason. However, the responsible body would need to have considered the extent to which the disabled pupil's behaviour could have been managed. It would also need to have considered whether reasonable adjustments could have been made to its policies and procedures before it could attempt to justify less favourable treatment.' Further: 'there were reasonable adjustments that were normally in place; the introduction of new ideas was carefully managed, as were time pressures. Left unmanaged, both of these tended to exacerbate the effects of the pupil's impairment. In this case, a supply teacher was taking the class and failed to make the adjustments that were normally made. Reasonable adjustments might have been made but were not, and therefore the responsible body is unlikely to be able to justify the less favourable treatment.'

As to the academic standards defence, the Post 16 Education Code of Practice gives the following guidance (paras 4.26–4.27):

> The Act does not require a responsible body to do anything that would undermine the academic standards of a particular course. A responsible body may be able to justify less favourable treatment if it is necessary to maintain these standards. [s 28S(6)(a)]
> • A young man with learning difficulties applies to do a biology degree. He does not meet the entry requirements for the course. The university talks to the college where the man had previously been studying and concludes that, even if reasonable steps were taken to eliminate any disadvantage caused by his disability, there would be no prospect of his completing the degree course successfully. Although the lack of entry requirements is related to the man's disability, the institution is likely to be justified in rejecting his application because to accept him would be to undermine the academic standards of the course.
> The academic standards reason should not be used spuriously. Where elements are not central or core to a course, they are unlikely to provide a reason to justify discrimination based on academic standards. Nor can academic standards be used as justification for barring whole groups of disabled people from courses or services. Any justification has to be relevant to the academic standards of a particular course and to the abilities of an individual person.

- A severely dyslexic student applies to take a course in journalism. She does not have the literacy necessary to complete the course because of her dyslexia. The college rejects her, using the justification of academic standards. This is likely to be lawful.
- The college now introduces a policy of rejecting all dyslexic applicants to Journalism. The policy does not allow course selectors to consider different levels of dyslexia, the ability of individual applicants or the range of possible adjustments. This is likely to be unlawful.

Discrimination in the education field (whether it consists of less favourable treatment or a failure to make reasonable adjustments) is also justified (in common with discrimination under Part II of the Act) if it is for a 'material and substantial' reason. There is little appellate case law other than under the employment-related provisions of the DDA but the decisions in *Jones* and *Collins* are equally applicable in the education context with the effect that (a) less favourable treatment is subject to a low threshold for justification but (b) a failure to make reasonable adjustments cannot be justified by reference to factors relevant to whether an adjustment would have been reasonable. Further, as is the case elsewhere under the DDA, less favourable treatment in the education context will be justified, in a case in which there is a duty to make reasonable adjustments, only if it would be justified even had the adjustment(s) been made.[56]

The Post 16 Education Code of Practice gives a number of examples of circumstances in which discrimination is (and is not) likely to be regarded as justified under the DDA (paras 4.30–4.3).

> To be material to the circumstances of the particular case, the reasons have to relate to the individual circumstances.
> - A student with emotional and behavioural difficulties applies for a college course. He has previously been on a link course to the college and staff know that he is extremely disruptive and makes a great deal of noise during classes which prevents other students from learning. During his previous periods in the college, tutors tried to make adjustments for him, but these were not successful. The college approaches the school, which confirms there has been no change in his behaviour. The college decides that they cannot accept him on to the course. The reasons for the failure to admit him relate to this particular student and his particular behaviour patterns. For this reason, the college is likely to be acting lawfully in rejecting the student.
> A reason also has to be substantial and not just minor or trivial.
> - A student with autistic spectrum disorder applies for a course. The student can be disruptive, and sometimes will talk inappropriately during classes. However, her interruptions are not much more than those made by other students, and when she has an assistant with her, her behaviour improves. There is unlikely to be any material and substantial reason to justify not admitting this student.
> - A blind woman applies to do a forensic science degree. Although she can undertake some parts of the course, she cannot see enough to undertake the parts of the course which involve visual analysis of materials. This is a core component of the course. The college is likely to have a substantial reason to justify not accepting this student . . .
> - A student has decided not to tell his institution that he has dyslexia despite several opportunities to do so. The course tutor notices that his test results are poor, and asks the student whether he might like to consider having a diagnostic assessment to see whether he has dyslexia. The student tells the tutor that he was just feeling tired that day and this

[56] Ss.28B(8), 28S(9).

appears a satisfactory explanation. While chatting to another member of staff, however, the student tells her in strictest confidence that he is dyslexic and is finding it difficult to write his essays. Because she has been asked to keep the information confidential, the staff member does not pass this information on. The tutor gives a low mark for the student's test. The institution is likely to have a material and substantial reason to justify the less favourable treatment.

Finally, the proposed regulation of disability-related discrimination by public authorities was mentioned above. New s.21D DDA, inserted by the DDA 2005, provides that discrimination (whether consisting of less favourable treatment or a failure to make reasonable adjustment) is justified if (s.21D):

> (3)(a) in the opinion of the public authority, one or more of the conditions specified in sub-section (4) are satisfied; and
> (b) it is reasonable, in all the circumstances of the case, for it to hold that opinion.
> (4) The conditions are—
> (a) that the treatment, or non-compliance with the duty, is necessary in order not to endanger the health or safety of any person (which may include that of the disabled person);
> (b) that the disabled person is incapable of entering into an enforceable agreement, or of giving an informed consent, and for that reason the treatment, or non-compliance with the duty, is reasonable in the particular case;
> (c) that, in the case of treatment mentioned in subsection (1), treating the disabled person equally favourably would in the particular case involve substantial extra costs and, having regard to resources, the extra costs in that particular case would be too great;
> (d) that the treatment, or non-compliance with the duty, is necessary for the protection of rights and freedoms of other persons.

According to the explanatory notes to the Bill: 'It is envisaged that a public authority will be able to rely on [s.21D(5)] only in relation to matters of public interest (for example, the detection of crime) that, subject to an assessment of proportionality, can be said to be sufficiently important to override the right conferred by new section 21B.' There are regulation-making powers in new section 21D(6) and (7) to restrict the operation of the justification defence.

9

Religion and Belief

Introduction

Prior to December 2003 Northern Ireland was unique in the UK in having legislation (the Fair Employment and Treatment Order (FETO)) which explicitly regulated discrimination on grounds of religion. Attempts had been made in Britain to pass such legislation by means of Private Members' Bills: in 1998, for example, MP John Austin introduced the Religious Discrimination and Remedies Bill in the House of Commons. The Bill, which would have applied to employment, goods, services and facilities, failed to become law as did Lord Ahmed's Race Relations (Religious Discrimination) Bill 1999 which would have amended the RRA to afford protection against discrimination on grounds of religion (see further the discussion of the RRA below). Not until 2003, with the passage of the Employment Equality (Religion or Belief) Regulations, did Britain have anti-discrimination legislation aimed specifically at discrimination on grounds of religion or belief. As their title suggests, the RB Regs deal only with discrimination in the context of employment, albeit broadly defined (see further Chapter 4).

The regulation of discrimination on grounds of religion and belief gives rise to difficulties not generated by other types of discrimination. Whereas one person's right not to be subjected to race discrimination is unlikely to conflict with another person's such right (the same being true in relation to sex, sexual orientation, disability, etc), anti-discrimination rights connected with religion and belief may well clash with each other, and with anti-discrimination rights connected with other grounds such as sex and sexual orientation. This 'clash of rights' arises in part from the fact that religious bodies, as well as individuals, claim protection for freedom of religion and belief. In order to maintain its religious ethos, a body may wish to exclude others who do not share that ethos, or whose behaviour is otherwise considered not to be in conformity with the ethos of the collective. This is relatively uncontroversial where, for example, a church or religious organisation wishes to discriminate, on grounds of religion, in the appointment of a minister. Most would agree that such discrimination is an exercise of the organisation's religious freedom and that any state interference with that decision would be an unwarranted intrusion into the organisation's autonomy. Certainly interference by the state in the selection of religious ministers is an interference with rights protected by Article 9 of the European Convention, and is likely to breach that provision absent very compelling justification (though such justification might be present in the case of established churches). It follows that any prohibition on religious discrimination will almost inevitably contain qualifications relating to the appointment of ministers, etc. Certainly the RB Regs, discussed below, contain a Genuine Occupational Requirement defence which would permit discrimination in these and similar circumstances. The SDA is also qualified in this context (see s.19), the restriction of religious positions to men being a feature of many religions. And even where no exception as such applies the courts are unlikely readily to intervene in disputes as to the suitability of candidates for religious ministry. In *R v Chief Rabbi, ex parte Wachman* [1993] 2 All ER 249, for example, an application for judicial review of the Chief Rabbi's decision to expel someone from the Jewish ministry on religious grounds was rejected on the basis (*per* Simon Brown J, as he then was) that:

> the court is hardly in a position to regulate what is essentially a religious function—the determination whether someone is morally and religiously fit to carry out the spiritual and pastoral duties of his office. The court must inevitably be wary of entering so self-evidently sensitive an area, straying across the well-recognised divide between church and state.
>
> One cannot, therefore, escape the conclusion that if judicial review lies here, then one way or another this secular court must inevitably be drawn into adjudicating upon matters intimate to a religious community.

The termination of the claimant's position as a rabbi resulted from the Chief Rabbi's declaration that he was 'no longer religiously and morally fit to occupy his position as rabbi' following allegations of adultery with members of his congregation. A similar approach would be expected where, for example, a Catholic priest was removed from the priesthood on the grounds that he was sexually active (celibacy being required of members of the priesthood), or a Presbyterian minister on the grounds that he was an active homosexual and therefore sexually active other than within marriage.

Judicial reluctance to intervene is evident also in the approach to unfair dismissal claims by ministers of religion which are met, almost invariably, with the response that no contract exists between the minister and the church. Typical of this approach is the dicta of Dillon LJ in *President of the Methodist Conference v Parfitt* [1984] QB 368:

> I do not think it is right to say that any contract, let alone a contract of service, comes into being between the church and the minister when the minister accepts an invitation from a circuit steward to become a minister on a particular circuit . . . it seems to me that it follows, from a correct appreciation of the spiritual nature of the minister's position and relationship with the church, that the arrangements between the minister and the church in relation to his stationing throughout his ministry and the spiritual discipline which the church is entitled to exercise over the minister in relation to his career remain non-contractual . . .
>
> . . . the spiritual nature of the work to be done by a person and the spiritual discipline to which that person is subject may not necessarily, in an appropriate context, exclude a contractual relationship under which work which is of a spiritual nature is to be done for others by a person who is subject to spiritual discipline. On any view the spiritual nature of the work and the spiritual discipline under which it is performed must be very relevant considerations when it has to be decided whether or not there is a contractual relationship.

The courts have declined to find contracts in existence between Presbyterian ministers, Anglican curates, Sikh priests and Muslim khateebs and their churches/ congregations,[1] although the House of Lords insisted in *Davies v Presbyterian Church of Wales* [1986] ICR 280 that it was possible that an intention to create contractual relations could be found in an individual case. This appears to be honoured wholly in the breach, however, and courts and tribunals are overwhelmingly unlikely to find that no contract exists. This being the

---

[1] Respectively *Davies v Presbyterian Church of Wales* [1986] ICR 280 (HL), *Diocese of Southwark v Coker* [1998] ICR 140 (CA), *Santokh Singh v Guru Nanak Gurdwara* [1990] ICR 309 (CA), *Birmingham Mosque Trust Ltd. v Alavi* [1992] ICR 435 (EAT).

case, ministers of religion are unlikely even to qualify for protection under the wide approach to 'employees' taken by the RB Regs (anyone 'employed' (reg 2) 'under a contract of service or of apprenticeship or a contract personally to do any work'). But the Regs also apply (reg 10) in relation to 'any office or post to which persons are appointed to discharge functions personally under the direction of another person, and in respect of which they are entitled to remuneration.' It is this provision which extends the protection of the RB Regs to many (though probably not all) ministers of religion. The recognition by those regulations of the GOR defence is the factor which will permit the courts to intervene without unduly interfering with the religious freedoms of religious collectives.

More problematic is the case in which a religious organisation, or an organisation with a religious ethos, seeks to rely on its own religious freedom to refuse employment to, or otherwise to subject to detriment, someone whose role is not that of a minister. Thus to take an example from the caselaw, should a Catholic school be permitted to sack an unmarried teacher because she is pregnant by a Catholic priest? The answer in *O'Neill v Governors of St Thomas More Roman Catholic School* [1997] ICR 33 was 'no,' this because (see Chapter 6) a dismissal on grounds of pregnancy is a dismissal on grounds of sex and no exception applied. But nothing in the SDA would prevent a school from requiring particular standards of sexual behaviour from staff, as long as these standards did not differentiate between men and women. Dismissals connected with private sexual behaviour might, of course, breach the unfair dismissal provisions of the Employment Rights Act 1996 or, in the case of a state school, Article 8 of the European Convention on Human Rights and, accordingly, the Human Rights Act 1998. But this will not necessarily be the case. Detailed discussion of the European Convention and HRA is outside the scope of this book. But we saw in Chapter 1 that the HRA does not fully apply the Convention rights where the discriminator is a private body. Further, the jurisprudence which has developed under Article 9 of the Convention provides very limited protection especially in cases in which religious adherence requires the accommodation of, for example, prayer time or dress codes. This is discussed briefly below.

The RB Regs permit some discrimination on grounds of religion where the 'employer has an ethos based on religion or belief and, having regard to that ethos and to the nature of the employment or the context in which it is carried out being of a particular religion or belief is a genuine occupational requirement for the job.' But this would not permit sex discrimination such as that which occurred in *O'Neill*, that discrimination (even if it could be regarded as being 'on grounds of religion or belief') nevertheless breaching *primary* legislation which takes precedence over the Regs. Special provision is made by the SO Regs in relation to discrimination connected with sexual behaviour. This is considered in Chapter 10.

The complexities associated with the regulation of discrimination on grounds of religion and belief have not given rise to particular difficulties in the operation of the religious belief provisions of FETO, perhaps given the extraordinarily homogeneous nature (until recently) of Northern Ireland's society. Race relations legislation was not extended to Northern Ireland until 1997 when the Race Relations (NI) Order was finally passed. The problem targeted by FETO, which is considered further below, was primarily that of discrimination and disadvantage experienced by the Catholic, largely politically nationalist, Northern Irish community. The Order prohibits discrimination on grounds of 'religious belief' and 'political opinion.' It is of particular interest, however, because of its structural approach to entrenched discrimination. Whereas, as was discussed in Chapter 5, British anti-discrimination legislation adopts a primarily individualistic approach to problems of discrimination, Part VII FETO imposes registration, monitoring and review obligations upon employers in relation to the religious composition of their workforces.

These obligations, as we shall see below, are directed towards ensuring that the Catholic and Protestant communities in Northern Ireland are accorded 'equality of opportunity' in employment in Northern Ireland (what this means is further considered below).

The nature of Northern Irish society has changed in the last few decades and FETO has become the vehicle for transposition of the religion or belief provisions of the Employment Equality Directive (Council Directive 2000/78/EC). It is worth making the point, however, that the experience of decades of anti-religious discrimination provisions in Northern Ireland has by no means generated all of the issues which can be expected to arise in the UK post implementation of the RB Regs. Some sense of the richness of the UK's religious composition is provided by the ACAS guide, *Religion or Belief and the Workplace* (Appendix 2) which lists 'some of the most commonly practised religions and beliefs in Britain' as 'Baha'I, Buddhism, Christianity, Hinduism, Islam, Jainism, Judaism, Other Ancient Religions including Druidry, Paganism, Wicca, Astaru, Odinism and Shamanism, Rastafarianism, Sikhism and Zoroastrians.'[2] Some aspects of these religions are considered below.

FETO is also considered below. But it does not stand alone in regulating religious discrimination in the UK. We saw, in Chapter 7, that the protections of the RRA extend to discrimination which, though related to religion, is sufficiently closely connected with race to amount to 'race' discrimination for the purposes of that Act. This form of protection remains very significant notwithstanding the recent transposition into the UK of the religion or belief provisions of the Employment Equality Directive: whereas the RRA prohibits discrimination across a wide range of grounds (and, see Chapter 3, imposes positive obligations on public authorities to promote racial equality), the RB Regs impact at present only on 'employment,' albeit broadly defined.[3] In this chapter we consider, in turn, the RRA, the RB Regs and FETO.

'Race' and 'Religion'

In Chapter 7 we considered the decision of the House of Lords in *Mandla & Anor v Dowell Lee & Anor* [1983] 2 AC 548, in which their Lordships ruled that Sikhs were properly considered a 'racial group' within the RRA on the grounds, that they shared (per Lord Fraser) a long shared history and a cultural tradition of their own, together with a number of additional useful but nor obligatory factors (per Lord Templeman, who agreed with Lord Fraser) 'group descent, a group of geographical origin and a group history.' The flaws in that decision have been considered in Chapter 7. Here we are concerned with the question

[2] According to the Judicial Studies 'Equal Treatment Benchbook' para 3.1.2: 'The 2001 Census show that 71.6 per cent of respondents (37 million) stated their religion as Christian, while 15.5 per cent (9.1 million) stated they have no religion and a further 7.3 per cent (4.2 million) did not respond to the question. Some 3.1 per cent of England's population and 0.7 per cent of the Welsh population give their religion as Muslim, making this the most common religion after Christianity. Some 8.5 per cent of London's population give their religion as Muslim; 4.1 per cent are Hindu and 2.1 per cent are Jewish . . . Among non-Christian faiths the largest groups were Pakistani Muslims (658,000), Indian Hindus (467,000), Indian Sikhs (301,000) Bangladeshi Muslims (260,000) and White Jews (252,000). 45 per cent of Indians were Hindu, 29 per cent Sikh and 13 per cent Muslim. 92 per cent of both the Pakistani and Bangladeshi groups were Muslim. There was variation by ethnicity among those saying they had no religion: over half of Chinese people and a quarter of those with mixed backgrounds said this.'

[3] The Equality Bill 2005 would have prohibited discrimination on grounds of religion and belief in access to goods, facilities and services and in relation to education. Its proposals are mentioned throughout the book and are very likely to be introduced in the event of a Labour victory in the May 2005 general election.

when discrimination on grounds of religion will also amount to discrimination on grounds of race.

Prior to the decision in *Mandla* it had been accepted that Jews were a racial group for the purposes of the RRA (*Seide v Gillette* [1980] IRLR 427, EAT). In *Dawkins v Department of the Environment* the Court of Appeal ruled that Rastafarians did not comprise a racial group for the purposes of the RRA. The claimant, whose job application had been rejected because he refused to cut his hair, claimed that he had been discriminated against on grounds of race. His claim had been accepted by a tribunal but rejected by EAT on the ground that, Rastafarians having existed as a group for only 60 years, they did not have a 'long shared history' which, in the EAT's view, was required in order that Rastafarians might be regarded as an 'ethnic' group. (Unless Rastafarians could be regarded as such a group they could not qualify as a 'racial group' within s.3(1): Rastafarians, who comprise only a small subsection of black people and African Caribbeans, a subsection of those of Jamaican or African origin, cannot be identified by reference to colour, race, nationality or national origins.)

Before the Court of Appeal, counsel for Mr Dawkins argued that the tribunal's acceptance of 60 years as a 'long' shared history was a question of fact which was not amenable to review. He also drew attention to the conflicts between Lord Fraser's and Lord Templeman's speeches in order to argue that, the decision in *Mandla* having obscured rather than clarified the meaning of s.3(1), the Court should rely on the intervening decision in *Pepper v Hart* [1993] AC 593 and look to the parliamentary debates in determining the question whether Rastafarians should be regarded as an ethnic group. These, he claimed, supported the understanding of ethnicity in the following terms:

> A group is identifiable in terms of its ethnic origins if it is a segment of the population distinguished from others by a sufficient combination of shared customs, beliefs, traditions and characteristics derived from a common or presumed common past, even if not drawn from what in biological terms is a common racial stock. It is that combination which gives them an historically determined social identity in their own eyes and in the eyes of those outside the group. They have a distinct social identity based not simply on group cohesion and solidarity but also on their belief as to their historical antecedents.

In *Dawkins v Department of the Environment* Lord Justice Neill rejected the argument that there was sufficient ambiguity between the speeches of Lord Templeman and Lord Fraser to justify recourse to parliamentary material, declaring that counsel for Mr Dawkins:

Dawkins v Department of the Environment [1993] ICR 517

falls into the error of equating the language used in speeches or judgments with that of a statute. In giving reasons for a decision a judge seeks to explain the basis on which he has reached his conclusion. The speech or judgment has to be read as a whole. It is very often possible to find one passage in a judgment which, because different language is used, gives a slightly different impression or has a slightly different nuance when compared with another passage. For my part, however, I cannot detect any real difference in substance between what Lord Fraser said and what Lord Templeman said. Both of them stressed that the words 'ethnic origins' had to be construed in the light of the fact that they occurred as part of a definition of 'a racial group.' Lord Fraser . . . said that the word 'ethnic' still retained a racial flavour. Lord Templeman . . . agreed that in the context ethnic origins had a good deal in common with the concept of race.

I am satisfied therefore that in these circumstances this was not a case where it would have been appropriate for the court to be referred to statements in Hansard . . .

I am unable to accept that the Industrial Tribunal's decision by a majority that Rastafarians had a sufficiently long shared history to satisfy Lord Fraser's first condition was merely a finding of fact with which an appellate court cannot interfere. The finding that the group originated in 1930 was indeed a finding of fact, but a decision as to the length of a shared history, which is necessary for the purpose of satisfying a statutory test, is a very different matter. In any event it is important to remember that the relevant words in the statute are 'ethnic origins' . . .

It is clear that Rastafarians have certain identifiable characteristics. They have a strong cultural tradition which includes a distinctive form of music known as reggae music. They adopt a distinctive form of hairstyle by wearing dreadlocks. They have other shared characteristics of which both the . . . Tribunal and [EAT] were satisfied. But the crucial question is whether they have established some separate identity by reference to their ethnic origins. In speaking about Rastafarians in this context I am referring to the core group, because I am satisfied that a core group can exist even though not all the adherents of the group could, if considered separately, satisfy any of the relevant tests.

It is at this stage that one has to take account of both the racial flavour of the word 'ethnic' and Lord Fraser's requirement of a long shared history. Lord Meston submitted that if one compared Rastafarians with the rest of the Jamaican community in England, or indeed with the rest of the Afro-Caribbean community in this country, there was nothing to set them aside as a separate ethnic group. They are a separate group but not a separate group defined by reference to their ethnic origins. I see no answer to this submission . . .

In my judgment it is not enough for Rastafarians now to look back to a past when their ancestors, in common with other peoples in the Caribbean, were taken there from Africa. They were not a separate group then. The shared history of Rastafarians goes back only 60 years or so. One can understand and admire the deep affection which Rastafarians feel for Africa and their longing for it as their real home. But, as Mr Riza recognises, the court is concerned with the language of the statute. In the light of the guidance given by the House of Lords in *Mandla*, I am unable to say that they are a separate racial group.

One of the problems which has become apparent with *Mandla* in recent years is its application to discrimination, whether direct or indirect, against Muslims. Such discrimination will sometimes, and sometimes not, amount to discrimination on racial grounds.

S Poulter, 'Muslim Headscarves in School: Contrasting Approaches in England and France' (1997) 17 *Oxford Journal of Legal Studies* 43, 64, footnotes omitted

So far,—in four cases decided by industrial tribunals and the Employment Appeal Tribunal, it has been held that Muslims are not an ethnic group but a religious one. As the South London Industrial Tribunal explained in *Nyazi v Rymans Ltd*:

'Muslims include people of many nations and colours, who speak many languages and whose only common denominator is religion and religious culture.'

More importantly, perhaps, Muslims worldwide do not possess a 'shared history' and many perceive themselves not as members of an ethnic group but as part of an essentially religious community or 'ummah.' To some extent, this definitional hurdle can be circumvented through a plaintiff's reliance on membership of a group which does fall clearly within the terms of the Act. A Muslim pupil whose parents came to Britain from Pakistan could plead, for example, that any discrimination against her was based on her Pakistani nationality, her Pakistani 'national origin' (if she was a British citizen) or her Asian 'race.' On the other hand, the daughter of one of the growing number of white or black (Afro-Caribbean) British converts to Islam could not take advantage of this approach.

Nyazi v Rymans Ltd concerned a complaint from a Muslim woman who had been denied leave to celebrate Eid. The tribunal found itself:

Nyazi v Rymans Ltd, App. No. EAT/6/88 (unreported)

unable to conclude that Muslims . . . come within the meaning of 'ethnic group.' All we can say is that Muslims profess a common religion in a belief in the Oneness of God and the prophethood of Muhammed. No doubt there is a profound cultural and historical background and there are traditions of dress, family life and social behaviour. There is a common literature in the sense that the Holy Quaran is a sacred book. Even so, many of the other relevant characteristics would seem to be missing.

The Muslim faith is widespread, covering many nations, indeed many colours and languages, and it seems to us that the common denominator is religion and a religious culture. In other words we believe Muslims are a group defined mainly by reference to religion and that being so we must find that we have no jurisdiction under the Act.

EAT rejected the claimant's appeal, ruling that the tribunal had not 'erred either in the exercise of its discretion, or in the conclusion it reached on the facts which were before it.' In *Walker v Hussain*, however, a tribunal accepted that discrimination against Muslims amounted to discrimination against Asians and thence to race discrimination.[4] There, Asians were less able to comply with a requirement to work through the summer than were non-Asians in the workplace. Eid fell during the summer months and observant Muslims could not work during that period. Their race discrimination claim succeeded because, most Asians in the workplace being Muslim and the tribunal adopting a workplace pool for comparison, the claimants could demonstrate that Asians were significantly less likely than non-Asian employees to be in a position to comply.

The reasoning adopted by the tribunal in *Walker* would not have applied in a workplace in which the majority of Asian workers were not Muslim, and, if a tribunal were to select the pool from the general population, rather than the workplace, Asians may not be significantly more likely than non-Asians to be devout Muslims so as to be unable to comply, for example, with a requirement to work through Eid. So, for example, in *Safouane v Bouterfas* (1996), the dismissal of two Muslim employees for praying during work breaks did not constitute indirect race discrimination because they were from the same North African ethnic Arab minority as the respondents.[5] 'In any event,' as Hepple and Choudhury point out: 'Even if a finding of indirect race discrimination is made, the legislation does not at present allow for an award of compensation . . . where there is no intention to discriminate.'[6]

Where direct discrimination against Muslims is at issue, the question whether indirect race discrimination has occurred depends upon whether people of the claimant's racial group are put at a particular disadvantage by a requirement not to be Muslim (what the relevant 'racial group' is will differ from case to case).[7] But where the discrimination against

---

[4] This aspect of the decision was not appealed to EAT whose decision in the case is at [1996] ICR 291.

[5] Discussed in B Hepple and T Choudhury, 'Tackling religious discrimination: practical implications for policy-makers and legislators' (Home Office Research Study 221), para 1.8.

[6] *Ibid.*

[7] In *Walker*, for example, it was 'Asians' while in *CRE v Precision Manufacturing Services Ltd* COIT 4106/91, 26 July 1991 a tribunal categorised direct discrimination against Muslims as indirect discrimination against 'coloureds'. The term is no longer acceptable but, as the CRE draft revised Code of Practice points out (para 2.4) a 'Nigerian' may be defined by up to four grounds: 'race,' 'colour,' 'ethnic or national origin' and 'nationality.' Claims based on nationality or colour are perhaps to be avoided, where there is a choice, given that the improved provisions of the RRA apply only to discrimination on the other grounds.

Muslims takes the indirect form (as in the discussion of hijab wearing, below), the RRA will be breached only where the relationship between religion and race is so close that the provision, criterion or practice complained of places people of the claimant's 'racial group' at a particular disadvantage, as well as disadvantaging the claimant herself.

The absence of any clear legal relationship between Islam and 'race' as it is conceived in the RRA has left Muslims without legal protection from discrimination aimed at them *as Muslims*, rather than, for example, as Asians or black Britons. Muslims are not the only religious group unprotected by the RRA (Jehovah's Witnesses, for example, were regarded as falling outwith the Act by a tribunal in *Lovell-Badge v Norwich City College of Further and Higher Education*).[8] But the patchy applicability of the RRA to discrimination against Muslims is particularly problematic given the rise of 'Islamophobia' in the wake of the Salman Rushdie affair and, more recently, September 11, 2001.[9]

BBC Online, Thursday, 29 August 2002

Earlier in the year, a European Union anti-racism research agency warned there was anecdotal evidence of a rise in Islamophobia. . . research by the University of Leicester is the first detailed study into the actual effects of 11 September on a Muslim community. Racist and religious attacks in Leicester rose dramatically after 11 September, the university's research found, before dropping back during 2002. Attacks included abuse hurled at children on their way to school or women shopping, to one reported incident where a baby was tipped out of a pram. One man reported that he had eggs thrown at him outside a supermarket and then had to run as a car was driven at him. Another victim reported that he had had to get off a bus after another passenger screamed accusations that he was a bomber. The research found that Hindus and Sikhs also suffered increased abuse after 11 September, although not to the same degree.

Dr Lorraine Sheridan who conducted the research for the university, said that she had been shocked by what she had found.

'The attacks are being carried out by people who don't like Islam, the abuse is more about the religion than the race. They think that it victimises women and that Muslims refuse to integrate. The people behind the attacks think that Muslims are outside of society and they are different. What is of most concern is that this is happening in Leicester, a leading multi-ethnic city which is supposed to be a model for the rest of the UK.'

Suleman Nagdi of the Federation of Muslim Organisations in Leicester, said that while incidences of attacks had now fallen, the community had been shaken by attacks—but many remained reluctant to report them.

'Many of the attacks that came after 11 September were against women in the street,' said Mr Nagdi. 'They presented an easy target because people could identify their religion by their headscarves.'

---

[8] Noted in Hepple and Choudhury, n 4 above, n 22 to para 1.8.

[9] See the Runnymede Trust, 'Islamophobia: a Challenge for us all' (1997), 'Addressing the Challenge of Islamophobia' (2001), 'The Nature of Islamophobia' (1997) and 'Islamophobia as a Form of Racism' (2000).

W Dalrymple, 'Islamophobia', *The New Statesman,* **January 2004**

There are moments when it is possible to believe that Britain is beginning to shed its racist past, and to hope that we do now live in a genuinely tolerant, colour-blind and multicultural society. Yet it is still clearly acceptable to most people in Britain to make the sort of straightforwardly racist remarks about Arabs and Muslims that would now be considered quite unacceptable if made about Jews, Catholics or blacks. At the very least, the furore has shown how badly the British need to be educated about Islam and the Arab world. At the moment, the Islamic contribution to world civilisation is completely ignored in the British school curriculum: at my own school, I came across Islam only in the negative and confrontational context of the Crusades. But the problem is bigger than that. Islam has now replaced Judaism as Britain's second religion, and it sometimes feels as if Islamophobia is replacing anti-Semitism as the principal western statement of bigotry against 'the Other': the pre-war Blackshirts attacked the newly arrived East End Jews, and today we have their modern equivalents going 'Paki-bashing.' The massacre of more than 7000 Muslims at Srebrenica in 1995 never led to a stream of articles in the press about the violent tendencies of Christianity. Yet every act of al-Qaeda terrorism brings to the surface a great raft of criticism of Islam as a religion, and dark mutterings about the sympathies of British Muslims . . .

Today, we have a situation in London where the number of mosque-going Muslims is fast catching up with the number of church-going Christians. Nor is there any obvious drop-off in the faith of second-generation British Muslims. There are now nearly a thousand mosques serving Britain's 1.8 million Muslims, the great bulk of them having opened within the past 15 years. Islam is the fastest-growing religion not only in Britain but also in France and the US, and this is as much to do with conversion as immigration. The constant media refrain about 'what went wrong' with Islam—to paraphrase Bernard Lewis—ignores its self-evident success and its increasing popularity.

Indeed, in the past few years Britain, and especially London, has become one of the world's principal centres of Islamic publishing, as well as a major Muslim intellectual and cultural centre. According to Fuad Nahdi, founder editor and publisher of the Muslim magazine *Q-News,* 'There's no other place in the world where you get quite as global a variety of Islam as here, and the result is the beginnings here of a cosmopolitan and distinctively British form of Islam.'

Yet for all this, British Muslims remain firmly on the margins of our national life. Britons of Bangladeshi and Pakistani origin are two and a half times more likely to be unemployed than the white population, and three times more likely to be on low pay. Considering the size of our Muslim community, it is scandalous that there are only four Islamic schools in the state sector. It is even more alarming that there are only four Muslim peers, two Muslim MPs and one lone British Muslim MEP. One of Tony Blair's most senior advisers recently told me that Labour did not take Muslim sentiment seriously as there was yet to emerge a serious lobby for Islam, capable of reacting in a politically coherent manner.

British Muslims are used by now to endless abuse, discrimination and violence. Little of this gets reported, whether to newspapers, monitoring groups or the police . . . perhaps the most worrying thing about this trend is the extent to which it has gone largely unrecognised and uncriticised: indeed, despite centuries of prejudice and violence against Muslims, the term Islamophobia was coined only within the past decade. Moreover, intellectualised versions of this anti-Islamic revulsion have come to find acceptance in defence and political circles . . . Significantly, one of the best-selling non-fiction books in both France and Germany last year was the horribly anti-Islamic *Who Killed Daniel Pearl?*, by the French salon philosopher Bernard-Henri Levy. The book was well reviewed in both countries, and few reviewers bothered to note Levy's profound and rather disturbing hatred of ordinary Pakistanis, whom Levy portrayed throughout as fanatical Orientals who 'scowl' as he passes and 'narrow their eyes . . . with a tarantula-like stare.'

Yet almost as worrying as the way Levy managed to get away with his crudely anti-Muslim comments was the true story of the abduction of Pearl, a journalist. The man who kidnapped Pearl in Karachi was a highly educated British Pakistani, Ahmed Omar Sheikh. Sheikh attended the same public school as the film-maker Peter Greenaway and later studied at the London School of Economics. Yet such was the racism he suffered, that he was drawn towards extreme jehadi groups and eventually came to be associated with both Harkat ul-Mujahideen and al-Qaeda. If intelligent, successful and well-educated British Muslims such as Omar Sheikh can be so readily drawn in to the world of the jehadis, we are in for trouble. The combination of widespread hostility to the Muslims in our midst, pervasive discrimination against them and huge ignorance is a potentially lethal cocktail . . .

Attempts to prohibit incitement to religious hatred floundered in December 2001 after the then Home Secretary David Blunkett suffered a second defeat in the House of Lords. The Law Lords were concerned about the implications for freedom of expression, In March 2002 a select committee of the House of Lords was set up to consider Lord Avebury's Religious Offences Bill which would abolish the common law against blasphemy and miscellaneous religious offences, and prohibit incitement to religious hatred.

The committee reported in June 2003 that outlawing incitement to religious hatred and amending other legislations relating to religious offences would be a 'threat to freedom of expression' and 'likely to be controversial.' According to the Muslim News, Secretary General of the Muslim Council of Britain, Iqbal Sacranie, was 'greatly disappointed with the outcome of the Report. Overwhelming evidence was provided which confirmed that the evil of Islamophobia is now broadly acknowledged as a pervasive and negative force in the society.' Proposals to criminalise incitement to religious hatred were included in the Serious and Organised Crime Bill 2004 but did not survive that Bill's passage into law.

The RB Regs, discussed below, now regulate discrimination against Muslims and others defined on grounds of religion in the context of employment and third level education. But Muslims are at present unprotected from discrimination in other areas of life, except where it amounts to race discrimination for the purposes of the RRA. The question addressed by Poulter below is whether a 'considerably smaller proportion' of (say) Pakistani girls than of non-Pakistanis or non-Asians could comply with a 'no scarf' requirement:

Poulter (1997) *Oxford Journal of Legal Studies* 65, footnotes omitted

. . . In practice, the general impression is that very few Muslim girls in England, of whatever nationality or national origin, wear the *hijab* as part of their normal clothing out of school. Certainly, the figure seems unlikely to be anywhere near twenty per cent of any national group, save possibly in the case of those pupils from states in the Arabian Gulf, of whom there are extremely few. The crucial point is that, in statistical terms, the wearing of

Muslim headscarves by girls in this country appears to be just as rare a phenomenon as it is in France, where it has been estimated at below two per cent. There is a stark contrast here with the wearing of *shalwars*, the loose-fitting trousers worn by large numbers of Asian women and girls in this country in pursuance of religious norms or cultural traditions. With *shalwars*, the proportionality test could easily be satisfied and therefore a school rule which prescribed the wearing of skirts certainly could constitute indirect indiscrimination.

Some of the difficulties mentioned by Poulter have eased somewhat as a result of recent amendments to the RRA, the new test for indirect discrimination being easier to satisfy (see Chapter 2). The recent controversy over headscarf bans in France and Germany is considered below, as are the implications of the RB Regs for discrimination against Muslims. It is sufficient here to say that a claimant no longer has to establish—where the alleged discrimination is on grounds of race or ethnic or national origin—that a 'requirement or condition' has been applied to her with which she is unable to comply and with which a considerably smaller proportion of those from her racial group than of others can comply; rather that a 'provision, criterion or practice' has been applied to her which is to her disadvantage and which 'puts or would put persons' of the same racial group 'at a particular disadvantage when compared with other persons.' It is no longer necessary for the claimant to establish that she is unable to comply with a requirement, for example, not to wear a headscarf (this would have rendered her vulnerable to investigation as to the extent of her adherence to the particular rule relied upon[10]); or to put forward statistical evidence of the extent of headscarf wearing in her particular racial group (though such evidence might help to establish that persons of that group would be 'put at a particular disadvantage' by the disputed provision, criterion or practice). But even if a prima facie case of indirect discrimination is established, discrimination against Muslims can be justified under the RRA. Whereas this is true only in respect of indirect discrimination against Jews and Sikhs (in the form, for example, of a requirement to work on Saturday, for men to be clean shaven or women to have short hair); both direct and indirect discrimination against Muslims may be justified under the RRA (this because such *direct* religious discrimination would amount at best to *indirect* race discrimination).

Poulter (1997) *Oxford Journal of Legal Studies* 66–7, footnotes omitted

Even if a Muslim pupil, necessarily relying on her national origins overseas, did manage to satisfy the court on the proportionality test, her school would still not be acting unlawfully if it could establish the statutory defence that its general headwear regulation was 'justifiable irrespective of the colour, race, nationality or ethnic or national origins' of the pupil concerned. In recent years this defence of justifiability has been considerably tightened and a test of objective necessity has been developed. A balance now has to be struck between the discriminatory effect of the rule and the reasonable needs of the school. The school would have to demonstrate that the rule corresponded to a real need, rather than mere convenience, and that there was no viable alternative solution available to meet that need. Such necessity might be established in cases where a *hijab* could put the health or safety of a pupil at risk, for instance in some scientific experiments or activities involving vigorous physical exercise . . .

If the foregoing analysis leads to the inexorable conclusion that Muslims, as such, have no legal right to wear headscarves at school and that there is only a remote prospect of even a pupil of Pakistani or Bangladeshi origin succeeding in a claim under the 1976 Act, the

---

[10] As in the *Nyazi* case in which there was some dispute as to whether the claimant was an observant Muslim (this being relevant to whether she could comply with a requirement to work during Eid).

irony of the situation should at least be noted at this stage. Any triumph in court would be derived from reliance upon national origins, whereas the whole reason for wearing the headscarf would be totally unconnected with such origins and be derived in fact from religious beliefs. It would indeed be a hollow victory for Islam in those circumstances. By contrast, the turban is invariably portrayed by Sikhs as a communal religious symbol and the decision in *Mandla v Dowell Lee* is thus perceived as upholding their religious freedom [though see below] rather than protecting them from racial discrimination.

The test for justification discussed by Poulter has been replaced, where the indirect discrimination is on grounds of 'race or ethnic or national origin' with the question whether the discrimination can be shown to be a proportionate means of achieving a legitimate aim. This is unlikely significantly to change the approach of the courts to justification (see further Chapter 2).

The headscarf issue has generated great controversy over recent months, the French Government having adopted a ban (effective from September 2004) on the wearing of all 'ostentatious signs of religion' including Jewish yarmulkes and large Christian crosses, in French public schools. The ban, which was aimed at Muslim headscarves, resulted in widespread protest and a debate as to the appropriate balance between secularism (a guiding principle of the French state) and a duty to accommodate religious obligations. There are five million Muslims in France which has the biggest Muslim population in the EU. Press reports suggest that 50 per cent of France's Muslim community (70 per cent of French generally) voted in favour of the ban. The *Daily Telegraph* reported (31 December 2003) that the French ban had gained the support of Sheikh Mohammed Sayyed Tantawi, the Grand Mufti of the al-Azhar mosque in Cairo and the foremost authority in Sunni Islam, who said that France had the right to pass a law banning all 'conspicuous' religious symbols in state schools and institutions. According to the *Telegraph* report:

Wearing the headscarf was 'a divine obligation for all Muslim women' that no governing Muslim could deny . . .

But, he added, that obligation only applied 'if the woman lives in a Muslim country.' He quoted verses from the Koran stipulating that any Muslim who conforms to the laws of a non-Muslim country need not fear divine punishment. Until yesterday the sheikh had remained silent over the issue, describing it as 'an internal French affair'.

Human Rights Watch, however, condemned the French ban: 'For many Muslims, wearing a headscarf is not only about religious expectation, it is about religious obligation.'[11] Many of the concerns expressed about the headscarf ban concern its potential for resulting in the exclusion of Muslim girls in France from mainstream education, though Catholic weekly *The Tablet* claimed in January 2004 that 'of [France's] 250,000 Muslim pupils, only 1256 schoolgirls insist on wearing the headscarf; of these, a mere 20 have caused problems, and just four have been expelled.' The French ban followed those imposed by a number of German Länder following a ruling by Germany's Constitutional Court in 2003 that states could ban headscarves if they were deemed to 'unduly influence' pupils.[12] According to a BBC report in April 2004, a further five of Germany's 16 Länder 'are in the process of passing similar bans.'

[11] Quote on www.humanrightwatch.org.
[12] The German case is discussed by Dagmar Schiek at (2004) 33 *Industrial Law Journal* 68.

Particular concerns have been expressed as to the impact of the ban on France's tiny Sikh community.

The *New York Times*, 12 January 2004

No one, it seems, thought about the Sikhs and their turbans . . .

After all, France is home to only several thousand Sikhs, compared with about a hundred times as many Jews and a thousand times as many Muslims. Historically, the Sikh community is quiet, law-abiding, apolitical and almost invisible, living, working and worshiping mainly in a few isolated pockets of suburban Paris.

Now the Sikhs have suddenly found their voice, demanding that they be exempted from the anticipated prohibition on religious symbols in schools.

Sitting bare-footed and cross-legged in a large worship room in the Gurdwara Singh Sabha temple in the working-class Paris suburb of Bobigny, two dozen Sikhs sounded a chorus of protest.

'I'm 100 per cent French, I speak French, I was born here,' said Dharmvir Singh, a 17-year-old student who wears a dark blue turban knotted in front to school every-day. 'But it's impossible for me to take off my turban. If they force me, I'll have to drop out, and never be able to do anything except a job that no one else wants.'

He said that he has no identity card—a violation of French law—because he refuses to remove his turban for the official photo. . .

The Sikhs' situation underscores the perils that confront a state when it ventures into the complicated world of religious practice. The impetus for the law stems largely from the phenomenon in recent years of more and more Muslim girls turning up at their public schools in head scarves or in long black veils that hide their chins, foreheads and the shape of their bodies. . .

Most Jewish students who wear yarmulkes attend private Jewish schools; Catholic students' wearing crosses that Chirac described as 'obviously of an excessive dimension' and therefore unacceptable have never posed a problem.

In a letter to Chirac last week seeking an exemption from the law, Chain Singh, a leader of the Bobigny temple said that if Sikhs could not wear their turbans to school, 'This will not only be a failure of our freedom to practice our religion here in France but also of the attitude of the French toward the Sikh community.'

The outcry of the Sikhs so late in the game has both stunned and dismayed French officials and experts involved in the blue ribbon panel, and many had no idea that Sikhs live in France . . .

An official at the Ministry of National Education, which is responsible for negotiating the law with Parliament, declined comment, except to say, 'What? There are Sikhs in France?' A senior official at the Ministry of the Interior responsible for religious matters said, 'I know nothing about the Sikh problem. Are there many Sikhs in France?'

The ideal of the secular Republican state in which all Frenchmen are equal is so strong that the census does not count people according to race, religion or ethnic origins.

Even though the vast majority of Sikh students are French citizens, the Sikh community has also sent a letter of protest to the Indian Embassy in Paris asking the Indian government to intercede on its behalf. The Sikh letter to Chirac injects a new twist into the debate, arguing that the turban should be allowed because it is a cultural not a religious symbol. "Different from a Muslim veil or a Jewish yarmulke, a turban has no religious symbolism,' the letter said. One of the tenets of the Sikh religion require Sikh men never to cut their hair, but says nothing per se about wearing turbans. . . .

The distinction between cultural and religious dress cuts both ways. On the one hand, the French government could argue if the garment is purely cultural, there is no reason why Sikhs must wear it, just as schools traditionally ban students from wearing baseball caps and other head coverings. Denis Matringe, one of France's leading specialists on India, said, however, that 'For Sikhs to remove their turbans and show their long hair would be to humiliate them.' On the other hand, the Sikhs could claim that there is nothing intrinsically religious about the turban and recommend that French school principals continue to turn a blind eye to the practice, as some do when Muslim girls turn up in veils.

Discrimination against Sikhs would be actionable in the UK because—as we saw in Chapter 7—Sikhs constitute a racial group for the purposes of the RRA. It is interesting, however, to note the different reactions generated by anti-Sikh and anti-Muslim measures. It should, of course, be noted that prohibitions on the wearing of head-covering, or the imposition of rigid rules regarding working time, amount at best to indirect rather than to direct discrimination (unless deliberately used as mechanisms by which to target members of particular religious groups). The extent to which employers and others can be required to accommodate religious needs and obligations, rather than merely refraining from subjecting adherents of particular religious groups to differential and less favourable treatment, is further considered below.

The Religion or Belief Regulations

The RB Regs, considered throughout the preceding chapters, form part of the transposition in Britain of the religion and belief provisions of the Employment Equality Directive. The Directive, so far as is relevant here, provides:

Article 2
1. For the purposes of this Directive, the 'principle of equal treatment' shall mean that there shall be no direct or indirect discrimination whatsoever on any of the grounds referred to in Article 1 [these include 'religion or belief'].

Article 4
1. Notwithstanding Article 2(1) and (2), Member States may provide that a difference of treatment which is based on a characteristic related to any of the grounds referred to in Article 1 shall not constitute discrimination where, by reason of the nature of the particular occupational activities concerned or of the context in which they are carried out, such a characteristic constitutes a genuine and determining occupational requirement, provided that the objective is legitimate and the requirement is proportionate.

2. Member States may maintain national legislation in force at the date of adoption of this Directive or provide for future legislation incorporating national practices existing at the date of adoption of this Directive pursuant to which, in the case of occupational activities within churches and other public or private organisations the ethos of which is based on religion or belief, a difference of treatment based on a person's religion or belief shall not constitute discrimination where, by reason of the nature of these activities or of the context in which they are carried out, a person's religion or belief constitute a genuine, legitimate and justified occupational requirement, having regard to the organisation's ethos. This difference of treatment shall be implemented taking account of Member States' constitutional provisions and principles, as well as the general principles of Community law, and should not justify discrimination on another ground.

Provided that its provisions are otherwise complied with, this Directive shall thus not prejudice the right of churches and other public or private organisations, the ethos of which is based on religion or belief, acting in conformity with national constitutions and laws, to require individuals working for them to act in good faith and with loyalty to the organisation's ethos.

Article 14

1. In order to tackle the under-representation of one of the major religious communities in the police service of Northern Ireland, differences in treatment regarding recruitment into that service, including its support staff, shall not constitute discrimination insofar as those differences in treatment are expressly authorised by national legislation.
2. In order to maintain a balance of opportunity in employment for teachers in Northern Ireland while furthering the reconciliation of historical divisions between the major religious communities there, the provisions on religion or belief in this Directive shall not apply to the recruitment of teachers in schools in Northern Ireland in so far as this is expressly authorised by national legislation.

We have considered the definitions of discrimination contained in the Regs in Chapter 2 (namely, direct and indirect discrimination, victimisation, harassment, the issue of instructions and the provision of assistance to discriminate). In Chapter 3 we considered the extent to which the Employment Equality Directive and its implementing regulations permit positive discrimination while the scope of the regulations (as of the other anti-discrimination provisions) was dealt with in Chapter 4 and enforcement issues in Chapter 5. Here we consider those aspects of the RB Regs which are unique to them. These consist of the meaning of 'religion or belief,' and the application in this particular context of the prohibition on indirect discrimination on grounds of religion and belief: to what extent are employers required to accommodate the needs or adherents of particular religions.[13] In addition, we consider the Genuine Occupational Requirements applicable under the RB Regs. We will then turn to FETO as it has been amended, in its application in Northern Ireland, to transpose the religion or belief provisions of the Employment Equality Directive and will, finally, consider Article 9 of the European Convention on Human Rights.

---

[13] On this point it is worth noting that reg 26 provides (1) that requiring a Sikh (man) to wear turbans on building sites is not justifiable under the Regs unless there are reasonable grounds to believe that the man will not wear a turban at all times on site, and (2) that any special treatment afforded to Sikhs by virtue of their exemption (under the Employment Act 1989) from the requirement to wear a safety helmets on a construction site 'shall not be regarded as giving rise, in relation to any other person, to any discrimination.'

'Religion or Belief'

The Employment Equality Directive does not define 'religion or belief.' Some sense of the width of the intended scope of the term is apparent from recital 13 of the preamble to the original proposal for the Directive, which referred to the EU's Declaration on the status of churches and non-confessional organisations, attached to the Amsterdam Treaty, which 'has explicitly recognised that it respects and does not prejudice the status which churches and religious associations or communities enjoy in the Member States under national law *and that it equally respects the status of philosophical and non-confessional organisations*' (my emphasis).

According to Mme Quintin of the European Commission, in her evidence to the House of Lords Select Committee on the EU (Social and Consumer Affairs (Sub-Committee G) in 1999: 'we have deliberately chosen not to define the various grounds of discrimination but to leave it for the definition of Member States . . . because we know all the differences and all the difficulties which have been encountered . . . when it has been discussed to come to a common definition.'[14] Bob Hepple was: 'not sure that given the great differences among the 15 Member States and the enlarged Union one could really begin to have a definition [of 'religion or belief'] which would satisfy all Member States. It may therefore be better to leave this . . . to case law development.'[15] The Committee, in its Ninth Report of 1998–99, however, found it 'notable . . . that Professor Hepple envisaged definitions evolving in the courts: "Ultimately the European Court of Justice has to decide the question." ' Thus even those witnesses who supported the Commission's decision not to provide definitions of key concepts, including the grounds of discrimination, did so on the understanding that 'definitions produced by Member States would be subjected to the scrutiny of the ECJ.'[16]

The possible approaches to the transposition of the religion and belief provisions of the Employment Equality Directive were discussed by Bob Hepple QC and Tufyal Choudhury in 2001:

B Hepple and T Choudhury, 'Tackling religious discrimination: practical implications for policy-makers and legislators' (Home Office Research Study 221) 25–30, footnotes omitted

For those framing [anti-discrimination] legislation there are three options. The *first* option is to attempt a definition within the legislation or through a statutory code of practice. A starting point may be the classical sociological definition of religion set out by Durkheim:

> [A] unified system of beliefs and practices relative to sacred things, that is to say, things set apart and forbidden—beliefs and practices which unite into one single moral community called a Church, all those who adhere to them.

Alternatively one could take the Oxford English Dictionary definition of religion as 'action or conduct indicating a belief in, reverence for, and desire to please, a divine ruling power; the exercise or practice of rites or observances implying this . . . a particular system of faith and worship' . . . Another broader formulation is that adopted by Ontario Human Rights Commission. The Ontario Human Rights Code prohibits discrimination on the grounds of 'creed.' Creed is not a defined term in the Code. The Commission's guidance states that:

---

[14] Para 62 of the Ninth Report of the Committee for the 1998–99 session, 'EU Proposals to Combat Discrimination', HL 68.

[15] *Ibid*, para 63.

[16] *Ibid*, paras 63–64.

Creed is interpreted to mean 'religious creed' or 'religion.' It is defined as a professed system and confession of faith, including both beliefs and observances or worship. A belief in a God or gods, or a single Supreme Being or deity is not a pre-requisite. Religion is broadly accepted by the Commission to include, for example, non-deistic bodies of faith, such as the spiritual faiths/practices of aboriginal cultures, as well as bona fide newer religions (assessed on a case by case basis). The existence of religious beliefs and practices are both necessary and sufficient to the meaning of creed, if the beliefs and practices are sincerely held and/or observed. 'Creed' is defined subjectively. The Code protects personal religious beliefs, practices or observances, even if they are not essential elements of the creed, provided they are sincerely held.

The advantage of utilising a statutory code of practice, to which the courts must have regard, is that it provides guidance to users of the legislation on where to draw the line while leaving flexibility to deal sensitively with individual cases. However any definition will inevitably exclude some groups and would require further interpretation.

A *second option* is to have a list of recognised religions with a process and criteria for such recognition. The list system is operated to an extent in Germany, where certain religions are given the status of legal person in public law, through procedures in force under Article 140 of the Constitution. The status of legal person gives rise to certain rights, in particular the right to levy church taxes through the services of the State and the right to tax advantages and tax exemptions. A 'cult' is granted the status of a legal person in public law when, in light of its statute and its membership, it gives every indication of durability.

Recognition requires a 'measure of internal organisation, adequate financing, and a certain period of existence; in practice, existence for thirty or forty years is required before a religious community can be considered to have shown sufficient durability.' Jehovah's Witnesses and the Church of Scientology and the Muslim Community are among those that have so far not received recognition as legal persons in public law in Germany.

The creation of lists of accepted religions raises the issue of the recognition of new religious movements. Those who favour an official list system claim a number of advantages. It provides a system of executive supervision to prevent protection being given to fleeting beliefs, or ones which are believed to present a threat to other human rights and values. It also allows for a high degree of certainty as regards the scope of legislation for various purposes. If utilised in the case of anti-discrimination legislation, it would reduce the need for litigation to decide whether a religious group came within the scope of the Act. There is already some experience of official listing of religions in the UK. The prison chaplaincy service carries out an Annual Religious Census on which Scientologists, Black Muslims and Rastafarians are recorded as 'non-permitted religions' . . .

The main *disadvantages* of a list system are that it would require an administrative or judicial procedure in order to determine the status of a particular religion . . . Certainty may be outweighed by rigidity, and the possibly unfair exclusion of new and unpopular beliefs. A law against religious discrimination is primarily concerned with conferring protection on individuals in respect of their own sincerely held beliefs, rather than protecting or legitimating any particular religion.

The *third option* is to leave the definition of religion for the courts to develop. Article 14 of the ECHR prohibits discrimination on the grounds of religion without providing a definition of religion. Most anti-discrimination legislation in Australia, Canada and the United States which prohibits discrimination on the grounds of religion adopts this approach. The definition has been left to the courts, in some cases with guidance provided by the enforcement commission.

The definition of religion by charitable trusts has been considered . . . by the Charity Commissioners in the light of the HRA. In determining an application by the Church of

Scientology the Commissioners reviewed the existing case law and concluded that the 'English authorities were neither clear nor unambiguous as to the definition of religion in English Charity law, and at best the cases are of persuasive value with the result that a positive and constructive approach and one which conforms to the ECHR principle, to identifying what is a religion in charity law could and should be adopted.'[17] They concluded that while belief in a supreme being was a necessary characteristic of religion for the purposes of English charity law it would not 'be proper to specify the nature of that supreme being or to require it to be analogous to the deity or supreme being of a particular religion.' The Commissioners concluded that the Church of Scientology did claim to profess a belief in a supreme being. However the Church of Scientology was not recognised as a religion because their core religious service of 'auditing and training' was not sufficient for the 'reverence and veneration for a supreme being' which the Commissioners considered 'necessary to constitute worship in English charity law.' ...

Courts and tribunals in the UK had some experience in the 1970s of interpreting 'religious belief' and also 'conscience' in the context of exemptions from closed shop arrangements. The Industrial Relations Act 1971, s.9 granted an exemption to a worker who genuinely objected on grounds of 'conscience' to union membership. The National Industrial Relations Court held that, in the context of an individual's reasons for refusing to join a trade union, this 'necessarily points to and involves a belief or conviction based on religion in the broadest sense as contrasted with personal feeling, however strongly held, or intellectual creed.'[18] However, the Employment Appeal Tribunal later disagreed and said that grounds of conscience do not necessarily involve religious belief.[19] The 1971 Act was amended in 1974 so as to limit the exemption to objections to 'grounds of religious belief.' The Employment Appeal Tribunal held that the belief which falls to be considered is that which is held by the person whose belief is under consideration, rather than an established body of creed or dogma appertaining to the individual as well as a number of other persons.

It can be seen from this discussion that the third option has the advantage of allowing the courts to interpret 'religion' in a way which accords with the purposes of the legislation. The main purpose of anti-discrimination legislation is to protect the individual from arbitrary treatment based on stereotypes or unjustified practices. The courts will not be concerned with the legitimacy of a particular creed, but rather with whether or not there has been discrimination because an individual is believed, rightly or wrongly, to subscribe to those beliefs.

The Employment Equality Directive does not, of course, confine its protection to 'religion' but extends also to 'belief.'

Hepple and Choudhury 31–2, footnotes omitted

No one argues that there should be an official list of recognised beliefs. But is some definition necessary? The House of Lords Select Committee looking at the Article 13 draft employment directive expressed concern that belief 'would appear to encompass a wide range of political or ideological views.' The issues and options raised by the definition of 'belief' are similar to those surrounding the definition of religion.

Again, the *first option* would be to provide a definition in the legislation or a statutory code of practice. The *second option* would be to leave this to the courts. The ECHR may be

---

[17] Citing Application for Registration as a charity by the Church of Scientology—decision of the Charity Commissioners for England and Wales made on 17 November 1999.
[18] Citing *Hynds v Spillers-French Baking Ltd* [1974] IRLR 281.
[19] Citing *Saggers v British Railways Board* [1977] ICR 809.

of some assistance here. The broad approach of the Convention organs to the interpretation of Article 9 has enabled them to accept, in principle, that its protection extends to Druidism, pacifism, veganism, the Divine Light Zentrum and the Church of Scientology.[20] The European Court of Human Rights has said that Article 9 is a 'precious asset for atheists, agnostics, sceptics and the unconcerned.'[21]

This does not, however, mean that every individual opinion or preference constitutes a religion or belief. To come within the protection of this article the views must attain a certain level of cogency, seriousness, cohesion and importance.[22] In *McFeely v UK* the Commission said that 'belief' in Article 9 'means more than just "mere opinions or deeply held feelings"; there must be a holding of spiritual or philosophical convictions which have an identifiable formal content' [[1981] 3 EHRR 161]. The courts may in future be guided, when interpreting the Article 13 employment directive, by the EU Charter of Fundamental Rights, Article 1 of which says that 'the dignity of the person must be respected and protected.' Those beliefs which are essential to the dignity and integrity of the individual are likely to be protected as an aspect of freedom of belief. On the other hand, the courts may be unwilling to allow political or ideological views (eg, against the criminalisation of drugs or against genetically modified foods) to qualify as a 'belief.'

The UN Human Rights Committee has also recognised that the definition of 'religion or belief' should be subjected to certain limits. In the case of *M.A.B .; W.A.T. and A.Y.T. v Canada*[23] the applicants argued that the Canadian *Narcotics Control Act* violated their right to freedom of thought, conscience and religion under Article 18 of the ICCPR because it prohibited the use of marijuana. The applicants were associated with the Assembly of the Church of the Universe. Their beliefs and practices included the care, cultivation, possession, distribution, maintenance, integrity and worship of marijuana, which they referred to as the 'sacrament' of the Church. The Committee said that the expression 'religion or belief' does not encompass a belief which consists primarily or exclusively of the worship of and distribution of a narcotic drug. [Even where the religion or belief is protected, religious observances (such as the use of prohibited drugs) may be restricted if this is objectively justified and reasonable (eg, because of the harm caused by drugs): see *Price v President of the Law Society of the Cape of Good Hope* 1998 (8) Butterworths Constitutional Law Reports 976 (C)]. A further safeguard is provided by Article 9(2) of the ECHR which allows for limitations on the manifestation of beliefs to be prescribed by law provided that the test of necessity is met . . . This would mean that although an employee could not be dismissed simply for holding extreme beliefs, dismissal or other discriminatory treatment for the manifestation of those beliefs, for example by proselytising other employees or engaging in disruptive behaviour, could be justified if this could be shown to be necessary for the protection of public order or health or morals or to protect 'the rights and freedoms of others.'

The original consultation document on the implementation of the Employment Equality Directive suggested that, because of 'the wide variety of different faiths and beliefs in this country, we have reached the view that we should not attempt to define "religion or belief," and that it would be better to leave it to the Courts to resolve definitional issues as they arise

---

[20] Citing, respectively, *Chappell v UK* (1987) 53 DR 241, *Arrowsmith v UK* (1978) 19 DR 5, 109 *X v UK* (Commission) App. 18187/91, 10 February 1993, *Omkarananda and the Divine Light Zentrum v Switzerland* (1981) 25 DR 105 and *X & Church of Scientology v Sweden* (1979) 16 DR 68.

[21] Citing *Kokkinakis v Greece* (1994) 17 EHRR 397.

[22] Citing *Campbell & Cosans v UK* (1982) 4 EHRR 293.

[23] Citing Comm No. 570/1993, Inadmissibility Decision of April 8 1994, cited in *Article 18—Freedom of Religion and Belief* (Human Rights and Equal Opportunities Commission, 1998) 11.

[nevertheless] we do intend to make it clear that the term "belief" does not apply to political belief—which is not covered by the Directive. In our view, "belief" extends only to religious beliefs and profound philosophical convictions similar to religious belief which deserve society's respect.'[24] A number of respondents pointed out that there were difficulties with this approach; not least the fact that 'Article 9 of the European Convention on Human Rights, which is given effect to in the UK by the Human Rights Act 1998, protects "freedom of thought, conscience and religion," as well as a qualified right to manifest "religion or belief." ' . . .

By the second round of consultation (*Equality and Diversity: The Way Ahead*) the Government had decided 'not . . . to give any further definition of these terms except to say that "belief" should be taken to refer to a religious or similar belief, but not a political belief more generally.' In the event, the RB Regs themselves provide (reg 2(1)) that: ' "religion or belief" means any religion, religious belief, or similar philosophical belief.'

DTI, 'Explanatory Notes for the Employment Equality (Sexual Orientation) Regulations and the Employment Equality (Religion and Belief) Regulations', paras 10–15 and 28–30

It will be for the courts and tribunals to determine, in accordance with the Directive's requirements, whether a religion or belief falls within this definition.

The reference to 'religion' is a broad one, and is in line with the freedom of religion guaranteed by Article 9. It includes those religions widely recognized in this country such as Christianity, Islam, Hinduism, Judaism, Buddhism, Sikhism, Rastafarianism, Baha'is, Zoroastrians and Jains. Equally, branches or sects within a religion can be considered as a religion or religious belief, such as Catholics or Protestants within the Christian church, for example. The European Court of Human Rights has recognized other collective religions including Druidism, the Church of Scientology as the Divine Light Zentrum. The main limitation on what constitutes a 'religion' for the purposes of Article 9 is that it must have a clear structure and belief system . . . Even if a belief does not constitute a religion for these purposes, it may constitute a 'similar philosophical belief' (see below).

The reference to 'similar philosophical belief' does not include any philosophical or political belief unless it is similar to a religious belief. This does not mean that a belief must include a faith in God/Gods or worship of a God/Gods to be 'similar' to a religious belief. It means that the belief in question should be a profound belief affecting a person's way of life, or perception of the world. Effectively, that belief should occupy a place in the person's life parallel to that filled by the God/Gods of those holding a particular religious belief. As with a religious belief, a similar philosophical belief must attain a certain level of cogency, seriousness, cohesion and importance, be worthy of respect in a democratic society, and not incompatible with human dignity . . . Examples of beliefs which generally meet this description are atheism and humanism; examples of beliefs which generally do not are support for a political party, support for a football team.

References to 'religious belief' and 'similar philosophical belief' include references to a person's belief structure involving the absence of particular beliefs, because these are two sides of the same coin. This is in line with Article 9 ECHR . . . For example, if a Christian employer refuses an individual a job, because he is not a Christian, regardless of whether he is Muslim, Hindu, atheist (etc), that would be direct discrimination on grounds of the individual's religious belief, which can be described as 'non-Christian.' It is not necessary to identify the individual as an atheist or a Hindu for the purposes of the Regulations in such circumstances if he can be identified as a 'non-Christian.' The same is true of persons who might describe themselves as 'unconcerned' by religious beliefs, or 'unsure' of them.

[24] *Towards Equality and Diversity.*

The definition of 'religion or belief' does not include the 'manifestation' of, or conduct based on or expressing a religion or belief (see also the distinction made in Article 9 ECHR). For example, a person may wear certain clothing, or pray at certain times in accordance with the tenets of her religion, or she may express views, and say or do other things reflecting her beliefs. In such a case it would not in itself constitute direct discrimination on grounds of religion or belief under the Regulations . . . if a person suffers a disadvantage because she has said or done something in this way. It would only be direct discrimination if a person with different beliefs (or no beliefs) was treated more favourably in similar circumstances. However, if an employer does set down requirements about (for example) clothing or breaks for prayers, these may constitute indirect discrimination . . . under the Regulations unless they are justified. . . .

The phrase '*on grounds of . . . religion or belief*' in the Regulations does not cover direct discrimination by the discriminator against another person because of his (the discriminator's) . . . religion or belief. When court or a tribunal considers if direct discrimination has taken place it must decide, from an objective viewpoint, if . . . religion or belief was the substantive cause of the different of treatment in question (see *O'Neill* [considered above] . . . For example, if an employer discriminates against a job applicant because of her sex or race, the objective cause for the difference in treatment derives from the applicant's characteristics, not those of the employer. It cannot be said that the employer acts unlawfully because of his or her own sex or race.

The same reasoning applies to direct discrimination on grounds of religion . . . For example, an employer with strong religious views who refuses to employ an applicant because she is female or gay does not discriminate on grounds of religion or belief. The cause of the difference of treatment, objectively considered, is the sex or sexual orientation of the applicant. The employer's religious views are not the cause of the difference of treatment; an employer without such views might refuse to employ a female or gay applicant in exactly the same way. The motivation for the act of discrimination (whether religious or otherwise) is not relevant.

The assertion that the RB Regs protect those who have no religious beliefs did not go unchallenged.

M Rubenstein, 'Is lack of belief protected?' (2004) 128 *Equal Opportunities Review*

In Britain, discrimination on grounds of religion or belief often takes the form of discrimination in favour of co-religionists or someone who shares the discriminator's particular belief rather than against someone because they are of a particular religion or espouse a particular belief.

If a Christian employer, for instance, decides that it will only employ someone who is Christian, can those who were turned down because they were not Christian claim that they were discriminated against because of their religious belief? Does it make a difference whether those who were turned down hold a particular religious or philosophical belief, or does the protection of the law extend to those who have no particular beliefs or who are uncertain?

If the Regulations do not protect those who are discriminated against because they do not hold a particular belief, there is a major gap in the statutory protection. Not being of a particular religion or belief is only supposed to be a potential ground for discrimination where a comparatively narrowly drawn genuine occupational requirement applies.

The Regulations do not expressly provide that absence of belief is covered. It is clear, however, that the government *intended* to protect non-believers against discrimination on grounds of their absence of belief. The Acas guide for employers and employees, *Religion or belief and the workplace*, unequivocally takes the position that the Regulations cover those who are not religious or who do not subscribe to a particular belief . . . The Department of Trade and Industry (DTI) explanatory notes . . . take the same position . . .

Yet it is difficult to reconcile the DTI's reasoning on this point with the guidance it gives as to the meaning of a 'religion or belief' in the Regulations. In explaining which philosophical beliefs are now protected, the DTI says that the phrase 'similar philosophical belief' 'does not include any philosophical or political belief unless it is similar to a religious belief.' According to the DTI: 'That does not mean that a belief must include faith in a god/gods or worship of a god/gods to be "similar" to a religious belief. It means that the belief in question should be a profound belief affecting a person's way of life or perception of the world. Effectively, the belief should occupy a place in the person's life parallel to that filled by the god/gods of those holding a particular religious belief.'

Where does that leave non-believers? Using this test, it is hard to see how 'non-Christian' can be a 'religious belief,' let alone how 'unsure' or 'don't know' can be regarded as a 'profound belief affecting a person's way of life or perception of the world.'

Because the legislation was introduced by way of Regulations, it could not be amended when it became apparent that this was a serious source of concern. Whether absence of belief was protected was one of the key issues probed during the House of Lords debate on the Regulations on 17 June 2003. The government spokesman Lord Sainsbury said that: 'It is clearly the intention that where people have strongly held views, which include humanism, or atheism or agnosticism, they would be covered under the phrase "or similar philosophical belief." ' Yet this is a rather different point, which far from providing parliamentary support for the proposition that discrimination on grounds of non-belief is covered, tends to undermine the argument: it is clear that the Regulations cover someone who is discriminated against because of their strongly held belief, such as atheism. What is not clear is whether the Regulations cover someone who is discriminated against because of their weakly held view, ie who is 'unsure' or, more importantly, whether they cover someone who is discriminated against because they do not share the discriminator's religious views.

In practice, the problem of absence of belief could have been avoided if the wording of the consultative draft Regulations on religion or belief had not been altered. Because the definition of direct discrimination simply refers to less favourable treatment 'on grounds of religion or belief,' the definition, on its own, would allow a claim where the discrimination was on grounds of the religion or belief of A, the discriminator, as well as where it was on grounds of B's religion or belief. That would have clearly covered the situation where an employer discriminates on grounds of religion in favour of his or her co-religionists.

However . . . it may well also have covered a situation where an employer, because of his or her religious beliefs, discriminates against someone because of their sexual orientation. This is clearly potentially actionable under the [SO Regs], because it is B's sexual orientation that leads to her or him being treated less favourably than someone of a different sexual orientation. But the government took a late decision to permit such discrimination in certain circumstances by adding a genuine occupational requirement exclusion to the Sexual Orientation Regulations. It then also added a further provision to the Religion or Belief Regulations, reg 3(2), which stipulates that the reference to discrimination on grounds of religion or belief 'does not include A's religion or belief', ie the religion or belief of the discriminator.

This means that it is not open to an applicant to argue that they have been discriminated against because of the employer's religion or belief. Instead, the tribunal will have to accept the government's view that an applicant will still be protected in such a case because there is no legal difference between being discriminated against because of the discriminator's religion or belief and being discriminated against because the applicant did not share that religion or belief. If there is a legal difference, it will drive a coach and horses through the legislation because employers will be able to say that discrimination against those who do not share their own religion or belief falls outside the scope of the Regulations.

When a tribunal or court comes to decide this issue, it will be confronted with two directly analogous areas where the government has legislated in respect of discrimination on grounds of religion or belief. Section 57(2) of the Fair Employment (Northern Ireland) Act 1976 provides: 'In this Act, references to a person's religious belief or political opinion include references to his supposed religious belief or political opinion and to the absence or supposed absence of any, or any particular, religious belief or political opinion.' Similarly, s.39 of the Anti-terrorism, Crime and Security Act 2001, which created the offence of religiously aggravated harassment, defines 'religious group' as meaning 'a group of persons defined by reference to religious belief or lack of religious belief.'

The fact that the drafters of the Religion or Belief Regulations did not choose to follow similar language will be a powerful argument that the 2003 Regulations do not cover absence or lack of belief. It will take a liberal interpretation to overcome this. Better drafting could have avoided this uncertainty.

The Equality Bill 2005 proposed the amendment of the RB Regs expressly to include lack of religion and lack of belief.[25] Reg 3(2) of the RB Regs provides that less favourable treatment on grounds of the *discriminator's* religion or belief does *not* amount to 'discrimination' for the purposes of the Regs. This, Lucy Vickers points out ('The Employment Equality (Religion or Belief) Regulations 2003' (2003) 32 *Industrial Law Journal* 188,188), was a change from the draft Regulations under which:

> discrimination could have been based on the *employer's* religious views, for example, a Catholic employer dismissing a (non-religious) employee for living in an extra-marital relationship, on the basis of his religious view[s] . . . However, this change may not be as significant as it looks, for two reasons. First, the refusal to employ B because he is living in a relationship outside of marriage could be said to be discrimination against B because of B's beliefs. If B shared exactly the same religious views as the employer he could be employed. Because he does not, he is discriminated against. In addition, if the religious view of the employer leads to discrimination against a person on another ground, that person may have a claim under the other regulations. For example, an employer who refuses to employ gay employees because of his own religious views, may be discriminating unlawfully under the [SO Regs].

In *Williams v South Central Limited* (Case No. 2306989/2003, June 2004, London South) an employment tribunal rejected a claim under the RB Regs by an American man whose employers objected to his wearing a small US flag stitched to his uniform, although he was told he could wear a lapel button on his jacket with the same representation. The claimant was eventually dismissed and claimed under the RRA (in respect of discrimination against him as an American) and the RB Regs. His RB Regs claim rested on the assertion that his loyalty to his native country amounted to a religious belief, an assertion rejected by the tribunal which noted that the dictionary definition of belief is 'persuasion of the truth of anything or opinion or doctrine or recognition of an awakened sense of a higher being controlling power or powers and the morality connected therewith, rights of worship or any

---

[25] The Bill would have inserted new regs 21(a)–(d) which provide, inter alia, that: '(c) a reference to religion includes a lack of religion, and (d) a reference to belief includes a reference to lack of belief". The fate of the Bill has been mentioned above.

system of such belief and worship.' The tribunal did not accept that loyalty to one's national flag or to one's native country could come within this definition and the application was struck out.[26]

Accommodating Difference

S Fredman, 'The Future of Equality in Britain' (EOC Working Series No 5, 2002) 19, footnotes omitted

The principle of equality in relation to religion has many complex dimensions. First, it comes against a background of a continuing strong link between Church and State. The Church of England enjoys a privileged position in many walks of life, from schools to the House of Lords. Even more fundamentally, many apparently secular practices are in fact Christian, whether it is the working week, the day of rest, the mode of dressing or the dietary laws. Thus, an approach which purports to be neutral and ignores the imbalances of power between minority religions and the majority will fail to address the real issues. This is seen clearly in the approach of the ECHR [in *Ahmad v UK*, further discussed below] which rejected a discrimination claim by a Muslim teacher who asked for time off for Friday prayers on the grounds that all minorities had to conform to the dominant Christian working week.

Instead, an important function of equality laws is to make sure that all religious groups are equally capable of expressing their religious identity. This receives legal expression through a duty to accommodate, and applies to differences in dress, religious holidays, days of rest and times of prayer, diet and so on. At the same time, equality extends to the interaction between different minority religions, as well as to those who choose to have no religion.

ACAS, 'Religion or Belief and the Workplace', Appendix 2

Baha'is should say one of three obligatory prayers during the day. Prayers need to be recited in a quiet place where the Baha'i will wish to face the Qiblih (the Shrine of Baha'u'llah, near Akka, Israel), which is in a southeasterly direction from the UK. Two of the prayers require movement and prostrations. . . Baha'i festivals take place from sunset to sunset and followers may wish to leave work early in order to be home for sunset on the day prior to the festival date. Baha'is will wish to refrain from working on the key festival dates.
The Baha'i Fast 2 March–20 March
Baha'is refrain from eating or drinking from sunrise to sunset during this period. Baha'is working evening or night shifts will appreciate the opportunity to prepare food at sundown [lists two other festivals including a number of days (21 April, 29 April, 2 May) on which Baha'is would prefer to refrain from working].

There are a number of different traditions in Buddhism arising from different cultural and ethnic backgrounds. Different traditions will celebrate different festivals. Some Buddhist traditions do not celebrate any festivals. Buddhist members of staff should be asked which festivals are important to them. Festivals follow the lunar calendar and will therefore not take place on the same day each year [lists 16 festivals] . . . Most Buddhists are vegetarian reflecting their adherence to the precept of non-harm to self and others. Many would not want to prepare or serve meat for others. Buddhists upholding the precept to avoid intoxication may not wish to drink alcohol, or serve it . . . Many Buddhists would prefer to wear clothing which reflects their adherence to non-harm eg not wearing leather clothing and leather shoes.

---

[26] This example kindly provided by Lucy Anderson of the TUC.

Hinduism is a diverse religion and not all Hindus will celebrate the same festivals [lists 12 festivals] . . . There are a number of occasions through the year when some Hindus fast. Hindu women will often wear a *bindi* which is a red spot worn on the forehead and denotes that she is of the Hindu faith. In addition, many married Hindu women wear a necklace (*mangal sutra*) which is placed around their necks during the marriage ceremony and is in addition to a wedding ring. A few Orthodox Hindu men wear a small tuft of hair (*shikha*) similar to a ponytail but this is often hidden beneath the remaining hair. Some Orthodox Hindu men also wear a clay marking on their foreheads known as a tilak. Most Hindus are vegetarian and will not eat meat, fish or eggs. None eat beef.

Observant Muslims are required to pray five times a day. Each prayer time takes about 15 minutes and can take place anywhere clean and quiet. Prayer times are: At dawn[, a]t mid-day[, l]ate Afternoon[, a]fter Sunset[, l]ate Evening. Friday mid-day prayers are particularly important to Muslims and may take a little longer than other prayer times. Friday prayers must be said in congregation and may require Muslims to travel to the nearest mosque or prayer gathering. Before prayers, observant Muslims undertake a ritual act of purification. This involves the use of running water to wash hands, face, mouth, nose, arms up to the elbows and feet up to the ankles, although often the washing of the feet will be performed symbolically . . . The dates of festivals are reliant on a sighting of the new moon and will therefore vary from year to year. Whilst approximate dates will be known well in advance, it is not always possible to give a definitive date until much nearer to the time.

- Ramadan, which takes place in the ninth month of the Muslim lunar calendar, is a particularly significant time for Muslims. Fasting is required between dawn and sunset. Most Muslims will attend work in the normal way but in the winter they may wish to break fast with other Muslims at sunset. This could be seen as a delayed lunch break. For those working evening or night shifts, the opportunity to heat food at sunset and/or sunrise will be appreciated.
- Eid Al-Fitr—three days to mark the end of Ramadan—most Muslims will only seek annual leave for the first of the three days.
- Eid al-Adha takes place two months and 10 days after Eid Al-Fitr and is a three-day festival. Again, most Muslims will usually only seek leave for the first of the three days.

All Muslims are required to make a pilgrimage to Mecca once in their lifetime. Muslims may therefore seek one extended leave period in which to make such a pilgrimage. Muslims are required to cover the body. Men may therefore be unwilling to wear shorts. Women may wish to cover their whole body, except their face, hands and feet. Muslims are forbidden to eat any food which is derived from the pig, this includes lard which may be present in bread or even ice cream. In addition they are forbidden to eat any food which is derived from a carnivorous animal. Meat that may be consumed must be slaughtered by the Halal method. Islam also forbids the consumption of alcohol which includes its presence in dishes such as risotto or fruit salad . . .

Any form of gambling is forbidden under Islam. Observant Muslims are required to wash following use of the toilet and will therefore appreciate access to water in the toilet cubicle, often Muslims will carry a small container of water into the cubicle for this purpose. By agreement with other staff and cleaners, these containers could be kept in the cubicle. Physical contact between the sexes is discouraged and some Muslims may politely refuse to shake hands with the opposite sex. This should not be viewed negatively.

Jains are required to worship three times daily, before dawn, at sunset and at night. Jains working evening or night shifts may wish to take time out to worship or take their meals before sunset. Jain festivals are spiritual in nature

- Oli—April and October. Eight days semi-fasting twice a year when some take one bland, tasteless meal during day time

- Mahavira Jayanti—April. Birth anniversary of Lord Mahavira
- Paryusan—August/September. During this sacred period of fasting and forgiveness for eight days Jains fast, observe spiritual rituals, meditate and live a pious life taking only boiled water during day time
- Samvatsari—September/the last day of Paryushan when Jains ask for forgiveness and forgive one another
- Diwali—October/November. Death anniversary of Lord Mahavira, includes a two-day fast and listening to the last message of Mahavira

Jains practice avoidance of harm to all life—self and others. They are, therefore, strict vegetarians including the avoidance of eggs; some may take milk products. Many also avoid root vegetables. Jains do not eat between sunset and sunrise. Jains do not drink alcohol.

Observant Jews are required to refrain from work on the Sabbath and Festivals, except where life is at risk. This includes travelling (except on foot), writing, carrying, switching on and off electricity, using a telephone and transactions of a commercial nature (that is buying and selling). The Sabbath and all other Festivals begin one hour before dusk and so practising Jews need to be home by then. Sabbath begins one hour before dusk on Friday. [Lists 5 festivals]

Orthodox Jewish men keep their head covered at all times. Orthodox Jewish women will wish to dress modestly and may not want to wear trousers, short skirts or short sleeves; some may wish to keep their heads covered by a scarf or beret. Jews are required to eat only kosher food (which has been treated and prepared in a particular manner).

Rastafarian festivals [lists 5]. [Rastafarians are v]egetarian [and] avoid . . . eggs. Many Rastafarians eat only organic food as close to its raw state as possible. Hair is worn uncut and plaited into 'dreadlocks'. It is often covered by a hat which is usually red, green and gold. Whilst the faith supports the smoking of ganga (marijuana) this practice remains unlawful in the UK, and is unaffected by the [RB Regs].

Sikh festivals [lists 7] . . . Sikhs do not eat Halal meat. Some do not eat beef and many are vegetarian. Practising male Sikhs observe the 5 Ks of the faith. These are:

- Kesh—Uncut hair. Observant Sikhs do not remove or cut any hair from their body. Sikh men and some women will wear a turban
- Kangha—Wooden comb usually worn in the hair
- Kara—Metal bracelet worn on the wrist
- Kachhahera—Knee length underpants
- Kirpan—Short sword worn under the clothing so that it is not visible.

Zoroastrians are required to pray five times during the day, saying a special prayer for each part of the day.

Prayers should be said in front of a fire—or a symbolic replica of fire. In addition, a ritual is performed each time a Zorostrain washes his/her hands although the ritual is not always strictly performed in all its detail. When it is performed, the individual will stand on the same spot and must speak to no one during the ritual. No special facilities are required.

A prayer will also be said before eating.

Festival dates follow the lunar calendar and will therefore vary from year to year [lists 16 festivals] . . . Zoroastrians, both male and female, wear two pieces of sacred clothing. The Sudreh (shirt) and the Kusti (cord) which is a string which passes loosely around the waist three times and is tied in a double knot at the back. It is the Kusti which is ritualistically retied each time the hands are washed.

It is clear from these extracts that any meaningful attempt to render 'equal' in the workplace those who adhere to minority religions will require not merely the prohibition of direct discrimination on grounds of religion and belief, but also the imposition of requirements to accommodate difference. The concept of indirect discrimination has been discussed in Chapter 2, and many examples given of its application in the case law there and in Chapter 4. The RB Regs follow the normal pattern of UK anti-discrimination legislation (to which the DDA is the only exception) by regulating 'indirect' and 'direct' discrimination. But for reasons which included the complexities of the original definition of indirect discrimination and the extent to which true equality requires the accommodation of difference in this context, Hepple and Choudhury floated, in 2001, the idea that transposition of the religion and belief provisions of the Employment Equality Directive might include the imposition of explicit duties to accommodate.

Hepple and Choudhury 37–40, footnotes omitted

Introducing the idea of reasonable adjustment or accommodation signifies an important shift in the understanding of equality. In the DDA the concept of indirect discrimination is not used but there is a primary duty to make reasonable adjustments where arrangements or physical features of premises place a disabled person at a substantial disadvantage compared with persons who are not disabled. In Northern Ireland, in the case of discrimination on grounds of religion or political opinion, the duty to promote equality of opportunity includes affirmative action defined in terms of steps to increase fair participation and fair access [see below]. In the context of religious discrimination in Britain it is argued that there is a need to accommodate diversity because our society is already structured around basic Christian assumptions and therefore already accommodates the needs of Christians, for example Christmas and Easter are recognised as public holidays, and shop workers and betting workers have the right to object to Sunday working [ERA]. In a multi-faith multicultural society, the needs of individuals with different religious faiths should be met. This was something understood by Lord Scarman in 1978 when, in [Ahmad,] a case involving a dispute between a Muslim teacher who requested time to attend Friday prayers and the local education authority, he argued[27] that 'room has to be found for teachers and pupils of the new religions in the educational system, if discrimination is to be avoided. This calls not for a policy of the blind eye but for one of understanding. The system must be made flexible to accommodate their beliefs and their observances. Otherwise they will suffer discrimination.' Justice McIntyre in the Canadian Supreme Court also recognised that 'the accommodation of differences . . . is the essence of true equality.'[28] Others have pointed towards the dangers of reasonable accommodation. Lord Denning in Ahmad took the view that it would do a minority group 'no good, if they were to be given preferential treatment over the great majority of people. If it should happen that, in the name of religious freedom, they were given special privileges or advantages, it would provoke discontent, and even resentment among those with whom they work . . . and so the cause of racial integration would suffer. So, whilst upholding religious freedom to the full, I would suggest that it should be applied with caution, especially having regard to the setting in which it is sought.' Lord Justice Orr also objected to pursuing a policy of reasonable accommodation. He argued that this would lead to 'resentment among non-Moslem staff at having to assume additional burdens and possibly to a situation in which education authorities would have been reluctant to employ more Moslem teachers.' More recently, Gay Moon and Robin Allen QC have argued that 'too great an emphasis on an obligation to make adjustments could lead to a more restrictive interpretation of religion or belief. This might cause the adjustments necessary for a fundamental right to be inappropriately limited in practice.'[29]

---

[27] Citing *Ahmad v Inner London Education Authority* [1978] QB 36.
[28] Citing *Andrews v Law Society of British Columbia* 10 CHRR D/5719.
[29] 'Substantive Rights and Equal Treatment in Respect of Religion and Belief: Towards a Better Understanding of the Rights and their Implications' [2000] *European Human Rights Law Review* 580, 601.

There are several *disadvantages* to the approach in the DDA of not utilising the concept of indirect discrimination. The issues in DDA cases revolve initially around whether or not the employer knew that the disabled person needed a reasonable adjustment. This does not arise with indirect discrimination. There the question is whether or not the apparently neutral provision, criterion or practice can be shown to have an adverse impact on a particular group, and if it does, whether the provision is objectively justifiable. The reasonable adjustment approach therefore places the onus on the individual to disclose a disability and explain that the arrangements place him or her at a substantial disadvantage. If he or she succeeds in doing this the result will be an individualised solution. The next disabled person will have to go though the same process of disclosure and negotiating reasonableness. The indirect discrimination approach, on the other hand, requires 'equality proofing'. The onus is on the employer or service provider to consider in advance whether or not a provision or practice indirectly discriminates and, if so, whether it is objectively justifiable. The indirect discrimination approach is easier for the individual and can have a much more significant impact in terms of promoting participation and access by the disadvantaged group. The absence of a concept of indirect discrimination in the DDA means that until a disabled person interacts with an employer or service provider, there is no incentive to make adjustments. Moreover, it is by no means clear that all the situations covered by indirect discrimination will be covered by duty to make reasonable adjustments . . .

The *Ontario Human Rights Code* has . . . attempted to combine the concept of reasonable adjustment within the concept of indirect discrimination. It goes further than the Article 13 employment directive by applying this to religious discrimination. The Code introduces the concept of 'constructive discrimination' which is similar to indirect discrimination. Section 11 of the Code provides a defence to claims of constructive discrimination where 'the requirement, qualification or factor is reasonable and bona fide in the circumstances.' The provision goes on to state that 'a court shall not find that a requirement, qualification or factor is reasonable and bona fide in the circumstances unless it is satisfied that the needs of the group of which the person is a member *cannot be accommodated without undue hardship* on the person responsible for accommodating those needs, considering the cost, outside sources of funding, if any, and health and safety requirements, if any.' This formulation has the advantage of clarifying the relationship between indirect discrimination and the duty to make reasonable adjustments. The Independent Review of the Enforcement of UK Anti-Discrimination Legislation proposed that this approach should be adopted in the UK.[30]

The RB Regs have not imposed an express duty to make reasonable accommodation but the prohibition of indirect discrimination does, as the following extract makes clear, require a degree of accommodation.

ACAS, 'Religion or Belief and the Workplace', paras 1.3–4.11

Indirect discrimination means that an organisation must not have selection criteria, policies, employment rules or any other practices which although they are applied to all employees, have the effect of disadvantaging people of a particular religion or belief unless the practice can be justified. Indirect discrimination is unlawful whether it is intentional or not.

---

[30] B Hepple, M Coussey and T Choudhury, *Equality: A New Framework—The Report of the Independent Review of the Enforcement of UK Anti-Discrimination Legislation*, (Oxford, Hart Publishing, 2000) para 2.33.

- Disliking the baseball caps his delivery drivers like to wear, a Chief Executive applies a 'no headwear' policy to all his staff. The policy, although applied to all employees, disadvantages his Sikh staff who wear turbans for religious reasons. This policy is indirect discrimination.

The example above is already well recognised. However, there are less well documented examples which are equally important to the followers of particular religions.

- An organisation has a dress code which states that men may not wear ponytails. This may indirectly disadvantage Hindu men some of whom wear a Shika, (a small knotted tuft of hair worn at the back of the head, as a symbol of their belief). Such a policy could be discriminatory if it cannot be justified.

In contrast to direct discrimination, indirect discrimination will not be unlawful if it can be justified. To justify it, an employer must show that there is a legitimate aim, (ie a real business need) and that the practice is proportionate to that aim (ie necessary and there is no alternative means available).

A small finance company needs its staff to work late on a Friday afternoon to analyse stock prices in the American finance market. The figures arrive late on Friday because of the global time differences. During the winter months some staff would like to be released early on Friday afternoon in order to be home before nightfall—a requirement of their religion. They propose to make the time up later during the remainder of the week. The company is not able to agree to this request because the American figures are necessary to the business, they need to be worked on immediately and the company is too small to have anyone else able to do the work. The requirement to work on Friday afternoon is not unlawful discrimination as it meets a legitimate business aim and there is no alternative means available . . .

- An advertisement placed only in a particular religious magazine may constitute indirect discrimination as it is unlikely to be seen by people of other religions or beliefs. Although the magazine may be available to all potential applicants, it effectively disadvantages groups of people who for religious or belief reasons may not subscribe to that particular publication . . .

Where it is reasonable to do so, organisations should adapt their methods of recruitment so that anyone who is suitably qualified can apply and attend for selection. Some flexibility around interview/selection times allowing avoidance of significant religious times (for example Friday afternoons) is good practice.

- Where the recruitment process includes a social gathering, care should be taken to avoid disadvantaging anyone for whom alcohol is prohibited on the grounds of religion or belief. For instance, holding the gathering in a hotel bar may pose particular difficulties for those whose religion forbids association with alcohol.

Invitations should make it clear that applicants with specific dietary requirements (which may be associated with their religion or belief) will not be disadvantaged by the process or the venue. Employers do not have to provide specific food such as Halal or Kosher if it is not proportionate for them to do so but they should ensure that there is some appropriate food available (eg vegetarian) . . .

If it is reasonable to do so, organisations should consider adapting their methods of delivering training if current arrangements have the effect of disadvantaging someone because of religion or belief. This may be particularly relevant if training takes place outside normal working hours, work place or in a residential environment.

Some things to consider:

- times within work schedules for religious observance
- special dietary requirements, for example kosher, halal and vegetarian food

- avoid ice breakers and training activities that use language or physical contact that might be inappropriate for some beliefs
- avoid exercises which require the exchange of personal information
- related social activities do not exclude people by choice of venue
- avoid significant religious festivals such as Ramadan.

Whilst organisations should be sensitive to the needs of their staff, staff have a responsibility to ensure that their managers and training departments are aware of their individual needs in good time so that there is an opportunity for them to be met . . .

The Regulations do not say that employers must provide time and facilities for religious or belief observance in the workplace. However, employers should consider whether their policies, rules and procedures indirectly discriminate against staff of particular religions or beliefs and if so whether reasonable changes might be made.

Many religions or beliefs have special festival or spiritual observance days. A worker may request holiday in order to celebrate festivals or attend ceremonies. An employer should sympathetically consider such a request where it is reasonable and practical for the employee to be away from work, and they have sufficient holiday entitlement in hand. While it may be practical for one or a small number to be absent it might be difficult if numerous such requests are made. In these circumstances the employer should discuss the matter with the employees affected, and with any recognised trade union, with the aim of balancing the needs of the business and those of other employees. Employers should carefully consider whether their criteria for deciding who should and who should not be granted leave may indirectly discriminate . . .

- A small toy shop employing four staff may be unable to release an individual for a religious festival in the busy pre-Christmas period. It may be justifiable to refuse a request for such absence. A large department store employing 250 staff would probably be unable to justify refusing the same absence for one person because it would not substantially impact on the business as other staff would be able to cover for the absence.

Employers who operate a holiday system whereby the organisation closes for specific periods when all staff must take their annual leave should consider whether such closures are justified as they may prevent individuals taking annual leave at times of specific religious significance to them. Such closures may be justified by the business need to undertake machinery maintenance for instance. However, it would be good practice for such employers to consider how they might balance the needs of the business and those of their staff.

Organisations should have clear, reasonable procedures for handling requests for leave and ensure that all staff are aware of and adhere to the procedures. Staff should give as much notice as possible when requesting leave and in doing so should also consider that there may be a number of their colleagues who would like leave at the same time. Employers should be aware that some religious or belief festivals are aligned with lunar phases and therefore dates change from year to year; the dates for some festivals do not become clear until quite close to the actual day. Discussion and flexibility between staff and managers will usually result in a mutually acceptable compromise. Organisations should take care not to disadvantage those workers who do not hold any specific religion or belief.

Some religions or beliefs have specific dietary requirements. If staff bring food into the workplace they may need to store and heat food separately from other food, for example Muslims will wish to ensure their food is not in contact with pork (or anything that may have been in contact with pork, such as cloths or sponges). It is good practice to consult your employees on such issues and find a mutually acceptable solution to any dietary problems.

- A worker who, for religious reasons, is vegetarian felt unable to store her lunch in a refrigerator next to the meat sandwiches belonging to a co-worker. Following consultation with the staff and their representatives, the organisation introduced a policy by which all food must be stored in sealed containers and shelves were separately designated 'meat' and 'vegetarian'. This arrangement met the needs of all staff and at no cost to the employer. Some religions require their followers to pray at specific times during the day. Staff may therefore request access to an appropriate quiet place (or prayer room) to undertake their religious observance. Employers are not required to provide a prayer room. However, if a quiet place is available and allowing its use for prayer does not cause problems for other workers or the business, organisations should agree to the request.

Where possible, it is good employee relations practice for organisations to set aside a quiet room or area for prayer or private contemplation. In consultation with staff, it may be possible to designate an area for all staff for the specific purpose of prayer or contemplation rather than just a general rest room. Such a room might also be welcomed by those for whom prayer is a religious obligation and also by those who, for example, have suffered a recent bereavement. Organisations should consider providing separate storage facilities for ceremonial objects.

Employers are not required to enter into significant expenditure and/or building alterations to meet religious needs. In any event many needs will involve little or no change. For instance some religions or beliefs require a person to wash before prayer. This is often done symbolically or by using the existing facilities. However, it is good practice to consult with staff and to consider whether there is anything reasonable and practical which can be done to help staff meet the ritual requirements of their religion. It may help, for example, if all workers understand the religious observances of their colleagues thus avoiding embarrassment or difficulties for those practising their religious obligations.

Some religions or beliefs do not allow individuals to undress or shower in the company of others. If an organisation requires its staff, for reasons of health and safety, to change their clothing and/or shower, it is good employee relations practice to explore how such needs can be met. Insistence upon same-sex communal shower and changing facilities could constitute indirect discrimination (or harassment) as it may disadvantage or offend staff of a particular religion or belief whose requirement for modesty extend to changing their clothing in the presence of others, even of the same sex.

Some religions require extended periods of fasting. Employers may wish to consider how they can support staff through such a period.

However, employers should take care to ensure that they do not place unreasonable extra burdens on other workers which may cause conflict between workers or claims of discrimination. If it is practical and safe to do so, staff may welcome the opportunity to wear clothing consistent with their religion. Where organisations adopt a specific dress code, careful consideration should be given to the proposed code to ensure it does not conflict with the dress requirements of some religions. General dress codes which have the effect of conflicting with religious requirements may constitute indirect discrimination unless they can be justified for example, on the grounds of health and safety.

- Some religions require their female followers to dress particularly modestly. A dress code which requires a blouse to be tucked inside a skirt may conflict with that requirement as it accentuates body shape. However, if the individual is allowed to wear the blouse over the outside of the skirt it may be quite acceptable.

If organisations have a policy on the wearing of jewellery, having tattoos or other markings, they should try and be flexible and reasonable concerning items of jewellery and markings which are traditional within some religions or beliefs. Unjustifiable policies and rules may constitute indirect discrimination.

- In addition to a wedding ring, many Hindu women wear a necklace (Mangal Sutra) which is placed around their neck during the wedding ceremony and is therefore highly symbolic. Some may find it distressing if they are not allowed to wear it in their place of work, unless the rule was for health and safety or other justifiable reasons.

The Genuine Occupational Requirement Defences

The concept of a 'clash of rights' was mentioned above. Churches, religious organisations and individuals are entitled to freedom of religion and belief (which includes a qualified entitlement to *manifest* religion and belief, as well as an *absolute* right to hold it. The question will, from time to time, arise: where are the boundaries to be drawn between one person or organisation's entitlement to manifest religion or belief and another person's entitlement not to be disadvantaged, whether on grounds of religion or belief or otherwise, by that manifestation.

Hepple and Choudhury 51–2, footnotes omitted

Particular issues arise in relation to exemptions from the legislation for religious schools. The approach in Northern Ireland, reflecting the particular sectarian issues in that jurisdiction, is to exclude schools entirely from FETO, so they are free to discriminate in respect of teachers from the Protestant and Roman Catholic communities. Article 15(2) of the employment directive has expressly preserved this exemption. In Scotland the management of denominational schools is regulated by the Education (Scotland) Act 1980. Section 21 of the Act provides that 'a teacher appointed to any post on the staff of any such school by the education authority . . . shall be required to be approved as regards his religious belief and character by representatives of the church or denominational body in whose interest the school has been conducted'. Employment in religious schools in England and Wales in regulated by the School Standards Framework Act 1998. Section 59 of the Act provides firstly that, in community, secular foundation or voluntary or special schools, no one can be disqualified from employment by reasons of his religious opinions, or of attending or omitting to attend religious worship. But s.60 provides that foundation or voluntary schools that have a 'religious character' can give preference in employment, remuneration and promotion to teachers 'whose religious beliefs are in accordance with the tenets' of that religion. Furthermore, 'regard may be had, in connection with the termination of the employment of any teacher at that school, to any conduct on his part which is incompatible with the precepts, or with the upholding of the tenets, of the religion or religious denomination so specified.' The provisions do not extend to cover employment beyond teaching. The House of Lords Committee indicated that these provisions go beyond those permitted by a 'genuine occupational qualification' found in the Article 13 draft employment directive [now the Employment Equality Directive]. Responding to these concerns the Government said that they were negotiating to 'ensure that the employment directive would permit s.60 of the Schools Standards and Framework Act 1998 to be maintained.' The final text of the employment directive was amended to ensure that the directive did not prejudice the rights of religious schools (above, 8.9, 8.12). The directive as amended 'allows Member States considerable latitude in implementing its provisions in relation to staff policies of religious organisations. In particular the agreed text allows the UK to protect the right of church schools to give preference to teachers of their faith in line with the provisions of the Schools Standards and Framework Act 1998.'

Lucy Vickers, 'The Employment Equality (Religion or Belief) Regulations 2003' (2003) 32 *Industrial Law Journal* 188, 191, footnotes omitted

It is evident that at times, the rights created under the Religion and Belief Regulations will come into conflict with the rights created under other discrimination provisions, such as the Sex Discrimination Act 1975 and the Sexual Orientation Regulations 2003. For example, a requirement that a priest be male directly discriminates against women. A Muslim medical partnership may indirectly discriminate against gay people if it requires staff to share its faith. However, despite the potential conflict, it is clear that the protection created under the Religion and Belief Regulations will rarely take precedence over the rights created elsewhere. Although there is no statement in the Religion and Belief Regulations to this effect, the regulations do need to be read together with the legislation prohibiting other forms of discrimination.

Direct discrimination on grounds of religion or belief, as on other grounds, can be justified both in EU and domestic law. In Chapter 4 we considered the scope of the RB Regs and some of the exceptions to their coverage (these included, for example, national security and geographical limitations). Here we consider the cases in which discrimination within the scope of the Regs can be justified by reference to the genuine occupational requirement defences.

Article 4 of the Employment Equality Directive was extracted above. It permits Member States to provide that less favourable treatment based on a characteristic related to religion or belief 'shall not constitute discrimination where, by reason of the nature of the particular occupational activities concerned or of the context in which they are carried out, such a characteristic constitutes a genuine and determining occupational requirement, provided that the objective is legitimate and the requirement is proportionate.' This aspect of the GOR is materially identical as it applies to religion or belief, on the one hand; sexual orientation, age and disability on the other.

Article 4(1) is transposed into domestic law by reg 7 of the RB Regs which applies across 'employment,' widely defined to include contract-workers, office holders and the police, partnerships, providers of vocational training, employment agencies etc and institutions of further and higher education (see further Chapter 4). It provides that the prohibitions on discrimination in relation to recruitment arrangements and offers of employment, promotion or transfer to, or training for, any employment; and dismissal from any employment shall not apply where:

(2) ... having regard to the nature of the employment or the context in which it is carried out—
    (a) being of a particular religion or belief is a genuine and determining occupational requirement;
    (b) it is proportionate to apply that requirement in the particular case; and
    (c) either –
        (i) the person to whom that requirement is applied does not meet it, or
        (ii) the employer is not satisfied, and in all the circumstances it is reasonable for him not to be satisfied, that that person meets it,

and this paragraph applies whether or not the employer has an ethos based on religion or belief.

(3) ... where an employer has an ethos based on religion or belief and, having regard to that ethos and to the nature of the employment or the context in which it is carried out—
    (a) being of a particular religion or belief is a genuine occupational requirement for the job;
    (b) it is proportionate to apply that requirement in the particular case; and
    (c) either –
        (i) the person to whom that requirement is applied does not meet it, or
        (ii) the employer is not satisfied, and in all the circumstances it is reasonable for him not to be satisfied, that that person meets it.

DTI, 'Explanatory Notes', paras 76–81

It is . . . rare for a particular religion or belief to be a genuine occupational requirement for a job under regulation 7(2) of the religion or belief Regulations . . . However, there are some jobs where a GOR could apply.

- For example, if a hospital were to employ a chaplain to minister to patients and staff, it might specify that he or she must be a Christian, because almost all the patients and staff are Christian. If the patients and staff represented a number of different faiths, the hospital might need to give consideration to whether a minister of a different faith could also carry out the job, including ministering to those of faiths other than his or her own. Even in that case, the hospital could probably specify that the chaplain must be a minister of a religion, rather than an atheist, for example . . .
- . . . it would not be proportionate for an employer to rely on a GOR to exclude persons of a particular . . . religion or belief when filling a vacancy if he already has other employees of that . . . religion or belief who could reasonably carry out those duties . . .

If challenged, it is the employer who faces the burden of proving . . . that the criteria in regulation 7 are met, if he wishes to rely on the exception. If the employee or applicant acknowledges that she is not of the particular . . . religion or belief specified by the employer, then the employer should have no difficulty in establishing that (i) the employee or applicant does not in fact meet the requirement. In other situations that may be difficult for the employer to establish, because the . . . religion or belief of the employee is usually something which would be in her exclusive knowledge. Therefore, the employer may instead seek to establish that (ii) he is not satisfied and in all the circumstances it is reasonable for him not to be satisfied, that employee or applicant meets the requirement.

- For example, when an employer is recruiting for a job to which a GOR applies, if the job applicant refused to disclose her . . . religion or belief, the employer could seek to demonstrate that he was not satisfied that she was of the specified . . . religion or belief required for that job, and that it was reasonable for him not to be satisfied.

This does not mean that an employer could refuse to offer an applicant a job, merely because he suspects that the applicant is not of the specified . . . religion or belief.

- . . . if the applicant states that she is of the specified . . . religion or belief, it is very unlikely that a mere suspicion on the part of the employer that this was not correct would be sufficient to establish that it was reasonable of him not to be satisfied that the requirement was met. The employer would probably need a good reason.which cast doubt on the applicant's statement if he were to prove to a tribunal that it was reasonable for him not to be satisfied.

Article 4(1) and reg. 7(2) are relatively uncontroversial. But Article 4(2), which provides an additional GOR applicable *only* to 'churches and other public or private organisations the ethos of which is based on religion or belief,' is not. That provision allows Member States to 'maintain national legislation in force at the date of adoption of this Directive [November 2000] or provide for future legislation incorporating national practices existing at the date of adoption of this Directive' which permits such organisations to discriminate on grounds of religion or belief in relation to occupational activities within the organisations in which, by reason of their nature or of the context in which they are carried out, 'a person's religion or belief constitute a genuine, legitimate and justified occupational requirement, having regard to the organisation's ethos.' This GOR is wider than the standard GOR inasmuch as there is no requirement that the person's religion or belief is a *determining* requirement for the job, that the objective pursued by the discrimination is legitimate, or that the requirement is proportionate to that objective. Rather, the requirement that someone be [or, perhaps, not be] of a certain religion or belief must only be 'legitimate and justified having regard to the organisation's ethos,' there being no need, it would appear, to justify that ethos. The second paragraph of Article 4(2) then goes on to state that the effect of the provision is that the Employment Equality Directive 'shall thus not prejudice the right of churches and other public or private organisations, the ethos of which is based on religion or belief, acting in conformity with national constitutions and laws, to require individuals working for them to act in good faith and with loyalty to the organisation's ethos.'

Article 4(2) went through a number of changes during the period preceding the adoption of the Employment Equality Directive. The original Article 4 was weaker, providing for a defence in cases in which a difference of treatment based on any of the protected grounds 'where, by reason of the nature of the particular occupational activities concerned or of the context in which they are carried out, such a characteristic constitutes a genuine occupational qualification.' The originally proposed Article 4(2) provided that:

> in the case of public or private organisations which pursue directly and essentially the aim of ideological guidance in the field of religion or belief with respect to education, information and the expression of opinions, and for the particular occupational activities within those organisations which are directly and essentially related to that aim, a difference of treatment based on a relevant characteristic related to religion or belief shall not constitute discrimination where, by reason of the nature of these activities, the characteristic constitutes a genuine occupational qualification.

The Explanatory Notes asserted that 'in organisations which promote certain religious values, certain jobs or occupations need to be performed by employees who share the relevant religious opinion,' and that 'Article 4(2) allows these organisations to require occupational qualifications which are necessary for the fulfilment of the duties attached to the relevant post.'

The original Article 4(2) was described by a Commission spokeswoman as 'an awful provision which is impossible to read . . . because it reflects the complexity of these issues.'[31] In evidence to the House of Lords Select Committee on the EU (Sub-Committee G) she stated that, as a derogation from the principle of equal treatment it had be read narrowly, and that 'It has to relate to the specific occupation.' Thus, according to the Committee (para 109):

> a Roman Catholic school would be entitled to appoint only Catholics to teach religious education; the entitlement would certainly not extend to the cleaners, and probably not to the teachers of other subjects. Stonewall confirmed that in their view the test might be used to bar homosexuals from such employment: they supported the proviso as long as it was narrowly read. . . . it is unclear how much Article 4(2) adds to Article 4(1).

The Committee noted the evidence of the former chairman of Northern Ireland's Fair Employment Commission that FETO contained no similar provision, although the Order did not apply to schools (see further below): 'no broader exemption was granted to the churches—organisations such as orphanages, as well as schools where non-teaching staff were concerned, were covered by the Act: "if the job is one which involves a representa-

---

[31] HL 68, n14, para 109.

tional role or proselytising then religion could be a genuine occupational qualification, but ... if it was a janitor then clearly it could not be." ' Sir Robert told the Committee that this provision had not led to 'any cases at all. It has not given rise to any significant difficulty.' The Committee recommended that:

> Article 4(1) ... should provide, as it stands, a sufficient safeguard for religious organisations. The narrow and convoluted wording of Article 4(2), as drafted, would seem to add nothing to this safeguard. In fact we believe that it is likely to limit the ability of religious organisations to apply the 'genuine occupational qualification' principle. We doubt that this can have been the Commission's intention. If Article 4(2) is to be retained, its meaning and scope should be clarified.
>
> There might still be problems in subjecting the employment practices of religious or denominational schools to the 'genuine occupational qualification' provision ... section 60 of the School Standards and Framework Act 1998 provides that voluntary schools in England and Wales which have a 'religious character' are permitted to give preference in employment, remuneration or promotion to teachers 'whose religious opinions are in accordance with the tenets' of that religion. Such schools may also terminate the employment of teachers whose conduct is 'incompatible with the precepts' of that religion. This is an extremely sensitive issue, which needs to be examined in much more detail, and the Committee has not received enough evidence on it to reach a firm conclusion. We urge the Government to explore with the Commission ways to provide effective protection (possibly by means of an express exemption from the provisions of the Directive) for the rights of religious organisations, particularly schools.

After comments from the European Parliament, the Economic and Social Committee and the Committee of Regions the Commission's proposal was amended, so far as is relevant here to provide as follows:

1. Notwithstanding Article 2(1) and (2), Member States may provide that a difference of treatment which is based on a characteristic related to any of the discriminatory grounds referred to in Article 1 shall not constitute discrimination where, by reason of the nature of the particular occupational activities concerned or of the context in which they are carried out, such a characteristic constitutes a genuine occupational requirement, provided that the objective is legitimate and the requirement is proportionate.
2. Notwithstanding paragraph 1, the Member States may provide that in the case of public or private organisations based on religion or belief, and for the particular occupational activities within those organisations which are directly and essentially related to religion or belief, a difference in treatment based on a person's religion or belief shall not constitute discrimination where, by reason of the nature of these activities or the context in which they are carried out, a person's religion or belief constitute a genuine occupational requirement. This difference of treatment may not, however, give rise to any discrimination on the other grounds referred to in Article 13 of the EC Treaty.

According to the Explanatory Notes, the amendments were designed 'to cover social work undertaken by religious organisations ... [and] to underline the fact that this provision will not justify discrimination on any other grounds.' The text of the final version adopted by the Council of Ministers (see above) granted more scope to religious organisations to discriminate, this as a result of pressure by the UK and Irish governments.

Article 4(2) expressly applies only to discrimination on grounds of religion. Much of the concern that has been expressed in relation to it has been concerned with the scope it may permit for religious organisations to discriminate against, for example, gay men and lesbian women on the grounds that active homosexuality is inconsistent with 'good faith and . . . loyalty to [their] ethos.' This aspect of the Directive is considered further in Chapter 4. Here we concentrate on the transposition of Article 4(1) and (2) by the RB Regs, and their implications for discrimination on grounds of religion or belief.

Concern was expressed by many who contributed to the government's consultation exercise on the implementation of the Employment Equality Directive that Article 4(2) might be abused.

Justice, 'Towards Equality and Diversity: Implementing the Employment and Race Directives—responding to the Government's Consultation Paper' (2002)

The [Government does] not intend to define which organisations have an ethos based on religion or belief nor which posts within any organisation are essential to underpin that organisation's ethos. We believe that this is the correct approach, however, it is an area where a Code of Practice similar to that prepared by the NI Fair Employment Commission could be very helpful.

A relevant part of this guidance explains how it works in greater detail. It says:

'If you are an employer who is considering recruiting for such a job then you should ensure that its essential nature is such that it must be done by someone of a particular religious belief, or none. It would be difficult to argue, for example, that the essential nature of cooking or gardening would require either the cook or the gardener to hold a particular religious belief even if that cooking or gardening was being done for the members of the particular religious group or church body. But when the cook or gardener had other duties of a religious or evangelising nature associated with their cooking or gardening functions—such as inducting members of a home hostel or community into a particular set of religious values—then you could reasonably claim that the essential nature of that particular job required to be done by someone of a specific religious belief.'

Clearly in a GB context, where the provision of cooks for Jewish or Muslim nursing homes would need to be considered, the example of cook may not be the most appropriate one, perhaps a kitchen cleaner could be substituted.

JUSTICE believes that the underlying purpose of these Directives is to counter unjustified discrimination hence that it is important that it is made very clear that no genuine or determining occupational requirement should amount to discrimination on another ground. This is clearly a difficult area where there is significant overlap between competing rights which are likely to surface when an organisation with a religious ethos wishes to discriminate against someone because of their membership of one of the other categories for which discrimination is prohibited such as racial origin or sexuality. An example of this sort of clash was provided in the American case of *Bob Jones University v United States*[32] where a private Christian university prohibited interracial dating or marriage and was consequently refused a tax exemption. Alternatively, if, for example, a religious school set up by a white supremacist religion, would it be able to discriminate on grounds of race because their religious beliefs entailed racial discrimination?

These are difficult questions of construction of the provisions of the Directive that are likely to be resolved ultimately by the European Court of Justice. In view of these difficulties we would propose that the government adopted the wording of article 4(2) of the Employment Directive as closely as possible, however, it should be accompanied by a Code

---

[32] 461 U.S. 574 (1983).

of Practice making clear what the limits of 'to require individuals working for them to act in good faith and with loyalty to the organisations ethos' should mean. It should spell out the types of activities that would amount to a breach of this duty and in particular that passive membership of one of the discriminated classes protected by the Directives should be insufficient to justify such discrimination. The Code of Practice should warn employers that these provisions do not permit them to ask intrusive questions about their employee's private life and they should be reminded of their duties under Article 8 of the ECHR in this respect. We believe that such a Code of Practice should be arrived at after consultation with organisations involved in advising people who are regularly confronted with discrimination.

Article 4(2) is given effect to in domestic law by Reg 7(3) (see above) in relation to which the DTI has the following advice.

DTI, 'Explanatory Notes' para 82

It is for the employer to show that his organisation has *'an ethos based on religion or belief.'* To do so, he may seek to rely on evidence such as the organisation's founding constitution or similar documents, provisions in contracts of employment used by the employer, or other evidence about the practices of the employer's organisation and the way it is run . . .

Under regulation 7(3) it is not necessary to establish that the GOR is a determining requirement. This means that it is slightly broader than the GOR in regulation 7(2), because the employer is not required to show that religion or belief is a determining (ie decisive) factor in selection for the post in question. However, the employer must still show that the religion or belief is a requirement, and not just one of many relevant factors.

- For example, a Christian hospice could probably show that it was a requirement for its chief executive to adhere to that faith, because of the leadership which a chief executive must give in relation to maintaining and developing the religious ethos. It could only establish that a similar requirement applied to a nurse in the hospice if there were aspects of the job or its context going beyond the medical care of patients which required that the person must adhere to the particular faith.
- On the other hand, it would not be a GOR for a shop assistant to be of a particular faith in order to work in a bookshop with a religious ethos, if for all practical purposes the nature and context of the job are the same as for a shop assistant in any other bookshop. The fact that the employer or customers may prefer a person of the same faith is not relevant to whether or not a GOR applies to the job.

If the ethos of the employer relates not only to adherence to a religion, but to a specific belief based in that religion, it is unlikely that having that belief will be a GOR for the job, unless the belief has particular relevance to the nature or context of the job.

- For example, in the Christian hospice . . . the ethos might not only be based on Christianity, but more specifically on Christian beliefs to the effect that gay sex is not acceptable. It would only be a GOR for the chief executive to hold these beliefs, if the nature or context of the job required it. The hospital would also have to consider its position under the [SO Regs, considered in Chapter 10] . . .

L Vickers, 'The Employment Equality (Religion or Belief) Regulations 2003' (2003) 32 *Industrial Law Journal* 188, 192–3, footnotes omitted

it may be possible to argue that the acceptance in the Directive of a wider exemption for religious ethos organisations indicates that the preservation of a religious ethos is a legitimate aim for an employer to pursue. Yet, even if it is accepted that imposing a preference for religious employees is legitimate, it is not clear that it would be viewed as proportionate. It remains possible that in very specialist cases such a requirement could be proportionate, for example where not to allow it makes an individual virtually unemployable because of his or her extreme religious beliefs.

Taken together, the genuine occupational requirements in the Religion and Belief Regulations and the Sexual Orientation Regulations mean that religious employers can create workplaces which are largely homogenous in religious terms where to do so does not result in discrimination on other grounds. However, where discrimination on other grounds does result, other legislation would give a cause for a discrimination claim (direct or indirect) and the attempt to create a religiously homogenous workplace would almost certainly be unlawful.

FETO

Introduction

The RB Regs do not apply in Northern Ireland which has for decades had legislation regulating discrimination on grounds of 'religion or political belief.' FETO, and the Fair Employment Acts of 1976 and 1989 which it amends and consolidates, have their roots in Northern Ireland's troubled sectarian history. Until relatively recently, Northern Irish society was (to the outsider at least) extraordinarily homogeneous. Decades of political unrest and its economic repercussions had deterred anything more than minimal immigration and, for most, 'religious' discrimination meant discrimination in favour of, or against, Catholics on the one hand, Protestants on the other. FETO protects not only in relation to discrimination on grounds of religion but also to political opinion encompassing, inter alia, 'left' and 'right' politics (*McKay v Northern Ireland Public Service Alliance* [1994] NI 103), but excluding opinions (Article 2(4)) 'which consist of [or include] approval or acceptance of the use of violence for political ends connected with the affairs of Northern Ireland, including the use of violence for the purpose of putting the public or any section of the public in fear.' *In Gill v Northern Ireland Council for Ethnic Minorities* [2002] IRLR 74 Northern Ireland's Court of Appeal ruled that the 'political opinions' protected by FETO were those concerned with the conduct of the government of the state or matters of public policy rather than (as was there claimed) differences between 'anti-racist' and 'culturally sensitive' approaches to race relations problems.

By contrast with the other discrimination provisions, FETO explicitly provides (reg 2(3) that 'references to a person's religious belief or polotocal opinion include references to (a) his supposed religious belief or political opinion.' From its creation, the Northern Irish 'state' prohibited religious discrimination, the Government of Ireland Act 1920 providing that Northern Ireland's Parliament must not 'give a preference, privilege or advantage, or impose any disability or disadvantage, on account of religious belief.'[33] From the outset, however, such discrimination was and remained endemic both in the private sector (Protestants and Catholics living largely separate lives) and in government, broadly defined.

---

[33] The Constitution Act 1973, which abolished the Stormont Parliament and created an Assembly with lesser powers, also prohibited (direct) discrimination by that body and by public authorities. The Assembly was short-lived, however, and direct rule was re-imposed in 1974. S.2 has been replaced by s.76 Northern Ireland Act 1998, discussed below.

Much of the difficulty arises from the intertwined nature of religion and Northern Irish political affiliation. Very broadly speaking, Northern Irish Catholics tend to favour the creation of a single Ireland, while their Protestant compatriots prefer the continued position of Northern Ireland as part of the UK. The close relationship between religion and political affiliation (and between religion and perceived political affiliation) has resulted in the construction of Catholics as disloyal to the state. This, predictably, has had repercussions in terms of their employment in the public sector and, in particular, in the security forces.[34]

K McEvoy and C White, 'Security Vetting in Northern Ireland: Loyalty, Redress and Citizenship' (1998) 61 *Modern Law Review* 341, 343–5, footnotes omitted

Since its inception, the Northern Ireland state has placed a great deal of emphasis on ensuring the loyalty of its employees. After the partition of Ireland and the creation of a devolved parliament in the six North Eastern counties, the new government viewed itself as under threat from the Nationalist government in the South and the potentially seditious minority of Catholic/Nationalists in the North who made up approximately one third of the population of Northern Ireland.

. . . Unsurprisingly, it was viewed as crucial by members of the new government that the loyalty of civil servants could be relied upon. In 1923 the Promissory Oaths Act was introduced which required civil servants and teachers (Catholic educational establishments were viewed as particularly worthy of suspicion in the Stormont era) to swear an Oath of Allegiance to 'His Majesty King George the Fifth, his heirs and successors according to Law and to his Government of Northern Ireland.' Section 1(3) required all government departments to keep a record of people who had taken the Oath and section 1(5) empowered the Minister of Finance to apply the oath to full or part time duties in all departments or authorities as he thought fit.

While a similar Oath had been required in Great Britain during the first World War, it had expired, as far as the Civil Service was concerned, by the time of the introduction of this Act in Northern Ireland. However as the then Prime Minister of Northern Ireland, Sir James Craig, explained, it was felt necessary: '. . . to leave no loophole for people to crawl into departments . . . those who were not favourable to British Rule, for instance, to use their positions in the Civil Service, to undermine the loyalty of those departments towards the Crown and the Government.' . . . the fear of disloyalty and mistrust of the Catholic minority, confirmed in the minds of the majority by the periodic outburst of Republican violence, became deeply embedded in the political and social fabric of the state. Catholic/Nationalist disloyalty was viewed as axiomatic, synonymous with those who were against the British connection and wanted to withdraw from the Union, whereas Protestant Unionists were by definition loyal.

These high levels of distrust were demonstrated in security terms in the enactment of Emergency legislation—namely the 1922 Special Powers Act—with extraordinarily wide powers and the maintenance of a paramilitary police force (the RUC) backed up by auxiliary units (the 'B' Specials), both of which were specifically designed to deal with the potential threat from seditious Catholics. On a political level, the guaranteed inbuilt Unionist majority ensured that the Unionist Party, dominated by 'a laager mentality,' remained in power uninterrupted for fifty years without any great incentive to attract Catholic votes.

---

[34] A Hegarty, 'Examining Equality: The Fair Employment Act (NI) 1989 and Its Review' [1995] 2 *Web Journal of Current Legal Issues* points out that two other recent Prime Ministers (Captain Terence O'Neill and Lord Brookeborough respectively) 'stood by while his wife advertised for a Protestant domestic help . . . and . . . publicly declared that [Roman Catholics] . . . ought not to be employed as they are not to be trusted and in any event are enemies of the state.'

. . . There are a number of references to the question of the loyalty of Civil Servants recorded in the Northern Ireland Hansard during [the Cold War] period. However the concerns expressed by the Unionist government remain consistent throughout with no noticeable shift of emphasis in the Cold War era. The exchange below between Minister of Finance Maginess and a member of the Nationalist opposition, at the beginning of the Cold War era, is worth reproducing.

Mr Maginess

It is not a question of one religion or another; it is a question of loyalty or disloyalty and that is just the way it should be . . . it is degrading, to my mind, to bring religion into politics, just as it is degrading to bring politics into religion.

Mr Diamond

Then to get employment in the Civil Service you must be a Unionist?

Mr Maginess

If the honourable member complains that not sufficient of his supporters are employed by the Government, then the person most to blame for it is the honourable Member himself who has taught these people disloyalty . . . We have heard proverbs about nursing vipers in the bosom and that sort of thing. If the honourable member would say to his own followers—Look here, Northern Ireland is established under law, and whether you like it or not, act as a citizen of Northern Ireland, and so long as it is in existence do your best for it—then you would see a great change in this country.

McEvoy and White go on to report that in 1969, by which stage Catholics accounted for one third of the population, they occupied 6 per cent, 7 per cent and 14 per cent respectively of technical and professional civil service posts, higher administrative civil service positions and government nominated public body appointments. In the same year political violence broke out leading to the imposition, in 1972, of direct rule (Northern Ireland having been governed, since its inception, from Belfast).

FETO differs most significantly from the other discrimination provisions in the monitoring and review obligations it places upon employers (save private sector employers of 10 or fewer). These obligations were first imposed by the FEA 1989, the 1976 FEA having merely encouraged monitoring (the same encouragement is provided, in the context of the SDA and the RRA, by the relevant Codes of Practice).

During the 1980s, evidence that the 1976 legislation had been largely ineffective, coupled with pressure from US investors, led to the demand for reform.

C McCrudden, 'The Northern Ireland Fair Employment White Paper: a Critical Assessment' (1988) 17 *Industrial Law Journal* 162, 162–3

The most authoritative recent study of the effectiveness of this legislation in reducing the extent of inequality of opportunity in Northern Ireland between the two sections of the community was published in 1987 by the Policy Studies Institute. The single most dramatic illustration of the continuing dimensions of the inequality is to be found in comparing the Catholic and Protestant unemployment rates. According to the P.S.I. study, Catholic male unemployment remains at a staggering 35 per cent, two-and-a-half times that of Protestant male unemployment. This has continued despite 10 years of legislation, and despite there being over 100,000 job changes a year. Religion remains a major determinant of this differential unemployment rate.

This P.S.I. study also found that the legislation passed in the mid-1970s had little effect on employers' practices. The vast majority of employers interviewed for the P.S.I. study believed that the Act had made little, if any, impact on their practices and procedures. Job discrimination was still thought to be justifiable in certain circumstances by a considerable number of employers. Informal recruitment and appointment procedures contributed to continuing levels of segregation. Investigations by the F.E.A . . . did not appear to have made an impact beyond the individual organisation investigated. Very few establishments were formally monitoring the religious composition of the workforce. Indeed, very few establishments were carrying out any type of equal opportunity measure.

There were a number of reasons for the ineffectiveness of the legislation. There was an almost complete lack of interest in the issue of both Labour and Conservative Governments between the mid-1970s and the mid-1980s, despite the limited effect that the legislation was having. The F.E.A. adopted a restrained approach to enforcement; negotiation rather than litigation was the dominant approach even when it delivered relatively little. Employers' organisations, soon after the legislation came into effect, adopted a belligerent approach to the Agency and to the issue. The main constitutional party representing Catholics (the Social Democratic and Labour Party), and the trade unions, seldom adverted to the issue.

Since the mid-1980s, however, inequality of opportunity between Catholics and Protestants in Northern Ireland has again become a key political issue, largely due to pressure from outside the Province. A campaign in the United States was begun to bring pressure to bear on American corporations, state legislatures and municipal governments with investments in Northern Ireland to adopt a set of anti-discrimination principles (inspired by the Sullivan Principles) called the 'MacBride Principles.' The MacBride campaign, despite well-orchestrated opposition from the British and American Governments, has proved popular with state legislators. By July 1988 eight States had already enacted legislation requiring American companies in which they invest to ensure fair employment practices in their Northern Ireland subsidiaries, and many more were considering similar moves.

This American campaign began to fill, however partially and inadequately, the political vacuum caused by the failure of Northern Ireland's political institutions to address the issue adequately.

The Standing Advisory Commission on Human Rights (SACHR), whose task it was to 'advis[e] the Secretary of State on the adequacy and effectiveness of the law for the time being in force in preventing discrimination on the ground of religious belief or political opinion and in providing redress for persons aggrieved by discrimination on either ground'[35] announced in 1985 that it intended to review the effectiveness of the 1979 Act. The review was welcomed by Douglas Hurd MP, at the time Secretary of State for Northern Ireland, and in the same year the government itself published statistics which showed:

marked differences between the characteristics of the Protestant and Catholic sections of the community in Northern Ireland. The statistics illustrated differences in such areas as employment, educational background and housing. They underlined the fact that, in spite of the institutional safeguards in place and the action taken over recent years, substantial differences between Catholics and Protestants continued to exist, notably in terms of employment and unemployment . . .[36]

[35] S.20 Northern Ireland Constitution Act 1923.
[36] SACHR, Religious and Political Discrimination and Equality of Opportunity in Northern Ireland—Report on Fair Employment.

The Policy Studies Institute conducted more detailed research, the results of which are mentioned by Christopher McCrudden in the extract above, and SACHR made a number of recommendations for amendments to the FEA 1976.[37] As McCrudden goes on to note, the White Paper (and the ensuing 1989 Act) did not wholly embrace the SACHR proposals. But it did introduce the compulsory monitoring mentioned above, and this obligation is now to be found in Articles 52–4 FETO, discussed below.

The Government announced during the passage of the 1989 FEA that a comprehensive review of the legislation would be carried out after five years. In the event, this was conducted by the SACHR. The Government had initially entrusted the process of review to the Central Community Relations Unit of the Northern Ireland Office, but concerns over this body's lack of independence resulted in responsibility for the review being transferred to SACHR which reported in 1997.[38] Subsequent amendment of the fair employment legislation by FETO took place in haste, as part of the legislative package associated with the Good Friday peace agreement and ensuing moves towards devolution in Northern Ireland.[39]

The decision of the Government to legislate in 1998 by way of an Order in Council (resulting in very curtailed parliamentary scrutiny) was criticised by the Northern Ireland Select Committee.

'The Operation of The Fair Employment (Northern Ireland) Act 1989—Ten Years On', HC 95-I, paras 26–8.

. . . the [FETO] . . . contained substantial changes from the earlier legislation. In contrast to the previous occasions, the House had no opportunity to seek to amend the proposals. Originally, indeed, the Government proposed taking the Order in the Standing Committee before [the Minister for Northern Ireland] gave evidence to us.

Our concern was, if anything, intensified by the way in which the draft Order in Council was presented to Parliament . . . In other circumstances in which an Order in Council approach to legislating for Northern Ireland had been adopted, the Government frequently published a proposal for the draft Order in Council before the draft itself was published, in order to enable interested parties to comment on the proposal before it was finalised. The 1998 Order was not first published as a proposal and so even that possibility of influencing the draft was substantially reduced . . .

While we appreciate that the Government wanted to make 'rapid progress' with the legislation in order to ensure that the terms of its obligations under the [Good Friday] Agreement were fulfilled, we do not consider that the procedures used in this case provided for adequate Parliamentary scrutiny of important new legislation in a sensitive policy area where, hitherto, primary legislation has been the norm. We regret that Government felt it should proceed by way of an Order in this case.

The Government did not in 1998 accept all of SACHR's submissions. In particular, it rejected the imposition of a statutory obligation on employers to consult employees and recognised trade unions as part of the tri-annual review (discussed below), and the exten-

---

[37] SACHR was abolished by the NIA which created the EC and the Human Rights Commission.

[38] See C Bell, 'The Employment Equality Review and Fair Employment in Northern Ireland' (1996) 2 *International Journal of Discrimination and Law* 53, 53.

[39] Lord Blease, speaking in the House of Lords debates on FETO (HL Debs 7 Dec 1998, col. 763), stated that it was 'one of the main pillars upon which the real function and work of the Northern Ireland Assembly will be built.' Also evidence given by the CAJ to the Northern Ireland Select Committee (and appended to that Committee's Fourth Report of the 1998–99 session, The Operation of the Fair Employment (HC 95-II)) was to the effect that fair employment legislation was central to the peace process—see, for example, answer to question 453.

sion of legal aid to the Fair Employment Tribunal (FET, the specialist tribunal established to deal with fair employment cases). It also declined to amend the definition of 'victimisation' to include victimisation of A by virtue FETO-related action by B; to extend contract compliance and to permit the award of exemplary damages by the FET.[40] But it did take into account SACHR's finding that 'disadvantage'—in particular, long-term unemployment—was the main obstacle to fair employment.

In 1997, Catholic men were 2.9 times more likely to be unemployed than Protestant men, Catholic women 1.4 times more likely to be unemployed than their Protestant counterparts. Catholics comprised 40 per cent of those employed in Northern Ireland, 41 per cent of the economically active but 62 per cent of the unemployed. The 'unemployment differential' (the unequal impact of unemployment between Catholics and Protestants) had actually increased for Catholic men from 2.0 to 2.9 in the seven years to 1997 (for all Catholics, from 1.9 to 2.4 in the same period)—this despite a substantial reduction in unemployment rates (from 9 per cent to 5 per cent for Protestants, 17 per cent to 12 per cent for Catholics). According to Adam Ingram MP, Minister of State for Northern Ireland, in his evidence to the Select Committee on Northern Ireland Affairs in its review of the fair employment legislation (December 1998): 'there remains a gap between the Catholic share of employment and the Catholic share of the economically active population . . . There is also evidence of continuing imbalances at the top of large organisations, not least the civil service.'

The reasons behind the differential unemployment rates of Catholics and Protestants in Northern Ireland are a matter of some controversy.[41] The differential was not, however, explained by relative levels of education.[42] The Committee for the Administration of Justice (CAJ) declared in 1997 that:

> the single most important contribution that government can make to ensuring equality of opportunity is to show by its words and actions that it considers inequality in Northern Irish society to be totally unacceptable. It must accordingly be prepared to put energy and resources into ensuring change . . . in particular . . . a culture of equality [must] be signalled by establishing specific equality goals along with the introduction of appropriate measures and funding to ensure that these goals can be met within a clearly defined time frame. The setting of goals and timetables is particularly important in those public services where representation from across the community is lacking . . . specific and public goals and timetables should be set in the achievement of lesser differentials in unemployment figures (as recommended by SACHR in its 1987 report). Specific (financial) incentives should be made available both to encourage employers to recruit from the long term unemployed and to enable the [latter] to compete on a realistic basis for employment opportunities.[43]

The issue of public service goals and timetables was considered in Chapter 3, in the discussion of s.75 of the Northern Ireland Act. Government spokespersons went out of their way to emphasise the Government's commitment to reducing the unemployment differential. But for all of the importance expressly placed on this matter by the Government, the time-frame set for the elimination of the differential was 13 years and the task was

---

[40] *Partnership for Equality* (Northern Ireland Office, 1998), responding to SACHR, 'Employment Equality: Building for the Future' (HMSO, Cmnd 3684, June 1997). 77 *Equal Opportunities Review* 8–9 quoted SACHR Chair Michael Lavery QC to the effect that 'it did not augur well for the future of Northern Ireland if the Government could not accept . . . SACHR's "modest proposals." '

[41] While SACHR was satisfied, in its review, that some discrimination was involved, one of its members (Ulster Unionist Dermott Nesbitt) disagreed and published a dissenting note on the matter.

[42] FEC, 'The Key Facts' (1995).

[43] Submission to SACHR's Employment Equality Review (1996).

established as one for the new Equality Commission (of which more below), rather than government itself. SACHR criticised the pace of proposed change as well as the delegation by the Government of responsibility for the establishment of goals and timetables.[44] The report of the Select Committee on Northern Ireland Affairs was also critical of the time frame imposed by the Government, and recommended that the first review of FETO, which was to take place no later than 2005, should 'consider any deviations between the benchmarks established and the available data. This would provide a suitable opportunity for appropriate policy initiatives on the unemployment differential.'

In addition to the issues already touched upon, FETO and the Northern Ireland Act 1998 made substantial changes to the law as it relates to discrimination on grounds of religious belief or political opinion. The most significant of these were:

- the replacement of the notorious s.42 FEA (discussed below), by which the issue of an unchallengeable 'national security' certificate by the Secretary of State could block action under the FEA, by Article 80 FETO and s.91 Northern Ireland Act 1998, which provide a review mechanism for such certificates;[45]
- the merger of all four Northern Irish equality bodies (the Fair Employment Commission, the EOC for Northern Ireland, the CRE for Northern Ireland—itself established only in August 1997—and the Northern Ireland Disability Council) into a super 'Equality Commission';[46]
- the imposition upon all public authorities of a statutory duty to promote equality of opportunity. This duty, the first to be imposed in the UK, is implemented by equality schemes enforced by the ECNI and extends beyond religion/political opinion to race, sex and disability to age, marital status, sexual orientation and the presence or absence of dependants;[47]
- the consolidation of the previously unwieldy FEAs 1976 and 1989 into a single piece of legislation—FETO;
- the extension of the fair employment legislation to cover the provision of goods, facilities, services and premises as well as employment (hence the change of name from Fair Employment Act(s) to Fair Employment and Treatment Order.

These changes are further discussed, where relevant, below. In addition to the very major changes introduced by FETO and the Northern Ireland Act 1998, a substantial number of 'housekeeping' amendments were made to the fair employment legislation which had the effect of bringing it more into line with the race and sex discrimination provisions. Many of these changes had been called for by the EEC. Among them were Articles 26 and 32, which respectively prohibit discrimination by partnerships of at least six partners and by

---

[44] SACHR response to the White Paper, discussed in SACHR's submissions to the Northern Ireland Affairs Committee, appended to the Report of that Committee, above.

[45] The RRA as amended by the RR(A)A does the same in the race relations context where, by contrast with the position under the FEAs, it has not been frequently used.

[46] Northern Ireland Act 1998. This was done despite strong opposition with 29 respondents to the White Paper Partnership for Equality supporting merger and only 29 in favour. The FEC was in favour but there is a fear, voiced, inter alia, by SACHR, the EOC and CRE for Northern Ireland and the NI Disability Council, that the other forms of discrimination will lose out to fair employment (see HL Debs 5 Oct 1998, cols 183ff). The creation of an Equality Commission for Northern Ireland, as one of three new commissions including a Commission on Policing and a Human Rights Commission, was seen as an important step in the peace process and formed part of the Belfast Agreement of Easter 1999.

[47] Northern Ireland Act 1998, s.75. Though the Government set out, for the first time in 1998, targets for the achievement of equal/pro-rata representation of women and ethnic minorities in public appointments (and proper consideration for the disabled)—see Quangos: Opening up Public Appointments. The plans published by each department under this scheme are not legally binding.

and in respect of barristers; Articles 41 and 34, which empowered the EC to take action against 'persistent discrimination' and in respect of discriminatory advertisements;[48] Article 7(d), which imposed upon the EC an obligation to review FETO; Article 39, which permitted the award of compensation in cases of employment-related unintentional indirect discrimination and Article 46(6), which recognised contractual discrimination as continuing for the purposes of time-limits. By contrast, Article 39(1)(d) created a new distinction between the fair employment regime and those imposed by the other Acts by permitting the FET, on making a finding of unlawful discrimination, to make 'a recommendation that the respondent take within a specified period action appearing to the Tribunal to be practicable for the purpose of obviating or reducing the adverse effect on a person other than the complainant of any unlawful discrimination to which the complaint relates.' This power is in addition to those of declarations, compensation and recommendations (Article 39(1)(c)) 'that the respondent take . . . action . . . for the purpose of obviating or reducing the adverse effect on the complainant of any unlawful discrimination . . .'. It is further discussed in Chapter 5.

In many respects FETO resembles the SDA or RRA with the addition of what might be termed 'collective' measures such as workforce monitoring, contract compliance and a form of affirmative action, discussed below. By contrast with the other discrimination legislation, the employment provisions of FETO are enforced by a specialist tribunal (FET). (SACHR's proposals that non-employment aspects of the legislation went to the FET were rejected by the Government in 1998.)

FETO has had a significant impact on the Catholic/ Protestant dimension of Northern Ireland's workforce. In summer 2000, the ECNI reported that Catholic participation in Northern Ireland's workforce had increased steadily over the past decade, Catholics accounting for 39.6 per cent of the workforce in 1999 (up from 34.9 per cent in 1990). Further, Catholic representation was proportionate in six of the nine occupational classifications, though they were still very under-represented in security-related occupations (8.5 per cent) and in the senior Civil Service. Research published in 2004 found a continued improvement in the position of Catholics, though they remained disproportionately likely to be unemployed, and found that the number of people working in integrated workplaces has increased while pockets of Protestant under-representation were emerging in the public sector and Protestants from poorer backgrounds were doing less well than their Catholic counterparts. The 2004 research found that education was the main factor determining social mobility rather than, as was the case before, 'community background.'[49]

FETO and the Employment Equality Directive

FETO has now become the vehicle for the transposition into law in Northern Ireland of the religion and belief provisions of the Employment Equality Directive. Those provisions, as we saw above, are directed at 'religion, religious belief, or similar philosophical belief.' Nevertheless, their transposition by the Fair Employment and Treatment Order (Amendment) Regulations (Northern Ireland) 2003 (Statutory Rule 2003 No. 520) has avoided the creation of a fault line in FETO similar to that created in the RRA by the transposition of the Racial Equality Directive. Whereas, in the latter case, the RRA now

---

[48] S.33 FEA forbade discriminatory advertisements but the FEC had no power to apply to the FET for a ruling.

[49] B Osborne (ed), *Fair Employment in Northern Ireland: A Generation On* (ECNI & Blackstaff Press).

adopts different definitions of indirect discrimination and harassment and a different burden of proof (to list just the most obvious) to discrimination on grounds of 'race or ethnic or national origin,' on the one hand; 'colour' or 'nationality' on the other; FETO applies the provisions of the directive to discrimination on grounds of 'religious belief or political opinion.' Thus, for example, the new provisions FETO which deal with discrimination against office-holders, harassment, constructive dismissal, discrimination by vocational organisations, etc, and to discrimination after the end of an employment relationship, all apply to discrimination on grounds of 'political opinion' as well as 'religious belief.'[50] Further, while FETO refers only to 'religious beliefs' and 'political opinion,' the definition of 'religious belief' it adopts (reg 2(2)) 'includes any religion or similar philosophical belief.'

A fault line has, however, been created in FETO along the same lines as that in the SDA between discrimination in the employment context (broadly defined to include all that falls within the Employment Equality Directive) on the one hand, and the other contexts in which FETO applies. This fissure is not exactly the same as that in the SDA because the Employment Equality Directive's coverage of 'employment' is wider than that of the Burden of Proof Directive on the basis of which the SDA's amendments were made. Some of the difficulties associated with this are considered below. Even more problematically, FETO imposes monitoring and other collective obligations considered immediately below. These apply only in relation to 'religion or political belief' as originally protected by FETO, and therefore not to beliefs which fall within the Directive, on the one hand, but are not regarded either as 'religions' or 'political' beliefs, on the other.

Exceptions to the Prohibition on Discrimination

FETO does not apply, for obvious reasons, to ministers of religion. The registration, monitoring, review and other obligations imposed by Part VII of the Order (see below) do not apply 'to or in relation to employment as a teacher in a school,' while the other provisions do not apply in relation to the *recruitment* of school teachers. Segregated schooling is the norm in Northern Ireland and prior to the implementation of the religion and belief provisions of the Employment Equality Directive the order did not apply in relation to school teachers at all. The Directive (Article 15) makes specific provision for Northern Ireland:

1. In order to tackle the under-representation of one of the major religious communities in the police service of Northern Ireland, differences in treatment regarding recruitment into that service, including its support staff, shall not constitute discrimination insofar as those differences in treatment are expressly authorised by national legislation.
2. In order to maintain a balance of opportunity in employment for teachers in Northern Ireland while furthering the reconciliation of historical divisions between the major religious communities there, the provisions on religion or belief in this Directive shall not apply to the recruitment of teachers in schools in Northern Ireland in so far as this is expressly authorised by national legislation.

Article 15(2) required the narrowing of the former complete exemption from the Order of school teachers. The Equality Commission, which is obliged by Article 71(2) FETO, to 'keep under review' the exception, recommended its removal in 2002. A research report commissioned by the EC explained the rationale for the exception as follows:

---

[50] Article 2(3) provides that 'references to a person's religious belief or political opinion include references to . . . (b) the absence or supposed absence of any, or any particular, religious belief or political opinion'.

S Dunn and T Gallagher, 'The Exception of Teachers from the Fair Employment & Treatment (Northern Ireland) Order 1998' (2002)

Roman Catholic educational interests were concerned that, without an exception for teachers, the [FEA] 1976 could eventually lead to a system of non-denominational education, with a resulting loss of Catholic ethos. On the other hand, Protestant educational interests had a very different concern. They were concerned that, without an exception, Protestant teachers would be placed in an unduly unfavourable position. They believed that the state education system would come within the scope of the legislation, while the maintained schools, which are in the main Catholic, would not come within the scope of the legislation, as they could conceivably claim that religion was a bona fide occupational qualification. In other words, Roman Catholics would have a right to equality of opportunity in state schools but Protestants would not have the right to equality of opportunity in Catholic schools.

Notwithstanding the wide support found by the report for the continuation of the exception the Commission recommended its abolition (paras 8–9 of the research report).

The key themes which emerged from the study are as follows:
    Within the educational sector, the exception of teachers from the religious discrimination provisions is widely accepted, and the support for change is a minority view. Indeed, it is widely recognised that the exception is a consequence of separate religion schools in Northern Ireland, and in twin there is widespread acceptance of a 'chill factor' for teachers.
    The Commission gave detailed consideration to the results of the research. It is particularly aware that its review duty has the express purpose of furthering equality of opportunity in the employment of teachers. However, in contrast to the findings of the research, the Commission does not consider that the continuation of the exception will so further equality of opportunity.

The Government of Northern Ireland did not take the opportunity afforded by the 2003 amendments to FETO to do away with the exception, and in October 2003 the Commission announced an investigation into it. The final report favoured the retention of the exception for primary school teachers only.[51] No action has been taken at the time of writing.
    Prior to its amendment by the 2003 Regs FETO did not apply in relation to employment in a private household. That exception has been removed to give effect to the obligations imposed by the religion and belief provisions of the Employment Equality Directive. The exemption (Article 77) applied to charitable 'provision[s] for conferring benefits on persons of a particular religious belief or a particular political opinion (disregarding any benefits to persons not of that belief or opinion which are exceptional or are relatively insignificant)' has been disapplied in relation to 'employment,' broadly defined as has Article 78's exemption of acts done under statutory authority.
    Article 79 FETO provides that:

No act done by any person shall be treated . . . as unlawfully discriminating if—
(a) the act is done for the purpose of safeguarding national security or protecting public safety or public order; and
(b) the doing of the act is justified by that purpose (my emphasis).

---

[51] ECNI, 'The Exception of Teachers from the Fair Employment and Treatment (NI) Order 1998 (2004).

Under s.42(2) FEA, which predated Article 80 FETO, the issue of a certificate by the Secretary of State to the effect that an act challenged under the FEA was 'an act done for the purpose of safeguarding national security or of protecting public safety or public order' (there being no equivalent to Article 79(b)), was conclusive evidence that the act was done for the stated purpose. Article 80, however, provides that a certificate may be challenged before a special tribunal set up for that purpose under the Northern Ireland Act 1998. The tribunal may uphold such a certificate only if satisfied that the disputed act fulfilled the requirements of Article 79. The new system for the scrutiny of national security certificates was established in the wake of *Tinnelly & Sons Ltd and McElduff v United Kingdom*,[51a] in which the European Court of Human Rights ruled that s.42 FEA breached Article 6(1) of the European Convention on Human Rights, in denying claimants in respect of whom certificates were served access to the courts.[52]

The *Tinnelly* case was brought by a building firm which had tendered unsuccessfully for demolition work with the Northern Ireland Electricity Service (NIE), despite having entered the lowest bid. The firm had initially been led to believe that its tender had been successful, but was subsequently informed that the work had been awarded to another firm with more experience. Tinnelly had then been told by the successful bidder that his (Tinnelly's) bid was rejected because 'the unions would not let [his firm] on to the site . . . because they believed them to be terrorists or sympathetic to terrorists'. Such an attitude on the part of the NIE workers could only have resulted from the fact that Tinnelly was Catholic.

Tinnelly complained to the FEA whose investigation of the complaint the NIE attempted (unsuccessfully) to prohibit by judicial review. Two months later, a s.42 certificate was issued by the Secretary of State with the effect that Tinnelly's challenge had to fail. A s.42 certificate was also issued in respect of a complaint to the FET by the McElduffs, who were denied the security clearance necessary to undertake work for the Department of the Environment.

The FEA (as it then was) sought judicial review of the Tinnelly certificate, arguing it 'was procured and issued in bad faith, was irrational, unfair and unreasonable and made for an improper collateral purpose, namely to prevent the FEA from investigating a complaint of unlawful discrimination.' The application was refused.

Mr Justice McCollum[53] castigated the NIE for the 'deep hostility' it had displayed to the objectives and activities of the FEA. Nevertheless, he was not satisfied that the decision had not been reached on the basis of security reports by the RUC, at least some of which 'appear[ed] not to give security clearance' to workers employed by Tinnelly. And if it was appropriate for NIE to seek a s.42 certificate, the issue of the certificate could not be challenged as long as proper procedures were followed by the Secretary of State. McCollum J took the view that he was unable to go behind the s.42 certificate in order to ascertain whether, as a matter of fact, there were grounds to consider Tinnelly a risk to national security.

The ECHR ruled that the s.42 certificates issued in the *Tinnelly and McElduff* case were 'a disproportionate restriction on the claimants' right of access to a court or tribunal.'[54] According to the Court:

[51a] (1998) 27 EHRR 249.

[52]   This followed a similar judgement made some 12 years before by the ECJ in *Johnson*, below.

[53]   *In re the Fair Employment Agency for Northern Ireland*, Queen's Bench Division MCCD 0590.T, unreported, 12 November 1991.

[54]   It awarded the Tinnellys and the McElduffs £10,000 and £15,000 respectively in compensation. The McElduffs, who had no criminal convictions save for minor motoring offences, and who had never been involved in any criminal or terrorist activity, claimed that they were discriminated against on the grounds of their perceived nationalist views, although they were not members of any political party and were not engaged in any form of political activity. They had in the past been mistaken by members of the security forces for different persons of the same name, and they suspected that this was a case of mistaken identity.

The conclusive nature of the section 42 Certificates had the effect of preventing a judicial determination on the merits of the applicants' complaints that they were victims of unlawful discrimination. The court would observe that such a complaint can properly be submitted for an independent judicial determination even if national security considerations are present and constitute a highly material aspect of the case. The right guaranteed to an applicant under Article 6 §1 of the Convention to submit a dispute to a court or Tribunal in order to have a determination on questions of both fact and law cannot be displaced by the 'ipse dixit' of the executive . . .

The introduction of a procedure, regardless of the framework which would allow an adjudicator or tribunal fully satisfying the . . . requirements of independence and impartiality to examine in complete cognisance of all relevant evidence documentary or other, merits of the submissions of both sides, may indeed serve to enhance public confidence . . . Mr Justice McCollum was unable under the present arrangements to dispel his own doubts about certain disturbing features of the Tinnelly case since he, like Tinnelly and the Fair Employment Agency, was precluded from having cognisance of all relevant material in the possession of [NIE] . . .

This situation cannot be said to be conducive to public confidence in the administration of justice.

Under the FEA regime, the issue of s.42 certificates was commonplace. Many jobs in Northern Ireland's public sector required, until very recently, that applicants be security-vetted by the RUC, as did jobs in British Telecom (Northern Ireland), the NIE, and some BBC jobs.[55] Where the outcome of such vetting was negative and an FEA complaint ensued, s.42 certificates were frequently issued to protect respondents' appointment procedures from scrutiny.

On the one hand, terrorist allegiances are clearly undesirable among employees in security-sensitive jobs. But the operation of s.42 was not even-handed. McEvoy and White point out that, of the 39 certificates issued between 1976 and 1993, 33 (85 per cent) were in respect of Catholic applicants (Catholics comprise around 40 per cent of the population).[56] The FEC's 'Review of Fair Employment Acts' (1998) stated (para 1.114) the 'strongly held belief' of that body that 'security checks may have an adverse impact of the employment of Roman Catholics in particular.' Further, there is evidence that s.42 certificates have been issued in order to disguise errors on the part of employers.[57] Vetting arrangements changed in 1993 to bring them more into line with those which operate in Great Britain. But McEvoy and White argue that:

'Security Vetting in Northern Ireland' (1998) 61 _Modern Law Review_ 341, 353–7, footnotes omitted

. . . the ideology and practice which continue to inform the process of information-gathering remains a major flaw in the security vetting system in Northern Ireland. . . . vetting is intended to uncover anyone who is or has been involved in, or associated with:

. . . terrorism, espionage, sabotage, actions intended to overthrow or undermine Parliamentary democracy by political, industrial or violent means, or who is or has been a member of any organisation advocating such activities, associated with any

[55] Recognition of the discriminatory impact of vetting contributed to an announcement in December 2003 that vetting would subsequently be restricted to security sensitive positions as in Great Britain (HC Debs 15 December 2003 Col. 125 WS).
[56] McEvoy & White, 352.
[57] _Ibid._

such organisation, or any of its members in such a way as to raise reasonable doubts about his or her reliability; or is susceptible to pressure or improper influence . . .

Information gathering for the purpose of security vetting in Developed Vetting cases and in Extended Security Check cases, where interviews are not normally conducted, are carried out by investigation officers working within the 'Security Branch' of the Department of Finance and Personnel. These officers are normally former policy officers with investigative experience who liaise with the RUC in carrying out the necessary checks. As Sir Patrick Wall has opined with regard to the similar process within the Ministry of Defence, '. . . a great deal depends upon the vetting officer.' Linn has argued with regard to the equivalent investigative officer in Great Britain that there are inherent dangers in having such a body staffed exclusively by former male police officers in their mid 50s, in so far as it is unlikely that such a group would reflect the plurality of political views and experiences of those being investigated. We would argue that in the context of the RUC, with over 90 per cent of the officers both male and Protestant, and substantial evidence of a difficult relationship between the police and sections of the Catholic community, those concerns are considerably enhanced.

In a community such as Northern Ireland, a more complete understanding of the realities of community life amongst those who gather information for security vetting purpose sic crucial. Poor quality intelligence, and a failure to understand the complexities of the minority community, have previously been attributed as significant factors in some of the most noteworthy failures in security policy in Northern Ireland. However, any analysis criticising the quality of intelligence provided by the RUC must go beyond superficial notions of sectarianism amongst former or serving police officers. While there is considerable literature to suggest that such attitudes do exist amongst some officers, it is more fruitful to locate our analysis in the ideological and practical mechanics of information gathering in the Northern Ireland context.

It has been suggested repeatedly that family and extended family networks are closer, more important and more extensive in Northern Ireland. Northern Ireland's predominantly rural heritage, small geographical size, large families, high unemployment and relative poverty have all been referred to as factors to be included in analysing this phenomenon. With the largest rate of imprisonment in Europe per capita, it has been estimated that Northern Ireland has the largest proportionate number of families which have been directly affected by imprisonment of a family member.

McEvoy and White explored the notions of 'loyalty' which served to exclude Catholics from many jobs long before the introduction of formal or 'overt' vetting, and concluded that:

In this context a new form of 'loyalty' may have emerged with regard to security vetting. The old system, of in effect excluding Catholics unless they could demonstrate sufficient 'loyalty' to Crown and government, has been replaced by one whereby none will be excluded other than those with 'an association with terrorism.' While such a formulation may have a superficial attractiveness, it is arguable that it may disproportionately disadvantage those from working class Catholic backgrounds. It may for example lead to an implicit reversal of the onus of proof, whereby people from certain postal districts have to demonstrate their 'bona fides' because of where they live, or their family or community backgrounds rather than any specific incident for which they are responsible. These are the areas where Sinn Fein are politically strongest. As noted above, these are also the areas in which police/community relationships are most strained. And these are also often the areas with the highest levels of unemployment where access to employment in the public sector (in its broadest sense) is crucial for the economic and social regeneration of the jurisdiction.

. . . the current system of security vetting is flawed because of a number of historical features. It is a system which grew from an exclusionary notion of loyalty in the public sector as synonymous with Unionism. It was refined during a period of violent political conflict where the avenues of redress which should protect the citizen from discriminatory practices were demonstrated to be wholly inadequate. Finally . . . the practical mechanisms for the gathering and assessment of information for security vetting purposes continue to have the potential to operate in a discriminatory fashion against the Catholic community. While Northern Ireland will undoubtedly continue to require some system of security vetting, it is one which will require a range of legal, practical and ideological changes in the administration of the system.

The Northern Ireland Affairs Select Committee's report on the fair employment legislation took the view that the changes introduced in this regard might be inadequate to comply with the ECHR protections:

'The Operation of The Fair Employment (Northern Ireland) Act 1989—Ten Years On', HC 95-I paras 109–12

The [national security] Tribunal is appointed by the Lord Chancellor: the chairman must be a current or former judge of the High Court or the Court of Appeal in England or Northern Ireland. The legislation authorises Rules which will enable proceedings before the Tribunal to take place without a party being given full particulars of the reasons for the issue of the certificate, and enable the Tribunal to hold proceedings in the absence of any person, including a party and any legal representative appointed by a party. Further provisions permit the Attorney General for Northern Ireland to appoint a Member of the Bar of Northern Ireland to represent the interests of a party to proceedings before the tribunal in any proceedings from which he and any legal representative of his are excluded, but the Order further provides that the person so appointed 'shall not be responsible to the party whose interests he represents.'

These provisions might be thought to represent a reasonable compromise between the need to ensure that the certificates are properly reviewed by an independent body and the need to ensure that information is not disclosed contrary to the public interest . . . On the other hand, these provisions might be thought to enable the Government to have the best of both worlds, enabling the appearance of independent adjudication to take place, but so interfering with the usual adversarial process as to render the process unacceptable. SACHR expressed the view to us that 'individuals who are affected by these certificates may not be happy at the end of the day that they have been fully and independently and properly represented by the tribunal. . . . And we feel that these provisions, while enabling some sort of independent scrutiny, do not go far enough, certainly with regard to winning the confidence of the person who is affected by them that he has been properly dealt with.'

If these provisions are ever used, it is possible that the issue of their compatibility with the European Convention on Human Rights will come before the European Court of Human Rights or, indeed, our own courts once the Human Rights Act 1998 is fully in force. SACHR considered 'there must be some reservations' about whether the provisions comply. We hope that the new Northern Ireland Human Rights Commission will consider this issue in due course, and also the desirability of an alternative approach. . . .

In the interim, another issue has arisen which needs to be resolved. The Northern Ireland Bar Council, which represents the practising Bar, has taken the preliminary view that counsel appointed to represent a person in these proceedings, while not being responsible to that party, may be at risk of being in breach of Bar ethics requirements. Since the legislation requires such counsel to be a member of the Northern Ireland Bar, and thus subject to Northern Ireland Bar Council ethics rules, this is a serious issue.[58]

In 1996 the CAJ had called for the immediate repeal of s.42, and in its submissions to the Select Committee on Northern Ireland Affairs in 1999 it favoured an approach such as that adopted in the sex discrimination context. There, the equivalent of s.42 had been declared in breach of the Equal Treatment Directive by the ECJ in *Johnston v Chief Constable of the RUC* Case C–224/84 [1986] ECR 651 (see Chapter 4). As a result of the *Johnston* decision the UK Government simply disapplied the relevant provisions of the sex discrimination legislation insofar as they applied to employment cases. The Fair Employment Commission's Review of the Fair Employment Acts (1997) criticised the ensuing inconsistency between the FEA (as it then was) and the race relations legislation, on the one hand, and the sex discrimination legislation on the other. That position remains.

Perhaps the most interesting exception from FETO is Article 70 which provides that:

(1) This Order does not apply to or in relation to—
(a) any employment or occupation as a clergyman or minister of a religious denomination [this has been mentioned above].
(2) Part VII [see below] does not apply to or in relation to any employment or occupation where the essential nature of the job requires it to be done by a person holding, or not holding, a particular religious belief.
(3) So far as they relate to discrimination on the ground of religious belief, Parts III and V [employment] do not apply to or in relation to any employment or occupation where the essential nature of the job requires it to be done by a person holding, or not holding, a particular religious belief.
(4) So far as they relate to discrimination on the ground of political opinion, Parts III and V [employment] do not apply to or in relation to an employment or occupation where the essential nature of the job requires it to be done by a person holding, or not holding, a particular political opinion.

This exception *substitutes* the GOR defence found in other anti-discrimination legislation, FETO containing no equivalent of reg 7 of the RB Regs, considered at length above.[59] Thus the only circumstances in which employment-related direct discrimination not falling within one of the particular exceptions outlined above, and not within the affirmative action provisions considered in Chapter 3 and below, can be justified under FETO is where 'where the essential nature of the job requires it to be done by a person holding, or not holding, a particular religious belief.' It is evident from the discussion of reg 7(3), in particular, that the scope for discrimination by religious organisations in Northern Ireland is considerably narrower than that in Great Britain. The evidence of the former chairman of Northern Ireland's Fair Employment Commission to the House of Lords Select Committee on the EU has been referred to above. According to that Committee's Ninth Report of 1999–2000: Article 70 'had not led to "any cases at all. It has not given rise to any significant difficulty."' It was this evidence in part which led the committee to suggest that there was no need for Article 4(2) of the Employment Equality Directive,

---

[58] The use of 'special advocates' has come under significant scrutiny in the terrorism context in the wake of the House of Lords' decision in *A v Secretary of State for the Home Department* [2005] 2 WLR 87 and the resultant Prevention of Terrorism Act 2005.

[59] The Employment Equality Directive contains a non-regression clause which would have been breached by the introduction of a wider exception.

which provides the basis for the broad qualification of the prohibition on 'religion or belief' discrimination by 'organizations whose ethos is based on religion or belief.' As that committee noted, however, the narrow GOR-equivalent in FETO was coupled at the time with a complete exception from its provisions of schoolteachers. It remains to be seen what will be the impact of the narrowing of the exception to recruitment alone.

Investigations of Practices, Monitoring and Review Obligations

We saw in Chapter 5 that the investigative powers of the EC in relation to FETO are broader than those of the other commissions (or, indeed, of the EC in relation to sex and race). We noted also there, however, that FETO provides no investigative powers in relation to discrimination outside the area of employment (broadly defined).

Turning to those collective dimensions of FETO which are unique to that legislation, the Order, by contrast with the SDA, RRA and DDA, imposes statutory obligations on employers (albeit only those having more than 10 employees) to monitor their workforces and applicants by religion (as distinct from political opinion), and to submit records to the Equality Commission. In addition, all public sector employers and those in the private sector having at least 250 employees must monitor the religion of their promotees and of those ceasing to be employed. FETO introduced the obligation to monitor promotees and those ceasing to be employed, and extended the obligation to monitor applicants to private sector employers of between 11 and 250 staff. It also extended the monitoring obligation to cover part-time workers (although these workers, defined as those working less than 16 hours per week, are not counted for the purposes of establishing the size of the workforce).

Failure to supply the EC with monitoring returns is a criminal offence. The Fair Employment (Monitoring) Regulations (Northern Ireland) 1999 provide the method by which the religious affiliation of employees, applicants, etc, may be determined and require that monitoring returns classify employees not only by religion but also by sex and, within this, by part-time/full-time status[60] and occupational group.[61] The Regulations provide that (save for specified uses) information gathered for monitoring purposes is to be treated as confidential.

Article 55 FETO requires that employers 'review the composition of those employed . . . and the employment practices of the concern for the purposes of determining whether members of each community [Protestant and Catholic] are enjoying, and are likely to continue to enjoy, fair participation in employment in the concern.' 'Fair participation' which, in the words of the FEC in 1997, was 'arguably the most novel departure' of the FEA 1989, is not defined.[62] These reviews must take place at least once every three years and must include review of practices relating to recruitment, training and promotion. Where it appears to an employer, as a result of such a review, that 'members of a particular community are not enjoying, or are not likely to continue to enjoy' 'fair participation', Article 55 FETO provides that the employer 'shall . . . determine the affirmative action (if any) which would be reasonable and appropriate.'

---

[60] FETO, for the first time, included part-time workers amongst those who must be monitored by race.

[61] Ie, 'managers and administrators, professional occupations, associate professional and technical occupations, clerical and secretarial occupations, craft and related occupations, personal and protective service occupations, sales occupations, plant and machine operatives and other occupations.'

[62] The Government did not act on the FEC's 1997 proposal (FEC's *Review of Fair Employment Acts,* para 3.34) that the legislation ought to 'clarify that fair participation will not be present where there is an under-representation of one community defined as "fewer members of that community than might be expected." '

Tri-annual reviews are not subject to an automatic obligation of return to the EC (SACHR's 1997 proposal that such an obligation should be imposed having been rejected by the Government). Also rejected by the Government was SACHR's proposal that employers should be obliged to consult with recognised trade union or employee representatives during the review process and the FEC's proposal (para 3.29) that reviews should consider 'the extent to which a harmonious working environment is being provided by staff'. The issue of affirmative action was considered in Chapter 3. Here it is useful to note once again that affirmative action obligations may be imposed by the ECNI where an Article 55 review demonstrates an absence of fair participation (discussed in Chapter 3) or may be pursued by employers, whether voluntarily (after an employment review or otherwise). Article 56(5) requires the ECNI 'where a review discloses that members of a particular community are not enjoying fair participation [to] make such recommendations as it thinks fit as to the affirmative action to be taken and . . . the progress . . . that can reasonably be expected' (again by way of goals and timetables). Although employers are under no general obligation to submit reviews to the Commission, the latter may require information from employers regarding such reviews (in particular, whether an employer has determined that fair participation is not occurring and, if such a determination has been made and a programme of affirmative action decided upon, any goals and timetables set). Where the ECNI has recommended affirmative action (which may include goals and timetables by which progress towards 'fair participation' may be measured), it is empowered to require follow-up information (not more than once every six months) as to the progress being made. And where the Commission is of the view that an employer's monitoring or review processes are not adequate, it may seek written undertakings from the employer as to changes to those processes and may, in the absence or breach of such undertaking, issue mandatory directions to the employer (Article 58). These may, in the final analysis, be enforced by the FET.

The monitoring requirement was imposed by the FEA 1989, in respect of the religious composition of workforces, after the widely acknowledged failure of the voluntary system established under the FEA 1976. It is impossible to judge conclusively how effective the monitoring and review obligations imposed by FETO are in eradicating discrimination. But what is noticeable is the decline in workplace segregation in Northern Ireland and the degree of consensus which exists as to the decline in religious discrimination. As the Northern Ireland Select Committee noted.

'The Operation of The Fair Employment (Northern Ireland) Act 1989—Ten Years On', HC 95-I, para 38.

. . . the general view from all the witnesses we heard [was] that unlawful employment discrimination on the grounds of religious belief and political opinion appears to have declined . . . Significant improvement appears to have occurred with lessening segregation of predominantly Roman Catholic firms, and predominantly Protestant firms . . . FEC statistics show that the overall Roman Catholic share of employment has risen by 4.3 percentage points over the period 1990 to 1998. . . The employment shifts described above are welcome, but the question arises as to how far they are the result of fair employment legislation. [The Chairman of the FEC] commented that:

It is very difficult to give an answer to that and very difficult to disentangle the situation. All I would say is that, during the previous period when the legislation was much weaker . . . there was not as great a change over the previous 15 or 20 years. So I believe that a considerable part of the changes has been as a result of the legislation but I would by no means argue . . . that the changes have been exclusively because of that.

Others shared that basic viewpoint, arguing that the legislation 'has created an environment within which the values that legislation encapsulates have been accepted by employers. . . .'[63] The Northern Irish CBI considers that the changes in employment 'are largely attributable [to the legislation], because [it] would suspect a lot of the changes are due to improved . . . recruitment selection procedures.' The Committee went on to endorse the fair employment legislation's regulatory regime (para 66):

> It has been argued that it might be preferable to reduce the regulatory functions of the FEC, and concentrate resources on resolving individual complaints, making them a more effective mechanism of deterrence.[[64]] However, it appears to us that such an approach does not recognise the different functions of the individual complaint and the FEC regulatory systems. The former is restricted to dealing with allegations of discrimination, while the latter has a much broader role in encouraging (and ultimately enforcing) fair participation, affirmative action, and equality of opportunity, which (as we have seen above) goes considerably beyond simply eradicating unlawful discrimination. We agree with SACHR, when it said that 'you do not necessarily arrive at [fairness and equality] simply by abandoning or abolishing or getting rid of discrimination . . .'
>
> While we welcome the extent to which individual complaints have been used by the [FEC] as the basis for strategic work with employers, we agree with the Commission that if this was the 'sole method of dealing strategically with employers then it would be a failure.' We recommend that the existing regulatory functions of the Commission be retained in their entirety.

Contract Compliance

Article 62 empowers the EC to declare 'unqualified' employers who either fail to register (a prerequisite to the monitoring obligations of all but private sector employers of no more than 10 employees) or to submit a monitoring return, or who fail to comply with an order issued by the EC after an investigation such as that described above. Article 64 provides that public authorities 'shall not enter into [a relevant] contract with' an unqualified person, and 'shall take all such steps as are reasonable to secure that no work is executed or goods or services supplied for the purposes of [a relevant] contract by any unqualified person.'[65] But Article 64(6) provides that '(6) Nothing in this Article affects the validity of any contract.'

Writing in 1996, Christine Bell remarked that:

---

[63] Evidence from SACHR to the Select Committee on Northern Ireland, appended to the Committee's Fourth Report of the 1998–99 session, (HC 95-II).

[64] Such a contract is either (Art 64(2): 'a contract made by the public authority accepting an offer to execute any work or supply any goods or services where the offer is made . . . (b) in response to an invitation by the public authority to submit offers' or (Art 64(3)) 'a contract falling within a class or description for the time being specified in an order made by the Department, where work is to be executed or goods or services supplied by any unqualified person'. The Local Government (Miscellaneous Provisions) (Northern Ireland) Order 1992, which prohibits local authorities from taking into account 'non-commercial matters' in awarding contracts, has an exemption in relation to employers in default.

[65] Prior to FETO, the FEA permitted contracts with unqualified persons if the alternative was either disproportionately expensive or not in the public interest. These qualifications were repealed but Art 64(7) provides that 'This Article does not apply to the execution of any work, or the provision of any goods or services, by any person which is certified in writing by the Secretary of State to be necessary or desirable for the purpose of safeguarding national security or protecting public safety or public order.'

**'The Employment Equality Review and Fair Employment in Northern Ireland' (1996) 2
International Journal of Discrimination and Law 53, 63–64, footnotes omitted**

Since the legislation was introduced in 1989 the disqualification provisions have only been
applied on one occasion and then only for a short period. This occurred after an employer
failed to register. However, the employer registered quickly thereafter and the disqualification was lifted. As no non-compliance findings have been made by the FET no opportunity has arisen to utilize that route of disqualification. The fact that recourse has only been
made to the disqualification provisions on one occasion does not mean that these
provisions have had no impact. Contract compliance does much of its work as a deterrent
and the threat of disqualification may have been one factor which led so many companies
to register and send in monitoring returns.

There are several ways in which this regime could be strengthened. Under the present system the contract compliance requirements operate as a penalty mechanism where grants
and contracts are removed after evidence of discriminatory practice. They could operate as
an incentive scheme whereby to be eligible for a grant or contract one must demonstrate
compliance with equality goals or good practice. Incentive operated schemes as utilized in
the U.S. and by some local authorities in England (prior to the Local Government Act
1988), have proved a successful tool for increasing the proportion of an under-represented
group in the workforce.

Even if the present scheme is not amended SACHR's Employment Equality Review
should examine to what extent equality considerations are taken into account by public
entities . . . which exercise significant powers to make grants or award contracts. Have pressures towards greater 'value for money' and cost reduction in the public sector led to the
marginalization of equality concerns when grants or contracts are awarded? Further, the
penalty scheme model could be extended. The possibility of disqualification could be added
to enforce the present remedy available in an individual complaint, whereby the FET can
order the employer to take action to reduce the affect of discrimination on the complainant,
within a specified period. An employer who fails to do this could be disqualified. This would
make the deterrent of disqualification for maintenance of discriminatory practices a more
visible one than it is under the present provisions.

SACHR made proposals in 1997 for the extensive amendment of the FEA's contract
compliance provisions,[66] suggesting that prospective contractors should be required to provide information on their 'policies, procedures and practices in relation to fair employment
and equal opportunities,' and that contracts could specify terms which contractors would
be obliged to meet. These proposals received short shrift in the White Paper which preceded
FETO. The White Paper, together with the response of the Select Committee on Northern
Ireland (HC 95-I) thereto and the wider issue of collective methods of enforcement, is considered in Chapter 5.

---

[66] Its first report in 1987 had also proposed extensive contract compliance provisions.

The European Convention on Human Rights

The Convention Provisions

Article 9 of the European Convention on Human Rights provides as follows:

1. Everyone has the right to freedom of thought, conscience and religion; this right includes freedom to change his religion or belief and freedom, either alone or in community with others and in public or private, to manifest his religion or belief, in worship, teaching, practice and observance.
2. Freedom to manifest one's religion or beliefs shall be subject only to such limitations as are prescribed by law and are necessary in a democratic society in the interests of public safety, for the protection of public order, health or morals, or for the protection of the rights and freedoms of others.

Also relevant where religious and other beliefs are concerned is Article 10:

1. Everyone has the right to freedom of expression. this right shall include freedom to hold opinions and to receive and impart information and ideas without interference by public authority and regardless of frontiers. This article shall not prevent States from requiring the licensing of broadcasting, television or cinema enterprises.
2. The exercise of these freedoms, since it carries with it duties and responsibilities, may be subject to such formalities, conditions, restrictions or penalties as are prescribed by law and are necessary in a democratic society, in the interests of national security, territorial integrity or public safety, for the prevention of disorder or crime, for the protection of health or morals, for the protection of the reputation or the rights of others, for preventing the disclosure of information received in confidence, or for maintaining the authority and impartiality of the judiciary.

Articles 9 and 10 can be read in isolation or in combination with Article 14 of the Convention (also discussed in Chapter 1) which provides that:

The enjoyment of the rights and freedoms set forth in this Convention shall be secured without discrimination on any ground such as sex, race, colour, language, religion, political or other opinion, national or social origin, association with a national minority, property, birth or other status.

The partial incorporation of Articles 9, 10 and 14 into domestic law by the Human Rights Act 1998 is considered in Chapter 1, the focus there being on the operation of the 1998 Act. Here we are concerned with the jurisprudence which has developed under Article 9 (read in conjunction, where relevant, with Article 14), and the extent to which these provisions might provide an additional source of protection against discrimination in connection with religion and belief.

The protection afforded by Article 9 to 'to freedom of thought, conscience and religion' including the 'right to change religion or belief' is unqualified. The right to *manifest* religion is, however, subject to 'such limitations as are prescribed by law and are necessary in a democratic society in the interests of public safety, for the protection of public order, health or morals, or for the protection of the rights and freedoms of others.'

Where someone is discriminated against solely on grounds of their religious or other beliefs, the question whether Article 9 has been breached will turn on (1) whether the discrimination is classified as 'interference' with the right and, if so, (2) whether the state can be held responsible for any interference either directly (where the state itself has interfered) or indirectly (where its failure to prevent or remedy the intereference is sufficiently culpable to make it appropriate for the state to be held liable for the interference). In cases where the discrimination has been in connection with the *manifestation* of religious or other beliefs there is an third question: whether the interference was 'necessary in a democratic society in the interests of public safety, for the protection of public order, health or morals, or for the protection of the rights and freedoms of others'. A similar test applies under Article 10. Where the interference with religious or other beliefs has been discriminatory, Article 14 may also come into play.

The second of the questions outlined above is not unique to Article 9 and has been considered in Chapter 1 in which the extent of the positive obligations imposed by the Convention was discussed.

The European Court's Approach

The general approach of the Convention organs in employment cases is set out in *Ahmad v UK* (1982) 4 EHRR 126 in which the claimant, a Muslim schoolteacher, claimed a breach of Article 9 after he was refused time-off work on a Friday afternoon in order to attend prayers at the mosque. The European Commission of Human Rights, which at the time had a sifting role in Convention claims, dismissed the claim as manifestly unfounded.

Ahmad v UK (1982) 4 EHRR 126 (Commission)

Judgment:

With regard to the applicant's claim, that the school authorities should have arranged their time-table so that he could attend Friday prayers, the Commission observes that the object of Article 9 is essentially that of protecting the individual against unjustified interference by the State, but that there may also be positive obligations inherent in an effective 'respect' for the individual's freedom of religion.

Article 9 of the Convention:

The freedom of religion guaranteed by Article 9(1) of the Convention includes the right of everyone to manifest his religion in worship 'either alone or in community with others'. The applicant's complaint is confined to the freedom to manifest his religion in worship 'in community with others'. The Government accept that attending the mosque amounts to manifesting religion in worship 'in community with others' but suggest that it may suffice to satisfy Article 9(1) if the right to manifest one's religion 'alone' is granted; the interpretation that both possibilities must always be available would have serious implications for the employment of persons belonging to religious minorities which do not have many places of worship. The applicant contests this interpretation.

The Commission has examined the ordinary meaning of the guarantee of the freedom of religion in paragraph (1) in the context both of Article 9 and of the Convention as a whole, taking into account the object and purpose of the Convention. It notes that the right to manifest one's religion 'in community with others' has always been regarded as an essential part of the freedom of religion and finds that the two alternatives 'either alone or in community with others' in Article 9(1) cannot be considered as mutually exclusive, or as leaving a choice to the authorities, but only as recognising that religion may be practised in either form. It observes at the same time that the freedom of religion is not absolute but under the Convention subject to the limitations of Article 9(2). The Commission concludes that the applicant may under Article 9(1) claim the right to manifest his religion 'in community with others'.

The applicant states that it is the religious duty of every Muslim to offer prayers on Fridays and, if considerations of distance permit, to attend a mosque for this purpose. A mere contractual obligation cannot excuse absence—a man cannot willingly put himself into a position where he cannot attend. When the applicant commenced his employment with the ILEA in 1968 there was only one mosque in the London area and it was physically impossible for him to work with the ILEA and to attend Friday prayers. After his transfer, in February 1974, to Division 5 he found himself nearer to mosques. He was then obliged by his religion to attend Friday prayers . . .

In its interpretation and application of Article 9 of the Convention, the Commission considers that, even if such a religious obligation were assumed, it could not, for the reasons given below, justify the applicant's claim under this provision in the circumstances of the present case.

The Commission has already stated that the freedom of religion, as guaranteed by Article 9, is not absolute, but subject to the limitations set out in Article 9(2). Moreover, it may, as regards the modality of a particular religious manifestation, be influenced by the situation of the person claiming that freedom . . .

The Commission here notes that the applicant did not, when he was first interviewed for his teaching position, nor during the first six years of his employment with the ILEA, disclose the fact that he might require time off during normal school hours for attending prayers at the mosque. The Government state that such a disclosure might have resulted in the applicant being offered only part-time employment. The applicant submits that the United Kingdom should not operate a system in which a job applicant must indicate his religion and thus risk not to be appointed because of his religious obligations. The Commission observes that the present case does not raise the general issue of the confidentiality of information concerning one's religion, but the question whether an employee should inform his employer in advance that he will be absent during a part of the time for which he is engaged. It considers it relevant for the appreciation of the parties' position during the relevant period that the applicant had at no time before and during the first six years of his employment brought to the attention of the ILEA his wish to have time off during normal school hours for attending prayers at the mosque.

The Commission further observes that, throughout his employment with the ILEA between 1968 and 1975, the applicant remained free to resign if and when he found that his teaching obligations conflicted with his religious duties. It notes that, in 1975, the applicant did in fact resign from his five-day employment and that he subsequently accepted a four-and-a-half day employment enabling him to comply with his duties as a Muslim on Fridays.

The applicant points out that his present employment means less not only as regards his pay but also concerning his pension rights, chances of promotion and security of employment. He submits that his case could have been better solved by a re-arrangement of the school time-table permitting his absence for about 45 minutes at the beginning of the afternoon sessions on Fridays. The Government contest this possibility.

The Commission, in its consideration of the parties' submissions, has had regard not only to the particular circumstances of the applicant's case but also to its background, as described in the pleadings. It notes that, during the relevant period, the United Kingdom society was with its increasing Muslim community in a period of transition. New and complex problems arose, inter alia, in the field of education, both as regards teachers and students. The parties agree that the applicant's case is not an isolated one and that it raises questions of general importance.

The Government state that separate education systems are administered in England, Wales, Scotland and Northern Ireland and that in none of these countries is the system a centralised one. Teachers are employed either by individual local education authorities or by individual schools and there appears to be no generally agreed practice for dealing with requests by teachers of any religious group (including Muslim teachers) for leave of absence from work in order to meet the requirements of their religion. The Council of Local Education Authorities in England and Wales are at present considering whether to issue guidelines on the subject.

The Commission accepts that the school authorities, in their treatment of the applicant's case on the basis of his contract with the ILEA, had to have regard not only to his religious position, but also to the requirements of the education system as a whole; it notes that the complex education system of the United Kingdom was during the relevant time faced with the task of gradual adaptation to new developments in its society. The Commission is not called upon to substitute for the assessment by the national authorities of what might be the best policy in this field but only to examine whether the school authorities, in relying on the applicant's contract, arbitrarily disregarded his freedom of religion . . .

Having regard also to the requirements of the education system as described by the Government, the Commission does not find that in 1974/75 the ILEA—or, in their independent capacity, the schools of its Division at which he was employed—in their treatment of the applicant's case on the basis of his contract did not give due consideration to his freedom of religion.

The Commission concludes that there has been no interference with the applicant's freedom of religion under Article 9(1) of the Convention.

The European Commission reached a similar decision more recently, in the case of *Stedman v UK*, in which a woman was dismissed for refusing to accept a contractual variation requiring her to work on Sundays. She, like Mr Ahmad, relied on her right to freedom of religion under Article 9. Unlike Ahmad, she was employed in the private sector, the alleged obligation on the part of the state being to protect her rights from interference by others, rather than to abstain itself from interference with them (see further Chapter 1). Unlike Mr Ahmad, she had not 'voluntarily' accepted employment inconsistent with her religious obligations.

Stedman v UK (1997) 23 EHRR CD (Commission)

Judgment:

The Commission notes that the applicant was employed and subsequently dismissed by a private company. The respondent State is thus not directly responsible for her dismissal.

The Commission however recalls that under Article 1 of the Convention, each Contracting State 'shall secure to everyone within [its] jurisdiction the rights and freedoms defined in . . . [the] Convention'. Hence, if a violation of one of those rights and freedoms is the result of non-observance of that obligation in the domestic legislation, the responsibility of the State is engaged (*Young, James and Webster* (1982) 4 EHRR 38, para 49). With specific reference to the rights of Article 9 of the Convention, the State has a responsibility to 'ensure the peaceful enjoyment of the right guaranteed under Article 9 to the holders of those beliefs and doctrines' (*Otto-Preminger Institut v Austria* (1995) 19 EHRR 34, para 47).

The Commission must first consider whether the fact the applicant was dismissed for refusing on religious grounds to accept a contract which meant she would have to work on Sundays, constituted a prima facie interference with her rights guaranteed under Article 9 of the Convention. Only in circumstance where such a dismissal would constitute such a prima facie interference with her rights under Article 9 of the Convention could the responsibility of the State be engaged.

The Commission recalls that in Application No 24949/94, Dec. 3.12.96, unpublished, an employee of the Finnish State Railways was dismissed for failing to respect his working hours on the basis that to work after sunset on a Friday was forbidden by the Seventh-Day Adventist Church, of which he was a member. The Commission held in this case that the applicant was not dismissed because of his religious convictions but for having refused to respect his working hours. In these circumstances the Commission considered that although the refusal was motivated by religious convictions, such a situation did not give rise to protection under Article 9(1). Further the Commission held in that case, that the applicant had failed to show that he was pressured to change his religious views or prevented from manifesting his religion or belief (inter alia, he was free to resign). Likewise in the present case the applicant was dismissed for failing to agree to work certain hours rather than for her religious belief as such and was free to resign and did in effect resign from her employment.

The Commission thus considers that, had the applicant been employed by the State and dismissed in similar circumstances, such dismissal would not have amounted to an interference with her rights under Article 9(1). A fortiori the United Kingdom cannot be expected to have legislation that would protect employees against such dismissals by private employers. In the absence of the dismissal itself constituting an interference with the applicant's rights under Article 9, the fact the applicant was not able to claim unfair dismissal before an Industrial Tribunal (who only had jurisdiction over employees of two years' standing), cannot, of itself, constitute a breach of Article 9 of the Convention.

It follows that this part of the application is manifestly ill-founded within the meaning of Article 27(2) of the Convention.

The applicant complains that the requirement to work on a Sunday constituted an interference with her right to family life and as such constituted a violation of Article 8 of the Convention.

The Commission notes that the applicant was obliged to work on a Sunday on a rota basis rather than every Sunday and was given time off in lieu during the week. The Commission notes that the applicant's husband worked from Monday to Friday and thus on weekends where the applicant was obliged to work on Saturday and Sunday her time with her husband was limited. However, given the almost inevitable compromise and balance between work and family commitments, particularly in families where both partners work, the Commission does not consider that the requirement that the applicant work a five day week to include Sundays on a rota basis, amounted to an interference with her family life such as to constitute a violation of Article 8 of the Convention.

It follows that this part of the application is manifestly ill-founded within the meaning of Article 27(2) of the Convention.

The difficulty illustrated by the Commission decisions in *Ahmad* and in *Stedman* lies in the refusal to demand that employers take steps to accommodate religious beliefs, rather than merely refrain from discriminating against the holders of such beliefs on that ground alone. Keith Ewing was, accordingly, pessimistic about the implications of incorporation.

K Ewing, 'The Human Rights Act and Labour Law' (1998) 27 *Industrial Law Journal* 275, 288–9, footnotes omitted

. . . it would be a mistake to be over optimistic [about the implications of incorporation] for there are several reasons for thinking that the progress will be measured in inches rather than miles.

The first of these is the very narrow approach to the construction of the Convention adopted by the Strasbourg authorities, at least in relation to its application to employees. In *Ahmad* the Commission held that there had been no violation of the applicant's article 9 right to freedom of religion, partly because the content of the right could 'as regards the modality of a particular manifestation, be influenced by the situation of the personclaiming that freedom', including any employment contract to which he or she was a party. And in *Stedman v United Kingdom*, where the applicant was dismissed by her employer 'for refusing on religious grounds to accept a contract which meant that she would have to work on Sundays,' the Commission concluded that the applicant had been dismissed 'for failing to agree to work certain hours rather than for her religious belief as such and was free to resign and did in effect resign from her employment.' Although directed to take these decisions into account, controversially the British courts are not bound by the Strasbourg jurisprudence, which they are free to disregard. It would indeed be disappointing if the courts were to take the view that Convention rights could be qualified by contract, and they would be rightly excoriated were they to adopt the formalism of the Commission's reasoning in *Stedman*.

The second reason for caution, however, is that the rights in the Convention are by no means unqualified. Indeed as the Commission reminded us in *Ahmad* 'the freedom of religion, as guaranteed by Article 9, is not absolute, but subject to the limitations set out in Article 9(2).' This has important implications for any court or tribunal faced with a complaint that a dismissal breaches a Convention right. The applicant will first have to establish that the right claimed is in fact a Convention right, a not inconsiderable obstacle in view of the fact that much of the jurisprudence is so embryonic, and in view of the fact that the content of the right can be determined by the contract itself. Consideration will then have to be given to the second paragraph in cases relating to articles 8–11 which permit restrictions where 'prescribed by law' and 'necessary' in 'a democratic society,' on a number of grounds including in each case 'the rights and freedoms of others.' Assuming that restrictions imposed by the contract of employment are restrictions 'imposed by law' (though *quaere* the position of implied terms where there is a self evident lack of transparency), the rights and freedoms in whose interests restrictions may be imposed presumably will include those of employers: it is a fair bet that commercial and business considerations will not always take second place.

The application of the Convention rights in the employment context is particularly problematic. In *Ahmad* and in *Stedman* the Commission refused even to accept that the claimants had suffered interference with their private lives. Similar reluctance to find interferences with Convention rights has been displayed where workers have been discriminated against in connection with their political beliefs: in *Kosiek v Germany* (1987) 9 EHRR 328 and in *Glasenapp v Germany* (1987) 9 EHRR 25, for example, the European Court of Human Rights ruled that the dismissals of an extreme right wing activist from a probationary academic position, and of a communist activist from a probationary teaching appointment respectively, did not amount to 'interferences' with their rights to freedom of expression. More recently, however, there has been evidence of a more robust approach on the part of the Court. In *Vogt v Germany* (1996) 21 EHRR 205 the Court ruled that the dismissal of a long-serving communist teacher interfered with her freedom of expression and, further, that the discrimination was not justified under Article 10. And in *Lustig-Prean & Beckett v UK* (1999) 29 EHRR 548 and *Smith & Grady v UK* (1999) 29 EHRR 493 the Court ruled that the dismissal of gay servicemen and women breached the UK's obligations under Article 8 of the European Convention (which protects the right to privacy).

Vogt, Thlimmenos (see below) and the MOD cases signal a movement away from the restrictive approach adopted to employment by the European Court in *Kosiek* and *Glasenapp*, and 'interference' might now be established in a case in which a worker was discriminated against directly because of his or her religious or other beliefs (though—see Chapter 1—it remains necessary to consider whether the *state* can be held responsible for this in order to establish an actionable interference). More problematic, however, is the jurisprudence of the Court and Commission on *indirect* discrimination: that is, on finding interferences with Articles 9 and/or 10 in cases in which religious or other beliefs and practices place the claimant in a position in which he or she needs *special* treatment in order to enjoy a level playing field with others.

Some indication of the approach taken under the Convention to *indirect* discrimination of this sort is seen in *Ahmad* and *Stedman*. More recently, in *Thlimmenos v Greece* (2001) 31 EHRR 14, the European Court ruled that discrimination contrary to Articles 9 and 14 had occurred when a man who had been criminalised because of his refusal (as a Jehovah's Witness) to wear a military uniform during compulsory military service, was refused access to the chartered accountancy profession because of his criminal conviction:

> The Court has so far considered that the right under Article 14 not to be discriminated against in the enjoyment of the rights guaranteed under the Convention is violated when States treat differently persons in analogous situations without providing an objective and reasonable justification . . . this is not the only facet of the prohibition of discrimination in Article 14. The right not to be discriminated against in the enjoyment of the rights guaranteed under the Convention is also violated when States without an objective and reasonable justification fail to treat differently persons whose situations are significantly different.

More recently still, in *Jordan v UK* (2003) 37 EHRR 2, the Court ruled that: 'Where a general policy or measure has disproportionately prejudicial effects on a particular group, it is not excluded that this may be considered as discriminatory notwithstanding that it is not specifically aimed or directed at that group'. The claim arose out of the killing by the security forces of an unarmed Catholic man, the man's father basing an alleged breach of Articles 14 and 2 on the fact that, of the 347 people killed by the security forces in Northern Ireland up to the point of his son's shooting, the overwhelming majority had been Catholic. Having accepted the possibility that an indirect discrimination claim might succeed under Article 14, however, the Court rejected such a claim in the instant case: 'the statistics . . . [could not] in themselves disclose a practice which could be classified as discriminatory within the meaning of Article 14. There is no evidence before the Court which would entitle it to conclude that any of the killings, save the four which resulted in convictions, involved the unlawful or excessive use of force by members of the security forces.' With the exception of *Thlimmenos*, which was not a case in which an accommodation of a religious or other belief was sought, the European Court has yet to uphold a complaint based on *indirect* discrimination.

A further difficulty with the Convention jurisprudence concerns the question what amounts to a manifestation of religion or belief. A requirement relating directly to religion, as in *Ahmad* and *Stedman*, will readily be accepted as such a manifestation. But this is not invariably the case. In *Arrowsmith v UK* (1978) 3 EHRR 110 the European Commission dismissed as manifestly unfounded a claim by a pacifist that her prosecution for handing out leaflets to soldiers urging them not to serve in Northern Ireland breached her Article 9 rights. According to the Commission, her action in handing out these leaflets was not a 'manifestation' of her pacifist beliefs: 'where actions of individuals do not actually express the belief concerned they cannot be considered to be as such protected by Article 9(1), even when they are motivated by it.'

B Hepple and T Choudhury, *Tackling religious discrimination: practical implications for policy-makers and legislators* (Home Office Research Study 221) 4–5, footnotes omitted

In the *Arrowsmith* case the applicant argued that under Article 9 she had a right to hand out leaflets to soldiers advocating that they should not serve in Northern Ireland because this was a manifestation of her pacifist beliefs. The Commission held that 'when actions of individuals do not actually express the belief concerned they cannot be considered to be as such protected by Article 9(1), even when they are motivated by it.' The Commission has also rejected attempts by conscientious objectors to prevent payment of taxes that may be used on military expenditure. It held that only acts 'which are aspects of the practice of a religion or belief in a generally recognised form are protected by Article 9' Van Dijk and van Hoof argue that an objective approach to this question is inevitable even if problematic:

> [A] restrictive interpretation may in general be unavoidable. A legal system consisting of general binding rules cannot afford to leave to (the subjective convictions of) [a] person the answer to the question whether a person manifests his religion or belief and can rely on Article 9. It should answer the question itself on the basis of objective criteria, primarily related to the outward appearance of the expression.
>
> However, for less known minorities who are not linked up with one of the world religions or ideologies this entails the danger that a behaviour will only be considered the expression of a belief, in case a sufficient resemblance can be found with the known patterns of familiar spiritual movements.

The European Court of Human Rights took a similar approach when deciding if a rule conflicted with a person's beliefs or religious practice. In the cases of *Valsamis v Greece* and *Efstratiou v Greece*[67] the applicants, who were Jehovah's Witnesses, complained that a rule allowing schools to require pupils, under threat of a disciplinary penalty, to take part in the National Day Parade, was in violation of their freedom to manifest their pacifist beliefs. The Court and Commission rejected their applications. The Court held that it could 'discern nothing, either in the purpose of the parade or in the arrangements for it, which could offend the applicants' pacifist conviction.' Other commentators have argued that there are many dangers in attempting to substitute a court's own interpretation of a particular set of beliefs to that of their holder.

By contrast to the ECHR, the US Supreme Court has held that it is not within the power of the judiciary to question a litigants' interpretation of their religious claim except where the claim 'is so bizarre, so clearly non-religious in motivation, as not to be entitled to protection under the Free Exercise Clause.'[68] Thus the Supreme Court does not normally question the litigant's claim that engaging in a particular activity would be contrary to his or her religious belief. Under the Ontario Human Rights Commission's policy on creed, personal religious beliefs, practices or observances are protected, even if they are not essential elements of the creed, provided they are sincerely held.

The European Commission and Court have proven particularly unsympathetic to challenges to clothing and appearance rules. In *Karaduman v Turkey* (1993) 74 DR 93 the Commission rejected a challenge to a Turkish rule prohibiting the claimant from graduating university unless she was photographed without a scarf. Similar decisions were reached in *Tekin v Turquie* (2001) 31 EHRR 4 and *Dahlab v Switzerland* [2001] ECHR 42393/98.

---

[67] Both judgments of 18 December 1996, Comm reports 6 July 1995 and 11 April 1996 respectively.
[68] Citing *Thomas v Review Board of the Indiana Employment Security Decision* 67 L Ed 2d 624, 632.

Most recently, in *Sahin v Turkey* the Court considered a challenge to a university rule prohibiting the wearing of headscarves on campus.

Sahin v Turkey, App No 44774/98, 22 June 2004

Judgment:

The Court reiterates that as enshrined in art 9, freedom of thought, conscience and religion is one of the foundations of a 'democratic society' within the meaning of the Convention. This freedom is, in its religious dimension, one of the most vital elements that go to make up the identity of believers and their conception of life, but it is also a precious asset for atheists, agnostics, sceptics and the unconcerned. The pluralism indissociable from a democratic society, which has been dearly won over the centuries, depends on it. That freedom entails, inter alia, freedom to hold or not to hold religious beliefs and to practise or not to practise a religion . . .

While religious freedom is primarily a matter of individual conscience, it also implies, *inter alia*, freedom to manifest one's religion, alone and in private, or in community with others, in public and within the circle of those whose faith one shares . . . Article 9 does not protect every act motivated or inspired by a religion or belief and does not in all cases guarantee the right to behave in the public sphere in a way which is dictated by a belief . . .

The applicant said that, by wearing the headscarf, she was obeying a religious precept and thereby manifesting her desire to comply strictly with the duties imposed by the Islamic faith. Accordingly, her decision to wear the headscarf may be regarded as motivated or inspired by a religion or belief and, without deciding whether such decisions are in every case taken to fulfil a religious duty, the Court proceeds on the assumption that the regulations in issue, which placed restrictions of place and manner on the right to wear the Islamic headscarf in universities, constituted an interference with the applicant's right to manifest her religion . . .

[Having decided that the interference was 'prescribed by law' (see further Chapter 1) and aimed at protecting the rights and freedoms of others and of protecting public order.]

In democratic societies, in which several religions coexist within one and the same population, it may be necessary to place restrictions on freedom to manifest one's religion or belief in order to reconcile the interests of the various groups and ensure that everyone's beliefs are respected . . .

The Court notes that, in the decisions of *Karaduman v Turkey* and *Dahlab v Switzerland*, the Convention institutions found that in a democratic society the State was entitled to place restrictions on the wearing of the Islamic headscarf if it was incompatible with the pursued aim of protecting the rights and freedoms of others, public order and public safety. In *Dahlab v Switzerland*, in which the applicant was a schoolteacher in charge of a class of small children, it stressed among other matters the impact that the 'powerful external symbol' conveyed by her wearing a headscarf could have and questioned whether it might have some kind of proselytising effect, seeing that it appeared to be imposed on women by a precept laid down in the Koran that was hard to reconcile with the principle of gender equality.

Likewise, the Court has also previously stated that the principle of secularism in Turkey is undoubtedly one of the fundamental principles of the State, which are in harmony with the rule of law and respect for human rights . . .. In a country like Turkey, where the great majority of the population belong to a particular religion, measures taken in universities to prevent certain fundamentalist religious movements from exerting pressure on students who do not practise that religion or on those who belong to another religion may be justified under art 9 § 2 of the Convention. In that context, secular universities may regulate manifestation of the rites and symbols of the said religion by imposing restrictions as to the place and manner of such manifestation with the aim of ensuring peaceful co-existence between students of various faiths and thus protecting public order and the beliefs of others . . .

In order to assess the 'necessity' of the interference caused by the circular of 23 February 1998 imposing restrictions as to place and manner on the rights of students such as Ms Sahin to wear the Islamic headscarf on university premises, the Court must put the circular in its legal and social context and examine it in the light of the circumstances of the case. Regard being had to the principles applicable in the instant case, the Court's task is confined to determining whether the reasons given for the interference were relevant and sufficient and the measures taken at the national level proportionate to the aims pursued.

It must first be observed that the interference was based, in particular, on two principles—secularism and equality—which reinforce and complement each other . . .

This notion of secularism appears to the Court to be consistent with the values underpinning the Convention and it accepts that upholding that principle may be regarded as necessary for the protection of the democratic system in Turkey. The Court further notes the emphasis placed in the Turkish constitutional system on the protection of the rights of women . . . Gender equality—recognised by the European Court as one of the key principles underlying the Convention and a goal to be achieved by member States of the Council of Europe . . . was also found by the Turkish Constitutional Court to be a principle implicit in the values underlying the Constitution . . . In addition, like the Constitutional Court . . . the Court considers that, when examining the question of the Islamic headscarf in the Turkish context, there must be borne in mind the impact which wearing such a symbol, which is presented or perceived as a compulsory religious duty, may have on those who choose not to wear it. As has already been noted . . . the issues at stake include the protection of the 'rights and freedoms of others' and the 'maintenance of public order' in a country in which the majority of the population, while professing a strong attachment to the rights of women and a secular way of life, adhere to the Islamic faith. Imposing limitations on freedom in this sphere may, therefore, be regarded as meeting a pressing social need by seeking to achieve those two legitimate aims, especially since, as the Turkish courts stated . . . this religious symbol has taken on political significance in Turkey in recent years.

The Court does not lose sight of the fact that there are extremist political movements in Turkey which seek to impose on society as a whole their religious symbols and conception of a society founded on religious precepts . . . It has previously said that each Contracting State may, in accordance with the Convention provisions, take a stance against such political movements, based on its historical experience . . . The regulations concerned have to be viewed in that context and constitute a measure intended to achieve the legitimate aims referred to above and thereby to preserve pluralism in the university.

Having regard to the above background, it is the principle of secularism, as elucidated by the Constitutional Court . . . which is the paramount consideration underlying the ban on the wearing of religious insignia in universities. It is understandable in such a context where the values of pluralism, respect for the rights of others and, in particular, equality before the law of men and women, are being taught and applied in practice, that the relevant authorities would consider that it ran counter to the furtherance of such values to accept the wearing of religious insignia, including as in the present case, that women students cover their heads with a headscarf while on university premises.

In the light of the foregoing and having regard in particular to the margin of appreciation left to the Contracting States, the Court finds that the University of Istanbul's regulations imposing restrictions on the wearing of Islamic headscarves and the measures taken to implement them were justified in principle and proportionate to the aims pursued and, therefore, could be regarded as 'necessary in a democratic society.' Consequently, there has been no breach of art 9 of the Convention.

The decision in *Sahin* perhaps indicates a willingness on the part of the European Court to engage with questions of substance, the Court having at least accepted that the headscarf ban was (a) an interference with (b) the manifestation of religious belief. But in employment-related cases, as in *Sahin*, even where the Convention organs have found employment-related interferences with claimants' Convention rights, those interferences have frequently been accepted as justified. Not untypical are the following decisions. In the first of these (*X v UK*) the Commission dismissed as manifestly ill-founded a complaint brought under Article 10 brought by a teacher who was dismissed for 'proselytising' after he gave religious instruction during school hours, held 'evangelical clubs' on school premises and wore religious and anti-abortion stickers. In the second (*Kara v UK*) the Commission dismissed a challenge by a bisexual male transvestite to a rule prohibiting him from wearing 'female.' He argued that his employer's policy discriminated against him on grounds of his religious beliefs (he described himself as a 'Berdache Shaman'—an American indigenous tradition in which certain men express themselves through dressing in conventionally female clothing).

X v UK (1979) 16 DR 101 (Commission)

Judgment:

It is clear . . . that [the Claimant] was dismissed because of his refusal to comply with specific instructions, not to advertise by posters or stickers on school premises his political, moral or religious beliefs.

The Commission considers that this instruction constitutes an interference with the applicant's freedom of expression. However the Commission is of the opinion that school teachers in non-denominational schools should have regard to the rights of parents so as to respect their religious and philosophical convictions in the education of their children. This requirement assumes particular importance in a non-denominational school where the governing legislation provides that parents can seek to have their children excused from attendance at religious instruction and further that any religious instruction given shall not include 'any catechism or formulary which is distinctive of any particular religious denomination' (see Education Act 1944, Sections 25 and 26).

In the present case the posters and 'stickers' objected to, reflected the applicant's strong Evangelical beliefs and his opposition to abortion. The Commission notes from the observations of the respondent Government that some of the 'stickers' worn on the applicant's lapel and on his briefcase were considered offensive to female members of staff and disturbing to children. Having regard to the particular circumstances of the case, the Commission considers that the interference with the applicant's freedom of expression is justified as being necessary in a democratic society for the protection of the rights of others within the meaning of Article 10, paragraph 2, of the Convention.

Kara v UK, App No 36528/97, 22 October 1998, unreported (Commission)

Judgment:

The Commission finds that constraints imposed on a person's choice of mode of dress constitute an interference with the private life as ensured by Article 8 para 1 of the Convention [citing *McFeely v UK*, DR 20, p 91]. It is therefore necessary to examine whether this interference was justified under Article 8 para 2 . . .

The Commission recalls that the Council's restriction on the choice of mode of dress of its employees was based on its internal policy which was confirmed by the Industrial Tribunal to be lawful. Accordingly, the Commission considers that the interference was 'in accordance with the law' within the meaning of Article 8 para 2 of the Convention.

The Commission further recalls that the aim of its dress policy as stated by the Council in April 1994 was to enable it to enhance its image in its dealings with the public, the business community and representatives of Government. Accordingly, the Commission considers that the interference could be said to pursue the legitimate aim of 'the protection of the rights of others', in the sense of protecting its own proper functioning and carrying out of its duties on behalf of the public.

As to whether the interference was 'necessary in a democratic society', the Commission recalls that this phrase corresponds to the existence of a 'pressing social need' in particular, the interference must be proportionate to the legitimate aim pursued [citing *Beldjoudi v France* (1992) 14 EHRR 801]. The Contracting States however, have a certain margin of appreciation in assessing whether such a need exits, but this goes hand in hand with a European supervision [citing *Silver v UK* (1983) 5 EHRR 345].

The Commission notes that the rules as to the mode of dress at work affected the applicant during work hours on work premises and that at other times he remained at liberty to dress as he wished. The Commission considers that employers may require their employees to conform to certain dress requirements which are reasonably related to the type of work being undertaken eg. safety helmets, hygienic coverings, uniforms. This may also involve requiring employees, who come into contact with the public or other organisations to conform to a dress code which may reasonably be regarded as enhancing the employer's public image and facilitating its external contacts. While the applicant has disputed that the Council provided support for its claims that the way he dressed prejudiced its external image and the extent to which he came into contact with members of the public and the representatives of other bodies in his daily work, the Commission notes that the applicant did not deny that he had contacts outside his own office and it is satisfied that the requirements in this case, that employees dress 'appropriately' to their gender, may be reasonably regarded by the employer as necessary to safeguard their public image. Having regard to the circumstances of the case, any restrictions on the applicant's ability to dress at work in the manner which he perceives as expressing his personality and fostering personal relationships was not disproportionate.

The Commission finds that the interference in this case may be regarded as necessary in a democratic society for the aim of protecting the rights of others within the meaning of Article 8 para 2 of the Convention. This complaint must therefore be rejected as manifestly ill-founded . . .

X v UK and *Kara* can be regarded as more favourable to employees than the decisions in *Ahmad* and *Stedman*, in the sense that the Commission was prepared at least to accept that interferences with the Convention rights had occurred. But while, in these cases, the employees were not regarded in terms as having left their Convention rights on the doorstep on their entry into the workplace, the Commission decisions illustrate how low the threshold of justification for interference with Convention rights can be in the employment context. And it appears from the following case that the early impact of the HRA in this context is relatively slight.

Impact of the HRA

M Rubenstein, 'In the Courts' 128 *Equal Opportunities Review* **(discussing** *Copsey v WBB Devon Clays,* **13 February 2004))**

The employers had introduced a seven-day shift system after a surge in demand, following consultation with the unions and with the support of a majority of the employees. Mr Copsey refused to work on Sundays, and was dismissed after he rejected offers of alternative employment that did not have a working pattern requiring Sunday work. An employment tribunal found that this was a fair dismissal on grounds that the employee would not agree to work a seven-day shift. When the case got to the Employment Appeal Tribunal (EAT), two main arguments were put forward. The first was that the real reason for dismissal was the employee's religious beliefs. The EAT (Mr Justice Rimer presiding) rejected this. It said: 'There was no evidence to suggest that [Devon Clays] did not respect his religious beliefs. On the contrary, the evidence was that it fully respected them and sought to accommodate Mr Copsey in alternative positions within the company that would enable him to practice and manifest them as he wishes . . . Had Mr Copsey chosen to take up the offered alternatives, he would have remained in Devon Clays' employment, and the continued holding by him of his Christian beliefs would have represented no bar to his doing so. The reason he was dismissed was not because he held, or wished to manifest, particular religious beliefs. It was because he declined to work seven-day shifts.'

It was also argued that whether the employers acted reasonably in dismissing now had to be interpreted in light of the right to freedom of religion under Article 9 of the European Convention on Human Rights. The EAT said that even if that were the case, account had to be taken of the 1987 decision of the European Commission on Human Rights in *Stedman v United Kingdom*. In that case, in which a Sunday working requirement was challenged, the European Commission on Human Rights took the narrow view that the employee's rights under the Convention were not infringed because she could seek alternative employment elsewhere that would allow her to observe the Sabbath. It might have been thought that a British court in 2004 would take a more liberal approach, but the EAT instead said that 'we regard it as sound in principle.' 'That decision is directly in point. The circumstances the Commission was considering are, in essence, identical to those relating to Mr Copsey's dismissal as found by the tribunal. The Commission held that a dismissal in such circumstances involves no interference with the employee's Article 9 rights. If the employee takes the view that his employer's work requirements are incompatible with the due exercise and manifestation of his religious beliefs, he is entitled to resign . . . Mr Copsey was not obliged to agree to the seven-day shift pattern, or indeed to work for Devon Clays at all, and was free to resign if he concluded that his religious commitments were incompatible with the hours of work that Devon Clays wanted of him. As he had that choice, nothing that Devon Clays did or proposed amounted to an infringement of his Article 9 rights.' This is a decision that is entirely out of keeping with the spirit of the new Religion or Belief Regulations, and it is to be hoped that it is not a harbinger of the way those Regulations will be interpreted by the EAT.

Perhaps more interesting is the decision in *R (Begum) v Headteacher and Governors of Denbigh High School* [2005] EWCA Civ 199 in which the Court of Appeal considered a complaint by a Muslim schoolgirl whose school, although it permitted the wearing of *shalwar kameeze* (mid calf length loose tunic and tapered full length trousers, plus a headscarf) as part of school uniform, refused to permit the claimant to attend school dressed in a *jilbab*— a dress which leaves only the hands and face exposed. She complained that she had been excluded from the school in breach of her Convention rights. The High Court rejected her claim ([2004] EWHC 1389 (Admin)) on the basis that she had not been excluded from the school and that, following *Stedman*, her Article 9 rights had not been interfered with. Even had there been such an interference, Bennett J ruled that it was 'necessary in a democratic society':

It is clear from the evidence that there is a not insignificant number of Muslim female pupils at Denbigh High School who do not wish to wear the jilbab and either do, or will, feel pressure on them either from inside or outside the school. The present school uniform policy aims to protect their rights and freedoms . . . Although it appears that there is a body of opinion within the Muslim faith that only the jilbab meets the requirements of its dress code, there is also a body of opinion that the shalwar kameeze does as well. In my judgment, the adoption of the shalwar kameeze by the defendant as the school uniform for Muslim (and other faiths) female pupils was and continues to be a reasoned, balanced, proportionate policy.

The Court of Appeal allowed Miss Begum's appeal, overturning the decision of the Administrative Court on all three issues. Lord Justice Brooke, who delivered the leading judgment, noted that children at the respondent school spoke no fewer than 40 languages and came from 21 different ethnic groups and 10 different religious groups, and that 79% were Muslim. He also recorded the history of the school's uniform policy which had been developed in consultation with parents, students, and the local mosques as well as staff, which was regarded by the school as satisfying the religious requirement that Muslim girls should wear modest dress, and which was designed to have regard to health and safety considerations and to be suitable for all school activities. The uniform policy was supported by the school's governors, seven of whom were Muslim and one of whom chaired the Luton Council of Mosques.

Lord Justice Brooke:

The claimant's family came to England from Bangladesh. She has two older sisters and two older brothers. She was born in this country in September 1988. Her father died in 1992, and through most of the history of the dispute she was living at home with her mother (who did not speak English) and one sister and one brother: the others had moved out. Her mother died in 2004. One of her brothers is acting as her litigation friend in these proceedings.

She first attended the School in September 2000, and during her first two years there she wore the shalwar kameeze without complaint. As she grew older, however, she took an increasing interest in her religion, and she formed the view that the shalwar kameeze was not an acceptable form of dress for mature Muslim women in public places. In her brother's view the shalwar kameeze originated as a Pakistani cultural dress without any particular religious foundation, and she believed that the Islamic Shari'a required women over the age of 13 to cover their bodies completely, apart from their face and hands. The shalwar kameeze was not acceptable, because the white shirt (which at the School is covered by a jumper except in hot weather) revealed too much of the arms, and the skirt length (which at the School may extend to the mid-calf) should go down to the ankles . . .

Brooke LJ ruled that the school had excluded the claimant by allowing her to attend only if she complied with the uniform policy and turned to consider whether this amounted to an interference under Article 9 of the Convention. He set out the decision of the school's governing body's complaint committee which had dealt with the claimant's case, and which had found (having considered the advice taken by the school from the Islamic Cultural Centre, the Muslim Council of Britain and the London Central Mosque) that the school uniform policy satisfied all the requirements of the Islamic dress code. He also noted the differing views amongst Muslim scholars as to appropriate women's clothing, South Asian Muslim mainstream opinion accepting the *shalwar kameeze* coupled with a headscarf while a smaller body of opinion regarded the *jilbab* as required. Having accepted the sincerity of the claimant's view as to the appropriate clothing for a Muslim woman, he ruled that her freedom to manifest her religion or belief in public was limited by the school uniform policy and that 'as a matter of Convention law it would be for the School, as an emanation of the state, to justify the limitation on her freedom created by the School's uniform code and by the way in which it was enforced' and continued.

SB's freedom to manifest her religion or beliefs may only be subject to limitations that are prescribed by law and are necessary in a democratic society in the interests of public safety, for the protection of public morals, or for the protection of the rights and freedoms of others. There was no suggestion that the protection of public morals had any relevance, and a justification on health and safety grounds was dismissed by the judge and not resurrected on the appeal once evidence had showed that other schools (including the local school which the claimant now attends) had been able to accommodate girls wearing the jilbab without any serious concern being raised on that ground . . .

The judge accepted the School's case that the limitations on the claimant's right to manifest her religion or beliefs were necessary for the protection of the rights and freedoms of others. His reasons can be summarised in this way: i) The School is a multi-cultural, multi-faith secular school; ii) The school uniform policy clearly promoted a positive ethos and a sense of communal identity; iii) There was no outward distinction between Muslim, Hindu and Sikh female students, and the shalwar kameeze also satisfied the right of Muslim female students to manifest their religion; iv) Any distinction between Muslim students who wore the jilbab and those who wore the shalwar kameeze was avoided; v) The present policy protects the rights and freedoms of not an insignificant number of Muslim female pupils who do not wish to wear the jilbab and either do, or will feel pressure on them to do so from inside or outside the school; vi) If the choice of two uniforms were permitted for Muslim female pupils, it could be readily understood that other pupils of different or no faiths might well see this as favouring a particular religion . . .

In *Dahlab v Switzerland* . . . the need to protect the principle of denominational neutrality in Swiss schools was treated as a very important factor which militated successfully against the applicant's case . . .

I have considered the case of *Sahin* in some detail for four main reasons. First, it is a recent judgment in which the European Court of Justice has set out carefully the structured way in which issues of this kind are to be considered under the Convention. Secondly, it shows that context is all-important: there are considerations to be applied in a state which professes the value of secularism in its Constitution which are not necessarily to be applied in the United Kingdom. Thirdly—and we did not receive any argument on this issue—there are clearly potential tensions between the rights and freedoms set out in a Convention agreed more than 50 years ago between Western European countries which on the whole adhered to Judaeo-Christian traditions, and some of the tenets of the Islamic faith that relate to the position of women in society. And fourthly, it is clear that a decision-maker is entitled to take into account worries like those expressed by the senior teaching staff of the School when it is deciding whether it is necessary to prohibit a person like the claimant from manifesting her religion or beliefs in public in the way in which she would wish.

The United Kingdom is very different from Turkey. It is not a secular state, and although the Human Rights Act is now part of our law we have no written Constitution. In England and Wales express provision is made for religious education and worship in schools in Chapter VI of the 1998 Act. Schools are under a duty to secure that religious education in schools is given to pupils, and that each pupil should take part in an act of collective worship every day, unless withdrawn by their parent. Sections 80(1)(a) and 101(1)(a) of the 2002 Act require the inclusion of religious education in the basic curriculum.

The position of the School is already distinctive in the sense that despite its policy of inclusiveness it permits girls to wear a headscarf which is likely to identify them as Muslim. The central issue is therefore the more subtle one of whether, given that Muslim girls can already be identified in this way, it is necessary in a democratic society to place a particular restriction on those Muslim girls at this school who sincerely believe that when they arrive at the age of puberty they should cover themselves more comprehensively than is permitted by the school uniform policy.

The decision-making structure should therefore go along the following lines:

1) Has the claimant established that she has a relevant Convention right which qualifies for protection under Article 9(1)?
2) Subject to any justification that is established under Article 9(2), has that Convention right been violated?
3) Was the interference with her Convention right prescribed by law in the Convention sense of that expression?
4) Did the interference have a legitimate arm?
5) What are the considerations that need to be balanced against each other when determining whether the interference was necessary in a democratic society for the purpose of achieving that aim?
6) Was the interference justified under Article 9(2)?

The School did not approach the matter in this way at all. Nobody who considered the issues on its behalf started from the premise that the claimant had a right which is recognised by English law, and that the onus lay on the School to justify its interference with that right. Instead, it started from the premise that its uniform policy was there to be obeyed: if the claimant did not like it, she could go to a different school . . .

Nothing in this judgment should be taken as meaning that it would be impossible for the School to justify its stance if it were to reconsider its uniform policy in the light of this judgment and were to determine not to alter it in any significant respect. Matters which it (and other schools facing a similar question) would no doubt need to consider include these:

i) Whether the members of any further religious groups (other than very strict Muslims) might wish to be free to manifest their religion or beliefs by wearing clothing not currently permitted by the school's uniform policy, and the effect that a larger variety of different clothes being worn by students for religious reasons would have on the School's policy of inclusiveness;

ii) Whether it is appropriate to override the beliefs of very strict Muslims given that liberal Muslims have been permitted the dress code of their choice and the School's uniform policy is not entirely secular;

iii) Whether it is appropriate to take into account any, and if so which, of the concerns expressed by the School's three witnesses as good reasons for depriving a student like the claimant of her right to manifest her beliefs by the clothing she wears at school, and the weight which should be accorded to each of these concerns;

iv) Whether there is any way in which the School can do more to reconcile its wish to retain something resembling its current uniform policy with the beliefs of those like the claimant who consider that it exposes more of their bodies than they are permitted by their beliefs to show.

All this is for the future, and this case has achieved the result of ensuring that schools will set about deciding issues of this kind in the manner now required of them by the Human Rights Act. It may be thought desirable for the DfES to give schools further guidance in the light of this judgment: one is bound to sympathise with the teachers and governors of this school when they have had to try and understand quite complex and novel considerations of human rights law in the absence of authoritative written guidance. For the present, however, I would allow this appeal and grant the claimant the three declarations she seeks.

Mummery and Scott Baker LJJ agreed, the latter expressing 'considerable sympathy with the School and its governors in the predicament that they faced' and opining that 'Had the School approached the problem on the basis it should have done, that the claimant had a right under Article 9(1) to manifest her religion, it may very well have concluded that interference with that right was justified under Article 9(2) and that its uniform policy could thus have been maintained. Regrettably, however, it decided that because the shalwar kameeze was acceptable for the majority of Muslims the claimant should be required to toe the line'.

The judgment in *Begum* has been extracted at very considerable length because it shows the potential of the HRA in the discrimination/equality context. Many commentators were critical of the decision of the Court of Appeal, and it is perhaps ironic that a school that made so many efforts to accommodate the diverse religious views of its pupils should have found itself at the wrong end of this judgment. Their Lordships were all keen to stress that the decision in *Begum* did not spell the end of school uniform policies. But the Court decided that enforcing the policy by making the claimant's return to school conditional on her compliance with it was tantamount to excluding her from school. Since schools can only exclude pupils either permanently or for periods of less than 45 days in any school year, this has the effect of tying headteachers' hands when it comes to enforcing such policy. Disciplinary action will have to wait, presumably, until a school has gone through the steps outlined by Brooke LJ above, the pupil meanwhile being free to interpret the uniform policy as he or she sees fit.

The decision of the Court of Appeal appears to disregard the fact that the respondent school had in this case gone through the balancing act required by Brooke LJ when it *adopted* the policy, rather than at the point of enforcement. It could be said, in fact, that the approach taken by the school to the adoption of a uniform policy was a model of good practice as regards 'mainstreaming' inasmuch as it attempted to feed equality considerations into policy development rather than ignoring them at this stage and then having to respond to them on an ad hoc basis as they subsequently arose. The decision of the Court of Appeal comes very close to demanding continual reinvention of the wheel. If, acknowledgment of the legitimacy of an individual pupil's religious views is required then it is difficult to imagine that the outcome in the *Begum* case would have been any different had the school gone through the correct procedure.

The issues raised in the preceding paragraphs are perhaps specific to the particular facts of *Begum*. More broadly, the willingness of the Court of Appeal to embrace a broad and generous approach to the question whether there has been an interference with the rights protected by Article 9(1) is to be welcomed. A similar approach has recently been adopted by the House of Lords in *R (Williamson) v Secretary of State for Education and Employment* [2005] 2 WLR 590.

10

Gender Identity and Sexual Orientation

Introduction

MIND, 'Lesbians, gay men, bisexuals and mental health' (1996)

In 1885 all male homosexual relationships were declared illegal. Many gay men were given prison sentences simply because they had homosexual relationships. This often resulted in blackmail and suicides. The first change in the law followed from the recommendations of the 1957 Wolfenden Report. In 1967 the Sexual Offences Act came into force. The Act did not incorporate all the recommendations made in the report. It decriminalised a small number of 'offences' and extended tolerance of homosexuality only slightly.

The Wolfenden Report and the resulting Sexual Offences Act did not refer to lesbianism. In fact, lesbians have never been directly legislated against and relationships between women have never been officially illegal. Lesbianism was last discussed in Parliament as a distinct issue in 1921 when The Criminal Law Amendment Act attempted to legislate with regard to the age of consent. However, the absence of legislation does not mean that lesbian relationships have been more acceptable. Lesbians have been discriminated against indirectly simply because of their invisibility in any legislation. Their relationships have remained largely unrecognised and the law offers scant protection in many areas of their lives. Throughout history the social climate has made it extremely difficult for women to live together independently of men. Lesbians have been seen as a threat to the traditional notions of the nuclear family and to the assigned gender roles men and women in modern western society are supposed to adopt. Society has suppressed lesbianism by making these roles very difficult to break, and women who have not conformed to society's expectations have found themselves considerably disadvantaged, socially, personally and economically.

Following the 1967 Act, men over the age of 21 were permitted to have sexual relationships with each other. The law only applied to England, although Scotland and Northern Ireland passed similar legislation some time after this. In 1992 the Isle of Man finally brought its law into line with the rest of the UK after its autonomy was threatened because of its consistent refusal to implement even the 1967 Sexual Offences Act.

The 1967 Act does not address many of the legal issues facing lesbians and gay men in Britain today. There is no legal framework for lesbian and gay partnerships and no law against the unequal treatment in society of lesbians and gay men.

Legal discrimination still remains in the 1956 Sexual Offences Act and the 1967 Sexual Offences Act. Other legislation, whilst it does not directly discriminate against gay men and lesbians, does not afford the same privileges to gay partnerships as it does to heterosexual ones. This reflects a general lack of civil rights throughout the legislative framework . . .

The introduction of the 1983 Mental Health Act did not take into account lesbian and gay relationships. This Act grants the 'nearest relative' specific rights: for example, the right to make an application for the patient to be admitted to hospital against their will under Section 2 of the Act, or to be discharged or to be given certain important information. The Act identifies the nearest relative according to a hierarchy: first choice is husband or wife (which can include common law heterosexual spouse of six months standing), then son or daughter, then other family members ending with nephew or niece. This order can only be altered if the 'patient' has lived with someone else for at least 5 years. As Sayce (1995) points out, this means that if a lesbian or gay man has lived with a partner for 4 years, the 'nearest relative' could be a nephew whom they hardly know. Meanwhile a heterosexual partner would gain nearest relative status after only six months and a married heterosexual partner immediately.

This discrimination was deliberate. In 1982 Parliament debated an amendment to the Act which would have given gay and lesbian partners equal rights with heterosexuals. David Ennals MP argued that gay men and lesbians often do not have very good relationships with their families because of their sexuality, and therefore family members should not automatically be given nearest relative status over a partner. Others argued against the amendment along the lines of strengthening family relationships and ties, some expressed outright moral censure, and others were worried that affording gay partners equal rights within the Mental Health Act would mean that other areas of law would be challenged, thus 'opening up the floodgates.' Despite these weak arguments and unsubstantiated claims the 1982 amendment was defeated.

Section 28 of the Local Government Act, introduced in 1987, was largely seen as an attempt by the Government to curtail the growing inclusion of lesbians and gay men in equal opportunities policies. The Act prevented 'a local authority from giving financial or other assistance to any person for the purpose of publishing or promoting homosexuality as an acceptable family relationship, or for the purpose of teaching acceptability in any maintained school.' Despite the mass efforts of lesbians and gay men, Section 28 passed into law and remains there today.

In fact, Section 28 works mainly as a deterrent to local authorities. Many have drastically cut funding for projects set up specifically for gay men and lesbians, and local authorities who wish to review their equal opportunities policies to include discrimination on the basis of sexuality are put off by the clause. Even though the legislation applies only to local government and grant maintained schools, many local authorities have applied it to other areas and some voluntary organisations have been discouraged from expanding their equal opportunities policies to include sexual orientation.

No legal proceedings have ever taken place on the interpretation of the concepts enshrined in Section 28. Many lawyers believe that 'promoting homosexuality' would mean local authorities directly persuading their populations to become homosexual—something that is very difficult, and arguably impossible, to do.

Until 1994 the age of consent for sexual relations between homosexuals remained at 21. The House of Commons voted to equalise this with heterosexual relationships by bringing the age of consent down to 16. The outcome of this vote was to lower the age from 21 to 18, still not granting gay people the same rights as heterosexuals. A bill to lower the age of consent to 16 was defeated by the House of Lords in the summer of 1998 [but see below].

'Equality for Lesbians and Gay Men in the Workplace' (1997) 74 *Equal Opportunities Review* 20, 20–1

In 1992, the Labour Research Department (LRD) carried out a questionnaire survey ['Out at work: lesbian and gay workers' rights' LRD 1992] distributed by several unions to their branch members. Of the 362 respondents, 61 per cent were lesbians, gay men or bisexual. A key finding was that nearly a quarter of respondents had personally experienced, or knew cases of, harassment or victimisation of lesbian and gay workers. Although 90 per cent said that there was an equal opportunities policy at their workplace, only 62 per cent of this group said that the policy covered sexuality. The proportion who were 'out' at work about their sexuality was higher among union post-holders (80 per cent), than among lesbian, gay or bisexual respondents as a whole (60 per cent).

A survey of nearly 2000 lesbians, gay men and bisexuals at work—the largest survey of its type to be carried out in Britain—was conducted by Stonewall in 1993. The questionnaire was distributed via mailing lists of gay businesses, publications, and social groups. The report [A Palmer, 'Less Equal than Others. A Survey of Lesbians and Gay Men at Work' (London, Stonewall, 1993)] found that one in six respondents (15 per cent) had at least one experience of discrimination; a further 21 per cent suspected that they had; and 8 per cent had been dismissed because of their sexuality. But the findings indicated that 'discrimination by employers is only part of the problem. Harassment is a much bigger problem, and discrimination avoidance, including the closet, is the biggest problem of all.' In the area of recruitment, 5 per cent said they knew that they had been discriminated against and 17 per cent suspected that they had been. A similar proportion (5 per cent) said they knew they had been denied promotion because of discrimination and 19 per cent suspected they had been.

Almost half the respondents (48 per cent) considered that they had been harassed because of their sexuality. A high proportion concealed their sexual orientation at work to avoid discrimination or harassment. Only 11 per cent said they had never concealed their sexuality at work, compared with over half (56 per cent) who had concealed it in some jobs, and 33 per cent in all jobs.

As in the LRD survey, the majority (79 per cent) said that their employer had an equal opportunities policy. But just over a quarter of private sector employees said that the policy covered sexual orientation, compared with nearly two-thirds of public sector employees, and around nine out of 10 voluntary sector employees.

The most recent study, published by Social and Community Research in 1995 [D Snape, K Thompson and M Chitwynd, 'Discrimination against gay men and lesbians' SCPR 1995], found that discrimination was 'widespread' against gay men and lesbians. The findings are based on the first representative sample of lesbians and gay men, drawn randomly from the National Survey of Sexual Attitudes and Lifestyles. Of the respondents, 116 defined themselves as homosexual, or as having been homosexual in the past, and 619 people as heterosexual. In the sphere of employment, 21 per cent of those who defined themselves as homosexual had been harassed at work; 8 per cent had been refused promotion because of their sexuality, 6 per cent had tried to get a job and failed, and 4 per cent had been dismissed.

To avoid discrimination many respondents said that they concealed their sexuality. Over half said that none of their work colleagues knew about their sexuality, and one one-fifth said that all their colleagues knew. The report suggests that those who concealed their sexuality were less likely to experience some form of discrimination, but pointed out that 'the strain and indignity of keeping such an integral part of their lives a secret is one of the most insidious forms of discrimination that homosexual people experience.'

Press for Change, 'The A to Z of Trans People's Discrimination' (1999)

B is for . . . Birth certificates . . . which, the government has repeatedly told the European Court of Human Rights, are not a proof of identity. However, many government agencies insist that they will not accept any other document instead. All but four of the 39 Council of Europe states has provision to correct the birth certificates of their trans citizens, and hence accord them a legal status which matches the reality of their lives. Britain, along with Ireland, Andorra and Albania has so far refused to concede that a mechanism to do this can be found...

C is for Children ... to whom transsexual parents are still regularly denied access. The only scientific studies that have been conducted into the effects of a transsexual parent upon young children have shown that there are no problems associated with such parents continuing to have normal access and an active involvement in the upbringing of their children. Any 'problems' tend to be those created by other adults, and based on ignorance and fear of the unfamiliar. The Press for Change Birth Parents Working Party is helping parents resist the attempts of others to subvert the law into denying them access to the children they love...

D if for Degree certificates ... which many colleges and universities still refuse to re-issue for graduates who have changed gender roles. Such refusal means that a trans person may either have to apply for jobs with employers who aren't going to ask to see their certificates, or voluntarily disclose their medical history during application. Needless to say, the latter will very often be the end of any prospect of a job offer ... and even if this is not the case, the forced declaration is humiliating for the applicant ... Sadly **D** also stands for **Death**, which haunts all British trans people. The law does not define how sex is to be recorded, but the Office of National Statistics informs us in correspondence that 'the registrar would generally expect this information to correspond with the sex recorded on the medical certificate of cause of death issued by the doctor who certified the cause of death.' So we're all in the hands of the doctor ... he may record sex as it was recorded at birth.' A dilemma also awaits living trans people, however, if they go to register the death of a friend or relative. The law demands that they identify themselves, and that the information given is 'true to the best of the informant's knowledge and belief.' A trans person knows what sex they are, but the law believes the opposite ... so we are left with a choice between a declaration we know to be false and one the law believes to be false. Finally, **D** stands for **DSS** ... which does not alter its records to truly reflect a change of official gender. New names are merely treated as aliases and the gender of the person concerned is unchanged ... Files can be flagged as private, so that only local managers can see the contents but, for many, this results in tremendous inconvenience dealing with benefit claims. Either way, many trans people ... report cases of correspondence being sent to them in their original names and with the wrong title ...

E is for evidence ... which spells a risk of a breach of privacy for any trans person involved in Court proceedings, whether they are involved in civil proceedings, charged with an offence, giving evidence, or standing surety for a friend. A Commons written answer from the Lord Chancellors' Dept in November 1999 confirms ... that the courts have discretion to require disclosure of any former name(s) if they decide it is relevant to the proceedings. Whatever the likelihood of this actually happening, the risk of forced disclosure may deter some trans people from seeking justice through the courts ...

I is for Insurance ... which is a legal minefield for British trans people. The fact that a trans person's legal sex is contrary to what they appear to be means that an obligation is created for them to disclose the 'facts' when taking out any of a range of insurance products in which sex may conceivably be a relevant factor. Even when the relevance is not obvious, trans people may still be at risk, in an industry where the insurer has the ultimate say in what they consider to be 'relevant.' The risk with non-disclosure is that the trans person may find that they are uninsured when it comes to the crunch.

M is for Marriage ... Paradoxically, British trans women can marry other women (and trans men can marry other men), but since [*Corbett v Corbett* [1971] P 83] ... it has not been legal for a trans person to marry a person of what appears to be the opposite sex ...

N is for National Health Service . . . whose local bodies, the health authorities and trusts have gone to ever increasing lengths over the past few years to do everything in their power to deny treatment to trans people, whilst staying just within the letter of the law. Most trans people who cannot afford private treatment are offered grossly inadequate psychological counselling at overcrowded and substandard centres and, after many years of hormonal treatment and having jumped through every hoop may then find that surgery is denied to them, or is subjected to absurdly low quotas . . . leaving them in limbo, half way between the sexes. Waiting times of ten years are not uncommon.

O is for Office of National Statistics . . . formerly the Office of Population, Censuses and Surveys . . . whose job it is to receive and reject hundreds of applications from British trans people to correct their birth certificates. Such is the absurdity of the regulations that a child born with malformed genitals, initially registered as a boy and then reassigned as a girl a few months later (after medical reassessment), could not have her birth certificate corrected. The child, now eight years old, thus technically became Britain's youngest trans-sexual woman, although at the very end of 1998 the government has belatedly acquiesced and agreed to alter the document for her, proving that the unalterable is really nothing of the kind when there is a will.

P is for . . . Passports. British trans people can have a new ten year passport appropriate to their presentation issued to them following surgery, but are cautioned against using the sex indicator on the document as a means of avoiding the problems created by their birth certificate. Prior to surgery, trans people can have a one year passport issued to them with similar details, under the bizarre logic that 'they may decide to change back.' Instead of having to deal with an extremely rare and unlikely possibility once in a blue moon, there-fore, the passport office has to reissue a new passport to every pre-operative trans person, every year until they've managed to jump through sufficient medical hoops to be treated (a process which can take ten years or more, given the deliberate delaying tactics adopted by some health authorities). For travel to countries which require visas, there is often a require-ment for a minimum period of remaining validity of the passport . . . which means that trans people may be effectively barred for much of the time from travel to certain destina-tions. **P** is for **Pensions** too. Any trans person taking out a private pension is obliged to reveal their legal sex, otherwise they may find, when the policy matures, that they are enti-tled to no more than the value of their contributions. The reason is simple . . . the govern-ment insist that trans people must retire at the age implied by the sex recorded on their birth certificate, 65 for men and 60 for women. Recent changes to the law mean that people under the age of about forty will retire at the same age, so this isn't a universal problem and will automatically resolve itself in 15–20 years time. In the meantime, for those trans people already in middle age, the difference means they must ensure that a pension company treats them 'correctly' in their records and, of course, their circumstances will become obvious when they are forced to retire at a different age to their contemporaries. Finally, **P** is for **Prison** . . . a frightening prospect for British trans people . . . who have no guarantee of being sent to an appropriate institution, nor of being allowed to continue their treatment if preoperative.

Q is for . . . Queues . . . which are absurdly long for trans people seeking treatment through the National Health Service. It is not uncommon for some people to patiently attend a Gender Identity clinic in their own area, see the clinic closed by cuts, be referred to a dis-tant centre such as the Charing Cross Hospital in London . . . and then be told that their 'evaluation' then has to start all over again, disregarding everything that has gone before. Finally, approved for surgery, the hapless trans person . . . now halfway between the sexes after years of hormone administration . . . can then find themselves at the tail end of a surgery waiting list, made long by a local health authority quota which arbitrarily dictates that only one or two procedures will be funded each year. With at least 100 trans people in every million of the population, it is little wonder that some reach this point seriously contemplating suicide. It isn't 'gender dysphoria' (or whatever fancy name you give it) that drives people to such despair, however, but aggravated neglect.

R is for . . . Rape . . . which couldn't officially happen to British trans women until very recently, because they are legally men. . . There is a means now, at least, for a trans woman to charge an attacker with what he had in mind, rather than the lesser charge of sexual assualt . . . due mostly to the fact that the courts have also belatedly recognised the reality of male rape too. It would be inconsistent to argue that trans people should be covered neither as women, nor as men. Yet the strength of such an argument still has to be proven . . . the only case to have been brought so far found the alleged attacker not guilty . . . Then there is **R v Tan** [[1983] QB 1053] . . . one of many employment discrimination cases, which . . . established that male sexual offence law, with its generally higher tariffs, should apply to trans sex workers . . . sending transsexual prostitutes to jail for gross indecency rather than soliciting.

U is for . . . Unemployment . . . Academic research undertaken by Press for Change co-founder, Dr Stephen Whittle has demonstrated that, after transition, trans people are regularly forced into far lower paid jobs, assuming they find jobs at all. The discrimination examples cited in this A to Z guide show just the tip of the iceberg as to why this should be. Yet ironically, many trans people are also very high achievers: . . . In spite of this, the British government's Department for Education and Employment published, in all seriousness, a consultation paper in January 1998 suggesting changes to the law which, if enacted, would have thrown teachers out of work (as unfit to work with children) and would have jeopardised the employment prospects of any trans people involved in working with the public in any state of undress (changing room attendants, shop staff, beauticians, . . . the list is endless).

X is for X, Y and Z . . . the case brought to the European Court of Human Rights in 1997 by Stephen Whittle and Sarah Rutherford, on behalf of their children. None of the children can have Stephen's name recorded on their birth certificates as father, because Stephen is legally a woman. Yet any other man could have his name recorded in Stephen's place, through rules designed to allow non genetic parents to take a responsibility for their partners' offspring . . .

It is clear from the extracts above that gay men, lesbian women, bisexuals and the UK's estimated 5000 trans people suffer significant disadvantage and discrimination. Prior to December 2003 the UK had no legislation regulating discrimination on grounds of sexual orientation and, despite the campaigning efforts of a number of organisations and individuals, transsexualism has until recent years generally been regarded more as a cause for mirth, at best a medical oddity, than a civil rights issue. Since May 1999 the SDA has, to some extent, regulated employment-related discrimination on the basis of gender-reassignment. This amendment was made as a result of the ECJ's decision, in *P v S & Cornwall* Case C–13/94 [1996] ECR I–2143, that discrimination on the grounds of gender reassignment amounted to sex discrimination contrary to the Equal Treatment Directive. More recently, the decision of the European Court of Human Rights in *Goodwin v UK* (2002) 35 EHRR 447 established that the failure of the UK fully to recognise the chosen sexual identity of gender-reassigned trans people, and to permit them to marry in that sex, breached Articles 8 and 12 of the European Convention on Human Rights. The Gender Recognition Act 2004 (discussed below) was introduced to give effect to the decision but trans people remain significantly unprotected from discrimination.

There have been a number of recent developments in relation to such discrimination. The age of consent for gay sex was reduced to 16 in January 2001, bringing it into line with that

applicable to heterosexual sex. The Adoption and Children Act 2002 permits gay and lesbian couples to adopt as couples. Section 28 was finally repealed in 2003 and the Sexual
Offences Act 2003 removed much discrimination against men in the criminal law context.
In December 2003 the Employment Equality (Sexual Orientation) Regulations came into
force, prohibiting much discrimination on grounds of sexual orientation in employment
and third level education. The Regulations do not, however, outlaw discrimination outside
this context (for example, in housing, education other than third level education, or access
to goods and services). And the Housing Act 2004 permits civil partners to inherit
statutory tenancies. We shall see, below, that the decent decision of the House of Lords in
Mendoza v Ghaidan [2004] AC 557 has rendered this particular reform unnecessary.

The Civil Partnerships Bill, which was introduced in the House of Lords in 2002 by Lord
Lester, would have extended the obligations and benefits of marriage to those (mixed or
same sex) couples registered as civil partners. This Bill was withdrawn after second reading
in the Lords when the Government undertook 'to conduct an inter-departmental review in
relation to civil partnerships and formulate its position on the proposed civil partnership
registration scheme.'[1] This review and consultation resulted in the Civil Partnership Bill,
introduced in the Lords in 2004, which proposed to permit the legal recognition of same-
sex (but not heterosexual) couples. The Bill proved controversial, and wrecking amendments in the House of Lords included its expansion to cover family members and carers.
According to Jacqui Smith, Minister for Women and Equality: 'For some people, raising
the spectre of two elderly sisters living together—who of course already have a legally
recognised relationship, unlike two gay men who may have been living with each other for
50 years—is a way of opposing the legislation without being open about their opposition.'[2]
The amendments, which failed, were introduced by Conservative peer Baroness O'Cathain
and supported by senior Tories including Lord Tebbit who, a month previously, had
'implied that 'buggery' was to blame for the break down in family relationships (and child-
hood obesity), and accused the Government of 'doing everything it can to promote' gay
sex.'[3] The Civil Partnership Act was passed in November 2004 and is further discussed
below.

Questions of sexual orientation and gender identity are considered in this chapter. It is
important, however, to draw a clear distinction between them.

Press for Change, 'The A to Z of Trans People's Discrimination' (1999)

G is for . . . Gender . . . which is what this is all about. Many are confused by the term 'transsexual,' which implies a condition that has something to do with sexuality . . . the sort of
relationships which people seek. In reality, however, trans people have as broad a range of
sexual preferences as anyone else. Some are straight, some are gay or lesbian, some are
bisexual. A large number profess to be, in fact, asexual . . . having no interest in sex at all.
Gender is something more essential . . . it concerns each individual's sense of who they are
and what sort of people they identify with as 'like me' or 'different to me.' To emphasise
this, and to try and end the confusion created by the terminology Press for Change, along
with other groups worldwide, now advocate the use of the adjective 'trans' to describe
people who, in expressing their sense of identity, come into conflict with the contemporary
gender behaviour norms of their society. We stress however that whether you use the word
'trans' or older, more prescriptive, terms like 'transsexual' these are adjectives not nouns. It
is no more polite to say that somebody is 'a transsexual' than 'he is a blind' or 'she is a deaf.'

---

[1] The Odysseus Trust, 'Civil Partnerships Bill 2002'.
[2] This in an interview with Gay.com reported at http://uk.gay.com/headlines/6452.
[3] According to a report at Gay.com.

Please remember that trans people, transsexual people, transgender people . . . or whatever description you use . . . are people first, and the 'T' adjective describes only one of the many interesting and individual characteristics which make up that person.

In this chapter I will consider first the protection given by the law to trans people, then that provided in relation to sexual orientation. In each case I will deal both with the statutory provisions directed at 'discrimination' as such (whether 'discrimination' on grounds of 'sex,' or discrimination on grounds of 'gender reassignment' or 'sexual orientation' in particular), and with the broader statutory provisions dealing, for example, with the recognition of trans persons' chosen gender identities, or of same-sex relationships. The impact of the Human Rights Act 1998 in this context cannot be separated out from the discussion of the various statutory provisions and so will be commented on where relevant to the discussion.

Discrimination on Grounds of Gender Reassignment: The SDA

The decision in *P v S* was mentioned above. Its effect was to entitle those employed by the state, broadly defined, to protection from discrimination on grounds of gender reassignment. In *Chessington World of Adventures Ltd v Reed* [1998] ICR 97, [1997] IRLR 556, EAT found itself able to interpret the SDA so as to provide the same protection to private sector employees. Shortly thereafter, the Sex Discrimination (Gender Reassignment) Regulations 1999[4] incorporated this approach expressly into the SDA by inserting into that Act the new s.2A:

(1) A person ('A') discriminates against another person ('B') in any circumstances relevant for the purposes of—
  (a) any provision of Part II [employment],
  (b) section 35A or 35B [discrimination against barristers and advocates], or
  (c) any other provision of Part III, so far as it applies to vocational training;
  if he treats B less favourably than he treats or would treat other persons, and does so on the ground that B intends to undergo, is undergoing or has undergone gender reassignment.
(2) Subsection (3) applies to arrangements made by any person in relation to another's absence from work or from vocational training.
(3) For the purposes of subsection (1), B is treated less favourably than others under such arrangements if, in the application of the arrangements to any absence due to B undergoing gender reassignment–
  (a) he is treated less favourably than he would be if the absence was due to sickness or injury, or . . .
  (b) he is treated less favourably than he would be if the absence was due to some other cause and, having regard to the circumstances of the case, it is reasonable for him to be treated no less favourably.
(4) In subsections (2) and (3) 'arrangements' includes terms, conditions or arrangements on which employment, a pupillage or tenancy or vocational training is offered.

---

[4] SI 1999 No 1102.

(5) For the purposes of subsection (1), a provision mentioned in that subsection framed with reference to discrimination against women shall be treated as applying equally to the treatment of men with such modifications as are requisite.

Section 2(2) of the Regulations amends s.5(3) SDA to the effect that:

A comparison of the cases of persons of different sex . . . under section 1(1) or 3(1) or a comparison of persons required for the purposes of s.2A must be such that the relevant circumstances in the one case are the same, or not materially different, in the other.

In addition to the genuine occupational qualification defence discussed below, s.19(3) and (4) SDA permit discrimination against trans people in relation to 'employment for purposes of an organised religion' and training for such employment. Section 2A(2) SDA provides that subsection (1) applies in relation to absence related to gender-reassignment but s.2A(3) states that discrimination will be made out, in relation to absence, only if 'he is treated less favourably than he would be if (a) the absence was due to sickness or injury' or (b) 'to some other cause and, having regard to the circumstances of the case, it is reasonable for him to be treated no less favourably.' This is clearly intended to avoid the application of an approach analogous to that which has finally prevailed in relation to pregnancy-related absence (see *Webb (No.2)* [1994] QB 718, discussed in Chapter 6) in the context of gender reassignment. Protection against discrimination on this ground starts at the point when a person indicates an intention to undergo gender reassignment, the original proposal to make protection contingent on the person formally having sought medical intervention being dropped after the consultation stage. Section 2(3) provides that pay-related discrimination against transsexuals shall be dealt with under the SDA rather than the EqPA.

The Gender Reassignment Regulations were, as was noted above, intended to bring the UK law into line with European Community requirements. In order to determine whether the new s.2A SDA has that effect it is necessary to consider the decisions of the ECJ in *P v S* and in the subsequently decided *KB* case (below). Prior to the decision of the Court in *P v S* Advocate-General Tesauro, while expressly accepting that the Equal Treatment Directive had not originally been intended to prohibit discrimination in connection with gender reassignment, urged that the ECJ interpret the Directive 'as the expression of a more general principle, on the basis of which sex should be irrelevant to the treatment everyone receives . . . [to include] all situations in which sex appears as a discriminatory factor.'[5] The ECJ responded to the Advocate-General's plea, ruling that:

The principle of equal treatment 'for men and women' to which the Directive refers in its title, preamble and provisions means, as Articles 2(1) and 3(1) in particular indicate, that there should be 'no discrimination whatsoever on grounds of sex' . . . the Directive is simply the expression, in the relevant field, of the principle of equality, which is one of the fundamental principles of Community law. Moreover, as the Court has repeatedly held, the right not to be discriminated against on grounds of sex is one of the fundamental human rights whose observance the Court has a duty to ensure . . .

Accordingly, the scope of the Directive cannot be confined simply to discrimination based on the fact that a person is one or other sex. In view of its purpose and the nature of the rights which it seeks to safeguard, the scope of the Directive is also such as to apply to discrimination arising, as in this case, from the gender reassignment of the person concerned.

[5] Calling in support the fact that the European Parliament expressed itself to the same effect in a Resolution on discrimination against transsexuals of 9 October 1989.

Such discrimination is based, essentially, if not exclusively, on the sex of the person concerned. Where a person is dismissed on the ground that he or she intends to undergo, or has undergone, gender reassignment, he or she is treated unfavourably by comparison with persons of the sex to which he or she was deemed to belong before undergoing gender reassignment.

To tolerate such discrimination would be tantamount, as regards such a person, to a failure to respect the dignity and freedom to which he or she is entitled, and which the Court has a duty to safeguard.

The ECJ was called to consider the position of trans persons once again in *KB v The NHS Trust Pensions Agency* in which the applicant challenged the unavailability to her partner of many years' standing (a female to male trans person) of benefits under the NHS scheme. Survivors' benefits were available under the scheme only to married partners, the claimant (a woman) being prevented by law from marrying her partner. She brought her claim under Article 141 TEC, considered in more detail in Chapter 1, which prohibits sex discrimination in relation to pay. An employment tribunal and EAT rejected her claim, the latter ruling (*per* Morrison LJ) that:

> *P v S* does not carry the argument . . . In that case, P was treated less favourably than he would have been had he not indicated a desire to undergo gender re-assignment. In other words, he was treated worse than he would have been had he not given that indication. Thus he was treated less favourably than an 'ordinary' male or a transsexual who did not intend, or announce an intention, to undergo the surgery. The case did not establish that transsexuals were entitled to equal rights with those of the sex to which they were seeking re-assignment.

The Court of Appeal referred to the ECJ the question 'Whether the exclusion of the female-to-male transsexual partner of a female member of the National Health Service Pension Scheme, which limited the material dependant's benefit to her widower, constituted sex discrimination in contravention of Article 141 EC.'

KB v The NHS Trust Pensions Agency, **Case C–117/01 [2004] ECR I–00000**

Judgment:

The decision to restrict certain benefits to married couples while excluding all persons who live together without being married is either a matter for the legislature to decide or as matter for the national courts as to the interpretation of domestic legal rules, and individuals cannot claim that there is discrimination on grounds of sex, prohibited by Community law . . .

In this instance, such a requirement cannot be regarded per se as discriminatory on grounds of sex and, accordingly, as contrary to Article 141 EC or Directive 75/117, since for the purposes of awarding the survivor's pension it is irrelevant whether the applicant is a man or a woman.

However, in a situation such as that before the national court, there is inequality of treatment which, although it does not directly undermine enjoyment of a right protected by Community law, affects one of the conditions for the grant of that right . . . the inequality of treatment does not relate to the award of a widower's pension but to a necessary precondition for the grant of such a pension: namely, the capacity to marry.

In the United Kingdom, by comparison with a heterosexual couple where neither partner's identity is the result of gender reassignment surgery and the couple are therefore able to marry and, as the case may be, have the benefit of a survivor's pension which forms part of the pay of one of them, a couple such as KB and R are quite unable to satisfy the marriage requirement, as laid down by the NHS Pension Scheme for the purpose of the award of a survivor's pension.

The fact that it is impossible for them to marry is due to the fact, first, that the Matrimonial Causes Act 1973 deems a marriage void if the parties are not respectively male and female; second, that a person's sex is deemed to be that appearing on his or her birth certificate; and, third, that the Births and Deaths Registration Act does not allow for any alteration of the register of births, except in the case of clerical error or an error of fact.

The European Court of Human Rights has held that the fact that it is impossible for a transsexual to marry a person of the sex to which he or she belonged prior to gender reassignment surgery, which arises because, for the purposes of the registers of civil status, they belong to the same sex [citing *Goodwin*] . . .

Legislation, such as that at issue in the main proceedings, which, in breach of the ECHR, prevents a couple such as KB and R from fulfilling the marriage requirement which must be met for one of them to be able to benefit from part of the pay of the other must be regarded as being, in principle, incompatible with the requirements of Article 141 EC.

Since it is for the Member States to determine the conditions under which legal recognition is given to the change of gender of a person in R's situation—as the European Court of Human Rights has accepted [citing *Goodwin*]—it is for the national court to determine whether in a case such as that in the main proceedings a person in KB's situation can rely on Article 141 EC in order to gain recognition of her right to nominate her partner as the beneficiary of a survivor's pension.

The decisions in *P v S* and in *KB* cast doubt on the compatibility of the SDA as it was amended in 1999 with EU law. The additional GOQs provided in this context are considered below. But it was noted above that s.2A excludes the *Dekker/Webb* approach to time off in connection with gender-reassignment, and that it does not prohibit indirect discrimination. As a commentary in the *Equal Opportunities Review* stated of the exclusion of the *Dekker/Webb* approach: 'Once it is accepted that discrimination based on a person's change of sex is equivalent to discrimination based on a person's belonging to a particular sex, treatment by the employer which would not take place but for the fact that the person was undergoing a gender reassignment must be regarded as treatment on grounds of sex, and thus unlawful.'[6] The Equal Treatment Directive expressly prohibits indirect as well as direct discrimination (this was recognised also by the Government in its Consultation Paper, *Legislation Regarding Discrimination on Grounds of Transsexualism in Employment*), and the decision of the ECJ in *P v S* defines gender-reassignment as 'sex' for the purposes of the Directive. It would appear, accordingly, that the express provisions of the SDA, as amended, may fall short of what is required to secure compliance. This conclusion is strengthened by the decision in *KB*. Scope remains, however, for purposive interpretation of the Act to achieve compliance with the demands of the Directive.

Section 7A SDA provides that employment-related discrimination in connection with gender reassignment is not unlawful if:

---

[6] Transsexual legislation proposed, 78 *Equal Opportunities Review* 30, 30, considering the consultation document. *Cf* 'Sex Discrimination (Gender Reassignment) Regulations: an EOR Guide' 85 *Equal Opportunities Review* 36, 37: 'the government has pragmatically—and arguably sensibly—adopted special rules in the case of absence due to a transsexual undergoing gender reassignment,' though this is contradicted on the next page, the special rules being categorised as a 'dilution of the principle of nondiscrimination.'

(a) in relation to the employment in question—
    (i) being a man is a genuine occupational qualification for the job, or
    (ii) being a woman is a genuine occupational qualification for the job, and
(b) the employer can show that the treatment is reasonable in view of the circumstances described in the relevant paragraph of section 7(2) and any other relevant circumstances.

Section 7A(4), introduced by the Gender Recognition Act, provides that the GOQ does not apply where a person's acquired sex has been recognised under the 2004 Act. The SDA's standard GOQ defence is considered in Chapter 6. By contrast with the position where straightforward sex discrimination (as distinct from that connected with gender reassignment) is at issue, the GOQs applicable in connection with gender reassignment cover dismissal as well as failure to recruit (this being necessary to cover gender reassignments which take place after recruitment).

S.7A is not problematic in principle, serving as it does simply to apply the GOQ defence in the context of gender reassignment rather than singling out trans people for special disadvantage. Different considerations apply in relation to s.7B SDA which provides 'supplementary [GOQs] relating to gender reassignment' where:

(2) (a) the job involves the holder of the job being liable to be called upon to perform intimate physical searches pursuant to statutory powers;
    (b) the job is likely to involve the holder of the job doing his work, or living, in a private home and needs to be held otherwise than by a person who is undergoing or has undergone gender reassignment, because objection might reasonable be taken to allowing such a person—
        (i) the degree of physical or social contact with a person living in the home, or
        (ii) the knowledge of intimate details of such a person's life, which is likely, because of the nature or circumstances of the job or of the home, to be allowed to, or available to, the holder of the job;
    (c) the nature or location of the establishment makes it impracticable for the holder of the job to live elsewhere than in premises provided by the employer, and—
        (i) the only such premises which are available for persons holding that kind of job are such that reasonable objection could be taken, for the purpose of preserving decency or privacy, to the holder of the job sharing accommodation and facilities with either sex whilst undergoing gender reassignment, and
        (ii) it is not reasonable to expect the employer either to equip those premises with suitable accommodation or to make alternative arrangements; or
    (d) the holder of the job provides vulnerable individuals with personal services promoting their welfare, or similar personal services, and in the reasonable view of the employer those services cannot be effectively provided by a person whilst that person is undergoing gender reassignment.[7]

The GOQs established by s.7B do not apply to those whose acquired gender has been recognised under the 2004 Act. Section 7B, unlike ss.7 and 7A SDA, applies whether or not there are other employees capable of carrying out the duties in question.[8]

---

[7] Reg 5 amends s.19 of the SDA to permit discrimination on the basis of gender reassignment in employment for the purposes of organised religion and reg 7 amends the EOC's responsibilities to include those who 'intend to undergo, are undergoing or have undergone gender reassignment.'

[8] The draft Employment Equality (Sex Discrimination) Regulations 2005 propose to amend s.7B(2)(a) to this end.

Turning to (b), the supplementary GOQs provided in the Regulations are considerably narrower than those originally suggested (the Government having originally countenanced, inter alia, an exclusion from the principle of non-discrimination in respect of all work with children). But s.7B(2)(a) was capable of operating as an effective bar to trans people in the police force, a situation regarded as unacceptable by an employment tribunal in the (pre-Regulations) *A v Chief Constable of the West Yorkshire Police*,[9] which involved a challenge to a refusal to recruit a male-to-female trans person into the police on the grounds that she would have to conduct intimate searches.

The tribunal took the view that, the police being under no obligation to disclose the claimant's status to those undergoing body searches, this should not be allowed to operate as a bar to such employment. The alternative approach 'would preclude transsexuals from ever becoming police constables and might have a similar effect in those other occupations and in the training leading thereto where close personal interraction is a prerequisite of the job . . . the risks to the respondent in permitting the applicant as a transsexual to carry out the full range of duties including the searching of women are so small that to give effect to them by denying the applicant access to the office of constable would be wholly disproportionate to the denial of the applicant's fundamental right to equal treatment.'

EAT overruled the tribunal decision on the basis that A had to be regarded legally as a man and could not properly be held out as a woman by the respondents. There was no obligation on the Chief Constable to disclose that the applicant was transsexual, but he was obliged not to authorise or condone a representation that she was a woman. Between the date of EAT's decision and the Court of Appeal's subsequent hearing the ECtHR decided *Goodwin*. The Court of Appeal overruled EAT's decision and the House of Lords rejected the chief constable's appeal. The decision of their Lordships turned not on the HRA, the discrimination in question having predated the implementation of that Act, but rather on the Equal Treatment Directive as it had been applied in *P v S* and in the more recent *KB*.

Lords Bingham and Rodger gave speeches as did Baroness Hale. All accepted that the case had to be determined absent reference to the HRA. Notwithstanding this, the decision in *Goodwin* was binding in domestic law through the medium of the Equal Treatment Directive.

A v Chief Constable of the West Yorkshire Police [2005] AC 51

Lord Bingham (for the majority):

The sheet-anchor of Ms A's case was the important judgment of the European Court of Justice in *P v S* . . . The Court adopted a similar approach in *KB* . . . That case concerned equal pay, not equal treatment, and judgment was given years after the chief constable's decision to reject Ms A's application. But there is nothing here to displace the ordinary principle that a ruling on the interpretation of Community law takes effect from the date on which the rule interpreted entered into force . . .

The question then arises whether the decisions of the European Court of Justice in *P v S* and *KB*, and the philosophical principles on which they rest, can cohabit with a rule of domestic law which either precludes the employment of a post-operative male-to-female transsexual as a constable of whom routine section 54 searching duties are required, or requires such a person to be willing to disclose her transsexual identity to working colleagues and, perhaps, members of the public. The first of these alternatives cannot be reconciled with the principle of equality: the exclusion is not one which applies to men or women but only to those who have changed their gender. Yet they also are entitled to be

---

[9] 18 March 1999, Case 1802020/98, discussed in 85 *Equal Opportunities Review*, above n 6, 39.

treated, so far as possible, equally with non-transsexual men or women. The second alternative derogates from the dignity and freedom to which a transsexual individual, like any other, is entitled. In my opinion, effect can be given to the clear thrust of Community law only by reading 'the same sex' in section 54(9) [PACE], and 'woman,' 'man' and 'men' in sections 1, 2, 6 and 7 [SDA], as referring to the acquired gender of a post-operative transsexual who is visually and for all practical purposes indistinguishable from non-transsexual members of that gender. No one of that gender searched by such a person could reasonably object to the search.

Lord Bingham went on to state that the decision in *A* should not be regarded as calling into question or the very recent decision of the House in *Bellinger v Bellinger* [2003] 2 AC 467 in which their Lordships had refused to interpret the Matrimonial Causes Act 1973 so as to to permit trans persons to marry in their chosen gender (although their Lordships did issue a declaration of incompatibility under s.4 HRA). Lord Bingham had 'no doubt that the decision was wholly correct, and there was a prompt legislative response to it. But the case concerned marriage, perhaps the most important and sensitive of human relationships. It lacked any Community dimension, so that *P v S* was not cited and there was no need to consider it.'

Baroness Hale (with whom Lord Carswell agreed):

It might be possible to regard [*P v S*] as simply a decision that discrimination on grounds of transsexuality is discrimination 'on grounds of sex' for the purpose of the Directive. But there are many reasons to think that it is not so simple. The purpose of the Directive, set out in Article 1(1), is to 'put into effect in the Member States the principle of equal treatment for men and women . . .'. The opinion of Advocate General Tesauro was emphatic that 'transsexuals certainly do not constitute a third sex, so it should be considered as a matter of principle that they are covered by the directive, having regard also to the above-mentioned recognition of their right to a sexual identity.' The 'right to a sexual identity' referred to is clearly the right to the identity of a man or a woman rather than of some 'third sex.' Equally clearly it is a right to the identity of the sex into which the trans person has changed or is changing. In sex discrimination cases it is necessary to compare the applicant's treatment with that afforded to a member of the opposite sex. In gender reassignment cases it must be necessary to compare the applicant's treatment with that afforded to a member of the sex to which he or she used to belong. Hence the Court of Justice observed that the transsexual 'is treated unfavourably by comparison with persons of the sex to which he or she was deemed to belong before undergoing gender reassignment.' Thus, for the purposes of discrimination between men and women in the fields covered by the directive, a trans person is to be regarded as having the sexual identity of the gender to which he or she has been reassigned.

That this is the correct interpretation of *P v S* emerges clearly from the recent decision in *KB* [which] . . . confirms the right of the trans person to be recognised in the reassigned gender, not only for the purpose of the direct enjoyment of community rights, but also for the purpose of the pre-conditions of such a right. . . .

If in principle the trans partner of an employee must be recognised in the reassigned gender for the purpose of death benefits, the employee herself must in principle be recognised in the reassigned gender for the purpose of carrying out the duties of the post. This means that section 54(9) of PACE must be interpreted as applying to her in her reassigned gender, unless, as was acknowledged in *P v S*, there are strong public policy reasons to the contrary. It is difficult to argue that such public policy reasons existed in this case even in 1998. Intimate searches were expressly recognised as a supplementary genuine occupational qualification under section 7B [SDA], but the Chief Constable accepts that they do not present a practical problem to which exclusion from the Force would be a proportionate response. If the Gender [Rea]ssignment Bill becomes law, they will cease to be recognised as such at all. Section 54 searches were not expressly recognised in section 7B, which was introduced in 1999 but in response to the decision in *P v S* in 1996. This is not surprising. By that time, the United Kingdom authorities were already doing everything they could to enable a trans person to live a normal life in her reassigned gender. There are many occupations which involve physical contact with members of the opposite sex. Although these are not usually in the circumstances of compulsion entailed in a section 54 search, they are often not truly voluntary—as for example in hospital wards where there are doctors and nurses of both sexes. And there are some, such as compulsory hospital patients, who have no choice. We generally depend upon the professionalism of the individual, backed up by the ordinary law and complaints mechanisms, to protect people's sensibilities. Those sensibilities may be rational as well as real. For example, it may well be rational to object to being nursed by a heterosexual person of the opposite sex. It may also be rational to object to being nursed by a homosexual person of the same sex. But it would not be rational to object on similar grounds to being nursed by a trans person of the same sex. In those circumstances it is not surprising that the Employment Tribunal held that an objection to being searched by a trans person would not be reasonable.

Until the matter is resolved by legislation, there will of course be questions of demarcation and definition. Some of these, for the reasons explained in *Bellinger*, will be sensitive and difficult. That is presumably why the Court of Justice in *KB* acknowledged the role of the national court in deciding whether the principle did in fact apply in the particular case. One can well envisage a person who claims to have gender dysphoria but who has not successfully achieved the transition to the acquired gender. (One could also envisage a relationship which was not as close to marriage as the relationship in that case.) The Gender Recognition Bill provides a definition and a mechanism for resolving these demarcation questions. But until then it would be for the Employment Tribunals to make that judgment in a borderline case.

In this case, however, Ms A has done everything that she possibly could do to align her physical identity with her psychological identity. She has lived successfully as a woman for many years. She has taken the appropriate hormone treatment and concluded a programme of surgery. She believes that she presents as a woman in every respect.

She meets entirely the plea of Advocate General Ruiz-Jarabo Colomer in *KB*, at para 79:

'Transsexuals suffer the anguish of being convinced that they are victims of an error on the part of nature. Many have chosen suicide. At the end of a long and painful process, in which hormone treatment is followed by delicate surgery, medical science can offer them partial relief by making their external physical features correspond so far as possible to those of the sex to which they feel they belong. To my mind it is wrong that the law should take refuge in purely technical expedients in order to deny full recognition of an assimilation which has been so painfully won.'

In my view community law required in 1998 that such a person be recognised in her reassigned gender for the purposes covered by the Equal Treatment Directive This conclusion does not depend upon *Goodwin* and this case can readily be distinguished from *Bellinger*. I would dismiss this appeal.

Baroness Hale refers to 'questions of demarcation and definition' which would arise prior to the implementation of the Gender Recognition Bill (now the Act). As mentioned above, the GOQs apply to those whose acquired gender has been recognised under the Act as they do to those who have never gender reassigned. But some questions of demarcation remain.

One such question arose in *Croft v Royal Mail Group plc* [2003] ICR 1425, which involved a challenge brought by a male-to-female pre-operative trans person who was denied permission by her employers to use a female toilet. The Court of Appeal accepted that persons at any stage of gender reassignment who are under medical supervision are entitled not to be discriminated against on grounds of gender reassignment (this because s.2A prohibits discrimination on grounds of gender reassignment and s.82 SDA provides that ' "gender reassignment" means a process which is undertaken under medical supervision for the purpose of reassigning a person's sex by changing physiological or other characteristics of sex, *and includes any part of such a process*' (my emphasis). But the Court of Appeal did not accept that the refusal to permit a gender-reassigned person access to the toilets of her choice amounted to less favourable treatment of her on grounds of gender reassignment. A permanent refusal of the choice of toilets to someone presenting as a woman could be an act of discrimination even if the person had not undergone the final surgical intervention. But it did not follow that a refusal immediately to treat a person presenting as female as a woman amounted to less favourable treatment. The employer and the tribunal had to take a view as to when a male-to-female transsexual became a woman and was entitled to the same facilities as other women. This decision depended 'on all the circumstances,' including the stage reached in treatment, how the employee presents, and the views of other employees.[10]

The changes to the SDA made by the Gender Recognition Act are considered below.

Gender Identity and Recognition Rights

The foregoing section deals with the existing legislation as it regulates *discrimination* against gender-reassigning or reassigned trans persons. This subject will be returned to below. But here I consider recent developments, resulting from the decision of the ECtHR in *Goodwin*, relating to the *recognition* of the chosen gender identity of trans persons. We saw, above, that the ECtHR in *Goodwin* ruled that UK law breached Articles 8 and 12 of the ECHR because it did not provide for the full legal recognition of gender reassigned trans people. The Gender Recognition Act gives effect to the decision of the ECtHR in *Goodwin* by providing for such full legal recognition. Sections 1 and 2 provide that:

1(1) A person of either gender who is aged at least 18 may make an application for a gender recognition certificate on the basis of—
    (a) living in the other gender, or
    (b) having changed gender under the law of a country or territory outside the United Kingdom . . .
(3) An application under subsection (1) is to be determined by a Gender Recognition Panel
    . . .
2(1) In the case of an application under section 1(1)(a), the Panel must grant the application if satisfied that the applicant—
    (a) has or has had gender dysphoria,
    (b) has lived in the acquired gender throughout the period of two years ending with the date on which the application is made,

---

[10] See, by contrast, the position under the Gender Recognition Act, discussed below.

(c) intends to continue to live in the acquired gender until death, and

(d) complies with the [evidential] requirements imposed by and under section 3.

(2) In the case of an application under section 1(1)(b), the Panel must grant the application if satisfied—

(a) that the country or territory under the law of which the applicant has changed gender is an approved country or territory, and

(b) that the applicant complies with the [evidential] requirements imposed by and under section 3.

Section 3 provides that an application to the Gender Recognition Panel must include reports from two medical practitioners at least one of whom practices in the field of gender dysphoria, or from a medical practitioner and a chartered psychologist one of whom practices in the field. One report must contain details of the applicant's gender dysphoria and any reassignment treatment the applicant is undergoing. Calls by the religious right Evangelical Alliance for the panels to hear applications for registration in public (to allow for objections to be made, inter alia, by applicants' relations *and employers*) fell on stony ground and panel proceedings are in private.

A full certificate cannot be issued to a married applicant, but an otherwise qualified applicant who is married at the time of the application must be issued with an interim certificate. The issue of such a certificate amounts to grounds for divorce which, if granted, must be accompanied by a full gender recognition certificate. Section 9 provides as follows:

(1) Where a full gender recognition certificate is issued to a person, the person's gender becomes for all purposes the acquired gender (so that, if the acquired gender is the male gender, the person's sex becomes that of a man and, if it is the female gender, the person's sex becomes that of a woman).

(2) Subsection (1) does not affect things done, or events occurring, before the certificate is issued; but it does operate for the interpretation of enactments passed, and instruments and other documents made, before the certificate is issued (as well as those passed or made afterwards).

(3) Subsection (1) is subject to provision made by this Act or any other enactment or any subordinate legislation.

In its original form the Bill would have permitted female to male gender-reassigned persons to be recognised as the fathers of their partners' children. This provision was removed, though such man will still be able to obtain parental recognition by marrying and then jointly adopting the children concerned with their partners.

Section 10 provides for the issue of what are in effect amended birth certificates to persons with such certificates. Section 12 provides that a person will retain his or her original status as either father or mother of a child. Various other exceptions are provided in relation to succession to peerages and competitive sports in which the fact of gender-reassignment would provide a competitor with an unfair competitive advantage or would endanger the safety of other competitors. Section 22 makes it an offence for a person to disclose information acquired in an official capacity about a person's application for a gender recognition certificate or about the gender history of a successful applicant unless, for example, the person to be identified consented to the disclosure or the disclosure is for the purposes of proceedings before a court or tribunal.

A gender-reassigned person who has been issued with a full certificate is entitled to marry in his or her acquired gender. A conscience clause is provided for ministers from the Church of England and the Church of Wales who might otherwise be required (as ministers of established churches) to solemnise marriages one or both parties to which were gender-reassigned, and the failure of a gender-reassigned person to inform his or her spouse about the fact of the gender reassignment provides grounds for annulment of any marriage (s. 11 and schedule 4).

One of the noteworthy things about the Gender Recognition Act is that it does not, by contrast with *Goodwin*, restrict its protection to trans people who have completed gender reassignment, in particularly by undergoing surgery. Section 2 provides, as a condition for the issue of a gender recognition certificate, that the trans person has 'lived in the acquired gender' for at least two years. But, while surgery may be taken into account as evidence of transition, it is not a necessary aspect of it. According to David Lammy MP, who spoke on the Government's behalf during the Bill's second reading in the Commons, the test was 'whether a person has taken decisive steps to live fully and permanently in their acquired gender . . . not whether the person's physiology fully conforms to the acquired gender and not whether they 'look the part'.[11] In this the Government's line is consistent with the observation of Lord Nicholls in *Bellinger v Bellinger* that gender reassignment surgery does not itself change a person's sex but serves merely to achieve congruence between a person's own perceived sex or gender and his or her physical appearance.

The Gender Recognition Bill received very wide support, attracting only 26 dissenting votes on second reading (of 361 cast), this despite a free vote being accorded to opposition MPs. Many of the concerns expressed in debate related to the fact that a gender-reassigned person who is married must divorce prior to issue of a full certificate: this was regarded by a significant number of politicians as setting up a 'conflict' between the rights of the trans person and those of the original spouse[12] or, as the EOC put it in its response to the draft Bill, between the right to full legal recognition of the trans person's acquired sex and his or her right to a private life. The EOC was also concerned about the plight of spouses who may have provided significant emotional and other support to the reassigning person and whose financial position, together with those of their spouses, might be seriously jeopardised by divorce. Both Press for Change and the Joint Committee on Human Rights were also very critical of this aspect of the Bill but the Government stood firm on the basis that 'marriage is of course an institution for opposite sex couples.'[13] There was also before Parliament at the time of the debate on the Bill the Civil Partnership Bill, which provides for the official recognition of same-sex relationships. The Bill, now Act, is further considered below. But despite the urgings of the Joint Committee, the Government has made no provision for the transformation of marriages to civil partnerships in the event of gender reassignment, still less taken any steps to comply with the Committee's recommendation that (former) spouses should suffer no financial disadvantage because of the gender reassignment of a spouse. The Joint Committee suggested that this aspect of the Bill was of doubtful legality given the decision in *K.B.* Nor did the Government accede to pressure from the Joint Committee to provide for the retrospective recognition of marriages entered into prior to the implementation of the Bill into law. The Committee argued that *Goodwin* required recognition at least for the marriages of those engaged in litigation at the date of the decision.[14] But the Government again insisted on the principle that the Bill was

---

[11] HC Debs 23 February 2004 Col. 53.
[12] See, eg, Hugh Bayley (Lab) HC Debs, 23 February 2004, cols 80–1.
[13] Above n 11, *per* David Lammy for the Government.
[14] 19th Report of 2002–3 on the draft Bill (HL 188-I, HC 1276-I). See also the 4th Report of 2003–4 (HL 34/HC 303) on the Bill.

concerned only with prospective change and (David Lammy at the Second Reading) 'does not seek to rewrite history.'

The final aspect of the Gender Recognition Act which has attracted criticism is its failure to prohibit discrimination on grounds of gender reassignment. We saw, above, that such discrimination is regulated in the employment context. But the Joint Committee on Human Rights and others urged the Government to take the opportunity afforded by the Bill to legislate more broadly. The Government responded to the effect that 'this Bill is specifically about gender recognition. It is not about wider issues of discrimination relating to transsexual people,' taking the view that 'the most pressing need had been to amend the law in relation to employment and vocational training' and—somewhat surprisingly—that there was no evidence 'of a pressing need to protect transsexual people against discrimination in other fields.'[15] The Joint Committee stated in its 19th Report (on the then draft Bill) its satisfaction with the evidence that there was a 'significant amount of discrimination against transsexual people in the supply of goods and services, particularly pubs and clubs, and in housing, where homeless people may be left without access to a hostel because the people in charge of hostels for men and women respectively refuse to take in people on account of their status as transsexuals.'

The Committee's view was that there was a 'pressing need to protect transsexual people against discrimination in fields other than employment and vocational training. We note that the difficulty of deciding whether a person falls into the category of transsexual person would be no greater than that involved in deciding whether transsexual people, or transvestites, are men or women, but that is not considered to justify refusing protection to men and women against discrimination on the ground of sex.' The Committee's Fourth Report of 2003–4, on the Bill in its final form, reiterated its call for wider anti-discrimination provisions in its later report on the Bill. But that call has so far gone unheeded by Government with the effect that—save in the employment context—trans people will remain vulnerable to discrimination should their status be known or suspected. Some legal protection will be available as a result of the HRA. Discrimination by a public authority would likely breach Article 8 and, accordingly, be unlawful under s.6 HRA (see further Chapter 1). But the position as regards private actors is less clear cut. Egregious discrimination on the part of private bodies may well, if it goes unchecked and unremedied in domestic law, found a breach *by the state* of its positive obligations under the Convention. The possibility of such a breach may give rise to obligations on the courts both under s.3 HRA (as regards the interpretation of statutory provisions) and s.6 of the Act (as regards the incremental development of the common law). So, for example, the courts might regard themselves bound to interpret the SDA so as to regulate discrimination against (at any rate fully gender-reassigned)[16] trans people across the full breadth of its provisions. Certainly, as we saw above, EAT in the *Chessington* case regarded such an approach to the SDA as mandated by the interpretive obligations imposed by the Equal Treatment Directive. That the HRA's interpretive obligations are no less robust is indicated by the recent decision of the House of Lords in *Mendoza v Ghaidan*, extracted below. But that this will not necessarily be the case is evidenced by the unwillingness of the House of Lords in *Bellinger* to rely on s.3 HRA to avoid a Convention breach, though this perhaps restricted to the particular case of marriage.

Goodwin applies to trans people who have completed gender-reassignment. Both it and the Gender Recognition Act by which it is to be given effect in domestic law, create a dis-

---

[15] *Ibid*, para 100.
[16] See below for the *Goodwin* dicta on this point.

tinction for the purposes of legal protection between gender reassigned and other trans people (although the Act is more generous than *Goodwin* inasmuch as it does not require 'full', in the sense of surgical, reassignment). The SDA, by virtue of its specific provisions on gender reassignment, provides some protection to trans people from the point at which gender reassignment is begun, subject to the additional GOQs which will cease to have effect once a gender-reassigned person acquires a full gender recognition certificate. It may be that the European Court will in the future rule on the application of Article 8 in the context of *ongoing* gender reassignment. Article 8 would certainly entitle the gender-reassigning person to the same protections in respect of private life as those others enjoyed. But the provision is a qualified one and the privacy and other rights of other persons may tip the balance against full recognition prior to the completion of gender reassignment. And in *Goodwin* the European Court, having recognised (at para 91) 'the difficulties posed [and] the important repercussions' of its decision in relation to 'birth registration . . . access to records, family law, affiliation, inheritance, criminal justice, employment, social security and insurance,' went on to state that 'any 'special difficulties,' particularly in the field of family law, are both manageable and acceptable *if confined to the case of fully achieved and post-operative transsexuals*' (my emphasis).

Discrimination on Grounds of Sexual Orientation: (I) The SO Regulations

Introduction

The SO Regs, considered throughout the preceding chapters, form part of the transposition in Britain of the religion and belief provisions of the Employment Equality Directive (their Northern Irish equivalents are the Employment Equality (Sexual Orientation) Regulations (Northern Ireland) 2003[17] which are materially identical save for the addition of a provision (reg 7) which regulates discrimination 'by persons with statutory power to select employees for others' and the ensuing difference in regulation numbering.

The Employment Equality Directive, so far as is relevant here, provides:

Article 2
1. For the purposes of this Directive, the 'principle of equal treatment' shall mean that there shall be no direct or indirect discrimination whatsoever on any of the grounds referred to in Article 1 [these include 'sexual orientation'].

Article 4
1. Notwithstanding Article 2(1) and (2), Member States may provide that a difference of treatment which is based on a characteristic related to any of the grounds referred to in Article 1 shall not constitute discrimination where, by reason of the nature of the particular occupational activities concerned or of the context in which they are carried out, such a characteristic constitutes a genuine and determining occupational requirement, provided that the objective is legitimate and the requirement is proportionate.

---

[17] Statutory Rule 2003 No. 497.

2. Member States may maintain national legislation in force at the date of adoption of this Directive or provide for future legislation incorporating national practices existing at the date of adoption of this Directive pursuant to which, in the case of occupational activities within churches and other public or private organisations the ethos of which is based on religion or belief, a difference of treatment based on a person's religion or belief shall not constitute discrimination where, by reason of the nature of these activities or of the context in which they are carried out, a person's religion or belief constitute a genuine, legitimate and justified occupational requirement, having regard to the organisation's ethos. This difference of treatment shall be implemented taking account of Member States' constitutional provisions and principles, as well as the general principles of Community law, and should not justify discrimination on another ground.

Provided that its provisions are otherwise complied with, this Directive shall thus not prejudice the right of churches and other public or private organisations, the ethos of which is based on religion or belief, acting in conformity with national constitutions and laws, to require individuals working for them to act in good faith and with loyalty to the organisation's ethos.

We have considered the definitions of discrimination contained in the Regs in Chapter 2 (direct and indirect discrimination, victimisation, harassment, the issue of instructions and the provision of assistance to discriminate). In Chapter 3 we considered the extent to which the Directive and its implementing Regulations permit positive discrimination while the scope of the Regs (as of the other anti-discrimination provisions) was dealt with in Chapter 4 and enforcement issues in Chapter 5. Here we consider those aspects of the SO Regs which are unique to them. These consist, in particular, of the exclusion from the scope of the Regs of benefits access to which is restricted by reference to marital status, and the GOQs applicable to sexual orientation. Before we turn to these, however, it is worth making a few more minor points.

'Sexual orientation' is not defined by the Employment Equality Directive or by most other instruments which prohibit discrimination on this ground. The Regulations, by contrast, provide (reg 2(1)) that 'sexual orientation means a sexual orientation towards—(a) persons of the same sex; (b) persons of the opposite sex; or (c) persons of the same sex and of the opposite sex'. The rationale for defining 'sexual orientation' was explained by the Government as follows:

Department of Trade and Industry, *Towards Equality and Diversity*, para 12.6

A concern voiced by some during negotiations on the text of the Directive last year was that—in addition to outlawing discrimination against people on the basis of their heterosexual, homosexual or bisexual orientation—it could also be used to protect those who have unlawful sex, in particular paedophiles. We do not believe that this is the intention of the Directive. Moreover, Article 2(5) allows member states to 'take measures . . . which, in a democratic society, are necessary for public security, for the maintenance of public order and the prevention of criminal offences, for the protection of health and for the protection of the rights and freedoms of others.'

The *Towards Equality* consultation paper which predated the draft Regs proposed outlawing orientation discrimination on grounds of 'heterosexual, homosexual or bisexual orientation.' This approach did not escape criticism:

H Oliver, 'Sexual Orientation Discrimination: Perceptions, Definitions and Genuine Occupational Requirements' (2004) 33 *Industrial Law Journal* 1, 18–19, footnotes omitted

The concept of sexual orientation is in fact a very fluid one. Sexual orientation will often change over time, as people try out different sexual experiences. Although many individuals will clearly define themselves as heterosexual or homosexual, many others may not, and still more will have had experiences in the past that depart from their present sexual identity . . . the idea of requiring individuals to 'label' their own sexuality in this way can be criticised. The 1980s saw the development of a movement which challenged the importance of sexual orientation to an individual's identity and showed the limits of the categories of gay, lesbian and straight in defining sexual identity. This unwillingness to fit sexuality into rigid categories continues today, in particular within the gay, lesbian, bisexual and transgendered communities. Queer theory explores further this problem of defining sexual orientation and identity. Queer theory is difficult to define in itself, and different writers have different conceptions of its meaning, but at a basic level it can be summarised as an approach which deconstructs categories of identity as applied to human sexuality and gender. It should be noted that queer theory is not solely relevant to sexual orientation, and it is beyond the scope of this article to explore the applications of the theory in any detail. However, a queer theory analysis can be used to challenge the binary opposition of the categories heterosexual and homosexual, such that 'sexual identities might be conceived as multiplicitous, shifting, fluid and fragmented'. If a queer theory approach is applied to a GOR, it appears to become impossible to state with any certainty whether a person is of a 'particular' sexual orientation, as is required by the Regulations.

In this respect, sexual orientation is somewhat different from other types of discrimination, where it is generally clear what category the individual belongs to.

'On grounds of sexual orientation' is sufficiently wide to cover discrimination on grounds of someone *else's* sexual orientation (the child of an employee, for example, or (as in the RRA case of *Weathersfield v Sargent* [1999] ICR 425, discussed in Chapters 2 and 7), the sexual orientation of a customer against whom a worker is instructed to discriminate.

'Benefits Attendant on Marriage'

Recital 22 of the preamble to the Equal Treatment Directive provides that the Directive 'is without prejudice to national laws on marital status and the benefits dependent thereon.' The Directive is otherwise silent on the question of marriage. The SO Regs, however, provide (reg 25) that:

Nothing in Part II or III [which shall render unlawful anything which prevents or restricts access to a benefit by reference to marital status.

The effect of this is that the Regs do not regulate discrimination in relation to, for example, surviving spouses' pensions, although they will prohibit discrimination between same sex and opposite sex *unmarried* couples. This provision was unsuccessfully challenged in a judicial review claim brought against the Government by a number of trade unions. The case is also considered below in the GOR context. Insofar as relevant here, however, the claimants argued that the Regs were ultra vires the European Communities Act 1972 (under which they were passed) because they were incompatible with the obligations imposed by the Directive. Richards J ruled that the legislative intention behind the

Directive was clear from recital 22 of the preamble notwithstanding the decision of the ECJ in *KB*. According to Richards J, reg 25 did not interfere with Article 8 ECHR or breach the non-discrimination guarantee laid down by Article 14 of the Convention.

R (Amicus) v Secretary of State for Trade & Industry [2004] IRLR 430

Richards J:

Regulation 25 provides that nothing in Part II or Part III of the Regulations, including therefore the prohibition on discrimination, 'shall render unlawful anything which prevents or restricts access to a benefit by reference to marital status.' Its effect is that employment benefits defined by reference to marital status, such as a surviving spouse's pension, are not prohibited by the Regulations. The Amicus applicants submit that this is in breach of the Directive. Article 3(1)(c) of the Directive prohibits discrimination on grounds of sexual orientation in 'working conditions, including . . . pay.' That applies to employment benefits, including benefits under occupational pension schemes, which have been held to be a form of pay. Under domestic law same-sex partners are prohibited from marrying. To make employment benefits dependent on marital status is therefore either directly discriminatory or at the very least indirectly discriminatory and requiring to be justified in each individual case. There is no provision in the Directive authorising the general exception contained in regulation 25. It follows that the regulation is *ultra vires* . . .

The recital states in terms that the Directive 'is without prejudice to national laws on marital status and the benefits dependent thereon.' I accept Miss Carss-Frisk's submissions [for the Secretary of State] as to the proper interpretation of the recital. In my judgment it is of general application, covering all benefits that are dependent on marital status, including benefits such as surviving spouses' benefits under occupational pension schemes. It is not limited to State benefits, which are dealt with separately in recital (13) and article 3(3). . . . The troubling feature about recital (22) is that it is only a recital and . . . it has no parallel in the substantive provisions of the Directive. Although it is common ground that recitals can assist in the interpretation of the substantive provisions of a directive, it is a different matter to rely on a recital alone as establishing an important limitation on the scope of a directive. I was not directed to any authority that assists on this point. Nor was I invited to consider making a reference to the ECJ under article 234 of the EC Treaty for a preliminary ruling on the general issue or on the specific question of the scope of the Directive. Those are matters that may need to be looked at further if the case goes higher. For the present, however, I take the view that I should decide the point as best I can.

The conclusion I have reached is that the Secretary of State's submissions concerning the scope of the Directive should prevail. To hold otherwise would be to frustrate the legislative intention as it appears in recital (22). What makes me particularly cautious in that respect is that this is an area of considerable sensitivity in social and financial terms, as explained below when considering the alternative submissions on objective justification (though my conclusion that regulation 25 would in any event be lawful on that alternative basis may be thought to weaken the force of this consideration).

On the basis that regulation 25 reflects a limitation in the scope of the Directive itself, I reject Mr Singh's attempt [for the trace unions] to circumvent that limitation by reference to the reasoning of the ECJ in the later part of its judgment in *KB*. The reasoning in that passage relates specifically to transsexuals and to rules on marriage that have been held to be in breach the Convention. It cannot be applied automatically to the position of homosexuals even though they, too, are unable to marry. In any event I am not satisfied that it can be applied across to a situation that the Community legislature has, *ex hypothesi*, decided to exclude from the scope of the Directive . . .

Richards J went on to rule that (1) differentiation based on marital status did not in any event discriminate on grounds of sexual orientation either directly—because 'the ground of the difference in treatment is marriage, not sexual orientation'—or indirectly, 'since married and unmarried couples are not in a materially similar situation'; and (2) that any discrimination was in any event objectively justified by (a) the Government's policy of supporting marriage as a social, (b) the difficulty of distinguishing between same-sex and opposite-sex unmarried couples if benefits conditional on marriage were to be extended to the former; (c) the practical difficulties for employers of extending, to unmarried employees and their partners benefits currently limited to married couples; and (d) considerations of cost (estimated at between £300 million and £1.8 billion per annum).[18] The appeal from this decision was dropped when the Government agreed to treat civil partners in the same way as spouses for the purposes of public sector pension schemes in respect of rights accrued since 1988. The Civil Partnership Act also provides a basis for regulations to be made amending legislation in order to make provision for surviving civil partners of their dependants.

Genuine Occupational Requirements

The 'clash of rights' between the manifestation of religion and belief, on the one hand, and freedom from discrimination on grounds of sexual orientation, on the other, has been touched upon in Chapter 9. The compromise struck in this regard by the SO Regs is controversial, a significant aspect of it having been inserted at the eleventh hour, without consultation, after intense lobbying by religious bodies.

Reg 7 applies across 'employment,' widely defined to include contract-workers, office holders and the police, partnerships, providers of vocational training, employment agencies etc. and institutions of further and higher education (see further Chapter 4). It provides that the prohibitions on discrimination in relation to recruitment arrangements and offers of employment, promotion or transfer to, or training for, any employment; and dismissal from any employment shall not apply where:

(2) . . . having regard to the nature of the employment or the context in which it is carried out—
   (a) being of a particular sexual orientation is a genuine and determining occupational requirement;
   (b) it is proportionate to apply that requirement in the particular case; and
   (c) either—
     (i) the person to whom that requirement is applied does not meet it, or
     (ii) the employer is not satisfied, and in all the circumstances it is reasonable for him not to be satisfied, that that person meets it,
and this paragraph applies whether or not the employment is for purposes of an organised religion.
(3) This paragraph applies where—
   (a) the employment is for purposes of an organised religion;
   (b) the employer applies a requirement related to sexual orientation—
     (i) so as to comply with the doctrines of the religion, or

---

[18] *Cf* the decision of the Canadian Human Rights Tribunal in *Attorney General of Canada v Moore* 98 CLLC 230–033, in which the denial of same-sex benefits was held to be discriminatory. Judicial review of that decision was refused by the federal court.

(ii) because of the nature of the employment and the context in which it is carried out, so as to avoid conflicting with the strongly held religious convictions of a significant number of the religion's followers; and

(c) either—

(i) the person to whom that requirement is applied does not meet it, or

(ii) the employer is not satisfied, and in all the circumstances it is reasonable for him not to be satisfied, that that person meets it.

DTI, 'Explanatory Notes for the Employment Equality (Sexual Orientation) Regulations and the Employment Equality (Religion and Belief) Regulations', paras 75, 77–81[19]

It is very rare indeed that being of a particular sexual orientation is a genuine occupational requirement for a job under regulation 7(2) of the sexual orientation Regulations. In the vast majority of jobs, a person's sexual orientation has no bearing on whether or not they can carry out the job in question. However, a GOR may be justified in a small number of cases.

• For example, it may be possible to establish a GOR to be gay or lesbian, having regard to the context of the work, for persons in a position of leadership in, or representing the public face of, an organisation concerned with advising gay men and lesbians about their rights, or promoting those rights. In those circumstances there may be an issue of credibility which makes it a GOR for the person to be gay or lesbian in order to perform the functions of the post. On the other hand, for posts in the organisation which simply involve advising gays and lesbians about their legal rights, no GOR would apply because it is not essential to be gay or lesbian in order to offer good legal advice to gays and lesbians. The mere fact that the people receiving the advice might prefer to deal with a gay or lesbian adviser does not make it a GOR for the job.

In practice, if an employer already employs a person who does not have the required sexual orientation / religion or belief in a particular post, this will provide a very strong indication that having that sexual orientation / religion or belief is not a GOR for the post. Also, in many jobs, it will be sufficient that employees have some understanding of, and respect for, the religion or belief in question, or persons of the particular sexual orientation, as the case may be. If that is the case, then being of that particular sexual orientation / religion or belief would not be a genuine occupational requirement for the job.

Proportionate application

Regulation 7(2)(b) requires the employer to show that the GOR is applied proportionately in the particular case . . . for the application of the requirement to be proportionate means that it must be an appropriate and necessary means of achieving the legitimate aim in question—namely that the employer needs to recruit a person able to perform the functions of the job. Proportionality will depend on the facts of each case. But generally, an appropriate means is one which is suitable to achieve the aim in question, and which actually does so. A necessary means is one without which the aim could not be achieved; it is not simply a convenient means. This will include consideration of whether the aim could be achieved by other means which have lesser discriminatory effects.

• For example, it would not be proportionate for an employer to rely on a GOR to exclude persons of a particular sexual orientation . . . when filling a vacancy if he already has other employees of that sexual orientation . . . who could reasonably carry out those duties. (If it caused the employer excessive difficulties to make such arrangements, it would be justified not to do so). In this way an employer could recruit a new employee to a post with duties to which no GOR applied.

[19] Available at http://www.dti.gov.uk/er/equality/so_rb_longexplan.pdf.

Meeting the genuine occupational requirement

Regulation 7(2)(c) provides that the GOR exception applies either (i) where the employee or job applicant does not meet the requirement, or (ii) where the employer is not satisfied and in all the circumstances it is reasonable for him not to be satisfied, that the employee or applicant meets it.

If challenged, it is the employer who faces the burden of proving before a tribunal that the criteria in regulation 7 are met, if he wishes to rely on the exception. If the employee or applicant acknowledges that she is not of the particular sexual orientation . . . specified by the employer, then the employer should have no difficulty in establishing that (i) the employee or applicant does not in fact meet the requirement. In other situations that may be difficult for the employer to establish, because the sexual orientation . . . of the employee is usually something which would be in her exclusive knowledge. Therefore, the employer may instead seek to establish that (ii) he is not satisfied and in all the circumstances it is reasonable for him not to be satisfied, that the employee or applicant meets the requirement.

This does not mean that an employer could refuse to offer an applicant a job, merely because he suspects that the applicant is not of the specified sexual orientation . . .

Witness statement of the Director of the Selected Employment Rights Branch, DTI, in the *Amicus* case

Regulation 7(2)(c)(ii) was included in order to cater for cases in which there may be some uncertainty as to the sexual orientation of the complainant, or in which the complainant may prefer not to disclose his or her sexual orientation. The provision is intended to enable an employer to rely on the GOR [genuine occupational requirement] where the applicant refuses to disclose his or her sexual orientation, without having to impinge on the applicant's privacy unnecessarily. In the absence of this provision, it would be very difficult for the respondent to show that the complainant did not meet a GOR, because the complainant's sexual orientation may be something which is in his or her exclusive knowledge. The respondent might even feel compelled, in those circumstances, to collect as much evidence as possible about the private life of the complainant with or without his or her consent. Regulation 7(2)(c)(ii) is intended to prevent this situation arising. An employer is not required to prove the actual sexual orientation of a job applicant or employee.

The Government recognised that the inclusion of Regulation 7 was likely nevertheless to result in employers asking questions about sexual orientation which some complainants would consider personal and intrusive. However, once it is accepted (as the Directive envisages) that there are some cases (however rare) in which sexual orientation truly is a GOR for a particular post, some such inquiry is inevitable and, in the Government's view, justified. The Government has thus sought in Regulation 7(2) to strike a balance between the protection of privacy and the availability of a GOR defence.

The application of the GOR in this context has not gone uncriticised.

Oliver (2004) 33 *Industrial Law Journal* 1, 15–18, footnotes omitted

. . . the [GOQ] exception can be seen as directly contradictory to the idea that an individual's sexual orientation can be kept private. Where an employer uses a GOR to require employees in a particular post to be of a particular sexual orientation, the employer is effectively imposing an additional requirement that sexual orientation must be revealed. How else is the employer to know whether or not the employee is of the 'correct' orientation? Although the requirement could be made clear in the initial advertisement for the post, so allowing individuals the choice not to apply at all, it also appears to be possible for employers to ask an individual direct questions about sexual orientation before making a decision—particularly as the exception can be used for promotion, transfer and training, as well as for recruitment. This is clearly incompatible with the concept of a definition of direct discrimination that recognises the intensely private nature of such issues . . .

[Reg 7] appears to allow the employer to make a decision without being aware of the individual's actual sexual orientation, relying instead on the employer's own view of the individual. This does remove the need for the employer to ask about actual sexual orientation, and so could be seen as supporting a policy of allowing employees to keep this private. However, when one considers the effect of this provision, the alternative is hardly more desirable. The test it appears to legitimise the use of mere assumptions made by an employer about sexual orientation in denying an individual employment, promotion or training. It is entirely unclear as to what would be regarded as leading an employer to be 'satisfied' that an individual does or does not meet a GOR. Although the test involves an objective element, requiring the employer's lack of satisfaction with an individual's ability to meet the requirement to be 'reasonable' in all the circumstances, there is no need for the employer's assumption to be correct. It therefore seems that the employer's reasonable perception of orientation can be used, whether right or wrong.

The ability of employers to rely on perceptions of sexual orientation in this way seems particularly contradictory when it is compared with the fact that the definition of direct discrimination expressly covers discrimination and harassment based on such perceptions. As argued above, this recognises the fact that sexual orientation discrimination is often based on stereotypical assumptions drawn from an individual's appearance or conduct. However, in deciding that an individual does not meet a GOR, what can an employer take into account? In the absence of actual knowledge of an individual's sexual orientation, presumably this can only be perceptions based on dress, appearance, presentation, and other conduct—the very stereotyping that discrimination law is supposed to address. This is inappropriate, whether or not the employer's perception is actually right. If the employer is wrong, the individual is denied a job for no good reason. If the employer is right, the individual suffers the humiliation of the employer having made assumptions based on stereotypical views about his or her sexual orientation. This does avoid the need for individuals to disclose their orientation, and therefore promotes privacy. However, it is puzzling as to how an employer could ever make such a judgement without resorting to stereotyping, which creates a clear tension with any privacy-promoting policy.

. . . the same test is used in the new regulations dealing with discrimination on the grounds of religion or belief, as well as in the new race discrimination legislation, and therefore it seems that this drafting is not in fact designed to address a particular issue relating to sexual orientation (such as the promotion of privacy). It has been suggested that this is appropriate in relation to religion and belief, as it may be difficult for an employer to determine whether or not a prospective employee meets specific religious requirements. However, although there may well be some very fundamental problems with definitions of sexual orientation, as discussed below, the solution to this problem hardly seems to be to allow the employer to impose their own view of the individual's orientation. As already explored, it can be argued that sexual orientation is a uniquely private characteristic that is particularly susceptible to such stereotyping, and therefore the inclusion of such a test in these Regulations is particularly inappropriate. Although employers are constrained in their assessments to some extent by a requirement of 'reasonableness', this imprecise concept tends not to operate as a significant constraint on employer conduct in other areas of employment law—as been shown by the development of the 'range of reasonable responses' test in the context of unfair dismissal. It may be that this provision will not survive scrutiny under the HRA, particularly in relation to whether it is 'proportionate' to discriminate against an individual on the grounds of sexual orientation where this is based solely on the employer's assumptions about that orientation. However, the inclusion of this test is clear evidence of an inconsistent approach towards perceptions of sexual orientation and recognition of the uniqueness of sexual orientation as a protected characteristic.

But the High Court in the *Amicus* case rejected a challenge to reg 7(2)(c)(ii), Richards J stating that the provision had 'a sensible rationale':

> . . . In those cases where being of a particular sexual orientation is a genuine and deter-mining occupational requirement, it cannot be right that an employer, having asked the plainly permissible initial question whether a person meets that requirement, is bound in all circumstances to accept at face value the answer given or is precluded from forming his own assessment if no answer is given. At the same time the provision limits the risk of unduly intrusive inquiry. If the employer is not satisfied that the person meets the requirement, and if it is reasonable in all the circumstances for him to do so, the employer can decline to employ the person without having to make the same degree of inquiry as might be called for if it were necessary to gather sufficient evidence by way of proof of sexual orientation to meet a potential complaint of unlawful discrimination.

Regulation 7(2) is of general application. Regulation 7(3) applies only to employment 'for purposes of an organised religion'. The last-minute inclusion of the provision was widely condemned.

Changing Attitude,[20] 'UK Secular News' (2003)

Following representations from the Archbishop's Council and other church groups, the government agreed to include a clause in the British version of the European employment directive granting religious organisations the legal right to exclude gay and lesbian people from employment for the first time . . . The decision was criticised by MPs from all parties as well as liberal sections of the church and gay rights groups. The legislation will enshrine in British law for the first time the right to discriminate against gays and lesbians in employ-ment. It will allow any religious organisation to sack or refuse to employ a person on the grounds of 'sexual orientation.'

In a four-page submission to government, the Archbishops' Council argued the European directive would mean that 'actions taken by the church to enforce its own doc-trines and beliefs in relation to sexual conduct could be found unlawful. For example a bishop who denied ordination to someone in a gay or lesbian relationship might be found to be discriminating unlawfully on grounds of sexual orientation.' . . . The Department of Trade and Industry conceded that the new clause would affect not only clergy but also teachers in church schools and employees of religious charities or hospitals. Sources close to the DTI claim Downing Street forced it to accept the clauses.

The Lesbian and Gay Christian Movement said the move would institutionalise homo-phobia in a way that 'makes section 28 look like a tea party.' LGCM's general secretary, the Revd Richard Kirker, said it would give Churches protection and privilege if they chose not to employ lesbian or gay people and added that government ministers had allowed them-selves to become 'apologists for the most intolerant religious bigots'. LGCM accused the

---

[20] An Anglican lesbian, gay, bisexual, transgender and heterosexual network.

Government of capitulating to right-wing fundamentalists: the concessions won now allowed them to discriminate against lesbian and gay people.

DTI, 'Explanatory Notes', paras 91–4

Regulation 7(3) thus applies to a limited range of employment. Its scope includes members of the clergy or other ministers of religion, but also other staff working for an organised religion. They may work in a local body or place of worship such as a church, temple, or mosque, or in a body which coordinates the work of such bodies or places of worship throughout the country. For example, this may include: a General Secretary, official spokesperson, typists, support staff, cleaners (though only if the other criteria in regulation 7(3) described below are also met).

The scope of regulation 7(3) does not include employment where the employer simply has some form of religious ethos. In this respect, it is narrower than regulation 7(3) of the religion or belief Regulations (see above). So it would not generally apply in relation to a care home or a school with a religious ethos because the employment is for purposes of a home providing healthcare, or a school providing education; the employees do not work for an organised religion. Only in exceptional circumstances might it be the case that an organised religion runs such an organisation (rather than simply having a representative on a board of management, or contributing to funding), such that employment there was for purposes of the religion.

In contrast to regulation 7(2), regulation 7(3) refers to the employer applying '*a requirement related to sexual orientation*,' rather than to the situation where '*being of a particular sexual orientation*' is a requirement. In this respect, regulation 7(3) is slightly broader. For example, a requirement not to engage in sex with a same-sex partner would be a requirement related to sexual orientation, which would be covered by regulation 7(3) but not regulation 7(2).

Doctrines of religion

Regulation 7(3)(b)(i) permits an employer to rely on the exception if he applies a requirement related to sexual orientation '*so as to comply with the doctrines of the religion.*' In other words, the employer may apply a requirement related to sexual orientation if the religion's doctrine requires him to do so. The doctrines of a religion are the core concepts and articles of faith laid down by a religion in its teachings as true. As such, doctrine must represent the established teachings of a religion which is authoritative, commanding a wide, if not universal, acceptance within the religion.

It is unlikely that this element of regulation 7(3) will be applicable in most cases of employment for purposes of an organised religion. Few religious doctrines have anything to say about heterosexuals, bisexuals, gay men or lesbians which necessitates the application of a requirement related to sexual orientation to those working for the religion. Where there are such doctrines, they are likely to apply to ministers of religion, rather than to other employees whose work is not of a spiritual nature (eg cleaners).

Religious convictions of followers

Regulation 7(3)(b)(ii) is an alternative which permits an employer to rely on the exception if he applies a requirement related to sexual orientation '*because of the nature of the employment and the context in which it is carried out, so as to avoid conflicting with the strongly held religious convictions of a significant number of the religion's followers.*' It does not cover any work for an organised religion that a requirement is applied to; it only covers work for an organised religion if the requirement is applied to it because of the nature and context of the work. What are *'strongly held convictions of a significant number'* of the followers will need to be assessed in the context of each case, but it may be a significant number of followers in a local context, or a regional, national or international context. It does not mean a majority of followers, but it does mean a substantial number—more than a few. In practice, there will be very few cases under regulation 7(3)(b)(ii) where a requirement for a job related to sexual orientation will be required by both the convictions of followers and the nature and context of the work.

- For example, a large number of followers of a particular faith may have strongly held religious convictions that ministers of religion must be heterosexual or, if they are gay, that they must be celibate. The employer could apply a requirement under regulation 7(3) to avoid conflicting with the followers' convictions, if that were required by the nat ure and context of the work—perhaps because it is essential that the minister of religion should have the confidence of the followers. However, the employer could not apply the same requirement to a church cleaner by reason of the same convictions of the followers, if that is not required by the nature and context of the work. It is very unlikely that the nature and context of work as a cleaner would require the application of such a requirement.

The legality of Reg 7(3) was challenged in the *Amicus* litigation referred to above.

R (Amicus) v Secretary of State for Trade & Industry [2004] IRLR 430

Richards J:

The Secretary of State has made clear that [Reg 7(3)] is intended to form part of the implementation of article 4(1) of the Directive (the general derogation for occupational requirements) rather than of article 4(2) (the derogation in respect of differences of treatment based on a person's religion or belief where religion or belief constitutes an occupational requirement) . . . In his submissions for the Amicus applicants, Mr Singh contends that regulation 7(3) is unduly broad. It is additional to regulation 7(2), which applies to employment whether or not for the purposes of an organised religion, and it would be unnecessary unless it were capable of applying to a wider range of circumstances than regulation 7(2). A requirement related to sexual orientation can be applied, under regulation 7(3)(b), either (i) so as to comply with the doctrines of an organised religion or (ii) so as to avoid conflicting with the strongly held religious convictions of a significant number of the religion's followers. It thereby permits discrimination on grounds of sexual orientation in circumstances where the requirement does not pursue a legitimate objective or is not proportionate. The very absence of a specific requirement of proportionality, to be applied by the courts by reference to the facts of individual cases, is a particular ground of complaint. In addition, issue is taken with the authorising of discrimination on grounds of *perceived* sexual orientation, by regulation 7(3)(c)(ii), ie the same point as that already considered in relation to regulation 7(2)(c)(ii). All these matters, it is submitted, mean that the exception fails to meet the strict requirements of the derogation in article 4(1) of the Directive.

To illustrate those concerns, Mr Singh submits that regulation 7(3) appears to authorise discrimination in the following cases, among many others: (a) a church is unwilling to engage a homosexual man as a cleaner in a building in which he is liable to handle religious artefacts, to avoid offending the strongly-held religious convictions of a significant number of adherents; (b) a school for girls managed by a Catholic Order dismisses a science teacher on learning that she has been in a lesbian relationship, reasoning that such a relationship is contrary to the doctrines of the Order; (c) a shop selling scriptural books and tracts on behalf of an organisation formed for the purpose of upholding and promoting a fundamentalist interpretation of the Bible is unwilling to employ a lesbian as a sales assistant since her sexual orientation conflicts with the strongly held religious convictions of a significant number of Christians and/or of that particular organisation; (d) an Islamic institute open to the general public but frequented in particular by Muslims is unwilling to employ as a librarian a man appearing to the employer to be homosexual, reasoning that his sexual orientation will conflict with the strongly held religious convictions of a significant number of Muslims. In each of those cases, it is submitted, it is doubtful whether the characteristic of sexual orientation could be said to be a genuine and determining occupational requirement and in accordance with the principle of proportionality; and if those conditions *were* satisfied, the case would fall within regulation 7(2) and it would not be necessary to rely on regulation 7(3) . . .

The case for the Secretary of State is in summary that the concerns expressed about the width of regulation 7(3) are misplaced. The exception has a very narrow scope. The criteria are tightly drawn and are to be construed strictly (since this is a derogation from the principle of equal treatment). The exception represents a proportionate striking of the balance between the competing interests involved. Without prejudice to the decisions that might be reached by employment tribunals in individual cases, Miss Carss-Frisk suggests that it is unlikely that any of the examples put forward by Mr Singh would meet the conditions in regulation 7(3) . . .

The main question, as it seems to me, concerns the scope of the exception. If it had as wide a scope as was submitted by Mr Singh and Mr O'Neill [who appeared for the NUT], then it would be open to serious objection on the grounds that they put forward. But if it is as narrow in scope as contended for by Miss Carss-Frisk, the objection advanced loses much of its force. I think it clear from the Parliamentary material that the exception was intended to be very narrow; and in my view it is, on its proper construction, very narrow. It has to be construed strictly since it is a derogation from the principle of equal treatment; and it has to be construed purposively so as to ensure, so far as possible, compatibility with the Directive. When its terms are considered in the light of those interpretative principles, they can be seen to afford an exception only in very limited circumstances.

The fact that the exception applies, by regulation 7(3)(a), only to employment 'for purposes of an organised religion' is an important initial limitation. I accept Miss Carss-Frisk's submission that that is a narrower expression than 'for purposes of a religious organisation,' or the expression 'where an employer has an ethos based on religion or belief,' as used in the corresponding regulations relating to discrimination on grounds of religion or belief. I also accept the example she gave, that employment as a teacher in a faith school is likely to be 'for purposes of a religious organisation' but not 'for purposes of an organised religion.'

The conditions in regulation 7(3)(b) impose very real additional limitations. In my view the condition in regulation 7(3)(b)(i), that the employer must apply the requirement 'so as to comply with the doctrines of the religion,' is to be read not as a subjective test concerning the motivation of the employer, but as an objective test whereby it must be shown that employment of a person not meeting the requirement would be incompatible with the doctrines of the religion. That is very narrow in scope. Admittedly the alternative in regulation 7(3)(b)(ii) is wider; but even that is hemmed about by restrictive language. The condition must be applied 'because of the nature of the employment and the context in which it is carried out'—which requires careful examination of the precise nature of the employment—'so as to avoid conflicting with the strongly held religious convictions of a significant number of the religion's followers.' Again this is in my view an objective, not subjective, test. Further, the conflict to be avoided is with *religious convictions*, which must be *strongly held*; and they must be the convictions of a *significant number* of the religion's followers. This is going to be a very far from easy test to satisfy in practice . . .

One further point I should deal with in connection with regulation 7(3)(b) concerns its opening words, which refer to an employer applying 'a requirement related to sexual orientation.' Those words may in one way make the provision wider in scope than the regulation 7(2), where the relevant occupational requirement is expressed in terms of 'being of a particular sexual orientation.' I note that the choice of wording in regulation 7(3) was deliberate, so as to accommodate the concerns of some Churches about certain forms of sexual *behaviour* rather than sexuality as such. In my view the wording is apt to cover the point, and it may have been prudent to use such wording in order to avoid argument about the scope of the expression 'being of a particular sexual orientation.' I do not consider, however, that the point has a material effect on the present analysis. The protection against discrimination on grounds of sexual orientation relates as much to the manifestation of that orientation in the form of sexual behaviour as it does to sexuality as such. I have already mentioned this when looking generally at the fundamental rights in issue in this case. The wording of the derogation in article 4(1) of the Directive, which refers to a difference of treatment 'which is based on a characteristic related to' sexual orientation, is wide enough to embrace a difference of treatment based on sexual behaviour related to sexual orientation . . .

Richards J also rejected a challenge to the legality of the GOR's application where the employer was not satisfied as to the sexual orientation of the worker, but he ruled that a decision based on mere assumptions or social stereotyping would not be reasonable for the purpose of the Regs. This, and the approach taken by Richards J to reg 7(3), robs the provisions of much of their sting and these aspects of the decision have not been appealed.

'A good loss: *R (Amicus–MSF section) v Secretary of State for Trade and Industry'* 130 *Equal Opportunities Review*

The main challenge to reg 7(2), which applies where sexual orientation is a genuine and determining occupational requirement, and it is proportionate to apply the requirement, is that the GOR covers not only where a person does not in fact meet the requirement as to sexual orientation, but also where it is 'reasonable' for the employer 'not to be satisfied' that the person meets it. It was argued that allowing discrimination to be based on perceived sexual orientation could lead to employers stereotyping, such as acting on the basis of appearance. Mr Justice Richards helpfully holds that if a decision is based on mere assumptions or social stereotyping, then it will not meet the requirement of reasonableness.

Regulation 7(3) contains a specific exception from the prohibition on discrimination where the employment is 'for the purposes of an organised religion' and the requirement is applied 'so as to comply with the doctrines of the religion' or 'because of the nature of the employment and the context in which it is carried out, so as to avoid conflicting with the strongly held religious convictions of a significant number of the religion's followers.'

The scope of this GOR was a major concern of the trade unions bringing the judicial review application, and they succeeded in securing a ruling that will protect the overwhelming majority of their gay and lesbian members . . . The result of the ruling in this case is that there will be very few jobs in which it will be permissible to discriminate on grounds of sexual orientation. Neither of the GOR exceptions are likely to be applicable outside a religious or counselling environment, and even in such a context, following the High Court's ruling, it will be difficult for the employer to establish that discrimination on grounds of sexual orientation falls within the scope of the exception. To establish this interpretation entirely vindicates the decision by the TUC-coordinated group of trade unions to bring the complaint.

There is a further bonus in the High Court's judgment, the importance of which may transcend all the other points decided. EOR readers will know that one of the major concerns we have had with the Sexual Orientation Regulations is the distinction the government has tried to draw between a person's 'orientation', which is protected, and manifestations of their orientation. The DTI's explanatory notes state unequivocally: 'The definition does not include sexual practices or sexual conduct. As the definition says, a sexual orientation is simply an orientation towards persons of the same sex, the opposite sex, or both sexes.' [But] . . . if orientation 'is simply an orientation,', it does not necessarily cover behaviour of any kind which manifests that orientation. That would mean that it would not be direct discrimination on grounds of sexual orientation for an employer to refuse to employ someone, for example, because they looked 'too gay' or because they were overt as to their sexual preferences.

The point arose in the judicial review application in the context of the meaning of a requirement 'related to' sexual orientation in reg 7(3)(b). Mr Justice Richards rules that 'the protection against discrimination on grounds of sexual orientation relates as much to the manifestation of that orientation in the form of sexual behaviour as it does to sexuality as such.' He adds that 'sexual orientation and its manifestation in sexual behaviour are both inextricably connected with a person's private life and identity.'

There have only been a handful of tribunal cases since the SO Regs came into force.[21] In *Imbrahim v T. Butcher Mastics Ltd* (Case No. 1100425/04, Ashford Tribunal, May 2004) a tribunal held that being called a 'poofter' did not amount to discrimination under the Regs where the word was used as a general term of abuse and not directed at the actual or perceived sexual orientation of the recipient (who was understood to be heterosexual). The decision should not be taken to mean that only a gay person could complain of discrimination on grounds of gay sexual orientation: as Hazel Oliver points out (p 5) the Regs do not require claimants to self-identify in terms of their sexual orientation as their protection applies equally to discrimination on grounds of perceived as of actual sexual orientation. In *Smith v Biffa Waste Services* (Case No. 1200400/04, Bedford Tribunal, July 2004) a tribunal accepted that it had jurisdiction to hear a complaint of ongoing discrimination against a man who had been called 'pretty boy' and been exposed to a homophobic poster in his workplace. 139 *Equal Opportunities Review* (March 2005) reported an award of almost £35,000 to a gay man who left his managerial job at Cleanaway UK following verbal harassment by senior managers who referred to him as 'queer', 'queen' and 'dear'.

Discrimination on Grounds of Sexual Orientation: (II) The SDA and the HRA

The SO Regs fall far short of prohibiting all discrimination on grounds of sexual orientation, limited as they are to the field of employment and third level education. It remains necessary, for this reason, to consider the extent to which sexual orientation discrimination is or may be captured by the SDA's prohibition on sex discrimination which extends beyond employment to cover education more generally, the provisions of goods and services etc. (see further Chapter 4).

---

[21] Thanks to Lucy Anderson at the TUC for these.

The ECJ's ruling, in *P v S*, that 'the scope of the [Equal Treatment] Directive cannot be confined simply to discrimination based on the fact that a person is one or other sex' suggests that the provisions of the Equal Treatment Directive [and, accordingly, the SDA] might extend also to prohibit discrimination on grounds of sexual orientation. As early as 1983, David Pannick suggested that the SDA ought to be interpreted to this effect:

D Pannick, 'Homosexuals, Transsexuals and the Law' [1983] *Public Law*, 279, 281–4, footnotes omitted

Adverse treatment of an individual by reason of his or her sexual preferences may constitute sex discrimination notwithstanding that sex discrimination can only be established by comparing the treatment of the complainant with the treatment of a person of the opposite sex. . . .

The simplest case is where the employer refuses to employ male homosexuals but is willing to employ lesbians. A male homosexual who is refused employment by reason of his sexual preferences can establish direct discrimination contrary to the 1975 Act: he has been less favourably treated by reason of his sex than a woman whose 'relevant circumstances . . . are the same, or not materially different,' the comparison required by section 5(3) [SDA]. The Employment Appeal Tribunal has emphasised that 'in deciding whether the circumstances of the two cases are the same, or not materially different, one must put out of the picture any circumstances which necessarily follow from the fact that one is comparing the case of a man and of a woman.' . . .

A claim of direct sex discrimination can also be formulated if the defendant adversely treats homosexuals of each sex because of their sexual preferences. The less favourable treatment of the complainant on the ground of his or her sex compared with a person of the other sex might, again, be established. Suppose the employer dismisses a male homosexual from employment because he has a rule that he will employ neither men or women who have sexual preferences for persons of their own sex. The complainant can argue that this is sex discrimination because if two employees—one male, and one female—are romantically or sexually attached to the same actual or hypothetical male non-employee, the employer treats the male employee less favourably on the ground of his sex than he treats the female employee. . . . The California Supreme Court, in deciding a case under the state Fair Employment Practices Act (which prohibits discrimination on the ground of 'sex') rejected a similar analysis. While recognising that 'as a semantic argument, the contention may have some appeal,' the court concluded that the legislation did not contemplate discrimination against homosexuals [*Gay Law Students Association v Pacific Telephone & Telegraph Co* 19 FEP Cases 1419 (1979)]. In *DeSantis v Pacific Telephone and Telegraph Co. Inc.* [608 F2d 327 (1979)], the US Court of Appeals considered the argument that discrimination against homosexuals breached Title VII because 'if a male employee prefers males as sexual partners, he will be treated differently from a female who prefers male partners . . . [T]he employer thus uses different employment criteria for men and women.' The court firmly rejected the 'appellants' efforts to "bootstrap' Title VII protection for homosexuals . . . [W]e note that whether dealing with men or women the employer is using the same criterion: it will not hire or promote a person who prefers sexual partners of the same sex. Thus this policy does not involve different decisional criteria for the sexes.'

The judgment of the US Court of Appeals in *DeSantis* emphasises that one's conclusion on the validity of this claim of sex discrimination depends on the classification of the problem and the precise comparison one adopts with regard to the treatment of a man and a woman. Should one conclude that if a male employee is adversely treated for his sexual relationship with a third party X (a male) when a female employee is not so treated for her sexual relationship with the same X, such a disparity in treatment is by reason of the sex of the employee? Or should one conclude that the comparison is false as one of the employees is a homosexual and the other is not. This difficult issue will be determined by an English court or tribunal pursuant to section 5(3) of the 1975 Act. In making the comparison between the treatment of the male employee and the female employee, are we dealing with cases which are 'such that the relevant circumstances in the one case are the same, or not materially different, in the other?' The problem is that the 1975 Act provides no criteria of 'relevance.' The Employment Appeal Tribunal held in *Grieg v Community Industry* [[1979] ICR 356] that section 5(3) is 'principally although not exclusively talking about . . . the personal qualifications of the person involved as compared with some other person.' It is arguable that, on this criterion, the private sexual preferences of the complainant are not 'relevant circumstances' unless the employer can establish that the sexual preferences of his staff are material to their ability to perform the job. This argument is strengthened by the fact that section 5(3) applies an objective test and does not provide for the comparison to be made by reference to those circumstances that the employer deems relevant.

Pannick's argument was made pre-*James v Eastleigh* [1990] 2 AC 751 (see further Chapter 2), at a point where it was thought that sex had to be 'the activating cause,' rather than simply 'a *causa sine qua non*' of the less favourable treatment. Nevertheless:

The homosexual who suffers a detriment by reason of his sexual orientation can, by comparing his treatment with the more favourable treatment of the person of the sex opposite to his, show that he has been less favourably treated on the ground of his sex. . . . In the case of sexual preferences, the sex of the complainant (and the sexual stereotypes which the employer associates with that sex) is very much in the foreground as the activating cause of the less favourable treatment of which complaint is made. The employer who has said that a sexual relationship with Mr X is conduct permissible in a female employee but conduct impermissible in a male employee has clearly differentiated in treatment of male and female employees. The differentiation is on the ground of sex: women may have relationships with Mr X and retain their jobs; if men have such relationships they will be sacked. The employer may well believe that he has good reason for differentiating between men and women in this respect. But, subject to the express exceptions contained in the 1975 Act, it is no defence for the employer to say that 'what was done was done with good motives or was done, even objectively, in the best interests of the person concerned or in the best interests of the business with which the case is concerned.' That the employer has an ulterior motive for differentiating in his treatment of men and women cannot abrogate the conclusion that such differentiation is on the ground of sex.

Pannick's approach has been echoed by Robert Wintemute in a number of articles but has not found favour with the courts. *R v Ministry of Defence, ex parte Smith* [1996] QB 517 concerned a discrimination claim brought by a number of ex-servicemen and women who were dismissed on grounds of their homosexuality. The applicants claimed, inter alia, that the policy excluding homosexuals from the armed forces breached the Equal Treatment Directive, the provisions of which were directly enforceable by them in respect of their employment by the state. Their claims failed, both High Court and Court of Appeal being so confident of the non-application of the Directive to discrimination on the grounds of sexuality as to refuse to refer the case to the ECJ (both decisions were reached prior to *P v S*). According to Simon Brown LJ (in the High Court), the Directive 'says everything about gender discrimination, but to my mind nothing about orientation discrimination . . . I have no doubt that the ordinary and natural meaning of 'sex' in this context is gender. Of course

the word is apt to encompass human characteristics as well as people's anatomical qualities
. . . Orientation . . . is another thing.'

Lord Bingham MR, in the Court of Appeal, found 'nothing whatever in the EEC Treaty
or in the Equal Treatment Directive which suggests that the draftsmen of those instruments
were addressing their minds in any way whatever to problems of discrimination on grounds
of sexual orientation,' a conclusion agreed with by Thorpe LJ on the grounds that 'any
common-sense construction of the Directive in the year of its issue leads in my judgment
to the inevitable conclusion that it was solely directed to gender discrimination and not to
discrimination against sexual orientation.' . . . Noting, as the Master of the Rolls had done,
more recent concern on the part of the European Commission with discrimination on the
grounds of sexual orientation, Thorpe LJ continued: 'if the European Union is to proscribe
discrimination on the grounds of sexual orientation that must be achieved by a specific
Directive and not by an extended construction of the 1976 Directive.'

It was clear from the decision of the ECJ in *Garland v British Rail* Case C–12/81 [1982]
ECR 359 (see Chapter 6) that the travel concessions amounted to 'pay' within Article 141.
The question for the court in *Grant v South West Trains* was whether discrimination on
grounds of sexual orientation fell within the principle enunciated by that court in *P v S*.
Advocate General Elmer recognised the significance of the decision in *P v S*, citing the ECJ's
ruling in it that 'the right not to be discriminated against on grounds of sex is one of the fundamental human rights whose observance the court has a duty to ensure . . . Accordingly,
the scope of the directive cannot be confined simply to discrimination based on the fact that
a person is of one or other sex. In view of its purpose and the nature of the rights which it
seeks to safeguard, the scope of the directive is also such as to apply to discrimination arising, as in this case, from the gender reassignment of the person concerned . . . Such
discrimination is based, essentially if not exclusively, on the sex of the person concerned.'

Advocate-General Elmer interpreted the decision in *P v S* as 'a decisive step away from
an interpretation of the principle of equal treatment based on the traditional comparison
between a female and a male employee. The Court of Justice thus held that it did not
matter that there was no reason to think that a woman who wished to undergo gender
reassignment would have been treated more favourably than a man who wished to do so
. . . The essential point was that the discrimination was based exclusively, or essentially, on
gender.' The Advocate General pressed the Court to apply the logic of *P v S* to the facts
before it in *Grant*, a position opposed by the European Commission whose approach the
Court chose to adopt:

Grant v South-West Trains Ltd, Case C–249/96, [1998] ECR I–3739

Judgment:

The refusal to allow Ms Grant the concessions is based on the fact that . . . she does not
live with a 'spouse' or a person of the opposite sex with whom she has had a 'meaningful'
relationship for at least two years.

That condition, the effect of which is that the worker must live in a stable relationship
with a person of the opposite sex in order to benefit from the travel concessions, is . . .
applied regardless of the sex of the worker concerned. Thus, travel concessions are refused
to a male worker if he is living with a person of the same sex, just as they are to a female
worker if she is living with a person of the same sex.

Since the condition imposed by the undertaking's regulations applies in the same way to
female and male workers, it cannot be regarded as constituting discrimination directly
based on sex.

The ECJ's decision did not seek to explain the apparent inconsistency between it and that in *P v S*, stating baldly that its reasoning in the earlier case '. . . is limited to the case of a worker's gender reassignment and does not therefore apply to differences of treatment based on a person's sexual orientation.'

The Pannick approach to s.5(3) SDA was adopted by Beldam LJ in *Smith v Gardner Merchant* [1999] ICR 134 but did not find favour with the majority in that case, Ward LJ and Sir Christopher Slade insisting that the correct comparator for s.5(3) purposes, in a case in which a gay man alleged discrimination connected with his sexual orientation, was a lesbian woman.

But in *Smith & Grady* and in *Lustig-Prean & Beckett v UK* the ECtHR ruled that the UK's ban on gays in the military breached Article 8 of the ECHR. The applicants in this case appealed to the European Court after their application for judicial review of the prohibition on gays in the UK armed services was rejected (see *ex parte Smith*, above). Before being dismissed from the service they were subjected to intense and invasive investigation and questioning by the military on the subject of their sexual inclinations, tastes and relationships and their HIV status. The ECtHR not only ruled against the UK in respect of the nature of the investigations carried out on the plaintiffs, but also in respect of the ban itself:

Smith & Grady v UK (1999) 29 EHRR 493

. . . the investigations by the military police into the applicants' homosexuality, which included detailed interviews with each of them and with third parties on matters relating to their sexual orientation and practices, together with the preparation of a final report for the armed forces' authorities on the investigations, constituted a direct interference with the applicants' right to respect for their private lives. *Their consequent administrative discharge on the sole ground of their sexual orientation also constituted an interference with that right* [my emphasis].

The judgment in *Lustig-Prean & Beckett v United Kingdom* (1999) 29 EHRR 548 was in similar terms, while in *Mouta v Portugal* (1999) 31 EHRR 47 the Court ruled that sexual orientation discrimination breached Article 14.

With the implementation in October 2000 of the Human Rights Act, judges were required '[s]o far as it is possible to do so. . . [to] read and given effect' to legislation 'in a way which is compatible with the Convention rights' (s.3). This obligation is imposed in relation to both primary and secondary legislation 'whenever enacted', and must be read in conjunction with section 6's provision that: '(1) It is unlawful for a public authority [defined to include the courts] to act in a way which is incompatible with a Convention right' (s.6(6) defining 'act' to include 'a failure to act').

In *MacDonald v Ministry of Defence* [2002] ICR 174 and in *Pearce v Governing Body of Mayfield School* [2002] ICR 198 the Court of Sessions and the Court of Appeal respectively were given the opportunity to apply s.3 HRA so as to reinterpret the SDA in order to regulate discrimination connected with sexual orientation. That such an interpretation was possible was clear from the Pannick/ Beldam approach set out above. But in both *MacDonald* and in *Pearce* the courts, in each case by a majority, rejected that approach.

MacDonald arose as a result of the compulsory resignation from the Air Force of the applicant prior to the removal of the ban on gays in the military. His SDA claim was dismissed by an employment tribunal. Both the tribunal decision and that of EAT preceded the implementation of the HRA. But EAT allowed his appeal on the (mistaken) basis that the ECHR treated sexual orientation as 'sex' with the effect that the word 'sex' in the SDA was ambiguous and, accordingly, could be construed so as to give effect to the UK's

Treaty obligations (there to protect the applicant from discrimination on grounds of sexual orientation).

The Ministry of Defence appealed against EAT's decision. By the time the case came to be heard by the Court of Sessions the HRA was in force. The reasoning upon which EAT had reached its conclusion was flawed, but it might have been expected that its decision would be upheld by the Court of Sessions on the grounds that s.3 required the interpretation of the SDA to regulate discrimination connected with sexual orientation where that discrimination breached the Convention and in circumstances in which (in line with the Pannick/ Beldam approach) such interpretation of the SDA was 'possible.'

Their Lordships accepted (*Secretary of State for Defence v MacDonald*) that such discrimination contravened the European Convention. But the Court, by a majority, refused to interpret the SDA so as to prohibit it. According to Lord Kirkwood, 'like' must be compared with 'like' under s.(3) SDA and the applicant's homosexuality 'was a very important circumstance to be taken into account' in applying that provision. Lord Caplan went further, stating that the applicant's homosexuality was the 'critical circumstance' for the purpose of the s.5(3) comparison, this because it formed the basis for his adverse treatment

Lord Caplan expressed the view that MacDonald's Convention rights had been breached. But he found it:

> difficult to see how section 3(1) will assist the respondent's case. The critical requirement for any introduction of the Convention is that there should be incompatibility with the Convention rights. The problem . . . the 1975 Act is merely concerned with unlawful inequality of treatment between men and women which is based on gender alone . . . It will be difficult in reading the 1975 Act to pinpoint where it is incompatible with the Convention. If it has deficiencies in relation to the Convention it may be that it does not deal with areas of discrimination which are separately definable from the issue of gender. However, I do not see the 1998 Act as requiring the insertion of omitted provisions so as to enhance the legislation under consideration. If there is a collision between that legislation and the Convention then one would look for a possible approach that may resolve the problem. However, that does not mean that omitted provisions should be added where no ambiguity exists and the scope of the Act is clearly not intended to deal with what is omitted. The incompatibility declaration is intended to apply to legislation which is contrary to a Convention provision.

Lord Prosser's powerful dissent adopted the Pannick/Beldam approach and expressed the view, further, that the use of terms such as sexual 'orientation' and 'homosexuality' in this context served only to obfuscate, as would the use of terms such as 'homoethnicity' and 'heteroethnicity' in relation to a veto on mixed marriage. Such a veto could:

> scarcely be justified by saying that black and white are treated alike because each is permitted to marry a person of the same, or their own, colour. There is discrimination on the ground of colour in such a situation despite the 'equal' treatment of persons of either colour. And that would not be altered by recourse to linguistic obfuscation, by inventing concepts of homoethnicity or heteroethnicity. These are not extra circumstances. Similarly in a situation such as the present, it appears to me that one must consider whether the man and the hypothetical woman are in fact being allowed to do the same thing. To say that they are allowed, or not allowed, to do some equivalent or analogous thing is in my opinion to import a test which is not that required by section 5(3). Indeed, that kind of comparison, with supposedly

equivalent but objectively different circumstances, is in my view likely to be destructive of one of the fundamental aims of the Act—that women should be able to do things previously or traditionally or conventionally regarded as the preserve of men, and *vice versa*.

The *Pearce* case was brought by a teacher subjected to homophobic abuse by her pupils. She claimed that her employers' failure adequately to deal with such abuse amounted to a breach of the SDA. Once more the argument relevant to present purposes was whether discrimination on grounds of sexual orientation could breach that Act. Both employment tribunal and EAT ruled that it could not. By the time the matter came before the Court of Appeal the Human Rights Act was in force but, by contrast with the position in *MacDonald*, the House of Lords had by this stage ruled in *R v Lambert* [2002] 2 AC 545, that the Human Rights Act did not have retrospective effect in these circumstances. In other words, an applicant could not appeal against a decision reached prior to the implementation of the Human Rights Act on the ground that, had the Act been in force at the time of that decision, s.3 would have required that the relevant legislation be interpreted in a manner more favourable to the applicant.

The timing proved fatal to Ms Pearce's SDA claim. But both Lady Justice Hale (as she then was) and Lord Justice Judge went on to consider what would have been the position had s.3 applied. Like the majority of the Court of Sessions in *MacDonald*, Judge LJ was of the view that s.3 would not in any event have required that the SDA be interpreted to regulate discrimination connected with sexual orientation. Lady Justice Hale appeared to favour the Pannick/ Beldam/ Prosser approach on the basis that, although *Smith v Gardner Merchant* [1999] ICR 134 was binding upon the courts prior to the implementation of the HRA, s.3 of that Act imposed an 'extremely strong interpretative obligation' upon the courts which 'enabled, indeed required [them], to give the legislation a different meaning from that which it has previously been held, even by binding authority, to have' in a case in which Convention rights were at issue. Judge LJ, with the apparent support of Henry LJ, indicated his disagreement with Lady Justice Hale on this issue while pointing out that her comments were, in any event, *obiter*.

Pearce and *MacDonald* went to the House of Lords ([2003] ICR 937). The decision there was to the effect that the SDA could not be interpreted to prohibit sexual orientation discrimination (their Lordships expressly disagreed with the analysis adopted by Lord Prosser in *MacDonald*). But it was made absent consideration of the HRA since their Lordships maintained the *Lambert* approach to retrosopectivity and all the discrimination alleged in the cases pre-dated the coming into force of the Act. Typical of the speeches was that of Lord Hope who declared that the Pannick/Prosser approach 'involves changing not only the sex of the comparator but also her sexual orientation. One cannot avoid the issue by saying that, as sexual orientation consists in being attracted by one gender or the other, to describe him as a homosexual is merely a comment on his orientation which can be dismissed as irrelevant as it adds no new fact. The search is for a comparator whose circumstances are the same as those of the applicant except for his sex. The comparator's circumstances are not the same as that of the homosexual if her sexual orientation is towards persons of the opposite sex.' Lord Rodger declared that the 'no gays in the military' policy:

is not to be compared with the racial discrimination legislation which the United States Supreme Court struck down in *Loving v Virginia* 388 US 1 (1967). The intention of the Virginian legislature was to maintain white supremacy by preventing a white person from marrying an 'inferior' black person. In that situation the Supreme Court had no difficulty in rejecting Virginia's argument that there was no racial discrimination because a white man wanting to marry a black woman and a black man wanting to marry a white woman were both punished. The argument was fallacious since both cases involved deliberate racial discrimination . . . By contrast, since in adopting their policy the RAF's aim was not to treat persons of one sex less favourably than persons of the other, it is legitimate, when considering whether the policy did none the less involve discrimination on the ground of sex, to have regard to the fact that a female homosexual was to be dismissed just like a male homosexual.

The position under the SDA pre-HRA implementation is clear. But that the interpretive obligation imposed by s.3 is very robust indeed is demonstrated by the decision of the House of Lords in *Mendoza*. The applicant challenged the failure of the Rent Act to provide full rights of succession to same-sex partners of tenants enjoying statutorily protected tenancies. A mere three years before, in *Fitzpatrick v Sterling Housing Association Ltd* [2001] 1 AC 27, the House of Lords had ruled that it was not possible to interpret the Act's 'person who was living with the original tenant as his or her wife or husband' to include same-sex partners 'shall be treated as the spouse of the original tenant.' In *Mendoza* the House of Lords, having accepted that discrimination in this context between same-sex and opposite-sex couples breached Articles 8 and 14 of the Convention, went on to rule (Lord Millet dissenting) that s.3 HRA required the interpretation of the Rent Act that they had refused to adopt in *Fitzpatrick*. According to Lord Nicholls (with whom Lords Steyn and Rodger: agreed):

Mendoza v Ghaidan [2004] 2 AC 557

Lord Nicholls:

It is now generally accepted that the application of section 3 does not depend upon the presence of ambiguity in the legislation being interpreted. Even if, construed according to the ordinary principles of interpretation, the meaning of the legislation admits of no doubt, section 3 may nonetheless require the legislation to be given a different meaning [citing *R v A (No 2)* [2002] 1 AC 45] . . .

From this it follows that the interpretative obligation decreed by section 3 is of an unusual and far-reaching character. Section 3 may require a court to depart from the unambiguous meaning the legislation would otherwise bear. In the ordinary course the interpretation of legislation involves seeking the intention reasonably to be attributed to Parliament in using the language in question. Section 3 may require the court to depart from this legislative intention, that is, depart from the intention of the Parliament which enacted the legislation. The question of difficulty is how far, and in what circumstances, section 3 requires a court to depart from the intention of the enacting Parliament. The answer to this question depends upon the intention reasonably to be attributed to Parliament in enacting section 3.

On this the first point to be considered is how far, when enacting section 3, Parliament intended that the actual language of a statute, as distinct from the concept expressed in that language, should be determinative. Since section 3 relates to the 'interpretation' of legislation, it is natural to focus attention initially on the language used in the legislative provision being considered. But once it is accepted that section 3 may require legislation to bear a meaning which departs from the unambiguous meaning the legislation would otherwise bear, it becomes impossible to suppose Parliament intended that the operation of section 3 should depend critically upon the particular form of words adopted by the parliamentary draftsman in the statutory provision under consideration. That would make the application of section 3 something of a semantic lottery. If the draftsman chose to express the concept being enacted in one form of words, section 3 would be available to achieve Convention-compliance. If he chose a different form of words, section 3 would be impotent.

From this the conclusion which seems inescapable is that the mere fact the language under consideration is inconsistent with a Convention-compliant meaning does not of itself make a Convention-compliant interpretation under section 3 impossible. Section 3 enables language to be interpreted restrictively or expansively. But section 3 goes further than this. It is also apt to require a court to read in words which change the meaning of the enacted legislation, so as to make it Convention-compliant. In other words, the intention of Parliament in enacting section 3 was that, to an extent bounded only by what is 'possible,' a court can modify the meaning, and hence the effect, of primary and secondary legislation.

Parliament, however, cannot have intended that in the discharge of this extended interpretative function the courts should adopt a meaning inconsistent with a fundamental feature of legislation. That would be to cross the constitutional boundary section 3 seeks to demarcate and preserve. Parliament has retained the right to enact legislation in terms which are not Convention-compliant. The meaning imported by application of section 3 must be compatible with the underlying thrust of the legislation being construed. Words implied must, in the phrase of my noble and learned friend Lord Rodger of Earlsferry, 'go with the grain of the legislation.' Nor can Parliament have intended that section 3 should require courts to make decisions for which they are not equipped. There may be several ways of making a provision Convention-compliant, and the choice may involve issues calling for legislative deliberation . . .

In some cases difficult problems may arise. No difficulty arises in the present case. Paragraph 2 of Schedule 1 to the Rent Act 1977 is unambiguous. But the social policy underlying the 1988 extension of security of tenure under paragraph 2 to the survivor of couples living together as husband and wife is equally applicable to the survivor of homosexual couples living together in a close and stable relationship. In this circumstance I see no reason to doubt that application of section 3 to paragraph 2 has the effect that paragraph 2 should be read and given effect to as though the survivor of such a homosexual couple were the surviving spouse of the original tenant. Reading paragraph 2 in this way would have the result that cohabiting heterosexual couples and cohabiting heterosexual couples would be treated alike for the purposes of succession as a statutory tenant. This would eliminate the discriminatory effect of paragraph 2 and would do so consistently with the social policy underlying paragraph 2. The precise form of words read in for this purpose is of no significance. It is their substantive effect which matters . . .

Lord Steyn (who agreed with Lord Nicholls and with whom Lord Rodger agreed), went further in his suggestion that the courts had to date been too ready to issue declarations of incompatibility which should, in his words, be 'a measure of last resort.' It is certainly possible to interpret the SDA to cover sexual orientation discrimination. Whether s.3 will require this result in a case in which the threat to the Convention right does not come from the legislation itself but where, rather, the interpretive feat would be to carve a *remedy* for extra-legislative discrimination from an Act not originally intended to provide such a remedy, is a question which remains unanswered for the moment by the House of Lords. Some guidance may be gleaned from the decision of the High Court in *Regina (J) v Enfield London Borough Council* [2002] EWHC 432 (Admin) in which, albeit *obiter*, Elias J took the view that s.3 could require the interpretation of a statutory power to permit a local authority to provide assistance in circumstances in which absent s.3 such interpretation was not possible but in which a failure to grant the assistance would result in a breach of Article 8. He went on, however, to state that, had such an interpretation not been possible, no declaration of incompatibility could have been issued since:

the alleged failure here would be the fact that legislation in general does not allow in these circumstances for assistance to be given . . . But it is not just the Children Act which, on this premise, would be failing to confer such a power. That would not matter if the power were conferred elsewhere. Strictly it is the body of legislation taken together. In these circumstances I am far from convinced that the court could properly be satisfied that any particular statutory provision is incompatible with a Convention right, as section 4(2) requires.

Any HRA argument that the SDA would have to be interpreted so as to prohibit sexual orientation discrimination would entail acceptance of two propositions:

(1) that the discrimination at issue breaches Article 8 and/or Article 14, and
(2) that s.3 (perhaps read with s.6) HRA imposes an obligation on the court as a public authority to remedy that quasi breach (in order to prevent a breach by the state of which, for these purposes, the court is an element).

Where the discriminator is a public authority the first of these requirements will generally not be problematic (see the decision in *Ghaidan* and, in particular, Baroness Hale's speech, though *cf X v Y* below). Where, however, the discriminator is a private body the Convention breach has to consist in the state's failure to prevent or remedy the 'quasi breach' by the private body.

In *Enfield* the public authority which was required to take positive action to prevent a breach of Article 8 was not the court itself but, rather, a local authority. Elias J took the view that s.3 could be used to interpret a statutory provision to grant the power to take such action even when it was not capable properly of being so interpreted. It might be possible to argue, similarly, that the courts, armed with legislation which could (by virtue of s.3 HRA) be interpreted so as to remedy a quasi breach of a Convention right (ie, a 'breach' by a private actor) and thus avoid a breach by the state, are obliged as public authorities by s.6 HRA so to interpret it.

In *X v Y* the Court of Appeal considered whether ss.3 and 6 HRA required the interpretation of the unfair dismissal provisions so as to give a remedy for a dismissal which amounted to a breach or quasi breach of a Convention right. The case arose from the applicant's dismissal from his position with a young offender's charity after it was discovered that he had been arrested and cautioned for committing a sex offence with another man in a toilet. The dismissal was said to be by reason of the applicant's misconduct in (a) having committed a significant criminal offence and (b) having deliberately concealed it. X claimed unfair dismissal, asserting that the dismissal had been inconsistent with Articles 8 and 14 of the Convention.

An Employment Tribunal rejected X's claim and both EAT and the Court of Appeal dismissed his appeals. According to the Court, Brooke LJ dissenting, Article 8 was not engaged. That decision will not further be discussed save to say that it is highly questionable given a number of ECtHR decisions which accept that the criminalisation of sexual contact in a 'public–private' context may breach Article 8. Of more significance here is the framework for consideration of Convention arguments which the Court of Appeal Mummery LJ went on to propose in cases in which the employer was a private body.

X v Y [2004] ICR 1634

Mummery LJ (with whom Brooke and Dyson LJJ agreed):

Ms Monaghan submitted [for the applicant] that the combined impact of s.3 and s.6 of the HRA was that it was not open to the employment tribunal to find that the dismissal of the applicant was fair and reasonable under the ERA without first determining whether his dismissal engaged a Convention right and, if so, whether any interference with the applicant's Convention rights was justified . . .The essence of the respondent's position was that it was never relevant for the employment tribunal to address issues under the HRA when determining a claim for unfair dismissal against a private sector employer under the ERA. As the respondent is not a 'public authority' within s.6 of the HRA, it is not unlawful for it to act (for example, in dismissing an employee for a conduct reason) in a way which is incompatible with a Convention right . . .

The starting point in this case, as with all private law cases, is the applicant's cause of action.

(1) The only cause of action asserted by the applicant was under s.94 of the ERA: he had a right not to be unfairly dismissed by the respondent . . . (2) The applicant did not assert any cause of action against the respondent under the HRA. He does not have an HRA cause of action. The respondent is not a public authority within s.6 of the HRA. It was not unlawful under s.6 of the HRA for the respondent, as a private sector employer, to act in a way which was incompatible with article 8 . . .

The applicant invoked articles 8 and 14 of the Convention in relation to his cause of action in private law. (1) . . article 8 is not confined in its effect to relations between individuals and the state and public authorities. It has been interpreted by the Strasbourg court as imposing a positive obligation on the state to secure the observance and enjoyment of the right between private individuals. (2) If the facts of the case fall within the ambit of article 8, the state is also under a positive obligation under article 14 to secure to private individuals the enjoyment of the right without discrimination, including discrimination on the ground of sexual orientation . . .

In the case of private employers s.3 is more relevant than s.6 of the HRA, which expressly applies only to the case of a public authority.

(1) Under s 3 of the HRA the employment tribunal, so far as it is possible to do so, must read and give effect to s.98 and the other relevant provisions in Part X of the ERA in a way which is compatible with the Convention right in article 8 and article 14.

(2) Section 3 of the HRA applies to all primary legislation and subordinate legislation . . . Section 3 draws no distinction between legislation governing public authorities and legislation governing private individuals.

(3) The ERA applies to all claims for unfair dismissal. S.98 of the ERA draws no distinction between an employer in the private sector and a public authority employer.

(4) In many cases it would be difficult to draw, let alone justify, a distinction between public authority and private employers. In the case of such a basic employment right there would normally be no sensible grounds for treating public and private employees differently in respect of unfair dismissal, especially in these times of widespread contracting out by public authorities to private contractors.

(5) If, for example, the applicant in this case had been an employee of the Probation Service, he could have brought an unfair dismissal claim against it and, as it is a public authority, he would also have been entitled under s6 of the HRA to rely directly on article 8, if the facts had fallen within its ambit. If the employment tribunal only had to consider article 8 and article 14 where the employer was a public authority within s.6 of the HRA, a surprising situation would have arisen in a case such as this: the applicant's unfair dismissal claim might be determined differently according to whether his employer was in the private sector, working closely with the Probation Service, or was a public authority, such as the Probation Service itself. It is unlikely that the HRA was intended to produce different results.

The employment tribunal as a public authority

There is a public authority aspect to the determination of every unfair dismissal case.

(1) The employment tribunal is itself a 'public authority' within s. 6(2) of the HRA.

(2) Section 6(1) makes it unlawful for the tribunal itself to act in a way which is incompatible with article 8 and article 14.

(3) Those features of s.6 do not, however, give the applicant any cause of action under the HRA against a respondent which is not a public authority. In that sense the HRA does not have the same full horizontal effect as between private individuals as it has between individuals and public authorities.

(4) The effect of s.6 in the case of a claim against a private employer is to reinforce the extremely strong interpretative obligation imposed on the employment tribunal by s.3 of the HRA. That is especially so in a case such as this, where the Strasbourg court has held that article 8 imposes a positive obligation on the state to secure the enjoyment of that right between private individuals. Article 14 also imposes that positive obligation in cases falling within the ambit of article 8 . . .

it is advisable for employment tribunals to deal with points raised under the HRA in unfair dismissal cases between private litigants in a more structured way than was adopted in this case. The following framework of questions is suggested:

(1) Do the circumstances of the dismissal fall within the ambit of one or more of the articles of the Convention? If they do not, the Convention right is not engaged and need not be considered.

(2) If they do, does the state have a positive obligation to secure enjoyment of the relevant Convention right between private persons? If it does not, the Convention right is unlikely to affect the outcome of an unfair dismissal claim against a private employer.

(3) If it does, is the interference with the employee's Convention right by dismissal justified? If it is, proceed to (5) below.

(4) If it is not, was there a permissible reason for the dismissal under the ERA, which does not involve unjustified interference with a Convention right? If there was not, the dismissal will be unfair for the absence of a permissible reason to justify it.

(5) If there was, is the dismissal fair, tested by the provisions of s.98 of the ERA, reading and giving effect to them under s.3 of the HRA so as to be compatible with the Convention right?

The facts in *X v Y* predated the SO Regs and so the claimant had to rely on the ERA read with the HRA. If the same case were to arise today the question would be whether X had been subject to direct or indirect discrimination on grounds of his sexual orientation, and the outcome may well have been different. The relative significance of the HRA and of specific discrimination legislation in regulating discrimination on grounds of sexual orientation will be greatly influenced by any future extension of the SO Regs or related legislation beyond the employment field. There are no current plans for such extension, but one of the very interesting features of the Parliamentary Debate on the Equality Bill 2005, which failed to become law prior to the dissolution of Parliament in advance of the May 2005 general election, was the concern expressed by politicians across the political divide about the failure of that Bill to treat sexual orientation discrimination in like manner to religion and belief discrimination, which it proposed to prohibit in access to goods, facilities and services. It is by no means impossible that a resurrected Equality Bill might contain such provision failing which it might reasonably be expected to feature in any single equality legislation which ought to be passed in the next Parliament, in the event of another (New) Labour Government.

Index

NOTE: The following abbreviations are used throughout this index.

CRE (Commission for Racial Equality); DDA (Disability Discrimination Act); DRC (Disability Rights Commission); ECNI (Equality Commission for Northern Ireland); EOC (Equal Opportunities Commission); FETO (Fair Employment and Treatment (Northern Ireland) Order); GOQ (Genuine Occupational Qualification); GOR (Genuine Occupational Requirement); RB Regulations (Employment Equality (Religion or Belief) Regulations 2003); RRA (Race Relations Act); SDA (Sex Discrimination Act); SO Regulations (Employment Equality (Sexual Orientation) Regulations 2003).